The Outer

Its Interpretations and Implications

The Impact of Eschatological Misthology on Soteriology
With a Special Focus on the Outer Darkness

Volume Two

By
Marty A. Cauley

Misthological Press
1231 Monteith Branch Road
Sylva, NC 28779

For the author's online articles and for updates concerning his coming releases, see www.UnconditionalSecurity.org. The author's email address is: Misthologist@misthology.org.

"Unless otherwise noted, all Scripture quotations are taken from the New American Standard Bible®. Copyright © 1960, 1962, 1963, 1968, 1971, 1972, 1973, 1975, 1977, 1995 by The Lockman Foundation
Used by permission." (www.Lockman.org)

Unless otherwise noted, the 1977 edition of New American Standard Bible is the edition used in the present book and abbreviated as the NAS.

All emphases in quoted material are added unless otherwise noted.

Special Notes:
All emphases in normal quotations are added unless otherwise noted. The original italics in lexical quotations may be retained without notification since italics are frequently used by lexicographers for formal or translational equivalents.
Abbreviations implemented by grammars and lexicons may be spelled out without notification in material quoted from these technical sources.
Transliterations will not differentiate between long and short vowels, even in quoted material.

Part 7.
Misthological Context Versus Gehenna

Chapter 26.
Gehenna Versus Kingdom Entrance

Introduction

In the previous chapter, reasons were given for agreeing with ultraists rather than with conservatives concerning the identity of the Bride of Christ. In this chapter, the reverse will be done concerning Gehenna. Grounds will be presented in favor of the conservative rather than the ultraistic stance concerning the possibility of a believer literally spending any metaphysical time in Gehenna.

The ultraists have two primary sets of arguments by which to conclude that subcomers will spend the millennium in Gehenna. Eight passages of Scripture specifically use the phrase *enter the kingdom of heaven*, and some of these passages do seem to indicate that subcomers may not enter the millennial kingdom but rather spend the millennium in Gehenna. The eight primary verses used in this connection are: Mt 5:20; 7:21; 18:3; 19:23; 19:24 (parallels in Mk 10:23-24 and Lk 18:24-25); Mk 9:47 (cf. Mt 18:9); Jn 3:5; and Acts 14:22. The ultraistic argument concerning Gehenna itself is based primarily on Mt 5:22,29-30; 10:28 (cf. Lk 12:5); 18:8-9 (parallel in Mk 9:43-47). In order to briefly state the reasons herein for preferring the conservative position, it will be necessary to deal with the ultraistic argument concerning these eight passages (and their parallels): Mt 5:20-22, 29-30; 7:21-23; 10:28; 18:3-9; 19:23-24; Jn 3:5; and Acts 14:22. The second principal argument that ultraists employ to argue that not all believers will enter the millennial kingdom is based on taking the requirements for inheriting the kingdom and making them requirements for entering the kingdom. They consider inheriting the kingdom synonymous with entering it.

The Entrance of Mt 5:20

Concerning the first passage, Mt 5:20, conservatives argue that what is being required is the imputed righteousness of justification for soteriological entrance into the kingdom. Ultraists, on the other hand, believe that Jesus is requiring the imparted righteousness of practical sanctification for misthological entrance into the millennial kingdom. Advocates from both parties belong to the FG camp and thus recognize that entrance into the future eternal kingdom is granted freely, being conditioned upon a simple response of faith alone in Christ alone. Therefore, although LS teaches a false gospel of works-righteousness, this accusation should not be leveled against our ultraistic brethren in the FG camp. The ultraistic point of contention is over the millennial expression of God's kingdom. They believe that good works are required for entrance into the millennial aspect of His kingdom, but works are not required for entrance into the eternal kingdom.[1064] Ultraism affirms unconditional security in relation to the eternal kingdom and, therefore, is not an accursed soteriology.

> [19]Whoever then annuls one of the least of these commandments, and so teaches others, shall be called **least in** the kingdom of heaven; but whoever keeps and teaches them, he shall be called **great in** the kingdom of heaven. [20]For I say to you, that unless your righteousness surpasses that of the scribes and Pharisees, you shall **not enter** the kingdom of heaven. (Mt 5:19-20)

Dillow argues that the righteousness being referred to in Mt 5:20 is the **imputed** righteousness of justification (cf. 2Cor 5:21). His defense is based on the context: "Therefore you are to be perfect, as your heavenly Father is perfect" (Mt 5:48).[1065] However, Dillow's conservative argument is far from persuasive. He elsewhere makes the excellent observation that the type of sonship described in Mt 5:9,44-45 is conditioned upon **practical** righteousness.[1066] But Mt 5:46-47 continues the exhortation for practical righteousness and, therefore, would lead to the conclusion that the perfection of Mt 5:48 is perfection in practical righteousness. Our Father's intention is that all His children attain maturity in practical righteousness, and indeed some do so (Mt 5:48; 1Cor 2:6; 14:20; Eph 4:13; Col 1:28; 4:12; Phil 3:15; Heb 5:14; Jam 1:4; 3:2). The same Greek word for maturity in practical righteousness is used in all these verses (*teleios*). Thus, the perfection in question is not that of imputation.

Illustration 204. Two Mediating Neo-Misthological Positions

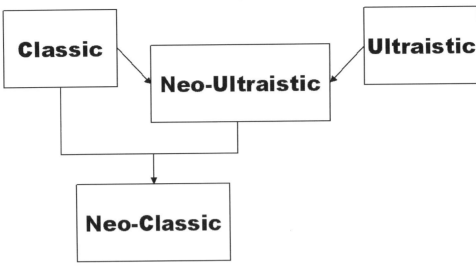

More recently, in 2003, Dillow discussed the variety of interpretations of Mt 5:20 and apparently, at that time, still found this verse to represent soteriological entrance (and basically the imputation of the active and passive righteousness of Christ to the believer).[1067] However, as of that writing, he now has taken what would be akin to a preterist view of Gehenna (focusing on the temporal wrath [in 70 A.D.], and thus denying that *aionios* necessarily means *eternal*), yet he has applied a misthological twist to the typical preterist view so that Gehenna now metaphorically refers to the temporal and misthological loss of one's soul in his modified view. Correspondingly, Gehenna would be misthologically and metaphorically equivalent to the *bema* fire of 1Cor 3:15.[1068] I would label this approach as the *Preteristic Gehenna-Bema* position—a mediating position between the classical position and the ultraistic position. For short, one might call it the *neo-ultraistic position.* Some more recent contemporary neo-ultraistic writers have contended that all entrance-passages are mistholic, even Jn 3:3-5.

For those who feel that the classic position needs to accommodate Gehenna-Bema applicability to believers, a *neoclassic* position is suggested as a mediating position between the classical and the neo-ultraistic positions that would entertain a dualism in which both the classic and neo-ultraistic positions are affirmed as being simultaneously and intentionally applicable in many passages.

Illustration 205. Neo-Mistholic Views

FG Views	Entrance	Gehenna
Classic	Soteric	Eternal
Ultraistic	Mistholic	Millennial
Neo-Ultraistic	Mistholic/Soteric	Preteristic Millennial
Neo-Classic	Soteric-Mistholic	Preteristic Eternal

Understandably, as in any system of thought, variance will be found among writers holding that perspective. (1) *Classic* misthologists will tend to regard traditional texts denoting unqualified* entrance into the kingdom as soteric. Typically, Gehenna is perceived as a picture of eternal damnation of the lost. (2) *Ultraistic* misthologists will tend to regard such entry texts as mistholic and Gehenna as merely millennial. Believers can be punished in Gehenna during the millennium. (3) *Neo-ultraistic* misthologists would regard some, if not all, of the typical entry texts as mistholic and Gehenna as millennial. But Gehenna threats to believers only anticipate the suffering at the Bema and may be prefigured by the preteristic burning of Jerusalem in A.D. 70. (4) *Neoclassic* misthologists would tend to regard some, if not most, of the entry texts as intentionally having dual soteric and mistholic applicability. The preteristic burning can be used dualistically to picture hell for unbelievers and the Bema for unfaithful believers. Gehenna is eternal or at least represents an eternal result.

---

* An entry text such as 2Pet 1:11 is not part of this consideration. Because this entrance is qualified by the word *abundantly*, the exclusively misthological nature of this entrance is readily apparent to misthologists of all persuasions. The quality of entrance is misthological.

Nevertheless, the present book, for the most part, will be content to compare and contrast the older views. A foundational understanding of the classic and ultraistic views would make serious interaction with the neoclassic and neo-ultraistic views more comprehensible. The neo-mistholic views will be interacted with briefly, primarily in the appendixes. Hodges, taking a more typical, conservative route (i.e., the classical view), believes that the righteousness of Mt 5:20 is imputational and that the Gehenna of Mt 5:22 is the Lake of Fire. Gehenna is thus soteriological and an intermediate and immediate possibility for the lost during the millennium.[1069] Gehenna is an intermediate possibility in that those sent there (during the millennium) will have to be taken out of it to stand before the Great White Throne Judgment (after the millennium) before being cast back into Gehenna permanently (Heb 9:27; Rev 20:11-15). Gehenna is immediate in that the beast and false prophet are thrown bodily into it at the end of the millennium (Rev 19:20). Equating Gehenna with the eternal fire of the Lake of Fire also allows Hodges to maintain that the lost may be cast into the Lake of Fire during the millennium (Mt 5:22; 5:46).[1070] Following Wilkin's example, the verse may be broken down into its three constituent parts in order to note the differentiation concerning Gehenna:

Illustration 206. Same Crime—Different Penalties

Whoever is angry **with his brother**		will be in danger of the court.
Whoever will say **to his brother**,	"Raca,"	will be in danger of the supreme court.
Whoever will say,	"You fool,"	will be in danger of Gehenna's fire. (TM)

The absence of any reference to *his brother* in the third statement strongly suggests that this potential penalty applies only to unbelievers, not to believers. From the first statement, we learn that angry believers will be in danger of court fines during the millennium. From the second statement, we find that vocal angry believers will be in danger of capital punishment. But the third statement reveals that vocal angry unbelievers (i.e., non-brethren) will be in danger of Gehenna if they receive the death penalty. In other words, if believers and unbelievers commit equivalent capital crimes, the punishment of the unbeliever will be worse in that it soteriologically will result in Gehenna.[1071] This combined soteriological approach by Hodges and Wilkin concerning Gehenna in 5:22 certainly would seem superior—if it can be shown that the conservative interpretation of soteriological entrance in 5:20 is correct. As noted above, Dillow advocates a soteriological entrance in 5:20 but then tries to take Gehenna as metaphorical and misthological. Either the conservative approach (in taking both as soteriological) or the neo-ultraistic adaptation (as taking both as misthological) would appear to be more natural than the ultraistic interpretation.

The immediate context favors the conservative understanding that soteriological entrance is in view, as Dillow demonstrates in some detail. For present purposes, however, I simply will note that in Mt 5:19 Jesus teaches that some "shall be called least in the kingdom of heaven," while others "shall be called great in the kingdom of heaven." Certainly, in this context, Jesus is affirming ranking within the kingdom. This is compatible with His teaching concerning the presence of those who are first and last (Mt 19:30; 20:16; Mk 9:35; 10:31; Lk13:30). Evidently, first, last, and least place believers are inside the kingdom. Having just described first and least place believers within the kingdom of heaven in v. 19, Jesus immediately proceeds in v. 20 to say that there will be others who have no entrance into the kingdom of heaven. The Lord, therefore, is teaching multiple possibilities in regard to the kingdom: no place, least place, last place, and first place.[*] This would seem to correspond to: noncomers, subcomers, midcomers, and overcomers.[1072] If that is the case, then Mt 5:20 is not talking about subcomers not entering the millennial kingdom, since Jesus has just pictured these least place kingdom believers (subcomers) as being inside the kingdom in v. 19.

Conservatives thus could contend that ultraists are mistaken in thinking that v. 20 teaches that least place believers will have no entrance into this kingdom. Verse 19 affirms that such believers will be in this kingdom. This argument is not invalidated by the ultraistic claim that the kingdom from which subcomers are excluded in v. 20 is the millennial kingdom—unless ultraists can show that v. 19 is talking about the eternal kingdom and v. 20 is talking about the millennial kingdom. These two verses cannot be talking about the same place and the same group—if those ultraists are correct who believe that those who are least in the kingdom are excluded from the kingdom. Obviously, subcomers cannot be both in it and excluded from it. The most natural reading is that these verses are describing the *same place* (i.e., some aspect of the kingdom) but *different groups* within the kingdom. Conservatives would say that noncomers and subcomers are excluded from the table, but least place believers are not excluded from the kingdom.

---

[*] See *Illustration 153. Sequence and Significance of Casting*, 467; *Illustration 231. Last is not Least*, 683.

On the other hand, the ultraistic position cannot be dismissed so easily because Faust rescues it from the above internal inconsistency. Instead of saying that least place believers are excluded from the kingdom, Faust argues that a ranking occurs within the kingdom from first to least. The least place believers inside the kingdom are those who break the *least* commandments. But those believers who follow the practice of the Pharisees and break the greatest commandments will not enter the millennial kingdom at all. This proposal by Faust is exegetically and internally consistent and thus an attractive interpretation in the immediate context. However, it presupposes that there will be those in the millennial kingdom who break the greatest commandments. Yet in such a strict millennial environment, where even the smallest infraction can be lethal, it is highly unlikely that there will be teachers like the Pharisees or people living in gross immorality. If calling someone a fool is a capital millennial offense, then teaching that it is okay to break the least commandments may be the greatest offense that one could commit without being subject to capital punishment during the millennial kingdom.

If during the millennial kingdom anyone is committing an offense greater than (privately) breaking the least commandments and (vocally) teaching others to do the same, then they will be subjected to premature death and thus removed from the kingdom by means of capital punishment. Faust fails to give adequate reason to conclude that believers living during the millennial kingdom will commit infractions greater than that described in Mt 5:19. Rather, it appears that unbelievers who commit even minor offenses may be thrown into Gehenna, but believers are not liable to the same punishment when committing similar offenses (Mt 5:22). No contextual reason is provided to think that Jesus is contemplating believers committing anything worse than minor offenses during the millennial kingdom. And even if they did, they might simply be subjected to capital punishment without being subjected to Gehenna. If such believers are removed from the millennial kingdom via premature death, they may join the other righteous dead who die during the millennium in awaiting their resurrection and judgment at the conclusion of the millennium.

As to the broader context, Jesus parabolically will locate the outer darkness within the kingdom in subsequent discourses. Church-age believers who wind up in the outer darkness break more than the least commandments during the present age. Therefore, the outer darkness imagery refutes a misthological exclusion from the kingdom. Granted, the ultraist may respond that table exclusion in the outer darkness is for lower infractions: for merely hiding your talent rather than spending it, for merely dressing inappropriately, and for having a low degree of faith and faithfulness. True, but moving to the opposite end of possibilities, these parabolic activities could be taken just as easily as picturing a believer burying his talents in the world and being dressed in worldly clothing. If so, those believers who exhibit immoral behavior would be thrown into the outer darkness rather than Gehenna. This is in harmony with the argument that immoral behavior disqualifies one from inheriting the kingdom, not from entering it. Ultraists will contest this proposal of course. But it is incumbent upon them to demonstrate that believers who are thrown into the outer darkness have enough misthological righteousness to qualify them for inheriting (and thus entering) the kingdom!

In all likelihood, Jesus is not trying to minimize the misthological impact of poor teaching in Mt 5:19. Rather, He is stressing how important it is to be a good teacher, because even teaching others to break the least of the commandments will disqualify one from kingdom rulership and table fellowship. Certainly, this understanding is in harmony with James' warning (Jam 3:1). Moreover, many of the severe misthological warnings in the NT (such as those in the book of Hebrews) certainly would seem applicable to those described by these parables. Consequently, minimizing the consequences for those who are unfaithful in the parables is not prudent. Can the ultraist prove that the misthological ***shortcomer*** in Hebrews (4:1; 12:15) is anyone significantly different than the misthological ***subcomer*** in the outer-darkness texts?[*] If the outer darkness is in the kingdom (as demonstrated herein) and if the shortcomer of Heb 4:1 is in reality the subcomer thrown into the outer darkness, then the severe punishment of Hebrews is the outer darkness, not Gehenna. The conservative view of the outer darkness makes the ultraistic view of Gehenna implausible.

The preference herein, consequently, will be for a misthological ranking but soteriological exclusion for these Gehenna texts. Singular imputational righteousness may be contrasted with plural *righteousnesses* (to use an awkward English rendition of the Greek) in such texts as Lk 1:6 and Rev 19:8. Indeed, even Jesus' half-brother, James, acknowledges the reality of singular imputational righteousness (Jam 2:23). Granted, the use of the singular form of righteousness is not conclusive, but had Jesus meant practical righteousness He easily could have clarified with the plural form to signify righteous deeds. As it is, the singular form of righteousness found in Mt 5:20 is in harmony with a soteriological entrance conditioned on imputational righteousness. We will return to this passage

---

[*] ***Shortcomer*** is a coined term for the believer who *comes short* (Heb 4:1; 12:15) of the level of misthological grace necessary to enter the kingdom rest by inheriting the kingdom.

after a discussion of Mt 18:3, but for now we will progress following Matthew's sequence with a preference for the conservative understanding of Mt 5:20.

The Entrance of Mt 7:21

The next Matthean text, Mt 7:21, that must be consulted is also from the Sermon on the Mount. Since the same type of entrance evidently is being described in both 5:20 and 7:21, the interpretation of the one will determine the meaning of the other.

Notes on Lukan Parallel

Before proceeding to the chart of this verse, however, a few comments concerning the parallels in that chart are in order. To recline at Jesus' table is to eat and drink at His table, which in turn means to rule in His kingdom (Lk 22:27-30). This privilege is granted only to those faithful believers who have made themselves ready by being appropriately *dressed in readiness* (Lk 12:35). Those seeking entrance into the kingdom in this manner will be rewarded with an abundant entrance (Lk 12:31-40).

Notes on Matthean Parallel

Although some of the same language is used in Mt 25:10-12 as in Lk 13:25 (and Mt 7:23), two different but related truths are being illustrated. In Mt 25:10-12, Jesus deals with exclusion from the feast, not from the kingdom. In Lk 13:25 (and Mt 7:23), He deals with exclusion from the kingdom, not from the feast.

Other Parallels

Other parallels that may be cited in reference to what it may mean to strive or seek to enter or to do God's will in order to enter the kingdom include the following:

- The work of God (i.e., the will of His Father) is that we believe in order to enter the kingdom, that is, in order to have eternal life (cf. Jn 6:26-40 with Mt 21:28-32).
- Grope for God and find Him (Acts 17:27).
- God is a rewarder of those who seek Him (Heb 11:6).

Illustration 207. Parallels for Mt 7:21

Lk 13:23-30	Mt 7:13-23	Jn 6:27-40
[23]And someone said to Him, "Lord, are there just a ***few*** who are being saved?" And He said to them, [24]"Strive to ***enter by the narrow*** door; for ***many***, I tell you, will seek to enter and will not be able. [25]Once the head of the house gets up and shuts the door, and you begin to stand outside and knock on the door, saying, 'Lord, open up to us!' then He will answer and say to you, '**I do not know** where **you** are from.' [26]Then you will begin to say, 'We ate and drank in Your presence, and You taught in our streets'; [27]and He will say, 'I tell you, **I do not know** where **you** are from; **depart from Me**, all you evildoers.' [28]There will be weeping and gnashing of teeth there when you see *Abraham and Isaac and Jacob* and all the prophets in the kingdom of God, but yourselves being *cast out*. [29]And they will ***come from east and west***, and from north and south, ***and*** will ***recline at the table in the kingdom*** of God. [30]And behold, some are last who will be first and some are first who will be last."	[13]***Enter by the narrow*** gate; for the gate is wide, and the way is broad that leads to destruction, and ***many*** are those who ***enter by*** it. [14]For the gate is small, and the way is ***narrow*** that leads to life, and ***few*** are those who find it....[21]Not everyone who says to Me, "Lord, Lord," will enter the kingdom of heaven; but he who does **THE WILL OF MY FATHER** who is in heaven. [22]Many will say to Me on that day, "Lord, Lord, did we not prophesy in Your name, and in Your name cast out demons, and in Your name perform many miracles?" [23]And then I will declare to them, '**I never knew you; depart from Me**, you who practice lawlessness." Mt 8:11-12 [11]And I say to you, that many shall ***come from east and west, and recline at the table*** with *Abraham, and Isaac, and Jacob*, ***in the kingdom*** of heaven; [12]but the sons of the kingdom shall be *cast out* into the outer darkness; in that place there shall be weeping and gnashing of teeth.	[27]Do not work for the food which perishes, but for the food which endures to eternal life..." [28]They said therefore to Him, "What shall we do, that we may work the works of God?" [29]Jesus answered and said to them, "This is the work of God, that you believe in Him whom He has sent."...[38]For I have come down from heaven, not to do My own will, but **THE WILL OF** Him who sent Me. [39]And this is **THE WILL OF** Him who sent Me, that of all that He has given Me I lose nothing, but raise it up on the last day. [40]For this is **THE WILL OF MY FATHER**, that everyone who beholds the Son and believes in Him, may have eternal life; and I Myself will raise him up on the last day."

The Will of the Father

Finley rejects the conservative FG interpretation of 7:21 by saying, "To interpret doing 'the will of My Father' here as simply believing in Christ violates the principle of interpretation according to the context. Nothing in the context of the Sermon on the Mount remotely stresses trusting in Christ or the gospel."[1073]

Actually, the immediate context suggests that understanding the will of the Father to be a reference to performing good works is faulty (Mt 7:22); the broader context of the sermon suggests that the issue of works is relative to having first versus least place in the kingdom but that entrance itself into the kingdom requires absolute rather than relative goodness (Mt 5:19-20). Doing the will of the Father in 7:21 is delimited within the verse to the Father's will regarding entering the kingdom. Realistically, this entrance is contingent upon believing in Christ. The broader context of the book links entrance into the kingdom with believing the testimony of a true prophet such as John the Baptist (Mt 21:31-32). These and related matters will be discussed as we proceed.

At this point, it is appropriate to note that Finley is not alone in his understanding. While the present writer was working on the rough draft of this chapter, two Jehovah's Witnesses came to his door. Upon inviting them in and asking them what was required to enter the kingdom, the author was given the same response as presented by Finley above. They turned to Mt 7:20-21, and like Finley, maintained that it is not enough to believe in Jesus for eternal life. If you really believe, then you will do God's will, that is, keep His commandments. Thus, the requirement to enter heaven, accordingly, is to keep His commands from the JW perspective. Although Finley and the Jehovah's Witnesses evidently have the same soteriology (i.e., Lordship Salvation), the same is not true of ultraists. For ultraists, doing God's will in this passage does indeed refer to practical righteousness, as LS maintains, but in distinction to the accursed LS soteriology, ultraists limit this requirement to millennial entrance.

The ultraists treat the verbs for *know* (*ginosko* and *oida*) as synonyms with the same misthological meaning in these passages (cp. Mt 25:12). Jesus does not acknowledge their claim to have served Him faithfully. In this sense the Lord does not know them. As a result, in ultraistic thought they are told to depart from Him into the outer darkness or Gehenna.

Strive to Enter

The ultraistic position can find further support from the parallel passage in Lk 13:23-30, where Jesus says that we must strive to enter and that what is at stake is entrance or exclusion from the kingdom. There is also further support for the ultraistic position in that the same verb (*oida*) is used in both Lk 13:25,27 and Mt 25:12. And the usage of *oida* in Lk 13:25,27 appears to be identical to the usage of *ginosko* in Mt 7:23. If entrance into the (millennial) kingdom is free, as conservatives believe, then why do we have to strive (work) to enter it? Further, if the basis of the exclusion of the lost from the kingdom in both Lk 13:23-30 and Mt 7:13-23 is that Jesus does not *know* them (*oida* and *ginosko*), as conservatives maintain, then can it legitimately be argued that the saved merely are excluded from the millennial feast (rulership) rather than from the millennial kingdom itself since they are excluded on the same basis (Mt 25:12)? Would it not seem that the same groups are being excluded from the same thing for the same reason (as ultraists maintain)? The saved are being excluded from the millennial kingdom, according to ultraists, because Jesus does not know them—that is, He does not acknowledge the worthiness of their works to enter.

In response to those ultraistic questions, observe that Jesus' discussion is launched by a question in Lk 13:23, which may be paraphrased as, 'Why are so few being saved in our churches today?" Jesus' answer is really common sense. At first glance, though, it appears to contradict what He taught on other occasions and what Paul teaches concerning salvation. In Lk 13:23-30, for example, it appears that in order to enter the kingdom of God we must *strive* (*agonizomai*), that is, work to enter it. Entrance appears to be based on works! As a matter of fact, Paul uses this very word in 1Cor 9:25 of an athlete doing his best to win. In 1Tim 6:12, he uses it to urge Christians to fight the good fight. This word for striving means to fight, that is, to do one's best. (So much for the passive nikology that claims that we are never told to do our best!) Jesus is definitely saying that salvation, in terms of entrance into the kingdom, may take earnest effort. In other words, He is saying that salvation for many will require hard work. The reason many are not being saved is because they are not doing the work that is necessary. Jesus is teaching that if you do not do the necessary work to enter the kingdom, you may be cast out of the kingdom. You will have no place in the kingdom.

Is Jesus, therefore, teaching salvation by works? No. But He is teaching that salvation may require works. What is the difference? Years ago while talking to a young man, whom I will call Matt, the author learned that this young man was from an Arminian background, and consequently that Matt believed he could lose his salvation, since in Matt's perspective salvation was ultimately by works. Naturally, Matt could not have a firm assurance of final salvation. To defend his position, he quoted the passage from Mt 7:21-23.

Why were these people lost in Mt 7:21-23? In response one may ask, "On what did they base the assurance of their salvation?" They based it on the same thing that Matt did, the same thing that many Southern Baptist do, and the same thing that Jehovah's Witness do—their works. Being from a Southern Baptist background, the author has asked many fellow Southern Baptists why God should let them into heaven, and the vast majority of them have given the wrong answer. They give the same answer as Matt and the Jehovah's Witnesses—a modern day paraphrase of Mt 7:22. They say that the reason God should let them into heaven is because they live a good life. Instead of saying, "We prophesied in your name, and we cast out demons in your name, and we performed miracles in your name," they phrase it as, "We lived a good life in your name." They base their salvation and their assurance of salvation on what they do rather than what Jesus has done. There will be *many* people who sincerely did many good things in Jesus' name (and who lived good lives in Jesus' name) who will be cast into hell. Why? Because salvation from hell is not by works. It is not based on living for Jesus. What is the response to Jesus' name that the Bible requires for salvation from hell? It is that we believe in His name (Jn 1:12; 3:18; 20:31; 1Jn 5:13; Acts 8:12; 10:43).

In this last passage referenced, "all the prophets bear witness that through His name everyone who believes in Him receives forgiveness of sins" (Acts 10:43). Biblical prophets, such as John the Baptist, teach that soteric salvation is through faith in Christ's name (Mt 21:31-32; Jn 1:6-7). False prophets teach such salvation is through something other than simple faith in His name. The false prophets in Mt 7:15 worked in Jesus' name rather than believed in Jesus' name. Oh, to be sure, they believed in Jesus' name in some sense of the word, but not in the biblical sense of the word. They did not believe that they were saved by simply believing in Christ's name. Perhaps the soteric sense of the word *believe* is best expressed in Jn 20:31. It means to believe that simply by believing in Him for eternal life you have eternal life. Conversely, it means to believe that works are not required for the gift of eternal life. To summarize, the will of the Father is that we believe in Jesus' name for eternal life.

Work to Enter

Nonetheless, it may take work to arrive at this conclusion. This is the case in Jn 6:26-40. From the context, it may be ascertained that *work* in Jn 6:27 does not mean to *believe* but to *do whatever is necessary to believe*. For some people, it may take a lot of work for them to come to the place where they can believe what they are being told. For example, although repentance is technically not required for the reception of eternal life, nevertheless, there may be those who would never come to faith if they had not first repented. For such people, discipleship may be a necessary psychological prerequisite to their becoming believers. Likewise, in this instance, some of Jesus' disciples were lost (Jn 6:60-66). But the best chance they had of coming to a saving knowledge of Jesus as the Christ was to stick it out as His followers in order to continue to see the signs, hear His teaching, and receive further illumination and drawing. In 6:26-27, Jesus is urging the crowd to seek for non-perishable food, that is, the food of eternal life. *Work* in 6:27 is a metaphor for *seek* (in 6:26), as is easily illustrated by substituting the word *seek* for the word *work* in v. 27—"Do not *seek* for the food which perishes, but for the food which endures to eternal life, which the Son of Man shall give to you." For some people, seeking may indeed involve working.

For example, since Matt had a faulty view of the gospel, the author wrote a three-page letter to him suggesting some books for him to read. If Matt is going to change his mind and accept the fact that eternal life is based on simply believing in Jesus, then he is probably going to have to get the books and read them. In other words, he is going to have to do some striving, seeking, and working to come to that conclusion. He is going to have to work to be persuaded that salvation from hell is not by works. We should encourage lost people to strive, seek, work, and grope for God.

As another example, at a plant where the author once worked, there was an unsaved man by the name of John who made fun of the Bible, saying that it was written in the second century. The author shared a book with him concerning the reliability of the Scriptures. John read it and apologized for making fun of the Bible. That work which John did in reading that book brought him a step closer to believing in Jesus' name. Next, the author gave him a copy of the Gospel of John and asked him to read it. He did so. That effort on his part brought him even a step closer to Jesus.

The current writer is also an example. It personally took me years of work—reading and studying the Scripture, and reading various books about the Scripture—before I permanently and decisively settled the issue that works have absolutely nothing to do with salvation from hell. It took me a lot of work to find the narrow gate—faith alone in Christ alone (Jn 10:9; 14:6). It took a lot of work for me to believe that salvation is not by works. It required a lot of work on my part to believe that believing is the only response necessary. A person may have to do a lot of work to accept the fact that salvation is not by works. This is Jesus' point. In Jn 6:27, Jesus uses *work* as a synonym for *seek*. In Jn 6:29 He uses it differently, as a synonym for *believe*—in order to clarify that the *work* (i.e., the requirement) is simply to believe.[*] He used the same word, *work*, to cover both the precondition and condition. The precondition is that we work. The condition is that we believe. Jesus holds His audience responsible for perceiving the transition from precondition to condition.

Believe to Enter

Mt 21:28-32 is another case in point. There will be harlots who will enter heaven because they did the *work*, that is, they did *the will of His Father* (Mt 21:31), which is merely to *believe*. Note that Matthew is possibly just as clear as John (Jn 6:40) in stressing that the *work* (i.e., the requirement, which is the will of the Father) is that we believe in order to enter the kingdom.[†] In any case, **three times in Mt 21:31-32, Matthew stresses that the response required to do the will of the Father, in terms of entering the kingdom, is simply to believe**.

If you believe that good works are required to enter the kingdom, then you will have no place in the kingdom. The Jehovah's Witnesses responded, as they bolted for the door, "Well, good works can't hurt you." To which I responded by warning, "They certainly can hurt you if you are trusting in them as your means for entering the kingdom. They can send you to hell." Does that mean that good works are unimportant? Those who ask such questions (as did the Jehovah's Witnesses) show a lack of appreciation for the Judgment Seat of Christ.

These Jehovah's Witnesses (JW) said they had never even heard of the Judgment Seat of Christ (although *bema* is explicitly translated as such in their New World Translation of 2Cor 5:10). Unfortunately, when it comes to discussing the importance of good works, many Lordship Salvationists act as if they have never heard of the Judgment Seat of Christ either. Understandably, the JSC has little impact on their theology since LS and JW share the same basic soteriology. If you have to do good works to enter heaven (according to LS and JW), then everyone who enters heaven is basically being rewarded for having enough good works to get inside. Heaven is essentially the same for everyone since everyone who enters it will have persevered in living a good life. Ongoing carnality is impossible from their perspective. At the very least, you will persevere in the end, if not till end. Thus, heaven itself is the real reward for living a good life from their mutual perspective.

Many Mansions Prepared for You

In counterpoint to this false LS-JW assessment of Mt 7:21, I believe that good works are not required to have a place in the kingdom, but they are required to have first place in the kingdom. On one occasion, while having lunch with a group of pastors, one pastor brought up Jn 14:1-3 to counter the idea of kingdom ranking.

> In My Father's house are many mansions; if it were not so, I would have told you. I go to prepare a place for you. [3] And if I go and prepare a place for you, I will come again and receive you to Myself; that where I am, there you may be also. (Jn 14:2-3; NKJ)

All Believers

For the sake of argument and conceptual parallels, a broad application will be allowed in order to respond to those pastors who use John 14:1-3 to say that rewards do not really matter. Their argument is that **all** believers have a place prepared for them in heaven, so no substantial distinction exists in heaven between the faithful and unfaithful. Such a premise is likely false (see below), but in any case, the conclusion certainly is wrong. Granted, the passage may be taken as applying to all believers, at least by broad implication. Jesus is referring to coming in the rapture, and since the rapture is for all believers, it could be argued that every believer has a place prepared for him or her (in some sense of the word) in the kingdom. Still, even this broader application in no way proves that all believers have the same identical place prepared for them. Even if the Father's house refers to His future kingdom, it is a place in His future kingdom that is being prepared, not the kingdom itself. Every believer will be in this future kingdom. Thus, in that sense they will all be in the same place—in the same kingdom. But within that kingdom there will be distinctions, as this very passage itself indicates. In this kingdom there are *many dwelling places,* which suggests that there is an **individualization of the preparation:** individual places, not identical places.[1074] Unfaithful believers will find that the place in the kingdom prepared for them is the outer darkness.

I referred the pastor at the luncheon to the passage in Mt 20:20-28, which deals with first and last place at the table. The place prepared for you in His kingdom is dependent upon your service. Your service, that is, your

---

[*] See *Work to Enter* in *Salvation: A Categorical Analysis* for an extended discussion about the psychological requirement for eternal life beginning with *Prerequisites for Gift*.
[†] This statement is true if Matthew is using work soteriologically, but he may be using it misthologically. See *First Parable*, 928.

good works, determine whether the place being prepared for you is first, last, or least place in His kingdom. The place prepared for you is dependent upon your preparation for that place. The building project is still going on and is dependent upon the building materials that you are sending ahead of you. That dwelling place, for some believers, may be a trailer park rather than a mansion. Or if Alcorn is correct, some might not even get a trailer:

> We might imagine that some of us are sending ahead sufficient materials for **pup tents**, some for studio apartments, some for trailer homes, some for ranch houses, and others for great mansions....
> If this seems too fantastic, remember that we are simply trying to put together and understand Christ's own words. Obviously he meant something—if not this, then what?
> The reason these concepts seem so foreign is that we tend to be so preoccupied with our life here that we never stop to think about life in heaven. And we overlook the fact that heaven is consistently described in the Bible not in ethereal, vague, or abstract means, but in very tangible and surprisingly earthly ways.[1075]

The pastor at the luncheon said that Jesus finished the preparation of the place for us in His death. Nonsense. When Jesus finishes preparing that place for us, He is coming back for us. It is still being prepared. As I pointed out to this pastor, the reason Jesus has not returned is because the place is still being prepared. It is a reward concept. If you want a mansion, you better work for it. There will be a mansion for every overcomer. The more overcomers there are, the more work that must be done. Even from this limited misthological perspective, it still would be concluded that the reasons there are so many places is because Jesus is preparing them one by one.

Reward City

More specifically, however, the manner in which Seymour ties together Jn 14:2 with Rev 22:14 is highly anticipatory of the position developed herein:

> The city is not Heaven; it is only a part of Heaven....The New Jerusalem is obviously the most glorious mansion of Heaven, but it is not the only one. And those who know the Lord and are obedient to Him will have the right to enter in through the gates of the New Jerusalem and also to eat the 12 manner of fruit of the tree of life.[1076]

Seymour is on the brink of suggesting that this city is itself a reward. He certainly implies that living in this city is a reward limited to faithful believers since he pictures it as the mansion prepared for obedient believers. Unfaithful believers will be given other mansions (i.e., other cities) in which to live. Multiple reasons have been provided herein for coming to a similar conclusion.[*]

The New Jerusalem is a city of rest that unfaithful believers are prohibited from even entering at all (Num 14:23; Ps 95:11; 132:13-14; Heb 3:11; 4:3,5). Special entrance by the gates is reserved for the faithful (Is 26:1-2). Because the unfaithful are barred from any and all entrances, the special entrance of the faithful must not be taken to mean that the unfaithful will be able to enter by some other means. Since the city is a reward (Heb 11:14,16; 13:14), those who lose their right to this reward completely lose their right to this city. Just as we would not picture a subcomer being allowed to borrow an overcomer's crown, we should not picture subcomers as being able to take subways into the city. When Jesus threatens to take away the unfaithful believer's portion in this city, we are left to conclude that this means that their participation in this city will be revoked completely since they will not have access to the fruit and springs of this city (Rev 7:17; 19:7-8). This bridal city is the reward for bridal saints (Rev 21:2,9-10; 22:2,12, 14,19), not a gift for all believers. It is the festive city (Is 25:6-9) from which unfaithful believers will be expelled (Mt 8:11-12). Their expulsion is the parabolic and telolic end[†] of the misthological story. We have no right to try to rewrite the end of the story. Yet Hodges objects:

> A parable, after all, has its natural limits and these we must be careful not to breach.
> We are not to deduce, either, that the failing Christian will spend an anguished eternity in some darkened corner of God's kingdom with nothing meaningful at all to do. That, too, would be a grotesque distortion of our Lord's teaching.[1077]

---

[*] See *Rev 21:2—City*, 542.
[†] See *Telology*, 675.

In counterpoint, why would it be a grotesque distortion of our Lord's teaching to picture the failing Christian as spending an anguished eternity in some darkened corner of God's kingdom with nothing meaningful at all to do? What Scripture indicates otherwise? To be sure, all believers will have the joy of being with the Lord in His kingdom. But that joy commences with the feast. And if those cast into the outer darkness can cry when the feast begins, why not later? Where does the Scripture suggest that they will be given something meaningful to do later? It appears that they will be given something menial to do instead.[*] Hodges himself acknowledges a few pages later that **the first passage dealing with the outer darkness is not a parable** and, therefore, interprets the feast from which they are excluded literally.[1078] However, if the feast is literal, as he himself acknowledges and as the OT affirms, then why can there not be a literal zone of darkness.[†] In any case, an eternal outer darkness certainly would seem to be implied by the eternal nature of rewards and corresponding loss of rewards. Moreover, I have not built my case upon the limitations of parables.

The New Jerusalem is a literal city and a bridal city. The city is pictured as the Bride of Christ. We have found numerous reasons for affirming the misthology of this city. Faithful believers will be allowed to participate in the city; unfaithful believers will not. For those who may wish a coined termed to describe *city misthology*, I offer *misthopology*: the study of the *reward city* (*misthopolis*). The similar English word *metropolis* is composed of two Greek words: *mother* (*meter*) and *city* (*polis*). Just as *metropolis* means *mother city*, so *misthopolis* means *reward city* (*misthos + polis*). As metropolitan refers to the composition of the metropolis, so misthopolitan correspondingly would refer to the population of the misthopolis. **Misthopology**[‡] is therefore the study of the reward city, and *misthopoligists* are those who affirm the misthological nature of the *polis*.

Bridal City

In terms of technical precision, though, the focus of Jesus' promise in Jn 14:2 is not on the many mansions (regardless as to whether these dwellings are cities, trailer parks, or pup tents) but on the special mansion for His Bride—those believers who prepare themselves for His coming. There are a number of reasons to conclude that He is only preparing one place out of many. This does not limit the rapture to faithful believers; all believers will have *places* (*monai*) in the kingdom. But it appears that the special place that Jesus is still preparing will be available only to those who are preparing for Him. Although many *dwelling places* (*monai*) are already in existence, the particular place that Jesus is still working on and preparing is a special *place* (*topos*). The Father's house already has many dwelling places (in the sense of ample room for all believers) already ready. Jesus did accomplish this for us in His death. All believers go to be with the Lord (in some connection with the Father's house) when they die or are raptured. Nevertheless, a new addition is being added on to these rooms for the Bride—the bridal suite. Jesus is still preparing the bridal suite.

In the context immediately preceding this passage, Jesus limited the *you* to those believers who are not only soteriologically bathed but subsequently washed in practical sanctification. Those believers are the ones who will have a misthological *part* (*meros*) with Him (Jn 13:8-10).[§] Jesus promises these bathed believers, who have been subsequently washed, that He is preparing a bridal suite for them and that they will be the ones who will be **with Him** in His Father's house (Jn 14:1-3). Only those believers who submit to the prenuptial washing of practical sanctification will be worthy of being presented to the Lord as His Bride.[**] If this *taking* (*paralambano*) refers to the nuptial taking of a bride, as previously was suggested, then the promise of a place that actively is being prepared is limited to overcomers.[††] Just as Joseph was told to *take* (*paralambano*) Mary as his wife (Mt 1:20), with the result that he *took* (*paralambano*) her as his wife (Mt 1:24), so Jesus will come to *take* (*paralambano*) us to Himself as His Bride (cp. Dt 25:5; 1Sam 25:39).

The Father's house would be the kingdom. Inside the kingdom there are many *dwelling places* (*monai*). There are rooms for all God's children in His kingdom. The rapture is not limited to overcomers, but the preparation of the bridal suite (i.e., the *topos* referring to the Heavenly City) within the Father's house will be restricted to overcomers who compose the Bride. In contrast, the carnal believers who are confined to the outer

---

[*] See *Fire*, 665; endnote 609.

[†] See *Illustration 181. Zone of Darkness*, 546.

[‡] **Misthopology** is a coined term derived from the Greek words *misthos* (*reward*) and *polis* (*city*) and refers to the study of the *reward city*. It is principally concerned with the capital city, that is, the bridal city. This city is properly called *Heavenly Jerusalem* during the millennium (when it hovers as a satellite city above the earth during the millennium) and *New Jerusalem* (when it possibly comes down to rest upon the new earth during the eternal state).

[§] See *Portion* in Jn 13:8, 110.

[**] See *Eph 5:26*, 584.

[††] See *Taken*, 337.

darkness in the kingdom will be outside the Heavenly City. Their *dwelling places* (*monai*) will be in the outer darkness. Although according to Paul both groups of believers will always be with the Lord as a result of the rapture (1Thess 4:17), one group simply will be with Him in His kingdom whereas the other group will be more closely associated with Him as His Bride in the Heavenly City co-ruling His kingdom.

In contrast to the many *dwelling places* (*monai*) that already are present within the Father's *house* (*oikia*), the Lord says that He is preparing a *place* (*topos*). Why is He preparing one *place* (*topos*) in distinction to the many *dwelling places* (*monai*)? Why did He say He is preparing one place rather than many? Tenney answers: "The imagery of a dwelling place ('rooms') is taken from the oriental house which the sons and daughters have apartments under the same roof as their parents."[1079] His answer is well taken since it corresponds to the historical background. For example, when Abraham's servant met Rebekah at the well, he asked her, "Please tell me, is there *room* [*topos*] for us to lodge in your father's house?" (Gen 24:23) She answered that they have such a room. It was one room among many. Yet Tenney's assumption that Jesus is preparing many such rooms in His Father's house or that all the rooms in the Father's house are such rooms is contrary to the text and, therefore, contrary to the probable bridal imagery. Jesus tells the disciples that there are lots of rooms, but He is going to prepare one room. The picture would appear to be that of a large oriental house in which one special room is being prepared for the Bride-to-be. Or as Chumney surmises: "Jesus said that there were many rooms (mansions) in heaven. One of these rooms is the room where the spiritual marriage will be consummated between Jesus and His bride."[1080]

Several passages use this same Greek word to talk of the Lord *preparing* (*hetoimazo*) an eschatological place/experience for believers (Mt 20:23; 25:34; Mk 10:40; Jn 14:2-3; 1Cor 2:9; Heb 11:16; Rev 21:2).[*] Also, two passages talk about believers preparing themselves for an eschatological place/experience (Lk 12:47; Rev 19:7). Even though the misthological nature of *hetoimazo* may be maintained, and even if the Johannine passage were broadened by way of conceptual application to include those believers who receive least place (see above), it is highly unlikely that the least are included at all in the preparation. This word for *prepare* (*hetoimazo*), when used eschatologically, is always misthological—meaning that all eschatological usages of this word for *prepare* refer to a reward concept.

The New Jerusalem is a reward as already noted. "And I saw the holy city, New Jerusalem, coming down out of heaven from God, *prepared* as a bride adorned for her husband" (Rev 21:2; TM). The city was prepared for her because she was prepared for Him. "Let us rejoice and be glad and give the glory to Him, for the marriage of the Lamb has come and His bride has *prepared* herself" (Rev 19:7; TM). His Bride is composed of those believers who have prepared themselves for the wedding by adorning themselves in good works. Good works are certainly important, but they are not to be taken for granted. We are not to assume that every genuine believer will so prepare him or herself. Nor are we to assume that these good works are required for entrance into the kingdom. Works (i.e., self preparation) are required for entrance into the city, not into the kingdom. The place being prepared is the Holy City, not the millennial kingdom or the New Earth. If you want a place in that city during the millennium and eternity, then you must prepare for it. You must be experientially holy.

The only other place that *monai* (*dwelling places*) is used in the NT is in this very chapter (Jn 14:23), where Jesus uses the singular form: *mone* (*dwelling place*). The conditional communion that believers experience with the Lord now (Jn 14:21,23) is in anticipation of the conditional consummation they will experience with Him then (Jn 14:2-3).[†] The world and worldly Christians are not offered this level of intimacy. The conditional nature of the singular *dwelling place* (*mone*) is suggestive that the singular *place* (*topos*) is being prepared for faithful believers.

The foundation for this conclusion already had been set in the conclusion of Jesus public ministry, where Jesus made this promise: "If anyone serves Me, let him follow Me; and *where I am*, there shall My servant also be; if anyone serves Me, the Father will honor him" (Jn 12:26). Note carefully the conditionalism and parallelism embedded in this verse:

---

[*] Since Is 65:17 is part of the source for Paul's statement in 1Cor 2:9, I deduce that the preparation within the new heavens and new earth (Is 65:17) of the New Jerusalem (Is 65:18) and the holy mountain (Is 65:25) is envisioned by Paul as the reward he has in mind for those who lovingly serve God. Yet in contrast to the present-future preparation found in this particular OT text, Paul indicates that God already *has prepared* this reward. The already-not-yet nature of this preparation would accord well with understanding this city (which already exists) to be our future reward. Paul already had visited this Paradise City (2Cor 12:4) but was not permitted to provide details. This crescendo was reserved for John in Revelation, who explicitly affirms its misthological nature. Yet for those who have eyes to see it, the writer of Hebrews builds to this point as well, although with not as much detail concerning the actual appearance of the city. The promised rest that we are exhorted to seek as a reward within Hebrews is obviously this misthological City of Rest. As you read through Hebrews, keep your eye on the promised rewards. The rest/rulership we are to seek is tied to the city. Exclusion from one would entail exclusion from the other. Like Paul, the writer of Hebrews confirms that God already *has prepared* this city (Heb 11:16). Yet the reward we are seeking is *the city which is to come* (Heb 13:14). The reward already prepared is yet to come.

[†] See *Love as Reward for Love*, 736.

- If we serve/follow Jesus, then we will be with Him in a place called *where I am*.
- If we serve Jesus, then the Father will honor us.

This futuristic place known as *where I am* (Jn 7:34,36; 12:26; 14:3; 17:24) also appears as *where I am from/going* (Jn 7:28; 8:14, 21-22; 13:33; 14:4). The two phrases are equated in Jn 14:3-4. From a comparison of the explicit confirmation in Jn 12:26 with contextual indications of 14:3-4, this conclusion necessarily follows: Being with Jesus in a place He describes as *where I am* (going to prepare for you), at least in these two passages, is a misthological honor conditioned on the believer's service to Jesus.[1081]

- **If anyone serves Me**, let him follow Me; and *where I am*, there shall My servant also be; **if anyone serves Me**, the Father will honor him (Jn 12:26).
- And if I go and prepare a place for you, I will come again, and receive you to Myself; that *where I am*, there you may be also. And you know the way *where I am* going (Jn 14:3-4).

If we serve Jesus, we will be with Him where He is in a place He is currently preparing for us. The place which Jesus is preparing for those believers who serve Him is a place of honor conditioned on their service to Jesus. It is a reward, not a gift. This place mystified both Jesus' adversaries and admirers. They did not know what He was talking about. This is still the case today. LS mentality tends to equate the *where I am* in both passages and to conclude that we earn heaven by our service. FG theology has the opposite propensity and seeks to disassociate the passages by assuming that they are talking about two different places: one earned, one unearned. The Marrowistic conclusion, in contrast, is that the same mistholic place is being described by both passages, and it is earned. A special place of intimacy in the kingdom of heaven reserved for those believers who serve the Lord, namely, the Heavenly City (with individual apartments for overcoming believers).

In summary, concerning our place/position in the kingdom, there are four possibilities: *no place, least place, last place,* or *first place*. First place is a place of bridal intimacy. In Mt 20:20-28, the concern of the mother of James and John was not that her sons would have no place in His kingdom. Jesus already had promised them a place. Rather, she was concerned with what place they would have within it. She wanted them to get first place, to sit at His right and left. They mistakenly thought they could obtain first place by merely asking for it. Jesus responds that it can only be obtained by having it prepared for them, which would recall His teaching that first place must be earned. He clarifies, "To sit on my right hand, and on my left, is not mine to give" (Mt 20:23). Jesus is not free to give away such exalted positions freely because He already has obligated Himself misthologically. These positions are reserved for those for whom they are prepared misthologically.

Likewise, the Heavenly City is *prepared* (as a reward) for those of whom *God is not ashamed to be called their God* (Heb 11:16). Consequently, this city is not prepared for those believers of whom the Lord will be ashamed. They will not live there. Otherwise, what would be the point of saying that the city is prepared for faithful believers if unfaithful believers will also be allowed to live there? Just as sitting at Jesus right and left is reserved for those for whom it is prepared, so living with Jesus in that city is reserved for those for whom it has been prepared. It might be objected that since inheriting *the kingdom prepared for* faithful believers (Mt 25:34) does not mean that unfaithful believers will be excluded from living in the kingdom, the preparation of the city for one group does not entail exclusion of another group. Yet this reply would fail to take into consideration that rendering *basileia* as *kingship* would necessarily entail complete exclusion (since the unfaithful will not participate in rulership) and that more than entrance into the spatial kingdom is being prepared for the faithful in that they will have the experience of inheriting it (from which the unfaithful will be excluded).

First vs Last vs Least

First place in the future is based on service in the present, as Luke pictures with the kingdom and its table. Believers might have no place, least place, last place, or first place. In Lk 13:23-28, the Lord deals with no place. Believing that good works are required to enter the kingdom fails to qualify one for having a place in that kingdom. For some it will take a lot of work to accept the truth that entrance into the kingdom is not by works. So the acknowledgement that works may be required as preconditions on the part of some of the lost to enter the kingdom and that works are required of all the saved to have first place in the kingdom does not rule out the conservative position concerning Gehenna.

Having a place in heaven—basic entrance into heaven—is by faith alone. Contrastively, an abundant entrance into heaven, that is, having first place in heaven, is by works. Having dealt with basic entrance, Luke proceeds to describe an abundant entrance in 13:29-30.[1082] Many believers will get first place. They will have the privilege of having supreme intimacy with Jesus in heaven, pictured as dining with Him, and thus ruling with Jesus over His kingdom. Other believers will get last place at the table. They will not be excluded from the table but sit at the lower end of it. So their place in heaven will be one of lower rulership. Still, they will have special intimacy with the Lord. Albeit, there is yet another group. Luke had expanded this same misthological truth pertaining to the table in the previous chapter (Lk 12:35-48; esp. vv. 35-39).

Only those believers who are dressed appropriately and have lit lamps will have a place at the table in Lk 12:37. Of course, this recalls the imagery in Matthew about the man thrown into the outer darkness because he was not dressed appropriately and also recalls the virgins left in the outer darkness because their lamps were not lit (cp. Lk 12:35 with Mt 22:11; 25:8). Only those believers who serve their master will be served by their master at the table. Those servants who do not serve, but rather are abusive, will not have a place at the table.

Do Not Know You

The remaining argument that must be addressed pertains to the fact that exclusion from the kingdom is based on Jesus not knowing the person. As stated above, it can be argued in favor of the ultraistic position that since His not *knowing* (*oida*) the person in Mt 25:12 is used misthologically, the same might be assumed concerning His not *knowing* (*oida*) the person in Lk 13:25,27. And since Lk 13:25,27 is parallel to Mt 7:23, His not *knowing* (*oida*) the person in the Lukan parallel is equivalent to His not *knowing* (*ginosko*) the person in Matthean passage.[*] Therefore, it might be argued, on this basis, that His not knowing the person in Mt 7:23 does not establish that such a person is lost and that *oida* is used in a similar manner to *ginosko* in these texts.

Dillow gives a conservative rejection of this type of argument by saying that the usage of *oida* in Lk 13:27 is "irrelevant to the usage in Mt. 25:12. Knowing where a man is from and knowing him in a saving sense are not equivalent."[1083] The safest procedure would be to allow the context of each passage to determine the author's intended meaning of the words *oida* and *ginosko* in each respective passage. In other words, it would be best to determine one's understanding of the words based on each of the contexts. Probably, neither the conservative nor the ultraistic positions can be proven or disproven by the words *oida* and *ginosko* in and of themselves.

The use of the word *never* in the Mt 7:23, however, would seem to give a decided advantage to the conservative interpretation of this passage. In Mt 7:23, Jesus says, *I **never** knew you* (*oudepote ginosko*). On the other hand, in Mt 25:12 and Lk 13:25,27, He simply says, *I do not know you* (*ouk oida*). The contrast in the Matthean usage appears to be between relative and absolute denial. The Matthean text uses the word *never* to denote the absolute soteriological nature of this rejection in 7:23, but this is softened in 25:12 to a misthological rejection with the absence of the absolute negation. To be sure, the Lukan parallel presents Jesus using this same teaching that He used in Mt 7:23 with *I do not know you* (*ouk oida*) rather than *I never knew you*. From this comparison, we learn that the more ambiguous *do not know* can be equated with *never knew* **if the context justifies this association**. But this does not necessarily prove that the reverse is true. The fact that the softer negation can be intensified contextually to the equivalency of absolute negation does not necessarily prove that the absolute negation can be so easily softened to a misthological rejection, especially when looking to the past rather than the future.

Jesus denies any past relationship with them. His saying that He never knew them any time in the past is a stronger negation than simply saying that He does not know them in the present. This stronger negation would appear to be absolute and soteriological. The softer negation could be either soteriological or misthological, depending on its context. As a result, acceptance of the ultraistic argument is hindered by Jesus' choice of the word *never* in Mt 7:23. And the absence of the word *never* in Lk 13:25,27 does not necessarily help the ultraistic case. Quite simply, on the occasion when Jesus spoke the parallel saying, as recorded by Matthew (7:23), He used a stronger negation to denote the absoluteness of rejection.[†]

Hodges and Dillow have given excellent discussions of these parallel texts.[1084] To briefly summarize what is evident from the passages themselves, the fruits in these passages refer to what a prophet speaks or teaches. The word *fruits* refers to his doctrine. False prophets produce bad doctrine. Even though they look good and act like sheep, their words reveal that they are wolves. Thus, the fruits refer to their words, not their works. Unfortunately, not only do they deceive others into thinking they were sheep, they also deceive themselves into thinking they are sheep! These wolves think that because they look like sheep, they must be sheep. In all sincerity, they appeal to

---

[*] The present treatment needs only prove that similarity does not prove equivalence. A principle of correlativity need not be denied. See *Theory of Correlativity*, 911.
[†] For an extended discussion of the different forms of casting out in the Matthean and Lukan parallels, also see *Matthew's Outer Darkness*, 463.

their works when they stand before Christ. They point to their works; He points to their sins. Soteriological assurance based on works is a very dangerous thing. We are not saved from our sins by working but by believing. We must enter the narrow gate in order to have life and avoid destruction. Since this destruction is the opposite of having life by merely entering the gate, it is a soteriological destruction rather than a misthological destruction.[1085] These prophets point to their work of prophesying in Jesus name as a reason they should be allowed into the kingdom. But why should Jesus let us into heaven? It is not because of what we do (in terms of performance)[*] but because of what we believe. He will not let us in because we work or teach in His name but because we have believed in His name. He is the only way (cf. Acts 4:12).[1086]

Know Them by Their Fruits

Two Free Grace Views

Bing questions Hodges' identification of the fruits as referring exclusively to the false prophet's words by pointing out that, although words are the primary test, works were also sometimes used to detect false prophets. Additionally, fruit can sometimes refer to works in the NT. Bing is correct, but that does not necessarily mean that both words and works are intended in this particular passage. Further, it should also be clarified that, although Bing takes what might be construed as a LS interpretation of fruits, he rejects the LS interpretation of the passage: "This passage, therefore, only teaches how to discern a false prophet, not how to discern whether one is lost or saved."[1087] Thus, we have two competing, conservative FG views concerning the meaning of fruits in this passage.

Two Lordship Views

Let it not be assumed that FG interpreters are the only ones who have differences of opinion concerning the meaning of fruits, however. Even Pagenkemper hesitates to insist that Jesus is using fruits to refer to good works in His parables, admitting, "The issue may be unresolvable....Thus one might maintain a certain amount of agnosticism about this issue because of the nature of the parables, for the fruit might not have any significance at all."[1088] On the other hand, Lenski shares Pagenkemper's soteriological perspective of the separation-parables, even to the point of understanding the workers in the vineyard as representing soteriological distinctions, which is a rather rare perspective. But even so, Lenski has no trouble coming to the conclusion that the fruits refers to words rather than works:

> Commentators are divided in their opinions as to what Jesus means by "the fruits" of the false prophets. Some say, their doctrines; others, their works; still others, doctrines and works combined. The answer is found in Isa. 8:20; I John 4:1; Heb. 13:9; II John 9, 11; Matt. 15:9; Titus 1:9-12: the fruits of the prophet are undoubtedly the doctrines he teaches. The fact that his own personal works are not the criterion by which we can without fail judge him is established by 24:24 ("great signs and wonders"); Deut. 13:1-3 (to the same effect)...True prophets often manifest sins and faults in their lives; false prophets often have the appearance of holiness as a part of their sheep's clothing. God alone is able to judge men's hearts and to distinguish hypocritical from genuine works.[1089]

In other words, how can counterfeit works be used to discern counterfeit faith? If Satan is able to counterfeit religious emotions and works in the lives of those whom he deceives to such an extent that even those who are performing them and experiencing them think that they are saved, then how can their salvation be denied on that basis?[†]

Examine False Prophets

Further, the fact that fruits can refer to works in some passages does not prove that it does so in every passage. Similarly, it is not necessary to conclude that false prophets can never be discerned as such to some extent by their works. Indeed, some false **prophets** can be discerned *as such* (as false prophets not as false believers) by their works. However, there are other false prophets who cannot be so detected. They can only be discerned as false teachers by what they teach. This particular passage deals exclusively with this type of doctrinal test. Not all false teachers can be detected as such based on how they live, but they certainly can be detected as false teachers

---

[*] See "Efficient Versus Instrumental Means" in *Soteric and Mistholic Faith*.
[†] For more information on counterfeit works, see *Theory of Misthological* Relativity, 687.

on the basis of what they teach. In developing our *karpology*[*] (doctrine of fruitfulness), we must be aware of the various possible types, sources, degrees, and results of fruit. The Jehovah's Witnesses who came to the author's door appealed to their good works as proof that they were saved. They welcomed an examination of their works. The author had no reason to question their claim to living good lives. Nor was it necessary to examine their good works to see if their teaching was false. They honestly thought they were the Lord's sheep because of their good works and because of their seeking to do the Lord's will. How tragic it is that they could not see themselves for what they really were—wolves in sheep's clothing. Their teaching is what identified them as such.

Illustration 208. Howl of the Wolf

The passage is not talking about discerning **your** own salvation. Rather, Mt 7:16,20 says, "You will know **them** by **their** fruits." Fruit inspection in this passage is not introspection. The people described in Mt 7:22 share the belief of the false prophets that salvation is based on works. Since they honestly, but unknowingly, believe in salvation by works, they are blind to the falsification of their profession. They base the assurance of their salvation on their works. To base the assurance of salvation on works is very dangerous indeed. To make good fruits (i.e., a life of good works) the inevitable consequence of having saving faith, as the Jehovah's Witnesses and others in LS do, is to make good works a requirement for salvation from eternal damnation. Faith is assurance (Heb 11:1). If your assurance is based on your works, then your faith is in your works.

Postconversional Performance

Calvinists are quick to charge FG advocates with falsely accusing Calvinists of mixing *how a person gets saved* with *the results of that salvation*. A simple examination of the allegation will reveal that FG correctly distinguishes the requirement from the results, or the root from its fruit. The verse is generally translated as: "Every tree that does not bear good fruit is cut down and thrown into the fire" (Mt 7:19). Yet it seems that some of those from a Reformed perspective want to treat the verse as if the temporal sequence were: "Every tree not thrown into the fire bears good fruit." They want it to mean that if you are genuinely saved (i.e., not thrown into the fire), then you bear good fruit. According to their theology, if you are genuinely saved from the fire, you will bear good fruits. However, the biblical sequence is: If you bear good fruit, then you will be saved from the fire. Since the verse must be read in reverse to support the Reformed view, they are the ones who are mixing the results with the requirement. Bearing good fruit is a *requirement for* (not a *result of*) not being thrown into the fire in this passage.[†] Nevertheless, Reformed Arminian, Picirilli, denies that these good works are a condition of salvation and instead expresses the standard Reformed claim that "we may even call them 'essential,' just as bearing apples is 'essential' to an apple tree but manifests what the tree is instead of making the tree what it is."[1090] Arminian theology,

---

[*] ***Karpology*** is a coined term derived from *karpos* (*fruit*) used to refer to the doctrine of fruitfulness. It is spelled as *carpology* in English. In accordance with my transliterative preference and to underscore that I am concerned about the biblical aspect of fruitfulness, I have chosen this alternative spelling.
[†] My interpretation is that the person is the tree and saving faith is the response the individual must produce to be saved from the fire.

Reformed theology, and Reformed Arminian theology can find common ground in asserting that good works are not necessary to become a believer but to be a believer. Postconversional good works are, therefore, logically necessary to be classified as a believer and reach heaven in such theologies. In their mutual perspective, salvation from the fire is in reality made contingent on faith and works, which makes good works a condition for reaching heaven. Calminianism makes good works essential for reaching heaven and therefore conditional. Postconversional performance becomes a postconditional requirement.*

A paraphrase of Mt 7:19 from the Calvinistic premise (that good fruits are inevitable) could be rendered as: *Every professing believer who does not bear good works is thrown into hell.* If this were the case, then good works are required for salvation from hell. To teach assurance based on works is to teach salvation by works. To say that salvation is by faith and assurance is by works is to be inconsistent. To try to discern the salvation of these teachers on the basis of their works is to fall into the very deception that Satan is using to deceive these lost teachers into thinking they are saved.

It does not matter that the Calvinist says that these are postconversional good works. Postconversional good works are a part of our sanctification. Such a claim by Calvinists makes our glorification conditioned on our sanctification. Justification by faith alone becomes a myth. In such a scheme, although justification initially might have been by faith alone (without any preconversional works), ultimately it is made dependent upon faith plus postconversional works for its fulfillment. But according to Pauline theology, to seek a justification by grace that even partially necessities postconversion works to reach heaven is to fall from grace (Gal 5:4).

Jesus also affirms the authenticity of justification in the absence of any promise to do better or perform postconversional works (Lk 18:13-14). In this parable of the Pharisee and tax collector, a contrast is seen between LS and FG. The Pharisees "trusted in themselves that they were righteous, and viewed others with contempt" (Lk 18:9). Like those in the modern LS movement who trust in their commitments (to perform good works and to turn from bad works) as conditions of coming into a saving relation with God and who view their follow-through in producing good fruits as proof of the genuineness of their commitment, they pride themselves that they are better than those who, like the tax collector, simply trust in God for mercy. They excuse their pride as being monergistically justifiable and pretend to be the tax collector by portraying him as if he were saying, "God, I promise to become morally upright like the Pharisee." They twist the humble cry of the tax collector into a promise to turn from bad works and to perform good works in order to Pharisaically try to turn him into one of them.

Like the Pharisees of old, whom Paul called dogs (Phil 3:2) because of their performance-based soteriology, Pagenkemper likewise asserts, **"The justification for acceptance or exclusion in the kingdom is found once again**, not simply in a claim, but **in** the evidence of that claim—one's works."[1091] According to Pagenkemper's proveitism, **your justification is found in your works**. Your exclusion from heaven is based on your works. Quite simply, his theology is justification by works. Making works the inevitable evidence of justification results in those works being made the grounds for justification in the end. He has followed his theology to its logical conclusion in finding his justification in his works. With such a Pharisaical attitude, one would have no trouble picturing Pagenkemper walking over to the tax collector and telling him that his lack of fruits proves his lack of justification.

Virgins and Oil

This understanding of Pagenkemper's soteriology is not derived from an isolated slip of the pen on his part. For example, concerning the identity of the oil in the parable of the ten virgins, he concludes that the connection "with good deeds is unmistakable in the broader strokes of the parable's message."[1092] He acknowledges that the foolish virgins do not represent those who outright reject the gospel but those who are rejected despite their interest in entering the kingdom and despite their initial appearance of being prepared to enter and notwithstanding their expectation of entering. (So much for the Calvinistic portrayal that those who are spiritually dead in sin cannot respond positively to God. Evidently, the Calvinistic God granted them temporary faith and works in this passage.) If the oil represents good works, as Pagenkemper believes, then those who had the additional oil evidently had enough good works to tip the scales in their favor, allowing them to enter. Or they persevered in good works to the end and were granted entry as a result. In either case, their eventual soteriological entrance is conditioned on their linear degree of works. If this is a soteriological passage (as Pagenkemper supposes), and if the oil represents good works (as he concludes), then the parable is best understood from an Arminian perspective: They lost their salvation.

Jesus does not teach that if you are a pure virgin, you *will* persevere. The Calvinistic *will* is in error. Jesus does not guarantee that regeneration *will* result in perseverance. Quite the opposite, you *must* persevere. The

---

* See "Believe and Live" in *Ordo Salutis*; "NOSAS Objection" and "Postconditions" in *Soteric and Mistholic Faith*.

Arminian *must* is correct—if the passage is in fact describing soteriological entrance as Pagenkemper believes. Being a regenerate virgin does not guarantee that you will persevere in the end. The right to enter may be forfeited. If the passage is describing soteriological entrance, then it is conditioned on perseverance, and the Arminian interpretation should be adopted. Likewise, concerning the parables of the talents and minas, the criterion of judgment is the works of the servants.

According to Pagenkemper, "their works demonstrate the reality of their trust in the master." In other words, if you do not work, then you do not really believe. Or in light of Pagenkemper's above comments, if you do not work long enough, then you were never really a believer to begin with: "Disciples *must* faithfully be waiting, and true servants *will* be productive."[1093] Here, Pagenkemper combines *must* with *will* in his soteriology, which is not uncommon since they are really one and the same in Calvinism: You *must* persevere in good works, or you *will* go to hell.[*] No real difference exists between the Arminian (*must*) and Calvinistic (*will*) in requiring good works to escape from hell.[†]

Pagenkemper's Full Salvation is Narrow

In seeking to harmonize his works-based soteriology with Paul, Pagenkemper continues: "When Paul discussed **justification** by faith, he was specifically identifying the 'entrance' requirements. But when Jesus discussed discipleship, He viewed **salvation** from a full-orbed perspective—not just entrance, but the life of commitment to His lordship."[1094] This is Pagenkemper's implicit affirmation of Lordship/Discipleship Salvation. He regards submission (in terms of performance) to the Lordship of Christ as a requirement for full-orbed salvation, which in his opinion is simple soteriological salvation from hell. Full-orbed salvation would just be another way of saying genuine salvation from his perspective. Faith might initially be enough for justification, but salvation from hell ultimately is based on the life one lives. He is advocating justification by faith but salvation by works.

> Salvation in these parables is viewed as a "whole," not simply as a point of entry. The "sons of the kingdom" and the "sons of the evil one" (Matt. 13:38) are on opposite sides of the soteriological divide. **There is no room for** purgatory, universalism, or a view that some may miss the heavenly "banquet" while yet retaining a right to entry into the kingdom (i.e. **"salvation," in Pauline terms**). Those who are rejected are permanently excluded.
>
> Third, **the basis for this eternal judgment is the individual's works**. In some cases the emphasis is on faithfulness to a job assigned: perhaps in a picture of preparation for an event, or a picture of the fruit (καρπός) of the believer. But however it was pictured, works were the key to the judgment. [1095]

Certainly, Pagenkemper is correct that these parables exclude purgatory, since the rejection is permanent. Further, some of the parables (e.g., dragnet, sheep and goats) are soteriological, so universalism is ruled out. Alarmingly, however, the fact that Pagenkemper can find no room for Pauline soteriology should raise more than an eyebrow, especially considering Pagenkemper's subsequent statements:

> **Works are not separated from the faith** one exercises **for entrance to the kingdom** for works are evidence of that faith. A true change of heart will be reflected in a person's life. **A lack of that change is apparently enough to prevent entrance** into the eschatological kingdom (the goats are prohibited from entrance because of their actions while the sheep are **given entrance because of their works**); but works are never ultimately separated from the faith of the individual, for it was also shown that works are not in themselves enough to impress the Son of Man positively in His role as judge (cf. Matt. 7:21-23).
>
> Paul wrote with different emphases in mind, focusing clearly on the entrance requirements into salvation, namely, justification by faith."[1096]

In Pagenkemper's soteriology, believers are "given entrance [into heaven] because of their works." Entrance into (initial) salvation is by faith, to be sure, but entrance into heaven is by works. Faith is not enough in his mutation of soteriological salvation.

---

[*] See *Illustration 248. Cross-Eyed Calvinism*, 709.
[†] See *Illustration 96. Three Major Soteriological Positions*, 266.

Keathley's Rejection of Pauline Harmonization

Although Keathley does not credit Pagenkemper on the two citations above, Keathley quotes him at length.[1097] Both he and Pagenkemper have rejected salvation by faith without any works. Keathley seems to be content to portray Matthew and Paul as teaching two different gospels, since Keathley acknowledges, on the basis of 1Cor 3:11-15, "that works don't always follow" in Pauline theology.[1098] Apparently in Keathley's estimation, poor Matthew evidently did not realize that a person could receive eternal life by simply believing in Jesus. If Keathley's perception of Matthew is correct, perhaps Matthew should have borrowed John's gospel! From Keathley's analysis, one would deduce that for Matthew the evidence of faith in the production of good works is required for salvation from hell.[1099] In Keathley's opinion, Matthew teaches salvation by faith that works (= faith and works). His karpology is so intertwined with his soteriology as to make the two inseparable. Keathley already had said that Matthew did not have a very well developed eschatology. According to Keathley, one should not try to harmonize Matthew's eschatology with that of Paul. Evidently, Keathley believes Matthew's soteriology was not much better than his eschatology, so one should not expect too much in way of agreement between Matthew and Paul here either. The problem is not that a harmony between Matthew and Paul is hard to conceive. After all, if the outer darkness represents the Pauline misthology expressed in 1Cor 3:11-15, then Matthew and Paul agree with one another both soteriologically and misthologically. Keathley just finds it ridiculous to conclude that these two biblical writers are in agreement.

Pagenkemper's Rejection of Pauline Gospel

Pagenkemper is more consistent in his denial of salvation by faith alone and wants to limit even the Pauline entrance requirements to mean nothing more than the initial requirement. In other words, salvation by faith alone is a necessary first step, but ultimately soteric salvation is determined by the second step—works. Works cannot be separated from faith as a requirement to enter the kingdom. A lack of works is enough to prevent entrance into heaven. Those who are given entrance into heaven will be given it because of their faith and works. Pagenkemper expects us to accept his assessment based on what he calls "a relatively brief element in Paul's corpus" in which "Paul spoke of the rejection of the unrighteous based on their lack of good works (Rom. 2:6-10; Titus 1:16)."[1100] But the fact that works can condemn one soteriologically to hell in Pauline soteriology does not prove that works can justify one soteriologically for heaven in Pauline thought. Pagenkemper's argument is logically unsound. That works can condemn a person to hell does not prove that they can justify a person for heaven.

Had Pagenkemper not tried to force all these parables into a soteriological grid, there would have been no need to stand Pauline soteriology on its head. The LS premise that Jesus taught that all believers will produce good works/fruits in His parables is easily refuted by a simple reading of the parable of the sower in the Gospel of Luke, in which the latter three soil types represent believers. The second soil type represents the first category of carnal believers—they produce no good fruits/works. The second category of carnal believers produces no mature fruits/works. Only the last group of believers produces good fruits/works. The conclusion should be that not all believers produce good fruits in terms of good works.* Regeneration does not inevitably result in good fruits/works. Indeed, to be saved without good works is quite possible. Pagenkemper is blind to this possibility and to parabolic soteriology, as is evidenced in his criticism of Ryrie for "making the decision to enter the banquet separate from the life of discipleship."[1101] According to Pagenkemper,

> Luke put these two elements one after the other to highlight **two sides of the same coin**. The banquet shows the broadness of the invitation and the **free cost** of attending (though the banquet clearly cost the master greatly). While the entrance is open to each one who will enter at **no cost**, the life of the disciple, assumed of all who enter the kingdom, will itself expect much and be **costly**. The first pericope [Luke 14:16-24] looks strictly at the entrance point, while the second [Lk 14:25-33] looks at salvation in its full-orbed perspective. **Separation takes place only at the semantic and conceptual level.**[1102]

Pagenkemper's coin-theology is really a two-headed monstrosity, which teaches that salvation from hell is free but costs you everything.† According to this soteriology, our salvation is not only costly to our Master; it is also costly to us. Supposedly, this "free cost" is both costly and not costly to us. This contradiction is utter

---

* See "The Nature of the Soil" in *Breaking the Rocking Horse*.
† See illustration for "Two Different Sides of the Same Coin?" in *Salvation: A Categorical Analysis*. A Marrowistic implementation of the two-sided illustration is certainly possible, however. See "Two Sides of the Same Coin" at www.unconditonalsecurity.org.

nonsense. Pagenkemper's separation between non-costly and costly, between faith and works, is only a **semantic** word play at the **conceptual** level, amounting to nothing more than theoretical rhetoric. It is no better than Shank's rank equating of a gift with a reward:[*]

> It is true that eternal life is the free gift of God to undeserving sinners. But just as the acceptance of the gift is costly (as we considered in Chapter 2), so is the retention of that gift, once received. There is therefore a sense in which eternal life, though God's gracious gift to undeserving men, is yet a reward to those who faithfully endure.[1103]

Shank's second chapter is entitled *The High Cost of a Free Gift* and is devoted to a defense of LS. Therein he claims, "The acceptance of the gift, like its provision, is costly. It costs the renunciation of self....One cannot accept Christ and His salvation on lesser terms than the complete surrender of self to Him." "The lordship of Jesus of self, life, and possessions must be acknowledged if we are to know Him as Saviour." "Receiving Jesus Christ as Saviour is not a matter of 'just' accepting Him—'no strings attached.' There must be full surrender to the lordship of Christ." "Salvation costs men nothing...and everything."[1104] Shank cannot tell the difference between a gift and a reward, between what is free and what is costly. To him, they are one and the same.

Whereas Shank makes discipleship a front door requirement to enter heaven, Pagenkemper brings discipleship in the back door as a requirement to enter heaven. Without a doubt, Pagenkemper's Judaic friends in the book of Galatians and his contemporary Arminian counterparts certainly would welcome his Calvinistically making final justification dependent upon postconversion performance, but Paul will have none of this perversion and maintains that those who make postconversional performance a soteriological necessity have fallen from grace as a theological principle and practical way of life. Paul emphatically asserts that they have denounced justification by faith alone (Gal 5:4). Justification by faith already has resulted in a judicial standing before God, in which all of a believer's sins already have been forgiven soteriologically as a result of the believer's position in Christ (Eph 1:7, Col 1:14; 2:13; Heb 10:10-14). Our soteriological future and entrance into the kingdom is assured by faith alone. Pagenkemper's superficial dichotomy between justification and full-orbed salvation is false since he misconstrues full-orbed salvation to be simple salvation from hell. He would have done much better if he had accepted the fact that both Paul and Jesus agree on the nature of justification and salvation and that full-orbed salvation is more than simple salvation from hell. The NT writers and Jesus are in agreement that full-orbed salvation is a misthological co-glorification by works. But such works are not required for simple soteriological glorification by faith alone.[†]

Secondary Assurance

Initially, it was taken for granted in FG theology that works can play a secondary, supplementary role in assurance or evidence of justification. Previously, FG camp advocates (myself included) argued that works can give additional, non-essential evidence for believing that we have experienced regeneration. Making this evidence non-essential distinguished this FG view from proveitism. Even so, this older FG view has now been abandoned by many in the FG camp, including Wilkin and myself, and the statement of the GES *Affirmation* was changed to reflect this shift.[1105]

For the sake of those in FG who still may hold this earlier view, it must be stressed that works at the very most provide a **secondary role, not a necessary role** for assurance. Good works are not necessary for salvation nor for the assurance of salvation. Such works can give positive evidence, but not negative evidence. We cannot deny someone's regeneration on the basis of his or her performance, even if he or she is not producing the good fruits we would normally expect. For example, when we go to a car lot, we do not have to drive the car to know that it is a car. The fact that it is a car is evident from the nature of the case apart from its performance. If we purchase the automobile and drive it home, we have additional confirmation that it is indeed a vehicle. But that drive home is not necessary in order to have absolute assurance that what we have purchased actually is a car. Even if it should fail to crank the next morning, we do not have grounds for concluding that it is not a genuine vehicle or that it never was a genuine car in the beginning. Temporary performance or lack of performance does not invalidate the reality of its genuine identity. The identity is guaranteed by the presence of the manufacturer's name on the vehicle, not by its operation. The genuineness of believer's identity in Christ is proven by the seal of the Spirit, a seal which is clearly visible to God but invisible to us.

---

[*] See "Gift ≠ Reward" in *Soteric and Mistholic Faith*.
[†] See *Salvation: A Categorical Analysis*.

Perhaps a similar automotive example will further clarify the auxiliary nature of works in relation to assurance. Suppose you and your friend carpool to work. You drove that morning. When you arrive back at the car that evening, you walk around to the driver side and immediately notice that you have a flat tire. You stand there pondering what to do since you do not have a spare. It is a long, four mile walk to the house. The reason the flat tire was immediately noticeable to you was due to the rim being all the way down to the pavement, so you know you cannot drive it, and there is no question about it being flat. Your friend sees you standing there looking at the car, so he walks around to see what is the problem. When he sees it, he remarks that you have a flat tire. Did you need his remark to know that you have a flat tire? No. Did his remark add anything to your assurance of the fact that you have a flat tire? No. His statement was completely unnecessary and is a simple restatement of the obvious. Your friend, representing works, has nothing to add to your assurance.

For the sake of illustration, allow the metaphor to be used in a dual capacity. Suppose that your friend is an automotive repair enthusiast, and due to his lack of confidence in your old car, he keeps a few items in your trunk, like a toolbox with a tire repair kit and a container of compressed air. He jacks up the car, patches the tire, and puts air back into it, enabling you to drive home. Works can pump life back into our faith and make it useful. Our works (such as what we do and say) can be an indication as to what we believe, as in the first part of this illustration. Yet this confirmation is not necessary for soteriological salvation. And the absence of this additional confirmation would in no way subtract from our assurance. Still, our works can enliven our faith and give it visible expression, allowing us to reach home in style. Some believers will reach home by the skin of their teeth, or by the soles of their shoes, so to speak, as they walk wearily along as a result of a flat, deflated faith. Nevertheless, they will be allowed into heaven. Entrance into heaven is not dependent on the assurance of good works. Good works are required for rewards in heaven but not for entrance into heaven.

What makes a person a believer is what that person believes, not what he or she does. What makes a person a new creature in Christ is experiencing the new birth ontologically and thus being created in Christ, not one's performance in Christ. Paul's affirmation in Eph 2:10 is a guarantee from the manufacturer that believers are "His workmanship." His seal guarantees that they are genuinely His product, but it does not guarantee their performance. They *should* run well, but they may not. They are not passive objects but creations with minds of their own. Technology is now capable of making cars with computers within them, in hopes of enabling such cars to drive themselves, but sometimes these brainy cars may drive themselves right off the pier and into the lake. Nevertheless, they are still cars, even though they do not always perform up to the manufacturer's expectations.

Fruit = Words

[31] Therefore I say to you, any sin and blasphemy shall be forgiven men, but blasphemy against the Spirit shall not be forgiven. [32] And whoever shall speak a **word** against the Son of Man, it shall be forgiven him; but whoever shall **speak** against the Holy Spirit, it shall not be forgiven him, either in this age, or in the *age* to come. [33] Either make the tree good, and its **fruit** good; or make the tree bad, and its **fruit** bad; for **the tree is known by its fruit**. [34] You brood of vipers, how can you, being evil, **speak** what is good? For the **mouth speaks** out of that which fills the heart. [35] The good man out of his good treasure brings forth what is good; and the evil man out of his evil treasure brings forth what is evil. [36] And I say to you, that every careless **word** that men shall **speak**, they shall render account for it in the day of judgment. [37] For by your **words** you shall be **justified**, and by your **words** you shall be **condemned**. (Mt 12:31-37)

In this parallel passage in Matthew, the tree is again known by its fruit. Jesus explicitly equates this fruit with the words that are spoken. In this passage fruit refers to what they say rather than what they do. Fruit does not refer to their lifestyle or their appearance. Jesus is saying that if you want to lift up the hood and take a look at a person's justification, then the words being spoken are the latch we should use. Admittedly, the justification in Mt 12:37 probably goes beyond mere soteriological justification to include misthological justification as well. That is, the judgment in Mt 12:36 most likely includes the judgment of the lost and the saved. Believers will be judged on the basis of what they have said in terms of misthological acquittal or condemnation (Mt 10:32-33). For believers, the possibility of mistholic justification is in view. For unbelievers, the severity of their soteric condemnation will be determined by their performance.

So there is a sense in which our words can be associated with our works, and fruits can refer to oral performance.[*] Although there are occasions in which the word *fruit* (as sg. common = *fruits*; cp. Lk 3:8) refers to

---

[*] See illustration of "The Words We Speak" in *Salvation: A Categorical Analysis.*

performance in general (Mt 3:8; Jn 15:2-8), at other times the meaning of fruit is limited to oral performance. Jesus moves from a generalization concerning **works** to a verbal specification regarding **words** in certain contexts, such as Mt 7:16-20 and 12:33-37. Likewise, although Jesus' warning is in harmony with Scripture against false teachers in general, He also gives an illustration that is particular to those false teachers who teach a false gospel.

Illustration 209. Contextual Specification of Fruit

Those who are lost will be judged on the basis of what they have said in terms of soteriological rejection. Their fruit (oral performance/works) soteriologically will condemn them for two reasons. First, what one says gives evidence as to what one believes. Those who teach soteriological justification by works (or by faith and works) demonstrate that they do not believe in justification by faith alone. Secondly, all of our works provide the basis for our soteriological conviction. All our righteous deeds, whether they are verbal or nonverbal, are like a filthy garment and demonstrate our soteriological guilt, when we consider those so-called good deeds the grounds (or means) for entrance into heaven. Words can be viewed as a partial subgroup of works, but it is a subgroup that more than anything else reveals what one truly believes.

Leaven = Doctrine

The same is true in the context of Mt 7:20-21.[1106] Jesus is warning about false teachers (Mt 7:15). The false teachers from whom He experienced daily opposition were the Pharisees and Sadducees. Jesus warned His disciples, "Watch out and beware of the **leaven** of the Pharisees and Sadducees" (Mt 16:6). His disciples thought that He was talking about bread. So He went on to explain, "How is it that you do not understand that I did not speak to you concerning bread? But beware of the **leaven** of the Pharisees and Sadducees. Then they understood that He did not say to beware of the **leaven** of bread, but of the **teaching** of the Pharisees and Sadducees" (Mt 16:11-12). False teachers are discerned by false teaching.[1107]

Illustration 210. Matthean Fruits

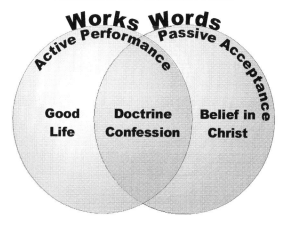

Narrow and Broad Fruits

Contextually, in this particular passage (Mt 7:16,20), fruits do not refer to works (as such) but to words, that is, doctrine as an indication of belief. If doing the Father's will refers to living a good life in Mt 7:21, then the passage teaches that works are required for entrance into the kingdom of heaven. However, if doing the Father's will refers to believing in Jesus (cf. Jn 6:40; Mt 21:32), then the passage is consistent with other NT soteriological teaching. False prophets teach false doctrine—in this passage specifically the false doctrine of salvation by works and assurance of salvation based on works. They are condemned by their works because all of us are sinners who fall short of salvation based on works. Their false belief system of salvation by works is to be discerned by their words (i.e., fruits) which reveal that they are trusting in their works and thus that they are lost. Good fruit, understood as true doctrine (= believing in Jesus), is required to escape the fire in Mt 7:19.

Teaching sound doctrine is a misthological work in the NT. Jesus, however, is not teaching that we can earn entrance into heaven as a reward by teaching sound doctrine, much less is He demanding a good life for entrance into the kingdom. He is rejecting good works as a basis for such entrance, demonstrating that those who strive for a performance-based soteriological entrance will be rejected on the basis of the very fruit that they offer in hopes of gaining such entrance. He rejects typical karpologically-based soteriology. Their fruits (in both the broad and narrow sense of nonverbal and verbal performance) will be found to be soteriologically rotten. The distinction between sheep and wolves in this passage is not between the teachers and practitioners of this doctrine of self-righteousness. Rather, Jesus points out that their practice nullifies their doctrinal claim that it is possible to be saved on the basis of one's practice.

Illustration 211. Fruits in Matthew 7:15-20

To be sure, Pagenkemper is correct that in certain contexts fruits may refer to good works, as has been indicated herein in noting that not all believers produce good works in the Lukan parable of the sower. Matthew also clearly links *fruits* (sg. common) with works on occasion (Mt 3:8; 13:8,26). The Marrowistic contention is that works in this broad sense cannot be made an infallible indication of salvation in any context. Further, in this particular context of Mt 7, Jesus is indicating that these false prophets are rejected because of their fruits in terms of the theology they teach, since this theology is one that appeals to one's fruits in terms of their works for kingdom entrance. What Jesus wants in relation to kingdom entrance is fruit in terms of trust in Him as the Messiah (the King who grants entrance into His kingdom to those who simply trust in Him for it). If at judgment some were to say that the reason God should let them into heaven is because they have trusted in Christ for eternal life, such words would denote passive reliance upon Christ for eternal life. But those who respond that their soteriological entrance should be granted because they have performed good works will thereby demonstrate by their words that they do not rely upon Christ alone for such entrance. Our words, then as now, reflect what we believe and in whom we trust.

To illustrate LS thought, consider the following parallelism. In FG, faith is a requirement—one cannot have salvation without having saving faith; thus, saving faith is required for salvation. In LS, works are also required—you cannot have salvation without having good works (fruits); thus, good works (fruits) are required for salvation. Or stated differently, in LS one cannot enter heaven without a life of good works; good works are required to enter heaven. In contrast, in FG theology good works are neither initially or subsequently required to be saved from hell or to enter heaven. Congdon has well stated the fallacy of the Calvinistic equivalency:

To be fair, Classical Calvinists usually object to this [claim that they make postconversional good works the *inevitable result* that is necessary for salvation] by describing the gospel message as *not* "faith + works = justification," but "faith = justification + works." I submit that anyone with a basic knowledge of logic can easily demonstrate that these two end up in the same place.

In the first equation, faith alone does not lead to justification; works must be added. But in the second, once again faith alone does not lead to justification; if works do not follow, then there was no faith. This is no more than a word game. It is best seen in the old Calvinist saying: "You are saved by faith alone, but the faith that saves you is never alone." Let me complete it: "You are saved by faith alone (apart from works), but the faith that saves you is never alone (apart from works)." This is internally inconsistent.

Suppose you go to a car lot to buy a used car, and purchase a car for $5,000. If you have the $5,000, you may pay it right then. If you don't, the salesman may arrange a loan for you to pay it back over a period of years. But does the fact that you don't pay anything up front mean that you got the car free? Absolutely not. You are paying for it—the payment is just an inevitable result of your buying the car. To paraphrase the Classical Calvinist saying: "You are a car-owner by signing a sales agreement alone (apart from any money changing hands), but the signing of a sales agreement by which you are a car-owner is never alone (apart from money changing hands)." If the money doesn't change hands, you lose the car (this wording reflects Arminian theology; in Calvinist theology, you never had the car in the first place!). (Emphasis his.)[1108]

LS Mathematics

Splendid analogy, yet having a mathematical background, I would like to engage LS mathematics from a mathematical orientation using a few abbreviations: (F) *faith*, (W) *works*, and (J) *justification*. Both FG and LS acknowledge that F + W = J is false. Yet Lordship Salvationists argue that F = J + W. Algebraically, this equation would seem reasonable since this statement is mathematically equivalent to F - W = J.[1109] However, the fallacy of this reasoning is evident when it is carried one step further. The full LS equation is F = J + W = S (*salvation* from hell). Works, as an expression of submission to the Lordship of Christ, are ultimately required for final salvation from hell in LS thought. The reason this Lordship mathematical expression fails is because it uses the wrong mathematical symbol. Faith, justification, works, and salvation are different concepts. They are not equivalent; they cannot be connected with equal marks.

The mathematical symbol $\Rightarrow$ (*if-then*) is better able to represent the logical relationship. If A then B (A $\Rightarrow$ B) means that A logically (inevitably) results in B. Free Grace mathematics could thus be expressed as, F $\Rightarrow$ J $\Rightarrow$ S. Faith alone results in justification alone which results in salvation alone (i.e., simple salvation from hell). Those believers who only have faith will enter heaven by the skin of their teeth. But in FG theology, if a believer works for the Lord, then he or she will have (R) *rewards* in heaven. Works results in rewards (W $\Rightarrow$ R). Works are required for a full-orbed salvation that includes rewards, but works are not necessary for basic salvation form hell.

In contrast, the Lordship position is F $\Rightarrow$ J + W $\Rightarrow$ S. Faith inevitably results in justification and good works (J + W). In turn, J + W is required for soteriological salvation. Consequently, faith and works are both required to be saved from hell. Faith is the condition for justification, but works are the postcondition (in relation to justification) upon which salvation from eternal damnation is conditioned. Accordingly, you cannot escape hell without good works in LS. Although Lordship Salvationists may acknowledge that justification is initially by faith alone, in the end they make salvation dependent upon works. By making full-orbed salvation semantically equivalent to basic salvation, LS makes basic salvation from hell dependent upon the believer's production of good works.

Illustration 212. Levels of Fruitfulness for Believer

Narrow Fruit	Broad Fruits	Narrow Entrance	Abundant Entrance
Justification: passive positional imputation of righteousness	*Sanctification*: active practical impartation of righteousness	*Simple Salvation*: Salvation from Hell	*Full Salvation*: Salvation from Outer Darkness
Regeneration: Impartation of life	*Communication*: Abundant Life	Book of Life	Crown of Life

Narrow and Broad Entrance

Within his gospel, Matthew calls for fruit (in both the narrow and broad sense) for full salvation from God's temporal, soteriological, and misthological wrath. The seeming conflict with Pauline karpology and soteriology results from a failure to perceive that fruit in the narrow sense (of trust in Christ for eternal life) is the single requirement for entrance in the narrow sense, but fruits in the broad sense (in the production of much fruit) is necessary for salvation in its fullest capacity. As has been noted in the parable of the sower, not all those in whom life was imparted went on to produce much fruit. They did not produce abundant fruit nor experience the abundant life; although, they had life imparted to them. In the immediate context preceding the fruit pericope of Mt 7:15-20, Jesus had given the invitation to enter by the narrow way that leads to life rather than the broad gate that leads to destruction, saying that many would try to enter by the broad gate (Mt 7:13-14).

Illustration 213. Sequence of Believer's Fruitfulness

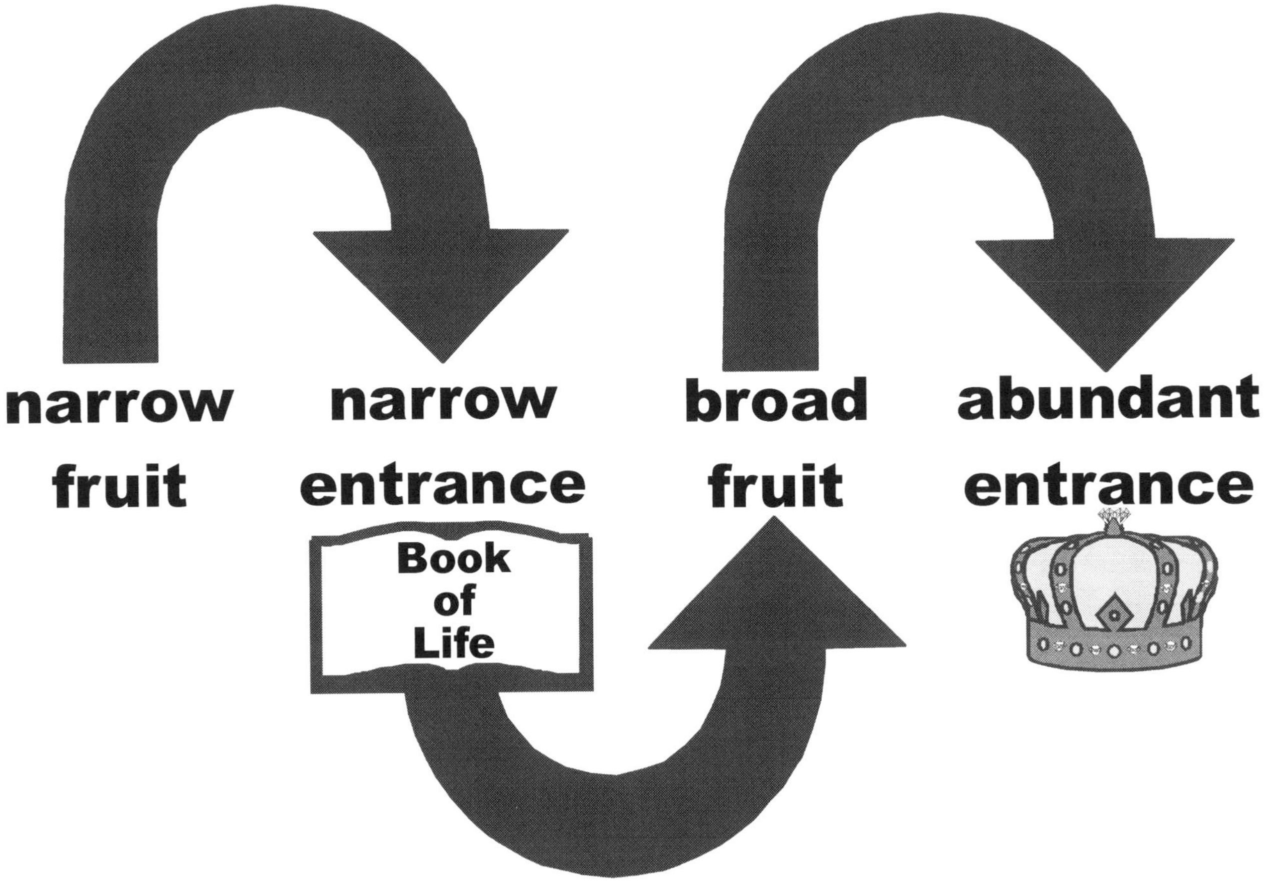

narrow fruit   narrow entrance   broad fruit   abundant entrance

Book of Life

In the pericope immediately following the fruit discourse, Jesus explains that many will be denied entrance. Those who are denied entrance are those who point to their postconversion works as a basis (necessary requirement) for their entrance. Like Pagenkemper, they believe that their conversion is indicated by their good works which they have done in Jesus' name. They would not do works in Jesus' name unless they had first come to have faith in Jesus' name. The problem is that it was not saving faith. These false prophets thought that their postconversional performance proved the genuineness of their faith, which is a proveitistic fallacy shared by both Arminianism and Calvinism. In Marrowism, in contrast, it is asserted that faith alone in Christ alone for eternal life will secure eternal life (Jn 1:12; 3:18; 20:31). These people, on the other hand, had trusted in Jesus and their postconversional performance for kingdom entrance rather than trust in Christ alone.

The irony is that Jesus certainly calls for fruits in terms of postconversional works, but He refuses to allow such fruits to form any part of the basis for soteriological entrance. Postconditional performance is a misthological issue, not a soteriological one. Those who trust in fruits in the broad sense for soteriological entrance are those who seek to enter by the broad gate. In these parabolic sayings about gates and fruits, Jesus cryptically is limiting the narrow gate to fruit in the narrow sense. To summarize, fruit in the narrow sense (of trust in Christ) is required for entrance through the narrow gate. Fruits in the broad sense (of works for Christ) are required for an abundant entrance into the kingdom (2Pet 2:11). Making fruit in the broad sense a requirement for entrance in the narrow sense is in reality an attempt to enter by the broad gate and reveals a lack of saving faith. Pagenkemper's attempt to understand this parabolic material through the superficial perspective of the masses misses the meaning intended by Jesus and embedded in the details.[*]

> [10] And the disciples came and said to Him, "Why do You speak to them in **parables**?" [11] And He answered and said to them, "To you it has been granted to know the mysteries of the kingdom of heaven, but **to them it has not been granted**. [13] Therefore I speak to them in **parables; because** while seeing **they do not see**, and while hearing they do not hear, **nor do they understand**. [14] And in their case the prophecy of Isaiah is being fulfilled, which says, 'You will keep on hearing, but will not understand; And you will keep on seeing, but will not perceive; [15] For the heart of this people has become dull, and with their ears they scarcely hear, and they have closed their eyes lest they should see with their eyes, and hear with their ears, and understand with their heart and return, and I should heal them.'" (Mt 10:13-15)

The crowds assumed that their performance had some part to play in their entrance into the kingdom. After all, Jesus called for fruits in terms of changed performance to escape the temporal fires of God's wrath and His misthological displeasure. Even the lost can produce that broad kind of fruit, however.[†] Many naturally assumed that such fruits would also be necessary for salvation from the soteriological fires of Gehenna. Jesus' warning in Mt 7:21-23 is an attempt to shock those who hold such naturalistic and simplistic assumptions into reconsidering their performance-based soteriology. He confronts them with fruit in a narrow sense that cannot be produced by the lost (cp. Mt 7:13-14). Any soteriological interpretation that equates saving fruit with works in this pericope must be rejected since this is the very theology being warned against in the context. The mentality which assumes that just because fruit refers to work in some passages it must do so in this passage is confounded by the fact that Jesus rejects the people in this passage on that very basis—their works. If fruit (singular) means work, then the people in this passage were correct to appeal to their work.

The problem is that the people in this passage offer their fruits in the broad sense as the basis for their entrance and were rejected by the Fruit Inspector because to offer fruit in the broad sense opens it up to soteriological inspection. Our works will not pass soteriological inspection. It would be far better to offer up fruit in the narrow sense and tell the Fruit Inspector that your only fruit worth inspecting in terms of entering heaven is your trust in Him. Faith in Him will pass inspection because He Himself passes inspection. Such a request is to ask Him to inspect His righteousness imputed to us. His righteousness passes the test. We must avoid the common misperception that fruitfulness in the broad sense is a requirement for soteriological entrance in the narrow sense. Broad fruit will not make it through the narrow gate. To limit our understanding to that of the masses is to take the broad gate taken by many to destruction.

Illustration 214. Common Misperception of Fruitfulness

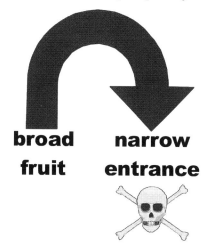

**broad   narrow
fruit   entrance**

---

[*] See *Inductive* and *Adductive*, 8-9.
[†] See *Fruitless Fig Tree*, 29.

Admittedly, the ultraistic interpretation of this passage, in which fruit is equated with works, does not result in a false gospel because the ultraistic interpretation bases one's rewards upon those works. Ultraists do not condition one's **final** entrance into the **eternal** kingdom on works. In the end, salvation from hell is not by works according to ultraistic theology. Nevertheless, the ultraistic perception is not plausible. The people in this passage are seeking entrance on the basis of their works. If kingdom entrance were by works, then they had a right to appeal to their works and expect admittance. If the passage were talking about a misthological entrance, then they had a right to appeal to their works for a karpologically-based entrance. But if it is talking about soteriological entrance, then their appeal is rightly rejected. In a soteriological context, works would disqualify rather than qualify one pertaining to entrance. And their words show that they are appealing to their works. This mistaken appeal matches Jesus' point that you will be able to discern the object of their faith by the mistaken words they say. You will know them by the fruits of their mistaken doctrine as expressed by their words.

Proverbial Limitations

A little sanctified common sense can go a long way in formulating a conclusion for this discussion of fruits in Mt 7:13-23. The proverbial premise for Jesus' didactical summations is based on the statement that "a good tree cannot produce bad fruit, nor can a bad tree produce good fruit" (Mt 7:18). Does this mean that a lost person cannot do anything relatively morally good in the broad sense of the word? No. Some lost people live morally better lives than some saved people (1Cor 5:1; 1Tim 5:8). If you were to judge such lost people on the basis of their fruits in terms of their moral performance, then you would be judging by appearance rather than with a righteous judgment, which is the very fallacy Jesus warns against (Jn 7:24). Jesus likewise cautions that in the world there would be tares that looked like wheat (Mt 13:24-30). This again makes it unwise to judge a person's regeneration by appearance and makes it intrinsically unlikely that Jesus would be advising us to judge soteriological salvation by appearance in this passage. Paul also teaches that some believers live as if they were lost (1Cor 3:3); whereas, some of the lost disguise themselves as if they were saved (2Cor 11:15). As a result, it is impossible to judge a person's soteriological status based on the broad fruits he or she produces in terms of good works. That unbelievers cannot perform any soteriologically good works in the absolute narrow sense does not mean that they cannot perform any type of good works in the broad relative sense.[*] Conversely, believers can produce bad works (2Cor 5:10). If Mt 7:20 is talking about works being infallible indications of regeneration, then it teaches instantaneous, practical, sinless perfection at the moment of regeneration, which is a blatant distortion of the Scripture.

Not only must fruits be limited to words in this passage, further boundaries limit how absolutely we can take such proverbial and parabolic images.[†] James, who is highly dependent upon the Sermon on the Mount in his epistle, uses similar parabolic allusions in describing inconsistent Christians as fig trees that produce olives rather than figs or as fountains that produce both good and bad water (Jam 3:9-12). The surprising contrast, however, is that James is not talking about inconsistency in terms of practice. In this passage, he is not referring to a discrepancy between what we do versus what we say, which is the classical definition of a hypocrite. Rather, he is dealing with the problem of inconsistency in proclamation. They were verbally blessing and verbally assaulting one another. The positive verbal response flows from our new nature; the negative one stems from our old nature.[‡] Since believers have both natures, they can produce dynamically opposed fruits. James urges believers to live lives consistent with their new natures.

Correspondingly, it is not even possible to tell with absolute certainty if someone is lost or saved based on what he or she may do or say. A believer who lives a life dominated by his or her old nature might be indistinguishable from an unbeliever who only has an old nature. Then how do we reconcile this observation with what Jesus is saying about discernment? Some would say that the *good tree* refers to our good nature. Our regenerate nature can only produce good fruit. So it is possible to maintain that a good tree only produces good fruit. Although this is true, Jesus is referring to a whole person, not just his or her nature that produces the fruit. The passage is dealing with false teachers, not contrasting natures within the same teacher. It is the person who is told to depart from Him, not just the person's nature. A holistic interpretation is preferable. Moreover, even the lost can produce good fruits in the broad, moral, relative sense of the word *good*.

A plausible explanation would be that Jesus is using a proverbial example and, as such, His analogy should be taken proverbially rather than absolutely. In this case, it would be asserted that false teachers generally teach

---

[*] See *Theory of Misthological* Relativity, 687.
[†] See also "Colloquial Proverbs-Proverbial Expectations" in *Fallen from Grace but Not from Perfection.*
[‡] See "Source Analysis" in *Soteric and Mistholic Faith.*

false doctrine but not always. In response it may be also pointed out that there is no such thing as a false teacher who does not teach false doctrine to some degree, some of the time. False teaching is the definite indicator of false teachers. Sound teaching denotes a sound teacher.

James is working from the premise that a fig tree cannot produce olives, that a good fountain cannot produce bad water, and that salt water cannot produce fresh water. Yet James acknowledges that this proverbial expectation was not being flawlessly expressed in the lives of these regenerate believers. Likewise, Jesus says that *a good tree cannot produce bad fruit*, and conversely, a bad tree cannot produce good fruit. To recast the problem in Jacobean form, "Is it possible for false teaching and sound teaching to come forth from the same teacher?" Proverbially, the answer is, "No," but experientially speaking, the answer is, "Yes." Even good teachers sometimes make mistakes. Jesus is not exhorting us to conclude naively that just because a teacher gets a number of things right that everything he or she teaches is correct. Most lies are wrapped in a deceptive amount of truth.

Jesus said concerning Satan: "Whenever he speaks a lie, he speaks from his own nature; for he is a liar, and the father of lies" (Jn 8:44). This verse does not say that whenever Satan speaks, he speaks a lie. Simply, whenever he speaks a lie, he is showing who he truly is—a liar. Likewise, whenever a wolf in sheep's clothing speaks false doctrine, he or she is revealing him or herself for what he or she really is—a false teacher. For example, when we hear someone accurately say, "Salvation is free," we should not jump to the conclusion that this teacher actually believes this is the case or that such a person is a sound teacher. A holistic interpretation means evaluating the teacher's doctrine holistically, refusing to be fooled by isolated statements. We must wait for the other proverbial shoe to drop and assess his or her doctrine systematically as a whole. If such a person were to proceed and say, "It costs you everything," then we certainly should be concerned with his or her theological consistency and biblical accuracy. It is contradictory to say that something is free but costs you everything.

With these warnings in mind, one may affirm that false doctrine infallibly indicates false belief. If you believe a false doctrine, then what you believe is false. And those who **never** have believed the true gospel are false believers. Whenever we consistently hear sound teaching from a teacher, we can correctly perceive that the teacher is sound. Whenever we hear unsound teaching, we should recognize that the teacher is unsound. Whenever someone buys into the false gospel of an unsound teacher, and as a result **never** comes to believe the true gospel, we must conclude that he or she never became a true believer. The people in this passage were duped into believing the false gospel of these false teachers and as a result never came to believe the gospel of salvation by grace apart form works. It comes as no surprise that Jesus responds to them with the words, "Depart from Me."

Singular Versus Plural Fruit

Marrowists could leave the matter at this point and be content to understand both *fruit* and *fruits* in this particular context as referring to one's words as an indication as to whether one has come to saving faith. However, this particular context strongly suggests a fine distinction between plural *fruits* and singular *fruit* so that the singular fruit produced by the good tree refers to *saving faith* as opposed to the *non-saving* faith produced by the bad tree.[*] This explains why the lost cannot produce good fruit, and why the saved cannot produce bad fruit: "A good tree *cannot produce* bad fruit, nor can a bad tree produce good fruit" (Mt 7:18). Singular good fruit is the narrow fruit that shows that one has entered the narrow gate (Mt 7:13-14). The plural good fruits do not reveal a different kind of fruit (such as a broad fruit) but multiple verbal attestations to the narrow fruit.[†]

Saving faith is the singular response to the gospel that results in the linear classification of being a good tree. Non-saving faith is a defective response to the gospel in which one remains unsaved and thus classified as a bad tree. Naturally, an unsaved person cannot exhibit saving faith. A bad tree cannot produce this good fruit. By definition, when a person exercises saving faith, that individual is saved. On the other hand, a good tree cannot exhibit *unsaving* faith. It is impossible for those who have become believers to exercise a faith that would *unsave* them. Just as there is no such word as *unsaving*, there is no such thing as *unsaving* faith—a faith that can unsave a person who has become saved. A good tree (i.e., someone who has become a believer) cannot produce a response that soteriologically will classify him or her as an unbeliever. The singular (and punctiliar) response of good fruit is associated permanently with the linear classification of being a good tree soteriologically. Anyone who has

---

[*] For discussion of cross references, see *Mere Christianity and Moral Christianity* and *Karpology*.

[†] The majority of the English texts do not concur with the Greek texts on the matter of plurality, so my comments must be judged by which text is being used as a frame of reference. My statement that plural fruits refer to multiple verbal attestations is made regarding the typical plural English rendering of Mt 7:16,20. However, the Greek plurality in Mt 7:17-18 is actually a distributive singularity. In these verses, the Greek text is referring to the singular faith of each individual with collective plurality. In other words, when attention is focused on each individual composing that collective unit, plural fruit can refer to singular fruit and thus to saving faith or to its absence. See *Mere Christianity and Moral Christianity*.

produced the good fruit (singular) of saving faith is permanently considered a good tree. Such a person cannot be reclassified as a bad tree or declassified as a good tree even if he or she stops believing.

The Arminian will object that if a bad tree can become a good tree by producing good fruit (i.e., by responding in saving faith), then a good tree can become a bad tree by producing bad fruit (i.e., by defecting from the faith). As to the protasis of this statement, certainly a bad tree can become a good tree by responding in saving faith to the gospel. An unsaved person can become saved in other words. The unsaved are no longer considered a bad tree when they respond in saving faith to the gospel. The first part of the Arminian statement is accurate.

At first glance, one might think that the Arminian objection in the apodosis would follow by logical implication and that the reverse could also be true: The saved person can become unsaved by responding with defective faith to the gospel. Marrowists will acknowledge that it is certainly possible for a saved person's faith to become defective (e.g., Gal 5:4). However, this does not mean that the saved person becomes unsaved. In logic it is well known that A $\Rightarrow$ B does not necessarily imply A $\Leftarrow$ B. In this context, the inverse is not implied. If the purpose of singular fruit is to denote whether saving faith has *ever* occurred, as seems to be the case, then the Arminian inversion is a perversion. If they had *ever* produced good fruit (singular, i.e., saving faith), then Jesus would not have said, "I *never* knew you" (Mt 7:23). A bad tree can become a good tree; otherwise, no one would ever be saved. Conversely, though, a good tree cannot become a bad tree; otherwise, Jesus would not have said, "I *never* knew you." You can never go back to being a bad tree because Jesus could never say, "I *never* knew you," if He *ever* knew you.

Multiple fruits, such as numerous apples on a single tree, do not indicate more than one kind of fruit. The typical English plural *fruits* in this context refer to the verbal expressions which indicate what kind of faith one has. The kind of faith is singular *fruit*; it is either saving or non-saving. Just as multiple fruits on a single tree indicate a singular kind of fruit tree, so multiple articulations of one's faith indicate what kind of faith one has. It is the multiple articulations by which we discern the faith of another person. Hence, it makes sense for Jesus to refer to the plurality of their fruit when He says that we *will know them by their fruits* (Mt 7:16,20). However, salvation itself is conditioned on the singular form of fruit in this context: "Every tree that does not bear good *fruit* [singular] is cut down and thrown into the fire" (Mt 7:19). Discernment is based on the plurality of one's fruit; contrastively, salvation is conditioned on the singularity of one's fruit. Naturally, salvation from eternal damnation is conditioned on saving faith, so the only reasonable deduction is that the singular form of fruit refers to saving faith.

Illustration 215. Different Kinds of Fruit

- Good fruit singular = saving faith.
- Good fruit plural = multiple, consistent, articulations of saving faith.[*]
- Good fruit narrow = saving faith (singular or plural).[†]
- Broad fruit = misthological responses to God's enabling grace (by lost or saved).[‡]

This distinction between plural fruits and singular fruit opens the door to two competing FG understandings of the passage. Plural fruits could be taken as referring either to (1) words or to (2) words and works. My bear-or-burn objection to the standard LS interpretation would not be directly applicable to this second FG approach. Salvation from burning in Mt 7:19 is conditioned on the singular fruit (i.e., saving faith). Thus, it might be tempting for some in FG to use this distinction between plural and singular fruit to pose an alternate FG view in which salvation is conditioned on faith alone (singular fruit), but to take both works and words as joint indicators as to whether a teacher believes the message of faith alone. In other words, entrance into the narrow gate would be conditioned exclusively on the narrow, singular fruit of salvation by faith alone, but the discernment of false teachers would be based on both their faith and works. In view of the discussion above, however, I find this FG alternative incompatible with the context. Why would Jesus use works as an indicator of saving faith in a passage in which He is denouncing works as an object of saving faith? How can you base your discernment of another person's salvation on his or her works and yet not base your own assurance on works? Since works play no role in discerning your own salvation, they cannot be expected to have a role in discerning the salvation of another.

---

[*] In the typical English text.
[†] Narrow fruit would include saving faith itself and the verbal affirmations of saving faith.
[‡] See *Illustration 11. Broad Fruit*, 29.

Illustration 216. Narrow Fruit

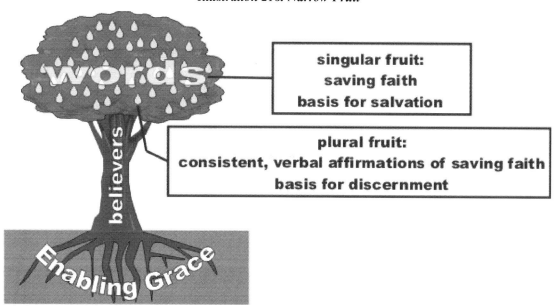

It is better to stick with the view that plural fruits refers exclusively to the words as the indicator as to what kind of singular fruit is being proclaimed or believed. Our **words** indicate what kind of faith we have: saving faith or non-saving faith. **Works** would not be an appropriate indicator as to whether one believes in salvation by faith alone. It is inconsistent to claim that works determine if one believes in salvation by faith without works. Saving faith is something we produce.[*] The moment we produce this passive response we are considered good trees who have done the will of the Father by having done everything necessary to enter the narrow gate.

Sunday School Summary

While attending a Sunday School class at a Southern Baptist church that was teaching through the Sermon on the Mount, the author was not surprised to hear the teacher assert that the narrow gate and path refer to the way we live as Christians. This Sunday School teacher then supported her conclusion from the next section in the Sermon on the Mount by claiming that the fruit of the good tree is the way we live as Christians. No surprise there. This is the standard type of teaching the present author has heard time and again for many years from many Southern Baptist pulpits and in corresponding Sunday School classes.

After this standard overview by the Sunday School teacher, the author posed a series of questions, such as: "If the narrow gate and path and the good fruits refer to the way we live as Christians, then is not our salvation from hell in this passage conditioned on the way we live as Christians?" After all, what is at stake in the context is destruction and fire versus life and kingdom entrance. "And if it is true in this passage that the way we live as Christians determines whether we will go to heaven versus hell, then is it not also true that the passage teaches salvation by works?" Of course, such questions sent the Sunday School presentation into a tailspin. It is interesting to watch the creative maneuvering that teachers invoke in order to avoid the logical conclusions of their own interpretations. Oh, what a tangled web had been spun by this *way-we-live* interpretation, as evidenced by the confusing tailspin that ensued! When the Sunday School teacher's argument crashed into the conclusion to which it was heading, she acknowledged that she did not believe in eternal security. Doing so was the only way she could maintain the presentation she had given. She then appealed to another lady in the class who was very clear in her denunciation of OSAS. They, like other members in the class and church, claimed that this passage rules out the possibility of carnal believers. As an alternative, the author then offered a simple Sunday-School-level interpretation of the passage that would be in harmony with unconditional security:

- Narrow Gate = Saving Faith (in the narrow path)
- Narrow Path = Christ
- Good Tree = person who produces saving faith
- Good Fruit = Saving Faith (i.e., trust in Christ alone for unconditional security)

---

[*] See "Not of Yourselves" in *Soteric and Mistholic Faith*.

Illustration 217. Narrow Gate

The narrow gate is faith in the narrow path, and the narrow path is Christ alone. Therefore, entrance is conditioned on faith alone in Christ alone. This simplistic summary resulted in some in the class acknowledging that the passage could be interpreted in a manner consistent with unconditional security. In this *what-we-believe* interpretation, whether a person goes to heaven or hell would not be conditioned on the way he or she lives after he or she becomes a believer. Thus, to speak at a Sunday School level, as the author did on that occasion, Jesus conditions entering into life (Mt 7:13-14) and into the kingdom of heaven (Mt 7:21) on the narrow way we take and on the fruit we produce. This poses no problem for FG theology. Those who enter the narrow gate by trusting in the narrow path for eternal life will enter the kingdom of heaven. In other words, those who come to saving faith by trusting in Christ alone for eternal life will enter heaven. The narrow gate is saving faith, and the narrow path is Christ. Those who come to saving faith in Christ are saved unconditionally from hell the moment they enter that gate (i.e., the moment they come to trust in Christ alone for unconditional security). In contrast, those who trust in the way they live the Christian life for entrance into heaven are indeed seeking entrance by the *broad gate* and the *broad path* (i.e., by non-saving faith in salvation by works).

- Broad Gate = Non-saving Faith (in the broad path)
- Broad Path = salvation by works
- Bad Tree = person who produces non-saving faith
- Bad Fruit = Non-saving Faith (i.e., trust in Christ for conditional security)

Illustration 218. Broad Gate

The broad gate is faith in the broad path, and the broad path is Christ plus performance. Therefore, entrance is conditioned on faith in both Christ and the way one lives. This *way-we-live* interpretation is the broad path that leads to hell. The author told the class that he did not believe that his security was conditioned on the way he lives or the fruits he produces. Unfortunately, most of the author's fellow Southern Baptists see the matter quite differently. Although they would deny that they are wolves in sheep's clothing who are conditioning entrance into heaven on the way they live as Christians, this is the conclusion to which their teaching logically leads. They are producing bad fruits (i.e., bad doctrine that leads to hell) by teaching salvation by works even though they emphatically will claim that their *way-we-live* interpretation is not salvation by works.[*]

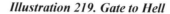

Illustration 219. Gate to Hell

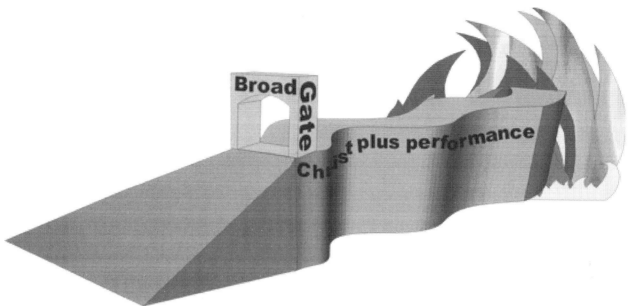

In teaching that carnal believers go to hell because there is no place in heaven for carnal believers, such teachers of works-righteousness have consigned themselves to a path that leads to hell. At least on this occasion, those present in the class could see that their position required a rejection of unconditional security. However, this is more than many wolves in sheep's clothing can perceive. Quite frequently, when the mirror of logical deduction from God's word is held up in front of many Baptist wolves in sheep's clothing, they tend look in the mirror and only see a sheep—a sheep that believes OSAS at that! They cannot see themselves for what they are: Wolves that believe in a security conditioned on their works.

Judas' Apparent Apostasy

Apostate Friend

When Zeller pulls Judas out as his ace in an attempt to refute unconditional security, he imagines that he has posed an insurmountable objection to the unconditional security approach taken by Hodges and Dillow. Hodges had related an instance in which he had a good friend who defected from the faith and left the doctrinal position he once held, after his wife died as a result of a prolonged illness. This friend eventually denied the Christian faith because of his wife's death. From the FG perspective, a believer who later defects from the path of the straight and narrow remains saved. Zeller objects by claiming that consistency requires that those taking the FG interpretation must reject Hodges' affirmation that his friend was saved: "If we consistently apply this [doctrinal] test, then the man given in Hodges' example must be unregenerate....Why was Judas more of an apostate than the man in Hodges' illustration?"[1110]

Zeller's objection is rather shortsighted in that it fails to consider the full scope of possibilities and scriptural implications. Those who teach false doctrine are false teachers. Those who teach a false gospel show by that teaching that they do not believe the genuine gospel. On the other hand, those who teach a true gospel thereby indicate that they believe the gospel and are genuine believers. Hodges' assessment of his friend's condition is

---

[*] Also, see applications of these illustrations to a related discussion in Appendix 1 of *Wooly Wolves and Woolless Sheep.*

consistent with Mt 7:20. At the point in his life when Hodges' friend taught and believed the gospel, Mt 7:20 would lead one to conclude that his friend was indeed a true believer. Only a good tree can produce good fruit. Only a genuine believer can produce saving faith. As far as Mt 7:20 is concerned, when Hodges' friend later rejected the gospel, one would likewise conclude that his friend was functionally **no longer** a true believer but had now become a false teacher.*

A bad teacher produces bad teaching. Nothing in Mt 7:20 itself precludes the understanding that the friend in question believed at one time and then stopped believing. After all, the question will be asked, "If a bad tree can become a good tree, then could not a good tree become a bad tree?" That is, since an unbeliever can become a believer could not a believer become an unbeliever? If the verse is taken in isolation, perhaps one might see how it would be possible to derive an Arminian interpretation. Nevertheless, even if there is some potential truth to the Arminian argument previously considered about the possibility of a good tree becoming a bad tree, it is not the whole truth, especially when the verse is interpreted in its context.

Ontological Wolves

The soteriological rejection in Mt 7:23 is limited to those who *never* believed. After all, Jesus said, "I never knew you." Such a statement could not be applicable to those who used to believe. This Matthean passage is not intended to depict every possible permutation of false teaching. Those teachers who abandon the true gospel of salvation by faith alone for a false gospel of salvation by faith and works are sheep who become **functional wolves** in sheep's clothing. The passage does not address this possibility but rather is limited to describing those who are **ontological wolves** in sheep's clothing, since it is dealing with those who *never* came to saving faith.

On the other hand, other passages describe the alternate reality of carnivorous sheep who "bite and devour one another" (Gal 5:15). According to Paul, wolves are not the only creatures capable of biting the sheep. In functional terms, believers are quite capable of becoming wolves either morally or theologically. To enjoin both possibilities, one might say: "Beware not only of wolves in sheep's clothing but also of sheep in wolves' clothing." Both bite! Regenerate sheep can turn into functional wolves: *regenerate werewolves*. They are sheep that function like wolves. These sheep in wolf's skin bite. One wonders if Paul does not envision some such monstrosities in Acts 20:28-30. The BBE translates the latter two verses of that passage as, "I am conscious that after I am gone, evil wolves will come in among you [i.e., from the outside], doing damage to the flock; and from among yourselves [i.e., from the inside] will come men who will *give wrong teaching* [*diastrepho*], turning away the disciples after them."[1111]

Illustration 220. Carnivorous Sheep

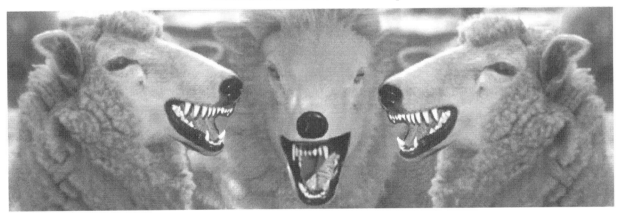

According to Paul, wolves would not only attack the flock from without but, additionally, from within their own ranks (i.e., within the flock). Defectors would become infectors who would draw away disciples to follow them. When someone leaves FG to become a teacher of LS, he or she becomes such a creature—a theological hybrid—a regenerate sheep in wolf's skin that acts like a wolf in sheep's skin. This functional wolf now infects other believers with his or her venomous teaching. A flock of sheep can become a pack of wolves—functionally speaking. Nevertheless, as noted above concerning Mt 7:18, they cannot produce bad fruit [singular] in that they

---

* From the premise of unconditional security adopted within this book, such a person would still retain regeneration even if that person no longer truly believes, and therefore still be classified as a believer (in terms of regenerative result) even if he no longer believes.

cannot do anything that would cause them to lose their regeneration. Ontologically, they remain a good tree. Otherwise, Jesus could not say, "I **never** knew you" (Mt 7:23). They cannot produce unsaving fruit.

Hodges' friend must still be considered a good tree because he had produced good fruit (singular), as evidenced by his initial good fruits (plural). The fact that he functionally produced bad fruits (plural) subsequently should not be taken to indicate that he had never produced good fruit previously or that he was now producing bad fruit ontologically. A good tree cannot produce bad fruit. This soteriological inability demonstrates ontological irreversibility—a fact which Jesus highlights with the word *never*.

To be sure, it will still be objected that since Jesus says, "You will know them by their fruits," one can indeed know whether others are saved soteriologically (from the destruction and fire in this passage) by the plural fruits they bear. The Arminian will say that those believers who go from producing good fruits to producing bad fruits cease to be good trees. And the Calvinist will claim that those believers who fall into this category were never good trees to start with. The Arminian is refuted by Jesus' word *never*, and the Calvinist is refuted by Jesus' affirmation that you will know them by their fruits. Jesus' statement of discernment does not exclude initial fruits.

The tension encountered by both theological approaches is found in those cases where the good tree becomes a bad tree in terms of the plural fruits it produces. The Marrowistic solution is to recognize that functional discernment cannot always be equated with ontological identity. Certainly, Jesus would expect us to recognize this fact (knowing that we pragmatically would encounter such occasions of inconsistency), and He supplies us with the word *never* to put us on the right path so that we may resolve the apparent conflict with logical coherency. Functional discernment can only reveal functional identity. The pragmatic discrepancy that we encounter when a good tree becomes a bad tree is to be explained by the divergence of the functional form from the immutable ontological reality. Christ's words remain true both functionally and ontologically. A believer can be a functional wolf in sheep's clothing. But a good tree cannot ontologically produce bad fruit. The problems interpreters seek to impose upon the text when they try to apply it to a situation Christ did not intend (as in the case of a good tree becoming bad) are self-imposed and rejected by Christ's use of the word *never*. By this word, the Lord signifies that He does not intend for His equivalence between functional and ontological identity to be applied to such cases. Jesus Himself thus provides an internal interpretive clue by which to limit the scope of His application to those situations in which it may be reasonably assumed that the verbal affirmations matches the reality of the internal transformation that takes place when one enters Him as the door that leads to heaven. Unfortunately, however, although those participating in that Sunday School class could perceive that Jesus is the door that is entered by saving faith (Jn 10:9), they could not bring themselves to acknowledge that Christ is the narrow path that one enters by the narrow gate of saving faith.

Some ≠ Many

As to Judas, sufficient grounds from Scripture are available for concluding that Judas *never* believed, as John informs us: "'But there are **some** of you who do not believe.' For Jesus knew from the beginning who they were who did not believe, and who it was that would betray Him" (Jn 6:64). On this occasion, Jesus is addressing a large group of His disciples, (1) some who believe, (2) some who are beginning to disbelieve (Jn 6:60-61), and (3) some who never believed *from the beginning* (Jn 6:64). "**Many** of His disciples" abandon Him at this juncture (Jn 6:66). The most natural inference, therefore, is that of the **many** who apostatized, only **some** of them never had believed. The others who abandoned Him stopped believing. Judas is a subset of the some who did not believe from the beginning. They, in turn, are a partial subset of those who abandon Jesus.[*] This conclusion concerning Judas is confirmed when Jesus indicates that Judas had not previously experienced the bath of regeneration (Jn 13:10-11). The logical deduction is that Judas *never* had believed.

Apparent Apostasy

From the beginning, Jesus knew which of His followers were unbelievers. These followers were not believers from the beginning, meaning they never believed. The articular participle used in this verse for those who do not believe may be taken simply as a substantive and translated as *not believers* or *unbelievers*. Jesus knew which of them were not believers (i.e., unbelievers) from the beginning. Judas was classified as an unbeliever from the beginning. This deduction is supported by John's later use of *apoleia* and *apollumi* in reference to Judas in a soteriological context as the son of *perdition* who *perished* (Jn 17:12). Zeller misconstrues these terms in thinking that since these words soteriologically pertain to Judas, they must be soteriological when used elsewhere regardless

---

[*] See *Unbelieving Judas*, 350. Also, see the Judas exception clause in *The Race of Grace*.

of the context (e.g., Heb 10:39).[*] To the contrary, it is a fallacy to conclude that anyone who commits apostasy or experiences destruction must be lumped together with Judas to either the same degree or kind. Judas is an example of *apparent apostasy*, not *real apostasy*. Judas never really believed, so he never really left his faith. He never had saving faith in Jesus at the beginning. On the other hand, Marrowists recognize that real apostasy is a real possibility in Scripture. Genuine believers can stop believing and thereby commit real apostasy.

Stop ≠ Never

Can believers read the Bible and then stop reading it? Of course. Is it possible to memorize the Bible and then stop memorizing it? Certainly. Can one believe the Bible and then stop believing it? Definitely. Yet Zeller would have us believe something quite strange: If a believer stops believing, then the believer never believed. Does this mean that if a believer stops memorizing the Bible, the believer never memorized it? Or if a believer stops reading the Bible, does this prove that he or she had never read the Bible before? Zeller's proveitistic conclusion is as illogical as it is unbiblical. The genuine biblical conclusion would be that genuine believers can stop believing. Hodges' friend who left the faith may indeed have experienced genuine apostasy and may end up in the outer darkness as a result. Judas, though, only experienced apparent apostasy and is in hell as a result. False believers can only experience false apostasy; genuine believers can experience genuine apostasy. The warnings in the Bible urging believers not to commit apostasy are not addressed to unbelievers. The concern in such passages is that genuine believers might commit genuine apostasy, not that false believers might commit false apostasy.

Conclusion

The contrast between the *many* and the *few* in Mt 7:13-14,22 shows that the **majority** of professing believers within the church will be excluded from life in the kingdom. The majority will have been duped into believing the false gospel of Lordship Salvation, seeking a performance-based entrance. To those who never believed the true gospel, Jesus will say, "I never knew you."

Illustration 221. Broad Way

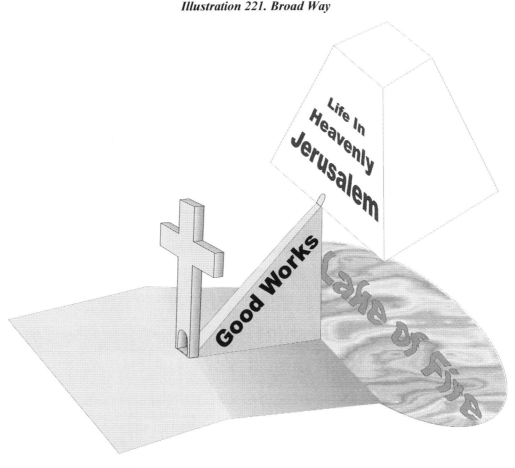

---

[*] For interaction with Zeller's assessment of *apollumi* and *apoleia*, see endnote 265.

The typical impression one receives from LS teachers is that Christ is the entrance into a grueling straight and narrow uphill climb that one must successfully complete in order to eventually reach life in heaven.* Arminians believe that if you fall off the straight and narrow path, then you must reenter the gate and start all over again; otherwise, you ultimately will be cast into the Lake of Fire. But this fall may be fatal. For example, depending on how high the cliff is from which one falls, one might twist an ankle or break a leg, making it difficult to return to the climb. Or even worse, climbers might break their backs or their necks and not be able to return to climbing. Likewise, it might be impossible for believers to be converted again (Heb 6:4-6). This Arminian theology might picture the straight and narrow path as having cliffs on both sides.

Advocates of eternal security frequently point out that Jesus says to those cast into the fire, "I **never** knew you." The problem is not that those cast into the fire were saved and then lost their salvation. On the contrary, they were never saved to begin with. For this reason, Calvinists will claim that if a believer falls from the straight and narrow path, then that believer was never saved to start with. But this answer is no better than that of the Arminians. To fall from something that one has never been on is impossible. For example, when the author was younger, he rode a horse on which the saddle had not been fastened securely. As the horse began galloping, the saddle began twisting further and further to the side until the author finally fell off. His wife, on the contrary, has never fallen off a horse. Does mean that she is a better rider? No, just that she has never been on a horse! You cannot fall off of something you have never been on. The Calvinistic gospel of perseverance is just as performance based as that of the Arminians, but it further suffers from the absurdity of warning us against falling from something that we were never on to start with. Calvinists picture the straight and narrow path as having psychological cliffs on both sides. If you fall off the path, then you were never on the path to start with—you just thought you were.

To avoid this psycho-absurdity, Calvinists will sometimes water down their theology by claiming that true believers may lapse temporary into a carnal lifestyle but not permanently so. Their claim is that genuine believers will not permanently or completely fall from the straight and narrow way. This theology conceives of the straight and narrow path as a slippery slope that only genuine believers eventually will climb successfully. You might slide back down when you hit a slick spot, but you will not slide back out of the gate. God will give you helpful boosts to make sure you eventually make it. Evidently, He does not give these boosts to the nonelect. Yet one wonders, "What are the nonelect doing on this Calvinistic synergistic treadmill since in Calvinistic theology the gate is only open to the elect?" It is very inconsistent for Calvinists to say that God gives those who are spiritually dead the temporary desire to be saved and then claim that the spiritually dead cannot desire to be saved.

Illustration 222. Narrow Way

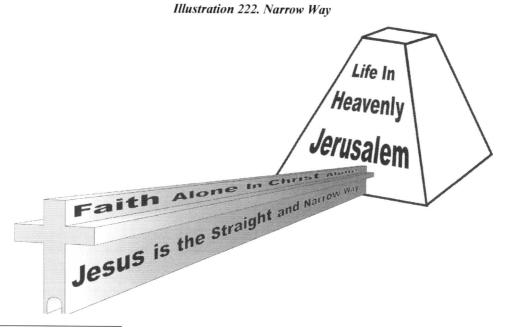

_____

* In accordance with the typical soteriological assumptions made within conditionalism, Heavenly Jerusalem is being used strictly in a soteric capacity in this faulty illustration. By adding the outer darkness as a misthological option, however, a misthologist might use a similar illustration correctly. In that case, reaching Heavenly Jerusalem would be a mistholic attainment. For such an illustration, see *Like a Tree Planted by the Water.*

   A far superior representation of this passage is readily available in picturing Jesus Himself as the straight and narrow way through which one enters heaven.* After all, He did identify Himself as such on other occasions, with similar metaphors pertaining to kingdom entrance. "Jesus said to him, '**I am the way**, and the truth, and the life; no one comes to the Father, but through Me'" (Jn 14:6). "Truly, truly, I say to you, **I am the door** of the sheep.... **I am the door**; if anyone enters through Me, he shall be saved" (Jn 10:7-9). We may likewise understand Jesus as saying, "I am the straight and narrow way through which one enters heaven." As soon as a person enters this gate, he or she has eternal life (Jn 5:24). A believer does not have to wait until he or she reaches heaven to receive it. Believers are assured of reaching heaven because of their position in Christ, rather than because of their performance in Christ. They are placed on a conveyor belt from which they cannot fall and from which they cannot escape that will take them straight to heaven because they have eternal life. It is a conveyor belt, not a treadmill, much less an uphill treadmill. As far as their position (security) in Christ and their entrance into heaven are concerned, believers passively let the conveyor belt do all the work in taking them to heaven.

   This passage is well suited to FG theology. Arminian and Calvinistic schemes, in contrast, find it impossible to deny a synergistic performance-based soteriological entrance into heaven and trip over the word *never*. Ultraists are also refuted by the absoluteness of the word *never*. Jesus is not talking about believers who used to be faithful and then slipped in that faithfulness. The people in this passage never had a relationship with the Lord. Granted, ultraists can respond that these people are carnal and never reached mature sonship status, so Jesus is here disavowing any intimate association with them. On the other hand, a performance-based misthological entrance is rendered unlikely since this is the very type of entrance that is being rejected. If works were the basis for entrance, then we would have expected this sincere appeal to works to have resulted in entrance. Since works are the basis for the exclusion instead, a misthological entrance is highly unlikely. As a result, the conservative FG soteriological understanding of this passage is strongly to be preferred.

---

* Even a misthopoligist can allow the soteric implementation of Heavenly Jerusalem in this illustration if it is acknowledged that all raptured believers freely enter the city at the time of the rapture. Expulsion from the city only becomes a misthological issue after the Bema. Therefore, for sake of simplicity, the city is being allowed to represent heaven in this illustration in accordance with this working model of the interim state.

Chapter 27.
Cut It Off to Enter the Kingdom

Introduction

In the previous chapter, mention was made that a response to the ultraistic position concerning Gehenna would require treatment of eight passages: Mt 5:20-22, 29-30; 7:21-23; 10:28; 18:3-9; 19:23-24; Jn 3:5; Acts 14:22. Two of these passages from the Sermon on the Mount were then discussed. It was noted that what is at stake is either entrance into the kingdom or Gehenna (Mt 5:19-22). The impression derived from Mt 5:19-20 was that entrance into the kingdom saves one from entrance into Gehenna. The ultraistic position is that (1) only overcomers enter the kingdom (since what is being referred to is the millennial kingdom) and (2) subcomers enter Gehenna. The conservative position is that all believers enter the kingdom, and no believer enters Gehenna. The conservative position was taken because at least three basic groups are referred to in the passage: noncomers, subcomers, and overcomers. Subcomers are least in the kingdom, but at least they are in the kingdom. So unfaithful believers are not excluded from being in the kingdom.

Whipple assumes that those who are least *in* the kingdom are *outside* the kingdom.[1112] However, maintaining that they are both in and outside the same location appears contradictory. It might be presumed that they were in it initially, as in the case of the man in the wedding feast who subsequently was thrown out of the feast, yet the antithetical parallelism between being called *great* versus *least* in the kingdom suggests that both groups are in the kingdom.

Faust, on the other hand, is self-consistent in posing two different groups of subcomers: one group who breaks the least commandments and another group who breaks the greater commandments. From this vantage point he can argue that those who break the least commandments will be in the kingdom, but those who break the greater commandments will be excluded from the kingdom. Still, even his perspective is refuted by the parabolic description in which the unfaithful slave is thrown into the darkness outside the banquet hall, not outside the kingdom. Also, the time periods in which the infractions occur would suggest that breaking some of the least commands in the millennial kingdom could be equivalent to breaking some of the greatest commandments in the present church age. If the former is not punishable with Gehenna, as Faust concedes, then it is reasonable to conclude that the latter is not also.

The better option is to contrast the three basic groups as: faithful, unfaithful, and faithless (using *faithless* to mean without faith, i.e., unbeliever). The parallelism of Mt 7:13-20 with similar texts (i.e., Mt 12:33-37; 16:6-12; Jn 6:26-40; 10:7-13) strongly indicates that the entrance in question is accomplished by a singular response of faith rather than by a life of faithfulness. This conclusion is further supported by Mt 21:21-32 and probably by Mt 18:3 as well. Although Matthew is a gospel of discipleship, the presupposition of its soteriological harmony with GJ leads to a conservative FG misthology.

Progressing now to the context of Mt 18:3, we encounter one of the famous *cut it off* passages. Also, within Mt 5:19-22 and its context (5:28-30) is a similar *cut it off* passage. A discussion of *cut it off* in Mt 18:1-11 basically will suffice for a discussion of Mt 5:28-30 and also be adequate for a discussion of the parallel passage in Mk 9:42-49. These texts, particularly Mt 18:1-11, are where the ultraists have their strongest case—since these passages seem to indicate that it is possible for believers to be cast into Gehenna.[1113] For this reason, I can sympathize with Dillow's more recent attempt to make Gehenna a misthological, albeit metaphorical, theme.[*] And it should be recalled, first of all, that not all of the Lord's sayings were intended to be taken literally (e.g. Jn 2:18-21; 6:51-58; 10:6; 11:11-14; 16:25). Literal interpretation is not the major problem in most passages, though, at least not in this passage. The passage is to be taken seriously but not literally. Still, in order to take it seriously, we must have an idea of what it means. There are four major interpretations: Arminian, Calvinistic, ultraistic FG, and conservative FG.

[1]At that time the disciples came to Jesus, saying, "Who then is **greatest in the kingdom** of heaven?" [2]And He called a child to Himself and set him before them, [3]and said, "Truly I say to you, unless you are **converted** and become like children, you shall not **enter the kingdom** of heaven. [4]Whoever then humbles himself as this child, he is the **greatest in the kingdom** of heaven. [5]And whoever receives one such child in My name receives Me; [6]but whoever causes one of these little

---

[*] See *The Entrance of Mt 5:20*, 595.

ones who **believe** in Me to stumble, it is better for him that a heavy millstone be hung around his neck, and that he be drowned in the depth of the sea.

⁷Woe to the world because of its stumbling blocks! For it is inevitable that stumbling blocks come; but woe to that man through whom the stumbling block comes! ⁸And if your hand or your foot causes you to stumble, **cut it off** and throw it from you; it is better for you to **enter life** crippled or lame, than having two hands or two feet, to be **cast into the eternal fire**. ⁹And if your eye causes you to stumble, pluck it out, and throw it from you. It is better for you to **enter life** with one eye, than having two eyes, to be **cast into the fiery hell [Gehenna]**. ¹⁰See that you do not despise one of these little ones, for I say to you, that their angels in heaven continually behold the face of My Father who is in heaven. ¹¹For the Son of Man has come to **save** that which was **lost**." (Mt 18:1-11)

Calvinistic

The first interpretation pictured below (*Earn It*) notices who is being addressed and assumes that some of the disciples are lost (v. 11). Accordingly, Jn 6:64-65 would be appropriate to keep in mind here. Some things Jesus spoke to His followers were due to the presence of unbelieving disciples. At the very least, this was a warning to Judas about the danger of hell. So Jesus is presumed frequently to be calling for radical discipleship as necessary evidence of regeneration. The problem with this proveitistic interpretation is that it teaches that the gift of eternal life is not a gift. Retaining this gift is Calvinistically costly. To *enter life*, and thus into heaven, in this passage may cost you your hand, foot, or eye. The gift is costly (and thus not a gift). This Calvinistic interpretation is an accursed gospel. Biblically and logically, works cannot be required to earn the free gift of eternal life.

Illustration 223. The Crippled Life

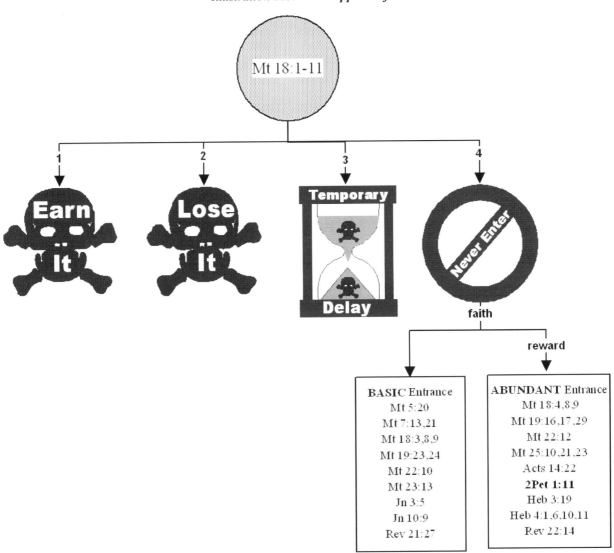

BASIC Entrance
Mt 5:20
Mt 7:13,21
Mt 18:3,8,9
Mt 19:23,24
Mt 22:10
Mt 23:13
Jn 3:5
Jn 10:9
Rev 21:27

ABUNDANT Entrance
Mt 18:4,8,9
Mt 19:16,17,29
Mt 22:12
Mt 25:10,21,23
Acts 14:22
2Pet 1:11
Heb 3:19
Heb 4:1,6,10,11
Rev 22:14

Arminian

To the credit of the second interpretation pictured above (*Lose It*), attention is given to who is being addressed—the disciples (v. 1). Thus, *you* and *your* throughout Mt 18:1-11 refer to the disciples. Arminians claim that Jesus is warning them that they might lose the gift of eternal life. But if that is the case, then eternal life is not eternal. The problem with the Arminian interpretation is that it teaches that the reception of the gift of eternal life does not impart eternal benefits. Entrance into heaven is conditioned on one's perseverance and thus is based on works. Therefore, the Arminian version is an accursed gospel and must be rejected. We cannot lose the gift of eternal life.

NOSAS certainly will persist in insisting that we can lose or return the gift of eternal life, along with other soteriological gifts. Nevertheless, the very nature of the gifts and the Giver make this impossible. The life God gives us is eternal life. Therefore, it cannot be lost. To be sure, eternal life has dual dimensions of quality and quantity.[*] Although the quality may fluctuate and be experienced in degrees, the same is not true of its quantity. Quantitatively, this life is eternal in its duration. Qualitatively, eternal life is misthological in its variation, yet there is a limitation to its minimization so that it cannot be reduced to something less than vivification. The qualitative-quantitative bond is wrongly dissolved to form conditional security when one illegitimately poses eternal life as one without the other.[1114] Better soteriological options are available for interpreting this passage.

- The present quantitative possession of *eternal* life given in response to initial faith is a gift.
- The future qualitative experience of eternal *life* given in response to linear works is a reward.

Works are not required to keep the gift of eternal life. Unconditional security maintains that eternal life is quantitatively eternal and qualitatively life. Moreover, since this duality is bestowed as a free gift independent of performance, separating them because of performance is impossible. One is not free to reduce eternal life to something that is not eternal or that is not life. Eternal life must be eternal, and it must be life. If it is missing either component, then it is not eternal life. If either component is removed because of performance (by setting that dimension to zero for example), then this life was never a free gift.

- The qualitative dimension is dynamic but never reduces to zero.
- The quantitative dimension is static and never approaches zero.

Ultraistic Grace

The first two interpretations (#1 and #2) *Illustration 223* are deadly distortions of the gospel, since they teach that salvation from eternal damnation is conditioned on works. In this perversion, eternal life reduces to zero if you fail to persevere. This theology is promoted by wolves in sheep's clothing. They have good works but bad theology. The second two interpretations (#3 and #4) are offered by those in the FG camp, in recognition that the gift of eternal salvation is by grace rather than by works. The first of these two FG interpretations (the third interpretation on the chart—*Temporary Delay*) teaches that the gift of eternal life will save a believer from the eternal flames of the Lake of Fire, but not from the flames of Gehenna (or Hades). Entrance into the kingdom may be delayed by 1000 years for such a believer. This ultraistic interpretation is rejected herein for the following reasons.

Never

Jesus has said that He will never abandon us, and Hades is a place of abandonment. The NT quotes David's description of Hades as a place of abandonment, "Thou shalt not abandon my soul to Hades" (Acts 2:27). Prophetically, David was looking to Christ's death on the cross and claiming that Christ would not be abandoned when He reached Hades. Jesus did not have to wait until He got to Hades to experience this abandonment. This is the same Greek word (*egkataleipo*) that Jesus used when He cried out on the cross, "My God, My God, why hast Thou *forsaken* [*abandoned*] Me" (Mt 27:46). Jesus experienced this abandonment on the cross so that we never would have to experience it.

The writer of Hebrews confirms this to be the case when he uses the same Greek word to record Jesus' promise to us, "I will **never** leave you, nor will I ever *forsake* [*abandon*] you" (Heb 13:5).[1115] The Greek here for *never* is the emphatic negative *ou me*. As was shown previously, this construction can be used as a litotetic

---

[*] See *Illustration 258. Quality versus Quantity*, 725.

affirmation of eternal security for those who have *eternal (aionios)* life.[*] They will never perish. Even if it merely meant *millennial* life, then it would still affirm assurance of millennial security! Millennial exclusion would be ruled out. From the moment of inception of this life, those who possess it are assured that they will never perish—not even for one day, much less for 1000 years!

Plainly put, **never** means *never*. The Lord will never abandon us to Hades or Gehenna. He already has finished His business in Hades and led the captives free. It is finished. He is not going to have to do it twice. Paradise has been removed from Hades so that Hades no longer has two compartments.[†] Seemingly, the ultraistic view would have to equate being thrown into Hades with being thrown into Gehenna now during the current time or at the Bema. But believers no longer go to a subterranean compartment in the center of the earth. Instead, they go to be with Lord in paradise in the Heavenly Jerusalem.

The problem for the ultraistic position is even more pronounced, however, by the presence of *ou me* in supposedly supporting ultraistic texts. I follow BDAG in translating *ou me* as *never* in Mt 5:20. For that matter, in both Mt 5:20 and 18:3, Jesus says that we will *never* enter the kingdom unless we meet these requirements. This emphatic negation bars the door on ultraists making these requirements misthological conditions to enter the kingdom eventually. No! Those who fail to meet these soteriological requirements will never enter the kingdom—neither the millennial or eternal form of the kingdom.

Jesus uses *ou me* soteriologically to promise believers that they will *never* thirst (Jn 4:14; 6:35), *never* be cast out (Jn 6:37), *never* die (8:51-52; 11:26), and *never* perish (Jn 10:28). Likewise, Jesus uses *ou me* soteriologically to warn those who do not believe that they will never enter the kingdom. To be sure, Jesus can use *ou me* to warn of misthological exclusion—because it is permanent! The believer who refuses to submit to practical sanctification will *never* have a misthological portion with Jesus (Jn 13:8).

Always

Not only does *never* mean *never*, but **always** means *always*. Paul has promised that when we are united with the Lord Jesus immediately after death or after the rapture, "We shall *always* [*pantote*] be with the Lord" (1Thess 4:17). Jesus is not taking us back to heaven to be with Him and then throw some of us into Gehenna after the Judgment Seat of Christ. The Greek word used here means *always*, that is, at *all times*. A 1000-year exception is not envisioned.

Eternal

Not only does *always* mean *always*, but **eternal** means *eternal*. Matthew (18:8) says that this fire is *eternal (aionios)*.[‡] *Eternal* means *forever*. Matthew earlier had described this fire in 3:12 as being unquenchable. This fire cannot be put out and what is put into it cannot get out. And in Mt 13:40 He said that this fire is a consuming fire. Consuming does not mean that what is put into it ceases to exist, as Jesus makes clear two verses later when He says that there is weeping and gnashing of teeth going on in that furnace of fire. Consuming means that nothing is saved from it. What is put into it is in it to stay eternally. It never gets out. This is confirmed by the picture of fire in Rev 14:11, "And the smoke of their torment goes up forever and ever; and they have no rest day and night." There is no escape.[§]

No Exceptions

Further confirmation of this truth may be found in Rev 20:13-14, which pictures the dead in Hades being thrown into the fire of the lake. They have not ceased to exist in spite of the fact that they were in the fire of Hades. They are still present to be thrown into the Lake of Fire. Rev 20:13-14 tells us that those who are in Hades at the end of the Millennium are thrown into the Lake of Fire. No exceptions are mentioned. So why think that some of them are carnal believers being allowed to come back to the Lord? On the contrary, those who are in Hades (and thus eventually thrown into Hell) are said specifically not to have had their name in the Book of Life in Rev 20:15. They were never believers. Their name was never written there.

---

[*] See *The Believer's Security*, 486.
[†] See *Appendix 9. Hades Versus Paradise*, p. 825.
[‡] See discussion surrounding *Aionios*, 520.
[§] See *Fire*, 665. Or for full discussion, see *Appendix 7. The Unquenchable Eternal Fire*, 803.

No Burning Wheat

That believers are not thrown into this literal fire is also confirmed by Mt 3:12, where it is said that the wheat goes into the barn and the chaff into the fire. The wheat goes to one place and the chaff to another. There is no idea of casting some of the wheat into the fire and then later taking it out to put into the barn. The same can be said of Mt 13:39. The fire is for the tares, not for the wheat nor for the sons of the kingdom (Mt 13:38). As Paul affirmed of all believers, you become a "son of God through faith in Christ" (Gal 3:26). Those who have come to faith in Christ are not tares or chaff; their names are in the Book of Life; they will never be thrown into the literal fire of Hades or Hell. God never will be guilty of child abandonment! Not for a day, a month, a year, much less for a 1000 years.

Secure in His Hand

Some ultraists acknowledge that believers either mystically or positionally enter the kingdom the moment we believe. In that moment, we are given eternal life and thus eternally placed in Jesus' kingdom and in His hand (Jn 10:28-29). Consequently, the natural conclusion would be that we are not thrown out of the kingdom at the Bema for 1000 years before being let back into it. God does not take eternal life from us for 1000 years or throw us out of His hand or kingdom for 1000 years. Even if we get out of hand morally, we *never* get out of His hand soteriologically (Jn 10:28). He will never cast us out soteriologically (Jn 6:37). We never experience the same eschatological judgment that the lost do (Jn 5:24). Therefore, this ultra-misthological position is garbled in that it teaches that we can share the same soteriological fate as unbelievers do for 1000 years because of poor performance. Even so, ultraism is not nearly as perverted as the Arminian or Calvinistic interpretations that teach that we can share the fate of the lost for eternity.

Conservative Grace

All three of these above interpretations are distortions of the saving efficacy of the gospel. Simple faith in Christ will save believers from sharing the same fate as unbelievers. Those in the misthological camp can acknowledge that in some passages eternal life is a gift and in some passages eternal life is not a gift. This is not a contradiction because two different aspects of eternal life are in view. The same is true of entrance into the kingdom. Sometimes entrance is a soteriological **gift** (Jn 3:5; 10:9; **Mt 18:3**), and sometimes entrance is a misthological **reward** (Mt 25:10,21; 2Pet 1:11; **Mt 18:4**).

Dual Entrance

This passage in Mt 18:3-4 is an invitation both to saving faith and radical discipleship. A problem arises in determining what is meant by the phrase *enter life* in Mt 18:8-9, which is equated with entering the kingdom (Mt 18:3; Mk 9:47). How do we enter the kingdom? We enter it by faith (Mt 18:3,6; Mt 9:42). In this passage, the equivalence between entering the kingdom in Mk 9:47 and entering life in Mt 18:9 makes it difficult to accept the ultraistic position that entering the kingdom cannot mean entering into possession of eternal life by a simple faith. The characteristic of children that Jesus has in mind, and that He describes as humility, is defined as faith. The *little ones* (i.e., the children, the humble ones) are those *who believe in* Jesus (Mt 18:6; Mk 9:42). Perhaps this can be explained by noting that children are not known for their obedience or sacrifice but for their dependency and confidence in another—humility. Simple entrance into the kingdom through new birth is humanly impossible; much less is the abundant entrance through radical discipleship humanly possible (2Pet 1:11). Both, however, can be accomplished only through relying on Jesus in faith. In addition to obtaining life by faith, we can live by faith. Imitating a child's faith not only results in entrance into the kingdom, but in first-place status within the kingdom (Mt 18:3-4). Dependency on the Lord to live His life through us in the power of the Holy Spirit is the key to the victorious Christian life.

This passage is also similar to the passage where Jesus tells us to fear Him who is able to destroy both soul and body in Gehenna (Mt 10:28). This need not necessarily mean that believers are to fear Gehenna, but they are to fear Him who deals with sin in such a manner and will deal with their sins in a correlative manner. Those believers who do not fear Him will be saved from Gehenna, yet they will have to pass through the misthological and metaphorical fire of the Bema (1Cor 3:15). Correlative fear makes sense.

The fact that both soul and body are cast into Gehenna in Mt 10:28 poses another difficulty for the ultraistic position. Granted, ultraists might be able to argue that since (according to their perspective) subcomers are cast into Gehenna after the Bema (and thus after their resurrection), they are thrown both soul and body into Gehenna. Nevertheless, the same argument cannot be made concerning the lost. They are not resurrected until after the millennium and thus cannot be thrown both soul and body into Gehenna until after the millennium. Consequently,

Gehenna apparently refers to a place of punishment of both the soul and body. In contrast, the suffering experienced in Hades is by disembodied spirits.* As a general rule, those in Hades will not be thrown into the Lake of Fire until after the millennium, that is, until after they receive resurrected bodies (Rev 20:14). The Lake of Fire is the place of torment for those whose souls have been reunited with their bodies. Torment of those in resurrected bodies does not commence until after the millennium. As a result, when the treat of Gehenna is perceived as describing metaphysical suffering therein, as it is by both classic and ultraistic writers, equating Gehenna with the Lake of Fire—eternal hell— is necessary, at least in the cases of those who already have died. The traditional understanding of Gehenna as eternal soteriological punishment after the millennium is superior to the ultraistic interpretation. Literally suffering in metaphysical Gehenna entails an eternal, unquenchable, place of undying agony—as pictured by undying worms (Mt 18:8; Mk 9:43-44,46,48)—and a place where both soul and body suffer (Mt 10:28). If Gehenna is a place of bodily suffering, it must refer to post-millennial suffering. Unbelievers in Hades cannot be thrown into Gehenna until after the millennium.

Although ultraists could respond that believers can be thrown into Gehenna during the millennium since they have resurrected bodies, it would seem more likely that Jesus is using Gehenna to describe the eternal suffering of the resurrected lost rather than the temporary suffering of the resurrected saved. Since Paul says that unworthy believers who have built upon the foundation of Christ *will be saved* in 1Cor 3:15, it is very doubtful that unworthy believers will undergo the same punishment that unbelievers go through who do not build upon the foundation. Conversely, that Paul's meaning is that such believers merely would be saved eventually is very unlikely.

Inclusive Invitation

Jesus is giving an invitation that applies to everyone—lost and saved. The disciples limit the discussion to rewards in heaven (Mt 18:1). Yet Jesus also wants to incorporate the more basic issue of entrance into heaven (Mt 18:3) with the discussion of rewards (Mt 18:4). He does this by contrasting the extremes, but this does not mean that there is no middle ground. Jesus is not saying that our only two options are radical discipleship or hell. If that were the case, then the passage would, in fact, teach a soteriological LS salvation by works or an ultraistic misthological salvation by works. Such is not the case, however. As noted previously, those passages that contrast spiritual and carnal believers do not disprove the existence of nonbelievers. Likewise, the contrast of spiritual believers with nonbelievers does not disprove the existence of carnal believers. In sports, when we urge people to play on a team, we do not point to the quitters or benchwarmers but to the starters for inspiration. Nonetheless, pointing to the starters does not mean that there are no quitters or benchwarmers. Similarly, in pointing to the spiritual believer as an example of what we can be does not mean that there are no carnal believers. On the other hand, some passages (e.g., the sower) contrast all three possibilities: lost, carnal, and spiritual.†

Minimum Versus Maximum Entrance

Jesus tells us how to become a starter in this passage: by entering life right here and now as a cripple—someone who needs a crutch. Just as children need their father and trust him to supply their needs, so God wants His children to trust Him to meet their needs. Only a child needs a daddy, and only a cripple needs a crutch. Only believers who recognize their need will recognize their need for God. Jesus is using childlike faith to illustrate the importance of dependency. Only those believers who supernaturally have surrendered their lives to the Lordship of Christ will find Him abundantly meeting their needs. They must cut off any sin that makes them independent (i.e., self-dependent, relying upon themselves) rather than dependent upon the Holy Spirit. To receive the basic entrance, you must trust the Lord as your Savior. To receive the maximum entrance, you must then trust the Savior as your Lord.

To summarize the fourth interpretation (i.e., the *Never Enter* interpretation), this passage is not teaching that we soteriologically can lose eternal life or that we must soteriologically earn it. Nor is it misthologically describing a temporary delay of 1000 years in terms of entering the kingdom. Rather, it teaches that soteriological entrance into life (and thus into the kingdom) is by faith. Without this simple faith in Jesus, the lost will never enter the kingdom; instead, they will spend eternity in the eternal Lake of Fire. However, this punctiliar, passive response of saving faith only results in receiving eternal life as a gift; it only results in basic entrance into the kingdom. In order to obtain maximum entrance into the kingdom, which Jesus describes as being greatest in the kingdom, progressing to radical discipleship that is rooted in living by faith is necessary.

---

* See *Appendix 9. Hades Versus Paradise*, p. 825.
† See *Illustration 234. Misthological Range of Fruitfulness*, 692.

That the *you* and *your* is addressed to the twelve (Mk 9:35) does not mean that soteriological concerns about one's eternal destiny cannot be in view. The twelve included Judas, and the fact that the twelve were summoned and addressed does not mean that no one else was around. John devotes an extended discussion that illustrates this point, attesting to the fact that many unbelievers were following Jesus earlier in His ministry (Jn 6:36,64). Some of the things which Jesus spoke to His disciples were spoken *because* they did not believe. Even so, He spoke these things to His disciples that they might believe and be saved.

> [64] "But there are **some of you who do not believe**." For Jesus knew from the beginning who they were who did not believe, and who it was that would betray Him. [65] And He was saying, "**Because of this, I have said to you**, that no one can come to Me, unless it has been granted him from the Father." (John 6:64-65; TM)

Jesus spoke these words, not merely to explain His followers' unbelief but to confront them with their unbelief. In the previous chapter, He confronted the antagonistic Jews with their unwillingness to believe (Jn 5:40) in an attempt to save them: "But the witness which I receive is not from man, but I say these things that you may be saved" (Jn 5:34). His salvific intent may be deduced in the next Johannine chapter as well (Jn 6:60-70); only this time it is extended to His unsaved followers.

If these warnings about Gehenna in the Sermon on the Mount were likewise intended for these unbelieving disciples (Mt 4:25; 5:1,22,29-30), then the warnings are concerned with soteriological issues. In his discussion of various levels of discipleship, Bing notes the ambiguity of the term:

> The broadest meaning of *disciple* in relation to Jesus Christ comes from those instances where the term may be used of the multitudes who followed Him. For example, in Matt 5:1 it is unclear whether the multitude is identified synonymously with the disciples or the disciples are a smaller group within the multitude. (Emphasis his.)[1116]

Likewise, the subsequent Gehenna warnings evidently were intended for the same group—unbelieving followers. This would certainly include Mt 10:28. Granted, Jesus subsequently reduced the number of His followers in the Johannine account. Yet we still are informed that not all of this remaining group of followers was composed of believers—not even all the twelve were believers (Jn 6:70). Jesus' words are intended to bring His followers—His disciples—to faith. Thus, it would be most natural to take His subsequent warning about Gehenna in Mt 10:28 as addressing unbelieving disciples as well.

The presence of unbelievers, who frequently were present (even at times when one would have thought otherwise, e.g., Jn 9:40), may be inferred. Further, it would be appropriate for Jesus to instruct genuine believers in matters related to evangelism. Surely, most of the twelve already were converted, yet Jesus addresses the twelve with the word *you*, which would mean that they were not converted if the *you* is interpreted too strictly (Mt 18:3). Those in the group who needed conversion and who needed to believe were those in danger of being cast into the fire. Nevertheless, an application is also made to those who already have believed and thus who are not in danger of being cast into that particular fire: Fear a God who deals with sin in such a corresponding manner (Mt 10:28).

The principle of correlativity provides plenty of motivation for believers to fear such a God—who throws unbelievers into Gehenna. Since a corresponding (not identical) fate is applicable to unfaithful believers, such a fear on the part of believers is prudent. Unmistakably, the Scripture is warning believers as to the applicability of correlative fear. Conditionalists treat the passage as if Jesus is warning believers, "Soteriologically fear God." To be sure, soteriological imagery is used and soteric fear would be applicable to any unbelieving disciples (such as Judas) who are listening to Jesus, but this is not the type of fear that Jesus is trying to instill into His believing disciples. Rather, He gives a warning that is applicable to both His unbelieving and believing disciples. For His believing disciples, and thus for Matthew's intended audience, the warning is, "Correlatively fear God." Because believers are expected to see a correlation between being cast into the outer darkness and Gehenna, they should fear a God who cast unbelievers into Gehenna, knowing that they, as believers, can suffer a correlative fate.

Radical discipleship is certainly much better than hell, but this does not mean that radical discipleship is required to escape hell. Although the *you* should not be interpreted too strictly, it should not be interpreted too simplistically either, that is, in a Calvinistic manner in which the issue is simply whether you are lost or saved. There is a sense in which genuine believers may fail to enter life. All believers enter into possession of eternal life, but not all believers enter into the fullest experience of eternal life, which is denoted by eternal possession of the kingdom. All believers will be in the kingdom, but not all of them will be great in the kingdom. Some will be least.

The challenge is to enter life and the kingdom as a cripple by trusting Jesus as Savior and then to enter the kingship by trusting Him as Lord.

Strictly Classic Soteriology

Wilkin argues that Jesus used this same type of illustration earlier in Mt 5:28-30, in a strictly classic soteriological manner to demonstrate that it is not possible to enter the kingdom by any amount of self effort or sacrifice and thus that imputed righteousness is needed in Mt 5:20. Entrance into the kingdom is consequently by faith rather than by works. This is one possibility. Or, as Wilkin also notes, it could be that Jesus was demonstrating the truth that anything that "hinders a person from coming to faith in Christ must be eliminated."[1117] Nothing must be allowed to prevent you from entering the kingdom by faith.[*] Some people have to work to discover that salvation is not by works.[†] Likewise, some people may have to give up something if it is preventing them from entering the kingdom by faith alone. Jesus appears to be using this same illustration in the same manner in Mt 18 and Mk 9. In all three passages the contrast is between entering the kingdom and entering the fire. In all three passages there are three possibilities: not entering the kingdom, entering the kingdom in least place, and entering the kingdom in first place. In all three passages the invitation is to *cut it off.* Thus, it certainly can be argued that the same type of entrance is being referred to in all three contexts—an exclusively soteriological entrance.

Joint Neoclassical Soteriology and Misthology

On the other hand, the context of Mt 5:19-20 demonstrates the need for imputed righteousness to enter the kingdom **and** the need for imparted righteousness to be great in the kingdom. (Mt 5:19 is parallel in thought to Mt 18:4, and Mt 5:20 is parallel to Mt 18:3.) In its context, there is not only a call to saving faith but to radical discipleship as well. Therefore, it is improbable that what is being denoted by the repeated emphasis on entrance in Mt 18:8-9 is an exclusively soteriological entrance into life. Rather, in this particular context, Matthew appears to use the phrase *enter the kingdom* (18:3) to describe a mere soteriological entrance, but the phrase *enter life* (18:8-9) is used to point to an entrance that is both soteriological and misthological. Mt 5:20 is to be interpreted in the same manner as Mt 18:3. Both verses are talking exclusively about soteriological entrance into the kingdom. Likewise, in the Markan parallel, entering life (Mk 9:43,45) should be taken as equivalent to entering the kingdom (Mk 9:47).

The dual *neoclassical* entrance into the kingdom being offered is entrance into the **kingdom** by an act of faith and entrance into the **kingship** by a walk of faith.[‡] In short, the contrast between entering the kingdom and entering the eternal fire contextually indicates that classic soteriological entrance is in view in Mt 18:1-11. This understanding of the passage is further supported by the parallel in Mt 5:17-20, where being least or greatest in the kingdom is contrasted with not entering the kingdom at all. Yet, at the same time, the fact that the entrance of Mt 18:8-9 may be costly seems to indicate that these verses picture a fuller neo-ultraistic misthological entrance in addition to a soteriological entrance. This understanding of these verses is further supported by the fact that 18:3-4 includes both the soteriological and misthological aspects of the kingdom. The entrance of Mt 18:8-9 incorporates both the soteriological and misthological aspects of 18:3-4 and is thus a neoclassical text.

Limited Agreement between Conservatives and Ultraists

Further support for the assertion that Jesus is using children to illustrate both the requirement of faith for basic entrance into the kingdom and the requirement of walking by faith for abundant entrance may be found in the introduction (Mt 19:13-15) to the account concerning the rich young ruler (Mt 19:16-30). Its introduction and its parallels (Mk 10:13-16; Lk 18:15-17) have an application to the present discussion of Mt 18:3. Conservatives and ultraists alike can agree with Finley's conclusion concerning the children in Mk 10:15. "Whoever does not receive the kingdom of God as a child will by no means enter it." He concludes:

> The Kingdom which the "children" receive (and thus enter) is the present Kingdom (the *present stage* of the Kingdom of God). Jesus pointed out that the quality of childlikeness is needed to *receive* the Kingdom. Everyone can be like a child: simple, trusting, unconfident, even timid. Any such person, whether an actual little child or not, can simply *come to Jesus, receive* the Kingdom (as a gift), and be taken in by Him, being blessed. This is the Kingdom according to grace. Reception of

---

[*] See "Cut it Off to Enter" in *Salvation: A Categorical Analysis.*
[†] See *Work to Enter*, 601.
[‡] See *Appendix 19. Neo-ultraistic and Neoclassic Entrance*, 947.

this Kingdom now also guarantees us a place in the eternal Kingdom of God (Jn. 6:37-40). The children were blessed by Jesus **not because of their merit**; He just wanted to bless them! (Emphasis his.)[1118]

Traditional Interpretation

Wessel's comment typifies the traditional interpretation: "The kingdom is both a gift to be received and a realm to enter."[1119] This simplistic interpretation would seem, however, to pose a problem for the ultraistic position concerning Mt 18:3. If Jesus simply uses children to illustrate possession and entry into the kingdom without merit in Mt 19:14, then it is very difficult to believe that He uses them to denote entry into the kingdom based on merit in Mt 18:3. Yet, having taken this simplistic interpretation of Mk 10:14-15, Finley accepts Govett's position that Mt 18:3 teaches exclusion from the kingdom based on merit.[1120] The ultraistic position seems somewhat inconsistent in using children to illustrate both unmerited entry and merited entry into the kingdom.

Children Represent Merited and Unmerited Entrance

This premature assessment of the ultraistic inconsistency is weak, however. Although the analysis herein rejects the ultraistic position, it does not do so for this reason. Indeed, it is reasonable to suppose that Jesus does in fact use children to illustrate unmerited basic entrance into the kingdom in Mt 18:3 and merited abundant entrance in Mt 18:4. The ultraistic position is not without merit. On the other hand, what is at stake is not exclusion from basic entry into the kingdom based on merit but exclusion from the fuller meritorious abundant entrance. Also, very likely, Jesus intends the same dual *neoclassical* aspect in Mk 10:14-15 as He does in Mt 18:3-4.

[14]But when Jesus saw this, He was indignant and said to them, "Permit the children to come to Me; do not hinder them; for the kingdom of God **belongs to** such as these. [15]Truly I say to you, whoever does not receive the kingdom of God like a child shall not **enter** it at all [*ou me*]." (Mk 10:14-15)

[3]Unless you are converted and become like children, you shall not **enter** the kingdom of heaven **at all** [*ou me*]. [4]Whoever then humbles himself as this child, he is the **greatest** in the kingdom of heaven. (Mt 18:3-4; TM)

The phrase *shall not enter at all into* in both passages is identical in Greek. In these passages what is being contrasted is having no entrance *at all* into the kingdom (i.e., a soteriological exclusion) versus being greatest in the kingdom and having the kingdom belong to you (as a misthological possession). Due to the parallel with Mt 18:3-4 and due to the fact that what is contrasted in Mk 10:14-15 is no entry into the kingdom of any type versus possession of the kingdom, it is best to interpret both passages similarly.[1121] A singular response of childlike faith to the gospel of the kingdom is the only requirement to enter the kingdom soteriologically.[1122] A life of childlike faith is necessary to possess the kingdom and to be greatest in the kingdom misthologically. Jesus is using children to teach us how to obtain both unmerited soteriological entry **and** merited misthological entry.

Exclusive Exclusion

Faust is misthologically consistent, however, in taking everything as referring to merited entrance. Concerning the children being converted, he states, "The word 'converted' is simply a reference to a practical change in the Christian's *walk*" (emphasis his).[1123] His point, then, is that unless the disciples imitate childlike humility in their practice, they will miss the millennial kingdom. In his view, the children do not represent soteriological entrance in either Mt 18:3 or Mk 10:15.

On the other hand, although *converted* can be used soteriologically, this is not its normal usage. It simply means *to turn*. In fact, Mt 18:3 and Jn 12:40 are the only two NT passages for which BDAG defines *converted* as: "To experience an inward change" (*strepho,* 5). An inner turning to God in faith is meant. Consequently, the LS claim that a person must turn from his or her sins in order to be saved soteriologically is unnecessary. Simply turning to God in faith for eternal life suffices lexically and contextually. In Jn 12:40, to be converted is used metaphorically to picture faith. And in Mt 18:3, it is used parabolically to picture faith—passive, childlike, humble, trusting dependency upon another for the necessities of life. After all, as already pointed out, the *little ones* (i.e., the children, the humble ones) are those *who believe in* Jesus (Mt 18:6; Mk 9:42), and children are not noted for their obedience or sacrifice but for their dependency and confidence in another (i.e., humility).

In contrast to the passive conversion in 18:3, an active humbling of yourself is urged in 18:4. The aorist passive subjunctive of *strepho* in 18:3 would suggest a punctiliar passive conversion. Yet the future active indicative of *humble* (*tapeinoo*) followed by the personal pronoun, in contradistinction, indicates a reflexive action (i.e., an action you perform on yourself). You humble yourself in 18:4 so that you can be great in the kingdom of God. These words were spoken inclusively to Peter, who later shares with others that this exultation is available to those believers who likewise humble themselves: "*Humble* [*tapeinoo*] yourselves, therefore, under the mighty hand of God, that He may exalt you at the proper time" (1Pet 5:7).

If the lexical definition and contextual contrast is accepted, then Faust's equating of the two verses must be rejected. Therefore, even though I do not find fault with Faust's misthological consistency, nevertheless, lexical and contextual evidence calls for a more conservative approach. The *turn* in Mt 18:3 is not a change in external action but in internal attitude. It is to turn to God in faith. Matthew (13:15) also had referred to such conversion earlier, where he provides a quotation from Jesus which draws upon the OT prophecy that the Jews "should understand with their heart, and should be *converted* [*epistrepho*], and I should heal them" (KJV). This is the same statement found in Jn 12:40, where John likewise had stated that the Jews should "understand with their heart, and be *converted* [*strepho*], and I should heal them" (KJV). *Epistrepho* is a compound form of *strepho* and can be used interchangeably with the simple form, and this compound form frequently is used to denote a soteriological response to God (e.g., Is 45:22; Acts 3:19; 9:35; 11:21; 15:19; 26:18, 20; 28:27; 2Cor 3:16; 1Thess 1:9). In believing the gospel, they were turning to the Lord in faith to be saved. Just as the NT teaches that we should repent and *believe* in the gospel (Mk 1:15), so it also teaches that we should repent and *turn* to God (Acts 26:20). Correspondingly, Mt 18:3 should be understood as saying that we should *believe* and become like children in doing so. The opening picture, therefore, illustrated by the children, is that of receiving soteriological entrance into the kingdom by simple faith (Mt 18:3; Mk 10:15; Lk 18:17), not that of earning misthological entrance. This entrance is received by faith rather than earned by works. Wessel was correct in stating that we enter this realm by receiving it as a gift. Entrance is a gift to be received, not a prize to be won.

Conclusion

Rejection of the simplistic interpretation concerning possession of the kingdom in Mk 10:14-15 does not mean acceptance of the ultraistic position concerning entry into the kingdom in Mt 18:3-4. On the contrary, both the classical interpretation of Mk 10:14-15 and the neoclassical one proposed herein are counterarguments to the ultraistic conclusion. The basic entrance into the kingdom being referred to in these passages is based on faith alone and is contrasted with misthological themes. Basic entrance is soteriological rather than misthological. Taking these passages as denoting misthological entrance is not necessary, so there is no need to take the warnings pertaining to Gehenna as misthological either. Unbelievers who fail to enter the kingdom by simple faith are those who are in danger of the fires of Gehenna. Contrary to Faust, there is a sense in which it may be said that unbelievers are to strive to enter—by doing whatever is necessary to reach the point of understanding that entrance into the kingdom is by faith rather than works. The lost may indeed need to cut out things in their lives that psychologically are preventing them from receiving this gracious entrance into the kingdom by simple faith. The tears shed in the outer darkness are consequently not shed in Gehenna. Those who entered the kingdom but failed to enter the kingship shed these tears within the kingdom, not outside of it in Gehenna.

Part 8.
Objections to Misthological Interpretation

Chapter 28.
Objections Based on the Eternal State

Introduction

This last section will be devoted to answering remaining objections to some of the presuppositions employed thus far in developing the misthological implications of the outer darkness. This chapter in particular will deal with potential objections arising from implications drawn concerning the eternal state. The next chapter will consider the punitive nature of the Bema. Further response will then be provided to the simplistic rejection-imagery theory. First, however, the misthological ramifications that overcoming has upon one's welfare in the eternal state will be considered.

Fleshly or Eternal

One interesting observation that immediately arises concerning the eternal state revolves around identifying the nations and kings of the New Earth in Rev 21:24-26 and 22:4 who dwell outside the New Jerusalem. Many interpreters believe that Rev 21:9-22:7 is a recapitulation of the millennium and consequently will object to my understanding this passage as a description of the eternal state. One of their major arguments used in defense of recapitulation is the fact that these verses appear to be describing people (i.e., nations) in flesh and blood bodies. Assuming that no one will have flesh and blood bodies in the eternal state leads the presumption that this passage would be referring back to a previous state of affairs. Other interpreters argue that the passage refers to the eternal state but assume that the nations are not composed of people in flesh and blood bodies.

The first of these two arguments is advanced by interpreters who believe that the nations refer to people in flesh and blood bodies in the millennial age. Their assessment that such people are genuinely in physical bodies is sound, but it is presumptuous to assume that this must refer to the millennial state. The second of these two arguments, promoted by interpreters who believe that it is referring to the eternal state rather than the millennium, is much more reasonable. Pentecost's solution is to say that the passage is a mix of millennial and eternal descriptions: The nations (inhabitants of the earth) refer to people in the millennial age; whereas, the inhabitants of the city refer to the eternal age.[1124]

Fleshly and Millennial

A better solution is to acknowledge the strengths of both positions without mixing them together. My proposition is that the passage is to be understood as referring to the eternal state and to nations in flesh and blood bodies in the eternal state. These nations not only exist in flesh and blood bodies, but they also reproduce sexually. Larkin is an advocate of this procreation position:

> Where did the people who inhabited the earth **after the Flood** come from? They were the lineal descendants of Noah, how did they escape the Flood? They were saved in an Ark which **God Provided**. Gen. 6:13-16. Shall not God then during the "Renovation of the Earth by Fire," in some manner, not as yet revealed, take off righteous representatives of the Millennial nations that He purposes to save, and when the earth is again fit to be the abode of men, place them back on the New Earth, that they may increase and multiply and **replenish** it, as Adam (Gen. 1:27,28), and Noah (Gen 9:1), were told to **multiply and replenish** the present earth....
>
> ...surely God can take off representative men from the nations and put them back again on the New Earth to **repopulate** it. If this is not God's plan then we have one type in the Scriptures that has no antitype, for Noah's Ark, which is a type, has no antitype unless it be this....
>
> It seems clear from the presence of the Tree of Life in the Garden of Eden, that God intended the human race to populate the Earth, and when it became too thickly populated, to use the surplus population to colonize other spheres....
>
> ...the representatives of the "Saved Nations" (Rev. 21:24) will be men and women in whom no taint of sin will remain, and who cannot therefore impart it to their offspring, who will be like the offspring of Adam and Eve would have been if they had not sinned. (Emphasis his.)[1125]

Walvoord dismisses this interpretation with these words:

> Larkin **introduces** the startling point of view that children will be born in the eternal state who unlike the posterity of Adam and Eve will be sinless. There is **no indication** whatever in Scripture

that **resurrected and translated** beings have the quality of human sex, much less the capacity to produce offspring. (Emphasis added.)[1126]

First Error

Walvoord makes three errors in this two-sentence statement. First, Larkin was not the one who originally introduced this point of view. Larkin's commentary was published in 1919. But Watson's book, *The Bridehood Saints*, was published six years before (in 1913) and takes this position as well: "The Church of the Firstborn…shall sit on thrones and reign with Christ a thousand years over the nations on earth, and then in the new heavens and new earth it is to reign over **the nations that shall be born in the ongoing ages of the new earth** (emphasis added)."[1127]

Alexander Patterson's, *The Greater Life and Work of Christ*, takes the same position and was published even earlier (in 1896). Walvoord's bibliography does not make reference to the works by either Watson or Patterson. However, Patterson cites the American editor, Craven, from Lange's commentary on Revelation, which was published in 1874, in support of this position.[1128] Walvoord's bibliography does contain reference to Lange's commentary, but Walvoord fails to note this earlier citation.

As early as 1874, Craven had concluded that the citizens of the city were risen glorified believers who composed the Bride of Christ, that the nations probably were composed of men in flesh and blood bodies who reproduced throughout eternity, and that the Bride of Christ likely was composed of only overcomers who are the governors (rulers) of the New Creation.[1129] Splendid assessment! Concerning procreation Craven says,

> Even after the new creation, the human race is to be continued (ever propagating a holy seed, such as would have been begotten had Adam never sinned)…
>
> The *nations*…will consist (probably) of *men in the flesh*, freed from sin and the curse, begetting a holy seed, and dwelling in blessedness under the government of the New Jerusalem. They will be, not the offspring of the glorified Saints, who "neither marry nor are given in marriage" (Matt. xxii. 30), but the descendants of those who live in the flesh during the period of the Millennial Kingdom.…The same Almighty power that conveyed Noah and his family across the waters of the first deluge, can bear other families across the fiery floods of the second, to be progenitors of the continued race. It may be retorted that there is no promise of such a miracle. That there is no expressed promise is admitted—but the Divine prediction of an event ever implies the promise of a sufficient cause.[1130]

It appears that this understanding of the nations in the eternal state as being composed of people in flesh and blood bodies who continue to have children was widespread enough (at least in certain circles) at the turn of the century that certain writers felt at ease just to mention it with little or no defense. Patterson can even cite Bickersteth's poetic expressions concerning the New Earth in support of this position:

> The wastes of ocean only were no more…
> And yet the earth through all her vast expanse…
> Already seemed to narrow for the growth
> Or her great family; so quick…
> when once Sin's crushing interdict was disannulled,
> That primal law, "Be fruitful; multiply…
> replenish and subdue the earth.[1131]

The oceans and sin are gone in the New Earth and eternal state. But the command to be fruitful, multiply, replenish, and rule the earth remains in force. Patterson's further citation of Bickersteth is a picturesque presentation of Larkin's position that these saints, who are translated without death from the millennial kingdom into the eternal kingdom, will be sinless like Adam and grow so vast in number that they shall populate other planets:

> Translated without death, for death was not,
> As Enoch joined the glorified in light…
> Like Adam, in some paradise of fruits
> The ancestors of many a newborn world,

Like Adam, but far different issue now,
Sin and the curse and death forever crushed.
And thus from planet on to planet spread.[1132]

Second Error

The second error Walvoord makes is to assume that there is no indication of Larkin's position in Scripture. To be sure, Larkin's two-page presentation has limited biblical citation in support of his position (Gen 1:28; 6:13-16; Dt 7:9; Is 66:12), but Patterson's majestic twenty-two page defense of this position demonstrates that these biblical texts should be considered carefully rather than ignored superficially.[1133]

Third Error

Third, Walvoord misrepresents the position. This position does not argue that "resurrected and translated" human beings will have offspring. On the contrary, it is acknowledged that resurrected human beings will not be involved sexually or have offspring (Mk 12:25). What is argued, by the advocates of this position, is that some human beings who survive the millennium in flesh and blood bodies will be translated into the eternal state without undergoing death and thus without experiencing the resurrection or receiving glorified bodies. The change they undergo will be the removal of their sin nature, not the removal of their flesh and blood status or sexual ability.

Larkin was neither the first nor the last interpreter to suggest this solution. Seiss takes it as well. Pentecost mistakenly cites Seiss as believing that Rev 21:9-22:7 is a recapitulation of the millennial age.[1134] However, Seiss is clearly affirming that children are born throughout eternity and that the passage is thus describing eternity. That Seiss understands John as describing the eternal state is confirmed in his discussion of Rev 22:1-5.

In Ezekiel's visions of the renewed earthly Jerusalem, a similar presentation is made....But that relates to an order of things on earth, which comes into being during the thousand years. What John describes is the order of things in the heavenly Jerusalem, which comes into existence only after the thousand years have passed away.[1135]

Internal Considerations

Seiss bases some of his arguments that children are born in the eternal state from the passage itself:

And the still ongoing race redeemed is there.... Who are these people...[in Rev 21:3]? Who can they be, if not the nations of the ongoing race, dwelling in the new earth in flesh....There is not a word [of Scripture] which asserts any purpose of God to terminate the perpetuity of humanity as ever-expanding race....Ransomed nations in the flesh are therefore among the occupants of the new earth...as Adam and Eve dwelt in Paradise.[1136]

This argument is basically an argument from silence and therefore is weak. On the other hand, Patterson's line of argument demonstrates that an appeal to this text is not without merit:

When the New Jerusalem descends to the new earth, it finds people already there. It is an inhabited earth to which it comes. It does not bring this population with it. They are evidently not a part of the great body who are in the city....the city comes from heaven, while this company is of the earth.[1137]

Based on what John is describing, the inference appears to be that the inhabitants of the New Earth are transported to the New Earth before the New Jerusalem descends to rest on it. That is, the millennial nations who survive the millennium and who enter the eternal kingdom in their flesh and blood bodies are transported to the New Earth before the overcomers in the city join them on the New Earth. Seiss continues by appealing to the implication concerning rulership in Rev 22:5.

If they are to be kings forever, they must have subjects forever..."*the nations*"....Either, then, their kingdom must come to an end for want of subjects, or nations...must continue in the flesh, as Adam and Eve before the fall...They [the rulers, i.e., glorified saints] neither marry, nor are given in marriage; for they are as the angels of God; but their subjects [i.e., the nations] are of a different order, and their [i.e., the rulers] dominion and glory shall grow forever, by the ceaseless augmentation of the number of their subjects throughout unending generations.[1138]

Admittedly, Seiss' argument in this verse is not entirely persuasive. The subjects of the kingdom in the eternal state could be the vast majority of believers (subcomers) in glorified bodies. If the subjects of the kingdom are limited to subcomers, then the kingdom will not end, but the growth of the kingdom will end. However, as will be shown, such a conclusion is unacceptable, and consequently the subjects of the kingdom cannot be limited to subcomers in glorified bodies but must include people in fleshly bodies who reproduce.

Internal Parallelism

As already noted, the millennial nations in Rev 20:8 are composed of those born during the millennium.[*] This conclusion must be accepted since they are contrasted with the saints inside the city in Rev 20:9 and because the OT teaches that children will be born during the millennium (Is 65:17-25; Eze 36:10-11,37-38; Zech 8:5). Certain believers and their children who live until the end of the tribulation will enter the millennial kingdom in flesh and blood bodies and reproduce sexually. Walvoord, as well as other dispensationalists, acknowledge that the millennial nations of Rev 20:8 are not composed of glorified saints but of people in flesh and blood bodies who reproduce. The most reasonable deduction, therefore, is that the eternal nations in Rev 21:24 also are composed of believers and their children who live until the end of the millennium and who enter the eternal kingdom in flesh and blood bodies and reproduce.

Internal Contrast

Not only does the parallel with Rev 20:8 (between the millennium and eternal nations) suggest that this is the case, but the contrast in Rev 21:24-27 (between the nations of Earth outside the city versus the inhabitants of the city who are inside it) imply that the inhabitants of the city (who inherit the kingdom in glorified bodies, 1Cor 15:50) are to be distinguished from the inhabitants of Earth in flesh and blood bodies. Moreover, Rev 22:2 also indicates that the nations in eternity represent humanity in flesh and blood bodies, as Govett states:

> It must indeed be allowed, that in the eternal state there is no death, nor pain. xxi, 4. But still there may be weakness and the painless decay of the body.
> The nations are still in the flesh. It is thought by some, that the tree of life, ere Adam fell, was designated to renovate his life from time to time, so as to prevent all necessity of death. It may be so now. The bodies of the nations may be invigorated by the application of the leaves of the tree of life. It may be that they may employ them against mechanical injuries to parts of their frame....
> ...The leaves of the tree of life do not fall, and rot disregarded on the ground: they supply the need of the dwellers outside. The priests need them not. They are not in the flesh.[1139]

The contrast is between the earth dwellers and the city dwellers. The nations live outside the city, give homage to the residents within the city, and are perhaps in need of healing. This contrast implies that the city dwellers are glorified saints whereas the nations are people in flesh and blood bodies, just as was the case in Rev 20:8-9. If it is accepted that the nations are composed of people in flesh and blood bodies, then there is no reason for not also accepting the fact that they can reproduce sexually.

OT Background

Governmental Increase

Not only does the context in Revelation point to this conclusion, but the promises within the OT background require that children will be born throughout eternity. For example, Is 9:7 says, "There will be no end to the **increase** of His government." If the increase of the population of His kingdom comes to a screeching halt, the increase of His kingdom will also. Infinite increase in His government requires infinite increase in the population. In Gen 1:28, human rulership of the planet presupposes human population of that planet: "Be fruitful and multiply, and fill the earth, and subdue it; and rule...the earth." But why limit infinite growth in population to just one planet? His kingdom will increase eternally as the population increases and occupies more space, even outer space.

If Adam and Eve had not sinned, then during the course of time they eventually would have populated this planet to such an extent that it would have been necessary for most of their offspring to be moved to other planets

---

[*] See *Procreation in the Millennial Kingdom*, 60; *What about the children?*, 65.

and populate those planets. Of course, this could have been accomplished supernaturally, but had their mental abilities not been impaired by sin, their offspring surely would have advanced in scientific knowledge at such an incredible rate that they would have discovered space travel and implemented it to solve their need for more territory long before the need was acute. Accomplishing this feat would have been humanly possible. In the eternal state, this human potential will become a realization. Those entering the eternal state in sinless flesh and blood bodies will not have to start from scratch. They will have the scientific knowledge and ability of space travel that exists not merely at the close of the church age but also at the end of the millennial age. Human achievement will continue to advance in music, art, literature, architecture, science, athletics, and worship. Heaven will be anything but a dull, stagnant, monotonous routine.

Infinite Growth

As Patterson points out, the ever-increasing population in eternity is clearly implied in the promise to Abraham, which was repeated five times. In Gen 13:16, the promise was made: "And I will make your descendants as the dust of the earth; so that if anyone can number the dust of the earth, then your descendants can also be numbered." If the human population of heaven is stagnate, then it is finite and can be numbered. However, if it is increasing eternally throughout infinity, it cannot be numbered. In Gen 15:5, the field of reference for the promise moves from this planet to the stars: "And He took him outside and said, 'Now look toward the heavens, and count the stars, if you are able to count them.' And He said to him, 'So shall your descendants be.'" As the population continues to increase from one star system to another, from one solar system to another, this promise will find literal fulfillment.

The next expression of this promise in Gen 22:17 combines this planet and the stars as the basis for the imagery of the promise: "Indeed I will greatly bless you, and I will greatly multiply your seed as the stars of the heavens, and as the sand which is on the seashore." In Gen 26:4, the promise also uses the combined reference to this planet and the stars: "And I will multiply your descendants as the stars of heaven, and will give your descendants all these lands; and by your descendants all the nations of the earth shall be blessed." In view of the foregoing discussion, the promise in Gen 28:14 should not be understood as referring two dimensionally to a flat earth or three dimensionally to a spherical globe but three dimensionally to the entire universe: "Your descendants shall also be like the dust of the earth, and you shall spread out to the west and to the east and to the north and to the south; and in you and in your descendants shall all the families of the earth be blessed." Up, down, and sideways his descendants will spread upon and from this planet throughout countless galaxies.[1140] The poetic call for those from the stars of the heavens to praise and worship the Lord will find literal fulfillment (Ps 19:1; 148:1-3; Phil 2:10).

The Extent of Redemption

Seiss argues from the implication of Gen 1:28 that mankind will multiply eternally after the thousand years:

> HUMANITY was created and constituted a self-multiply order of existence...God created man in his own image; male and female created he them, and said to them, Be fruitful, and multiply, and replenish the earth, and subdue it, and have dominion over it....the redemption must necessarily involve the restitution and perpetuation of the race...for if the redemption does not go as far as the consequences of sin, it is a misnomer, and fails to be redemption. The salvation of any number of individuals, if the race is stopped and disinherited, is not the redemption of what fell, but only the gathering up of a few splinters...
>
> ...our race, as a self-multiplying order of beings, will never cease either to exist or to possess the earth. (Emphasis his.)[1141]

Thus, on the basis of creation and redemption, Seiss argues that humanity as a race will continue to multiply throughout eternity. As pointed out above, the implication of this verse is that for humanity to exercise dominion over a planet, that planet must be thoroughly inhabited by humanity. One would not picture one lonely overcomer ruling this planet and another one ruling that planet. The planets over which they rule will be inhabited by people.

A possible objection could be raised that the planet is not eternal. After dealing with this objection at length and arguing that the earth will be redeemed and continue forever (see Ecc 1:4; Ps 37:29; 119:90; Is 60:21; 66:22), Seiss then returns to his discussion of race, defines it, and introduces another argument for eternal procreation:

> And with the continuity and redemption of the earth, goes the repopulation and redemption of *the race*. For why is the one continued if not for the other? As surely as the "earth abideth forever,"

so surely shall there be eternal generations upon it [Ps 119:90]. Paul speaks with all boldness of the "*generations of the age of the ages*." (Eph. 3:21) After the termination of the present Aeon, he contemplates many more Aeons, even Aeon of Aeons; and those interminable years he fills up with generations and generations. The covenant which God made with Noah, and all living things...is, by its own terms, unending in duration; but that duration is at the same time described as filled in with *unceasing generations.* (Gen. 8:22,23 [sic]; 9:8-16.) Joel tells of generations and generations for Jerusalem through all that "*forever*"...(Joel 3:20,21; Ezek. 37:25,26.) Eternal generations were certainly provided for when humanity was originally constituted...eternal generations certainly would have been the effect...had sin not come in to interfere with the wonderful creation; and as surely as Christ's redemption-work is commensurate with the ruinous effects of the fall, *eternal generations* must necessarily be. Earth and multiplying man upon it surely would never have passed from living fact into mere legend had sin never come in. Much less, then, can they now pass into mere legend....

We thus reach the underlying foundations and background of the sublime presentations of the text. The Apostle beholds here the final redemption of our earth and race. (Emphasis his.) [1142]

Seiss' limited citations fail to do full justice to the force of his argument. Numerous passages indicate eternal generations: Ex 3:15; 31:16; Lev 3:17; 7:36; 17:7; 23:14,31; 24:3; Num 10:8; 15:15; 18:23; 1Chron 16:15; Ps 33:11;[1143] 49:11; 72:5; 102:12,24; 105:8; 106:31; 119:90; 135:13; 145:13; 146:10; Is 13:20; 34:10; 34:17; Lam 5:19; Dan 4:3,34; Joel 3:20; Eph 3:21. Likewise, a number of passages seem to indicate the eternal generation of children: Gen 9:12 (cp. 9:16); 13:15; Ex 12:24; Dt 5:29; 12:28; 28:46; 29:29; Josh 14:9; 1Sam 20:42; 1Chron 23:13; 1Chron 28:8; Ezr 9:12; Ps 89:29,36; Is 66:22; Jer 33:22; Eze 37:25-26; Lk 1:55.

Although some of the passages in the second group are open to debate (cp. 1Kgs 2:33 and 2Kgs 5:27), it would seem that the former passages clearly indicate that generations will continue to be born throughout eternity. For example, eternity is often expressed in terms of generations, with the clear expectation that generations will continue throughout eternity (e.g., Ps 33:11; 49:11; 106:31; 146:10). As long as there is an earth, sun, and moon, there will be generations (Ps 72:5; cp. 119:90). Since the former will exist in the eternal state, so will the latter. Generations will continue to exist just as long as God and His name exist (Ps 102:12,24). Generations, of course, are one group of people giving birth to the next generation of people who in turn continue the propagation of the next generation. Generations will continue to be born just as long as God's everlasting kingdom and dominion endures (Ps 145:13; 146:10). To say that God's promise is to a thousand generations is a way of saying it is forever (Ps 105:8; cp. 1Chron 16:15; Dt 7:9). It is like saying that it is to the nth degree or n^{th} generation; it will last throughout eternal generations, infinite generations.[1144]

Paul's expression in Eph 3:21 may be bold when compared to Platonic ideas but not when compared to the OT. Paul simply is affirming what the OT already has indicated. Generations will be born throughout eternity. Wuest translates Eph 3:21 as, "Into all the generations of the age of the ages."[1145] This is a very literal translation, and it is to be commended for indicating the genitive with the word *of*, but a better translation would paraphrase the idiom and retain the *of*: "All the generations **of eternity**." In other words, it means, "Throughout the eternal generations." Or as Ezekiel expresses it, their sons will continue to have sons and multiply throughout eternity (Eze 37:25-26). The millennial multiplication of the race promised in Eze 36:11,37-38 is to continue throughout eternity (Eze 37:25-26). Accordingly, God's promise in Eze 37:25-26 is that He will multiply them forever. The OT affirms the perpetual increase of humanity throughout eternity.

NT Background

The logical implication of NT teaching would also indicate procreation in eternity. Not only will overcomers rule this planet, they also will rule the angels. Surely the domain of the angels exceeds the terrestrial boundaries of this planet (1Cor 6:2-3; cp. Heb 2:7). Will overcomers not rule these other angelic domains also? Since angels apparently have the power of flight and since overcomers are glorified humans who will rule angels (Heb 2:7), overcomers evidently will not only be a higher order of being than the angels but also will have greater powers than the angels over whom they exercise rule. Certainly, overcomers will have the power of flight. Indeed, if overcomers are to rule far away galaxies and still have unlimited access to the capital city on the New Earth, their power of flight would include the power to move at the speed of thought, that is, to teleport from one place to another. Apparently, our Lord used this ability when He appeared to the disciples in His glorified body (Jn 20:19,26). It is commonly believed that there will be a correlation between His glorified body and ours; hence, we may assume that those who rule with Him will share this capacity with Him.

We will only be able to be in one place at a time, however, as Alcorn notes. Still, his more important observation is: "There's no suggestion that even the resurrected Jesus was in two places at once."[1146] Suppose you are a ruler over a galaxy that is a billion light years away from New Jerusalem. How often are you going to be able to visit the place prepared for you there by Jesus? How often will you be able to see Jesus? Only once every million years? Hardly. It is impossible to believe that Christ would only see the members composing His Bride on such an infrequent basis. Their reward is to be able to see His face (Rev 22:4). They will have unlimited access to Him. Neither time nor space, both of which will exist, will be a hindrance. How can this be? By teleportation and time bubbles. The overcomer could teleport to the city to attend a party with Jesus and some friends. If that room were in a ***time bubble***,* then they could spend all day together and yet have used only a millisecond of time relative to another point of reference. Computational considerations make such deductions logically necessary.

Of course, overcomers may have varying degrees of teleportational abilities depending on their degree of reward. One might conjecture as to distance, location, or frequency of teleportation. In any case, it would seem improbable that subcomers would have any power of flight or teleportation. Unfaithful believers will have forfeited their rule and probably their ability to fly as well. They will not rule the angels nor rule with Christ, so there is no reason to postulate that they will have abilities superior to the angels or share Christ's abilities. Indeed, one could conjecture that one eternally confining aspect of the outer darkness is the eternal inability to fly. Those believers who want to fly like angels in the future must first learn to fly like eagles now by waiting on the Lord (Is 40:31). Since overcomers are to rule angels, surely overcomers will also rule their angelic domains, which would include other planets. At the very least, since all believers are to be like angels in certain ways, is it too much to deem it probable that overcomers will fly like angels (Mt 22:30; Mk 12:25)?

Jesus is *heir of all things* (Heb 1:2), and all things will be made subject to Him (1Cor 15:25-28), but having been made *head over all things*, He is given to us—His Bride, the church (Eph 1:22). Overcomers will reign over all things as His queen. Victorious humanity has been appointed over the works of His hands; He has "put all things in subjection under his [humanity's] feet....He left nothing that is not subject to him [humanity]. But now we do not see all things subject to him [humanity]" (Heb 2:7-8). The OT passage being referred to by the writer of Hebrews specifies that the creation over which overcomers are to rule includes the stars (Ps 8:3-6). The millennium will not be sufficient time to see this accomplished—it will take eternity. Those who attempt to limit rewards to the millennial age are overlooking some very significant data. Jesus promises that the faithful believer will be put in charge of *all His possessions* (Lk 12:47). Solid ground exists for thinking that those possessions are not limited to this planet. His dominion cannot be limited to this one planet, so neither can ours.

By necessity, the expansion of our dominion to encompass *all His possessions* will be a universal rule that will be exercised by overcomers over all the universe. An infinite amount of people and time will be involved as the subjects over whom overcomers are to rule spread across the stars. Ruling the universe will require procreation and eternity for the entire universe to be ruled by humanity. Since Jesus' heirship is to all things, our co-heirship with Him must include all things (Rom 8:17). Our co-glory with Him will encompass *the whole creation* (Rom 8:17-22), which would include the sun and stars. As Dillow says, "One day mankind will conquer the galaxies!"[1147] Lutzer concurs with Dillow and exclaims: "We will be ruling over all the galaxies, affirming Christ's Lordship over the whole universe."[1148] Appreciably, Keathley (senior) acknowledges this possibility: "Many will be perhaps in various parts of the new universe carrying out responsibilities for the Lord."[1149] Alcorn concurs: "If Christ expands his rule by creating new worlds, whom will he send to govern them on his behalf? His redeemed people. **Some may rule over** towns, some cities, some planets, some solar systems or **galaxies**. Sound far-fetched? Not if we understand both Scripture and science."[1150]

Beirnes devotes his book to the thesis that the Bride is only composed of overcomers and correctly distinguishes these overcomers from those of the millennium:

> There is every evidence that these Millennial overcomers will be placed in the new earth, and that the human family will go on propagating for all eternity....The promise that the seed of Abraham would be as the sands that are upon the seashore and as the stars of heaven will literally take an eternity to fulfill....

---

* A ***time bubble*** is a temporal sphere in time, in which time may be experienced at vastly different rates by those in the sphere as opposed to those outside of it. Although the bubble may be restricted spatially to a certain location (see "*Jerusalem* Cloaked in Time Bubble" in *Predestination and the Open View*), it is not to be thought of as being a different place in time as if one spatially could visit another place in time, whether past or future, by means of such a bubble. Nevertheless, experiential time travel probably would be possible in such a bubble even though spatial time travel would not be.

The new earth and the multiplied millions of other planets in His universe will be conditioned for human life....God will never again create angels, but He will continue creating worlds for redeemed men to inhabit in an eternal, holy oneness, over which glorified saints will reign.[1151]

Carmical is to be commended for portraying these theological truths in a fictional format that excites the imagination.[1152] Heaven will be exciting, buzzing with activity. What makes the outer darkness so tragic for those who miss out on the excitement of the feast is that they will be missing out completely on these ongoing, joyous festivities forever. Evans likewise believes that procreation continues in the eternal state:

> There is only one group of people left on earth to go into eternity in their physical bodies—those who were true to Jesus Christ and served Him during His millennial kingdom. They go into eternity after the millennium with physical glorified bodies, not spiritual glorified bodies like we will have, because they did not experience death and resurrection....
>
> The Bible indicates that the new, renovated earth will be occupied in eternity. This group from the millennium will fill the earth because they will be able to procreate. These will make up the nations who do not live in the New Jerusalem, but will have access to the city.
>
> Why? To pay homage to God and bring Him their worship, and because they will need the leaves of the tree of life for their continued health and well-being.[1153]

In conclusion, procreation will continue so that mankind can inhabit and rule the whole creation. No rulership can exist without subjects to be ruled. A distinction must be made between the nations and those who rule over them in the millennial age (Rev 2:26). This distinction extends into the eternal age. Yet the transition from one age to the other will bring a change. Whereas the millennial nations will be composed of men and women in *sinful* fleshly bodies who reproduce offspring with sin natures, the eternal nations will be composed of men and women in *sinless* flesh and blood bodies who likewise reproduce sinless offspring. Correspondingly, a change in the nature of the rule will occur that reflects the change in the nature of the subjects. Ruling with a rod of iron and forcing submission will no longer be necessary (Rev 2:26). In eternity their subjects will submit joyfully to the serving rulership of their rulers.

Minor Objections

No Sun

Several potential objections to this conclusion concerning the eternal state need to be addressed. Some erroneously assume that there will be no sun or stars in the eternal state. However, the fact that the capital city needs no sun (Rev 20:23) does not mean that no sun exists or that the New Earth needs no sun. John makes it clear that day and night continue eternally (Rev 20:10), so the new heavens and New Earth must have a new sun. This particular city (i.e., New Jerusalem) will not experience night (Rev 20:24), but the rest of the planet will. Exclusion from this reward city could thus entail habitation of those parts of the planet that experience literal darkness every night. The gates of the city may or may not be closed when that part of the planet is experiencing night.[1154] Day and night, as well as seasons and years, will continue. As Govett notes, the fact that the tree bears fruit every month and that there are only twelve different months (Rev 22:2) proves "that the New Earth will possess both a sun and a moon, as now. The year will be divided into 'months' by the moon; and the year will consist of twelve of them, determined by the earth's course around the sun, as now."[1155]

No Stars

Not only is the star of this planet to be involved in the renovation, but the Bible tells us that the whole creation awaits the transformation, will be set free by it, and groans just as we do in our anticipation of participation in it (Rom 8:18-23). The New Heavens will not be limited to our sun. The other stars will be included as well. The stars will last forever as well (Dan 12:3). And the promises in passages such as Gen 15:5; 22:17; 26:4; Dt 1:10; 28:62; 1Chron 27:23; Neh 9:23 will find literal fulfillment as Abraham's descendants populate the stars. As Patterson says: "This was figuratively fulfilled in the age of Solomon when, as the scripture says, the children of Israel were as the sand of the sea, and later when Paul tells us the same. But here in this eternal view is the literal fulfillment....It is not rhetoric. It is not hyperbole. It is actual."[1156]

Although David's census was ill-conceived, he shows better sense concerning these biblical promises in his census than many contemporary interpreters do in their interpretation of these promises. David did not count those under the age of twenty since he realized that these promises concerning the innumerable composition of Israel meant that God would multiply the descendants of Israel as the stars of heaven so that it would be impossible to count them (1Chron 27:23; cp. Gen 22:17). However, if the human race ceases to multiply in eternity, then humanity does not infinitely grow. If procreation were to cease, Abraham's descendants would be finite and capable of being counted. Those who rule out eternal procreation go even further than David did in numbering the sons of Israel. The logical implication of their position is that it will be possible to count the sons of Israel. In contrast, David recognizes that the promises point to a literal fulfillment that will transcend any metaphorical fulfillment in that it will be literally impossible to count his descendants. To count them in eternity will be impossible because they will reproduce infinitely.

No Flesh

Another potential objection that could be raised, on the basis of 1Cor 15:50, is that there will be no people in flesh and blood bodies in the eternal state: "Flesh and blood cannot inherit the kingdom of God; nor does the perishable inherit the imperishable." On the other hand, it must be carefully noted that the verse rules out flesh and blood inheriting the kingdom; it does not rule out flesh and blood entering or inhabiting the kingdom. The position being advocated herein is that the flesh and blood bodies of those who enter the eternal state will be sinless and, therefore, be completely free from corruption and thus imperishable (Rom 8:20-21). The objection that is raised from 1Cor 15:50 is invalid since the fleshly, imperishable people who compose the nations will inhabit rather than inherit the kingdom. Further, it would be inconsistent for a premillennialist to use this verse to argue that flesh and blood cannot enter the **eternal** kingdom and then claim that flesh and blood can enter the **millennial** kingdom. Consistency would dictate that those in flesh and blood bodies cannot inherit the millennial or eternal kingdom, but those in flesh and blood bodies can enter both the millennial and eternal kingdom.

No Marriage

Similar comments can be made concerning marriage in the eternal state. "For in the resurrection they neither marry, nor are given in marriage, but are like angels in heaven" (Mt 22:30). "For when they rise from the dead, they neither marry, nor are given in marriage, but are like angels in heaven" (Mk 12:25). If these verses rule out marriage and sex in the eternal age, then they also rule out marriage in the millennial age and tribulational period since both are preceded by a resurrection. Yet we know that children will be born in both the tribulation and millennium, even though both time periods are preceded by a resurrection. These two verses do not say that there will be no marriage or sex in the tribulational, millennial, or eternal periods. What is ruled out is sex and marriage for those who participate in the resurrection, that is, for those who are raised from the dead.

This does not apply to those who do not participate in the resurrection at the rapture and who thus continue to populate the earth during the tribulation. It does not apply to those who do not participate in the resurrection at the second coming and who thus continue to populate the Earth during the millennium. It does not apply to those who do not participate in the resurrection at the end of the millennium and who thus continue to populate the Earth and other planets during eternity. There will be men and women who are alive at the time of each of these respective resurrections. Since they are alive, they do not have to be resurrected. They may continue to live on in flesh and blood bodies rather than undergo a transformation into glorified bodies. In many cases, they will be able even to maintain their marital status. The resurrection does not dissolve the marriages of those who do not participate in it. The resurrected already have been parted by death. Those who are not parted by death need not be parted by the resurrection since they do not participate in it.

No Free Will

Baughman objects to Seiss' proposal that procreation will continue in the eternal state and finds it improbable on the basis of free will: "If man is created with a will and permitted to have freedom of choice, he has proven time and time again…that he will fall into sin….If man is created without a will he would not be of the same 'kind of man' but a subnormal type of being."[1157] Baughman acknowledges that "mankind will be what theologians call 'confirmed in holiness,' or no longer subject to sin." Mankind will have a "crystallized character."[1158] This objection is weak, however. Most theologians would also apply this crystallization and confirmation to holy angels. They are no longer able to sin. If this is true, does this mean that holy angels are subnormal angels? How about God? Can God sin? No. Does this mean that God is a subnormal God? Of course not! Many theologians believe that if Adam and Eve had proven faithful, God would have confirmed them in a state of holiness. Does this mean that they would have been subhuman at that point? Obviously not. Even Baughman would acknowledge that resurrected believers are no longer capable of sin, but he would not describe them as being subnormal. What is removed is sin, not free will.[*]

Kings

As demonstrated above, there are many reasons for concluding that the nations of the New Earth represent mankind in flesh and blood bodies who reproduce sexually throughout eternity. But the question still remains as to the identity of the kings of those nations. Both Patterson and Govett believe that the kings of the earth in Rev 21:24 refer to subordinate rulers in flesh and blood bodies.[1159] Seiss acknowledges this possibility but prefers to regard them as glorified saints who will live in the New Jerusalem and exercise their rule primarily from this city.[1160] Baughman is undecided.[1161]

This discussion is complicated by the fact that the Greek word for *kingdom* (*basileia*) can mean *king*. The plausibility of translating basileia as *kingship* or *kingdom of kings* has been demonstrated already.[†] And Govett gives credible cause for simply translating it as *king*.[1162] Admittedly, it can be difficult at times to know for certain if the reference is to the king(s) of the kingdom or to the kingdom of the king(s). Govett's definition is acceptable, and the interpretation by Petterson and Govett is attractive. Yet it is possible to accept Govett's definition without adopting his interpretation.

In discussing the identity of the nations in Rev 20:8, the conclusion has been reached that these nations are the descendants of those who enter the millennium in flesh and blood bodies. Walvoord's suggestion that Gog and Magog refer to the millennium kings and kingdoms was rejected since the millennial kings will be those who inherit (rule) the earth. The millennial kings (of the nations of the earth) will be overcomers who have received their glorified and sinless bodies. These kings will not be deceived by Satan or participate in his rebellion. Unfortunately, their kingdoms (i.e., the subordinate nations over which they rule) will rebel at the conclusion of the millennium. These kings will rule their kingdoms (i.e., these nations) with a rod of iron (Rev 2:26-27), and their kingdoms will rebel against this iron rule. Contrary to my expectation, Seiss may be correct to conceive of the primary residence of these rulers as being in the capital city.[‡] In any case, these rulers will travel both to and from the city. The rebellion by the populous at the end of the millennium will be against these kings and their capital city.

Gog and Magog

The background for Gog and Magog is Eze 38-39, where the reference is to the tribulational kings and kingdoms of the earth who rebel against God in the battle of Armageddon (Rev 19:17-21). John uses the same terminology in Rev 20:8 in order to indicate that the **same type** of battle will occur at the end of the millennium as happened at the beginning of it. The battles are similar but not identical since the details are different. Again, inductive logic applied to the details is useful in making deductive comparisons and conclusions. These battles have the same nature, not the same time nor same participants. Whereas Gog referred to the kings of the earth in the premillennial battle, it refers to Satan himself in the postmillennial battle.

Gate Guards

Satan will not be able to deceive the kings of the earth after the battle of Armageddon because these overcoming kings will no longer have flesh and blood bodies or sin natures. These millennial kings come to the light of the city (Is 60:3) to bring the wealth of their kingdoms into it (Is 60:5). These rulers will fly like the clouds and doves (Is 60:8) in ministering to the inhabitants of the city (Is 60:10) and in bringing the wealth of their kingdoms into the gates of the city (Is 60:11). We probably can picture them as having the literal ability to fly since they are overcomers. But when they are loaded down with treasures from the nations, they will use the highways and enter the city by its gates and be honored by the angelic honor guards at the gates when these kingdom rulers enter in this kingly manner. Those nations and kingdoms who rebel against these kings will perish (in the battle of

---

[*] *Adam's Free Will*, 218.

[†] For example, see *Present—Future*, 54.

[‡] Given the background in Is 60:10-16, one mediation posed herein is that the kings of the earth are faithful Gentile overcomers from the tribulational period who are granted glorified bodies when they come into their inheritance of the kingdom (Mt 25:34) and who live (in terms of their principle residence) among the nations. As an alternate or second mediation, to their number might be added those believers who (like the repentant prodigal son) failed to qualify for living in the *Heavenly City* (HC) but who still qualify as rulers in the *twilight zone* (TZ). See *Illustration 370. Twilight Zone*, 960.

Armageddon, Is 60:12). However, the kings of those nations will not rebel against the city; they are its guardians (Is 49:23).

Gate Entrance

Although Govett defends this position at length—that the millennial kings are risen saints and that Satan has "no king with him" in the rebellion—Govett strangely concludes that the eternal kings are fleshly kings rather than risen saints.[1163] More likely, the eternal kings are glorified overcomers; however, I would concede to Govett that they may be low ranking kings who dwell on Earth (as opposed to Heavenly City kings), and these earthly kings may have to pay homage in order to enter the city.[1164] For the moment, though, let it simply be assumed that the kings of the earth in Rev 21:24 are overcomers.[*] After reigning with Christ over fleshly millennial nations that still had their sin natures (in Rev 20:4,6), overcomers will then rule with Christ over fleshly eternal nations that no longer have a sin nature. As these nations in the eternal state multiply and spread throughout the universe, these kings (overcomers) will spread throughout the universe with them. Even though the overcomers' citizenship remains in the city of the New Jerusalem, they and their rule are not confined to the city. As they enter the gates of this city, they bring the wealth of the universe into it through the city gates. Truly, it will be a great reward to be able to "enter by the gates into the city" in this fashion (Rev 22:14). They will enter as kings in joyful procession rather than forced subjection, as they bring their glory and the wealth of their domain into the city (Is 60:11; Rev 21:24). Their right to enter by the gates into the city in Rev 22:14 is no small reward! In view of the OT and Johannine background, it means that they enter as glorious kings who are bringing tremendous wealth into the city.

This reward will be limited to overcomers, but overcomers will not be limited by the reward. The fact that they alone have this type of entrance need not be taken to mean that this is the only type of entrance they have. Surely, overcomers will come and go as they please to the city, even teleporting into it and thus bypassing the gates if they desire. They are the pillars of the community, supporting its thriving economy by the wealth they bring into it. They will have unlimited access to the city and to the King of kings. As the population continues to grow infinitely, the greatest reward then will be the same as it is now—intimate fellowship with the Lord.

My anticipation, then, in consideration of the literal dimensions of the city, is that the general population of the eternal kingdom (who are born during the millennium and eternal state) will be able to enter the city in numerous ways: railways, subways, expressways, and airways. Entrance by the city gates may be reserved for overcomers on special occasions when they bring the *wealth of the nations* (Is 60:5,11) so that they may enter the city in this manner: The kings of the earth..."will bring the glory and the honor of the nations into it [the city] **in order that they may enter it** [the city]" (Rev 21:24-26; TM; Hodgian MT).[†]

On the other hand, perhaps it could be that the general populace might have access even through this honorific route on non-honorific occasions when the kings of the earth are not using it for parading their kingly entrances. This alternative is suggested because the symbolic contrast in both Rev 21:24-27 and 22:14-15 is not between kingly entrance and general entrance but between kingly entrance and non-entrance. Kingly admission is contrasted with not being able to enter the city at all, not with being able to enter it as a citizen of the nations (i.e., a member of the general populace). While it may be assumed that the nations will be able to enter the city (and one presumably would think that this includes entry through the gates in Rev 21:24-27), John makes it clear that it must not be assumed that the lost will have any entrance—by its gates or otherwise. The purpose of the symbolic contrast between entry and non-entry in Rev 22:14-15 suggests that if one is not allowed to enter by the gates, then one is not allowed to enter the city at all. I propose, therefore, that entrance by the gate serves dually for honorific entrance and general entrance. One purpose of the parallelism of the two passages and the contrast within both passages would seem to be to specify symbolically that those who are not able to enter the city by its gates are not allowed to enter the city at all. The nations would be able to enter by its gates, but not as kings. Only kings would be able to enter as kings by its gates. Subcomers and noncomers would not be able to enter by its gates and thus would be excluded from the city. The *ou me* is emphatic and prevents me from making the following parenthetical exception: "But there shall *by no means* enter it [**by the gates**] anything that defiles, or causes an abomination or a lie, but only those who are written in the Lamb's Book of Life." (Rev 21:27; NKJ)

One is not at liberty to impose parenthetically (from Rev 22:14) that those whose names are not in the Book of Life may enter the city by some other means than its gates. Universalists might try to insert *by the gates* into the

---

[*] These kings of the earth are at least overcomers in the end (such as the prodigal son) if not overcomers until the end. *Heavenly City overcomers* (HCO) will have their principle residence in the HC. T*wilight zone overcomers* (TZO) will have their principle residence in the TZ. See discussion surrounding *Illustration 370. Twilight Zone*, 960. The above discussion is not implementing the TZO model.

[†] Alternately, TZO might have to pay this tribute in order to enter the HC at all. They may not have the right to enter the city but may be allowed to enter it by paying homage to those who do have the right to live there.

verse parenthetically so as to suggest that the lost can enter the city by some other means, but I will not take such liberties with the text. I also would question conservative misthologists who may make such an insertion in order to try to read the text as making entrance into the city by some other means possible to those believers who subcome. Although I suspect multiple means of entrance (due to literal considerations), I also expect (due to the symbolic contrasts and correlative considerations) that those who are excluded from entering by the gates into the city are excluded from all forms of entrance into the city.

If this theory is correct, then the general populace may be allowed to enter by the gates into the city on general occasions, but only overcomers will have a right to enter by the gates on special occasions, such as kingly parades. Since the nations will have access to the leaves of the tree (Rev 22:2), without having a right to the tree, it is reasonable to suppose that they may have some type of entrance by the gates into the city as well. Nevertheless, only overcomers will have the actual *right* to the tree and gates. Most translations, however, render the subjunctive as if the word *right* applies only to the tree.

Illustration 224. Singular Right

Blessed are those who wash their robes, in order that

> *(1) they may have the **right to** the tree of life,*
> *and*
> *(2) **they may** enter by the gates into the city (TM).*

Leedy's diagrams certainly favor this traditional arrangement in which the only *right* given to the faithful is the tree of life. However, the *hina*-subjunctive clause, when denoting purpose (as it does here), may be translated appropriately with a simple infinitive (i.e., with *to*, GGBB, 472), as is done by Tatford and TEV.[1165]

Illustration 225. Dual Right

*Blessed are those who wash their robes, in order that they may **have the right***

> *(1) **to** the tree of life,*
> *and*
> *(2) **to** enter by the gates into the city (TM).*

This translation appears grammatically and contextually preferable. The context specifies that the city itself is a reward (Rev 22:19). Therefore, the right to enter by the city gates would appear to be a reward as well. Even assuming the accuracy of the traditional translation, though, I have had no difficulty in presenting my misthological interpretation of the verse as applying to overcomers.[*] Nevertheless, the context and grammar do appear to allow for a misthological alternative in which John is understood as indicating:

- Only overcomers have the right to the tree and city.
- Those not allowed entrance by the gates are not allowed any entrance.
- The nations are allowed entrance although they do not have a right to it.

When diagramming sentences in Greek, the break between multiple phrases following *hina* (*in order that*) and joined by *kai* (*and*) does not necessarily come immediately after the *hina*. Rather, the break may come later in the phrase, as Leedy acknowledges (e.g., Mt 17:27; Lk 21:36) and as suggested in *Illustration 225. Dual Right*.

Illustration 226. Parallel Breaks

Lk 21:36	Rev 22:14
In order that you may be counted worthy	In order that they may have the right
(1) to escape	(1) to the tree
and	and
(2) to stand	(2) to the gates

---

[*] For my principle discussions of misthopology, see *Tree and City Inclusion*, 527; *Misthologically Seeing God*, 528; *Tree and City Exclusion*, 530; *Rev 21:2—City*, 542; *Part*, 548; *Limited Accessibility*, 549; *Portion in the City*, 551; *City of Rest*, 551; *Gates of Honor and Limitation*, 551; *Limited Entrance*, 570; *Reward City*, 603; *Bridal City*, 604.

The conceptual parallel with Lk 21:36 is interesting for a number of reasons. Not all those who *escape* the tribulational wrath (i.e., who live until the end of the tribulation) will be considered *worthy* of having done so. The goats (i.e., the lost) who live until the end of the tribulation will not be considered worthy of having survived until the end of the tribulation although they will, in fact, have done so. The same may be said of gray sheep who live until the end of the tribulation. Even so, according to the text, living to the end of the tribulation is a misthological privilege granted to some faithful believers who will be considered worthy of having done so. Just as having a portion in the resurrection or being worthy of the resurrection means more than merely experiencing the resurrection (Lk 20:35; Rev 20:6), and just as inheriting the kingdom or being worthy of the kingdom refers to more than merely entering the kingdom (Mt 25:34; 1Cor 6:9-10; 15:50; Gal 5:21; Eph 5:5; 1Thess 2:12; 2Thess 1:5), and just as being worthy to escape and stand before the Lord refers to more than simply doing so (Lk 21:36),[*] so **having the right** to enter by the gates into the city probably means more than simply *entering by the gates*.

This observation is in harmony with my proposal that black sheep are killed during the tribulation. Living to the end of the tribulation will be a misthological attainment for some believers who are unwilling to take the mark of the beast. Moreover, although everyone will appear before the Lord, not everyone will be considered worthy of doing so, have the strength to *stand* before Him as a result, and be able to withstand shrinking away in shame.[†] Therefore, to some extent unspecified by the text, those who experience the benefits in both Lk 21:36 and Rev 22:14 exceed the number of those who are *worthy* of doing so or who have the *right* to do so. This acknowledgement does not detract from the blessedness of the benefits but underscores their richness—these benefits will be experienced to varying degrees. The highest degree (i.e., experiencing the benefit as a reward) is reserved for those who misthologically qualify for the benefit. There is a gray area in which some of those experiencing the result may not be qualified misthologically for the fullness of the experience.[1166] Nevertheless, there is also a black and white dimension in that some will be qualified and some will be disqualified. Neither black sheep nor goats will have access to the tree or city.

As for the text from Revelation, entrance by the gates is the only entrance entertained by the text. One would tend to think that one who is denied entrance by the gates is denied entrance by any other means. After all, the parallel passage in Rev 21:24-27 does not suggest entrance by the gates as an alternate means of entry. The contrast is absolute—between entry and non-entry. Jesus has this to say about those who seek some other entrance than the rightful one: "He who does not enter by the door into the fold of the sheep, but climbs up some other way, he is a thief and a robber" (Jn 10:1). The symbolic intent is not to suggest multiple means of entry in either Jn 10:1 or Rev 22:14. The symbolic intent is to show that those not allowed the proper form of entry are not allowed any entry. Subcomers will no more be able to climb mistholic walls than unbelievers will be able to climb soteric walls. Correlatively, the exclusion of the latter from the city is just as complete as the exclusion of the former. On the other hand, just as the sheep are allowed to come and go in the context of Jn 10:1, so one may infer from the literal dimensions of the city that those who are qualified for the symbolic entrance will be allowed to come and go through other means as well. Subcomers will not eat of the tree of life or have access to the tree of life. Indeed, subcomers will be excluded from the holy city which houses the tree of life (Rev 2:7; 22:14,19).

Misthological Intimacy

Betz relates this quote from C. S. Lewis: "Money is not the natural reward of love; that is why we call a man a mercenary if he married a woman for the sake of her money. But marriage is the proper reward for a real lover, and he is not a mercenary for desiring it."[1167] We are not mercenaries seeking rewards when we see that the natural connection between them and our enjoyment of them as consummation with Christ.[‡] We get to rule *with Him* in His kingdom, dine *with Him* at His table, sit *with Him* on His throne, and walk *with Him* in white. As the author writes this paragraph, he is wanting to go watch a movie with either of his sons, but they want to go with their friends instead. So he is staying home typing this paragraph, because he has no desire to go watch that movie alone. Let there be no doubt that if the Lord came to the door and asked the author if he would like to go watch the movie *with Him*, the author literally would jump at the chance. Maybe when the author gets to heaven, he and the Lord will be able to go watch a movie together then, maybe even that particular movie. In the interim, he finds the words of Chris Rice's song coming to mind:

---

[*] See *Misthological Worthiness*, 73.
[†] See *Before (emprosthen)*, 663.
[‡] See *Love as Reward for Love*, 736.

> I just want to be with You
> I want this waiting to be over
> I just want to be with You
> And it helps to know the day is getting closer.
> But every minute takes an hour
> Every inch feels like a mile
> Till I won't have to imagine
> And I finally get to see You smile!

Trillions upon zillions of people scattered throughout the stars will be longing to see Jesus in an up-close, personal, extended, face-to-face fellowship in eternity future, but only overcomers will have this privilege—the greatest of rewards. As humanity increases in number, seeing Jesus face-to-face will become an increasingly rare opportunity. The greatest privilege Moses had was to know the Lord face-to-face (Dt 5:4; 34:10). It is also the greatest privilege overcomers will experience (1Cor 13:12). Conversely, the greatest tragedy would be to look into His eyes and experience shame rather than joy (1Jn 2:28).

Conclusion

Imagine being born in the far distant eternity future. Your planet may now be one of the trillions of planets that has a population that exceeds billions of people. Many of the other planets only have thousands or millions. A few people on your planet actually may have seen the Lord Jesus face-to-face, and perhaps even a handful of them actually were able to touch the nail scars on His hands in person. Still, being only a few thousand years old yourself, you are still very young and have not yet seen the Lord face-to-face. Oh, to be sure, you have seen Him on the interplanetary communication networks countless times, but now, in just fifty years, the Lord Himself is scheduled to come to your planet for a personal appearance since your planet is the capital planet of your galaxy. Your planet is buzzing with excitement over the anticipation of the event. Super bowls or Olympics on old earth would be tame by comparison to the excitement that is being generated and the preparations being set in motion. Naturally, accommodations will need to be made for the many other people on nearby planets in your galaxy who will wish to attend.

Needless to say, everyone would like to see Jesus face-to-face when He comes, but that would be impossible. Nevertheless, He will attempt to personally see as many as possible. Your planetary ruler, however, being an overcomer, has often sat down face-to-face with Jesus via teleportation in a time bubble and personally and privately had fellowship with the Lord in discussing the affairs of your planet. They reminisce about the past as they discuss the present and plan for the future. It has actually been rumored on your planet that Jesus takes time to watch an occasional movie with your planetary ruler. The implications of that type of intimacy with the Lord are almost too mind boggling to comprehend. How could Jesus possibly have time for movies when He is so busy doing so many things and traveling to remote galaxies like yours as time permits? There is no doubt in your mind that the greatest joy in your planetary ruler's heart is not the joy of ruling for Jesus; rather, it is the ecstasy of spending time with Jesus. Little do you know that before your planetary overcomer ever saw Jesus' face for the first time in the rapture eons ago, he was singing,

> Uppy, Daddy, Uppy, let me see your face;
> Uppy, Daddy, Uppy, let me feel your embrace;
> Uppy, Daddy, Uppy, my feet are tired;
> Uppy, Daddy, Uppy, I want to go home;
>
> Uppy, Daddy, Uppy, kiss my cheek;
> Uppy, Daddy, Uppy, you're not weak;
> Uppy, Daddy, Uppy, my feet are tired;
> Uppy, Daddy, Uppy, I want to go home;
>
> Uppy, Daddy, Uppy, let me rest on you;
> Uppy, Daddy, Uppy, I love you too;
> Uppy, Daddy, Uppy, my feet are tired;
> Uppy, Daddy, Uppy, come Lord, come.[1168]

Chapter 29.
Punitive Podium

Introduction

The present work has provided evidence that the outer darkness is a picture of the negative misthological outcome at the Bema for unfaithful Christians. One common misperception that frequently is raised against such a position is the assertion that the Bema must be positive. This objection may be posed in the form of a question: "Can believers actually be judged and perhaps even punished at the Bema, or must their experience at the Bema be limited to a positive outcome?" The present chapter will respond to the mindset that asserts that believers cannot have a negative experience at the Bema. At the same time, it will be shown why the conservative reluctance to describe this negative experience as punishment has been rejected in favor of the ultraistic terminology. The question really boils down to asking, "Is it accurate to say that believers actually are punished at the Bema?"

An article by Sproule, "Judgment Seat or Awards Podium," starts with the premise that the Bema was both a judgment seat **and** an awards podium.[1169] The article then proceeds to give support for the inclusion of the judgment seat motif. In contrast, others (such as Hoyt) start with the premise that the Bema cannot be both a judgment seat and an awards podium. It exclusively refers to awards from this perspective. Sumner defends Hoyt's position against Faust's misthological claims concerning the punitive aspects of the Bema. While the present work does not share Faust's literal inclusion of Gehenna in the punitive misthological range, the forthright manner in which Faust defends the punitive position is appreciated.[1170] In the ensuing discussion, the exclusively positive **pro-awards** position will be denoted as **PA** and the potentially punitive **pro-judgment** position as **PJ**.*

According to FB (Friberg), *bema* has two basic meanings: a (1) step or (2) platform ascended by steps. The point of contention between PA and PJ is not the range of meaning or the basic meaning of the Greek word *bema*; rather, the disagreement is concerning the meaning of *bema* in the Pauline texts (Rom 14:10; 2Cor 5:10). Specifically, what is the resultant nature of the believer's judgment? PA advocates attempt to limit the meaning of *bema* in these passage to one type of platform (i.e., an awards podium), whereas PJ advocates believe that the *bema* has a *judicial* nature to it as well,† in which the positive and negative works of a believer are weighed, and corresponding positive and negative consequences are rendered.

PA (Pro-Awards) Arguments

Hoyt begins his discussion of *the Judgment Seat and Punishment* by noting that Dollar takes a misthological view of the outer darkness, to which Hoyt responds: "Such a view misinterprets and misapplies this parable, for the unprofitable servant is not a saved individual, but is an unsaved person facing eternal damnation. To apply this to a Christian, even to a carnal Christian, is contrary to the whole tenor of biblical revelation."[1171] My reply will begin with a summation of the arguments employed by such PA advocates against the misthological position. Some of these points are from Hoyt's article and book; some are from my personal interaction with PA advocates. I will then show why it is necessary to reject this PA response due to lexical, contextual, and theological evidence. The arguments advanced against the PJ interpretation typically run as follows.

Forgiveness

Perhaps the most common PA objection is that judicial forgiveness of sins is so complete as to render judicial punishment of sin impossible (Is 38:17; 44:22; Ps 103:12; Micah 7:19; Col 2:13; Heb 8:12).[1172] Thus, a judicial understanding of the Bema is impossible. The judgment of the believer cannot include the judgment of his or her sins. We cannot be punished for our sin, so we cannot be punished for our sinful works. Forgiveness and chastisement are familial rather than judicial (cp. 1Jn 1:9; Heb 12:6). Our sin and sin nature are removed completely in heaven, so there is no longer any need for forgiveness or chastisement.

---

* **PA** (pro-award)—takes the Bema as an awards podium rather than a judgment seat, which is a *Toothless Bema* perception.

  PJ (pro-judgment)—takes the Bema as both a judgment seat and an awards podium.

† The word *judicial* is being used in a more comprehensive manner in this chapter than that used elsewhere in this book. Elsewhere, the popular usage has been adopted in which judicial righteousness means to be forensically righteous in terms of soteriologically-imputed righteousness. In this popular capacity, judicial and misthological terminology were contrasted. However, in the present chapter, it will be demonstrated that there is a sense in which misthology is judicial, but the judicial aspect of misthology must still be clearly distinguished from that of soteriology. The Bema is misthologically judicial, but it is most definitely not soteriologically judicial for the believer. The purpose of the judgment for the believer is to determine judicially the believer's positive or negative rewards in heaven, not to determine whether the believer's fate is heaven versus hell.

No Condemnation, Judgment, or Punishment

A similar PA protest against the Marrowistic viewpoint is the objection that the judgment of the believer cannot result in condemnation (Rom 8:1). We cannot be condemned on the basis of our performance. Consequently, our performance cannot result in any type of negative response. Believers cannot come into judgment (Jn 3:18; 5:24; 6:37; Rom 5:1; 8:1; 1Cor 11:32). Stanford clarifies, on the basis of 2Cor 5:10, that the believer's works rather than the believer himself is judged: "Although the believer's <u>works</u> are both judged and rewarded at the Bema, he himself is in no way judged or condemned" (emphasis his).[1173]

Dual Meaning is Impossible

Granted, Stanford overstates his PA case when he claims: "'Judgment seat' refers to the place where winners of contests were rewarded; it was called the 'reward seat,' or Bema, and never was used as a judicial bench."[1174] This statement is patently false, if the NT as a whole is taken into consideration. To assist Stanford in his criticism of the PJ position, I will offer a more sophisticated representation of the point Stanford is trying to make with the following rewording. Although the Bema can have either a misthological or judicial meaning, these two meanings are so radically different in nature that it cannot have both meanings at the same time. Thus, from this PA perspective, misthologists who assume both meanings of *bema* in one context are guilty of illegitimate totality transfer.

2Cor 5:10 and Unconditional Love

The misthological result is described as receiving back from the Lord, which is in harmony with the awards view. According to PA advocates, judgment was to determine innocence or guilt, not to give something. Stanford says, "Paul did not use the word for 'bad' which would signify that which is morally evil, but rather the word which means 'unacceptable.'"[1175] Others who share the PA perspective with Stanford believe that *bad* may be taken merely to mean the loss of reward. Supposedly, the bad feelings or disappointment believers may feel will be self-imposed rather than imposed by the Lord. Believers may be ashamed of their behavior, but the Lord will not be ashamed of them because He unconditionally loves believers. Thus, the Lord will not express disappointment with us, although we may be disappointed with ourselves. In the PA perspective, the Lord will not express disappointment with us because of His unconditional love for us.

No fear

PA believes that we have nothing to fear from the Lord's coming (1Jn 4:18), so it cannot be punitive. We have nothing to fear from the Lord. We are to serve Him out of love rather than out of fear. Those who fear the Lord are being very immature in their understanding of His loving nature.

Krima

If Paul had used *krima* instead of *bema*, then he clearly would have been denoting judgment. Thus, PA adherents stipulate that if Paul had meant judgment, then he could have specified that meaning with *krima* rather than *bema*.

Historical Background

The Isthmian Games played a part in how one is to understand the Pauline Bema, certainly in the Corinthian reference. Considering the fact that Paul was writing to believers at Corinth and his usage of athletic terminology, the Award's Platform at the Olympic Games probably is intended in the reference. The judge at the Bema rewarded the winners. Hoyt remarks from a PA perspective: "He did not whip the losers."[1176] Losers were merely left unrewarded.

Rewards are Positive

The very word *reward* suggests something positive rather than something negative. According to Stanford, "It is not the Lord's purpose there to chasten His beloved Bride for her already forgiven sins, but to <u>reward</u> her service and way of life" (emphasis his).[1177] Christ will reward everyone according to his or her works (Rev 22:12). This is in verbal harmony with 2Cor 5:10; hence, PA would have us believe that Christ will reward us according to our works, not punish us. After all, Paul earlier had told the Corinthians that God would praise every one (1Cor 4:5). Since rewards are positive rather than punitive, PA maintains that rewards must be equated with the

Olympian *bema*, which was strictly positive. Rewards are awards. They cannot be associated with the judicial *bema*, which was negative.

PJ (Pro-Judgment) Response

Illegitimate Totality Transfer

Having outlined the typical PA arguments above, against the implementation of a negative judicial misthology, I now will render my judgment. The present work takes the dual approach in which the Bema is taken to be both positive and negative. I thus advocate the PJ position rather than the PA opposition. In response to the preceding PA arguments, I will begin by stating that the PA rejection of the dual meaning of the Bema is guilty of a false dichotomy. Just as it was not beyond Paul to create new words, it is not beyond him to combine two meanings into one word. At one time, I would have told my children that a football and a Nerf ball are two different kinds of balls and that the word *ball* could not possibly refer to both. Yet today they have Nerf footballs. Someone combined the two. Likewise, it would be false to conclude that since golf balls are round and Frisbees are flat that there could be no such sport as Frisbee golf. There is reason to believe that Paul combined the concepts of awards and judgment into one word.

The PA charge of illegitimate totality transfer must not only demonstrate that the Bema **can** have two radically different meanings; it is also obligated to prove that it **must** have two different meanings and that both meanings are not intended by Paul. In other words, the PA argument is that Bema can mean two radically different things, and in texts where so employed, both meanings are impossible. But this argument may be guilty of a jump in logic. That the same word *may* have two separate meanings in two separate contexts does not necessarily prove that it *must* have two separate meanings in a given context. *May have* is not the same as *must have*. The proof as to whether a dual PA-PJ position is possible will involve considering whether both meanings are represented by the word in that particular context. The presentation of positive rewards combined with the historical background of the Olympic Games favor a PA understanding in the Corinthian epistle. Nevertheless, this does not prove that PA is exclusively or even primarily in Paul's mind, especially in the book of Romans.

Bema

In defining the various meanings of *bema*, BDAG lists both Rom 14:10 and 2Cor 5:10 under the section of tribunal, especially judicial bench, more specifically "the judgment seat" of God and Christ. Therefore, BDAG defines Bema from a PJ perspective concerning the Pauline texts. Likewise, Louw-Nida (L-N) states concerning the *bema*:

> There is almost always an important component of judicial function associated with this term. Therefore in translating *bema*, it is often best to use a phrase such as 'a place where a judge decides' or 'a place where decisions are made' or 'a judge's seat.' The focus upon judgment is particularly important in those passages which refer to the judgment seat of God (Ro 14.10) and of Christ (2 Cor 5.10).

Thus, this Greek lexicon also agrees with the PJ position. An extra biblical example, such as the Sibylline Oracles (2:216-220), illustrates this as well: "What evils anyone did previously, lead all the souls of men from the murky dark to judgment, to the tribunal of the great immortal God...who will be the judge of mortals." Here, we find corroboration of the association of the *bema* with God's judgment. God's *bema* is judicial, not merely an awards podium. This understanding of *bema* in extra biblical Greek literature appears to be in substantial harmony with that of the lexical information seen above for the Greek NT.

Romans 14:10-13

A very strong case for the connection of the *bema* with judgment can also be made from the context of Paul's use in Romans 14:10.

> [10] But you, why do you *judge* [*krino*] your brother? Or you again, why do you regard your brother with contempt? For we shall all *stand before* [*paristemi*] the *judgment seat* [*bema*] of God. [11] For it is written, "As I live, says the Lord, every knee shall bow to Me, and every tongue shall give praise to God." [12] So then each one of us shall give *account* [*logos*] of himself to God. [13] Therefore let us not *judge* [*krino*] one another anymore. (Rom 14:10-13)

The association of *bema* with *krino* (*judge*) and *paristemi* (*stand before*) in this passage would suggest a legal scene: *bema* seems to be offset with *krino*. Believers should not judge one another because God will do the judging. The *bema* is equated with the verb *krino* (*judge*). The PA argument that Paul would have used *bema's* nominal cognate—*krima* (*judgment*) rather than *bema*—is shown to be superficial. Paul does, in fact, associate the *bema* with this type of judgment.

Rom 14:10

As noted above, the fact that believers *stand before* (*paristemi*) the *bema* indicates a legal scene. BDAG and FB note that *paristemi* can be used as a legal technical term. FB states that it can mean to "legally, *prove, show to be true* (AC 24.13)...as a legal technical term *stand before* (AC 27.24)." BDAG (1.e) defines it "as a legal technical term [to] bring before (a judge)," and likewise as a legal technical term in Acts 27:24, meaning "you must stand before the Emperor (as [your] judge)," and BDAG (2.a.α) also considers it to have the same judicial meaning in Rom 14:10. Since this judgment seat is one before which all Christians will appear, it must be the Judgment Seat of Christ and is explicitly referred to as such by the MT and rendered as such by a number of translations (e.g., KJV, NKJ). This passage is referring to standing before a judge in a court scene.

Rom 14:11

The next verse in the context of Romans continues the judgment scene and depicts a universal acknowledgment that God is the righteous and sovereign Judge of all. We see God as *Judge* (*krites*) of all in Acts 10:42. He will exercise *judgment* (*krisis*) on all (Jn 5:22). Or as Paul says in Romans, God will *judge* (*krino*) everybody (Rom 2:16). Of course, if judgment is universal, it must include Christians. This is Paul's assumption in Rom 14:10-12. That judgment will be universal (v. 11) means that it includes Christians (vv. 10,12). This universal judgment cannot be limited to PA. It is judicial. It is punitive. The lost will be punished in hell as a result of this judgment. Therefore, the judicial and punitive dimension of this judgment is beyond question. Verse 11 certainly argues in favor of the PJ understanding of this passage. Everyone, including Christians, will stand before God in judgment. The judgment of Christians in verses 10 and 12 is based on the universal nature of God's judicial judgment in verse 11. One certainly would be inclined to think that the judgment of Christians consequently would share this judicial aspect.

The present author, therefore, would question Hodges' disassociation of *krisis* with *bema*. Even Hodges admits that *bema* may refer to *judicial* bench in Rom 14:10 and 2Cor 5:10.[1178] *Bema* is certainly associated with the verbal form *krino* in the context of Rom 14:10. For that matter, does Jesus not refer to Christians being subject to *krino* in Mt 7:1-2, and would this not be at the *bema*? Paul certainly associated *bema* with *krino* (Acts 25:10). He acknowledges that believers are subject to the Lord's *krino* (1Cor 11:32; cp. 2Tim 4:1). Moreover, Hodges' statement that Paul never uses *krisis* to refer to the believer's experience is open to question in 2Thess 1:5. If being counted misthologically worthy in this verse is the result of a successful outcome at God's *krisis* (as Wilkin correctly perceives in GNTC), then Paul indeed does link the two words. In any event, the two concepts are related, and *krisis* is used by other biblical writers to describe the Bema experience of believers (Heb 9:27; 10:27; Jam 2:13; 5:12).

Rom 14:12

FB also says *logos* is used "in a somewhat legal or technical sense; (a) *accusation, matter, charge; (b) account, reckoning* (RO 14.12)." A courtroom scene is envisioned, not an awards podium. Since this judgment of accountability will include everyone (v. 11), certainly it must include Christians. This is Paul's point (vv. 10,12). There is no reason to judge one another because we will be judged by God (cp. 1Cor 4:5). We each will take the witness stand and give account of how we have lived. Believers, like everyone else, will be held accountable for the way they have lived and be called on the carpet, so to speak, to give a verbal accounting for their behavior.

When Paul appeared before Gallio's judgment seat, he fully expected that he would have to open his mouth and give a verbal defense for his actions (Acts 18:14). When Paul stood before Festus' judgment seat, charges were made against him, and he was given a chance verbally to *speak in his own defense* (Acts 25:8). The verb used in this instance is *apologeomai*, which means, "to give an account of oneself, hence *to defend oneself*" (TY). Paul was his own defense attorney.

Apologeomai is a verbal compound of the word *logos*, used by Paul in Rom 14:12. When Polycarp entered the stadium to stand trial before the proconsul for his faith, Polycarp boldly confessed that he was a Christian, despite being threatened with lions and burning. And in response to the inquisition, he responded to the proconsul,

"To thee I have thought it right *to offer an account* [*logos*] of my faith; for we are taught to give all due honor (which entails no injury upon ourselves) to the powers and authorities which are ordained of God. But as for these, I do not deem them worthy of receiving any *account* [*apologeomai*] from me" (Mpol 10:2). Polycarp did not consider it necessary to give an account to the bloodthirsty populace sitting in the stadium crying for his death, but he did deem it obligatory to offer an account to the proconsul. Polycarp used *logos* and *apologeomai* interchangeably for *giving an account* in this legal setting. He was burned alive for the account that he rendered. These stadiums were not merely places for handing out awards. Paul tells us that we must give an account to God as well.

When Jesus was brought up on charges before His accusers, Pilate (Jesus' judge), was amazed that Jesus offered no defense and made no answer, not even a word (Mt 27:14; Mk 15:5). The expected norm was for the defendant to offer a verbal defense. Paul knew what it was like to stand before a *bema* and have to offer a verbal defense in behalf of his actions. He told Christians that they could expect to do the same before God's *bema*. This judgment must be judicial in nature. **When an athlete stood on a *bema*, it was not to be judged or to make a verbal defense of his actions but to be rewarded on the basis of the examination that he already had passed. Since we are to perform these actions at the JSC, this *bema* must be something other than an awards podium.** In contrast to the PA equation, we must give a confession and explanation: "As I live, says the Lord, every knee will bow to Me, and every tongue will confess to God. So then each one of us will give an account of himself to God." (Rom 14:11-12; TM). These activities did not occur at an athletic podium. Any perception of this *bema* as a PA is a misperception. This *bema* is thoroughly PJ. This *bema* is misthologically judicial.

NIDNTT concurs with the lexical descriptions by FB and BDAG of the *bema* in Rom 14:10 and 2Cor 5:10 as denoting a **judgment** seat. It was the platform from which the civil officials decided certain legal cases and rendered judgment (Mt 27:19; Jn 19:13; Acts 18:12,16; 25:6,10,17), as in the case of Jesus before Pilate or Paul before Gallio and Festus. There will be a role reversal. Just as Jesus stood before the judgment seat of men, men will stand before the Judgment Seat of God.

Krima

The PA statement concerning *krima* is true as far as it goes, but it does not demonstrate the PA contention. If Paul had used *krima*, the judicial nature of the judgment would have been specified. The PA position, however, requires something much stronger than this simple acknowledgement. The PA position is wrong to imply that Paul would have had to use the word *krima* rather than *bema* if he had meant judgment. The common meaning of *bema* in the NT is judgment seat, not awards podium. Jesus did not stand before Pilate's awards podium. In fact, there are no passages in the NT where *bema* clearly refers to awards podium, but multiple places where it clearly refers to judgment seat. And it is this latter meaning that most naturally suggests itself in the context of Rom 14:10. For that matter, the PA understanding of *bema* in Rom 14:10 is contextually impossible to accept. The entire world will stand before God in judgment (Rom 14:11), not before His awards podium.

Illustration 227. The Bema is a Judicial Subset

The Bema of Christ for believers in 14:10 is but a subset of the accountability which the entire human race must render to God as each human being stands before God in judgment (Bema ⊂ judgment). This is not to say that every human being will be judged at the same time or that believers must necessarily be judged at the same time as unbelievers. What it does demonstrate, however, is that the Bema partakes of the judicial nature of the judgment rendered in this context. The world will not stand on God's awards podium to hear His voice of praise for their sins! The Bema is not an awards podium in this context. Everyone, lost and saved, will be judged judicially. For the lost, this judgment will focus on the soteriological outcome. For the saved, this judgment will be limited to the misthological sphere. In *Illustration 227*, think of the white area as being soteriological. The gray strips are misthological. Within this larger circle of gray and white strips, resides a smaller sphere that is composed exclusively of gray misthological matter.

Illustration 228. Misthological Sphere Within Judicial Context

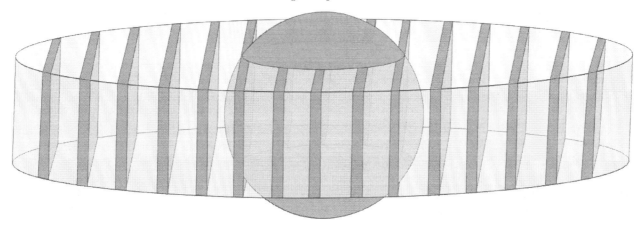

Or if one were to turn the illustration sideways, as in *Illustration 228*, the three-dimensional nature might be easier to grasp. The sphere represents the Bema. The judicial context of Rom 14 is pictured as the disk round about it. In this three-dimensional view, I have not embedded the misthological sphere within the judicial dimension. While completely immersing the Bema within a judicial semantic range would seem preferable in Rom 14, I am leaving part of the sphere out of the judicial range. This protruding misthological material might be gleaned from non-judicial elements in other texts that focus on the athletic imagery of the Olympian games. After all, the PJ position is not that the Bema is exclusively judicial in every misthological context. Rather, the judicial element is present within certain misthological contexts. The sphere for the semantic range as to what the Bema entails for believers draws its source from both judicial and non-judicial texts.

Judgment is a prominent theme in Romans

Katakrima (*condemnation*) is used 3 times in the NT, all in the book of Romans. Experiential salvation in the present temporal period from this condemnation is limited to those Christians who walk according to the Spirit (Rom 8:1). Those Christians who walk according to the flesh will not experience salvation from this death sentence (Rom 8:6). The reasonable deduction is that those believers who do not walk according to the Spirit will experience condemnation. The MT confirms this contextual impression: "There is therefore now no condemnation to those who are in Christ Jesus, who do not walk according to the flesh, but according to the Spirit" (Rom 8:1; NKJ). There are two requirements for a person not to be under condemnation. The applicability of the promise is limited to those (1) *who are in Christ* **and** (2) *who walk according to the Spirit*. All believers meet the first qualification positionally, but not all believers meet the second qualification experientially. Consequently, this usage of *condemnation* indicates that believers who do not walk according to the Spirit are condemned. They are subject to experiential condemnation. This position is not incompatible with Marrowism.

On the other hand, some conditionalists insist that Rom 8:1 refers to soteriological condemnation and then condition salvation from that condemnation on two things: being in Christ and walking in Christ. In this Calvinistic scheme of things, your walk (i.e., your experience) determines whether you were ever genuinely saved. Those who walk in Christ really are saved; those who do not are not. Thomas holds this view:

> The claim that you are in Christ Jesus, and under no condemnation because you have been redeemed, is only valid if it is vindicated by a walk that indicates your new relationship to God.

I know of no gospel in the Bible that offers you salvation from the condemnation of your sin, that does not at the same time demand a radical change of walk![1179]

This hermeneutical approach claims that your justification is validated by your performance. Your justification is invalid if it is not stamped with good works. Proveitistic salvation from hell demands a radical change in your performance according to such backdoor LS. Ultimately, your salvation from hell is conditioned on works according to this Thomanistic hermeneutic. Perhaps Thomas doubts the gospel of grace since it does not demand a radical change in one's performance for entrance into heaven. In any case, Thomas is his own worst enemy. In his chapter (*Three Categories of Men*) which immediately precedes his statement above, Thomas affirms the existence of carnal Christians. He acknowledges that these wilderness Christians are indeed saved.[1180] And in the chapter before that one, he confirms the existence of two classes of carnal Christians, whom he likewise insists are saved.[1181] Since his understanding of Rom 8:1 effectively rules out the existence of carnal Christians, his interpretation of this verse is refuted by his own analysis and results in a schizophrenic questioning of conversion based on personal holiness.[1182] Had he simply acknowledged that carnal believers could be condemned, he easily could have avoided such conflicting statements.

The recognition of the *condemnation* of believers is self-evident not only in the context of Rom 8:1, but also in the cognate forms found elsewhere in Romans. *Katakrino* (*condemn*) is used 6 times. Believers can be condemned (Rom 14:23). *Krino* (*judge/condemn*) is used 18 times. This judgment is universal (Rom 2:16; 3:6). Believers can be condemned (Rom 14:22). *Krima* (*judgment/condemnation*) is used 6 times. Believers can be condemned (Rom 13:2).

Nine of these thirty-three references, using various forms of the word *condemnation* in Romans, are found in ch. 14, a chapter that is concerned with the judgment of believers. That *bema* in Rom 14:10 is dealing with the **judgment** of believers is not surprising since (1) the immediate context of 14:10-12 is using legal terminology, (2) the immediate context of 14:10-13 uses the universal judgment as the basis for the exhortation concerning the judgment of believers, (3) the broad context of the chapter is dealing with the judgment of believers, not the awarding of believers, and (4) the broader context of the book is dealing with the universal judgment that includes the judgment of believers. What evidence does PA find in the book of Romans that *bema* means awards podium rather than judgment seat? None. Sensitivity to the literary context appears to be lacking in the PA assault on punitive misthology. According to the book of Romans, believers will be judged, not merely positively rewarded.

2Cor 5:10

Having dealt with lexical considerations of Rom 14:10, the same will now be done for the other Pauline usage of *bema*, which is in 2Cor 5:10: "For we must all appear *before* [*emprosthen*] the *judgment seat* [*bema*] of Christ, that each one may be *repaid* [*komizo*] for his deeds in the body, according to what he has done, whether good or *bad* [*phaulos*]" (TM).

Before (*emprosthen*)

FB says that *emprosthen* (*before*) may be used "as a legal technical term of appearing before a judge or high official (MT 27:11)." BDAG (1.b.β) says that *emprosthen* may mean to appear "before, in the presence of….Especially of appearing before a judge Mt 27:11; also before the divine judge 25:32; Lk 21:36; 1Th 2:19; 3:13; GPt 11:48; cp. 2Cor 5:10. But the judicial element is not decisive in all the passages…[i.e.] 1Th 1:3; 3:9; 1Jn 3:19." Although BDAG acknowledges that not all passages are decisively judicial, it considers the passages such as 2Cor 5:10 to be **decisively judicial**.

Emprosthen is used in a misthological sense in Mt 10:32-33 (cf. Lk 12:8-9). When we appear *before God*, Jesus will deny us or confess us, depending on whether we denied or confessed Him. The universality of this judgment is indicated in Mt 25:32, where both the sheep and goats will be gathered before Him for judgment. Believers and unbelievers both experience the same type of judgment in that both are judged according to their works—that is, both groups are rewarded and punished according to their works. However, the parameters are different for believers and unbelievers. Believers cannot come into soteriological judgment. They cannot be judged soteriologically. That is, they cannot be sent to hell. Unbelievers will be punished and rewarded in hell as a result of the judgment; believers will be punished and rewarded in heaven as a result of the judgment. Unbelievers will have different degrees of rewards in hell; whereas, believers will have different degrees of rewards in heaven.

In Mt 27:11, Jesus *stood before* (*emprosthen*) the governor and charges were made against Him. Again, we have a legal setting. In Lk 19:27, we see punitive judgment executed on God's enemies who are made to come before Him. In Lk 21:36, Jesus urges believers to pray "in order that you may have strength to escape all these things that are about to take place, and to *stand before* the Son of Man." Again, believers *standing before* Jesus is apparently judicial. One does not worry about having strength to stand before an awards podium! All believers will appear before the *bema*, but not all believers will be able to stand it. Many will shrink away in shame since they are unworthy of reward (1Jn 2:28).[1183] We need to pray that we will have the misthological strength to stand before the Lord so that we will be misthologically blameless when presented before Him at the *bema* (Col 1:22), rather than shrink away from Him in misthological shame (cp. Ps 1:5; Jude 1:24).

In Acts 18:17, "all the Greeks took Sosthenes, the ruler of the synagogue, and beat him before the judgment seat." Here *before* is used of an action that took place "before the *bema*," which is verbally identical to 2Cor 5:10. Paul seems to associate his crown with how his converts would appear before Jesus. "For who is our hope or joy or crown of exultation? Is it not even you, *before* our Lord Jesus at His coming?" (1Thess 2:19) It is little wonder that Paul is concerned that God would establish their "hearts unblamable in holiness *before* our God and Father at the coming of our Lord Jesus" (1Thess 3:13). How well they do when they were called on the carpet *before* God was not taken for granted, and it will affect how well Paul does when he gives account for what he has done.

Apparently, awards will be rendered **upon** (*epi*) the *bema*, but judgment will be rendered **upon or before** the *bema*. (*Epi* is used in connection with the *bema* in a judicial sense, as is *emprosthen*.) Evidently, the defendant would step up on the *bema* platform to stand before the judge who was seated on the *bema* seat. To stand before the judge would indicate a judicial *bema*. To stand on the *bema* could denote either a judicial or Olympic *bema*. Using this as my working hypothesis, I merely will note that in an excellent chapter on the Olympic Games, Sauer states that when the victor's name "was announced by the herald, he had to appear before the raised seat of the Umpire" to receive the "victor's wreath."[1184] My tentative proposal is that the victor appeared **on** the *bema* **platform** to stand **before** the *bema* **seat**; whereas, those who *stood before* (*emprosthen*) the *bema* were there to be judged judicially, not simply awarded. Even so, Sauer has no qualms with identifying the *bema* as a judgment seat in spite of the Olympian background.[1185]

Repaid (*komizo*)

The lexical information concerning *bema* in the discussion of Rom 14:10 already has been found to be supportive of the judicial understanding of judgment seat in 2Cor 5:10. Proceeding to the next major word *komizo*,[*] note that L-N defines it as,

> to cause someone to experience something on the basis of what that person has already done – 'to cause to experience in return, to **cause to suffer** for, to cause to experience in proportion to, to be repaid for....'for the one who has done wrong will be **caused to suffer** for what he has done' Col 3.25;... 'in order that each one may be repaid in proportion to those things which he has done in his bodily life' 2 Cor 5.10.

The UBS sums up these explanations rather nicely with its definition: *be paid back*. The *bema*, as Paul presents it, is payback time. It is time for God to pay back good for good, and bad for bad. The Lord will pay back in like kind. If one accepts the L-N definition (and this current study has given considerable reason for doing so), then God will pay back those who have caused suffering by causing them to suffer. The *bema* is definitely punitive. This is the only sense that does justice to Paul's use of this word in Col 3:25. "He who does wrong will be repaid the wrong which he has done" (TM).

PA Counterargument #1

The PA counterargument is that *bad for bad* simply means *no reward for bad*. The bad works are burnt up leaving nothing to be rewarded. This counterargument is weak in that it practically pictures God as ignoring the misbehavior: The Lord simply does not reward the bad things we do since He finds them unacceptable. This PA rejoinder falls short of the force of the verb. Biblically, God is depicted as rendering harm for harm and evil for evil. Those familiar with the OT background should have no qualms about God rewarding evil with evil.

Evil for Evil

"The Lord shall repay the evildoer according to his wickedness" (2Sam 3:39; NKJ). Will the Lord repay the evildoer by ignoring his wickedness? Not hardly. The Lord says, "I will repay Babylon and all the inhabitants of

---

[*] See *Col 3:23-25*, 122, *NT Usage*, 177. Also see 1Pet 1:9 in *Salvation: A Categorical Analysis*

Chaldea for all the evil they have done in Zion in your sight" (Jer 28:24). Will the Lord repay the Babylonians by doing nothing about their evil? Far to the contrary. Again the Lord says, 'Behold, **I bring evil** on this place and on its inhabitants'" (2Kgs 22:16). Just as the Lord can repay the evil/bad with evil/bad, so He can repay the Christian who does evil/bad with evil/bad in 2Cor 5:10.

The Lord promises, "**I will bring evil** upon you" (1Kgs 21:21). Of course, the intent of this warning is that those being warned will turn from their evil and thus avoid being repaid with evil. "If that nation, against whom I have pronounced, turn from their evil, **I will repent of the evil** that I thought to do unto them" (Jer 18:8; KJV). If they did not repent of doing evil, then the Lord would not repent of bringing evil upon them. The Lord clearly dealt in this manner with His own people when they did evil in the OT. "I, the Lord, have spoken, surely this **I will do to all this evil** congregation who are gathered together against Me. In this wilderness they shall be destroyed, and there they shall die" (Num 14:35). God brought evil upon His own people when they deserved it (Jer 11:17; also see 1Sam 17:14; 19:9; 1Kgs 14:10; 21:21; 2Chron 34:24; Job 42:11; Jer 6:19; 11:11; 16:10; 36:3).

Numerous translations render Is 45:7 as saying that God creates *evil* (*rah*). Other translations render it as creating *calamity*, *bad times*, *disaster*, *trouble*, or *woe*. Certainly, God does not cause moral evil, but He certainly causes unpleasant experiences, both temporally and misthologically, on His OT people. So why do some find it so surprising that God will do the same to His NT people if they will not repent? Sometimes the Lord repented of the evil He planned to bring (2Sam 24:16; Jonah 3:10); sometimes He did not (Zech 8:14). If we repent, we will find that the Bema is not nearly as bad as it would have been otherwise. If we refuse to repent, we will not find any repentance on God's part at the Bema. Just as God can punish His children with temporal evil in the present, He can punish them with misthological evil in the future.

Fire

To be sure, some passages indicate that those believers whose lives are characterized by moral failure will have their works burnt up: "If any man's work is burned up, he shall *suffer loss* [*zemioo*]; but he himself shall be saved, yet so as **through fire**" (1Cor 3:15). "But if it yields thorns and thistles, it is worthless and close to being cursed, and it ends up being burned" (Heb 6:8). For sake of argument, assume for the moment that this just pictures God depriving you of rewards for poor service, as PA insists. Is that not enough to conclude that a punitive aspect is intended? PA seems to picture God as saying, "Please set outside while I burn your house down, and please don't mistake this as being an indication that I am upset with you or are punishing you. It's just that your house is not up to code for this neighborhood, and I am responsible for enforcing that code." The Lord stands there emotionally neutral while burning your house down. Such PA impassivity is not a suitable picture of this excruciating activity, however.

Moreover, the biblical imagery does not necessarily prove that this burning has nothing to do with the believers themselves. To be sure, the Bema fire does not necessarily singe the believers. "Shadrach, Meshach and Abed-nego came out of the midst of the fire. And the satraps, the prefects, the governors and the king's high officials gathered around and saw in regard to these men that the fire had no effect on the bodies of these men nor was the hair of their head singed, nor were their trousers damaged, nor had the smell of fire even come upon them" (Dan 3:26-27).

These particular believers passed through the fire unharmed and without suffering because they were faithful. In contrast, the believers in 1Cor 3:15 and Heb 6:8, who suffer as a result of the flames, are unfaithful. God burns the believer's house down (so to speak) while the believer is still in it. God does not tell the believer to step outside while He burns down his or her house. God sets the house aflame while the believer is still morally asleep in it. Let the fire be the wakeup call! The believer escapes, but one would suspect that he or she does so with burned hair and clothing, and perhaps second and third degree burns. Similarly, in the second passage, the field lays charred. They did not cut the thorns down and cart them off to the fire. They burned the thorns while they were still in the field. God's fiery wrath is not limited to the believer's works. It touches the person in the house and scorches the field as well. The believer does not escape unscathed.

"If anyone does not abide in Me, he is thrown away as a branch, and dries up; and they gather them, and cast them into the fire, and they are burned" (Jn 15:6). The branches are identified in the context as believers. Parabolically, believers themselves are thrown into the fire. Also, the context of Heb 10:27 addresses this warning to believers: "A certain terrifying expectation of judgment, and the fury of a **fire** which will consume the adversaries." The adversaries themselves experience the fury of the fire.

Illustration 229. Flaming Soul at Bema

Certainly, God's people can misthologically put themselves in an adversarial position.* The application of God's fiery wrath to the believers' works is not pictured as having no application to the believers themselves though. They themselves are cast into the misthological fire and consumed in the loss of their souls (cp. Heb 10:39). They are not let out a day or two later, or after death, or after the Bema, or even after a thousand years. The misthological results are eternal. Their **souls** (i.e., earthly lives) are lost for eternity in terms of their life's work. Their spirits are saved soteriologically, but their souls are lost misthologically at the Bema (cp. 1Cor 5:5). Granted, some conservative misthologists may prefer a temporal understanding of God's fiery wrath. But the context teaches that the misthological results will be eternal in both John (12:25) and Hebrews (3:11; 4:3,5). Misthologically, Dillow is quite justified to link 1Cor 3:15 with Jn 15:6 so as to conclude: "The apostle obviously sees an intimate connection between the believer and his work. To apply the fire of judgment to the believer is the same as applying it to his work. Indeed the believer's works are simply a metonymy for the believer himself."[1186]

Some have sought to find justification in Dillow's statement for concluding that the sin nature of a believer is burned up and consumed by the fires of the Bema. To the contrary, although 1Cor 3:15 is "a metonymy for the believer himself," the verse is not teaching an annihilation of that part of the person producing that defective behavior. The purpose of the passage is to show penalization rather than purification. A trope is being used for the painful punishment inflicted upon believers as they are deprived of their trophy. The person him or herself, not some part of the person, is saved. Paul is making a soteriological distinction between the believer and his or her works to show that a person is not saved from hell by works. At the same time, Paul is making a misthological association between the workers and their works (both undergoing the fire) to show that faithful believers are saved by works from painful, personal loss at the Bema. The identification of believers with their works is a misthological metonymy, not a soteriological metonymy. Paul's point in 2Cor 5:10 is not merely that the works are judged, but that the workers receive the results of their judged works.

Radmacher and Derickson reject Dillow's metonymy, seeking to maintain the distinction between the workers and their works. I find no such misthological distinction. This compositional duo also stipulates that Jn 15:6 must be limited to a temporal punishment by claiming that this is the only valid option for those who hold to eternal security. I find no such necessity. Strangest of all, these two authors argue that *they* in this verse must refer to people rather than angels: "To find angels, then, one must see Jesus referring back to the Olivet Discourse."[1187] Radmacher and Derickson presume that understanding this Johannine text as talking about angels would necessitate a **soteriological** fire. To the contrary, casting by angels does not prove that a soteriological

---

* See *Misthological Wrath*, 676.

casting is necessarily in view. Nor does the fact that those doing the casting are not explicitly identified as angels prevent one from understanding the plural *they* to refer to the servants of the husbandman/vinedresser, and thus to angels.

I concur with Radmacher and Derickson that in this parable *they* means *people*. But the question then becomes, "Who do these **parabolic** people represent?" The vinedresser in the parable is a person who represents someone else, namely God. The branches represent someone else, namely believers. Why is it necessary to presume that the people merely represent people (i.e., human beings), as Radmacher and Derickson suppose? Why assume that *they* literally refers to people in general or to people of the world? Would not Radmacher and Derickson's own horticultural analysis lead to a different conclusion than the one they themselves draw? In the horticulture of that day, who were the people who carried out the fall purging? Was it not the servants? It is natural, therefore, to conclude from the parable itself and from the practice of that time period that the vinedresser's **servants** are the ones who will be participating in the fall purging. The *they* refers to people parabolically, and these parabolic people are servants. It is unreasonable to maintain that those people merely passing by, with no interest in the vineyard, are the people working in the vineyard to gather the branches and cast them into the fire. These parabolic people would be better understood to be workers in the vineyard and, therefore, the servants of the vinedresser. One need not defer to the Olivet Discourse to make this deduction.

On the other hand, having made the deduction from the context itself that servants are the ones dealing with the unfruitful believers, it is natural to ask if there are other parables in which Jesus implements plural attendees as dealing with unfaithful believers. From that perspective, the Olivet Discourse does provide a natural cross-reference since the parabolic master there commands, "Therefore take away the talent from him [the unfaithful believer], and give it to the one who has the ten talents" (Mt 25:28). Again, a group of people in the parable are being ordered to perform the specified action, namely take away the talent. Certainly, this unspecified group of people is not to be understood as being the world at large. This master then issues a further command to his parabolic attendees, "And cast out the worthless slave into the outer darkness; in that place there shall be weeping and gnashing of teeth" (Mt 25:30). Naturally, one would assume that it is the master's servants who are being ordered to perform this action. In fact, the accuracy of this hypothesis is verifiable since Jesus told a similar parable in which this missing detail is provided: "Then the king said to the *servants*, 'Bind him hand and foot, and cast him into the outer darkness; in that place there shall be weeping and gnashing of teeth'" (Mt 22:13). The servants perform this action, not someone merely passing by.

Perhaps some would wish to offer the rejoinder that mere bystanders or spectators perform this action in a similar parable: "And he said to those who *stood by* [*ho paristemi*], 'Take the mina from him, and give it to him who has ten minas'" (Lk 19:24; NKJ). However, this articular participle (*ho paristemi*) is used of **servants** who stand by, in the presence of their king (1Kgs 10:8; 1Chron 9:7). From this background, we see that these servants are on standby to do the will of their king. Since in this parable Jesus is talking about a nobleman who has returned after receiving a kingdom (Lk 19:12), this passage likewise should be understood as talking about the king's servants who stand by to do his will. This is particularly true since the king orders them, "But these enemies of mine, who did not want me to reign over them, bring them here and slay them in my presence" (Lk 19:27). These servants can also function as soldiers and kill those whom the king orders to be killed. Such texts describe those who are on standby, not someone who is a mere passerby. Surely, no question arises as to the identity of the ones performing these actions. These parabolic servants should be understood to be angels. As a matter of fact, the only other time Luke uses this articular construction (*ho paristemi*) in his gospel, he clarifies this angelic association: "And the angel answered and said to him, 'I am Gabriel, who *stands* [*by*] in the presence of God; and I have been sent to speak to you, and to bring you this good news'" (Lk 1:19).

To restate, in the Olivet Discourse, along with other texts, the king gives orders to his servants standing nearby to do such things as bind the worthless slave, take away his talents, and throw him into the outer darkness (Mt 22:13; 25:28,30; cp. Lk 19:24). In both Mt 22:13 and 25:30, the *outcast* (*ekballo*) are cast *into* (*eis*) the outer darkness. In Jn 15:6, those *cast out* (*ballo exo*) are cast *into* (*eis*) the fire. The identity of those servants who cast believers into the fire would be best gleaned from related parables where God's servants cast the outcast into something. That something is identified by Matthew as the outer darkness, and the identity of those servants doing the casting is understood to be angels. Contextually, the *they* in Jn 15:6 refers to servants. Cross-references confirm both this understanding regarding the casting and the assessment regarding the casters. These servants are angels.

Unlike Mt 5:13, where the text explicitly says that **men** trample those *cast out* (*ballo exo*) under foot, this Johannine parable in Jn 15:6 leads to the supposition that the *servants* are the ones who do the casting. The two concepts need not be mutually exclusive, however. Angels will cast the unfruitful believers into the outer darkness, and then men will trample these unfaithful believers under foot. The menial servitude that unfaithful believers will have to render to men throughout eternity may be pictured in part by the fire. Angels are the casters, and men are the burners.*

Regardless, these parabolic servants are angels. They are our fellow servants (Rev 19:10; 22:9) who stand around God's throne (Rev 5:11; 7:11). They will throw unfaithful believers into the outer darkness outside the city. Then, angels will stand guard at the gates of the city (Rev 21:12), as a solemn reminder of that exclusion. It may be deduced from such passages that the **angels** are the servants who cast worthless **Christians** into the outer darkness at God's command. *They* (i.e., the angels)—whether they be parabolically identified as servants, bystanders, or an ambiguous *they*—gather the withered *branches* (i.e., the believers who did not abide in Christ) and throw them into the *fire* (which is misthologically equivalent to the outer darkness) to suffer the eternal consequences of their misthological judgment (in menial servitude to men). A painless expulsion is not envisioned.

Be Punished (zemioo)

This position will certainly not be palatable for most readers, not even for conservative misthologists. Yet one should not be so quick to throw hermeneutical water on these misthological fires and water down the warning. "If any man's work is burned up, he will be *punished* [*zemioo*]; but he himself will be saved, yet so as through fire" (1Cor 3:15; TM). BDAG states that *zemioo* generally means "to cause injury or inflict punishment." The verb is used in the passive in our literature and thus means to "suffer damage or loss, forfeit, sustain injury." More specifically, as BDAG points out, in 1Cor 3:15 it means to "be punished."

One definition L-N offers for *zemioo* in 1Cor 3:15 is: "To be punished, with the implication of suffering damage–'to be punished, to suffer punishment." Additionally, it provides an alternative definition: "To suffer loss." But L-N qualifies this alternative by saying that the implication is "that the loss involves considerable hardship or suffering." An expanded translation thus would be: *He will suffer the punishment of painful loss.*

Zemioo is used in six passages in the NT. In Phil 3:8, Paul said that he had "suffered the loss of all things" in order to gain Christ. Gaining Christ was not a painless experience: No pain, no gain. In 2Cor 7:9, Paul is relieved that the temporary pain his first letter had caused the Corinthian believers would not cause them permanent pain. The inference is rather clear that had these believers not repented, they would have suffered a permanent, painful loss. In view of how Paul uses this same verb in his first epistle to this church, there is no need to speculate as to what he means in his second epistle. Had they failed to repent, they would have suffered the permanent loss of rewards. This is not a painless experience. It is indeed very painful: No gain, then pain.

After describing the *bema* in 2Cor 5:10, Paul immediately goes on to state in the next verse: "Therefore knowing **the terror of the Lord**, we persuade men" (2Cor 5:11; TM). The *bema* is something that an awards podium is not—terrifying. The *bema* will be a terrifying experience for those believers who do not prepare for it. Jesus also uses *zemioo* in connection with the possibility of losing your soul. "For what will a man be profited, if he gains the whole world, and forfeits his soul?" (Mt 16:26) The lost person who suffers the loss of his or her soul-life will find it a very painful experience but so will the saved person. Forfeiture of one's soul-life is painful. It is compared to taking up one's cross.

"For what is a man profited if he gains the whole world, and *loses* (*apollumi*) or *forfeits* (*zemioo*) himself?" (Lk 9:25) Here, *zemioo* is equated with *apollumi*. Perhaps this usage is simply repetitive. More likely, the repetition is used in order to more powerfully convey the punitive aspect. The PA argument, that it cannot be punitive because it refers to loss, is simply not persuasive. One week, when my children were very young, I told them that if they missed the school bus any day that week, they could not watch TV the rest of the week. They easily understood that the potential loss of this privilege was to be a punitive measure if they failed to get ready in time. They got ready. Perhaps, if Christians were better informed of the punitive nature of the Bema, they would be more inclined to get ready for it as well. Parental and punitive discipline are not incompatible.

PA Counterargument #2

Another PA objection raised concerning 2Cor 5:10 is that since the purpose of a judicial *bema* was to determine innocence or guilt in order to decree punishment when the verdict of guilty was pronounced, a judicial *bema* could not be in view since what is given is positive rather than negative. Positive rewards were administered at the Olympic *bema* rather than at the judicial *bema*. Supposedly, if any positive association is made with the *bema*, no negative consequences could be considered. In contrast, Dillow believes that dual aspects of the *bema* are to be understood in 2Cor 5:10 because it has both positive and negative aspects.[1188] It already has been demonstrated that the inclusion of the negative is certainly possible; in fact, it is probable. If this conclusion is

---

* See endnote 609.

accepted, then PJ is proven. The question now is, "Does the inclusion of the positive rule out a judicial *bema* as PA assumes?"

Rewards May Be Positive or Negative

First, note in 2Tim 4:8 that Paul says that the person who will make the presentation of the reward at the *bema* is God as *Judge* (*krites*). "In the future there is laid up for me the crown of righteousness, which the Lord, the righteous **Judge**, will award to me on that day; and not only to me, but also to all who have loved His appearing." When Paul appears before God, the Lord will be acting as Paul's Judge. The Judge at the judgment seat will be *krites*. The judge had the power to act punitively: "For while you are going with your opponent to appear before the magistrate, on your way there make an effort to settle with him, in order that he may not drag you before the judge, and the judge turn you over to the constable, and the constable throw you into prison" (Lk 12:58). No question as to the judicial power of the judge is permissible, as is displayed by the negative sentence he pronounces. The judge also had power to act positively: "And someone in the crowd said to Him, 'Teacher, tell my brother to divide the family inheritance with me.' But He said to him, 'Man, who appointed Me a judge or arbiter over you?'" (Lk 12:13-14). That judgment may result in a positive outcome does not necessarily prove that it is not judicial.

As already noted, appearing before the Lord's throne in the judgment of the sheep and the goats is judicial (Mt 25:31-41). God sits on His throne and administers judgment with the result that the goats go to hell and the sheep inherit the kingdom. To stipulate that this judgment cannot be judicial because it results in positive and punitive consequences would be foolish. Positive and negative implications of God's judgment are also seen in Paul's writings. In 1Thess 1:5, potential positive ramifications are manifest. Paul hopes that as a result of "God's righteous judgment" these believers "may be considered worthy of the kingdom of God," for which indeed they were suffering. They were suffering to be counted worthy. The negative aspect is seen a few verses later: "Dealing out retribution to those who do not know God and to those who do not obey the gospel of our Lord Jesus" (2Thess 1:8). Again, the fact that judgment can be positive or negative does not prove that it is not judicial.

In the NT, rewards/repayment can be both positive and negative (e.g., Rev 22:12). Consequently, the fact that the judgment results in positive rewards by no means rules out its judicial aspect. The positive nature of the *bema* in 2Cor 5:10 may certainly include the positive idea of the Olympian *bema*, but the *bema* of 2Cor 5:10 is not limited to the positive aspect of the Olympian *bema*.

Rewards May Be Negative

Paul candidly remarks that God will *reward/repay* (*apodidomi*) Alexander according to his evil works (2Tim 4:14). Does this mean that God will give Alexander a positive reward for the evil Alexander did in opposing Paul? Of course not! Yet *apodidomi* is the same verb used in Rev 22:12 to say that God will *repay/reward* (*apodidomi*) everyone according to his or her work. This verse explicitly connects the *repayment* (*apodidomi*) with *reward* (*misthos*). Rewards are not necessarily positive. All people will be judged according to their works. This is a common NT teaching (Mt 16:27; Rom 2:6; 2Cor 11:15; Rev 2:23; 18:6; 20:12-13; 22:12). The fact that unbelievers will be rewarded according to their works proves that the judgment/reward may be punitive. Similarly, all believers will be judged according to their works (1Cor 3:13-15; 2Cor 5:10). One likewise would presume that this judgment could be punitive. Stanford poses a false dichotomy between the person and his works. Rather than make a sharp distinction between the two, it should be noted that it is the person him or herself who is judged and punished on the basis of his or her works.

The assumption that everyone will be praised in 1Cor 4:5 is just as erroneous. The **preceding** context rules out praise for certain believers (1Cor 3:13-15). The **proceeding** context acknowledges that even Paul may be disqualified for praise if he fails to finish well (1Cor 9:27). The thought is that each and every believer will get the praise he or she deserves, not that all believers will be praised regardless of their works.[*] Even if 1Cor 4:5 is understood to speak of Christians collectively, this does not mean that it refers to each believer indiscriminately or individually. Taking it as referring to Christians collectively is open to serious challenge, however. Niemelä gives an extended contextual justification for concluding that it is not referring to Christians in general, but at most to the apostles (if taken broadly), but much more likely it refers exclusively to Apollos and Paul (1Cor 3:22; 4:6).[1189] A large part of Niemelä's defense is the contrast between the first person and second person pronouns throughout the passage, a contrast that the present author also acknowledges.[†] Even granting secondary application to all believers

---

[*] See *Illustration 197. The Assumed All*, 577.
[†] See exclusive we in *Carnal Corinth*.

potentially, this does not mean that it applies unconditionally. No doubt, Paul is included in the verse as being a potential candidate for praise, and yet he himself may be excluded from praise (1Cor 9:27). If Paul seriously can entertain the possibility that he himself may be disqualified from praise, then how can anyone seriously suppose that all believers automatically will be praised?

The Greek lexicons agree that the reward may be punitive. The verb for *reward* (*apodidomi*) means "to recompense, whether in a good or bad sense, *render, reward, recompense*" (BDAG, 4). God will reward the lost with wrath and indignation (Rom 2:6-8). It can be used of paying back evil for evil (Rom 12:17; 1Thess 5:15; 1Pet 3:9), to pay back in like kind (Rev 18:6). Concerning the noun for *reward* (*misthos*), BDAG (2.c) says that it refers to "*reward or punishment* as the case may be." FB notes that *misthos* may be positive or negative and that in Rev 22:12 it has the negative meaning of "divine payback for disobedience to God's will *punishment.*" In other words, God will reward those who disobey Him with punishment. L-N defines *misthos* as, "A recompense based upon what a person has earned and thus deserves, the nature of the recompense being either positive or negative...may be understood as either a positive or negative reward [in Rev 22:12]."

Paul's meaning, then, in 2Cor 5:10 should be understood in a manner consistent with other passages which teach that God rewards good for good and bad for bad. He will do so in either a positive or negative manner as the case may warrant. God will not ignore the bad. The bad we have done will not simply go unrewarded. The Lord actively will reward the bad we have done with punishment. A believer's reward may be punitive, so the believer's *bema* should not be simply equated with the Olympian *bema*.

Misthological Forgiveness

Admittedly, judicial forgiveness (of the type described in those passages cited by PA) rules out any soteriological judgment of sin, as described in those particular passages. But the fact that all believers are forgiven in one sense does not mean that all believers are forgiven in every sense, contrary to Stanford. The PA advocates themselves frequently acknowledge that judicial forgiveness does not prevent the need for familial forgiveness. Although all believers have been forgiven of all sins soteriologically, this does not rule out the need for daily familial forgiveness, which is conditioned on our daily walk, confession, and forgiveness of others (Mt 6:12,15; 1Jn 1:6-9). Likewise, it may be concluded that misthological forgiveness is dependent upon such things (Mt 18:34-35). This conclusion is confirmed by those texts which teach that judgment will include our worthless works (1Cor 3:11-15), our bad works (2Cor 5:10), and our harmful works (Col 3:25). The fact that the shameful elements of our lives will be revealed (Mt 10:26; 1Cor 3:13; 4:5; Rev 3:18; cp. Heb 4:13) presupposes that, although these sins are forgiven, these sinful works will be dealt with publicly and misthologically. What is ruled out for the believer is judicial-soteriological judgment, not judicial-misthological punishment. Or as Lutzer surmises: "Even if our sins are represented as forgiven, we cannot escape the conclusion that our lifestyle is under **judicial** review, with appropriate rewards and **penalties**."[1190] Even ultra-conservative misthologists, such as Lutzer, thus admit the judicial nature of the penalties. No hesitation to call them punishment is necessary.[1191]

Misthological Judgment and Condemnation

As noted above, the fact no believer will be judged in one sense does not prove that he or she will not be judged in any sense. The citation of 1Cor 11:32 in defense of the PA position is self-defeating: "But when **we are judged** [*krino*], we are disciplined by the Lord in order that we may not be *condemned* [*katakrino*] along with the world." This verse explicitly teaches that we are, in fact, judged and punished temporally by the Lord. So much for the PA argument that we cannot be judged or punished by the Lord! Granted, the verse in conjunction with other considerations rule out soteriological condemnation in that we cannot share the same fate that the world shares. We cannot share the same fate as unbelievers. The possibility of other types of condemnation cannot be ruled out, however. Paul uses the nominal cognate in Rom 8:1 and reaffirms that some believers have no *condemnation* (*katakrima*). Yet he later, in the same epistle, uses the verbs *krino* and *katakrino* to indicate that a believer's sin may indeed invite God's misthological *judgment* and *condemnation* (Rom 14:22-23).

Jesus teaches that believers cannot be judged in one sense (Jn 3:18; 5:24), yet He also teaches they may be judged in other senses (Mt 5:25; 7:1-2; 12:36-37; Lk 6:36-37; 12:58). In Mt 12:36-37, the words *judgment*, *justified*, and *condemned* are as equally applicable to the lost as they are to the saved. These terms apply soteriologically to the lost and misthologically to the saved. A correlation exists between the judgment of the lost and saved. These statements are just as judicial for the lost as they are for the saved, but the sentence pronounced on the two groups will be different. From the wider Matthean context, one may specify that the unbelieving lost will be sentenced to hell, but the unfaithful believers to the outer darkness. Similarly, in Luke we find that our condemnation as believers is conditioned on our performance: "Be merciful, just as your Father is merciful. And do not judge and you will not be judged; and do not condemn, and you will not be condemned; pardon, and you will be pardoned" (Lk 6:36-37). The passage is talking about those who legitimately can call God their Father. They may experience judgment, condemnation, or pardon depending on how they treat others. Again, this biblical representation of the believer's misthological standing is definitely judicial.

The writer of Hebrews explicitly affirms, "The Lord shall *judge* [*krino*] his people" (Heb 10:30). Then he proceeds to warn Christians not to be adulterers because God will *judge* (*krino*) adulterers (Heb 13:4). The clear implication is that God will judge Christian adulterers. James cautions that Christian teachers will experience a "stricter *judgment*" (*krima*) (Jam 3:1). He also warns believers that they may be *judged* (*krino*) when the Lord returns as Judge (*krites*), if they grumble against each other (Jam 5:9). The PJ acknowledgment that the *bema* has a judicial nature if it is referred to by *krima* causes the PJ argument to crash on these Jacobean shores. James interweaves *krima* and its cognates together to picture the judgment that will take place upon believers when the Lord comes at the time of the rapture.

Stanford would have us believe that Christians who currently are engaged to be wedded to the Lord will be rewarded with white garments and become His Bride even if they crawl in bed with the devil in the interim. After all, Christ supposedly would not chastise His beloved Bride for such behavior since He already has forgiven her completely. Bridal misthologists acknowledge that Christ will not punish His Bride but insist that misthological conservatives are wrong to picture Christ as publicly stripping His Bride so that she is half naked. Contrary to Stanford and others (even within our own ranks), the reason that Christ's Bride is not so chastised is because only overcomers will compose His Bride. Overcomers have responded positively to His chastisement on earth, so there is no need for Him to chastise them in heaven. Since the Bride is not composed of all believers, Stanford's objection that Christ will not chastise any believers at the Bema because He will not chastise His Bride is groundless.[*] Naturally, the Lord will not chastise His Bride. However, those believers being punished are not His Bride, only His betrothed. Believers who had the potential to become a part of that bridal company and yet forfeited that potential as a result of their unfaithfulness are the ones being punished. Indeed, this forfeiture is a keen part of that punishment.

The notion that God judges a believer's actions but not the believer's sins fails to do justice to the fact that the Bible teaches that God will judge believers because of their sins. He will judge the adultery of the adulterer, the teaching of the teacher, the murder of the murderer, the grumbling of the grumbler, the apostasy of the apostate, and the apathy of the lukewarm apathetic. Furthermore, the punishment of the sin necessarily entails the punishment of the sinner. That Christians can be called sinners is seen in Jam 5:20 where a straying brother, in danger of the punishment of losing his soul in premature death, is referred to as a *sinner*.

Peter says that Christians fearfully should anticipate God's judgment of their works (1Pet 1:17) and that God's judgment would begin with the judgment of believers (1Pet 4:17-18). In contrast to Stanford, Peter sees no dichotomy between the judgment of the believer's works and the judgment of the believer him or herself. The thought that believers cannot be temporally or misthologically punished because of their sins is quite foreign to Scripture. The way one punishes adultery, murder, grumbling, and apostasy is by punishing those who are guilty of such behavior. It would be ridiculous in a court of law to declare that the criminal's crime will be punished but the criminal will not be punished.

Stanford's objection to this position evidences little comprehension concerning what the word *reward* entails. The believer himself or herself (not his or her works) receives the payback in 2Cor 5:10. Of course, the substitutional benefits of Christ's death are not called into question. Christ did not die to save us from the Bema; He died to save us from hell. No appeal to the benefits of Christ's death can be made at the Bema to escape God's misthological wrath when we trample Christ's blood under our feet by the way we live (Heb 10:26-31). Christ did not die in our place in order to save us from appearing at the Bema. Since believers are to be **judged** judicially in the misthological arena, there is no reason to assume that Bema cannot mean judgment seat in the legal sense of the word.

Do we say that we will punish the murder but not the murderer? The imagery of the believer's works being burnt up is not meant to be taken as an indication that the judgment is limited to the works and not to the worker. On the contrary, punishing a shoddy worker by burning his house down to the ground while he barely escapes being consumed in the flames himself (as in 1Cor 3:15) is picturesque of the simple truth that the punishment of the workmanship necessarily includes the punishment of the worker.[192] The punishment of the sin necessitates the punishment of the sinner. As noted above, Dillow is quite justified to link 1Cor 3:15 with Jn 15:6 as a metonymy.[†] After all, the branch itself, representing the fruitless believer, is cast into the fire (Jn 15:6).

---

[*] See *Chapter 25. The Bride*, 565.
[†] See *Misthological Fire*, 678.

Misthological Fear

In the context of 1Jn 4:18, those believers who experientially abide in love will have a mature love that will give them confidence before God on judgment day. By implication, those believers who do not love one another should fearfully anticipate punishment on that day. The Bema should be fearfully anticipated by those believers who do not prepare for it. Hodges responds to the PA argument concerning this verse by affirming, "The Judgment Seat of Christ should not be thought of as simply some kind of great awards celebration."[1193] Jesus tells us to fear God (Mt 10:28; Lk 12:5). As believers, we should have no fear of hell, but it is wise to fear One who deals with sin in such a manner. Paul teaches believers to fear God's Bema (2Cor 5:10-11), to mature in holiness in fear of God (2Cor 7:1), to live godly lives out of fear of God (Eph 5:21), and to work to bring about our misthological "salvation with fear and trembling" (Phil 2:12). The writer of Hebrews warns believers to fear exclusion from God's misthological rest (Heb 4:1); in fact, it has absolutely terrifying ramifications (Heb 10:27,31). Peter warns us to conduct ourselves in fear since God will judge our works (1Pet 1:17). Such fear would indicate a punitive aspect of the judgment. One does not fear getting a pat on the back. The PA argument that we should not fear the Lord is grounded in fantasy.

Misthological Punishment

Can this response by God to His people actually be labeled *punishment*? Certainly. In Heb 10:29, the Scripture teaches that NT believers who turn their back on Jesus will receive a *punishment* (*timoria*) that is severer than the OT death penalty that God inflicted upon His OT people. This theme of punishment upon the people of God continues in the next verse. Most versions translate *ekdikesis* in Heb 10:30 in a manner similar to the NAS: "'*Vengeance* is Mine, I will repay.' And again, 'The Lord will judge His people.'" If one were to consult the lexicons concerning *ekdikesis* in this verse, however, it would be readily apparent that it also may be translated as *punishment*. In fact, this is how the BBE translates it both here and in Rom 12:19: "*Punishment* is mine, I will give reward." (Incidentally, *ekdikesis* is normally translated as *punishment* in 1Pet 2:14). *Punishment* is the *reward* that God will give to His disobedient children in ch. 10 of Hebrews.

God's love for us does not prevent Him from disciplining us, and that discipline may be regarded as a form of punishment. God's love for us compels Him to punish our sinful actions by whipping us if necessary. The Greek word *mastigoo* means to *whip* or *punish* in Heb 12:6 (see FB, L-N, UBS, BDAG). Also, BDAG (2.b) confirms that *paideuo* means "**to discipline with punishment**" and puts Heb 12:6 in this category, explaining that this type of discipline is used "mostly of divine discipline" (2.b.α). "For the Lord sends *punishment* [*paideuo*] on his loved ones" (Heb 12:6a; BBE) "and he *punishes* [*mastigoo*] everyone he accepts as a son" (Heb 12:6b; NIV). Jesus also uses the same verb (*paideuo*) in Rev 3:19 when He says, "Those whom I love, I rebuke and discipline," or as the BBE translates it, "I give sharp words and *punishment*."[*]

Misthological Rebuke

Jesus warns these Christians in Rev 3:19 that He will rebuke them with sharp words if they do not repent. So much for the false idea that God will not express disappointment with us because He loves us! The Bible teaches exactly the opposite. Because God loves us, He will express His disappointment with us. Jesus' misthological rebuke of us may include misthological denial (Mt 10:33; 2Tim 2:12). Certainly, we will be ashamed of ourselves when He does rebuke us (1Jn 2:28). In contrast to our modern culture, our self-esteem is not God's highest concern.

Misthological Shame

The fact that we shrink away from God in shame does not mean that the shame is self-imposed. Quite the contrary, the verb for *be ashamed* (*aischuno*) in 1Jn 2:28 is passive and thus would mean to be put to shame or disgraced (see FB). In his *Word Pictures*, Robertson concurs that it means to *be put to shame* since it is passive. Paul likewise uses the passive form in 2Cor 10:8 and Phil 1:20, where the NAS correctly translates it as, "Be put to shame." Unfortunately, the NAS failed to translate the passive properly in 1Jn 2:28. This shame is not self-inflicted. This shame is God-inflicted. Such believers will be put to shame by God, before God, and shrink away in shame from God. Various translations bring out different nuances of what is being said. The DBY tries to bring out several subtleties: "Be put to shame **from before** him at his coming." The preposition *apo* is best translated as *from*. I would translate it thus as: "Be shamefully put away from Him." He will shamefully have us cast away from

---

[*] See *Illustration 323. Discipline is Punishment*, 899.

His presence into the outer darkness when He returns if we fail to abide in Him. The outer darkness is a place for the outcasts who are cast out *from before* Him at the execution of the Bema judgment associated with the rapture.

Genuine believers can be ashamed of Jesus and His words. Otherwise, Paul would have no need to warn Timothy, his beloved child in the faith, "Do not be ashamed of the testimony of our Lord" (2Tim 1:8). In turn, it is equally possible for Jesus to be ashamed of such believers. Jesus said that if we are ashamed of Him and His words on earth, then He will be ashamed of us when He returns to earth (Mk 8:38). He is the active agent; we are the passive objects. He will shame us. His judgment will result in our shame being revealed when He returns if we refuse to repent (Rev 3:18; 16:15). He puts such believers to open and public shame. Certainly, the proper conclusion is that this punitive judgment He inflicts will be inaugurated at the Bema.

Jesus taught believers, "Everyone who exalts himself shall be *humbled* (*tapeinoo*), and he who humbles himself shall be exalted" (Lk 14:11). The passive form of this verb is used both here and in Mt 23:12 to show that believers who refuse to humble themselves will be humbled by God. The Lord will cause them to "become disgraced and humiliated, with the implication of embarrassment and shame"; He will "put to shame" those believers who refuse to suffer shame for Him (L-N 25.198). The context is dealing with a man in a wedding banquet that is forced to take last place when the host says: "Give your place to this man." Jesus continues to elaborate on the consequence, "Then in *disgrace* [*aischune*] you [will] proceed to occupy the last place" (Lk 14:9). By putting such believers in last place, Jesus will disgrace them and cause them to experience shame. This might be seen "idiomatically as 'to hang the head' or 'to turn away the eyes' or 'to hide from people's stares'" (L-N 25.189).[1194] If the Lord is going to do this to midcomers, how much greater will be the shame for subcomers!

Probably, many people have had a nightmare in which they dreamed that they were naked in a public place and were trying to find a way to hide. In heaven, this nightmare will become a reality. This same word for *disgrace* is used in Rev 3:18 of those believers who failed to overcome and, consequently, have the shame of their nakedness publicly revealed. Clothes, like crowns (Rev 3:11), can be lost. Jesus warns, "Behold, I am coming like a thief. Blessed is the one who stays awake and keeps his garments, lest he walk about naked and men see his *shame* [*aschemosune*]" (Rev 16:15). Being embarrassed by the Lord and publicly having to stand before Him in naked shame will be no fun. The metaphorical rock you will want to crawl under will be found in the misthological darkness outside the feast.

The passive verb for *ashamed* (*epaischunomai*) takes a direct transitive object in both Mk 8:38 and Lk 9:26, where Jesus will be ashamed of those believers who are ashamed of Him. Where commentators frequently err is not in equating this response with Jesus denying those who deny Him, but in regarding this denial as an absolute soteriological denial rather than a relative misthological denial. Jesus will deny such believers. He will publicly deny them rewards in heaven. Their unfaithfulness will not merely invoke an emotional reaction from Him but a punitive reaction as well. The thought is not that He merely will feel shame; rather, He will inflict shame. Those believers who put Jesus to "open shame" (Heb 6:6) can themselves expect to be put to open shame by Jesus.

Hoyt acknowledges that the passive voice in 1Jn 2:28 could be understood grammatically as Christ "putting the believer to shame" and thus "driving the unfaithful Christian away from Him in shame." Yet he objects: "This seems contrary to the whole tenor of the New Testament Scripture which pictures the church as the bride of Christ who will be ushered into His presence to enjoy His presence throughout eternity." Hoyt's objection demonstrates that he has misunderstood the whole tenor of the NT regarding the Bride of Christ. Of course, the Lord does not drive His Bride away from Him in shame. Instead, He drives those believers away in shame who fail to comprise the Bride because they slept with the devil. The logical extension of Hoyt's lukewarm doctrine of rewards is that all believers will have unhindered, joyful bridal intimacy with Christ throughout eternity even though they suffered the minor inconvenience of losing some rewards. Perhaps Hoyt should have given further consideration to his earlier statement: "God was not only viewed as the Giver of rewards but as the ultimate reward Himself" (Gen 15:1).[1195] According to Hoyt, the only thing at stake is the *loss of rewards*. However, as even Hoyt unwittingly admits, God Himself is the *ultimate reward*. Accordingly, what is at stake is losing God—losing out on the bridal intimacy that one could have with the Lord. Just because believers are betrothed virgins does not mean that even if they lose their virginity to the devil, they still will become married brides of Christ (2Cor 11:2).

We/Us

The author of Hebrews is particularly forceful in the way in which he pictures the punitive nature of the Lord's reaction toward such believers. No doubt the warnings are addressed to regenerate believers, since the author of Hebrews includes himself in the warnings with the first person plural pronoun: "**We** must pay much closer attention to what **we** have heard, lest **we** drift away (2:1). "How shall **we** escape if **we** neglect so great a salvation?" (2:3). "Therefore, let **us** fear lest" (4:1). "Much less shall **we** escape who turn away" (12:25). The nature of these sins, warnings, and conditions are only applicable to genuine believers. "If **we** hold fast our confidence" (3:6) and "if **we** hold fast the beginning of our assurance firm until the end" (3:14), presumes we have something we already genuinely have received to which we should hold fast. You cannot *hold fast* to something you have not yet received. These believers can achieve the realization of this misthological salvation in the end by holding fast to the misthological potential which already has been given them. Soteriological salvation is not conditioned on holding fast to what you have, and counterfeit believers could not be saved by holding on to a counterfeit gospel. False believers are not being addressed or warned. Clearly, the warnings are intended for believers.

"If **we** go on sinning willfully after receiving the knowledge of the truth, there no longer remains a sacrifice for sins....The Lord will judge His people" (10:26,30). As seen in this passage, even Christians can be **misthologically** guilty of the unpardonable sin.* Those Christians in danger of committing this unpardonable sin are the genuine believers included in the sanctified group of 10:10: "**We** have been sanctified through the offering of the body of Jesus Christ once for all." We, the brethren, can have confidence that the blood of Jesus applies to us: "since therefore, brethren, **we** have confidence to enter the holy place by the blood of Jesus" (10:19). The earlier reference to these sanctified brethren in Heb 2:11-13 is very descriptive.

Positional Sanctification

[11] For both He who sanctifies and **those who are sanctified are all from one Father**; for which reason He is not ashamed to call them **brethren**, [12] saying, "I will proclaim Thy name to **My brethren**, In the midst of the congregation I will sing Thy praise." [13] And again, "I will put My trust in Him." And again, "Behold, I and the **children whom God has given Me**." (Heb 2:11-13)

Jesus is the active agent in our positional sanctification; we are the passive recipients. According to the context of Hebrews, the believers he is addressing are "all from one Father." In other words, they are begotten of God; they are born again (2:11). Like Jesus, they have *put* their *trust in* the Father (2:12-13). They are God's children (2:13). They are *given* to Jesus (2:13). They are thus the same group described in Jn 6:37, "All that the Father **gives Me** shall come to Me, and the one who comes to Me I will certainly not cast out." Positionally, they are sanctified permanently.

Correspondingly, the statement that such a believer may regard "as unclean the blood of the covenant by which **he was sanctified**" in 10:29 is not referring to Jesus being passively sanctified, as some presume. The one who is sanctified is the believer, not Jesus. In this verse, Jesus is the sanctifier, not the sanctified. This passage is presenting the passive, positional sanctification of the believer who tramples underfoot the blood that sanctified him. In the very context of the warning in 10:29-31, the writer of Hebrews denotes it as being sanctified "once for all" (10:10), affirming that "He has perfected **for all time** those who are sanctified" (10:14).

Retrogressive Sanctification

The writer of Hebrews warns that permanently sanctified believers may be **punished severely** (Heb 10:29). Then he proceeds to say that such believers will be repaid with God's vengeance. Their payment will be God's vengeance applied directly against them when He exercises terrifying judgment upon them.

[29] How much **severer punishment** do you think he will deserve who has trampled under foot the Son of God, and has regarded as unclean the blood of the covenant by which he was sanctified, and has insulted the Spirit of grace? [30] For we know Him who said, "**Vengeance is Mine, I will repay**." And again, "The Lord will **judge His people**." [31] It is a **terrifying** thing to **fall into the hands** of the living God. (Heb 10:29-31)

Believers can grieve and quench the Spirit. Rather than progress in their sanctification, they may regress instead. They cannot retrogress from their perfect positional state, but they certainly can retrogress in terms of their practical sanctification. An example of retrogressive, practical sanctification is seen in the book of Galatians, where Paul said that, although they were running well initially, they now had fallen from grace.† Other examples of retrogressive sanctification include believers becoming: unsalty (Mt 5:13), thorny (Mt 13:7), thistly (Heb 6:8), and falling into moral or theological apostasy. In Heb 10:29, a sanctified believer insults the Spirit. Naturally, the Lord will judge the lost, but this passage is not dealing with the judgment of the lost (i.e., the unsanctified). It is dealing

---

* See *Appendix 10. The Unpardonable Sin*, 831.
† See *Fallen from Grace but Not from Perfection*.

with the Lord judging *His people* (Heb 10:30), His people whom He positionally and permanently already has sanctified as belonging to Him, as noted earlier in this same chapter (Heb 10:10,14). According to Heb 10:29, what happens to Christians who commit such a hideous sin after being sanctified? They will be punished severely. Understandably, those who have been conditioned to read the NT through a soteriological lens will have difficulty seeing the misthological nature of this passage, but the passage is talking about the judgment of genuine believers.

Warnings

These sanctified scum are permanently sanctified positionally and thus are eternally secure—soteriologically. These *sanctified brethren* (Heb 3:1; TM) are nevertheless the objects of the warnings of Hebrews and in real danger (cf. 3:12-13; 4:1,7). To be sure, they are subject to God's temporal paternal discipline (12:4-7). Yet if God's discipline of His people in the present is not heeded, it will give way to God's judgment of His people in the future (10:30). Running away from God's discipline is expressed as drifting away (2:1; *pararreo*), being lead away (3:12; *aphistemi*), falling away (4:1; *pipto*), falling aside (6:6; *parapipto*), throwing away (10:25; *apoballo*) turning away (12:25; *apostrepho*), and being carried away (13:9; *paraphero*). The nature of the warnings presumes the genuine, saved status of these believers. Can a ship drift away from shore if it has not first been brought to shore? No. Neither can a person drift away from the faith if he or she has not first been brought to faith.

Exhortations

The character of the exhortations also signifies that genuine believers are in view. They are to hold fast (4:14; 10:23), press on to maturity (6:1), endure (10:36), run with endurance (12:1), and not grow weary (12:3). In short, they are warned and exhorted misthologically so that they may gain the payment of a great reward (10:35; *misthapodosia*; cf. 11:26). The exhortations are to hold on to what they have and move forward. Claiming that they are not genuine believers make no sense. If that were the case, then where in the Epistle of Hebrews are the exhortations to believe in Christ for eternal life? They are missing. Instead, repeated evidence is found that they already had believed in Christ.

Telology

The Greek word for *end* in the phrase, "if we hold fast our confidence...firm until the **end**," is *telos* (Heb 3:6; MT). The importance of holding fast to the end is again reiterated a few verses later: "If we hold fast the beginning of our assurance firm until the **end**" (3:14; *telos*). It is also found at the conclusion of the famous warning in chapter 6. "Show the same diligence so as to realize the full assurance of hope until the **end**" (6:11, *telos*). What is gained in the end by holding this assurance and confidence fast to the end is the payment of the great reward mentioned above: "Therefore, do not throw away your confidence, which has a *great* [*megas*] reward" (10:35). This mega reward is the end result—if the outcome is positive. The end result may be negative, however: "If it yields thorns and thistles, it is worthless and close to being cursed, and it **ends** up being burned" (6:8; *telos*). Considering the nature of the warnings and promises and the writer's usage of *telos*, the necessary conclusion is that what is at stake is an eschatological experience of God's judgment. The writer of Hebrew's **telology** in these verses is equivalent to the present writer's *misthology*. Telological perseverance results in misthological results. What is at stake is millennial and eternal misthological salvation and judgment. Failure may result in a terrifying, severe, burning, misthological punishment.[*]

The writer of Hebrews wants them to advance beyond an immature temporal misthology to a mature eschatological misthology that recognizes the tragic reality of a believer's heart becoming so hardened as to make these eschatological rewards impossible to obtain. The burning in Heb 6:8 is not temporal, and its results are not temporary. Rather, the burning is eschatological, and its results are eternal—just as it is in Jn 15:6 and 1Cor 3:15. In both Jn 15:6 and Heb 6:8, the agricultural burning is the end result of lack of fruitfulness. This burning is not referring to clearing the land so that it may become fruitful. If one must impose some similar fanciful interpretation upon Heb 6:8, it would not represent the preparation of the land for fruitfulness, it would picture perfect sanctification. The sin nature (i.e., the thorns) that caused the failure to produce fruit is removed. Even if this were the case (which it is not),[†] it would not indicate that the land will now produce misthological fruit. As in the

---

[*] **Telology** is a coined expression derived from *telos* and refers to doctrine of the end of time. It is the nominal cognate of the verb *teleo*, concerning which I have noted my preference for misthology, over teleology, in reference to the doctrine of rewards despite the preference of some others for teleology. Misthology is not limited to the doctrine of rewards in the end of time but includes the millennium and eternal state. To avoid confusion, misthology has been used herein in preference to telology.

[†] The sin nature is removed before the Bema, not at the Bema.

parable of the sower, the last picture we have of this type of ground is that it is thorny. The writer of Hebrews tells us what misthologically happens to this type of ground in the end of time. Those so pictured never ever enter the misthological rest for the rest of eternity. Like Esau, they are rejected forever from the full inheritance that could have been theirs (Heb 12:16-17). Tears after the fire or in the fire are too late. In accordance with the broader didactical context, the fire should be recognized as symbolizing the eschatological judgment and punishment of believers, rather than misperceived as the preparation or sanctification of believers. This particular metaphorical detail is one more way of picturing the same truth signified by the outer darkness—misthological punishment of unfaithful believers.

Just as being thrown into the furnace of fire pictures the end of the story for the lost (and their eternal fate), so the misthological fire to which believers are subject is the closing chapter on their lives. We have no more right to try to change the fate of the one than the other. Certainly, unfaithful believers will be better able to cope with their fate than unbelievers will be able to cope with theirs since believers will be able to counterbalance their loss with the positive aspects of their situation. Nevertheless, the loss they experience will be literal and eternal.

Misthological Wrath

The reiteration of the nature of this punishment will be from a summarization of the word *wrath/anger* (*orge*). If you are wronged by a fellow believer and refuse to take your own revenge and refuse to pay back evil, as instructed in Rom 12:17-19, is not the implication of Rom 12:19 that God will revenge you by bringing wrath on your fellow believer? Consider the similar statement concerning vengeance in Heb 10:30-31. Jointly, these passages would read as: *"Never take your own revenge, beloved, but leave room for the **wrath** of God, for it is written, '**Vengeance is Mine, I will repay**,' says the Lord. And again, '**The Lord will judge His people**.' It is a terrifying thing to fall into the hands of the living God"* (Rom 12:19 & Heb 10:30-31). Believers can be the objects of God's *wrath* or *punishment*.[*] In 1Thess 4:6, Paul explicitly warns that the believer who defrauds his fellow believer will be the object of God's vengeance: "The Lord is the avenger." He is the one who *punishes* (*ekdikos*). The avenger will judge the offending brother. God is the avenger for the believer, even if it means executing His revenge on a fellow believer. The terror and wrath that God has promised renders foolish our doing anything in a vindictive manner. We should pray that our fellow believers will realize this fact and repent. A believer is not exempt from the divine avenger.

When our evil brothers and sisters in Christ treat us in an abusive manner (like the evil slave in Mt 24:49), we should not seek vengeance. God will repay (Mt 24:50-51). We should allow the Holy Spirit to use the doctrine of rewards to dispel wrath from our hearts and replace it with love. At the same time, we lovingly should respond to the abuse we suffer by seeking to use the doctrine of rewards to reawaken love in the hearts of our abusive brothers and sisters, warning them that they are putting themselves in danger of their Father's wrath.

Undoubtedly, God's people are the object of God's wrath in Heb 10:26-39. Nothing prevents us from understanding God's adversaries in Heb 10:27 as referring to God's people. God's people can be His enemies (Jam 4:4).[1196] And Heb 10:29 assures us that the person in danger is sanctified positionally and permanently (Heb 10:10,14). Furthermore, Heb 10:38 clearly states that it is the righteous one who may shrink back and become the object of God's displeasure. Contextually, this displeasure certainly must be an understatement, a litotes meaning, "God will be severely angered."[1197] Believers themselves are in danger of being the object of God's anger/wrath. The only real question is whether the judgment of this passage refers to temporal wrath or eschatological wrath or both.

Hodges apparently considers this judgment to be exclusively temporal, and, to be sure, temporal judgment is a strong biblical theme.[1198] Dillow appears to consider it as referring primarily to temporal judgment and secondarily to misthological (eschatological) judgment.[1199] The present work agrees with Dillow that both are in view but perceives the emphasis differently. Dillow has well said, "The parallel of the exodus generation's failure and their destruction in the wilderness is the controlling thought of the warnings."[1200] However, in Heb 3:11 and 4:3, believers are the objects of God's **eschatological** (misthological) wrath, when He swears that those believers who do not live by faith will not enter into His eschatological rest.[1201] The eschatological consequences of failure form the controlling thought of the warnings. In the context of Heb 10 itself, the displeasure and destruction of Heb 10:38-39 are contrasted with the eschatological reward in Heb 10:35. Additionally, the implied wrath of Heb 10:38 is associated eschatologically with His coming in Heb 10:37. This wrath is to be associated with the coming *day of* 10:25. The *Day of the Lord*, and its attendant judgment day for the Christian, is drawing near (cp. Rom 13:12; Jam 5:8-9) and provides the basis for the exhortation in Heb 10:25. The writer of the epistle is showing

---

[*] See *Misthological Punishment*, 672.

that God's temporal wrath, as described in the OT, has a strong eschatological dimension as well, as he proves from the OT itself. Their failure to enter the rest is an OT example of God's temporal wrath on His children. The writer of Hebrews demonstrates from the OT that God intends for us to see an eschatological application of this temporal wrath. This temporal wrath was intended by God in the OT to illustrate His eschatological and misthological wrath typologically, as the OT itself demonstrates. God's children are not only the objects of His temporal wrath; they are also the objects of His misthological wrath (but not objects of His soteriological wrath—Jn 3:36).

Tanner has written an excellent defense of the misthological position for Heb 10, in which he argues that even if a temporal sense is permitted, the eschatological dimension is certainly paramount. Briefly, Heb 10:27 is alluding to Is 26:11, which is embedded in the description of God's fiery wrath in the coming *Day of the Lord* in Is 24-27.

> The song of Isa 26 begins by stating: "We have a strong **city** . . . Open the gates, that the righteous nation may enter, the one that remains faithful" (26:1-2). The author of Hebrews held out the **eschatological heavenly Jerusalem as the ultimate hope** of New Covenant believers: "For here we do not have a lasting **city**, but we are seeking the **city** which is to come" (13:14; cf. 11:16; 12:22).[1202]

This accords well with the misthological understanding that the eschatological Jerusalem is a city which believers are to seek (Heb 11:14,16) as their reward by *going to Jesus outside the camp* (Heb 13:14) *in laying hold of the hope set before us* (Heb 6:18)—a misthological *hope* to be sure.* Tanner continues,

> In both the Hebrew text as well as the Septuagint translation, the prophet seems to have in mind the wicked among Israel who fall under God's judgment at the time of the "Day of the Lord." They are in contrast to those in the nation who are trusting in the Lord (26:3-4) and waiting eagerly for Him (26:8). The "fire" depicts God's judgment against His covenant people (recall 24:6; cf. 5:24-25; 9:19; 29:6; 33:14)….
> …At the very least, however, we could conclude: if God does not withhold His awesome judgment against His own covenant people as depicted in Isaiah 24–27, there is no reason to think He would spare those who forsook the New Covenant. That is, if <u>rebellious</u> Jews of the Tribulation will certainly receive God's judgment, so will those who <u>rebel</u> in the days when the author of Hebrews writes.[1203] (Emphasis his.)

To recap, the writer of Hebrews is alluding to an eschatological text in which those of God's covenant people who are wicked are prevented from participating in the millennial festivities, such as entering the city, and the writer is applying this backdrop as a warning to his saved readership.† Therefore, Tanner concludes,

> The judgment seat of Christ will not only determine whether one receives praise from the Lord and whether or not one's work is rewarded, but will also determine whether one enters the *eschatological rest*, i.e., is allowed to share in the Son's inheritance and exercise dominion with Him. This would suggest that the "worse punishment" for the apostates in Heb 10:26-31 *will at least include* a denial of the latter opportunity of the *eschatological rest*…a punishment that they will have to live with for all eternity.[1204] (Emphasis his.)

Thus, when a text like Eph 5:7 is encountered, one should not be shocked to find that the children of God may partake of God's wrath. Just as it was possible for God's people to partake of His wrath under the old covenant, so it is possible for them to do so under the new one as well. Paul does not take it for granted that children of light will live like children of light. They might partake of immorality and its attend wrath along with the children of the darkness.

> But do not let **immorality** or any impurity or greed even be named **among you**, as is proper **among saints**; ⁴and there must be no filthiness and silly talk, or coarse jesting, which are not fitting, but rather giving of thanks. ⁵For this you know with certainty, that **no immoral** or impure person or

---

* See *Misthological Hope and Glory*, 92; *Heb 6:17*, 246; *Jesus' Love Motivated By Rewards*, 744.
† See *Misthological Support of OT Background*, 557.

covetous man, who is an idolater, **has an inheritance in the kingdom** of Christ and God. [6]Let no one deceive you with empty words, for because of these things the **wrath of God comes upon the sons of disobedience**. [7]**Therefore do not be partakers with them**; [8]for you **were** formerly darkness, but **now** you are light in the Lord; walk as children of light. (Eph 5:3-8)

Why does Paul warn these saints against allowing any immorality among them? Why must believers not be immoral? Soft Lordship Salvationists like Zeller, who backload the gospel, would say that they must not be immoral because otherwise they will not enter the kingdom. In Arminianism, Calvinism, and Catholicism, entrance into heaven is dependent upon how good you are after your conversion. The Marrowistic answer, in contrast, is that Paul is not warning believers in order to threaten them with hell but to inform them that immorality prohibits them from inheriting the kingdom. All those who participate in immorality invite God's wrath upon themselves, whether they are believers or unbelievers. If believers partake of the immorality of the darkness, they also will partake of God's wrath. Children of darkness will partake of God's soteriological wrath. Correlatively, children of light will partake of God's misthological wrath, if they live like children of darkness. Living like the unsaved will prevent children of light from achieving full salvation. If children of light live like children of darkness, God will cast them into the outer darkness.

The sons of disobedience is articular in all three NT passages in which it occurs (Eph 2:2; 5:6; Col 3:6) and refers **categorically** to those who are lost. However, the occurrence of this expression in the text before us makes it clear that believers can participate with the lost in God's wrath. The sons of disobedience participate in this wrath *by nature* (Eph 2:3). Obviously, the regenerate can only participate **characteristically** in this unregenerate behavior.[*] Nevertheless, as Paul warns, the regenerate can participate correlatively in this wrath.[†] No immoral person (i.e., no one who is characteristically immoral) will inherit the kingdom. If God's children (who by nature are of light) fall into this dark classification by means of their behavior, they will fail to inherit the kingdom. Likewise, in Gal 5:21 those who are characteristically unrighteous will not inherit the kingdom.

Misthological Fire

Similarly, the severe punishment to which His people are liable in Heb 10:29 is misthological (i.e., eschatological), as is the *fire* (*pur*) to which they are subject in Heb 10:27. In addition to the context demanding this conclusion, the eschatological parallel in Lk 17:33 indicates this perspective as well. The *burning* (*pur*) coals of Rom 12:20 probably have misthological application to the burning of abusive believers. Numerous other texts dealing with *fire—pur* (Mk 9:49; Jn 15:6; 1Cor 3:15; Heb 6:7-8; 10:27; Jam 5:3; Jude 1:23)—would have such application. Being a believer does not save us from the misthological fire. The wheat (all of it) goes into the barn; it never goes into the soteriological fire of Gehenna or the Lake of Fire (Lk 3:17). Yet once in the barn, its maturity will be judged, and its usefulness accordingly determined. In view of the doctrinal and parabolic material concerning the negative results of immaturity, let us encourage each other to press on toward the goal of maturity. Let us not be ashamed of the gospel of the kingdom; rather, let us proclaim the whole council of God concerning this kingdom. Let us not ignore or water down the misthological punishment of carnal believers that Jesus describes in such forceful language with a *Toothless Bema*.[‡] If we do so, their immaturity will be on our hands, and neither they nor we will escape the temporal and misthological consequences.

Misthological Flogging

Hoyt's PA argument is that losers were not penalized in the Olympics; that is, the losers were not beaten. However, this is not an entirely inaccurate assessment of what actually happened at the games. Paul said that it was necessary to compete according to the rules (2Tim 2:5), meaning likewise in 1Cor 9:27 that he did not want to be *disqualified* in this athletic endeavor.[§] (See *adokimos*, FB.) The NIV is correct in its interpretation of the verse that the disqualification is for the reward described in the context: "No, I beat my body and make it my slave so that after I have preached to others, I myself will not be disqualified **for the prize**" (1Cor 9:27). The passage is describing misthological disqualification, not soteriological rejection.

In 2Cor 5:10 Paul entertains the idea that both good and bad will be taken into account. What happened if the athlete did not compete according to the rules? What happened if he cheated? He was punished by being

---

[*] See *Illustration 336. Hoi Adikoi versus Adikoi*, 914.
[†] See *Theory of Correlativity*, 911.
[‡] See *Warning to Soteriologists*, 959.
[§] See *Appendix 14. Adokimos in 1Cor 9:27*, 865.

flogged at the stadium. As BDAG (1.a) notes, this *flogging (mastigoo)* was used "as a punishment for cheating in athletic contests." The same word for this flogging is used of our being punished in Heb 12:6. From Miller's description, flogging would appear to be a generally associated part of the games.

> A *Hellanodikes* (judge) enters the tent when it is time for the next group of runners. He will be dressed in a black *himation* (long robe) as were the judges at the ancient Nemean Games, and he will be holding a switch of olive with which **he will flog anyone who commits a foul** or does not obey his orders....
>
> ...if both feet [of the runners at the beginning of the race] are not in the groove **the switch of the *Hellanodikes* will be felt**....
>
> ...Unless one starts too early, gets tangled in the barrier-cords, and **is flogged**, and the race has to begin over, all the runners sprint straight down the track.[1205]

Since the games assumed the punishment of the cheaters, it is not surprising that Paul broadens the analogy to include the punishment of the unfaithful, especially considering the fact that the NT teaches such punishment in numerous passages. Instead of blowing whistles, they flogged the offenders.

Even if a flogging were not a consideration, the PA argument still would self-destruct. Kroll observes that the *bema* was used as both a judgment seat and award's podium in the NT. Concerning that latter usage, he states: "This was not a judicial bench of condemnation. The winner was not determined here. The contest was won on the playing field. The loser was not brought to the *bema* for condemnation. Only the winner stood before the judge and here he was commended." Therefore, equating the NT Bema with the Olympic Award's Podium is out of the question. Concerning 2Jn 2:28, Kroll also correctly acknowledges, "Losing a reward is not just the absence of a reward. At the judgment seat each of our works that abide will bring reward, and in addition, much rejoicing. Likewise, each of our works that are burned will bring more than loss. There will accompany that loss a great sense of shame." Winners are not the only ones who will be present at the NT Bema; losers will be present as well. By necessity the *bema* imagery cannot be limited to the awards podium. Losers as well as winners will be present: those receiving crowns and those have their potential crowns publically stripped away from them and given to others at this time (Rev 3:11; cp. Lk 19:24).[1206]

PJ Arguments

This examination of Rom 14:10 and 2Cor 5:10 has found PA arguments counterproductive to the PA conclusion. In this last section, arguments in favor of the PJ will be presented. The heart of this issue is that PA wants to avoid any negative judgment of believers. On the other hand, PJ maintains that judgment can be negative; consequently, the *bema* is not to be equated simply with an awards podium. The passages in support of this key PJ presupposition will be listed below in summary fashion. It is not necessary that the PJ interpretation be accepted regarding all these passages. Conversely, it will be necessary for PA advocates to demonstrate that the PJ position is untenable in practically all of such passages.[1207]

Further, even if the punishment is limited objectively to a verbal reprimand and loss of certain rights and privileges (which may indeed be the case), the psychological impact still may be devastating emotionally. One may well wonder if Peter would not have preferred a physical whipping instead of Jesus' nonverbal rebuke (Lk 22:61-62). Those who have suffered severe emotional pain know how real it can be. That it can be described metaphorically rather than literally makes it no less painful. The metaphorical picture may be the best way to convey what it actually feels like. Although the beating may be metaphorical, it may feel just as real as a physical thrashing. The real question, then, is whether the Scripture intends for us to understand this outcome as punitive, not whether it is literally limited to loss of positive rewards. If Scripture presents it as punitive, and the biblical interpreter attempts to argue that it is not punitive (because it is limited or is not literal), then the interpreter has rejected the way Scripture intents for us to understand the Bema.

The Lord's refusal to grant a positive reward also may legitimately be considered punitive. The following list of negative rewards could be extended considerably if many of these types of references were included. Yet since PA does not consider lack of rewards to be punitive, such references have been limited to some of the most potent (implicit) negative warnings concerning positive rewards. Those who are familiar with the FG treatment of these themes and contexts will recognize readily the misthological value of most of these items. In any case, the treatment of the contexts for these proof texts may be readily gathered from the GES website or other published FG sources for those items not covered in the present work. After all, the present work is rather limited in its scope. Its focus is not on positive misthological passages, nor does it even treat all negative misthological passages. My focal point is the subset of negative misthological passages and themes that deal most directly with the outer darkness.

Even so, the following list will help the reader see the outer darkness in its broader thematic misthological context. The outer darkness is only one of the numerous negative rewards promised to unfaithful believers.

Temporal and eschatological passages are included in this particular lineup. Passages that apply to both unbelievers and believers will not be differentiated, since they correlatively have application to believers. Thus, these references should not be taken as absolutes or taken soteriologically when applied to believers. For example, just because believers are cast out in one sense does not prove that they are cast out in every sense. That all believers are heirs in one sense does not prove that all believers are heirs in every sense. Nevertheless, God's judgment of believers is punitive since believers can experience the following negative rewards.

Illustration 230. Negative Rewards, Believers May Be

1. Cast out (Mt 5:13)
2. Called least (Mt 5:19)
3. Thrown into prison (Mt 5:25)
4. Not forgiven (Mt 6:15)
5. Judged in like manner (Mt 7:1-2)
6. Cast away from the table into the darkness outside (Mt 8:11-12)
7. Denied before the Father (Mt 10:33)
8. Counted unworthy of Jesus (Mt 10:37-38)
9. Condemned on the basis of their words (Mt 12:36-37)
10. Paid back with the loss of their souls (Mt 16:24-27)
11. Handed over to torturers (Mt 18:34-35)
12. Last (Mt 19:30)
13. Last (Mt 20:16)
14. Bound hand and foot (Mt 22:13)
15. Cast outside the wedding feast into the darkness outside (Mt 22:13)
16. Pictured as weeping and gnashing their teeth (Mt 22:13)
17. Not chosen (Mt 22:14)
18. Humbled rather than exalted (Mt 23:12)
19. Whipped (Mt 24:51)
20. Assigned a place with the hypocrites (Mt 24:51)
21. Pictured as weeping and gnashing their teeth (Mt 24:51)
22. Denied entrance into the feast and left in the darkness outside (Mt 25:12)
23. Rebuked (Mt 25:26)
24. Penalized (Mt 25:28)
25. Cast into the darkness outside (Mt 25:30)
26. Pictured as weeping and gnashing their teeth (Mt 25:30)
27. Pictured as losing their lives (Mk 8:35)
28. Made objects of shame (Mt 8:38)
29. Last (Mk 10:31)
30. Ruined (Lk 6:49)
31. Exposed (Lk 8:17)
32. Warned of losing their souls when Jesus returns (Lk 9:24-26)
33. Made objects of shame (Lk 9:26)
34. Not fit for the kingdom (Lk 9:62)
35. Exposed (Lk 12:2)
36. Told to fear God who casts people into hell (Lk 12:5)
37. Publicly denied by Jesus (Lk 12:9)
38. Called fools in the loss of their souls (Lk 12:20)
39. Whipped (Lk 12:46)
40. Assigned a place with the unfaithful (Lk 12:46)
41. Subject to many lashes rather than just a few (Lk 12:47-48)
42. Thrown into prison (Lk 12:58)
43. Last (Lk 13:30)
44. Publicly disgraced and humbled by being put in last place (Lk 14:9-11)
45. Thrown out as worthless (Lk 14:35)
46. Humbled rather than exalted (Lk 18:14)
47. Penalized (Lk 20:24-26)

48.   Cast into the fire and burned (Jn 15:6)
49.   Killed (Acts 5:5-10)
50.   Threatened with death (Acts 8:20)
51.   Not forgiven (Acts 8:22)
52.   Rewarded with God's wrath and indignation (Rom 2:6)
53.   Subject to death (Rom 8:13)
54.   Severely cut off (Rom 11:22)
55.   Condemned (Rom 13:2)
56.   Subject to wrath (Rom 13:4)
57.   Condemned (Rom 14:22-23)
58.   Revealed for the negative they do (1Cor 3:13)
59.   Punished with loss (1Cor 3:15)
60.   Destroyed (1Cor 3:17)
61.   Revealed for the negative they think (1Cor 4:5)
62.   Delivered over to Satan for physical destruction (1Cor 5:5)
63.   Rejected as kingdom heirs (1Cor 6:9-10)
64.   Rejected as losers (1Cor 9:24-27)
65.   Afflicted with God's judgment of weakness and sickness (1Cor 11:30-31)
66.   Judged and disciplined (1Cor 11:32-34)
67.   Accursed (1Cor 16:22)
68.   Punished (2Cor 2:6)
69.   Paid back with evil for the evil they do (2Cor 5:10)
70.   Punished with suffering loss (2Cor 7:9)
71.   Not profited by Christ (Gal 5:2)
72.   Severed from Christ (Gal 5:4)
73.   Fallen from grace (Gal 5:4)
74.   Rejected as kingdom heirs (Gal 5:21)
75.   Reapers of corruption rather than eternal life (Gal 6:8)
76.   Rejected as kingdom heirs (Eph 5:5)
77.   Partakers of God's wrath (Eph 5:6-7)
78.   Considered unholy objects of blame and reproach [at the Bema] (Col 1:22-23)
79.   Rewarded with harm rather than the inheritance (Col 3:24-25)
80.   Objects of God's vengeance (1Thess 4:6)
81.   Put to shame (2Thess 3:14)
82.   Condemned (1Tim 5:12)
83.   Publicly rebuked (1Tim 5:20)
84.   Plunged into ruin and destruction (1Tim 6:9-10)
85.   Denied (2Tim 2:12)
86.   Ruined (2Tim 2:14)
87.   Dishonored (2Tim 2:20)
88.   Self-condemned (Tit 3:11)
89.   Subject to a negative payback (Heb 2:2-3)
90.   Objects of God's wrath and anger (Heb 3:11-17)
91.   Rejected from God's rest (Heb 3:18-4:11)
92.   Burned (Heb 6:8)
93.   Subject to a terrifying fiery judgment (Heb 10:27)
94.   Subject to server punishment (Heb 10:29)
95.   Subject to God's vengeance (Heb 10:30)
96.   Subject to God's judgment (Heb 10:30)
97.   Subject to a terrifying experience at God's hands (Heb 10:31)
98.   Subject to God's displeasure (Heb 10:38)
99.   Subject to destruction (Heb 10:39)
100. Subject to God's discipline (Heb 12:5-8)
101. Subject to God's reproving (Heb 12:5)
102. Subject to God's whipping (Heb 12:6)
103. Disinherited as illegitimate children (Heb 12:8)

104.   Rejected concerning the inheritance (Heb 12:17)
105.   Unable to escape God's fiery judgment (Heb 12:25-29)
106.   Subject to potentially harmful or detrimental consequences (Heb 12:17)
107.   Subject to God's judgment (Heb 13:4)
108.   Susceptible to merciless judgment (Jam 2:13)
109.   Not be saved from this merciless judgment (Jam 2:14)
110.   Susceptible to strict judgment (Jam 3:1)
111.   Opposed by God (Jam 4:6)
112.   Susceptible to miseries on judgment day (Jam 5:1)
113.   Susceptible to being burned with fire (Jam 5:3)
114.   Susceptible to condemnation when the Lord returns (Jam 5:9)
115.   Susceptible to judgment (Jam 5:12)
116.   Susceptible to premature death (Jam 5:20)
117.   Justifiably afraid of God's judgment (1Pet 1:17)
118.   Opposed by God (1Pet 3:12)
119.   Opposed by God (1Pet 5:5)
120.   Worse off because they are believers (2Pet 2:20-21)
121.   Fallen from grace (2Pet 3:17-18)
122.   Out of fellowship with God (1Jn 1:6)
123.   Put to shame by Jesus (1Jn 2:28)
124.   Subject to premature death (1Jn 5:16)
125.   Removed (Rev 2:5)
126.   Subject to having their crowns taken away (Rev 3:11)
127.   Punished with sickness (Rev 2:22)
128.   Cast into great tribulation (Rev 2:22)
129.   Killed (Rev 2:23)
130.   Spit out (Rev 3:16)
131.   Reproved (Rev 3:19)
132.   Disciplined by God (Rev 3:19)
133.   Plagued by God (Rev 22:18)[1208]
134.   Subject to having God take away their portion in the tree of life (Rev 22:29)
135.   Subject to having God take away their portion in the holy city (Rev 22:29)

Conclusion

Considerable evidence exists that God's judgment is punitive and correspondingly judicial. The judicial nature of the *bema* in Rom 14:10 is contextually proven beyond question. The fact that the *bema* of 2Cor 5:10 will include the negative things believers have done implies that they may receive negative consequences in a punitive form, as confirmed by Col 3:25. Related misthological themes confirm these exegetically-derived conclusions. There is no reason for extrapolating the notion, from the historical background concerning the Olympian *bema*, that the *bema* as applied to Christians is strictly positive nor even merely neutral. It will indeed be a very negative for many believers. The *bema* is a judgment seat, not a mere awards podium. Rather than deny the punitive rewards, a biblical perspective would balance this negative list with a positive one. A positive list would definitely be longer than the negative one presented above. Admittedly, the emphasis in Scripture is on positive rewards rather than on negative ones.* Certainly, believers should be encouraged by positive rewards. What must be avoided is the all-too-prevailing tendency to assert the positive to the exclusion of the negative. Both aspects of the *bema* are scriptural, and we can only ignore either aspect to our own peril.

Comparatively speaking, the outer darkness is a rather mild picture of the punitive aspect of judgment, considering the fact that believers are also described as being whipped and burned. Nevertheless, the outer darkness provides a suitable point of reference from which one can interact with passages which appear more severe in nature. The triple repetition of this particular punitive reward in Scripture, when coupled with the splendid visual parabolic imagery and details, makes the outer darkness a reasonable vehicle of choice by which to relate the didactic and parabolic material found elsewhere in the NT concerning this punitive misthological outcome for those who subcome.

---

* One of the most encouraging positive reward is probably *Misthological Sinlessness, 772.*

Chapter 30.
Misthological Rejection

Introduction

Comments from Pagenkemper's two-part article have been responded to in a number of places in the preceding discussion. His thesis is that the outer darkness and other such parables are limited to soteriological rejection. Keathley's two articles adopted Pagenkemper's approach concerning the outer darkness and the Mount Olivet discourse in rejecting the misthological interpretation. Limited interaction also has been provided with Keathley's objections. This chapter will deal more directly with some of their remaining arguments (and those of others) against a misthological understanding of the outer darkness. A response to each of their arguments in the present chapter is unnecessary since the present work already has addressed many of their objections (both indirectly and implicitly) in the foregoing discussion without necessarily citing their works on every occasion. Even so, the author index of the present work will make it apparent that explicit interaction with their criticism is by no means lacking.

Workers in Vineyard (Mt 20:1-16)

The most common parabolic objection to the doctrine of rewards is derived from the workers in the vineyard in Mt 20:1-16 who receive the same reward. Different groups work a different number of hours, being called at different times of the day. Yet at the end of the day, they all receive the same wage.[*] Indeed, Blomberg uses this parable to begin his article, in which he denies that believers get different rewards in heaven. He assumes that the parable teaches that all genuine believers work and get the same reward since false believers are excluded from the kingdom. Thus, he takes the reference to having last place in Mt 20:16 to mean "excluded from the kingdom" so that there is no ranking "among genuine believers."[1209] This assessment is rather strange for a verse that concludes a kingdom parable by saying, "Thus the last shall be first, and the first last." One would be inclined to suppose a misthological ranking within the kingdom according to this parabolic conclusion. Even broadly speaking, Blomberg's understanding of how the word *last* is used is open to serious question.

First versus Last

A more careful observation of how the word *last* (*eschatos*) is used parabolically could lead to the conclusion that those who are last are misthologically last at the **table** in the kingdom. Those paid last in this parable are given the same reward as those hired last. Both groups work faithfully and are paid the same accordingly. The natural inference, therefore, is that the first-versus-last distinction that concludes the parable is a ranking of faithful workers. This ranking is relative to the table rather than to the kingdom per se.

Illustration 231. Last is not Least

	First	**Last**	**Least**
Kingdom	✓	✓	✓
Table	✓	✓	NA

Luke implicitly makes this first-last table distinction (Lk 13:29-30) and then follows up with a parable that explicitly pictures this as a ranking in terms of priority of seating at the table (Lk 14:9).[†] In contrast, those cast into the outer darkness would be the misthologically *least* (*elachistos*) in the kingdom (cp. Mt 5:19), since they are not even allowed a place at the table. The table is reserved for kingdom rulers. Therefore, kingdom ranking is: first, last, and least.

---

[*] For charts and further discussion of this parable, see "The Ruler and the Parable" in *Salvation*.
[†] See *Illustration 153. Sequence and Significance of Casting*, 467; *First vs Last vs Least*, 606.

Illustration 232. Kingdom Ranking

Those who receive last place at the table are certainly within the kingdom. They are the semi-faithful who get lower positions of rulership in the kingdom and are labeled as midcomers herein due to their midrange degree of faith and faithfulness. As kingdom rulers, they cannot be least in the kingdom. The least in the kingdom are unfaithful believers thrown into the outer darkness. So in comparison to overcomers (who get first place at the table and in the kingdom) and to subcomers (who get no place at the table and least place in the kingdom), midcomers are those who get last place at the table but not least place in the kingdom. Midcomers are ranked in-between overcomers and subcomers.

Called Versus Chosen

As already noted, the MT gives a more complete reading, "So the last will be first, and the first last. **For many are called, but few chosen**" (Mt 20:16, NKJ). This latter phrase is repeated shortly thereafter in Matthew's gospel: "For many are called, but few are chosen" (Mt 22:14). This verse forms the conclusion for the second parable concerning the outer darkness, coming just after the second mention of the outer darkness in Mt 22:13. If this MT reading is accepted (which is the case in the present work), then the arguments and conclusions concerning misthological election in 22:14 are also applicable to the text of 20:16.[*] In short, the election is honorific rather than salvific. For the sake of those who do not share the author's textual preference, however, the argument below will not implement that earlier analysis. The insufficiency of Blomberg's soteriology is still apparent. For that matter, interaction will be provided with Blomberg's assumption that this is kingdom ranking rather than table ranking.

---

[*] See *Misthological Sequence of* Election, 298; *Comer = Believer*, 426; *Chosen = Misthologically Prepared*, 427.

Interpretation

Contrary to Blomberg, to have last place should not be construed as having no place. Last place believers in the kingdom still will be in the kingdom. More pointedly, why does this parable conclude with the statement in Mt 20:16 which shows ranking within the kingdom? Why does a parable that shows no distinction in the vineyard conclude with a warning of distinctions within the kingdom? As already suggested herein, they receive the same categorical reward as a result of their actions but a different subcategorization of their rewards based on their attitudes.* The *inclusio* in 19:30 and 20:16, about being first and last, certainly suggests the subcategorization amidst the parabolic standardization in which each laborer receives the standard wage for a day's wage.

The two most popular interpretations of this parable are based on the single premise that the reward pictured therein is based on faithfulness and not on the timing of one's entrance into Christian service. Believers who come to Christ (1) late in their lives or (2) late in the Christian era have the opportunity to earn the same reward as do those who come to Christ early in their lives or early in the church age. Rewards are based on faithfulness subsequent to coming to Christ, not on how long one has been a Christian or when one became a Christian. Being rewarded according to one's faithfulness certainly explains the standardization.

Yet does it not take great faith to believe that you can receive the same reward as those who have served the Lord longer or earlier than you have? Certainly. Believing that the Lord will reward our late efforts is hard, yet this is precisely what the Lord is encouraging us to believe within this parable. Gregg has written a splendid article demonstrating the exegetical basis for concluding that these believers are rewarded on the basis of their faith, not merely on the basis of their faithfulness. His contribution explains the subcategorization.

This parable is a beautiful picture of misthological faith. As Gregg shows, the first group that was hired did not need very much faith. They had an implied *contract*. The second group needed more faith that their faithfulness would be worthwhile, yet they could trust the landowner's verbal *commitment* that he would pay them what was right. The last group did not even have the promise of personal remuneration by the landowner himself. Hallelujah, God rewards faith! Or as Gregg expresses it, "Laboring faith is especially rewarded by the Rewarder of this service." His thesis "is that the degree of faith exercised, and not the grief endured, is the overarching principle in God's compensation of his servants....Greater trust in His just reward is justly rewarded with greater honor in the end....the greater faith of the later-day workers becomes evident." God rewards the greater faith of the later workers by paying them first. This reward is based on the merit of their character in believing rather than on the merit of their economic contribution.[1210] Soteric faith has no mistholic value. However, this parable implicitly is dealing with misthological faith, not soteriological faith.

Those believers who serve the Lord faithfully will receive the reward of the inheritance and become the Bride of Christ. All the believers in this particular parable qualify since they work till the end of the day. They endure to the end. Still, this does not in any way establish that all believers will work faithfully in the vineyard. The parable demonstrates God's grace in that He gives us an opportunity to earn rewards and even allows those who work for shorter or later periods of time to earn the same privileges as those who served longer and in the hotter and harder periods of His kingdom building project.

Jesus concludes His parable with the misthological warning to those who presently have prominent or prestigious places in His kingdom work. In the parable, those who have worked the hardest grumble about the amount of reward they have received. They do not feel that they have received adequate compensation in comparison to others who served the Lord just as faithfully in more limited capacities. The rebuke in Mt 20:13-15 is addressed to the Lord's more prominent servants who have served Him longer and more strenuously. Likewise, the warning in Mt 20:16 is addressed to this same group of servants, signifying that those who presently are considered as being in first place in the kingdom may find themselves in last place (at the table). Thus, a dual application is discernible for those in service to the Lord. They are rebuked for an attitude of pride and warned that their service may not be rewarded with eternal prominence over those who have served the Lord just as faithfully for shorter periods. Indeed, those who were called first were paid last in the parable. They had to wait longer to get their paycheck. In fact, in light of other Scripture (e.g., 1Cor 3:11-15), it could be surmised that some who have served the Lord with temporal prominence may not get any paycheck. Their service may be found defective.

Application

As a potential illustration of a worker who has worked through the heat of the day, note that Blomberg not only has advocated a false misthology; he also bases that false misthology on the false premise of LS soteriology. He advocates the Reformed position in which eternal security only applies to saints who persevere.[1211] And he

---

* Also see *Theory of Misthological Relativity*, 687.

applies his LS theology to Paul as well: "In 1 Corinthians 9, Paul wants to make sure that he perseveres in his faith so that he does receive eternal life."[1212] Blomberg claims, "One of the main reasons for trying to live as good a Christian life as possible is to make sure that we do in fact persevere, so that we do not lose out on eternal life altogether (as in 1 Cor 9:24-27; Phil 3:10-14, discussed above)."[1213] He considers this the

> crucial contribution of those who today advocate lordship salvation….The major spokespersons for historic Calvinism and Arminianism agree that people commit apostasy and are lost for all eternity…true, saving faith does over time lead to visible transformation in lifestyle and to growth in holiness.[1214]

In Blomberg, we may have an example of a Lordship Salvationist who is considered a prominent parabolic expert, serving the Lord through the heat of the day, only to find himself disqualified for any prominence in the kingdom because he has taught a false gospel that conditions one's eternal security upon one's performance. This is of course assuming that sometime in the past Blomberg believed the true gospel before he fell from grace into legalism.

Refutation

Blomberg's assumption that the parable teaches that all true disciples will receive the same reward is refuted by a host of passages. The parable of the minas in Lk 19:16-26, for example, portrays some believers ruling over ten cities, and some over five, and others over none. A balanced perspective would have deduced that the **workers in the vineyard show a basic equality among those who serve the Lord faithfully. But this is not an absolute equality**. All such believers will rule, but they will not be given equal spheres of rulership. A holistic misthology would not use this rather obscure parable of the vineyard laborers in an attempt to overturn the clear misthology regarding misthological ranking found in other parables. Further, that all believers are rewarded positively in this parable does not prove that all believers in every parable are rewarded positively. All the laborers in this parable labor, but this is not the case in every parable. This parable does not teach that all **genuine** believers are rewarded alike, as Blomberg assumes. On the contrary, it teaches that all **faithful** believers will experience basic misthological equality.

Pagenkemper cites Blomberg in support of his conclusion that the outer darkness is soteriological.[1215] But as badly as Blomberg misconstrues the parable, his assessment is superior to that of Pagenkemper, who believes the parable of the workers in the vineyard pictures "the free gift of grace."[1216] At least Blomberg could recognize that the passage is talking about rewards rather than a free gift! The laborers in the parable work for their wage: no work, no pay. One should be able to deduce that since the payment that is given is response to work, it is merited and therefore not a *free gift of grace*.* Yet following Pagenkemper in this error, Keathley quips: "Because this parable starts off with 'the kingdom of heaven is like…' I think it is a salvation parable. Matthew uses this phrase eleven times and in the other parables where this phrase is used, the parables are about salvation and getting into the kingdom of heaven."[1217] On the contrary, as is commonly recognized, the parable of the workers in the vineyard is talking about rewards in heaven, not entrance into heaven. The parable is not picturing absolute equality of rewards, nor is it picturing heaven as a reward. It is not talking about the requirements for entering the kingdom. It is not talking about a gift. Jesus is presenting one of the many misthological dimensions of the kingdom rather than a soteriological description.

Affirmation

The parable announces its misthological nature in the opening verse: "For the kingdom of heaven is like a landowner who went out early in the morning to *misthologically hire* [*misthoo*] workers for his vineyard" (Mt 20:1; TM). *Misthoo* is the verbal root for *misthos*, from which the term *misthology* is derived. When the landowner asked a group later that day why they were not working, they respond: "Because no one *misthologically hired* [*misthoo*] us" (20:7; TM). Later, when it is time to *pay* (*apodidomi*) the *workers* (*ergatns*), he tells his foreman to pay the workers their *misthological wage* (*misthos*). This parable is dripping wet with misthological details. The nominal and verbal forms of misthology are used to indicate that it is dealing with something that is paid to those who work.

For LS soteriologists, such as Pagenkemper and Keathley, to come along and try to turn this parable into a description of a gift freely given to those who do nothing to earn it (except work for it!) is to ignore just about every detail in the parable. Misthologists need only point out the numerous details, which stress through

---

* For charts and further discussion of this parable in relation to merit, see "The Ruler and the Parable" in *Salvation*.

redundancy that the payment is paid to those workers who work. Soteriologists, on the other hand, in trying to ignore the details in order to derive one major soteriological truth, miss the richness of this misthological vineyard. There is a major truth, to be sure, but it is misthological in nature. Properly inducing the fact that this parable is conveying misthological truth will allow us to compare it deductively with other misthological parables, as well as with didactic material, in order to determine what major misthological truth is being expressed in comparison with and in relation to other such illustrations.

Theory of Misthological Relativity

Exegetically Fruitless

Does the parable of the workers in the vineyard necessarily teach that all believers will work, that is, produce good works in terms of good fruits? No. Various degrees of carnality are portrayed in other parables.[*] Jesus indicates that some carnal believers bear no fruit (Lk 8:13); these are contrasted with believers who bear no fruits to maturity (Lk 8:14). The immature believer fails to produce mature fruit. He fails to produce fruit to the same quality and quantity as the mature believer (Lk 8:15). In another parable, Jesus represents believers as vines who may produce no fruit, some fruit, or much fruit (Jn 15:2). Despite the Lord's persistent care and discipline, no fruit may be produced (Lk 13:6-9). The Lord may not be able to get any interest back on His investment in the lives of some believers (Mt 25:26-27). This unfaithful slave does not bear any fruit in terms of producing even one talent.

Likewise, in the parable of the minas, one group of believers will be very faithful, others partially faithful, and still others will be totally unfaithful and not even yield an increase of one mina (Lk 19:11-27). Some believers produce zero fruit, minas, or talents. Certainly, many believers will serve money instead of Jesus (Mt 6:24). According to John, a number of believers have a dead love that does not express itself in good works (1Jn 3:17-19), and James concurs that believers may have a dead faith that fails to express itself in good work (Jam 2:14-27). Peter indicates that believers may lack good works (2Pet 1:8-9). The Greek word that Peter uses to describe the reality of *unfruitful* (*akarpos*) believers in this passage is the same word that Paul uses to describe the possibility of unfruitful believers in Tit 3:14, which in turn is the same word that Jesus used to describe believers who become unfruitful after initially bringing forth immature fruit (Mt 13:22; Mk 4:19).

In fact, *akarpos* is the same word Paul uses to tell believers, "Stop participating in the *unfruitful* deeds of darkness" (Eph 5:11; TM). If believers cannot be unfruitful, then why does Paul command them to stop being unfruitful? Lest anyone say this is just a temporary condition, Paul teaches that it is as equally possible for a believer to not have any works worthy of reward at the conclusion of his or her life as it is for another believer to have many works worthy of being rewarded (1Cor 3:11-15). Equal possibility rules out mere hypotheticality. In this passage, a believer can be considered barren even when his or her whole life is under review. The writer of Hebrews also relates the possibility of believers yielding thorns rather than fruit and consequently experiencing a fiery judgment as their concluding result (Heb 6:8). According to Jesus, Peter, Paul, John, James, and the author of Hebrews, believers may be unfruitful.

Theologically Fruitful

An inductive analysis of the passages above indicates that it is indeed possible for believers to be unfruitful. Nevertheless, a balanced discussion of the *doctrine of fruitfulness* (*karpology*) must not only take into account the various passages that exegetically indicate (at a categorical level) that believers may be unfruitful; it must also be open to a possible theological counterbalance at a broader thematic level if deductive considerations demand it. For this reason, Ryrie's chapter devoted to this subject may be received warmly, even though he argues that all believers will be fruitful—despite the biblical evidence to the contrary. The few proof texts he offers fail miserably at sustaining his assertion that all believers bear good fruits.[1218] Therefore, his argument is being received cordially herein without his being able to offer a shred of inductive support in support of his position. For logical rather than exegetical reasons, then, his premise may be adopted that all believers will produce good fruit.

Evidently, the theological difficulties of affirming fruitfulness and the exegetical inability of proving it lead Ryrie to qualify his position to such an extent as to make fruitfulness a useless criterion upon which to base a doctrine of assurance. By and large, others in the FG camp would agree with Ryrie's approach, but in contrast to the LS camp, they insist that assurance should not be based on works. According to Ryrie, the fruit may not be produced until after the believer already has died and gone to heaven. Consider the example of a deathbed

---

[*] See "Expression of the Spirit" in *Trichotomy*.

confession that may produce fruit after the believer's death. One might regard the thief on the cross as an example. Suppose, however, that the thief had kept his mouth shut and privately believed in Jesus for eternal life. He would not have born any visible fruit whatsoever—no public testimony. Would he still have produced any fruit?

According to Ryrie, the fruits may not be visible, so evidently the invisible fruit of a changed heart would suffice for Ryrie's definition of fruitfulness. The fruits may be private rather than public, perhaps only discernible by the Lord and maybe by His angels. The fruits may be weak, erratic, and invisible. Hodges likewise states,

> Finally, we must add that there is no need to quarrel with the Reformer's view that where there is justifying faith, works will undoubtedly exist too. This is a reasonable assumption for any Christian unless he has been converted on his death bed! But it is quite wrong to claim that a life of dedicated obedience is guaranteed by regeneration, or even that such works as there are must be visible to a human observer. God alone may be able to detect the fruits of regeneration in some of His children.[1219]

Similarly, Wilkin believes that all believers will produce good works. But the qualifications he adds are that even believers who are very carnal and dominated by a life of sin generally can be expected to produce good works. And he acknowledges, "It is hypothetically possible for a believer never to produce even one good work."[1220] Hodges, likewise, states:

> Of course, there is every reason to believe that there *will* be good works in the life of each believer in Christ. The idea that one may believe in Him and live for years totally unaffected by the amazing miracle of regeneration, or by the instruction and/or discipline of God his heavenly Father, is a fantastic notion—even bizarre. *We reject it categorically.* (Emphasis his.)[1221]

Even so, Hodges' statement is made in the midst of his insistence that our assurance should not be based on our works. And he adds an extremely important clarification:

> We believe that all born-again Christians will do good works. We believe it, however, because it appears to be the only rational inference from the scriptural data. But, let it be also said clearly, it *is* an inference. No text of Scripture (certainly not Jas 2:14-26!) declares that all believers will perform good works....*No text says that!* (Emphasis his.)[1222]

Apparently, Wilkin shares Hodges' theological assessment but not his exegetical denouncement:

> Does this mean [in Lk 8:6-8] that every born-again person "springs up" in the sense of doing some good works? Yes, I believe it does. Except for those who die at the moment of the new birth, some changes occur in every believer that are capable of observation. However, we must be careful to avoid two erroneous applications of this truth. First, we may not be infallible observers. Thus we may not see the changes in a person. Even the person himself may not identify them. Second, these changes are not the basis of assurance. Assurance is found in believing in Jesus.[1223]

For Wilkin, the springing up of all three seed types in the parable of the sower represents both the germination of the new nature and the production of good works. Consequently, his comments would lead to the conclusion that this text of Scripture (contrary to Hodges) pictures all believers as producing good works. My preference, however, will be for Hodges' emphatic articulation. There is no need to see the production of works in the springing up, particularly since the first seed type that springs up bears no fruit. If one wishes to press the temporary joy in Lk 8:13 in support of Wilkin's assessment, it may be countered that this is illustrative and descriptive but not necessarily conclusive in that it is contrasted with the other two occasions of germination by its complete lack of fruit. Foliage is not fruit.

In any event, the two FG perspectives are in theological agreement, and my Hodgian preference does not distract from Wilkin's excellent discussion of assurance. Not only does the Calvinistic doctrine of temporary faith make absolute assurance absolutely impossible for soteriological fruit inspectors, the tendency in Calvinistic circles to regard those who bring forth immature fruits as lost, even in Lk 8:14, makes it impossible to find assurance within LS even if you persevere in the faith to the end. According to this parable, not only must your faith persevere to the end, it must persevere to maturity. You must persevere in faith and faithfulness both quantitatively and qualitatively. If you are a consistent Calvinist, not only must your faith and faithfulness persevere, they must progress. And not only must they progress, they must progress sufficiently; otherwise, you will burn soteriologically.

Positive Expectations

A favorite ploy among Lordship Salvationists is to represent themselves as merely **expecting** some change in a person's life. **Demanding** changes in a person's life is quite different from expecting them, however. LS exegetically and pragmatically demands radical changes. Those in FG generally expect fruits (i.e., positive changes) in the lives of the regenerate, but FG does not confuse expectations with conditions by demanding works as conditions or as necessary proof of regeneration. The general expectation that regeneration makes a positive difference in a person's life is not the point in question. The point of contention is not with this general expectation but with making this expectation into a scriptural condition for salvation. FG theology does not turn what a person does into a litmus test for regeneration. Good works, or lack thereof, are not infallible indicators of regeneration. Moreover, the Bible provides numerous exhortations to do good works. These are exhortations, not promises.

When those in FG encounter a professing believer who is living a life that is substantially substandard, the FG advocate would do well to question the salvation of the professing believer on the basis of general positive expectations. The primary difference between LS and FG would be what happens at that point of examination. Suppose the individual being questioned gives clear articulation of the fact that he or she indeed has trusted in Christ alone for eternal life. LS would continue to doubt, if not outright deny, such a person's salvation due to the LS insistence on a visible turning in a saved person's life; whereas, those from FG more readily accept the person's testimony. Secondarily, the FG advocate would not encourage such individuals to base their soteriological assurance on their performance but to be assured that they will be judged severely at the Bema due to such performance. The FG message to such believers is to repent, not to become believers since they already are believers.

Invisible Fruit

The wedge that Zeller seeks to drive between Ryrie and others in the FG camp concerning fruitfulness is not as pronounced as Zeller would make it out to be, at least at the theoretical and theological level. Interestingly, Zeller fails to mention the caveats that Ryrie stresses. On the same page from which Zeller begins his quote to prove that Ryrie asserts that all believers will be fruitful, Ryrie himself states that both Tit 3:14 and 2Pet 1:8 "indicate that a true believer might be unfruitful…believers are *not always fruitful*."[1224] In that same chapter, Ryrie considers Jn 15:6 as dealing with "fruitless believers," who are either taken away in judgment or lifted up in hopes that they might eventually bear fruit. Ryrie also notes, concerning this passage, that some believers actually may retrogress "to a fruitless condition for a period of time." And then Ryrie concludes with 2Pet 1:5-7 and surmises that "barrenness and fruitfulness may both be a believer's experience" with the result that "we *are* unfruitful" (emphasis his).[1225] All in all, this chapter by Ryrie is excellent and very much in harmony with FG theology, a fact very conveniently overlooked by Zeller, who wants to make **visible** fruits a soteriological necessity; whereas, Ryrie indicated that **invisible** fruit would suffice. Nevertheless, Ryrie's chapter is rather inconsistent with his exegetical comments in his other writings that Zeller cites. Therefore, exegetical preference must be given to FG writers other than Ryrie regarding alleged LS proof texts where fruitfulness is turned into a soteriological signpost. Other FG writers are much more consistent in harmonizing their exegesis with their theology.

Generally and practically speaking, all believers will produce some good works: sometime, somewhere, somehow. Nevertheless, my earlier description of the Arminian, Marrowistic, and Calvinistic views as *must*, *should*, and *will* is still valid. All believers probably will produce some good works. But Eph 2:10 says that we should **walk** in good works. Although all Christians should *walk* in good works, many do not and will not. Relative to such verses and in terms of overall lifestyle and concerning the biblical descriptions cited above concerning fruitlessness, the *must-should-will* categorization is indeed very useful. Some believers will manifest good works; some will not. Exegetically and comparatively speaking, all believers do not produce good works.

Most importantly, neither soteric salvation nor assurance of that salvation can be based on good works since the quality and quantity of such good works may be so poor as to be visible only to God. Even though Dillow's articulation on this particular matter is very disappointing, to his credit he does correctly acknowledge: "A total unbeliever can live a loving life full of good works."[1226] In similar fashion, Wilkin perceptively states, "It is a mistake of the first order to think that the Holy Spirit can only work in the lives of believers."[1227] Unbelievers (false believers) may love Jesus, confess Jesus, live for Jesus, die for Jesus, and go to hell because they failed to trust in Jesus alone for eternal life. To base one's salvation or assurance of salvation on one's works is foolhardy. Unbelievers may live lives that are morally superior to believers, but this does not prove that unbelievers are saved or that believers are lost.

Blind Wolves

Will all believers produce good works ? Yes. But so what! Unbelievers will produce good works also! Just as the unholy spirit prompts both unbelievers and believers to do evil works, so the Holy Spirit prompts both unbelievers and believers to do good works. The observable presence or absence of good works proves nothing in regard to regeneration. Indeed, some lost people may produce more good works than some saved people. In many cases, the unbeliever may be prompted even by unholy forces to do good. Satan disguises himself as an angel of light, and his servants also disguise "themselves as servants of righteousness" (2Cor 11:14-15). If Satan prompts his servants to disguise themselves as servants of righteousness, would he not do so by prompting them to perform works of righteousness in order to conceal their true nature from both themselves and from others? False assurance of salvation is a dreadful reality. Certainly, in blinding the hearts of unbelievers (2Cor 4:3-4), Satan first blinds the hearts of wolves in sheep clothing into thinking they are saved, when in fact they are not. He fools them into looking at their works.[*]

Tragically, in the end, when Satan's masquerading servants are judged by their works from the Books of Works at the Great White Throne judgment, they will find that their good works have contributed nothing to their having their names in the Book of Life. Little wonder that Jesus condemns these LS fruit inspectors in Mt 7:20-23 on the very basis of what they sought to base their entrance—their works. Unbelievers can be prompted at times by demonic forces to do good and be duped as a result into trusting in their good works for their justification. Such victims may not necessarily be intentionally performing good works to mask their satanic gospel. They may be performing their good works out of (what they perceive to be) genuine love for Jesus and to demonstrate the reality of their regeneration to themselves and others. Nevertheless, demonic forces may be compelling them to perform these good works in order to have them unknowingly mask their lack of regeneration from both themselves and others. Not only do the good works fool those who believe the LS gospel into thinking they are saved, these good works also lead others to believe the LS gospel. Thus, those performing good works may be ambassadors for Satan's false gospel of salvation based on good works. As a result, those in LS might be prompted by both holy and unholy forces to do good works.

Lost people can believe a counterfeit gospel, produce counterfeit good works, and experience counterfeit victory. A soteriological assurance based on works is wide open to Satanic forgery. To base assurance on something that can be counterfeited so easily is utterly precarious. Since faith is assurance, those who base their assurance on their works are foolishly basing their faith on their works. Faith in works will not work; it will not save; it cannot save. Our faith (assurance) must be in Christ alone.

Contrary to proveitism, good works do not prove regeneration. Even aside from such considerations as those above, Paul teaches that some believers live in a manner that is morally worse than unbelievers (1Cor 5:1; 1Tim 5:8). Believers need to learn to engage in good deeds (Tit 3:14). Christians need to learn to do good works. Doing good is learned behavior, not an automatic or inevitable response. Many lost people can put carnal believers to shame in the amount of good works that they—the lost—do. Even if unholy forces do not promote good works, it is still possible that the Holy Spirit finds greater success in promoting good works in the lives of some unbelievers, in His restraining ministry of common grace, than He does in the lives of certain believers who have experienced saving grace.

To be sure, some passages of Scripture seem to indicate that unbelievers cannot produce good works, and understandably so since unbelievers cannot produce any good works that count toward their justification. Relative to their justification, their good works are categorically dead works rather than good works.[1228] Naturally, it is impossible for unbelievers to perform good works in the absolute sense of the word. Even so, different degrees of punishment will be meted out in hell for unbelievers based on their works. Relative to one another, some sinners are worse than others. Likewise, some sins are worse than others. Relative to hell, some unbelievers are worse than others and will be rewarded accordingly. But relative to heaven, unbelievers produce no good works at all and receive no rewards at all.

In the same manner, different degrees of rewards will exist in heaven, different degrees of punishment in the outer darkness, and various positions of authority in the rulership of heaven. Although all overcomers will enter the feast, they will not all be seated at His right and left; there will be a ranking in positions of authority at the kingdom table. Noncomers, subcomers, and overcomers are to be treated individually as well as corporately. Relative to the outer darkness, some carnal Christians produce more good works than other subcomers and will be rewarded accordingly. Yet relative to the feast, subcomers produce no good works at all and receive no rewards at all. Thus, the degree of reward is relative to the corporate and individual experience of that reward.

---

[*] See *Illustration 208. Howl of the Wolf*, 609.

Illustration 233. Relativity Chart

Theory of Relativity	CATEGORY not one-to-one correspondence ↔		
	Noncomer (natural)	Comer	
		subcomer (carnal)	overcomer (spiritual)
one-to-one correspondence ↕	first ↕ last	first ↕ last	first ↕ last

Unlike my previous charts,[*] the above chart does not contrast *first* versus **least** for the simple reason that the scale from *first* to **last** runs vertically rather than horizontally. It runs relative to its self-contained category. If these results are compared horizontally, then certainly first place in hell is less desirable than least place in the outer darkness. And naturally, first place in the outer darkness would not measure up to last place at the table. Horizontally, unbelievers categorically produce no good works. All their righteous deeds are like a filthy rag. Similarly, in terms of horizontal classification, believers who fail to inherit the kingdom may be considered completely barren.

On the other hand, relative to inheriting the kingdom or not inheriting the kingdom, all believers receive the same reward or lack of reward. They either merit the inheritance, or they do not. It is all or nothing. In response to the claim that all believers receive the same reward in this parable, Govett rightly notes, "No one is rewarded who did not work at all." The theory of equalization in the parable of the laborers is contradicted by the misthological distinction in its conclusion, which pictures misthological ranking of first and last inside the kingdom feast, which more specifically would be the kingdom banquet table (Mt 20:16). Govett is right on target: "The parable deals with *classes*, not with *individuals*."[1229] The classifications are horizontally noted above, whereas the individualization is pictured vertically.

One objection that Zeller raises in regard to the FG misthological division of believers into two distinct categories, such as overcomers versus subcomers (i.e., those who rule versus those who do not), is to ask, "How carnal does a saved person need to be in order to be placed in Group 2?"[1230] One might well respond, "How carnal does a believer have to be before Zeller considers that believer lost?" After all, in Zeller's analysis, if you are too carnal, you go to hell. His shortsighted question throws his own categorization into a quandary and shows a very shallow perception of FG misthology. In Zeller's perseverance-based soteriology, absolute soteriological assurance is logically impossible. Correspondingly, absolute misthological assurance is likewise impossible. In Marrowism, on the other hand, absolute soteriological assurance is a given (i.e., a natural inference), which makes relative misthological assurance possible. Marrowists have no soteriological fear and need not have misthological fear. Lordship Salvationists, in contrast, cannot maintain soteriological assurance with logical consistency; hence their misthological assurance suffers from the cracks of doubts found in the LS soteriological foundation.

Zeller seeks to nullify class distinctions in heaven: no upper class versus lower class, no rulers versus sweepers, no partakers versus non-partakers, no cheerful versus sorrowful, no co-heirs versus heirs, none in the lighted room versus those in the outer darkness, and the like. But even a basic misthological text such as 1Cor 3:11-15 makes a sharp distinction between those who build with good quality workmanship versus those who are satisfied with shoddy workmanship. The one saved so as through fire is not going to have anywhere near the same rank as the one who served with honor. A private is not going to be mistaken for a general in heaven.

---

[*] See *Illustration 153. Sequence and Significance of Casting*, 467; *Illustration 231. Last is not Least*, 683.

Illustration 234. Misthological Range of Fruitfulness

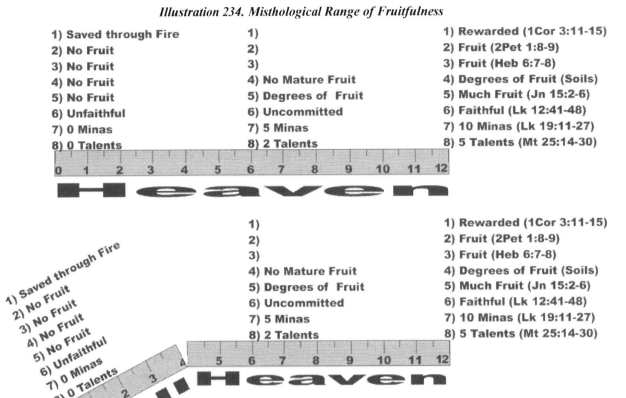

Niemelä has a splendid discussion, complete with two helpful diagrams, to show that Paul is contrasting two extremes from zero rewards to a full reward as a standard for the full range of rewardability. I have adapted and modified Niemelä's diagrams above. The correct ruler for NT misthology is pictured in the first ruler. Calvinists break this ruler (i.e., this misthological standard) for faithfulness in trying to maintain the perseverance of the saints. The second ruler represents their broken standard. Calvinistically speaking, if saints are to persevere in holiness, then surely they will produce good fruits during their lives. Realistically, since in the Calvinistic scheme true believers persevere until the end of their lives and progress in sanctification, believers should be most fruitful as their lives approach their culmination. Those believers who fail in this regard are relegated to the realm of the lost by Calvinistic theology. For Calvinists to admit that believers may die prematurely in a backslidden condition is inconsistent with their theology. This inconsistency aside, however, their view is soteriologically defective in that in consigning the poorest performing believers to hell, Calvinists are basing salvation from hell on the believer's performance. So much for salvation by grace apart from works! Salvation by faith apart from works is a myth in Calvinistic soteriology. Calvinists are synergists.

Their broken ruler is also misthologically defective in that the very first contrast listed in the above diagram is that found in 1Cor 3:11-15, where Paul makes a stark contrast between two workers: the one has much worthy of reward, the other has nothing worth rewarding. This contrast is strictly misthological. It is not a combination of soteriology and misthology. Hell is not part of the contrast. Niemelä explains the significance and necessity of an unbroken standard:

> The entire range is a standard for measuring rewardability. (Nothing short of an entire range will suffice.)…
> …The very nature of rewards suggests intermediate levels between the extremities. This resembles a yardstick, not an on-off switch. Paul does not deny the existence of such a range of rewards. The most reasonable application of his teaching is that all levels of reward will exist. This includes: (1) no reward, (2) full reward, and (3) all intermediate values.[1231]

In a footnote to this material, Niemelä appropriately points out that the parable of the minas depicts this very truth. One slave receives no rewards; another slave receives rulership over five cites, and the most highly-rewarded slave initially receives rulership over ten cites. Then the most fruitful slave is given a bonus when Jesus makes a strong contrast between *first* and *least* place in the kingdom (i.e., between a full reward versus no reward) and when the talent of the slave who receives nothing loses what he did have. His talent is taken away and given to the slave who received rulership over ten cities. Jesus makes a stark contrast between the *haves* and the *have-nots* in heaven (Lk 19:12-26). The parable of the minas shows a one-to-one correspondence, since it portrays not only categories but sub-categories as well. On the other hand, as is seen in the parable of the vineyard (Mt 20:1-16), the payment given in response to the work is not rewarded in a one-to-one correspondence. So in terms of *Illustration 233. Relativity Chart,* a one-to-one correspondence is stressed at times while at other times it is not.

Generally speaking, when the contrast is between one category versus another category, as when moving horizontally across the chart, a one-to-one correspondence is not being stressed. Rather, opposite ends of the soteriological or misthological continuums are being contrasted. Therefore, when Jesus uses a soteriological gulf between sheep with goats or Paul employs a sharp misthological differentiation being saved through fire versus being rewarded, they are both affirming the poles of those reference points rather than denying the full intervening range of the spectrum. The existence of such poles, in either a soteriological or misthological standard, is not to be taken to an extreme polarization that would deny that some situations fall in-between (such as lost people who act like they are saved or saved people who live like they are lost). Consider a bar magnet. It has poles that are labeled N and S. Yet the bulk of the magnet is made up of the intervening material that has characteristics of both poles.

The acknowledgement that the parable of the sheep and goats contrasts unbelievers with believers does not break the misthological ruler above since it is not a part of that ruler. It is not part of *Illustration 234*. The relativity chart in *Illustration 233* would better portray the sheep and goats since it includes the soteriological spectrum. Everyone, lost and saved, will be rewarded according to their works. The relativity chart in *Illustration 233* pictures that truth. The misthological relativity chart (i.e., the ruler in *Illustration 234*), in contrast, acknowledges that (comparatively speaking) many believers will have no works worthy of misthological mention. Nevertheless, they are saved soteriologically. For this reason, the parable of the soils is included in the misthological chart above, since it depicts three types of believers: the zero, the runt, and the mature. The misthological section spans the complete misthological spectrum. To break the misthological ruler at the second soil, or even worse at the third soil, limits the misthological range in an attempt to make perseverance a soteriological requirement. Maintaining the full misthological span, across all three soil types, allows one honestly to affirm that soteriological salvation is by faith apart form works. After all, germination pictures regeneration as taking place in all three soils. If one wishes to picture the full range in this parable of the soils, including the soteriological component, it would be through means of the relativity chart in *Illustration 233*.

Even unbelievers as vile as Judas and Hitler probably performed a number of good deeds in their lives in response to the supernatural prompting they received. Judas was a disciple of Jesus, so he certainly did many good works. Yet he and Hitler will be much worse off in hell than a morally good person who never heard the gospel. Unfaithful believers such as Hymenaeus and Demas probably did a number of good works before they apostatized and may have done many more good works after they left the faith. Nonetheless, believers who turn their back on the Lord and bring the greatest shame to the Christian faith will be in last place in the outer darkness, even if they do good works after they leave the faith. On the other hand, those believers who do the best they can to live the Christian life, but do so in the strength of the flesh, may fail to be considered victorious, but certainly they will not receive as many lashes as those who put forth no effort to serve the Lord or as those who desert the Lord (cp. Lk 12:48). Believers will be given authority based on their faithfulness. Speculatively, one may suggest that aborted babies will grow up in heaven, become believers, and be given positions of authority. They are not disqualified from rulership on the basis of unfaithfulness. Still, having never fought the fight, they will not be qualified for the highest positions of authority that are attained by the most faithful. Faithfulness in the midst of earthly adversity counts for a lot in heaven.

You must have the Spirit before you can walk by the Spirit. Only believers can obey the Spirit by the power of the Spirit in supernaturally demonstrating the Spirit-filled life in a manifestation of good works beyond the normal range of human experience from God's perspective. LS believes that such an observable change in the quality and quantity of good works will be manifested that these works can be relied upon for soteriological assurance. FG does not believe this is the case. As a matter of fact, FG would acknowledge that it is possible that a morally good, legalistic person trying to work his or her way to heaven might accept the gospel of grace and then do a role reversal and go into an antinomian lifestyle. His or her conversion could result in a worse lifestyle rather than a better one, in fewer good works rather than more. He or she might go from a nomian LS position to an antinomian FG lifestyle.[*] Such a believer would be saved from hell, although not from the outer darkness.

Misthological Relativity

A related question might be asked concerning believers who advance in their walk with the Lord and then turn away from the Lord. Do they lose all their rewards for the good they had previously done? In other words, can negative works completely nullify positive works (Eze 3:20; 18:24)? Conversely, can positive works completely nullify negative works (Mt 5:7; Jam 2:13)? The Bible does indicate that negative works can wipe out positive ones:

> Again, **when a righteous man turns away** from his righteousness and commits iniquity, and I place an obstacle before him, he shall die; since you have not warned him, he shall die in his sin, and **his righteous deeds which he has done shall not be remembered**; but his blood I will require at your hand. (Eze 3:20)

> But **when a righteous man turns away** from his righteousness, commits iniquity, and does according to all the abominations that a wicked man does, will he live? **All his righteous deeds which he has done will not be remembered** for his treachery which he has committed and his sin which he has committed; for them he will die. (Eze 18:24)

At first glance, this would seem to indicate that when those who are righteous turn away from the path of righteousness, all of their previous righteous works will be wiped out, making it impossible for them to receive any reward for their former good works. However, passages such as Mt 10:42 and Mk 9:41 teach that you cannot lose your reward for doing something so simple as giving a cup of water. Suppose a righteous man gave a cup of water and then turned from his righteousness. Which passages would hold true? Will his righteous works not be remembered, as Ezekiel warns, or will they not be forgotten, as Jesus promises? If we take our cue from a mediating passage, such as 2Jn 1:8, which teaches that what is at stake is the forfeiture of a full reward (cp. Rev 3:11), we may hold that both sets of passages are true. Positive and negative works can offset one another— but not necessarily completely, depending upon the frame of reference. For example, all rewards may be lost in regard to receiving a full reward.

Righteous believers who turn away from the Lord can indeed fail to have their righteous works remembered **relative to the subject matter at hand**, whether it be deliverance from temporal and/or misthological wrath or inheriting the kingdom. In the above passages, relative to saving one's life (i.e., soul), righteous believers who subsequently become unrighteous will find that their righteousness will count for nothing. Some rewards, like ruling/inheriting the kingdom are conditioned on faithfulness till the end of one's life (cf. 2Tim 4:7-8; Rev 2:10). Naturally, any good thing believers do previous to that point will count for nothing in terms of inheriting the kingdom if they do not persevere to the end. Those believers who fail to persevere will find that nothing they did will count for anything in terms of inheriting the kingdom. In that sense, whether one's righteous deeds are remembered is all or nothing. However, this need not be ripped out of context and applied indiscriminately to passages which teach that all our works will count for some type of evaluation. There will be varying degrees of loss of reward in the outer darkness. Although the righteous works a subcomer performs will count for nothing in regard to inheriting the kingdom, at least such works will count for something in regards to not receiving as many lashes in the outer darkness (cp. Lk 12:47-48). On the positive side, an overall positive performance may result in misthological sinlessness, in which negative works do not prevent a believer from being found spotless.[†] All overcomers will be spotless in terms of composing the Bride of Christ. Yet not all overcomers will have the same degree of prominence in that bridal company. Therefore, the little things as well as the big things we do for the Lord have eternal significance. All in all, Marrowism is the proper antidote for antinomianism. All our good works count for something, whether good or bad. Each and every work we perform as believers has eternal significance. Marrowism is not nomian in that it does not teach that good works are soteriologically necessary to reach heaven, nor is it antinomian in that Marrowists believe the good works are misthologically necessary to have rewards in heaven.

---

[*] Licentious FG antinomians are denounced very strongly in the present book. See *Warning to Soteriologists*, 959.
[†] See *Misthological Sinlessness*, 772. Also see, discussions of *misthological mercy*.

Chronic Depression

Keathley objects to the misthological interpretation of the outer darkness because he finds it too depressing, alleging that it contradicts the joy that the Bible promises in heaven:

> If Hodges and Huber are correct, then we need to change all our sermons which hold out hope for the chronically depressed person that their condition is not going to last forever. I seriously doubt that either of them would teach that a person better get with it, stop being depressed and start trusting God and walking by the power of the Holy Spirit or they are going to be stuck in that **depression for eternity**.[1232]

Double Standard

Interestingly, Keathley does not object to Pagenkemper requiring submission to the Lordship of Christ to escape the outer darkness, but he does find it repulsive for those in the FG camp to require submission to the Lordship of Christ to escape it. Why the double standard? Both LS and FG promote submission to the Lordship of Christ. Both believe that submission to His Lordship is required for salvation from the outer darkness. The difference is that LS requires this full, subjective submission for salvation from hell; whereas, those in FG do not. LS is much more gloomy than FG theology in this respect in that LS is telling those with substandard performance that they are in danger of hell.

Granted, it is depressing to tell people that unless they victoriously submit to Christ's Lordship, they will be excluded from the highest privileges in heaven. In counterpoint, how much more depressing is the LS doctrine, espoused by those such as Pagenkemper, who believe that unless you are victorious you will burn in hell forever? At least in FG theology, those in the outer darkness will have some joy and happiness. They will have sorrow over what they have failed to achieve but joy over what they graciously have been given. Further, we have seen evidence above that even those in the outer darkness still can receive a reduced reward and be thankful for this reduced privilege. Contrastively, those in hell will be in severe physical and emotional pain with no joy or happiness whatsoever. Certainly, LS is far more depressing to the depressed than is FG theology.

False Dichotomy

Not only is Keathley guilty of a double standard, he also makes a false dichotomy between sorrow and joy, arguing as if both cannot occur simultaneously in the human heart. The requirement posed by both LS and FG for salvation from the outer darkness is a life of faithful submission to the Lordship of Christ that expresses itself in good works. The requirement is not an absence of sorrow or depression, as Keathley erroneously attempts to paint the FG canvas. Keathley's caricature of the FG position is ridiculous. One of the best books on the victorious Christian life from a FG perspective is that by Charles Stanley. In relation to the above discussion concerning the theory of relativity, Stanley acknowledges, "I have met some nonbelievers who demonstrate more 'fruit type' character than many Christians I know."[1233] Stanley believes that the thing that distinguishes genuine fruits of the Spirit from the counterfeit fruits is that the latter is deeply grounded in its environment. Pertaining to the particular fruit of joy experienced by the victorious believer, it is effected by the Spirit and only temporally affected by shifts in their circumstances. "They don't allow disappointment and sorrow to control them."[1234] This is excellent FG nikology, insofar as it goes. It would seem, however, that Keathley wants to push it further than is intended by those in the FG camp.

Those in FG would concur with Dobson's perspective that the wonderful victorious Christian life for certain believers, such as Joni Eareckson, may mean "life in a wheelchair as a quadriplegic. For others it means early death, poverty, or the scorn of society."[1235] After grappling with some less than joyful illustrations, Dobson asks, "So tell me, where did we get the notion that the Christian life is a piece of cake?" Then, with a few concluding passages (Jn 16:33, 2Cor 7:4-5, 1Pet 4:12-13), he surmises, "Note that in each of these references the coexistence of both joy and pain."[1236] I might also add 1Pet 1:6: "In this you greatly **rejoice**, though now for a little while, if need be, you have been **grieved** [*lupeo*] by various trials" (NKJV). These believers were not merely experience objective distress; they were experiencing the emotional distress that accompanies it. They were not merely hurting on the outside but on the inside also. They were experiencing sadness and grief, not just hard times through which they were sailing effortless. They were not keeping a stiff upper lip, nor did Peter reprove them for not doing so. Rather, despite their sorrow, he commends them for rejoicing during their sorrowing. Wilkin likewise acknowledges the coexistence of both sorrow and joy in the life of the believer:

Though a believer who dwells on these truths will experience joy, he may not necessarily be *happy*. Joy and happiness are not the same thing. Happiness is dependent on circumstances. Joy is independent of our circumstances. So a believer might be discouraged, or even depressed, and yet experience joy if he abides in Christ and in the certainty of his eternal salvation.[1237]

Keathley's emotional objection is false and directed toward the wrong camp. The abiding life can be one in which the victorious Christian experiences joy and depression simultaneously. Wilkin's distinction between joy and happiness is well taken, as long as it is remembered that he is using these words in their popular usage rather than providing a word study of the biblical terms. To rephrase in the vocabulary of popular usage, biblical words such as *chara* may refer to a joy that is experienced independently of present circumstances. However, this joy is frequently dependent on the anticipation of a change in one's future circumstances. The reference to joy may be used, depending on the context, to refer to a present or future happiness that is dependent upon, or influenced by, one's temporal or eschatological environment and circumstances. Unfortunately, studies in nikology frequently ignore passages that depict ongoing unhappiness as part of the Spirit-filled life. Such one-sided studies give the false impression that Spirit-filled believers do not suffer negative emotions on a recurring basis.

Worry or fear is often mistakenly seen as a negative emotion depicting lack of victory. The author heard a speaker on the Spirit-filled life give the impression to a church audience that concern is worry in disguise. The implication was that since Spirit-filled believers are not to worry, they are not to be concerned! Although it is true that worry may be disguised as concern, it is false to say that all concern is worry. *Anxious concern (merimnao)* can be either good or bad (Phil 2:20; 4:6). Paul said that he himself was *concerned/anxious/worried (alupos)*, depending on which translation you read, about his converts (Phil 2:28). In fact, being distressed over the well-being of others is a positive attribute (Phil 2:26). Paul certainly was motivated by fearful concern (2Cor 11:3; 12:20; Gal 2:2; 4:11; 1Thess 3:5). The NAS translates *me pos* as *for fear* in Gal 2:2; 4:11; 1Thess 3:5. The verb for *fear (phobeo)* is used in conjunction with this construction in both 2Cor 11:3; 12:20; Gal 4:11. This is the verbal root from which we derive the word *phobia*.

Paul was motivated by phobia, not an irrational fear but a rational one. He realized that Satan could overthrow the work he was seeking to carry out in the hearts and lives of believers. Not to fear a coiled rattlesnake that is ready and able to strike a deadly blow would be foolish. Satan is not a foe to be taken lightly. One might well speculate that Paul was not unaccustomed to experiencing this human emotion of worry while at the same time experiencing the power of the Spirit: "And I was with you in weakness and in fear and in much trembling. And my message and my preaching were not in persuasive words of wisdom, but in demonstration of the Spirit and of power" (1 Cor 2:3-4). He asks others to pray for him that he would be bold in proclaiming the gospel (Eph 6:19-20). Evidently, this was a real need because he experienced real fear. To be sure, at times courage can dispel fear (Phil 1:14). Yet at other times the Spirit empowers believers to do the right thing despite their fears.

Emotions are a false barometer of one's spirituality. The better books on the victorious Christian life stress that we live by faith not by emotions. Gillham likewise devotes an excellent chapter to this topic, with a subsection entitled, *Christ Could Not Control His Emotions*, and he uses Lk 22:44 to prove his point.[1238] This does not mean that Christ lost His peace according to Gillham; rather, peace is a persuasion rather than an emotion. Gillham's conviction is that the formula for victory is basically to trust and obey and don't let the rain ruin your parade. **Do not base your victory on your emotional response to your circumstances**. To offset Keathley's misperception, the following passages are cited as examples of the sorrow and happiness being experienced by Spirit-filled believers.

Circumstantial Joy of Victorious Christians

Paul, the same man who said to *rejoice always* (1Thess 6:16), acknowledges that he has *great sorrow and **unceasing** grief* (Rom 9:2). Paul suffered from chronic depression. Yet this need not mean that his countenance was always one of depression. He experiences sorrow and joy simultaneously (2Cor 6:10). Not only does he rejoice always, he also experiences tremendous, unceasing grief and sorrow. The intensity of his emotional pain was such that he evidently would have been willing to die and go to hell because of it (Rom 9:3)! Paul's concern for others moved him to tears the entire three years he ministered in one city (Acts 20:31; cp. 2Cor 2:4). Indeed, he does not hesitate to admit that God's working in the circumstances of his life is to spare him from having *sorrow upon sorrow* (Phil 2:27). In short, his emotional stability is dependent, to some degree, upon his circumstances. The Greek word he uses in 2:27 for *sorrow* is *lupe*. And he uses a derivative of it (*alupos*) in the next verse (2:28) to say that his having less sorrow is contingent on the reactions of others. Paul is comforted in his distress by the hearing of good news from Titus about the positive response of his converts (2Cor 7:4-7). Paul even went so far as to condition his experience of the abundant life (in terms of happiness) upon whether or not his converts were faithful to the Lord (1Thess 3:7-9). His being filled with happiness was dependent upon his fellowship with other believers (2Tim 1:4). He is cheered up or grieved by fellow believers (2Cor 2:2-3). Whether his happiness is complete is dependent upon how people respond to his instructions (Phil 2:2,19).

John's happiness is likewise dependent upon his fellowship with other believers and their obedience to his instructions (1Jn 1:3-4). He experiences great happiness because of a positive response by other believers (2Jn 1:4; 3Jn 1:3). The writer of Hebrews takes it for granted that whether a pastor experiences happiness or sorrow as he leads his congregation is largely dependent upon how his congregation responds to his ministry (Heb 13:17). Objective success in the ministry brings great subjective happiness (Acts 15:3). Jesus also teaches that the fullness of our happiness is dependent upon our receiving answered prayers (Jn 16:24). Of course, answered prayer frequently involves a change in our circumstances or in the people around us. Prayer does, in fact, change things and people and in doing so affects our attitude. The happiness being described is dependent upon present circumstances, upon what is presently happening in one's own life or in the lives of others.

The writer of Hebrews has no problem encouraging believers to accept joyfully their present circumstances in view of the future misthological changes that God would make in their circumstances (Heb 10:34). James gives the same exhortation (Jam 1:2). The biblical writers encourage a present joy based on an anticipated change in future circumstances. Faithful believers will enter into the eschatological happiness of their master; unfaithful believers will be cast into the outer darkness instead and weep (Mt 25:21,23,30). Jesus teaches that those who weep now because of their allegiance to Him will have the last laugh (Lk 6:21). He teaches them to leap for joy despite their present sorrow because of the future misthological happiness that awaits them as His faithful servants (Lk 6:23). Jesus contrasts present unhappiness with future misthological happiness: "Blessed are you when men cast insults at you, and persecute you, and say all kinds of evil against you falsely, on account of Me. Rejoice, and be glad, for your reward in heaven is great, for so they persecuted the prophets who were before you" (Mt 5:11-12). Yet the list of requirements for this future blessing has a reference to negative emotions in its introduction: "Blessed are those who mourn, for they shall be comforted" (Mt 5:4).

Yes, we are to rejoice now—have joy now—because of the future misthological happiness that we are earning in terms of a change in our future circumstances. This present heavenly joy is based on anticipated circumstantial change and is expected to take place simultaneously with our earthly mourning. Rejection now and present sorrow for Jesus' sake results in rulership then—a major turn of events. We are expected to mourn as we rejoice and rejoice as we mourn. Those hurting internally and subjectively at the beginning of the Matthean misthological list of the beatitudes (Mt 5:4) are those being hurt externally and objectively at its conclusion (Mt 5:11). Lest someone try to ignore the emotional depth of this mourning, let it be pointed out that to *mourn* (*pentheo*) means "to experience sadness as the result of some condition or circumstance" (BDAG). Or stated more fully, it means "to experience sadness or grief as the result of depressing circumstances....The reference in Mt 5.4 is not to grieving or mourning for the dead but rather sadness and grief because of wickedness and oppression" (L-N). It is depression based on depressing circumstances. Stoic Christianity is not from Christ. If having a pure heart is a virtue in Mt 5:8, then should a hurting heart be considered any less a virtue in Mt 5:4? In the battle with sin, a wounded heart is certainly to be preferred to a callous heart or an indulgent heart. Those with wounded hearts will be awarded the Lord's Purple Heart.

Cure for Depression

If Spirit-filled believers can experience depression and unhappiness now because of their service for the Lord, then why can carnal believers not experience regret and remorse in the future because of their lack of service for the Lord? Unfaithful believers frequently experience little internal joy now as they seek to maximize their temporal circumstantial happiness. In contrast, faithful believers sometimes have to be satisfied with internal joy rather than temporal circumstantial happiness while on earth. Such internal joy is independent of present circumstances and anticipatory of future eschatological happiness. In eternity, those who have been unfaithful will experience a minimal joy and happiness, while those who have been faithful will experience the maximum of both internal and external joy and happiness.

Corner devotes ch. 17 of his book to *OSAS and Suicide*. His two major objections are that OSAS would encourage suicide as an easy way out for those who are depressed. Second, since suicide is self-murder, those who die in that state would die as murderers since they would not have an opportunity to confess their sin afterward. Consequently they would be confined to the Lake of Fire which is for murderers.

The flaw with his first objection is that it underrates the doctrine of rewards. The Marrowistic assessment is that suicide eternalizes the depression. Tears and gnashing of teeth will occur in the outer darkness. Let the suicidal be informed that they will be making the emotional torment permanent if they commit suicide. People in both hell and the outer darkness will weep and gnash their teeth. This is something that people in hell and some people in heaven will have in common. Suicide is not the means to rid oneself of this hellish emotion. **The only complete cure to eternal depression is full, unadulterated submission to the Lordship of Christ.**

Misthologists, therefore, would encourage someone who is longing for suicide to leave the timing of their death prayerfully in the Lord's hand. We would not respond by teaching works-righteousness as a means of escaping hell, as Corner would have us do. Marrowists would not tell the suicidal to tough it out in order to avoid hell. But we would encourage them to do everything necessary to escape the outer darkness. And if that means bearing emotional pain through the power of the Spirit, then so be it.

As to self-murder, it is true that suicide is self-murder, and there will be no murderers in heaven. Then how can we claim that believers who commit suicide will be cast into the outer darkness within heaven? Simple. Their murder will be a thing of the past not of the present. Believers who reach heaven will not be considered murderers any more than they would be considered sinners. It is a matter of classification. Alcorn deals with the past versus present in this manner:

> "Nothing impure will ever enter it [the New Jerusalem], nor will anyone who **does** what is shameful or deceitful, but only those whose names are written in the Lamb's book of life" (Revelation 21:27). This passage doesn't say: "If someone becomes impure or deceitful, that person will be evicted." There is an absolute contrast between sinners and the righteous....Three times in the final two chapters of Scripture, we're told that those **still** in their sins have no access to Heaven, and never will (Rev 21:8, 27; 22:15).[1239]

Alcorn's point is well taken. When unbelievers die, they are *still* in their sins. When believers die, they are no longer in their sins (Jn 8:24; 1Cor 15:17). In fact, Rev 22:11 might be saying something similar: "Let the one who does wrong, still do wrong; and let the one who is filthy, still be filthy." Regardless, those described in these other three passages are unbelievers who died in their sins and consequently are still regarded as sinners. Corner should be able to recognize this truth since he believes that David is in heaven because David confessed his sin. Marrowists simply perceive a different condition than Corner for not dying in one's sin. In Marrowism the condition is belief, not confession (Jn 8:24). In any event, Corner would have to admit that just because someone commits murder on earth, this does not mean that this person still will be considered a murderer in heaven.

Moreover, Corner's *Appendix A* is devoted to passages from the YLT which use the continuous tense for *believe*. Corner uses this to argue that one must continue to believe in order to reach heaven. I have dedicated books to refuting this type of argument.[*] Yet the point of curiosity at this juncture is that the YLT likewise translates Rev 21:27 in a manner similar to Alcorn: "And there may not at all enter into it anything defiling and **doing** abomination, and a lie." If this present participle is indeed anarthrous (BYZ[†]), then perhaps YLT and Alcorn are right in this case. Those in hell are still *doing* shameful things. There is no reason to think otherwise. If so, then John is saying that those in eternity future who are in hell outside the kingdom are still sinning. If that is the case, then they not only died in their sins, they still will be sinning.

On the other hand, this possibility has zero applicability to a believer—even if such a believer were to commit suicide. Believers would not still be in their sins after death, nor would they still be sinning. On the other hand, even if the participle were articular (HMT; CT?) or the present tense were not denoting continuous action, the adjectival and substantival classifications coalesce to confirm that the people in these passages are outside because they still are considered sinners.[‡] They are still labeled with this classification. Consequently, it has no application to a believer. Believers are not still classified as sinners in heaven. There will be no sins or sinners there. To be sure, believers will be judged for their works, and thus have to pay the misthological price for their unconfessed sinful actions. However, the price they pay is not soteriological. Those who, like Corner, teach otherwise are teaching soteriological salvation by works.

Since Corner, by his own theology, acknowledges that David is in heaven and that murderers are not allowed into heaven, it must be concluded that Corner does not believe that David is still classified as a murderer. Moreover, since Corner provides an extended quote from Hodges, which makes much the same point as I have just made (e.g. "If they had been liars, they are liars no more."), one is left to wonder if Corner is lying when he then turns around and says, "While the popular *grace* teachers previously cited [including Hodges]...say grace does

---

[*] See *Believe: An Aspectual and Metaphorical Analysis of the Gospel of John.* Also see *John in Living Color.*
[†] I do not always check the *Hodgian MT* (HMT) as opposed to the BYZ since the majority of the time when I consult them, they are in agreement. Yet Rev 21:27 is one of those occasions where they do not agree. The HMT has the article; whereas, the BYZ omits it. CT parenthetically interjects it.
[‡] See "Substantival Categorization" in *Believe: An Aspectual and Metaphorical Analysis from the Gospel of John.*

allow the sexually immoral in heaven, the real grace teachers of the Bible categorically say **no** to the exact same question" (emphasis his).[1240] Very well, let FG teachers ask Corner the question: "Is King David in heaven?" "Yes," is the mutual answer. Does this mean that God allows murderers into heaven? Like Corner, those in FG say, "No." Corner will agree with us that David is in heaven and that he is no longer considered a liar, immoral, or a murderer. So is Corner intentionally lying when he says that FG teaches otherwise? If not, then at the very least he appears to be blind to the weakness of his own argument.

Conclusion

The present author is now even more emphatic about submission to the Lordship of Christ from a FG perspective than he was as a Lordship Salvationist. One problem with LS is that it tends to water down submission to the Lordship of Christ with theological inconsistencies. For example, if deliverance from depression is a free gift, then you do not have to submit to the Lordship of Christ in order to get it. Alternatively, if it is not a free gift, then you have to submit to the Lordship of Christ in order to achieve it. By trying to picture salvation from depression as both free and not free, LS conceives of it as earned and unearned. In combining soteriology and misthology, LS waters down its misthology and poisons its soteriology. If you want to be free from depression in eternity, then embrace the soteriological and misthological distinctions concerning Christ's Lordship found within FG and live accordingly. There is a cure to eternal depression—this cure is none other and no less than submission to the Lordship of Christ. Suicide is not a cure; it does not eliminate the pain; it only eternalizes it. GRAPE theology is the antidote to painful existence. As rewards are eternal and our enjoyment of them is as well, it is reasonable to conclude that our loss of rewards and sense of loss will be just as eternal. Those who suffer such loss will in fact suffer (1Cor 3:15). Presumably, in time they will learn to cope with the loss considerably. Yet I find no evidence that their pain of that loss will ever simply go away completely.

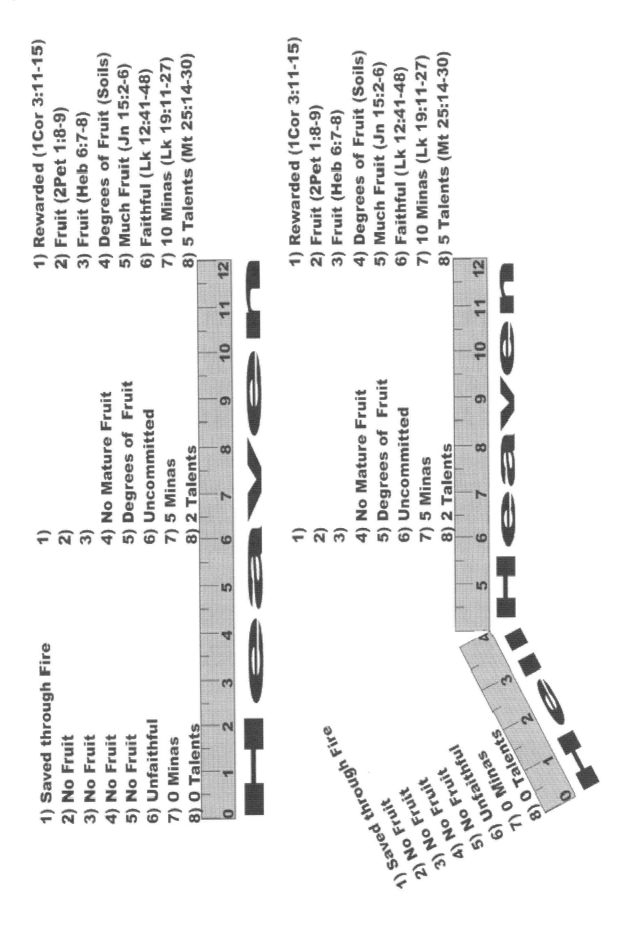

Chapter 31.
Conclusion

Introduction

Rather than go through and summarize the conclusions from all the preceding chapters into this centralized location, this concluding chapter will highlight and clarify some of the most significant findings. Since this study of the outer darkness has interacted with the other primary soteric camps, reviewing the interaction with Calvinism and Arminianism is certainly in order. In particular, doctrinal findings regarding the outer darkness should be compatible with one's views regarding eternal security, which in turn necessitates a harmonization with predestination that explains how those who have been predestined for glory can, nevertheless, end up in the outer darkness. An explanation as to the difference between soteriological security and misthological security is also necessitated.

Predestination Objection

The Calvinistic and Arminian objections to a misthological understanding of the outer darkness have been examined and found soteriologically defective and misthologically deficient. Ventilato, for example, claimed that election unconditionally guarantees our inheritance (Jam 2:5) as well as our salvation (2Thess 2:13).[*] According to Calvinists, predestination guarantees perseverance. Naturally, from that mindset it is understandable that Ventilato would assume that election guarantees the result, in this case, the richness of our faith, with its attendant inheritance of the kingdom.

Illustration 235. Predestined Perseverance

Ventilato's appeal to Jam 2:5 as a soteriological example is ill-advised, however, and certainly counterproductive to the very point he is trying to make. The text itself is quite resistant to both Calvinistic and Arminian manipulation: "Listen, my beloved brethren: did not God choose the poor of this world to be rich in faith and heirs of the kingdom which He promised to those who love Him?" Are all *the poor of this world* rich in faith? Of course not. The most natural conclusion from the text is that God has not unconditionally elected the poor to be rich in faith; otherwise, not only would all the poor be believers, they would also all be strong believers without exception. Therefore, this verse is not describing unconditional election. Nor is the verse talking about a soteriological inheritance. Salvation from eternal damnation is not conditioned on our love for God but on His love for us. Nor is soteric salvation conditioned on the magnitude of our faith in God. The object of saving faith is God, not our faith. Consequently, the Calvinistic approach to the text yields unsatisfactory results for multiple reasons.[1241]

---

[*] See *Introduction*, 181.

Illustration 236. Perseverance-Based Predestination

The Arminian fares no better than the Calvinist in dealing with Jam 2:5. In Arminianism, election is based on foreseen perseverance in faith. God elects those who will persevere in the faith, and these are the ones whom He has predestined to reach heaven. James, in contrast, teaches the exact opposite in this verse. God elected the poor to be rich in faith. They are rich in faith because they are elected; they are not elected because they are rich in faith. The Arminian is correct, however, to insist on the acknowledgement of free will. Whether the poor will develop a rich faith is contingent upon their response to the gospel of the kingdom. In this text, we find that God has held an election, and He has given us the deciding vote. The poor are not unconditionally or irresistibly chosen to be rich in faith; rather, they are contingently chosen to be rich in faith so that they may inherit the kingdom.[1242]

Eternal Security

This overview leaves Marrowism as the most straightforward treatment of a text such as Jam 2:5. Only this approach is prepared to deal with the contingent nature of misthological predestination. As an expression of conditional election and through the means of providential inclination, God has chosen the poor to be rich in faith. Their free response is the basis for His misthological selection. Marrowism is first and foremost a sophisticated, soteriological defense of unconditional eternal security, and secondarily, yet significantly, a misthological defense of the conditional nature of rewards. One of the strongest passages in the Bible typically used in defense of eternal security is the golden chain of Rom 8:29-30.

Illustration 237. Perkins' Perversion

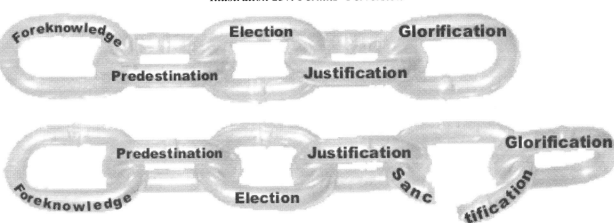

The five verbs of this passage have been considered an unbreakable golden chain by Calvinists since the time of Calvin's son-in-law and successor, Theodore Beza (1519-1605). William Perkins wrote *A Golden Chain* in 1591 and dedicated it to Beza. The primary thrust of Perkins' argument is that the chain of events conveyed by the verbs of Rom 8:29-30 assures that the elect will persevere and thus reach heaven. In actuality, this is an argument for conditional security since the realization of one's glorification is contingent upon one's perseverance in such a chain. The way Perkins implemented this contingency was to insert sanctification as an additional link into the chain, as Anderson explains: "Perkins writes about four degrees of God's love: effectual calling, justification,

sanctification, and glorification. Notice how conveniently he [Perkins] slips 'sanctification' into the mix, when Rom 8:30 quite obviously omits sanctification in its 'golden chain.' It is, in fact, conspicuous by its absence."[1243]

Rather than adopt Perkin's modification, which results in conditional security, Marrowists insist upon the Pauline version, which is a strong affirmation of unconditional security.* *In any event, whereas Perkins asserted that the elect will persevere and thus reach heaven, Arminius reversed these essential elements and provided a rebuttal by claiming that those who persevere would be elected and thus reach heaven.* The essential difference between these two men and their respective camps has been condensed by Reasoner to a cause-and-effect relationship between predestination and perseverance: "According to both Perkins and Arminius, if the believer does not persevere, such a person proves to be non-elect. The difference is that Perkins taught that believers persevere because they were elected. Arminius taught that God elects believers whom he foresees will persevere."[1244]

To restate this observation pictured in the above hand illustrations, according to Perkins, if you are predestined, then you will persevere.† The rejoinder by Arminius is the converse: If you persevere, then you are predestined. According to Calvinists, predestination causes perseverance, while Arminians claim that perseverance is the basis for predestination.‡ To Arminius' credit, he does not insert an additional link into the chain in doing so. Or does he?

Illustration 238. Arminius' Abrogation

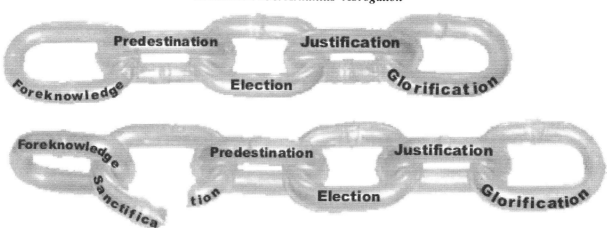

In *Illustration 237. Perkins' Perversion*, securitists are quick to point out that Perkins perverts the Pauline chain by inserting sanctification as an additional link. Perkins' progressive sanctification is just another name for perseverance. Therefore, in teaching that predestination results in sanctification as a condition for glorification, Perkins is presenting a predestination-based perseverance as his additional link. Arminius is doing much the same thing in making a prescience-based perseverance (i.e. practical sanctification) his additional link. However, Arminius' arrangement results in an absurd order in which sanctification logically precedes justification![1245] Consequently, it must be stressed emphatically that **Marrowism differs fundamentally from Arminianism in that Marrowism does not have the perverted insertion and inversion found in Arminianism.**

Within Marrowism, believers are justified by faith, not by faithfulness. Moreover, it cannot be linear faith because this soteric justification is granted permanently (not prematurely) the moment a person comes to faith. As a result, Marrowism affirms the unconditional security of anyone who comes to faith, and it does so the very moment such a person comes to faith. Both Calvinism and Arminianism (and their combined Calminianism) condition soteric glorification upon perseverance. Whether a believer reaches heaven is contingent upon the believer's perseverance according to both of these camps. Granted, Calvinists and Arminians might both agree that those who persevere will be secure when they reach heaven. Thus, believers who persevere will be granted unconditional security eventually. But such soteriology amounts to conditional security for believers who have not yet reached heaven.

---

* See *Illustration 89. Golden Chain of Rom* 8:29-30, 236.
† See *Illustration 235. Predestined* , 701.
‡ See *Illustration 236. Perseverance-Based Predestination*, 702.

Illustration 239. Calvinistic Conditional Security

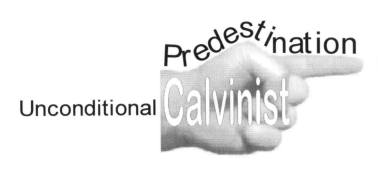

Unconditional   Unconditional

In this Calvinistic model, God is pictured by the hand on the left. He unconditionally elects certain people to become believers and persevere in the faith so that they will reach heaven. The first occurrence of the word *unconditional* represents the fact that God's selection in the Calvinistic model is not based on any foreseen faith or faithfulness on the part of the individual. God simply chooses the ones whom He wants to be saved as those who will be saved. God then unconditionally predetermines that they will believe and persevere and reach heaven as a result. So the first occurrence of *unconditional* to the left of the first hand represents the unconditional **basis** for predestination, while the second occurrence of *unconditional* to the right of the hand represents the unconditional **result** of predestination.

The raised hand on the right represents the Marrowistic objection to this scheme of things. The foremost Marrowistic objection is that Calvinism teaches synergistic salvation by works. Calvinistic faith is synergistic. Suppose you were to reach heaven's gates, and God were to raise His hand and motion for you to stop (as indicated by the hand on the right), and He were to ask you, "Why should I let you into My heaven?" What would your answer be? The consistent Calvinist would have to answer, "Because I believed and persevered in faith and faithfulness." After all, you cannot enter the Calvinistic heaven without both. Yet this is salvation by faith and works, and such a soteriology will condemn a person to hell.

Suppose a slightly less consistent Calvinist were simply to answer, "Because I believed and persevered in my belief." By not mentioning his perseverance in faithfulness, he has not explicitly made his works a condition to enter heaven. Is this answer then acceptable? Unfortunately not. By mentioning his perseverance in faith as a reason, he unwittingly and implicitly has admitted that he is trusting in his works as a means to enter heaven and that he did not believe the promises in Scripture that he was eternally secure the moment he came to faith in Christ because of his simple faith in Christ for eternal life. By pointing to his perseverance in faith as part of his reason he should be allowed to enter heaven, he implicitly has pointed to his good works as part of the basis for his hope to enter heaven and therefore will fail to enter as a result. Perseverance in faith is a misthological consideration and thus a work. However, we are not saved from hell by works or by faith and works.

Could not the Calvinist respond that his perseverance was produced monergistically by God and thus a gift? He could try, but it would be to no avail. God could easily point out that, by the Calvinist's own admission, he is trusting in these works as part of the reason he should be allowed into heaven. Thus, he would not be allowed to enter heaven because works are disallowed as a reason to enter heaven. We are not saved from eternal damnation by postconversion works.

Second, God could point out that He repeatedly has indicated in His word that these works are produced synergistically and, consequently, cannot be considered a monergistically-excused basis by which to enter heaven. Works are works. Trying to be saved from eternal damnation on the basis of works or by means of works is clearly forbidden in Scripture. Just because the Calvinist claims that postconversion works are produced monergistically, so that we supposedly get no credit for them, does not mean that God is obligated to agree, especially when He has stated in His word that He considers these works rewardable.

Third, God could point out the inconsistency of the person's claim. If the Calvinist's works were not required because they were produced monergistically, then Calvinistically his faith was not required either since his faith reputedly was produced monergistically. Calvinism reduces both faith and works to a description of those who are the genuine objects of election and in doing so rejects faith as a condition for salvation. But to deny that faith is a condition is to claim that one is saved through election rather than through faith. To the contrary, God has required that we believe that our salvation is contingent upon our faith. If we fail to believe that this is the biblical condition, then we fail to believe what the Scripture teaches concerning the requirement to enter heaven.

Fourth, God could point out that the person did not believe what he was required to believe. Saving faith is believing that one is unconditionally secure the moment one believes in Jesus for eternal life. By believing in Jesus for probation rather than for eternal life, such a person would have failed to receive eternal life and therefore remained spiritually dead. Calvinism can be quite deadly.

Illustration 240. Arminian Conditional Security

Marrowism appreciates the fact that Arminianism affirms free will. In the Arminian model above, the word to the left of the hand is *conditional* and therefore indicates that the basis for predestation is our free persuasional response. This is much better than the previous Calvinistic model which based predestation on some mysterious decree. However, Marrowists must still raise their hand in objection to this Arminian model since the Arminian model (in similar fashion to the Calvinistic model) claims that we cannot enter heaven apart from our good works. At the very least, the good work of perseverance in faith is considered a condition for entering heaven by the Arminian. In contrast, the Scripture demands that we not seek entrance on a performance basis. Furthermore, Scripture repeatedly indicates that we must trust in Christ for eternal life. Believing in Him for probation is not the same thing as believing in Him for a gift of eternal life that delivers one from eternal damnation the moment one receives this gift of life.

Both Arminianism and Calvinism teach conditional security for the justified believer, and thus the insecurity of the believer. Calvinists are insecuritists. At the very least, the believer must continue to believe in order to reach heaven. Both systems are designed to prevent one from embracing eternal life as a free gift, as presented by both John and Paul. In John's invitations we are urged repeatedly to take the water of life without cost by believing in Jesus for eternal life and, therefore, to be eternally safe and sound as a result. In Paul's writings we, likewise, are implored to believe in Jesus for eternal life and not to believe in our works in any shape, form, or degree whatsoever for salvation from eternal damnation.

Illustration 241. Persevering in Faith Syllogism

1. Perseverance in faith is rewarded.
2. Rewards are always based on works.
3. Therefore, perseverance in faith is a work.

Perseverance in faith is not the only contributing factor towards our rewards in heaven, of course, but it is certainly one such factor and, consequently, is a misthological contingency. Since personal acceptance of one's own personal security is the essence of saving faith, we must adopt a model that meets this requirement without conditioning our security on our perseverance. Unfortunately, many popular arguments for eternal security fare little better than the Calvinistic and Arminian systems above.

Illustration 242. Simplistic Eternal Security

Unlike the Arminian model, the basis for the selection in this simplistic OSAS model is the punctiliar appropriation of eternal life, represented by the dot rather than a line to the left of the hand. Just as the Arminian model was a considerable advancement over the Calvinistic model regarding free agency, this OSAS model is a considerable advancement over the Arminian model regarding soteriology. Advocates of this simplistic model of eternal security include Norman Geisler, Gordon Olson, and Steven Waterhouse.[1246]

Unfortunately, advocates of this view of OSAS tend to view perseverance in faith as guaranteed by God. From their perspective, perseverance is more frequently described as a *demonstration* or *manifestation* of one's regeneration rather than a *condition* of one's final salvation. But those holding this view still tend to think that you are not saved by faith and works but by faith that works. Or restated in terms of perseverance, you are not saved by perseverance in faith but by faith that perseveres. This useless rhetoric does little to conceal the fact that works are being brought in the back door as a basis of entering heaven. Granted, such works are not considered a basis for predestination in this watered-down Calvinism; nevertheless, these postconversion works logically remain a basis for entering heaven. Even in this simplistic scheme, you would not be allowed into heaven apart from persevering.

Geisler, for example, thinks that in 1Pet 1:5 we are saved through persevering faith.[1247] Olson fares little better.* To his credit, Olson does acknowledge the punctiliar nature of the appropriation, so the illustration with the dot correctly portrays his position of simplistic security.[1248] Additionally, when discussing the golden chain, he says that loving God is a description rather than condition of those who meet the chain's soteriological application.[1249] Further, he seems to regard 1Pet 1:5 as a promise of a protected faith rather than a condition of (i.e., for) protection by faith.[1250] Nevertheless, it still would seem that if you were to lose your faith, then you would lose your salvation in Olson's theology. Olson assures us that it is impossible. However, perseverance in faith appears prescriptive rather than merely descriptive in texts such as 1Cor 15:1-2 and Col 1:22-23. So Olson's assurance would tend to drift toward lack of assurance.†

Tragically, Olson seeks to divorce faith from assurance so that he can affirm perseverance in faith for those who lose present assurance.[1251] This is an exceedingly awkward arrangement. Faith is assurance. Additionally, of the five warnings in Hebrews, the only one Olson applies to genuine believers is the third one in Heb 6:4-6. How can he apply only one out of five of these tightly integrated warnings to believers? Although both Geisler and Olson (to their credit) can affirm that this particular warning in Hebrews is to genuine believers, their view on perseverance causes them to shrink back from admitting that apostasy is a possibility and thus leads them astray into exegetical inconsistency.

The same basic objection may be raised in response to this simplistic Calminian security as was raised above concerning Calvinism and Arminianism. According to simplistic securitists, you cannot reach heaven (not even hypothetically) apart from perseverance in faith. To be sure, advocates of this simplistic position will say that those who fail to persevere were never genuine believers to begin with. Yet this is the same evasive maneuver used by Calvinists, and it fails to circumvent the problem. As the rudder of the Titanic was too small to save the ship from its collision with the iceberg, so this evasive maneuver is too weak to avoid the conclusion that entrance into heaven is conditioned on perseverance for those who hold this perspective. So one must object to it for the same

---

* For other examples of those holding this view and problems inherent in it, see endnote 499.
† Olson's weakness regarding assurance aside, his perspective regarding 1Pet 1:5 and his appeal to the descriptive nature of works can be harmonized with unconditional security with some measure of success if one is careful with the terms and conditions and avoids making the descriptive also necessitative. See *soft regeneration-oriented securitists* (SROS) in *3D Unconditional Security.*

primary soteriological reasons that required the objection to the other two positions. This Calminian solution conditions salvation from eternal damnation upon one's work.

Even aside from such objections, this simplistic view of predestination will still not work. It fails to deal adequately with Ventilato's comments regarding Jam 2:5 and 2Thess 2:13. As to Ventilato's objection itself, his position is not a viable alternative in that it does not allow the most straightforward understanding of such texts. The most natural perception of Jam 2:5 is not that God unconditionally or irresistibly has elected the poor (or certain ones among the poor) to be rich in faith and love Him. Instead, the result of God's election in this verse is contingent upon the free response of the poor. In these verses, God has held an election and has given believers the deciding vote.

Olson correctly perceives that the calling in 2Thess 2:13-14 is not accomplished immediately through irresistible grace; rather, it is brought about intermediately through faith in the gospel which was preached to them, and this calling is thus conditioned on their free response for its fulfillment.[1252] Whereas Olson stands on the threshold of correctly acknowledging that the outcome of election is contingent upon the free response of the believer, Eaton clearly steps through the doorway when he affirms both an irresistible soteriological predestination and a resistible misthological predestination to inherit the kingdom.[*] Lopez is also clearly thinking along the same lines when he identifies the misthological nature of predestination in the second link of the golden chain as predestination to co-glorification as firstborn sons with special status in the kingdom.[†] The present book has presented this as a general model of predestination[‡] and would prefer it for the golden chain as well.[§]

Illustration 243. Marrowistic Predestination

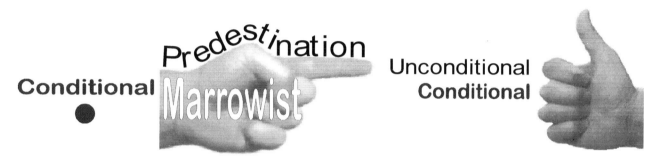

God foreknew who would believe in Jesus for eternal life and has predestined that these believers will unconditionally reach heaven, even if they do not continue to believe. Believers are thus assured of unconditional security the very moment they come to faith in Christ. After all, the essence of saving faith is being personally assured of one's own unconditional eternal security as a result of coming to faith in Christ. No further stipulations must be met, such as continuing in faith, in order to live with Christ forever in His kingdom.

Subsequently, in the process of discipleship, these new believers should be taken to texts such as Jam 2:5 and shown that they need to develop a rich faith so that they can inherit the kingdom of God and thus co-rule with Christ over this kingdom. This fuller realization of their salvation is misthologically conditional. On the positive side, this means that they can earn the privilege of ruling with Christ. Still, one should be frank about the dark side of misthology as well. Salvation from the outer darkness is conditional for the believer. Thus, unconditional security from eternal damnation is balanced with conditional security from negative rewards (such as the outer darkness) in the Marrowistic illustration above.

God not only has predetermined what *should* happen, but He also has predetermined that some things *would* happen. Particular prescient predestination is both positive and negative. God has predetermined that those who believe in Jesus will go to heaven and that those believers who live for Jesus will rule in heaven. On the flipside, God also has predetermined that those who fail to believe in Jesus will go to hell and that those believers who refuse to live for Jesus will be cast into the outer darkness. Nevertheless, no believer will be cast out of the kingdom. This misthological view of predestination is, therefore, genuinely compatibilistic with free agency.

---

[*] See *Working Model of Would & Should*, 188.
[†] See "Rom 8:28-30" in *Ordo Salutis*. Although the present book adopts an exclusively soteriological view of the golden chain, the discussion in *Ordo Salutis* (in which I interact with Lopez) will set forth my preference for viewing two links of the chain as misthological.
[‡] See *Illustration 77. Predestination*, 189, *Illustration 86. Should/Would*, 227.
[§] See "Golden Chain with Two Misthological Links" in *Ordo Salutis*.

Unlike Calvinistic compatibilism, in which you cannot act contrary to your desires, in Marrowism you can act contrary to your desires. The unbeliever can be saved from hell by believing in Jesus, despite his or her sinful inclinations otherwise. The believer, on the other hand, can resist the righteous inclinations of his or her new nature and still end up in the outer darkness as a result. With freedom comes responsibility. Unbelievers have the responsibility to believe in Jesus; believers have the responsibility to live for Jesus.

What God has predetermined **should** happen, He has made possible. He has taken the steps necessary to make freewill responses contingently possible by means of prevenient grace for the unbeliever and by means of enabling grace for the believer. This context in which the golden chain occurs has a special promise to those believers who love Christ. Not all believers love Christ in the manner described by such passages as Jn 14:15; Rom 8:28; and Jam 2:5. Regardless as to whether believers love Christ or live for Christ, they will live with Christ since the golden chain culminates in the simple soteriological glorification of all those who have experienced regeneration. When one becomes persuaded that he or she has become eternally saved from eternal damnation by faith alone in Christ alone, simple glorification is assured. Eternal security is thus guaranteed; misthological rulership is not.

Syllogistic Summations

The conditional nature of the regenerate believer's security in Calvinism and Arminianism can be summarized by the following hypothetical syllogisms.

Illustration 244. Calvinistic Conditional Security

1. If you are one of the elect, then you will persevere.
2. If you persevere, then you will retain your regeneration.
3. Therefore, if you are one of the elect, then you will retain your regeneration.

Illustration 245. Arminian Conditional Security

1. If you persevere, then you are one of the elect.
2. If you are one of the elect, then you will retain your regeneration.
3. Therefore, if you persevere, then you will retain your regeneration.

Many are fooled into thinking that Calvinism teaches OSAS because of its syllogistic conclusion. However, the minor premise of the above Calvinistic syllogism is the same as the conclusion of Arminian syllogism: *if you persevere, then you will retain your regeneration.* Both systems of theology teach conditional security for the regenerate believer. Both go back to Augustine's conditionalism in which it is possible, at least hypothetically speaking, for believers to lose their regeneration.

Illustration 246. Augustinian Conditional Security

1. If you do not persevere, then you lose your regeneration.
2. If you lose your regeneration, then you are not one of the elect.
3. Therefore, if you do not persevere, then you are not one of the elect.

Unlike the other syllogisms, the Marrowistic syllogism affirms that once a person comes to saving faith that person no longer has any condition to meet in order to remain saved from eternal damnation or in order to retain one's regeneration ontologically or one's justification legally.

Illustration 247. Marrowian Unconditional Security

1. If you ever come to believe, then you become regenerate.
2. If you become regenerate, then you retain your regeneration.
3. Therefore, if you ever come to believe, then you retain your regeneration.

The saved cannot become unsaved. The regenerate cannot become unregenerate. The justified cannot become unjustified. Those who have believed cannot revert to the same state they were before they believed, even if they cease to believe. To be sure, they may not experience the fuller dimensions or aspects of their salvation, regeneration, or justification. But they cannot become unsaved, unregenerate, or unjustified in the same sense in which they were before they became saved, regenerate, and justified. As far as soteriological security, the question is, "Did the person ever believe?" not "Did he or she ever cease to believe?"

COSAS

The general assumption that OSAS is affirmed by TULIP has been shown to be a misrepresentation. Popularly, Calvinists are misbelieved to affirm *Once Saved Always Saved* (OSAS).[*] Indeed, Calvinists use this popular misperception to cloak themselves as advocates of OSAS in order to give themselves a hearing among those who are not more discerning in their theology and who think that Calvinists actually believe in eternal security. But in reality Calvinists believe in insecurity—conditional security. The claim made by some Calvinists, that they believe in *OSAS*, is open to strenuous objection. After all, Calvinists do not believe in the synonymous terms *Once Saved Always Secure* or *Once Saved Always Safe*, so why must we fall for their centrifuge in claiming to believe in *Once Saved Always Saved*? Calvinists cannot separate their OSAS from their NOSAS. Therefore, an informed perspective would conclude that the Reformed camp does not believe in OSAS. Instead they believe in a COSAS (*Conditional Once Saved Always Saved*), which is no better (and perhaps worse) than NOSAS.

Illustration 248. Cross-Eyed Calvinism

Calvinism takes a cross-eyed view at our retention of regeneration. On the one hand, as pictured on the right, retention of regeneration is said to be guaranteed from the perspective of predestination, so OSAS is affirmed. On the other hand, as seen on the left, retention of regeneration is also said not to be guaranteed from the perspective of God's condition of perseverance so that NOSAS is also affirmed. Unfortunately, the logical impossibility of this dualistic Calvinistic perspective is shrouded by the claim that it is not a contradiction since it is supposedly looking at the same truth from two different, yet supposedly compatible, perspectives.

To be sure, various concepts may be viewed harmoniously from different perspectives. For example, Marrowists speak of soteriological versus misthological salvation, of imputational versus impartational justification, and of positional versus practical righteousness. However, we do not speak of gifts that are free but costly from the same perspective—that of the recipient. Although a gift may be costly to the giver, it is free to the recipient. The LS claim that the free gift is offered at a price to the recipient is logically contradictory and biblically deadly.

Something is a contradiction if it affirms both A and non-A in the same way at the same time. Calvinists will claim that retention of regeneration is both conditional and unconditional at the same time without being contradictory because it is being viewed from two different perspectives: predestination and condition. But this assessment is false since the same agent (God) is looking at the same object (retention of regeneration) in the same way (soteriologically). One may speak of different kinds of justification, sanctification, and glorification. Personal regeneration, however, is only one of a kind. Soteriological regeneration (i.e., the regeneration of one's spirit) is not both conditional and unconditional.

The Calvinistic claim that our retention of regeneration is both secure and insecure is an antinomy and, therefore, false since our retention of regeneration is only capable of being viewed from a singular perspective. Retention of regeneration is singularly a soteriological issue. One simultaneously may have soteriological security and misthological insecurity (since soteriology and misthology are two different concepts), but one cannot have both soteriological security and soteriological insecurity concerning the same issue—retention of regeneration. One cannot be both soteriologically secure and insecure. These two concepts are mutually exclusive. Soteriological security cannot logically overlap with soteriological insecurity.

---

[*] See *Arminian Equalizers*, 281.

Illustration 249. 3D Calvinism

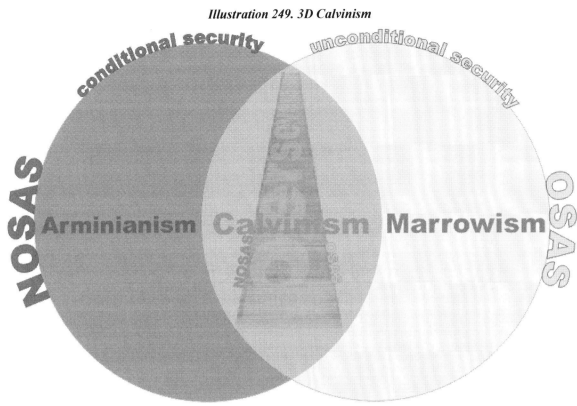

Calvinists ask us to put on their theological 3D glass so that we can see their fictional reality and walk their nonexistent bridge of soteriological perseverance to heaven. But logically, this bridge does not exist. The author took his children to Universal Studios for a family vacation. The 3D effects were spectacular, but not real. It would be a tragic mistake to try to escape the fires of hell by stepping out on the 3D bridge of perseverance-based soteriology provided by Calvinism. This bridge is an optical illusion that cannot logically exist and which is biblically accursed. Illusions are fun at a magic show or an amusement park, but in the desert it can be fatal to wander off after a mirage in search of life-giving water. In theology it can be equally and eternally fatal to attempt to walk on the nonexistent bridge of works-righteousness fabricated by Calvinism.

Illustration 250. Calvinistic Square Circle

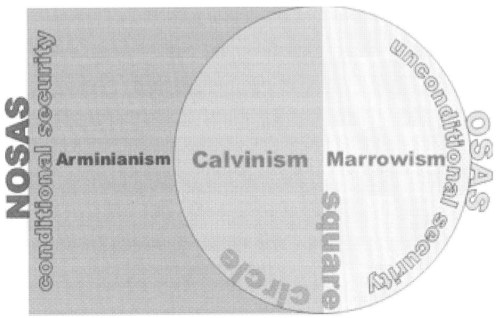

The previous illustration, using overlapping circles, may fail to adequately convey the fact that these two circles cannot logically overlap since they are picturing two mutually exclusive possibilities. Either the NOSAS of Arminianism is true, or the OSAS of Marrowism is true. Calvinists cannot combine these two possibilities. The Calvinistic equation in which NOSAS + OSAS = COSAS is in actuality misleading because it pictures something that cannot exist. In actuality, NOSAS ∩ OSAS = ∅. The intersection of these two theologies is an empty set. The circles may overlap in my illustration used to picture the Calvinistic illusion, but in a field of logic they cannot overlap.

To picture the illogical nature of this overlapping intersection, I have combined the NOSAS square with the OSAS circle to produce the Calvinistic square circle. Some Calvinists, when asked whether they believe in OSAS, affirm that they do. However, such an unqualified answer by such Calvinists is also a request from those Calvinists that we turn a blind eye to the fact that Calvinism does not believe in a OSAS that is not simultaneously NOSAS. Questioning some Calvinists about OSAS could be likened to asking a group of people who believe that circles are square if they believe in the existence of circles. Of course, from their perspective, they could answer that they believe in circles. But in reality they do not genuinely believe in circles because they deny the existence of round circles. Likewise, when Calvinists respond that they believe in OSAS, it must be understood that they believe in a fictional form of OSAS that cannot possibly exist. The P of TULIP makes their OSAS conditioned on their perseverance and proves that they do not believe in unconditional security. Calvinists believe in COSAS, not OSAS.

Incompatibilism of Compatibilism

Calvinistic compatibilism is another popular example of Calvinists trying to combine concepts that are mutually exclusive. Calvinistic compatibilism regards the determinism of Calvinism mysteriously compatible with libertarian freedom. Walls and Dongell rightly challenge the claim to compatibility made by the Reformed camp by showing that the TULIP of Augustinian antinomy is a contradiction.

Illustration 251. Forms of Determinism

Without repeating all the illustrations above regarding the futility of the antinomy, we may content ourselves with the illustration which Calvinistically looks at self-determination through the eye of divine determinism and simultaneously through the other eye of libertarianism. In libertarianism many of our actions are self-determined. In divine determinism none of our actions are self-determined. God determines what we will do and will not do. Obviously, both cannot be logically true. So Walls and Dongell have no trouble pointing out the inconsistencies of Calvinists who try to maintain the compatibility of both.

Yet some Calvinists try to make these mutually exclusive possibilities compatible by redefining freedom so that self-determinism is no longer seen through the eye of libertarianism but exclusively in a deterministic fashion. Freedom is mysteriously claimed to exist, but it is a caged freedom that only allows us to do what our God-caused desires make us do. Whether God causes these desires immediately or intermediately makes no difference as to the certainty and irresistibility of the outcome and the fact that we cannot do otherwise.

Ironically, Calvinism, which loves to appeal to mystery, has logically given itself no room to do so. In Arminianism and Marrowism, an appeal can legitimately be made to mystery in that we do not know exactly how God foreknows the future. We can affirm that He foreknows our freewill responses contingently by looking within His creative potential, but we cannot provide the mechanics by which this is accomplished. Calvinists, in contrast, by claiming that God deterministically causes the future with causative foreknowledge have left no room for mystery, only for logical inconsistency when they appeal to compatibility.

Illustration 252. Calvinistic Dominos

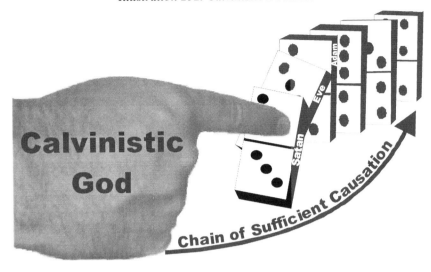

Logically, then, from a consistent Calvinistic vantage point, the reason Adam fell was because God set in order a chain of events that made him fall. Adam fell because he was pushed—by God as the initiator of the chain of events that led up to his fall. Adam could not have done otherwise. The reason Adam fell was because he was pushed by the domino behind him, which was pushed by the domino behind it. Since in Calvinistic thought, God causes everything, the logically consistent Calvinist would have to trace the domino effect to God, who irresistibly caused Satan to fall, knowing that Satan irresistibly would cause Eve to fall, knowing that she irresistibly would cause Adam to fall, and so on. Adam had to fall because he was acted upon by an irresistible chain of events (set in motion by God) that irresistibly caused Adam to have an internal desire that irresistibly made him fall. No mystery here.

Calvin apparently concurs that his system leaves no room for mystery when he objects to those who "say that, in accordance with free-will, he [Adam] was to be the architect of his own fortune, that God had decreed nothing but to treat him according to his desert." Calvin did not believe Adam had any such libertine free will. On the contrary, according to Calvin, "**The decree, I admit, is, dreadful; and yet it is impossible to deny that God foreknow [sic] what the end of man was to be before he made him, and foreknew, because he had so ordained by his decree....God not only foresaw the fall of the first man, and in him the ruin of his posterity; but also at his own pleasure arranged it.**"[1253] The Calvinistic decree is not mysterious; it is monstrous. This horrendous decree is attributed to God by Calvin.

According to Calvin, God sovereignly arranged for Adam to fall. Thus, Adam's domino was arranged in such a way by God's dominion so that Adam could do nothing other than fall. Adam fell because he was pushed—ultimately by God. The Calvinist seems to think this is okay because he was not pushed directly by God. But what about the original fall—that of Lucifer. Was Lucifer not directly pushed by God. Calvinism cannot allow the lead domino to fall on its own. For one thing, Calvinists believe that God's sovereignty demands that we understand that everything that will happen does so in that exact manner because God determined that it must happen in that exact manner. In addition to this conclusion being demanded by the Calvinistic view of sovereignty, their view of foreknowledge also requires that they deny that Lucifer or Adam could do otherwise than what they did. Calvinists believe that the reason God knows the future is because God sovereignly has determined everything that will take place. From their viewpoint, if God truly had granted Lucifer libertarian freedom, then Lucifer would have caught God by surprise. God would not have been able to see it coming. At best, God would have had an educated guess. Calvinists takes the guesswork out, yet somehow think they can appeal to mystery, when in fact they have left no room for mystery—only for inconsistency.

At the very least, consistent Calvinism would have to picture God as putting Lucifer in a position where God knew that Lucifer would be tempted irresistibly to rebel. Oh sure, Lucifer fell because his desires were corrupted, but compatibilistically speaking, the reason they were corrupted was because God put Lucifer in a position where Lucifer's desire would be corrupted irresistibly by God's sovereign control of history. God overcame Lucifer's original goodness with temptations that caused Lucifer irresistibly to desire to be like God. The Creator created Lucifer in such a way that Lucifer could not help but do what his desires dictated, and then the

Creator tempted Lucifer with His creation beyond what Lucifer was able to resist. God created Lucifer and then made him Satan.

Libertarians can object and assert that God made Lucifer (originally a good angel) but that God did not subsequently make Satan (an adversarial angel). God did not corrupt Lucifer; rather, Lucifer corrupted himself of his own free will. To put it another way, God did not create Satan. Lucifer created Satan. Through the God-given power of self-determinism, Lucifer turned himself against God and made himself an adversarial being. Divine determinism, in contrast, cannot attribute Lucifer's fall to his power to act otherwise than how God acted upon him. Calvinistically speaking, Lucifer had to respond in the manner in which God determined he would respond. Calvinistically, therefore, the devil is able to say, "God made me do it." Consistency with the Calvinistic premises would lead to the logical, but unbiblical, conclusion that God created Lucifer and then turned him into the devil without giving him any power of contrary choice in the matter.

Incompatibilism

Like the fabled apple hitting Sir Isaac Newton on the head, resulting in his brilliant insight regarding the law of universal attraction, so the illustration of a falling rock strikes C. S. Lewis with an insightful deduction as to why we cannot blame God, fate, the devil, or our circumstances for our decisions. (Nor for that matter would Satan be able to blame God for his fall.) Lewis suggests that the *Law of Human Nature* (LHN) is not like the *laws of nature* (LN).[*] The latter only tells us what *will* happen. A rock *will* fall if you drop it, such is the law of gravity. The laws of nature do not tell what the rock *ought to* do, only what a rock *will do* under certain circumstances.

Lewis, therefore, reasons that the *Law of **Human** Nature* (*LHN*) is not like the *Law of Nature* (*LN*). LN tells us what its objects *will* do. A rock *will* fall if you drop it. LN does not tell us what *ought to* take place, only *will* take place under certain circumstances. In contrast, LHN does not tell us what we *will* do but only what we *ought to* do. A rock does not have free will; a human being does, and therein lies the difference between the *LN* and *LHN*. The missing ingredient (the *H* in other words) that makes us (morally accountable) **human** beings is free will. The *Law of **Human** Nature* appeals to our moral conscience to do what we *ought to* do. It does not determine what we *will* do, only what we *ought to* do. As free moral agents, we are the ones who determine what we *will* do.

The Moral Law (another name for LHN) will often tell us to follow our weaker impulse. We must decide whether or not we are going to obey this weaker *ought-to* desire. If Lewis were using philosophical jargon, his argument would be a clear affirmation of *incompatibilism* (i.e., libertarian freedom). Incompatibilism teaches that determinism is *not compatible* with libertarianism. Lewis' deduction means more than claiming that we are not a rock controlled by **external** factors. More precisely, his appeal to our freedom to choose to obey the weaker impulse means that we are not mechanically (or chemically) controlled by our **internal** desires.

The opposing view, *compatibilism*, is a form of determinism which believes that divine determinism is *compatible* with libertarianism. In other words, God's dictating everything we will do can, supposedly, be made compatible with our free will. The way compatibilists try to pull this off is by saying that God controls us by controlling our internal desires. We are free to do what we want to do. God simply controls what we do by controlling what we want to do. Lewis asserts otherwise. We control what we are going to do by deciding which of our desires we will obey. We can choose to obey the weaker desire, which will quite often be the ought-to desire of the Moral Law.

True free will, not some compatibilistic imitation, is crucial to Lewis' argument. His entire contention collapses without it. In the absence of incompatibilism, there would be no difference between *ought to* and *will*. Our reactions would be chemically controlled just as a rock's actions are mechanically controlled. The difference between LHN and LN would disappear without *free will—the power of contrary choice*. Without it, the Law of Human Nature which internally prompts us with suggestions would control us. It would be an unmerciful dictator whose every desire we would carry out to the letter. Lewis' freewill argument, therefore, would be an affront to both materialistic and theistic determinism. And it is a frontal assault to the soft determinism of compatibilism. When faced with two competing impulses, one to help others in danger versus the contending desire to help yourself by fleeing from danger, Lewis finds support for libertarianism (free will) in the arbitration that occurs between these opposing motivations:

---

[*] When Lewis refers to the singular *Law of Nature*, he does not mean the plural *laws of nature* (1.3.16-17). Rather, he intends for *Law of Nature* to refer to the *Law of Human Nature* (i.e., the *Moral Law*). For sake of abbreviation and clarification, I will not rely on this differentiation between the two laws with a singular versus plural designation but rather use the abbreviation *LN* for *law(s) of nature* in contradistinction to *LHN* (*Law of Human Nature*).

You will find inside you, in addition to these two impulses [to help and flee], a third thing which tells you that you ought to follow the impulse to help, and suppress the impulse to run away. Now *this thing* that judges between two instincts, that decides which should be encouraged, cannot itself be either of them....If two instincts are in conflict, and there is nothing in a creature's mind except those two instincts, obviously the stronger of the two must win.[1254]

So what is *this third thing* that decides which impulse to obey and sometimes chooses to obey the weaker impulse. The only one conclusion left is that it is you yourself—your self. Philosophically speaking, this is an affirmation of self-determinism. We determine our own course of action. This is not to say that we decide what we will do in the absence of desires. Simply, our desires do not dictate which course of action we will take.

Lewis will return to this argument again in the second section of his book to affirm: "God created things which had free will....Some people think they can imagine a creature which was free but had no possibility of going wrong; I cannot. If a thing is free to be good it is also free to be bad. And free will is what has made evil possible."[1255] This is the classic freewill explanation as to why there is evil in the world. God created us with free will so that we could love Him voluntarily rather than involuntarily as robots. I concur with this classic conclusion but question its premise.

Let us ask two questions of Lewis' statement. First, can God sin? If not, then how can it be said that God has free will? If God is not free to be bad, then how can God be free to be good according to Lewis' explanation? Second, will people be able to sin in heaven? If they cannot sin in heaven, does that mean that their free will is taken away in heaven and that they love God involuntarily when they reach heaven? Philosophically, Lewis' response is satisfactory, even if elementary, and his freewill argument can be strengthened theologically by considering the source of the first evil desire, as I am doing here. But as far as Lewis' contribution to the present discussion, note that no one can blame a rock for falling down a hill and hurting someone. The rock has no choice in the matter. One can blame a human being, though, for pushing the rock because the human being has a choice. With the ability to choose comes the culpability for the choice made as to whether or not to hurt someone else.

Chain of Sufficient Causation

Compatibilists Peterson and Williams define incompatibilists as those who object to the view that "God controls the flow of history in such a way that he has sovereignly ordained who will come to faith and who will not." Incompatibilists are said to find the idea that God sovereignly decides everything we will do incompatible with free will. The rationale given for the incompatibilistic response is that they believe "there cannot be two sufficient causes for any one event, one divine and one human; either God causes Jackie to believe, or Jackie chooses to believe." Peterson and Williams go on to say that the libertarian objection to compatibilism is that there cannot be any sufficient condition prior to the free agent choice.[1256] In other words, if a sufficient condition caused Jackie to believe, then Jackie was not free to respond to the contrary. It would be a forced faith rather than free faith. I have no quarrel with this definition and description by Peterson and Williams of the incompatibilistic position. In affirming irresistible grace (both in the classic form regarding perseverance and the contemporary form regarding saving faith), Calvinists, by their own admission, have made faith irresistible and God culpable. They effectively have undercut the biblical affirmation of human ability, responsibility, and freedom.

In response, Peterson and Williams try to deflect this charge by asserting "the motives of the human agents provide the sufficient condition for the entire event. And the sovereign will and action of God provide the sufficient condition for the event as well."[1257] Although "every choice we make and every act we perform is determined by forces outside ourselves, and ultimately by God's ordaining guidance, we are still free, for we still act according to our desires."[1258] In other words, (A) God determines our external circumstances; (B) our external circumstances determine our internal desires; (C) our internal desires determine our action. Compatibilism provides a domino effect: A ⇒ B ⇒ C.

Purportedly, this Calvinistic chain of causation makes us free (and avoids making God culpable for our sin) because our actions are free in the sense that they arise from our own hearts, nature, desires, motives, and character. We are not coerced directly by external factors. Within compatibilism, the link in the chain of causation that reputedly lets God off the hook for causing sin is the fact that our internal desires determine our actions. We are supposed to believe that compatibilism does not reduce us to puppets or pawns since God ultimately controls us internally rather than externally. The last domino is internal causation. Since God is not pulling external strings but using our internal desires to control us, God is not at all responsible for the bad we do, yet somehow He is totally (i.e., monergistically) responsible for the good we do.

Why Lucifer would have fallen under this model is left unexplained. Peterson and Williams claim that it is an irrational mystery for which they have no logical explanation in the present state of their compatibilistic scheme of events. How God's internally causing us to sin does not make God culpable for our sin is similarly left unexplained as being unfathomable.[1259] Quite frankly, they are failing to own up to the logical implications of their own system. Like the materialists who leave the question as to what caused the Big Bang unanswered because they have no room for God, so these compatibilists leave the question as to what left the Big Fall unanswered because they have no room for free will. They create a Frankensteinish picture of God but want us to consider it a masterpiece. Yet leaving such matters aside for the moment, the logical reduction of their argument to a chain of sufficient causation will suffice for present purposes. Compatibilism leaves us with a picture of God sovereignly placing in motion a causal chain of events by His sovereign control of history that causes us to do everything that we do. We must do what we do. We cannot do otherwise. And that is what we are free to do. This is compatibilistic freedom. God determines our desires, and our desires determine our actions. God is the sufficient cause for our desires, and our desires are the sufficient cause for our actions. We are left with nothing but Calvinistic dominos. We are not mindless pawns and puppets in compatibilism, just pawns and puppets under God's mind control.[1260]

Infralapsarianism

In their chapter on predestination, Calvinists Peterson and Williams object to the claim that Calvinism reduces people to puppets. They counterclaim that humans retain considerable freedom in Calvinism.[1261] Yet later, when the rubber meets the road, they admit: "Beza subjects even the first sin, the disobedience of the garden, to the divine decree. The **Adamic fall into sin was ordained by the divine will**. Man was created to sin. Beza's doctrine of the decree became known as *supralapsarianism*, meaning '**before** the fall'" (bold mine).[1262] Peterson and Williams further confess: "It is difficult to imagine how God escapes culpability for human sin in his thought....**God is ultimately responsible for the existence of sin and unbelief. Even the fall of Adam and Eve took place in conformity to the predetermining will of God.**"[1263]

Nevertheless, for some reason Peterson and Williams imagine that their affirmation of the more popular Calvinistic *infralapsarianism* (**after** the fall) avoids this difficulty. Yet they acknowledge that Arminius rejected this form of Calvinism as also making "the fall necessary and God its author" and thus making "God the author of sin."[1264]

According to *supralapsarianism* God decided that He would save the elect **before** He decided that man would fall (i.e., the decree of election and perdition comes **before** the decree of the fall). Therefore, in supralapsarianism God decided He would save some and damn others **before** He decided they would all fall. Subsequently, God decided that they would fall. Consequently, the reason God created mankind was so that He could damn some of them to hell. The damnation of unfallen humanity was not because of human sin.

According to *infralapsarianism*, on the other hand, God first decided that man would fall and then **afterward** God decided that He would only save the elect (i.e., the decree of election and perdition comes **after** the decree of the fall). Therefore, in infralapsarianism God decided He would save some and damn others **after** He decided they would all fall. Supposedly, according to Peterson and Williams, this sequence makes God's condemnation "conditional upon human sinfulness and unbelief."[1265]

The reason I interject the word *supposedly* is because Peterson and Williams interject, contrary to consistent expectations, that God's election is not conditioned upon human belief. Reprobation is conditional; election is not conditional. Why are both not conditional? Peterson and Williams do not explain why this is the case, so one is left with the impression that infralapsarian confirms "an asymmetric relationship" between election and condemnation out of theological necessity rather than logical consistency.[1266] Somehow election supposedly is unconditional while condemnation supposedly is conditional. Their affirmation of an *asymmetrical* relationship seems to be a Calvinistic code word for *contradictory* relationship.

Permit the Fall?

Even aside from the seemingly contradictory nature of infralapsarianism, I fail to see how Peterson and Williams have successfully assailed Arminius' contention that infralapsarianism makes God responsible for sin. Undoubtedly, the Calvinist will object to the above wording by pointing out that the standard articulation of both supralapsarianism and infralapsarianism is not merely that *God decreed the fall* but that *God decreed **to permit** the fall*. Supposedly (I again use this word out of concern for logical consistency), the above articulation which portrays infralapsarianism as simply asserting that *God decreed the fall* is faulty. I purposefully, however, did not describe God as merely **permitting** the fall because the Calvinistic terminology is misleading or at least logically inconsistent. To be sure, for those outside of the Calvinistic camp, a difference truly exists between merely permitting the fall and decreeing the fall. Contrastively, in Calvinism one has to ask if there is any real difference between God permitting evil and causing evil? Given the confines of their own theological construction, can

Peterson and Williams really affirm that God merely allowed the fall without causing the destruction of their Calvinism?[*]

Peterson and Williams already have conceded that supralapsarianism results in the very thing they are trying to avoid—making God the cause of the fall. However, supralapsarianism also teaches *God decreed **to permit** the fall*. If God's permitting the fall is fatalistically deterministic in supralapsarianism, why is it any less deterministic in infralapsarianism? Both forms of Calvinism assert that *God decreed **to permit** the fall*. Therefore, in condemning supralapsarianism as being deterministic, Peterson and Williams unwittingly, or at least without argumentation, have undermined infralapsarianism which uses the same articulation.

Perhaps Peterson and Williams intend for us to see infralapsarianism as affirming that *God decreed to permit the fall through self-determinism* (cp. EDT). Yet such an answer would be counter to their denial of libertarian self-determinism. In any event, neither form of Calvinism can allow God to permit something to occur that He does not cause. For God to permit the fall, He had to decide to cause the fall. After all, in Calvinism God is the cause of it all. The reason God foreknows the future in Calvinism is because He predetermined what necessarily would take place. God only foreknows what will occur because He has predetermined that it must occur. He arranged the dominos, gave them a push, and now **permits** them to fall according to His plan. They are permitted to fall because God already has decided that they must fall and has taken action to cause them to fall. They have no choice to do otherwise. Permissive will is, therefore, a misnomer for the Calvinist. God does not permit His creatures to do otherwise than what He already has decided that they must do. God simply is pulling their strings and only permitting them to move in accord with the external and internal compulsions He creates about them and within them.

As Walls and Dongell point out, "They [Calvinists] cannot properly use *permission* to suggest that we are free in the libertarian sense or that God permits some choices he has not determined." Consequently, Calvinists

> must either say that God cannot foreknow those choices or say that his knowledge of them is contingent on what his creatures, independent of his determinism, will choose to do. If they take this latter option, they no longer enjoy the advantage of having a readily intelligible account of how God can foreknow these choices.
>
> This dilemma is part of what motivates many Calvinists to "bite the bullet" and embrace a thoroughgoing determinism.[1267]

Preterition

The only real difference between the lapsarian systems is the order of decrees. Still, if we were to look more closely, we would find that *infralapsarians* try to pull a rabbit out of their mysterious hat by asserting that *God passed over the nonelect* (with **unconditional** *preterition*), with the result that the nonelect could not believe, so that *He might condemn the nonelect for not believing* (with **conditional** *condemnation*). Thus, not only are election and reprobation not symmetrical, reprobation is also broken up into asymmetrical components as well. Reprobation is both conditional and unconditional. If the infralapsarian subcomponents are put into the mix, it would look like this:

Illustration 253. Infralapsarian Sequence

1) Decree to create human beings.
2) Decree to *permit* the fall (i.e., actually to *cause* the fall through intermediate means).
3) Decree to
   a) unconditionally elect some.
      i) Decree to *unconditionally* regenerate the elect.
      ii) Decree to *conditionally* justify the elect.
   b) conditionally reprobate nonelect others.
      i) **Decree to *unconditionally* pass by the nonelect (i.e., preterition).**
      ii) Decree to *conditionally* condemn the nonelect.
4) Decree to provide salvation for the elect.

The monkey wrench in the Calvinistic machine (not mentioned by Peterson and Williams in their affirmation of conditional condemnation) is that perdition is predicated upon God's preterition. For clarification

---

[*] See *Permissive Will*, 263.

and balance, I also have added the Calvinistic affirmations of regeneration and justification from their *ordo salutis* to the above outline.[*] As may be seen in the above infralapsarian sequence, unconditional election is comprised of unconditional regeneration followed by conditional justification. Supposedly, so-called conditional reprobation is comprised of unconditional preterition followed by conditional condemnation. Yet how can reprobation be *conditional* when the same corresponding components and sequence result in an election that is *unconditional*? It cannot be. Reprobation must be just as unconditional as election. The infralapsarian mirror is logically broken.

Illustration 254. Broken Infralapsarian Mirror

*Un*conditional election	=	unconditional regeneration	+	conditional justification
? conditional reprobation	=	unconditional preterition	+	conditional condemnation

First, in this model God decided that He would create man. Second, God decided that He would *permit* (i.e., *cause* through deterministic secondary causes) man to fall. Third, God decided He would select certain men to save, not because of their faith but simply because of His prerogative to select whomever He wishes. And then He decided that He would save them by unconditionally causing them to believe, by regenerating them so that they would irresistibly believe (via their own freewill response which would be dictated by their new nature) so that He could condition their justification on this resultant faith. God simultaneously decided that He would condition the reprobation of the nonelect on their failure to believe by not making it possible for them to believe so that He might condition their condemnation on their failure to believe. Fourth, God decided to provide salvation for the elect but not for the nonelect.

Some of the parts that Peterson and Williams leave out of their explanation are that God only conditioned His condemnation on human sinfulness and unbelief after God first decided that He unconditionally would cause this sin and unbelief through irresistible forces and further decided that He would do nothing to make belief (faith) possible for the nonelect. However, the last point might rightly be contested. God does, in fact, make temporary faith (which is indistinguishable from saving faith) possible to the nonelect so that He might fool the nonelect into thinking they are saved. Still, if the nonelect can believe, even temporarily, as Calvinists acknowledge with their affirmation of temporary faith, then regeneration is not really necessary for faith after all. What really is needed is election so that faith might persevere and keep regeneration alive. When the smoke and mirrors are removed, *infralapsarianism* is no less deterministic than *supralapsarianism* and no more compatible with human freedom. Humans are merely automations. In supralapsarianism, nonelect babies are *created to be cursed*. In infralapsarianism, nonelect babies are merely *doomed from the womb*. The latter statement is of course Calvin's infamous affirmation, but the former is grounded in his theology as well.

Calvinists can debate among themselves as to which articulation they prefer, but the bottom line is the same. What really matters is election in their system. In fact, it is the only thing that really matters. The supposed free will of the elect cannot be distinguished from that of the nonelect. Both believe. Logically, one is led to conclude from consistent Calvinism that God capriciously lines up His dominos and knocks them all down, and then arbitrarily decides to stand some of them up. But one is not to complain because they are His dominos, and He can do with them as He pleases. The logical sequence and structure gives Calvinists no room to appeal to some mysterious libertarian free will. We must do what God has decided we will do.

Sphere of Security

Of course, Marrowists affirm the biblical doctrine of election; we just find no reason to accept the Calvinistic perversion of election. Eternal security is not dependent upon the Calvinistic view of election. Far from it! Paul's implicit affirmation of OSAS in Rom 8:10 prevents one from deducing that the dynamic death that awaits the disobedient believer in Rom 8:13 is the static death of his or her regenerate spirit.[†] Also, I have pointed out Paul's reaffirmation of eternal security in the golden chain of events which he depicts in Rom 8:29-30. Further, unconditional security is demonstrable whether the election in this chain is soteriological or misthological. All those who are *called* are in turn *justified*. The elect are those who are justified. Confirmation comes in Rom 8:33, where Paul makes a rhetorical inquiry, "Who will bring a charge against God's elect? God is the one who justifies." Whether the election is a soteriological selection based on foreseen faith or a misthological invitation implementing a contingent realization, those so selected or invited, as the case may be respectively, are justified by

---

[*] See "Ordo Salutis—Calvinistic" in *Ordo Salutis*. For further illustration and rebuttal of infralapsarianism, see *Woolly Wolves and Woolless Sheep*.
[†] See *Contextual Analysis*, 286.

faith. In v. 33, the elect are those who already have responded in saving faith since no charge can be brought against them.

Election

As a result, the Arminian attempt to circumvent the classic conclusion of unconditional security in Rom 8:35-39 is doomed to failure. Even if the passage is talking about the elect, the reason the elect cannot be separated from Christ is because of their justification. Their preservation is not conditioned on their perseverance. Even if Paul were speaking of their being elected misthologically to persevere in order to attain contingent co-glorification with Christ, the fact still remains that they are justified soteriologically. Furthermore, they are soteriologically inseparable from Christ. Otherwise, the devil would be able to glory in their soteriological separation, which Paul rules out in this particular context.[*] The same deduction nullifies perseverance in faith as a possible soteriological condition. To be sure, a believer can be separated from Christ temporally and misthologically. A variety of passages affirm that very fact. The outer darkness is a very graphic picture of such a misthological possibility. But this particular Pauline context is dealing with the impossibility of soteriological separation for those who are justified by faith, which is why Paul is so emphatic as to the absolute impossibility regarding even the hypothetical nullification of justification.

Love of God

The Arminian evasion of eternal security is not limited to a consideration of election. Corner seeks to pose a less sophisticated objection: "OSAS defenders equate the love of God to the life of God by using Rom 8:38,39. Since unsaved people are loved by God (Mk. 10:21), yet without the life of God (Eph. 4:18) to equate the two is a definite fallacy."[1268] Perhaps we should defer Corner to the latter pages in his book where he approvingly quotes Wesley: "The love of God is everlasting life. It is, in substance, the life of heaven."[1269]

Wesley seemingly equates "the love of God" with "everlasting life" since he says one *is* the other. In Corner's defense, Wesley apparently is talking about our love for God rather than God's love for us, since Corner extends this quote from Wesley as saying, "Now, everyone believes, loves God, and therefore, hath everlasting life."[1270] According to Wesley, our love for God results in our soteriologically having eternal life. This is terrible soteriology. Nevertheless, since Corner espouses this perspective, might we be so bold as to suggest that if Arminians are going to equate our love for God with the life of God, then they are certainly being very shortsighted in criticizing their opponents for equating God's love for us with the life of God! If our love for God allows us to experience the life of God, then certainly it is because God's love for us provides us with the life of God!

I agree with Corner that God loves every lost person in the world (Jn 3:16). But does this mean that God will love every lost person in hell? Do the lost not cease to be objects of God's love once He casts them into hell? If so, then the logical outcome of Paul's declaration is that no believer will be thrown into hell. On the other hand, for the sake of argument, suppose that God does love those in hell so that even hell will not separate them from His love (cp. Ps 139:8). Does Corner intend to reduce Paul's crescendo to a tautological whisper in which Paul is merely pointing out that he is convinced that nothing will be able to separate the lost or saved from the love of God? Of course not. To ask the question is to answer it. Paul makes a polarization in this context between being in Christ versus being in the flesh (Rom 8:8-9). Corner is blinded by his theology when he tries to make a polarization between love and life in this context and to make an equation between being in Christ versus being in the flesh.

Obviously, a differentiation is intended in this context between the love which God has for His children versus those who are not His children. Paul makes this crystal clear in the verse itself. Paul is not describing God's love for those in hell or even for the lost people still alive in the world. No! It is "the love of God, which is in Christ Jesus" (Rom 8:39). The context is talking about the love of God for those in Christ since it is the love of God which is located in Christ. It is a love for those who are in the Spirit as opposed to being located in the flesh and thus do not belong to Christ (Rom 8:9).

---

[*] See "Devil's Glory" in *Sealed and Secure*.

Illustration 255. Unconditionally Loved in Christ

In the above illustration, my younger son, Jonathan, is entrapped in a sphere of God's love from which there is no escape. The sphere represents Christ. Believers have been sealed permanently in Christ (Eph 1:13). Likewise, according to Paul, when believers are baptized by the Spirit into Christ, they are clothed with Christ (Gal 3:27). Elsewhere I illustrate this as being in a picture of Christ, but for present purposes a sphere will serve nicely for this dative of sphere as long as it is kept in mind that Christ is the soteriological sphere in which believers are located.[*] Paul uses this phrase *in Christ Jesus our Lord* twice in Romans.

On the first occasion in which Paul uses this phrase, he assures us that the free gift of God is ***eternal life*** *in Christ Jesus our Lord* (Rom 6:23). On this second occasion, Paul affirms that nothing can separate us from *the **love of God** which is in Christ our Lord* (Rom 8:39). In both instances, Christ is the sphere. Both eternal life and this specialized dimension of God's love are located *in Christ Jesus our Lord*. The lost can no more have this love outside of Christ than they can have eternal life outside of Christ. If a person is outside of this sphere, that individual does not have *the love of God which is in Christ our Lord,* and such a person does not have *eternal life in Christ Jesus our Lord*. Conversely, if you are in Christ, then you have both the love of God and the eternal life which are *in Christ our Lord*.

1. Nothing can separate the believer from the love of God in Christ.
2. The love of God in Christ is limited to those who are in Christ.
3. Therefore, nothing can separate the believer from being in Christ.

Since nothing can separate the person who has been justified by faith from the love of God (which is in Christ) and since this love only exists in Christ, nothing can take the justified believer out of Christ. Death is separation. Since the believer cannot be separated soteriologically from Christ, the believer cannot die soteriologically. Moreover, since eternal life is in Christ and since the believer cannot be taken out of Christ, the believer cannot be taken out of this soteriological sphere of life.

---

[*] See "Spherical Security" in *Sealed and Secure*. The *dative of sphere* is also known as the *locative of sphere*. The former refers to its form; the latter to its case. Those using the eight case Greek classification will use the latter term while those using the five form Greek system will use the former term. Regardless, both terms are referring to the same syntactic relationship.

Conditionally Loved In Christ

To be sure, the Arminian will point out that Jude instructs us: "Keep yourselves in the love of God, waiting anxiously for the mercy of our Lord Jesus Christ to eternal life" (Jude 1:21). The parallel to Jn 15:10 is obvious and often cited: "If you keep My commandments, you will abide in My love." Marrowists have no quarrel with Shank's comment: "Those who *keep* are kept" (emphasis his).[1271] The biblical deduction is rather straightforward: Those believers who *keep* Christ's commandments are *kept* in God's love. In these contexts, we keep ourselves in the love of God by our works—by keeping His word on an ongoing basis. Shank is correct on this matter, but he errors in thinking that this is a soteriological keeping that is conditioned on works. Any keeping that is conditioned on works is misthological, as Jude proceeds to indicate: "Now to Him who is able to keep you from stumbling, and to make you stand in the presence of His glory blameless with great joy" (Jude 1:24). God wants to keep believers from stumbling out of the sphere of His misthological love (i.e., love that results in rewards) so that they will be able to stand misthologically blameless at the Bema.[*] Constable is correct in regard to its spherical nature: "We should keep ourselves in the sphere of God's love."[1272] Jude's dative of sphere is misthological. Paul, in contrast, describes a soteriological sphere in which the believer is unconditionally secure. Paul and Jude are talking about two different spheres of God's love.

Illustration 256. Conditionally Loved by God in Christ

A more precise translation of the Judean text would be: "But you, beloved, building yourselves up in your most holy faith; praying in the Holy Spirit; keep yourselves in the love of God, waiting anxiously for the mercy of our Lord Jesus Christ resulting in eternal life" (Jude 1:20-21; TM). *Beloved* (*agapetos*) is the adjective form of the noun and verb for *love* (*agape and agapao* respectively). In other words, *beloved* means *agaped ones*. Believers are beloved. Jude commences his letter to these believers with the affirmation that they are "beloved in God the Father, and kept for Jesus Christ" (Jude 1:1; MT). Paul says that the *beloved* are the elect, so does Jude (Col 3:12; 1Thess 1:4; Jude 1:1—*eklektos, ekloge,* and *kletos* respectively). While it might be noted that Rom 11:28 makes it impossible to invert our statement and claim that all beloved are believers, it is nevertheless true that even in this verse the beloved are the elect. Thus, with this exception noted, Jude's harmony with Paul (and with the rest of the NT writers) may be inferred so that Jude 1:1 is to be understood as affirming that these believers are beloved because they are unconditionally loved in Christ and unconditionally kept in Christ. Or as the KJV expresses Jude 1:1, they are *preserved in Jesus Christ*. The beloved are the preserved. With his affirmation of their status as

---

[*] Misthological love describes a love that results in reward or a love that constitutes the reward. Sometimes it is both. See *Love as Reward for Love*, 736.

beloved, Jude wishes to confirm their unconditional security as objects of God's loving protection. John expresses it this way: "Beloved, we are God's children" (1Jn 3:2; NAB). The term *beloved* is used in the NT to convey the sense of God's unconditional love and security to those who are believers because they are loved as God's children.

Naturally, it will be asked, "Then why does Jude urge these believers to keep themselves in the love of God in 1:21?" Such a question is, however, quite unnatural. Jude is using the same technique exhibited in John's writing: "Beloved, let us love one another" (1Jn 4:7). John supplies the cohortative to love one another after providing the indicative that we are loved as God's children. John's thought, like that of Jude, is clearly: *You are loved so love.* Be what you are! You are loved so be loving. God's unconditional love for us is the basis for our unconditional love for others. God wants us to be like Him and follow His example. The reason parents should unconditionally love their children is because their heavenly Father unconditionally loves them. It would be foolish for conditionalists to assert parents should unconditionally love their children, much less each other and their enemies, if it were not for the fact that God unconditionally loves them. We are to love others unconditionally because this is the manner in which God loves us. The affirmation of God's unconditional love for us in Christ necessarily carries with it the realization of our unconditional security in Christ.

Neil Anderson relates how much of his success as a Christian counselor has come from tying these two twin truths together. Believers are unconditionally secure in Christ because they are unconditionally loved in Christ. Understandably, these powerful truths can be expected to have profound impacts in our lives. Anderson does well to interlace OSAS with God's unconditional love for us. A popular Christian song, *What If*, keeps asking God, "Would You love me even more?"—if I could perform up to various expectations. The obvious answer expected by the song is, "No." Having hit upon the powerful positive results that come from unconditional love, our Christian subculture pragmatically demands that love be unconditional. Unfortunately, in doing so, a half truth is being perpetuated as if it were the whole truth. The whole truth of the matter is that believers are not only loved unconditionally, they are also loved conditionally. Imagine how much more powerful and positive the whole truth would be than just a half truth.

Anderson asserts, "We don't follow Him in order to be loved; we are loved, so we follow Him."[1273] According to Christ, however, we follow Him in order to be honored by Him (Jn 12:26). From this statement, one would deduce that if we wish to be lovingly honored as a follower of Christ, we must be a follower of Christ. If one wishes simply to be loved as a believer in Christ, one needs only to believe in Christ. But if one wishes to be loved as a follower of Christ, then one needs to follow Christ. These two truths are not expected to act independently of one another. For example, the author's realization as a child that Christ loved him so much as to die for him was the primary motivating factor that led him to believe in Christ for eternal life. He was lead to believe in Christ as a result of contemplating Christ's unconditional love for him as a lost child. However, after believing in Christ, he became a child of God. Instantly, he was no longer loved unconditionally as a lost child; rather, he now was loved unconditionally as a saved child. Furthermore, having tasted of Christ's unconditional love for him as a redeemed child, the author wanted to experience the depth of Christ's love for him as an obedient child. The truth of the matter is that God cannot love His disobedient children as His obedient children anymore than He can love the children of the devil as His own children. To be sure, God unconditionally loves the lost children of the devil. But let us not imagine that God loves them as His own children. He does not. His own children are loved in Christ and protected in Christ for the day of redemption. The lost children of the devil are not. If you want to be loved as a child of God, you must be a child of God.

Likewise, if you want to be loved as an obedient child of God, you must be an obedient child of God. Such children are loved as Christ's friends. Jesus asserts, "If you keep My commandments, you will abide in My love…You are My friends, if you do what I command you" (Jn 15:10,14). If we want to be loved as Christ's friend, then we must be Christ's friend. Being loved in this manner is conditioned on keeping Christ's word. For this reason, Jonathan is pictured in *Illustration 256. Conditionally Loved by God in Christ* as standing on Christ's word and grasping Christ's word. To the degree he does so, he is loved as Christ's friend. Yet one foot is pictured outside this loving sphere to depict various truths:

- Some areas of our lives may be outside the bounds of God loving us as His friends.
- Being loved as God's friend is experienced in degrees.
- Being loved as God's friend is not necessarily all or nothing.

Yet in a *Who-Am-I* list, Anderson lists Jn 15:15 as if it means that all believers are unconditionally friends of God because they are in Christ.[1274] The truth of the matter, to the contrary, is that not all believers are friends of God. Some believers are in fact *enemies of God* (Jam 4:4). Granted, God unconditionally loves His children who are at enmity with Him, but let us not suppose that God loves them as His friends. Being loved as God's friend is conditioned on being God's friend. As parents we hope that when our children grow up, we will be able to love them not only as our children but also as our friends. God has similar aspirations for His children. Should this not motivate us to be friends of God? Of course it should. Will the conditional nature of this love cause some to brood? Perhaps.

Illustration 257. Unconditionally and Conditionally Loved in Christ

If we want to be loved as Christ's Bride, then we must be Christ's Bride. Those believers who live their lives in a love affair with the world will not be loved as Christ's Bride since they will not be a part of that bridal company. Will those believers who fail to attain to this experience of love brood over not being loved in this manner? Yes, they will. They will weep and gnash their teeth over being rejected from this experience of intimacy. Will they be able to cry out to God that it is not fair for Him to love His obedient children more than He loves His disobedient children? No, they will not. First, God already has clearly stated the terms of being loved in this conditional manner in His word. Christians who wish to ignore the conditional aspects of God's love in favor of pop music and pop psychology have no right to blame God. Second, God loves all His children equally and infinitely when it comes to their position in Christ. Even if believers step completely out of the conditional sphere of God's love, they may rest in the knowledge that they cannot step out of the larger unconditional sphere of God's love, which encompasses the smaller conditional sphere. As believers, we can rest psychologically in knowing that we are loved unconditionally in Christ. God is gracious. As obedient believers, we can further rejoice in realizing that we have a fuller experience of God's love than we would have had as disobedient believers. God is fair.

Jude gives believers two means by which to keep themselves in the conditional sphere of God's love: building themselves up in their faith and praying in the Holy Spirit. Remaining in this mistholic sphere is conditioned on believers' performance—their works. The Greek verb for *building* is *epoikodomeo*, the same verb

Paul uses three times in 1Cor 3:11-15 to describe believers as building upon Christ in a manner worthy of being rewarded. In both contexts, believers are the ones actively engaged in the building process. They are not passive pawns in God's building program. Their active participation in building themselves up in the faith through energized prayer is likewise to be compensated with two rewards: misthological mercy *resulting in (eis)* misthological life. Like Jesus and James, Jude indicates that the future mercy, which such believers eagerly anticipate, is a reward for their present performance (Mt 5:7; Jam 2:13). That this future acquisition of eternal life as a reward is a crowning experience on the part of loving believers who already have received eternal life as a gift is straightforward inference:

1. Keeping the faith results in eternal life (Jude 1:20-21).
2. Keeping the faith results in a reward (2Tim 4:7-8).
3. The eternal life that comes as a result of keeping the faith is a reward.

To reiterate, OSAS is the foundational truth for Jude. All believers have become *beloved* (MT) and positionally *sanctified* (CT) so that they are perfectly *protected* in Christ (Jude 1:1). Jude originally had planned on writing about this aspect of their *salvation* shared in *common* by the *beloved* (Jude 1:3) before he decided to advance to another matter. Even so, he provides enough information to justify the deduction that the beloved are unconditionally secure believers. In the soteric sphere, such believers are loved unconditionally by their heavenly Father. Yet rather than limit his discussion to an affirmation of loving security that is true of all believers regardless of their performance, Jude advances beyond this elementary truth to warn these soteriologically secure believers that false teachers, nevertheless, pose a real danger in that even soterically secure believers can be lead astray from the purity of their devotion to Christ and fail to experience the full depths of God's love in the mistholic sphere. It almost goes without saying that one must first become a beloved child of God before one can become loved as an obedient child of God. Nevertheless, Jude does not leave the matter unsaid. He clearly indicates that before one can engage actively in keeping oneself in the love of God (that results in the reward of eternal life), one must first be numbered among those who are beloved unconditionally in Christ (as a result of having received the gift of unconditional security). For John, being beloved is the precursor to being loving. For Jude, being beloved soterically is the grounds for being loved mistholically.

A children's song at the opposite end of the spectrum from *What If* misrepresents God's soteric love for His children as if it were conditional with its lyric: "If I love Him till I die, He will take me home on high." Reaching heaven and remaining an object of God's saving love is conditioned on the believer's preserving in love according to this accursed stanza. *What If* is a far superior song and completely accurate in regards to the soteric sphere which it is clearly addressing, as noted in its chorus line: *I belong to You apart from the things I do.* In terms of belonging to God, our Daddy could not love us any more, regardless of how good we are. He cannot love us any more than He already does because He loves us infinitely. Nor can He love us any less. He will always be our loving Daddy, and we will remain His children, even if we do not love Him the way we should, even if we lose our first love. Nevertheless, the Bible clearly indicates that a reciprocal and misthological dimension to God's love is experienced by those of His children who love Him. A biblical harmony between these two songs and these two truths is attained easily by a modification to the children's song. When the chorus is first sung, it should express the unconditional security that is granted when a believer first believes. When the chorus is repeated, it should stress the additional conditional security that is available if a believer expresses undying love. Together, these two affirmations would be:

*   If I trust Him before I die, He will take me home on high.
*   If I love Him till I die, He will give me a throne on high.

Necessity of OSAS

GRAPE is OSAS at its core. Unconditional security is foundational for the FG gospel. One can no more rip the necessity to believe eternal security out of the gospel of grace (and expect it to still save) than one can rip the heart out of a person (and expect that person to still live).[1275] One cannot believe in Christ for eternal life and yet not believe that one has eternal life as a result.[*] The realization that one has eternal life must necessarily involve the persuasion that one is unconditionally and eternally secure soteriologically. Therefore, the personal assurance of one's own eternal security is a soteriological necessity at the point of saving faith.

---

[*] See "Soteriological Believe in = Believe That in GJ" in *Dad, can I be sure I am really saved?*

Symmetry

It is foolish to suppose that one can believe in Christ for probation and expect to get salvation instead. Conversely, those who only believe in Christ for probation have not believed in Him for salvation. For a person to become saved, that individual must understand that the condition for eternal life is that he or she believes in Christ for eternal life. The consequence, in turn, of believing in Christ for eternal life is eternal life. A symmetrical relationship may be seen between the condition and consequence. The condition is that we believe that we have the stated consequence. Since eternal life is the stated consequence of believing in Christ for eternal life, we cannot believe in Christ for eternal life and yet not believe that we have eternal life in Christ. If we believe that we have something other than eternal life in Christ, then we do not have eternal life in Christ because we have not met the condition of believing that we have eternal life in Christ.

To make this easier to digest, a candy bar will be used to illustrate the point. If you believe in Christ for a candy bar, then you have no right to believe that you will be given eternal life as a result. The consequence does not match the condition. If you believe in Christ for impartational righteousness, then you have no right to believe that you have been given imputational righteousness as a result. If you believe in Christ for sanctification, then you have no right to believe that you have been given justification as a result. In the same fashion, if you believe in Christ for probation, then you have no right to believe that you have been given salvation as a result.[1276]

Yet at a *Free Grace Alliance* (FGA) conference a number of years back, in which the present author questioned the notion that one could believe in Christ for probation and get salvation instead, the FGA panelists at that conference took an opposing view (that was counter to the position that had been presented at the FG conference by GES). Panelists at this FGA conference opposed the necessity of believing in OSAS by trying to divorce assurance from faith and by claiming that those in FG who believe in the necessity of OSAS are confusing the protasis with the apodosis (i.e., the condition with the result). This FGA perspective simplistically presumed that belief is the condition and eternal life is the consequence. After all, we are to believe in Christ for eternal life. But their response misstates the protasis. The condition is not merely that we believe in Christ; it is that we believe in Christ for eternal life. As already noted, believing in Christ for a candy bar will not result in eternal life. We must believe in Christ for eternal life. Moreover, to believe in Christ for eternal life necessarily means that one believes that one has eternal life in Christ.

For example, if you believe in your bank account for a thousand dollars, it is because you believe that you have a thousand dollars in your bank account. You cannot believe in your bank account for a thousand dollars and yet not believe that you have a thousand dollars in your bank account. Likewise, you cannot believe in Christ for eternal life and yet not believe that you have eternal life in Christ. Therefore, the condition for eternal life is that one must believe that he or she has eternal life in Christ as a result of believing in Christ for eternal life. The consequence of believing this proposition is that the believer has eternal life in Christ. In banking, you can trust in your account for that money just as soon as you put that money in the bank. In Christianity, the benefit is imputed to your account the moment you believe. The moment you believe that you have eternal life in Christ as a result of believing in Christ for eternal life—in that moment—you receive this life.

The question the author asked the FGA panel was, "In light of Jn 6:47, is it possible to believe in Christ for probation and get salvation instead?" The panel declined to answer and asked for clarification instead. So the author clarified by asking if it were possible to believe in Christ for something less than eternal life and get eternal life as a result. Unfortunately, the panel responded affirmatively.

Let the implications of Jn 6:47 be considered by misquoting it as: "He who believes in Me has a candy bar." Would a person who believes this misquote of Christ's words still get eternal life? Of course not! The verse must be understood as saying, "He who believes in Me has eternal life," and it must be believed as such in order to result in the possession of eternal life. (A) The condition is that a person believes that he or she who believes in Christ **has eternal life**. (B) The result is that the individual **has eternal life**. The fact that the phrase *has eternal life* appears in both the condition and the consequence (i.e., in both A and B) does not mean that I have confused the condition with the consequence (or the protasis with the apodosis). It simply means that I have stated the full condition. The panel has misunderstood the full condition. Furthermore, in the context of GJ, Jesus expects one to understand that His promise of eternal life guarantees the recipients of such life that they will never perish: "I give eternal life to them, and they will never perish" (Jn 10:28). Jesus expects to be trusted as the guarantor of eternal security to the one who trusts Him for eternal life. Jesus is our Savior, not our probation officer. To trust in Him as your probation officer falls short of trusting in Him as your Savior.

To the present writer's chagrin, the panel objected to the necessity of believing OSAS by asserting that believing in Christ for eternal life does not entail trusting Him with one's eternal security. According to the panel, eternal life is just a quality of life. A prospective convert would not need to understand eternal life quantitatively (i.e., linearly as a duration of spiritual life that logically results in OSAS). The purpose of the panel's objection was to make belief in OSAS optional. One problem with such a response is that it leaves potential converts with the false impression that they can trust Christ to better their quality of life and still believe that they might go to hell. Secondly, if merely trusting in Christ for a better quality of life qualifies for saving faith, then one can argue that those who believe in Christ for health and wealth are given eternal life as a result. Therefore, I reject the panel's notion that one can simply believe in Christ for a better life and get eternal life. One cannot trust in Christ for health and wealth (i.e., a better quality of life) and expect to be given a quantity of life instead.

Simply trusting Christ to improve your quality of life does not mean that you have believed in Christ for eternal life. Whether you are trusting Christ to improve your quality of life (1) by giving you health and wealth, or (2) by helping you with your problems, or (3) by bringing you into a fellowship with God, or (4) by taking the control of your life so that you can stop making a mess out of it—none of these things constitutes saving faith. Even trusting in Jesus for a non-linear relationship with God does not qualify one for a linear relationship with God. One must realize that there is a durative nature to the life which Jesus is giving. Certainly, it is qualitative—it is called *life* after all. But it is also quantitative—it is not called *eternal* for nothing. Simply believing in Christ for a *better life* does not necessarily qualify one as having believed in Christ for *eternal life.*[*] Since Jesus equates being given eternal life with never thirsting (Jn 4:14; 6:35), never dying (Jn 8:51-52), and never perishing (Jn 10:28), it must be concluded that Jesus intends to be understood as guaranteeing a linear result to those who believe in Him for eternal life.

Illustration 258. Quality versus Quantity

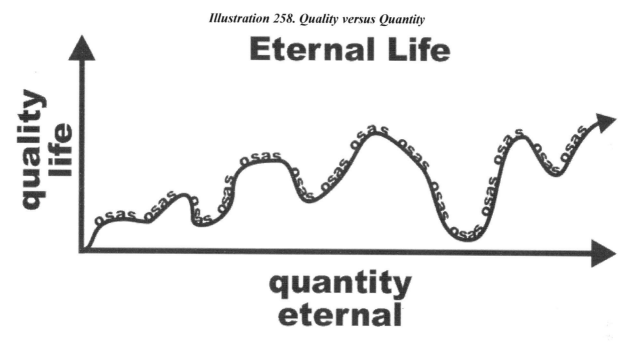

The panel justified their rejection of the necessity of OSAS by claiming that eternal life is dynamic rather than static, which incidentally is a common claim by Arminians who also reject eternal security.[†] The irony is that this FGA panel, which affirmed the fact rather than necessity of eternal security, was using the same argument employed by those who deny the fact of eternal security. In response, I would contend that the quality of eternal life is dynamic but the possession of eternal life is static. One does not have eternal life one moment and then not have it at all the next. Eternal life does not come and go. Possession does not fluctuate. Eternal life quantitatively stretches linearly into eternity future and must be graphed with an unbroken line.[1277] We have been born again of an imperishable seed that has imparted an imperishable nature to us that makes it impossible for us to perish soteriologically. Everlasting life is better pictured by an evergreen than by a plant that keeps dying and coming back to life with each passing season.

One of the panelists at this FGA conference (who rejected the necessity of believing in eternal security) responded that even the lost have eternal life in the durative sense. The fallacy of this statement is seen in the fact that the lost do not have their names in the Book of Life. The reason is because they do not have eternal life. Jesus

---

[*] See "Soteriological Believe in = Believe That in GJ" in *Dad, can I be sure I am really saved?*
[†] See *Illustration 104. Dynamic Lamp*, 288. Also see "Dynamic Classification" and "Static Classification" in *Believe: An Aspectual and Metaphorical Analysis from the Gospel of John.*

promised eternal life to believers, not to unbelievers. The lost have endless existence in the form of eternal death. They do not have eternal life. The panelist who made this remark should have known better than to reject the need of recognizing the durative nature of eternal life by asserting that even the lost have eternal life!

At the point of conversion a person is either going to believe OSAS or NOSAS. Those who believe NOSAS will certainly do so because they believe that their reaching heaven is somehow conditioned on their performance. Consequently, the panel's reaction to those who believe in a performance-based security would logically be one of condoning it. By not demanding OSAS at the point of conversion, the panel was allowing NOSAS with its attendant works-based security. In essence the panel was rejecting NOSAS as false gospel for themselves but affirming that others who believe this accursed gospel can be assured of heaven. I disagree. A false gospel is a deadly gospel. Those infected with this deadly soteriological virus must take the OSAS vaccine if they are to reach heaven.[*] To insist otherwise is to lull the infected into self-righteous complacency.

Reaching heaven is conditioned many times in Scripture on believing in Christ for either regeneration (i.e., eternal life), justification, or salvation. If you believe in Christ alone for any one of these consequences, then you have met the condition for receiving that consequence. However, if you do not believe that you permanently have that consequence, then you have misunderstood the condition and consequence and thereby have failed to meet the condition. An objection that might be raised at this point would be to claim that I am being inconsistent by asserting that you can believe in Christ for regeneration and be given a different result (i.e., justification) instead. After all, I have denied that you can believe in Christ for a candy bar and expect eternal life instead. My response to this potential criticism is that one can believe in Christ for regeneration and be given justification and salvation in addition, not as substitutions.

Suppose a father were to tell his son, "If you feed the dog, I will give you a candy bar." Further, suppose that after the son fed the dog, his father not only gave him a candy bar but a cookie and cup of milk also. Would anyone accuse the father of having falsified the original condition-consequence arrangement? No. In the same manner, God's children do not need to know all the benefits of soteriology in order to receive those benefits.[1278]

On the other hand, suppose that after his son fed the dog, his father divided the candy bar up into seven pieces and gave his son one piece and then clarified that he meant that his son had to feed the dog all week in order to get the whole candy bar. The father would certainly be guilty of having given his son a false impression. Those who say that we can picture God as dividing our soteriological candy bar up into pieces that are received on the basis of our daily performance have not only misconstrued the nature of the condition, they also have misconceived the nature of the consequence and slandered God's character in the process. Neither regeneration nor justification or salvation are soteriological concepts which can be cut asunder theologically into little earned pieces without destroying the saving nature of the proposition and making God out to be a liar. God has not given us a soteriological candy bar that can be cut into contingent pieces. Being given regeneration, justification, and salvation is more akin to being given a baseball glove, bat, and ball. You do not cut them up.

OSAS cannot be optional since those who deny it have failed to meet the condition and have denied the consequence. Eternal security is foundational to both the condition and consequence. Eternal security is not the caboose. It is the engine. We will not get to heaven without it. The object of our faith is Christ's proposition that we have eternal life in Him by simply entrusting Him with our eternal welfare. This does not mean that we necessarily will live on welfare for eternity. It means that we are entrusting Him with our eternal security. To entrust Him with something less is to trust Him for something less than what He demands. To trust Him for something less is to fall short of meeting the stated condition. Those who do so will fail to receive the promised appropriation of regeneration, justification, or salvation.

Sufficiency

In his gospel, John repeatedly stresses the necessity and sufficiency of believing in Christ for eternal life. Doing so leaves no room for us to believe in Christ plus something else for our eternal security. Nor does it leave room for us to believe that we are not eternally secure. With considerable narrative skill, John brings these affirmations concerning the implications of having eternal life to a climax in Jesus' dialogue with Martha: "Jesus said to her, 'I am the resurrection and the life; he who believes in Me shall live even if he dies, and everyone who lives and believes in Me shall never die. Do you believe this?'" (Jn 11:25-26).

Martha responded, "Yes, Lord" (Jn 11:27). Unfortunately, most within Christendom respond, "No, Lord." Many would say, "Well, Lord. If he believes in You and is at least willing to make you Lord of his life, then yes, I believe that such a person will be eternally secure." But such frontloading of the gospel, even though mild, is still a

---

[*] See endnote 1275. Also see *3D Unconditional Security.*

rejection of the eternal security that Jesus offers to all who simply believe in Him. It is to say, "No, Lord. I do not believe the promise as You have stated it." Others, such as Gordon Olson, risk backloading the gospel with at least this addition, "Well, Lord. If he believes in You and continues to believe in You, then yes, I believe that such a person will be eternally secure." Again, this evasive rewording falls short of positive affirmation and risks failing to secure eternal security. The Arminian would say, "No, Lord. There will be some who believe in You but who, nevertheless, will die spiritually because they do not continue to believe in You eternally." Although Geisler and Olson would perhaps limit this to no more than a hypothetical possibility, they still (seemingly) condition eternal life on eternal faith. In doing so, they seemingly deny the unconditional security that Jesus promises to everyone who simply believes in Him.[*] Jesus promises eternal life to those who come to faith in Him. The Lord did not condition eternal life on eternal faith.

According to Jesus' conversation with the woman at the well, we must know that the gift He offers is eternal life if we are to receive eternal life (Jn 4:10). Certainly, if we mistake the gift for a reward, then we have no hope of receiving the gift. Pseudo advocates for OSAS are the ones who would slip up to the woman at the well, listen in on the conversation, and polity nod in agreement as Jesus tells her, "Everyone who drinks of this water shall thirst again; but whoever drinks of the water that I shall give him shall never thirst; but the water that I shall give him shall become in him a well of water springing up to eternal life" (Jn 4:13-14). But then they would whisper in her ear, "Don't believe that one drink is enough though. You can drink and still be thirsty again if you stop believing."

In contrast to such naysayers, Marrowists accept the uncomplicated promise, just as Jesus has made it. We are aware that some mediators deny that it is possible to see the matter in such black and white terms. They would like to picture the unconditional security of FG theology as being an extreme position at one end of the spectrum and costly grace at the other and then locate themselves as the supposed balanced view in the middle by adding just a little performance, rather than a lot of performance, as necessary to reach heaven. Nevertheless, even adding a little performance-based poison to the pure milk of the gospel can be deadly.

Illustration 259. Accursed Mediation of Lordship Salvation

	Front end	Back end
Free Grace	**None**	**None**
Mediation 1	**None**	**Some**
Mediation 2	**Some**	**None**
Mediation 3	**Some**	**Some**
Costly Grace	**Many**	**Many**

The mildest form of mediation that can be made to the pure milk of FG theology is to add just a little work on the back end of what is required to reach heaven. This is pictured as *mediation 1*. Soft conditionalists add just a single drop of poison to the FG gospel by making perseverance in faith a soteriological necessity to reach heaven. However, if the implications of even this mild form of mediation are followed through to their logical conclusion, then two disastrous outcomes are realistically possible. People who are exposed to such a gospel may never be persuaded that their unconditional eternal security has been guaranteed as a result of simply believing in Christ for eternal life. How can they be persuaded that they are unconditionally secure as a result of one drink if they are told that certain passages exegetically condition their security on their perseverance or that such perseverance is at least a logical necessity? If such potential converts are logically consistent, they cannot believe that a single drink is all that is required. Even this mild mediation poisons the well from which the potential convert is supposed to be able to take one drink of living water and live forever as a result.[1279]

Others will add more requirements—some to the front end and others to the back end. In doing so, they will say that, since they do not add as many requirements as someone else, they are really advocating free grace by way

---

[*] This assessment might be challenged, perhaps even successfully, in the case of soft-shelled securitists who condition unconditional security (as ironic as that sounds) upon preservation in the faith rather than on perseverance in the faith. Hopefully, Olson would qualify as a soft-shelled securitist. See my book, *3D Unconditional Security*, for further discussion regarding strong and soft securitists.

of comparison. Many will be deceived by such lies. Comparing themselves to one another is not the accurate standard by which to determine if they are teaching a false gospel. Even a diluted form of an accursed gospel is still an accursed gospel and could still be quite deadly for two reasons. Those drinking this dilution might fail to believe the true gospel and believe a false gospel instead. It is a delusion to think that this dilution is an acceptable mediation. Rather than accept the unconditional security of the punctiliar believer, this perversion teaches the conditional security of the fruity, linear believer. Such theologically, queer fruition is a monstrous variation. Regardless of the degree of deviation by any such mutation, it makes it logically impossible to believe the promise of eternal life as Christ has offered it. Such mediators make it impossible to believe what is necessary to be believed in order to experience regeneration. Mediation is not always healthy. In this case, it is downright deadly.

Illustration 260. Mediated Mutation

Rom 11:6; Gal 2:16   Rom 3:22-24,28; 4:4-5; Eph 2:8-9   Jn 6:47; 1Tim 1:16

Such adaptations lead a person to look to his or her performance for personal assurance. However, one cannot be saved by trusting in Christ and in one's performance for eternal life. We cannot be saved by works. Those who offer their works as **the** reason they should be allowed into heaven will be rejected. We must therefore draw an X through the first category in the chart above. Neither can one be saved by faith and works. Those who offer their works as **a** reason they should be allowed into heaven will be rejected also. An X must be drawn through the second category as well. There is no room for any mediation that turns unconditional security into conditional insecurity or that bases one's salvation from eternal damnation on one's performance. Despite good intentions otherwise, those who make such modifications are dressing themselves up in sheep's clothing and entering as ravenous wolves into the discussion.

Salvation from Sin

Can a person believe in Christ for a candy bar and expect to be given eternal life as a result?[*] Of course not. It is a ridiculous question. Yet many evangelistic invitations seem to be just as ludicrous. One often hears messages that address felt needs by talking about the tragic results sin may have in our lives. We are then presented with an evangelistic invitation to trust Christ to save us from our sins as our means of getting to heaven. With considerable subtlety, evangelists thus twist their invitations into a false gospel. The falsity of their appeal is evident in that we cannot trust in Christ for practical sanctification (i.e., salvation from the practice of sin) and rightfully expect to be given soteriological justification (i.e., salvation from the penalty of sin) instead.

Evangelistic appeals often assert that we can have a better life (in the sense of not doing the bad things we do not want to do) by coming to Christ. But trusting Christ to save us from our practice of sin is different from trusting Him to save us from the penalty of sin. Those evangelists who exhort lost sinners to trust Christ to deliver them experientially from sin in order to reach heaven are making imparted righteousness the means of imputed righteousness. In short, they are teaching salvation by works. LS makes submission to Christ's instructions for a better life the requirement for a linear life. Biblical requirements for experiencing the abundant life are turned into requirements for possessing eternal life by these wolves in sheep's clothing.

GMR

Years later, after having attended the FGA conference described above, I attended a Bible study in which this discussion came up again. One of the attendees took the position taken years before by the FGA panel. When I

---

[*] See "Soteriological Believe in = Believe That in GJ" in *Dad, can I be sure I am really saved?*

asked him if one could trust in Christ for probation and be given salvation instead, he had to ask for clarification also. My fuller explanation would entail explaining GMR: grounds, means, and result.[*]

> G: Faith in **Christ** alone as the *grounds*/benefactor.
> M: Faith in punctiliar **faith** alone as the sufficient instrumental *means* of being benefitted.
> R: Faith in the gift of **unconditional security** alone as the *result*/benefit.

Rather than give a technical explanation, I used a practical illustration instead and asked, "Can you believe in Jesus for a hamburger and expect to get to heaven as a result?" The point I was making with this question is that you cannot make eternal life anything you wish and claim to have experienced saving faith. Eternal life must be understood to guarantee unconditional security. The attendee objected that I was making getting into heaven too difficult. Children, he insisted, should not have to understand that they get unconditional security as a result of believing in Jesus for eternal life.

To the contrary, a childlike misunderstanding of that magnitude does not qualify as a saving understanding. Suppose six-year-old Johnny is at the lake for a family cookout. After Johnny's dad finishes grilling the burgers, his dad leans back at the picnic table, holds the grilled burger up in his hand, and remarks with relish, "This is the life." Later, during the meal, Johnny's dad tells his young son that it is important to believe in Jesus for eternal life. His dad assures Johnny that if he will just believe in Jesus for eternal life, he will be given eternal life as a result.

Johnny reasons that eternal life must consist of an endless supply of hamburgers. He informs his dad that he believes in Jesus for eternal life and is baptized the next Sunday. Has Johnny experienced saving faith? No, he has not. His childish misunderstanding, although limited to R (result), is preventing him from experiencing saving faith. The unconditional expectation of heaven, not of hamburgers, is necessary for the bestowal of eternal life. Likewise, we are not given salvation by believing in Christ for probation. We are not given unconditional security by believing in Christ for conditional security. Even children must understand that in believing in Jesus for eternal life, they are trusting Christ to give them life with Him forever in heaven.

Some conditionalists contend that as long as their faith is grounded in Christ, it does not matter if they believe that good works are necessary to reach heaven. They misconstrue both the means and the result (M and R). If asked, "Why should God let you into heaven?" they purposefully would leave out any mention of works and simply respond, "Because Jesus died for me." By making Jesus the sole consideration (the ground, G), they believe that they should be acquitted of trusting in their works. Nevertheless, God will not be fooled by such calculations or responses. He knows that they mean, "Because Jesus died for me [G] and because I lived a good life [M]." They have trusted in their good life as a means (M) to eternal life with Him in heaven. As a result, they are disqualified for life in heaven. They misconstrued GMR: what (G) Jesus did and what (M) they do in terms of their performance to (R) result in their entrance into heaven. $G + M \Rightarrow R$.

In the above scenario concerning Johnny, however, I am not posing a misunderstanding on Johnny's part regarding the *means* (M), only concerning the *result* (R). Johnny thinks that he will be given the endless supply of burgers simply because he believed in Jesus for *eternal life* (which he misbelieves to be an endless supply of burgers). Misbelieving in Jesus for eternal life does not qualify as believing in Jesus for eternal life. Johnny cannot misconstrue eternal life to be an endless supply of ground beef and be expected (by Johnny's dad or anyone else) to reach heaven as a result. Someone must clarify in Johnny's thinking that by believing in Jesus for eternal life, he is believing in Jesus for life forever with Jesus in heaven. Eternal life cannot be made whatever you wish and still be considered eternal life. To believe in Jesus for eternal life cannot licitly be made to believe in Him for hamburger.

Johnny's eight-year-old sister, Susie, is much more perceptive than her brother. She realizes that when her dad says, "This is life," he means much more than just the burger. Surely, he means to include being with them by the lake on a beautiful day. In theological terms, she correctly has sensed that her dad is referring to a quality of life in the present. Johnny thought that the quality of life to be gained by believing in Jesus was literally to have all the burgers he could eat. She is more perceptive and intuitively perceives that her dad is talking much more comprehensively about being able to enjoy life. So she thinks that if she believes in Jesus for eternal life, then this means that she will be able to enjoy her life. Life with Jesus in heaven is not in the picture, only a wonderful life on earth for as long as she may live. She too tells her father that she believes in Jesus and is baptized with Johnny the following Sunday. Unfortunately, she is no more saved than her brother.

---

[*] For fuller explanation, see GMR in *Dad, can I be sure I am really saved?*

    Both children need to realize that what they are being urged to believe is that they will be with Jesus in heaven as a result of believing in Him for eternal life. Is this concept to difficult for children to grasp? Of course not. One of my favorite children's tracts is the *Am I Going to Heaven?* tract by Phil Myers.

Illustration 261. Am I Going To Heaven?

    With this focal point before us, pictured by the front of Myer's tract above, let me recast this illustration with some significant clarifications and with a dad who teaches his children eternal security at a rudimentary level. Picture little Johnny laying on his back at the lake with his dad, talking about the importance of believing in Jesus for eternal life, looking up into the clouds, musing the question, "Am I going to heaven?" His dad has just read Jn 11:25-26 to him and Susie and explained that what it means to believe in Jesus for eternal life is summarized by the question Jesus asked Martha: "Jesus said to her, 'I am the resurrection and the life; he who believes in Me shall live even if he dies, and everyone who lives and believes in Me shall never die. Do you believe this?'" (Jn 11:25-26). As their dad explains, Jesus is asking Martha if she believes that the life He offers extends beyond the present life to what comes next. Those who believe in Jesus for eternal life will live with Him forever in heaven. Their dad asks them if they are going to heaven, and he lets them lie on the grass and ponder the question.

    To be sure, their dad could have said many more things. He could have pointed out that they are sinners and need forgiveness, or that eternal life is a gift and thus not earned, or that that they do not have to be good to go to heaven. Myers adds these considerations in a way children can understand in his little tract. Doing so is commendable. If I were Johnny's dad, I would have added that one does not need to keep believing in order to keep eternal life. However, Johnny's dad chooses a simpler path. He will allow his children the opportunity to discern for themselves that going to heaven is conditioned on simply believing in Jesus for eternal life.

    If they do not connect that believing with having to continue to believe (which would be counterintuitive anyway), then he does not have to explain that it does not mean having to continue to believe. Belief in *incipient eternal security* qualifies as saving faith. Such questions as, "What happens if I stop believing?" or "What happens if I deny Christ?" have not even entered Johnny's mind. Nevertheless, he implicitly believes that as a result of simply believing in Jesus that he will spend eternity with Jesus. At this rudimentary level, eternal security instinctively will be unconditional security in his mind. Although he would not be able to articulate it as such without further instruction, his faith is logically consistent with unconditional security and counted as such.[*]

Consider an alternative scenario, however, in which Johnny was raised in a family that denied eternal security. Johnny is now nine years old. When the rapture occurred, his family and the other families in his church were left behind. Various speculations were given as to why. Some families determined that they could not trust Christ any longer. After all, they had trusted Him, and He left them behind. Better to turn to the antichrist. Johnny's family, though, came upon a book that explained that only those who believed in unconditional security would be taken; others who thought themselves believers would be left behind. His dad explained to Johnny and Susie that if they believed in Jesus, then taking the mark of the beast was not an option, even if they starved. Those who took the mark would go to hell according to the Bible. Yet according to the Bible one had to believe in a security not conditioned on performance in order to be saved from hell. What could they do? Not taking the mark is a performance issue. His dad throws up his hands in despair.

Johnny lies on the grass in the backyard contemplating the question of going to heaven. If he regards not taking the mark a condition to reach heaven, then he realizes that, in doing so, he still believes in conditional security. So that is not an option. He puzzles over the situation all afternoon. If he does not take the mark, the beast will kill him. If he does take the mark, then God will damn him. Then a solution occurs to him. If he believes in Christ, God will not damn him, because he is unconditionally secure. But if he were to try to take the mark of the beast after believing in Christ, then God would kill him—not to keep him out of hell, for he would be unconditionally secure from hell, but because God would not tolerate a believer taking the mark of the beast.[†] So he has two basic options: (1) take the mark and be damned by God, or (2) believe in Christ and risk being killed by beast and by God.[‡] The second option—believing in Christ—is the only way to heaven. So believing in Christ is the smart thing to do. The beast would seek to kill him for not taking the mark, and God would kill him if he decided to take the mark. Even so, it would be better to risk being killed by the beast and by God than to spend eternity in hell. So he trusts in Christ. He might not have very many burgers on earth as a result, but eating from the tree of life sounds like a great compensation. Time to go discuss his decision with dad.

Outer Darkness Summation

I will now summarize these findings concerning the outer darkness in relation to both the soteriological and misthological spectrum by filling in the misthological axis with a few more details. Along the horizontal axis, I have shown that Marrowism (GRAPE) is a soteriologically mediating position between Arminianism (PEARS) and Calvinism (TULIP). This mediation is healthy since it allows one to believe the promise of eternal life, as Christ has made it, and since it moves one away from trusting in one's performance to trusting in Christ alone for salvation from eternal damnation. This true soteriological mediation is necessary to avoid the false gospel presented on the opposing ends of the soteriological spectrum. To move away from this Marrowistic mediating position toward either the left or right would be a fatal migration from the truth of the gospel. Marrowists, therefore, must warn, as I have above, against horizontal mediation from the central position.

---

[*] The issue being addressed in this illustration is not merely theoretical. Shortly after adding this note, I attended a Kingdom Conference, at which unconditional security would be considered a given. After the conference, however, a group of us were sitting around a table sharing our backgrounds. One of the people at the table shared that he had a Catholic background. This lead to an inquiry as to his assurance of salvation. He shared that he did not have firm assurance that he would reach heaven because in his perspective reaching heaven was conditioned on the way he lived and his perseverance. **He believed that he had eternal life, but the thought had never occurred to him that there was a connection between having eternal life and reaching heaven.** (Evidently, he had an exclusively qualitative view of eternal life, which is a common conditionalistic perspective that unfortunately also was shared at the FGA panel I had questioned years before.) This kingdom attendee believed that in addition to believing in Jesus, he had to follow Jesus in a life of obedience in order to reach heaven. As a result he was trusting in his righteousness works (i.e., his works-righteousness) as a necessary means of reaching heaven. To the rest of us sitting at the table, this was cause for serious alarm because, in our perspective, trusting in one's works-righteousness as a necessary means of reaching heaven means that one is trusting in a false gospel that leads to hell.

[†] Although he would not be able to articulate it as such, Johnny correctly has discerned that not taking the mark is a precondition to believing in Christ. The precondition must be distinguished from the condition. Additionally, not taking the mark is a postcondition for living—at least in terms of not being killed by God because of the mark. Not taking the mark is a precondition for believing and a postcondition for surviving.

[‡] If he believes in Christ, then he receives eternal life as a free gift, but he risks (A) being killed by the beast if he does not take the mark and (B) being killed by God if he subcomes to the intent to take the mark.

Illustration 262. Soteriological and Misthological Poles

In addition to the horizontal mediation regarding soteriology, the present work also has adopted a vertical mediation regarding the doctrine of rewards. Deviation from this mediation would not be soteriologically disastrous, in that migration long the vertical axis still keeps one in the center of the soteriological axis. Although correct placement on the vertical axis is not as nearly as critical, the impact of proper misthology on soteriology has been demonstrated repeatedly. For example, the acknowledgement that the outer darkness is a punishment rendered to carnal believers at the Bema forcibly argues against the false soteriology that would limit entrance into heaven to faithful believers. Misthologists are, therefore, better equipped to defend FG soteriology.

So starting with the outer darkness at the top of the vertical axis, I have defined a Marrowist as a FG soteriologist who affirms the misthological nature of the outer darkness. Meeting this basic requirement is necessary to be properly labeled a FG misthologist. Some FG misthologists will not proceed any further down the misthological scale than this very conservative misthological assessment. They will be content to conceive of the outer darkness simply as a metaphorical picture of losing rewards. I wish them well.

For those misthologists who advance further down the scale, I have added a misthological picture of the church to represent those misthologists who acknowledge that the church of the firstborn is a misthological concept. That affirmation, in and of itself, is a rather elementary assessment—a conservative *church misthology*. A more advanced realization would be to acknowledge that the eschatological church will be composed of firstborn sons and is thus a rewards issue. Those in the outer darkness will not be included misthologically in the church. In other words, the *out-cast* (*ekballo*) will not be included in the *out-called* (*ekklesia*).[*]

Moving further down the axis, into the heart of misthology, brings us to the picture of the Bride. Misthologists who progress to this point in the chart will affirm that those cast out of the marriage celebration will certainly not compose the Bride of Christ. The Bride will not be cast out of her own wedding! Rather, the Bride will be composed of the out-called, that is, the misthological church. Bridal misthology is the mediating position held by moderate misthologists of the more conservative persuasion and hence is regarded as a conservative-moderate position. Eschatologically speaking, the church and Bride are misthological concepts. Yet bridal misthology is a little more advanced and thus is located halfway between the conservative misthology at the top of the misthological axis and the ultraistic misthology at the bottom of the axis.

Next comes the picture of the bridal city (i.e., New Jerusalem) and represents yet another advancement in the degree of one's misthological understanding. Still, it is located in the middle of the chart, in close association with the Bride. Those holding this misthological position concerning the city still would be considered conservative-moderate misthologists. *City misthology* affirms that at the beginning of the millennium, after the satellite city is stationed in orbit above the planet, believers who are in the city (but who have been judged as unfaithful at the JSC) will be cast out of the city to dwell on the planet below (i.e., on Earth). These outcasts may live among the nations, but they will not **inhabit** the capital city. The coined term used herein to describe *city misthology* is *misthopolis* since the similar English word *metropolis* is composed of two Greek words: *mother* (*meter*) and *city* (*polis*). *Metropolis* simply means *mother city*, and metropolitan refers to the composition of the metropolis. Likewise, *misthopolis* means *reward city*, and misthopolitan refers to the population of the misthopolis. I identified myself as a *misthopoligist*—a misthologist who affirms the misthological nature of the *polis*.[†]

Many Marrowists will probably not agree with the full ramifications of my strong misthopology. They will contend that those who are cast out of the city into the outer darkness may, on occasion, still enter the city, although such outcasts will not be allowed to live there. Perhaps such subcomers could enter the city through the subway. Those taking this perspective may be labeled as soft misthopoligists. This position apparently is held by some very conservative misthologists. This present book, however, goes one step further and argues that those cast into the outer darkness (i.e., outside of the bridal city) will not be allowed to enter the capital city ever again, not even in the eternal state. The affirmation of eternal misthological exclusion from the bridal city is herein regarded as hardcore misthopology.

The classic moderate position was pictured initially as being in the center of the axis.[‡] It was subsequently moved to the lower center to make room for bridal misthology.[§] Now, in the illustration above,[**] the moderate position of kingdom exclusion has been moved even further down the misthological axis to make room for misthopology. This migration, as reflected in these three illustrations, shows progression along the misthological axis and reflects a shift in focus for the present writer over the years as well. He would today regard himself as a misthological moderate despite the fact that he does not hold to the classical moderate view of kingdom exclusion. The present writer might be regarded as a ***progressive moderate*** in that he has shown, in this progression, that kingdom exclusion is not the central focus of misthology. Rather, bridal misthology and its related corollary of misthopology would be better regarded as the mediating view. Therefore, when the present book argues in favor of a mediating position or for a moderate understanding, it is not to be understood as arguing for what has been technically labeled herein as the classical moderate view of kingdom exclusion.

The next item on the scale represents the ***classical moderate*** view of kingdom exclusion. This is the view that the present work technically has labeled as the moderate view of the kingdom. The present book does not affirm kingdom exclusion. Granted, *basileia* can be translated either spatially as *kingdom* or experientially as *kingship*. So stated more exactly, the present work does concede to the affirmation of experiential exclusion from the kingdom, but this is as far as the present work progresses into the classical moderate view. The present work does not concede to spatial exclusion. In other words, no believer will be cast out of the kingdom, but unfaithful believers will be denied the kingship. Understandably, kingdom exclusionists will note that the logical progression of placing the outer darkness outside the city could be taken to mean outside the kingdom. But the present book would contend that, while such a position is logically possible in terms of the above illustration, it is exegetically improbable, if not impossible. Just because the outer darkness is outside the city does not logically necessitate that

---

[*] See *Illustration 200. The Post-Temporal Church*, 582.
[†] See *Reward City*, 603.
[‡] See *Illustration 151. What is a Classic Moderate* Misthologist? 458.
[§] See *Illustration 203. Bridal Misthology*, 589.
[**] See *Illustration 262. Soteriological and Misthological Poles*, 732.

it is outside the kingdom. Kingdom exclusion proper (i.e. spatial exclusion from the kingdom) is a moderate position to which the present book does not adhere.

Some kingdom exclusionists would advance to *ultraism*, which is the next and final item at the bottom of the misthological scale. These misthologists teach that, in addition to being cast out of the kingdom, unfaithful believers can be cast into Gehenna for one thousand years. The present book does not agree with this ultraistic position, but the writer would like to stress that he has pictured *Gehenna misthology* on the misthological axis. Ultraism (i.e., Gehenna misthology) is, therefore, considered a FG position in the present book. Gehenna misthology is not a LS position or an accursed gospel. By and large, the proponents of Gehenna misthology are very much in harmony with FG soteriology.

As to the severity of punishment, the present writer has conceded to his friends within the Gehenna misthological ranks that his own view is more severe than some of theirs.[*] Some Gehenna misthologists tend to limit rewards to one thousand years. According to their limited perspective, rewards are only affirmed to be millennial in scope. Thus, in the minds of some Gehenna misthologists, after unfaithful believers are allowed out of Gehenna (after the millennium), they may be treated as faithful believers for the rest of eternity.

If the present writer had to choose between suffering negative misthological punishment as perceived by these Gehenna misthologists versus the manner in which he perceives it, then he would choose to undergo their perception of punishment. Their dip-in-the-lake view is, in his opinion and theirs, less harsh than the view adopted herein. After all, would not a thousand years in Gehenna be less severe than eternity in the outer darkness? Both this author and Gehenna misthologists think so. Even if the outer darkness were to be understood as simply referring metaphorically to the loss of rewards, which is the case in conservative misthology, a thousand years in Gehenna would be preferable to missing out on those rewards for eternity.

Conclusion

To be sure, none of us will be faced with such a choice—between a thousand years in Gehenna versus eternity in the outer darkness. God is not going to ask us for our preference. Nonetheless, there is a twofold reason for pointing out this theoretical preference. First, the rejection of metaphysical Gehenna misthology herein is due to exegetical and theological objections, not to emotional reservations. As even admitted by some Gehenna misthologists, the views taken herein are more harsh than their own. Second, as a note to those who emotionally shrink back from Gehenna misthology as being too severe, it is not.

The views expressed herein are conceded by parties on both sides as being more severe than millennial Gehenna misthology. Those in the know (i.e., misthologists who seriously have considered what is at stake) would rather spend a thousand years in Gehenna than undergo an eternal loss of rewards. Naturally, we do not want to spend eternity in the outer darkness or a thousand years in Gehenna. Biblically, there is no need to live our lives in fear of either a rock or a hard place, that is, in fear of the outer darkness or of Gehenna. Having already been saved from eternal damnation by grace, we desire to serve the Lord so that we may hear His voice of praise and experience intimacy with Him throughout eternity. The same Lord who saved us from eternal damnation can and will save us from dire misthological consequences—if we trust and obey Him. The Lord wants to reward us, not punish us.

Marrowists believe in misthological LS. Misthologically, submission to the Lordship of Christ is absolutely essential to Marrowists. But pity the poor soteriological Lordship Salvationist who cannot tell the difference between a gift and a reward and who merges them together by saying that eternal life is a gift that costs you everything. Such false teachers bring down the anathema of God upon themselves by teaching an accursed gospel.

The Arminian PEARS and Calvinistic TUPLIP treat the gift as if it were a reward. They threaten unfaithful believers with eternal damnation. The dark side of both of these systems is that perseverance is turned into a requirement to reach heaven. But perseverance is a work. Consequently, those who trust in their perseverance to reach heaven are trying to earn entrance by their works. They are going to be in for a sad, sad surprise. Those who trust in their perseverance for salvation from eternal damnation cannot receive the free gift of life. Most emphatically, the free gift of eternal life must be received as a gift. By conditioning our final salvation from eternal damnation on perseverance, PEARS and TULIP both teach a false gospel that leads to eternal damnation.

Marrowists can only beg and plead that pseudo Lordship Salvationists consider GRAPE. The first two letters of this Marrowistic acronym clearly distinguish *gift* from *reward*. And the acronym concludes with an affirmation of *eternal security*, apart from perseverance, for all those who personally are persuaded of their own eternal security as a result of having simply trusted in Christ alone for eternal life.

---

[*] See endnote 609.

Appendix 1.
Misthological Love

Introduction

False notions regarding mythological love prove a hindrance to a mature misthological love. However, these perpetual myths regarding love can be dispelled with a careful examination as to what God has to say about the matter. Popular and psychological sentiments should not be considered the ultimate authority on the nature of love. God is love. When He talks about love, He knows what He is talking about. We would do well to listen.

Love for Enemies

Jesus presents a parable regarding an abusive servant in Mt 24:45-51 that James articulates later (Jam 2:13ff) regarding loveless believers. Jesus presents the fate of a believer whose practice does not match his position in that this believer does not practice love. Practicing loving deeds of mercy is the last thing on his mind. Notice how his practice degenerates. When his master first put him in charge of his household and other servants, he was a "faithful and sensible" servant (Mt 24:45; Lk 12:42). Surely he was loving at first. Yet he first loses his sense of imminency of his master's return (Mt 24:48; Lk 12:45). He next loses his sense of accountability and his love for his fellow slaves and **begins** to mistreat them (Mt 24:49; Lk 12:45). Like the Christians in Rev 2:4, he had lost his first love—the love he had at first for his lord and his fellow servants. Many believers lose their love for fellow believers and begin to mistreat them. What is our biblical incentive to love one another and the Lord? Gratitude? Yes. Scripture makes it clear that our love should be based on gratitude (Lk 7:42). But is gratitude the only biblical incentive given for love? No. What is our God-given motivation for loving our enemies according to Mt 5:44-45? Jesus says, "Love your enemies…in order that you may be sons of your Father." The motivation that Jesus gives us to love our enemies is in order to obtain the reward of being a son of God.[*] Why love those who do not love you according to Mt 5:46? Jesus expresses the question this way, "If you love those who love you, what **reward** have you?" The clear implication is that we are to love our enemies in order to receive a reward.

The parallel account in Lk 6:32-35 reinforces this understanding of Jesus' words. In Lk 6:35, Jesus says, "Love your enemies…and your **reward** will be great." We may not receive anything back in return from the one whom we love, but we will receive something back from the Father for such love. We love in order to get something back from the Father in return. In Lk 6:38, Jesus augments His promises of credit and rewards with the picture of giving to others in order to receive an abundant reward which overruns **your** own lap. In other words, Jesus teaches that we should give to others in order to be rewarded personally in return. That rewards are a basis for our love is also pictured in the present parables. According to the parables in Mt 18:21-35, 24:45-51, and Lk 12:41-48, we are to serve one another lovingly so that we will not receive a negative recompense. Why show mercy to others according to Jam 2:13? In order to be shown mercy yourself. Do unto others as you would have **the Lord** do unto you (cf. Mt 6:14-15). But the servant in this parable lost his love for his fellow servants and his master.

Focus of Love Determined by Location of Treasure

Of course, Mt 5:44-46 is part of the Sermon on the Mount, which Jesus began in Mt 5:3-12 with promises of rewards for certain actions and attitudes. Mt 5:19 also discusses the reward of greatness in the kingdom. After using rewards in Mt 5:3-12,19 to motivate certain actions and attitudes, Jesus then continues in His sermon to give rewards as the incentive for loving others in 5:44-46. This, in turn, is followed by His discussion of rewards in Mt 6:1-24 where He promises that the Father will **repay (reward) you with eternal treasure in heaven** if you perform according to the rules. In Mt 6:2-4 Jesus says that some have their temporal **reward** from others in full, but you can have **payment** from the Father if you perform your contributions according to His rules. In Mt 6:5-6, Jesus continues with His discussion of reward (repayment) for prayer if it is performed according to the guidelines He gives. In Mt 6:16-18, Jesus promises reward (repayment) for fasting if it is done according to His regulations. Then He proceeds to link this reward (repayment) in Mt 6:19-20 with future eternal treasure in heaven, in contrast to present temporal treasure on earth. As Jesus affirms all through the discussion, these rewards are personal; they are for **you**. He orders **you** to lay up treasure (rewards) for **yourself**. He proceeds in Mt 6:21 to explain why: Treasure determines affection. The location of your treasure determines where your heart is.

---

[*] See *Sons of God*, 77.

Alcorn devotes the second part of his book (five chapters) to a discussion of the relationship between eternal rewards and tithing. Even though Alcorn does occasionally use LS terminology, his overall discussion is superb, and his section on rewards is outstanding. His comments concerning this verse are fully appropriate:

> We must realize Jesus didn't tell us we are wrong in wanting to lay up treasures. On the contrary, he commanded us to lay up treasures. He was simply saying, "Stop laying them up in the wrong place, and start laying them up in the right place....
>
> But what we do with our money is more than an indicator of where our heart is. According to Jesus, it is a *determiner* of where our heart is. This is an amazing and exciting prospect. If I want my heart to be in one particular place and not in another, then I need to put my money in that place and not in the other.
>
> Do you wish you had a great heart for missions like other people you know? You can, according to Jesus. Put your money into missions and your heart will follow. (Emphasis his.)[1280]

Jesus did not say in Mt 6:21, "Where your **heart** is, there will your **treasure** be also." Yet that is how most people interpret it. They interpret it as if Jesus is saying that you need affection in order to have treasure. But Jesus is teaching the opposite: "Where your **treasure** is, there will your **heart** be also." We need treasure in order to have affection. We need rewards in order to have love. We may confidently assume that Jesus knows our human nature well enough to be considered a reliable source of information as to what is required for us to experience love and be motivated to love. Sadly, most Christians think they are better psychologists than Jesus, as attested by how they shrink in shame from the real implications of His words on this subject. Jesus continues with this discussion of heart/love/affection in Mt 6:24 where He says that we cannot love God and the world (cf. 1Jn 2:15). We must either love God or the world. But He promises us rewards in order to enable us to love Him rather than the world.

Love as Fruit of Spirit

Jesus knows our human nature better than we do, and He appeals to both our **human** nature and our **new** nature. Jesus is not using rewards to appeal to our **sin** nature. He does not appeal to our sin nature for love, which is the highest Christian attribute. Love is the fruit of the Spirit (Gal 5:22) and is produced by the Spirit in our new nature as we yield to the Holy Spirit. Personal rewards are the major biblical incentives given to yield to the Spirit and to allow Him to produce that love within us. The Lord appeals to our human nature created in His image in motivating us by rewards. As we will see, even the Lord is motivated by rewards.

Cold Love

What do you do when the love of a fellow believer goes cold? The believers in Ephesus lost the freshness of their love for the Lord according to Rev 2:4, where Jesus rebuked these believers: "But I have this against you, that you have left your first love." What does the Lord use to reawaken that love in this passage? An appeal to gratitude? Not at all. He appeals to temporal and eternal rewards in Rev 2:4-7. This is the same manner in which He dealt with the problem of cold love earlier in His ministry in Mt 24:12-13. In v. 12 He says that the love of many will grow cold, but in v. 13 He promises salvation to those who will endure without letting this happen to their love. Jesus promises salvation as a reward. Of course, this is a misthological salvation. In both cases, He deals with the problem of cold love by promising rewards.

Perhaps one reason there is so much cold love among Christians is because we do not treat this heart disease with the same treatment that Jesus does—rewards. Jesus uses rewards as a very powerful misthological antioxidant to prevent spiritual arteriosclerosis. If you want to avoid hardening of the heart, take the doctrine of rewards to heart. It is such a powerful chelation therapy that it may not only help prevent heart disease, it is capable of reversing some of the hardening that already may have developed.

Love as Reward for Love

Jesus promises us rewards **for loving Him**. In Jn 14:21-23, the reason Jesus gives that we should love Him is so that He will love us in return. His *agape* love for us in these verses, in the form of a special degree of intimacy with Him, is conditioned upon our love for Him.

> He who has My commandments and keeps them, he it is who loves Me; and **he who loves Me shall be loved [***agapao***] by My Father, and I will love [***agapao***] him**, and will disclose Myself to him....**If anyone loves Me**, he will keep My word; and **My Father will love [***agapao***] him**. (Jn 14:21-23)

Thus, His love for us in these verses is a reward for our loving Him. His love is a misthological love. It is conditioned on our keeping His commandments. We earn this level of His love. Although we should love Him because He first loved us, there is also a derivative sense, according to these verses, in which it is true that He loves us because we first love Him. Simplistically, this might be pictured as a love cycle: He loves us; we love Him in return; He loves us in return; we love Him in return; etc.

Illustration 263. Love Cycle

The reward for responding to His love with love is an intimate rewarding experience of His love. He has first loved us. His soteriological love is original and unconditional (Rom 5:8), but His familial love is conditioned on our response to His love. We are to respond to His love by loving Him. If we do so, the reward we will experience will be a greater experience of His love: "If you keep My commandments, you will *abide* [*meno*] in My *love* [*agape*]" (Jn 15:10).* *Meno* is used dynamically and conditionally in this verse. Here, God's *agape* love is conditional on our familial obedience. The typical non-Calvinistic notion that God's *agape* love is necessarily equal and unconditional is fictional. But Calvinists do no better in alleging that God's love cannot be responsive to what it finds in us. Certainly, in a passage such as Jn 3:16, God unconditionally loves unlovable humanity because of His omnibenevolence. In such passages, God's soteriological love may be initially equal and unconditional and not based on any response from us. This is not the end of the story, however.

The short comings of the *love cycle* include: (1) not showing that God started the love cycle, and (2) failing to show increased closeness and depth in the love dynamic. Therefore, a *love spiral* would better convey these aspects.

Illustration 264. 3D Love Spiral

---

* The conditional nature of God's love is certainly pictured in the OT: God shows His *steadfast love, faithful love, lovingkindness, love, unfailing love* (depending on the translation consulted) to those who love Him and keep His commandments (Ex 20:6; Dt 5:10; 7:9; Dan 9:4). According to such translations, if you love God, He will love you. Such texts may provide the background for the NT exhortation: "Keep yourselves in the love of God" (Jude 1:21). "If you keep My commandments, you will *abide* [*remain, stay*] in My love" (Jn 15:10). Staying in this sphere of God's love is conditioned on lovingly obeying God. This agape love is conditional. The OT teaches the same truth: God's people are told that if they keep God's commandments, God will *love* them (Dt 7:12-13). The Hebrew word for love in Dt 7:9,12 is *aheb*. In Greek it is *agapao*. The bottom line is that in this passage, God's agape love for His people is conditioned on their agape love for Him.

The love-spiral model still has a considerable shortcoming of its own, however, in that it does not distinguish between conditional and unconditional love. Therefore, a better model would take the infinite 3D love spiral and place it inside a 4D container that provides this differentiation. The only point of entry into this multidimensional experience of God's love is found in the unconditional plane.

Illustration 265. 4D Love Spiral

His *agape* love in Jn 15:10 is associated contextually with His conditional *phileo* love: "You are My *friends* [*philos*] if you do whatever I command you" (Jn 15:14). Although the adjectival form of *phileo* is used in this verse, the verbal form is used in the same capacity in the next chapter: "For the Father Himself *loves* [*phileo*] you, because you have loved Me" (Jn 16:27). The reason the Father loves these believers in this capacity is because these believers love His Son. The verbal from is also used in Prov 8:17: "I love those who love me." Our love should be ongoing and dynamic rather than static. It should be growing. If we continue to love Him by keeping His commandments, then we will continue to be objects of His *agape* love and experience His *agape* love. Moreover, the more we love Him, the more He will love us. In turn, the more He loves us, the more we should love Him.

According to James, the Lord has promised us the crown of life **for loving Him** (Jam 1:12). James also affirms that the Lord has promised us the inheritance of the kingdom **for loving Him** (Jam 2:5). Of course, to love the Lord means to obey the Lord (Jn 14:15,23; 2Jn 1:6). Since rewards are given for our attitude and actions, it only makes sense that genuine love must be rewarded since it expresses itself in action (cf. 1Jn 3:16-18). On the other hand, it is also evident that the rewards are promised in order to produce love. Jesus promises us rewards for loving Him so that we will love Him. In 2Tim 4:8, Paul promises rewards to those believers who love Jesus' appearing. But is there any substantial difference between loving Him and loving His appearing? No. Paul implicitly promises rewards **to** those who love Jesus, which in turn is very close to saying that Paul promises rewards **for** loving Jesus. Rewards are an incentive to love Jesus. Yet this acknowledgment does not promote a mercenary spirit since the driving force of our desire for rewards is the desire to be loved by the Lord and to express love for the Lord.[*]

Rewards for Husbands' Love

In Eph 5:28, Paul instructs that husbands should love their own wives because doing so really is to love themselves. One implication seems to be that the reward husbands can expect for loving their wives is that their wives will love them in return. This is modeled after Christ's example in Eph 5:25-27, where we find that the reason Christ died for us was so that He could have the reward of a loving, holy Bride. In the parallel passage in Col 3:17, Paul says that whatever you do, do it in the name of the Lord. He then proceeds to exhort wives to obey their husbands; husbands to love their wives; children to obey their parents; and slaves to obey their masters. The incentive that Paul gives for doing all these things in the name of the Lord (i.e., in a Christian manner) is that whatever you do, if you do it as for the Lord, you will be rewarded (Col 3:23-24). Thus, the incentive that Paul

---

[*] See *Misthological Intimacy*, 655.

gives for husbands to love their wives in this passage is rewards. Paul is teaching husbands to love their wives because by doing so they will earn a reward from the Lord.

Rewards Used to Promote Love

Paul makes the pursuit of love equivalent to fighting the good fight: "Pursue righteousness, godliness, faith, **love**, perseverance and gentleness. Fight the good fight of faith; take **hold of the eternal life** to which you were called" (1Tim 6:11-12). The incentive Paul gives for this love is the reward of eternal life in the misthological dimension. We are to love so that we can earn eternal life and salvation. Yet again, rewards are the given incentive to love. Paul likewise urges Christians to put on love as a breastplate so that they can earn a misthological salvation: "Put on the breastplate of faith and **love**, and as a helmet, the hope of salvation. For God has not destined us for wrath, but **for earning salvation** through our Lord Jesus Christ" (1Thess 5:8-9; TM).

In 2Pet 1:7-11, Peter exhorts us to practice love so that we can obtain the reward of an abundant entrance into the kingdom. Our receiving a rich entrance into the kingdom is conditioned on our practicing Christian love. According to Peter, the incentive for Christian love is rewards. In Heb 6:10, the writer of Hebrews likewise promises that God will not forget our labor of love. The writer then proceeds in Heb 6:11-12 to urge us to show this loving labor so that we may obtain the promised reward: "For God is not unjust so as to forget your work and the love which you have shown toward His name…And we desire that each one of you show the same diligence so as to…inherit the promises." We are to do loving works so that we can inherit the promised rewards. In Heb 10:24, he exhorts that we should "consider how to stimulate one another to love." Probably, the major reason we see so little love in our churches is because we have neglected one of the major biblical stimulus for love—rewards. We have failed to follow the example of the writer of Hebrews who uses rewards as the incentive to love.

Personal Good

What is the greatest commandment? To love God of course. At the same time, if we love Him, we will keep His commandments. Yet is serving God out of love and seeking our own good at odds with one another? Far from it! "And now, Israel, what does the Lord your God require from you, but to fear the Lord your God, to walk in all His ways and **love Him**, and to serve the Lord your God with all your heart and with all your soul, and to keep the Lord's commandments and His statutes which I am commanding you today **for your good**?" (Dt 10:12-13) We lovingly are to serve Him for our good. Seeking our good by loving the Lord is biblical. "The Lord commanded us to observe all these statutes, to fear the Lord our God **for our good always**" (Dt 6:24). Biblically, Christians are taught to *rejoice always* (1Thess 5:16) and *pray always* (1Thess 5:17). Given today's climate, they also need to be taught that it is biblical for us to *seek our good always*. The Good Book tells us that it is good to seek our own good. Seeking one's own good is loving and smart when done in a biblical manner.

In fact, God does not forgive our sins merely for our sakes, but for His own sake: "I, even I, am the one who wipes out your transgressions for My own sake; and I will not remember your sins" (Is 43:25). For the sake of His love which compels Him to act on our behalf, for the glory of His grace, and for the sake of His holy name, He forgives us. Sometimes our sake is not even a factor: "It is not for your sake, O house of Israel, that I am about to act, but for My holy name, which you have profaned" (Eze 36:22). Sometimes God acts on our behalf with mixed motives, acting for both His sake and ours. At other times, He simply is motivated to act on our behalf for His own sake. For what He gets out of it. So is it selfish to help others for the good you get out of it? If so, is God acting selfishly? Since God is good and since being selfish is not good, perhaps we should rethink what it means to be selfish. Obviously, helping someone else for your own sake cannot automatically be marked as being selfish.

Love Versus Selfishness

Alcorn gives a simple definition for selfishness as the pursuit of gain "at the expense of others" but points out that pursuing rewards is not selfish since "God doesn't have a limited number of treasures to distribute."[1281] Those who perceive it as being selfish to seek for rewards portray God as if He had a piggy bank with limited resources by which to reward His children. Like siblings at the breakfast table telling one another to not be a pig and drink all the milk in the almost empty container because they think that is all the milk available, they fail to realize that three more gallons are in the refrigerator and plenty more besides. Why should God's children squabble over the milk when their Father owns the dairy?

To expand on Faust's definition of selfishness, it may be defined as "seeking the wrong things at the wrong time" in the wrong way for the wrong reason.[1282] Dillow's observation concerning the relationship between a desire for rewards and being motivated by love is very good, in as far as it goes: "It is impossible to separate the motivation of love and the motivation derived from reward. They are, in the Bible at least, inextricably interrelated.

This is so because to strive for the biblical inheritance requires that one strive 'according to the rules.'"[1283] Perman, a Reformed writer, would answer the charge of misthological selfishness this way:

> Seeking your own delight in helping others does not ruin the moral value of your good deeds. In fact, a good deed is only moral to the extent that you are motivated by your own delight!...
> *Selfishness is not seeking your own happiness*. It is seeking your own happiness at that *exclusion* or *expense* of others. (Emphasis his.)[1284]

Concerning Mt 6:19-21 and Lk 12:32-34, Hodges deals with the objection of selfishness by clarifying,

> It is not selfish to take an interest in matters Jesus Himself has told us to be concerned about. It is not wrong to seek what He tells us to seek.
> It is wrong not to seek. It is, in fact, a sin to refuse to lay up heavenly treasure when we are explicitly commanded to do it. Moreover, the effects on our hearts of *not* doing it will be calamitous. For where our treasures are, there our hearts will be also! (Emphasis his.)[1285]

Indeed, Hodges' further response to the charge of selfishness ties it in with our discussion of love,

> Selfishness ought not to be defined simply as the pursuit of our self-interest. Instead, it should be defined as the pursuit of our self-interest *in our own way*, rather than in God's way. Since "love" is a preeminent virtue in Christianity, true selfishness often involves a pursuit of self-interest that violates the law of love.
> But no one who seriously pursues heavenly treasure can afford to be unloving. As Paul pointed out in his great chapter on love, all seemingly spiritual and sacrificial activities are reduced to nothing in the absence of love (1Cor 13:1-3). Loveless activity will no doubt go up in billows of smoke at the Judgment Seat of Christ as though it were so much wood, hay, or stubble (1Cor 3:11-15). (Emphasis his.)[1286]

Granted, some will object that we should serve the Lord out of love rather than out of a desire to be rewarded. This sentiment sounds very pious until it is unmasked for the pious fraud that it really is. As Alcorn puts it, "We flatter ourselves—and insult God—when we say, 'I don't care about reward.'"[1287] Those who denounce rewards in the name of love are denouncing the teaching of the Bible and of Jesus concerning love. In actuality they are claiming to be morally superior to Jesus in two ways. They are saying that we should follow their example and their teaching rather than Jesus' example and His teaching.

Atheistic Ethic

The above pious-sounding sentiment (that we should just do the right thing because it is the loving thing to do) is actually derived from atheists and agnostics rather than from Christianity. Dillow calls it an *atheistic ethic* to think "that good should be done only for the sake of good and with no [thought of] reward for the doing of it." "We should, according to the atheist, do something only because it is right and not because some benefit will accrue to us if we do it."[1288] In response to the agnostic Kant, who says that we should obey God only because it is our duty, Faust rightly counters, "It is our *duty* to seek holy rewards." Faust further points out that C. S. Lewis likewise noted the Kantian connection with those who despise rewards, pointing out that the real problem is that "**our Lord finds our desires** [for rewards]**, not too strong, but too weak**" (emphasis his).[1289] Let us not mince words. The equation of self's interest with selfishness is from Kant, not from Christ. Those who despise rewards as being selfish are followers of Kant rather than of Christ. They are Kantian not Christian in their perspective. According to Kant, if your motive is to get a reward, then you are acting immorally. If Kant is right, then Christ teaches immorality. Christians therefore must insist that it is not selfish to perform an action to benefit ourselves as well as others. Kant is wrong, and Christ is right.[1290] Those who despise rewards despise the One who offers the rewards. They are despisers of Christ rather than followers of Christ.

Platonic Ethic

This anti-reward thread can be traced much further back beyond contemporary atheists and agnostics to the Greeks. As Böttger relates, "In the religious sphere, *misthos* was not used, since Greek religion did not rest on the basis of rewards. In general, too, it was not reward that was the goal of ethical endeavor but honour."[1291] In a lengthy appendix dealing with rewards, Ron Barnes expounds upon Böttger's comments:

> In fact, Plato rejects the Orphic doctrine of reward and punishment, using the term misthos more so in the sense of recognition and honor. For Plato, righteousness carried with it its own reward.
> Thus moral acts are to be done for their own sake, not with the motive of some reward. The denial of future reward is even more prominent in Aristotle and Stoicism.[1292]

Whether this distaste for heavenly rewards is atheistic or Platonic, the aversion to seeking eternal rewards is not Christian. To genuinely embrace the full message of Christ, one must encourage a strong desire for heavenly rewards. Unfortunately, this NT emphasis is often downplayed by those who should be defending it.

Nonmeritorious Ethic

Although Barnes' overall book is very commendable, even he is tainted by Böttger's negative reaction to the development of rewards in the OT and NT, however. Concerning Mt 20:1-16, Barnes summarizes that the point of the parable of laborers in the vineyard is to teach that "too much focus on rewards is wrong!"[1293] In contradiction to Lewis, does Barnes find our desires for heavenly rewards too strong? In any case, Barnes is wrong. Actually, this parable teaches that one should think carefully about rewards. Too many scholars completely misconstrue the entire point of this parable. Without going into the technical detail I have provided elsewhere, here I simply will note that these hired laborers were hired laborers. The summation made by both Jesus and Paul (possibly quoting Jesus) is: "The laborer is worthy of his wages" (Lk 10:7; 1Tim 5:18). The laborers were worthy of their payment.

Slaves are not Hired

Slaves may be rewarded, but they are not paid. A slave does not contract with his master for payment. A slave is not a hired hand. Nor does a slave deserve payment. However, a master still might chose to reward his slave. Even in the case of a slave being rewarded, though, the reward is based on the slave's performance. A master might graciously allow his slave the opportunity to earn/merit a reward. A slave is not able to take the initiative, of course, in obligating his master to reward him. His master is completely gracious in taking the initiative to reward his slave; nevertheless, the slave merits the reward. This derivative merit is merit that is derived from the gracious promise in which the master makes it possible for the slave to earn/merit a reward to which the slave otherwise would not be entitled.

Master's Initiative

For that matter, a contractual worker cannot take the initiative in obligating his potential employer to pay him. Potential employees cannot obligate their potential bosses to give them jobs. The landowner was not under obligation to hire laborers for his vineyard. He simply could have chosen to let his slaves do the harvesting and foregone having to pay any wages to hired laborers. Yet the master of the slaves freely chose to become an employer and to offer the opportunity to work to a number of potential workers. Those workers who chose to take him up on his offer and work were entitled to the wage they received though. For the master not to give them the full payment to which they were entitled would have been wrong, as James graphically portrays: "Behold, the pay of the laborers who mowed your fields, and which has been withheld by you, cries out against you; and the outcry of those who did the harvesting has reached the ears of the Lord of Sabaoth" (Jam 5:4).

God is not Unjust

Unlike such employers, "God is not unjust so as to forget your work" (Heb 6:10). God would be unjust if He were not to pay His laborers the full payment which He has promised them. In the parable, the master instructs: "Call the laborers and pay them their wages" (Mt 20:8). The reward on this occasion is an obligatory payment, not an optional reward. While a slave normally has no right to expect payment or to demand a reward (Lk 17:10), these laborers in the vineyard do have that right. They are hired hands, not slaves. Laborers have such rights at the end of the workday. The problem for these particular parabolic laborers was not that they had thought too much about rewards but that they had thought too shallowly. Like Böttger, and so many other Protestants, the laborers whom Jesus criticizes failed to factor in the possibility of congruent merit.

Rewards are not Gifts

Böttger commences his subversion of the biblical perspective by claiming that God's rewards are gifts. The first OT passage he cites to prove his point is, "Behold, children are a *gift* of the Lord; the fruit of the womb is a *reward*" (Ps 127:3).[1294] To his credit, Böttger does not use this questionable translation by the NAS. Better translations of this verse would say that children are a *heritage* or *inheritance*. This *inheritance* is a *reward*. Even without the unsupported NAS translation of the parallel for *gift* as *reward* though, Böttger thinks that the only conceivable recourse is to interpret the reward "against the background of ancient social relations—[as] a free gift from a generous king." In actuality, given the OT background, one should not be so quick to conclude that Jewish children in the OT economy were regarded as gifts. To some extent, Constable makes the same mistake but supplies the grounds for a correction:

> Many of life's best blessings come as gifts from God. Children are one of these great gifts. God gives them to a couple or withholds them as He chooses regardless of how much a husband and a wife may strive to obtain them. Under the Mosaic economy God promised to bless the godly with children (Deut. 28:4), but He gave no such promise to Christians. Therefore it is a mistake to conclude that the more children a Christian couple has the more godly they are.[1295]

If the godly Jewish parents under the Mosaic economy (in which Ps 127:3 was written) were given children because of their godly behavior, then indeed those children were rewards, rather than gifts, given by their King. In this case, one could even make an argument for merit, in which God is understood as saying, "If you are godly, I will reward you with children." In such a case, God obligates Himself to reward faithful Jewish parents with children. Although no such obligation exists today, children still may be given as a reward. God is not obligated to reward couples with children; nevertheless, when He does choose to do so, He is rewarding a couple's faithfulness to His original command: "Be fruitful and multiply, and fill the earth, and subdue it" (Gen 1:28). Whether it be the fruit of the womb or the fruit of the field, the fruit God gives can be considered a reward for one's labor. When a woman decides to go the full term of pregnancy and through the agonies of labor to give birth to a child, she is rewarded with a child for her faithfulness to God's command and for the pains of her labor.

Condign and Congruent Merit

Even aside from the OT background, if one insists that the ability and opportunity to have children is a gift from God, the argument is still valid that actually following through on the opportunity to have children is a reward for one's labor. Condign merit is still pictured. If and when God decides to reward a couple today with children, those children are a condign reward. We cannot obligate God to give us children anymore than the laborers in the vineyard could obligate the vineyard owner to give them a job. Yet we can earn children and wages from God as rewards for our labor when He graciously gives us this opportunity. Condign merit is seen in the fact that the opportunity must originate with God. Solely on the basis of God's gracious initiative, He makes it possible for us to earn rewards. God must take the initiative to obligate Himself to give us rewards.[1296] Congruent merit, on the other hand, is apparent in that the reward is much greater than the effort.*

OT and NT Rewards

The enjoining of rewards with works, so that the latter results in the former, even from God, is the understood OT perception: "May the Lord reward your work, and your wages be full from the Lord, the God of Israel, under whose wings you have come to seek refuge" (Ruth 2:12). The OT anticipation is that God will reward good behavior and punish bad behavior; although, the OT perspective is focused mostly on getting one's just deserts in this life: "If the righteous will be rewarded in the earth, how much more the wicked and the sinner!" (Prov 11:31). Even so, the OT lays principles and imagery that is picked up by the NT and shown to be applicable eschatologically: "He who sows righteousness gets a true reward" (Prov 11:18). Specifically, in this context, "The fruit of the righteous is a tree of life" (Prov 11:30). Of course, the theme—you reap what you sow—is given an eschatological dimension in the NT: "Do not be deceived, God is not mocked; for whatever a man sows, this he will also reap. For the one who sows to his own flesh shall from the flesh reap corruption, but the one who sows to the Spirit shall from the Spirit reap eternal life" (Gal 6:7-8). Reaping eternal life, even in the form of the tree of life, is an eschatological reward for one's work (Rev 2:7; 22:14,19).

---

* Also see discussion of Ps 127:3 in *The Race of Grace*.

Congruent Merit

Understandably, Böttger is concerned about opening "the flood-gates to 'works-righteousness.'"[1297] What he fails to perceive is that in denying that rewards have merit, he is the one opening those very flood-gates. He conditions the final soteric "bestowment of eternal life" on works. Calling these works *gifts* and denying that they have merit does nothing to deter from the conclusion that Böttger is teaching salvation by works. Like so many other short-sighted Reformed writers, he thinks that in ruling out strict merit he has ruled out all merit. Far from it, he unwittingly is making heaven out to be an earned reward, attributable to condign and congruent merit rather than to strict merit.[*]

Aside from obvious soteriological deficiencies, misthological inadequacies are glaringly apparent as well. For example, Böttger claims: "God does not only repay far beyond any merit (cf. Lk. 19:17,19); payment of reward is simply independent of the worker's achievement."[1298] To the contrary, repaying far beyond the normal range of merit but in a manner congruent with the merit smacks of congruent merit—not no merit. In Lk 19:16-19, the servant who was faithful and fruitful to the point of producing a tenfold increase was given rulership over ten cities; the servant who produced a fivefold increase was given rulership over five cities. A congruent correspondence is obvious. Böttger's remarks are oblivious to the true character of the very passage he cites as his proof text. If the payment of the reward was independent of the worker's work, then why is there a congruent correspondence? Moreover, why is the servant who produced no increase reprimanded rather than rewarded? The passage is dripping wet with congruent merit. For Böttger to claim that it is bone dry of any merit is inexcusable. His theological commitment to Calvinism has led to his failure as a lexicographer. His Calvinistic premises precluded his fulfilling his lexical responsibilities.

Unworthy Slaves can be Worthy of Reward

Despite the scriptural emphasis on our congruently receiving our just deserts and the biblical acknowledgement that God would be unjust not to pay them, Böttger claims: "Every claim to one's deserts must fall silent in the face of the demand for total obedience" (Lk 17:10).[1299] Actually, every claim to just deserts is not silenced by this parable because Scripture teaches elsewhere that laborers are worthy of their wages and that God would be unjust to withhold those wages. The Lord Jesus Himself considers His good workers to be worthy of their wages (Rev 3:4). God counts those who endure as worthy (2Thess 1:11). Once again, let it be noted that laborers are contractual workers, not slaves. If you contract to work for a day's wage, you are entitled to that day's wage, even if the contract is with God. Conversely, slaves are not contractual workers. The slaves in this Lukan parable have no bargaining power. Their master is their master, not a potential employer. Slaves are not employees.

Slaves are Slaves

Harmonization between this parable and numerous other passages is easily attainable by observing that God has to take the initiative to reward His slaves. If a master promised to reward his slave for a certain action, then the master has obligated himself to do so. Obviously, the master would have exhibited great grace in making such an obligation since he simply could have commanded his slaves to perform the action without any promise of a reward. Slaves are unworthy of the opportunity to earn rewards. Slaves have no right to demand such an opportunity. Nevertheless, having been graciously given an opportunity that they do not deserve, even slaves certainly have a right to expect their master to follow through on his promise.

Let it not escape notice that the parable in question, that of Lk 17:7-10, is not talking about rewards. These slaves are not portrayed as saying, "We are unworthy *of our reward*." Rather, the thrust of the passage is that as slaves we are under obligation to obey our Master. In terms of obligation, we are not potential laborers standing in the market place being offered a job to work in the vineyard, with a right to determine whether we will take the job offer. Slaves are not offered a job, but given a command. In this context, the Lord commands us to forgive those who sin against us if they repent. We cannot squirm out of our obligation to forgive by acting as though we need more faith in order to obey. *We are unworthy slaves* in the sense of being obligated to forgive (and do whatever else our Master commands) just because He is our Master. As our Master, He has every right to make such a demand and expect our full, unconditional compliance. Thus, independent of any other consideration, we *ought to* forgive simply because our Master has commanded us to forgive. The absence of reward and the stress on unworthiness in this parable complement each other to emphasize the obligatory nature of our service. This coherency does nothing to undermine the obligatory nature of the promised reward in those passages dealing with

---

[*] See my discussion of Jonathan Edwards in *Mere Christianity and Moral Christianity* for an example of a Reformed writer who slays strict merit while unwittingly allowing condign and congruent merit.

promised rewards. When rewards are offered, Scripture encourages us to do what is necessary to be considered worthy of those rewards by God. Accordingly, we should consider ourselves as **worthy of reward in a derivative sense** if we perform the required task. Worthiness that is derivative must spring from God's gracious initiative.

Contractual Workers Still Paid

In summary, Lk 17:10 teaches that we should have the attitude: "We have done that which was our duty to do" (KJV). Yet the Bible also commands us to work hard for the reward (Col 3:23-24) and run for the prize (Phil 3:14). These statements can be reconciled by noting that we do not deserve the opportunity to earn rewards. Rewards themselves are not gifts, but the opportunity to earn them is a gift. God graciously obligates Himself to reward us by graciously making a promise to do so. It is not a contract in which God is attempting to get some service from us that He needs in exchange for the goods He offers. A simple contractual exchange of goods and services is not intended. Those believers who have this mistaken contractual attitude are rebuked in Mt 20:1-16. Nevertheless, even they still get the reward for which they contracted! Amazingly, even those believers who misconstrue the gracious nature of the reward[*] still are rewarded with the same basic reward as those who simply trusted the Lord to give them whatever is right. What will the Lord give? He will reward every believer who is faithful until death with the crown of life (Rev 2:10). Each of the laborers in the vineyard (Mt 20:1-16) worked faithfully till the end of the day. Presumably, then, each received the same categorical reward. However, we would expect that not only their actions but also their attitudes would be taken into consideration for sub-categorical rewards.[†]

Misthological Disbelief

When the author was a child, he was taught a little saying that was used to help children distinguish Sadducees from Pharisees: The *Sadducees* were *sad-you-see*, because they did not believe in the resurrection (Mk 12:18)—or angels, or eternal life for that matter. More specifically, Panton relates "that Sadoc, the founder of the Sadducees, started off his career of unbelief by denying the doctrine of rewards."[1300] Misthological unbelief in Sadoc's case led to a widespread disbelief in other areas as well. More pragmatically for the Christian, denying the existence or value of rewards can lead to depression when one comes to believe that his or her service for the Lord will go unnoticed and unrewarded. Misthological disbelief can lead easily to a skeptical attitude in which a person keeps asking him or herself questions expressing internal doubt: "What difference does it make? If the Lord really loves me, then why do I have to endure this mediocre job or painful trial?"

Soteriologically, it does not make any difference if you serve the Lord. The reason is because your salvation from hell is not dependent upon your service. Misthologically speaking, though, it makes a tremendous difference because your salvation from the outer darkness and your rulership of heaven are conditioned on your service. So if you are serving the Lord, you can be *glad-you-see* because your effort will not be in vain. Even working hard as a menial laborer at a mediocre job still can qualify you to rule in heaven (Col 3:23-25). You will tend to love the Lord more because He makes your life misthologically meaningful and thus bearable.

Jesus' Love Motivated By Rewards

Jesus endured the cross for the joyful reward of ruling (cp. Heb 12:1-2 with Heb 1:8-9). If we follow His example, we will endure so that we may rule. Paul followed Jesus' example of enduring in order to rule. In 2Tim 2:12, he exhorts us to endure so that we can also rule: "If we endure, we shall also rule with Him." Jesus exhorts us to endure like Him so that we can rule like Him. In Rev 3:21, He promises, "He who overcomes, I will grant to him to sit down with Me on My throne, as I also overcame and sat down with My Father on His throne." Jesus was motivated by this reward, and He expects us to be as well.

Peter likewise follows Jesus' example, and in 1Pet 2:19-21 he says that we should follow Jesus' example in enduring suffering so that we can gain God's favor. In 1Pet 3:9, he said that the reason we should do this is to gain the inheritance. In 1Pet 5:6, the incentive that Peter gives for us to humble ourselves is in order to have God exalt us. James affirms the same truth: "Humble yourselves…and He will exalt you" (Jam 4:10). The reason you should humble yourself is so that God will exalt you. If you want to be exalted, let God do so. He will do a much better job of it than you will. Does this sound selfish? Then consider Paul's words in Phil 2:3-11. He tells us to do

---

[*] See *Derivative Merit*, 31.
[†] See *Workers in Vineyard (Mt 20:1-16)*, 683.

nothing form selfishness or empty conceit, to look out for the interests of others, and to follow Jesus' example by having the same attitude that Jesus had.

What was Jesus' attitude? Paul continues in Phil 2:8-9 to say that Jesus humbled Himself; therefore, God exalted Him. Did Jesus humble Himself in order to be exalted? Yes. This answer is consistent with the teaching of Jam 4:10 and 1Pet 5:6. The principle that humbling yourself results in God exalting you did not originate with Peter and James. It is a principle that Jesus Himself taught (Mt 23:12; Lk 14:11). The motive Jesus gives others for humbling themselves in these verses is to have God exalt them. Personal exaltation is the motive that Jesus gives us for humbling ourselves. He practiced what He preached. Jesus humbled Himself in order to have God exalt Him. In doing so, He gave us an example to follow. This is the example that the writer of Heb 12:1-2 exhorts us to follow.

It appears quite evident from the book of Hebrews itself that rewards are an incentive for Jesus' love and that rewards are a reason that He died on the cross. In Heb 1:9, we are told that the reason Jesus was anointed with the oil of gladness was because He **loved** righteousness. This misthological gladness is associated in Heb 1:8 with rulership. His joy is referred to again in Heb 12:1-2. In 12:1 we are urged to run the race with *patience* that is **set before us**. Earlier in Heb 6:12, the writer urged us to be diligent and *patient* so that we can inherit the hope (promises/rewards). In Heb 6:18, he urges us to flee "for refuge in laying hold of the hope **set before** us." What is *set before us* in Heb 6:18 and Heb 12:1 is the same thing set before Jesus in 12:2—a reward. Likewise, in Heb 10:35-36 he urges us to **endure** so that we may obtain the promise which is a reward. In other words, the imagery and message of Heb 12:1 is the same as 1Cor 9:24-27. We are to run (endure) in order to win the reward. This is the same reason that Jesus endured in Heb 12:2. He endured the cross in order to obtain the joy, the reward. As in Heb 1:8-9, the joy is associated in 12:2 with sitting on a throne at the Father's right hand, which recalls the promise recorded in v. 13. "Sit at My right hand, until I make Thine enemies a footstool for Thy feet" (Heb 1:13; cp. 10:12-13). Jesus lovingly died for us on the cross in order to obtain this exaltation.

Morris (EBC) is correct concerning Heb 12:2 when he comments that "Jesus went to the Cross because of the joy it would bring"; however, Morris is incorrect in simply defining this as the "joy of bringing salvation to those he loves."[1301] Guthrie is closer to the truth when he says that "there is some correlation between the race set before us and the joy set before Jesus....[It] echoes the idea expressed in 1:3 and 8:1. The passion is seen as part of the path to the throne....the cross is at once linked with exaltation."[1302] Even so, Lenski's articulation of this correlation is superior:

> "The joy lying before him" is the **glorification** that followed the sufferings **plus his kingship** over all believers....in order to get this joy Christ paid the price of the cross...
>
> ...this seating himself at the right hand of the throne of God...is the infinite **exaltation** of the human nature of Christ and thus the **crowning** of all his saving work for all eternity.[1303]

Christ died on the cross because of the joy—the glorification and exaltation—this would bring to Himself. It was for the joy set before Him personally that He endured in Heb 12:2, and it is for the joy set before us personally that we should endure in Heb 12:1. If we follow Jesus' example, we will be motivated by rewards since He was so motivated. Haldeman does well to connect this joy with the joy of the Mount Olivet Discourse expressed in Mt 25:21,23:

> The Christian who has passed his civil service examination at the Judgment Seat of Christ will be invited to share that joy.
>
> The Lord will say to him:
>
> "Well done, good and faithful servant: thou hast been faithful over a few things, I will make thee ruler over many things: *enter thou into the joy of the Lord.*"
>
> *Here* as plainly as language can put it, the Lord's power and authority to appoint rulers on the earth is His joy. That appointment of rulership is the declaration that He is acting in His office as King...*Acting as King on the earth then is His joy.*
>
> The faithful Christian will share this joy by being appointed ruler in the earthly or millennial kingdom. (Emphasis his.)[1304]

As I have noted above, the writer of Hebrews uses this same expression on one other occasion: "We may have strong encouragement, we who have fled for refuge in laying hold of the *hope set before us*" (Heb 6:18). The *hope set before us* is parallel to the *joy set before Him* (Heb 12:2). This joyful hope is realized by running "with patience the race that is set before us" (Heb 12:1). Sauer notes that this word for *set before* (*prokeimai*) could even be considered a technical term for the rewards and prizes publicly displayed at the Greek races: "These gifts were used as prizes in the Greek races and were publicly exhibited, *i.e.*, 'set before' the eyes of all onlookers."[1305] The joy set before the Lord is the same joy set before us—rulership (cp. Heb 2:9).

The purpose of a ship's *anchor* (*agkura*) is to save that ship from destruction on the rocky reefs (Acts 27:29-30). The writer of Hebrews identifies the *anchor* of our soul as this misthological **hope** *set before us* (Heb 6:18-19). The purpose of this misthological anchor is to save our souls from misthological destruction.[*] For this reason, he exhorts us to flee for refuge from the rocky reefs that would destroy our souls by laying hold on this misthological hope as our anchor.[†] Grasping the misthological potential of this reward has the potential to save our souls from misthological loss. Peter also links misthological hope with the salvation of our souls (1Pet 1:3,9). The Greek word used in Heb 6:18 for *grasping* or *laying hold of* this hope is *krateo*. It is the same word used by Jesus when He says, "*Hold fast* what you have, so that no one will take your crown" (Rev 3:11). Our hope of being crowned victor and saving our soul from loss is at stake. We dare not let go of this misthological hope! This hope of future reward is our present anchor. Of course, we need pneumatological rope to hold on to this misthological hope. It is only by the power of the Spirit that we can save our souls.

NT Teaches Rewards as Incentive to Love

Not only was Jesus personally motivated by rewards, He also uses rewards as an incentive for our loving service in His teaching. As a result, those who claim that using rewards as a motivation for service promotes a selfish and an unloving spirit are in reality accusing Jesus of promoting selfishness and an unloving spirit. Rather than accuse Jesus of being unloving or selfish (because He was motivated by rewards), and rather than accuse Jesus of promoting unloving or selfish attitudes (because He teaches others also to be motivated by rewards), it is necessary to accept the biblical assessment given in 1Cor 13:3, where Paul warns: "And if I give all my possessions to feed the poor, and if I deliver my body to be burned, but do not have love, it profits **me** nothing." According to this verse, **our works are to be motivated by love, and our love is to be motivated by rewards.**

Rewards as Motive Purifier

1Cor 13:3 is one of the most famous verses in the Bible concerning loving others. It is obvious that the motive for our actions is to be love. Consequently, many people say that we should serve the Lord out of love and not for rewards.[1306] Nonsense! Earlier in this same epistle Paul had used rewards as an incentive to serve the Lord (see 1Cor **3:8-15**; **4:5**; 6:2-3,**9-10**; **9:24-27**; 15:2,50). He also uses rewards as an incentive for serving the Lord in his second epistle to the Corinthians (see 2Cor **4:17-18**; **5:10**; 6:2; 7:10; 9:6). Paul does not appeal to improper motives to motivate his readers since he is concerned about their motives. In 1Cor 4:5, Paul announces that the Lord will judge our motives and base our rewards on our motives. Paul appeals to rewards to motivate us and warns us that proper motives are required for rewards. He would be blatantly inconsistent to turn around in 1Cor 13:3 and say that rewards are an improper motivation! On the contrary, in 1Cor 4:5 he uses the doctrine of rewards as a motive purifier. He is far from being inconsistent. In 1Cor 13:3, Paul does exactly the same thing he had done earlier in 1Cor 4:5. He appeals to rewards as an incentive for pure motives. He does not appeal to ungodly motives for godly actions or attitudes. The desire for rewards cannot be an ungodly motive in and of itself. However, the desire for rewards can be an ungodly motive if it does not involve love, as Paul demonstrates in 1Cor 13:3.

According to 1Cor 13:3 what is the incentive for our love? It is rewards. Why are we to serve others out of love? We are to lovingly serve others in order to reap profit for ourselves. The danger of unlovingly serving others is that it will profit us nothing. Thus, we should serve one another out of love so that it may profit **us**. Biblically, the reason we are lovingly to serve others is for personal profit; that is, for heavenly rewards. The present author quoted 1Cor 13:3 to a pastor friend one day to prove this point, but that pastor could not believe that the verse was being quoting correctly: "And if I give all my possessions to feed the poor, and if I deliver my body to be burned, but do not have love, it profits **me** nothing." He said that the present writer must have been mistaken in putting the word *me* in the verse.

Yet this type of rendering is the standard one given by the translators and commentators. More importantly, in Greek the verb *profit* is first person passive and can also be translated as, "**I** am profited nothing." Just as verse 2 concludes by saying, "I am nothing," (that is, a nobody) so verse 3 concludes with, "I am profited nothing." I am expected to perform my actions out of love in order that **I** may obtain profit for **myself**, that is, for **me**. If I want to be a misthological somebody in God's kingdom, I must love. We are to serve out of love for others and a desire for

---

[*] See illustrations for "Anchor of the Soul," 1847 and "Loss of the Soul" in *Salvation: A Categorical Analysis*.

[†] See *Illustration 229. Flaming Soul at Bema*, 666..

profit for ourselves. As Alcorn relates, "This isn't a matter of *mixed* motives (some good, some bad) but of *multiple* motives—multiple righteous motives."[1307]

Personal Profit Basis for Loving Others

Paul definitely uses personal profit as the motive for profiting others. If you unlovingly give your possessions to feed the poor, it will profit them. Paul is not denying that there is no profit for them; rather, he denies it is profitable for you. It is possible to profit others without profiting yourself. If you want to profit yourself as well, you must do it out of love. The word translated as *profited* (*opheleo*) in 1Cor 13:3 is also translated as *profited* in Mk 8:36, where Jesus said that the profit is the reward of gaining your own soul, not the souls of others. The point is not that your actions or testimony will be unprofitable to others; it is that it will be unprofitable to you if not done out of love. Indeed, it is possible that the background for Paul's statement in 1Cor 13:3 comes from another passage in Mark. "Jesus felt a love" for the rich young ruler and said to him, "Go and sell all you possess, and give to the poor, and you shall have treasure in heaven" (Mk 10:21).

What incentive does Jesus give for the young ruler to give all his possessions to feed the poor? It is treasure in heaven—personal profit. The incentive Jesus gives to feed the poor is rewards. Paul uses this same theme but makes explicit what Mark made implicit: Our actions, like Jesus' words on that occasion, must be based on love. Paul, in essence, is stating that if you succeed in doing what the rich young ruler failed to do (i.e., if you give your possessions to feed the poor), you must do so out of love if you want to obtain the reward that was promised to the rich young ruler. Paul points out that both the proper attitude and the proper action are mutually required in order to obtain the reward. Rewards are the incentive that both Paul and Jesus use. Those who say that rewards are an improper motive to feed the poor are refuted by both Paul and Jesus.

Misthological Profit for Serving Others

The eschatological nature of this reward is seen in the fact that the personal profit promised extends beyond the grave, beyond giving your body to be burned in martyrdom in 1Cor 13:3. Even if we make the ultimate sacrifice to the Lord, it will not profit us if we do not do it out of love for the Lord. In 1Cor 13:3, we see that it is possible to serve others and serve the Lord without love. Paul warns us that unloving service, whether to others or to the Lord, will not profit us.

When Jesus uses *profit* (*opheleo*) in Lk 9:25, He immediately links it in Lk 9:26 with shame experienced by those who are not *profited* when He returns with the angels. The profit (or lack thereof) is eschatological. Paul's warning in Gal 5:2 certainly includes the misthological dimension, where he uses *opheleo* to warn these legalistic, carnal believers: "Christ will *profit* you nothing," (NKJ). After all, Paul proceeds to warn them about the eschatological possibility of not inheriting the kingdom (Gal 5:21).

Likewise, when Paul mentions being "made heirs according to the hope of eternal life" in Tit 3:7, he immediately follows with the adjectival form to remind them of the faithful saying that good works are *profitable* (*ophelimos*). His use of this adjective to Timothy is a parallel: "Godliness is *profitable* for all things, since it holds promise for the present life and also for the life to come" (1Tim 4:8). Obviously, Paul's interest in personal profit is not limited to the present. In 1Cor 13:3, we must therefore surmise that it is possible to serve others and serve the Lord without love. Paul warns us that unloving service, whether to others or to the Lord, will not profit us misthologically. Cold, legalistic, unloving sacrifice will not profit us anything misthologically in 1Cor 3:2, just as Christ will not profit us anything misthologically in Gal 5:2 if our sacrifice is not an expression of "faith working through love" (Gal 5:6). Paul exhorts us to obtain **personal** profit that lasts beyond the grave by **lovingly** serving others and the Lord in obedience empowered by the Holy Spirit. We thus should be concerned that others benefit by our actions.

Love Motivated by Personal Glory

But how is God benefited by our service? Everything we do (including our service) should be done for the glory of God (1Cor 10:31). If we endure for our own glory without love for God, and thus without any concern for His glory, it will profit us nothing. Conversely, if we let our light shine in such a way that He is glorified (Mt 5:16), then we will obtain eternal glory for enduring (2Cor 4:17). Thus, personal glory is the motive for loving God, for seeking to glorify Him. The motive for love is personal glory, which is praise from Him (1Cor 4:5). It should be assumed that if God wants us to do everything for His glory, as 1Cor 10:31 tells us, then He does everything for His own glory as well. And this is the way it should be since we are to be like Him. We are to follow His example in glorifying Him.

God sent His Son to die for us and His Spirit to seal us for the **praise of His glory** (Rom 9:23; Eph 1:6,14). God sacrificed His Son so that He would be glorified by it. And His Son accepts us for the purpose of glory (Rom 15:7). And yet other passages (such as Jn 3:16, Rom 5:8, and Eph 2:4-5) state that the reason God sent His Son to die for us is because He loves us. Which is true? Did God send His Son to die for us because He loves us or in order to glorify His name, as Jesus prayed in Jn 12:28? Obviously, both statements are true. God sent His Son to die for us because He loves us and in order to glorify Himself. The either/or mentality is ruled out.

So why is it that so many think that one cannot perform an action **both** out of love **and** in order to glorify oneself? They believe that one must **either** perform an action out of love **or** out of a desire for rewards. They are mistaken. As shown above, in sacrificing His Son for us, God was motivated out of love for Himself (in the form of personal glory) as well as out of love for us. Our actions, likewise, are expected to be performed both out of love and out of a desire for personal rewards in the form of glory. The proper mentality is both/and. The Holy Spirit gave us the instructions contained in 1Cor 13:3 because they help us be like Jesus. What Jesus does for others is out of love for them. But as we have seen, personal glory is the motive for love.

God lovingly gave His Son to die for us in order that His name might be glorified. He did it for personal glory. **The motive for His death was love; the motive for His love was personal glory.** He was motivated by both. For example, when we exercise and diet for God's glory, we also do it for our own personal benefit (e.g., health). At the same time, the Bible tells us to take care of our family (1Tim 5:8). Could taking care of ourselves not be one way of taking care of our family? Since the Bible tells us that our eating and drinking, as well as everything else we do, are to be done for the glory of God (1Cor 10:31), are we to conclude that it is wrong or impossible to take good care of our body because we love God and our family? In other words, it is not improper to want to live long, healthy lives in order to provide for our family's financial and emotional security **and** because at the same time we want to offer the Lord more years of service. Are we to consider our motives impure if we are motivated to diet and exercise both because we love God and our family? How about if we do it because we love God and our family and because it makes us feel and look better? Does it then become wrong to diet and exercise since we do it because we love God **and** ourselves? Hopefully, the conclusion is apparent. If most of us need as many complementary, positive motivations as possible to do something that even the world would approve of, such as dieting and exercising, then we would be wise to use as many biblical motivations as possible in carrying out biblical mandates to win God's approval in the face of the world's disapproval. Positive motivations need not be exclusive; we need to include as many as possible. It is just as possible and permissible to serve God out of love for ourselves and out of a desire for personal benefit as it is to exercise for His glory and our own good health.

Likewise, the motive for our works should be love, and the motive for our love should be personal glory. In relation to God's glory, this means that the motive for our works should be the desire to glorify God, and the motive for our desire to glorify God should be the desire that He will glorify us. The incentive the Bible uses to urge us to live lives that glorify God is that **we may obtain personal glory as our reward** (e.g., see Rom 2:5-10; 8:17-18; 2Cor 4:17-18; 1Thess 2:12; 2Thess 2:14; 2Tim 2:10; 1Pet 1:7; 5:4,10). In other words, our desire to hear His words, "Well done," should motivate us to love Him and others.

Conclusion

A young man trying to win a young lady's heart or win her hand in marriage is not considered mercantile. Rather, his efforts are regarded as noble, and many love stories are based on the theme of the noble prince trying to win the heart of a young maiden. Is it so strange that the Lord would want us to win His heart as well? Do we regard the young maiden in such love tales to be unloving in nature because she limits her special affection to the one young man who admires her the most and desires her enough to demonstrate his desire to be loved by her as his one and only love? Of course not. Her desire to be loved is natural and reciprocal. The sleeping beauty in such tales is not only lovely but loving. She would have to have a loving disposition to be fond of grumpy dwarfs! Still, she is expected to withhold special expressions of her love for her lover—her Prince Charming. The Lord also withholds special expressions of His love for those believers who love Him enough to want to be His Bride. They win His hand in marriage by demonstrating a loving disposition towards others in general and believers in particular (especially the grumpy ones) and thereby demonstrating that they love Hm. Like the fair maiden, the Lord's love for grumpy believers is unconditional. But let us not begrudge Him the right to hold a special place in His heart for those loving believers who, like Him, love the grumpy believers. Let us not demand that He marry the grumpy believers in His biblical love tale. Our Prince Charming is looking for companionship in the hearts of those who are loving. He will not find it in the hearts of those who are unloving.

Appendix 2.
Kingdom and Kingship Entrance

Introduction

The distinction between entering and inheriting the kingdom has been maintained in the present work, in response to the false soteriology of the traditionalists and the errant misthology of the ultraists. As a result, the kingdom has been understood as a kingship in certain contexts. This appendix will further demonstrate the soundness of this approach by examining the two remaining texts used by ultraists in their claim that entrance and inheritance are synonymous (Jn 3:5; Acts 4:22). Also, in connection to kingdom entrance, I will delve into the typological role that Achan plays in this discussion of kingdom entrance and exclusion.

Overview

There appear to be at least fourteen texts where the word *kingdom* (*basileia*) is used in connection with its entrance. Of these fourteen texts, the classic conservative position is preferable the majority of the time in that the entrance being described is soteriological rather than misthological. However, although the conservative argument concerning Mk 9:47 is strong, it probably does not rule out an ultraistic interpretation altogether. Rather than taking an either/or approach and interpret this verse conservatively or ultraistically, it appears best, in this passage at least, to take the reference to *basileia* on the chart as denoting both a soteriological and misthological neoclassical entrance into the kingdom.[*] However, as was conceded earlier, the ultraistic interpretation of the text in Acts 14:22 is superior to the conservative argument.[†] This passage is definitely describing a misthological entrance. Still, it is an ultraistic entrance with a conservative meaning—a neo-ultraistic entrance. It is entrance into the kingdom as a kingship which is in view. No believer will be excluded from the kingdom, but many believers will be excluded from the kingship.

Illustration 266. Kingdom Entrance

	Passage "into the kingdom" (*eis ten basileian*)				Type:	
					sot.	mist.
1.	Mt 5:20				✓	
2.	Mt 7:21				✓	
3.		Mk 9:47			✓	✓
4.	Mt 18:3	Mk 10:15	Lk 18:17		✓	
5.	Mt 19:23-24	Mk 10:23-25	Lk 18:24-25		✓	
6.	Mt 21:31				✓	
7.	Mt 23:13				✓	
8.			Lk 23:42		✓	
9.				Jn 3:5	✓	
10.				Acts 14:22		✓
11.				Col 1:13	✓	
12.				1Thess 2:12		✓
13.				2Tim 4:18		✓
14.				2Pet 1:11		✓

Misthological Entrance Expanded

This assessment does not mean that Acts 14:22 is to be regarded as a unique case of misthological entrance into the kingdom. To expand upon the previous discussion,[‡] in his first letter to the Thessalonians, Paul exhorts believers to *walk* in a manner *worthy* of entering *into* the *kingdom* (1Thess 2:11-12). This is misthological worthiness. In his next letter to the Thessalonians, Paul again picks up on this same theme, urging believers to

---

[*] Entrance into life in Mt 18:9-9 and Mk 9:43,45 parallels entrance into the kingdom in Mk 9:47 and therefore would be neoclassical entrance as well.

[†] See *Limited Entrance*, 570.

[‡] See *Misthological Entrance*, 571.

persevere in walking by faith during their sufferings so that they may be considered *worthy of* the kingdom (2Thess 1:5). Worthy entrance into the kingdom is what Paul personally is looking forward to in 2Tim 4:18 when he assures, "The Lord will deliver me from every evil deed, and will bring me safely *to* [*into, eis*] His heavenly kingdom." As noted in the above chart, these references to the *kingdom* are misthological; hence, *basileia* may be translated as *kingship* (as has been shown repeatedly in the course of this study). Similarly, in 2Tim 3:11 to be delivered from evil is not to be delivered from being persecuted by evil (cf. 2Tim 3:12), it is to be given wisdom to endure evil for misthological salvation (2Tim 3:15). There is a sense in which it is necessary to endure hardship in order to experience a full entrance into the kingdom and misthological salvation. This misthological entrance into the kingdom may be denoted as entrance into the kingship of the kingdom.

That deliverance from evil is not deliverance from being killed by evil in 2Tim 4:18 is made evident by the fact that Paul is about to be martyred (2Tim 4:6-7). Deliverance from evil means victory over evil in the present for rulership in the future, as Paul beautifully expresses in the preceding verses: "I have fought the good fight, I have finished the course, I have kept the faith; in the future there is laid up for me the crown of righteousness, which the Lord, the righteous Judge, will award to me on that day; and not only to me, but also to all who have loved His appearing" (2Tim 4:7-8). This future crown/rulership is the subject of 2Tim 4:18, "The Lord will deliver me **from** every evil deed, and will save me **for** His heavenly **kingship**" (TM.) Salvation is not only from something; it is for something. It is to be saved for His kingship, to exercise His rulership.

Salvation from evil is achieved by victoriously enduring evil for the sake of the kingdom (2Thess 1:4-5). Such endurance is necessary to be worthy of and fit for the kingdom (Lk 9:62). Likewise, in Mt 6:13 we should pray that the Lord will save us from evil and for His kingdom, that is, His future kingdom (Mt 6:9). The Lord has not promised to deliver us from the experience of evil but from the necessity to subcome to it. Through His enabling grace we can endure the evil that confronts us (1Cor 10:13). It is possible for believers to overcome evil or to be overcome by evil—to be overcomers or subcomers (Rom 12:21). Those believers who are overcome by evil will not enter His future kingdom in the sense of entering His future rule of that kingdom. They will be in the future kingdom as subjects of the kingdom rather than sovereigns of the kingdom. As has been stated previously, while most people principally think of the kingdom as a place, Paul primarily thought of it as an experience.

The compound verbal form of this word for kingship/rulership is found in 2Tim 2:12 where Paul promises, "If we endure, we will also **co-rule** [*sumbasileuo*] with Him" (TM). The salvation of 2Tim 2:10 is also associated with kingship in 2Tim 2:12. This meaning of salvation is self evident in Rev 7:10. The salvation being ascribed to God who sits on the throne is certainly not salvation from hell. It is the salvation of rulership: *Rulership to our God who sits on the throne*. Paul then proceeds to say that he has endured (2Tim 4:7), and the Lord will save him for **rulership** (2Tim 4:18). The co-kings of 2Tim 2:12 are those who experience salvation in terms of kingship in 2Tim 4:18. We are saved misthologically by enduring, as Jesus states when He stipulates that the person who endures will be saved (Mk 13:13). Paul teaches the same thing. They both promise a misthological salvation (i.e., kingship, rulership) for those who endure. Paul announces that it is this type of entrance into the kingdom that God *calls* believers to become worthy of by earning it (1Thess 2:12).[*] Peter also declares that it is this abundant entrance into the kingdom that God is misthologically *calling* believers to obtain by practicing holiness—that is, by practical sanctification (2Pet 1:10-11).[†] Practical sanctification determines the degree of a believer's entrance. Abundant entrance into the kingdom is entrance into the kingship of that kingdom.

Soteriological Entrance

On the other hand, basic entrance into the kingdom is not determined by practical holiness; it is determined exclusively by faith. In Lk 23:42 the dying thief requested, "Remember me when You enter into Your kingdom" (TM). He was relying upon Jesus' mercy rather than his own practical sanctification for entrance into Jesus' kingdom. As a little child relies upon his parents, so this thief relied upon Jesus and thereby received entrance into this kingdom (cf. Lk 18:17). Just before he died, the thief believed that Jesus is King, as he testified by saying, "**Your** kingdom." That is, "The kingdom which belongs to You." The thief's entrance was based on his faith in King Jesus, not on any faith in his good works. This is the type of entrance that all believers already have received by a simple passive response of faith, even before they die (cf. Col 1:13-14). Yet it covers entrance into the kingdom both before and after death.

Jesus made it very clear that this type of entrance into the kingdom is based upon faith, not works, when He asserted, "Truly I say to you that the tax-gatherers and harlots will **enter into the kingdom** of God before you. For

---

[*] See *Misthological Worthiness*, 73.
[†] See *Misthological Sequence of Election*, 298.

John came to you in the way of righteousness and you did not **believe** him; but the tax-gatherers and harlots did **believe** him; and you, seeing this, did not even feel remorse afterward so as to **believe** him" (Mt 21:31-32). Many morally good people are slow to believe in Jesus. They prefer to believe in themselves. However, the thief knew that he could not believe in himself, and he evidently was acquainted well enough with Jesus' teaching concerning the kingdom to know that even tax-gatherers and harlots could enter it if they simply believed Jesus. If even harlots could enter Jesus' kingdom by faith, then the thief reckoned he could also.

Soteriological Baptism

When morally-good Nicodemus came to Jesus, he was presented with this same truth. The structure of the two repetitive statements suggests that the latter explains the former: "Unless one is **born again**, he cannot **see** the kingdom of God....unless one is **born of water and Spirit**, he cannot **enter** into the kingdom of God" (Jn 3:3-5). There are numerous ways to interpret these verses. For grammatical reasons, the reference to water should probably be taken just as literally as the reference to Spirit in Jn 3:5. Therefore, water could refer to water baptism, rain, female water, male water, or spiritual water. Beckwith takes the typical position saying that "although some commentators see in this a contrast between natural and spiritual birth (cf. L. Morris, *John*, 1972, 215 ff.), most see in it a reference to baptism and spiritual regeneration...To enter the kingdom of God implies joining the church."[1308] He is joined in this definition of water in Jn 3:5 by Beasley-Murray who "affirms the necessity of a 'new beginning' from God ('from above') through submission to baptism and through the recreative work of the Holy Spirit."[1309]

The typical interpretation correspondingly taken by most commentators is that water refers to water baptism and is required to enter the kingdom and escape hell. This interpretation is the one logically required by the Lordship Salvationist camp. Submission to baptism and church membership are required for submission to the Lordship of Christ. Therefore, if submission to the Lordship of Christ is required for salvation and regeneration, then baptism and church membership are required for salvation and regeneration. Not only does such an interpretation teach salvation by works, it also teaches that baptism is required for regeneration. According to the passage, before you can enter the kingdom, you must be born again, that is, born of water. If being born of water refers to water baptism, then baptism is required to be born again. Thus, if you take the expression *born again* in v. 3 to be parallel with the expression *born of water and the Spirit* in v. 5, then water baptism certainly precedes regeneration. But this interpretation inverts the biblical order: faith, then regeneration, and then water baptism.

Thus, the soteriological interpretation of baptism in Jn 3:5 is rendered implausible by the (1) broader context of the NT. Water baptism is a work which we do, and our regeneration is not by works. (2) The immediate context also provides problems for the soteriological view of water baptism. In the later part of this conversation, which Jesus is having with Nicodemus, the single requirement for eternal life is belief (vv. 15-18). Water baptism is contextually not a necessary agent. Whatever being born of water means, it therefore would not be referring to baptism as a necessary agent.

The agent of regeneration is to be found in comparing *born again* with *being born of water and Spirit* (vv. 3,5) and with the summation (v. 8) that it is to be *born of the Spirit*. There is no reference to water in Jesus' summary statement in the latter verse. There is only one agent—the Spirit. This accords well with the grammar of verse 5 in which the word *of (ek)* only occurs once: "Born **of** water and Spirit." Jesus does not say, "Born **of** water and **of** Spirit." There are not two agents—only one. There is only one agent causing the new birth, not two. The anarthrous coupling of these agents under the roof of one preposition suggests that we treat them jointly as either symbolic or literal, as either essential or nonessential.

This singularity of agency also refutes the notion that *born of water* refers to baptism as a nonessential representation of what is actually necessary—spiritual birth. Being born of water is just as much an intermediate means as the being born of Spirit. Being born of water is not an outward sign of an inward reality in this passage. It is part of the means necessary to experience the new reality. The single preposition unites these agents grammatically in type and rank into one agent. Even if this were not the case, it should be remembered that Christian baptism does not represent birth. It pictures death (Rom 6:4). Granted, baptism may picture being raised to new life, but not apart from the prerequisite death (Col 2:12). Thus, water baptism would be a picture of death-followed-by-life rather than a simple picture of life-imparting-life in the new birth experience. Contextually, grammatically, and logically, it must be concluded that water baptism is not in view in the passage describing being born again.

Illustration 267. Born of Water in Jn 3:5

| Unless one is | **born again,** | he cannot | **see** | the kingdom of God (Jn 3:3). |
| Unless one is | **born of water and Spirit,** | he cannot | **enter into** | the kingdom of God (Jn 3:5). |

Categorization	Interpretation	Confirmation	Explanation	Evaluation
Baptism	of John	Jn 1:25-26; 3:23	Essential/Nonessential	L
	of Jesus	Jn 3:22		L
	of repentance		outward sign	L
	of Christianity			L
Birth	embryonic fluid (female water)	Jn 3:6	flesh & Spirit = physical & spiritual	L,S,P
	male semen (male water)	Pirke Aboth 3:1; 3En 6:2	flesh & Spirit = physical & spiritual	L,S,P
	spiritual semen (spiritual water)	1Jn 3:9; 1Pet 1:23	God gives begets us through His seed	L,S,P,A✔
Symbol	word	Ps 119:9; Jn 6:63,68; 15:3; Eph 5:26; 1Pet 1:23; Jam 1:18	cleansing resulting from gospel	S
	living water	Jn 4:10-14; 7:37-39	symbol used to explain a symbol	S,A
	Spirit	Is 44:3; Jn 4:10-14; 7:37-39; Tit 3:5	and = even (i.e., born of water even the Spirit)	S,A
	rain	Is 44:3-5; Prov 30:4-5	rain & wind = above	S,A

L (literal)   S (soteriology)   P (parallelism)   A (singleness of agent in type and rank

Misthological Baptism

Marrowists believe that regeneration is required for baptism. Regeneration should precede Christian baptism and church membership. Therefore, even the ultraistic interpretation in which baptism is required to enter the millennial kingdom (but not required for regeneration, or for entrance into the eternal kingdom, or for salvation from eternal damnation) is superior to the typical interpretation in which water baptism is required to reach heaven. Basically, the FG position represented by Chitwood and also by ultraists is that all believers will *see* the millennial kingdom but not all believers will *enter* it.[*] Thus, v. 3 is not parallel with v. 5.[1310] From their perspective, the only requirement for being able to see the millennial kingdom is spiritual birth. However, both water baptism and spiritual birth are required to enter the millennial kingdom. Entrance into the eternal kingdom is free a gift in this Free Grace perspective. From this neo-ultraistic and ultraistic vantage point, then, Jesus is giving the requirements for misthological entrance into the millennial kingdom.

If there is no distinction between seeing and entering the kingdom in these verses, however, the ultraistic interpretation suffers a decisive setback. Admittedly, scholars come out on both sides of this issue. Although Morris sees no significant difference between the two words, he notes that some scholars such as Westcott do see a distinct difference and that a writer of antiquity (i.e., Hermas) also made a distinction.[1311] Although such interpreters may not agree as to the significance of the difference, they nevertheless perceive that a difference actually exists. In the same citation, Morris notes that other scholars such as Barret find no distinction between the two words in this context.

---

[*] Chitwood is not an ultraist, though at times he seems to write as one and sometimes is mistaken for being one. Although he removed this section on *Seeing and Entering the Kingdom* (dealing with the necessity of baptism to enter the kingdom) from his 2011 edition of *Judgment*, I will still site from his 1986 edition of this book as his current position because in a personal correspondence (2-9-2012) he has confirmed that he understands entering the kingdom in Jn 3:3,5 to be a misthological entrance in terms of inheriting the kingdom (e.g., 1Cor 6:10). Indeed, I would agree with him that this is the case in Acts 14:22. Thus, although I am not opposed to such an equation conceptually when justified contextually, nevertheless, I disagree that this misthological interpretation is warranted in Jn 3:3,5. To his credit, Chitwood affirms that all believers will be in the millennial kingdom, as he has clarified in this 2011 edition: "All Christians, faithful and unfaithful alike, will be in the kingdom" (p. 100). Therefore, Chitwood is not a kingdom exclusionist. Nevertheless, he apparently interprets all the typical entrance passages as being misthological. Consequently, interacting with his interpretation is still applicable to the exclusionist argument. For they both make entrance a reward in this context.

Arguing distinction, Chitwood says that "this passage is not dealing with the issue of eternal life, but with the issue of entrance into the kingdom."[1312] However, it is questionable that there is any real difference between seeing the kingdom in 3:3 and seeing life in 3:36. "He who **believes** in the Son **has eternal life**; but he who does not obey [i.e., disbelieves] the Son shall not **see life**, but the wrath of God abides on him" (Jn 3:36). Seeing life in Jn 3:36 is based on faith and is equivalent to having eternal life. However, both spiritual life and seeing the kingdom are the result of the spiritual birth mentioned in Jn 3:3. Therefore, seeing life, having eternal life, and seeing the kingdom appear to be synonymous and interchangeable in this passage.

To see life is to escape God's soteriological wrath (Jn 3:36).[1313] One can either see life or see death (Jn 8:51). To see death is to taste death (Jn 8:52). To taste death is to experience death (Mt 16:28; Mk 9:1; Lk 9:27; Heb 2:9). It is to enter into the realm of death. The supposed distinction between seeing and entering in Jn 3:3,5 may be more imagined than real. To see the kingdom may simply mean to experience the kingdom and thus to enter the kingdom.

Entering the kingdom, entering life, and having eternal life can be used synonymously. Having eternal life and entering into life appear to be used somewhat synonymously in Mt 19:16-17. This is certainly the case in Jn 5:24, where John records Jesus as saying, "Truly, truly, I say to you, he who hears My word, and believes Him who sent Me, **has eternal life**, and does not come into judgment, but has **passed** out of death **into life**." Having eternal life is equated with entering life in John's gospel. A comparison of Mt 18:8-9 with its parallel in Mk 9:43-47 shows that entering life and entering the kingdom can also be used synonymously. Therefore, to enter the kingdom can mean to enter life, which in turn can mean to have eternal life. To enter the kingdom can simply mean to have eternal life. This conclusion is further supported by the discussion above in which it was shown that some verses of Scripture show a soteriological entrance into the kingdom that is based exclusively upon believing.

Types of Water

Consequently, it appears best to conclude that seeing the kingdom in Jn 3:3 is synonymous with entering the kingdom in Jn 3:5. In like manner, it is better to take *anothen*—being born *again* (also translatable as *from above*)—in Jn 3:3 synonymously with being born *of the water and Spirit* in Jn 3:5. The words and phrases employed in Jn 3:3 and Jn 3:5 are being used congruently. Grace interpreters are free to choose any one of the four remaining possibilities for water: embryonic fluid, rain, male semen, or spiritual semen.

Female Water

Wilkin (GNTC) prefers the first option. In Jn 3:6, Jesus informs Nicodemus that natural birth and spiritual birth are both necessary. In Jn 3:5, Jesus may be alluding to the same thing, and thus the female bag of waters is a good possibility.

Rainwater

Hodges rejects the natural birth interpretation (taken by Wilkin), citing Guthrie that "no parallel exists to support the connection of water-birth with physical birth."[1314] Hodges argues that the water is rainwater from above; after all, *Spirit* can be interpreted as *wind*. The primary passages in support of this option are Is 44:3-5 and Prov 30:4-5.[1315] However, concerning another matter, Reisser informs us regarding the Baal cult, Baal "is the mythical generative power that fructifies the earth by means of the **sperm of rain**."[1316] Even if the reference is to rain, one correspondingly might wonder if rain could be thought of as a picture of sperm.

Male Water

Indeed, rainwater can be taken as a reference to sperm. In fact, there are very good reasons for believing that water is being used as a metaphor for sperm in this passage. Morris agrees with Odeberg in this regard: "Odeberg has gathered an impressive array of passages from Rabbinic, Mandaean, and Hermetic sources to show that terms like 'water,' 'rain,' 'dew,' and 'drop' are often used of male semen"; he has many citations from Rabbinic material that would seem to indicate that water, particularly water from above, can refer to male semen.[1317] Terms like 'water' are often used by rabbis and others in antiquity to refer to male semen. Thus, Jesus could be contrasting being born of human sperm with being born of the Holy Spirit. This interpretation would be very similar to that offered by Wilkin above, in which Jn 3:5 is pictured as contrasting physical birth with spiritual birth. The difference between Wilkin's interpretation and this one is that water associated with physical birth is male water (semen) rather than the female water (bag of waters).

Spiritual Water

Morris, however, appears to be correct in considering the better option as taking "'water' and 'Spirit' closely together to give a meaning like 'spiritual seed.'"[1318] Indeed, this is Odeberg's position.[1319] The verb for born in Jn 3:3-8 is *gennao*. This verb is generally, although not always, associated with the male parent's role in birth. John uses this verb in this way in 1Jn 3:9 where he declares that everyone who has been *begotten* (*gennao*, in contrast to the female role in birth—*conceived*) of God has His *seed* (*sperma*, sperm) permanently within him. Physical birth is a result of physical sperm, and spiritual birth is a result of spiritual sperm.

Jesus is using this figurative language to make a very good analogy since even in physical birth it is impossible to take the father's sperm out of the child. Once the egg and the sperm have been united and resulted in birth, it is absolutely impossible to go back and separate the sperm from the egg. That egg has become something new—a new creature. It has permanently been made a new creature as an act of procreation. It cannot be uncreated. Likewise, anyone who has been procreated by God has been created a new creature eternally. To take the father's sperm out of the newborn child is impossible. Nor can the child grow up and lose his father's sperm, which has permanently become a part of his or her genetic makeup. The father's nature has been implanted permanently in his child through his transfer of DNA.* This *water* is thus a beautiful picture of living water (of the father's sperm living on in his child) and thus OSAS.

John records many images of this spiritual water, that is, this living water that gives life. In Jn 4:14, it is pictured as an internal well. In Jn 7:38, it is an internal river. In Rev 7:17 and 21:6, it is an external spring. In Rev 22:1, it is an external river. In Jn 3:5, it is internal sperm. The water in Jn 3:5 results in birth. It gives life. It is not baptismal water but spiritual water. This spiritual water in Jn 3:5 is pictured as spiritual seed, that is, spiritual sperm. The life-giving seed in Lk 8:5,11 and 1Pet 1:23 is plant seed (*sporos*).[1320] (*Sperma* can refer to plant seed, male seed, or divine seed.) In Lk 8:5,11 and 1Pet 1:23, the word of God is pictured as the plant seed. In Jn 3:5, living water is pictured as the divine seed. Or as Odeberg says,

> That which is to become spirit must be born spiritually from a spiritual semen…[the water of Jn 3:5] is that which in the spiritual process corresponds to the semen in the sarcical process. …Nevertheless it shall be maintained that the sense of the term 'water' is not restricted to that of (spiritual) 'semen,' but there are certainly, after [Johannine] fashion, allusions to other ideas, and, may it be said, a whole world of ideas.…These ideas may be summed up…waters from above—Life-giving, Living Water— the Divine Gift coming down from on high—waters of Eternal Life.[1321]

This water-birth does not refer to physical birth (female or male water); it refers to spiritual birth. The impartation of spiritual life by the Spirit is likened to water in Jn 3:5 and wind in Jn 3:8. Rain certainly would be included in the sphere of ideas to which Jesus refers in Jn 3:5. But the specific imagery being employed in Jn 3:5 in reference to that sphere is water/rain as spiritual sperm. The studies by Hodges and Odeberg appear to be more complementary than contradictory. Hodges' rainwater may be taken as Odeberg's spiritual semen. Spiritual birth requires a spiritual Father who spiritually begets His children with spiritual semen. This spiritual birth is the only requirement for this soteriological entrance into the kingdom.

Misthological Inheritance

Spiritual birth makes a believer a child of God who is thus qualified to enter the kingdom of God. A difference must be maintained between soteriologically entering the kingdom and inheriting it, however. Although all children of God are heirs of God (Rom 8:17), not all heirs of God are heirs of the kingdom (Jam 2:5). Being an heir of the kingdom or inheriting the kingdom deals strictly with misthological concepts. These are some of the ways used in the Bible to describe owning the kingdom rather than merely entering it.

Illustration 268. Kingdom Inheritance

Mt 25:34		
1Cor 6:9-10	Gal 5:21	Eph 5:5
1Cor 15:50		
Jam 2:5		

---

* See *Ontological Sinlessness*, 771; *Person versus Nature*, 792.

Jesus pronounces a misthological blessing upon the sheep who inherit the kingdom saying, "Come, you who are blessed of My Father, inherit the kingdom prepared for you from the foundation of the world....**because**...you gave...you gave...you invited...you clothed...and you visited" (Mt 25:34-36). Jesus tells them that the reason they are inheriting it is **because** of the works they have done on His behalf. The preparation (*hetoimazo*) of this inheritance for them in the Matthean text is conditioned on their works (cf. Jn 14:2-3). Their performance has qualified them for this inheritance. Incidentally, the fact that this inheritance of the kingdom is *from the foundation of the world* would denote its permanence just as the presence of one's name in the Book of Life *from the foundation of the world* denotes its permanence (Rev 13:8). Whereas the latter provides soteriological security, the former describes misthological security. The misthological significance of this statement is that the inheritance is eternal. Rewards are eternal.

On three separate occasions, Paul warned believers in three different churches that they would fail to inherit the kingdom if their practice was substandard.[*] Subcomers will not inherit the kingdom. The significance of the first of these three passages has been adequately presented as being a warning addressed to genuine believers who were genuinely guilty of practicing the very sins that would disqualify them from inheriting the kingdom.[†] The other two Pauline passages are conceptual parallels.

Concerning the passage in Gal 5:21, Zeller backloads the gospel while at the same time conceding: "**Admittedly a believer can walk in the flesh at times and struggle with carnality, but** because of the indwelling presence of the Spirit, his whole life is **not** dominated by the flesh **as it once was**."[1322] In other words, as a believer you can walk in the flesh and struggle with the flesh as long as you do it less frequently and less intensely than you did before you became saved; otherwise, you are not really saved. Your entrance into heaven is ultimately determined by how much you walk according to the flesh. If you are excessively carnal, then you are lost. If you are mildly carnal, then you are saved. Zeller conditions your entrance into heaven upon your walk on earth. This is nothing less than the typical backloading of the gospel in soft LS. Justification must result in a pronounced degree of practical sanctification, or it will fail to result in soteriological glorification. This is the necessary conclusion for those who take inheritance of the kingdom as soteriologically equivalent to entrance into the kingdom in Gal 5:21.[‡]

Wilkin, on the other hand, devotes an entire article to this verse, defending the FG interpretation that the passage is talking about inheriting the kingdom as a reward rather than receiving it as a gift.[1323] The misthological nature of the inheritance is the natural reading since it is based on their practice—that is, their practical sanctification:

> [19]Now the **deeds** of the flesh are evident, which are: immorality, impurity, sensuality, [20]idolatry, sorcery, enmities, strife, jealousy, outbursts of anger, disputes, dissensions, factions, [21]envying, drunkenness, carousing, and things like these, of which **I forewarn you** just as I have forewarned you that those who practice such things shall not **inherit** the kingdom of God. (Gal 5:19-21)

The inheritance is based on *deeds*, that is, on their works. The warning about the potential failure to inherit the kingdom is addressed to the Galatians, thus to genuine believers.[§] Believers are the ones being warned about the potential danger of not inheriting the kingdom. The warning is that those believers who walk according to the flesh, that is, who practice sin, merely will enter the kingdom, not inherit it. Zeller attempts to counter the FG position by pointing out that believers "have crucified the flesh" (Gal 5:24). However, in doing so he fails to consider the difference between having crucified the flesh positionally versus experientially. Some Calvinists have used this verse to say that all true believers "**will** crucify the flesh," in an attempt to turn this positional affirmation into a practical confirmation of perseverance in faithfulness. This is a fallacy. The text says that they *have* not *will* crucify the flesh. Although the context is talking about practice, the point of the passage is that their practice was not matching their position, so they will not inherit the kingdom.

Zeller cites Rom 8:9 in support of his supposition that practice matches position. Here, Paul states, "Believers are not **in** the flesh." Again, Zeller presumes that positional truth determines the believer's practical walk. However, the context again runs counter to such claim. Paul immediately goes on to caution these believers: "If you are living according to the flesh, you must die" (Rom 8:13). This warning is addressed to believers

---

[*] See second line in *Illustration 268*, which provides three parallel passages.
[†] See *Three Options Concerning Portion*, 118.
[‡] See "Misthological Warning to Soteriological Heirs" in *Fallen from Grace but Not from Perfection*.
[§] See "Eternal Security in Galatians" in *Fallen from Grace but Not from Perfection*.

concerning the peril of walking, or in this case *living*, according to the flesh. Believers may live and walk according to the flesh.

In characteristic fashion, Zeller glosses over Paul's statement in 1Cor 3:3 much too quickly: "**You are still fleshly**. For since there is jealousy and strife among you, are you not fleshly, and are you not walking like mere men?" According to Paul, believers might not only walk according to the flesh, they might be labeled as fleshly (i.e., carnal) in terms of their practice. As to the doctrine of co-crucifixion in Romans, immediately after affirming that the believer's old self has been crucified with Christ (Rom 6:6), Paul goes on to exhort the believers: "Therefore do not let sin reign in your mortal body that you should obey its lusts" (Rom 6:12). Obviously, Paul was concerned that sin might rule in their fleshly bodies. It is just as possible for believers to live a defeated Christian life as it is for them to live a victorious Christian life.

James also concurs with Paul that only those believers who genuinely love the Lord will inherit the kingdom (Jam 2:5). Those genuine believers who do not genuinely love the Lord will be temporally and misthologically accursed.[*] They will be rejected from inheriting the kingdom in the future when as believers they will have resurrected bodies (1Cor 15:50).

There will be those within the millennial kingdom who are in their flesh and blood bodies. Either they or their parents enter the kingdom in their physical bodies. Consequently, there must be a difference between entering and inheriting the kingdom. Some will **enter** it in their flesh and blood bodies and procreate in the millennial kingdom, but others not only enter it but inherit it. They will thus not be in their flesh and blood bodies but have glorified bodies. Since some enter the kingdom in physical bodies while others inherit it, we cannot simplistically equate entering with inheriting. Again, the ultraistic solution is misthologically unsatisfactory.

Inheriting the Kingdom

Since some passages of Scripture refer exclusively to soteriological **entrance** into the kingdom by faith alone and since **inheriting** the kingdom is a misthological concept dependent upon works, entrance into the kingdom is not necessarily synonymous with inheriting the kingdom. The ultraistic position must be rejected which equates entering the kingdom with inheriting the kingdom. These concepts are not always synonymous. When misthological entrance into the kingdom is in view, then misthological inheritance of the kingdom is likewise understood. Conversely, when a strictly soteriological entrance into the kingdom is solely in view, then misthological inheritance of the kingdom cannot be the intended meaning.

There are a variety of ways in which the Bible describes possession of the kingdom; inheritance is just one of them. In the flow chart (*Illustration 269*), the wording of Mt 5:3,10 in the NAS has been changed to agree with its rendition of the similar phrase in Mt 19:14. To say that the *kingdom is yours* is the same as saying that *it belongs to you*. In Lk 12:31-34, it is readily apparent that the kingdom in this passage is given as a reward rather than a gift.

The Greek word for *give* in Lk 12:32 is *didomi*, concerning which it already has noted that the context determines whether what is being given is merited or unmerited.[†] That which is given may be a reward—a payment. The kingdom in Lk 12:32 is a treasure to be bought—earned. The unfailing nature of this treasure again suggests its unending character. Rewards are eternal.

As has also been pointed out in the previous discussion of Heb 12:28, the kingdom can be received as a gift or a reward depending on the context.[‡] It is one thing to receive a paycheck and quite another to receive a gift. That both are received does not mean that both are free. The blessing that is earned in Mt 25:34-36 is the inheritance of the kingdom based on what they have done. In Jam 2:5 the reward promised for loving the Lord is the kingdom as an inheritance. In 1Cor 6:9-10, Gal 5:21, and Eph 5:5, those believers who practice evil will not inherit the kingdom. They will enter it but not possess it. Soteriological entrance is free. Misthological entrance (i.e., possession) is not free. There is also an interesting parallel concerning misthological entrance in 2Pet 1:10-11. Both inheritance of the kingdom and misthological entrance are based on our practice, and both concepts describe the same thing—possession/rulership of the kingdom.

---

[*] See author's discussion of *1Cor 16:22* in *Carnal Corinth*.
[†] See *The Tree is not Free*, 509.
[‡] See *Reception of the Unshakable Kingdom*, 525.

Illustration 269. Expressions of Possession

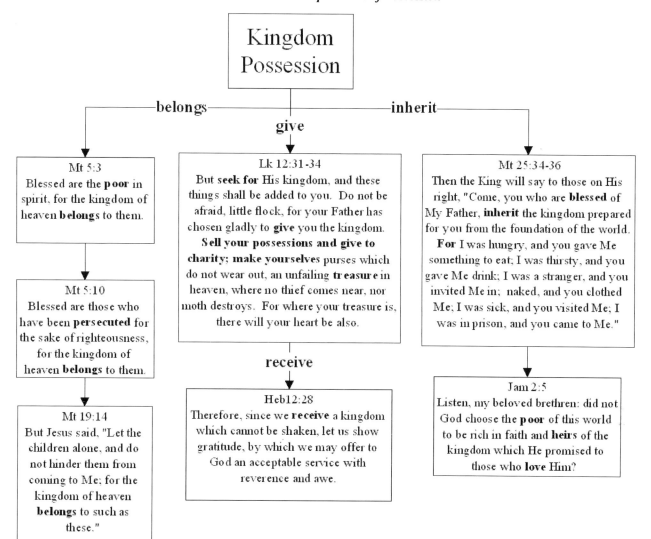

This overview of the kingdom has interacted with the principal texts and arguments for the exclusionist position concerning the kingdom and has found them lacking. However, complete rejection of the ultraistic position or absolute acceptance of the conservative position has been considered unwise. There are some texts where entrance into the kingdom is not free. However, what is at stake is not millennial exclusion from the kingdom, as the ultraists claim, but permanent exclusion. It is permanent exclusion from an experiential reign rather than a spatial realm. Just as rewards are eternal so lack of rewards is eternal. All believers will enter the kingdom but not all will enter the kingship. As can be seen in a related appendix, there are numerous texts where kingdom may actually mean kingship.

---

* See *Illustration 274. Statistical Basis for Kingdom/Kingship*, 765.

Illustration 270. Statistical Summation of Kingdom

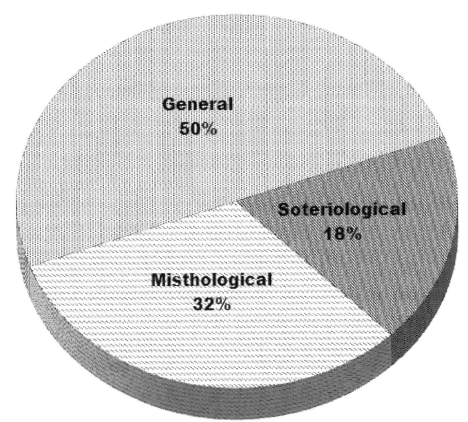

Primary & Secondary

About half the time the kingdom is referred to in the NT, it might be regarded as generic or ambiguous as to its misthological versus soteriological status. However, as seen above, when specificity is contextually permissible, the ratio is three to two in favor of a misthological understanding of the kingdom. In other words, the kingdom is a reward much more often than it is a simple gift. The previous discussions of kingship have delved into the Johannine[*] and Pauline[†] dimensions of this topic. To recapitulate the earlier findings concerning the dual nature of *basileia* as meaning either *kingship* or *kingdom*, this time we will hear from Peter as attested by two writers. Klappert and Best point out the harmony between these three biblical writers: John, Paul, and Peter. But since I already have noted the misthological agreement of the Johannine and Pauline material, I will allow this pair of writers (a commentator and a lexicographer) to illustrate the Petrine concord this time. Klappert defines *basileia* as "kingship, kingly rule, kingdom" and then proceeds to explain:

> The thought of the people of God sharing in **kingship** goes back to the OT. Exod. 19:6 contains the promise…"And you shall be to me a kingdom of priests…(cf. Isa. 61:6). This thought is applied to Christian believers in Rev. 1:6 and 5:10 (where *basileia* is used in both cases)….
>
> The same thought occurs in 1 Pet. 2:9: "But you are a chosen race, a royal priesthood…[royal/*basileios*] can be taken either as a neut. adj.…or as a noun, i.e. **group of kings** (cf. E. Best, 1 Peter, 1971, 107 f.). Although there is no actual occurrence of the word in this sense, Best holds that its form indicates that such meaning is possible. Moreover, it accords with the Targumic interpretation of Exod. 19:6 and the Christian tradition of Rev. 5:10, where the glorified saints "shall reign [*basileusousin = basileuo*] on earth" (cf. Rev. 1:6).
>
> The vb. *basileuo,* reign, is used of the **reign of believers** in Rom 5:17…and Rev. 20:4, 6; 20:5 (of the reign of the saints on earth and in glory).[1324]

---

[*] See *Present—Future*, 54.
[†] See *Misthological Entrance*, 571.

Best, therefore, concludes "that the word 'royal' is to be taken as a noun, preferably with the meaning 'group of kings.'"[1325] But what makes these kings one group? It is the fact that they co-rule over one kingdom in service to one King, who is King of kings. Therefore, the best way to define Best's *group of kings* is *kingship*, that is, a group of kings co-ruling with and under one King over one kingdom. Or as was stated previously, in these particular contexts, *basileia* would be well translated, "a rulership of rulers" (a kingdom ruled over by one group of kings, cf. 2Tim 2:12). In those contexts in which *basileia* refers to priests in this manner, it is best translated, "a rulership of priests" or "priestly kings." All believers will enter the territorial kingdom, but not all believers will enter the experiential kingship. To be in the outer darkness is to be excluded from the *basileia* (kingdom/kingship) in one sense of the word but not the other. Thus, in contrast to ultraistic misthologists who advocate spatial kingdom exclusion, the present writer only affirms experiential kingdom exclusion.

Achan's Entrance into the Kingdom

Surprisingly perhaps, Achan plays a very interesting role in typological discussions about kingdom entrance and exclusion, especially in relation to kingdom *rest*. In a personal correspondence with Finley, a very gracious ultraistic writer, the present author and he accessed the present state of the conservative misthological argument at that time, which was that all believers enter the millennial kingdom.[1326] Finley's manuscript, *Worthy Of The Kingdom*, had precipitated an inquiry on his part concerning the typological problem that Achan might present in regard to kingdom entrance and the conservative view of *rest*. The present author pointed out that Hodges had dealt with this *rest* Heb 3-4 in BKC and basically had presented three arguments that inheriting the kingdom is not equated with entering it or inhabiting it but refers to the greater experience of ruling it. Hodges' three arguments are: (1) *inherit ≠ enter*, (2) *inherit > enter*, and (3) *inherit > inhabit*.[1327] That is, (1) the inheritance is not to be equated with entering the kingdom. (2) Inheriting the kingdom refers to a greater experience than merely entering the kingdom or (3) inhabiting the kingdom. Hodges' conclusions were based on 1Cor 15:50 and the OT background. His arguments are solid but limited. They do not actually prove that unfaithful believers will enter the millennial kingdom.

Hodges further argues that the *inheritance*, *rest*, and *rulership* of the millennial kingdom are merited. Most readers thereby would assume that this *rest* is different from entrance into the millennial kingdom, since it is popularly assumed that entrance into the millennial kingdom is unmerited. Nevertheless, Hodges does not prove this assumption. His unproven underlying argument is that unmerited entrance into the present kingdom results in unmerited entrance into the future millennial kingdom (i.e., *present ⇒ future*). His unspoken premise is that if a believer has entrance into the present kingdom, then he or she will have entrance into all forms of the future kingdom, including the millennial kingdom.

Dillow presents the same arguments with the same shortcomings.[1328] He assumes that his citations of Jn 3:3,5 establish his point that entrance into the millennial kingdom is unmerited (i.e., *present ⇒ future*) and that such entrance is based simply upon the new birth. Therefore, the conservative position that all believers will enter the millennial kingdom was based at that point in time on these four points: (1) inherit ≠ enter; (2) inherit > enter; (3) inherit > inhabit, (4) present ⇒ future. Dillow did not add a fifth argument (i.e., *Achan = enter*), which was what prompted Finley's inquiry. Since the present appendix is interacting with the ultraistic understanding of the kingdom entrance, the present author's interaction with Finley will be included here. Albeit, due to its condensed and technical nature, the general reader may wish to skip to the conclusion of this appendix.

Ultraistic Argument

Achan ≠ Enter

Even though Dillow did not add the fifth argument, he nevertheless does resume his argument that unfaithful believers will enter the millennial kingdom with the **example** of Achan.[1329] Dillow considers Achan as representative of unfaithful believers who enter the millennial kingdom (*Achan = enter*). Obviously, I am allowing the equal sign to serve as an abbreviation for typological equality. But it would probably be too strong of an assessment to assert that Dillow claims that the example of Achan proves that subcomers can enter the kingdom but not inherit it. He does not base this claim on the example of Achan. If he had taken an *Achan = enter* as being typological proof that subcomers will enter the kingdom, then ultraists easily could respond to his argument by claiming that Dillow is outside of the typological boundaries of Heb 3-4 in including Achan.

Illustration 271. Achan's Lack of Rest

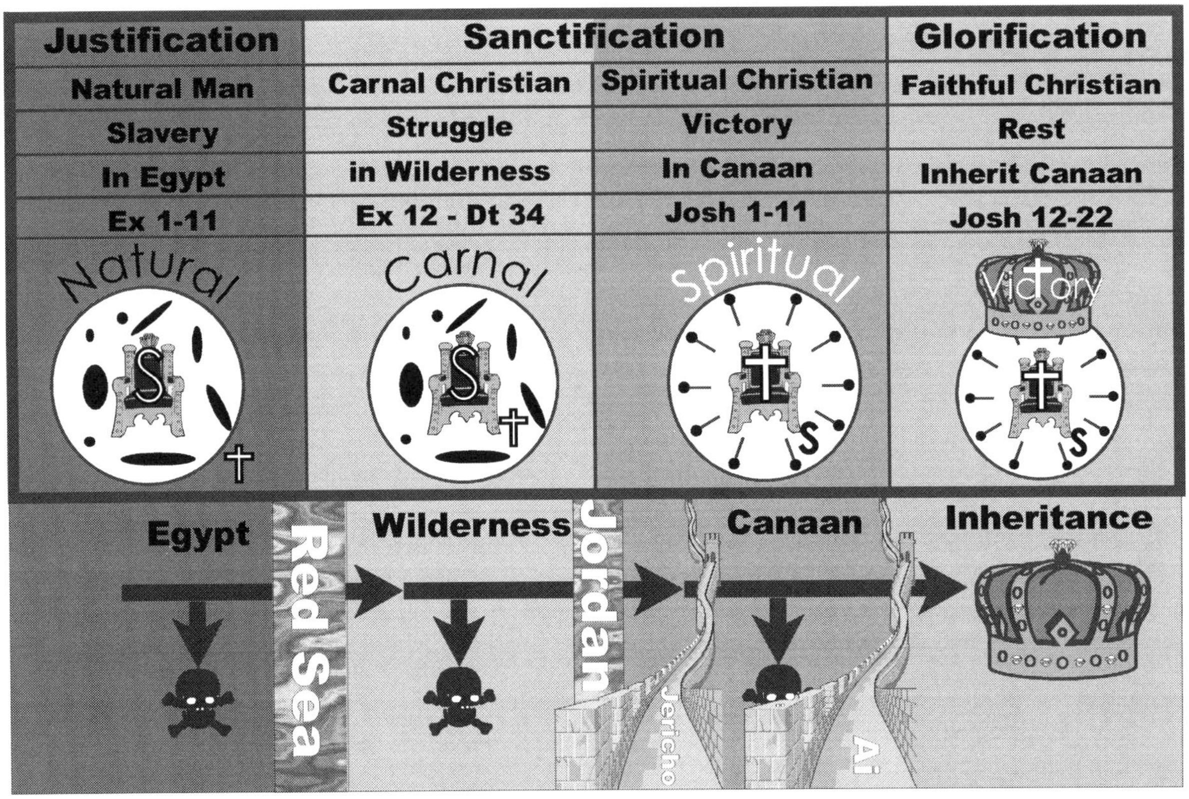
Justification
Sanctification
Glorification
Natural Man
Carnal Christian
Spiritual Christian
Faithful Christian
Slavery
Struggle
Victory
Rest
In Egypt
in Wilderness
In Canaan
Inherit Canaan
Ex 1-11
Ex 12 - Dt 34
Josh 1-11
Josh 12-22
Natural
Carnal
Spiritual
Victory
Egypt
Red Sea
Wilderness
Jordan
Canaan
Inheritance
Jericho
Ai

The difficulty the ultraists still face, however, is that of explaining Heb 4:8 and the OT background to which the writer of Hebrews is referring. "For if Joshua had given *them* rest, He would not have spoken of another day after that." Achan was part of those (the *them*) who entered the land with Joshua in Heb 4:8. But the *rest* was not experienced when the Israelites entered the land. Rest was not experienced until much later (Josh 11:23; cp. 22:4; 23:1). To *inherit* the land is to *possess* it (Josh 18:2-3). To *possess* the land is to have *rest* (Josh 21:43-45). Therefore, to *inherit* the land means to *possess* it and have *rest*; these terms mean more than merely to enter the land. This was anticipated in Dt 3:18-20 where the Israelites were told in advance that they would not have rest when they entered the land but when they took possession of it (so also Dt 1:8; Num 13:30; 14:24). Therefore, Dt 12:8-10 is not referring merely to entering a place; it is referring to entering that place and taking possession of it so that it may become a place of rest—a resting place and an inheritance. For these reasons, it is reasonable to agree with Dillow that Achan is a legitimate part of the typological background. Still, even so, although Achan strengthens and greatly illustrates the conservative position, it is doubtful that Achan's inclusion in the typology is actually necessary for the conservative understanding of the passage.

Achan causes considerable trouble for the ultraists if they believe that *the rest* = ***the land of Canaan*** = *the millennial kingdom* because then they have a subcomer like Achan in the millennial kingdom. But they need not take such a position. Ultraists need only prove that *the rest* = *the millennial kingdom*. Ultraists do not need to include *the land of Canaan* in their equation. On the other hand, if conservatives were unperceptive enough to say that *the land of Canaan* = *the millennial kingdom*, then they could easily be refuted from the ultraistic perspective (without even rejecting the typological reference to Achan). If *the land of Canaan* = *the millennial kingdom* and Achan's entrance into the land of Canaan proves that those who fail to overcome will enter the millennial kingdom, then the exclusion of those who died in the wilderness from that land proves that there will be other believers who fail to enter the millennial kingdom at all. The result would be that some believers who fail to overcome are allowed into the kingdom while others are not. Rather than adopt such an inconsistent conclusion, it would be better to admit that Achan does not prove that unfaithful believers enter the millennial kingdom because *the land of Canaan* ≠ *the millennial kingdom*. If he represents an unfaithful believer who enters the millennial kingdom, it must be for another reason. One would think that conservatives, ultraists, and moderates should be able to agree that *the land of Canaan* ≠ *the millennial kingdom*.

Ultraists would have a better line of attack if they agreed with Dillow that Achan is part of the typological illustration and then turned to the references that Dillow himself gives concerning the land and to his definition of the rest and from these show that Achan (as well as other unfaithful believers) never enters the land of rest. They could argue that *the rest = the millennial kingdom* and conclude on the basis of Dillow's references and definition that Achan represents those who enter into spiritual warfare but fail to win that war. Ultraists could then conclude that those who died in the wilderness show that carnal believers will not enter the millennial kingdom, and Achan shows that it is possible for spiritual believers to fail to enter it as well. The typology shows Achan's entrance into the land of war, not into the land of rest (*Achan ≠ enter*). As the present writer pointed out to Finley, if the present author were persuaded by the ultraistic position, this is the type of argument he would employ since Achan is evidently a legitimate part of the typology. Dillow's example of Achan is based upon his previous conclusion that one can enter the kingdom but not inherit it. He draws this conclusion from Jn 3:3.[1330] It is the *present ⇒ future* argument.

Dillow does not claim that *the land of Canaan = the millennial kingdom*; rather, "entering Canaan is not to be equated with entering the kingdom," since a believer enters the kingdom at the point of spiritual birth (Jn 3:3).[1331] Entering Canaan pictures a believer entering into submission to the Lordship of Christ in spiritual warfare. According to Dillow, entrance into Canaan does not picture entrance into the kingdom or the millennial kingdom. Therefore, Achan's entrance into the land would not prove that one can enter the millennial kingdom without inheriting it. *Achan = enter* not because Achan entered Canaan but because Achan had entered the inaugurated form of the kingdom, since he is typologically a part of those who had come out of Egypt. Achan entered the kingdom typologically in the same manner in which those who died in the wilderness did without entering Canaan. Dillow uses Achan as part of his argument to prove the nature of the *rest*. He does not use Achan to prove that unfaithful believers enter the millennial kingdom. He does not argue that Achan's entrance into the land proves that those who fail to overcome will enter the millennial kingdom. He relies exclusively on the conservative *present ⇒ future* assumption for this aspect of his argument. His *Achan = enter* applies only to the nature of the rest; Achan entered the land without entering the rest.

Ultraists could respond that *the rest = the millennial kingdom ≠ the land* and that Achan is simply another picture of an unfaithful believer who does not enter the millennial kingdom. Dillow's argument concerning Achan does not advance the conservative argument that unfaithful believers enter the millennial kingdom beyond its fourth argument (*present ⇒ future*). It is based on this conservative assumption, so ultraists need only assail this assumption rather than Achan's inclusion. In other words, Dillow's *Achan = enter* is equivalent to *present ⇒ future* concerning the issue of whether unfaithful believers enter into the millennial kingdom. An ultraist could accept Dillow's *Achan = enter* (land) and still maintain *Achan ≠ enter* (millennial kingdom).

Present ⇏ Future

The conservatives assume that present entrance into the kingdom guarantees millennial entrance into the kingdom (i.e., *present ⇒ future*). Ultraists can challenge this conservative assumption concerning Jn 3:5 by pointing out that being co-seated with Christ at the right hand of the Father presently and positionally (Eph 1:20; 2:6; Col 3:1) does not guarantee that the believer will be co-seated with Him millennially or experientially (Rev 3:21).[1332] Certain things are true of us positionally (and potentially) that will only become true of us experientially if we overcome. Thus, the conservative assumption—if you enter the kingdom in the present, you will enter it in the future millennium (*present ⇒ future*)—does not necessarily follow. As a result, present positional entrance does not necessarily guarantee future millennial or experiential entrance (*present ⇏ future*).

Provisional Entrance

Moreover, Faust counters the conservative argument by contending that there is no such thing as present entrance (which would not only rule out positional but mystical entrance as well) and cites Peters in support of concluding that any present entrance is merely potential, provisional, allegorical, parabolic, and figurative.[1333] He would thus treat Col 1:13 as talking about provisional entrance into the kingdom: "For He delivered us from the domain of darkness, and **transferred us into the kingdom** of His beloved Son" (TM). The present work, on the other hand, would be more inclined to take the conservative route that the transference into the kingdom and deliverance from darkness are both positional in this verse, as Paul explains with a temporal marker. "For you were formerly darkness, but **now** you are light in the Lord" (Eph 5:8). However, this does not mean that Faust's ultraistic argument is without force. The present work agrees with Faust that Rev 1:6 is indeed provisional; where the NKJ says that God "has made us kings." As was explained previously, this verse does indeed picture a potential and thus conditional rulership.[*] The present work is also sympathetic with the provisional nature of other truths such as the inheritance, atonement, and victory.[†]

My minor quibble with Faust on some of these matters would be over my preference to describe such truths as positional **and** potential, rather than just strictly potential. The present positional truth of being seated with Christ provides us with spiritual authority right now, providing we appropriate that authority through faith. Our being seated with Christ is not exclusively future. It already has occurred (Eph 2:6; Col 3:1), and the positional reality of that event is supposed to be the dynamic by which we live in the present. Of course, we could not be seated positionally with Him in His kingdom if we were not already positionally in that kingdom.

Inherit > Enter/Inhabit

Ultraists would be much better off agreeing with the conservatives that inherit ≠ enter, inherit > enter, and inherit > inhabit. That is, there will be people in the millennial kingdom who enter it and who live there as inhabitants of the millennial kingdom who do not have the greater privilege of inheriting the millennial kingdom. They could then claim that these observations do not prove that those who merely enter the millennial kingdom and inhabit it are unfaithful believers. On the contrary, they could acknowledge that those who enter the millennial kingdom are the children. Further, they could agree that the descendants who compose the millennial nations of Rev 20:8 are descendants of those children who merely enter the millennial kingdom. These two groups merely inhabit the kingdom without inheriting it. Therefore, there is no reason to conclude on the basis of these three conservative arguments that unfaithful believers will enter or inhabit the kingdom. Rather, those who merely enter the millennial kingdom and inhabit it are the children and their descendants, not unfaithful believers. In summary, if the present writer were an ultraist, he would take these positions: (1) *inherit ≠ enter*; (2) *inherit > enter*; (3) *inherit > inhabit*; (4) *present ≠> future*; and (5) *Achan ≠ enter*.

Conclusion

The author has given thought to the ultraistic position and sought to envision what the terrain would look like through their eyes. Hopefully, in doing so the present work has found common ground where conservatives and ultraists can agree that entrance into the kingdom is both soteriological and misthological, but it is not soteriological in the traditional sense, which results in one having to work his or her way into heaven. Instead, entrance into the **kingdom** is free to all who believe, but entrance into the **kingship** is limited to the faithful.

Although Achan is a legitimate part of the typology, the differentiation between entering and inheriting the rest does not require his inclusion. If he is not included, then those who died in the wilderness failed to achieve misthological entrance into the kingdom, but this does not prove that they failed to enter the millennial kingdom any more than it proves they failed to enter the eternal kingdom. What they failed to enter is the rest, that is, the rulership of the land. If Achan is included in the typological consideration of what it means to enter the rest (which is the present author's preference), then Achan is part of a two-part typological illustration of the fact that unfaithful believers will not inherit the millennial kingdom or the eternal kingdom, and they will be excluded from certain places within both.

In this case, as depicted in *Illustration 271. Achan's Lack of Rest*, those who died in the **wilderness** typologically highlight the doctrinal fact that unfaithful believers will not enter the place or the experience of rest. Those like Achan who died in **Canaan** further show that even if one progresses in the practical sanctification to the point of experiencing the victorious Christian life, he or she still may fail to achieve the intended goal if he or she fails to persevere. Faithfulness is required for entrance into the heavenly rest, that is, the rulership of heaven. But such victorious perseverance is not required for entrance into the land of heaven itself. Taken together, these groups picture the fact that all blood-bought believers will enter the kingdom, but unfaithful believers will be limited spatially and experientially in both its millennial and eternal expressions. They will never obtain the rest either spatially or experientially. The outer darkness is permanent exclusion from this type of *rest*. As already demonstrated, the rest is a reward.[‡] This conclusion is not dependent upon the inclusion of Achan.

---

[*] See *Present—Future*, 54.
[†] See *Co-Life* 89. Also see author's discussion of "Three Types of Reconciliation" in *Carnal Corinth* and "Misthological Warning to Soteriological Heirs" in *Fallen from Grace but Not from Perfection*.
[‡] See *Rewarded Rest at Revelation*, 149. *Ever, Never, and Forever*, 525. *Rest*, 526. *City of Rest*, 551.

Appendix 3.
Kingdom and Kingship Statistics

Introduction

The distinction between the use of *basileia* as a soteriological place (*kingdom*) versus misthological experience (*kingship*) has been demonstrated repeatedly herein. At the same time, ongoing interaction with the differences of opinion among misthologists also has been provided. This appendix will summarize this material for easy statistical reference.

Conservative approach

The check marks on the following chart (*Illustration 274. Statistical Basis for Kingdom/Kingship*, 765) indicate that Acts 14:22 is an example of misthological entrance into the *kingship*, whereas Jn 3:5 is an example of soteriological entrance into the *kingdom*. Thus, the general distinction between *kingship* and *kingdom* is readily displayed. Even so, this distinction is not absolute in that Mk 9:47 is the singular exception, marked as both soteriological and misthological. In this verse, *basileia* soteriologically means kingdom; it misthologically means kingship. This particular verse has been counted twice.[1334] Thus, the statistical information was compiled by counting Mk 9:47 as a double occurrence: once as referring soteriologically to the kingdom and once as referring misthologically to the kingship. As a result, the percentage of the occurrences that *basileia* appears to mean *kingdom* is 52/164 not 52/163, although there are only 163 actual occurrences of the word. This unique marking of Mk 9:47 is due to the impression that the context does not leave the term ambiguous enough merely to mark it in the general category. Rather, the context indicates that both meanings are intended. Even as a classical misthologist, I interpret this verse in a neoclassical manner as having both meanings. Of course, neoclassicalists will insist, and perhaps rightly so, that this opens up the dike to other passages being understood in this dual manner. I would not disagree, but my present purpose is not to expand the neoclassical horizon so much as to view the terrain from as much a classical position as reasonably possible. After all, one needs a strong classical foundation if one is to build a case for a neoclassical position on top of it.

John the Baptist preaches repentance (Lk 3:3,7-14) as preparation for belief (Acts 19:4). Nevertheless, the single requirement for eternal life according to John the Baptist is belief (Jn 1:7; 3:34,36—KJV & NKJ). Jesus preaches the same message of repentance as John the Baptist (cf. Mt 3:2; 4:17). The summons for the lost to repent is a summons for unbelievers to change their behavior, which would aid them in becoming believers and thus in receiving soteriological entrance (cf. Mk 1:15). The repentance in Mk 1:15 is accompanied by a call to believe and thus could be understood as urging unbelievers to receive this soteriological kingdom experience. Repentance can take place before, during, or after saving faith. In my actual *ordo salutis*, however, repentance is relegated strictly to taking place after saving faith as a theological requirement for misthological salvation. Such distinctions are not in conflict since repentance is being viewed from different perspectives, on the one hand, as pertaining to temporal salvation and on other occasions as psychological preparation or as misthological necessitation. Jesus urges full repentance (of behavior and belief). Repentance results in temporal salvation and prepares the way for faith—faith being the single requirement for soteriological salvation. Once a person has believed, repentance becomes the requirement for misthological salvation. However, since the call in this verse is addressed to unbelievers rather than unbelievers, it is not marked misthologically.

The proclamation of the kingdom can be used to encourage a soteriological (Mk 1:15) and/or a misthological response (Mt 24:13).[1335] The general sense in which it is used in Mt 9:35 is not decisive as to which sense is intended. It is used in connection with a variety of kingdom parables, some of which are soteriological and some of which are misthological in the parallel passages of Mt 13 and Mk 4 (cf. Lk 13:18,20).

Illustration 272. The Gospel of the Kingdom

The *gospel of grace* in Acts 20:24 is a part of, not the sum total of, the *gospel of the kingdom*. The gospel of the kingdom includes this soteriological aspect but is not limited to it. The gospel of the kingdom is the whole message (Acts 20:27), and thus includes the soteriological plus misthological dimensions of the kingdom message. Consequently, the gospel of the kingdom concerns not only what is freely offered though grace, but also what is profitable (Acts 20:20). This fuller message encompasses the misthological message of inheriting the kingdom as well (Acts 20:32).

The denial of entrance in Mt 5:20 is the very emphatic Greek *ou me* and is translated as *at all* on the chart. This emphatic negative is used in regard to entrance of the kingdom in Mt 5:20; 18:3; Mk 10:15; Lk 18:17. In the later three usages of this emphatic negative concerning entrance, this emphatic negation is apparently used to deny soteriological entrance. The same appears true of Mt 5:20. Some believers will enter heaven by the skin of their teeth. Unbelievers will not enter it *at all*. Mt 5:20 is not saying that practical (i.e., imparted) righteousness is required for misthological entrance into the kingship. Rather, it appears to be saying that imputed righteousness is required for soteriological entrance into the kingdom.[*]

The Greek text in 2Tim 4:8 actually reads, "And will save me for/into His kingdom/kingship." Paul could be understood as describing **salvation** as misthological entrance into the kingship. Or he could be describing the **entrance** as misthological salvation. Salvation is not only from something (i.e., hell); it is also for something (i.e., heavenly rulership). In either case, the meaning is the same: Paul will be rewarded with misthological salvation/entrance pertaining to the kingship. Those who seek for (Mt 6:33) and hunger for (Mt 5:6) righteousness will be satisfied with the crown of righteousness (2Tim 4:8).[1336] They will be able to administer righteously.[1337]

---

[*] In this statement, only the classical view is being considered. For the neoclassical view to be applicable to this text, the classical view must also be applicable. For the neoclassical view is a combination, not convolution, of the classical and neo-ultraistic views. Writing predominately as a classical misthologist in this appendix, and for the most part throughout this book, I am allowing the classical view to stand on its own two feet without any assistance from the neoclassical view. The best defense for the neoclassic view is a strong offense for both the classic and neo-ultraistic views. I currently am writing more so as an offensive coordinator for the classic position, leaving the offensive coordination for the neo-ultraistic position to others, as well as the defensive coordination of the neoclassical combination. For example, if I were trying to formulate a neo-ultraistic position to complement the position taken above, I would point out that I also have taken *ou me* as meaning *never*. (See *Ou Me*, 487; *Never*, 633.) Elsewhere in my writings, I have shown a fondness for translating *ou me + an aorist subjunctive* emphatically as *never ever*. This is the same construction as found in Mt 5:20; 18:3; Mk 10:15; Lk 18:17. **Thus, these texts might be understood as simply affirming that unfaithful believers will *never ever* enter into the kingship, which is natural since loss of rewards is eternal. In that case,** instead of interpreting these passages as denying *any type* of entrance whatsoever (soteric and mistholic), **one might argue neo-ultraistically that any type of misthological entrance (last and first) is denied eternally. But if that is the case, then one in turn could further entertain the possibility that the duality of *ou me* (*at all, never*) is being used** purposefully to suggest both the classical and neo-ultraistic positions **so that a neoclassical combination is best**. At least I will set the hermeneutical ball up for the spike by pointing out this possibility for those misthologists who might like to follow through on that recourse. Even as a classical writer, I at least find this neoclassical position tempting and am willing to hold it out as a theoretical possibility. If this position should prove persuasive, it would combine the strengths of the classical and neo-ultraistic positions on some texts that are highly debated within misthological circles. Dogmatically insisting that my friends who hold a misthological view of Mt 5:20 and 7:21 are wrong is much more difficult when the possibility exists that we both may be right. Such is the principle of correlativity. For brief consideration of the neoclassical position, see *Joint Neoclassical Soteriology and Misthology*, 638; *Appendix 19. Neo-ultraistic and Neoclassic Entrance*, 947.

Illustration 273. Classical Pie Chart of Kingdom

Primary & Secondary

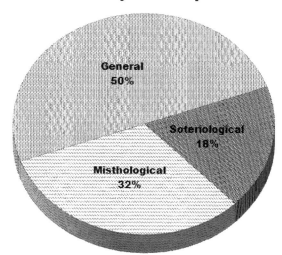

Illustration 274. Statistical Basis for Kingdom/Kingship

#	Ref.	*Basileia—Abbreviated Paraphrastic Translations*	G	S	M	K	E	I	Comment
1.	Mt 3:2	**Repent** for the *kingdom* is at hand.			✓				Mt 4:17
2.	Mt 4:8	The devil showed Jesus all the *kingdoms* of the world, and their glory.	✓						
3.	Mt 4:17	Jesus began to preach and say, "**Repent**, for the *kingdom* is at hand."			✓				Mk 1:15 -believe
4.	Mt 4:23	And Jesus was proclaiming the **gospel** of the *kingdom*.	✓						
5.	Mt 5:3	Blessed are the **poor** in spirit, for theirs **is** the *kingdom*.			✓	✓			possession
6.	Mt 5:10	Blessed are those who have been **persecuted** for theirs **is** the *kingdom*.			✓	✓			possession
7.	Mt 5:19a	Whoever annuls one of the least commandments will be **least** in the *kingdom*.			✓				status
8.	Mt 5:19b	Whoever keeps and teaches them, he will be **great** in the *kingdom*.			✓				status
9.	Mt 5:20	Unless your **righteousness** surpasses, you will not **enter** the *kingdom* at all.		✓			✓		
10.	Mt 6:10	Your *kingdom* come. Your will be done.	✓						Rev 17:12
11.	Mt 6:13	For Yours is the *kingdom* forever.	✓			✓			Rev 17:12
12.	Mt 6:33	**Seek** first His *kingdom* and His righteousness.			✓	✓			
13.	Mt 7:21	Those saying Lord will not **enter** the *kingdom*, but he who **does My ...will**.		✓			✓		Mt 21:31
14.	Mt 8:11	Many will **recline at the table** with Abraham…in the *kingdom*.			✓				
15.	Mt 8:12	The sons of the *kingdom* will be **cast out** into the **outer darkness**.			✓				out
16.	Mt 9:35	Jesus was proclaiming the **gospel** of the *kingdom*.	✓						
17.	Mt 10:7	Preach, saying, "The *kingdom* is at hand."	✓						
18.	Mt 11:11	He who is **least** in the *kingdom* is greater than John.			✓				status
19.	Mt 11:12	The *kingdom* suffers violence, and violent men **take it** by force.	✓						
20.	Mt 12:25	Any *kingdom* divided against itself is laid waste.	✓						
21.	Mt 12:26	If Satan is divided against himself, how will his *kingdom* stand?	✓						
22.	Mt 12:28	If I cast out demons by the Spirit, then the *kingdom* has come upon you.	✓						
23.	Mt 13:11	To you it has been granted to know the mysteries of the *kingdom*.	✓						
24.	Mt 13:19	Anyone hearing of the *kingdom* and not understanding…snatches away.		✓					
25.	Mt 13:24	The *kingdom* may be compared to a man who sowed good seed.		✓					
26.	Mt 13:31	The *kingdom* is like a mustard seed.	✓						
27.	Mt 13:33	The *kingdom* is like leaven.	✓						
28.	Mt 13:38	The good seed are the **sons of** the *kingdom*, and the tares are the sons of evil.		✓					
29.	Mt 13:41	All stumbling blocks and the lawlessness will **gather out** of His *kingdom*.		✓					out
30.	Mt 13:43	The **righteous** will shine as the sun in the *kingdom* of their Father.			✓	✓			
31.	Mt 13:44	The *kingdom* is like a hidden treasure, and he sells all that he has to buy it.	✓						
32.	Mt 13:45	The *kingdom* is like a merchant seeking fine pearls.	✓						
33.	Mt 13:47	The *kingdom* is like a dragnet…gathering fish of every kind.		✓					out; Mt 13:47
34.	Mt 13:52	Every…**disciple of** the *kingdom* is like the head of a household.	✓						
35.	Mt 16:19	I will give you the keys of the *kingdom*.	✓			✓			
36.	Mt 16:28	Some will not taste death until they **see** the Son coming in His *kingdom*.	✓						
37.	Mt 18:1	The disciples asked Jesus, "Who then is **greatest** in the *kingdom*?"			✓				status
38.	Mt 18:3	Unless you become like **children**, you will not **enter** the *kingdom* at all		✓			✓		
39.	Mt 18:4	Whoever humbles himself as this **child** is the **greatest** in the *kingdom*.			✓				status
40.	Mt 18:23	The *kingdom* is like a king who wished to settle accounts with his slaves.			✓				
41.	Mt 19:12	Have made themselves eunuchs for the **sake of** the *kingdom*.			✓	✓			Lk 18:29
42.	Mt 19:14	Let the **children** alone, for the *kingdom* **belongs to** such as these.			✓	✓			possession

#	Ref	Text	1	2	3	4	5	Notes
43.	Mt 19:23	It is hard for a rich man to **enter** the *kingdom*.		✓		✓		
44.	Mt 19:24	A camel cannot enter the eye of a needle, nor can the rich **enter** the *kingdom*.		✓		✓		
45.	Mt 20:1	The *kingdom* is like a landowner who **hired laborers for** his vineyard.			✓			
46.	Mt 20:21	Command that my sons may **sit** on Your **right** and **left** in Your *kingdom*.			✓	✓		status
47.	Mt 21:31	Which **did the will** of his father? Harlots are entering **into** the *kingdom*.		✓			✓	Jn 6:40
48.	Mt 21:43	The *kingdom* will be taken from you and given to a nation producing fruit.			✓	✓		
49.	Mt 22:2	The *kingdom* is like a king, who gave a **wedding feast** for his son.			✓	✓		
50.	Mt 23:13	You shut off the *kingdom* and do not **enter** nor allow those **entering** to **go in**.		✓		✓		
51.	Mt 24:7a	For nation will rise against nation, and *kingdom*	✓					
52.	Mt 24:7b	against *kingdom*, and there will be famines and earthquakes.	✓					
53.	Mt 24:14	And **this** gospel of the *kingdom* will be preached in the whole world.			✓	✓		Mt 24:13
54.	Mt 25:1	The *kingdom* is like **ten virgins**.			✓	✓		
55.	Mt 25:34	Come, you who are **blessed**, **inherit** the *kingdom* prepared for you.			✓	✓	✓	Possession
56.	Mt 26:29	I will never drink of this wine until I drink it new in My Father's *kingdom*.	✓					
57.	Mk 1:15	The *kingdom* is at hand; **repent and believe** in the gospel.		✓				Jn 1:7
58.	Mk 3:24a	If a *kingdom* is divided against itself.	✓					
59.	Mk 3:24b	that *kingdom* cannot stand.	✓					
60.	Mk 4:11	You have been granted the mysteries of the *kingdom*, but parables to the rest.	✓					
61.	Mk 4:26	The *kingdom* is like a man who casts seed upon the soil.		✓				
62.	Mk 4:30	How will we picture the *kingdom*, or by what parable will we present it?	✓					
63.	Mk 6:23	Whatever you ask of me, I will give it to you; up to half of my *kingdom*.	✓					
64.	Mk 9:1	Some will not taste death until they **see** the *kingdom*.	✓					
65.	Mk 9:47	It is better to **enter** the *kingdom* with one eye, than to be cast into Gehenna,		✓	✓	✓	✓	
66.	Mk 10:14	Permit the **children** to come to Me for the *kingdom* **belongs** to such as these.			✓			Possession
67.	Mk 10:15	Whoever does not **receive** the *kingdom* like a **child** will not **enter** it **at all**.		✓		✓		
68.	Mk 10:23	How hard it will be for those who are wealthy to **enter** the *kingdom*!		✓		✓		
69.	Mk 10:24	How hard it is to **enter** the *kingdom*!		✓		✓		
70.	Mk 10:25	A camel cannot enter the eye of a needle, nor can the rich **enter** the *kingdom*.		✓		✓		
71.	Mk 11:10	Blessed is the coming *kingdom* of our father David.	✓					
72.	Mk 12:34	You are **not far from** the *kingdom*.		✓				
73.	Mk 13:8a	For nation will arise against nation, and *kingdom*.	✓					
74.	Mk 13:8b	against *kingdom*.	✓					
75.	Mk 14:25	I will never again drink of this wine until I drink it new in the *kingdom*.	✓					
76.	Mk 15:43	Joseph of Arimathea was **waiting for** the *kingdom*.	✓					
77.	Lk 1:33	He will **reign** forever, and His *kingdom* will have no end.	✓			✓		
78.	Lk 4:5	And the Devil showed Jesus all the *kingdoms* of the world in a moment of time.	✓					
79.	Lk 4:43	I must preach the *kingdom* to the other cities also.	✓					
80.	Lk 6:20	Blessed are you who are **poor**, for yours **is** the *kingdom*.			✓	✓		Possession
81.	Lk 7:28	He who is **least** in the *kingdom* is greater than John.			✓			Status
82.	Lk 8:1	He was proclaiming and preaching the *kingdom*.	✓					Lk 8:10
83.	Lk 8:10	You have been granted the mysteries of the *kingdom*, but parables to the rest.	✓					Mt 13:11; Mk 4:11
84.	Lk 9:2	He sent them out to proclaim the *kingdom*.	✓					
85.	Lk 9:11	He began speaking to them about the *kingdom*.	✓					
86.	Lk 9:27	Some will not taste death until they **see** the *kingdom*.	✓					
87.	Lk 9:60	Go and proclaim the *kingdom* everywhere.	✓					
88.	Lk 9:62	No one who looks back is **fit for** the *kingdom*.			✓	✓		
89.	Lk 10:9	Heal the sick and say, "The *kingdom* has come near to you."	✓					
90.	Lk 10:11	We wipe off in protest against you; the *kingdom* has come near.		✓				
91.	Lk 11:2	Father, hallowed be Thy name. Thy *kingdom* come.	✓					
92.	Lk 11:17	Any *kingdom* divided against itself is laid waste.	✓					
93.	Lk 11:18	If Satan also is divided against himself, how will his *kingdom* stand?	✓					
94.	Lk 11:20	If I cast out demons by the finger, then the *kingdom* has come upon you.	✓					
95.	Lk 12:31	**Seek for** His *kingdom*, and these things will be added to you.			✓	✓		Lk 12:33
96.	Lk 12:32	Do not be afraid, for your Father has chosen gladly to **give** you the *kingdom*.			✓	✓		Lk 12:33
97.	Lk 13:18	What is the *kingdom* like, and to what will I compare it?	✓					
98.	Lk 13:20	To what will I compare the *kingdom*?	✓					
99.	Lk 13:28	You will see Abraham…**in** the *kingdom*, but yourselves **cast out**.		✓				out
100.	Lk 13:29	And they will come and **recline at the table** in the *kingdom*.			✓			Lk 14:30; status
101.	Lk 14:15	**One reclining** said, "**Blessed** is everyone who **eats** bread in the *kingdom*."			✓			
102.	Lk 16:16	The gospel of the *kingdom* is preached, and everyone is **forcing** his way **in**.	✓					
103.	Lk 17:20a	Now being questioned by the Pharisees as to when the *kingdom* was coming,	✓					
104.	Lk 17:20b	He answered, "The *kingdom* is not coming with signs to be observed."	✓					
105.	Lk 17:21	Behold, the *kingdom* is in your midst.	✓					
106.	Lk 18:16	Permit the **children** to come to Me for the *kingdom* **belongs** to such as these.			✓	✓		Possession
107.	Lk 18:17	Whoever does not **receive** the *kingdom* like a **child** will not **enter** it **at all**.		✓		✓		
108.	Lk 18:24	How hard it is for those who are wealthy to **enter** the *kingdom*!		✓		✓		
109.	Lk 18:25	A camel cannot enter the eye of a needle, nor can the rich **enter** the *kingdom*.		✓		✓		
110.	Lk 18:29	He who has left house or wife or brothers for the **sake of** the *kingdom*.			✓	✓		

#	Ref	Text	G	S	M	K	E	I	Notes
111.	Lk 19:11	They supposed that the *kingdom* was going to appear immediately.	✓						
112.	Lk 19:12	A certain nobleman went to a distant country to receive a *kingdom*.	✓						
113.	Lk 19:15	After receiving the *kingdom*, he questioned his slaves' service.	✓						
114.	Lk 21:10a	Nation will rise against nation, and *kingdom*	✓						
115.	Lk 21:10b	against *kingdom*.	✓						
116.	Lk 21:31	When you see these things happening, recognize that the *kingdom* is near.	✓						
117.	Lk 22:16	I will never again eat it until it is fulfilled in the *kingdom*.	✓						
118.	Lk 22:18	I will not drink it until the *kingdom* comes.	✓						
119.	Lk 22:29	Just as My Father has granted Me a *kingdom*, I grant you	✓			✓			
120.	Lk 22:30	**eat and drink at my table** in My *kingdom*, and you will **sit on thrones**.			✓	✓			
121.	Lk 23:42	Remember me when You **come in** Your *kingdom*!		✓		✓			
122.	Lk 23:51	Joseph was waiting for the *kingdom*.	✓						
123.	Jn 3:3	Unless one is **born again**, he cannot **see** the *kingdom*.		✓					
124.	Jn 3:5	Unless one is **born of water and the Spirit**, he cannot **enter** into the *kingdom*.		✓			✓		
125.	Jn 18:36a	My *kingdom* is not of this world.	✓			✓			
126.	Jn 18:36b	If My *kingdom* were of this world, then My servants would be fighting.	✓			✓			
127.	Jn 18:36c	My *kingdom* is not of this realm.	✓			✓			
128.	Acts 1:3	He presented Himself alive speaking of the things concerning the *kingdom*.	✓						
129.	Acts 1:6	Lord, is it at this time You are restoring the *kingdom* to Israel?	✓			✓			
130.	Acts 8:12	They believed Philip's gospel about the *kingdom*.	✓						
131.	Acts 14:22	**Through many tribulations** we **must enter** the *kingdom*.			✓	✓	✓		
132.	Acts 19:8	He was reasoning and persuading them about the *kingdom*.	✓						
133.	Acts 20:25	I went about preaching the *kingdom*.	✓						
134.	Acts 28:23	He was testifying about the *kingdom*, trying to persuade them about Jesus.		✓					Acts 28:24-28
135.	Acts 28:31	He was preaching the *kingdom* and teaching about the Lord Jesus Christ.	✓						
136.	Rom 14:17	The *kingdom* is not eating and drinking, but righteousness and peace and joy.	✓						
137.	1Cor 4:20	For the *kingdom* does not consist in words, but in power.	✓						
138.	1Cor 6:9	The **unrighteous** will not **inherit** the *kingdom*?			✓	✓		✓	Possession
139.	1Cor 6:10	Neither thieves… nor swindlers will **inherit** the *kingdom*.			✓	✓		✓	Possession
140.	1Cor 15:24	In the end He will deliver up the *kingdom* to the Father.	✓						
141.	1Cor 15:50	Flesh and blood cannot **inherit** the *kingdom*.			✓	✓		✓	Possession
142.	Gal 5:21	Those who practice such things will not **inherit** the *kingdom*.			✓	✓		✓	Possession
143.	Eph 5:5	No **immoral** or impure person…has an **inheritance** in the *kingdom*.			✓	✓		✓	Possession
144.	Col 1:13	He delivered us from darkness and **transferred us to** His *kingdom*.		✓		✓			
145.	Col 4:11	These are fellow **workers for** the *kingdom*.			✓	✓			
146.	1Thess 2:12	**Walk** in a manner **worthy of** His call **into** His *kingdom* and glory.			✓	✓	✓		2Thess 1:5
147.	2Thess 1:5	So that you may be **worthy of** the *kingdom*, for which you are **suffering**.			✓	✓			
148.	2Tim 4:1	I solemnly **charge** you in the presence of the Judge and by His *kingdom*.			✓	✓			
149.	2Tim 4:18	The Lord will **deliver** me and **bring** me **safely to** His *kingdom*.			✓	✓	✓		
150.	Heb 1:8	Your throne, O God, is forever, and the scepter is the scepter of His Kingdom.	✓			✓			
151.	Heb 11:33	Who by faith conquered *kingdoms*.	✓						
152.	Heb 12:28	Since we **receive** a *kingdom* which cannot be shaken, let us serve God.			✓	✓			possession
153.	Jam 2:5	The **poor are** to be **rich in faith** and **heirs** of the *kingdom* for His **lovers.**			✓	✓		✓	possession
154.	2Pet 1:11	**Entrance into** the eternal *kingdom* will be **abundantly** supplied to you.			✓	✓	✓		
155.	Rev 1:6	He has made us to be a *kingdom*, **priests** to His God and Father.			✓	✓			
156.	Rev 1:9	Your **fellow partaker** in the **tribulation** and *kingdom* and **perseverance**.			✓	✓			Rev 1:6; 5:10
157.	Rev 5:10	You made them a *kingdom* and **priests** to our God, and they will **reign**.			✓	✓			
158.	Rev 11:15	The *kingdom* of the world has become His *kingdom*, and He will **reign**.	✓						
159.	Rev 12:10	**Salvation**, power, and the *kingdom* and the authority of Christ have come.	✓						
160.	Rev 16:10	He poured out…upon beast's **throne,** and his *kingdom* became darkened.	✓						
161.	Rev 17:12	Ten have not yet **received** a *kingdom*, but they receive **authority** as **kings**.	✓						
162.	Rev 17:17	For God has executed His purpose by giving their *kingdom* to the beast.	✓						
163.	Rev 17:18	And the woman who *reigns [basileia]* over the **kings** of the earth.	✓						
	TOTAL	163 + Mk 9:47 twice = 164 references	82	30	52	46	22	7	

(G) General   (S) Soteriological   (M) Misthological   (K) Kingship   (E) Enter   (I) Inherit

Neo-Ultraistic Alternative

Receiving and entering the kingdom in several passages (i.e., Mt 19:23-24; Mk 10:15,23-24; Lk 18:17,24-25) possibly could be regarded misthologically (not in the ultraistic sense in which only overcomers enter the millennial kingdom but) in a conservative (thus neo-ultraistic) sense in which only overcomers enter the kingship. In other words, these verses could be treated just like Acts 14:22. If this be the case, then the disciples misunderstand Jesus and think He is using the expression soteriologically in Mt 19:25; Mk 10:26; Lk 18:26. If so, then Peter's insight is better than that of the other disciples. Instead of understanding it soteriologically, Peter correctly perceives that Jesus is talking misthologically and thus asks in effect, "What is in it for us?" In response, Jesus gives a misthological answer.

This interpretation could be supported by the observation that receiving the kingdom is normally a misthological concept and is associated practically with ownership of the kingdom in the respective contexts (i.e., Mt 19:14; Mk 10:14; and Lk 18:16). In fact, Matthew leaves out the potentially soteriological expression about receiving and entering the kingdom—found in the other two synoptic accounts (Mk 10:15; Lk 18:17)—and only uses the misthological expression about owning the kingdom. Matthew seemingly wants to highlight a misthologically understanding of Jesus' discussion about the children and the subsequent discussion that it introduces with the rich young ruler, which is why Matthew includes Jesus' words about inheriting eternal life in Mt 19:29, in contrast to Mark (10:30) and Luke (18:30) who only describe it as (futuristically) receiving eternal life (which by inference would be a misthological reception). The rich young ruler is concerned with meriting eternal life. Jesus first proves to this young ruler that there is a sense in which it is impossible to merit eternal life (Mt 19:17), before discussing the misthological manner in which such life can indeed be merited (Mt 19:21). If this is correct, then Jesus' point is that the way to inherit/receive/enter/obtain the **kingship** is to do what children are so good at, to trust and depend on their provider. If you want to rule in heaven, you must live in a manner worthy of it. You must depend on the King, just as the only way to bear fruits as a branch is to depend on the vine (Jn 15:4-6).

If this neo-ultraistic interpretation is adopted, then it might be best to understand the expression about not entering the kingdom *at all* in Mt 5:20 as a misthological reference to kingship as well, which in turn would result in taking Mt 7:21 similarly. Likewise, Mk 10:15 and Lk 18:17 would be taken as additional misthological references to the *kingship* and correspondingly mean: "Unless you receive the *kingship* as a child, you will not enter the *kingship* at all." In short, it is possible to mark these twelve verses (Mt 5:20; 7:21; 18:3; 19:23-24; Mk 10:15; 10:23-25; Lk 18:17,24-25) as misthological references to the **kingship** rather than as soteriological references to the **kingdom**. For those who prefer a misthological understanding of these verses, using *kingship* rather than *kingdom* would be preferable.

If ultraists want to take these passages misthologically, then let them do so in this neo-ultraistic manner. They would be on much stronger ground arguing that what is at stake is exclusion from the kingship rather than exclusion from the kingdom in these passages. Those who feel compelled to interpret these passages misthologically may argue that the emphatic double negative in Mt 5:20; 18:3; Mk 10:15; Lk 18:17 means that subcomers will not be allowed any entrance whatsoever into the **kingship.** It does not mean that subcomers will not be allowed any entrance whatsoever into the kingdom itself. Although the current study does not render this neo-ultraistic alternative impossible, it does consider it improbable. It is possible (although improbable) to understand Mt 5:20; 7:21; 18:3; 19:23-24; Mk 10:15; 10:23-25; Lk 18:17,24-25 as misthological references to entering the *kingship* rather than as soteriological references to entering the *kingdom*. If this alternative ultraistic approach is taken, then these twelve occurrences of the word *kingdom* would need to be marked as references to the *kingship*, resulting in an alternative statistical analysis.

Illustration 275. Neo-Ultraistic Alternative of Kingdom

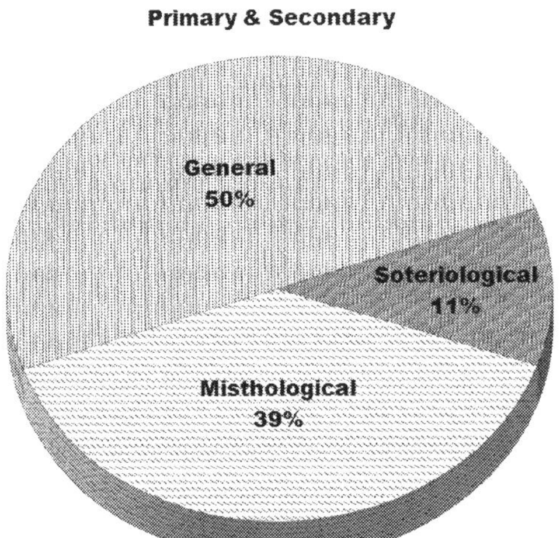

Primary & Secondary

General 50%

Soteriological 11%

Misthological 39%

Conclusion

Regardless of which route is taken, as may readily be seen on both pie charts, when specificity concerning the usage of *basileia* is contextually probable, misthological emphasis is discernibly more prominent. For those conservatives following Dillow's reconsideration of the possible misthological nature of several key texts or for ultraists seeking to embrace a more conservative posture, this latter approach is provided herein for consideration.

Appendix 4.
Johannine Anamartetology

Introduction

For the average reader, the problem proposed by ***anamartetology***[*] (the doctrine of sinlessness) is very basic. How can a believer be sinless? For those more familiar with the doctrine, the problem posed by 1Jn 3:6-10 is far more complex. Is John referring to multiple aspects of anamartetology? The Navigators' commentary on the Johannine epistles in the *Life Change Series* gives nine different interpretations of this passage. The ninth interpretation is the one it prefers, a common LS interpretation according to which one can "fairly accurately" judge one's own salvation and the salvation of others based on the amount of sin in one's life.[1338] In other words, performance determines which professing believers truly are saved. MacArthur also takes this position saying, "One who is truly saved cannot continue in a pattern of unbroken sin."[1339] This understanding of the text is based on the Calvinistic doctrine of perseverance and the present tense of the verbs used.

Rather than give numerous interpretive options, Wilkin simply follows Kubo's lead in dividing the interpretations of 1Jn 3:9 into two broad categories: **habitual** and **absolute**.[1340] The habitual interpretation is the one preferred above by MacArthur and the Navigators. This interpretation finds representation in the NIV and NAS translations. On the other hand, the absolute interpretation is popular in the FG camp and is also known as the *new nature interpretation*. The KJV and NKJ represent this understanding.

According to the new nature view, a believer's new nature does not sin. In this sense, all believers are sinless. This is interpretation #3 in the Navigator's material. Their criticism of this interpretation is that a believer would then be free to claim that he or she is not responsible for his or her sin since it is not done by the "real me." Such criticism is groundless since a believer is responsible for yielding to his or her old nature in committing sin. Will the Navigators argue that a believer's new nature sins? Is attributing sin to a believer's new nature the only way to make a believer accountable for his or her sin? If so, would this not make God the author of sin in a believer's life? The Navigators' criticism is open to some very critical questions and overlooks the simple answer. It is the person who sins, not simply his or her nature. Therefore, when a believer sins, this sin cannot be attributed to his or her new nature.

The Navigators admit that Hodges' interpretation of 1Jn 3:6 (BKC) "makes sense."[1341] His interpretation of 1Jn 3:6 is that sin is not an expression of a believer's abiding experience in Christ—that there is a sense in which a believer who is abiding in Christ is absolutely sinless. The Navigators reject Hodges' position saying that it would not make sense in 1Jn 3:9 because the latter verse is talking about whether you are born of God, not about your abiding in Christ. Evidently the Navigators have misunderstood Hodges. Many years ago, the present author wrote Hodges about his position and asked if his statements in BKC meant that 1Jn 3:6 views our experience as abiders (disciples) while 3:9 views our new nature (ontologically) as children? Hodges responded, "On 1Jn 3:6 and 9, I would say 'yes.' The former is experiential, the latter ontological."[1342] Unfortunately, the Navigators evidently did not understand Hodges' position well enough to pick up on this distinction. Granted, the Navigators' misunderstanding was based on Hodges' limited statements in BKC. They did not have access to his more recent work, *The Epistles of John*. Still, it is difficult to excuse their confusion. The present author's accurate assessments of Hodges' statements in BKC were also made before Hodges' more recent work. Hodges' articulation is comprehensible—if one is predisposed to giving it a fair hearing. John is expressing the absolute sinlessness of believers in a twofold manner. Wilkin adopts this twofold position as well.

Grammar makes the Navigator position improbable; theology makes it impossible. It is extremely improbable that John is stressing the tense of the verbs to mean habitual sin since he uses this same tense in 1Jn 1:8 concerning sin, and it does not mean habitual sin there. The same objection to the habitual interpretation may be raised from John's use of the present tense in 1Jn 5:16. Further, this tense argument is special pleading since this is not the manner in which the present tense is normally treated in NT translations or studies. Additional factors move beyond probability to certainty and make the tense argument impossible to accept. In the first two chapters of his epistle, John makes it clear that some believers do, in fact, practice sin. And he made this truth abundantly clear in his gospel. Also, the NT and OT give evidence that believers can and do practice sin.

John is not teaching in 1Jn 3:6-9 that all believers are relatively sinless in terms of their experience. Rather, he is teaching that all believers are absolutely sinless. The new birth results in sinlessness. There are at least seven

---

[*] ***Anamartetology*** is derived from the Greek word *sinless* (*anamartetos*) used by John in Jn 8:7 and is employed herein to refer to the doctrine of sinlessness.

ways in which the new birth may result in sinlessness. John uses all seven aspects in much the same way that the leader of a symphony would use trumpets, saxophones, clarinets, harps, drums, violins, and flutes to make a melody. The focus of attention may fluctuate from one featured theological instrument to another, but the other components are always present as well.

Topical

This investigation into *anamartetology* will first deal with the subject topically and then expound upon it exegetically in a running commentary.

Multiple Types of Sinlessness

Judicial Sinlessness

The NT teaches that believers have been justified and therefore made judicially sinless. The righteousness of Christ has been imputed to believers (e.g., Rom 4:22-24), and they have been made righteous in Him (2Cor 5:21). Although Pauline texts are perhaps the ones that come most readily to mind, this picture of sinlessness is not entirely absent from Johannine material. John, likewise, teaches that unrighteousness is sin (1Jn 5:17), yet believers are just as righteous as Jesus (1Jn 3:7) and therefore just as sinless. The judicial nature of this righteousness may be seen in the fact that believers do not come into judgment as sinners; they are not judged as sinners (Jn 5:24). Believers are judicially sinless in regard to this soteriological judgment. This is the type of forgiveness pictured by the *bath* (*louo*) of Jn 13:10. Since unbelievers die in their sins, the inverse must be true of believers—believers are sinless when they die (Jn 8:24).

Positional Sinlessness

The above Pauline truth that believers are righteous because they are in Christ is often referred to as positional righteousness. John also implements positional truth. Believers have moved fully and completely out of a sphere of death, darkness, and sin into a sphere of life, light, and sinlessness (Jn 5:24). When believers die, they will not die in their sins because their sins have been taken away by Jesus in His death (Jn 1:29). They do not move from death into sickness or from darkness into the shadows. The transition is absolute. Although believers are not just as sinless as Jesus in practice, they are just as sinless as He is in terms of position. The moment they trust in Jesus as Savior, it is like stepping out of a darkroom into a greenhouse full of bright sunlight. All Christians **are** sinless in this respect because they are in Him, and He is sinless (1Jn 2:12; 3:3,5,7; also see Col 2:13-14; Rom 5:1ff.).

All believers *abide* (*meno*) in the light (Jn 12:46). All believers remain (abide) in the light permanently and completely. The fact that all believers abide in Christ can also be seen in Jn 6:56. However, not all believers abide in Christ in Jn 15:1-6. *Abide* (*meno*) is used in different ways, determined by its various contexts. Most of the time, it refers to the experience of eternal life in fellowship with Christ. On the other hand, it is also used to refer to the present possession of eternal life independent of experience, which is the case in Jn 6:56. *Abide* in Jn 6:56 contextually refers to a **promise** concerning an eternal relationship: "He who eats My flesh and drinks My blood abides in Me, and I in him." Here *abide* means to remain in eternal union with Christ, to eternally have life (cf. Jn 6:27,56-58). In contrast, in Jn 15:4 *abide* is a **command** concerning temporal communion: "Abide in Me, and I in you." Therefore, Christ's abiding in us and us in Him is used in the Johannine writings both experientially and non-experientially.[1343]

This abiding, remaining, being kept *in Him* (or in the Father) is also the object of the Lord's prayer in Jn 17:11-12,21.[1344] This petition is best understood as dealing with both experiential and non-experiential unity. The eschatological dimension of this prayer allows us to affirm the experiential nature of Jesus' requests for our preservation and unity. Jesus requests both our experiential and essential unity and preservation. His prayer must be answered affirmatively, fully, and completely. Yet His request for our experiential preservation and unity is not fully answered in the present. This part of His prayer will be fully realized only eschatologically. On the other hand, His prayer for our essential unity is fully answered ontologically and positionally for all believers in the present. We organically share an oneness of life and sameness of nature derived from one source, as branches in a vine.

Jesus' request of the Father that we would be kept *in Him* certainly includes the idea of being kept from the devil (Jn 17:15). This keeping is both temporal and eschatological. The temporal nature of this preservation is clearly confirmed by 1Jn 5:18 where it is absolute. The devil cannot even touch us. We are sinless. The positional dimension of this sinlessness is highlighted by Jesus' repeated statement that we are not of the world just as He is not of the world (Jn 17:14,16). This statement is repeated immediately before and after His request that we be kept from the devil. We do not share the world's nature or position. Unfortunately, this dimension of His request does not mean that we are not of the world experientially in terms of our practice. These two verses should not be twisted to mean that our practice is not of the world just as Jesus' practice is not of the world! These verses are not talking about our practice but our position. Positionally, we are just as righteous as He is (1Jn 3:2-3,7). In begetting us, His seed has imparted to us an imperishable life and nature, neither of which can be defiled by the devil's sinful hands. We are new creatures who have a sinless new nature. The devil cannot touch what we are ontologically or where we are positionally. Obviously, the implications of this understanding naturally result in unconditional eternal security.

Ontological Sinlessness

Not only does John teach that we are in Jesus, he also teaches that Jesus is in us (e.g., Jn 6:56). His being in us has resulted in a permanent ontological change by virtue of our new birth and corresponding new nature (Jn 3:3-8; 1Jn 2:29; 3:1-2,9; 5:18).[1345] Our new birth really results in something new. We really are new creatures (2Cor 5:17). Our physical birth resulted in a physical being and nature; our spiritual birth results in a spiritual being and nature. Through the power of God's spoken word, we were created human beings with physical life; in similar fashion, through the power of God's proclaimed word in the gospel, we are created spiritual beings with spiritual life the moment we believe. Just as our physical birth passed on to us the sinful nature of our parents, our spiritual birth passed on to us the sinless nature of our new Parent. But even though we are new creatures ontologically, we may fail to be new creatures experientially.[1346] We are ontologically children of light (Jn 12:36) but may fail to live experientially as such (Jn 12:35)[1347] Like children who share their father's nature through DNA and yet do not necessarily share it in practice, so believers share their Father's nature even if they do not express that nature in their behavior. This pictures the biblical reality above. Consequently, using DNA to picture OSAS is a biblically accurate analogy.* And the Bible in general, and Jesus in particular, is certainly fond of analogies.

Eschatological Sinlessness

Although our present earthly experience is not sinlessness, our future experience will be. All believers will be sinless in terms of their future experience when their old sin nature is eradicated (1Jn 3:2,5; also see Rom 8:29). This aspect of sinlessness is sometimes referred to as *perfect sanctification*. When we reach heaven, God will completely remove our sin nature and our desire to sin. As believers we should look forward to that experience with great joy and anticipation. Unfortunately, there are many Christians who probably dread it. They love sin so much that they will hate to see it go! Nevertheless, many such Christians have had to kiss it good-bye as they departed this life, and now in heaven they **are** sinless.

Relational Sinlessness

Not only can the devil not touch *where* we are or *what* we are, he cannot touch *whose* we are. We are sinless is in terms of our relationship. We are relationally sinless since all of our sins have been forgiven in terms of being God's children. Jesus prayed that we would be kept in the Father's name. He remains our Father. This relationship is permanent.[1348]

This type of forgiveness can be illustrated by the play, *Annie*, in which an orphan is adopted by a rich loving father. Her new father does not say, "Annie, if you promise to be a good girl, I will adopt you." He does not say, "Annie, if you are a good girl, I will keep you." He did not demand that she agree to let him be lord of her life in order for him to adopt her. He was not a Lordship Adoptionist who conditions his keeping her on her ongoing obedience to him. On the contrary, his request was simply, "Annie, will you let me adopt you?"

In the same way, God asks us to let Him adopt us. He is not a Lordship Adoptionist. He knows how bad we are and how bad we will be, but He still wants us to be His children. The moment we say, "Yes," He adopts, keeps us, and forgives us of all our sins (past, present, and future), as far as the adoption is concerned. What happens when we sin afterward? Like a loving father, God spanks us if we need it because we are His children. When God forgives us afterward, it is not in order that we may stay His children (the relationship is permanent) but because, in addition to a relationship with us, He wants fellowship with us as well.

---

* See *Spiritual Water*, 754; *Person versus Nature*, 792.

Familial Sinlessness

The above aspects of anamartetology apply to all believers: judicial, positional, ontological, eschatological, and relational sinlessness. This next aspect of anamartetology does not apply unconditionally or indiscriminately to all believers. All Christians **can** be sinless in terms of their fellowship with God, but not all believers are sinless in this manner since some believers walk in darkness rather than the light. Many believers are out of fellowship with God. If a believer abides in Christ, by walking in obedience to God's word and confessing his or her sin, then God forgives and cleanses him or her of *all* his or her sins in terms of fellowship (1Jn 1:7,9; cf. 1Jn 3:6). In contrast to the relational forgiveness mentioned above, this type of forgiveness is familial (1Jn 2:1). It does not establish our relationship with God; rather, it is based on that pre-existing relationship. This type of forgiveness is pictured by the *washing* (*nipto*) of the feet in Jn 13:10 and pertains to communion rather than union. Only some believers walk in the light and therefore enjoy this dimension of sinlessness.

Misthological Sinlessness

This last category applies to even fewer believers because it is conditioned on perseverance in walking in the light. John implicitly acknowledges that believers can be sinless in terms of their misthological experience in 1Jn 2:28. If we abide in Christ, then we can have boldness and confidence rather than shame and dishonor when we stand before His Bema. This understanding of this verse is confirmed by John's promises of white garments to believers who overcome. It is possible to have white garments that are misthologically unsoiled by the defilement of sin (Rev 3:4). This white garment motif certainly represents the misthological blamelessness that believers can obtain by washing their robes in ongoing practical sanctification (Rev 3:5,18; 4:4; 6:11; 7:14; 19:14). Paul also describes the misthological sinlessness of Christ's Bride as "having no spot or wrinkle or any such thing; but that she should be holy and blameless" (Eph 5:26), and Paul clearly indicates that being presented in this manner is conditional for believers and is based on their performance (Col 1:22-23). Being misthologically blameless is possible but only if we diligently persevere (1Cor 1:8; Eph 1:4; Phil 1:10; 2:14-15; Col 1:22-23; 1Thess 3:12-13; 5:23; 2Pet 3:14; Jude 1:24; Rev 14:4-5).[*] Therefore, the white garments represent being clothed in the practical righteousness that Christ makes conditionally available to the believer. These white garments are contingent upon the believer's sacrifice, rather than on the imputational righteousness which Christ provides, which is Himself (Gal 3:27).

Of course, the realization of this potential possibility does not apply to all believers, in that not all believers compose the Bride. The writer of Hebrews says that Christ will "appear a second time for salvation without reference to sin, to those who eagerly await Him" (Heb 9:28). This misthological sinlessness, which Paul describes as misthological righteousness (2Tim 4:8), is only promised to those believers who love Jesus' appearing. Those believers who love His appearing are promised a foretaste of it temporally (Jn 14:21). Since some believers love the world rather than Jesus or His appearing, these passages do not apply to all believers. By the same token, some believers are merciful while some believers are merciless. Amazingly, mercy can triumph so completely over judgment at the Bema that the experience of being judged may be one of complete joy (Jam 2:13). Those believers who are sufficiently merciful will receive sufficient mercy to be misthologically clothed in white garments.

Two Types of People

In 1Jn 3:6-9, John informs his readers that there are two types of people. One type of person is by nature a child of God; the other is by nature a child of the devil. A child of God manifests his or her true nature by living righteously; a child of the devil manifests his or her true nature by living sinfully. What does sin reveal? It reveals nothing less than a satanic nature. What does an act or life of sin reveal in someone who is a child of God? It reveals a satanic nature. A child of God can live like a child of the devil, but in doing so he or she manifests his or her old nature rather than his or her new nature. All sin is of the devil. The devil is the origin of all sin. When people sin, whether they are lost or saved, whether they commit a big sin or a little sin, whether they commit a few sins or a lot of sins, they are manifesting their sin nature. This nature is satanic in origin. All sin should be recognized as being satanic in that it is of the devil. In contrast, when a saved person lives righteously, he or she is displaying his or her new and true nature.

---

[*] See *Illustration 198. Holy and Blameless,* 579. And consult discussion of *Eph 5:27,* 585.

Two Types of Sinfulness

Not only does John present us with at least seven types of sinlessness in his writings, he also teaches that there are at least two basic ways in which we are sinful: by nature and by action. The background for this aspect of his teaching can be found in Jn 8:44.[1349] Satan's sinful action is an expression of his sinful nature. Jesus rebukes those who want to kill Him rather than believe in Him by saying that Satan is the father of their nature and desires. In that regard, fruit shows root. If the fruit is sin, it stems from a sin nature and thus from Satan. This statement holds true for the sins expressed by both the lost and the saved. Thus, John acknowledges that believers are sinners in terms of their present experience (1Jn 1:6,8,10; 2:4,9,11,15,28; 3:4,6; also see Jn 2:23-24; 8:30-32; 12:42-43; 15:2).[1350] In doing so, he acknowledges the existence of their old sin nature (1Jn 2:16; 3:8,10; also see Rom 7:15-25; Gal 5:16-17; Eph 4:22-24; 5:8-11; Col 3:9-10; Jam 1:13-18; 3:9-18). Determining which aspect(s) of sinlessness and sinfulness John is referring to with each expression is difficult, if not impossible. Probably, he planned for his readers to see one meaning upon their first reading and then to see the fuller meaning with its multiple aspects as they considered his repetition and parallelism. John shows a fondness for using simple statements that lead to a deeper complexity because they can be interpreted in a variety of ways.

Illustration 276. Anamartetological Parallels (1Jn 3:4-10)

		4a	Everyone who produces sin	8a	Everyone who produces sin		
		4b	also produces lawlessness and sin is lawlessness.	8b	is **of the devil**,		
		5a	(And you know that) He was manifested in order to	8c	The Son of God was manifested for this purpose,		
		5b	take away sins (and in Him there is no sin).	8e	that He might destroy the produce of the devil		
		6a	Everyone who **ABIDES in Him**	9a	Everyone who has been **born of God**	5:18a	Everyone who has been **born of God**
		6b	does not sin.	9b	does not do produce sin,	5:18b	does not sin,
		6c	Everyone who sins				
		6d-e	has neither come to see Him nor come to know Him.				
				9c	because His seed **ABIDES in him**,	5:18c	but the **one born of God** keeps him,
				9d	and it is impossible to sin,	5:18d	and the evil does not touch him.
				9e	due to having been **born of God**.		
2:29	You know that	7a	Little children, let no one deceive you;	10a	By this are manifested		
2:29b	everyone who produces righteousness	7b	the one who produces righteousness				
2:29c	has been born of Him.	7c-d	is righteous, just as He is righteous.				
				10b	the children of God		
				10c	and the children of the devil.		
				10d	Everyone who does not produce righteousness		
				10e	is **not of God**.		

Illustration 277. Suggested versus Actual Parallels

TNTC's parallelism:			NTC adds vv. 7,10			Actual parallelism:		
4	=	8a-b	4	=	8a-b	4	‖	8a-b
5	=	8c-e	5	=	8c-e	5	‖	8c-e
6a-b	=	9a-b	6a-b	=	9a-b	6a-b	‖	9a-b
			7b-d	=	10d-e	7b-d	‖	10d-e

For technical accuracy, the equal marks (see NTC) have been replaced with parallel marks (∥) since 7b-d ≠ 10d-e. In this case, they are antonymous parallels rather than statements of equality. Further, the statements that are similar in meaning are not necessarily equivalent in meaning. There are often shifts and advances in thought. Thus, parallel marks are superior to equal marks. Nevertheless, even the parallel marks are too simplistic to do justice to the richness of this text. The diagram below represents agreement with those who begin this section with 1Jn 2:29. The first cycle (C1) is completed by 1Jn 3:7, which recapitulates 2:29 (and forms one cycle held together by three *just as He is* affirmations). And 1Jn 3:7 ends this section with the last of these three statements.

Illustration 278. Three Parallel Cycles

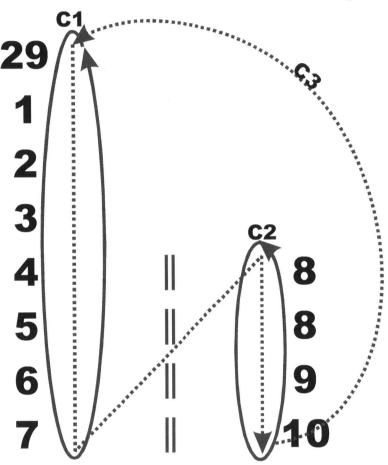

A second, but parallel, cycle (C2) is introduced by 1Jn 3:8, in which the devil is mentioned for the first time. Verse 10 should probably be treated as a litotes. *Everyone who does not produce righteousness* (v. 10d,) is a litotes for *everyone who produces sin* (vv. 8a). *Is not of God* (10e) is a litotes for *is of the devil* (8b). Verse 10d-e is a recapitulation of verse 8a-b and thus ends the second cycle.

These two cycles form a larger cycle (C3). Lenski and NIC note that 2:29b-c is opposite of v. 10d-e; thus, the entire passage makes a third cycle. Not only is 29b-c the opposite of 10d-e, but their parallels are also corresponding opposites. Thus, 7b-d is parallel to v. 10 and a polar opposite of 8a-b.

This arrangement is not intended to deny the chiasmic structure of the epistle or of 1Jn 3:9, as pictured by Ramey and McCoy respectively.[1351] Rather, these cycles function within the broader chiasm (in which the whole epistle is outlined as a macro chiasm) and incorporate the narrower micro chiasm of the verse. In a chiasm, the staircase parallelism climactically can build up to a pivotal point and then symmetrically descend from it. If we abbreviate the steps ascending and descending from the apex of 1Jn 3:9 to focus on the climax, it would yield the following.

Illustration 279. Chiasmic Staircase Parallelism of 1Jn 3:9

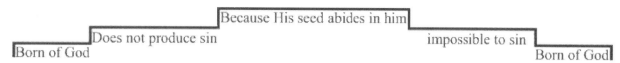

To express this structure more fully in classic (ABXB'A') format, and using my translation above, 1Jn 3:9 would be outlined as follows:

A	*Everyone who has been born of God*
B	*does not produce sin,*
X	*because His seed abides in him,*
B'	*and it is impossible to sin,*
A'	*due to having been born of God.*

The pivotal point (X) in the chiasm is the explanation: "*Because His seed abides in him.*" In Ramey's chiastic outline for the whole epistle, he has 1Jn 3:4-10 pictured as the thematic pinnacle for the epistle. The modification, as pictured above, presents the climax as extended and richer in parallelism than his classic model. This alternative model (sometimes described as ABXX'B'A') might be better suited for a harmonization between his outline and the above cycles. The pinnacle is composed of twin peaks in which 3:4-7 mirrors 3:8-10. The commentary herein will focus on the cycles that compose these peaks. However, in order to exegete the peaks in their theological and epistolary context, this Johannine theme in GJ will be considered, as well as a few prolegomenous and concluding verses.

Commentary

Jn 8:34

Everyone who commits sin is the slave of sin.[*]

Everyone who sins is in the position of being a slave; such a person belongs to sin. Only those who believe in Jesus are freed from this positional bondage to sin. The issue is whether a person is a sinner, not how much a person sins. All four of the following translations correctly convey this thought. The KJV, NKJ, and NAS all translate *poieo* by as everyone who *commits* sin is the slave of sin. The NIV says that everyone who sins is the slave of sin. None of these four translations suggests a habitual translation. They all translate the present tense in the absolute (or at least unmarked) sense. Excellent! This is the same wording found in 1Jn 3:4a and 8a. The KJV, NKJ, and NIV also translate these verses in the absolute sense. However, the NAS is inconsistent and inserts the word *practice* in both cases. The Greek tense certainly does not demand or even need this insertion. This insertion is based on a theological bias by the NAS translation rather than an aspect demanded by the Greek text.

Admittedly, the tense of the verb can denote the practice of sin, if contextually warranted. Indeed, it does so in a very similar passage in Rom 6:12-13. "Stop letting sin reign in your mortal bodies in order that you may obey its lust, and stop offering the members of your body to sin" (TM). The prohibition of a present imperative may mean to stop the continuance of the act. The tense of these verbs may indicate that these believers were practicing sin, and Paul tells them to stop it. The same is true in 1Cor 15:34 where Paul tells those believers to *stop practicing sin* (cp. Eph 4:26).[1352] If tense advocates wish to stress the linear aspect just because of tense, then the tense of these verbs indicate the very opposite of what tense advocates wish for them to prove. The tense of these verbs signify that believers do practice sin!

1Jn 1:6-7

If we say that we have fellowship with Him and walk in the darkness, then we lie and do not practice the truth; but if we walk in the light as He is in the light, then we have fellowship with one another, and the blood of Jesus His Son cleanses us from all sin.

John does not share the Calvinistic perspective that genuine believers cannot practice sin. In v. 6 he is talking about believers who *practice* (*poieo*) sin; they *walk* in it. The NAS and NKJ rendering of *poieo* as *practice* is reasonable in this context and calls into question the NAS translation of *poieo* as *practice* in 1Jn 3:9. If 1Jn 3:9 is

---

[*] The translation used in this running commentary is mine.

asserting that no believers practice sin, as the NAS alleges, then 1Jn 1:6 leads to the opposite conclusion. John entertains the possibility of some believers walking in the darkness in terms of their practice in 1:6.

Those believers who walk in the light are not sinless in terms of their experience since they have sins that need to be cleansed as they walk. Yet they are familially sinless, cleansed of all sin in regards to fellowship as they walk. Paul likewise does not take it for granted that all believers will walk in the light (Eph 4:1; 5:8; Col 2:6). To the contrary, he explicitly teaches that carnal Christians walk like mere men; that is, practice sin (1Cor 3:3; Eph 4:17; 2Thess 3:6,11). Paul teaches the Marrowistic view of the Christian walk. He does not believe that all Christians **will** inevitably walk in the light; rather, he believes they **should** walk in the light (Eph 2:10). In similar fashion, John does not teach that all believers **will** walk in the light; he teaches that they **should** walk in the light (1Jn 2:6; 2Jn 1:6). He gives specific examples of believers who do not walk in the light (1Jn 2:11).

1Jn 1:8

If we say that we do not have sin, then we deceive ourselves and the truth is not in us.

If the present tense proves the continuance of sin, as the habitual argument maintains, then this verse is saying, "If we say that we do not continually have sin, then we deceive ourselves." But this would refute the habitual argument since the verse would then be affirming that believers do in fact continually sin (i.e., they practice sin).

1Jn 1:9

If we confess our sins, then He is faithful and righteous to forgive us our sins and to cleanse us from all unrighteousness.

All of our sins already are forgiven in terms of relationship as believers (i.e., *little children*; 1Jn 2:12). We are completely sinless concerning relationship. As we confess what sins we are aware of as believers, we are forgiven of all sins, even the ones we are not aware of, in terms of fellowship. Thus, we can become completely sinless in terms of fellowship.

1Jn 1:10

If we say that we have not sinned, then we make Him a liar and His word is not in us.

The false claims of not having sin (1Jn 1:8) and not having sinned (1Jn 1:10) are parallel and perhaps even equivalent in meaning. Or perhaps the perfect aspect might signify that anyone who claims not to have sinned in the past with the result that they are still regarded as sinners in the present are delusional. They are still experientially sinners even if they are not sinning at the present second. In any event, all claims to experiential sinlessness are refuted by John. Such claims show that God's word is not experientially in the believer making such a claim. The rebuttals are parallel in thought: Neither God's word (v. 10) nor the truth is experientially in such believers (v. 8). Christians who claim to be abiding (living) in God experientially free of sin are in reality not abiding (living) in God experientially nor is God abiding (living) in them experientially. The truth of God's word is not living in them, and they are not living in it.

1Jn 2:1

My little children, I write these things to you in order that you may not sin, and if anyone sins, then we have an advocate with the Father.

John is not intending to discourage his Christian readers by telling them that they will sin experientially. A defeatist or flippant attitude is inexcusable. Christians should not have the attitude that since they will sin anyway committing sin or living in sin is no big deal. On the contrary, John writes to encourage them not to sin at all, much less to live in sin. John's point is not that a little bit of sin is okay as long as you do not live in it or practice it!

Tense advocates point to the use of the aorist in this verse and contrast it with the present tense used in 1Jn 3:6,9 and assert that John is contrasting the two tenses. They argue that if John had intended to rule out an act of sin, he would have used an aorist tense in those verses as well. This is a very shortsighted argument. If a contrast is intended between the tenses, then the most natural place to find it is in the present context. If a contrast is intended between the aorist tense of 2:1 and the present tense in 1:8, the contrast would be between the aorist of 2:1 and the present tense in its context—not the remote context of 3:6-9. If John means to contrast the tenses, then verse 8 says that all Christians practice sin! Verse 8 destroys the tense argument. John is not contrasting the present and aorist tenses to denote continuous action in the present tense or context.

The reason he uses the aorist in 1Jn 2:1 is quite natural. If he had used a present tense in the subjunctive mood, then it would have indicated linear action. In other words, he would have been telling his readers that their goal should be to not practice sin, which could be mistaken as saying that a little sin is okay but a lot of sin is not. To avoid such potential misunderstanding, he slams the door on all sin with the aorist tense. However, in 1Jn 3:6,9 (etc.) he returns to the present tense for a simple reason—he is describing their present experience (inclusively) rather than their past or future experience (exclusively). Unfortunately, there is no way to specify punctiliar action with the present tense. But this would pose no problem since he is not making any sharp distinction between the practice of sin and the act of sin in his discussion in ch. 3.

1Jn 2:12

I write to you, little children, because your sins have been forgiven.

All sins of all believers are forgiven in regards to their being a child of God. Their forgiveness in terms of this relationship is complete and already accomplished. This forgiveness is not conditioned upon confession of sin. These *little newborn children* (*teknion*, cp. *teknon* in Jn 1:2) stand in a perfectly forgiven state. The perfect tense of *forgiven* in 1Jn 2:12 is used concerning these *little children*. In the next verse (1Jn 2:13), the perfect tense of *know* is used in relation to their more mature knowledge as *children* (*paidion*) who are old enough to experience its cognate *discipline* (*paideia*; cp. Heb 12:7). Unfortunately, the KJV and NKJ fail to note the transition from *little children* to *children*. John uses this transition to mark a progression from infancy to early stages of Christian maturity in their moving from an infantile to a juvenile knowledge of God.

The use of the perfect tense for forgiveness in v. 12 also has significance regarding the scope of forgiveness. Some NT texts describe a forgiveness that is associated with reconciliation (Eph 1:7; Col 1:14). The scope of this soteriological/positional forgiveness is even stated to cover all sins in Col 2:13. To be sure, many conditional securitists object that such texts only indicate the forgiveness of all past sins. Such a restriction would make no sense in the present text, however. John is not indicating that only their past sins have been forgiven and that only those past sins remain in a forgiven state. What about their present sins which he just mentioned in the previous chapter? Are they not also being forgiven? Most certainly. John does not exclude these sins, yet he excludes the present action of forgiving in 2:12. John does not imply, "I write to you, little children, because your sins are *being* forgiven." Instead, he includes the present sins (that are being forgiven via 1:9) in the present state of already having been forgiven (in 2:12). The sins being forgiven presently from ch. 1 are subsumed in the perfect forgiveness of 2:12. The sins that we are confessing in order to be forgiven familially are already forgiven relationally in terms of state. All these sins already have been forgiven in terms of their state as little children.

1Jn 2:29

You know that everyone who produces righteousness has been born of Him.

John is not implying that everyone who lives a good life is born of God. He already has made it clear in his gospel that only believers are born of God. Considering the fact that John has just exhorted these believers to abide in Christ experientially (2:28), the righteousness in 2:29 probably refers primarily to experiential righteousness, that is, to practical righteous, practicing righteousness. Intrinsic probability also points to habitual action since this righteousness provides a basis for confirming the new birth of someone else. In other words, this verse is parallel to the thought of 3:10. Righteousness is the means of manifesting one's new birth and new nature. Conversely, sinfulness is the means of concealing one's new birth and new nature. Because of the parallelism that 1Jn 2:29 has with 1Jn 3:10, the NKJV rendering of *poieo* in both verses as *practice* to signify manifestative righteousness is reasonable.

On the other hand, Hodges' comments are not without merit. He prefers to translate *poieo* as *does* since the "one who to any extent reproduces His **righteous** nature is actually *manifesting* that nature" (emphasis his).[1353] If so, the production of one righteous act would qualify since Hodges says *to any extent*. Even the production of one genuinely righteous action would show a righteous nature. Hodges inclusion of righteousness *to any extent* is in harmony with the absolute statements that John makes in the material encapsulated between the *inclusio* found in 2:29 and 3:10. Anderson does very well to explain the interior use of the similar phrase in 1Jn 3:7 in terms of fruit production.[1354] *Poieo* is properly translated as *produce* in well-known passages using similar imagery. Like John, Jesus speaks absolutely: "Every tree that does not *produce* good fruit is cut down and thrown into the fire" (TM). The NAS correctly renders *poieo* as *produce* in a like-minded passage: "Can a fig tree, my brethren, *produce* olives, or a vine produce figs? Neither can salt water *produce* fresh" (Jam 3:12). *Poieo* also occurs twice in Mt 7:18, which the NAS renders as: "A good tree cannot *produce* bad fruit, nor can a bad tree *produce* good fruit."[*] If you find an apple growing on a tree, you may safely deduce that it is an apple tree. The fruit manifests the nature of the root. Just as in the case of the Matthean and Jacobean texts where fruit shows root, so in this Johannine imagery, fruit (what is produced) shows seed. If you bite into a fruit and find an apple seed, you can reasonably deduce that you have bitten an apple.

Anderson goes too far, however, when he suggests that the point John is making can be inverted so as to conclude that "God's nature *will produce* God's righteousness....A certain kind of root *will produce* a certain kind of fruit."[1355] To the contrary, just because you find a fig tree does not mean that you will find figs (Mk 11:13; Lk 13:7). John is not claiming that if you are born of God, then you necessarily will manifest that the new nature in terms of your behavior. To be sure, if you bite into an apple and find a seed, you can reasonably deduce that it will be an apple seed. Perhaps this is the point Anderson was trying to make. If so, it is logical. Even so, it is not contextual. This inverse point is not the point John is making. Most certainly, he is not making the inverse point articulated by Anderson.

Illustration 280. Produces Righteousness ⊂ Born of God

This verse (2:29), in conjunction with 2:28, teaches that **if** you abide in Him, **then** you are born of Him. This informal *if-then* conditional relation may be represented by the *if-then* symbol as: abide ⇒ born. Unfortunately, many interpreters stand it on its head to make it assert: If you are born of Him, then you will abide in Him (i.e., born ⇒ abide). But the verse does not teach this inverted logic. Practical righteousness in the life of a believer indicates positional righteousness. Lack of practical righteousness does not prove the absence of positional righteousness. Water coming up out of the ground proves there is water under the ground. Lack of water coming up out of the ground does not prove that there is no water under the ground. You may have to drill a well to find that underground water. This verse gives an auxiliary basis for affirming someone else's regeneration, not for denying it. This verse does not teach *no fruits* ⇒ *no root*; rather, it teaches *no root* ⇒ *no fruits*. Or stated positively, it teaches: *fruits* ⇒ *root*.[1356] In terms of the above illustration, all those (believers) who practice righteousness are born of God.[1357] This does not mean that all those who are born of God practice righteousness. The fact that some unbelievers do relatively righteous things is outside the scope of John's discussion. Even so, this consideration does make it impossible to make this verse a litmus test by which to determine whether someone is regenerate.

Believers *know* (*ginosko*) with deductive certainty that everyone who produces even one genuinely righteous action is born again. The insistence made by some that *ginosko* always denotes experiential knowledge rather than deductive knowledge in this epistle is certainly open to question. How can one know that someone is manifesting a genuine righteous work, much less discern their regenerative nature, from the observation of a singular action? Perhaps over a period of time of observing a practice of such works, one might have a degree of confirmative inductive probability. However, John certainly is not limiting his affirmation of knowledge to mere probability! The safest procedure is to allow the possibility that John permits some degree of inductivity during parts of his discussion but insists upon stressing the underlying deductive certainty. He intends for this level of

---

[*] Proveitism uses a false fruit-proves-root argument to assert that the way you live proves whether you are saved. Nevertheless, this does not mean that all fruit-proves-root arguments are false.

deductive certainty to be the basis for any inductions. This dual understanding of *ginosko* is superior. Correspondingly, the best translation for *poieo* within this section spanning from 2:29-3:10 is *produce*. This rendering leaves both the inductive and deductive possibilities open.

1Jn 3:1

See how great a love the Father has given us that we may be called children of God, and we are, for this reason the world does not know us because it did not know Him.

Believers are already God's children in fact. Unfortunately, we may fail to be God's children in practice. Our behavior may fail to reveal our heavenly and sinless parentage.

1Jn 3:2

Beloved, now we are children of God, and it has not been manifested what we will be; we know that when He is manifested we will be like Him, because we will see Him just as He is.

We will be like Him in terms of our behavior as well as our nature. When we are transformed by His appearance, we will be as sinless as He is in appearance and in experience when we see Him. (This universal transformative vision of God given to all believers is not to be confused with the misthological vision of God limited to overcomers.) All believers will be experientially sinless as a result of seeing God **at that time**. Presently, there is a tension between the *now* and the *not yet*. We are not yet in practice what we are now in nature—sinless. This eschatological tension paves the way for the ontological transition in 3:6. As Martin acknowledges, in reference to the immortality and incorruptibility we will receive in 1Cor 15:52-53, "We shall have a soul and body *incapable* of sin."[1358]

1Jn 3:3

And everyone who has this hope in Him purifies himself just as He is pure.

Verse 3 repeats the phrase *just as He is* and further explains in what sense this will be true. We will be just as pure as He is; we will be just as sinless as He is (1Jn 3:5b). Every believer (i.e., everyone who has set his or her hope on Him) will be sinless. Due to verse 2, we should not allow the present (and supposedly linear) tense of the verbs *has* and *purifies* to cause us to miss the punctiliar and futuristic dimension of the purification. The articular participle simply may be describing someone who has hope, that is, faith in Jesus.

To set your hope on someone is synonymous with depending on that person, to believe in that person (cf. Jn 5:45). The Greek phrase *hope in Him* (*ep auto*) is not far removed from the use of this expression (*ep auto*) in the phrase *believe in Him* (Rom 9:33; 10:11; 1Tim 1:16; 1Pet 2:6), or *trust in Him* (Heb 2:13). And the verbal form of *hope* with the corresponding *in Him* (*ep auto*) is found in Rom 15:12: "*In Him* shall the Gentiles *hope*." The Gentiles will *hope in Him*. This Johannine verse, therefore, may be understood as anticipating the perfect and permanent purification of our future eschatological sanctification that is guaranteed as a result of our regeneration. Hodges' understanding that the passage as a whole is talking about an ontological purification, equated with regeneration (cf. Tit 3:5), is not ruled out since John will soon come to this very conclusion in verse 9.[1359]

Nevertheless, as stated previously, there are a number of ways in which believers are already pure *just as He is pure*. The purification of which this verse speaks is probably not exclusively futuristic, that is, it is not merely anticipatory of the future purity of verse 2. More likely, John is thinking also of believers' present absolute sinlessness as well. Hodges' assessment that it refers to the sinless experience of verse 6 is possible at this point in the context if the hope of verse 3 is more than just the soteriological expectation of seeing God in heaven. If *this hope* (v. 3) includes the joyful expectation of being experientially pure in the future (v. 2), then one certainly may expect that those believers who joyfully anticipate being made sinless at that time will walk in the light in the present time period and thus be cleansed of all sin as a result of abiding in Him. It is a reasonable prospect that those believers who are looking forward to the eternal experiential purity of verse 2 will avail themselves of the temporal purity offered in the preceding context (1Jn 1:7,9) and in the proceeding context (1Jn 3:6) and thereby attain the potential misthological purity referred to in 1Jn 2:28.

On the other hand, those believers who are in a current love affair with present worldly lusts (1Jn 2:15-16) naturally would not be inclined to look forward to their complete experiential deliverance from sin in the future. They enjoy sin, so they have no joy at the thought of seeing it removed. For them, this passage is nothing more than soteriological faith—the hope of being in heaven rather than in hell as a result of soteriological forgiveness. Contrastively, for believers who long for experiential purity, this passage offers a very blessed hope. They finally will be rid of sin, never to sin again. This war against sinful impulses will not go on forever. Oh, the blessed thought of not merely seeing God but being absolutely sinless in all aspects—at last!

Unfortunately, Calvinistic LS maintains that all genuine believers are seeking to purify themselves in imitation of His sinless. According to their interpretation, if you are not seeking to purify yourself, then you are not a genuine believer. They use verse 3 as part of their litmus tests to determine if you are really regenerate. The LS position (that believers who fail to purify themselves experientially in the present time abandon all hopes of entering heaven in the future) does a grave injustice to the text. Their argument that this verse shows that all genuine believers live pure lives free of the practice of sin is fraudulent. The verse refers to being absolutely pure. The thought is not that they merely try to purify themselves; rather, they successfully and absolutely do so. Not only will they be just as sinless as He is, they are already sinless in multiple aspects. Second, confident expectation of His return does not guarantee confidence at His return, as John has just stressed four verses earlier (1Jn 2:28). Confidence that He will appear and that we will see Him does not inevitably rule out sinful and shameful behavior on our part or guarantee that we are abiding in Him experientially. In addition to expecting Him, we must abide in Him if we want to be misthologically sinless. This experiential abiding is commanded, not promised.

1Jn 3:4

Everyone who produces sin also produces lawlessness and sin is lawlessness.
All sin, not just the practice of sin, is lawlessness. We must be perfectly pure because all sin is perfectly awful. Sin is nothing less than rebellion against God. Whether one sin or a lot of sin is produced, it is completely sinful. John is not stressing linear production.

1Jn 3:5

And you know that He was manifested in order to take away sins, and in Him there is no sin.
Jesus appeared in His first coming to take away our sins by dying in our place (Jn 1:29; 11:50-52). He took away all our sins in His death. All our past, present, future, habitual, and occasional sins have been removed. He dealt with both the sinful root and sinful fruits. He has taken away all of our sins. This indicates our absolute sinlessness. The idea is not that He has only taken away the sins that we commit habitually and left those that we commit occasionally. When viewed in terms of what He has done rather than what we do, we are completely sinless.

The angelic announcement that Christ would *save His people from their sins* should not be watered down, as it is in LS theology, to mean that Christ merely will save believers from the habitual practice of sin (Mt 1:21). The LS ditty that *Christ came to save us from our sin but not in our sin* is intended to slap FG theology in the face by insinuating that FG theology considers sin okay. The truth of the matter, however, is that LS is trying to justify a little bit of sin in the life of the believer while FG theology is rejecting the notion that any sin falls outside of the range of Christ's saving sufficiency.

The statement that there is no sin in Christ is meant to be taken absolutely. In this passage, the thought is not that there is occasional sin rather than habitual sin in Him. Jesus died to save us from all sin, not just the practice of sin. He was not only partially successful. The statements *there is no sin*, (1Jn 3:5), *do not have sin* (1Jn 1:8), and *have not sinned* (1Jn 1:10) are parallel expressions referring to absolute sinlessness. What the proto-Gnostic Christians falsely claimed to have in their experience, believers actually have in their position. Logically, since there is no sin in Him, anyone who is in Him is sinless by virtue of his or her position in Him. Any sin in a believer's experience, whether occasional or habitual, is not an expression of his or her being in Christ. Any sin in a believer's life is not an expression of his or her life in Christ. Jesus has accomplished the objective of saving His people from their sins—all of their sins, not just some of them as in LS thought.

1Jn 3:6

Everyone who abides in Him does not sin; everyone who sins has neither come to see Him nor come to know Him.
The habitual argument is ruled out by the previous verse (1Jn 3:5) which describes absolute sinlessness. Since there is no sin in Him, no one who is in Him sins. Do Christians who abide in Christ sin? Yes. Those believers who experientially abide in Christ (i.e., who walk in the light in the experiential sense described in 1Jn 1:7) sin experientially (1Jn 1:7-8,10). But 3:6 is not describing experiential sinlessness (when that experience is made to encompass everything we do in our bodies); although, it may be referring to experiential abiding. Believers still have a sin nature resident in the members of their bodies that expresses itself in sinful actions through their bodies.

Three Anamartetological Dimensions

Three different aspects of anamartetology are probably contained in this verse. Those believers who positionally abide in Christ are **positionally** sinless. Because of the positional use of *in Him* in verse 5 and the positional use of *abide* in GJ (Jn 6:56; 12:46), it is possible to take *abide in Him* in a positional sense in verse 6. However, abide is certainly not limited to a positional sense in this verse. Most likely, it is being used primarily in an experiential sense. *Abide* normally is used experientially in John's writings, as it was in the preceding passage (1Jn 2:27-28). It also prepares the way for the practical expression of righteousness in 1Jn 3:7b. Abiding in Him is probably to be taken as an experiential equivalent to walking in Him (1Jn 1:7). As John pointed out in that previous passage, those who abide are **familially** sinless. In 1Jn 3:6-9, he advances beyond these earlier anamartetological affirmations to **ontological** anamartetology by showing that the eschatological anamartetology of 1Jn 3:2-3 already is fundamentally realized even in the present. In the present we are already pure, sinless children of God (cp. 1Jn 3:1-5).

John uses the future tense to state *what we will be* in 3:2. He simultaneously uses the present tense in 3:2, and throughout 2:29-3:10, to show *what we are*. What will be true of us in the future is already true of us in the present. We will be (and are) pure, sinless children of God in terms of who and what *we are* (3:1-2). As a result of our new birth (2:29), our nature is derived from Him. We are able to abide in Christ experientially by means of our new nature, which is completely sinless, not only in terms of being but also in terms of expression. Since the believer's new nature represents who and what he or she truly is in Christ (i.e., the true person him or herself), he or she is completely sinless in terms of genuine self-expression. Sin is not an expression of who he or she truly is in Christ, nor is it a representation of his or her abiding experience in Christ. Believers are sinless in regard to who they truly are and what they truly do as expressions of who they truly are (cf. Rom 7:17,20). Any sin found in a believer's experience at any time (much less while abiding in Christ) is not produced by his or her walk in Christ and is not traceable to that abiding experience. Sin is an expression of what a believer used to be and used to do. It is due to the old nature rather than the new nature. Sin represents the believer's experience outside of Christ, not any part of his or her experience within Christ. 1Jn 3:6 takes an ontological and positional look at the believer's abiding experience in Christ and finds that experience sinless.

For this reason, it would be quite possible to add an eighth area of Johannine anamartetology. A believer's experience **in Christ** is sinless, so there is a sense in which believers can be experientially sinless even though they are not sinless in terms of their earthly experience. In spite of the fact that it is logically necessary to concur with Hodges on this perspective, it has not been deemed advisable herein to list this as an eighth category due to potential misunderstanding and misrepresentation.

We are not sinless in terms of our earthly experience, but we are indeed sinless in terms of our Christly experience. All of our experience in Christ is sinless; none of our experience outside of Christ is sinless. Any part of our earthly experience lived in opposition to Christ or independently of Christ is sinful. Yet that part of our life lived in submission to Christ and in dependence on Christ may be said to be truly sinless.

In addition to participating ontologically in His sinless nature, it is also possible to share to a limited extent in His sinless experience. The present author therefore has no real quarrel with those who wish to employ this extra category as long as they clearly explain the difference between earthly and Christly experience, between experiences viewed partially versus holistically. When we stand before the Bema to be judged, we will be judged for both the good and bad we do. We will be judged holistically for what we did as a person. Judgment will not focus on a part of us, that is, the sinful part. We will not be judged for what a part of us did. We will be judged for what we did. If our earthly experience is taken holistically as referring to our entire experience in our earthly bodies, then the only part of the experience that is in Christ is sinless. Our sinless Christly experience is a subset of our total earthly experience. This relationship is pictured in the following illustration.

Illustration 281. Christly Experience ⊂ Earthly Experience

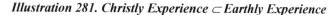

Nevertheless, John affirms that **everyone** who abides in Christ is sinless rather than stating that the **abiding** in Him is sinless (v. 6). Although the latter is true, it is a corollary to the main thought. Yes, the abiding itself is sinless, but John's articulation explicitly says that the person himself or herself is sinless. The sinless experience is an expression of who he or she is—a sinless person. As a result, in *Illustration 286. Anamartetological Emphasis* (p. 796), preference has been given to charting the person himself or herself as ontologically sinless rather than graph the person's experience as sinless. The person **himself** or **herself** who experientially abides in Christ is sinless: positionally, familially, and ontologically.

Transition

Everyone who experientially abides in Him (1Jn 2:28; Jn 15:4) is familially sinless (1Jn 1:7,9), born of Him (1Jn 2:29), and thus does not sin in the manner described in this verse (1Jn 3:9). Since 1Jn 3:6 encompasses both the experiential and nonexperiential aspects of *abiding*, it forms a transitional link between the experiential abiding of 1Jn 2:28 and the nonexperiential abiding of 1Jn 3:9c.

Exhortation to Continue to Abide

The context immediately preceding 3:6 makes it clear that not all regenerate believers experientially abide in Christ. John uses the present imperative three times in 1Jn 2:24,27-28 to exhort these believers to continue to abide in Christ. To be consistent, the habitual interpretation must interpret 1Jn 3:6 as if it were saying that everyone born of Him experientially and continually abides in Him. Obviously, such a position would be impossible to maintain in view of the contextual exhortations.

If all those born of Him abide in Him experientially and continually, then John would not need to exhort these believers to continue to abide in Him in 1Jn 2:24,27-28. That those being exhorted to abide in Him are already born of Him is proven by the fact that John exhorts them to abide in Him rather than believe in Him and by the fact that John uses the present imperative to urge them to continue to abide in Him rather than to start abiding in Him. The habitual interpretation ignores the implication of these exhortations.

The habitual interpretation must interpret the statement in 1Jn 3:6, "no one who abides in Him sins," to mean, (a) every regenerate believer experientially and continually abides in Him and (b) thus does not continually sin. But as just shown, the first part of this interpretation is contextually impossible to maintain. John does not take it for granted that all believers experientially and continually abide in Christ. Since the first part of the phrase (part *a*) does not apply experientially to all regenerate believers, the second part of the phrase (part *b*) does not either. The resulting conclusion would be that only those regenerate believers who experientially abide in Christ do not continually sin while they experientially abide in Christ. Yet even this watered down conclusion, based on the present tense of sin, still would have to be rejected in view of 1Jn 1:8, which acknowledges that we continually have sin. Thus, 1Jn 3:6 is not ruling out continuous sin; it is ruling out all sin.

Exhortations to Believers to Stop Practicing Sin

The habitual (continuous) argument also ignores the tense of the exhortation in 1Jn 2:15. As a present imperative, it can be taken as denoting continuous action and its negation as signifying to stop the habitual action—if one wants to be consistent with the present tense position. These believers were in the habit (to some degree) of loving the world, and John tells them to stop it. The habitual interpretation's argument that the present tense cannot be used to describe the sins of genuine believers runs counter to 1Jn 2:15 where, in fact, it is used to describe the sin of genuine believers. The same is true in 1Jn 3:18 where John tells these genuine believers to stop loving each other with mere words. Without a doubt, the intended recipients of his exhortation in 3:18 are genuine believers since John explicitly refers to them as *little children* whose sins are soteriologically forgiven (cf. 1Jn 2:12) and as *children* who have progressed beyond an infantile understanding of their Father to a juvenile knowledge (1Jn 2:13), even though they might (potentially or partially) not genuinely love one another (1Jn 3:17-18). He uses the present tense of love to describe their dead love for each other. Their verbal practice of love was experientially dead.

Believers with Dead Love do not Know God

This passage (1Jn 3:17-18) is parallel with Jam 2:16. Believers who have a love or faith that is merely verbal are practicing sins of omission. Yet in the next chapter (1Jn 4:8), John will say that such believers do not know God, if they fail to truly love. How can it be that his readers as little children both know God and yet may fail to know God if they do not have a mature love? Considering the comparison between 1Jn 3:17-18 and 4:8, it must be concluded that John does not rule out such believers having saving knowledge; rather, he denies that they have mature knowledge, or at least that their maturity needs to be complemented with greater consistency. A comparison of 1Jn 2:3-6 with 3:6 yields the same conclusion.

Failure to Know God in the Previous Context

Fellowship

1Jn 2:3 starts off with the word *and* connecting this paragraph (1Jn 2:3-11) with the proceeding one (1Jn 1:5-2:2). John is continuing his discussion of fellowship from the previous paragraph. Both paragraphs contain three claims. In the first paragraph, the claims represent believers with the first person plural: "If *we* say" (1Jn 1:6,8,9). In the third paragraph the claims represent believers with the third person: "The *one* who says" (1Jn 2:4,6,9).[1360] Both paragraphs start off by dealing with believers making a claim to fellowship with God. The claim to have fellowship with God in 1Jn 1:6 is now described as a claim to know God in 1Jn 2:4. John uses *knowing* (*ginosko*) God as a synonym for *having fellowship* with God. He is talking about experientially knowing God in terms of fellowship rather than soteriologically in terms of relationship in this passage. As a result, 1Jn 2:3 could be paraphrased as, "By this we know that we have fellowship with Him, if we keep His commandments."

Conditional

In 1Jn 2:3-5, experientially knowing God is conditioned upon keeping His commandments. You cannot know Him without keeping His commandments. If the passage were describing saving knowledge, then it would be conditioning soteric salvation on works, specifically on keeping His commandments. But this is not the case since the passage is not giving the requirement for knowing God in terms of relationship but in terms of fellowship. It is describing familial knowledge rather than soteriological knowledge. Just like Jn 14:20-23, these verses in 1Jn 2:3-5 condition knowledge and love on keeping His commandments. Both passages are addressed to those who already are saved and who thus know God at the rudimentary, soteriological level. In order to progress to a more mature level of knowledge and love, they must work. What is at stake is maturation rather than regeneration, as is proven by John's statement that the person who meets these requirements has a perfect, that is, mature love (1Jn 2:5). The knowledge being spoken of in this passage is closely identified with this maturation in love and thus should be understood as a mature knowledge. The accuracy of this identification is confirmed in the next paragraph in which John talks about believers having an immature knowledge of God corresponding to the childhood level. All believers have this fundamental soteric knowledge of God since they are His children. John next describes the possibility of believers advancing beyond this state to becoming obedient to the word and, in the process of time, developing a mature knowledge of God (1Jn 2:12-14). This potential progression in knowledge is thus: little children—children—young men—fathers.

Mature Knowledge

The believer who has reached a mature love (1Jn 2:5; 4:12,17-18) is not only born of God and therefore has saving knowledge, he or she also has mature knowledge. Just as works perfect faith (Jam 2:22), works also perfect love. In view of the context (3:17-18) and the statements in 3:5 and 4:12,17, a mature love is one that works. Works bring faith and love to full maturity, and works bring the believer who matures in them to a mature knowledge. Those believers who fail to keep His commandments fail to come to a mature knowledge of God.

Perfective Stative

Anderson, Eaton, and Hodges rightly reject the soteric *tests of conversion* interpretation for the Johannine epistles in their commentaries and jointly call attention to the perfect tense for 1Jn 2:3. Eaton's assessment of the perfect aspect is flawed, however, and results in an exegesis that is counterintuitive to the very point Eaton is trying to make. Like the other two commentators, Eaton correctly perceives that experiential knowledge is being stressed in this epistle. Yet he exegetes 1Jn 2:3 as calling believers to *look back* in order to determine whether the knowledge under discussion has been experienced in the past—based on the present fruit of obedience as the *effect* that allows them to determine who is one of the elect as opposed to a gnostic counterfeit. Such an approach is highly inconsistent with his arguments that the Johannine knowledge being discussed in this epistle is experiential rather than soteriological and with his assessment that John is not encouraging soteric introspection.[1361] John is not implying that those who have been soteriologically elect in the past necessarily demonstrate that reality in the present by their ongoing obedience. He is not providing litmus tests by which we become fruit inspectors of the lives of others to determine whether they are one of the Calvinistic elect. Those trying to make the fruit of obedience necessitative evidence for saving knowledge necessarily condition salvation on one's ongoing obedience. Ongoing obedience is necessary in this verse, but not for a past regenerative experience.

The syntax in 1Jn 2:3 is parallel to Heb 3:14. Believers *have become* (●—) partakers of Christ and remain in that state as long as they *hold fast* (→) their assurance (Heb 3:14). Similarly, believers know that they *have come to know* (●—) Christ and remain in that state of knowing Christ as long as they *keep* (→) His commandments (1Jn 2:3). Both verses place a conditional *if* after the perfect state. Placing the condition at the beginning of the sentence, as is normally done in English, may clarify the logical A ⇒ B relationship: "If (A) we keep His commandments, then (B) we have come to know Him." Eaton mistakenly writes as if the purpose of the perfect is to denote antecedent acknowledge: If we knew Him (●) in the past, then we obey (→) Him in the present. Not so. John is not expressing a sequential relation (●→). To the contrary, he is expressing a parallel contingency (●⇁).[1362] Even if John is including the past, his stress is on the present result and underlying contingency. The present and abiding state of knowing God (—) is conditioned on presently obeying (→) Him. Continuing to know Him is conditioned on continuing to obey Him. The stress is on the present state of knowing Him.

Those who teach that the fruit of obedience is necessary for a saving knowledge of Christ are teaching conditional security. The tests-of-conversion interpretation of these epistles presents a series of tests that a person must pass in order to reach heaven. If you fail to pass the tests, you go to hell. Such tests become tests-of-regeneration in which passing such tests is necessary to maintain regeneration. The soteric tests-of-life interpretation inevitably leads to conditional security. For example, conditionalism would make 1Jn 4:12 a soteric condition: "If we love one another, God remains in us" (Eaton's translation). Salvifically keeping God in us is conditioned on our love for one another in such a perspective. Having God abide in us is conditioned on our love for one another. If this is soteriological abiding, then it is conditional security in which staying born of God is conditioned on obeying God. Eaton rightly rejects this conclusion by interpreting *remain* (*meno*) in experiential rather than soteriological terms: "We consciously *enjoy* His blessing in our lives. His indwelling presence *becomes a reality*. Others become *aware* that God is with us and in us."* Experientially enjoying the dynamic reality of abiding in God is conditioned on loving the children of God. Being a child of God is not conditioned on loving the children of God. A soteric interpretation of 4:12 would be counter to such experiential affirmations.

A soteric interpretation of 1Jn 2:3 is equally unnecessary. Eaton's attempt to take this and similar statements in this epistle as litmus tests to determine whether others have been born of God implode on his attempts to avoid soteric introspection. Making subcoming to false doctrine the means of discerning the salvation of others, as Eaton does, necessarily will lead to soteric introspection in which one's personal assurance of salvation is based on his or her own theological perseverance.[1363] One cannot simply point one's finger at others and say that they must pass these tests in order to qualify for heaven and not point one's remaining three fingers at oneself in the process. Extrospection becomes introspection before one has finished Eaton's retrospection.

Aspectual and soteriological objections must be raised against Eaton's Calvinistic retrospection. John is teaching conditional knowledge but not conditional security. Unlike Eaton, Hodges is consistent: "The Christian who has *come to know* the Lord (**through** fellowship and obedience to His commandments) can be assured that he has attained this [experiential] knowledge" (italics his).[1364] John's *if* and Hodge's *through* harmonize to teach conditional experiential knowledge. Moreover, Hodges, quoting Zerwick, correctly notes that the perfect tense "is not a past tense but a present one, indicating not the past action as such but the present 'state of affairs resulting from the past action.'"[1365] Unlike Eaton, who makes having come into a saving knowing of God the sufficient condition for obeying God (so that obeying God is the *effect* of being one of the elect who has come into a saving knowledge of God), Hodges accurately notes that obedience is the *condition* for knowing. Obedience is the necessary means *through* which we know God.

Hodges' stress on the present is also superior to Eaton's soteric retrospection. Nevertheless, Hodges is content with the popular translation of the perfect tense: *we have come to know*. This rendering of the perfect tense is also adopted by Eaton. Does this mean that if we have come to know God salvifically, then we obey God experientially? No. Calvinistic theology misplaces the condition, acting as if (A) the condition is knowing God and (B) obeying God is the necessary effect of knowing God. To the contrary, John makes obeying God the condition for knowing God. The perfect tense does not make knowing God antecedent to obeying God. The logical sequence of the condition is: (A) obey ⇒ (B) know. It is not: (A) have come to know ⇒ (B) obey.

Anderson interprets the verse much the same as Hodges but believes that it is crucial to translate the perfect tense in this verse as *we know* in order to accurately convey the emphasis on the present state. A number of translations render it in this manner. Anderson moves yet a step further to insist: "A more accurate reflection of the emphasis on the intensified state of experiential knowledge here would be, 'And by this we *know* that we **know** Him **intensely**'" (italics his).[1366] Anderson appeals to a Greek aspectologist in defense: "McKay has written an

---

* Eaton, *1 John*, 153.

excellent article dealing with the perfect tense of stative verbs in which he demonstrates that putting a stative verb into the perfect tense has the effect of intensifying the basic meaning of the verb."[1367] Fanning, another aspectologist, cites McKay's article in apparent agreement (VANT, 139).

Pragmatically, since translating the verb in the manner suggested by Hodges (with the auxiliary verb *have*) still results in a faulty aspectual understanding by Eaton, the contracted translation *know* (as suggested by Anderson) is better than *have come to know*. Also, the aspectual support for translating the perfect exclusively in terms of present aspect may be expanded by including instances where the perfect result is expressed by other constructions rather than just conditions. For example, the perfect in 1Jn 1:4 is not translated as: "And these things we write, *so that* (*hina*) our joy may **have** been full."[1368] Translating the potential result with the auxiliary *have* is simply not possible in such a case. John is not saying that his present action (of writing) will change their past emotional state. He is not envisioning time travel, as if what he writes in the present affects the past. Likewise, the present condition of obeying in 2:3 does not determine one's past knowledge of God. Whether the potential result is expressed by *hina* (*so that*) or the third class condition *ean* (*if*), the purpose of the perfect is not to state that one's present actions determine one's past. The contracted translation (*know*) has a lot of merit in leaving out *have*. Still, an expanded interpretative translation is perhaps even better: *we know Him intimately*. Not only is the *have* left out, but the reader is alerted to the deeper aspect of the knowledge conveyed in the Greek by the perfective stative. A firm, intimate, present, experiential knowledge of God is maintained as a result of obeying God.

Despite Anderson's sound reasons for contracting the translation (so as to leave out *have*) and for expanding it (to stress the aspectual emphasis), I generally prefer for a translation to signify the perfect aspect with *have* when possible, at least as a rule of thumb. Therefore, I will adopt what might be regarded realistically as an inferior translation—the one advocated by Hodges and abused by Eaton. Consequently, clarification will have to be provided by means of education rather than translation regarding the contracted-expanded nature of the perfect aspect. I will do so with aspectual symbols. This approach allows me to compare and contrast the perfect found in Heb 3:14 (•⟶) with that found in 1Jn 2:3 (⟶).* In both verses, the typical dot (followed by the line) is retained to demonstrate the perfect aspect. However, the dot in 1Jn 2:3 is deemphasized (since it is a stative perfect) so that the emphasis may be seen to rest on the line (i.e., the state). In both cases, the arrow underneath (showing the underlying linear contingency) is only under the line, not under the dot. The past is not determined by the present, nor is the present determined by the past. Instead, maintaining the present perfect state is conditioned on meeting the present contingency. Maintaining the present experience of knowing God is conditioned on obeying God.

Calvinistic conditionalists are dead wrong when they insist that our present actions (i.e., effects or fruits) determine whether we have come to know God salvifically in the past. John is not saying that our past conversion determines our present performance (or inversely that our present determines our past). A Calvinistic *tests of conversion* interpretation is logically and aspectually impossible. Granted, a frontal assault on unconditional security by an Arminian *tests of conversion* interpretation is still technically permissible, but it is aspectually implausible since a deeper knowledge of God is aspectually indicated and contextually demanded. John is not saying that the way we keep a saving knowledge of God is by morally obeying God. Instead, the way we maintain an intimate knowledge of God is by obeying Him. Ongoing fellowship is conditional; an ongoing relationship is permanent. Union is static; communion is maintained dynamically.

---

* Using this technique also allows me to avoid any appearance of special pleading since I am not necessarily implementing translations and grammars that support my interpretation. Moreover, this translation can be used consistently throughout the epistle for the perfect tense of *know*: "In every case where he employs this tense, an appropriate translation would be *to come to know*" (Hodges, *1 John*, 99; emphasis his). This preference need not be followed slavishly, however. Hodges himself suggests an expanded translation for the perfect for both *see* and *know* in 1Jn 3:6: "Whoever sins is in a not-seeing and not-knowing condition [meaning state] with reference to God" (ibid., 136; emphasis his). The condition for remaining in the state of knowing God is that one obey God by not sinning against God. John is not saying that the one presently sinning has never known God in any saving capacity in the past. Rather, intimate knowledge of God in the present is under discussion. What Hodges endeavors to demonstrate with his translation and explanation, I am seeking to represent with my unmarked symbolization:

When we *sin* (⟶), we do not *know* (—) God.

(•⟶)

The past salvific dot (•) is not in question nor in the translation.

Placing the aspectual symbol for the present tense in light gray is used to deemphasize any necessary linear aspect. The action may be linear, but that is not the point. It is not necessarily linear. The linear action is not emphasized. John is not saying, "When we *are* sin*ning*, we do not know God," as if we have to sin continuously in order to break our fellowship with God. One sin can break it. The auxiliary verb and corresponding *ing* ending should not be used to mark this tense as denoting continuous action in this context.

Levels of Knowledge

Various levels of Johannine knowledge are suggested by the aspect and context. Saving knowledge of the Lord is conditioned upon being His child (1Jn 2:12-13; cf. Jn 10:14; 17:3). All believers know God as their Savior. Yet believers who do not experientially abide in God do not understand Him nor know Him intimately (1Jn 2:3-5). Intimate knowledge of the Lord is dependent upon obeying Him (Jn 8:30-32; 14:20-24; 1Jn 2:3-5). Intimacy moves beyond merely knowing Him in terms of relationship to knowing Him in terms of fellowship (cf. 1Jn 1:6; 2:4). Mature knowledge of the Lord is conditioned upon maturity; intimacy plus time is required to know Him as a father (1Jn 2:13-14; cf. Phil 3:8,10; Jn 14:9). Time in and of itself does not guarantee that immature (saving) knowledge will advance to a mature fatherly knowledge (Jn 14:9).

The abiding experience of 1Jn 2:6 is associated contextually with knowing and loving God in a mature fashion, which in turn refers back to the experiential fellowship of 1Jn 1:6. Through obedience and time, a believer's fluctuating fellowship may achieve the stability of maturity. To the degree we *abide in Him*, we experientially are *in Him* (1Jn 2:5-6). The statements concerning being in Christ, abiding in Christ, keeping His word, knowing Him, loving Him, and walking like Him in 1Jn 2:3-6 should be understood in terms of degrees and levels rather than as absolute statements.

Habitualists Take the Wrong Passage Absolutely

Strangely enough, those who reject the absolute interpretation in 1Jn 3:6-9 try to interpret 1Jn 2:2-6 in an absolute manner by insisting that those who habitually fail to keep His word, love Him, and walk like Him **never** knew Him, never were in Him, never abode in Him, and never loved Him **at all!** They try to interpret 1Jn 2:2-6 as if it were soteric and thus describing absolutes: you are either (absolutely) in Him or you are not in Him at all; you either (absolutely) know Him as your Savior or you do not know Him at all; you either (absolutely) abide in Him or you do not abide in Him at all; you either (absolutely) love Him or you do not love Him at all. Their reasoning is that you are either (absolutely) saved or you are not saved at all; He is either (absolutely) Lord of all or not your Lord at all. They take the wrong passage in absolute terms. There can be various degrees of loving and knowing Him, of abiding and walking in Him, and of keeping His word. Most emphatically, however, there cannot be various degrees of being born of Him (1Jn 3:9)! Just as a woman cannot be a little bit pregnant, a believer cannot be a little bit born of God. 1Jn 3:9 is the absolute passage.

Degrees of Knowledge

On the other hand, the denial in 1Jn 3:6 is basically 1Jn 2:3-6 recapitulated in a nutshell. The same concepts are involved: abiding, knowing, and sinning. The same thought is being expressed. If you abide in Him, you know Him. If you sin, you do not know Him or abide in Him. The matter of experiential degrees must be recalled. To the extent you sin, you do not know Him or abide in Him. (In the following table and discussion, ⊘ = *do not* or *not*). The statements in 1Jn 2:4, 3:6, and 4:8 are practical equivalents. The believer who sins via either sins of omission or commission does not know God.

Illustration 282. Knowing God

1Jn 2:4	1Jn 3:6	1Jn 4:7	1Jn 4:8
⊘ keep commandments ⇒ ⊘ know	sin ⇒ ⊘ know	love ⇒ born & know	⊘ love ⇒ ⊘ know

Observing the contexts of 2:4 and 4:7 is important. John does not announce that if a person sins (or has no love), then he or she is not born of God. In other words, John does not say, *sin ⇒ not born*, nor does he say, *no love ⇒ not born*. Likewise, in 4:8 John does not say that an unloving person is not born of God. Instead, John only negates part of 4:7 in 4:8, not all of it. He says that if you love, you are born of God and know God. However, when he gives the negative form of this statement in the next verse, he does not say that if you do not love, then you are not born of God and do not know God.[1369] He only denies that an unloving person knows God. He stops short of stating that an unloving person is not born of God. Apparently, he stops short of making the absolute negation because he is not speaking absolutely in these texts. That is, he is not saying that there is absolutely no sense in which a sinful or unloving person can know God. Whereas love and knowledge can be experienced in various degrees, birth cannot. Therefore, birth is not negated because denying birth would be an absolute denial of the unloving believer's regenerate experience, which is contrary to John's purpose. Any denial of birth by necessity would be absolute, so birth is not denied.

Love and knowledge can be denied in degrees, so they are expressed in the negation. To the degree a believer does not love, to that degree the believer does not know God.[1370] And 1Jn 3:6 correspondingly is dealing with such degrees. However, this is not strictly the case in its fuller context. In this expanded contextual discussion, John denies that sin can be associated with being born of God in 1Jn 3:9. Since this verse deals with birth, it is an absolute denial. He contextually combines a degree concept, *abiding*, with an absolute concept, *birth*, to show that there is a way in which the degree concept may be taken absolutely. And yet he does so, as he does in 2:4 and 4:8, without denying that a person who manifests a certain degree of sin or who fails to manifest a certain degree of virtue is born of God. John consistently refuses to question someone's regeneration based on the quality or quantity of the person's fruits.

With the previous contexts in mind, we can understand what and why John says what he does in 3:6. John had argued in 1Jn 1:5-2:2 that God is completely sinless (without any darkness), and the only way to have fellowship with Him is to be completely sinless. However, the only way we can be completely sinless in that passage is through familial forgiveness of all our sins, since it is impossible to walk/abide sinlessly in Christ in terms of our experience.

Then John proceeds immediately in the next passage to show that there are degrees of love, and, by necessary implication, degrees of abiding and knowing as well. From what John had said, the reader might be left with the impression that since it is impossible to abide sinlessly in Christ, sin must, in some degree, be a part of our abiding experience in Christ. John slams the door on this possible misunderstanding in 1Jn 3:6, where he again resumes his discussion of knowing in terms of abiding. Sin has no part of our abiding experience in Christ.

His opening phrase, "**everyone who abides in Him does not sin**," of v. 6 should be understood in terms of the degrees of abiding he presented in ch. 2 in conjunction with his discussion of sinlessness in ch. 1. To the extent/degree a believer abides (walks) in Christ (who is absolutely sinless 1:5; 3:5), to that extent/degree the believer is absolutely sinless. Sin is not a part of his or her abiding experience in Christ. Any sin found in a believer's experience cannot be attributed to his or her abiding experience in Christ.

The negative inverse of John's opening statement would be: "**Everyone who sins does not abide in Him**." Sin has absolutely no part in a believer's abiding experience in Christ. John's second statement in 1Jn 3:6 is simply the negative inverse of his first statement stated in slightly different words: "**Everyone who sins has neither come to see Him nor come to know Him**."[1371] To abide in Him is to see and know Him. Sin is absolutely not a part of our abiding in Him, seeing Him, or knowing Him. Sin can have no part in our fellowship with Him. To the degree we sin, we do not abide in Him, see Him, or know Him. And to the degree we abide in Him, see Him, and know Him, we absolutely do not sin. To the extent we experience one, we absolutely do not experience the other.[1372] Peter also talks of believers who lack knowledge, love, and sight (2Pet 1:5-9), so it is erroneous to assume that the failure to express the positive traits proves lack of regeneration.

1Jn 3:7

Little children, let no one deceive you; the one who produces righteousness is righteous, just as He is righteous.

The one who produces righteousness, that is, who experientially abides in Him to any degree, is relationally sinless. They have been born of God (1Jn 2:29) and thus are ontologically sinless. Believers are just as righteous, that is, as sinless, as He is. They are absolutely sinless. True righteousness can come only from a righteous nature. In other words, John is exhorting, "Christians, do not be deceived, anyone who produces any righteousness is absolutely righteous." They are absolutely righteous in some unspecified manner and therefore potentially in multiple aspects.

Tense advocates argue that this verse, coupled with the following verse, must be understood exclusively in terms of continuous action. Logically, their argument would require that one act of righteousness in a life marked by habitual sin is evidence of a sinful nature rather than a righteous nature. But this is a false dichotomy. One act of true righteousness is evidence of a righteous nature just as one act of sin is evidence of a sinful nature. Furthermore, one person can manifest both natures. Applying their same line of reasoning to 1Jn 3:8 allows one to see the folly of the habitual position. From the habitual perspective, we would conclude that one act of sin in a life marked by habitual righteousness is not evidence of a sinful nature; it is evidence of a righteous nature. Such reasoning is absurd. Any degree or amount of sin is evidence of a sinful nature rather than a righteous nature. Even if it were granted that John is thinking primarily in terms of continuous action, this does not prove that he is thinking exclusively in terms of continuous action. Rather, at most, he uses a tense that allows him to think primarily in terms of linear action without ruling out punctiliar action.

1Jn 3:8

Everyone who produces sin is of the devil, because the devil has sinned from the beginning. The Son of God was manifested for this purpose, in order that He might destroy the produce of the devil.

Sin in any degree is of the devil. The abiding believer who sins a little is participating, by means of his or her old nature, in the sphere of darkness. The issue is not simply a little sin versus a lot of sin. All sin is of the devil. Nevertheless, even if the sense of the passage is that of experiential abiding in Christ, what the verse teaches is that one who does not abide in God experientially is *of* the devil. The devil is the origin of his or her actions and nature. Nonetheless, John does not say that such a person is *born of* the devil. Birth is generally associated with the impartation of life. When birth is viewed as an expression of life, viewing someone as born of the devil is unnatural. Viewed from this perspective, one can understand why John does not say that those who sin are born of the devil.[1373] The devil does not impart life but death, and the impartation of death is not normally regarded as birth. In imparting death to the human race, the devil became the father of fallen human nature. Notwithstanding, John avoids associating birth with death. In terms of Johannine imagery, to be *of the devil* does not mean to be *born of the devil* (*of the devil* ≠ *born of the devil*).

Anyone, lost or saved, who sins is of the devil in nature and action (all sin is a work of the devil), since the devil is the source of sin (he started it and is still doing it). Jesus came to take away sin (1Jn 3:5). All sins are satanic in origin and rebellious in nature. Jesus destroys sins by taking them away (3:5). Although the anamartetology of v. 8 is parallel to v. 5 (cp. 5b & 8e), a slight shift in emphasis occurs. Whereas in v. 5 our sinlessness was said to be in God and thus positional, the present verse is used to introduce the sinlessness that is a result of our new birth in v. 9. He came to take away our sins and sin nature. The Lord has come to destroy everything produced by the devil: both our sinful nature and sinful actions. We already have been delivered ontologically from both and will be delivered experientially from both when we see Him. This deliverance is absolute. The question naturally arises, "If you can be the child of the devil without being born of the devil, then can one limit being a child of God to being born of God?" John's discussion suggests that one can be a child in a least two different senses and thus anticipates his statement in the next verse.

1Jn 3:9

Everyone who has been born of God does not produce sin, because His seed abides in him, and it is not possible to sin, due to having been born of God.

This verse stresses that being born of God results in sinlessness in terms of what it produces. Previously, this new birth was described by John in Jn 1:12-13 and 3:3-7. This birth and abiding seed result in a new being (child of God by spiritual childbirth) who is ontologically sinless. Everyone who has new birth does not sin because he or she has a new nature that ontologically abides in him or her (Jn 6:56). This new nature makes ontological sin impossible because begetting by a sinless Parent results in a sinless nature. However, the verse takes an ontological look at the person himself or herself, at who he or she is rather than at what he or she has. It does not limit its perspective to his or her new nature. Rather, it looks at who the believer is as a result of that nature. It does not merely affirm a sinless nature; it affirms a sinless person/child.

The distinctions between person and nature are made herein because in 1Jn 5:1,4 a differentiation is made between the new nature and the person who possesses that new nature. **Who**ever believes is born of God (1Jn 5:1). This refers to the person. **What**ever is born of God overcomes (1Jn 5:4). This refers to the new nature. *Whoever* believes has the *whatever*—the new nature—that overcomes. The *whoever* is the same as the *everyone* in 1Jn 3:9 and refers to the person him or herself. In contrast, the word for *what* in *whatever* is the same word that Jesus uses in Jn 3:6. "*What* is born of the flesh is flesh, and *what* is born of the Spirit is spirit" (TM). This refers to our nature. By a singular response of saving faith, we already have overcome the world because we have received a new nature that is already completely victorious over sin since it cannot sin.

Present Infinitive

The strongest argument for the habitual interpretation is the use of the present active infinitive in the phrase *it is not possible to sin.* The present active infinitive normally denotes linear action. Still, as noted above, even if it were granted that John is thinking primarily in terms of continuous action, this does not establish that he is thinking exclusively in such terms. Rather, he uses a tense that allows him to think primarily in terms of linear action without ruling out punctiliar action. This would explain his use of a present infinitive rather than an aorist infinitive.

His use of an active infinitive with this construction (*ou dunamai;* **not possible**) certainly does not prove that he had linear action exclusively in view. John sometimes uses this expression with an aorist infinitive (Jn 3:3,5; 7:34,36; 8:21-22; 10:35; 13:33,36-37; 5:19 14:17). However, he also frequently uses the present infinitive with this construction (Jn 3:27; 5:19,30; 7:7; 8:43; 9:33; 12:39; 15:4-5; 16:12; 1Jn 3:9; 4:20). John's use of *ou dunamai* (*not possible*) with the present infinitive is demonstrated below.

- John answered and said, "A man **cannot receive** even one thing unless it has been given him from heaven" (Jn 3:27; TM).
- Jesus therefore answered and was saying to them, "Truly, truly, I say to you, the Son can do nothing [lit. **cannot do anything**] of Himself, unless it is something He sees the Father doing." (Jn 5:19).
- I can do nothing [lit. **cannot do anything**] on My own. (Jn 5:30)
- The world **cannot hate** you; but it hates Me because I testify of it, that its deeds are evil. (Jn 7:7)
- You **cannot hear** My word. (Jn 8:43)
- If this man were not from God, He **could do nothing**. (Jn 9:33)
- They **could not believe**. (Jn 12:39)
- Abide in Me, and I in you. As the branch **cannot bear fruit** of itself, unless it abides in the vine, so neither can you, unless you abide in Me. (Jn 15:4)
- For apart from Me you can do nothing [lit. **cannot do anything**]. (Jn 15:5)
- You **cannot bear** them now. (Jn 16:12)
- No one who is born of God practices sin, because His seed abides in him; and he **cannot sin**, because he is born of God. (1Jn 3:9)
- If someone says, "I love God," and hates his brother, he is a liar; for the one who does not love his brother whom he has seen, **cannot love** God whom he has not seen. (1Jn 4:20)

Not even one occurrence of this construction in Johannine literature is translated by NAS or NIV in a manner to denote continuous action other than 1Jn 3:9.[*] Like the NAS, the NIV translates every other occurrence in an unmarked manner. Therefore, neither the NAS or the NIV are marking the linear aspect of the verb simply based on the tense of the verb in 3:9 but on their understanding of the passage. In other words, those who use the tense argument are not basing their understanding of the passage on the tense of the verb; they are basing their understanding of the tense of the verb on their understanding of the passage. They are guilty of circular reasoning: The passage shows that the verb is linear because the verb shows the passage is linear. The linear translation is based on theological presuppositions rather than on Johannine usage. Nowhere else does John limit the present active infinitive in this negative construction to linear action.

Jn 3:27 does not mean that a man may continually rather than occasionally receive something independently of heaven. Rather, a man cannot receive anything independently of heaven. In like fashion, Jn 5:19,30 does not mean that the Son may continually rather than occasionally do something independently of His Father. Rather, the Son cannot do anything independently of His Father. The stress in Jn 7:7 is not that the world may continually rather than occasionally hate unbelievers. Rather, the world cannot hate unbelievers—period. The thought in Jn 8:43 is not that unbelievers occasionally rather than continually savingly hear Jesus. Likewise, in Jn 12:39, their ongoing problem was that they could not believe, not that they could not believe continuously.[†] Jesus is not to be misconstrued as indicating that the unregenerate can occasionally rather than continually believe. In Jn 9:33, the blind man whom Jesus healed does not mean to imply that if Jesus were not from God, He could occasionally rather than continuously heal a man blind from birth! Similarly, Jn 15:4-5 does not mean that a branch may continually rather than occasionally bear fruit independently of the vine. Rather, a branch cannot continually or occasionally bear fruit independently of the vine. Likewise, **1Jn 3:9 does not mean that one born of God may continually rather than occasionally sin. Rather, it means that one born of God cannot continually or occasionally sin.** In the same manner, 1Jn 4:20 does not mean that a believer may continually rather than occasionally love God while simultaneously hating his brother. Rather, a believer can neither continually nor occasionally love God while simultaneously hating his brother. **John never limits the present active infinitive in this construction to linear action. It always refers to both linear and punctiliar action. It is always used for absolute denial, never for merely denying habitual action.**

---

[*] The similar construction of *oudeis dunamai* (*no one is able*) + the present infinitive in Jn 9:4 and 10:29 is likewise absolute. Jesus is not saying that one occasionally can work at night or that one occasionally can snatch the believer out of the Father's hand!

[†] For related examples and further discussion of Jn 12:39, see *John in Living Color*. Their linear inability to believe (even once) is the problem. Their problem is not that they cannot linearly believe but that linearly they cannot believe (at all). Linearly, they could not believe even once. Likewise, in 1Jn 3:9, what is being affirmed is that the one born of God linearly cannot sin even once. As an ongoing principle, a person hardened in unbelief cannot believe (even once) and a person born of God cannot sin (even once). As a matter of principle, an absolute (rather than partial) denial is being made.

Comparison with 1Jn 3:6

Whereas in 1Jn 3:6, John primarily is thinking in terms of degrees with his reference to *abide*, the same cannot be said in 1Jn 3:9 in reference to *birth*, since one is either born of God or not born of God. There are no degrees here. However, the two passages are not incompatible. The point in 3:6 is that to whatever the extent believers abides in Christ, to that extent they are **absolutely sinless**. In 3:9 the thought is that believers are absolutely sinless in terms of who they truly are—people born of God. These two verses combine to teach that sin is not a part of the **expression** of who a believer truly is because it is not a **part** of who he or she truly is. Everyone who has been born of God or who abides in Him does not sin in terms of being born of Him nor in terms of abiding in Him. Sin is not a part of his or her new birth or the expression of his or her new birth.[1374]

Negation and Inversion

As pointed out in the introduction to this appendix, the Navigators and MacArthur use verse 9 to question a person's salvation. In doing so, they use the negative inverse of what John has said. John states in 1Jn 3:9 that everyone who is born of God does not sin. In other words, if you are born of God, then you do not sin (born $\Rightarrow$ $\oslash$sin). The negative inverse would be: If you sin, then you are not born of God (sin $\Rightarrow$ $\oslash$born). From this negative inverse, they conclude that if there is a lot of sin in your life, then you are not born of God. The legitimacy of using a negative inverse (i.e., a contrapositive) already has been demonstrated. A number of John's statements could be expressed as simple negations even though they are not contrapositions.

Illustration 283. Negations

Simple Negation		
1Jn 2:3	keep $\Rightarrow$	know
1Jn 2:4	$\oslash$ keep $\Rightarrow$	$\oslash$ know

Contrapositive Inverse		
1Jn 3:6	abide $\Rightarrow$ $\oslash$ sin	
1Jn 3:6	sin $\Rightarrow$ $\oslash$ abide	

Potential Negation		
1Jn 2:29	does right $\Rightarrow$	born
1Jn 2:29	$\oslash$ right $\Rightarrow$ $\oslash$	born
1Jn 3:10	$\oslash$ right $\Rightarrow$ $\oslash$	____ of God
1Jn 4:7	love $\Rightarrow$	born & know
1Jn 4:8	$\oslash$ love $\Rightarrow$ $\oslash$	____ & $\oslash$ know

Potential Negative Inverse		
1Jn 3:9	born $\Rightarrow$ $\oslash$ sin	
1Jn 3:9	sin $\Rightarrow$ $\oslash$ born	

Unlike contrapositives, simple negations are sometimes true and sometimes not true. Whether or not simple negations are true must be confirmed. Just because something is potentially true does not mean that it is actually true. John informs his readers that the simple negation of 2:3 is actually true in 2:4. According to John, if you keep His commandments, then you know Him. If you do not keep His commandments, then you do not know Him. John affirms the truth of the negation, as he logically must in order for his readers to know that this negation is actually true. In 2:29, he assures that if you produce righteousness, then you are born of God. However, he does not give the negative form. That is, he did not affirm that if you do not produce righteousness, then you are **not born of God**. If that is what he meant, then he easily could have said so. To use this verse to question whether someone is born of God is to put words into John's mouth.

1Jn 2:29 begins this section, and 3:10 concludes it and parallels 2:29. As will be seen in 3:10, when John makes the parallel statement in 3:10, he states that *if you do not produce righteousness, then you are not of God*. He does not imply that *if you do not produce righteousness, then you are not* **born** *of God*. To use this verse to question whether someone is born of God is to fill in a blank that John purposefully leaves blank (see above chart). It is to give a negation that John did not give and that does not logically result from his statement. Likewise, in 4:7 he assures *that if you love, then you are born of God and know God*. Yet when he negates this statement in the next verse, he only negates part of it. He only confirms part of the negation: *If you do not love, then you do not know God*. He does not affirm: *If you do not love, then you are* **not born of God**. In the same manner, to use this verse to question whether someone is born of God is to fill in a blank that John purposefully leaves blank by sticking the word *born* in his mouth.

A discernible pattern emerges. Whenever John has the opportunity to deny that someone is *born of God* based on the amount or degree of sin in the individual's life, John passes up the opportunity to do so. It would seem that he refuses to question someone's salvation based on the amount or degree of sin in a believer's life. Granted, this is an argument from silence and therefore is limited in force. Nevertheless, observing this pattern is better than putting words into John's mouth. Moreover, this observation is not based on an isolated instance but forms a discernible pattern. Furthermore, this pattern is again found in the very verse where the Navigators, MacArthur, and Zeller take their stand.[1375] They use 1Jn 3:9 to question your salvation based on the amount of sin in your life, but this verse demonstrates the same pattern we have just seen in which John avoids using sin to question whether you are born of God. If John does not use inversion to question your conversion, why should you?

Concerning negative inverses, in 3:6 John states the positive: *if you abide in Him, then you do not sin.* He then confirms the negative inverse by affirming that if you sin, then you do not abide in Him. In 3:9 he positively states that if you are born of God, then you do not sin. Given his propensity for negations, one would not be surprised to have John turn right around and provide the inverse by confirming that if you sin, then you are **not born of God**. However, he does not do so. Why not? Why does he pass up such a golden opportunity to use sin to deny that a person is born of God? His refusal to do so is part of the discernible pattern just observed in which he always avoids denying someone's new birth on the basis of sin or the degree of sin in an individual's life. The most natural conclusion would be that his purpose is not to question whether a believer is born of God by means of performance. He is not a performatist or proveitist. He is not denying a believer's new birth because of substandard performance. What he is denying is that sin is a part of that new birth.

Double Explanatory Clauses

Saying that God's seed abides in you is equivalent to saying that you are born of God. Therefore, habitualists conclude that anyone who sins habitually is not born of God. Such a conclusion is counterintuitive to John's methodology. John is not merely denying habitual sin. To insist that *someone who sins occasionally is born of God but someone who sins habitually is not born of God* is just as absurd as thinking that *a little sin proves that you are born of God.*

The absolute interpretation has no problem with the negative inverse: If you sin, then you are not born of God. Sinlessness is the result of being born of a sinless Parent. Therefore, if you are born of a sinless Parent, you are sinless as a result. The habitual interpretation requires the negative inverse to be: If you sin a lot, then you are not born of God. However, if this is John's point, why did he avoid the inverse? Why does he consistently refuse to state his comments in a way that would question the believer's new birth? Further, why would being born of a sinless Parent result in a little sin? The better conclusion is that when a believer is viewed in terms of who he or she is by new birth, the believer is sinless. Believers are new creatures in Christ, are they not?

At times you can use a negative inverse. However, sometimes you cannot use a negative inverse. Someone might respond that when an explanation is given, it provides the conditions under which the statement is true and thus can be used to form a new conditional statement. Perhaps. But another factor makes a negative inverse unlikely in this particular verse. Unlike the other verses, in this verse John gives an explanation clause—two as a matter of fact (a double *hoti*). These explanation clauses further reduce the likelihood that John intends for his statement to be taken in reverse.

For a true representation of John's statement, *the condition* (part A) must be equivalent to *the explanation* (part C). In the following illustration, being a circle *is equivalent to* (≈) being symmetrical: A ≈ C.

Illustration 284. Absolute Explanation

(A) If you are born of God,	(B) you will not sin,	(C) because His seed abides in you.
	(B) You cannot sin,	(C) because you are born of God.
(A) If it is a circle,	(B) it is not a square,	(C) because it is symmetrical.
	(B) It cannot be square,	(C) because it is a circle.

The contrapositive inverse is true:

| (A) If it is a circle, | (B) it is not a square | (i.e., A ⇒ ⊗B). |
| (B) If it is a square, | (A) it is a not a circle | (i.e., B ⇒ ⊗A). |

The fact that the negative inverse is true, however, does not testify that what is being denied is degrees of sinfulness or squareness. What is being denied may still be absolute. It is either a square or a circle; you are either a sinner or a saint (i.e. born of God or not). Since part B is being contrasted with absolutes, the natural inclination would be to take it also as an absolute. That is, in part A, you are either born of God or you are not—no degrees. In part C, you either have His seed abiding in you or you do not—no degrees. In part B, you are either a sinner or you are not—no degrees.

Instead of giving the logical inverse of his statement, John proceeds to say that you cannot sin. His position is that you cannot sin **because** you have been born of God. His point is not that you cannot be born of God because you sin. His argument is that it is impossible for you to sin. Logically, to regard sin as part of your new birth experience or as derivable from your new birth experience is impossible. To indicate that this is the manner in which he wishes to be understood, John gives a double explanation as to why you cannot sin: because His seed abides in you and because you have been born of Him.

Person versus Nature

The distinction was made in the opening comments concerning this verse between person and nature, and it was pointed out that this verse is dealing with the new person rather than just his or her new nature. Nevertheless, although the verse is not viewing the person's new nature itself, it is viewing the person in terms of his or her new nature, or as stated previously, it views believers as who they are as a result of their new nature. The verb used for *born* normally is associated with the male parent's role in birth, and this is the manner in which it is used here. Everyone who has been born of God has His seed (*sperma*; sperm) living in them. The idea is that seed produces according to its kind (Gen 1:11; cf. Mt 13:24-37). Peter also describes new birth in terms of absolute purity in 1Pet 1:23 and 2Pet 1:4.

> *22Having purified your souls* (●—) by obedience to the truth for a sincere love of the brethren, ***start fervently loving*** (◐) one another from the heart, *23having been born again* (●—) not of seed which is corruptible but incorruptible, through the living and abiding word of God. (1Pet 1:22-23; TM)

> *3His divine power has granted* (●—) to us everything pertaining to life and godliness, through the true knowledge of Him who called us by His own glory and excellence. *4For by these He has granted* (●—) to us His precious and magnificent promises, in order that by them you *might become partakers* (●) of the divine nature, *having escaped* (●) the corruption that is in the world by lust.* (2Pet 1:3-4)

The perfect tense shows past action with present result (i.e., ●—). When we obeyed the truth (i.e., believed the gospel), we were purified and still are pure. Nevertheless, this purity may not be expressed in our lives. Peter urges these born again believers to allow their perfect (i.e., ●—) ontological purity to **start** (i.e., ◐) becoming experiential purity. Their ontological purity is expressed by the parallel expressions: having purified souls and having been born of incorruptible seed. Peter also uses the punctiliar form of escape, pertaining to corruption in 2Pet 1:4, to describe their ontological purity, saying that as believers they have escaped lustful corruption.

Hodges is of the opinion that Peter is again instructing his readers in 2Pet 1:4 to become experiential partakers in the purity of the divine nature that is already theirs ontologically.[1376] In other words, because they partake of God's nature ontologically, they should also partake of it experientially. Hodges may very well be correct, but if so, then it is perhaps a little surprising that Peter uses an aorist subjunctive in 2Pet 1:4.[1377] The manner in which Hodges interprets 2Pet 1:4 would seem to take the aorist subjunctive in the same way as the aorist imperative in 1Pet 1:22—meaning to *start* (i.e., ◐). Admittedly, I have taken a similar approach concerning the aorist **imperative** of *ginomai* (to become holy) in 1Pet 1:15, acknowledging that the *passive* form of *ginomai* may take a middle meaning. The aorist **subjunctive**, on the other hand, would seem to be punctiliar, as noted in my discussion pertaining to *believe* in Jn 20:31 and other related texts. Nevertheless, Meisinger has written an article that corroborates the experiential approach taken by Hodges in this context, and Meisinger explicitly states that he is taking the aorist subjective of *ginomai* in 2Pet 1:4 as an ingressive aorist and translates it accordingly: "You may start to become partakers."[1378] This approach is certainly suitable to the context and may even be preferable if *having escape* is regarded as antecedent action to becoming partakers.[1379]

Although the experiential interpretation concerning 2Pet 1:4 is plausible and provides a valid FG alternative, my inclination is to take the aorist subjunctive as denoting punctiliar action. Peter uses an aorist participle to denote the escape, which would seem to also indicate that he is referring to the new birth, which would be punctiliar. Also, both Wilkin and Dillow concur with the preference adopted in the present book in taking the aorist subjunctive in this construction as referring to imputed righteousness in 2Cor 5:21; therefore, it would be absolute and punctiliar. Consequently, it seems preferable to view it as punctiliar in 2Pet 1:4.[1380] Wallace also considers the imperatival use of *hina* with the subjunctive to be rare. So Hodges is appealing to a usage that is used seldom

---

* The perfect tense is conceived as past action with present result and is represented herein by ●— (which is a combination of punctiliar action [●] and resulting static state [—]). Ingressive action is represented by ◐ and can be translated as *start*. To translate Greek tenses woodenly without regard for their contexts is unwise. Nevertheless, this study is simply analyzing the tenses from a tense-advocate presupposition.

according to Wallace, who suggests that 2Pet 1:4 be taken as a purpose-result clause like Jn 3:16, in which *hina* is followed by an aorist subjunctive: *would not perish*. This usage may express both the intention and certainty of the event promised without any doubt (and might be best translated as *would* in certain contexts).[1381] We became partakers of the divine nature and escaped worldly lust the moment we believed—no doubt about it. This escape is perfect and permanent because the nature we received cannot be corrupted by sin. Again, this would be a beautiful OSAS picture of spiritual DNA.[*]

Regardless of which FG option is taken, Peter does affirm that we have been born again of incorruptible seed.[1382] This seed (and by implication the nature and life generated by it) is absolutely incorruptible. It cannot be corrupted by sin or lust. Whereas Peter assures that we are absolutely incorruptible as a result of our new birth, John insures that we are absolutely sinless as a result of our new birth. Whereas Peter looks at our sinless new nature, John looks at us in terms of our new nature. For both writers, God's seed results in absolute sinlessness. Neither writer would agree with the habitual interpretation that attributes a little sin rather than a lot of sin to our new nature.

Ontologically speaking, we are who we are as a result of our birth. Our nature is derived from our parent. A fish gives birth to a fish, a bird to a bird. Believers are new creatures; they have a new Parent; they have a new nature—the nature of their Parent. Since that new nature is derived from a sinless Parent, the new nature is sinless. Because the new nature is sinless, the new creature is sinless. Peter looks at the nature; John looks at the new creature. When viewed exclusively in terms of who we are as a new creature, we must be absolutely sinless because our Parent is absolutely sinless.

Paul, likewise, views us as absolutely sinless in 2Cor 5:17-21 and bases his experiential exhortation on what we are positionally and ontologically. Every believer is in Christ; every believer is a new creature. These statements are absolute. You are either in Christ, or you are not. You are either a new creature, or you are not. Paul is viewing our being in Christ in absolute terms in 2Cor 5:17:

> Therefore if any man is **in Christ**, he is a new creature; the old things passed away; behold, new things have come.

The believers whom Paul is addressing in this epistle in 2Cor 5:20 are new creatures positionally speaking and thus already are completely reconciled to God (2Cor 5:18-19). Nevertheless, he urges them to become experientially what they are positionally, that is, to become reconciled:

> Therefore, we are ambassadors for Christ, as though God were entreating through us; we beg you on behalf of Christ, ***start** being reconciled* (◑) to God.[†]

Positionally speaking, you are either in Christ, or you are not. Paul is not talking about degrees of sinlessness or righteousness in 2Cor 5:21. He is describing perfect imputed righteousness:

> He made Him who knew no sin to be sin on our behalf, that we *might become the righteousness* (●) of God **in Him**.

Paul affirms that God had reconciled (●) them in 2Cor 5:18. He uses punctiliar action to describe that reconciliation. This reconciliation was accomplished by making these believers absolutely sinless and righteous, as he again says in 2Cor 5:21 with the same punctiliar verb tense. This punctiliar verb tense is the same one that Peter used in 2Pet 1:4 to say that we have become partakers of the divine nature. It happened in an instant, the very moment they believed. A completed action is envisioned. Paul describes this in positional terms, "in Christ," and ontological terms, "new creatures." Paul views us as positionally and ontologically sinless. This sinlessness, which happened at the moment of regeneration, is described by all three writers. Likewise, all three (John, Peter, and Paul) urge believers to start becoming experientially what they already are ontologically (1Jn 5:21; 1Pet 1:22; 2Cor 5:20).[1383]

---

[*] See *Spiritual Water*, 754; *Ontological Sinlessness*, 771.

[†] See author's book *Carnal Corinth*. Alternatively, one might simply assume that these new creatures are being exhorted to become (●) something they are not—reconciled (2Cor 5:20). Nevertheless, in conjunction with the other biblical writers expressing a similar injunction, an ingressive understanding is reasonable.

Illustration 285. Ingressive Injunctions

Paul's emphasis is:
- "Start being in practice what you are in **position** and are by nature."

Peter's emphasis is:
- "Start being in practice what you are by **nature**."[1384]

John's emphasis is:
- "Start being in practice what **you** are by nature."

1Jn 3:10

By this the children of God and the children of the devil are manifested. Everyone who does not produce righteousness is not of God.

By producing righteousness versus producing lawlessness, God's sinless offspring and the devil's sinful offspring show their true nature and thus who they truly are: God's sinless offspring versus the devil's sinful offspring.[1385] Anyone, lost or saved, who produces sin is of Satan (i.e., Satan is the source of the sin and the nature that produced that sin). It should not be overlooked that this verse is a recapitulation of 1Jn 3:8, and the two verses taken together refer to sins of omission and commission. Anyone guilty of either type of sin *is not of God*. God is not the source of his or her sin or of the nature that produced that sin. Consequently, God is not the origin of his or her activity or inactivity. As noted in verse 8, although the devil is the father of the lost and they are his children, he is not their genitor. He has not begotten them. They received death rather than life from Satan. John carefully avoids saying that they are born of the devil: *of the devil ≠ born of the devil*. Likewise, *of God ≠ born of God*. That someone is not *of God* does not necessarily mean that they are not *born of God*.[1386]

Since to be a *child of* the devil cannot mean to be *born of* the devil and since it was pointed out in 3:8 that every sin in the life of the believer is of the devil, it is conceivable that the expression *children of the devil* could apply to those who are saved in addition to those who are lost. When believers sin, they are demonstrating a nature and action that is of the devil. They are children of the devil in terms of their behavior. On the other hand, *children of God* must refer to those who are regenerate since the only way to get the new nature is through new birth. Since both the lost and the saved have the old nature, *children of the devil* could refer to either the lost or the saved. Your behavior shows which parent you are acting like—your old parent or your new One. A believer can legally and ontologically be a child of God yet experientially be a child of the devil. In other words, a child of God can live like a child of the devil. Otherwise, John's point simply would be that children of the devil are lost and that the lost manifest their deprived nature by sinning. But regenerate children of God mask rather than manifest their true nature when they sin.

1Jn 5:16

If anyone sees his brother sin a sin not to death, he will ask, and He will give life to him, to those who sin not to death. There is a sin to death; not for this do I say that he should request.

Some sins are worse than others (Jn 19:11). *All sin* is soteriologically fatal to the lost person (Rom 6:23). Yet in the present passage it would be better to label this temporal *fatal sin* as a certain specific sin for which God prematurely would kill a Christian (Acts 5:1-11; 1Cor 5:5; 11:29-30). Nonetheless, the practice of *any sin* can be fatal (Gal 6:1; Heb 12:9; Jam 5:14-20). God has an individual sin scale. It varies according to the type of the sin, the type of sinner, and perhaps the duration of the sin (cf. Mk 9:19). We should warn our Christian brothers and pray for them. Sometimes when Christians take this action on behalf of other Christians, even fatal sin is not terminal (1Cor 5:5; 2Cor 2:6-8).

The inconsistency of the tense advocates is clear in this verse. The NIV gives the habitual translation of the verbs in question in 1Jn 3:6,9 by saying that no believer continues to sin, keeps on sinning, or goes on sinning. The NIV does the same thing in 1Jn 5:18. Yet it translates 5:16 in the absolute sense, in spite of the fact that this verse uses the same tense. If the habitual argument were consistent, it would need to translate verse 16 as, "If anyone sees his brother keep on continually practicing sin not to death, he will ask, and He will give life to him, to those who keep on continually practicing sin not to death." If the tense argument is correct, then tense advocates should correct their theology to say that Christians may in fact practice sin, but they do not practice sin unto death, in which case tense advocates would have to deny that sin can be fatal. Since they cannot do so, they should abandon their tense argument and the faulty theology upon which it is built. Even those who adopt the habitual solution acknowledge that believers can practice sin with the result that such believers die prematurely. This admission destroys the ability of tense advocates to deal consistently with the tense in 1Jn 5:16 and 3:9. Some Christians not only practice sin, they practice sin to such an extent that God takes them home prematurely. Rather than persevere in holiness, such believers persevere in sin—at least to the point of death.[*]

1Jn 5:17

All unrighteousness is sin, and there is a sin not to death.

Not all sin is fatal in the sense defined above. Ezekiel (3:17-21) wrote concerning his responsibility to warn God's children, Israel. A paraphrase of this OT passage is certainly appropriate here to bring out its applicability to those of the present time period:

[17] Christian, I have appointed you a watchman to the church; whenever you hear a word from My mouth, warn your brethren in the church.

[18] When I say to the wicked believer, "You shall surely die," and you do not warn him or speak out to warn the wicked believer from his wicked way that he may live, that wicked believer shall die prematurely in his sin, but you have delivered yourself.

[19] Yet if you have warned the wicked believer, and he does not repent, he shall die prematurely in his sin, but you have delivered yourself.

[20] Again, when a righteous believer turns from his righteousness and sins, and I place an obstacle before him, he will die prematurely; since you have not warned him, he shall die prematurely in his sin, and his righteous deeds which he has done shall not be remembered, but his blood I will require at your hand.

[21] However, if you have warned the righteous believer that righteous believers should not sin, he shall surely live because he took warning, and you have delivered yourself.

By way of immediate application, the passage tells us that we should warn our brothers, that is, our fellow believers, our fellow Christians. But by way of further application, if God is going to hold us accountable for failing to warn believers so that they may be saved from premature death and loss of reward, how much more accountable is He going to hold us for failing to warn unbelievers so that they may be saved from eternal death and suffering in hell.

1Jn 5:18

We know that everyone who has been born of God does not sin, but the one who was born of God keeps himself, and the evil one does not touch him.

This verse is describing absolute sinlessness. The devil cannot touch the believer with sin. Satan cannot induce the one born of God to sin nor accuse him or her of sin, either positionally or ontologically. For the background of being kept form the evil one, see Jn 17:11-12,15.[1387] This background passage describes the absolute unity and thus sinlessness of believers in Christ. This verse is true of all believers, whether they are wicked or righteous in action.

John could say of himself and this particular congregation, "We know that we are of God" (1Jn 5:19). Even so, 1Jn 5:19 is not true of all Christians. Not everyone who is *born of God* is *of God*. Some of those who are born of God fail to manifest the fact that they are born of God in their lifestyle and may die prematurely as a result of that sinful lifestyle. These particular Christians in this congregation had progressed beyond the infancy stage—of merely being born of God, having their sins forgiven (1Jn 2:12), and not being touched by Satan—to the stage of maturity in experientially overcoming Satan as young men (1Jn 2:13-14). As a result they had a mature knowledge of God as fathers (1Jn 2:13-14). This was a mature congregation (1Jn 2:20-21,27) that was experiencing spiritual victory in being *of God* (cf. 1Jn 4:4). Only believers can overcome (1Jn 5:5). Only those *born of God* can be *of*

---

[*] Saints who sin on earth will no longer be considered sinners in heaven. There will be no sinners in heaven. For one thing, John declares that we will be like Him when we see Him. Naturally, and especially in this context, this means that we will be purified of our sin nature. We will no longer be capable of sin, much less capable of practicing sin in heaven. Therefore, when John later indentifies those in the eternal state who are on the outside as liars and murderers, he is not saying that believers who lie or murder are excluded from heaven (Rev 22:15). They will not be liars or murderers in heaven. Therefore, I do not affirm that there will be liars or murderers (outside the city) inside heaven. Saints who are guilty of such sins will no longer be committing those sins or classified as sinners when they reach heaven. More to the point, those pictured on the outside of New Jerusalem will not be committing murder or sexual immorality either. No one will be having sex or committing murder in hell! Yet they are still classified on the basis of such sin due to having engaged in such activity while they were on earth. This articular classification has nothing to do with ongoing participation.

God. These particular believers were being all that they could be. Unfortunately, many believers fall far short of being what they truly are.

Conclusion

Briefly, to review the anamartetology leading up to the first cycle, 1Jn 1:5 pronounces that there is no sin (darkness) in God, and 1Jn 1:7,9 teaches that if we experientially abide in God, then we are familially sinless. Fellowship is dependent upon walking (abiding) in the light and thus upon the practice of righteousness. 1Jn 2:9-11 pictures some Christians as experientially abiding in the light (thus as familially sinless) and some Christians as experientially abiding (i.e., walking) in the darkness (thus as familially sinful). 1Jn 2:12 maintains the relational sinlessness of all believers. 1Jn 2:16 parallels Jam 1:13-17 in teaching that our sin is attributable to our own sinful worldly nature, not to our new nature. In 1Jn 3:1-9, righteousness reveals a new nature and thus a new parentage and new relationship. Sin reveals the old nature and old relationship without nullifying the potential existence of a new nature and new relationship. One sin resulted in Adam's spiritual death ontologically. In remarkable contradistinction, in response to Jesus' prayer (Jn 17:11,15) and promises of eternal life, God keeps sin from resulting in the believer's spiritual death ontologically, so that not even the practice of sin can taint the believer ontologically or eschatologically (1Jn 5:18). For quick reference and summary, the different aspects of anamartetology being set forth and emphasized might be charted as follows.

Illustration 286. Anamartetological Emphasis

1JN	Judicial	Positional	Ontological	Eschatological	Relational	Familial	Misthological
1:7						✓	
1:9						✓	
2:12					✓		
2:28							✓
3:2				✓			
3:3	✓	✓	✓	✓	✓	✓	✓
3:5	✓	✓	✓	✓	✓		
3:6		✓	✓			✓	
3:7	✓	✓	✓		✓	✓	
3:8	✓	✓	✓	✓	✓		
3:9			✓				
5:18			✓				

The simplistic tense argument advocated by LS against the FG position is demonstrably weak. Christians can and do practice sin. The sinlessness being set forth in 1Jn 3:9 does not teach that just because a person is a genuine believer he or she cannot be guilty of practicing sin at the experiential or fleshly level. Such believers are sinless judicially, positionally, ontologically, and relationally, but they are not sinless familially or misthologically. Consequently, pertaining to the eschatological consequences of practicing sin, the reasonable expectation is to find believers who practice sin in the outer darkness rather than in hell.

Appendix 5.
Gnostic Writings

Introduction

This appendix on Gnosticism will give readers a taste of this genre and enable them to understand how and why certain NT believers were caught up in this false theology. We may anticipate that those believers who subcome to this false theology will be consigned to the outer darkness.

Part A. Apocryphon of John

Author

The *Apocryphon of John* (*AJ*) claims to be a record of a secret revelation given to John the Apostle by Christ in which John is instructed by Christ secretly to share this writing only with his fellow spirits, that is, those who share his perspective. A curse is pronounced on anyone who fails to transmit this document secretly. Hence, this document is aptly called an *apocryphon* due to its secrecy in reception and transmission. The fact that it is a revelation of Christ to John which pronounces a curse on those who mistreat the revelation is, of course, reminiscent of the canonical book of Revelation. Both the Gnostic and canonical revelation to John is announced in the same manner: "I have come to teach you what is and what was and what will be" (*AJ* 2:15; cp. Rev 1:19). The reference to Jesus as "the only-begotten one of the Father" (*AJ* 6:15) also brings to mind John's writings.[1388] However, Irenaeus counters that "the Gnostics cannot trace their tradition to the apostles but must admit descent from the enemy of the apostles, Simon Magus."[1389]

Canonicity

Pearson believes that *Apocryphon of John* "very probably served as the basis for that [myth] developed by the Christian Gnostic teacher Valentinus, and further eleborated [sic] by his disciples."[1390] Valentinus was born in northern Egypt at the beginning of the second century A.D. and educated at Alexandria, where he served as a Christian teacher. He was later considered for the office of bishop in Rome. Scott finds it probable that Valentinus "never formally detached himself from orthodox Christianity" and "perhaps never regarded himself as alienated from the Church." Further, Scott states, "Valentinus was much more closely allied to orthodox Christianity than the records of the Fathers might lead us to suppose."[1391] If this be the case, then a favorable case can be made for the use of *AJ* as a Christian document.

On the other hand, although the savior in *AJ* is presented as Jesus Christ, he is not the Christian savior. This Gnostic savior needs salvation when he takes the form of a human body: he is saved when he remembers who he is (31:15). Man is awakened and redeemed by the message of what he really is. The incarnation of this Gnostic Jesus, although not really necessary for our salvation, provides us with an example to follow so that we can achieve our salvation as well. He was saved by following his root back to where he came from (31:15), and we will be saved if we follow our root back to where we came from—the *Pronoia*—the world of light. Jesus' cross was not necessary except evidently to serve as an example that we must endure whatever it takes to finish the good fight in order to achieve ultimate salvation.

This is neither the redemption nor the redeemer of the NT. Scholars have acknowledged that Irenaeus is correct in that this document was written by someone masquerading as John the Apostle. The author of *AJ* and the author of Revelation are two different people. Further, it should be recognized that Irenaeus was correct in considering *AJ* a heresy. Although the Christ of *AJ* masquerades as the Christ of the NT, they are two entirely different saviors. Whether the author was a Gnostic who became Christianized or a Christian who became Gnosticized, it is impossible to say. But it is impossible to regard this author's Christ as the Christ of Christianity.[1392] By advocating a false Christ and by teaching salvation by faith and works, the author of *AJ* certainly falls under Paul's curse as presenting a totally different gospel (Gal 1:6-9).

Conclusion

This Gnostic Christian writing may have influenced the Christian Valentinus (who became a Gnostic). In any case, it clearly pictures the influence of Christianity on Gnosticism or of Gnosticism on Christianity. Regardless of the sequence (Christian then Gnostic or Gnostic then Christian), this document fails to express the Christian faith and is evidence that Christianity cannot embrace Gnosticism.

Part B. Gospel of Philip

Author

Grant believes that "the title may have been an addition" since the *Gospel of Philip* (*GP*) itself does not claim to have been written by Philip.[1393] The only reference to Philip is an insignificant quotation where it is reported that Philip said Joseph the carpenter planted the trees from which he made the cross on which his offspring, Jesus, was crucified (*GP* 73:10,15).[1394] The title probably was added later as a "librarian's device to identify an untitled book."[1395]

Valentinus & Irenaeus

The general consensus is that *GP* represents Valentinian Gnosticism, and that *GP* comes from him or one of his students.[1396] Further, considering Valentinus' background, there is good reason to regard Valentinus as originally having been a believer in the NT sense of the word. The same is true of the author of *GP* in which, according to Wilson, there are some passages

> where the closest parallels are to be found not in Irenaeus' discussion of Gnostic theories but in his own Demonstration of the Christian faith. This is a reminder that the Gnostics were not always so far removed from 'orthodox' Christianity. In the early stages especially there was a good deal of common ground, and it was only gradually that the lines of division emerged.[1397]

Most of the Gnostics we are familiar with wanted to be considered Christians.[1398] And in the case of the *Gospel of Philip* (*GP*), there is reason to give the author of *GP* the benefit of a doubt and regard him as a Christian. Wilson acknowledges an obvious but important point when he says that the author considers himself and his readers Christians. And his concurrence with Grant seems reasonable:

> Here are signs of movement from Judaism through Christianity to Gnosticism, and it is difficult to avoid his conclusion that in Philip 'we find little reason to regard Gnosticism as a pre-Christian phenomenon. It looks like a special way of viewing materials which are largely Christian in origin.[1399]

The author and his readers were originally Christians before becoming Gnostic Christians.

Self-Identification

The author of *GP* refers to Christians seven times and always in a positive manner (52:24; 62:32; 64:24; 67:26; 74:14, 27; 75:32). He explicitly identifies himself and his readers as Christians. "When we were Hebrews we were orphans and had only our mother, but when we became Christians we had both father and mother'" (52:20). He is also very concerned that a person should not make a false claim to be a Christian: "If one go down into the water and come up without having received anything and says, 'I am a Christian,' he has borrowed the name at interest. But if he receives the Holy Spirit, he has the name as a gift. He who has received a gift does not have to give it back, but of him who borrowed it at interest, payment is demanded." In other words, the only one who legitimately can claim to be a Christian is the one who has received the Holy Spirit as a gift; those who borrow the name falsely will pay for it. Furthermore, we are born again through the Spirit (69:5-6).[1400] Apparently, not everyone remains a Christian since some regret it afterwards (74:25-29), but he and his readers have remained Christians (75:32).

Yet they have not been static Christians; in their opinion, their progression to Gnosticism is not an abandonment of Christianity. As already mentioned, Grant believes the progression in *GP* is from "Judaism to Christianity to Gnosticism."[1401] Siker, however, believes the movement is

> from Gentiles to Judaism or non-gnostic Christianity to gnostic Christianity. By becoming proselytes, Gentiles can move from one level to another, from hylic to psychic. Jews and non-gnostic Christians seem to operate on the psychic level, and may become pneumatics, true Christians.[1402]

The book opens (51:29-52:24) with a description of this movement:

> A Hebrew makes another Hebrew, and such a person is called "proselyte"...

A Gentile does not die, for he has never lived in order that he may die. **He who has believed in the truth has found life**, and this one is in danger of dying, for he is alive....When we were Hebrews we were orphans and had only our mother, but when **we became Christians** we had both father and mother (emphasis added).

Siker gives a number of arguments based on the six occurrences of the word "Hebrew" in *GP* as to why *Hebrew* means non-Gnostic Christians rather than simply a reference to their Jewish status. Although he acknowledges the position of Wilson and others, based on traditional presuppositions concerning the definition of key words (that the writer and his readers are Gnostic Christians who "were formerly Jews, and probably Jewish-Christians"), Siker does not commit himself to this position.[1403] However, he does entertain this possibility, which is based on the traditional understanding in his conclusion: "Since the Gospel of Philip refers to Gnostic Christians as former 'Hebrews,' this might be some indication that they themselves were initially Jewish-Christians."[1404] There are then two basic ways in which to understand the terminology:

Illustration 287. Gnostic Christians

	Traditional	Siker
Gentiles	non-Jews	non-Christians
Proselytes	Gentiles converted to Judaism	Gentiles converted to Christianity
Hebrews	Jews	non-Gnostic Christians
Christians	Christians	Gnostic Christians

A major point in Siker's favor is found in 55:29-30 where the apostles and apostolic men are called *Hebrews*. However, it could be countered that the apostles and many of the apostolic men were Hebrews in the traditional sense—they were Jews.[1405] But if apostolic men are of such low esteem, why does the author of *GP* quote from them (66:30-67:1)? Siker further argues that there is a distinction between being Hebrews and Jews based on 62:26-32, where it is said that no one will be disturbed if you say that you are a Jew, Roman, Greek, barbarian, slave, or a free man, but the whole world will tremble if you say that you are a *Christian*. Are we to assume that the pagan world was so sensitive to the distinction between Gnostic and non-Gnostic Christians that they could and would clearly distinguish between the two groups and would only be upset with Gnostic Christians? Of course not! As Wilson points out, "The pagan world, however, did not recognize the finer distinctions between 'orthodox' Christians and Gnostics; all alike were simply Christians."[1406] *GP* also says that "he who has not received the Lord is still a Hebrew" (62:6).

Grant cites this text in favor of his position that *Hebrew* means non-Christian **Jew**, not non-Gnostic Christian.[1407] Yet Siker fails to discuss this text in his treatment of the word *Hebrew*.[1408] Much of Siker's discussion is truly insightful; however, his redefinition of the terms employed must be rejected in favor of the more traditional interpretation. When the author of *GP* says that he and the community became Christians, he is not referring to what they are now (Gnostic Christians); he is affirming that they became believers in the NT sense of the word before becoming believers in the Gnostic sense of the word.

Consequently, *GP's* statement, quoted above, means that *Gentiles* (non-Christians) do not have life. However, they may have life (i.e., become Christians), if they simply believe in the truth. **Therefore, from the GP's perspective, the only requirement to have life in the Christian sense is to believe in the Christian Christ.** This aspect of *GP's* theological perspective is identical to Jn 20:31 and therefore meets the NT definition of a genuine believer. (Also, note the distinction between being an unbeliever and believer in *GP* 80:10.) As a result, it is very reasonable to assume as a working hypothesis that the author of *GP* and the community to which he writes were genuine believers in the NT sense of the word before becoming Gnostics. Any departures from genuine Christianity discovered in the document may be due to their (self-perceived) advancement to Gnosticism after becoming genuine Christians.

Illustration 288. Self-perceived Gnostic Progression

Gentile ⟶ Hebrew\Jew ⟶ Christian ⟶ Gnostic Christians

Gentiles are not destined by their nature to remain in death. They could become proselytes to the Hebrew faith, then become Christians, then Gnostic Christians (i.e., this sequence is: Gentile then Hebrew then Christian then Gnostic Christians). However, there is no reason to assume that the author intends to signify that Gentiles must become proselytes to Judaism before becoming Christians or Gnostic Christians. The author of *GP's* position is simply that a person, whether Jew or Gentile, must become a Christian before he or she can become a Gnostic Christian. *GP's* attitude toward circumcision originally may have been very close to that of the Antiochan church. Circumcision is positive but is not to be taken "as a sign of God's covenant with the Jews."[1409] The observance of the Sabbath and sacrifice are even presented in a negative anti-Judaic light.[1410] The author of *GP's* treatment of these items indicates a basic agreement with the Antiochan church in that in dealing with these Jewish matters, he does not fall under the Galatian curse.

Simon Magus

Borchert finds it incredible that the author of *GP* could have been a "true Christian."[1411] He believes that the author "deceptively uses Christian terminology."[1412] He points to Marcus as an example: "The Gnostic leader who seduced the wife of a prominent Christian by convincing her that God would have direct relations with her and thereby impart to her saving *gnosis*."[1413] Perhaps, Marcus was not a genuine Christian, and perhaps he deceptively used the terminology. But does not the example of this Christian's wife indicate that genuine believers were being deceived by Gnosticism? Borchert next points to Simon Magus in support of his argument. Yet again his argument backfires. According to the Bible, Simon was a genuine believer, who according to tradition became a Gnostic heretic.* Although Magus must biblically be considered a genuine believer, traditionally it was argued that he later became a leader, if not the very founder, of Gnostic Christianity. Since Simon Magus was a genuine believer, nothing rules out the possibility that the author of *GP* was a true believer before becoming a Gnostic believer.[1414]

Contents

To mention a few of the more interesting details presented in *GP*, Jesus is a redeemed redeemer (71:3-4). The story of the virginal conception of Christ is assumed to have been invented because the apostles, being Jewish-Christians, found Mary to be a great anathema (55:24-35). Gnostic believers already have become Christs and will become the Father (61:30ff; cp. 67:26-27). Jesus kisses Mary Magdalene, who is called His companion, often on the mouth (63:32ff) so that she would become spiritually pregnant (cp. 59:1ff). She was Jesus' companion/consort/spouse (59:9; 63:34 *koinonos*).[1415] As human beings have intercourse with one another (78:18,26; *koinonein*), if you become light, you will have intercourse with the light (79:1ff).[1416] The greatest sacrament is the bridal-chamber.

Canonicity

Borchert concurs with "the early Christian heresilogos' view of Gnosticism as a Christian heresy" and gives numerous reasons for concluding that *GP* is evidence of this Christian heresy.[1417] His argument is by and large accurate except for his presupposition that the Gnostic Christians were not genuine believers. At least in certain cases, such as Simon Magus and *GP*, it is possible to presume that they were genuine believers who, in seeking to move beyond the Christ of the NT, actually abandoned Christ. Although from their perspective (and from the prospective of pagans of that time, and from the perspective of many scholars today) they remained Christians in embracing Gnosticism, it must be concluded that in actuality they became apostates. Rather than being merely seen as an attempt to deceive genuine believers, *GP* is probably better understood as the actual deception of genuine believers. These Jewish-Christians in all actuality abandoned their functional status as Christians in their attempt to become Christs. Although their regeneration was not forfeited, their representation of Christ was distorted, and their hopes of Messianic rulership were destroyed.

Conclusion

The *GP* was written by a Jewish-Christian expressing the viewpoint of a Jewish-Christian community who had distorted their faith by moving beyond it to Gnosticism. Like Hymenaeus and Philetus (2Tim 2:18-19), these Gnostics destroyed their own faith and the faith of others by teaching, among other things, that they already had obtained to the resurrection in this life.[1418] As an expression of apostate Christianity, rather than genuine Christianity, the document is a Christian forgery that presents a false Christ. To say the least, it is completely unworthy of canonization. Nevertheless, it is quite likely that many of these apostates had experienced regeneration before abandoning the historic Christian faith for a more contemporary modification of it. As regenerate apostates, one would expect to find them in the outer darkness rather than in hell in eternity future.

---

* See *Portion in Acts 8:21 (meris)* and *Portion* in Acts 8:21 (*kleros*), 108, 110.

Appendix 6.
Eschatological Summation Chart

The PREMILLENNIAL option is correct because:

(I) there is a physical resurrection before the millennium—Rev 20:1-7 (*ezesan; anastasis; achri;* cf. 20:11-13)

(II) the PRETRIBULATIONAL option is correct because:

(A) the rapture (of 1Thess 4:13-18) will proceed and deliver us from the tribulation (of 1Thess 5:1-11):

- 1:10—order: rapture (ch. 4) ⇨ tribulation (ch. 5)
- 4:17 U-turn—cf. Jn 14:1-3
- 4:18—comfort rather than warn
- 5:1 cf. Acts 1:7—imminent
- 5:2 cf. 1:10 & 5:3 (cf. Mt 24:43)—imminent coming and commencement of wrath and destruction
- 5:3 cf. 5:2 (cf. Mt 24:8,9)—the beginning of the tribulation will be imminent and come in a peaceful time
- 5:4 you (believers) versus them (unbelievers)
- 5:5 all—even carnal believers are positionally in the light (cf. in of v. 4) and ontologically sons of light
- 5:6 position is basis for practice and exhortation: practice is not basis for position (cf. 1Thess 5:8; Eph 5:8)
- 5:6 alert (*gregoreo*) = morally awake 5:10 (cf. Mt 24:42-43; 25:13 Mk 13:34-37)
- 5:6-7,10 sleep (*katheudo*) ≠ physically asleep (*koimao*, 1Thess 4:13-15)
- 5:6-7,10 sleep = morally asleep (Mk 13:36)
- 5:8 = 5:4-6 & Eph 5:8: exhorted to be sober because they are positionally & ontologically *of the day*
- 5:9 cf. 1:10 (coming Son delivers from coming wrath)—tribulational salvation (or misthological salvation)
- 5:10 cf. 4:17—"with" as a result of the rapture
- 5:11 cf. 4:18—comfort and encourage rather than warn

(B) the second coming is in TWO STAGES because:

(1) the order is rapture, wrath, revelation (2Thess 2:1-15):

- 2:1   cf. 1Thess 4:13-18 (rapture)
- 2:3   cf. 1Thess 5:2-3,9—the day of the Lord = the future tribulation
  - ⇑ cf. 1Thess 1:10; 5:9 (deliverance promised form future tribulation)
  - ⇑ cf. 1Thess 1:6; 2:14; 3:3-4; 2Thess 1:4-7 (present tribulation ≠ future tribulation)
  - ⇑ the day of the Lord begins with the very beginning of the future seven year tribulation:
  - ⇑ cf. Mt 24:8-9 & 1Thess 5:2-3 it comes like birth pangs which mark the very beginning
  - ⇑ cf. Dan 9:27—it begins with the revealing of the antichrist which happens at the very beginning
  - ⇑ cf. Rev 6 (esp. 6:16-17; 7:14)—the (great) wrath begins with the seals in ch. 6 before chs. 8 or 11
- 2:7 restrainer = Spirit in the church is removed via rapture
- 2:8 then revelation of antichrist; then revelation of Christ
- rapture then tribulational apostasy (2Thess 2:3,11-12)

- cf. 1Thess 5:8-11 & 2Thess 2:13-16 salvation = tribulational (or misthological so be sober, take helmet)
  (2) the first stage is imminent (thus pretribulational):
- eagerly wait, watch, & look for Christ not antichrist (1Cor 1:7; 1Thess 1:10; Phil 3:20; Tit 2:13)
- His coming is at hand and He is at the door (Jam 5:7-9)
- His misthological judgment (Rev 2:25; 3:10-11; 22:12) will quickly take place
- His coming is sudden and the time of His coming cannot be discerned by signs (Mk 13:32-37)
- cf. Mt 24:36-51
  - ⇨ 24:36—Time is unknown and not indicated by signs
  - ⇨ 24:37-38—Life will be business as unusual proceeding His coming
  - ⇨ 24:39—It is sudden, unexpected, and not indicated by signs
  - ⇨ 24:40-41—Taken = paralambano = Jn 14:3 (rapture)
  - ⇨ 24:42—Be on alert now because He may come now
  - ⇨ 24:43—Like thief in the night the time of His coming is unknown (cf. 1Thess 5:2-4; Rev 3:3)
  - ⇨ 24:44—The time of His coming is unexpected (cf. Mt 24:50; Lk 12:40,46)
  - ⇨ 24:43-44—"Day" and/or "hour" = "time" (cf. Rev 3:3; Mt 24:36,42,44,50; Lk 12:39-40, 46)
  (3) the second stage is not imminent since it is proceeded by the revelation, worship, miracles, & teachings of the antichrist, and also by the signing of the peace treaty and destruction of the Jewish temple—(Dan 9; Mk 13:24-26; 2Thess 2:2-8).
  (C) Typology indicates the deliverance of believers before catastrophic judgment as was the case of Noah, and Lot & his wife (2Pet 2:5-9; Mt 24:37-41; Lk 17:26-32; Gen 18:17-19:26).
  (III) The rapture is **FULL** rather than partial because:
- 1Thess 4:16—it involves the resurrection of all dead believers, which includes carnal believers
- 1Thess 4:17—it implicitly involves the translation of all living believers
- 1Thess 5:5-10—explicitly teaches that the rapture is guaranteed regardless the moral quality of believers' lives
- 2Thess 2:6-8—the removal of the restrainer requires the removal of the church
- 1Cor 15:51-52—Paul explicitly teaches the rapture involves all believers
- Lot and his wife typologically indicate the pretribulational rapture of all believes (Lk 17:26-32; Gen 18:17-19:26)
- the judgment of all believers, faithful and unfaithful, occurs simultaneously and immediately after the rapture (Mt 24:42-51; 25:14-30; Lk 14:14; Lk 19:12-27; 1Cor 3:11-15; 2Cor 5:10; Jam 5:8-9; Rev 22:12)

Conclusion: the Bible teaches a FULL, PREtribulational, PREmillennial rapture.

All the points made under II A, II B, and II C argue for a premillennial interpretation. Of course, this means that practically every argument on the chart is an argument for the premillennial interpretation. Obviously, if the rapture is pretribulational, then it must be premillennial. The reasons for accepting the pretribulational position are summarized on the chart as II A (the nature of the rapture as proceeding and delivering from the tribulation). II B (the nature of the second coming as being in two stages), and II C (the nature of typology indicating deliverance of believers). The argument presented in II A is based on 1 Thessalonians; both the order presented in 1 Thessalonians and the details in 1 Thessalonians argue convincingly for accepting the fact that the rapture proceeds and delivers all believers from the tribulation. The order was anticipated in 1Thess 1:10 and in 1Thess 4:13-5:11, and that order is rapture then tribulation.

Appendix 7.
The Unquenchable Eternal Fire

Introduction

The preliminary response offered in the body of this book concerning Gehenna may be satisfactory for those who hold a traditional view. However, it is quite unlikely to suffice for those who hold to conditional immortality or restoration. To fully engage these alternate views is beyond the purpose of the current material. Nevertheless, since ultraists hold to a form of conditional misthological restoration, response to this misthological position will entail some level of response to the broader, soteriological conditional view of immortality or of restoration for the simple reason that misthological ultraists employ some of the same arguments for maintaining a limited duration of punishment. The author does not wish to use a guilt-by-association tactic, though, in responding to ultraists. Let it be clearly stated that ultraists are not conditional immortalitists. Notwithstanding, of necessity there must be an overlapping of their arguments and counterarguments because there are similarities in the view taken by both ultraists and annihilationists. Both groups believe that those put into the flames of hell may only suffer there temporarily.

My primary interaction with the meaning of *aionios* in the body of the text was with Whipple, who takes the adjective as either meaning *limited or unlimited* period of time for a believer's reward depending on the context. This oscillation resulted in an inconsistency in his argument. However, Faust dedicates *Chapter 22* and *Appendix A* of his book to defending the position that believers may suffer fiery punishment for 1000 years. His argument will have greater consistency than Whipple's since Faust rejects the eternal nature of all believers' rewards. By the same token, his argument will have greater problems dealing with the many indications in Scripture that rewards are eternal.

I already have pointed out these weaknesses in the ultraistic argument and need not repeat those arguments again here. Rather, in this section I will strengthen (but not necessarily agree with) Faust's argument by also considering additional passages normally used by conditional advocates in their attempt to prove that punishment in Gehenna may be temporary. My purpose in doing so is to be more thorough in my rebuttal. On the basis of the OT background, some argue that being submitted to unquenchable or eternal fire does not necessarily mean eternal burning. From an ultraistic point of view, this would mean that the OT provides evidence that being put into an eternal or unquenchable flame does not necessarily mean to stay there eternally. Therefore, in the material to follow, I will make what concessions that are possible to Faust and yet still demonstrate the implausibility of believers burning metaphysically in the unquenchable fires of Gehenna.

Unquenchable Fire in the Old Testament

2Kgs 22:17

Because they have forsaken Me and have burned incense to other gods that they might provoke Me to anger with all the work of their hands, therefore My wrath **burns** against *this place*, and it **shall not be quenched**.

The wrath of God was burning against Jerusalem and the people of Judah over the neglected scroll they had just found (2Kgs 22:13). Does the statement that His burning anger against them will *not be quenched* mean that God will be angry with them for eternity? Not necessarily. If His anger is that of the calamities in the scroll (e.g., Dt 28:15-68; Lev 26:14-39), then how can temporal judgments be equated with eternal wrath? Perhaps His wrath would not be quenched until it had run its course completely in executing the promised temporal judgments. Indeed, those taken away in captive would never see their homeland again but die in captivity instead (Dt 28:68). Further, it might be stipulated that the wrath could then be satiated subsequently with repentance on the part of their descendants (Lev 26:40-46). If this is the case, then there is justification in this passage and in the parallel in 2Chron 34:25 for entertaining the possibility that *unquenchable* does not necessarily denote *eternal* burning. If so, Faust would have a basis for using the OT background in this passage to limit the duration of burning.

On the other hand, it is not that easy to dismiss completely a more traditional interpretation that God's burning wrath against the wicked in this passage is eternal, since it may go beyond the temporal calamities that came upon the disobedient in the past. This burning in the past might possibly have a typological connection with a future burning. Further, the literal perpetual burning of that place is quite possible. The offering of one's children to Molech as a burnt offering was prevalent in that time period as an aspect of Baal worship. Although Solomon had built an idol for the worship of Molech in 1Kgs 11:7, it was Ahaz (king of Judea) who actually introduced this pagan practice of sacrificing Israeli children to Molech. "He burned incense in the **Valley of the Son of Hinnom**, and burned his children in the fire, according to the abominations of the nations whom the Lord had cast out before the children of Israel" (2Chron 28:3 NKJ; cf. 2Kgs 16:3).

After Ahaz's death, his son Hezekiah led reforms to do away with such practices in Judah. Yet following Hezekiah's death, his son Manasseh revived this abominable practice (2Kgs 21:6; cf. 2Chron 33:6). The sacrifice of one's children would in turn be stamped out subsequently by Josiah later in the next chapter: "And he defiled Topheth, which is in the **Valley of the Son of Hinnom**, that no man might make his son or his daughter pass through the fire to Molech" (2Kgs 23:20). Even so, it was revived again, evidently by Jehoiakim: "And they have built the high places of Topheth, which is in the **Valley of the Son of Hinnom**, to burn their sons and their daughters in the fire, which I did not command, nor did it come into My heart" (Jer 7:31). "My wrath burns against **this place**, and it shall not be quenched" (2Kgs 22:17). If *this place* in 2Kgs 22:17 includes a **typological** allusion to the *Valley of the Son of Hinnom* as *Gehenna*, as seems very likely, then it is very difficult to claim that the fires have been quenched typologically. The godless unbelievers who burned their children in the fire may indeed burn literally and eternally in the fires associated with that place.

Jeremiah 7:20

> Therefore thus says the Lord God, "Behold, My anger and My wrath will be poured out on this place, on man and on beast and on the trees of the field and on the fruit of the ground; and it will **burn and not be quenched**."

Constable replies: "His judgment would affect people, animals, trees, and crops; in other words, it would affect everything in the land. Nothing would put out the fires of His anger—except genuine repentance (cf. vv. 3, 5-7)."[1419] From this admission by Constable, it likewise would appear that the unquenchable fires can be quenched contextually in the case of repentance. If so, the unquenchable nature of the fire is understood contextually to be conditional. Those submitted to this fire need not suffer it eternally. Again, Faust would have OT justification for limiting the duration of God's unquenchable burning wrath against His people.

Then again, it would appear that Constable might have erred in saying that repentance could quench this fire. God says that if they repent, He will not pour out the fire. However, since they will not repent, He will pour out this unquenchable fire upon them. It would appear that once this fire is unleashed, it is humanly impossible to stop it. The fire may be limited in duration by God, but that duration cannot be cut short by human repentance. If repentance is to stop this fire, it must do so before the fire is lit. Otherwise, the fire will run the full duration that God intends for it to run. Thus, it is humanly impossible to quench this fire once it is kindled. Also, one may need not jump to the conclusion that the passage is describing the literal burning of every single beast and fruit, as will be seen below.

Before leaving this passage, though, my contextual counter that the traditional interpretation need not be dispensed with too quickly in favor of a conditional one may be reinforced theologically. Although Constable points out the contingent possibility of repentance in the early part of the chapter (7:3-7), God foreknows that they will not repent (7:27). As explained elsewhere, God's certainty of their future response did not make their repentance impossible.* On the contrary, their temporal stubbornness is what rendered their repentance impossible (Jer 7:26). Still, the point at present is that this judgment on the cities of Judah in general and Jerusalem in particular is focused contextually on the *Valley of the Son of Hinnom*.

> [31] And they have built the high places of Tophet, which is in the **Valley of the Son of Hinnom**, to burn their sons and their daughters in the fire, which I did not command, nor did it come into My heart. [32] "Therefore behold, the days are coming," says the Lord, "when it will no more be called Tophet, or the **Valley of the Son of Hinnom**, but the Valley of Slaughter; for they will bury in Tophet until there is no room. [33] The corpses of this people will be food for the birds of the heaven and for the beasts of the earth. And no one will frighten them away. [34] Then I will cause to cease from the cities of Judah and from the streets of Jerusalem the voice of mirth and the voice of gladness, the voice of the bridegroom and the voice of the bride. For the land shall be desolate." (Jer 7:31-34, NKJ)

---

* See illustration of "Two Types of Certainty" in *Predestination and the Open View*.

The *Valley of Hinnom* in Hebrew is *Ge Hinnom* and serves as the basis for the NT transliteration *Gehenna*. This word is translated as *hell* by the KJV in the NT. If the unquenchable fires of this literal valley are not eternal, then might it be stipulated that the fires of hell are not eternal either? Or if those fires do not eternally burn the bodies put into it, might it at least be assumed that the fires of hell do not eternally burn the bodies put into it? These are the types of objections raised by conditional immortalitists.

Jeremiah 17:27

But if you do not listen to Me to keep the Sabbath day holy by not carrying a load and coming in through the gates of Jerusalem on the Sabbath day, then I shall **kindle a fire** in its gates, and it will devour the palaces of Jerusalem and **not be quenched**.

As noted above, once this fire is kindled, it is unquenchable. Conditionalists are quick to respond that this does not mean that they will eternally burn the object submitted to their burning. Eby's comments are typical of the conditional point of view:

Since God said no person or thing would "quench" this fire, did that mean that it would *burn for ever*? Since it accomplished the work it was sent to do, and since it is NOT BURNING TODAY, it obviously went out *by itself* after accomplishing its purpose! Unquenchable fire is not eternal fire - it is simply fire that cannot be put out until it has consumed or changed everything it is possible for it to change! It then simply goes out, for there is nothing more to burn. Yet I hear the preachers ranting and raving about poor souls being cast into hell fire where "their worm dies not, and the fire is not quenched" and this, we are told, means eternal, unending torment. How foolish, illogical, and *deceptive*! Such a view contradicts the plain meaning of the term "unquenchable" and its use in the Word of God. (Emphasis his.)[1420]

Accordingly, *unquenchable* is taken by conditionalist immortalitists as simply meaning that no one is able to quench or put out the fire until it has done its work. For example, when the planes full of fuel hit the twin towers, the fire from the terrorists' attacks of 9-11 was unquenchable until it destroyed both skyscrapers. Stopping those fires was humanly impossible. Thus, *unquenchable* might just mean *humanly unquenchable*. The text is stressing human inability. After all, this needs to be stressed. The author once had someone tell him that if God ever tried to burn up the world that man would put it out! The absurdity of such a statement was utterly remarkable. Man could not even save those two buildings! All the king's horses and all the king's men would have a better chance of putting humpty dumpty back together again than for all the fire trucks and all the firemen in the world to quench God's fire even for a moment. God's fire is unstoppable. Man cannot extinguish it. But the question is, "Does God intend for those fires to burn eternally?" The terrorists did not intend for their fires to last throughout eternity, only long enough to destroy those buildings. The fire could not be stopped until it accomplished its purpose. The point Eby is making is intelligible.

Nevertheless, Eby makes a leap in logic to conclude that because the unquenchable fire is limited in duration in this particular context, it must be so limited in every context. Faust is more careful and notes that the expansion or limitation must be based on contextual determination. There are contexts, such as those above (cf. Amos 5:6), in which it might appear that there are limitations, at least to the duration of God's unquenchable fiery judgment upon the inhabitants of the land. But even so, it is very difficult to discount the traditional interpretation altogether, even in this passage.

[2] And go out to the **Valley of the Son of Hinnom**, which is by the entry of the Potsherd Gate; and proclaim there the words that I will tell you, [3] and say, "Hear the word of the Lord, O kings of Judah and inhabitants of Jerusalem. Thus says the Lord of hosts, the God of Israel: 'Behold, I will bring such a catastrophe on *this place*, that whoever hears of it, his ears will tingle. [4] Because they have forsaken Me and made this an alien place, because they have burned incense in it to other gods whom neither they, their fathers, nor the kings of Judah have known, and have filled *this place* with the blood of the innocents [5] (they have also built the high places of Baal, to burn their sons with fire for burnt offerings to Baal, which I did not command or speak, nor did it come into My mind), [6] therefore behold, the days are coming,' says the Lord, 'that *this place* shall no more be called Tophet or the **Valley of the Son of Hinnom**, but the Valley of Slaughter.'" (Jer 19:2-6 NKJ)

Again, the repetitious stress on the Valley of Hinnom is evident. Although the rest of the passage in Jer 7:7-14 does in fact expand upon the temporal expression of *this place* as the city and inhabitants of Jerusalem, the focus of the passage on the *Valley of the Son of Hinnom* does give pause for consideration. If the literal, temporal calamity pictured by the unquenchable fire above is a **typological** envisage of the literal eschatological fire of Gehenna, can it actually be claimed that those fires have long since gone out as Eby assumes? It would appear not.

Ezekiel 20:47-48

And say to the forest of the Negev, "Hear the word of the Lord: thus says the Lord God, 'Behold, I am about to kindle a fire in you, and it shall consume every green tree in you, as well as every dry tree; **the blazing flame will not be quenched**, and the whole surface from south to north will be burned by it. [48] And all flesh will see that I, the Lord, have kindled it; **it shall not be quenched**.'"

Ezekiel and Jeremiah were contemporaneous prophets, and concerning this similar passage from Ezekiel, Constable adds further clarification:

> Here it becomes clear that God was using the trees in the south to represent Judah's people. The Lord announced that He was going to judge the Judahites as when a fire sweeps through a forest. All types of people would suffer, the outwardly righteous (green tree) and the outwardly unrighteous (dry tree), and the judgment would affect the whole land. Everyone would eventually realize that Yahweh had brought this terrible judgment on the Judahites.[1421]

Ezekiel, as Constable notes, goes on in the next few verses (Eze 21:3-5) to explain that he is describing the fire of judgment (i.e., the sword) that would affect everyone: "Both the righteous (the green tree) and the wicked (the dry tree) throughout the whole land."[1422] While conditionalists are pointing out that the trees are not still literally burning, traditionalists could very well respond that the fire was **metaphorical** and may still be ongoing after death against those unrighteous persons (trees) who died in it. This association of God's fury with the sword is also picked up by Jeremiah:

> [35] And they built the high places of Baal which are in the **Valley of the Son of Hinnom**, to cause their sons and their daughters to pass through the fire to Molech, which I did not command them, nor did it come into My mind that they should do this abomination, to cause Judah to sin. [36] Now therefore, thus says the LORD, the God of Israel, concerning this city of which you say, "It shall be delivered into the hand of the king of Babylon by the sword, by the famine, and by the pestilence": [37] Behold, I will gather them out of all countries where I have driven them in My anger, in My fury, and in great wrath; I will bring them back to this place, and I will cause them to dwell safely. (Jer 32:35-37 NKJ)

Now, while it may be true that the fury of the Lord against the city would eventually go out, what about the inhabitants devoured by the sword who had sacrificed their children to Molech? If the green trees represent those who are truly righteous (Eze 21:3), then it may be supposed that they did not participate in such idolatrous sacrifices. Not that it is necessarily impossible for believers to do such a thing, but it may be assumed that such a possibility is not necessarily part of the intended contrast. As to the present discussion, the text appears to fall short of affirming that all aspects of this fire may be quenchable. The physical manifestation of it might be temporarily hidden from view only to be brought back into view in the future millennium.

Isaiah 34:8-15

[8] For it is the **day of the Lord's vengeance**, the year of recompense for the cause of Zion. [9] Its streams shall be turned into pitch, and its dust into brimstone; its land shall become burning pitch. [10] It shall **not be quenched** night or day; **its smoke shall ascend forever**, from generation to generation it shall lie waste; no one shall pass through it **forever and ever**. [11] But the pelican and the porcupine shall possess it, also the owl and the raven shall dwell in it. And He shall stretch out over it the line of confusion and the stones of emptiness. [12] They shall call its nobles to the kingdom, but none shall be there, and all its princes shall be nothing. [13] And thorns shall come up in its palaces, Nettles and brambles in its fortresses; it shall be a habitation of jackals, a courtyard for ostriches. [14] The wild beasts of the desert shall also meet with the jackals, and the wild goat shall bleat to its

companion; also the night creature shall rest there, and find for herself a place of rest. [15] There the arrow snake shall make her nest and lay eggs and hatch, and gather them under her shadow; there also shall the hawks be gathered, every one with her mate. (NKJ)

Unlike the other passages considered thus far, this passage clearly moves beyond the temporal present to the eschatological future—to the Day of the Lord. It is depicting the land of Edom as burning forever with an unquenchable fire at the end of the tribulation and throughout the millennial age. Relative to the existence of that land in the millennial age, the fire will be unquenchable. Evidently, this part of the earth will remain a desolate land of burning tar throughout the millennial age and will not experience the renovation described in later chapters of Isaiah during that time period (see Is 35, 40-66). Notwithstanding, at the end of such time, the whole earth will be made new, and this land as such will presumably cease to exist. Or more likely, it will be relocated to the place of eternal torment. The fire will continue to burn in that land as long as that land exists and then be merged with the eternal fires of the eternal state. Once again, it is possible for the traditionalist to maintain the everlasting nature of the fire in one form or another, whether it is typological or an eschatological merger with the ultimate reality to which it typologically points.

Isaiah 66:23-24

[23] "And it shall be from new moon to new moon and from Sabbath to Sabbath, all mankind will come to bow down before Me," says the Lord. [24] "Then they shall go forth and look on the corpses of the men who have transgressed against Me. **For their worm shall not die, and their fire shall not be quenched**; and they shall be an abhorrence to all mankind."

These verses form the conclusion of the book of Isaiah and again recap the conclusion of the tribulation and the beginning of the millennial kingdom. Whereas the above passage describes the inhabitation of the wicked at the beginning of the millennium, this final passage in Isaiah foretells the fate of the wicked at the beginning of the millennium. Concerning this passage, Constable states:

> The worshippers would be able to view the corpses of those whom the Lord will judge. This probably includes those **killed in the battle of Armageddon and those sentenced to eternal damnation**. The picture is of Jerusalem dwellers going outside the city to the Hinnom Valley where garbage and corpses burned constantly, where worms (corruption) and fire (holy wrath) were always working (cf. Matt. 5:22; Mark 9:43; Luke 12:5). As those who worship God rejoice before Him perpetually, so those who rebel against Him will die perpetually (cf. Matt. 25:46). (Emphasis added.)[1423]

This text is the one that Jesus quotes in the NT concerning the punishment of the wicked in Gehenna (Mk 9:44,46,48). There is certainly a problem in the conservative argument here that Faust may exploit in defense of his position concerning Gehenna. Dispensationalists of the conservative misthological camp would equate Gehenna with eternal suffering in the Lake of Fire. Impe summarizes the traditional view nicely:

> The two Greek words used for "hell" in the New Testament are *Hades* and *Gehenna*. The temporary holding place is Hades, while Gehenna refers to the final "penitentiary" for lost souls. The lake of fire is synonymous with Gehenna, which differs from Hades in that Gehenna is a place where there are degrees of suffering.[1424]

Impe then goes on to equate the undying worms and the outer darkness with the Lake of Fire. However, in the same study Bible, Evans refutes Impe's position: "The 'outer darkness' described in this passage is not hell, but is likely a lesser status in God's kingdom."[1425] The present work, of course, substantiates Evans' assessment. But if Impe is so mistaken about the outer darkness, how can we be so certain that he is not also mistaken about the worms? Here is the problem. If Gehenna refers to, or at least includes, the millennial age, as Isaiah surely seems to indicate, then Faust has a strong platform from which to launch his argument that the fires and worms of Gehenna are millennial rather than eternal and that unfaithful believers are only punished in the flames of Gehenna for a thousand years rather than in the eternal flames of the Lake of Fire for eternity.

Millennial or Eternal Fire

Let it further be noted on Faust's behalf that Carmical (in a misthologically conservative journal) pictures the above passage in Is 66:24 as finding millennial fulfillment: "Most distressing of all [during the millennial age] was the smoke that constantly rose from the Valley of Hinnom, smoke belching out of the dreaded entrance to Hell."[1426] In his footnote to this assessment, Carmical cites Is 66:24 and Rev 14:9-12 in support.[1427] In fact, he explicitly mentions the "unhappy sounds" coming from those suffering in "Gehenna" during the millennium.[1428] To be sure, other interpreters like Ryrie, Martin, and Archer all believe that Is 66:24 refers to eternal torment. Ryrie actually goes so far as to say that the passage "refers to the eternal state."[1429] But like Constable above, Archer combines the millennial with the eternal:

> The establishment of new heavens and a new earth will usher in the final, permanent, and unchanging state of both the redeemed and the dammed....Yet Jerusalem visits would still be a logical possibility for the duration of the Thousand Year period. The faithful will look on the corpses of those who have joined in the final assault of the World-Power on Jerusalem, as they litter the battlefield...Note that it is not said that the corpses will lie there forever. The souls of the wicked will be consigned to the eternal torments of hell (as Christ reaffirmed in Mk 9:48)."[1430]

However, if the corpses do not *lie there forever*, is there any reason to believe that the worms infesting their bodies will gnaw there forever? And if the worms do not gnaw eternally, then must it be concluded that the fire burns eternally? Martin concurs concerning the merger of eschatological periods denoted by *the new heavens and new earth* (Is 65:17; 66:22):

> In these verses the Lord described the millennial kingdom, which is seemingly identified here with the eternal state (**new heavens and a new earth**). In Revelation, however, the new heavens and new earth (Rev. 21:1) *follow* the Millennium (Rev. 20:4). Most likely Isaiah did not distinguish between these two aspects of God's rule; he saw them together as one. (Emphasis his.)[1431]

Constable makes similar remarks:

> Isaiah described the future generally as a new heaven and a new earth. In the New Testament, we have further particularization of what this will involve: the making of all things new for those in Christ presently (Gal. 2:20), the millennial kingdom (Rev. 20:4-6), and the "eternal state" (2 Pet. 3:13; Rev. 21:1). Thus Isaiah's use of "new heavens and a new earth" is not identical with the Apostle John's (Rev. 21:1). What Isaiah wrote about this new creation is true of various segments of it at various stages in the future; it is not all a description of what John identified as "new heavens and a new earth," namely, the eternal state.[1432]

Archer likewise summarizes: "The designation **new heavens and a new earth** is applied to the Millennial kingdom only as a stage preliminary to the eternal glories of heaven."[1433] Traditionalists, for the most part, evidently are willing to concede that the description of fire and worms in Is 66:24 may indeed be a preliminary reference to the millennial state. Even so, this millennial picture is simply "an early description of eternal punishment."[1434] Therefore, it is herein acknowledged that Faust would be justified in finding a millennial background for Gehenna in this OT passage. Carmical's description, depicting the OT Gehenna as the mouth to Hades during the millennial age, is thus accepted without abandoning the traditional position concerning Gehenna in the NT. Carmical was extremely astute in linking the millennial Gehenna to Is 66:24 and not citing its NT counterpart in Mk 9:44-48.

A misthologically conservative assessment would be that the NT Gehenna is distinguishable from its OT counterpart. Jesus takes the latent potential of Is 66:24 and brings out its full and final fulfillment in eternity future. John does the very same thing with the *new heavens and new earth*. Although Isaiah includes both the millennium and the eternal state under this inclusive terminology, John limits it to the eternal state in Rev 21:6. A defense of the traditional view will allow that Jesus did the same with Gehenna. The millennial Gehenna of the OT serves as a picture of the eternal Gehenna of the NT. The fire and worms of the *new heavens and new earth* during the millennial age will become the fire and worms of the Lake of Fire in the eternal state.

Illustration 289. Millennial and Eternal Worms

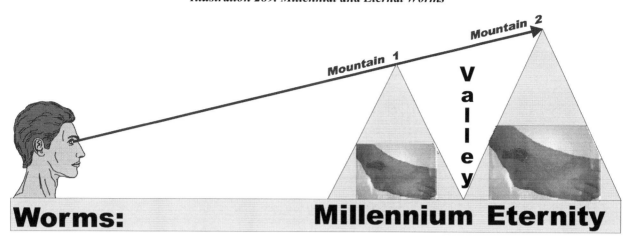

To restate in terms of the above illustration, Isaiah saw the worms in the unquenchable fire gnawing the bodies of those within it. This has been pictured in the above illustration by a foot in the flames of fire with a worm emerging from under the skin of the worm-infested foot. Isaiah saw the millennial and eternal aspects of this reality merged together. He could not distinguish the short period of time that would have taken place between the millennial state and eternal state in this prophetic picture that the Lord gave him at that time. But the picture becomes progressively clearer in the NT. The same type of fulfillment—literal fulfillment—will be experienced in both states. The flames will burn literally and the worms will gnaw literally. However, when it comes to the NT period, the eternal aspect of this punishment is exclusively in view. Jesus is only pointing to the second mountain peak, not to the first one.

Concessions to Faust

To this point, it has been conceded that Faust is correct that the terminology employed concerning the fire not being quenched need not necessarily mean that the fire will burn eternally if the context logically warrants such a limitation. However, this limited concession is nothing new. Walvoord already has pointed out the necessity of contextual sensitivity in conjunction with the above text and with the *devouring fire* and *everlasting burnings* of Is 33:14.

> To some, that the idea of "forever" does not always mean an infinite duration in time may seem to be an unnecessary concession to the opponents of eternal punishment. But like the word "all," this word has to be interpreted in its context: and where the context itself limits the duration, this needs to be recognized in fairness to the text. At the same time, however, an important principle must be observed all throughout the Scriptures: while the term "forever" may sometimes be curtailed in duration by its context, such termination is never once mentioned in either the Old or New Testament as relating to the punishment of the wicked. Accordingly, the term continues to mean "everlasting" or "unending in its duration." Unfortunately, this is not recognized by those who are opposed to eternal punishment.[1435]

Walvoord, as well as the present writer, are in agreement with Faust that a *relative all* is possible in certain contexts and that *forever* does not necessarily refer to eternity future in the OT. Nevertheless, the point of disagreement that Walvoord and I have with ultraists will be with their identification of Gehenna and their definition of *aionios* in the NT. Despite this concession in the OT usage, Walvoord insists that the NT Gehenna was "traditionally understood by the Jews as the place of the final punishment of the wicked….its usage in the New Testament is clearly a reference to the **everlasting** state of the wicked, and this seems to be the thought in every instance."[1436]

As to *aionios*, Walvoord correctly acknowledges that *aion* may or may not refer to eternity. This noun might be used to refer just to a limited portion of eternity, such as an *age*. Nevertheless, he contends that the adjectival form *aionios* always refers to that which is eternal in the NT. He defers the reader to Harry Buis' book *The Doctrine of Eternal Punishment* for lexical analysis.[1437] At the same time, a simple premise is noted that unless the context indicates otherwise, *all* is understood to mean absolutely *all* and *forever* is taken to mean *forever*. The burden of proof naturally will be on those who seek to limit these terms in any particular context.

Aionios and Forms of Eternity

Walvoord clarifies, nevertheless, that various forms of eternity must be acknowledged. If one pictures a number line extending in either direction or both directions, then one can easily see three different ways something can be eternal. It can extend into the eternal past. On a number line, eternity past would be pictured as an arrow pointing to the left in the direction of negative infinity. Or it can extend the opposite direction in an infinite positive direction into the eternal future, which is correspondingly depicted below as positive infinity. Or eternity can extend infinitely in both directions. Affirmations of eternity in the present and future are pretty straightforward. Eternity past is questionable, however. Some would assert that eternity past could refer to a finite amount of time.

Illustration 290. Three forms of Eternity

Eternity Past	Eternity Absolute	Eternity Future
$\longleftarrow -\infty \;\bullet$	$\longleftarrow \infty \longrightarrow$	$\bullet\; \infty + \longrightarrow$
or		
$\mathbf{A} \; \overset{?}{\rule{2cm}{0.4pt}} \; \mathbf{B}$		

Suppose you took infinity and divided it in two. You still would be left with an infinite amount of time, whether you are looking at the past or the future. Walvoord explains that those who try to restrict *aionios* to a finite duration typically challenge the eternalists on the basis of texts dealing with eternity past or eternity future. For example, L-N lists two ranges of meaning for *aionios*. (1) It can mean *eternal* in the sense of "unlimited duration of time" (67.96). And L-N explicitly lists the Gehenna passage of Mt 18:8 (cp. 18:9) in this category. (2) However, L-N also lists another possibility in which *aionios* may mean: "An exceedingly long period of time from an assumed beginning up to the present – 'since all time, from all ages past, from the beginning of time'" (67.133). This second meaning is the one pictured above by a question mark under eternity past. It is stigmatized with a question mark because I find this lexical alternative to be of questionable accuracy for the NT, at least when trying to move point A (the beginning point) to the beginning of time. Five sample passages for this second meaning are cited by L-N: Jn 9:32; Col 1:26; Rom 16:25; 2Tim 1:9; Jude 1:25. However, the first two are not applicable to our discussion because they use the nominal form (*aion*) rather than the adjectival form (*aionios*). This leaves three passages in which L-N says that *aionios* refers to a "period of time." However, Walvoord says that passages such as these (Rom 16:25; 2Tim 1:9; Tit 1:2) are describing **eternity** past, not a limited period of time. Of course, Walvoord's position is nothing new. In his chapter, *Is Future Punishment Everlasting?*, Wuest takes the same position concerning these texts and the adjectival use in the NT: "In all its occurrences in the New Testament, *aionios* never refers to a limited extent of time, but always to that which is eternal or everlasting."[1438]

Looking at the more contemporaneous lexical scene, BDAG lists three ranges of meaning for *aionios*. (1) BDAG basically concurs with L-N that it can refer "to a long period of time, *long ago*" and cites Rom 16:25. Again, note the "period of time" definition for *aionios*. In this same category, BDAG cites 2Tim 1:9 and Tit 1:2 and similarly defines their meaning as "*before time began*." (2) Another meaning is "a period of time without beginning or end, *eternal*." For example, God is eternal in the fullest sense. He does not have beginning or end. (3) However, the category for which BDAG cites numerous examples is the last one: "A period of unending duration, *without end*." The Gehenna passage of Mt 18:18 is one of many such examples cited by BDAG in this category. The italics in each of the three categories are those of BDAG and simply denote its translation for that respective category. Translations used for the third category also include *forever* and *everlasting*.

This lexical delineation by BDAG corresponds to my graphical representation above with the exception of the first category. BDAG and L-N are evidently content with the temporal definition of *aionios* regarding these questionable texts for the past. The NKJ concurs and translates Rom 16:25 as "since the world began." However, Walvoord treats them as dealing with eternity past. Of these three texts, the most difficult is Rom 16:25. Constable concurs with Walvoord on the meaning of this text: "The gospel had been hidden in **eternity past** until God revealed it first in the Old Testament and then fully in the New."[1439] Some translations also express this viewpoint (ASV; BBE; DRA; NJB). The literal translation provided by the first of these two translations is good: *through times eternal*. Still, a smoother alternative would be something more akin to: *from eternity past*.

Rather than simply base our preference on the stance taken by Walvoord and Constable, note that Rom 16:25 lexically falls into the same broad class of 2Tim 1:9; Tit 1:2; and Jude 1:25. The NAS renders 2Tim 1:9 as *from all eternity*. Obviously, this translation would be very conducive to my position, since I maintain that what is pictured is eternity past rather than a finite amount of time—the latter of which is represented by the time segment with the question mark above it. Nevertheless, since the wording of the NKJ is contrary to my position on Rom 16:25, I will adopt its translation of 2Tim 1:9, *before time began*, and interact with this rendition and demonstrate that even proceeding from this more difficult premise leads to my conclusion.

To use an oxymoron, if pre-temporal time is understood as being eternally timeless, then the NKJ (as well as L-N and BDAG) immediately encounter a problem. There is no point in *time before time began* to which the temporal line segment can be anchored. There is no such thing as *pre-temporal time*. On the eternally timeless view, no chronological sequence before time began exists to which we can anchor point A (the initial point of the line segment). In this view of time, the translation by NKJ and the definitions by L-N and BDAG are impossible.

Illustration 291. Eternally Timeless Line Segment

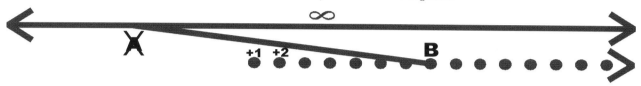

The same shortcoming is true if we adopt the initial timeless view. It is like trying to anchor your boat in a bottomless sea. The temporal line segment keeps sliding infinitely down the number line..

Illustration 292. Initially Timeless Line Segment

Either of these two above views automatically results in Walvoord's position. There is no initial point in time to which we can anchor this initial point (i.e., A) since we must anchor it *before time began*. The supposed line segment slides endlessly backwards into eternity past.

Illustration 293. A Timeless Beginning is Eternal

The present author's preference, as discussed elsewhere, allows the line segment to be anchored in both the metaphorical time on top and the temporal time on bottom. Thus, if L-N, BDAG, and NKJ are adopting a similar view of time as that held by the present author, then it is at least possible to graph this possibility.[*]

Illustration 294. Metaphysical-Temporal Time Segment

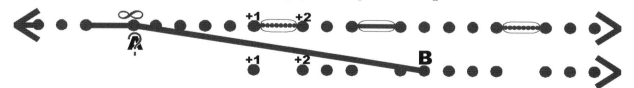

In this view of time, there is a point of beginning and ending, that is, a point A and B. But it is very speculative as to how a temporal line segment could be temporally anchored that far back in metaphysical reality.

---

[*] See illustration of "Elastically Temporal" in *Predestination and the Open View*.

It may not stretch our logic to extend the segment that far, but it does stretch our imagination, all most to the breaking point, to think that the biblical writers were using this pre-temporal terminology to denote a temporally limited time period. Even if *aionios* is technically not eternal in the strictest logical sense for these particular passages, it is still nevertheless eternal for all practical purposes, even in this model. The supposed time segment spans our time frame and moves somewhere into the great beyond of eternity past. Even if point A (the first terminal point of the segment) is not eternal in eternity past from a metaphysical perspective, it is pragmatically eternal from a temporal perspective. I am content to regard *aionios* as describing eternity past from a temporal perspective and thus concur with Walvoord.

Here is a lexical problem, then, that Faust must contend with: Although the primary Greek lexicons of our day do give credence to his view that *aionios* may be limited, they do this for the past, not for the present or future, which does not help his case at all. For this reason, Peterson is certainly justified in appealing to classic research in this area: "Shedd concludes that when applied to hell *aionios* means 'endless' since it pertains to the future infinite age."[1440] Conditionalists have long insisted on taking *aionios* as meaning *age-lasting* rather than *everlasting* for the **present** and **future** and have been resisted by traditionalists in this regard, apparently for good reason. It is even questionable whether the conditionalistic lexical assessment for *aionios* as limited to mean a temporal period of time in the **past** is even pragmatically possible when the past is moved to the beginning of time. Moreover, even if *aionios* does mean a limited period of time in the past, can ultraists demonstrate that it was limited in that capacity to one age, rather than two, three, four, or a practically unlimited number of ages?

Contrastive Passages

Daniel 12:2

And many of those who sleep in the dust of the ground will awake, some to *everlasting* (*aionios*) life,
but others to disgrace and *everlasting* (*aionios*) shame. (TM)

How would Faust answer conditionalists who argue that *everlasting* is only used relatively and does not denote everlasting burning **of the lost**? Probably, he would apply the same argument that is employed commonly by traditionalists: show a passage of Scripture in which the word *everlasting* is used to show that the everlasting benefit conferred upon the saved is eternal in contrast to the everlasting punishment inflicted upon the lost. Such parallelism would indicate that the lost will suffer eternally. I already have dealt with the immediate context of the above verse.* Since Faust is a dispensationalist, the first of the previous three options (simple soteriological) is really not suitable for his position. This realistically leaves two more possibilities.

Faust could take a soteriologically telescopic position discussed previously. Indeed, I have just taken a telescopic understanding of Is 66:23-24 above. And Faust concurs with the telescopic approach in general:

There are many Scriptures that speak of Christ's first and second comings at the same time. Therefore, it is possible that many passages that appear to be describing an eternal kingdom are in actuality, revealing the final and endless age *on top of* the millennial age. They read as one event (i.e., one kingdom), as if there is no division between the *two* different ages. (Emphasis his.)[1441]

I fully concur with Faust on this telescopic understanding. Constable applies this approach to this present passage and says that the resurrections are a thousand years apart.[1442] Yet the problem for conditionalists is that the LXX uses *aionios* for both *everlasting life* and *everlasting shame*. The everlasting shame lasts as long as the everlasting life and must therefore be eternal. If this passage is soteriological, as Constable believes, then it refutes conditional immortalitists. But it is not at all apparent that the ultraistic argument fares any better. Regarding the telescopic nature of Is 66:23-24 above, it was shown that the millennial age only serves to introduce the eternal state of affairs that will follow. The soteriological telescopic view militates against the millennial limitation that Faust seeks to impose upon unquenchable punishment. The lost burn forever. If Faust were to seek to counter by advocating a misthological understanding of the burning in Is 66:23-24, on the basis of the misthological understanding I supplied earlier concerning Dan 12:2, then I would clarify that I prefer an interpretation of Dan 12:2 that is both misthological and telescopic. That is, Dan 12:2 misthologically describes what will happen to faithful and unfaithful believers and telescopically describes this millennial result as lasting into the eternal state.

---

* See *Daniel 12:1-3*, 533.

Whether the passage is misthologically or soteriologically telescopic, it fails to limit the *aionios* as falling short of eternity future. Both the millennial and eternal life and shame are telescopically merged.

The results of this judgment are everlasting—spanning the millennium and encompassing the eternal state. It is a picture of eternity future. Faust's limitation of rewards to the millennium falters. Faust cannot limit the *shame* that the unfaithful believer experiences to the millennium without simultaneously limiting the affirmation of *life* for the obedient believer to the millennium as well. Therefore, whether *aionios* is used of a positive or negative recompense, it refers to an eternal consequence. This Danielic passage is very important for our transition to the NT. This verse is the first reference to eternal life in the OT, and it is the first description of a twofold resurrection. Regardless of which of the three interpretations are taken, it leads to the conclusion that the results of the resurrection are permanent for both parties being contrasted. Even Fudge, a conditionalist, concludes in his chapter on *aionios* that it means that the "outcome of the judgment will have no end." It is *everlasting* in that it denotes "a result which will never end."[1443]

Fudge, of course, takes such passages soteriologically and contends that the ultimate extinction of the mortal soul would satisfy this requirement. The judgment against that soul would not be extinguished or end because the soul permanently would cease to exist as a result of such judgment. However, Faust cannot retreat to such a claim because he, like the present author, to use nontechnical language, presumably holds to the immortality of the human soul. As Erickson summarizes, the biblical concept of this immortality differs from that of Greek philosophy in that the biblical view does not view the eternality of the soul as extending in "both directions, past and future, having neither beginning nor end."[1444] In other words, eternity absolute (pictured above) does not apply to the human soul. The human soul is not absolutely eternal; rather, its eternality is derived from the one who creates it—God. The soul therefore has a derivative eternality and is eternal in the sense of lasting throughout eternity future. Contrary to the criticisms launched by conditionalists, the reason traditionalists believe in the eternal torment of the lost soul is not because they believe in the immortality of the soul. Rather, the reverse is true; traditionalists believe in the immortality of the soul because they believe in the eternal torment of the lost soul.

The traditionalist believes that lost souls will be tormented throughout eternity future. Although Fudge would reject the notion of ongoing torment, he would acknowledge that everlasting results are demanded by *aionios*. Thus, both the traditionalist and conditionalist can join together in refuting Faust's contention that *aionios* denotes temporary results. For Faust to interject temporary punishment where the Bible uses *aionios*, he must mount a very convincing case indeed. The parallel contrast of the fate of the faithful and unfaithful in terms of *aionios* would appear to be a very fatal counterpoint to Faust's millennial limitation.

Matthew 25:46

> And these will go away into *eternal* (*aionios*) punishment, but the righteous into *eternal* (*aionios*) life.

The above passage is perhaps the most famous one in connecting and contrasting the fate of the believer with that of the unbeliever in parallel statements invoking the use of *aionios*. To quote Augustine on the matter is common, and his insight in this issue does in fact appear to be accurate:

> The Lord predicted that He would pronounce in the judgment, saying, "Depart from me, ye cursed, into everlasting fire, prepared for the devil and his angels." [Mt 25:41] For here it is evident that the devil and his angels shall burn in everlasting fire. And there is also that declaration in the Apocalypse, "The devil their deceiver was cast into the lake of fire and brimstone, where also are the beast and the false prophet. And they shall be tormented day and night for ever." [Rev 20:10] In the former passage "everlasting" is used, in the latter "for ever;" and by these words Scripture is wont to mean nothing else than endless duration….being reserved to the judgment of the last day, when eternal fire shall receive them, in which they shall be tormented world without end….How can this be believed without enervating our faith in the eternal punishment of the devils? For if all or some of those to whom it shall be said, "Depart from me, ye cursed, into everlasting fire, prepared for the devil and his angels," [Mt 25:41] are not to be always in that fire, then what reason is there for believing that the devil and his angels shall always be there?…Then what a fond fancy is it to suppose that eternal punishment means long continued punishment, while eternal life means life without end, since Christ in the very same passage spoke of both in similar terms in one and the same sentence, "These shall go away into eternal punishment, but the righteous into life eternal!" [Mt 25:46] **If both destinies are "eternal," then we must either understand both as long-continued but at last terminating, or both as endless. For they are correlative—on the one hand,**

punishment eternal, on the other hand, life eternal. And to say in one and the same sense, life eternal shall be endless, punishment eternal shall come to an end, is the height of absurdity. Wherefore, as the eternal life of the saints shall be endless, so too the eternal punishment of those who are doomed to it shall have no end.[1445]

Erickson likewise seeks to discredit the conditionalistic position on the basis of this parallelism,

> In an extensive argument Fudge attempts to show that when applied to nouns that speak of a resulting condition (such as punishment), αἰώνιος does not denote eternity as it does when modifying nouns that refer to activities (such as punish*ing*). Yet he does not discuss the matter of parallelism in verse 46, namely, that if in the one case (life) the adjective αἰώνιον means eternal, it must also mean eternal in the other phrase (punishment). The parallelism requires that if life for believers is of everlasting duration, punishment for unbelievers must be also. (Emphasis his.)[1446]

Although I am critical of Fudge, I will not fudge in my criticism of Fudge by uncritically accepting Erickson's criticism of Fudge. Erickson's response is an unfair assessment of Fudge. Granted, in Fudge's initial chapter concerning *aionios*, Fudge did not mention the parallelism. However, he certainly does in his subsequent and extended discussion of this passage: "In each case it is described as 'eternal.' That the language flows along parallel channels highlights the split into opposite directions looming just ahead." Fudge continues the explanation on the next page: "Whatever *aionios* means, one should have good cause for not translating it the same way when it appears twice in the same verse! The KJV translators betrayed theological bias by translating 'everlasting' punishment but 'eternal' life."[1447]

Erickson's assessment of Fudge is as inaccurate as it is insufficient. The necessity of pointing out this weakness is not to defend Fudge, the present author also rejects conditionalism, but to bring the problem that ultraists face into sharp focus. How will ultraists counter conditionalism if ultraists themselves try to limit the parallelism of the contrast? Soteriological conditionalism cannot adequately account for the parallelism (cp. Mt 25:41 & Rev 20:10), and it does not appear that misthological ultraism fares any better. The soteriological parallelism of the present passage conveys an everlasting qualitative experience of life in contrast to the everlasting punishment of the unbeliever. Likewise, the misthological parallelism of Dan 12:2 presents an everlasting result for the disobedient believer. The results of the judgment are just as lasting for both groups in both cases.

Faust repeatedly urges his conclusions as being necessary to successfully refute universalism. However, it would appear that the rejection of his conclusions might be even better suited to refute universalism. Erickson supplies a popular statement from an universalist, John A. T. Robinson:

> The genuine universalist will base nothing on the fact (which is a fact) that the New Testament word for eternal (*aionios*) does not necessarily mean everlasting, but enduring only for an indefinitely long period. For he can apply this signification to "eternal punishment" in Matt 25:46 only if he is willing to give exactly the same sense to "eternal life" in the same verse. As F. D. Maurice said many years ago now, writing to F. J. A. Hort: "I did not see how *aionios* could mean one thing when it was joined with *kolasis* [*punishment*] and another when it was joined with *zoe* [*life*]" (quoted, J. O. F. Murray, The Goodness and Severity of God, p. 195). To admit that the two phrases are not parallel is at once to treat them with unequal seriousness. And that a true universalism must refuse to do.[1448]

In other words, Robinson acknowledges that he must find a better argument for universalism than trying to limit the meaning of *aionios* to a limited period of time since the parallelism makes this impossible. However, in seeking to evade the parallelism misthologically, the ultraist would be handing the universalists their argument on a silver platter. The universalist need only reply to the ultraist that if the ultraist can ignore the parallelism and restrict *aionios* to a limited duration when it suites them to do so in misthological contexts, then there is nothing to prevent universalists from ignoring the parallelism and restricting *aionios* to a limited duration in soteriological contexts. The counter position taken herein is that a strong case can be made for taking *aionios* as always meaning *eternal* in the NT and thus for simultaneously rejecting conditionalism, universalism, and ultraism.

Granted, Faust is sensitive to the problem and anticipates the above rejection to his position: "One may object that the arguments of this book lend too much weight to Universalism. To the contrary, the view of this book actually *affirms* the truth of the endless destruction of the lost!" (Emphasis his.)[1449] However, it is questionable that Faust is able to make his affirmation with exegetical consistency. He responds to universalism by saying, "The

Bible reveals that the lost end up in the final Lake of Fire, with *no* hope of being delivered (Revelation 20:10, 15)." (Emphasis his).[1450] Moreover, he quotes Jn 6:40 and concludes:

> It therefore follows that those who do *not* believe must be condemned for absolute eternity. There are many promises such as this that do not have the future millennial age in view. Therefore, there is no contextual reason to take the word 'everlasting' in a limited or relative sense in such verses. If believers receive absolute eternal life, *unbelievers must receive the exact opposite.* (Emphasis his.)[1451]

Splendid statements. But can they be consistently maintained on the ultraistic premise? Do not the same statements apply to those thrown into Gehenna? Does the context indicate that the punishment is not eternal in the absolute sense? That is, to use our terminology, does this punishment not last throughout eternity future? Does the context indicate that there is *any* "hope of being delivered"? If Faust can read hope for deliverance into passages where no such hope is given, then what is to prevent universalists from doing the same? As a case in point, the present passage in Mt 25:46 has "the future millennial age in view," to use Faust's words. And yet it refers to the suffering the lost are to experience in the millennial age as eternal! This passage is dealing with the Sheep and Goat Judgment that comes at the end of the tribulation. Yet those cast into this fire will be there throughout eternity!

Telescopic Fiery Fusion

Mt 25:41

Faust references Rev 20:10 as indicating the eternal suffering of the lost: "And the devil who deceived them was thrown into the Lake of Fire and brimstone, where the beast and the false prophet are also; and they will be tormented day and night forever and ever." This is an excellent point that Faust makes. It is the same argument employed by traditionalists to counter conditionalism. But traditionalists also point out that this eternal suffering is linked with the suffering described by Jesus in the Sheep and Goat Judgment: "Then He will also say to those on His left, 'Depart from Me, accursed ones, into the eternal fire which has been prepared for the devil and his angels'" (Mt 25:41). When do they depart? A thousand years later? No.

They are cast into this fire immediately but suffer eternally, as Peterson specifies concerning the eternality: "That fate is plainly depicted in Revelation 20:10 as involving endless torment. So separation from Jesus' presence in Matthew 25:41 means suffering forever in hell, not annihilation."[1452] Lang concurs that they are cast in at this time instead of waiting for the devil to join them later, and Lang even goes on to say that any annihilationists who seeks to limit *aion* and *aionios* to mean something less than everlasting punishment "is a poor Greek scholar."[1453] Govett likewise pictures them as being immediately "led away to punishment, and that punishment eternal. For the infliction of the thousand years is no sooner over, than that of eternity begins."[1454] So not even these misthological Gehennalists limit *aionios* to mean *age lasting* in this verse. And Hodges concurs concerning the immediacy in the related passage of Mt 5:22, the "offender may be liable to **immediate** banishment into Gehenna, the lake of fire."[1455]

I, on the other hand, agree with my fellow dispensationalists, such as Pentecost and Constable, that the eternal fire is describing the Lake of Fire, which already has been prepared, **but the lost are not actually cast into the Lake of Fire until the end of the millennium**.[1456] Presently, at our current point in time, the eternal fire into which lost are thrown is the fire of Hades. This fire will later be poured into the Lake of Fire (Rev 20:14). But here is a problem for advocates of this point of view: How can the lost be cast into this fire immediately if this fire is not the eternal fire of the Lake of Fire but the intermediate fire of Hades? In response, it may be said that the colloquial expression describing from *bad to worse* as *jumping from the frying pan into the fire* is an apt description of the sequence of events. Jesus is not making a distinction between the frying pan and fire because there is no need to do so. The frying pan will be poured into the fire. The two fires are **telescopically** merged together and one day will actually be merged together. There is no need to posit a sharp distinction between them. The furnace of fire should be understood similarly.

Mt 13:40-43

[40] Therefore just as the tares are gathered up and burned with fire, so shall it be at the end of the age. [41] The Son of Man will send forth His angels, and they will gather out of His kingdom all stumbling blocks, and those who commit lawlessness, [42] and will cast them into the furnace of fire; in that place there shall be weeping and gnashing of teeth. [43] Then the righteous will shine forth as the sun in the kingdom of their Father. He who has ears, let him hear. (Mt 13:40-43)

The furnace of fire spans both Hades and Hell, both the millennial and eternal states. The reader will recall that I already have mentioned the latter verse (Mt 13:43) in that it is derived from Dan 12:3. Whereas the Danielic passage is describing a misthological contrast and the Matthean passage a soteriological contrast, they are both dealing with the same event and complement each other by showing that the *faithless* will experience everlasting torment, the *unfaithful* will experience everlasting shame, and the *faithful* will experience everlasting glory. A correlation rather than identification is to be observed in the everlasting torment/shame.

Rev 14:10-11

[10] He also will drink of the wine of the wrath of God, which is mixed in full strength in the cup of His anger; and he will be **tormented** with fire and brimstone in the presence of the holy angels and **in the presence** of the Lamb. [11] And the smoke of their **torment goes up forever and ever**; and they have no rest day and night, those who worship the beast and his image, and whoever receives the mark of his name. (Rev 14:10-11)

Dispensationalists offer different interpretations concerning the time and location of the torment in this passage. When commenting on this passage, Ryrie links it to eternity future.

> Throughout eternity, the Lake of Fire is **in the presence** of the Lord, for nothing can be outside His omnipresence, even the Lake of Fire. However, the wicked will be separated from His presence in the sense of contact and fellowship (see 2 Thess. 1:9, where a different preposition is used). Its extent is forever (v. 11).[1457]

Constable, on the other hand, appeals to 2Thess 1:9 to draw the opposite conclusion:

> This [Rev 14:10] is not a reference to their eternal torment. Their final torment will be in the lake of fire **removed from the presence** of the holy angels and the Lamb (19:20; 20:10; 21:8, 27; 22:14-15; cf. Matt. 25:41; Mark 9:43; 2 Thess. 1:8-9).[1458]

Ryrie notes that "a different preposition" is used in 2Thess 1:9, but Constable finds this an inadequate basis for advocating that the eternal state is in view. He believes that a different preposition is used because it is referring to a different temporal and spatial location. To restate the problem, according to Rev 14:10, they will be tormented *in the presence* (enopios) of the Lord and His angels, but according to 2Thess 1:9, they will be *away from the presence* (apo) of the Lord. This problem is compounded by the fact that the passages are dealing with the tribulational period and its conclusion and thus with the commencement of the millennial age, not the eternal state!

Not only are the timing and location important, the type of separation normally gets the lion's share of the attention and thus must certainly be evaluated as well. Peterson provides fuller explanation as to why it is necessary to differentiate that the type of separation in 2Thess 1:9 is not dealing with omnipresence: "'Eternal destruction' will entail the wicked being forever excluded from the gracious presence of the Lord. This cannot be annihilation, for their separation presupposes their existence. Some conditionalists contend that being shut out from Christ's presence means obliteration."[1459] At this point he quotes a footnote from Fudge, which I will restate in typical syllogistic format for the reader's convenience:

1. God's presence will fill all that is, in every place.
2. The wicked will not be in his presence.
3. Therefore, the wicked will no longer exist.[1460]

Quarles spends an entire article trying to weaken this syllogism with a causal understanding of *apo*.[1461] The Lord's face will cause them to be punished. They will be punished *because of* His appearance. Thus, their punishment would not entail separation from God. If this is correct, then the passage provides no support for Fudge's syllogism. On the other hand, as Morris notes, others would suggest a temporal understanding of *apo*. They would be punished *from the time of* His appearance.[1462] This approach would also break the syllogism. Like Morris, however, my preference will be for the spatial understanding. They would be punished *away from* the Lord. In other words, their punishment would consist of banishment. Since this is the prevalent view, I will be content to proceed with the continuation of Peterson's response to Fudge's syllogism:

This argument, however, is based on a faulty understanding of God's presence in 2 Thessalonians 1:9. Here the presence of God is not His general omnipresence, with the idea that separation from His presence would mean nonexistence. Rather, the verse refers to Christ's revealing His special presence as King to His people. [1463]

Nevertheless, such responses in terms of omnipresence on the part of Ryrie and Peterson, though well intended, are unlikely to be convincing to a diehard spatial separatist like Henry Morris: "They must be removed from the earth, since it will thenceforth be where God will dwell (Rev 21:3), and transported to some far-distant body of flaming darkness, forever."[1464] The present author prefers the approach by Morris but believes that it can be reconciled successfully with the comments by both Ryrie and Constable. The torment in the presence of the Lamb during the tribulation is **typologically and telescopically** merged with the torment to be experienced throughout eternity away from His visible presence. Some, such as Schwarze, have given a good scientific description of dwarf white stars, whose gravitational force will not allow them to burn out, as possible locations of the Lake of Fire. After all, Mt 25:41 indicates that the Lake of Fire already is prepared and thus in existence.[1465] Perhaps a black hole would be another possibility, an alternative scientific anomaly presenting an existing possibility. In any event, both Rev 14:11 and 2Thess 1:9 provide solid exegetical reasons to support the mergence of the millennial and eternal descriptions of the suffering of the wicked, just as we already have been led to believe concerning several other major passages considered above.

Incidentally, this would be a major problem for Fudge's syllogism. I grant Fudge that spatial separation is intended. However, by posing relative rather than absolute spatial separation, I make his major premise unnecessary. The lost will be separated from the visible manifestation of God's glory in eternity future, but this need not mean that they will be out of reach of His omnipresence. Even far worse for the conditionalist is the fact that this mergence of millennial and eternal suffering indicates that the suffering the lost experience in the flames during the millennial state will last throughout eternity. Conscious suffering throughout eternity nullifies annihilationism. This assessment is also detrimental to the ultraistic position in that millennial suffering is eternal. It is not limited to the millennial age.

Age to Come

Moreover, even taking *aionios* to mean *age-lasting* in 2Thess 1:9 does not necessarily support either Fudge or Faust. In denying that the verse teaches annihilationism, and thus a limited duration of suffering, Morris replies: "The adjective 'eternal' [*aionios*] means literally 'age-long,' and everything depends on the length of the age. In the New Testament there is never a hint that the coming age has an end—it is the continuing life of the world to come."[1466] Thus, when the Bible speaks of *the age to come* (Mt 12:32; Mk 10:30; Lk 18:30; Heb 6:5), this may be regarded as a summation of the eschatological future rather than a termination of this *age to come* at the conclusion of millennium. More specifically, when Jesus spoke of the unpardonable sin, for example, He was not limiting it to the millennial age. "And whoever shall speak a word against the Son of Man, it shall be forgiven him; but whoever shall speak against the Holy Spirit, it shall not be forgiven him, either in **this age**, or in **the age to come**" (Mt 12:32). The contrast of *this age* with *the age to come* was not to limit *the age* [*aion*] *to come* to a one thousand year period of time. The contrast here, fused with the combination of millennial and eternal suffering, nullifies the limitation imposed by the ultraist and conditionalist.

Jn 3:36

He who believes in the Son has **eternal life**; but he who does not obey the Son shall not see life, but the **wrath** of God **abides** on him.

In this passage a contrasting parallelism between the fate of the believer and unbeliever is again evidenced. One has eternal life; the other has abiding wrath. Yet how can God's wrath continue to abide on someone who has ceased to exist? The parallelism with eternal life suggests that the wrath is likewise eternal. Both the life and wrath are qualitative and quantitative. Further, the possession of this life rules out the experience of this wrath. This eternal wrath cannot be limited to the eternal state. Surely it encompasses the millennial age as well as the present age since it presently abides on the unbeliever. But if that is so, then the believer cannot experience this wrath during the millennium since the possession of this life prevents the believer from being the object of that wrath in both this age and the one to come.

Eternal Fire in the New Testament

Eternal (aionios) fire (pur) is found in three places in the NT (Mt 18:8; 25:41; Jude 1:7). The passage in Mt 25:41 has just been treated above in association with its contextual parallel in Mt 25:46, which calls it "eternal punishment." These two verses, as well as the furnace of fire in Mt 13:42 and the torment with fire in Rev 14:11, were found to be a combination of millennial and eternal fire. In fact, the latter verse emphatically affirms it will be "forever and ever." One would be inclined to presuppose that the same would be true of the two texts concerning this *eternal fire*.

Jude 1:7

Just as **Sodom and Gomorrah** and the cities around them, since they in the same way as these indulged in gross immorality and went after strange flesh, are exhibited as an example, in **undergoing the punishment of eternal fire**.

Fudge acknowledges that Bietenhard had called "attention to a contemporary Jewish idea that the people of Sodom and Gomorrah were even then suffering fiery punishment." Yet Fudge rejects this by claiming, "There is no biblical hint that Sodom and Gomorrah's inhabitants presently endure conscious torment; several passages, in fact, make a point of their abiding extinction." And he notes that the "OT allusions to Sodom's destruction include" the following passages: Dt 29:23; Is 13:19-22; 34:10; Jer 49:18; 50:40; Lam 4:6; Zeph 2:9.[1467]

However, none of these passages listed by Fudge refer to the metaphysical extinction of the people who inhabited those cities. Fudge has overstated his case. Not only that, his case overstates itself! As Peterson notes, it proves more than Fudge intends for it to prove. If the destruction of Sodom and Gomorrah prove that their inhabitants are not presently experiencing ongoing suffering, then it refutes "the teaching of evangelical annihilationism, which holds that the wicked dead will be resurrected to face terrible judgment before their extinction."[1468] Moreover, these passages are repetitive and thus my treatment of Is 34:10 above will suffice to show that the passages do not point to an eternal extinction but to an eternal exhibition, just as Jude 1:7 affirms. Biblically, therefore, we would be led to believe that just as that land remains a continuous exhibition of God's wrath today in the Dead Sea area, and will also be so in the future millennium, the inhabitants of that land remain even now and will remain forever as a continuous exhibition of God's wrath as well. They are still on exhibit in the burning eternal flames.

Mt 18:8-9

[8]And if your hand or your foot causes you to stumble, cut it off and throw it from you; it is better for you to enter life crippled or lame, than having two hands or two feet, to be cast into the **eternal fire**. [9]And if your eye causes you to stumble, pluck it out, and throw it from you. It is better for you to enter life with one eye, than having two eyes, to be cast into the **fiery hell** [Gehenna fire].

Having already dealt with this passage on multiple occasions and having devoted a chapter to it, I will be content here to deal with it in summary fashion. The eternal fire of Mt 18:8 is the fire of Gehenna in Mt 18:9. Entering it is contrasted with entering life and the kingdom. From the parallel *cut if off* passages, we learn that Gehenna is a place for the *whole body* (Mt 5:30; cp. 10:28) and its fire is unquenchable and filled with undying worms (Mk 9:43-45). This is in contrast to Hades, which is the intermediate location of disembodied souls. Since the fire of Gehenna is unquenchable, it is inconceivable that what is put into it can escape from it. As such, it is understood traditionally to be equivalent to the Lake of Fire into which the lost are cast, soul and body, at the conclusion of the millennium.

This fire is called eternal in the sense that it already has been prepared (Mt 25:41) and will extend into the future. Since *aionios* is being used to describe a place that exists in the present and future, the lexical basis by which to claim that it is merely *age-lasting* is annihilated. The debatable understanding of *age-lasting* for a past event is not even within the possible scope of consideration for the NT meaning for this present-future realm. The annihilationist argument is thus weakened by this observation and annihilated by the fact that the result of being cast into this fire is permanent. Annihilationists are fond of asserting that the action of the casting is not eternal; rather, it is the result of the casting that is everlasting. To be sure, the casting is punctiliar. However, the result is permanent. If what is cast into the fire ceases to exist at some point in time subsequent to being cast into the fire or is allowed to escape at some subsequent point, then the result is not eternal. It changes over a period of time. The eternality of the result argues with equal force against annihilationism and ultraism. This eternal fire does not denote the intermediate state but the final state and location of the damned.

Unquenchable Fire in the New Testament

The unquenchable nature of this fire in the *cut it off* parallel of Mk 9:43 was noted above. This word for *unquenchable* (*asbestos*) is also found in two other synoptically parallel passages in the NT:

> And His winnowing fork is in His hand, and He will thoroughly clear His threshing floor; and He will gather His wheat into the barn, but He will **burn up** the chaff with ***unquenchable*** fire. (Mt 3:12; cp. Lk 3:17)

The conditionalistic argument is that the fire is *unquenchable* until it completely has fulfilled its purpose of consuming (i.e., *burning up*) everything placed within it and has changed them to the fullest extent possible to their resultant ashen form. One weakness with this argument is that in the immediate context Jesus goes on to explain that the result of being cast into this furnace of fire is not cessation of existence but "weeping and gnashing of teeth" (Mt 13:42). Apparently, the purpose of the fire is not to extinguish ones' anguish but to perpetuate and intensify it. John is very explicit that those cast into this Lake of Fire "will be tormented day and night forever and ever" (Rev 20:10). The conditionalistic attempt to depersonalize the beast and false prophets by turning these individuals into institutions will not be very convincing to those of a dispensationalist persuasion. John specifies that it is people who are cast into this fire: "And the smoke of their torment goes up forever and ever; they have no rest day and night, those who worship the beast and his image, and whoever receives the mark of his name" (Rev 14:11). These two verses combine to picture a torment, not merely smoke, that continues day and night forever. This is the final state, but we also find fire carrying out this same purpose in the intermediate state, in which Hades is defined as a "place of torment" for the lost (Lk 16:28) and illustrated as such:

> [23] And in Hades he lifted up his eyes, **being in torment**, and saw Abraham far away, and Lazarus in his bosom. [24]And he cried out and said, "Father Abraham, have mercy on me, and send Lazarus, that he may dip the tip of his finger in water and cool off my tongue; for I am **in agony** in this flame." (Lk 16:23-24)

The purpose of this fire is not to terminate but to torment, not to exterminate but to excruciate. One strand of thought that emerged in the intermediate period of time between the OT and the NT was that the worms described in Is 66:24 would torment those cast into this unquenchable fire: "Humble yourself greatly, for **the punishment of the ungodly is fire and worms**" (Sirach 7:17; RSV). This came to be understood as eternal torment: "Woe to the nations that rise up against my kindred! The Lord Almighty will take vengeance on them in the day of judgment, in **putting fire and worms in their flesh; and they shall feel them, and weep for ever**" (Judith 16:17; KJA).

Now it is true that apocalyptic literature is not unanimous or consistent in its treatment of the damned or its understanding of Gehenna. On the other hand, it is also equally obvious that the traditional understanding of the OT background concerning the fiery worms in Is 66:24 (and thus Gehenna) was one of these strands of thought that existed in that time period. This strand of thought is most consistent with the NT texts above concerning the purpose of the fire—to torment. And if the purpose of the fire is to torment, then there is no reason for it not to burn perpetually. The purpose of this fire is not to alleviate pain by consuming those placed within it so that they cease to feel its flames eating their flesh, nor is its purpose to relieve their pain by purifying them so that they may be released from it. This punishment is not a purgatory but punitory. This understanding of the purpose of this fire argues decisively against annihilationism and ultraism.

But what is to be made of the fact that this fire is also stated to *burn up* or *consume* that which is placed within it? After all, the passage quoted above in Mt 3:12 easily could be understood from the conditionalist viewpoint to teach that the fire is unquenchable until it completely consumes what is placed within it so that it may be termed, *The Fire that Consumes*—to use the title of Fudge's book. One problem with this approach is that it proves more than conditionalism and ultraism want it to prove. Believers are submitted to a fire in Jn 15:6 that burns and thus consumes the branches placed within it. Yet believers do not cease to exist as a result. Believers are consumed by the fiery fury of Heb 10:27 (cp. 12:29), yet they are not annihilated. So then what is the significance of such passages? I will conclude by answering that question.

Conclusion

Paul Harvey was fond of saying, "And now you know the rest of the story." This figure of speech about being burnt up or consumed by fire is God's way of saying, "And now you know the end of the story." It is Jesus' way of saying that there is nothing more that really needs to be said about the matter. They have met their fiery fate in the end, and that is the end of the story. Speculation about their ceasing to exist or being released sometime later is needless. It is not going to happen. Their suffering a fiery fate is the last picture we have of them. No escape, no parole, no time off for good behavior, no termination or cessation of retribution are envisioned. No more need be said about their soteriology. Hell is their terminal point, but they do not terminate. The last stop their train makes to let off its passengers is at the gates of hell were they will weep forever.

As to believers cast into the fire of Jn 15:6, this is the end of the story pertaining to their misthology as well. These misthological fires, like those of 1Cor 3:15 and Heb 6:8, represent the *end* (*telos*)—the teleological Bema fate—for unfaithful believers. They weep in the outer darkness for eternity. To be sure, they will have a degree of glory and joy that is promised unconditionally to all believers. Yet their joy will be mixed with and interrupted by sorrow. The gospel of grace cries out for unbelievers to come freely and drink of the water of life so that they will never thirst in hell. The gospel of the kingdom calls out for believers to submit to the Lordship of Christ so that they will not subcome to the world and experience eternal shame and sorrow.

Appendix 8.
Judicial Hardening

Introduction

God's hardening of Pharaoh's heart is a watershed text from which Calvinists draw a number of conclusions: God unconditionally hardens the reprobate; foreordination is unconditional, Pharaoh never had a chance to act otherwise; free will is a fraud. Non-Calvinists appeal to the OT background and find instead that Pharaoh had a very active role to play in the hardening of his heart, so much so that it even appears that the hardening was contingent on his reaction. God foreknew Pharaoh's reaction, but Pharaoh (of his own free will) made the first of many moves down the slippery slope of no return.

Illustration 295. Pharaoh's Heart

Pharaoh's Heart Condition	Stem	Ex	God	Pharaoh	chazaq to strengthen	qashah to make stubborn	kabed to harden
God will strengthen Pharaoh's heart	P	4:21	✓		✓		
God will make Pharaoh's heart stubborn	H	7:3	✓			✓	
Pharaoh's heart was strong	Q	7:13	?		✓		
Pharaoh's heart is stubborn	na	7:14	✓				✓
Pharaoh's heart was strong	Q	7:22	?		✓		
Pharaoh hardened his heart	H	8:15	✓				✓
Pharaoh's heart was strong	Q	8:19	?		✓		
Pharaoh hardened his heart	H	8:32	✓				✓
Pharaoh's heart was hard	Q	9:7	?				✓
God strengthened Pharaoh's heart	P	**9:12**	✓		✓		
Pharaoh hardened his heart	H	9:34	✓				✓
Pharaoh's heart was strong	Q	9:35	?		✓		
God hardened Pharaoh's heart	H	**10:1**	✓				✓
God strengthened Pharaoh's heart	P	10:20	✓		✓		
God strengthened Pharaoh's heart	P	10:27	✓		✓		
God strengthened Pharaoh's heart	P	11:10	✓		✓		
Pharaoh was stubborn	H	13:15		✓		✓	
God will strengthened Pharaoh's heart	P	14:4	✓		✓		
God strengthened Pharaoh's heart	P	14:8	✓		✓		
God will strengthen the Egyptian's hearts	P	14:17	✓		✓		

Q = Qal (simple active)   P = Piel (intensive active)   H = Hiphil (causative active)

According to Forster, "the first instance of any act of God on Pharaoh's heart does not come until Exodus 9:12, after Pharaoh himself has repeatedly rejected God's request."[1469] This assessment poses a difficulty in that according to some translations several passages seemingly would describe God as already having acted upon Pharaoh's heart much earlier in the narrative (Ex 7:13,22; 8:19; 9:7), since these passages are translated as Pharaoh's heart *was hardened*. However, Forster's rendition finds corroboration among various other translations. In 7:13 for example, the verb is rendered: *became hard* (NIV), *was strengthened* (DBY), *is strong* (YLT), *was obstinate* (NAB), *remained hard* (NLT), and *remained obstinate* (NJB). Translating the Qal in each of these cases as *was strong* or some equivalent, rather than as *was hardened* or *was strengthened* avoids implying that God was the active agent or that Pharaoh was the passive agent on such occasions.

In the instances where the Qal stem is used, the agent is unnamed and the state is merely affirmed. This may be contrasted with the Piel, used in 9:12 for example, where the Lord explicitly is identified as the active agent acting upon Pharaoh's heart. Forster's analysis finds substantiation from verbal and contextual analysis and is thus acceptable. Although the Lord foreknew that He would act upon Pharaoh's heart (Ex 4:21; 7:3), God did not actually do so until 9:12, as is indicated by the change in stem and the explicit identification of the Lord as the agent at this juncture.

The verb used in 9:12 should be distinguished from the other two verbs used in the narrative. The Hebrew word *qashah* is used once for God's agency: *I will make Pharaoh's heart stubborn* (Ex 7:3; TM). And it is used once of Pharaoh as the agent: *Pharaoh was stubborn* (Ex 13:15). Otherwise, the verb used to describe God's role in making Pharaoh stubborn is *chazaq* (with the exception of *kabed* which is delayed until 10:1). God uses this verb *chazaq* to command the Israelites to be *strong and courageous* (Josh 1:9). He was not commanding them to be hardhearted! The basic meaning of *chazaq* is *to be strong* or *to strengthen* and can be used synonymously with *courage*—to encourage with courage. Thus, God does not even strengthen Pharaoh's heart until 9:12. But God did not actually *harden* (*kabed*) Pharaoh's heart until 10:1, after Pharaoh himself already had done so repeatedly. Pharaoh **caused** his own heart to be hard (note the repeated Hiphil in 8:15,32; 9:34) before God **caused** it to be hard (note the Hiphil in 10:1).

Geisler also adopts this approach to explaining the hardening of Pharaoh's heart and cites Forster approvingly, but Geisler is guilty of oversimplification when he says, "When Pharaoh is the agent of the hardening *kabed* is used. When God is the agent, *chazaq* is used."[1470] On the contrary, in 10:1 God is the agent and *kabed* is the verb that is used. Up unto this point in the narrative, Pharaoh repeatedly has hardened his own heart. Yet as Forster notes, the significance of this verb being delayed until this point in the narrative to describe God taking over this hardening activity may be understood by representing the Lord as saying: "Very well, if he is determined to be hard and unrepentant then I will make his heart hard, just as he wishes."[1471] It would appear that at this stage God's judicial hardening becomes irrevocable and irresistible. Up until now, God merely has strengthened Pharaoh's heart, but now God himself actually will harden Pharaoh's heart and then strengthen him in that resolve. Afterward, neither God nor Pharaoh needs to harden his heart. It has been completely and permanently petrified. Pharaoh wanted a hard heart, and now at last God gave him the desire of his heart—a heart made of stone.

I have been content to follow the typical trend in the above discussion of Pharaoh's hardening by beginning with 4:1 for the simple reason that this is the first reference in Exodus to Pharaoh's heart, and it has one of the three verbs used in the verbal analysis. On the other hand, Hunt wisely questions the wisdom of such an approach by noting that God's prescience of Pharaoh's disposition had been stated earlier in the narrative, where God said to Moses at the burning bush: "But **I know** that the king of Egypt will not permit you to go, except under compulsion" (Ex 3:19).[1472] God's predetermination is based on His foreknowledge of Pharaoh's predisposition. Nevertheless, in spite of this foreknowledge, God did not take any action to harden Pharaoh until long after Pharaoh already had done so himself.

Just as God can impart encouragement directly to the heart of the believer, so He can impart courage to the heart of the unbeliever. Such action on God's part does not nullify free will on the part of either the believer or the unbeliever. It does not make holy or unholy behavior inevitable. It neither guarantees the perseverance of the saints or the sinner. To encourage is to impart courage. To encourage is not to force. Having been content until this point to give Pharaoh the courage to do what he freely chose to do, God now confirms Pharaoh in the choice he has made with an unredeemable firmness of heart.

Granted, Forster questions the adequacy of the term *judicial hardening* to describe this process, wishing to clarify: "God did not give Pharaoh the wicked desire to rebel against him. What God did was to give him stubborn courage to carry out that desire."[1473] Forster's point is well received but only demonstrates the necessity of carefully defining one's terminology. Judicial hardening does not mean that God makes people sin or that He actively or directly intensifies their desire to sin. He simply gives them over to their own sinful desires. Geisler has a helpful chart in this regard, which serves as the basis for the following chart.[1474]

Illustration 296. God's Hardening

God Does Not Harden Hearts	God Does Harden Hearts
• initially	• subsequently
• directly?	• indirectly
• against free will	• in accordance with free will
• as to their cause	• as to their effect

My only minor quibble with Geisler's chart is to challenge his assertion that God never acts directly in the hardening process. Since Geisler failed to note that Ex 10:1 was an occasion where God is said to harden Pharaoh's heart, the completeness of his assessment is open to question. Seemingly, God can take a direct role in the hardening (cf. Jn 12:40; Rom 11:7-8). On the other hand, Vance also may be cited in affirmation of the judicial nature of Pharaoh's hardening.[1475] Yet Vance had earlier demonstrated that what God passively allows may be described by Scripture as if He caused it, when in fact He merely permitted it.[1476] God's passive will and agency can be presented as if He were the active agent. Not only must this realization be kept in mind, the distinction between ultimate and intermediate agency should also be retained. Vance illustrates these truths with the examples of David and Job. On the one hand, it is said that Satan incited David to number Israel (2Chron 21:1), but on the other hand, it is said that God is the one who did so (2Sam 24:1). In such cases, God would be the ultimate agent but Satan would be the intermediate agent. In the case of Pharaoh, God simply may have limited His active role to judicial hardening by giving Pharaoh over more fully to demonic influence.

Archer, like Vance, uses Job to elucidate how God and Satan could work jointly in what happened to David in his numbering the sons of Israel. Although Satan is the one who attacked Job (Job 1:12; 2:7), God is actually the one who instigated the test and permitted it—and in that sense caused it (Job 1:8,12,21; 2:5-6; 42:11). Archer goes on to cite other examples.[1477] Such examples certainly abound. To cite yet another illustration, that neither Forster, Geisler, nor Vance mentioned in this connection, we may turn to James, who says that God tests Christians by sending *trials* (*peirasmos*) upon them (Jam 1:3-4). And yet James uses the verbal form of *trials* (*peirazo*) a few verses later with the declaration that trials are not from God: "Let no one say when he is *tempted*, 'I am being *tempted* by God'; for God cannot be tempted by evil, and He Himself does not *tempt* anyone" (Jam 1:13). God tries us in one sense of the word, but not the other.

Hodges likewise uses the example of Job to explain this Jacobean passage.[1478] What God sends for a positive purpose is carried out by Satan for a negative purpose. A trial from God is a temptation from Satan. We must not confuse the intermediate agent or purpose with the ultimate agent or purpose. Jesus uses this same noun to exhort us to pray in the model prayer to God: "And do not lead us into *trials/temptation*, but deliver us from evil" (Mt 6:13). From personal experience, Jesus knew what it was like to be led by God into temptation: "Jesus was led up by the Spirit into the wilderness to be tempted by the devil" (Mt 4:1). Even so, God is the leader, not the tempter. James clarifies the matter. God does not try us by tempting us. Rather, God may try us by allowing us to be tempted. Pray that such trials do not come (especially judicial ones), but when some such (misthological) trials inevitably do come, joyfully endure them through the courage which God supplies. God must allow misthological trials to come so that we misthologically may overcome and be counted as worthy of kingdom rulership (cp. 1Cor 11:19). Our prayers cannot remove all trials, but all trials can be passed successfully through prayer.

In passing, it also may be stated that God's judicial hardening need not always be absolute or irrevocable. Those trice described as hardened by God's giving such people over to their sins (in Rom 1:24,26,28) does not necessarily demonstrate that such people are too hard to reach with the gospel. They may be harder to reach, but that does not mean they are impossible to reach. God will also lift the partial hardening in Rom 11:25 in due time. However, the fact that God's judicial hardening frequently is limited in duration or degree does not mean that it is never absolute. Those who take the mark of beast are hardened sovereignly beyond being able to believe. Still, even this sovereign hardening is not from eternity past. It is temporal and judicial. We might summarize 2Thess 1:10-11 as saying that God (as the ultimate agent) actively will allow an evil spirit (as an intermediate agent) to deceive those who take the mark of the beast so that they might not believe the gospel because they did not believe the gospel when they had the chance. In other words, God ultimately will harden them because they did not believe. They will reject the gospel before God makes it impossible for them to accept the gospel. They did not believe; they were hardened; they could not believe as a result. Taking the mark of the beast will be an unpardonable sin and will result in an unpardonable state.[1479]

Conclusion

God foreknew rather than foreordained Pharaoh's initial state and what his corresponding reaction would be. Once Pharaoh demonstrated his initial state and reaction and repeatedly persisted in that state and course of action, God strengthened Pharaoh in his resolve to continue in the path he had chosen for himself. While the objection might raised that God was giving Pharaoh the courage to do the wrong thing, the judicial nature of this hardening prevents us from saying that God was causing Pharaoh to sin. Even though Calvinists are sometimes wont to attribute our sins to God, Pharaoh's sin cannot be attributed to God because: (1) God did not cause Pharaoh's initial state or reaction. (2) Pharaoh could have done otherwise up until the point that God Himself hardened him in 10:1. (3) The only way any created being can exercise free will is through the enabling grace of God; therefore, it is necessary that He give us free will. But God's giving us the grace to exercise free will does not make Him responsible for our abuse of that free will. (4) This hardening was judicial rather than sovereignly unconditional. (5) It is not clear that God directly hardened Pharaoh; He may have simply given him over to the demonic influence as the intermediate agent since Pharaoh already had inclined himself to listen to this influence. (6) Regardless as to whether God acted directly, God did not tempt Pharaoh to sin. God strengthening Pharaoh's ability to act contrary to God's will made Pharaoh more culpable for his abuse of the courage he was given and more susceptible to plagues for acting contrary to God's will. (7) God's purpose for granting Pharaoh this courage was to increase Pharaoh's punishment and display the glory of God, not to cause more sin.

Appendix 9.
Hades Versus Paradise

Introduction

A basic understanding of the sequence of events regarding the intermediate state is helpful in developing one's misthology. Nevertheless, it must not be thought that the basic outline of events described below are limited to misthologists or even to one particular form of misthology. The position summarized below is a popular understanding of the sequence of events known as the *Descent into Hades*. Lange's commentary on Revelation has an extended *excursus on Hades* inserted at Rev 20:8 that gives a far more detailed defense of this position. Archer (a non-misthologist) and Whipple (a Gehenna misthologist) as well as I subscribe to the basic components of this popular view.

On Earth

The Hebrew word for *garden* is *gan*; the Greek word is *paradise* (*paradeisos*). Christians are familiar, of course, with the *Garden of Eden* in Gen 2:8-16. It also may be translated as *Paradise of Eden* in the Greek OT (i.e., LXX). Alternatively, it also is referred to as the *Paradise of God* (Eze 28:13; 31:8-9; LXX). Paradise, otherwise known as God's garden, originally was located on planet earth. After man sinned, man was removed from Paradise. Subsequently, Paradise was removed from earth, at least from the surface of earth.

Below Earth

Jesus said that the people of Capernaum would *descend to Hades* when they died: "And you, Capernaum, will not be exalted to heaven, will you? You will descend to Hades; for if the miracles had occurred in Sodom which occurred in you, it would have remained to this day" (Mt 11:23). In the time of the OT, the people of Sodom went to Hades. Thus, it may be concluded that lost people went to Hades in the past. Looking to the future, Jesus still affirms that people of Capernaum will go to Hades. Therefore, it may be deduced that lost people in the present and future still go to Hades. Thus, Hades is the abode of the lost dead.

The KJV unfortunately translates this reference as saying they would be in hell, thus translating both Gehenna and Hades as hell. But Gehenna and Hades do not refer to the same eschatological sphere of existence. They are not the same thing. Lost people and saved people went to Hades in OT times. *Hades* could be understood simply to mean *the abode of the dead*. Concerning the account of a certain rich man, Jesus relates, "In Hades he lifted up his eyes, being in torment, and saw Abraham far away and **Lazarus in his bosom**" (Lk 16:23). To be *in his bosom* would denote an intimate dining experience. This Semitism denotes table fellowship. Because of the use of cushions rather than chairs around the table, they could recline in proximity to each others' chests around the table. A great impassable chasm existed between the rich man and Lazarus (Lk 16:26).

What were Abraham and Lazarus eating around the table? They were eating fruit from the Garden of Paradise. Paradise had been moved to this location, as we learn a few chapters later in the Gospel of Luke, when Jesus promises the dying thief that both He and the believing thief would be in Paradise (the Garden) when they died: "And He said to him, 'Truly I say to you, today you shall be with Me in Paradise'" (Lk 23:43). Accordingly, when Jesus went to Hades, it was to Paradise.

Since we know that lost people descend to Hades when they die, we may conclude that the chamber of torment in which the rich man was imprisoned was a compartment within Hades. Since Lazarus and Abraham were in a neighboring compartment, having what appears to be a dining experience, the most natural deduction is that this is the section of Hades to which Jesus referred to as Paradise (thus the Garden) in His promise to the thief.[1480]

Illustration 297. Paradise Removed

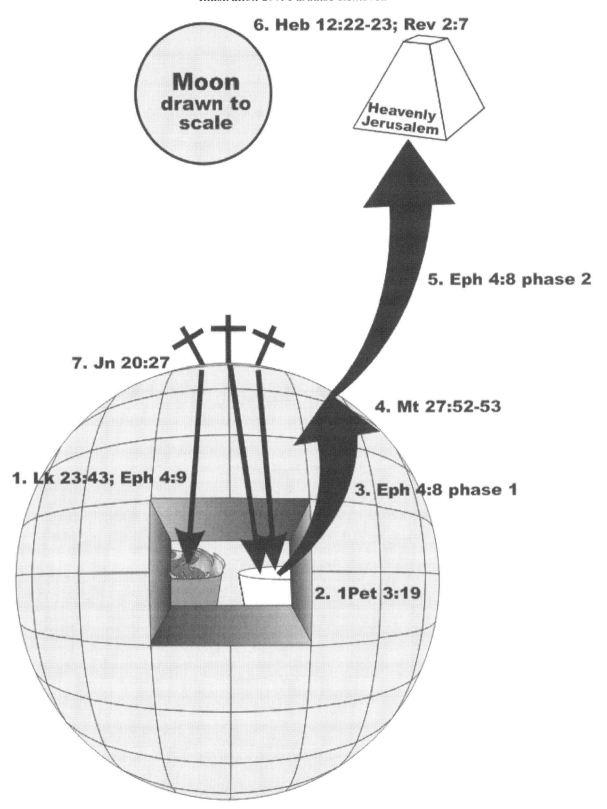

This impression is reinforced by several passages that indicate that Christ indeed did descend into Hades when He died on the cross. Christ was not abandoned to Hades when He died (Acts 2:30-31), meaning He was not left there. He went there and then left. Yet He did not leave alone, as we learn from Paul:

[8] When He ascended on high, He led captive a host of captives, And He gave gifts to men. [9] (Now this expression, "He ascended," what does it mean except that He also had descended into the lower parts of the earth? [10] He who descended is Himself also He who ascended far above all the heavens, that He might fill all things.)" (Eph 4:8-10)

It is quite possible that Peter also describes Christ's descent in 1Pet 3:18-19. If so, then Christ gave proclamation to the lost and liberation to the saved.[1481] He did not suffer there. When Jesus died on the cross, He declared, "'It is finished!' And He bowed His head, and gave up His spirit" (Jn 19:30). We are redeemed by His blood (His suffering on the cross), not by any suffering on His part in hell. Our redemption was paid in full by His sacrifice on the cross. But where did His spirit go? "And Jesus, crying out with a loud voice, said, 'Father, into Thy hands I commit My spirit.' And having said this, He breathed His last" (Lk 23:46). He committed His spirit to His Father, but this does not mean that He immediately went to His Father. Rather, His spirit was not abandoned in Hades by His Father. In His spirit Jesus went to Paradise before He went in His spirit to the Father. According to Paul, Jesus descended before He ascended. He went to Paradise before He went home to His Father.

David's prophecy about not being left in Hades reached out beyond himself to include the Messiah: "Thou wilt not abandon my soul to Sheol; neither wilt Thou allow Thy Holy One to undergo decay" (Ps 16:10). Prophetically, David referred to Jesus' soul inclusively: his/His soul was not abandoned to Sheol/Hades.[*] In the second half of the verse, David refers exclusively to Jesus' body.

Above the Earth

Phase One

Jesus did not go straight home to the Father when He ascended in spirit from Hades and lead the captives from the subterranean Paradise. He stopped to pick up His body on the way—via His resurrection. Evidently, He shared this experience with some of the captives whom He had just liberated as well. "And the tombs were opened; and many bodies of the saints who had fallen asleep were raised; and coming out of the tombs after His resurrection they entered the holy city and appeared to many" (Mt 27:52-53). They were resurrected also. Typically, three questions are asked about this event. (1) When were they raised—when Jesus died or when He was raised? Since Jesus was the first fruits (1Cor 15:20, cp. Rev 1:5), He probably was raised first and others were raised subsequently. (2) Who was raised—was it OT heroes or believers who had died recently? Since it was evidently a resurrection of those who had been buried around Jerusalem (who entered Jerusalem) and who were recognized when they entered the city, most likely they were recent inhabitants of Jerusalem: Believers who had died recently could appear in the city as witnesses to their friends of Jesus' liberating power. It is not beyond the range of possibility that the believing thief who died on the cross with Jesus could have been in that number and went and witnessed to his former associates. He could persuade them that it was really him by sharing inside information about the crimes they had committed together. (3) What kind of bodies did they receive—were they physical bodies that would die again (like Lazarus) or glorified bodies? Since Jesus was the first fruits, presumably they received glorified bodies. Such speculations aside, turning to Jesus for information, who is the focus of this biblical drama, results in a surprising find: "Jesus said to her, 'Stop clinging to Me [**stop touching Me**], **for I have not yet ascended to the Father**; but go to My brethren, and say to them, 'I ascend [I am ascending] to My Father and your Father, and My God and your God'" (Jn 20:17). This is an emotional reunion with one of His friends whom He loved deeply. One would think that hugs were certainly in order. Amazingly, Jesus did not want to be touched because He was on the way to the Father. He stayed a few minutes more to greet the other women described in Mt 28:9 before ascending.[1482]

Phase Two

After greeting them, He ascended, taking with Him to heaven all those who had been in Paradise (Eph 4:8-10). He not only moved the inhabitants of Paradise, He moved Paradise itself. According to Rev 2:7, the tree of life *is* (now—note the present tense) in the Paradise of God. The tree of life is in the Holy City (Rev 22:14). A simple deduction is that the Paradise of God is in the Holy City. It is there now and will be there in the future. Speaking of the present time period, Paul says that when he was caught up to the third heaven, it was to Paradise (2Cor 12:2,4). Where is the third heaven? The same place you will find Paradise—the Heavenly Jerusalem. Paul was caught up to Paradise; he did not descend down to Paradise. We may deduce that Paradise had been transferred

---

[*] Sheol is the Hebrew word; Hades is the Greek term.

to the Heavenly City. This deduction is confirmed by Heb 12:22-23 where the text explicitly confirms that the departed spirits of the righteous currently inhabit the Heavenly Jerusalem.

Round Trip

After seeing His Father and transferring Paradise and its inhabitants to the Heavenly Jerusalem, Jesus made a return trip to earth. He wanted to see select individuals and provide some hands-on experience. "Then He said to Thomas, 'Reach here with your finger, and see My hands; and reach here your hand and put it into My side; and do not be unbelieving, but believing'" (Jn 20:27). He demanded that Thomas touch Him. Before, when Jesus had talked with the ladies, He commanded them to stop touching Him. Now, He already has ascended to His Father and returns and demands that this doubting disciple touch Him.

Guaranteed Trip

In the OT, when believers died they went to Hades because the price for their redemption had not yet been paid. They were put on layaway so to speak. Once Jesus paid for their redemption with His blood, His first order of business was to liberate these believers from their subterranean department. In the present time period, when a believer dies, he or she still goes to be with the Lord in Paradise—although it is now Paradise relocated from the realm of the dead to the realm of heaven, the abode of God (cp. Acts 7:55-60; 2Cor 5:8; Phil 1:23). They are no longer put on layaway because Jesus already has paid the full price for their pardon. This guarantee of being with the Lord applies to all believers for all time (1Thess 4:13-18). Believers will always be with the Lord, if not in His city, then at least with Him in His kingdom. Gehenna is an impossibility.

With the Lord

As a Gehenna misthologist, Faust challenges this summation. At a kingdom conference at which Faust and I were both teaching, while we were answering questions from the audience in a symposium at the conclusion of the first day of the conference, I responded to a question regarding the intermediate state by surmising that *to be absent from the body is to be at home with the Lord*. Faust challenged this statement by reading the text in 2Cor 5:8 and noting that the exact wording does not make this explicit confirmation and by further pointing out that he already had expressed his counter in his book.[1483] In my session the next morning, I outlined my reasons for coming to the summation I had given. At the same time, with illustration below in *Illustration 298*, I also answered a question that had been raised regarding the Heavenly Jerusalem.

According to Faust's assessment of the intermediate state, Stephen's invocation suggests a condition when he prays: "Lord Jesus, receive my spirit!" (Acts 7:59). Stephen was a white sheep, accordingly white sheep can expect the Lord to receive their spirits. I conceded that Stephen was a white sheep, so I could not use this passage to prove that gray sheep or black sheep would be with the Lord in the intermediate state. This text, in and of itself, does not refute the contention made by Gehenna misthologists that the receiving of one's spirit by the Lord at the point of death is conditioned on being a white sheep. However, my assessment was not based on a simplistic assumption regarding this text. Turning to the principle text in question, I made an exegetical observation:

> [8] We are of good courage, I say, and prefer rather to be absent from the body and to be at home with the Lord. [9] Therefore *also* (*kai*) we have as our ambition, whether at home or absent, to be pleasing to Him. [10] For we must all appear before the judgment seat of Christ, that each one may be recompensed for his deeds in the body, according to what he has done, whether good or bad. (2Cor 5:8-10)

Even if Paul is using an exclusive *we*, so as to refer to the apostolic circle rather than to the Corinthian readers in vv. 8-9, the point is still valid that his *ambition* is to be pleasing to the Lord, not to be present with the Lord. The latter is presumed rather than pursued. Being *with the* Lord is an unqualified anticipation. Being *pleasing to* the Lord, in contrast, is an ambition. The *also* (*kai*) that introduces this ambition signifies addition. That is, in addition to the unqualified (and apparently unconditional) anticipation of being with the Lord, Paul also has the ambition of being pleasing to the Lord. In fact, the expression of *good courage* that prefaces the anticipation of being with the Lord is frequently translated as *confidence*: "*We are confident, yes, well pleased rather to be absent from the body and to be present with the Lord*" (NKJ). Paul expresses complete confidence that if he is absent from the body, he will be at home with the Lord. Moreover, this confidence is unconditional. The conditional component is reserved for the additional constituent found in the next verse and amplified in the verse following it. The ambition of be pleasing to the Lord is conditioned on a positive result at the Bema judgment. Together these two components may be expressed as:

Unconditional Anticipation (v. 8) + Conditional Ambition (v. 9)

The logical implication is that Paul anticipates the pleasure of being with the Lord even if he is not pleasing to the Lord. Naturally, however, Paul desires to be pleasing to the Lord because he will be judged before the Lord. A number of corollaries are naturally implied: (1) Even if they are not pleasing to the Lord, all the believers referred to in v. 10 will be with the Lord at the time they become absent from their bodies. (2) The judgment of all these believers apparently will take place at the Lord's home. And (3) the outcome of the judgment determines whether they are pleasing to the Lord, not whether they are present with the Lord—not even during the intermediate state. Implicitly, their presence with the Lord during the intermediate state is affirmed to be unconditional.

Indeed, Paul explicitly affirms that all believers will be raptured to be with the Lord: "For God has not destined us for [tribulational] wrath, but for earning [millennial] salvation through our Lord Jesus Christ, who died for us, that whether we are [morally] awake or asleep, we may live together with Him" (1Thess 5:9-10). Being with the Lord via the rapture is not conditioned on earthly performance. This is a word of comfort and applies to all raptured believers from the point of the rapture forward (1Thess 4:17-18). Even the judgment of believers by the Lord does not dampen this promise. All believers, even those not found pleasing to the Lord, will be with the Lord after the rapture, despite its attendant judgment. Taken together, these Thessalonian and Corinthian passages affirm that all believers (good and bad) will be with the Lord before and after the rapture. *To be absent from the body is to be at home with the Lord.* Also, to have a glorified body is to be at home with the Lord as well.

Although the above argument has not been based on the passage in Acts regarding Stephen, his prayer does exemplify the above interpretation derived from key Pauline passages. As specified in 1Thess 5:10, redemption is the Pauline basis for this unconditional union with the Lord in the intermediate state. We will be with the Lord because He died for us, not because we lived for Him. Stephen may very well link his being with the Lord to redemption as well. Luke is the only one of the gospel writers who records Jesus' appeal to the Father for the forgiveness of those who were crucifying Him: "Father, forgive them; for they do not know what they are doing" (Lk 23:34). Luke also uniquely records these closing words: "Jesus, crying out with a loud voice, said, "Father, into Thy hands I commit My spirit." And having said this, He breathed His last. (Lk 23:46). Surely in his Luke-Acts composition, Luke intends for us to see the connection between Jesus' dying statements and those of Stephen: "And they went on stoning Stephen as he called upon the Lord and said, 'Lord Jesus, receive my spirit!' And falling on his knees, he cried out with a loud voice, 'Lord, do not hold this sin against them!' And having said this, he fell asleep" (Acts 7:59-60). Whereas Jesus committed His spirit into the Father's care, Stephen (in a conceptually parallel fashion) committed his spirit into Jesus' care. Before the stoning started, Stephen saw Jesus standing at the Father's right hand (Acts 7:55-56). I dare suggest that Stephen had his eyes fixed on Jesus rather than on his performance as his hope of being with Jesus. Like David, he had his eyes on his Redeemer: "Into Thy hand I commit my spirit; Thou hast ransomed me, O Lord, God of truth" (Ps 31:5). Jesus quoted the first part of this verse as He was providing the ransom price on the cross. Jesus committed His spirit into the Father's care as He completed redemption. David and Stephen were able to commit their spirits into the Lord's care because of this redemption.

Although the conclusion that *to be absent from the body is to be at home with the Lord* is based primarily on the evidence from the key passages such as 2Cor 5:8-9 and 1Thess 5:10, circumstantial evidence is collaborative. Stephen is currently with the Lord, even before the rapture. As to the rapture, "God will bring with Him those who have fallen asleep in Jesus" (1Thess 4:14). They will be brought with Him at the rapture because they are with Him before the rapture. Those who have fallen asleep in the Lord already have preceded those who are yet to be rapture. In other words, those who have fallen asleep are already with the Lord (1Thess 4:15). As to after the rapture, those who will be waiting in their intermediate state for the results of the Bema are seen waiting in heaven (Rev 6:9-11). Granted, those who will be waiting with the Lord in that context are faithful believers who died during the tribulation. Still, the reasonable presumption is that believers are not presumed guilty until proven innocent. Faust's assumption that unfaithful believers are kept in Hades as a holding cell (as a result of some preliminary judgment awaiting their judgment at the Bema) is refuted by the evidence.

None of those who have fallen asleep in the Lord are in Hades waiting for the rapture. For that matter, unfaithful believers are not cast into the outer darkness until after the wedding feast starts. Not even the results of the Bema immediately go into effect. Unfaithful believers remain with the Lord in His city until such time as His kingdom expands to encompass the earth. Then they can be cast into the outer darkness. One reason the effects of the judgment are not carried out until this time is because their presence with the Lord in His kingdom is guaranteed unconditionally. Until that kingdom expands beyond the walls of the city, they are with Him in the city.

After the kingdom expands beyond the walls of the city, it is no longer necessary to keep unfaithful believers in the city in order to keep them within the kingdom. Instead, it is necessary to expel them from the reward city once kingdom rewards are realized because they have no part in the realization of that reward. Nevertheless, they remain in the kingdom because merely being present in the kingdom is not a reward.

Illustration 298. City Migration from Intermediate to Eternal State

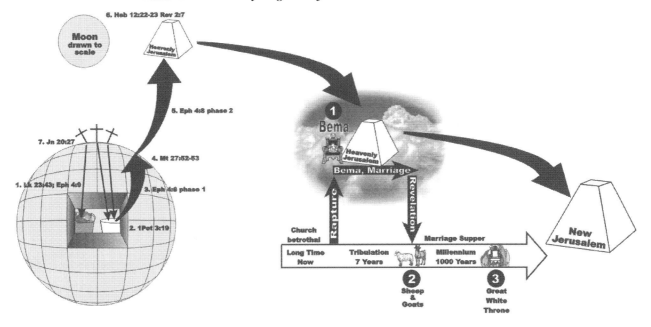

The sequence of events, then, is as follows. All believers in the intermediate state are currently with the Lord: OT as well as NT believers, good believers as well as bad believers. Presently, they are in the Heavenly City, presumably to the far north of this planet. At the rapture the Lord will bring all these believers with Him—by bringing the city to an orbit around this planet. (The city will be cloaked from view until the end of the tribulation.) During that seven year period of earth time, the Bema judgment (of at least all church-age believers) will take place at the Lord's home. Those church-age believers who are judged to be well pleasing to the Lord will hear the words, "Well done," and enter into permanent marital union with the Lord. Although they are given the proper attire at this time, they do not consummate the benefits of their rewards with the Lord until the marriage supper starts on earth during the millennial reign.

After the marriage supper starts, those believers who are disqualified from experiencing marital bliss with the Lord (because they previously were found to be displeasing to the Lord at the Bema) will be cast out of the bridal city to dwell on earth during the millennial kingdom. Instead of ruling with Christ, they will perform menial service for millennial inhabitants. At the conclusion of the millennium, the Heavenly City will descend to the surface of the planet. Unfaithful believers will be excluded from the city throughout eternity.

Conclusion

After the layaway transaction was completed in the act of redemption, the Lord's first order of business was to take His ransomed people home. Thereafter, they always will be with Him at home in His kingdom. However, His first order of business after He expands His kingdom to include the millennial earth will be to cast unfaithful believers into the outer expanse of His kingdom. One can only wonder as to what His first order of business will be after His kingdom rule expands to other planets. Will the exile of unfaithful believers become the outer expanse of His inhabited kingdom? As the kingdom expands, will the distance they are exiled from the capital city increase so that they inhabit the remotest parts of the universe? One can only wonder if they will wander from one star system to the next in the eternally expanding outer fringes of the kingdom. Although I will not appeal to Jude 1:13 to support this conclusion, what evidence we do have is suggestive that this indeed may be the case. In that case, Jude 1:13 would apply correlatively to those wandering from star to star in the outer darkness. As Earth becomes increasingly prime real estate in eternity future, why think that those cast into the outer darkness will have their homes on this planet? In eternity future, their recollections of their time in the capital city and on the capital planet may become increasingly distant yet haunting memories.

Appendix 10.
The Unpardonable Sin

Primary Texts

Mt 12:24-32

[24] But when the Pharisees heard it, they said, "This man casts out demons only by Beelzebul the ruler of the demons."... [30] "He who is not with Me is against Me; and he who does not gather with Me scatters. [31] "Therefore I say to you, any sin and blasphemy shall be forgiven men, but blasphemy against the Spirit shall not be forgiven. [32] And whoever shall speak a word against the Son of Man, it shall be forgiven him; but whoever shall speak against the Holy Spirit, it shall not be forgiven him, either in this age, or in the *age* to come."

Mk 3:28-30

[22] And the scribes who came down from Jerusalem **were saying**, "He is possessed by Beelzebul," and "He casts out the demons by the ruler of the demons."... [28] "Truly I say to you, all sins shall be forgiven the sons of men, and whatever blasphemies they utter; [29] but whoever blasphemes against the Holy Spirit never has forgiveness, but is guilty of an eternal *sin*"— [30] **because they were saying**, "He has an unclean spirit."

Lk 12:8-12

[8] "And I say to you, everyone who confesses Me before men, the Son of Man shall confess him also before the angels of God; [9] but he who denies Me before men shall be denied before the angels of God. [10] And everyone who will **speak a word** against the Son of Man, it shall be forgiven him; but he who **blasphemes** against the Holy Spirit, it shall not be forgiven him. [11] And when they bring you before the synagogues and the rulers and the authorities, do not become anxious about how or what you should speak in your defense, or what you should say; [12] for the Holy Spirit will teach you in that very hour what you ought to say."

Secondary Texts

Hebrews 6:4-6

[4] For in the case of those who have once been enlightened and have tasted of the heavenly gift and have been made partakers of the Holy Spirit, [5] and have tasted the good word of God and the powers of the age to come, [6] and then have fallen away, it is impossible to renew them again to repentance, since they again crucify to themselves the Son of God, and put Him to open shame.

Heb 10:26-31

[26] For if we go on sinning willfully after receiving the knowledge of the truth, there no longer remains a sacrifice for sins, [27] but a certain terrifying expectation of judgment, and the fury of a fire which will consume the adversaries. [28] Anyone who has set aside the Law of Moses dies without mercy on the testimony of two or three witnesses. [29] How much severer punishment do you think he will deserve who has trampled under foot the Son of God, and has regarded as unclean the blood of the covenant by which he was sanctified, and has insulted the Spirit of grace? [30] For we know Him who said, "Vengeance is Mine, I will repay." And again, "The Lord will judge His people." [31] It is a terrifying thing to fall into the hands of the living God.

1Jn 5:16

If anyone sees his brother committing a sin not leading to death, he shall ask and God will for him give life to those who commit sin not leading to death. There is a sin leading to death; I do not say that he should make request for this.

Comments by Others

Matthew and Mark ≠ Luke

In his *Word Pictures*, concerning both the Matthean and Markan passages, Robertson states his conviction that the unpardonable sin is attributing the work of the Holy Spirit to Satan and that this sin **can** be committed today. This is a common opinion, but more importantly, Robertson (WPNT) appropriately states that Matthew and Mark record this warning concerning the unpardonable sin

> immediately after the charge that Jesus was in league with Beelzebub. Luke here separates it from the same charge made in Judea (11:15-20). As frequently said, there is no sound reason for saying that Jesus only spoke his memorable sayings once. Luke apparently finds a different environment here.

Hardened Heart

Concerning Mt 12:31, Barbieri states the other side of the popular sentiment: "This specific sin **cannot** be reproduced today, for it required Jesus' presence on earth with His performing miracles through the Spirit's power."[1484] But Grassmick's comments concerning Mk 3:29 are more in harmony with Robertson:

> This refers to an attitude (not an isolated act or utterance) of defiant hostility toward God that rejects His saving power toward man, expressed in the Spirit-empowered person and work of Jesus. It is preference for darkness…Such a persistent attitude of willful disbelief can harden into a condition in which repentance and forgiveness…become impossible.[1485]

BKC is joined by the NIBC, concerning the Matthean and Markan passages, in thinking that stubborn, irrevocable continuance in a state of opposition is what results in the unpardonable sin rather than one defiant act. Lane appeals to support from the Greek text to derive the same conclusion, stating that the tense of the verb *were saying* in Mark "implies repetition and a fixed attitude of mind." "Only the man who sets himself against forgiveness is excluded from it."[1486] Morris takes the same position, "It is this continuing attitude that is the ultimate sin…this kind of sinner no longer has the capacity to repent and believe."[1487]

Unpardoned Believers

In his comments on Mark, Lenski states: "The unpardonable sin or the sin against the Holy Ghost may be committed, not only by former believers (Heb. 6:4-6; 10:26-31; I John 5:16), but also by men who have never believed."[1488] Thus, Lenski extends the argument from saying that the unpardonable sin can be committed today to saying that it may be committed today by believers and unbelievers. Due to his Arminian (actually Lutheran) perspective, one would think that Lenski is of the opinion that such believers lose eternal life. On the other hand, in the NIC Hendriksen claims, "The blasphemy against the Spirit is the result of gradual progress in sin. Grieving the Spirit (Eph. 4:30), if unrepented of, leads to resisting the Spirit (Acts 7:51), which, if persisted in, develops into quenching the Spirit (I Thess. 5:19)…'Harden not your hearts!' Cf. Heb. 3:7,8a."[1489]

Evidently, he would agree with Lenski that these passages describe a believer committing the unpardonable sin. Of course, given Hendriksen's Calvinistic presuppositions, this would prove they were never genuine believers to begin with. The important point, however, is that Lutherans and Calvinists potentially can agree that the harden heart syndrome is more wide spread than three passages. Further, it appears that believers as well as unbelievers can experience this same malady.

Berkhof provides the historical interpretive background detail that Jerome and Chrysostom believed the unpardonable sin could be committed only while Christ was on earth and that it was attributing Christ's works to Satan. However, Berkhof notes that the secondary passages listed above in Hebrews and 1John render this unlikely. Thus, he would agree with Lenski and Hendriksen concerning the applicability of these passages to believers today. He also surmises that Augustine and Lutherans believe that it was stubborn persistence in unbelief. Yet Berkhof wisely points out that the weakness with this position is that this would make all those who persist in unbelief until death guilty of the unpardonable sin, which seems to fall short of the nature of the sin that Jesus is warning against. Later, Lutherans "taught that only regenerate persons could commit this sin, and sought support for this view in Heb. 6:4-6."

Berkhof accepts the Reformed view, which is that it occurs when people harden their hearts "beyond the renewing power of the Holy Spirit." Thus, regeneration becomes impossible for such people because they no longer can repent or believe. Berkhof also argues that since all sins may be forgiven, except that which is classified as unpardonable sin in the gospel accounts, there is only "one unpardonable sin." And since Heb 6:4-6; 10:26-29; and 1Jn 5:16 also describe an unpardonable sin, "it is reasonable to conclude that these passages refer to the same sin." Although this "specific form of this sin…could only occur in the apostolic age."[1490]

FG Camp

In turning to the FG camp, some overlapping opinions are apparent, Hutson says, "It is rejecting the Holy Spirit's plea until the rejecting sinner loses all desire to be saved."[1491] In his chapter on the unpardonable sin, Hutson rejects Scofield's position that it "is ascribing the works of the Holy Spirit to Satan." He believes that the saved cannot commit it because the saved have all their sins pardoned. Yet he believes that Heb 6:4-6 describes the unpardonable sin, which would bring him into limited agreement with Berkhof. Hutson sees it as reaching an unpardonable state of not wanting pardon after continual rejection of the Spirit's conviction.

Stanley takes the typical approach in asserting that it is ascribing the works of the Holy Spirit to Satan and cannot be duplicated today because of the unique historical circumstances, but adds, "Although there is no unpardonable sin, there is an unpardonable state—the state of unbelief."[1492] In a very well written article, Wilkin prefers to designate it as an *unpardoned* sin rather than *unpardonable* sin and thinks it might be reached in a one-time act that would be of such proportions as to show a hardened heart. Considering the fact that the verb for *blaspheme* (*blasphemeo*) is an aorist subjective in Mark and an aorist participle in Luke and that the verb for *speak against* (*epo*) is an aorist subjective in Matthew, I would certainly not want to rule out that possibility.

Basically, Wilkin concedes that it represents a hardened heart that has crossed "the point of no return." He shows preference for limiting it to the period of the gospels since the NT epistles do not include it. Still, in deference to Berkhof, I might object: The fact that the epistles do not mention it by name does not prove that they do not indicate the phenomenon by other means. Certainly, taking the mark of the beast is an unpardonable sin, although it is not explicitly named as such (Rev 14:11). Even young adults and perhaps older teenagers could be susceptible. Taking the mark would be a punctiliar act that would result in a linear unpardonable state. This would be a good picture of the unpardonable sin. In my opinion, Jesus' use of the aorist is intuitive for this reason. Although the unpardonable sin may take a process of time to reach in certain cases, the fact that when one finally does reach this point of no return he or she does so permanently and punctiliarly makes the aorist choice natural.

If it be asked, "Why does John use a present tense in Rev 14:11 to describe taking the mark?" my answer is twofold. First, the use of the present tense in general and John's use in particular does not necessarily show linear action by the individual. Neither saving faith nor taking the mark are linear. Second, since both saving faith and taking the mark have eternal results, John could assume that the Greek speakers of his day would not try to condition the retention of eternal life on linear faith anymore than they would try to argue that one would continuously have to take the mark of the beast to be damned. The sheer nature of the case is that an irreversible result would not be expected to require parallel linear contingency (⇄) unless the writer indicates otherwise.[*] Therefore, it is a mistake to ask if the unpardonable sin is an act or state, as if it has to be one or the other. It is as much one as it is the other. It is an act-state that may be reached by an act/state.

Wilkin is absolutely certain that a Christian cannot commit the unpardonable sin due to eternal security. On the basis of the brief analysis above, a mutually exclusive relation between eternal security and the mark of the beast is certain. One necessarily precludes the other. If the unpardonable sin is limited to the soteriological realm, then logically Wilkin must be correct. He concludes by taking the almost universally held position that any unbeliever who desires to be saved has not committed the unpardonable sin.[1493] This completes the survey on some of the more prominent opinions. The following evaluation will come to an independent conclusion.

Comments by Present Author

Can the Unpardonable Sin be Committed Today?

The argument that the unpardonable sin cannot be committed today is weakened by the fact that Luke did not link it to the historical occasion of attributing the work of the Holy Spirit in the ministry of Jesus to Satan. Matthew and Mark do make this association, but Luke attributes these words to a different occasion, as Robertson has pointed out. Jesus evidently spoke this warning on multiple occasions and in different contexts. Interpreting it in context means not limiting it to one context in this particular case. Indeed, Luke's rendition seems to imply a futuristic and broader application of this warning.

---

[*] See *Illustration 162. Contingency and Consequence*, 488. Also see "Immutability and Conditionality" in *Sealed and Secure*.

Further, Berkhof's statements in favor of associating the primary and secondary texts seem logical. If the secondary texts are describing an unpardonable sin (which can be committed today) and if there is only one unpardonable sin, then the unpardonable sin can be committed today. There is only one type of unpardonable sin, although it may be reached and expressed by different means and forms. It is possible that the Matthean and Markan forms of the unpardonable sin could be expressed only while Jesus was physically present on earth. However, it is probably not true that the Lukan form of this sin could be committed only during Jesus' earthly ministry, and it is certainly true that the apostolic forms of this sin in the secondary passages can be committed today. Since both Lutherans and Calvinists can agree that both the primary and secondary passages describe different forms of the same type of sin, it would be advisable for FG to consider this possibility as well.

Can Believers Commit this Sin?

Luke's account provides an interesting parallel in associating one denying Jesus with speaking against Jesus. The former sin is not forgiven; the latter sin may be forgiven. The assumption that unbelief is the only sin that is unpardoned is false. Denying Jesus is also an unpardoned sin. As for that matter, there are many *unpardoned sins*. It is clear in Scripture that if a believer refuses to forgive others, that God will not forgive that believer (Mt 6:14-15). If a believer does not pardon others for their sins, then that believer will not be pardoned for his or her sins. Likewise, if believers do not walk in the light and confess their sins, they will not be forgiven (1Jn 1:6-9). The faulty assumption that unbelief is the only unpardoned sin is based on the simplistic notion that all forgiveness is soteriological. It is not. As is widely acknowledged, there are other types of forgiveness as well (e.g., familial, temporal, misthological). That a sin is forgiven in one aspect does not mean that it is forgiven in all aspects.

However, it would seem to trivialize Jesus' warning to say that all *unpardoned sin* is **unpardonable sin**. From the primary texts, we see that Jesus does not equate denying Him (which is an unpardoned sin) with the unpardonable sin. Concerning the secondary texts of Hebrews, in the context of that book (especially as seen in verses like 3:11; 4:3,5), God swears that a certain group of people would not enter His rest. The Lord made this decree before the people died. The unpardonable sin is not merely dying in an unpardoned state; it is reaching an unpardonable state before death.

For God's redeemed people to enter His inheritance rest was impossible because of the hardness of their heart (Heb 3:7-8). They had reached a point where they could not repent (Heb 6:6). Even worse, they could not get God to repent (Heb 12:17). They had reached an unpardonable state before death by persistence in sin. Many in FG have acknowledged that these passages are talking about believers. In fact, R. T. Kendall (*Stone Deaf*) has well demonstrated that such believers could never repent or find misthological forgiveness and that the book of Hebrews describes an unpardonable state that could be reached by believers before death. This unpardonable state was not merely dying in a state of unbelief. It was a hardening that accrued before death that made forgiveness impossible after death. God is not going to forgive such believers relative to the misthological sphere. Misthologically, He is going to judge and punish them. Their loss of rewards will be eternal.

Of course, those in the FG camp readily acknowledge that 1Jn 5:16 describes a genuine believer who has sinned so grievously as to be subject to God's judgment in the form of premature death. God does not (temporally) forgive such a believer; God kills him. A believer can reach a place where God decrees premature death and nothing can be done to change it. These secondary texts concerning the unpardonable sin shed light on the fact that it can be committed by believers and indicates a harden state where repentance is impossible.

Returning to the primary text as presented in Luke 12:8-12, it is possible for believers to deny Jesus and be denied misthologically by Jesus. Since Jesus' warning concerning denying Him is applicable to believers, it would seem sensible to presume that His warning against blaspheming against the Spirit is also applicable to believers. It is possible for believers to grieve (Eph 4:30), quench (1Thess 5:19), and insult the Spirit (Heb 10:29). Believers can harden their hearts to the point where repentance is impossible and punishment is certain. Chapters 3, 4, 6, 10, and 12 of Hebrews would seem to describe just such a possibility.

Definition

The unpardonable sin is hardening your heart against the convicting ministry of the Holy Spirit to the point that you reach an unpardonable state in which it is impossible to repent because God has given you over to the path you repeatedly have chosen. For unbelievers this means they cannot believe and will suffer eternal judgment in hell. For believers this means they cannot repent and will suffer eternal loss of rewards in the outer darkness, barred from being allowed to rule in heaven for all eternity.

Pastoral Principle

Only God knows who has reached the point where He has sworn in His wrath that they will persist in their stubborn state until the end. As is almost universally acknowledged, if an individual is concerned that he or she might have committed the unpardonable sin, then this person has not committed it. After all, if a person is still sensitive to the convicting ministry of the Holy Spirit, then how can it be said that the Holy Spirit is no longer convicting such a person?

The fact that Esau tearfully sought repentance and was rejected need not mean that those who tearfully seek repentance in this life may find that it is too late. Esau was in tears because he had forfeited his inheritance. He might be regarded as a picture of a believer who stands before the Bema and tearfully hopes that God may repent and decide to reward him even though he failed to live for God. It is not going to happen. God will not repent. It will be too late for our repentance at the Bema to move God to repentance. The misthological consequences are eternal. This aspect of the inheritance is forfeited forever. Our repentance needs to be in this life. If it does not occur now, it will occur then, but what a sad state of affairs it will be for those believers who wait to repent then.

Alternatively, Esau may be an example of the fact that those who repent in this life may find it impossible to undo completely the damage they have done so as to receive a full reward. Some Christians evidently reach a Kadesh Barnea point in their lives long before death. The Kadesh Barnea typology is certainly Bema related, but it may not be posthumously isolated.[*] In addition to OT typology exemplified by Esau and Kadesh Barnea (which is picked up by the NT and applied misthologically to church-age believers), Crawford also notes that the OT supplies the example of Saul:

> [24] Then Saul said to Samuel, "I have sinned; I have indeed transgressed the command of the Lord and your words, because I feared the people and listened to their voice. [25] "Now therefore, please pardon my sin and return with me, that I may worship the Lord." [26] But Samuel said to Saul, "I will not return with you; for you have rejected the word of the Lord, and **the Lord has rejected you from being king over Israel**." [27] And as Samuel turned to go, Saul seized the edge of his robe, and it tore. [28] So Samuel said to him, "**The Lord has torn the kingdom of Israel from you today**, and has given it to your neighbor who is better than you. [29] "And also the Glory of Israel will not lie or change His mind; for He is not a man that He should change His mind." [30] Then he said, "I have sinned; but please honor me now before the elders of my people and before Israel, and go back with me, that I may worship the Lord your God." [31] So Samuel went back following Saul, and Saul worshiped the Lord. (1Sam 15:24-31)

In personal dialogue with Crawford, he has suggested that believers who come to a mature understanding of kingdom truth and then reject it will be rejected permanently by God as kingdom rulers even if they should subsequently desire it.[1494] Saul was a believer who repented and yet found his repentance rejected misthologically. The possibility of extended rulership of the kingdom was taken away from him that very day despite his repentance. In conjunction with the misthological view of *epignosis* suggested herein (as dealing with mature kingdom knowledge), this view is favorably entertained herein: Misthological apostasy results in a permanent exclusion from kingdom rulership long before death and therefore results in a misthologically unpardonable state. A counter example might be offered. Since the offer of the kingdom was taken away from the Jewish generation that killed Jesus and then re-extended to them, perhaps there is hope that, at least in isolated instances, exceptions to this rule might exist. Seeing that Jesus has been raised never to die again (Rom 6:9), however, there appears to be nothing substantial enough to apply this corporate exception to the individual apostates who "again crucify to themselves the Son of God, and put Him to open shame" (Heb 6:6). Does the example of Saul, then, show that such posttraumatic repentance is completely null and vain? No. The example of Esau suggests that such repentance can find a limited blessing even in protracted and procrastinated cases.[†] If one is rejected from kingdom rulership because one has abandoned the misthological faith, one still would be advised to repent in order to avoid the darkest corners of the outer darkness. Fewer strips are still better than many strips (Lk 12:47-48).

Potential Objections

Two potential objections need to be addressed regarding the application of the unpardonable sin to believers. First, can a believer blaspheme the Holy Spirit? Curtis Hutson believes they can and states that "good preachers, have, out of jealousy, ascribed the works of the Holy Spirit to Satan." The example he shares is an evangelistic one

---

[*] See *Kadesh Barnea*, 874.
[†] See *Pastoral Concern*, 874.

in which many youth were saved, and some people in the community did not believe it was genuine. If you criticize genuine regeneration as being a deception of Satan, have you not attributed the work of the Holy Spirit to Satan?

One might also cite a controversial example, such as healings within the Charismatic movement. For the sake of illustration, assume for the moment that many Charismatic healings are genuine. In that case, those believers outside the Charismatic movement who criticize it as being false or demonic would be blaspheming the work of the Holy Spirit. On the other hand, suppose that many of the miracles that occur in the Charismatic movement are false or demonic. Then those believers inside the movement who claim that these miracles are genuine are blaspheming the Holy Spirit by ascribing false or demonic miracles to Him. After all, believers can be guilty of blasphemy (e.g., Eph 4:31; Col 3:8; esp. 1Tim 1:20). Believers can and do blaspheme the Holy Spirit by profaning His ministry in their own lives and in the lives of others. The objection that believers cannot blaspheme the Holy Spirit is groundless.

The second objection that might be raised concerns the possibility of believers being *guilty of an eternal sin* (Mk 3:29; CT). This reading by the Critical Text is possible, and this theological stumbling block already has been hurdled—believers can be guilty of eternal sin. The objection that this passage cannot be true of believers because all believers' sins have been forgiven is based on the presupposition that this passage must be soteriological and thus be limited to soteriological forgiveness. This presupposition has been found very questionable. Solid evidence exists for thinking that this forgiveness may entail misthological forgiveness in the case of believers.

The alternative reading of this text by both the Majority Text and Textus Receptus may be preferred, where it is said they are *in danger of eternal judgment* (Mk 3:29; MT; TR). The difference is in the last word *krisis*. The KJV translates it soteriologically as *damnation*. Yet it could be translated just as easily in a neutral sense as *condemnation* (NKJ) or *judgment*. If one must insist on taking the translation *damnation* soteriologically, then the KJV is providing an interpretation, not merely a translation. If this is the case, then the KJV wrongly asserts the damnation of believers in Rom 13:2; 14:23; 1Cor 11:29; and 1Tim 5:12. Just to translate the word in its normal and neutral sense as *judgment* would be far better. Believers cannot be damned soteriologically, but they can be judged temporally and misthologically. The results of the misthological judgment are eternal. Hence, those believers who commit the unpardonable sin are subject to eternal judgment.

If the *krisis* reading is accepted, then the closet verbal parallel to the phrase is Mt 5:21-22, where it is said that they are *in danger of judgment*. This judgment is distinguished from being in danger of hell in v. 22. Thus, evidence exists from the broad context to think that the phrase is not simplistically equated with soteriological judgment; rather, it may be applicable to believers.

The closet parallels to *eternal judgment* are Mt 25:46 and Heb 6:2. The first of these references is definitely soteriological, and the second one is also, but perhaps not exclusively soteriological. Tanner is of the persuasion that the *eternal judgment* of Heb 6:2 refers to **both** the Judgment Seat of Christ **and** the Great White Throne Judgment.[1495] He is joined in this assessment by IBC. In any case, the fact that the expression could be used soteriologically does not necessarily prove that it must be limited to this usage. That it has that usage in some contexts does not mean that it must have that meaning in every context. For example, even if it has that meaning in Mk 3:29, it must be remembered that the Lukan account occurs in a different context and omits this phrase. It could be that on the occasion recorded by Matthew and Mark, Jesus had one form of the unpardonable sin principally in mind, since in that historical context it was unbelievers who were being prevented from believing by their soteriological blasphemy. Yet on other occasions, such as that recorded by Luke, Jesus inclusively had other forms of this blasphemy in mind that may be applicable to believers today.

Conclusion

Unbelievers and believers can both be guilty of the unpardonable sin. Although it is possible that unbelievers were principally in view in two of the three gospel accounts, there is no compelling reason to conclude that Jesus limited this form of the unpardonable sin to unbelievers. The rest of the NT makes it clear that both unbelievers and believers can harden their hearts against the Holy Spirit to such an extent that they will suffer the eternal consequences of such hardening. Consequently, the most natural conclusion is that both unbelievers and believers can be guilty of the same sin—the unpardonable sin. Those who are so hardened before death will be subject to sever judgment after death. In such cases, unbelievers will be subject to hell, while hardhearted believers will be subject to the outer darkness. Jesus rebuked hardhearted believers while on earth (Mk 6:52; 8:17; 16:14), and the NT warns believers against becoming hardhearted today (Heb 3:8,15; 4:7). Let us heed this rebuke and warning while there is still time, if there is still time.

Appendix 11.
Light And Darkness

Introduction

Pagenkemper finds the sharp incongruence between light and darkness in the NT to be such that it is impossible to believe that true believers, who are sons of light, could possibly be cast into the outer darkness.

> The New Testament consistently affirms that belief in Christ unites an individual with God's kingdom of "light." Therefore the casting of a child of light into the outermost reaches of darkness contrasts with the motifs of light and darkness and the revealed realities of salvation. To be in outer darkness indicates that one is not related to light. They are incompatible. This separation is most clearly seen in the Gospel of John. Those who believe in Christ become "sons of light" (υἱοὶ φωτὸς, John 12:35-36) and no longer remain in darkness (v. 46; cf. Matt. 5:14, 16; Luke 16:8; John 1:4-9, 3:19-21; 8:12; 9:5).[1496]

The lack of precision in Pagenkemper's summation results in distortion. Certainly, all those who believe in the light become sons of light (Jn 12:36; cp. Eph 5:8; 1Thess 5:5). John also had used *believe* (and a synonym for it) to speak of appropriating the light in Jn 1:4-9. However, the NT is also clear that not all believers necessarily walk in the light (Eph 5:8; 1Thess 5:6-9). John himself acknowledges that it is possible for a believer to walk in the darkness (1Jn 1:6-7). Evidently, Pagenkemper and John do not agree on the implications of the Gospel of John. I suspect that John is in a better position to gauge whether his gospel rules out the possibility of a believer being in darkness! John's assessment that some believers walk in light while some believers walk in darkness is the understanding adopted herein.

John 8:12

Jesus' statement that those who follow Him will walk in the light should be understood also as probably describing the potential experience of believers. "Again therefore Jesus spoke to them, saying, 'I am the light of the world; he who follows Me shall not walk in the darkness, but shall have the light of life'" (Jn 8:12). The soteriological interpretation of this verse takes *follow* as a synonym for *believe*, as is the (probable) case in Jn 10:27. Accordingly, to *have the light* would denote the soteriological possession of eternal life (cp. Jn 10:28). Further support for this position could be derived from Jn 12:35-36 where *to walk in the light* seems to mean *believe in the light*. (However, this assumption will be rejected below.) Because of this seeming metaphorical equivalence, some would argue that the stated requirement for eternal life is to believe, and some of those advocating this position would then proceed to state that what is required is continuous belief since the metaphors used for believe are *follow* and *walk*. An aspectual and metaphorical analyses of *believe* in GJ would demonstrate that such a notion is very selective in the tenses and metaphors being used for such an appeal. Regardless, in the present case, it is probable that *follow* and *walk* denote linear action, but it is improbable that they should be taken as metaphors for *believe*.

These verses can be understood as describing experiential possession. Those believers who walk in the light will experience the light. They will have light in their daily experience. *Follow* in Jn 8:12 can be taken as it is in Jn 12:26 as referring to discipleship, which would be a conceptual parallel to the synoptic injunction to take up our cross and follow Jesus (Mt 10:38; 16:24; Mk 8:34; Lk 9:23). This promise of experiential possession, which Jesus makes to believers who follow Him in discipleship, is very reminiscent of what He had spoken earlier: "Jesus therefore was saying to those Jews who had believed Him, 'If you abide in My word, then you are truly disciples of Mine; and you shall know the truth, and the truth shall make you free'" (Jn 8:31-32).[1497] Practical knowledge of the truth and effective release of its power in a believer's life is conditioned upon the believer following the Lord's instructions. Jesus came that we might not only have eternal life soteriologically but also have it abundantly (Jn 10:10).* He wants believers to have freedom (8:32), to have a partnership with Him (Jn 13:8),† to have a

---

* Abundant life need not be limited to the temporal sphere but might very well reach to the misthological horizon.

† Conceptually, retaining partnership with Christ certainly reaches beyond the temporal present to the misthological future: "For we have become and remain (●━) partners with Christ, if we hold fast (→) the beginning of our assurance firm until the end" (Heb 3:14; TM). Continuation in this perfective state of partnership is conditioned on a parallel linear contingency (●➜). The contingency runs parallel to the perfective state and is necessary to maintain that state. See *Fallen from Grace but Not from Perfection*.

fullness of joy (Jn 17:13), to have fellowship with Him (1Jn 1:3,7) and with one another (1Jn 1:6), to have a vibrant knowledge of Him (1Jn 2:3), and to have life in their expression of love for one another (1Jn 3:14). He is not talking about having the gift of life, but about having the light of life in terms of our everyday walk.[1498] Believers who follow the Lord in discipleship will walk in light rather than darkness. The hymnist has so well expressed this truth: *When we walk with the Lord in the light of His word, what a glory He sheds on our way.*

Illustration 299. Logical Sequence of Experiencing Light

LIGHT		
1. Jn 1:4-5; 12:36,46	**BELIEVE**	in the light
2. Jn 3:19-21	**COME**	to the light
3. Jn 8:12; 11:9-10; 12:35	**WALK**	in the light

John urges three responses from his readership in relation to the light. They are invited to **believe in** the light, **come to** the light, and **walk in** the light. The sequence is important and is illuminated by Matthew. You are light so let your light shine (Mt 5:14,16).[1499] You have to be light before you can let it shine. Like John and Paul, Matthew indicates that although you may be a child of the light, you might not walk in the light. Your walk does not determine whether you are saved or whether you are a child of the light. You might hide the fact that you are light. You might be light ontologically but hide your light experientially. If so, then you will walk in the darkness. Your walk does not determine your regeneration; nor does your regeneration necessarily determine your walk.

John 12:46 (Believe in the Light)

Illustration 300. Type of Sequence of Light

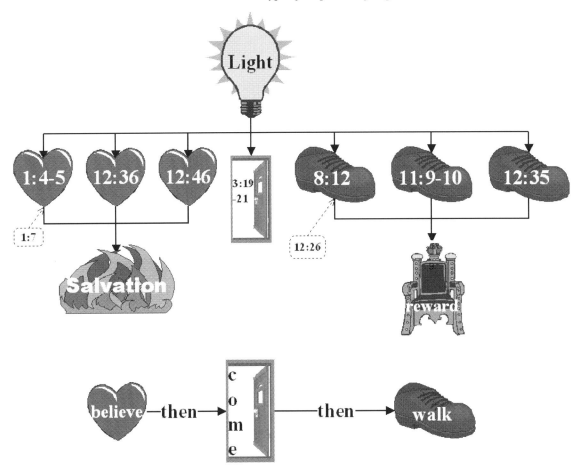

In Jn 8:12, the theme of *light* is presented in relationship to discipleship. Of course, this same imagery of light can also be used in relation to salvation: "I have come as light into the world, that everyone who believes in Me may not remain in darkness" (Jn 12:46). Everyone who appropriates the saving benefit of Jesus' death by soteriologically trusting Him for eternal life abides in the light permanently and completely. Believers have moved fully and forever out of one sphere into another (Jn 5:24). They do not move from death into sickness or from the darkness into the shadows. Pagenkemper is correct in his polar comparison in this aspect regarding those verses, which describe a believer's position rather than a believer's practice. Nevertheless, Pagenkemper is in error in equating practice with position. Although we are new creatures positionally and ontologically, we may fail to be new creatures experientially. Believers have moved spherically and ontologically into the realm of light and thus are exhorted to enter it experientially. Just because someone is a child of light does not guarantee that he or she will not live in darkness.

John 12:35 (Walk in the Light)

As mentioned above, *walk* in Jn **12:35** might conceivably be a metaphor (or precondition) for *believe* in Jn 12:36. However, there is a better option that would retain the consistency of the imagery of 12:35 with 3:19-21; 8:12; 11:9-10; and 1Jn 1:6-7. A call to discipleship in 12:35 is not out of place since the commencement of conversion anticipates an appeal to discipleship (Jn 12:25-26). Further, the call to take up your cross and follow Jesus in discipleship and possible death (Jn 12:25-26) is very reminiscent of His earlier appeal for discipleship in 8:12 where He used the light motif as an invitation to discipleship. Granted, the soteriological reference to believing in Jesus who is the light in 12:46 would seem to support a soteriological understanding of light in this context, but it must be remembered that **12:46 is not a part of the closing dialogue**. Instead, Jn 12:46 is part of a monologue in the mini epilogue (Jn 12:37-50) which follows this dialogue (Jn 12:20-36).

Illustration 301. Supper Outline of John

1. Prologue   (ch.1A)
2. Before Supper (chs.1B-12)
3. During Supper (chs.13-17)
4. After Supper   (chs.18-20)
5. Epilogue   (ch. 21)

Dual Invitation of the Dialogue

"Jesus therefore said to them, 'For a little while longer the light is among you. **Walk** while you have the light, that darkness may not overtake you; he who walks in the darkness does not know where he goes. [36] While you have the light, **believe** in the light, in order that you may become sons of light. These things Jesus spoke, **and He departed and hid Himself from them**." (Jn 12:35-36).

Dual Explanation of the Epilogue

[37] But though He had performed so many signs before them, yet they were **not believing** in Him that the word of Isaiah the prophet might be fulfilled, which he spoke, "Lord, who has believed our report? And to whom has the arm of the Lord been revealed?" [39] For this cause they **could not believe**, for Isaiah said again, [40] "He has blinded their eyes, and He hardened their heart...[42] Nevertheless many even of the rulers believed in Him, but because of the Pharisees they were **not confessing** Him, lest they should be put out of the synagogue; [43] for they loved the approval of men rather than the approval of God. [44] And Jesus cried out and said, "He who believes in Me does not believe in Me, but in Him who sent Me. [45] And he who beholds Me beholds the One who sent Me. [46] I have come as light into the world, that everyone who believes in Me may not remain in darkness." (Jn 12:37-46).

To reiterate and expand upon a point made previously, John not only closes his Gospel with an epilogue, he also closes this *Before Supper* section with an epilogue.[*] This sectional epilogue is given after the conclusion of Jesus' public ministry, which concludes with Jesus departing and hiding Himself from the masses (Jn 12:36). The verses following v. 36 are John's summary of what he has written so far (chs 1-12): a summary about Jesus' signs

---

[*] See "Sectional Epilogue" in *Believe: An Aspectual and Metaphorical Analysis from the Gospel of John.*

(v. 37), a summary about the results (vv. 37-43), and a summary about Jesus' teaching (vv. 44-50). Granted, this monologue in 12:44-50 was spoken publicly by Jesus (cp. v. 44). Yet how could Jesus have spoken these words publicly after His public teaching had ceased? Obviously, John is either using direct and indirect quotes from Jesus' teaching to compose it, or he records another speech, which Jesus had given earlier. Commentators are divided on these two options and either is reasonable. As John credits us with common sense to be able to anticipate such possibilities, so we may do the same for John in implementing such suggestions.

In John's summary, two problems are dealt with: the lack of faith **and** the lack of discipleship (cp. 12:42). Why did people by-and-large not believe in Jesus and why did those who believed in Him not confess Him? Since the closing epilogue of this section deals with both problems, it would be expected that the closing dialogue would emphasize both invitations. Thus, the statement in the epilogue of 12:42-43 is a strong parallel to the corresponding statement in the closing dialogue of 12:35. This latter verse is an invitation to discipleship and is followed by an explanation as to the limited response to the invitation in Jn 12:42-43. The fact that 12:35 and 12:36 occur side by side is not a convincing argument that they are both giving the same invitation. Rather, Jesus gives a dual invitation to step out into the light with public confession (v. 35), with the foundational understanding that one must believe in the light to experience regeneration (v. 36).

The explanation in the epilogue concerning the limited response to discipleship (vv. 42-43) is surrounded by references explaining the limited response to salvation. The rationalization concerning the lack of discipleship is preceded with illumination as to the lack of faith. The dual explanation for lack of faith and discipleship in the epilogue of 12:37-50 would presuppose a dual invitation to faith and discipleship in closing statements of the dialogue in 12:35-36. Certainly, this call to discipleship in v. 36 is compatible with the theme of discipleship—to which John's next section in the after-supper section will be dedicated. Finally, the broader biblical context of Eph 5:8 makes a beautiful Pauline parallel to this Johannine truth pictured in 12:35-36. You cannot walk in light until you become a child of the light.

Jn 12:35 is an invitation to the secret believers in the audience to step out into the light of public profession and discipleship right now. These secret believers are the subject of 12:42-43. Combined with 12:36, the invitation in 12:35-36 is to believe and become disciples without a moment to waste. Jesus had just given a call to discipleship in 12:26. He concludes by giving it again in 12:35. The call to discipleship is natural in view of the cross that He is about to bear. On the other hand, there are also many in the audience who had not yet even come to faith, much less to the light. Jesus also gives them the expected invitation to become children of the light (i.e., children of God) through a simple response of faith in 12:36. He does not expect unbelievers to walk in the light. Thus, the exhortation to walk in the light in 12:35 is an invitation to believers, not unbelievers.

John 3:19-21

In all probability, Nicodemus was one of these secret believers to whom John refers, who had come to believe in Jesus for eternal life.[*] Previously, Nicodemus had come to Jesus in the secrecy of night, and Jesus had given him a gospel presentation in Jn 3:16-18. Immediately afterwards in Jn 3:19-21, Jesus told Nicodemus that he should step out of the darkness of the night in which he had come to see Him and publicly declare his faith in Him. Nicodemus failed to do so; nevertheless, he had experienced spiritual regeneration that night (or shortly thereafter), and the Holy Spirit was working in his heart to move him beyond the realm of mere saving faith to a victorious, overcoming faith. The Holy Spirit's work was proving fruitful—growth was occurring.

By the time John's readers reaches Jn 7:50-51, they find that Nicodemus made a statement that was just shy of being a victorious confession; nevertheless, it was enough to result in his receiving public ridicule. What Nicodemus did in ch. 7 was extremely close to testifying "the good confession in the presence of many witnesses" (1Tim 6:12). Joseph of Arimathea also believed in Jesus, perhaps as a result of Nicodemus' influence. Both were suspected by the other rulers as being secret disciples of Jesus. Their witness behind the scenes probably helped other rulers believe as well. Still, these other rulers, who were brand-new converts, did not want to be branded as believers and thus risk being ostracized. They kept their faith a complete secret.

With considerable literary skill, John compels believers to step out of the dark closet into the light of public profession. John does not share Pagenkemper's view that as soon as a person becomes a believer he or she comes to the light and walks in the light. John paints a picture of theological realism that depicts believers who have undergone a metamorphosis into creatures of light who are struggling to escape their dark cocoon and spread their wings and fly in the light. His words are meant to be an encouragement as they fight the grave clothes that bind them so that they may experience the power of flight.

---

[*] See illustration of "Sequence of Events" in *Believe: An Aspectual and Metaphorical Analysis from the Gospel of John*.

Granted, although overcoming love for sin can be a psychological precondition for coming to faith for particular people, in which they require (of themselves) that they give up (or at least be willing to give up) the pleasure of sin before they are willing to come to saving faith, Jesus is speaking universally rather than particularly with His reference to *everyone* (v. 20). Jesus is not dealing with pre-evangelistic concerns in Jn 3:19-21 but with post-evangelistic ones instead. The one who *comes to the light* is the one who already has become a *doer of the truth* (v. 21). Certainly, this doer of the truth is one who is already a believer in the One who is the truth (Jn 14:6). Coming to the light in this context is not a metaphor for coming to saving faith but a metaphor for stepping out in public profession once one already has come to saving faith. In effect, Jesus is saying, "Believers who practice the truth step out into the light of public profession." Now that Nicodemus has become a believer, Jesus is exhorting him to step out of the closet and publically confess his belief in Jesus as the Christ.[*]

Reward for Walking in the Light

The flow chart in *Illustration 300* (p. 838) depicts a number of these texts dealing with light as culminating in reward. Theologically, one may deduce this to be the case since (in accordance with the conclusion reached herein) these texts are dealing with discipleship, and discipleship results in reward. Nonetheless, the Gospel of John (being an evangelistic gospel) does not frequently focus on the doctrine of rewards. Remarkably, however, two exceptions occur within the same chapter (ch. 12)—the final chapter that gives an invitation to secret believers to step out of the darkness and walk in the light of public profession and discipleship.

Tragically, *many* of these secret believers do not step out into the light of public identification with Jesus—the Light of the Word. Out of fear, they prefer to lurk in what they think is the safety of the shadows. Nevertheless, something is lurking there in the darkness with them; something they did not suspect; something behind them, waiting, watching, and straining against its chains. John only hints at it in his misthological explanation (Jn 12:42-43). Despite its ravenous desire, it cannot pounce just yet; it has to await the Bema. For now, it can only hungrily wait there with them and stare at them with hungry, steadfast eyes. Yet, it is there waiting. And if you listen carefully, you can hear it breathing, even now, in the background.

Illustration 302. Darkness may Overtake You

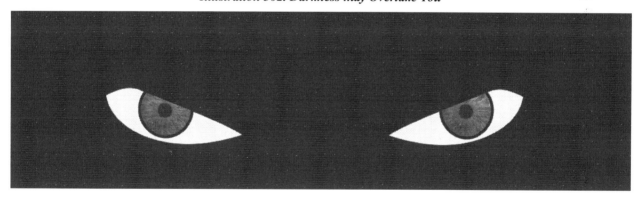

Jesus lets out a piercing warning in this contextual background. I can hear Him even now shouting: "Run for your lives! Get out of the darkness quickly while you still can! Run now! Step out in service to the Light, or you will lose your life to the creature of darkness" (cp. Jn 12:25-26). "Walk while you have the light, that darkness may not *overtake* [*katalambano*] you; he who walks in the darkness does not know where he goes" (Jn 12:35). Jesus practically points His finger at this thing of darkness that is straining against its chains: a misthological avenger that wants to slay them and take their lives (cp. *katalambano* in Dt 19:6); an accursed creature in that it invokes God's curses upon His disobedient children (cp. *katalambano* in Dt 28:15); a beast that seizes its victims with almost demonic frenzy as it causes them to weep and gnash their teeth (cp. *katalambano* in Mk 9:18). In other contexts, Jesus even gave this creature a name—*the outer darkness.*

---

[*] Some have objected by regarding Jesus as the light and assuming correspondingly that coming to the light must mean coming to faith in Jesus. Identifying Jesus as the light, however, poses no problem for the interpretation adopted herein. Those who have come to faith in Jesus (i.e., the light) are exhorted to come to Jesus (i.e., the light) in public association. Coming to the light would still denote stepping out in public discipleship. Coming to light would be the first step of public discipleship.

Additionally, coming to the light (i.e., coming to Jesus in public discipleship) may be regarded as one of the good deeds done by believers who practice the truth. Publically coming to Jesus would be consistent with practicing the truth (i.e., with the behavior expected of those who have become believers; 1Jn 1:8). Coming to the light would be a good work, not saving faith.

Mercy Came Running by Phillips, Craig, and Dean is a beautiful song that pictures mercy coming running as a prisoner set free at the point of redemption. Mercy is not the only thing, however, that may be pictured as eagerly waiting and then as coming running when set free. God's misthological disapproval may be pictured as watching them from the darkness with hungry, steadfast eyes—waiting to overtake them and avenge the blood of Christ which they have trampled underfoot (Jn 12:35,43; Heb 10:29-31).

Illustration 303. Judgment Came Running

Judgment came running.
Like a beast set free
Because of all my failures
Because I wouldn't heed
When my own preservation
Was all I could see
When I wouldn't stand for Jesus
Judgment came running for me.

Given the misthological context of Jn 12:35, the supposition is reasonable that Jesus is not limiting believers being overtaken by darkness to the temporal sphere of the experiential present. Indeed, the more reasonable supposition is that Jesus is warning that this darkness will overtake them misthologically. If being overtaken experientially were the exclusive (or even primary focus), would it not have been more fitting for Jesus to describe the darkness as already having overtaken them? Surely their present walking in the darkness had resulted in the darkness already overtaking them experientially in the present. Jesus is not warning about being overtaken in the present but in the future. Being *overtaken* by the outer darkness at the JSC is the most reasonable point of reference.

Reward of Walking in the Light

The temporal rewards for experientially walking in the light with Jesus (who is the Light) include: experientially having the light of life (Jn 8:12), present fellowship with Jesus (1Jn 1:7), and abiding continually in the light (1Jn 2:10). In short, the reward of walking with Jesus is being with Jesus. Naturally, this communion with the Light is in the sphere of light. Jesus is "the light of the world." He is also "the light of life" (Jn 8:12). Jesus is the reward. In this verse, being with Jesus now is the reward for following Jesus now. Yet Jesus goes on to show the misthological dimension of this reward. The reward for following Jesus is also being with Jesus then: "If anyone serves Me, let him follow Me; and where I am, there shall My servant also be [i.e., be with Jesus]; if anyone serves Me, the Father will honor him" (Jn 12:26).* Walking with Jesus in the light is a reward that bridges the present to the future. Believers have a choice to make: Walk with Jesus in the light, or weep in the outer darkness. Given such considerations, Jesus may not have intended for His reference to walking in the darkness to be limited to experiential darkness but to include the possibility of stumbling in misthological darkness as well. Regardless, those who walk in the darkness certainly will be overtaken by the outer darkness.

Conclusion

When John's gospel and epistle are duly considered, it is apparent that some believers, after having believed in the light and having become sons of light, may fail to come to the light, much less to walk in the light. Such believers will be cast out into the mistholic darkness of night when they reach the Bema. Those believers who prefer to lurk in the shadows or walk in the black night morally and temporally will be overtaken by the misthological darkness. This blackness is referred to as the outer darkness in Matthew's gospel. This metaphorical blackness is their eternal reward. Believers may be pictured as losing their lives there—misthologically (Jn 12:25).

---

* Those not interested in being with Jesus really should not pursue rewards. Conversely, those not interested in pursuing rewards really should not pretend to be interested in being with Jesus.

Appendix 12.
Ultra-Dispensational Objections

In his *Dispensational Disintegration* Stanford objects to the misthological distinctions maintained herein, criticizing Dillow, Hodges, and a host of others as abandoning traditional dispensational distinctions. Interaction has been provided already within the present book with what few statements Stanford made in part one of his attack against FG misthology that merited some response. Part Two of his assault has little, if anything, of substance to interact with since it amounts to little more than stringing together proof texts. The doctrine of the outer darkness in particular catches his attention.

> All Overcomer teaching is centered in Matthew: the Sermon on the Mount in general, and the Parable of the Wedding Celebration (22:1-14) in particular. Hence Gregory Sapaugh's Overcomer article is in "harmony with the context of Matthew," all right, but in what <u>portion</u> of "the teachings of the NT"? Certainly not in the grace realm of the Pauline Church Epistles! (Emphasis his).[1500]

Certainly, the doctrine of the outer darkness is centered in Matthew. Where else would it be centered since this is the only book of the NT that uses the term? However, Stanford's statement that "all overcomer teaching is centered in Matthew" is false. Overcomer is not a Matthean theme, in terms of terminology at least. This terminology is Johannine. Further, the misthological aspect of this subject is central to Rev 2-3, which John addresses to the NT church. Amazingly, Stanford admits that Sapaugh's misthological understanding is in harmony with Matthew. Yet Stanford objects to its applicability to the church on the grounds that he does not find this in harmony with Pauline doctrine. Evidently, Stanford supposes a disharmony between Matthew and Paul. Misthologists do not share his disposition, choosing rather to find the NT a harmonious whole. The endeavor herein has been to demonstrate this harmony throughout the entirety of the present book, demonstrating that parabolic and doctrinal harmony exists between the gospels and the epistles. Certainly, some details may be limited to the dispensation to which they are intended, but this does not mean that everything in the gospels may be outright rejected as not being applicable to the church just because the corresponding matter is not found verbatim in the Pauline corpus. This observation is especially true concerning the outer darkness since the eschatological framework in which Jesus gave the teaching regarding the outer darkness anticipated the church age, thus issuing a warning to believers of the current dispensation.

Admittedly, the present book does not retain the thoroughgoing distinctions between the kingdom of God and the kingdom of heaven that Stanford insists upon maintaining. He would limit kingdom-of-heaven truths to Israel, as a subset of kingdom-of-God truths which are only applicable to church. Thus, the church rules in heaven, and Israel will rule on earth. But why is kingdom-of-heaven truth limited to earth rather than inclusive of heaven? Why is the church excluded from the kingdom of heaven by being confined to heaven? Why does membership in the heavenly kingdom exclude the NT believer from participation in Stanford's kingdom of heaven? While Marrowists do share Stanford's concern that a distinction be made between the gospel of the kingdom and the gospel of grace, the latter being a subset of the former, we do not find a kingdom of heaven versus a kingdom of grace. Kingdom truths are applicable to both Jew and Gentile, as are grace truths. The same gospel is extended to both groups in all dispensations. Justification salvation always has been by faith in the promised Messiah. The co-glorification salvation of the out-resurrection, described as "a better resurrection," was anticipated by the OT believers in terms of their earning access to the heavenly city based on faith expressed in action—i.e., faithfulness (Heb 11:16,35).

Stanford also objects to finding works as a part of progressive sanctification. But his understanding of sovereign grace is substantially that of Calvinists and passive nikologists: God does it all. It is all of pure grace. In effect, he turns God's enabling grace into irresistible grace. We do nothing. In contrast, the present author rejects such simplistic monergistic nikology and perceives synergistic sanctification even within Pauline material. Nikology supports misthology. The vast majority of the passages Stanford cites have been dealt with already while developing the Marrowistic misthological thesis. Since he provides little more than mere citations of passages, which he assumes support his position, no further interaction is needed with his proof texting disregard of the contexts. For example, he quotes Rom 8:18 and 1Jn 1:5 and then exclaims: "Subject <u>that</u> to the Overcomer's 'outer darkness,' or any other darkness!"[1501] (Emphasis his.) In response, it already has been noted that Rom 8:18 contextually refers to misthological glory and is, therefore, limited to overcomers. His comment on 1Jn 1:5 is hardly worthy of comment. The very next Johannine verse notes that some believers walk in the darkness. Would it be so strange to think that those believers who walk in moral darkness will be cast into misthological darkness?

Stanford has difficulty discerning the difference between ontological and experiential darkness, between moral and misthological darkness, and between parabolic and literal darkness.

On the positive side, in agreement with Stanford, the parenthetical nature of the church as a dispensational distinction has been retained herein, at least to the extent as it is essential. The distinction between the guests and the Bride has thus been maintained. Part Three of Stanford's article further bemoans the ground that classic dispensationalism has given way to progressive dispensationalism. I do not wish to become embroiled in the arguments between classical, modified, and progressive dispensationalists any more than necessary. Still, since Stanford has challenged the misthological position on the basis of his classical dispensationalism approach, a limited response is in order.

Pentecost lists three premillennial views concerning the relation between the church and Israel regarding the new covenant. (1) In the Darby view there is only one covenant, and it has no relation to the church. (2) The Scofield view allows dual application of the covenant, primarily to Israel and secondarily to the church. (3) There are two new covenants; one to Israel and the other to the church.[1502]

Schmidtbleicher notes the popularity of the dual application approach and traces God's moral law through the dispensations. He finds God's moral law much more comprehensive than what typically is designated as such within the Mosaic economy, preferring to designate it as God's eternal law.[1503] God's eternal law predates the giving of the law by Moses. The believer is no longer under the external Mosaic law, which was derived from God's eternal law. The tithe, for example, was in effect before Moses. The eternalized law of God is now internalized by the Spirit in the church-age believer so that its fulfillment is no longer dependent upon the flesh. Although the temporal application of God's eternal law might be modified in subsequent dispensations, the eternal law remains in effect via eternal principle. Believers are to rely on the Spirit for wisdom in discerning the underlying principle[*] and applying it to their modern environment and act upon their convictions through the power of the Spirit.

Pentecost, on the other hand, does not attempt to settle the dispute but does devote a chapter to the matter that plagues Stanford, namely, the relationship between rewarded Jews and Christians during the millennium.[1504] Therein, Pentecost points out that Israelites would participate in the blessings associated with the new heavens and new earth (Is 65:17-18). This passage also describes their blessings in Jerusalem during that same period. Certainly, one might allow Stanford's misthological distinction between Israel and the church by speculating that the center of earthly rulership during the millennial kingdom will be the earthly Jerusalem, and the center of the heavenly rulership during that period will be the heavenly Jerusalem. But can these two spheres of rulership be so sharply segregated as to disallow any overlapping? After all, Abraham as well as other OT saints were looking for a heavenly country and city (Heb 11:16). And the writer of Hebrews also states that NT Christians have access to this "heavenly Jerusalem" (Heb 12:22). It is understandable that Pentecost and others, therefore, would find OT and NT believers in the Heavenly City. Naturally, Pentecost also finds corroboration in Rev 21:12-14 for this assessment, since the heavenly Jerusalem has the names of the twelve Israeli tribes on it. Are they excluded from the city bearing their name? Not likely. For such reasons, Pentecost concludes:

> The occupants of this city are from the Old Testament age, the New Testament age, as well as unfallen angels....The first resurrection is composed, not of church age saints alone, but of all individuals, of whatever age, who are raised to eternal life. While this resurrection takes place at different times in reference to different groups, the result is the same in each case—the resurrection to eternal life. These resurrected ones are said to be priests and to reign with Him....This must mean that all those who partake in the first resurrection have a common destination, the New Jerusalem.[1505]

All those who have a part in the first resurrection will reign with Him. "Blessed and holy is **the one who has a part in the first resurrection**; over these the second death has no power, but they will be priests of God and of Christ and **will reign with** Him for a thousand years" (Rev 20:6). The promise to sit with Jesus on His throne is extended to the church (Rev 3:21). Stanford, however, wants to make a sharp division between the pre-cross believers and post-cross believers. What will he do with trans-cross believers such as Peter and company to whom Jesus promised the thrones of Israel? "And Jesus said to them, 'Truly I say to you, that you who have followed Me, in the regeneration when the Son of Man will sit on His glorious throne, you also shall sit upon twelve thrones, judging the twelve tribes of Israel'" (Mt 19:28). If being with the Lord on His throne is to be in heaven, then the

---

[*] See *Principlism*, 887.

thrones of Israel are in heaven are they not? What are to be done with these believers who lived on both sides of the cross and who had been promised thrones on the other side of the cross?

In agreement with Pentecost, I already have shown that the OT promises to Israel to have her tears wiped away (Is 25:18; 65:19) is extended to the church (Rev 21:3). The church does not replace Israel but joins Israel in sharing these promises; although, I believe the distinction between the church and the nation of Israel will be retained. In his chapter concerning ultra-dispensationalism, Ryrie points out that ultra-dispensationalists tend to forget that within progressive revelation, **God may reveal information pertaining to a future dispensation before that dispensation arrives**. Thus, when Jesus spoke of mysteries pertaining to the church age in the Gospel of John that would commence when the Spirit was given on the day of Pentecost concerning a future flock and promised that they would be in Him and He in them, Jesus was revealing anticipatory information (Jn 7:39; 10:16; 14:20).[1506] Thus, we have considerable precedence for believing that when Jesus indicated in His warnings about the outer darkness that He was dealing with a time of judgment that would come without warning upon His servants, Jesus was prophesying concerning judgment awaiting believers of the church age. The question is not, "Did His disciples understand at the time He was speaking that He was giving a warning to the church?" rather, "Did He intend for them to understand later that at the time He was speaking that He was giving a warning to the church?"

In point of fact, some of the things that Jesus did and taught He did not expect for His disciples to understand at the time He originally gave this instruction: "Jesus answered and said to him, 'What I do you do not understand now, but you will understand later" (Jn 13:7; TM). To suppose that Jesus must have meant that all His parabolic warnings were addressed to Israel rather than to the church because His disciples did not know about the church at the time He gave the warnings overlooks the obvious fact that they would know about the church shortly thereafter and that Jesus could be understood as giving a warning that would take that future realization into account.

Paul himself expressed a similar sentiment: "For whatever was written in **earlier times** was written **for our** instruction, that through perseverance and the encouragement of the Scriptures **we** might have hope" (Rom 15:4). The OT anticipated the misthological hope in which church-age believers would share if they persevered.[*] These truths were given **to** them **for** us. As to the OT background for this misthological salvation of the NT believer, Paul assures Timothy: "You, however, continue in the things you have learned and become convinced of, knowing from whom you have learned them; and that from childhood you have known the sacred writings which are able to give you the wisdom that leads to salvation through faith which is in Christ Jesus" (2Tim 3:14-15). Persevere, NT believer, in the OT truth you have learned because the salvation you earn by faithful adherence to the Messiah has been foretold of old. Little wonder that Paul precedes to immediately say: "**All Scripture** is inspired by God and profitable for teaching, for reproof, for correction, for training in righteousness; that the man of God may be adequate, equipped for every good work" (2Tim 3:16-17). All Scripture, including that of the outer darkness, is profitable for teaching in our churches for the reproof of carnality and the motivation of the godly. Peter likewise urges believers, on the basis of OT prophesies, concerning a misthological gospel:

> [9] Obtaining as the outcome of your faith the salvation of your souls. [10] As to this salvation, **the prophets who prophesied of the grace that would come to you** made careful search and inquiry, [11] **seeking to know what person or time** the Spirit of Christ within them was indicating as He predicted the sufferings of Christ and the glories to follow. [12] It was revealed to them that **they were not serving themselves, but you**, in these things which now have been announced to you through those who preached the **gospel** to you by the Holy Spirit sent from heaven—things into which angels long to look. (1Pet 1:9-12)

Peter is just as clear, if not more so, that the misthological salvation of the church-age believer's soul, obtained by persevering faith, was the subject of OT prophecy. This salvation, envisioned by the OT prophets, was a misthological procurement to be obtained by the future believers of the church age. This was revealed to the prophets for the church. To use a NT illustration, the entire book of Revelation was written to the church, but chapters 2-3 of Revelation are directly for the current church age. Most of the other chapters are for the believers of the future tribulation period, and thus only indirectly applicable for the church today. Although most of Revelation refers to a time period that believers in the future tribulation will have to endure, the book was given to believers of the present age. Much of the material is **to** us **for** them, in terms of primary application. Similarly, the synoptic

---

[*] See *Misthological Hope and Glory*, 92.

material was spoken to the Jewish believers, but much of it was intended for the church. When the oral teaching was put into writing, it was given to the church. Even the Sermon on the Mount has truth applicable for church-age believers; although, it was not spoken to church-age believers. Some OT and synoptic material was written for the church indirectly and inclusively (rather than directly or exclusively).

The warning concerning the outer darkness is part of the truth given by Jesus which is to be taught to believers. Certainly, the gospel of the kingdom is different from the gospel of grace, but both aspects of the gospel are applicable both then and now. Paul preached kingdom truth (Acts 19:8; 20:25; 28:3,31): misthological inheritance of the kingdom (1Cor 6:9-10; Gal 5:21; Eph 5:5), misthological entrance into the kingdom (Acts 14:22; 1Thess 2:12), and misthological worthiness of the kingdom (2Thess 1:5). Paul's gospel included the message of misthological hope (Col 1:5,23) and misthological glory (2Thess 2:14). The gospel of grace was, is, and will remain a subcomponent of this broader gospel of the kingdom (Acts 20:24-25). This trans-dispensational truth transcends dispensational boundaries, arising in one dispensation but applying to all dispensations, and thus expressing an eternal truth. Does not the Great Commission apply to believers of the church age?

> [19] Go therefore and make disciples of all the nations, baptizing them in the name of the Father and the Son and the Holy Spirit, [20] teaching them to observe **all** that I commanded you; and lo, I am with you always, even to the end of the age. (Mt 28:19-20)

The first book of the NT ends with the injunction to teach all that Jesus taught. Why teach it if the underlying truths are not applicable? Surely, much of the synoptic material was intended for the church and all of it is applicable to the church, at least in terms of understanding and applying underlying principles. The last book of the NT concludes with this warning concerning those who would do otherwise with the word of God: "And if anyone takes away from the words of the book of this prophecy, God shall take away his part from the tree of life and from the holy city, which are written in this book" (Rev 22:19). It would be most unwise misthologically for an exegete to take away the message of the outer darkness hermeneutically from those to whom it was intended lest the message of the outer darkness become applicable misthologically to such an exegete.

Appendix 13.
Ventilato's Bridal Objections

Part One

Ventilato provides a long refutation of the FG misthological position, the first part of which is based on the premise that the body of Christ and the Bride form an organic unity with Christ. Part of His argument is that the body/Bride cannot be dismembered and cast into the outer darkness while the other part is allowed into the bridal chamber. Christ's body will not be divided into rejoicing rulers versus weeping non-rulers any more than Eve could have been so divided as Adam's queen. The body of Christ is one and thus jointly called Christ, just as Adam and Eve jointly were referred to as Adam (1Cor 12:12; Gen 5:2). All believers must share an "**indivisibility, unity, and universality of experience**" (emphasis his).[1507] His assumption that all believers will be presented holy and blameless is based largely on deductions rather than exegesis, however. He conveniently quotes 2Cor 11:2 and Eph 5:27 in this regard without discussing the conditional relationship for presentation in Col 1:22-23. Merely quoting Newell's opinion that those in Col 1:23 are lost is hardly adequate since in this passage Paul conditions their presentation on their continuation, not their regeneration—as Ventilato would have one believe. As to 2Cor 11:2, Paul is concerned that these betrothed believers may lose their virginal purity in 2Cor 11:3. The implicit condition for being presented to Christ, so as to become His Bride, is that we maintain our purity. As for the presentation in Eph 5:27, apparently it is conditioned upon one's practical sanctification as well.

As to Ventilato's typological appeal to Eve, it appears to backfire upon itself. It actually leads to the conclusion that not all believers form the Bride. His opinions might have some force in countering the conservative view of the Bride, but they actually reinforce the view maintained herein. He argues that because the Bride is composed of all believers, no believers can be in the outer darkness. Alternately, however, the deduction could be made just as well that since some believers are in the outer darkness, the Bride cannot be composed of all believers.

To briefly summarize arguments already employed herein, the fact that Christ is the organic head of the Federal body does not mean that all of His body is in heaven with Him.[*] The fact that we are part of Christ's organic body now (while He is in heaven and while we are on earth) illustrates that those believers in the outer darkness will not cease to be an organic part of His body then. The fact that only those believers who keep themselves pure actually will follow-through the betrothal to become His Bride does not mean that they are isolated from the rest or His body, that is, from that part of His organic body that is in the outer darkness. On the contrary, just as the head rules the body but does not compose the entire body, so His bridal body will rule His federal body and remain connected to His federal body through the exercise of that relationship.

I share much of Ventilato's assessment that all believers will be with Christ (Jn 17:24) and receive His glory (Jn 17:22), and that Jesus' prayer for organic unity and sharing His glory and location cannot be unanswered. But the deductions that he draws from this passage (that all believers must receive equal glory with Christ and equal accessibility to Christ due to their organic connection with Christ) fail exegetically and typologically.

Part Two

In the next section, Ventilato maintains that all saints will judge and thus rule (1Cor 6:2-3). The kingdom of priests represents all believers and is not based on merit (1Pet 2:9; Rev 1:5-6).[†] This royal priesthood of co-rulers represents His bridal queen and is comprised of all the redeemed (Rev 5:9-10). Thus, all believers will rule with Christ as His Bride. The same claim is made concerning "the church of the firstborn" (Heb 12:23). Although such texts already have been dealt with in the body of the present book, further interaction will be provided with some of his remarks.

Overcomers

Ventilato believes that all believers are overcomers because of the soteriological nature of the promises to overcomers. For example, the promises of not being hurt by the second death or having their names erased must be applicable to all believers (Rev 2:11; 3:5) because eternal security is applicable to all believers. Yet one will have to do better than appeal to eternal security as a basis for rejecting the FG interpretation since the FG interpretation is in complete harmony with eternal security. In regarding these promises as assuring eternal security, Ventilato

---

[*] See *Illustration 199. Two Bodies in One*, 581.
[†] See *Present—Future*; 54; *Kings or Kingdom*, 55; *Royal Priesthood*, 56.

rejects the litotes interpretation, calling it alchemy, hermeneutical gymnastics, as well as a transmutation and spiritualization of the text. Perhaps he is not aware that Greek grammarians recognize litotes as a standard literary device and that all three soteriological camps (including his own) recognize litotes in Johannine literature. Litotes are just one of many figures of speech found in the Bible along with: simile, metaphor, hyperbole, metonymy, synecdoche, personification, apostrophe, irony, and euphemism. If an interpreter fails to recognize these forms of literary expression, then distortion of the text is inevitable. The same is true when an interpreter fails to give due consideration to litotes. Ventilato's name-calling reaction to litotes would seem to say more about his failure as an exegete than the supposed failure of the misthological exegesis.

Another problem with Ventilato's defense is that it applies the definition of overcomer in 1Jn 5:4-5 to all believers regardless of the context. Similar claims are made from other texts (Jn 16:33; Rom 8:37; 1Jn 4:4). Further, by coupling 1Cor 6:2-3 with Rev 20:4-6, he seems to think that he has established that all believers will rule with Christ, claiming that there are no exceptions and that good works are not a condition. He mistakenly assumes that *the saints* means *all* saints characteristically.[*] Moreover, his assessment is dependent upon a point of view concerning overcomers in chapters 2 and 3 of Revelation that pictures carnal believers—who have lost their first love, who put up with false teaching, and who are described as dead, asleep, and lukewarm—as overcomers! Misthological blasphemy!

Ventilato approvingly quotes Newell that even the most wretched, lukewarm, defeated, half-heated believer is considered an overcomer with this assurance: "Let not the most wretched, defeated believer despair – if only there be the least yearning for Christ. The most tender plea of all the seven is made to a lukewarm assembly."[1508] One is reminded of a shampoo commercial in which it was claimed: "Just a little dab will do." It does not matter how little you do, according to Ventilato you still will be worthy of ruling with Christ if you have any desire at all to do something positive. Shockingly, the most miserable believer will make a worthy Bride. To the contrary, this watered-down view of overcoming flies directly in the face of the text! "So because you are lukewarm, and neither hot nor cold, I will spit you out of My mouth" (Rev 3:16). The Lord does not consider these lukewarm believers to be overcomers! He threatens to spit them out of His mouth like vomit, not kiss them on the mouth like a Bride! For that matter, Ventilato does not even believe his own writing since in this same section, he conditions one's bridal worthiness on persevering and enduring suffering.

Ventilato chides Hodges as being too harsh on non-persevering believers by relegating them to the outer darkness. Yet Ventilato would consign them to hell, claiming that those who fail to endure (1Cor 15:2; Col 1:13) or who are ashamed of Christ (Mk 8:38) are lost to an eternal hell. In reality, he conditions their preservation on their public perseverance. Whereas Hodges frankly would acknowledge that salvation from the outer darkness is conditioned on public perseverance, Ventilato inadvertently (covertly?) moves this requirement to what is necessary to escape hell. He cloaks his distinctions between persevering and non-persevering saints, when he says, concerning 2Tim 2:10-13, "No distinctions [are] made between faithful/worthy/persevering saints as over against unfaithful/unworthy/non-persevering saints."[1509] In reality, he himself is forced by his own theology to make an extremely sharp distinction between persevering and non-persevering saints. On the basis of his theology, he is forced to send non-persevering saints to hell! Not only does he fail to admit his severe distinction, he further claims that all saints will endure suffering and thereby rule with Christ "by virtue of *who* and *what* they are *in Christ*; thus all saints in Christ will reign with Him" (emphasis his).[1510] Somehow it escapes his attention, or at least his admission, that he has just inadvertently acknowledged that such rulership is conditioned on works after all (i.e., enduring suffering), despite all his previous denials to the contrary! Perhaps, he thought that he could implicitly avoid any meritorious association with suffering by calling it a gift, on the basis of Gaebelein' comments on Phil 1:29. But it will take more than such a simple appeal as this to overturn the obvious meritorious implications of 2Tim 2:12, which explicitly conditions our ruling with Christ with our enduring for Christ: "**If** we endure [*hupomeno*], we shall also reign with Him."

Phil 1:29

In Ventilato's quote of Gaebelein concerning Phil 1:29, he refers to suffering as a "God-given privilege."[1511] Yes, it is a God-given privilege to suffer with Christ so that you may **earn** the right to rule with Christ! The gracious opportunity to earn the reward of rulership does not nullify the fact that rulership is a reward! Ventilato's logic is highly flawed. Making suffering part of an "effectual call" or a "natural result" does nothing to lessen its meritable nature. For example, suppose for a moment that God gives us faith and faithfulness. Does this mean that faith is no longer required for salvation? Granted, Calvinists will deny that faith is required for regeneration. Still,

---

[*] See *Illustration 53. Unrighteous will not Inherit*, 121.

even they admit that faith is required for justification—the imputation of righteousness. Yet if the Calvinistic presupposition that faith is given does not prevent faith from being required, then the Calvinistic belief that faithfulness is given does not prevent it from being required either. Faithfulness is just as much a requirement as is faith—even given Calvinistic premises. In reality, salvation from hell is conditioned on both faith and faithfulness in Ventilato's view, and the argument by Calvinists that both are given in Phil 1:29 does nothing to change the fact that both are required to enter heaven in Calvinistic theology.* Moreover, what is given is the **opportunity** to *endure suffering* (*pascho*), not the guaranteed result that we will endure the suffering successfully.

Hupomeno

To build a wall around his crumbling sandcastle, Ventilato appeals to Heb 12:7, where the same word is used for *endure* (*hupomeno*) as Paul used in Philippians: "It is for discipline that you endure; God deals with you as with sons; for what son is there whom his father does not discipline?" He asserts, "*All* believers *endure suffering* in the form of chastening." Yet the very next verse puts his defense on a shaky foundation: "But if you are without discipline, of which all have become partakers, then you are illegitimate children and not sons" (Heb 12:8). The writer of Hebrews opens up the possibility that believers may be "without discipline" rather than endure discipline. Illegitimacy may indeed be a reward concept.† The writer of Hebrews had just indicated that some of his believing readership might faint and lose heart rather than endure (Heb 12:3).

James uses this same verb (*hupomeno*): "Blessed is a man who **perseveres** [endures] under trial; for once he has been approved, he will receive the crown of life, which the Lord has promised to those who love Him" (Jam 1:12). Obviously, this is a *conditional promise* based on our perseverance and thus on our merit. The same verb is used by Jesus on other occasions: "He who **endures** to the end will be saved" (Mt 10:22; 24:13; Mk 13:13). This perseverance-based promise is based on merit. Of course, some Calvinists are fond of standing such verses on their head and reading them backwards as if they said, "The saved will endure," when in fact the correct order is: "Those who endure will be saved." But if you have to flip a verse on its head to make it say what you want, have you not done violence to the text?

Acts 14:22

Ventilato has a simple technique to get around conditional statements. He simply denies that they are conditional. Compare Paul's statement in Acts 14:22, "through many tribulations we must enter the kingdom of God," with that of Ventilato's assessment:

> This is a statement of *fact* concerning all believers, not a *conditional* promise based on our merit or worthiness. It is *necessary* for us believers, by virtue of who and what we are in Christ, to enter into (equivalent here to "inherit") the Kingdom of God through many (varying degrees of) tribulations while yet in this wicked world of darkness that hates the Lord Jesus and His own. (Emphasis his.)[1512]

Even if one allows the first sentence of his position to go unchallenged in Acts 14:22 and regard it as a general expectation, it still flies in the face of his claim concerning 2Tim 2:12. "**If we endure, then** we will also reign with Him" (TM). This is a first class conditional sentence in Greek. It is a conditional promise! Further, it is based on our merit—our endurance. Furthermore, Ventilato's very next sentence in the above quote moves Acts 14:22 from the realm of general expectation to being a **necessity** to enter the kingdom of God! He implicitly makes it a *necessary* condition for entering heaven, after just denying its conditional nature! Inconsistencies in his statements abound. As to Ventilato's statement that Acts 14:22 is not a conditional promise based on personal merit, the following texts and diagrams illustrate his fallacy.

> [21] And after they had preached the **gospel** to that city and had made many **disciples**, they returned to Lystra and to Iconium and to Antioch, [22] strengthening the souls of the **disciples**, encouraging **them to continue in the faith**, and saying, "**Through** (*dia*) many tribulations we **must** (*dei*) **enter** (*eiserchomai*) into the **kingdom** (*basileia*) of God." [23] And when they had appointed elders for **them** in every church, having prayed with fasting, they commended **them** to the Lord **in whom they** had **believed**. (Acts 14:21-23)

---

* See *Gift of Faith ≠ Act of Faith*, 205; *Phil 1:28-29*, 211.
† See "Illegitimate Children" in *Fallen from Grace but Not from Perfection.*

We

Those who are being addressed in the third person in this passage and being told that they must enter the kingdom through many tribulations in Acts 14:21-23 are those disciples who had believed in the Lord and the gospel. They are being exhorted to persevere in the faith. Obviously, they already had come to saving faith. Consequently, the stipulation about tribulations is addressed unmistakably to those who already had been born again. Paul includes himself in that group with the first person plural, saying that this is the way "we" must enter the kingdom. He had recently been stoned in verses 19-20. Why does Luke mention Paul's stoning just before presenting this excerpt from Paul's preaching about tribulations as being necessary to enter the kingdom? Evidently, Luke expects his believing readers to see the logical connection between the tribulations that Paul endured and what they are expected to endure if they want to enter the kingdom. Ventilato is correct that only those believers who persevere will enter the kingdom in this passage. However, he fails to admit the obvious: Perseverance is the condition for such entrance.

Must (Dei)

Was Paul serious that believers "must" pass through tribulations in order to enter the kingdom? Luke records Peter using this word for *must* (*dei*) representing conditional necessity in Acts 4:12. "And there is salvation in no one else; for there is no other name under heaven that has been given among men, by which we **must** (*dei*) be saved." Is faith a necessary condition that one must meet in order to be saved? Yes. Yet an even closer parallel using *must* in relation to kingdom entrance may be found in the words of Jesus:

> Truly, truly, I say to you, **unless** one is born again, he **cannot...enter** (*eiserchomai*) **into the kingdom** (*basileia*) **of God**....Do not marvel that I said to you, "You **must** (*dei*) be born again" (Jn 3:3-7).

According to Jesus, the new birth is a conditional necessity to enter the kingdom. You *must* (*dei*) enter the kingdom through new birth. New birth qualifies you for kingdom entrance.

> [1]Truly, truly, I say to you, he who does not *enter* (*eiserchomai*) *through* (*dia*) the door into the fold of the sheep, but climbs up some other way, he is a thief and a robber...[7]Jesus therefore said to them again, "Truly, truly, I say to you, I am the door of the sheep"...[9] I am the door; if anyone *enters* (*eiserchomai*) *through* (*dia*) Me, he will be saved, and shall go in and out, and find pasture" (Jn 10:1-9; TM). Jesus said to him, "I am the way, and the truth, and the life; no one comes to the Father, but *through* (*dia*) Me" (Jn 14:6).

Obviously, it is necessary to enter through Jesus because entrance is conditioned on entrance through Jesus as the necessary means of entering the kingdom. Ventilato draws a false dichotomy between what is necessary and what is conditional. It is necessary because it is conditional. To imagine that it is necessary but not conditional is nonsensical. This word *must* (*dei*) is like a brick wall that will allow entrance *through* (*dia*) only one door. According to Jesus and Peter, the door through which one is saved in terms of kingdom entrance is through faith in the name of Jesus. Once you have believed in Jesus for eternal life, you thereby are qualified for kingdom entrance. So why does Paul posit another door to believers who already are qualified for kingdom entrance? Are there really two doors into the kingdom? Do believers have to jump through a series of hoops to make it into the kingdom? Is Paul saying being born again is not enough to enter the kingdom since those who have been born again must endure subsequent tribulations in order to enter in the end?

Illustration 304. Two Doors?

Basileia

No doubt two different doors are being described. New birth cannot be equated with perseverance in tribulations. The door through which believers enter in one case is regeneration; the door through which they enter in the other case is bulldog determination in continuation. Even if Ventilato's above Calvinistic presuppositions were granted, that new birth inevitably results in tribulations and that all believers will "*necessarily* endure by virtue of who and what we are in Christ," this still would be a conditional entrance into heaven based on personal worthiness. Not only does his statement lack internal consistence, it also is refuted by the context. Paul is encouraging these believers to persevere in the faith by saying that through maintaining their faith in the midst of persecutions they would qualify for kingdom entrance. Paul is not promising these believers that they would endure. Instead, he is urging them to endure because this is how these believers would qualify for kingdom entrance.

Illustration 305. Two Doors?

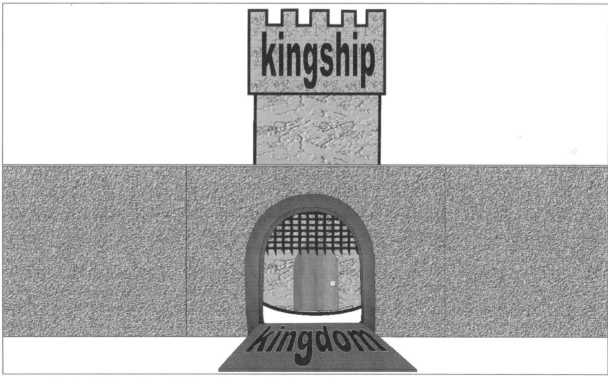

Dei is the brick wall, and *dia* points to the door. There are two doors into the kingdom because two different, but related, aspects of the kingdom are in view. Jesus Himself taught that the kingdom could be a reward in regard to rulership (Mt 5:3,10-12). Unbelievers enter the *kingdom* (*basileia*) as a place of salvation from hell by simple faith in Jesus for the gift of eternal life (which is the impartation of regeneration to one's spirit via new birth). They must enter this door (pictured as a drawbridge in the second illustration) before they enter the other door. Once they have entered the door of saving faith, they are then qualified as believers to enter the *rulership* or *kingship* (*basileia*) by continued faith in Jesus and by faithfulness in the face of opposition. A careful examination of this text that Ventilato cites in support of his thesis is actually detrimental to his position.

Stephanos

To Ventilato's credit, he does admit that rewards will vary for believers according to their degrees of faithfulness. While corporate soteriological blessings will be identical, individual rewards may vary. Misthologists can agree with him to a limited extent on this matter but would strongly disagree with him that believers only have one corporate identity or that crowns do not represent special privileges or positions (or access to special places). For him, crowns appear to be nothing more than nice head dressings. All believers will be driving the same car, so to speak, but some of them will just have a better hood ornament. From his point of view, the believer's crown (*stephanos*) does not entitle the believer to the imperial privileges of a ruler's crown (*diadema*).

His quote from Vine that diadem is always kingly and never used in the same capacity as *stephanos* is not impressive in the least. On the contrary, Hemer states that *diadema* is often used in the apocryphal books "in metaphorical senses otherwise confined to *stephanos*."[1513] In Wisd 5:16 it is a misthological reward given to the righteous in the form of a beautiful crown. Thus, in this passage it is an eschatological reward for the faithful followers of the Messiah and not limited to the Messiah alone. Likewise, it is called a "crown of glory" in Sir 47:6. Nevertheless, others (who tend to disassociate *stephanos* from regal rule) share Ventilato's presumption. So a more thorough interaction with another writer holding his viewpoint will be allowed.

Trench attributes the use of the word *stephanos* as used for the crown of thorns to the materials with which it was woven. On this basis, and the lack of usage of *stephanos* as a kingly crown in classical Greek, Trench concludes that *stephanos* does not denote a kingly crown in the NT. He further indicates that the *stephanos* and *diadem* do not overlap in the Septuagint and Apocrypha.[1514]

As already noted above, however, Hemer has a right to question this opinion based on the use of diadem in the Apocrypha. In response to the soldiers putting a *stephanos* on Jesus' head to mock Jesus' royalty as king of the Jews, Hemer likewise concludes, "The view that *stephanos* could never be used thus of kingship is overstated."[1515] His response has much to commend it. Ventilato and his ilk are much too quick to dismiss any regal connotation with *stephanos*.

First, admittedly, Ventilato is correct that *diadem* is only used in regard to Christ's kingly rule in the NT. Faithful believers only receive a *stephanos*, never a *diadem* (unlike Wisd 5:16 above.) However, what Ventilato fails to mention is the fact that diadem is ascribed to Christ only once (Rev 19:12)! In fact, it is only used three times in the NT. (The other two references are to the dragon and beast, Rev 12:3; 13:1). However, *stephanos* is also ascribed to Christ in this same book (Rev 14:14) and pictures the authority to exercise judgment on the earth. Revelation thus pictures Christ wearing both a *diadem* and a *stephanos* and uses the latter in a manner that would be associated with the former.

Second, Revelation also equates *stephanos* with victorious believers sitting on their thrones: "And around the throne were twenty-four thrones; and upon the **thrones** I saw twenty-four elders sitting, clothed in white garments, and golden **crowns** [*stephanos*] on their heads" (Rev 4:5). Overcomers are pictured sitting on their thrones wearing their *stephanos*. The notion that *stephanos* could not be associated with rulership is superficial indeed since here it is associated with sitting on thrones.

Furthermore, comparing the similar rewards given to those who meet the interchangeable requirements could easily challenge this simplistic notion that *stephanos* cannot be regal. For example, enduring in Jam 1:12 is rewarded with the crown. By Ventilato's own admission, enduring in 2Tim 2:12 is rewarded by ruling with Christ. Those who endure are rewarded with rulership pictured by a *stephanos*. The same verb for *enduring* is used (*hupomeno*) in both cases after all. Should we not consider these as overlapping promises? Those who receive this *crown* (*stephanos*) for enduring will rule regally. A regal *stephanos* is indicated. Cross-references require that *stephanos* be admitted as probably denoting rulership.

Historical background concurs with the above impression. As to the Septuagint and Apocrypha, the careful discrimination that Trench claims to exist between *diadem* and *stephanos* is not as sharp as he would have us believe. S*tephanos* (victor's crown) could be used in the same capacity as *diadema* (kingly crown): "He took the crown [*stephanos*] from Milcom's head. It weighed a talent, of gold and precious stones; it was placed on David's head" (2Sam 12:30; cp. 1Chron 20:2). This is not a wreath or even a golden crown shaped like a wreath. This *stephanos* is a diadem. Likewise, "Mordecai went out from the presence of the king in **royal** apparel of blue and white, and with a **great crown** [*stephanos*] **of gold**, and with a garment of fine linen and purple" (Est 8:15). Here, *stephanos* is again a regal crown, a crown denoting royal power. It is a kingly type crown. Similarly, of the high priest, the Apocrypha states: "And so we have appointed you today to be the high priest of your nation; you are to be called the king's friend (and he sent him a purple robe and a golden crown [*stephanos*]) and you are to take our side and keep friendship with us" (1Macc 10:20; RSV). Ruling authority is ascribed to *stephanos*. The *stephanos* is also associated with wearing purple in Sir 40:4 (cp. 45:12).

Returning to the OT, a *stephanos* of gold and silver is fashioned for the high priest. This time it is for Joshua who will typify Christ. There is a double reference to *stephanos* (Zech 6:11,14), but sandwiched in-between these references to the crown is a description of his role as a "priest on his throne" (Zech 6:13). Christ will unite the offices of priest and king in His future rule—pictured by the *stephanos*. In Ps 21:3, the king is given a *stephanos* of pure gold. It is thus a kingly crown. In Song of Solomon 3:11, King Solomon is *crowned* (*stephanoo*) with a *crown* (*stephanos*). Brenton's translation of the LXX in Is 22:21 reads, "And I will put on him thy robe, and I will grant him thy **crown with power**, and I will give thy stewardship into his hands" (LXE). Some other translations describe the *robe* as a *royal robe* and the *stewardship* as *authority* or *government*. Thus, in this verse the *stephanos* is associated by the LXX with royal governmental authority. Trench thinks that the reference to *stephanos* as a "crown of glory" is to be carefully discriminated from the "royal diadem" by the LXX in Is 62:3. But the reverse would seem more likely to be the case: "In that day the Lord of hosts will become a beautiful crown and a glorious diadem to the remnant of His people" (Is 28:5). Are a beautiful crown and a glorious crown to be sharply distinguished? It seems highly unlikely. These two crowns can be closely associated rather than sharply disassociated: "Remove the diadem, and take off the *crown* (*stephanos*)" (Eze 21:31). These terms can be used interchangeably to a considerable degree.

Concerning the underlying nature of *stephanos*, BDAG states, "Its primary significance [was] as a symbol of **exceptional merit**." Those who rule as a result of receiving this crown will do so because of their exceptional merit. It is not rulership passed on by virtue of being born into royalty. This rulership is not the result of being born with a silver spoon in one's mouth. Instead, it is a meritorious privilege, an earned royalty. By admitting that *stephanos* is a reward based on faithfulness, Ventilato unravels his argument about overcomers in Rev 2-3. If you want to be classified and rewarded as an overcomer, then you are going to have to earn the privilege by being faithful. This *crown* (*stephanos*) is twice listed as part of the reward promised to overcomers in these two chapters (Rev 2:10; 3:11). Since overcomers are promised rulership in this same context (Rev 2:26-27, 3:21), contextual association requires that we favorably consider this rulership attribute as applicable for *stephanos* as well. Earned rulership based on individual merit is represented.

Did Ventilato pause to consider the ramifications of referring to *stephanos* as a "victor's garland"? The Greek word for *victory* is *nike*. The Greek word for *overcome* is *nikao*—the verbal form of victory. Overcomers are the victors who earn the victor's crown. Overcomers are winners. This is a rulership you have to win by earning it, hence the use of the word *stephanos* to describe it. *Stephanos* is used of misthological regal authority. It is a reward-crown, not a gift-crown. It does not refer to authority you have simply by virtue of royal birth. The reference is to authority you earn. If you want this crown, you are going to have to merit it.

Part Three

Rom 8:32

In his next section, Ventilato frequently is satisfied to base his statements on innuendo. For example, Rom 8:31-32 is taken as proving that God will *freely* give (without merit) all believers (without exception) *all things* (including co-rulership with Christ). His position is faulty exegetically in that *charizomai* need not necessarily mean freely, it may simply mean graciously. God graciously gives overcomers rulership of the universe. Just as in Heb 2:8 we find God submitting all things to man, and yet understand this in context to be a limited class of men (i.e., faithful *brethren*), so too in Rom 8:32 we find contextual delineation of these co-rulers with Christ as the faithful elect who suffer with Christ.

Even apart from contextual sensitivity, logical consistency would have allowed Ventilato to derive this conclusion. If the *stephanos* (or any other reward for that matter) is not freely given to all believers, then Ventilato has misapplied the text. Or if the reward is even given in equal portions based on one's performance, then it is still misthologically given and thus not freely given. But Ventilato already has conceded the argument being made herein in the closing remarks of part two of his rebuttal: "**Some saints may indeed receive more or less rewards than others, according to their varying degrees of faithfulness**."[1516] Although he mistakenly believes that all believers will receive at least one of these "reward-crowns" (1Cor 4:5), he at least recognizes that not all believers will receive the same degree of **reward**. Most importantly, it will vary according to their personal faithfulness—their individual worthiness. Since the giving of the reward-crown (*stephanos*) is based on personal faithfulness, it is not freely given to all believers independently of their personal performance, nor is it given in equal portion. To be rewarded graciously in this manner is to be rewarded congruently in response to one's merit. Ventilato's argument from Rom 8:32 bleeds to death from the wounds that he himself inflicts upon it.

In like manner, he assumes that since all believers are heirs in certain passages, all believers must be equal heirs in all passages. Yet since by his own admission all believers do not receive an equal share pertaining to the *stephanos*, why must it be assumed that all believers must receive an equal share regarding the inheritance? In his defense he states, "Thus no part of it – neither the forgiveness nor the inheritance – is a matter of works or personal worthiness." In making this claim, he has rather conveniently forgotten about Col 3:23-25, in which the believer's inheritance is a reward based on his or her works and thus conditioned on personal worthiness. As to forgiveness, it does not rule out accountability for either the good or bad that we do (2Cor 5:10). His appeal to emotion rather than Scripture is repeatedly apparent: "What believer in their right mind will say that they are not *personally worthy* of being cast into outer darkness, let alone that they are, or ever can be, *personally worthy* of being a joint-heir with Christ?" (Emphasis his.)[1517]

Actually, if one consults the Bible, Jesus said that those who do not take up their cross are not worthy of Him (Mt 10:38). The implication is that those believers who do take up their cross are worthy in some sense of the word. Is it possible to take up your cross and follow Christ in the power of the Holy Spirit? Evidently, the NT believers thought so (Acts 5:41; Eph 4:1; Phil 1:27; Col 1:10; 1Thess 2:12; 2Thess 1:11). Paul taught that believers who endured suffering would be counted worthy of the kingdom of God (2Thess 1:5). Is Ventilato out of his mind to imply that Paul is not in his right mind for allowing the possibility of believers being personally worthy? Although Ventilato may be a scoffer of biblical misthological worthiness, it is plainly taught in Scripture.

2Pet 2:18-22

In attempting to make all believers experiential overcomers, Ventilato quotes from Newell again: "There are those who overcome, and there are those who *are* overcome. These latter are lost (II Peter 2:20)." This remark hardly settles the matter in Ventilato's favor. Actually, several interpretive options are available for this passage. Four basic views of 2Pet 2:18-22 are pictured below.

Illustration 306. Four Basic Approaches to 2Pet 2:20

	LS	FG
Unregenerate:	Arminian	Seymour
Regenerate:	Calvinistic	Wilkin

Both views in the LS camp teach that it is impossible to be saved in the end apart from perseverance to the end. Preservation requires perseverance. You cannot reach heaven apart from perseverance. At the very least, you must return to the Lord before you die. Final salvation is conditioned on final perseverance.

- Arminian: Those who fail to persevere lose eternal life.
- Reformed: Those who fail to persevere never had eternal life.
- Both LS views: Those who fail to persevere go to hell.

Lost Grace & Sovereign Grace

Arminians believe that you can lose life by falling from grace and thus become lost (punctiliar loss) or fail to attain life and thus be lost in the *end* (*telos*) because you did not persevere. You lose out on eternal life in the end (linear loss). We might label this persuasion, regardless of the timing of the loss, as the *lost grace* view (LG). God's saving grace can be resisted and be lost soteriologically. On the other hand, the Reformed view of Calvinism teaches that as a result of God's sovereign grace, a believer will persevere. This perspective might be called the *sovereign grace* view (SG). If you do not persevere, then you were never a genuine believer. The only way you can know for sure that you are a genuine believer is by persevering. Thus, they teach a perseverance-based preservation. To be sure, some in their camp might deny that perseverance is a requirement for reaching heaven and claim that perseverance is the result of regeneration. Nevertheless, they still show a strong tendency to make the expected result (i.e., perseverance) a requirement to reach heaven. They condition final salvation upon perseverance. The expected result is made a soteriologically necessary result. Even if they were to affirm that salvation is by grace initially, they backload the gospel by making perseverance a requirement subsequently. Those who fail to meet their expectation are consigned to hell. Their expectation is consequently a condition for salvation from hell. You must have both the root (regeneration) and the expected fruit (perseverance) in order to be saved from hell—obtain final salvation. In the final analysis, both forms of LS require perseverance to reach heaven.

The old rejoinder that perseverance is descriptive rather than prescriptive is just that—old.[*] It is not difficult to show that perseverance is commanded and therefore prescriptive. Nor is it difficult to demonstrate that it is conditional and therefore a teleological necessity for the end in view. If that end is soteriological, then perseverance is a soteriological condition. If the end being described is misthological, then perseverance is a misthological condition.

FG

The *free grace* (FG) camp, in contrast, teaches that preservation is not dependent on perseverance. In other words, you are eternally secure even if you fail to persevere. Conversely, not all professing believers who persevere are necessarily genuine believers. The FG view acknowledges that genuine believers genuinely can fall from grace (Gal 5:4). Thus, FG recognizes the validity of this aspect of the LS stance. Yet FG affirms the reality of SG concerning the permanence of regeneration, since FG maintains that when a believer falls from grace he or she does not lose the free gift of eternal life. God, in His sovereign grace, will preserve the believer as one of His own. Eternal security is an expression of God's sovereign grace. God is free to choose in what capacities He sovereignly will act in grace and in what ways He will allow His grace to be resisted. Regeneration and the present temporal behavioral resulting from regeneration are not caused by irresistible grace independent of the human response. The unregenerate may come to Christ or turn away from Christ of their own freed response. Likewise, the regenerate follow Christ or turn away from Christ of their own freed will. Thus, free grace is a combination of the other two views (FG=LG+SG).

Unregenerate

Context

As to 2Pet 2:18-22, the delightful FG book, *Gift of God*, by Richard Seymour takes the position that those addressed in this passage are the unregenerate false teachers of verse 1. In support of this understanding, several things are asserted. The contrast between *you* and *they* in verse 3 is pointed out: "And through covetousness shall *they* with feigned words make merchandise of *you*." The *they* refers to the lost false teachers and *their damnation* (v. 3). This third person reference of the false teachers is continued throughout the Petrine chapter and in this passage of 2:18-22 in particular.

Dog

Cross-references are then called into play to show that genuine believers are described as sheep and never as dogs. Believers are warned of false teachers who dress as wolves in sheep's clothing (Mt 7:15), and believers are told to beware of these unregenerate dogs (Phil 3:1-2). Most importantly, the dogs are rather clearly identified as the lost in Rev 22:15. Thus, the designation of those being led astray as *dogs* is taken by Seymour as an indication of their unregenerate nature.

Knowledge (Epignosis)

Seymour further argues that the Greek word for *know* (*epignosis*) does not mean personal knowledge. Although he does not mention Rom 1:28 as a corroborating text, it could indeed be cited in defense of his position.

Worse

According to this FG interpretation, the resultant state of these false believers is worse because hell will be even hotter for those who have rejected so much light. A person who turns away from Christianity, after being immersed in Christianity, will certainly be more accountable than someone who never even heard the Christian gospel. So there is no trouble understanding how Peter could say the end for such unbelievers would be worse than the beginning.

---

[*] See endnote 499 for a more technical elaboration as to why the appeal to descriptive perseverance is difficult to maintain..

Wallow

Also, the passage does not say that anyone who behaves like a prodigal pig is lost. Just because these particular prodigal pigs are lost does not mean that a true believer cannot return to acting in accordance with his or her old nature. Further, even if it were assumed that this passage is teaching some correspondence between what a person is and what a person does, it may be considered a general, rather than absolute, expectation. Actions are generally expected to reveal nature to a certain extent. For believers who subcome to their previous lifestyle, to wallow happily in it would be unnatural. One would anticipate that such a believer would be miserable. A sheep may fall into the mud, but one would be surprised to find a sheep wallowing in the mud. It would be acting contrary to its nature. Thus, according to this FG view, this passage is not denying that some muddy sheep act contrary to their new nature. (The passage does not prove proveitism.) Rather, the passage is concerned with those among the lost whose short-term transformation fails to prove regeneration.

Summary

This FG position, at least as I have articulated above, has much to commend it. First, moral reformation is not proof of regeneration. A dog or sow in nature remains a dog or sow in nature even if it has had a temporary change in conduct. It is not a new creature. Just because someone hears the gospel, gets baptized, and cleans up his or her act, this does not mean that such a person is saved. The lost who look at their works for assurance of salvation can fool themselves into thinking they are believers. To look to works as a necessary indication of regeneration is extremely precarious.

To clarify, this FG view should be distinguished carefully from the Reformed view. For the Reformed view would be quick to jump to the conclusion that **anyone** who commits apostasy, or at least final irremediable apostasy, thereby **proves** that he or she never was regenerate to begin with. This Reformed assumption must condition final salvation upon perseverance. Those in this Reformed camp would be inclined to insist that such behavior proves that the person is lost and in doing so condition final salvation on one's behavior.

An accurate articulation of this particular FG position, in contrast, would stipulate that, although these particular false teachers who committed apostasy were lost, this does not prove that all false teachers or all apostates are lost. Other passages address the reality of defection among those who truly have experienced regeneration. Genuine believers can become false teachers (2Tim 1:18-20; 2Tim 2:17-18). Simply, this particular passage is dealing with lost apostates rather than saved ones. Thus, one's behavior is not an infallible indicator of whether one is lost or saved. This differentiation between the FG and SG views is extremely important.

Regenerate

While the first FG view considered above is plausible and theologically permissible, it is exegetically improbable. The position taken by Wilkin is far more likely. He devotes a chapter to this text.[1518] A transition occurs in the passage from the false teachers to those who subcome to the false teachers. The false teachers are the ones who do the speaking, enticing, and promising in vv. 18-19.

Context

Seymour did well to appeal to the context, and it is true that the context makes a contrast between the unregenerate *they* and the regenerate *you*. However, it must be noted who is exploiting whom in this context.

Annotated Text of 2Pet 2:1-3

[1] But **false prophets** also arose among the people, just as there will also be **false teachers** among **you** [i.e., believers], who will secretly introduce destructive heresies, even denying the Master who bought **them**, bringing swift destruction upon **themselves**. [2] And many will follow their sensuality, and because of **them** the way of the truth will be maligned; [3] and in **their** greed **they** will exploit **you** [i.e., believers] with false words; **their** judgment from long ago is not idle, and **their** destruction is not asleep.

The context is clear: "They [i.e., false teachers] will exploit **you** [i.e., believers]" (v. 3). Those being exploited are identified explicitly by Peter by the second person plural *you* (*humas*). He is concerned about the exploitation of his saved readership, whom he addresses as *beloved*. His concern for his beloved readers is for genuine believers: "**You** therefore, **beloved**, knowing this beforehand, be on your guard lest, being carried away by the error of unprincipled men, **you** fall from your own steadfastness" (2Pet 3:17). He is concerned about genuine believers being *carried away* (*sunapago*) and *falling from* (*ekpipto*) their steadfastness. Paul uses this same combination of words in Galatians (2:13; 5:4) to say that Barnabus had been *carried away* (*sunapago*) by hypocrisy and that many of the Galatian believers had *fallen from* (*ekpipto*) grace. There is no reason to doubt that those being exploited in 2:3 by the false teachers are the same group being lead astray to "follow their sensuality" in 2:2. Thus, one reason the "way of the truth will be maligned" is because genuine believers will be duped into believing a lie. The Galatian context confirms, rather than questions, the expectation that those being lead astray from their steadfastness on the path of righteousness are genuine believers. Consistency with the Judean context would suggest a similar understanding for the passage under discussion.[1519]

In this passage, the danger is of blood bought **unbelievers** leading believers astray. The Greek verb that Peter uses above for *bought* is *agorazo*. It means to *buy, redeem, ransom*. These unbelievers have been bought by the Lord.[1520] Conversely, Paul and John use this verb to describe blood bought believers (1Cor 6:20; 7:3; Rev 5:9; 14:3-4). Peter, in contrast, uses this same verb to point out that this precious price has been paid even for those who reject it. Bryson does well to stress the clash between Calvinistic perseverance and limited atonement in this verse and to insist that the doctrine of the limited atonement should be abandoned since the Lord actually paid the purchase, the ransom price, for these unbelievers.[1521]

Conceptual parallels would, of course, include the complementary statements by Jesus and Paul in which they both use *ransom* (*lutron* and *antilutron* respectively) to affirm that the atonement was a ransom for *many* (*polus*) and for *all* (*pas*). See Mt 20:28; Mk 10:45; and 1Tim 2:6. Calvinists seek to limit the atonement by asserting that *all* may only be relative and mean *many*. Granted, *all* may be used relatively. Yet in this case, it appears to be used absolutely. In the broader theological context, advocates of unlimited atonement, such as Gordon Olson and Bryson, discuss the connection in which *many* (*polus*) refers to the whole rather than part in both Rom 5:15 and 19.[1522] *Many*, meaning *all*, of the human race have died spiritually and have sinned in v. 19 (cp. the *pas* of Rom 3:23). *Many* (*polus*) means *all* (*pas*) in this discussion of redemption. WBC puts it like this: "Has the apostle changed the extent of **the many** in either side of this comparison? No, because he is showing in what categories God puts men when he views them in terms of the *actual* effect of Adam's disobedience and the *potential* effect of Christ's obedience" (all emphasis original).

In other words, in Rom 5:19 the first *many* refers to **all in Adam**, and the second *many* refers to **all who will be in Christ**: "For as through the one man's disobedience the *many* were made sinners, even so through the obedience of the One the *many* will be made righteous." As the BKC notes in harmonious concord, the context leading up to this verse shows "the **provision** in the one righteous act, therefore, is **potential** and it comes to the entire human race as the offer and opportunity which are applied only to 'to those who receive' (v. 17). So those who *will be made righteous* in 5:19 are those who receive the *gift of righteousness* in 5:17, and this could potentially be anyone and everyone in that whosoever will may come. Those who come to saving faith will be made ontologically righteous on the inside and one day be made eschatologically righteous on the outside, but in the meantime they are imputed as being legally righteous.

Peter uses the verbal cognate to assure that believers have been *redeemed* (*lutroo*) by the blood of Christ (1Pet 1:18-19). The most natural conclusion is that Peter does not limit the atonement to the elect when his statement here is compared with his affirmation that these false teachers have been redeemed also. Peter's discussion of redemption in his first epistle would be a natural antecedent as to what he believed about redemption—it was by the blood of the Lamb—in his second epistle. Liberation from sin, which is the subject of Peter's context, is not by virtue of creation but redemption. Peter is not talking about God having purchased them by creating them. The only price the Lord could pay to buy these slaves from the market place of sin was His own blood, no covenant or church attendance would do. Moreover, Peter's acknowledgement in this very epistle (2Pet 3:15) that he had read Paul's epistles and considered them Scripture gives reason to believe that he probably had read Paul's statement in 1Tim 2:6, which was probably written about three years earlier, and thus concurs with Paul concerning the universal nature of the atonement. These men are referring to the universal atonement of all men, not merely to the creation of all men or to some covenant with all men. God is the Savior of all men (1Tim 4:10), not merely the Creator of all men. Chang devotes an article to the defense of this position, following in the footsteps of Chafer and Lightner, whom he quotes, in asserting that the payment made all men savable.[1523]

The most effective counter by advocates of limited atonement is their insistence that Peter is describing an actual rather than potential purchase of the people in question: *They* rather than *their redemption* is what is actually purchased. Escobedo, who is the executive vice president of the website where White is the director, uses an automotive illustration to drive this rebuttal home in his response to Chang:

> I sell parts for Chevrolet in my secular employment. It would be far fetched to suggest that someone could come into my store and "purchase" or "buy" a part and then leave my store without acquiring ownership of it. To buy necessitates subsequent and inevitable ownership of that which is

purchased. Moreover, it is equally important to underscore that ownership is not contingent upon physical possession. Again, someone can purchase a part from my store, leave without possession of it, but this does not relinquish his ownership of the product, nor does it give the store the right to sell what rightfully belongs to him.[1524]

It is a splendid illustration—when talking about physical objects that have no free will! And perhaps for Calvinists who deny free will, it will remain a convincing argument. But for those who recognize that the Scripture has made the application of redemption conditioned on one's reception of the provision, a second glance at the illustration is in order. Is it reasonable to expect a buyer to go into an automotive parts store and buy every part in the store and even buy the store itself and then announce to the parts that he will only walk out of the store with those parts that wish to be purchased and burn the rest with the store? Like Escobedo, the present author also has worked in a automotive parts store, and to his recollection no buyer ever gave any automotive part he was purchasing a choice over the matter. No buyer ever walked back to the alternators and announced that he would buy the alternate for his car that wished to be bought!

Perhaps Escobedo has forgotten that many of his readers might not be impressed by an argument that reduces free will to that of an automotive part. That argument aside, for the sake of interaction with his illustration, let us suppose that the buyer will only elect to buy some of the parts and leave the rest. He walks up to the counter and purchases all the parts he wants at once and then leaves, evidently waiting for the parts to be delivered. After all, Christ purchased all of His elect at once on the cross and then left for heaven. Even granting Escobedo this analogy and ignoring the fact that it fails to factor in any conditionality or self-determinability, two immediate problems arise for his illustration.

First, when Christ purchased us and left for heaven, did His purchase of us immediately and automatically make us a part of His body? No, just as a part left in the store does not become a part of the car body until put into the car, so we do not become a part of Christ's body until we are placed into Christ—after believing (Eph 1:13). Until the point of time in which we are taken out of the store and placed into that body, we do not become a part of that body. We must belong to that body potentially before we can belong to it positionally. Until we have a position in that body, we are not a part of that body, and the purpose for which that payment was made remains unrealized.

Second, not only is there a problem of timing with relation to Christ's payment in the past, there is also a problem of timing with relation to heresies in the future. Peter is using the future time and linear aspect in regard to their denying and teaching, but a punctiliar aspect and antecedent time in regard to their being purchased. Before this future action on their part to deny Him, there already has been a punctiliar action on the Lord's part to purchase them. This aorist participle for purchase is not referring to ongoing purchasing in the future as the Lord purchases more and more unbelievers as they superficially join themselves to the new covenant community of the church through false professions of faith. Rather, it refers to a punctiliar purchase that already has been made. This purchase already is completed and past before the additions of the false professions. The purchase is not through means of the false professions but antecedent to them. The contrast of aspects and time should not be ignored.

In this regard, the provisional nature of this atonement was demonstrated already in relation to 1Tim 2:6 and 4:10. When Christ gave Himself for us, many of us were not yet born, and yet our sins already have been nailed objectively to the cross. The price already has been paid. He is already the Savior of all men universally throughout all time and eternity in that provisional sense.* Hence, the Calvinistic limitation of the atonement to those who have received subjective application is theologically defective. As Olson comments on 2:6, in his lexical discussion of the various words used for atonement, "there would be a serious theological problem if the focus were to be on the liberation of the captive, since obviously all have not been liberated."[1525]

The price has been paid objectively and provisionally for all without exception. But these false teachers prefer to reject the price paid for them so that they might legally remain slaves in the market place of sin, favoring leniency in sin to liberty from sin. Their love of sin prevented them from accepting the payment for their sin. Instead of singing, "Redeemed how I love to proclaim it," they exclaim, "Redeemed how I love to deny it!" And they seek to entice believers, who have left the market place of sin by subjectively receiving the liberty offered to them in Christ, to return as slaves to the market place of sin with the false lure of licentiousness. The inherently illogical nature of this allurement is spelled out by Peter: Freedom to sin cannot be freedom from sin (2Pet 2:19). Those who pursue sin will be enslaved subjectively by it. These false teachers are unregenerate, blood-bought unbelievers who successfully are enticing genuine believers.

---

* See *Absolute All*, 240.

Annotated Text of 2Pet 2:17-22

¹⁷ **These** [i.e., false teachers] are springs without water, and mists driven by a storm, for whom the black darkness has been reserved. ¹⁸ For speaking out arrogant words of vanity **they** [i.e., false teachers] entice by fleshly desires, by sensuality, **those** [i.e., believers] *truly having escaped* from the ones who live in error, ¹⁹ promising **them** [i.e., believers] freedom while **they** themselves [i.e., false teachers] are slaves of corruption; for by what a man is overcome, by this he is enslaved [whether he is lost or saved]. ²⁰ For if after **they** [i.e., believers] have *escaped* the defilements of the world by the *true knowledge* [*epignosis*] of the Lord and Savior Jesus Christ, **they** [i.e., believers] are again entangled in them and are overcome, the last state has become worse for **them** [i.e., believers] than the first. ²¹ For it would be better for **them** [i.e., believers] not to *truly have known* [*epiginosko*] the way of righteousness, than *truly having known* [*epiginosko*] it, to turn away from the holy commandment delivered to **them** [i.e., believers]. ²² It has happened to **them** [i.e., believers] according to the true proverb, "A dog returns to its own vomit," and, "A sow, after *washing* [*louo*], returns to wallowing in the mire" (TM).

Escaped

Those who are enticed by the false teachers are those who have *escaped* "from the ones who live in error" (v. 18) and who have *escaped* "the defilements of the world" (v. 20). *Those* in v. 18 refers to the same group being exploited in v. 3—the saved readership. There is some question as to the reading of the text in v. 18. The CT has *oligos* before *escape* so that the verse is translated as *barely* or *scarcely escape* by some translations, while others render it as *just, newly,* or *for a little while*. In either case, the picture conveyed by the reading of the CT is that of new or immature believers who just recently have abandoned their former manner of life but made little positive progress in practical sanctification beyond that initial entry point.

The MRD misses the point entirely by translating it as, "*who have almost abandoned.*" To the contrary, there is no question of the fact that those who are duped by the false teachers actually made a *clean escape*. A number of translations render it in just that fashion. The YLT renders it as: *those who had truly escaped*. The NKJ stresses this certainty as well by translating it as: *who have actually escaped*. Now, although this translational certainty may be based in part on the presence of *ontos* (*actually, truly*) rather than *oligos* (*barely*) in the MT and on the MT aorist (*escaped*) rather than CT present tense (*escape*), the fact still remains that those who *barely escape* have *actually escaped*. Therefore, the logically clarity of the MT is preferable.

As to textual usage, this verb for *escape* (*apopheugo*) is an aorist participle in v. 20 and denotes a punctiliar, completed action that actually has taken place. The only other time this verb is found in the NT, other than these two verses, is in 2Pet 1:4, where Peter again uses the aorist to describe the regenerate.[*] The parallelism between the aorists therefore is very pronounced:

- *having escaped* the corruption that is in the world (1:4)
- *having escaped* from the ones who live in error (2:18; TM)
- *having escaped* the defilements of the world (2:20; TM)

Since both 1:4 and 2:20 use the aorist participle to describe a punctiliar escape that already has occurred and since the ambiguous reading of the CT logically gives way to the clarity of the MT in 2:18, I adopt the MT aorist and *ontos* in 2:18 and render this combination as: *truly having escaped*. They *truly have escaped* (2:18) by the *true knowledge* of the Lord and Savior Jesus Christ (2:20). To put it in different Petrine terms, they had *purified their souls* (1Pet 1:22) by the washing of regeneration. The perfect participle denotes a completed state of purification.

Washed

An aorist participle is used in 2Pet 2:22 where the escape is pictured as having been *washed*. Apparently, this washing is the punctiliar *washing of regeneration*, to use Paul's words (Tit 3:5). Of course, Peter was familiar with Paul's writings. In fact, he exalts Paul's epistles to the level of being Scripture in the very next chapter (2Pet 3:15-16). Paul uses *loutron* to describe this regenerational washing. This is the nominal form of the verb that Peter uses for washing (*louo*). Peter would not have to consult Paul to make this connection, however. Jesus used

---

[*] See *Person versus Nature*, 792.

this same verb to address Peter himself when Jesus washed Peter's feet. "Jesus said to him [Peter], 'He who has *washed* [*louo*] needs only to cleanse his feet to be completely clean" (Jn 13:10; TM). Punctiliar coming to faith is pictured as washing the body in a bath; subsequent cleansing of the believer's feet needs to be done on a daily basis so that the believer may be completely clean. Otherwise, the believer's feet become dirty in the mire of this world. The initial washing of regeneration, pictured by the verb *louo*, already has occurred. Peter uses this same imagery to describe the regenerational cleansing experienced by the sow. Consequently, the sow represents someone who is saved, having experienced the washing of regeneration. Subsequently, the sow became dirty when it went back to wallowing in the mire. Rather than just getting dirty feet thereafter, the sow wallowed in the mud, however.

Mature Knowledge (Epignosis)

The dog and sow make their initial escape from the defilement of the world "by the *knowledge* [*epignosis*] of the Lord and Savior Jesus Christ." Granted, it is possible to understand this verse and Rom 1:28 in a manner that would be consistent with Seymour's interpretation: "And just as they [i.e., the lost] did not see fit to keep God in their *knowledge* [*epignosis*], God gave them over to a depraved mind, to do those things which are not proper" (TM). Here, it could be argued, are **unregenerate** people who previously were experiencing moral restraint because of their knowledge of God. They subsequently lost that knowledge and were plunged into an even worse moral state as a result. As a result of abandoning their knowledge of God, their last state has become morally worse for them than the first. Hence, it could be assumed that *epignosis* does not necessary represent saving knowledge, and a parallel to 2Pet 2:20 could be made by those who prefer to understand these moral apostates as being lost.

There are several problems with this view, on the other hand. First, it is also possible to translate Rom 1:28 as, "They did not see fit to acknowledge God" (TM). Although the NAS adds the words *any longer*, BADG does not. The NAB and NRS do not add this qualification. The ASV says, "They refused to have God in their knowledge" (cp. DBY). Thus, it is possible to understand the verse as saying the lost never came to know God. If translated in this manner, Rom 1:28 would argue for understanding *epignosis* as an understanding of God only available to those who already have experienced regeneration. The lost in Rom 1:28, and in contrast to those in 2Pet 2:20, are those who have never come to a saving knowledge of God.

Although it is not necessary for present purposes to take a definitive stance, the second option is preferable: taking *epignosis* as having this meaning throughout the NT—if for no other reason than to accord with the Pauline usage of this word elsewhere. Thus, *epignosis* is taken as representing mature saving knowledge. God "desires all men to be saved and to come to the *mature knowledge* of the truth" (1Tim 2:4; cp. 2Tim 2:25). God wants everyone to experience saving knowledge and then move on to *mature knowledge* (*epignosis*). Indeed, it seems that some who are very religious are "always learning and never able to come to the *mature knowledge* of the truth" (2Tim 3:7; TM). Of course, the lost never attain to *epignosis.* Unfortunately, many of the saved apparently never reach it either.

The lost fail to come to this level of knowledge, and many of them may reach the point to where it becomes increasingly difficult, and perhaps even impossible, to attain it. This assessment could have a potentially strong parallel in Rom 1:28. The lost in this verse never come to a mature knowledge of God and subsequently are temporally hardened. As Lenski surmises, they did not let their *gnosis* (natural knowledge) advance to *epignosis* (full knowledge).[1526] The *epi* prefix may be used to intensify the verb, and this would appear to be the case here. The lost may *know* (*ginosko*) God in a basic way through nature (Rom 1:21) and even *fully know* (*epiginosko*) what His word teaches about judgment (Rom 1:32), but they have not come to a full knowledge of God Himself (Rom 1:28). The lost may have a zeal for God, but they do not have this knowledge of God (Rom 10:2). Lexically, *epignosis* could be defined as either "true knowledge" or as simply "to acknowledge God" (L-N 28.2). Accordingly, the verse is either saying that the lost never had a true knowledge of God or never truly acknowledged Him. The type of knowledge expressed by *epiginosko* of God is reserved for the regenerate in the NT. It is a saving knowledge of God that has progressed into a mature knowledge (Eph 1:17; 4:13; Phil 1:9; Col 1:9-10; 2:2; 3:10; etc.). This contrast between partial and full knowledge is also brought into play by Paul's description of mature eschatological knowledge: "Now I *know* [*ginosko*] in part, but then I will *fully know* [*epiginosko*] just as I also have been *fully known* [*epiginosko*]" (1Cor 13:12; TM).

The NAS justifiably translates it as *true knowledge* in 1Pet 1:3,8. Lenski is correct that consistency would require that *epignosis* in 1Pet 1:2 and 2:20 and *epiginosko* in 2Pet 2:21 be understood in the same manner.[1527] The passage is talking about those who truly have escaped by coming to a genuine saving knowledge of the gospel. Unfortunately, some among the regenerate do not allow this knowledge to progress in practical sanctification (Heb 10:26; 2Pet 2:20). The use of this Greek word in the NT reinforces the perception that those who escaped past corruption did so as a result of regeneration and its attendant practical sanctification. Like the writer of Hebrews, Peter acknowledges the realistic possibility that his saved readers may fall rather than grow (2Pet 3:17-18). Some believers become blind and stumble because they forget their cleansing from their former sins (2Pet 1:9-10) and return to the mire (2Pet 2:22). Consequently, since *epiginosko* appears to denote not merely saving knowledge but mature saving knowledge, especially in this context with its association regarding the *way of righteousness*, I prefer the reading of the MT over the CT. As a result, those being depicted as falling into moral apostasy are to be understood as mature believers who **truly** have escaped the mire, not immature or new believers who just barely or recently escaped.

Dog

Reformed advocates of perseverance would find the above analysis difficult to accept. From their perspective, the lack of perseverance is proof that the persons being so described were never regenerate to start with. Thus, the objections regarding these believers as genuine believers include the terminology, the applicability to the lost teachers, and the last state.

As to a believer being called a dog, the proverbial reference to the dog in Prov 26:11 would be just as applicable as a description of believers as it would be for unbelievers. Just because unbelievers are described as dogs in the eternal state in Rev 22 does not mean the believers cannot be described as such in their temporal conduct. Likewise, the comparison of a believer to a sow is proverbial, not ontological. The appeal to terminology is certainly not an insurmountable objection from the Reformed camp.

Applicability to the Lost

Much of what is said is generically true of all men, regardless of whether they are saved. Both the lost and the saved can become entangled and overcome by sinful desires. Moral reformation can result in a lost person becoming worse off than before (Mt 12:45; 27:64; Lk 11:24-25). The same Greek word for *worse* (*cheiron*), used of the lost in these three previous passages, is used also of the saved (2Tim 3:13; Heb 10:29). The saved can be morally worse than the lost. They also can be subject to a severer misthological punishment (as a result of trampling the blood of Christ under foot after being sanctified by it) than the temporal punishment that their typologically saved counterparts experienced in the OT. Peter applies this generic statement, "by what a man is overcome, by this he is enslaved," to these lost teachers in verse 19. Next, he shows that this statement is fully applicable to those saved believers who are duped by the false teaching of these unregenerate teachers (2:20). The *they* in verses 18-22 makes a transition at verse 20 from the false teachers to those believers who are duped by their false teaching. The fact that such descriptions may be used of the lost does not prevent them from having applicability to the saved, so the Reformed camp cannot voice a convincing objection on these grounds.

Last State

However, a seemingly valid objection to the understanding being advocated herein could be posed by the following question: "How can the last state be *worse* (*cheiron*) than the first?" Standard suggestions generally are limited to a worse types of temporal states: (1) They are in a worse state of entanglement. It has often been said that preacher's kids either turn out good or bad. A person who rejects light is left with darkness. Kids from a strong Christian background who reject that background are not likely to be morally neutral. Their degenerate behavior, however, does not prove an unregenerate status. In fact, this is one of the most important observations from the passage. Regeneration does not guarantee positive behavior. Behavior is not an infallible indication of regeneration or lack thereof. There are black sheep in God's family. Proveitism is proven false. (2) Another temporal option is to interpret the phrase to mean that they are in a worse state of temporal calamity. Only heartaches are ahead for those believers who steer their ships for immoral reefs. God may discipline believers more severely now that they have become His children than He would have otherwise. (3) Yet another option is to say that they will be in a worse state in terms of finding self-gratification since their old way of life will not be as pleasurable as before. The saved have an awakened conscience and will be miserable emotionally as a result of grieving the Holy Spirit who dwells within them. (4) Another temporal possibility is that they will be in a worse state in terms of finding pardon than before. It is possible for a believer to harden his heart beyond remediation and even reach an unpardonable state (Heb 6:4-6; 10:26-31).

The above four possibilities are sufficient to show that life for wayward believers may be worse off than before, if those believers reject the moral compass provided for them in the Bible. On the other hand, as noted above, the CT reading of *oligos,* seems quite unlikely. Peter's use of *epignosis* and *epiginosko* would be better suited to describe a mature believer rather than an immature believer or a new believer. Thus, my preference is for the MT reading and for translations which likewise emphasizes the completeness of their escape. They have *actually escaped* (NKJ). They made a *clean* escape (KJV). Peter is not describing immature believers who have just barely escaped, but mature believers who made a complete escape. These believers actually have made a clean escape from their past immoral state and progressed in sanctification to the point of maturity. Like the believers in Heb 6:4-6, they moved beyond both immorality and immaturity, but they subsequently subcomed to the seduction of the world. This process of progressive sanctification to the point of maturation took time. Peter describes this progressive sanctification as the *path*, *road*, or *way of righteousness* in 2:21 (also described as such in Prov 12:28; 16:31; Mt 21:32; cp. Ps 23:3).

Illustration 307. Falling from Path of Righteousness

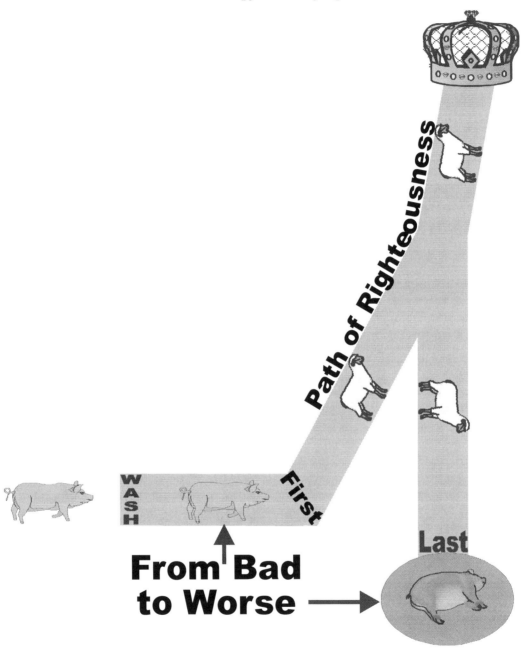

There is no need to constrict Peter's words to mean that their last state as believers is worse than their previous state as unbelievers. Peter is not contrasting their regenerate state with their previous unregenerate state. Rather, he is contrasting their beginning on this path, after they were saved, with their subsequent lapse from the path of righteousness. He is thus differentiating their latter state as lapsed believers with their initial state as immature believers. Even though I prefer a punctiliar understanding of the escape (2:20) and washing (2:22), this escape experientially was transformed from a positional to practical reality through the path of righteousness (2:21). Peter is not insinuating that it would be better for these believers never to have experienced regeneration.

Rather, in verse 21, he warns that it would have been better if they never had started off on this path than to stray from it afterwards.

Peter is not claiming that these moral apostates were better off originally as unbelievers. NOSAS is to be found here. Instead, what is found is an assertion by Peter that **they were better off as immature believers than as apostate believers**. Immature believers never make the trip up the path of righteousness. They never experientially escape the ways of the world. Mature believers, on the other hand, in starting on this upward climb, risk severe temporal and misthological consequences if they fall down. Wilkin likens this to the *death zone* in free soloing rock climbing. Not all believers decide to climb "the mountain of holiness on the path of righteousness." Such "discipleship is dangerous."[1528] Count the cost first (Lk 14:28-33). You and the cause of Christ will be mocked if you fall after you publicly identify yourself as a disciple of Christ.

For example, consider believers who go to seminary. Suppose they are led astray by false teaching and subsequently reject the faith. It happens. The misthological end for such believers will be worse than if they never had gone to seminary! Likewise, the more you study and know, the higher your accountability climbs (Lk 12:47). Some believers will be content never to even attempt to make the climb. They will point to those who have attempted and failed as reasons for not trying at all. They can refuse to take the risk and bury their talent (Mt 25:18). Parabolic accountability shows that to be a poor strategy.

The servant who refused to take a risk with his talent was thrown into the outer darkness. Better to risk losing the talent and receiving more lashes in the outer darkness, than not to take the risk and receive less lashes. Although to start and fall is worse than never to start at all, to start and finish is better than never to start at all. The only escape from the outer darkness is to climb the mountain. But for those who take the risk and fail, their last state (as fallen believers) is worse than their first state as immature believers (before they started the climb). There is no compelling reason to limit their worse state to temporal conduct and consequences. Their *last* (*eschatos*) state, as Peter calls it, will be worse eschatologically for them in terms of the misthological stripes they will receive (Lk 12:47). As believers, we have a choice between the crown of righteousness (2Tim 4:8) and the stripes of righteousness (Lk 12:47-48). Which one we receive will be determined by what we do with the path of righteousness.

The LS mentality would equate the washing with climbing. From the LS point of view, you must submit to the Lordship of Christ and commence climbing at the point you trust in Christ for eternal life. However, FG recognizes that many believers do not even really begin to submit their performance to the Lordship of Christ until sometime subsequently—if ever. To provide an actual example of delayed climbing, in his classic chapter opposing LS, "Must Christ be Lord to be Savior," Ryrie cites the example of believers in Acts 19:18-19 who "did not burn their books of magic as soon as they became believers....Yet their unwillingness to give it up did not prevent their becoming believers."[1529]

Whether through ignorance, inability, or insurrection, some believers simply do not start the climb as soon as they become believers. Now suppose that some of those believers who eventually got serious about living the Christian life subsequently had lapsed and fallen into a worse state morally. In that case, their last state would be worse for them misthologically than their first state as saved converts practicing magic. To have continued in their immature state as magic-practicing believers would have been better than for them to apostatize subsequently and plunge into even a worse state of moral degradation and receive even more lashes at the Bema. Ryrie conjectures that some of the initial converts may not have known that their practice of magic was something they should give up. As Paul continued to minister there for months, however, they could no longer plead ignorance, only reluctance. For them to have died in a rudimentary state would have been better than for them o die in a state of reluctance. Likewise, for them to have died in a state of reluctance would have been better than for them to die in a state of hard-core rebellion. Those believers who die in a rebellious state will receive more Bema lashes than immature believers who die in their initial rudimentary state. Morally and misthologically, for such believers to have never given up their magic would be better than, having given it up, to take it up again with even greater indulgence.

"And that slave who knew his master's will and did not get ready or act in accord with his will, shall receive many lashes, but the one who did not know it, and committed deeds worthy of a flogging, will receive but few" (Luke 12:47-48). Better to stay a rudimentary believer and receive fewer Bema lashes than to become a mature rebellious believer and receive many Bema lashes. But better still is to become a mature godly believer and escape the outer darkness and such lashes altogether. Those who are entangled and overcomed in this passage are believers. Such believers subcome to the world rather than overcome it. Hence, they may be designated as subcomers rather than overcomers. Subcomers earn lashes; overcomers earn crowns.[*]

Part Four

Ventilato has another section and an addendum with more remarks that largely are beside the point. Yet an interesting question is posed in this material in which the present author would find himself in agreement with Ventilato:

> Are those poor, unworthy, undeserving, non-persevering children of God, whom Hodges labels as "bastards," to remain as "bastards" in "outer darkness," "weeping and gnashing their teeth" *for all eternity*? If not, what Scripture do you have for the timing, circumstances and ultimate deliverance of these children of God from the Protestant-Purgatory of "outer darkness" and "bastardship"? (Emphasis his.)[1530]

Actually, in the conservative estimation of misthologists such as Hodges and Stanley, God's bastards will not cry for all eternity. Even ultra misthologists tend to deny that negative consequences, such as the outer darkness, will last beyond a thousand years. With Ventilato, the present author would ask, On what basis are his fellow misthologists limiting these negative rewards to anything short of eternity? Naturally, Ventilato intended for his question to drive people away from punitive misthology. The present author would intend just the opposite. The eternal consequences of what is at stake make it all the more imperative that we be diligent. Our temporal performance has eternal significance.

Ventilato would ask, What "*certainty*" can we have that we will not spend eternity in the outer darkness?[1531] In response, I would ask, "What certainty can Ventilato have that he will not?" In Reformed theology, absolute assurance of salvation is conditioned on one's perseverance. Thus, those in the Reformed camp who fail to persevere will, in terms of their own theological perspective, spend eternity burning in outer darkness of hell (since the Reformed camp believes the outer darkness is hell). Logically, If Ventilato is consistent with his destitute theology, he will not be able to offer his readers any absolute assurance that neither he nor they will not burn in hell forever.

In contrast, those in FG can offer absolute soteriological assurance that the believer will not burn forever, in fact, never. Believers can know with absolute certainty that they will not burn in the literal fires of hell. We can also point out that there are degrees of reward. Although we cannot be absolutely certain that we will rule in heaven, since it is conditioned on continuation in faith and faithfulness, those who do dedicate themselves to running the race can say with Pauline confidence: "I have fought the good fight, I have finished the course, I have kept the faith; in the future there is laid up for me the crown of righteousness, which the Lord, the righteous Judge, will award to me on that day; and not only to me, but also to all who have loved His appearing" (2Tim 4:7-8). When it came down to the end of his life, Paul knew he would win the prize, not because it was not based on his performance but because it was. Performance-based misthological assurance can become absolute when one is crossing the finish line if one has run well. Until that time we run with absolute soteriological assurance and relative misthological assurance. Because of Paul's comments pertaining to his own assurance in 1Cor 9:27, we cannot do otherwise. Those who reject FG theology and yet claim to have full soteriological assurance (despite the fact that they make it contingent on their perseverance) have made themselves superior to Paul. Misthologists will not follow their lead. Perseverance-based soteriology logically results in uncertainty. Misthology does not endorse such theology but rather opts for perseverance-based misthology.

---

[*] There is another sense in which their last state may be misthologically worse for them than their first if irremediable apostasy is taken into consideration. See *Misthological Knowledge (Epignosis*, 873.

Appendix 14.
Adokimos in 1Cor 9:27

Castaway

Illustration 308. Three Options for Castaway in 1Cor 9:27

Arminian	Eternal Security	Reformed
Some Assurance	Full Assurance	No Assurance
Conditional Security	Unconditional Security	Conditional Security

Arminian

The popularity of 1Cor 9:27 as an Arminian proof text is rather surprising: "But I keep under my body, and bring it into subjection: lest that by any means, when I have preached to others, I myself should be a castaway" (1Cor 9:27; KJV). Its popularity in the NOSAS camp is probably due to the fact that the key word translated as *castaway* (a*dokimos*) by the KJV is translated as *reprobate* by the KJV on every other occasion Paul uses this word in the NT. Thus, Arminians can refer readers who prefer the KJV to these cross-references and claim that by *castaway* Paul means that he could lose salvation and become *reprobate*.

Ashby takes this approach.[1532] Certainly, Paul entertains the possibility that he himself may be *adokimos* in 1Cor 9:27. Thus, according to the Arminian perspective, if Paul himself could not be absolutely sure that he would not be considered reprobate in the end, then neither can we. We might be able to test ourselves and be certain of our present salvation, but we cannot be sure that we will be saved in the end. Present assurance of salvation is possible as long as you are running well. But if you falter, then you lose the race and go to hell. Arminians who are running well can at least enjoy a measure of present assurance in their theology, but those who are running poorly cannot have absolute assurance.

Corner also insists upon the possibility of present assurance for the Arminian and criticizes OSAS advocates for asserting otherwise: "**It's a false accusation and misrepresentation to say that people who believe in a conditional security can't have assurance of salvation!**" "There is such a thing as a 'know-so salvation,' but only for those presently *believing* on Jesus." "John said [1Jn 5:13] *you may know that you have eternal life*—**not** 'you may know you will go to heaven when you die" (all emphasis his).[1533] Corner's insistence that present assurance is possible in Arminianism does contain a measure of truth. Certainly, the possibility of present assurance is greater in Arminianism than Calvinism. Unfortunately, a lack of frank admission on Corner's part is also detectable in that absolute present assurance is not possible for Arminians, at least not for all believers according to all Arminians.

To his credit, Shank acknowledges that Arminian believers may be saved yet carnal. Still, in the same chapter in which he makes this admission, he nullifies present assurance for carnal believers by using Samson as an example of those who could lose the Spirit (and regenerate life) without realizing it (Judges 16:20). The Spirit might "quietly abandon" them without their "being aware of his departure." "On his way to hell, he still imagines himself to be on the way to heaven. He still professes faith, and all seems well to him. **He is quite unaware of his apostasy.**"[1534] You think you are a believer, but in reality you really have committed apostasy from saving faith without knowing it. So assurance is limited to those with a high level of performance in Arminianism. However, Shank's approach leads to be a deadly trap, as even he anticipates:

> But when they [works] were deliberately embraced in a conscious effort to ensure justification, they contradicted faith in Jesus Christ, severing the individual from Him. The transfer of faith from Christ *alone* to Christ *plus other things* is fatal. Thus, things which of themselves are not wrong may yet constitute a deadly snare. (Emphasis his.)[1535]

Shank realizes that many will anticipate that his theology may be equated with this "deadly snare" of which he warns, and he understandably tries to offset this concern with emphatic emphasis on the deadly nature of the possibility:

> Christ Himself must be the sole object of one's faith and the exclusive ground of all his hope for heaven and eternity. To be wrong at this point is to miss the Way. Men who rest their faith on

foundations other than Christ, or in addition to Christ, are destined for everlasting disappointment and despair.[1536]

This is splendid FG theology! Unfortunately, I fear that Shank not only has backed himself into a corner (and bumped into Corner) with his frank admission and emphatic warning, he also has destined himself to "everlasting disappointment and despair." His theology logically leads to the very thing he warns against. By embracing FG theology on the one hand and denying it on the other hand, with CS (conditional security), he has condemned himself. With the CS hand, he reaches out to grab works as a soteriological necessity. He believes that you have to have good works to keep your faith alive; otherwise, it ceases to be saving faith. So hopefully you have enough good works to keep your faith alive and to keep yourself spiritually alive. Yet if your works are necessary to keep yourself alive, then how can you not trust them to keep you alive? How can it be claimed that works are not necessary "to ensure justification" in that case? If your assurance must be based on your works, then how can your faith not be based on your works? Can your faith be based on one thing and your assurance on another? FG answers, "No, what is faith if not assurance?"

Nonetheless, Shank continues with his claim that works "are only *the expression* of faith. They must never be *objects* of our faith. All our faith must rest in Christ alone" (emphasis his).[1537] Why? Because if your faith rests even in part on your works, then you lose eternal life according to Shank. Either way you lose. You cannot believe that your works are soteriologically necessary and yet soteriologically unnecessary. This NOSAS persuasion could be represented syllogistically as:

Illustration 309. Arminian Perseverance Syllogism

Major Premise: Paul's salvation is conditioned on his perseverance.
Minor Premise: Paul might not persevere.
Conclusion: Paul might lose his salvation.

Arminians would see the passage as talking about loss of soteriological salvation rather than loss of reward. At least Paul could be sure of his salvation as long as he was running well, but if he stopped running, he would lose his salvation. Thus, in denying the *unconditional security of the believer*, Arminianism realistically teaches the *insecurity of the believer*. By making perseverance a necessary expression of faith, Shank has made it the object of faith. As objectionable as this interpretation may be, another approach is even worse—yet just as popular—in the camp that is the polar opposite of the Arminian camp.

Calvinistic

The Calvinist will claim that Paul is saying that he could not be certain that he was saved even when he wrote these words! Blomberg articulates his position as thus:

A too simplistic understanding of "eternal security" has probably led many Christians to doubt that Paul could have seriously considered not "making it to heaven." But true Reformed doctrine recognizes that saints are those who persevere. No Biblical text offers assurance of salvation for people who flagrantly repudiate Christ without subsequent repentance.[1538]

Blomberg also quotes Hoekema in agreement, but this is just typical Reformed Calvinistic theology, in which Paul is afraid that he might prove to have never been regenerated or justified in the first place: no assurance apart from perseverance. No absolute assurance is available, not even for Paul. How ludicrous! Tragically, Calvinistic theology logically requires this proveitistic conclusion, as even many in their camp admit. If one pictured their reasoning syllogistically, it would be something like this:

Illustration 310. Calvinistic Perseverance Syllogism

Major Premise: Paul is saved if he perseveres in the race.
Minor Premise: Paul might not persevere in the race.
Conclusion: Paul might not be saved.

According to this camp, Paul could not be sure that he was saved and neither can you. You cannot be certain that you are saved right now, much less that you will be saved in the future. If one had to choose between these two camps, then Arminianism would be the better choice. Thankfully, there is an alternative. Although advocates within both these camps condition your assurance and thus your salvation on your perseverance, another option is available: the OSAS interpretation. According to advocates of unconditional security, the crown you are running to win is not salvation from hell; it is a reward in heaven. Consequently, you can have absolute assurance of your present and future soteriological security because it is not conditioned on your perseverance in either faith or faithfulness.

Unconditional Security

Alpha Privative

The word in question, *adokimos*, is the Greek word *dokimos* with the negative prefix *a* (*alpha*) attached to the front of it. It is called an alpha privative by Greek grammarians and would correspond to the English prefix *un* or *dis*. For example, **un***faithful* (*apistos*) is the antonym of *faithful* (*pistos*). Paul is fond of this construction. For example, in 2Tim 3:2 he lists three alpha privatives, one after another: **dis***obedient* (*apeithes*), **un***grateful* (*acharistos*), and **un***holy* (*anosios*). He breaks this record in Rom 1:31, where he lists five in a row in the MT. The whole verse is composed of alpha privatives: "Undiscerning, untrustworthy, unloving, unforgiving, unmerciful" (Rom 1:31; NKJ). We retain this usage in English. For example, a theist is someone who believes in God. An *a*theist is someone who does not believe in God. Putting the letter *a* on the front of the word may make it mean the opposite (e.g., *a*sexual, *a*millennial).

Dokimos

If we knew what *dokimos* meant, we would have a clear indicator as to what *adokimos* means. Since the KJV is so popular with its translation of *reprobate* for *adokimos*, it will be interesting to consult the KJV to see how it renders Paul's usage of *dokimos*. In each and every case, the KJV translates *dokimos* from Paul's pen as *approved* (Rom 14:18; 16:10; 1Cor 11:19; 2Cor 10:18; 2Cor 13:7; 2Tim 2:15). The last of these verses is the theme verse for AWANA: "Study to shew thyself **approved** unto God, a workman that needeth not to be ashamed, rightly dividing the word of truth" (2Tim 2:15; KJV). The AWANA motto correspondingly is: "Approved workmen are not ashamed." Good motto and good translation. *Dokimos* means *approved*. The most obvious translation for *adokimos*, therefore, would be **dis***approved* or **un***approved*. If *dokimos* means *approved*, then *adokimos* means **un***approved*. According to Paul, whether you are *approved* depends on how well you work. You either will be ashamed or approved based on the effort you put into your Bible study. The inverse of the AWANA motto would be: "Disapproved workmen are ashamed." Nobody wants to be in this DWANA group.

Is this verse teaching that the way we study our Bible determines whether we are genuine believers? A consistent Calvinistic response would say that it does and appeal to 2Cor 13:5-7 as cross-reference. Indeed, this is a good cross-reference in that 1Cor 13:7 is the only verse in the NT in which *adokimos* and *dokimos* both appear: "Now I pray to God that ye do no evil; not that we should appear *approved* [*dokimos*], but that ye should do that which is honest, though we be as *reprobates* [*adokimos*]" (KJV). Bad translation. A clash is apparent in translational consistency. Do our works determine whether we are reprobates, or do they determine whether we will be approved for rewards? Since Paul earlier had used the verbal form of this word (*dokimazo*) to teach the Corinthians that works result in rewards and that salvation could be had apart from works (1Cor 3:13-15), the translation more consistent with Pauline theology is that what is at stake is salvation, in terms of rewards, rather than in terms of heaven versus hell.

This misthological understanding is correct even if the most restrictive interpretation of 1Cor 3:13-15 were adopted so that it does not refer to believers in general but to preachers, such as Paul and Apollos in particular. Even if this point were granted for the sake of argument, the truth of that passage still applies to Paul. He knew that he would be saved, even if as through fire, and that the testing of his works would not determine his salvation from hell. Soteriological reprobation is not under consideration. Paul's applicability of 1Cor 3:13-15 to himself rules out the applicability of 1Cor 9:27 to hell! Paul did not question his salvation from hell even if he were to perform poorly, but he could question his salvation regarding rewards in heaven. Whether he built or ran poorly, he knew he still would be saved from hell. What is at stake is being a misthological castaway, not a soteriological one.

James agrees with Paul on this matter that what is at stake is salvation in terms of rewards rather than salvation from hell: "Blessed is a man who perseveres under trial; for once he has been *approved* [*dokimos*], he will receive the *crown* [*stephanos*] of life, which the Lord has promised to those who love Him" (Jam 1:12). Paul clarifies that the reason he is so concerned about being *approved* (*adokimos*) in 1Cor 9:27 is because of the *crown* (*stephanos*) he just mentioned in 9:25. What is at stake is misthological approval or disapproval rather than soteriological reprobation. Paul entertains the possibility that he himself may be *adokimos* in 1Cor 9:27. In doing so, the thought does not even cross his mind that the salvation which he has been given freely is one of probation. Soteriological reprobation is not part of the picture, as Krell explains:

> When Paul envisioned this "disqualification," what did he have in mind? The word translated "disqualified" is the Greek word *adokimos*. The letter *a* in *adokimos* is known in Greek grammar as the alpha privative, which gives the word the opposite meaning. *Dokimos* means "tested, and approved." Therefore, not to pass the test is to be *adokimos*. It means "not standing the test, disapproved."[1539]

An examination of such texts, then, leads to the conclusion that the best translation for *adokimos* would be *disapproved*, in terms of rewards, when talking about believers. Many translations so render it. On the other hand, if one prefers the KJV wording, this will result in a category of *saved reprobates*—reprobates saved from hell but not saved from the outer darkness. They are soteriologically saved but misthologically lost, qualified to enter into heaven but disqualified to rule in heaven. They will not be cast away from God into hell, but they will be cast away into the outer darkness. They would be misthological castaways.

Context

Ashby admits that the imagery of the race supports the rewards motif so that Paul is concerned about "being *disqualified* [*adokimos*] from receiving the prize-rewards."[1540] Some Arminians appeal to the broader context in which Paul is concerned about winning and saving the lost by preaching the gospel and, from that broader basis, assert that Paul is concerned that he would fail to win what he is offering to the lost in the gospel. This objection is valid to a point, in that Paul is indeed running and winning the lost by preaching the gospel so that he himself might have a share in the gospel: "And I do all things for the sake of the gospel, in order that I may become a co-partaker of it" (1Cor 9:23; TM)

The soteriological objection offered by Arminians who appeal to this text fails to take into account the misthological dimension of the gospel that Paul is preaching. His becoming a co-partaker of the gospel is contingent on how he runs the race in sharing the gospel with others. His active participation in this process is reflected by the middle voice of *ginomai* (*become*). The aorist tense might suggest punctiliar realization of this aspiration at the JSC. Paul's salvation from hell is not dependent on his saving others from hell. Rather, his salvation in heaven, in terms of rulership therein, is dependent upon his efforts to evangelize and disciple others so that they could become co-rulers as well. Paul's gospel starts with the gospel of grace, but it does not end there. It goes on in complete harmony with Jesus' gospel of kingdom. Jesus' gospel of the kingdom is a summons to endure and thus be saved (Mt 24:13-14). Paul's exhortation is likewise to endure and consequently co-rule (2Tim 2:12). Salvation from hell is by grace. Salvation in the kingdom, from the loss of rewards therein, is by works. Paul teaches a misthological gospel (Rom 2:16; Col 1:5,23; 2Thess 2:14). He wants to be saved from loss of reward in heaven. His eternal security is not the issue.

Cross-references

These considerations only leave the cross-references to this passage as potential objections to the Marrowistic interpretation. But at least five out of the seven times that the KJV renders *adokimos* as *reprobate*, the passage is talking about believers (1Cor 9:27; 2Cor 13:5-7; Tit 1:16). An extended defense for understanding 2Cor 13:5-7 as being applicable to genuine believers in the specifics of the passage and the broader context of the Corinthian epistles is available elsewhere.* Only Tit 1:16 is left for present consideration. As will be demonstrated below, it is best taken as referring to believers.

Only two other passages might be used in reference to unbelievers (Rom 1:28; 2Tim 3:8). These passages will be addressed below as well. The only other time *adokimos* is used in the NT, it refers to believers, and the KJV does not translate it as *reprobate* there (Heb 6:8). Therefore, anticipating the conclusions to follow, the majority of the time *adokimos* is used in the NT, it is talking about those who have been saved. Thus, it should not be translated as *reprobate*. Or if one is KJVO, then the doctrine of reprobation will have to be expanded to include misthological reprobation. And castaway will mean castaway into the outer darkness.

---

* See 2Cor 13:5 in *Carnal Corinth*.

Tit 1:16

Apistos

"They profess to know God, but by their deeds they deny Him, being detestable and disobedient, and *worthless* [*adokimos*] for any good deed" (Tit 1:16). To be sure, the Reformed camp will object to taking Tit 1:16 as a reference to believers and assume that the Greek word *apistos* in 1:15 proves that the passage is talking about unbelieving reprobates. In fact, Zeller criticizes Hodges for suggesting otherwise. Hodges had linked his discussion of Tit 1:16 with 2Tim 2:13 by mentioning the possibility of "faithless" believers. Zeller complains: "The immediate context [Tit 1:15] is speaking about those who are defiled and **unbelieving.**"[1541] In doing so, Zeller evidently fails to note at least two things underlying Hodges' discussion. The word used to describe *faithless* (*apisteo*) in 2Tim 2:13 is the verbal counterpart of the adjective (*apistos*) used in Tit 1:15. Due to Hodges' expertise in Greek, he probably is alluding to the Greek text in his association of these texts. The people being described in both passages are *faithless*. If the Greek text is consulted, it might be concluded in Hodges' defense that Tit 1:15 simply may be describing **unfaithful** believers, just as does 2Tim 2:13.

Aside from not recognizing this verbal-adjectival correspondence, Zeller also fails to deal with the possibility that *apistos* itself may be used to describe unfaithful believers elsewhere in the NT.[*] Although neither Hodges or Zeller explicitly deal with the Greek wording on this particular matter, it is rather apparent that Hodges' assessment is in harmony with the underlying Greek text. However, if Zeller has consulted the Greek text, then one is left to wonder why he acts as though the potential connection does not exist.

As the present author writes this note, he is preparing his older son, Jeremy, to quote the book of Titus for the AWANA program at their church. In addition to their normal AWANA activities, his children memorize books of the Bible and quote them verbatim for their local AWANA group. The author's son and he have been practicing by quoting Titus back and forth to one another. This practice has the benefit of increasing one's sensitivity to the context of any supposed proof text in a biblical book such as Titus. The LS notion that profession of regeneration is dependent upon behavioral modification for its validation is quite foreign to the situation as depicted by Paul in the book of Titus.

Good behavior is an exhorted and learned behavior in this epistle. Such behavior is not guaranteed or inevitable. Nor is it an infallible indicator of regeneration or lack thereof, as is also demonstrated by Paul's use of this same adjective in another pastoral epistle, where he says that some believers behave worse than *unbelievers* (*apistos*; 1Tim 5:8). Certainly, the word *apistos* may be used of lost unbelievers, as in 1Tim 5:8, but this does not prove that the word is limited to such usage, particularly since Paul is aghast that the behavior of some believers is worse than unbelievers! To turn around and use *apistos* in Tit 1:15 to say that behavior proves regeneration or lack thereof, as Zeller does, is indeed a shortsighted argument.

For the sake of discussion, however, let us suppose that Zeller is correct in that the word *apistos* refers to *unbelievers* in the present passage (Tit 1:15). Does this necessarily prove that Hodges is wrong? Not at all. First, one must consider the possibility that Paul might be describing **regenerate** unbelievers. Believers may become regenerate and then cease believing; nevertheless, they do not lose their regeneration. Phenomenally at least, such a person could be described as a *regenerate unbeliever*. Not all believers walk by faith. An even smaller percentage of believers who walk by faith do so long enough to mature in the faith. Only a fraction of believers who walk by faith follow through and persevere in the faith. In the immediate context, Paul had just given stringent instructions to Titus that would have to be carried out if the believers in Crete were to be sound in the faith: "Reprove them severely that they may be sound in the faith" (Tit 1:13). Why did Titus need to rebuke these believers so harshly for them to be sound in the faith? According to Paul, the reason is because "Cretans are always liars, evil beasts, lazy gluttons" (Tit 1:12). Their regeneration did not eradicate all effects of their degeneration. As Cretans, they were prone to very degenerate behavior, even though they had now become believers.

To interact briefly with a few commentators, Litfin seems to be of the opinion that those to be rebuked in hopes of becoming "sound in the faith" (Tit 1:13) are the false teachers (Tit 1:10). Lenski disagrees, saying the deceivers are to be silenced (Tit 1:11) and that it is the church members themselves who need to be rebuked, particularly if they are among those who fall prey to the false teachers (v. 11). Hendriksen is of the opinion that both "the errorists and those who listen to them must be reproved."[1542] Of the three possibilities, Lenski's proposal is the most persuasive. Concern for a healthy faith presupposes that they have come to genuine faith. Paul is concerned that believers be sound in the faith.

---

[*] See *Unfaithful*, 352.

Although it could be argued that these false teachers were once believers themselves who had had their own faith destroyed and were now destroying the faith of others (cp. 2Tim 2:18), for the time being the premise will be adopted that some of these false teachers are unregenerate unbelievers who turned away from the truth of the gospel after initially hearing it but never believing it (Tit 1:14; cp. 2Tim 3:7). Even so, they were infiltrating the homes of true believers and overthrowing the faith of these genuine believers (Tit 1:11). This verb for *overthrow* (*anatrepo*) is the same word used by John to describe Jesus overthrowing the tables of the money changers (Jn 2:15) and by Paul to describe the subversion of genuine believer's faith by genuine believers who had defected from the faith (2Tim 2:18). In this present context in Titus, as well as in the other two Pastoral Epistles, Paul is trying to salvage the faith of those who are being shipwrecked regarding their faith and wandering from the faith. Defection from the faith is of paramount concern in these Pastoral Epistles (1Tim 1:5-6,19; 4:1-3; 5:8,12,15; 6:10; 20-21; 2Tim 1:15; 2:12,14-18; 3:1-5; 4:3-4;10,16; Tit 1:11,13-14). For this reason, Guthrie is certainly justified to take *apistos* as a possible reference to weak Christians who are *paying attention* and *giving heed* (Tit 1:14; 1Tim 4:1) to this false doctrine and having their faith *overthrown* (Tit 1:11; 2Tim 2:18) as a result. "The *unbelieving*, as Lock suggests, could refer either to weak Jewish Christians, who did not believe that Christ was the end of the law, or to those who, like the later Gnostics, refused to admit the divine creation of matter."[1543] In other words, the unbelievers in question may refer to weak believers who subcomed to false doctrine and in doing so were departing from the faith. If this is correct, then Zeller's entire argument against Hodges collapses. The word *unbelieving* may be understood in a relative sense to refer to weak or apostate believers rather than as a technical term for the lost who never believed.

Given the concern that Paul has over the destruction of believer's faith in these epistles, it would seem best to take 2Tim 2:13 as affirming eternal security whether one becomes faithless or unfaithful. Paul denies that security is contingent on either perseverance in faith or faithfulness. Still, just suppose that Zeller is correct and *apistos* is being used in an absolute manner in Tit 1:15 to describe the unregenerate, does Zeller's interpretation of the passage necessarily follow in that case? The answer is still, "No."

Know God

A crucial component of Zeller's assessment lies in taking the phrase *they profess to know God* as a simple profession of salvation. In other words, they profess to know God, but they do not possess eternal life. Professors are not possessors. These professors are lost. I have no problem, either biblically or logically, affirming professors are not necessarily possessors. Indeed, I believe many in the LS camp would fall into this category. (They profess to believe in Christ for eternal life, but actually they believe in Christ plus their performance and thus fail to come into possession of eternal life.) The problem in this verse occurs when one makes this professor-possessor argument an exegetical necessity. The LS assertion from this passage is that those who profess to be saved but do not live a life in harmony with that profession thereby falsify their profession. This backdoor LS approach requires that you live a good life in order to enter heaven. Yet making good works necessary to enter heaven is an abuse of the professor-possessor argument, runs counter to Tit 3:5, and leaves numerous questions unanswered.

If Paul's point is that fruit proves root or that performance proves possession, then why does he expend so much energy in the book of Titus to urge regenerate believers to live a good life? If the root of regeneration automatically or inevitably results in the fruit of good works, then why does Paul present Titus with various checklists of good works for elders, older men, younger men, older women, younger women, and bondslaves? Why is it necessary for Titus to encourage, instruct, remind, and rebuke these believers in order to get them to produce good works—if good works are in fact an inevitable expression of their new nature? Why does Paul conclude that "those who have believed God" need to "be careful to engage in good deeds" if they automatically are going to do good works anyway? (Tit 3:8) Why does Paul find it necessary to use an imperative to command these believers to "engage in good works" if such good works are going to flow inevitably from their new nature? (Tit 3:14) And why, in this very verse, does Paul warn Titus that believers may be "unfruitful" if in fact believers inevitably bear good fruits? Sensitivity to the context slams the backdoor shut. Knowing God or not knowing God is not necessarily a simple affirmation or denial of generation. Context is king, and this context rules against taking it as simple soteriological knowledge.

Wilkin devotes a chapter to the thesis that there is a sense in which believers may fail to know God and cites Tit 1:16 in connection with his chapter *Believer, Do You Know God? 1 John 2:3-6.*[1544] Hodges has written an extended discussion of this Johannine text in his commentary on Johannine Epistles. Zeller, on the other hand, rejects the type of approach taken by FG writers such as Hodges and Dillow on the basis that knowing God is associated with eternal life in Jn 17:3, and the lost do not know God in 1Thess 4:5 and 2Thess 1:8.[1545]

Zeller's one-dimensional view of knowing God and having eternal life is evidentially something like turning a light switch on and off. If you turn on the switch (know God), you then have light (eternal life). In other words, if you are saved, you know God. If you are lost, you do not know God. To be sure, the Bible can speak of knowing God in such black and white, absolute terms. However, knowing God need not be restricted merely to having eternal life but may be broadened to experiencing God, to knowing Him intimately. Not all believers know Him in this capacity. Knowing God can be used relatively rather than absolutely or soteriologically. Certainly, the passages that Zeller cites in Thessalonians would indicate a lack of soteriological knowledge. But to conclude on such basis that knowing God must be a soteriological knowledge in Tit 1:16 is tantamount to claiming that because a cow eats grass and a horse eats grass, a cow must be a horse. Zeller deduces that since a group of people do not know God in one passage and a different group of people do not know God in another passage, they must be the same group of people—the same kind of theological animal—unregenerate people. Never mind that they are in different contexts, look differently, and sound differently. If a cow does not fly and a horse does not fly, the cow must be a horse, of course, using Zellerian logic. Just because one does not _____ and another group does not _____, does not mean that one-and-the-same group is intended.

Knowing God is not such a static concept that one can safely take such a jump in logic with Zeller. The sad reality is that Jesus still can ask many believers today, just as He asked Philip then: "Have I been so long with you, and yet you have not come to know Me"? (Jn 14:9) Paul even said that there is a sense in which lost unbelievers know God (Rom 1:18-21)! Since there is a sense in which Paul can affirm that lost unbelievers know God, how can Zeller be so certain that there is no sense in which faithless believers do not know God? Zeller's assumption would appear to be nonsense. If one equates knowing God with having eternal life in Jn 17:3, will one jump to the conclusion that demons have eternal life because they know Jesus (Acts 19:15)? Both verses use *ginosko* for *know*. Perhaps one should not be so hasty in equating knowing God with having eternal life independent of the context.

The underlying reason for Zeller's rejection of FG theology is revealed in his summation of the FG position as teaching that is possible to say: "I'm saved, but I refuse to do what my Saviour tells me to do!"[1546] Zeller finds such FG theology ludicrous. Why? Because in his theology you cannot be saved and refuse to do what your Savior tells you to do in terms of performance. His theology is LS pure and simple. Your salvation is conditioned on your performance-related submission to the Lordship of Christ. Jesus will not save you if you are not willing to obey Him. His salvation comes with a price tag, and you are the one who must be willing to pay that price. Persistent willful disobedience disqualifies you from entering Zellerian heaven. Conversely, persistent, willful obedience is necessary to reach Zellerian heaven. In contrast to Zeller, FG prefers to understand entrance into God's heaven being offered on the basis of free grace. Heaven is not a reward. This verse in Tit 1:16 can indeed be understood as referring to regenerate believers who fail to know God intimately or experientially. Consequently, the cross-references for *adokimos* support the point of view that *adokimos* can indeed refer to genuine believers.

Cognates

Cognates for *adokimos* lead to the same conclusion: Believers may be the ones so described. The verbal synonym **apo***dokimazo* is used of Esau in Heb 12:17. The preposition *apo* gives it the same essential meaning as does *a*. In this passage, Esau was *rejected* misthologically for the inheritance. The verbal antonym *dokimazo* is used in 1Cor 3:13 in connection with the misthological *test* of the believer's works. It is also used pertaining to deacons being *tested* in 1Tim 3:10. The results of the test will determine if they are able to serve as deacons, not if they are lost or saved. The misthological test of believers' faith is also used in 1Pet 1:7. The misthological salvation of their souls is at stake, not their salvation from hell.

Synonym

Quite likely, Paul's use of *katabrabeuo* in Col 2:18 parallels his use of *adokimos* in 1Cor 9:27. In the context of 1Cor 9:27, being *disqualified* (*adokimos*) is associated with failure to win the *prize* (*brabeion*) in the race. The *brabeion* (*prize*) is a cognate of *brabeus* (*judge*), who was the judge or umpire at a public game who awarded the prizes. The verbal form *brabeuo*, to judge or umpire at the games, occurs in Col 3:15, where the "peace of Christ" is to act as our umpire, qualifying us to receive the prize. Of course, just a few verses later Paul will refer to the inheritance as the potential "reward" (Col 3:24), as he already had done so previously: "Giving thanks to the Father who has qualified us to be partakers of the inheritance of the saints in the light" (Col 1:12). God already has qualified us to run in the race and win the prize that is potentially ours. Naturally, being qualified to win the prize does not mean that we actually will do so. We might refuse to run, or we might run poorly, or we might not follow the rules and be disqualified accordingly.

The prize is for the *victor*, that is, the *winner*,[*] otherwise known as the *overcomer*. Therefore, when the compound form of *katabrabeuo* is encountered in Col 2:18, one should be inclined to agree with those such as Bullinger and Constable, who understand it in terms of the Olympic games as meaning to judge as umpire against the competent as being unworthy of the prize. After all, *brabeuo* means *judge* and *kata* means *against*; *katabrabeuo* correspondingly means *judge against*. In terms of the historical background, it would mean to judge against in terms of receiving the reward and would thus be a misthological judgment. Those translations that render Col 2:18 as meaning disqualified for the prize or for the reward are to be preferred, such as: "Let no man rob you of your prize" (ASV); "Let no man take your reward from you" (BBE); "Let no man beguile you of your reward" (KJV); "Let no one cheat you of your reward" (NKJ).

Just as living a life that submits our conscience to the dictates of Christ can qualify us for this reward, so living a life that submits to the dictates of the ascetic consciences of others can disqualify us for the reward that could have been ours otherwise. One must chose one's coach carefully. Incidentally, this *katabrabeuo* is equated with *krino* in Col 2:16,18, which again shows the superficiality of the PA argument discussed previously.[†] The *bema* judgment, which may result in loss of reward for the believer, is interchangeably anticipated by both *katabrabeuo* and *krino*: "Let no one *judge* you (*krino*)…let no one *disqualify* you (*katabrabeuo*)." The *bema* is judicial. If you let others judge you now, you will be judged by Christ then.

Text

[23] And I do all things for the sake of the **gospel**, in order that I may become a co-partaker of it. [24] Do you not know that in a **race** all the runners run, but only one receives the **prize** (*brabeion*)? ***Run*** in such a way that you may **win** it. [25] And everyone who competes in the games exercises self-control in all things. They then do it to receive a perishable victor's **crown**, but we do it to receive an imperishable victor's **crown** (*stephanos*). [26] Therefore I ***run*** in such a way, as not without aim. I box in such a way, as not beating the air. [27] But I strictly discipline my body and bring it under control, lest, after I have preached to others, I myself should become disqualified (*adokimos*) for the prize (1Cor 9:23-27; TM).

Illustration 311. Run for the Brabeion and Stephanos

Summary of Castaway

Being a castaway in 1Cor 9:27 in no way detracts from objective or subjective assurance of soteric salvation. Paul was saved, and he knew he was saved. Earlier in this same epistle, he affirmed that he would be saved (1Cor 3:13-15), even if he built poorly. So running poorly has nothing to do with fear over whether one will be saved in that sense. Both texts are using different imagery in dealing with the doctrine of rewards. The text in 1Cor 9:27 uses the athletic imagery of Paul's day in scenes that would have to be understood easily by his readers. The umpire at the sporting event would cry *adokimos* if the athlete did not compete according to the rules.[1547] The

---

[*] See *Illustration 41. Parallelism of Out-Resurrection and Crown*, 94.
[†] See *Romans 14:10-13*, 659.

contestant was then disqualified from receiving the prize. In this context, the word must be understood as referring to loss of reward in the eschatological future at the Bema.

When we attend athletic events today, we are accustomed to referees blowing a whistle to signify a foul—the breaking of the rule. In Paul's day the referee would sit at the *bema* and cry *adokimos* if an athlete did not follow the rules. The rules had been broken and the contestant was rejected for the prize. Likewise, when we stand before the Bema, God may blow His misthological whistle on us and declare us *adokimos*, rejected for the prize of ruling with Christ.

Illustration 312. Athletic Adokimos

Alternative Misthological Adokimos Passages

Dillow limits the misthological usage of *adokimos* to the standard passages (1Cor 9:27; 2Cor 13:5-7; Heb 6:8).[1548] As noted above, Hodges adds Tit 1:16 to this list. Wilkin expands this list to the maximum extent and claims that this word is used exclusively of believers in the NT. Yet this would include Rom 1:28 and 2Tim 3:8. Thus far, the discussion has assumed that Wilkin is incorrect in adding these two additional references, especially Rom 1:28. However, Wilkin's suggestion is intriguing. At a kingdom conference dedicated to the subject of rewards, the present author pressed Chitwood on the issue, and Chitwood concurred with Wilkin that the reference in Rom 1:28 is, in fact, dealing with believers.

Since the above discussion on *adokimos* is rather elementary in terms of misthology, the reader might enjoy considering an alternate understanding of the term in relation to these two alternative texts. Although I do not necessarily adopt this alternate position, I will briefly outline an argument that could be used to defend Wilkin's inclusion of these two additional texts as pertaining to believers.

Misthological Knowledge (Epignosis)

It has been demonstrated that *epignosis* refers to more than saving knowledge in the following passage: "For if after they have escaped the defilements of the world by the *knowledge* of the Lord and Savior Jesus Christ, they are again entangled in them and are overcome, the last state has become worse for them than the first" (2Pet 2:20).[*] At the very least, *epignosis* refers to mature saving knowledge in this context. It is full knowledge, or more literally, knowledge upon knowledge. Perhaps, one could even go so far as to say that in certain contexts *epignosis* is misthological knowledge that has been laid upon the foundation of soteriological knowledge.

Worse State

This *epignosis* refers to knowledge that advances beyond entering the kingdom (by grace) to ruling the kingdom (as a reward). Those believers who obtained this mature knowledge and then fell from it ended up in a state worse than their original state. When they first became believers, they were immature baby believers—carnal Christians. They advanced beyond this state on the path toward inheriting the kingdom and becoming one of the *metochoi*. Subsequently, they rejected their pursuit of becoming one of the *metochoi*. As a result of their misthological apostasy from the path of righteousness, they were disqualified permanently from becoming one of the *metochoi*. Their last state is temporally worse than their original state because, at least initially, as carnal Christians, they had the opportunity to advance on to becoming one of the *metochoi*. That possibility no longer exists. Their misthological apostasy is irremediable. Their last state as misthological apostates has become worse for them than their previous state as carnal believers because in their initial state of immaturity they still had the hope of ruling the kingdom. Now, in their state as mistholic apostates, they have become misthologically hopeless.

---

[*] See *Mature Knowledge (Epignosis)*, 860.

Kadesh Barnea

Likewise, when one considers the children of Israel, one sees a typological parallel. They had wondered in the wilderness of carnal immaturity long enough. God brought them to the Promised Land with the intent of taking them to possess the land so that they could rule it. But at Kadesh Barnea, when Caleb challenged them to be overcomers, they shrank back in doubt and considered themselves to be grasshoppers instead, comparing themselves to their adversaries (Num 13:30-33). God's people rejected the kingdom offer, so God rejected them from inheriting the Promised Land. The next day, however, His people repented and went up to fight (Num 14:40). Too late. God already had sworn that His people would not enter into possession of the land (Num 14:22-23; Heb 3:9-11; 4:3). Typologically, a believer (someone related to God under the new covenant) who comes to understand kingdom truth (*epignosis*) and then apostasies from that truth is disqualified permanently for kingdom inheritance. Misthological apostasy is tragic. The same truth is seen in connection with Esau. He sold his birthright and could not get it back afterwards. He repented, but his father would not. Again, it was too late (Heb 12:16-17). God does not forgive apostasy pertaining to *metochoi* on the part of those who have reached *epignosis* (Heb 10:26-27). Those who reached this mature understanding (*epignosis*) and rejected it were disqualified permanently from becoming one of the *metochoi*. This sin is misthologically unpardonable.

If God Permits

If Heb 6:4-6 is describing those who similarly reached mature kingdom knowledge and then turned back, it would be just like the other warnings in Hebrews. Those who reject the kingdom message, once they fully understand it, are thereafter disqualified from becoming a kingdom ruler even if they subsequently try to become one. Those who object that God may renew them to repentance even if their fellow believers cannot renew them are missing the point. In Heb 6:1, the writer exhorts his readers to move on to maturity. He immediately goes on to stipulate that they can only do so *if God permits* (Heb 6:3). The plain fact of the matter is that God may not permit (Heb 4:3).

The writer of Hebrews already had stated repeatedly that God swore in His misthological wrath that many of His people would not enter this misthological rest even though they subsequently repented. The people could repent, but God would not. In Heb 6:4-6, a related case apparently occurs where God will not repent and, as a result, will not even allow the apostates to repent. Crawford draws upon the nature of all five warnings, the OT background, and the meaning of *epiginosko* to conclude:

> Those Israelites angered God so thoroughly He swore on His own name they would not enter the Promised Land. God made up His mind, and He would not repent....*They changed their mind—repented—but God did not. Therefore, they suffered defeat when they attempted to enter.* (Emphasis his.)[1549]

Barker likewise surmises that the rest is referring to the loss of reward and that because of their sin at Kadesh Barnea, "God would not let them enter the land *even when they desired to do so*" (emphasis his). He also observes that the expression, *if God permits*, indicates "the possibility that God will not permit some to go on to spiritual maturity."[1550] Lang concurs concerning the misthological impossibility.[1551] As already noted, Kendall's entire book, *Stone Deaf*, is written in defense of the thesis that believers can become irremediably stone deaf and thus incapable of repentance before death and consequently excluded permanently from the reward before they ever reach the grave, much less the Bema.[1552] Dillow expresses a similar outlook: "Those who have been hardened by sin (3:13) and who have unbelieving hearts which have turned away from God (3:12) are, like the exodus generation, apparently not permitted to go on."[1553] If this view of the phrase *if God permits* is correct, and the evidence certainly indicates that it is, then the misthological position concerning 2Pet 2:20 is even more ominous. Rejection of the doctrine of rewards pertaining to becoming one of the king's *metochoi* by those who clearly have understood what it entails may result in their inability to become one of the *metochoi* subsequently. Misthological apostasy may be irremediable. A straightforward deduction from the texts leads to this conclusion. Whether the individual may repent is open to debate, but the consensus of the above writers and this writer is that God will not repent.

Pastoral Concern

Ramifications of the application of Esau by the writer of Hebrews to this theme suggest that the typological implications may be more encompassing than many might suspect. For example, Moses, like those who sinned at Kadesh Barnea, was not allowed into the Promised Land either. Now certainly Moses will inherit the kingdom;

nevertheless, he typologically represents a group of people who will not do so. We must, at times, make a differentiation between personal and typological implications. On the other hand, Saul, like Esau, reached a point where his repentance failed to prevent him from losing the promised kingdom. Here we find personal and typological unification. Parabolically, the prodigal son also illustrates the fact that a believer may reach the point where his repentance is too late to salvage his inheritance.

Thankfully, for those like Esau and the prodigal son, who do respond positively even after such a repentance, positive blessings still are available even though the reward of the inheritance is lost. So from a pastoral perspective, repentance is always advisable, even on the part of those whose repentance might not qualify them for a full reward.* They may be assured that their repentance will have a positive impact. Equally important from a pastoral perspective, those who have come to a mature misthological knowledge must be warned that falling from such a position may have irreversible consequences. Repentance may not even be possible, and even in the cases where it is possible, the consequences may not be completely reversible. Even if God grants the individual repentance, He may not regard this penance a sufficient qualification for kingdom possession.

2Tim 3:8

It would also appear that *epignosis* in 2Tim 3:8 is knowledge in addition to and subsequent to being saved soteriologically. Those who "oppose the truth" in this passage are those who are "always learning and never able to come to the knowledge [*epignosis*] of the truth" (2Tim 3:7). Paul says that they must be rejected as presently useless regarding the faith: "And just as Jannes and Jambres opposed Moses, so these men also oppose the truth, men of depraved mind, *rejected* [*adokimos*] as regards the faith." But their situation may not yet be hopeless. Paul instructs Timothy how to deal with these opposing men: "With gentleness *correcting* [*paideuo*] those who are in opposition, if perhaps God may grant them repentance leading to the *knowledge* [*epignosis*] of the truth, and they may come to their senses and escape from the snare of the devil, having been held captive by him to do his will" (2Tim 2:25-26). *Paideuo* is not used of disciplining false believers. Consequently, those in opposition to the truth in 2Tim 2:25-26 are genuine believers who have not yet come to this *mature knowledge* (*epignosis*).

Dillow likewise states that those who need to repent in this passage are regenerate believers, and Litfin concurs that the passage is talking about "when brethren fall into false teaching they must be treated with gentleness and Christian love."[1554] He correctly cites 1Tim 3:7 and 6:9 from the broader context to show that this danger of falling into the devil's *snare* (*pagis*) is dealing with believers. Roy Aldrich's agreement has been noted already: The passage is dealing with believers who have fallen into the devil's snare. It is believers who need to *come to their senses*.

Actually, the NAS rendering, *come to their senses*, is a little weak. This is a translation of *ananepho* (*ana/again* + *nepho/sober*). But the verb actually means to be *sober **again***. For example, a little later in this same epistle, Paul tells Timothy to be *nepho/sober* (2Tim 4:5). The *ana/again* prefix is missing when Paul talks to Timothy because Paul is telling Timothy to stay sober. However, in 2Tim 2:26 Paul is instructing Timothy as to how to awaken fallen believers out of their theologically drunken stupor and return to theological soberness. Obviously, they could not return to a sober state, if they were not originally sober. As L-N (30.27) notes, *ananepho* should be translated, "to come back" to their senses. Timothy is to brew the black coffee of strong doctrine in 2Tim 2:24 in hopes that God will use this to sober up these theologically drunken believers. Naturally, these believers will have to co-operate with Timothy by drinking the doctrine he is teaching (2Tim 2:26).

Contextually, this passage refers to genuine believers, such as Hymenaeus and Philetus, who had gone astray from the truth (2Tim 2:17-18). They now need to be brought back to the truth. Paul had turned the theologically erring Hymenaeus "over to Satan" earlier, just like he did the morally erring brother in 1Cor 5:5, so that God could use Satan as His whip to *discipline* [*paideuo*] Hymenaeus (1Tim 1:20). God child-trains His children, not the devil's children. The fact that God (as the ultimate agent) uses Satan as an intermediate means of discipline does not mean that they are Satan's children. When a father takes a belt to his son's bottom, this does not mean that the belt becomes the son's father!

Another weakness in the NAS translation is the rendering of *held captive* for *zogreo*. Actually, the KJV and NKJ render it better as: *taken captive*. The picture is not of one born in captivity and who has been held in captivity all his or her life. The word means to *capture alive*. It is a combination of *zoos* (*alive*) and *agreuo* (*capture*). It is a picture of capturing something that is still alive yet once was free. In fact, the word for *snare* is that used of trapping animals. The animals they catch and put into cages for zoos are still alive and were once free before being captured. Correspondingly, the word is used of capturing animals alive. The only other time it is used in the NT is

---

* See *Pastoral Principle*, 835.

in Lk 5:10, where Jesus tells His disciples that He will make them fishers of men: catchers of men. The word was also used of capturing fish alive. Of course, in order to capture a fish alive, it has to be a live fish when you capture it. The imagery is not that of Satan finding some road kill, or swooping down on carrion, or finding a dead fish washed up on the beach. Rather, Satan finds those who are spiritually alive and who are not his captive and makes them his captive. He is not capturing those dead in their sins in this verse. Rather, he is capturing those alive in Christ. While Christ is fishing for the lost, Satan is fishing for the saved. These believers once were roaming free in Christ and now are in Satan's zoo.

Through the means of Timothy's teaching or the devil's affliction, Paul hopes that these erring believers will be delivered out of the devil's captivity into which they have fallen after becoming believers. Evidently, some misthological hope for these fallen believers still remained. God just might grant them repentance. This being the case, it could easily be postulated that those who are in opposition to the truth and who have not yet come to *epignosis* in 2Tim 3:7-8 are genuine believers. In chapter two, Paul is describing the obstinate believers in the *last days*, which would be the *last days* of the church age that began with Jesus' ministry (Heb 1:1-2). Hymenaeus was living in those *last days* and is an example of what can happen to believers in the last days. There is certainly no reason to exclude believers from what is being described in chapter three.

Paul tells us that the people in the church age will be morally corrupt. Such a description could be very well descriptive of those believers who are caught in Satan's snare. They proceed from "bad to worse" (2Tim 3:13), a description Peter applied to believers (2Pet 2:20). They always are learning and never able to come to this *mature knowledge* (*epignosis*) of the truth (2Tim 3:7). Such a fate would apply more readily to believers who have committed the sin of Kadesh Barnea, than to unbelievers who have not yet come to experience the saving knowledge of the gospel. Those believers who start off bad may come to a worse state in which it becomes impossible for them to ever come to an experiential knowledge of what it means to be one of God's kingdom rulers. Paul holds out hope that maybe some of these believers had not yet committed the sin of Kadesh Barnea but may regain their previous openness to the kingdom truth and become kingdom rulers—if they repent (2Tim 2:25-26). Even so, among these apostates would be those who have gone from bad to worse and become permanently disqualified for rulership. Consequently, those in 2Tim 3:7 (who are failing to come to this *epignosis* of the truth) presumably would be believers who, in their opposition to this kingdom *epignosis*, have become *adokimos* (2Tim 3:8). They may learn many wonderful theological truths, but they cannot bring themselves to accept the misthological truth of the kingdom. Wilkin's inclusion of *adokimos* in 2Tim 3:8 as referring to believers is very plausible indeed.

Rom 1:28

It might also be possible to take *adokimos* in Rom 1:28 as referring to believers. There are indications in the passage that lead one to at least consider Chitwood's position as plausible that this passage does in fact refer to believers who have committed apostasy from kingdom *epignosis* and become *adokimos* as a result. Chitwood's brief comments in defense of his position were basically that the book of Romans is not dealing with salvation from hell to the extent that is commonly thought and that the next chapter is dealing with rewards (e.g., Rom 2:6-7). The present author certainly can attest to the accuracy of those simple statements. However, it will take more than this to overturn the tide of traditional interpretation concerning Rom 1:28. Still, several things in the context make one pause for reflection.

First, before launching into his next section concerning rejection of *epignosis* in the introduction of his epistle, Paul makes his thematic statement: "But the righteous man shall live by faith" (Rom 1:17). However, the author of Hebrews went on to express this same statement more fully, "But My righteous one shall live by faith; and if he shrinks back, My soul has no pleasure in him. But we are not of those who shrink back to destruction, but of those who have faith to the preserving of the soul" (Heb 10:38-39). It is possible for the righteous man, that is, the justified believer to live by faith. Alternatively, it is just as possible for the justified believer to shrink back to destruction in unrighteous behavior and disbelief and suffer the misthological loss of his or her soul. This statement in verse 17, therefore, is certainly applicable to believers who are righteous in their behavior. Righteous believers are to live by faith. If believers want to live, then it will have to be through means of continuation in a living faith. Otherwise, they will be subject to a misthological forfeiture of their lives. In contrast to Arminians who use this verse to say that continuation in faith is soteriologically necessary, Marrowists may postulate a misthological necessity instead. Temporal death and misthological death are possible for the eternally secure believer.

Next, Paul goes on to add, "For the wrath of God is revealed from heaven against all ungodliness and unrighteousness of men, who suppress the truth in unrighteousness" (Rom 1:18). Could it be that this verse is describing just such an event described in Heb 10:38-39 where unrighteous believers shrink back from the truth and suppress it as a result? After all, believers can behave in a godless and unrighteous manner. Further, one most naturally would assume that those who suppress the truth in this verse are those who actually have it. In fact, the next verse informs us that they have the knowledge of God manifested in them. Not only did they have knowledge about God, Paul says in Rom 1:21 that "they *knew* [*ginosko*] God"! But how can a lost man know God? When Paul says in 1Cor 1:21 that the world through its wisdom did *know* (*ginosko*) God, this would seem to indicate that the lost do not know God. Many sermons are preached on the significance of the statement, "Adam knew Eve" (Gen 4:1). Where are the sermons about, "They knew God"? (Rom 1:21) The same Greek word for *know* is used in both verses—*ginosko*.

Oh, yes, we could launch into a traditional discussion of natural revelation giving the lost man a knowledge of God sufficient for his condemnation but insufficient for his justification apart from special revelation. In this case, Rom 1:19 might be rendered as simply saying that the revealed knowledge of God ascertainable through visible creation is within the unregenerate, and it is in this capacity that they know God. But should we be so quick to assume that those without eternal life actually know God when Jn 17:3 defines eternal life as knowing God? Knowing *about* God is one thing (Rom 1:19), but the text actually affirms that they knew God Himself (Rom 1:21). It just might be easier to explain Rom 1:21 as talking about believers who used to know God rather than to explain it away.

These believers became foolish in their thoughts about God (Rom 1:21). Their hearts became darkened, suggesting that there was a time when their hearts were not dark (1:21). They became fools (1:22). They "exchanged the truth of God for a lie" (1:25). Certainly, they would have to have the truth before they could exchange it for something else. Those being described in these verses appear to have gone from not being foolish to becoming foolish. A homily on the wise virgins who became foolish virgins would be tempting at this point. Or how about betrothed virgins who sold their bridal gowns for harlot's dresses?

Yet to stick with the text, when they rejected their *mature knowledge* (*epignosis*) of God, God rejected them and gave them over to their foolish sinful homosexual impulses. A play on words uses the verbal form of *adokimos* to describe their rejection of God in conjunction with the adjectival form of *adokimos* used to describe God's rejection of them. Sandwiched in-between these two occurrences of *adokimos* is the term *epignosis*, which one may suspect is a level of knowledge only attained by mature believers in the NT. If this is a misthological sandwich, then it has plenty of meat.

Perhaps one reason Paul is so adamant about believers not being unrighteous and committing homosexuality in 1Cor 6:9-10 is because he had seen what had happened to mature believers who had gone down that path in both his own day and in history. Perhaps what follows afterward in chapter one of Romans is Paul's detailed description of the moral filth that Peter described in 2Pet 2:22 as "mire." This conjecture is not so unreasonable since Peter affirms that the believer who rejects the mature message pertaining to the offer of the kingdom is liable to fall into just such mire once he sees the doctrine of rewards for what it truly is and then rejects it. The combination of past and present tenses in Rom 1:18-32, intertwined with the reference to an understanding that has existed "since the creation of the world" (Rom 1:20), allows one to formulate at least a tentative theory in defense of Wilkin's inclusion of Rom 1:28 as being a description of what happened to believers. Just as these believers did not see fit to retain God in a mature understanding any longer, God gave them over to misunderstanding and abuse.[1555]

The gospel of the kingdom, including its soteriological component (the gospel of grace), was known by Adam and Eve in its rudimentary form and passed on to their descendants; many of whom received imputational righteousness by faith in the coming Messiah and sought to live righteously in order that they might rule over the earth with the Messiah. Although Adam and Eve had forfeited rulership of the earth, they were aware, through the gospel of the kingdom, that such rulership could be reclaimed. But these believers failed to retain an interest in heavenly treasure and became more interested in temporal earthly pleasure. They stopped pursuing eternal rewards and were then given over to a *depraved* (*adokimos*) mind as a result of their misthological apostasy. Their morality quickly degenerated as the knowledge of both grace and the kingdom were suppressed. The human race became, by and large, composed of unbelieving descendants as a result of a failure of their depraved apostate parents to pass on the gospel. By the time of the flood, they were (at least for the most part) a race of unbelievers. Noah and his family were an exception, and God started all over again with them.

Men such as Noah, Abraham, and Moses were saved by grace and motivated by the gospel of the kingdom pertaining to future rewards (Heb 11). Still, throughout human history, whenever men have come to know God and subsequently have rejected His offer of the kingdom, God has redrawn that offer just like He did with the children of Israel during the ministry of Moses and Jesus. Nevertheless, as in Acts 14:16-17, God has not left Himself without witness in that creation still has testified to the existence of a Creator. Throughout history, and in Paul's day and these last days, God repeatedly has offered this misthological rulership time and time again to succeeding generations. But once a person comes to a mature knowledge of that kingdom and then walks away from it, he or she may never be able to return to the place of being able to inherit the kingdom. Believers may sink in the miry quagmire of moral degradation or wander in the wilderness of defeat or tearfully plead to be blessed with the fullness of the inheritance that otherwise could have been theirs, but it may have become too late for them completely to undo the damage they have done. If so, Rom 1:28 would be applicable to believers.

Conclusion

As attractive as the above synopsis may be in offering a misthological alternative, this misthological interpretation of Rom 1:28 has not been adopted herein at the present time, so my conclusion concerning *adokimos* is not dependent on this text for its formation. The overall typological and exegetical deductions from a variety of passages are clear, however. Believers can become *adokimos* and thereby fail to win the kingdom as a prize. Be careful what you do with the doctrine of rewards. Failure to deal with it truthfully might land one in the temporal mire and the misthological darkness. The outer darkness may loom ahead for those believers who clearly understand the misthological nature of this darkness and yet reject it.

Appendix 15.
Upward Call

Introduction

The *upward call* (*ano klesis*) in Phil 3:14 is subject to a wide variety of interpretations. Understandably, partial rapturists take it to be a reference to the rapture. Yet, full rapturists rightly reject the partial rapture interpretation because the rapture is not earned but unconditionally promised to all believers. Even so, some full rapturists, such as Constable, still believe that the out-resurrection refers to the rapture but the upward calling does not. The grammatical basis that would make such a distinction possible surfaces in other interpretations as well.

For example, Wilkin abandoned the reward view of out-resurrection while retaining the reward view of the prize of the upward call. To be sure, for those who equate the out-resurrection with the upward call, such a distinction would seem highly strained, if not simply artificial or inconsistent. Even though the present book is inclined to equate the out-resurrection with the upward call (as a reasonable proximity as to what Paul is saying), simply accusing Constable or Wilkin of logical inconsistency on this basis would be premature. A distinction between the call and the resurrection is grammatically possible. Pursuant to yet another interpretation of the upward call, deSilva adds this grammatical clarification:

> Collange has suggested that this imagery comes from the Panhellenic games, where the victor ascends at the summons of the judge to receive the prize. More recently, O'Brien has argued that κλῆσις is to be understood in the usual Pauline sense as "God's act of calling to salvation" in Christ. The genitive is then read as subjective, meaning the prize which belongs to or is announced by God's heavenward call.[1556]

This clarification regarding the type of genitive being used in Phil 3:14 allows one (grammatically at least) to reconcile distinctions being posed by Wilkin and Constable. Their interpretations would fail without such a distinction in interpreting the genitive as a substantive. Although their views of the out-resurrection are mutually exclusive (Wilkin thinking that the out-resurrection is spiritual resurrection, and Constable regarding it as a physical resurrection via the rapture), their interpretation of the upward call necessitates a substantive genitive since they correctly understand the prize to be an eschatological reward and therefore not equatable with their particular views of the out-resurrection. My overall misthological interpretation, on the other hand, is not dependent upon whether a distinction is made between the prize and upward call in that the out-resurrection is regarded as a reward herein. Still, thoroughness requires a further demonstration of the superior probability of a misthological interpretation by interacting with these considerations.

Subjective Genitive

To begin with, backing up to Phil 3:9, Paul's probable use of a subjective genitive regarding *faith of Christ* in that verse provides a springboard by which to consider the possibility of a subjective genitive in Phil 3:14 as well. The attractiveness of Eaton's argument for subjective genitive on that earlier occasion has been implemented in the present work with the understanding that believers in Christ are saved by the faith which Christ Himself exercises.[1557] In other words, Phil 3:9 could be understood as affirming that our soteriological righteousness is through the faith of Christ being given to us because of our faith in Christ. Believers get Christ's faith and faithfulness imputed to them when they come to faith in Christ.

- Faith *in* Christ (objective genitive)
- Faith/faithfulness *of* Christ (subjective genitive).[*]

In this connection, deSilva likewise mentions regarding this earlier verse: "The basis for the righteousness which Paul desires, therefore, is Christ's own faithfulness to God with respect to securing the promises given to Abraham for all who believe."[1558] Although my openness to the use of a subjective genitive in v. 9 causes me to give pause to the possibility of such usage in v. 14, my misthological interpretation of the out-resurrection or the

---

[*] For survey, see GGBB, 113-116.

upward call is not dependent on a distinction regarding the type of genitive in either verse. As to Constable's proposal, however, he could equate the rapture with the out-resurrection and the out-resurrection with the upward call and yet differentiate the prize as being a reward merely experienced at the rapture rather than the rapture itself by appealing to a subjective use of the genitive.

- The logic of Constable's approach would go something like this:

  Rapture = out-resurrection = upward call ≠ prize

- Wilkin's distinction might run something along the following lines:

  Spiritual resurrection = out-resurrection = upward call ≠ prize

- A soteriological understanding of the resurrection and call could argue for a misthological prize:

  Resurrection of believers = out-resurrection = upward call ≠ prize

Preliminary Views of the Call

Call ≠ Prize

Posing a distinction between the prize and the call in v. 14 is not uncommon in the commentary tradition: "Paul does not say that he is pressing on for the call of God but rather for the prize of that call" (NIBC, 1554). A popular soteriological/misthological distinction is to regard the call as the past soteriological call that Paul experienced at conversion and to assert that Paul is not pressing on for that past call but for the future prize associated with that call (cp. NIC, TNTC).

Call = Soteriological Prize

Conversely, those preferring to understand the call soterically and assuming that the prize is correspondingly soteriological (e.g. EBC) show a complete insensitivity to the potential subjective distinction and to the provable differentiation between a gift and a reward. Heaven is not the prize we are trying to earn! Even if one insists on making this *heavenly call* in Phil 3:14 conceptually synonymous with the *heavenly calling* in Heb 3:1, it still remains to be demonstrated that the prize is the calling. For that matter, it is by no means apparent that the *heavenly calling* in Heb 3:1 is a call to heaven. I would argue that it is a **misthological** calling to which believers already are invited that deals with obtaining heavenly rulership rather than entrance into heaven.* More exactly, as Tanner perceives correctly, a **misthopological** call to "participation in the New Jerusalem" is at stake (GNTC). In appealing to texts such as Eph 4:1 and 2Thess 1:11, as demonstrating that the call Paul has in mind must be an effective soteriological call, EBC completely overlooks the more probable likelihood of a misthological call in such texts. Regardless, even if one were to argue for a soteriological call in Phil 3:14, one still could argue for a misthological prize in distinction to the call (so NIBC above).

Call = Soteriological Christlikeness

A related soteriological misperception of the calling in Phil 3:14 is to equate it with simple participation in eschatological Christlikeness. Pyne, for example, interprets the call as an effective call to soteriological participation in eschatological glorification: "To fulfill one's calling is not simply to come to faith; it is to fulfill God's divine purpose in salvation. Ultimately that means becoming fully conformed to the image of Christ through glorification (Rom 8:30; 2 Cor 3:18)."[1559] I object. The *unconditional* promise in such verses as these (in which all believers will obtain soteriological glorification and transformation as children of God, cp. 1Jn 3:2) cannot provide the motivation for the *conditional* transformation that Paul is striving to obtain in Phil 3:14. Like Pyne, Holloman's misconstruing unconditional glorification with conditional glorification rings hollow:

I press on toward the goal for the prize of the upward call of God in Christ Jesus" (Phil. 3:13–14).
From the context of this passage and from other Pauline passages, it is evident that Paul pursues

---

* See *Misthological Call*, 299.

Christlikeness as the goal of his present Christian growth (1 Cor. 11:1; Phil. 3:10–14 cf. 2 Cor. 3:18), even though he will not attain ultimate or eschatological Christlikeness until Christ's coming (Phil. 3:11, 20–21 cf. Rom. 8:29).[1560]

No. Paul is not pursuing an eschatological Christlikeness that is assured unconditionally to him as a free gift. One does not strive to earn a gift! Soteriological participation in eschatological Christlikeness through simple glorification is a gift to be received, not a prize to be won. All believers will share freely in this basic degree of Christlikeness as children of God.

Call = Misthological Christlikeness

On the other hand, if a misthologist were to interpret Paul's intent to be regarding the possibility of eschatological Christlikeness, due consideration could be given to the possibility of misthological Christlikeness. Believers have to live like Christ to rule like Christ. Being like Christ in terms of rulership requires that believers behave like Christ in terms of performance. Temporal Christlikeness is the means to misthological Christlikeness. Co-rulership with Christ and co-glorification with Christ would be within the realm of misthological possibilities for the prize to be won. Despite my rejection of Wilkin's proposal that spiritual transformation into temporal Christlikeness is what Paul intends in the term out-resurrection in v. 11, I nevertheless appreciate the fact that Wilkin does not misconstrue this likeness into soteriological Christlikeness as a prize in v. 14. Acknowledging the possibility of a subjective genitive allows one to appreciate the proposals advanced by Wilkin, Constable, and NIBC as grammatically valid FG options.

- Nevertheless, my preferred interpretation of v. 14 is a subjective genitive:

misthological resurrection = out-resurrection = upward call ≠ prize

My primary preference is to adopt the subjective genitive and understand the prize as being something received at the time of the call rather than the call itself. Kent (EBC, 143) cites Blaiklock as taking this interpretation: "The 'upward calling' could then refer to the summons to the winner to approach the elevated stand of the judge and receive his prize." The upward call is the Bema call to come up and take your prize if you are a winner. Collange's agreement with this assessment has been noted already. Constable cites Hawthorne in mutual agreement. The imagery most likely intended by Paul is that of a winner being called up to the award's podium to receive his prize. Both the call and prize would be a misthological benefit, albeit distinguishable from one another.

- Alternately, one might simply regard it as an epexegetical genitive:

misthological resurrection = out-resurrection = upward call = prize

In this case, the prize is the upward call of the out-resurrection. As previously discussed, the imagery of the text would accommodate a reference to misthological inheritance as well as to the winner's purse. The prize purse would include the inheritance of the kingdom as a kingdom ruler. Regardless as to which of these routes are chosen, the bottom line still remains the same. Paul is pressing on for the *reward of the kingdom*. Whether that kingdom is the reward (epexegetical) or the reward is a misthological benefit in the kingdom (subjective) makes no difference as to the overall picture. Even so, a picture is composed of details, and the following flowchart factors those details into consideration in deriving the big picture.

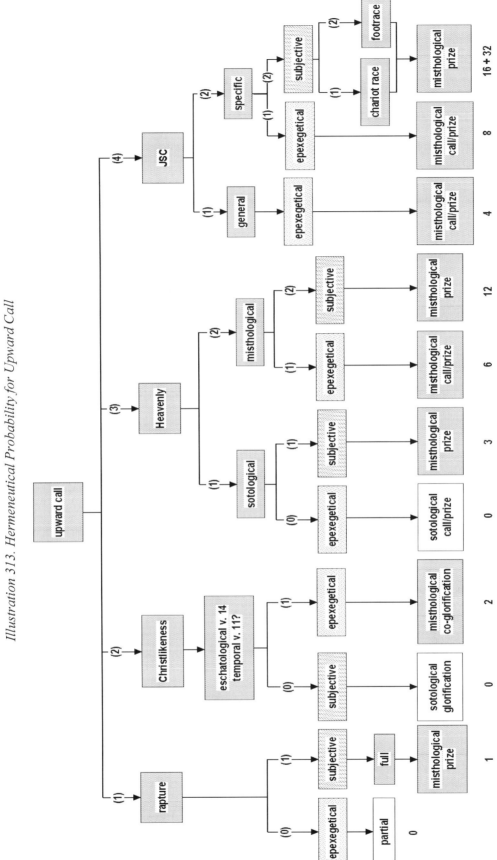

Illustration 313. Hermeneutical Probability for Upward Call

Primary Views of the Call

Rapture

To restate my assessment in terms of the chart, the major interpretations for upward call in terms of increasing probability are: (1) rapture, (2) Christlikeness, (3) heavenly calling, or (4) JSC. These interpretations have been ranked as such on the main trunks of the chart with four being the highest value on this corresponding scale. The rapture is presented first as being least likely.

Partial Rapture

As to the rapture options, if out-resurrection is a reference to the rapture and one interprets the upward call as also being another veiled reference to the rapture, then one is left with a choice as to how to take the genitive. If this genitive is epexegetical, then it would be translated as *that is*. Paul is striving to obtain the prize, *that is*, the upward call of the rapture. The rapture is the reward that Paul is striving to obtain, which logically results in a partial rapture interpretation.[*]

Full Rapture

On the other hand, under this option if it were a subjective genitive, then Paul is not talking about the prize which is the rapture but the rapture's prize—the prize received at the time of the rapture. In this case, Paul would be referring to the misthological prize that faithful believers will receive at the time of the rapture. The full rapture is to be distinguished from the partial prize. All believers will be raptured, but only some believers will obtain the Bema prize after the rapture. Such an interpretation is intelligible, so Constable's preference for this type of approach is not completely reprehensible. Nevertheless, the flow of the context is such that if one traces what Paul is *pressing on for* in v. 14 to what he is trying to *lay hold of* in v. 13 to what he is *pressing on for* and trying to *lay hold of* and *obtain* in v. 12, one finds that it is the *out-resurrection* of v. 11. Such continuity would disincline one to adopt an interpretation that relies so much on a sharp discontinuity between the obvious meritorious nature of the prize and the alleged non-meritorious nature of the calling to obtain that prize. The continuity flowing through the context, as well as the continuity between the nature of the calling and the prize, most strongly suggests that the calling itself participates in the misthological nature of the prize. If the out-resurrection itself is a reward, as I have argued, then this subjective rapture alternative collapses, since it is acknowledged by Constable that the rapture is not a reward.[†]

Christlikeness

Soteriological Interpretations for Call

Two routes for deriving a soteriological interpretation of the prize are provided in the chart, both of which are marked with zero probability because heaven is not a reward. The first route by which to derive a soteriological understanding is to treat the genitive as a subjective.[‡] The prize for which Paul is painfully laboring is eschatological glorification with Christ as a result of Christlikeness. Or one might conversely state this position, as Pyne does, by making this soteriological Christlikeness the result of glorification with Christ. In any event, this interpretation pictures Paul as pressing on so that he may reach heaven's glory. Reaching heaven is a result of perseverance. In this theological perspective, heaven is not a gift given in response to simple faith. Thus, this interpretation is rejected summarily in the chart.

The second route by which to try to make heaven a result of perseverance is simply to consider the upward call a heavenly calling—a calling to heaven.[§] With an epexegetical genitive, one may simply regard heaven as the

---

[*] Because this possibility of a partial rapture has been found to be an impossibility in my discussion, it has been marked with zero probability in the chart. To derive the total probability for any of the routes being traced in this chart, simply take the values leading to the respective conclusions and multiply those values together. Rapture only had a ranking of one to start with (since it was the least probable for the four major interpretations), and the epexegetical branch leading to the partial rapture position has been given zero probability since $1 \times 0 = 0$. The epexegetical rapture position is assigned zero as the value for its final product.

[†] As to our computation for the subjective rapture position, since the epexegetical branch for the rapture position was marked with a zero, the alternative subjective branch was only incremented one unit higher (i.e., with a 1). The multiplicative total for the subjective rapture position is thus: $1 \times 1 = 1$.

[‡] See *Christlikeness* branch.

[§] See *Heavenly* branch.

prize for which Paul is persevering. O'Brien, as deSilva noted, prefers to label it a subjective genitive which makes salvation in heaven the prize. Basically, the heavenly calling is distinguished from heaven itself. Still, the bottom line remains the same: Heaven is a reward for perseverance. So regardless of the subjective or epexegetical path chosen by those taking these soteriological routes, these interpretations are rated with zero probability since they make heaven a reward rather than a free gift. Soteric righteousness in this context is based on simple faith (Phil 3:9), not on perseverance. Thus, making the prize a soteric benefit does an injustice to the context.

Misthological Christlikeness

Admittedly, the context does include the temporal pursuit of Christlikeness. This point was conceded to Wilkin in the discussion of Phil 3:10. What was not conceded, however, was taking the out-resurrection in Phil 3:11 as being equatable with the temporal Christlikeness. The *resurrection* (*anastasis*) in both verses refers to a physical resurrection. Paul is not announcing that he wants to know Christ's spiritual resurrection in v. 10. Christ's resurrection was indeed a physical resurrection, as Paul himself insists in other contexts. Correspondingly, he should be understood as affirming the same perspective in this context. What Paul wants to experience in the here-and-now is the *power* of that resurrection. The reason he wants to do so is in order to obtain the physical out-resurrection in the eschatological future. Nevertheless, laying aside my insistence on this distinctive for the sake of expounding the possibilities outlined in the chart, those who (mistakenly) equate the out-resurrection with experiencing the power of Christ's resurrection in the here-and-now could argue that this temporal out-resurrection in v. 11 makes it possible to receive the misthological prize of co-glorification with Christ at the time of the eschatological transformation into Christlikeness in v. 14. The genitive would be understood most readily as epexegetical in this approach so that the prize would be distinguished from the timing of the event at which the prize is bestowed. In short, I do not have a theological objection to such a view since it would understand Paul as affirming that as a result of pursuing temporal Christlikeness, he will be rewarded with rulership of the kingdom when he experiences his eschatological transformation into Christlikeness. We need glorified bodies (which all believers will be given freely) as a prerequisite for exercising heavenly rulership (which only faithful believers will be rewarded meritoriously). Such an assessment is theologically accurate, but it is exegetically doubtful that this is all that Paul is revealing with this rich imagery. This approach is theologically possible but exegetically strained and only rated with a 2.

Heavenly Call

Soteriological Call

Taking the upward call simply as heavenly calling has been dismissed already as a possibility[*] when the prize is epexegetically equated with reaching heaven since heaven is a gift, not a reward. Still, several translations render the expression as *heavenly call*, and one could indeed take this route and regard it as a subjective genitive so that prize is a reward that one receives in heaven rather than heaven itself. Accordingly, what Paul is pressing on for is a reward in heaven rather than for heaven itself. The heavenly calling is soteriological, but the prize is misthological and experienced at the time one reaches heaven. This misthological interpretation has been ranked with a 3.

Misthological Call

Alternatively, the calling itself could be misthological. This misthological branch has been ranked with a 2 on the chart to represent it as being more probable than its soteriological counterpart (whose branch was ranked with a 1). Two valid options are then available. One could take it as epexegetical genitive and simply equate the prize with the calling (this branch is ranked with a 1). The misthological prize is the upward call and thus the out-resurrection. This simple interpretation is attractive, particularly in association of other passages which deal with a misthological call as our goal. The realization of this misthological call is the prize. The final product for this branch results in a ranking of 6.[†]

---

[*] See *Call = Soteriological Prize*, 880; *Soteriological Interpretations for Call*, 883.

[†] The ranking for this branch jumps to 6 because I am simply incrementing the values by one and then multiplying the results. Had I truly been weighting my preferences, I would have assigned higher values to these latter branches. Nevertheless, for the sake of consistency and objectivity, I have been content simply to increment the values by one. Even so, since I am moving up the scale to interpretations which are more valid and to branches that are paired with other valid branches, the values jump multiplicatively, which does provide at least some objective means by which to picture my subjective impression of the relative probability.

The other option under this hierarchy would be to take it as subjective genitive. Because this option is even more probable (in the case of this route), this branch is ranked with a 2. This value results in a final score of 12 since I am multiplying the values of its constitutive branches (3 x 2 x 2 = 12). Like its counterpart, this interpretation acknowledges that the call is a reward, but it regards the prize to be a distinguishable, yet related, reward that is experienced at the time that the misthological call is realized. One reason for giving preference to the subjective genitive is because of the attraction to that conclusion being exerted by the JSC to be considered next. These interpretations are not (necessarily) mutually exclusive in their gravitation toward a shared perspective of the nature of the call.

JSC

General

Last and most importantly, the JSC (Judgment Seat of Christ) is charted as the most probable event in Paul's mind. Some interpreters leave the matter there so that Paul is understood simply as declaring that he is pressing on for a misthological call/prize at the Bema. This generic epexegetical affirmation is ranked with a 4.

Specific

Realistically, however, the imagery of the passage is too rich to think that Paul only intends some ambiguous reference to the JSC. A dual reference to the inheritance motif and athletic imagery is much more likely in view. If the *inheritance* is included, then it would be epexegetical. Paul is pursuing the prize of the inheritance. This possibility is ranked with an 8. Even if the inheritance is in view (and it probably is), it is not exclusively in view. Paul certainly has some form of the Olympian Games in mind (even though he is quite possibly also alluding to the inheritance as well). Commentators differ as to whether the form of the contest might be a chariot race or a footrace, the latter being the more prevalent and probable suggestion. In any case, the prize that Paul is pursing is specifically the Bema prize that the successful athlete receives when he is called up on the awards podium (the Bema) to receive his prize purse as a result of winning the *race*. Of course, being called up on the podium to receive the prize would be a part of that misthological experience and thus would be a reward in its own right. Nevertheless, the calling was disguisable from the prize itself.[*]

Illustration 314. The Race-Inheritance Call

---

[*] A subjective genitive would distinguish (not disassociate) the two in this case. By multiplying the value of the branches together, the chariot race receives a score of 16 and the footrace a score of 32. In order to derive the total score for this athletic event being interpreted as what is in the forefront of Paul's mind, these values would have to be added together to yield a total of 48 for the race motif in contrast to the 8 for the inheritance perspective. Nevertheless, both these and the 4 for the general perspective give a combined weight of 60 for the JSC. This overall perspective wins hands down

In the above young-woman-old-lady illustration, the race motif is pictured as being most attractive, yet the inheritance perspective is just as salient. Both are present. All in all, a number of strong contenders for the misthological crown lend their collective weight to yield an impressive misthological composite and to reject soteriological abuses of the text. A *partial heaven* theory in which only some believers earn heaven is ruled out. Nor is there any warrant for affirming a *partial rapture* theory in which only some believers earn the rapture. Trying to reduce this passage into making either heaven or the rapture a reward is inexcusable when so many rich alternatives are available. Both soteric interpretations of the call were found to end in zero probability and thus impossible. Eight misthological interpretations are possible. A combined misthological perspective is most reasonable, in which the call pertains to the race and inheritance.

Conclusion

What is partial is the misthological experience which Paul is seeking to win. The upward call is misthological. Only faithful believers will experience it. This misthological call probably includes a reference to the misthological heritance. At the same time, it definitely refers to a call to go up on the awards podium and receive one's prize/reward for successfully having completed and won the contest. Consequently, this call simultaneously results in a prize that would include misthological co-glorification with Christ as a result of being granted misthological Christlikeness in terms of regal rulership at the resurrection. Only those believers who successfully compete according to the rules will rule with Christ.

Appendix 16.
Fulfilling the Law and the Prophets

Introduction

Discussions regarding initial and final justification naturally pivot on the type of righteousness necessary for final justification. Does mere imputational righteousness qualify one for entrance into heaven? Or does justification start off as being based on imputational righteousness and then finally require imparted righteousness to enter heaven? Understandably, the unique combination of righteousness with entrance into heaven on the lips of Jesus in Mt 5:20 must be given critical attention in answering such questions: "For I say to you, that unless your *righteousness* surpasses that of the scribes and Pharisees, you shall not *enter the kingdom of heaven*" (Mt 5:20). As with any passage, context is king. This context is the hinge between the Old and New Testaments and swings open to the entrance of heaven. Analyzing the relationship between the OT and NT, starting with the beginning of the paragraph in which verse 19 is embedded, will be necessary to grasp this context.

OT is still Applicable

"Do not think that I came to abolish the Law or the Prophets; I did not come to abolish, but to fulfill. For truly I say to you, **until heaven and earth pass away**, not the smallest letter or stroke shall pass away from the Law, **until all is accomplished**" (Mt 5:17-18).

Blomberg, Wilkins, and Hayes (among others) acknowledge that the OT is still normative, relevant, and valid as an expression of God's will for believers today. For that matter, Paul himself clearly indicates that this is the case: "All Scripture [OT too] is inspired by God and profitable for teaching for reproof, for correction for training in righteousness [even today]" (2Tim 3:16). Paul's NT affirmation applies to the entire OT: both its fulfilled and unfilled portions. These commentators wisely caution against avoiding two extremes: (1) One should not think that *none* of the OT applies unless explicitly *affirmed* in the NT, (2) nor should one conclude that *all* the OT applies unless *revoked* in the NT. So how does one achieve a balance between these two extremes?

Principlism

Expressed another way, how is the OT law applicable today? A solution is available in affirming that the principles of the law are still in effect. Martin states: "The **principle** underlying the moral laws of God is indeed eternal."[1561] Geisler and Rhodes concur that since the moral **principles** reflect the nature of an unchanging God, they are still binding, but we are not under the moral law.[1562] The moral principles are binding; the moral law is not. Wilkins uses the atonement as an example: The OT commandment to offer atoning sacrifices "is no longer legally binding as a practice. Nevertheless, the Old Testament **principle** of penalty and payment for sin remains valid."[1563] "**Principles** of the law are valid guidelines."[1564] The practice has been modified, but the underlying principle still applies. The application of underlying principles is called *principlism*. But how does principlism work in practice?

Unity of the OT Law

The *Westminster Confession of Faith* (WCF) breaks the law up into three parts (moral, legal, ceremonial) in order to claim that the moral parts are still binding for the NT believer today. Martin and Hayes (along with many others) demonstrate the unity of the law and thereby nullify such attempts to make certain parts of the law directly applicable today by means of such artificial distinctions. Surely Jesus fulfilled both the moral and ceremonial parts of the law. Jesus is not distinguishing between various parts of the law in this passage. Morris concurs that there is "no distinction between the ceremonial and moral law here."[1565] Of course, dispensationalists are known for insisting that the OT law is a unity and that NT believers are not under any part of the law. Since it is a unity, if believers are not under part of it, they are not under any of it. Schmidtbleicher suggests that the OT and NT laws are dispensational expressions of the *eternal law of God* under which humanity has lived from the beginning of time. In the chart below, I have adapted his chart and approach.

Illustration 315. Eternal Law

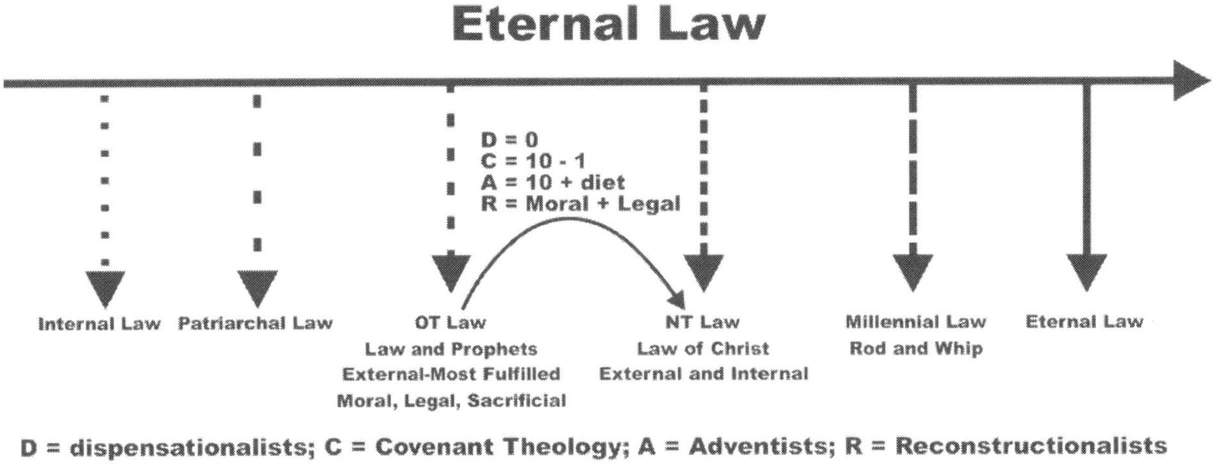

Eternal Law

D = dispensationalists; C = Covenant Theology; A = Adventists; R = Reconstructionalists

Paul tells us that the law has been written in hearts of those who do not have the written law (Rom 2:14). He also adds, "Where there is no law, neither is there violation" (Rom 4:15). Are we to conclude, then, that when Cain killed Able, Cain was not violating God's law just because God had not spelled it out for him: "Thou shalt not murder"? No! Cain was violating the moral law that God already had written in his heart. Even before that violation, Abel respected the Lord's sacrificial law, and the Lord respected him for doing so (Gen 4:4). Both the violation and respect of God's law was going on long before the Ten Commandments.

As to the continuity between the OT and NT expressions of this eternal law, dispensationalists are criticized for saying that NT believers are not under any of the OT law. Ultra-dispensationalists even go so far as to claim that the four NT Gospels do not apply to church age believers because the church did not come into existence until after the time period covered by the Gospels. These ultra-dispensationalists lump the NT Gospels with the OT. (Some would even lump the non-Pauline NT epistles in this list of non-applicable NT writings.) The Gospels refute such ultra-dispensationalistic handling of their pages, however. John, writing after the NT church already had been established, tells unbelievers that they can find eternal life by reading the words of Jesus contained within his Gospel (Jn 20:30-31). A verse like Jn 3:16 still applies directly today! Matthew, writing to NT believers, tells them that the way to make disciples is by teaching them to obey the words of Jesus contained within his Gospel. NT believers today are to obey all that Jesus commanded His disciples during His earthy ministry as recorded in the Gospels (Mt 28:19-2).

Going in the opposite direction, Covenant theology adopts the Reformed statement, as expressed in WCF, and brings over the Ten Commandments (minus the fourth one regarding Sabbath worship) to the NT period and places Christians under this part of the Mosaic law, despite the NT insistence that NT believers are not under the OT law. Adventists err even more by bringing over all Ten Commandments plus the dietary regulations, despite the fact that Jesus simultaneously nullified both their dietary error and ultra-dispensationalism in Mk 7:19 when "He declared all foods clean." There is no way an ultra-dispensationalist can make that part of the OT! Neither can the OT dietary regulations be brought over by Adventists from the OT and be made directly applicable today when they have to pole vault over such a statement to do so. In an even greater blunder, Reconstructionists bring over all the moral and legal laws. The Sermon on the Mount stands at the intersection of these colliding approaches. By paying attention to how the Lord handles the past, present, and future, collisions may be avoided, however.

Until heaven and earth pass away

Will Jesus throw away the OT when He returns? Some seem to think so. Admittedly, Jesus does say that *not the smallest letter or stroke shall pass away from the Law **until** heaven and earth pass away*. Still, heaven and earth will not pass away when He returns. So the OT will continue at least *until* then. Morris understands Jesus' statement to mean that Scripture will not pass away even though the physical universe will pass away. Similarly, France believes that Scripture will endure because the phrase is idiomatic for enduring forever. In any event, the proper interpretation is that the Scripture will abide forever (Ps 119:89; Is 40:8; 1Pet 1:25). The best explanation is that the principles of the eternal law as expressed in the Scripture will never pass away.

Until all is accomplished

How did Jesus fulfill the law in such a manner that it is still operative at least until He returns and evidently throughout eternity? There are three primary options:

Option 1. Jesus personally fills *up*, performs, carries out, completes by meeting the OT **demands**. The text may mean more than simple completion by Jesus' action, but it cannot mean less since even its smallest detail has eternal validity.

Option 2. Jesus fills *out* the full **meaning** of the OT by showing forth and bringing out its true meaning. MacArthur acknowledges, "There is a sense in which Jesus did that...But that cannot be the primary meaning of **fulfill**, because that is not what the word means. It does not mean *fill out* but *fill up*" (bold his).[1566] Regardless, this full meaning had to await Jesus' death and resurrection and the sending of the Spirit, so this fulfilling extends beyond Jesus' earthly ministry.

Option 3. Jesus brings the OT to its completion. Jesus brings the OT to its intended goal, bringing its complete **meaning** to fruition. With this approach, Blomberg effectively incorporates option two into option three, observing that the need for sacrifices already has been "brought to complete fruition," but "in other instances certain requirements of the law [such as loving God and others] endure until Christ's coming again."[1567] Superficially, Blomberg's statement might be taken to make the present day *application* of the law contingent upon whether or not it has been fulfilled. However, this would be a misunderstanding of Blomberg's intent since he states in the preceding paragraph that all the OT remains normative today. As an advocate of *principlism*,[1568] Blomberg probably should be understood as affirming that the unfilled proportions of the OT await direct application, but the fulfilled portions may only be made normative through indirect application. After all, unfilled prophesies still await literal fulfillment and therefore have direct application to a future age. Some dispensationalists even believe that OT sacrifices will be reinstated as memorials during the millennium. So I would qualify Blomberg's position by adding that those portions of the OT which still await fulfillment will have direct application in the day and age in which they are fulfilled. Even so, this direct application does not entail placing those in the future directly under the OT law.[*]

Blomberg seems to err, though, when he indicates that the application of the law will only endure until Christ comes again. For one thing, as already indicated, the physical universe does not pass away when the Lord returns at the beginning of the millennium. The application of the law would have to extend at least until the end of the millennium. The fulfilling of the Prophets certainly would include the literal fulfillment of unfilled prophesies during the millennial age. Moreover, Mt 5:22 (which is the first application that Jesus makes of what He is teaching in 5:17-18) finds its culmination in Jesus' millennial administration. Since Scripture affirms its own perpetuity, and since Jesus affirms Scripture, we may affirm the perpetuity of Scripture by Jesus' authority.

Whereas Blomberg combined the third option with the second one, France combines the third option with the first one (via v. 17):

> It is, then, Jesus' 'fulfillment' of the Old Testament which is in view here. The law remains valid until it reaches its intended culmination; this it is now doing in the ministry of Jesus. This verse does not state, therefore, as it is sometimes interpreted, that every regulation in the Old Testament law remains binding after the coming of Jesus. The law is unalterable, but that does not justify its **application** beyond the purpose for which it was intended."[1569]

France is correct to stress that Jesus is the one doing the fulfilling; however, in accordance with principlism, direct application of the OT is intended until its fulfillment. Subsequently, indirect application is still intended. All in all, option three is preferable and should entail options one and two. These options are not mutually exclusive.

Principlism

Principlism is the approach adopted herein to explain the means by which the OT principles are still applicable today. In this approach, one determines if the OT statement still has direct application by means of a consistent hermeneutic which simply asks, "Has the OT proposition been fulfilled?" If not, it still has direct application in the time period in which it is to be fulfilled. If it does not have direct application to the current time period, then indirect application is sought. The application of the moral principles may vary from one dispensation

---

[*] See *Then-Now-Then*, 891.

to another, but the underlying principles are still valid. All Scripture, even the fulfilled parts, are still useful for instruction when one discovers and applies the underlying principles (cp. 1Cor 9:9-10; 2Tim 3:16-17).

Kuhatschek suggests a three-step, pyramidal approach.[1570] For sake of simplicity, this approach will be adopted as a working model. As the level increases vertically upward, the level of the application becomes more general so that our love for God and love for others are the two capstone principles. As one proceeds vertically down to the base of the pyramid, the applications become more specific and numerous. Yet as will be explained subsequently, direct application of a principle as stated in the OT to the NT era does not mean that people in the NT era are under the OT law.

Illustration 316. General Versus Specific Application

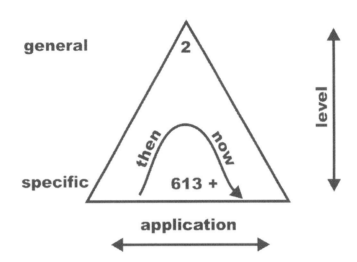

1. **Direct application**: Determine *what* the intended application was in the original situation at the ground level application. Ask yourself: "Is the OT application repeated in the NT as being applicable today?" If so, then you can apply it directly to your current situation today. If the OT application is not repeated or if it is revoked, then proceed through the pyramid to discover its indirect application for today.[1571]

2. **Underlying principle**: If direct application is not applicable, then move up the pyramid to seek the underlying principle from the ground level (original application) by discerning the broader principles at the higher levels. Asking *why* the original application was made will help you move up the scale to broader principles to discover key elements by considering the reason for the original application.

3. **Derivate application**: After finding the underlying principle, move back down the pyramid to make a specific application for today by asking *how* this principle can be applied to your specific situation. Use the same key elements from the original application as in the indirect application. In comparing key elements, avoid confusing these elements with variables.

Adventists

As an example in distinguishing key elements from variables, Kuhatschek notes that Paul objects that the Colossians were wrong in observing special days (Gal 4:10). Yet Paul allows the Christians in Rome to do so (Rom 14:5-6). Why? Because the Galatians were doing so as a means to *retain* justification (Gal 5:4).[1572] Consequently, Adventists are wrong in observing the Sabbath because they do so for the wrong reason.[1573] Adventists not only mistakenly believe that only parts of the law have been abolished,[1574] far worse, **they believe that obeying the moral law is necessary to *retain* salvation**. Adventists wrongly believe that they successfully have avoided being charged with trying to merit salvation since (according to Martin) they affirm that salvation *gained* by grace is *retained* by works.[1575]

Even so, the Adventists are no worse than many Arminians (such as Guy Duty) who uses a similar argument for *gaining* versus *retaining* salvation. Picirilli, also an Arminian, correctly notes that such an argument does not avoid meritorious legalism: **We cannot keep our salvation by works without conditioning our salvation on works.** Even more surprisingly to some perhaps, if Martin is correct, then Adventists are better than MacArthur, since MacArthur makes works necessary for both gaining and retaining salvation.[1576] Blomberg, a Baptist, considers heaven a reward! So my criticism herein of Adventists is not based on a bias against them just because they are cultists. To the contrary, this Adventist gain-by-grace-retain-by-works soteriology is better than that of many mainline Reformers and is no worse than that of many Arminians. This acknowledgement does not make their error any less serious, however. All these false gospels lead to hell since they condition either the reception or retention of justification on works. Soteric justification must be apart from works.

Then-Now-Then

In my adaptation of Kuhatschek's pyramidal model, I have proposed that OT prophecies which have not yet been fulfilled will be fulfilled literally in the future. If this literal fulfillment entails a return to the sacrificial system during the millennial kingdom, does this mean that people in the future will be placed directly under the OT law? No. For one thing, the nature of those sacrifices could be modified in this future dispensation so that they are no longer reconciliatory but only commemoratory, in a manner similar to the observance of the Lord's Supper. Even if these sacrifices are necessary for temporal forgiveness in the millennial kingdom (in a manner which is somewhat analogues to 1Jn 1:9), would this mean that those in the future are placed directly under the past moral code? No.

Illustration 317. Application Then-Now-Then

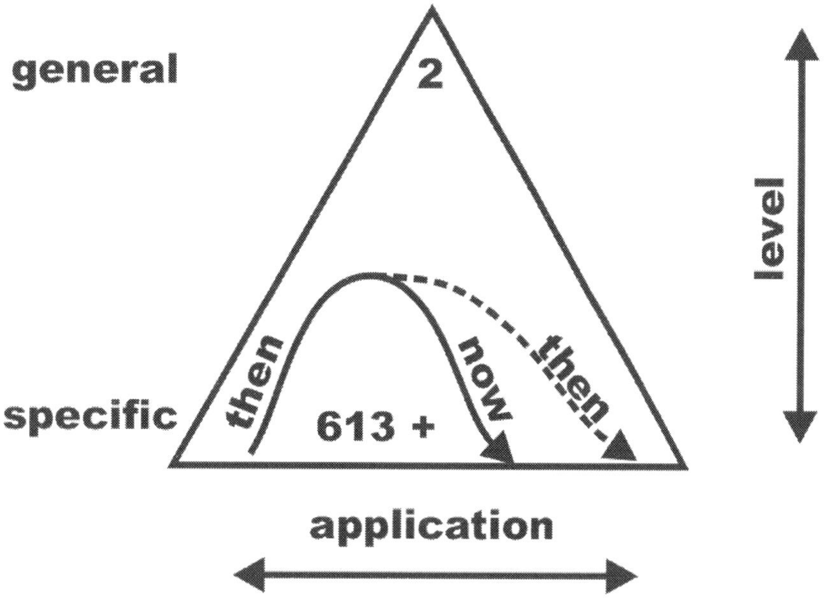

Suppose you were to leave your present country and move to another country and become a citizen of that country, and you were to commit murder in that country after moving there. Would you have violated the law in your original country prohibiting murder? No. You would have violated the law in your current country prohibiting murder; you would not have violated the law in your original country. You would be subject to the laws of the land in which you now reside, not subject to the law of the land in which you previously had resided. Your current country may impose the death penalty; your former country cannot. You would be subject only to the penalty of the country whose law you broke—your current country. Suppose the laws of both countries prescribe the death penalty. Even then, you still would be guilty only of breaking the law of your current country and subject to the death penalty under its law and by its administration. You would not be subject to the death penalty under the law of your former country. We might say that the prohibition against murder (as expressed by either country) is *directly applicable* to you, but you are only *under* the law of your current country. In the same way, laws from a past dispensation may apply to the current dispensation or future dispensation without placing one back under the laws of that past dispensation.

The OT prohibition against murder not only applied *then* but applies *now* also. Many have assumed that since it applies in both the OT and NT, the prohibition against murder is part of an OT moral law that transcends dispensational boundaries. They have chopped up the OT law into constituent parts and tried to port what they consider the moral part over into the current dispensation in an attempt to place believers directly under the OT law. Their surgery has been quite messy. NT believers are no longer under the OT law—any of it. Technically, although the same prohibition may *apply* in both dispensations, the people in the new dispensation are *under* a completely new law—the law of Christ (1Cor 9:21). Granted, the law from that old dispensation may apply just as directly to NT believers as before, but it is not because they are still under the law of that old dispensation.

Just as the prohibition against murder may apply to you in your new country also (since it expresses an underlying principle that has identical representation in both countries), the prohibition against murder in the OT would apply to you even though you are a NT believer. Still, this NT application does not place you under OT jurisdiction. The prohibition against murder in the OT applies just as directly to believers in the OT as it does now in the church age because this law expresses an underlying principle that finds identical expression in both dispensations.

Future

> "But I say to you that everyone who is angry with his brother **shall** *be guilty* before the court; and whoever shall say to his brother, 'Raca,' **shall** *be guilty* before the supreme court; and whoever shall say, 'You fool,' **shall** *be* guilty enough to go into the fiery hell" (Mt 5:22).

Many commentators (particularly of the non-dispensational persuasion) have failed to pay sufficient attention to the futuristic nature of Mt 5:22. The futuristic setting is not accidental, incidental, or merely logical. It is an eschatological future, not merely a logical future. Jesus is describing a future judicial system in this verse. Nevertheless, Jesus makes a present day application beginning with the next verse (Mt 5:23ff). Principlism applies to both the past and future. When examining a passage of Scripture regarding the past or future, believers are not to place themselves under the jurisdiction of that past or future administration. Rather, they are to take the underlying moral principles in that passage of Scripture and apply it to their current situation. They should follow Jesus' example (as exemplified in this context) by making proper, present day applications of past and future moral codes.

This principlistic approach, therefore, does not require that the Sermon on the Mount be placed on a pair of dispensational roller skates and shoved off into the future, contrary to the criticism expressed by some non-dispensationalists. As widely noted, James shows that the Sermon on the Mount has direct application for today. But for that matter, so does Jesus. After affirming the lasting validity of the law in Mt 5:17-18, Jesus starts off with a prohibition against murder as His first illustration (5:21) and demonstrates the full intent of the moral principle underlying that OT law by showing how it will be treated during the future millennial kingdom. Those who display a murderous attitude *shall be* guilty (5:22)—future tense.

Next, Jesus proceeds to deal with adultery. He does not speak in futuristic terms this time, however: "Everyone who looks on a woman to lust for her *has* committed adultery with her *already* in his heart" (Mt 5:28). Jesus does not say that the offender *shall be guilty* of committing adultery (in the millennial kingdom). Instead, the offender is *already* guilty of adultery. Likewise, when He deals with divorce, Jesus states that the one abusing the marriage relationship *commits adultery*—right now in the present dispensation (Mt 5:32). When dealing with the law of retaliation (Mt 5:38), Jesus gives present day application also. When dealing with love (Mt 5:43), the exhortation is that we should love now. Therefore, even though the brilliant writings of Hodges and Wilkin should be consulted for the eschatological dimension of this passage,[1577] the application is by no means limited to the future. Jesus is informing His present listeners, among other things, as to how they can enter that future kingdom.

Entrance into the Kingdom

> "For I say to you, that unless your righteousness surpasses that of the scribes and Pharisees, you **shall not** enter the kingdom of heaven" (Mt 5:20)

Commentators are quick to point out that Pharisees of Jesus' day were trusting futilely in their external righteousness as their means for justification (Lk 18:9). Yet many of these same commentators then lead their readers astray into thinking that internal righteousness is practically equivalent to something like a two-coupon ticket in which both faith and works are necessary to enter the kingdom in Mt 5:20. To the contrary, the righteousness necessary to enter the kingdom is exclusively that produced by Jesus in His fulfilling the law. Jesus states that He is the one who fulfills the law in 5:17: "I...fulfill." Next, He launches an immediate attack against any and all forms of self-righteousness as a means for entrance, whether it is external or internal. If anyone wants to try to enter the kingdom by means of his or her internal performance, then this is what that internal performance has to look like. Men have to never look at a woman with the intent to lust. Never, ever. If a man does so, even once, then he is guilty of internal adultery. Adultery was a capital offense in the OT and is punished with the Lake of Fire in the NT. Make no mistake about it, adulterous thoughts defile a person. But for that matter, so do murderous, lying, or unloving thoughts. Men and women alike fail to meet such standards. No one can make it into the kingdom by seeking entrance on the basis of his or her personal performance.

On the basis of OT standards, one would conclude that none of us are righteous (Is 64:6). And Jesus raises those standards, rather than lowers them, by demonstrating the underlying principles of those standards. Gaining absolute righteousness initially as a free gift is necessary because we certainly do not deserve it. By the same principle, none of us can retain such righteousness by our performance. We have to be able to retain it without having our postconversional performance brought into the picture since our performance is flawed. Judged by an absolute standard, we are lying, murdering, adulterers before conversion and after conversion. If we are to be considered righteous by an absolute standard, then such righteousness must come from another source and must not be based on our performance.

Could the righteousness of a transformed life that God produces through believers after their conversion be what is required for kingdom entrance? Hardly! The level of righteousness that God produces within believers does not rise to sinless perfection on this side of the grave. And even if it did, to base entrance on such postconversional performance-based righteousness would be to make entrance into heaven a reward because it would be based on the righteousness that we produced through God's enablement. Entrance would be gained by works of righteousness which we have done—a deadly fallacy (Tit 3:5).

Jesus has plenty to say about rewards in this Sermon, even rewards that come for being righteous externally (Mt 5:10,12) and secretly (Mt 6:1) and thus internally (Mt 5:6). However, entrance into the kingdom is not a reward; therefore, it is not based upon our external or internal righteousness, or upon our initial or subsequent righteousness. Admittedly, our level of internal righteousness can surpass the level of internal righteousness achieved by the scribes and Pharisees. So does this mean that we can follow the example of the Pharisees and trust in ourselves that we are righteous (Lk 18:9)? Not if we want justification (Lk 18:14). Those who experience justification are those who come to God in an attitude of hopelessness, not self-righteousness. By His life of obedience, Jesus fulfilled "all righteousness" (Mt 3:15). He did not do so for Himself, but for us. We must trust in His righteousness, not our own, in order to have His righteousness imputed to us.

Illustration 318. Gaining/Retaining Initial/Final Justification

In Mt 5:20 and 7:21, Jesus is talking about a future entrance into the kingdom—an eschatological entrance into the kingdom. Naturally, this entrance would require final justification. Such justification would be an eschatological justification. This justification must be granted apart from our performance since our performance would condemn us rather than justify us. Further, since this justification must be retained to the end by those who receive it in order to enter the kingdom "on that [eschatological] day" (Mt 7:22), it must be concluded that such justification (from start to finish) is not based on our performance. Jesus is not advising us in Lk 18:9-10 to follow the example of the publican in gaining justification and then to turn around and follow the example of the Pharisee in retaining it! From start to finish, this justification cannot be based on our performance.

Jesus implores the unbelievers in this mixed crowd to enter the narrow gate that leads to inclusion within this future kingdom. He wants them to do so without delay (Mt 7:13) so that they may enter on that day. That narrow gate is Jesus, not performance. By entering into Jesus, believers are clothed imputationally with His righteousness and thereby granted entrance into this kingdom. The broad gate that leads to destruction, in contrast, is the broad gate of human performance. Such Pharisaical performance, even if done in the name of Jesus, is a poor substitute for faith in Jesus and is destroyed by the demands of Jesus. Those trying to enter the kingdom by means of their performance (Mt 7:22) are excluded on that basis because their performance fails to meet the requirements of the law (Mt 7:23). Indeed, any attempt to gain entrance by means of performance is doomed to failure (Rom 3:20) so that one must be justified by faith in Christ's performance (Rom 3:28).

In James' epistle, which in many ways serves almost as a commentary on the Sermon on the Mount, James confirms that regeneration is a gift (Jam 1:17-18). Moreover, like Paul, James acknowledges that imputational righteousness is by faith: "Abraham believed God and it was imputed to him as righteousness" (Jam 2:23). James does not reduce retaining the gift of regeneration or retaining final imputational righteousness to doing one's best. James' demands are absolute: "Whoever keeps the whole law and yet stumbles in one point, he has become guilty of all" (Jam 2:20). Those trying to get into heaven by means of their performance must be able to keep the whole law, which is why Paul is so emphatic about the impossibility of Christians finding final justification by means of their performance (Gal 5:3-4). To stumble at even one point along the way would be deadly.

Least and Great in the Kingdom

> "Whoever then annuls one of the least of these commandments, and so teaches others, shall be called **least** in the kingdom of heaven; but whoever keeps and teaches them, he shall be called **great** in the kingdom of heaven" (Mt 5:19).

Porter pairs Mt 5:19 with Jam 2:20 in his list of forty-five statements from James that find corresponding parallels in the Sermon on the Mount.[1578] Recognition of this paring is not unusual, but its misthological significance is normally glossed over. Jesus is dealing with misthological ranking in the kingdom, and James properly applies this statement to believers concerning kingdom rewards. James does so by addressing believers and by warning them that they will need mercy when they stand before the Lord in judgment: "Judgment will be merciless to one who has shown no mercy" (Jam 2:13). Paul likewise warns believers: "We must all appear before the judgment seat of Christ, that each one may be recompensed for his deeds in the body, according to what he has done, whether good or bad" (2Cor 5:10). James and Paul are in complete agreement that believers will be judged by their works, so good works are necessary to do well at this judgment. James stresses that works of mercy are necessary to be shown mercy. Jesus teaches the exact same thing: "Blessed are the merciful, for they shall receive mercy" (Mt 5:7). Positive outcomes, on the basis of one's works at this judgment, are identified by Jesus, time and again during the course of the Sermon on the Mount, as rewards and treasures in heaven (Mt 5:12,46; 6:1-2,5,16,19-21).

The scope of Jesus' concern reaches far beyond mere entrance into the kingdom. In bringing the OT teaching to full fruition in the lives of His followers, Jesus touches upon the fact that there will be status ranking within that millennial kingdom. Hodges describes dispensationally what this will look like for those living in that future age. Various commentators, not just dispensationalists, concur that the issue is misthological ranking in the future kingdom, not exclusion from the kingdom.[1579]

Baxter rightly objects to those scholars who are so infatuated with Jesus' triple references to entering the kingdom in this Sermon (Mt 5:20; 7:13,21) that they think that "Jesus' main concern of the Sermon is the front-end of the kingdom (i.e., how to get in) and assume that this 'entrance' is based on good works." Baxter counters: "Much of Jesus' teaching is not 'evangelistic' per se, but presupposes a 'beyond-entry-level' discipleship."[1580] Jesus is addressing a mixed crowd that includes believers (who already have become light by entering into a relationship with God as their Father) and also addressing unbelievers who have not yet entered the narrow gate.

Jesus' repeated reference to the *Law* and *the Prophets* (Mt 5:17; 7:13) forms an *inclusio* for the main body of the Sermon. Since the Sermon includes the instructions for His disciples (the believers within the audience) as to how they should treat others (and their rewards for doing so), Jesus' fulfilling the Law and the Prophets would certainly seem to include His teaching on how His disciples should treat others and the impact that practical righteousness would have on their corresponding rewards. Truly, the Lord moves beyond entry-level discipleship.

Without making either the present or future entrance a reward, however, Jesus demonstrates the importance of His followers having their own personal righteousness. A rich entrance into His kingdom certainly will require that His followers meet His postconversional performance requirements to the best of their God-enabled ability. Peter, who was sitting in the audience, spells out this conclusion by exhorting believers to develop their Christian character so that they could qualify for a rich entrance into the kingdom: "For in this way the entrance into the eternal kingdom of our Lord and Savior Jesus Christ will be richly supplied to you" (2Pet 1:11; TM). Before, during, and after the antithetical section of His Sermon, Jesus stresses rewards. In His last antithesis, when responding to those who claim that meeting the letter of the law regarding love is good enough, Jesus counters by going to the spirit of the law and demanding much more than trying to do just enough to get by; His followers have to love even their enemies. And Jesus explains in Mt 5:48 that the reason believers (i.e., those who already have

God as their heavenly Father) need to meet this higher standard of love is in order to have heavenly rewards: Having God as their Heavenly Father is a gift rather than a reward, but being treated as mature *sons* (Mt 5:45) with full inheritance rights by their Heavenly Father is a *reward* (Mt 5:46). Immediately, upon concluding this antithesis (which is dealing with potential rewards for believers), the Lord commences a full blown discussion of such rewards (Mt 6:1-20). He wants these believers to practice their righteousness privately so that by laying up treasures for themselves in heaven they may have a reward from their Father who is in heaven. They are to lay up treasures *in* heaven, not the treasure *of* heaven. Heaven is not the treasure. Heaven is not the reward. Rewards in heaven are earned by practical righteousness; entrance into heaven is freely granted because of imputed righteousness.

Jacobean Parallels

As noted above, Porter lists forty-five parallels between the Epistle of James and the Sermon on the Mount. Unfortunately, Porter misaligns and misapplies some of these parallels. No doubt, Jam 2:10 does, in fact, parallel Mt 5:19 in that both passages show that one cannot trifle with the law. (For that matter, Mt 5:22 should have been included in Porter's chart for the same reason.) However, Jam 2:10 is absolute in its demands, and Mt 5:19 is relative in its rankings. (Mt 5:22 is relative in its punishments also.) The correspondence in Jacobean allusions to the Sermon on the Mount is not necessarily one-to-one in that one cannot equate absolute demands with relative results.

Even putting this concern aside, though, Porter does not prove to be a good matchmaker when he matches such texts as: Mt 7:21/Jam 2:26 and Mt 7:21-23/Jam 1:26-27&2:14-16. He pairs Matthean soteric texts with Jacobean mistholic texts. In doing so, Porter ends up making entrance into heaven a reward for one's works. Rather than equating soteric and mistholic texts, one should consider the possibility that James' absolute statement has application to both soteric and mistholic texts. The law cannot be trifled with ether in terms of what it demands for kingdom entrance or kingdom inheritance. Better matchmaking can be achieved as follows.

Illustration 319. Lawful Entrance

Matthew	James	Comment
Whoever then annuls one of the least of these commandments, and so teaches others, shall be called least in the kingdom of heaven; but whoever keeps and teaches them, he shall be called great in the kingdom of heaven. (Mt 5:19)	For whoever keeps the whole law and yet stumbles in one point, he has become guilty of all. (Jam 2:10)	You cannot trifle with any of the law, not even the least commandment.
But I say to you that everyone who is angry with his brother shall be guilty before the court; and whoever shall say to his brother, "Raca," shall be guilty before the supreme court; and whoever shall say, "You fool," shall be guilty enough to go into the fiery hell. (Mt 5:22)	For whoever keeps the whole law and yet stumbles in one point, he has become guilty of all. (Jam 2:10)	You cannot trifle with any of the law, not even the spirit of the law or one commandment of the law.
For I say to you, that unless your righteousness surpasses that of the scribes and Pharisees, you shall not enter the kingdom of heaven. (Mt 5:20)	For whoever keeps the whole law and yet stumbles in one point, he has become guilty of all. (Jam 2:10)	Absolute righteousness is required for entrance.
[21] Not everyone who says to Me, "Lord, Lord," will enter the kingdom of heaven; but he who does the will of My Father who is in heaven. [22] Many will say to Me on that day, "Lord, Lord, did we not prophesy in Your name, and in Your name cast out demons, and in Your name perform many miracles?" [23] And then I will declare to them, "I never knew you; depart from Me, you who practice lawlessness." (Mt 7:21-23)	For whoever keeps the whole law and yet stumbles in one point, he has become guilty of all. (Jam 2:10)	Absolute righteousness is required for entrance. Those who base their entrance into heaven on their submitting to God's will in terms of their Christian practice will be rejected because of their lawless practice. Regeneration is a gift (Jam 1:17-18) and imputational righteous is by faith rather than by works (Jam 2:23).

When Jesus deals with those already in the millennial kingdom, He shows that their degree of guilt will be relative (Mt 5:19, 5:22). James likewise shows that for those already justified by faith, there will be a subsequent, relative justification by works (Jam 2:21). They already have absolute imputational righteousness and, thereby, are qualified for entrance into the kingdom (Jam 2:23). But they will need justification by works in order to do well at the Judgment Seat of Christ and hear the words, "Well done."

As James surmises, "You see then that a man is justified by works, and not only justified by faith" (Jam 2:24; TM). Two types of justification are affirmed. Relative justification by works is the goal for those who already have absolute justification by faith. Justification by faith grants believers entrance into the kingdom and qualifies them to pursue justification by works so that they may obtain rewards within the millennial kingdom. Citizens of the kingdom are encouraged to lay up treasure in the kingdom now that they are citizens of that kingdom. How one will be treated within the kingdom will be dependent, to a certain extent, upon their performance as citizens of that kingdom—how much treasure they lay up in that kingdom for example. In contrast, entrance into the kingdom must be granted independent of their performance since James relegates postconversional works to misthological justification by works and affirms that imputational righteousness is based on faith (apart from works since works pertain to a different type of justification).

Conclusion

Entrance into the kingdom is based on Jesus' imputational righteousness. The demands are too high for it to be anything less than His imputational righteousness. It will not do for Adventists or Arminians to think that they gain entrance by faith but retain it by works or for those in the Reformed camp to argue that they gain initial justification by faith but retain finial justification by works. Soteric justification—all of it—is *by faith apart from works* (Rom 3:26). Justification for this Pauline statement in 3:26 not only goes back to the OT (as shown in Rom 4:6) but also is deduced logically straight from the words of Jesus in the Gospels.

Without a doubt, there is more to what Jesus is teaching in Mt 5:17-20 than mere imputational righteousness, but there is not less. By necessity, option one (and thus imputation by implication) is included in the third hermeneutical option for this passage. Jesus shows what it means to meet the OT demands, and His corresponding illustrations require that His listeners conclude that He is the only one who can fully meet such demands. His righteousness is the fruit demanded by OT law and provided by Him, in compliance with OT demands, to those who believe in Him. To believers who already are qualified for entrance into heaven because of His imputed righteousness, Jesus promises treasure in the kingdom if they will practice kingdom righteousness.

In the process, the Lord demonstrates hermeneutical genius, showing His mixed group of listeners how to apply princiglism—in deriving present day application from past and future dispensations—so that they may be qualified not only for entrance into heaven but for rewards in heaven. His words are too full of past, present, and future dispensational truth to be archived away on a dispensational bookshelf as being only applicable to another age.

Surprisingly, Porter omits Jam 2:23 from his chart. Yet the parallel appears to be rather obvious. In Mt 5:17, Jesus affirms that He came to *fulfill* (*pleroo*) the Scripture. James acknowledges: "The Scripture was *fulfilled* [*pleroo*] which says, 'And Abraham believed God, and it was reckoned to him as righteousness,' and he was called the friend of God." In the Sermon on the Mount, Jesus is fulfilling the Scripture and its demands for righteousness. He makes the righteousness necessary to enter the kingdom so high that He is absolutely the only one who can fulfill the scriptural demands. At the same time, He demonstrates the rewards for relative righteousness in the lives of His followers. Wiersbe compares this fulfilling in Mt 5:17 to an acorn seed that grows up into an oak tree.[1581] Righteousness is imputed, implanted, and imparted to the believer. This analogy is permissible as long as one does not make the tree a requirement to enter heaven, as some in the Reformed camp are prone to do. Only germination (picturing regeneration) via the seed is necessary for kingdom entrance; the full-grown tree is required for kingdom rulership. James urges believers to give this implanted word a humble reception so that it can save their souls from misthological loss (Jam 1:21). By implanting His word of righteousness in our heart, Jesus makes the full fruition of righteousness possible in our lives and urges us to build upon those words in order to save our lives from ruinous results (Mt 7:24-27). The Lord wants to bring out the full fruition of the OT demands for righteousness in the NT believer's life as well so that the NT believer may be called a *friend of God* in the kingdom of heaven.

Appendix 17.
Ezekiel's Millennial Temple

Introduction

The Misslers have one of the best illustrated books on misthology and nikology. Moreover, they take a spatial view of the outer darkness. Needless to say, much of their book is certainly appealing to the outlook adopted in the present book. The most interesting proposal found in their book regarding the outer darkness is their proposal that the outer darkness be equated with the *gizrah* of Ezekiel's Temple. At a kingdom's conference I was attending, and at which their book was being promoted, I was asked to look into this possible identification. This appendix will do so and offer a possible clarification.

Gizrah

The Hebrew word *gizrah* is found in nine verses in the OT (Lev 16:22; Lam 4:7; 41:12-15; 42:1,10,13). In relation to Ezekiel's Millennial Temple, the Misslers locate the Gizrah in the western building. Indeed, this is a plausible option. LaHaye and Ice, for example, concur with that location.[1582] If one were to search the internet for images of the millennial temple, this would be seen to be a popular option. In the illustration, below, I have scaled back the details typically shown for the temple so that we might focus on the key issues.

Illustration 320. Option One for Gizrah

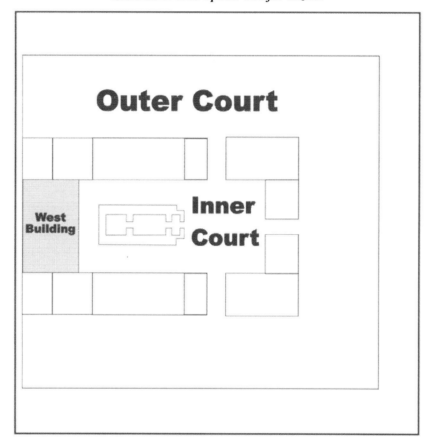

The Misslers cite *Strong's Concordance* as defining *gizrah* as "a place for 'polishing or making something smooth by friction." My edition of *Strong's Concordance* defines it as "an *enclosure* inclosure (as *separated*): — polishing, separate place." Thus, I can understand why one might assume that the enclosure of the West Building might be thought to have some such positive purpose as the Misslers pose. See the shaded area in *Illustration 320*. On the other hand, scholastic opinion is certainly not uniform in that assessment. Lange, for example, believes it was a place for garbage, the scraps left over from the bloody sacrifices. Moreover, he would include the separating courtyard as part of the Gizrah. So the shaded area in *Illustration 320* would have to be expanded as in *Illustration 321*.

Illustration 321. Option Two for Gizrah

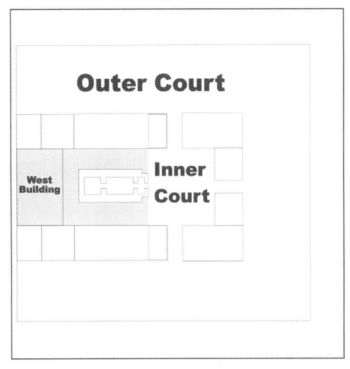

Indeed, if one searches the internet, one can find illustration of this possibility as well. No polishing, cleansing, or restoring would be occurring in this courtyard. So if the Gizrah includes the separating courtyard, then the basic function of the Gizrah that would pertain to the outer darkness would seem to be merely that of separation. As to the proposed *polishing*, yes, *gizrah* has that meaning in Lam 4:7. However, that is the meaning of the word used of sapphires. When the word is used of the temple, BDB defines it as a "separate place…i.e. yard, or space adjoining [the] temple on three sides."[1583]

Illustration 322. Option Three

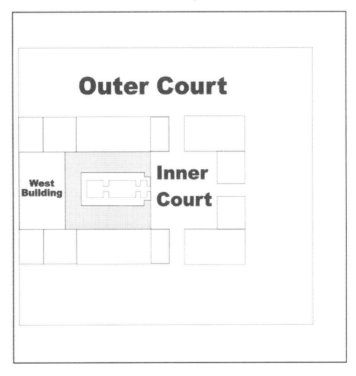

This understanding of Gizrah will be adopted herein. See *Illustration 322*. Wayne ODonnel has a beautiful, 3-D walk-through of Ezekiel's Temple available at his website that visually presents this perspective in 3-D. For those who would just like to see his images of the floor plain without walking through the whole temple, his online book may be quickly consulted.[1584] If this location of the separate place is correct, then the meaning that the Misslers have attributed to the Gizrah in relation to the temple is incorrect.

For that matter, even if one were to opt for *Option 1*, their projected meaning would still be suspect. They are employing a questionable illegitimate totality transfer in importing the word's full range of meaning into this context. Nevertheless, among the scholarly speculations as to what would be the purpose of this Gizrah building, one option is to pose that it would be a place where things that have become ritually unclean might be separated from the holy thing until these unclean items could be cleansed or discarded. So the Misslers are not alone in projecting a positive meaning. Still, they were on safer ground when they simply concluded: "*The Gizrah in Ezekiel's Temple will be a place where everything that is rejected or excluded from the worship service (because of defilement) will be kept. It is an unsanctified area, separate from the sanctified region*" (emphasis theirs).[1585] If one avoids the speculative notion of separation for the purpose of restoration, then even the Gizrah building can be defined in a manner suitable for the Gizrah courtyard and simply regarded as a means of separating the holy from the unholy. In this case, Gizrah separates the Holy of Holies and the Holy Place (the white area in the center of the Gizrah in *Option 3*) from the common area outside of the Gizrah. The shaded area pictures Gizrah in the three illustrations above.

Separation for Restoration

Apparently, the Misslers want to latch onto this speculative association of the Gizrah with the outer darkness so that they might use it to pose their remedial view of the outer darkness. They insist that the Lord disciplines us rather than punishes us, and they project this discipline into the hereafter.[1586] Supposedly, because the Lord disciplines us rather than punishes us, the outer darkness is "*not* a place of purging" and thus not a purgatory (emphasis theirs).[1587] However, their logic conveys the exact opposite impression than what they intend. According to the Bible, the Lord *disciplines* (indeed *punishes*) us because He loves us (Rev 3:19). *Paideuo*, which is used here, as well as in Heb 12:6, means to *discipline with punishment* (BDAG). As Heb 12:7 attests, to *discipline by whipping and scourging* is within its range of meaning.[*] The Lord's disciplining punishment of believers in this life is being affirmed by the biblical text. The Lord will temporally punish/discipline redeemed Israel (Jer 30:11).

In Lk 23:16,22, *paideuo* frequently is translated as *punish*. The misthological lashing of unfaithful believers in Lk 12:47 is not for the purpose of purging them in the hereafter but for punishing them in the hereafter so that they will purge themselves in the here and now. A believer's purgatory (purging in view of punishment) is now. If we are going to purge ourselves because of impending discipline, then we better do it now because it will be too late in the afterlife. Because of the punishment we are receiving now and will be receiving in the future, we should purge, purify, and cleanse ourselves now. The outer darkness is not a place of purging because it is a place of pure punishment.

Illustration 323. Discipline is Punishment

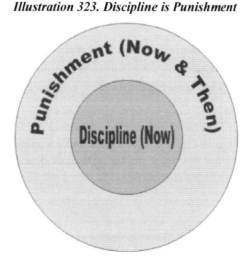

---

[*] See *Misthological Punishment*, 672. Also, see *Israel My Redeemed Punished Servant*, 377.

If one wishes to stretch the discipline in Rev 3:19 to include misthological scourging, then let it not be forgotten that the purging aspect of future punishment is to occur now and that such scourging is indeed punishment. Believers are subject to severe *punishment* (*timoria*, Heb 10:29). In Mt 25:46, the lost are subject to *punishment* (*kolasis*). Yet this same Greek word is used to express the judgment to which the saved who are not perfected in love are subject (1Jn 4:18). The Misslers insist that their view of the outer darkness is not purgatorial because "*God's judgment of believers is* not *punitive!*" (Emphasis theirs).[1588] Contrary to the Misslers, the outer darkness is not purgatorial in the hereafter because it is pure punishment and not remedial.[1589] Strangely, they claim that it is remedial and yet admit: "If we haven't learned 'holiness' *here*, unfortunately, it will be too late to learn it when we get *there*."[1590] By their own admission, deriving any training from the outer would be *too late* once one is cast into the outer darkness. Any positive instruction to be learned from the outer darkness must be learned in this life, not the next. Just as the lost will be punished in the hereafter because they did not believe, so believers will be punished in the hereafter because they did not love. The lost are not punished in the hereafter so that they may come to postmortem faith, and the saved are not punished in the hereafter so that they may be retrained to become more loving. Just as whatever positive value the lost may derive from hell must be derived before they are cast into hell (by believing), whatever positive lessons believers are going to learn from the outer darkness in the department of loving must be learned now (by loving).

One might go so far as to say that all discipline is a form of punishment, but this does not mean that all punishment is a form of discipline. Punishment in neither hell nor the outer darkness is corrective, only punitive, for those who thus have been sentenced. Also, to further differentiate between discipline and punishment, note that punishment can take place now or in the future. Discipline, though, is limited to the present. Unfaithful believers are warned about future punishment for the purpose of present discipline. Therefore, counter their intentions, by merging the outer darkness with future purging, the Misslers are using a questionable meaning (and location) of Gizrah to impose a purgatorial function upon the outer darkness. Furthermore, even if a purging meaning is conjectured for the Gizrah building (if in fact the West Building is a Gizrah building), this meaning would be foreign to the Gizrah courtyard and should not be imposed upon the outer darkness.

The Concept of the Outer Darkness

In the heart of their chapter *The Millennial Temple*, the Misslers bring Michael Huber to the stand as their star witness in their section called, "The Concept of the Outer Darkness." Huber is an authority on the outer darkness, so providing this extended quote from Misslers' book is justified, particularly since it is crucial to their argument regarding the Gizrah:

> Michael Huber form Dallas Theological Seminary wrote an article "The Concept of the Outer Darkness" in which he said: "The term **'outer darkness'** appears nowhere else in the New Testament outside of the three verses mentioned **(Matthew 8:12; 22:13; 25:30)**. However, it **does** occurs [sic] **20** times in the **Septuagint version of the Bible** and **it's** *always in relation to Ezekiel's Temple or* God." He continued: "Most significantly, the term is used **15** times in Ezekiel to describe the **O**uter **C**ourt of the temple (10:5; 40:19-20; 41:15, 17; 42:1, 3, 6, 7, 8, 9; 44:19; 46:20-21). It may be noteworthy, considering the eschatological imagery of the subject **of the** parable that the *dominant use of the term is in relation to the Millennial Temple*."[1591] (Italics original.)

A few problems with the Misslers' use of this quote must be mentioned, however. First, Huber did write a splendid article, but the name of that article was, "The 'Outer Darkness' in Matthew and Its Relationship to Grace." What the Misslers call "an article" was actually his thesis: "The Concept of the 'Outer Darkness' in the Gospel of Matthew." Apparently, they misidentified his thesis as an article. Second, they do not provide the page number for this reference. Nor evidently will they be able to do so since Huber did not write this quote that they attribute to him, at least not in the sources consulted.

Outer (*exoteros*)

As I scan back over Huber's thesis, I do not find the quote the Misslers attribute to Huber. However, their quote (or something close to it) does occur in Sapaugh's article:

> The term **translated "outside"** (*exoteros*) appears nowhere else in the **NT** outside of the three verses mentioned. However, it occurs **23** times in the **LXX** and always in relation to **the tabernacle**

or temple of God, or the palace of a king. Most significantly, the term is used **fifteen** times in Ezekiel to describe the outer court of the temple (**Ezek** 10:5; 40:19,20; 41:15, 17; 42:1, 3, 6, 7, 8, 9, **14**; 44:19; 46:20, 21). **Once, it describes the outer gate of the temple (Ezek 44:1).** It may be noteworthy, considering the eschatological imagery of the subject parable, that the dominant use of the term is in relation to the millennial temple in Ezekiel 40-48.[1592] (Bold mine.)

The Misslers did not provide documentation for the page they were citing, but evidently they have rather freely quoted Sapaugh and mistakenly cited Huber. In any event, I have used a bold font to highlight about a dozen differences between the quote I provided from Sapaugh and the one the Misslers attributed to Huber. By my count *exoteros* occurs 25 times in 25 verses: Ex 26:4; 1 Kings 6:29-30; Job 18:17; Eze 10:5; 40:19-21, 31, 37; 41:15, 17; 42:1, 3, 6-9, 14; 44:1, 19; 46:20-21; Mt 8:12; 22:13; 25:30. The difference in the count and other matters pales in significance to the omission made by the Misslers. They failed to provide the translated word *exoteros* as part of their quote. They are using this quote to equate the Greek *exoteros* with the Hebrew *gizrah*, but these words are talking about two different parts of the temple! Even if the *exoteros* of the temple pictures the outer darkness of the NT, *exoteros* is not *gizrah*. Correspondingly, the outer darkness is not Gizrah!

Even aside from Greek, one can derive this conclusion from the quote itself. *Exoteros* is used to describe the **outer court**, not the *separate place*! Since *gizrah* is not the *outer* (*exoteros*) darkness, all the speculation by the Misslers that the outer darkness serves a remedial purpose because Gizrah supposedly has a remedial purpose completely misses the point. The Misslers have completely confused the *outer court* with the *separate place*. So that there will be no mistaking what the quote is actually saying, yet another picture is provided. In *Illustration 324*, the shaded area pictures *exoteros*.

Illustration 324. Outer Court = Outer Darkness

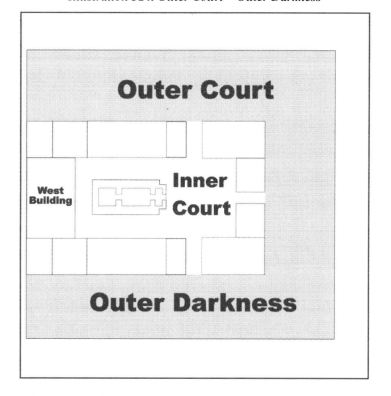

According to Sapaugh, since the dominant use of the term *exoteros* (*outer*) is in relation to the outer court of Ezekiel's temple, "it seems reasonable to conclude that the improperly clothed man of Matthew 22 is thrown into the outer court of the palace."[1593] Many years ago, when I first read this assessment by Sapaugh, and derived my own conclusions regarding the outer darkness, I did not factor this statement by Sapaugh into consideration for the simple reason that Ezekiel does not use the term *outer darkness.*

Yet the Misslers completely overlook this distinction and repeat the quote yet again. However, this time they change it and make this assessment, "We found this absolutely fascinating: "*The dominant use of the term* **outer darkness** *is in its relation to the Millennial Temple*" (italics theirs).[1594] Indeed, I would have found such a statement fascinating also—if such a statement actually had been made. But Sapaugh did not make such a statement because he was being more careful, factual, and accurate in his assessment. The term that Sapaugh is referring to is *outer*—not *outer darkness*. He is pointing out that the same Greek word used for the *outer* court of the temple is used of the *outer* darkness. Nevertheless, having called attention to numerous errors on the part of the Misslers, I would like to salvage the main point they are trying to make. Building upon Sapaugh's observation, let me distinguish fact from inference.

- Fact One: the dominant OT use of the term *outer* (used by Matthew to describe the *outer darkness*) is in relation to the millennial temple in Ezekiel 40-48.
- Fact Two: this dominant OT usage of this term for *outer* is of the *outer court* of the millennial temple.
- Fact Three: Matthew's parabolic imagery of being cast out of the wedding feast into the darkness outside most reasonably refers to the outer court of the palace.[*]
- Inference: the outer court of the temple typologically represents the outer darkness of the palace.

As a reasonable inference, the outer court of the millennial temple may be taken as picturing the outer darkness of the wedding feast in Mt 22:13, and thus the Matthean outer darkness in general.[1595] The basic point the Misslers was trying to make is sound, albeit they misidentified the part of the temple that provides the allusion. Further, their Gizrah hypothesis, although flawed, may serve a useful purpose yet, and my pointing out that correlation will provide opportunity to correct another potentially mistaken opinion.

When I first read the Misslers' Gizrah hypothesis, I was not impressed because my initial impression was that they were trying to squeeze all the carnal believers of all time into that tiny little building. Not even the old question, "How many angels can dance on the head of a pin?" could come to the aid of such a preposterous notion since these believers will have material bodies. Granted, they will have resurrected bodies. But are we really to think that all carnal believers are going to be packed into that little room in such a way as to make sardines in a can look like whales swimming in the vast ocean? Hardly!

Or, given my correction, so that the outer darkness is correctly seen to correlate to the outer court, one might make the mistake of thinking that the outer darkness is the outer court. No, it is not. You will not be able to pack all the unfaithful believers into that literal outer court. At this point, some will inject that just as all the faithful believers will not be in the inner court at the same time, so not all the unfaithful believers will be in the outer court at the same time. The erroneous projection then might be made that unfaithful believers will be allowed to visit the outer court—a few at a time.

ODonnel made the interesting proposal that those taking his walk-through of the 3-D model of the temple could meet him at a specified location of the millennial temple at a specified time in the future. I would like to take him up on that offer. Overcomers will be able to walk within that temple during the millennium, and they can make plans to meet one another at specified parts of that temple at specified times. However, I do not believe that subcomers will be allowed into that temple—any part of it.

When I visited the Grand Canyon and hiked down into it, I took lots of pictures. I even took pictures of the 3-D model that they had in the building overlooking the Grand Canyon. The only way to get to that 3-D model of the Grand Canyon, however, is to visit the Grand Canyon. Likewise, Ezekiel's Temple is a 3-D model of the millennial kingdom. The only way to get to that model is to visit the part of the kingdom where the model is kept, and that part of the kingdom is off limits to those in the outer darkness. When I took a picture of the 3-D model of the Grand Canyon, I could see what parts of the canyon looked like even though I did not hike to those parts of the canyon. That is one big canyon! And I did not hike all of it, not by a long shot. Similarly, the temple will allow one to grasp the significance of the various parts of the kingdom, even if one does not travel to all those parts. For overcomers to visit the temple and walk through the outer court on their way to the inner court will not mean that they walk through the outer darkness. Rather, in walking through the outer court, they will be walking through the 3-D representation of the outer darkness. They will be able to appreciate the fact that they lived for Christ so that they do not have to live in that part of the kingdom.

---

[*] While some might call this third point an inference, I am calling it a fact. It is a fact that this is the most reasonable inference. Sapaugh is using the data differently than I am. He is using facts one and two to make the logical inference that the outer darkness of Matthew is the outer court because this is the dominant OT usage of *outer*. I appreciate his argument but would prefer to argue instead that the outer darkness of Matthew is the outer court of the king's palace because that is what makes the most sense (for reasons that both he and I would provide, independently of the consideration of the temple). Therefore, having established this perspective as the most reasonable deduction, one is then free to conclude that the outer court of the temple and of the palace are typological parallels. Our two approaches complement one another.

Illustration 325. Separation from Outer Darkness

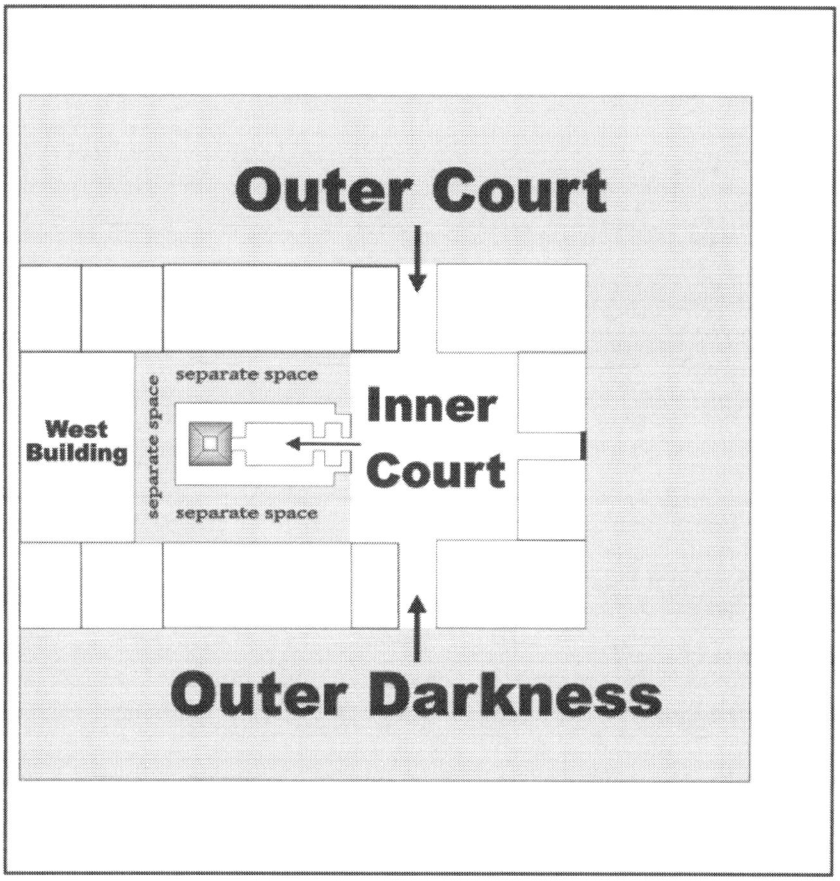

In *Illustration 325* the arrows denote avenues of entry. Some topologists have long recognized that the Holy of Holies of the tabernacle represents heaven (Heb 9:24-26), where Jesus entered through the veil of His flesh when He made atonement for us (Heb 9:1-10:20). More specifically, the Holy of Holies symbolizes where the presence of God resides. The typological correlation between the perfect cube of the Holy of Holies and New Jerusalem certainly has not gone unnoticed (1Kgs 6:20; 2Chron 3:8). Since the outer walls of Ezekiel's three-tiered temple become progressively smaller as one moves up the levels, some have thought that that the pyramidal shape of the Heavenly/New Jerusalem is suggested (cp. Eze 41:1). The Great Pyramid of Egypt is thought by many to represent the Heavenly City and thus to support the pyramidal perception. The OT and NT corner stone would be the capstone to such a pyramid.

Regardless of shape, the Holy Place is a place of fellowship with God. Previously a veil separated the Holy of Holies from the Holy Place. This veil has now been removed by the sacrifice of Jesus. I have pictured the *Holy of Holies* as the pyramidal Heavenly City in the model above and would suggest that the *Holy Place* represents the Promised Land (i.e., the millennial land of Israel on earth).

No entrance into the Holy of Holies is possible through the Gizrah—the separate space surrounding both the Holy of Holies and the Holy Place. One must enter these holy places through the Inner Court (which I would conceive as the northern hemisphere of the planet). Beyond the Inner Court lies the Outer Court (the southern hemisphere). To enter the Outer Court, one must enter through either the North Gate or South Gate, after the Eastern Gate is shut up because the Lord enters through it (Eze 44:1-3). Just as the Outer Court is part of the temple complex, so the outer darkness is part of the kingdom. This kingdom is entered by new birth. The *uncircumcised in heart* (i.e., unbelievers) will not enter the sanctuary at all (Eze 44:9).

Those priests who represent those guilty of apostasy will *bear the punishment* of serving in a state of shame, but they still will be within the complex (Eze 44:9-14); although, they will not be privy to the more intimate access granted as a reward to those priests who represent the faithful (Eze 44:15-16). Yet these faithful priests must change clothing when passing back and forth between the inner and outer court (Eze 44:17-19) so that holiness may not be transmitted to the Outer Court. In this perspective I am adopting the suggestion by the Misslers "that the original line of Levitical priests, who were once in charge of the worship services in Solomon's Temple, will *not* be able to approach the sanctuary in the future Millennium Temple because their **forefathers** did *not* remain faithful to the Lord" (bold mine).[1596] If the Misslers are correct in this particular assessment, and I believe they are, then those serving in this capacity are Levitical priests who enter the millennial kingdom in flesh and blood bodies.[1597] In commenting on Eze 44:10-16, *The Pulpit Commentary* (TPC) correctly perceives the typological correlation regarding the moral apostate priests and that of the unfaithful slave thrown into the outer darkness: "The loss of the Levites is the gain of the family of Zadok. The talent that is taken from the idle servant is given to the servant with ten talents [Mt 25:28]. We may here see a *hierarchy in the making.*"[1598] Unfortunately, TPC does not follow through when commenting on the Matthean counterpart and fails to note that a hierarchy is what is at stake. Still, to its credit, TPC resumes the hierarchal perspective when commenting on Lk 12:47-48:

> If these use the little knowledge and seize the few opportunities, they will, while occupying a lower grade in the *hierarchy of heaven*, still enjoy the perfect bliss of friendship with God. The punishment for failure here is designated by the few stripes. In this solemn passage it is notable that degrees or *grades in punishment* as well as degrees or grades in glory are distinctly spoken of. Merit and practical utility lie at the foundation of institutions that have subsequently become more formal.[1599]

Apostate priests are assigned lower positions in a hierarchy within the millennial kingdom of heaven (that correspond to being cast into the outer darkness) as their punishment. The typology is highly confirmatory of unconditional security. Even apostates are saved from hell, even during the millennium! Contrary to the Misslers, who shy away from the idea of merit and misthological punishment, this text explicitly affirms twice that these servants bear *the punishment for their iniquity* as their demerit (Eze 44:9,12).[1600] Moreover, the form of this punishment refutes both conditionalism and ultraism. These typological apostates are within Ezekiel's Temple. The millennial role of service performed by these unfaithful Levitical priests represents the punishment of the outer darkness within the kingdom. They serve the people rather than the Lord and take care of the animals. Presumably, not only are they responsible for sacrificing the animals but also for disposing of their carcasses and feces—a bloody, smelly job that depicts, on a small scale, the lowly service performed by those cast into the outer darkness.

The total picture, then, is one in which those believers whose only righteousness is soteriological justification will enter the kingdom but be limited to the outer darkness. Those believers who achieve misthological justification will have access to the remaining parts of the kingdom. Those living in natural bodies will occupy both the northern and southern hemispheres. Jews will live in the Promised Land. Unfaithful believers who are limited to the outer darkness will not have access to the Promised Land, much less to the Heavenly City.

Ezekiel's Misthopology

Misthopological implications may be traced even further. *Gizrah* is the Hebrew word for the *separating space* surrounding the temple. The Greek word used to translate it is *apoloipos* (*open space*) and is found only in the following passages: Eze 41:9, 11-15; 42:1, 10.* The separating space between the Heavenly City and the outer darkness literally will become the *open space* of *outer space* in eternity future. No Gizrah separates the Holy of Holies from the Holy Place or from the Inner Court. Some might want to press this to mean that the New Jerusalem will rest upon the planet, but this may be pressing the typology too far. Suffice it to say that those living in the area typified by the Holy Place and Inner Court will have unwavering visual and physical access to the Heavenly City. Those living in the Outer Court will have neither, at least not from the outer court.

Becker, on the other hand, thinks that unfaithful believers will live inside the city: "Those who are born again by the Spirit but fail to hear God and obey will live inside the heavenly city but receive no reward."[1601] By her own assessment, however, if living inside the city is a reward, then unfaithful believers will not live inside the city because they will receive *no reward*. Living inside the city would be a reward that they would not receive. Instead of entertaining this possibility, she divides the city into three cities, limits subcomers from to the lower one, and inconsistently assumes: "These will eat from the tree of life, but they will be denied the crown of life."[1602] To the contrary, they will lose all rights and access to the tree of life and to the entire holy city (Rev 22:14,19).

Nevertheless, something useful may be gleaned from Becker's misthopology, and her planetology is highly intriguing. Becker takes many of the events in Revelation very literally, as describing real-time events involving

---

* Note that Lev 16:22 and Lam 4:7 are excluded, where *gizrah* is not used in relation to the temple. These passages should have never been used for the Misslers' projection as to the role of the Gizrah of the temple. Also, the *free space* of Eze 41:9 is included in the LXX. This is *open space* where noting is built. I anticipate that in eternity future Gizrah literally will be the *open space* of *outer space*.

astral bodies.[1603] In her comments on Rev 6:12-14, she believes this could be explained by the earth turning upside down for the last time (cp. Is 24:1,20). The Hebrew word translated as describing the Lord *turning* the world *upside down* (ASV, BBE, CJB, DBY, ERV, JPS, KJV, WEB, cp. YLT) is *avah* and translated as *anakalupto* by the LXX. If this is the case, the idea seems to be *uncovering Earth's face by turning its face over*. Of course, turning a planet over is bound to cause considerable twisting, distress, devastation, and distortion of its surface, so the full semantic range of this word, as conveyed by those translations opting for these latter renderings, may be justified on this occasion.

True to his dispensational perspective, Walvoord is inclined toward a literal interpretation of this passage.[1604] The sun becoming black *like* (*hos*) sackcloth, the moon becoming red *like* (*hos*), the sky being rolled back *like* (*hos*) a scroll could be well taken as phenomenal (rather than symbolic) descriptions of what actually will take place. Therefore, Becker's thesis will be adopted as the working hypothesis in the present discussion.

That planetary rotation will take place during the tribulation. As the outer boundaries of the kingdom expand during the eternal sate, via space travel to other planets, those in the outer darkness can be expected to be deported from Earth to these remoter locations. As these boundaries continue to expand infinitely across the finite universe, Gizrah eventually may reach to the other side of the universe so that those on the fringe parts of the kingdom are finally confined to a planet called the Outer Darkness in the remotest region of the universe.

Based on reputed accounts of those who have visited heaven, some have entertained the possibility that the Heavenly City is really three-cities-in-one. The three-tiered Ezekiel Temple might support such a perception. Thus, those believers who have not matured are allowed into the lower realms. Such a hypothesis is attractive and in harmony with the proposal made herein. Indeed, Becker poses this interpretation because of extrabiblical testimonies.[1605] In any event, her preference for the pyramidal shape of the city is certainly justified. Her speculation about three cities in one will be entertained for sake of discussion. Unfortunately, Becker equates the outer darkness with being shut up **soteriologically** outside the city in Rev 22:14-15.[1606] Thus, she speculates that unfaithful believers are allowed into the lower city but not permitted access to the streets where the tree of life is located. This strained attempt to reconcile the misthological nature of the tree of life (Rev 2:7; 22:14,19) with soteriological access into the city would be much more convincing if she were to adopt a misthological understanding of the outer darkness.

To their credit, as a result of properly adopting a misthological understanding of this darkness, the Misslers are perceptive as to timing of the ejection: "Being thrown into the outer darkness is probably not something that occurs in heaven, but something that occurs on the earth at the beginning of the Millennial reign, perhaps just before the Marriage Feast."[1607] Given this timing of the expulsion, harmony with my exposition and with Becker's reporting of the visions is easily achievable. All believers when they die (or are raptured) are taken to the Heavenly City. The city is divided up into three main levels with innumerable planes in each level. Overcomers reside in the upper two levels, depending on their degree of maturity. The first level is for infants, children, immature believers, and subcomers. They will reside in this introductory first level, where they will receive instruction until they are mature enough to move up planes within their levels. (I do not believe they would be able to move from the first level to the second level, only to the top of the first level.) Some have suggested that subcomers may be spiritually retarded—imbeciles. Their capacity to mature may be so severely impaired so as to be nonexistent. However, to give the Becker-Missler remediation theory some credence,[1608] let it be supposed that even subcomers can experience some maturation within the city. In that case, what happens to them at the beginning of the millennium when the wedding feast starts? They are expelled from the lower level of the city to the lower hemisphere of the planet where they cannot even see the city. Whatever theoretical remediation they were experiencing ceases. The outer darkness is punitory, not purgatory. Believers cast into the outer darkness will reap and gnash their teeth as they are excluded from the feast.

Greenhouse

Becker and I hold very similar perspectives regarding the tree of life: "Innumerable trees line both sides of the river inside the divided street....The whole city is like a gigantic hydroponic greenhouse."[1609] "The ones who overcome...will be given access to the tree of life in the paradise of God."[1610] However, I would interject that since subcomers currently reside in the lowest levels of the city, even they will be able to partake of the tree of life before being cast out of the city. The misthopological implications are that access to both the tree and the city are taken away from the subcomer at the commencement of the wedding feast: "God shall *take away* his part from the tree of life and from the holy city" (Rev 22:19). To *take away* (*aphaireo*) means to *cause a state or condition to cease* (BDAG). All believers who have died or who have been raptured, even those believers who eventually and eternally will be cast into the outer darkness, are taken immediately to the Heavenly City where they have access to the tree of life when they die or are raptured. One does not have to await the Bema in order to be in the city or to have access to the tree of life. Rather, what is granted to the overcomer as a result of the Bema is the right to continue to abide in the city and to continue to partake of the tree of life.

Little wonder, then, that those cast into the outer darkness weep and gnash their teeth. Literally, they will have had a taste of heaven before that experience of abiding in the city and eating of the tree of life is taken away from them. Whatever (theoretical) maturation and education they will have experienced while in the city will not be taken away from them, but the opportunity for further maturation and education will be taken away from them during the millennial kingdom and eternal state. The outer darkness is punitive, not instructive or curative.

The application and exhortation are easily derived. Your spiritual capacity to increase your capacities and your spiritual opportunities are determined by your spiritual maturation in this life. If you want unlimited opportunities to increase your capacity throughout eternity, then put a premium on doing so now. A student studying at the university would not rejoice in being taken out of the university to be sent to wash dishes at a diner for the rest of his or her life. Studying is hard, but not nearly so harsh as the alternatives. Study to show yourself approved at the Bema (2Tim 2:15). As Becker says, "God is looking for those who will take enough interest in His plans for this earth that they will be helpful in organizing His future kingdom."[1611] Those believers who take His word seriously now will be given charge of implementing it then.

Where is the Heavenly City

Based on Is 60:19-20, Becker observes that "since the earthly Jerusalem will constantly be bathed in God's light, it is always in view of the heavenly city." She provides three options as to how this might be accomplished.

Illustration 326. Revolving Planet

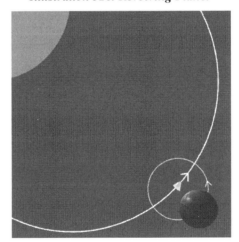

Becker's first option is: "One, the earth will revolve around the city with the same face always turned toward the city, like the moon which turns the same face to the earth."[1612] The city will revolve around the sun, and the Earth will revolve around the city. The Earth will become the city's moon.

Illustration 327. Geostationary City

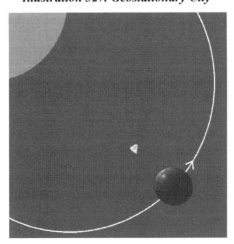

Her second option is: "Two, the city will revolve around the earth at a point in space (22,300 miles out) called by scientists geostationary, which will allow the satellite to match the earth's speed of rotation. Hence, the heavenly city will remain stationary over earthly Jerusalem…eleven times closer than the present moon." This option is more attractive than the previous one.

Illustration 328. Revolving City

Becker prefers the third option: "Three, the earth will turn that quarter turn on its axis, and the earthly Jerusalem will be the north pole with the New Jerusalem revolving above it and traveling with the earth around the sun."[1613] She gives three reasons for this northern preference: "Lucifer tried to sit on the mount in "the sides of the north" (Isa. 14:13).* Ezekiel saw the great whirlwind cloud of the glory of God come out of the north (Ezek. 1:4). Judgment armies were always sent from the north."[1614] Because this turn of the earth on its axis takes place during the events of the tribulation, and therefore does not pose an inconsistency between the millennium and eternal state, this position will be adopted as a tentative proposal in this second volume.[1615] Doing so will require that a slight tweak be made on the location of the outer darkness as I have pictured it elsewhere.

Illustration 329. Revised Location of Outer Darkness

Traditional	Tentative
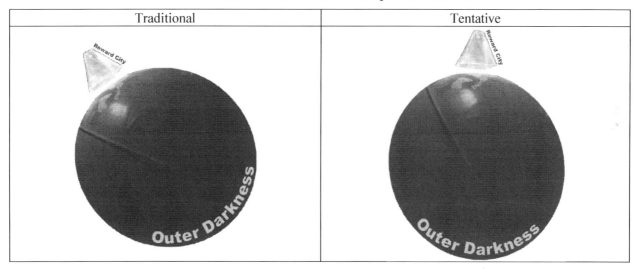	

Becker's planetary-rotation theory and her location of the city are well received herein. Unfortunately, however, although Becker has one of the most interesting descriptions of the outer darkness in regard to this rotation and location, she fails to realize that this is what she is describing:

> The city will turn at the same rate as the earth….Day and night will go on undisturbed in the southern hemisphere. The western hemisphere, which has basked in gospel light for years, will end up

---

* For collaboration of the location to the north and other misthopological matters from Psalms, see *Like a Tree Planted by the Water*.

underneath as the hemisphere subject to night, hidden from the supernatural light. Isaiah says that messages will have to be sent to some in the kingdom who have not seen the glory of God that they may come and see (Isa. 66:18-19). Therefore, a *place* will exist where the city cannot be observed.[1616]

That *place* on the planet where the city cannot be observed, is the outer darkness, at least during the millennium. During the millennium, *all flesh* (which I take to mean all people living in flesh and blood bodies) will be required to go to the North Pole and worship at earthly Jerusalem. As Becker notes, that will require amazing advancement in transportation. She provides a picture of the new earth with Jerusalem at the New North Pole and with the New Jerusalem suspended above it. She has removed the oceans from her depiction since the Scripture teaches that there will no longer be any seas (only large fresh water lakes).[1617] She is correct in that assessment; nevertheless, I have not removed the seas in my representation in *Illustration 330* so that the correlation with the present situation might be better perceived.

Illustration 330. Gizrah as Measured on Planet Earth

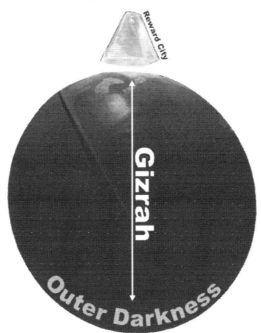

The Misslers' discussion of the outer darkness may be enjoined with Becker's discussion of New Jerusalem. The correction noted herein regarding Gizrah may also be made at the same time. The outer darkness is not Gizrah. Rather, the southern hemisphere of the planet comprises this darkness outside the city during the millennium. Gizrah is not the outer darkness but the free space between the Promised Land of Jerusalem and the outer darkness. Since believers cast into the outer darkness are pictured as being bound *hand and foot* (Mt 22:13), these amazing advancement in transportation to the North Pole to worship will not be applicable to them. While those living in flesh and blood bodies in the southern hemisphere will be able to travel to the New North Pole to worship, those resurrected believers who are bound in the outer darkness will not be able to travel to the New North Pole to worship. Instead, as a whole and as a rule, they will be confined to the southern hemisphere where they will not be able to see the light of the city where they formally lived in the lower level of the city before their expulsion.

As Becker admits, "Ezekiel tells us that the same trees [of life] will grow on earth and line the sides of the river flowing from the temple" (Eze 47:7,12). "The one condition seems to be their location. They will only be available in the middle of the 'the way' along the river of life."[1618] If these are indeed the same type of trees as the tree of life in Revelation, then the most natural supposition would be that the water will flow freely, and be freely available, but the fruit is only accessible to those who have the right to the middle of the streets where the trees grow by the river.[1619] Since subcomers do not have access to such trees after the millennium starts, it is doubtful that they will have access to the area where the trees grow after that point either. The trees will be confined to the New Jerusalem and the Promised Land (the Holy of Holies and the Holy Place). Those confined to the outer darkness will be confined to a location where the water of life may eventually reach—on the other side of the planet—but the tree of life will not be there.[1620]

Expanding Gizrah

To this point, the millennial location of the outer darkness, and thus Gizrah, has been confined to the study of this planet. Yet as Becker correctly perceives, "those in the heavenly city will have an ever-expanding universe to rule over."[1621] A word needs to be said about the outer darkness and Gizrah in relation to this ever-expanding rule throughout the universe. As this planet becomes more densely populated and humanity moves out in all directions from this planet, the most reasonable proposition is that those in the outer darkness will be ported to the outer fringes of this ever-expanding kingdom. The outer court literally will become outer space. "But where in outer space?" is a more speculative question.

Theory of General Relativity

Humphreys begins his book with a discussion as to how "*gravity affects time*" (emphasis his) in the theory of General Relativity (GR).[1622] The Misslers also have a page devoted to this topic in their book.[1623] Basically, God is said to "inhabit eternity" (Is 57:15), outside of time, from where He can declare, because He sees, "the end from the beginning" (Is 46:10). Certainly, GR (General Relative) is to be accepted as scientific fact, yet I would pose that the statement that God is outside of time should be understood as meaning outside of *our* time. Although our clock is affected by gravity, God's clock, so to speak, would not be affected by gravity. Just as space can exist in more than one dimension, so can time. We may experience time differently from the Lord, but we both experience time relative to one another (2Pet 3:8).

Illustration 331. Big Bang Gizrah

Assuming one adopts the closed-space version of the Big Bang theory, the universe is a finite, three-dimensional space being stretched out like as if on the surface of a balloon in fourth dimensional hyperspace. In that case, Gizrah eventually may point to the other side of the finite universe across the interior part of the fourth dimension of hyperspace. Just as an ant crawling around the 2-D surface of a balloon that has been blown out around 3-D space never reaches the edge of the 2-D surface, so one moving round the 3-D area of outer space would never reach the edge of outer space. Indeed, according to this theory, if one were to travel far enough, one eventually would return to one's point of origin. As humanity spreads out in all directions from earth, it eventually will converge from all directions on the other side of the universe. So Gizrah might be measured in 3-D around the circumference or in 4-D as passing through hyperspace. The above diagram depicts the latter. Conceivably, in infinity future, a planet on the other side of the universe could become the residence for those expelled from the city. The most fitting name for this planet would be *The Outer Darkness.*

Illustration 332. Creationist 4-D Gizrah

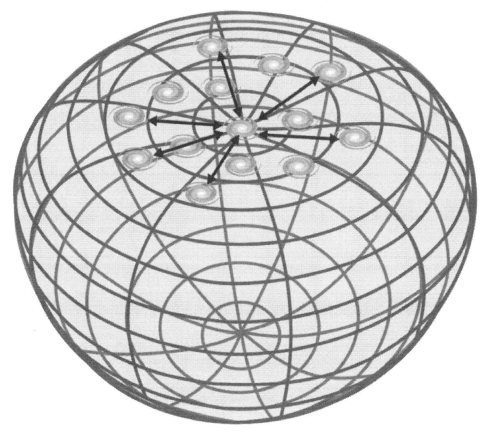

In Humphreys' creationist model, however, not only is space finite (1Kgs 8:27; Ps 147:4), but it is bound with a surface (Gen 1:2) and has an edge (that is now a spherical wall of ice).[1624] Earth is at the center of the universe. God stretched out the heavens (i.e., outer space) using this fourth dimension of space (Job 9:8; Ps 104:2; Is 40:22; Jer 10:12; Zech 12:1). God commenced the universe in a black hole and then expanded the universe by means of a white fountain* (which is a black hole running in reverse) until the white hole ceased to exist. Earth was at least roughly in the center, if not in the very center, of this ball of water and thus of the expansion. On day one of creation, God created a ball of water two light years in diameter. The gravitational force was so great that it immediately started compressing in on itself and thereby generated intense heat and light in a thermonuclear fusion. This black hole phenomenon lasted 24 hours, at which time, on day two, God intervened and converted it to a white hole. Cooling started to occur rapidly with this expansion. The laying of the foundations of the Earth (i.e., the core mantel), referred to in Job 38:4,† occurred on the second day.[1625] Dry land appeared on the surface of the cooling Earth on day three. The expanding universe (i.e., the expanse of the heavens, referring to interstellar space) reaches its event horizon "early on the morning of the fourth day" and started forming galaxies.[1626] Although physical matter cannot move through the fabric of space faster than the speed of light, this does not mean that *space itself* cannot travel faster than the speed of light.[1627] Because of GR, the newly formed galaxies (particularly the ones further out from Earth) traveling much faster than the speed of light aged billion of years during the 24-hour period of E.S.T. (Earth Standard Time) on the fourth day. This expansion and time dilation was strongest on the fourth day, faded during the fifth day, and came to a complete stop by the evening of the sixth day. When Adam and Eve looked up into the night sky at the end of the sixth day, these galaxies were now visible.‡

In this model, Gizrah eventually would be the distance to the galaxies on the outer edge of the universe. As humanity spreads to the outer edge, conceivably those in the outer darkness might be moved to the fringes of the universe.

---

* Although the term *white fountain* is more technically correct, most people would still call it a *white hole*.
† Therefore, the angels had to be created on the first day of creation since they were present to shout for joy at the foundation of the Earth (Job 38:7).
‡ For a picture of this cosmology in relation to the gap theory, see *Illustration 344. Neoclassical Creational Gap*, 919.

Illustration 333. Creationist 3-D Gizrah

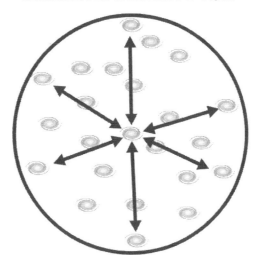

For those who would prefer a more traditional 3-D picture of the universe, the above diagram may be consulted. As already explained, Gizrah is not the outer darkness. Rather, in Ezekiel's model Gizrah represents the separate space (i.e., free space) between the holy places on this planet and the outer darkness in the southern hemisphere of the planet. Perhaps Gizrah will be defined in millennial text books as the space between the New North Pole and the New South Pole. As humanity continues to move out across the universe, though, Gizrah might be redefined in the textbooks of infinity future as (1) the 3-D distance between Earth and the outer wall of ice that separates the fabric of space in outer space from the external hyperspace which lies beyond the universe or (2) the 4-D distance that factors the hyperspace within the universe into consideration, as the distance from earth to the wall of ice is computed.

Theory of Correlativity

Just as Einstein proposed a theory of general relativity to explain the mathematical data he perceived to exist in the material universe, so the present work proposes a theory of correlativity to elucidate the intentional points of similarity and dissimilarity that may be seen to exist and be directly applicable to the judgment of both unbelievers and unfaithful believers within the hermeneutical arena. Since this field of study overlaps typology, some of the same rules that govern the latter will be found applicable to the former.

Illustration 334. Principle of Correlativity and Typology as Subsets of Biblical Correspondence

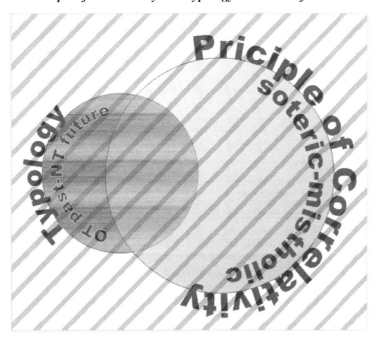

To clarify the relationship between typology and the ***principle of correlativity**** being proposed herein, when typology is defined narrowly as the intentional OT portrayal of a future NT event, then obviously many things that would fall within the range of typology would fall outside the range of the principle of correlativity and vice versa. Nevertheless, some overlap would occur in which an OT judgment that took place in regard to unbelievers might serve as a warning for NT believers. Moreover, OT-NT typology (pictured on the left) in *Illustration 334* and soteric-mistholic correlativity (pictured on the right) are but two forms of correspondences in the broader range of biblical correspondences (pictured by the slanted lines within the plane).

If some type of soteric-mistholic correlation exits between the soteriological *black darkness* of Jude 1:13 and the misthological outer darkness of Matthew, then the moving of those in the outer darkness from planet to planet, and even from star system to star system, might be entertained as correlative parallels. On the other hand, if a correlation exists between the stationary location of the Lake of Fire and an eventual static position of the outer darkness, a mediating possibility might be suggested. Rather than continually move those in the outer darkness from one planet to the next (until the outermost fringes of the universe are eventually met), eventually a planet might be designated for those cast into the outer darkness. Still, the most fitting name for this planet would be *The Outer Darkness*. Either conjecture would be within the scope of theoretical possibilities.

As to the correlativity hypothesized between the judgment pronounced on demons and unfaithful believers, several passages indicate that some type of connection exists between the judgment of (1) Satan, demons, and unbelievers as compared to that of (2) unfaithful believers. In Jude 1:11-13, being destroyed in the rebellion of Korah is linked (not equated) with spending eternity in the black darkness forever. But the destruction that took place at Korah would be presumed to represent misthological destruction. Thus, misthological destruction is purposely linked with (but not equated with) soteriological destruction (Korah ≅ Hell; Korah ≠ Hell). Not only do these two verses supply this link in back-to-back conjunction, but Jude uses the destruction (*apollumi*) that took place after the people were saved from Egypt to depict the *misthological* outcome for believers who subsequently disbelieved after being saved out of Egypt (Jude 1:5), and he links this destruction with the *soteriological* outcome for unbelievers who never believed (Jude 1:11).

- The Lord, after saving a people out of the land of Egypt, subsequently *destroyed* [*apollumi*] those who did not believe. (Jude 1:5)

The Lord saved them and then destroyed some of those whom He saved. One such occasion, in which He destroyed those whom He saved out of Egypt, was at the rebellion of Korah:

---

* The ***principle of correlativity*** is a subset of the broader field of correspondence that refers to a specific type of intentional correlation in which a broad soteric-mistholic or mistholic-soteric typological relation is perceived to exist between two different persons, events, or states. A mistholic-misthological correlation, therefore, such as that which exists between the out-resurrection and the outer darkness or between the priests that serve in the outer courts versus their typological counterparts, would be outside the scope of the type of correlation being described by the principle of correlativity.

Possible examples of such soteric-mistholic correlations include: exclusion from kingdom inheritance based on classification versus characterization, the covering of one's bets by Judas and the servant, the lost and saved being thrown into the outer darkness, weeping and gnashing their teeth, being outside the city, categorically black dogs versus characteristically black sheep, metaphysical black darkness as compared to the metaphorical outer darkness, outer darkness as compared to exclusion from the city, being cast out of the kingdom as compared to being cast out of the feast, exclusion from the kingdom versus from the city, expulsion of both unfaithful angels and servants from the city, being cast into the fire, being condemned, being hurt by the second death, partaking of God's wrath, not being known, experiencing eternal torment versus enduring eternal shame, and being subject to soteriological death as opposed to misthological death.

Correlative applicability is not to be limited to or confused with metaphorical applicability in that being hurt correlatively by the Lake of Fire, for example, is not to be equated with being cast metaphorically into the Lake of Fire. The principle of correlativity does not deduce that unfaithful believers are cast metaphorically into the Lake of Fire. Rather, the casting of (1) *unbelievers into the Lake of Fire* and (2) *unfaithful believers into the outer darkness* can be said to have a soteric-mistholic typological relation. At most being hurt by the second death would be a metaphorical picture of this correlation. Believers are not submitted to the Lake of Fire; although, a direct correlation exists between the Lake of Fire and the Outer Darkness. Even so, a direct correlation is not to be confused with a direct application. One should not confuse type and antitype.

The negative results meted out at the Bema can be compared in the broad typological sense (but not literally or metaphorically equated) with the negative results poured out at the GWT. The typological correlation is **direct**: *Bema ≅ GWT*.

- [11] Woe to them! For they [unregenerate false teachers] have gone the way of Cain, and for pay they have rushed headlong into the error of Balaam, and were *destroyed* [*apollumi*] in the rebellion of Korah. [12] These men are those who are hidden reefs in your love feasts when they feast with you without fear, caring for themselves; clouds without water, carried along by winds; autumn trees without fruit, doubly dead, uprooted; [13] wild waves of the sea, casting up their own shame like foam; wandering stars, **for whom the black darkness has been reserved forever**. (Jude 1:11-13; TM)

Since the destruction at Korah was part of the destruction that took place after the Israelites came out of Egypt, the *misthological* destruction that occurs in v. 5 is not only verbally linked, but also contextually linked, with the *soteriological* destruction that occurs in v. 11. This dual mistholic-soteric association makes it unmistakably clear that both subcomers and noncomers reap destruction as their outcome. Many who were saved out of Egypt perished in a manner similar to unbelievers.[*]

Illustration 335. Salvation Linked with Destruction

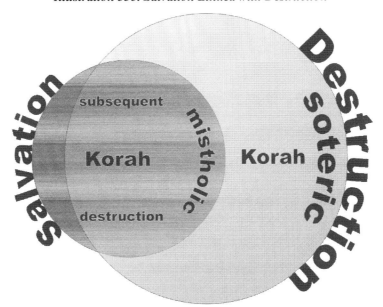

Dissimilarities must not be lost amidst similarities, however, in developing a principle of correlativity. In the study of typology, dissimilarities can be just as important as similarities. Jude is not saying that those saved typologically out of Egypt will be condemned soteriologically to the same black darkness as the unregenerate. Nevertheless, surely Jude intends for us to see a correlation between the misthological destruction that occurred at Korah and the soteriological destruction of the black darkness with which he links it. In addition, the plausible usage of the Enochian soteric outer darkness as a backdrop for the Matthean mistholic outer darkness has been noted already. Moreover, the fact that those cast into the outer darkness and the fires of eternal punishment both experience a *weeping and gnashing of teeth* is surely not incidental or coincidental, but neither is it identical (Mt 8:12; 13:42,50; 22:13; 24:51; 25:30; Lk 13:28).[†] Given this plausible Enochian linkage, the highly probable Judean linkage, and the provable verbal linkage made by Jesus, the position adopted herein is that some intentional mistholic-soteric correlation exists between the outer darkness and the black darkness. Although not identical, the darkness is applicable in some manner to both unbelievers and believers.

This type of correlation has been suggested already regarding the warning of not inheriting the kingdom. At the beginning of the Corinthian context in 1Cor 6:1, Paul categorically refers to *the lost* as *the unrighteous* (*hoi adikoi*). In this context, Paul uses this articular expression to refer to the identity of the lost as a class of people in differentiation to *the saints* (*hoi hagioi*) as a separate class of people (1Cor 6:2). He then uses the verbal form of

---

[*] Soteric fire ≅ mistholic fire (Jude 1:6,23). Correlations can either be soteric-mistholic or mistholic-soteric. Peter uses all of a chapter for a soteric-mistholic relation: soteric (2Pet 2:1-17) ≅ mistholic (2Pet 2:18-23). The soteric judgment of phenomenal apostates ≅ the mistholic judgment of moral apostates. On a smaller scale, believers are capable of falling correlatively from their secure position into the destruction of those who distort Scripture (2Pet 3:16-17).

[†] See *Weeping and Gnashing of Teeth*, 431.

behaving unrighteously (*adikeo*) to assert that some of the Corinthian sheep are *behaving unrighteously*. By characteristically lumping these vice-prone sheep in with categorically black goats, Paul establishes a correlation between the black sheep and black goats.[*]

Illustration 336. Hoi Adikoi versus Adikoi

- *Hoi adikoi*—categorically unrighteous
- *Adikoi*—characteristically unrighteous

Paul uses an anarthrous term (*adikoi* without the article) for *unrighteous* in 1Cor 6:9 to refer to the black character of those described by the vice list and warns that those so characterized will not inherit the kingdom—even if they are sheep. Paul is pointing out, most strongly, that those who *categorically* are righteous will not inherit the kingdom if they *characteristically* are unrighteous. In other words, the unrighteous righteous will not inherit the kingdom. Legal righteousness needs experiential righteousness to qualify for kingdom rulership.[†] To qualify for this qualitative experience in the kingdom, the believer must be morally righteous.

These black sheep used to be black goats before they *were justified*—i.e. before they were *declared legally righteous* (1Cor 6:11). Now they are no longer *hoi adikoi* (i.e., they are no longer classified as lost goats). Nevertheless, these justified believers still are acting like *adikoi* (*unrighteous*) people and thereby living in such a way that will disqualify them from inheriting the kingdom. Paul provides a similar vice list in Galatians (5:19-21); he likewise makes the same application and provides the same warning. The unrighteous, whether they are saved or lost, will not inherit the kingdom.

Illustration 337. Dogs and Sheep Outside the City

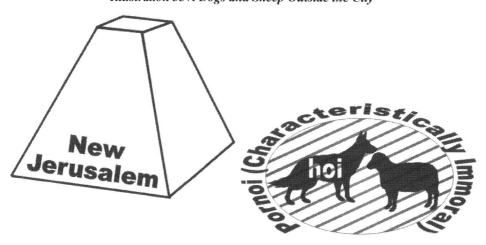

---

[*] See *Illustration 53. Unrighteous will not Inherit*, 121.
[†] For use of this same illustration in the context of a different discussion, namely that of the parable of the sheep and goats, see *Woolly Wolves and Woolless Sheep*.

Given such considerations, the proposal becomes very reasonable that John probably intents to bring this *misthological* truth to mind with his *soteriological* depiction in Rev 22:15: "Outside are the dogs and the sorcerers and the immoral persons and the murderers and the idolaters, and everyone who loves and practices lying." Both Paul and John include the *sexually immoral* (*pornoi*) in their vice lists. Whereas Paul uses the anarthrous form, John uses the articular form. Whereas Paul is talking about those who are characteristically immoral in the present, John is talking about those who are categorically immoral in the eternal state. John starts off his list by stating that the dogs are outside the city, depicting the lost as outside the city. However, John probably intents for us to see a correlation between the unregenerate being outside the city and the regenerate who are characterized by unregenerate behavior as being outside the city. For he immediately goes on to warn that those (believers) who add or take away from the words of his prophecy will have their portion in the city taken away. Apparently, a correlation is anticipated in which these regenerate believers will, in some capacity, be outside the city in a manner similar to the unregenerate.[*]

Illustration 338. Outside and Outcast

However, at least one major difference between the unregenerate dogs outside the city and the carnal believers outside the city is suggested by the context. Those cast outside the city lose their portion within the city. This portion will be taken away at the Bema. Subsequently, they will be cast outside the city. Yet not all those outside the city are outcast in the sense of having been previously in the city to be cast out of it. Those classified by John as dogs were never in the city; they never had a portion in the city to lose. Notwithstanding, John probably intends to use them to remind his readers that a similar fate awaits anyone who tampers with his words. Still, a similar fate is not an identical fate. Being soteriologically outside the city in the Lake of Fire is to be compared to, not equated with, being misthologically outside the city in the outer darkness. John expects his readers to see a correlation between soteriological exclusion and misthological exclusion, but he does not intend for them to equate the two. Misthological correlation must not be turned into a soteric equality but factored in a mistholic cosmology.

Gap Theories

The misthological cosmology being entertained intersects various views of the gap theory. Therefore, locating it on the cosmological map in relation to other gap theories is advisable. If the traditional gap theory is accepted, then Becker's proposal (that Heavenly Jerusalem will be located to the north of this planet) would seem to be rather conclusive, and the theory of correlativity between Satan's expulsion and that of unfaithful believers is more tenable. However, Humphreys' cosmology provides a creationist alternative to the classical gap theory. For ease of reference, the three major gap theories can be summarized in relation to the first three verses of Genesis.

- Gap 1 places the gap before Gen 1:1.
- Gap 2 places the gap after Gen 1:2.
- Gap 3 places the gap after Gen 1:3.

---

[*] Other examples of correlation might be mentioned. Jesus uses a similar expression to say that He does *not know* unbelievers and unfaithful believers (Mt 7:23; 25:12; Lk 12:25). Being *cast out* of the present kingdom is parallel (but not identical) to being cast out of the future feast (Mt 8:12; 22:13; 25:30; Lk 13:28). Believers may be *condemned* (*katakrino*) *along with the world* (1Cor 11:32). Subcomers come into the same *condemnation* (*krima*) as the devil (1Tim 3:6). *If God did not spare the* natural branches (Jewish unbelievers), then He will not spare believers (Rom 11:21). The judgments for unbelievers and believers are certainly not identical (Jn 5:24); nevertheless, a correlation might be anticipated (Jn 5:28-29). Being cast into Gehenna as an A.D. 70 event may picture both misthological and soteriological outcomes. See *Illustration 361. Neoclassical Preteristic Gehenna-Bema*, 950. Scripture expects us to see a correlation between the Lord's soteric judgment and His mistholic judgment.

The second position is the one typically called the *gap theory*. According to this theory, Satan fell between Gen 1:1 and Gen 1:2, and God brought judgment upon the Earth in consequence at that time. Yet all three theories pose a gap of time and will be considered briefly below.

Precreational Gap Theories

Metaphysical Gap Theory

On the basis of Job 38:4-7, some gap theorists have concluded that the angels were created before Gen 1:1. The angels were created before the Earth because they sang when the Earth was created. Moreover, according to this perspective, because Lucifer initially was blameless when he was created (Eze 28:15), his fall had to occur before the beginning of the creation of earth described in Gen 1:1. Satan was a murderer from the very beginning of the present creation (Jn 8:44). Thus, he must have fallen before creation.

Illustration 339. Precreational Metaphysical Universe

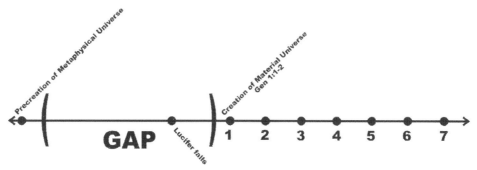

Lucifer fell within parenthetical the gap of time (GAP) denoted above, that is, between the time when he (along with the rest of the metaphysical universe) was created and when the material universe was created. This creation of the metaphysical universe would have included the creation of the third heavens and the angels (who are heavenly beings). Thus, God created the *heaven of heavens* (Neh 9:6), the *highest* realm of heaven (Lk 2:14), the *third heaven* (2Cor 12:2)—where angels abide (Rev 5:11) and where believers go to live with God when they die—before He created the astral heavens and the planet Earth. In this view, sin entered the immaterial universe before Gen 1:1, but sin did not enter the physical universe until the fall of man. God had created the immaterial heaven of heavens, that is, the third heavens, before He created the first and second heavens. Genesis only describes the creation of the first and second heavens—the atmosphere and the stellar universe. For simplicity's sake, let us assume this extra dimensional plane of existence is hyperspace. The gap of time in which Lucifer fell was before Gen 1:1 and occurred in hyperspace. One problem with this view, however, is in answering the question as to where Lucifer fell. If he fell from heaven, to where did he fall? Both Isaiah and Ezekiel say that it was *to the ground* (Is 14:12; Eze 28:17). The existence of a material universe seems to be supposed.

Physical Gap Theory

A more popular gap proposal is to suppose that the material universe already had been created, but left in a formless state, when Lucifer fell.

Illustration 340. Precreational Formless Universe with Pre-Formational Fall

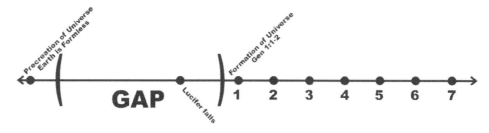

Since Earth was obviously formless when God first started working on it, like a potter working on a piece of clay, being formless is not necessarily an expression of judgment. The Earth initially was formless, in a state of chaos.

Still one is left to wonder if a formless universe would qualify as having ground, much less all the other precious stones associated with Lucifer's creation and coronation.

Illustration 341. Precreational Formless Universe with Post-Formational Fall

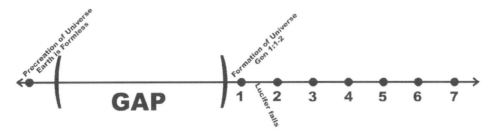

One way to resolve this problem is to adjust the precreational model so that the ground has been formed to which Lucifer will fall. As God started to form the chaos into the cosmos, Lucifer fell very early in the creation week, after Gen 1:2. But this model still has two immediately apparent problems: (1) No ground had been formed yet, and (2) creation was still good.

Illustration 342. Precreational Formless Universe with Post-Creational Fall

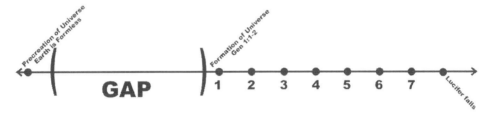

Some advocates of this precreational theory pose that Lucifer fell after the creation of man. Since God said *all that He had made was very good* (Gen 1:31) at the conclusion of the creational week, this view is preferable over the other models thus far surveyed. Additionally, it has the advantage of placing Lucifer's fall to the ground of this planet, presuming that the ground of this planet is intended, after the formation of dry land on Earth on the third day (Gen 1:9). This concludes the precreationist models being surveyed.

Classical Creational Gap Theory

Other gap theorists pose that Lucifer fell in the gap of time between Gen 1:1 and 1:2 and therefore after the commencement of the creational account in Genesis.[1628] In the Luciferian flood God judged the world during this time, and the world *became* formless and void (Is 34:11; Jer 4:23). Lucifer's flood predates Noah's flood, of course. Speculations about dinosaurs being killed in this Luciferian flood and demons finding their origin as disembodied spirits as a result of this flood are well known but beyond the scope of the present discussion.

Illustration 343. Classical Creational Gap

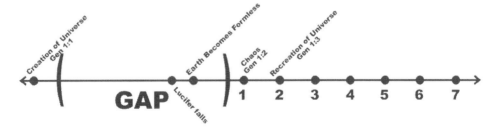

In both Is 14:12 and Eze 28:17, Satan was cast to the *ground/earth* (Heb. *eretes, Gr. ge*). The most pressing question now to be considered is, "To the ground of which planet?" These are the same Hebrew and Greek words used respectively in Gen 1:1 for the creation of Earth. Therefore, advocates of this classical gap theory appear to be on firm ground in posing that Lucifer's fall took place on this planet. Additional support might be derivable from Rev 12:4, the Dragon (Satan) with "his tail swept down a third of the stars of heaven and cast them to the *earth*

[*ge*]." The context is describing a war that took place in heaven (Rev 12:7-9). If this casting down to earth is a recapitulation of what happened in the past, then the case for this model is strengthened.*

Since Satan is called the god of this *world* (*aion*) in 2Cor 4:4 and the ruler of this *world* (*kosmos*) in Jn 12:31, presumably this planet is supposed. Unger advocates this traditional understanding: "Intimations are not lacking in Scripture that the highest of all God's created angels, 'the day star, son of the morning,' was placed in charge of the earth when this planet was originally created."[1629] Satan's fall occurred after creation and resulted in chaos on Earth in which this planet became formless and void:

> Satan's defection and fall occurred after the creation of the earth (Job 38:7) and apparently in connection with it. Although the subject is to a large extent wrapped in mystery, there are not lacking Scriptural intimations that suggest that Satan and certain angelic spirits were given suzerainty over the earth when it was primevally created and that it was in that high position of trust that "the day-star, son of the morning" planned his far-sweeping insurrection to usurp authority over the heavenly spheres and the earth that rightfully belonged only to "the Most High" as Creator and, therefore, "possessor of heaven and earth" (Gen 14:19, 22).
>
> If this interpretation is true, it would explain the cause of the fearful cataclysmic judgment that engulfed the pristine globe, reducing it to a chaotic ruin (Gen 1:2). It would also give meaning to Satan's specific use of the divine title "the Most High," which is descriptive of ownership by virtue of creation, in his original revolt against divine authority, when he cried: "I will make myself like the Most High" (Isa 14:14).[1630]

Yet weaknesses for even this streamlined version of this gap theory are well known. At the conclusion of the creation week, God said that creation was *very good*, so there could not have been a fall before that point in time (Gen 1:31).† Young-earth creationists insist that a planet full of dead dinosaurs (etc.) bones buried under the ground would have been an unclean planet. Moreover, Scripture attributes the entrance of death into the world through Adam's sin (Rom 5:12). Obviously, Lucifer fell (Is 14:12-14) before he induced Eve to fall, but there is no room for a gap in the creation account (Ex 20:11).

Neoclassical Creational Gap Theory

Traditionally, advocates of the creation model would not be considered gap theorists. Indeed, the typical form of this creationist model does not indicate any appreciable gap of time in Earth's calendar between the creation and Lucifer's fall. The Luciferian fall would have to occur after the end of the creation week but before Adam and Eve conceived a child. Whitcomb provides the classical creationist model:

> When God created the "heavens" at the beginning of the first day of creation week, He apparently created all the angelic beings (including unfallen Satan), who were thus on hand to sing together and shout for joy at the creation of the earth (Job 38:7). Sometime after the creation week and before the temptation of Eve, Satan rebelled against his Creator.[1631]

Some creationists suppose that many years could have occurred before Adam and Eve conceived their first child, perhaps even a hundred years. After all, their third child that is mentioned is Seth, and he was born when Adam and Eve were 130. This view is very weak though. Certainly, other unnamed children were born before and after Seth. Thus, one would be mistaken to think that Adam and Eve did not have their third child until they were 130 years old. Their children were not spaced out by large blocks of time. Undoubtedly, the prefect man and woman, without any genetic or physical problems preventing them from reproducing, and under divine command

---

* This war and casting down probably is future, however. Even if a past casting is in view, it could still be interpreted in harmony with other gap positions. The casting may have occurred when Satan rebelled, which would have taken place after Gen 1:31. Or the casting may have occurred at the incarnation when Satan sought to oppose the birth of Christ. Thus, this passage does not help pinpoint which gap theory is correct, other than to provide additional reason to reject precreational metaphysical gap.

† Creationists criticize classical gap theorists for posing that God calls this creation *very good* when Satan, as the god of this world, is hovering in the atmosphere overhead. Surely, Satan, overhearing this statement by God, would have reason to snicker if he already had fallen. Yet this same weakness would be inherent in the precreational theories. Those creationists adopting a precreational perspective are rightly refuted by those creationists adopting a post-creational perspective of Lucifer's fall. Whitcomb is thus consistent when he rejects Waltke's proposal along with the more traditional form of the gap theory.

to reproduce, would not have to wait beyond Eve's first ovulation for conception. Therefore, more reasonable proponents of this creationist model acknowledge that the fall had to occur within the first 45 days of creation.

Yet this leaves too small of a window of opportunity for the fall of Lucifer as it is depicted in the Scripture. The impression one gleans from Scripture is that Lucifer had been around quite some time before his fall. Notwithstanding, the creationist model can be rescued, however, by Humphrey's creational cosmology. The traditional creationist model can be amended with Humphreys' newer creational model[*] that gives a much larger window of time in terms of O.G.T. (Outlying Galaxies Time).

Illustration 344. Neoclassical Creational Gap

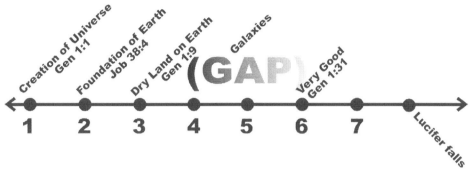

In this neoclassical creationist model, the angels could have been created on day one, as Whitcomb suggests, or perhaps they could have been created as late as the early morning of day four when the galaxies were formed. I will opt for Whitcomb's proposal. A few days later (E.S.T.), after the creation week was completed, Lucifer rebelled, as Whitcomb deduces. But this Luciferian fall was billion of years later O.G.T. The angels, being heavenly creatures, inhabit the second heavens and have access to the first heavens and third heavens. For billions of years (O.G.T.), they awaited the emergence of the last galaxy and for God to complete His creation. They sang for joy as the long-awaited event came to completion. The creation was only a few days old by E.S.T, yet it was billions of years old by O.G.T.

If the angels were created on the first day of creation and given jurisdiction over the galaxies coming from the white fountain, then they would have had billions of years by O.G.T. to await the foundation of the planet Earth. They would have rejoiced when Earth emerged from the white fountain as the center of the universe in the last galaxy to be created (Job 38:4,7). Therefore, contrary to the precreational models, this passage from Job does not prove that the angels were created before day one of creation, only before the foundation of the Earth (on day two). This founding of the Earth would have taken place on the second day of creation E.S.T. but possibly billion of years later in terms of O.G.T. In any event, Lucifer had all the time in the universe to rebel. Nevertheless, in deference to Gen 1:31, the most reasonable hypothesis is that Lucifer did not rebel until after day 7 E.S.T., as Whitcomb and other creationists maintain. Although the Earth was only a few days old, and even though the universe was a few days old by E.S.T, the outlying galaxies (where Lucifer and the other morning stars were awaiting the emergence of the last star) were billion of years old by O.G.T.

As to the appeal made to Jn 8:44 by metaphysical precreationists, this verse does not say that Satan was *a murderer from the beginning **of creation***. The beginning in mind may be from the beginning of his role as *the devil*. In other words, the beginning of his fall may be in view. Or his role as serpent in the fall of Adam and Eve may be in view. In this case, from the beginning of his role in the fall of man may be in view. Either of these perspectives is more intuitive than supposing that creation is the reference point. The more intuitive position is that Lucifer was one of the morning stars and sons of God who sang and shouted for joy when God laid the foundation of the Earth. They all sang and shouted for joy together. Within a matter of days, however, Lucifer had a change of heart. God had laid the foundation of the Earth, the last planet for angels to rule, or so Lucifer may have thought. But then God pulled a surprise. He created man in His image and gave him rulership over this new central planet of the universe. The angels had been created billions of years earlier and had been ruling the universe during that time. Now God slowly, but surely, was turning this rulership over to an upstart called *man*. Lucifer sang for joy at the foundation of the Earth, but he began to have a change of heart with the creation of man. He would not be mastered by man. Rather, he would set out to become the master of man. Therefore, this neoclassic creationist model is very attractive in posing that Lucifer fell after Gen 1:31.

---

[*] See *Illustration 332. Creationist 4-D Gizrah*, 910.

Lucifer's Fall

The timing of the Luciferian fall in this model is thus superior to other models that pose his fall before the creation week is completed. But what about the spatial location of Lucifer's fall? From where did he fall, and to where did he fall? Isaiah uses the king of Babylon to symbolize the fall of Satan, as Ron Rhodes notes, "We find a *dual* reference that includes not just the king of Babylon but a **typological** description of Lucifer as well" (italics his).[1632] While some scholars might object to considering this imagery an example of typology, it is more reasonably taken as a duality rather than mere apostrophe and thus best fits the picture of typology.[1633] Indeed, when typology is understood as the intentional shadowing of some metaphysical reality (antitype) by some physical entity (type), then this depiction of Lucifer's fall qualifies as an example of typology.* The type does not necessarily have to precede its antitype in time but would be expected to exceed by its antitype in significance.

[12] How you have *fallen* [past tense] from [third?] *heaven*, O *star of the morning* [Lucifer], son of the dawn! You have been cut down to the *earth* [Earth?], you who have weakened the nations! [13] But you said in your heart, "I will ascend to [third?] *heaven*; I will raise my throne above the stars of God [astral or angels?], and I will sit on the mount of assembly in the *recesses of the north* [north of which planet?]. [14] I will ascend *above the heights of the clouds* [of which planet?]; I will make myself like the Most High." [15] Nevertheless you *will be* [future tense] thrust down to Sheol, to the recesses of the pit. (Is 14:12-15)

Lucifer fell (aorist) from heaven down to the ground, but from which heaven: one (terrestrial), two (astral), or three (celestial)? Presumably, Lucifer, like other angels, had his abode in the astral heavens (of the stars and planets), but he wanted to establish his throne in the celestial heavens above the other angels. He was cut down to earth/Earth (cp. Gen 1:1). But is the passage talking about the ground of this planet or of some other planet? Unger (a classical gap theorist) thinks that Satan was cast down from the third heaven to Earth and adds: "In his use of the term *heaven* Satan evidently means the third or highest heaven, where God Himself and the redeemed have their abode" (emphasis his).[1634] This traditional interpretation is very attractive if one enjoins the third heaven with this planet.

A number of references in this passage from Isaiah could refer easily to Satellite Jerusalem in the atmosphere, above the North Pole, of an unnamed planet: the far/farthest recesses of the north, on the mount of assembly, above the clouds. The reference to *above the stars* might be a reference to the atmosphere of this unnamed planet. Then again, this statement might only refer to ascending above the angels of the mount of assembly (i.e., to the top of Satellite Jerusalem). In the future, according to Isaiah, Satan will be brought down to the pit. Thus, the evidence from Isaiah seems split between two primarily possibilities.

The quote from Ezekiel helps fill in some missing details, where the king of Tyre is used to symbolize the fall of Lucifer:

You had the seal of perfection, full of wisdom and perfect in beauty. [13] You were in *Eden* [on or above what planet?], the *garden of God*; every precious stone was your covering: the ruby, the topaz, and the diamond; the beryl, the onyx, and the jasper; the lapis lazuli, the turquoise, and the *emerald*; and the gold, the workmanship of your settings and sockets, was in you. On the day that you were created they were prepared. [14] You were the anointed cherub who covers, and I placed you there. You were on *the holy mountain of God* [the Heavenly Eden]; you walked in the midst of the stones of fire. [15] You were blameless in your ways from the day you were created, until unrighteousness was found in you. [16] By the abundance of your trade you were internally filled with violence, and you sinned; therefore I have cast you as profane from *the mountain of God* [the Heavenly Eden]. And I have destroyed you, O covering cherub, from the midst of the stones of fire. [17] Your heart was lifted up because of your beauty; you corrupted your wisdom by reason of your splendor. I [have] cast† you to the *ground* [of which planet?]. (Eze 28:12-17)

"Why should someone as beautiful as he serve someone as frail as man?" would be the question that ran through Lucifer's mind. "Why should the whole universe eventually be placed in subjection to such a puny

---

* Some taking the point of view adopted herein regarding a typological relation between Lucifer and the king of Babylon would call Satan the type and the king of Babylon the antitype because the antitype is expected to come later in time. I prefer the reverse labeling because the antitype is expected also to exceed the type in significance. The king of Babylon is the earthly type of the metaphysical cherub who fell. The fall of Lucifer both preceded and exceeded the picture conveyed by the king of Babylon.

† Hebrew: perfect. Greek: aorist indicative. Completed past action, not future action (contra KJV).

creation as man?" In conjunction with other Scripture, combining the fall from heaven (so Isaiah) with the fall from the mountain of God (so Ezekiel) so as to derive a fall from the Heavenly Mountain Eden is the most reasonable explanation. Apparently, Satan was cast from the Heavenly Eden (which was a satellite mountain residence to the north of some planet) to the ground of the planet below that residence—a residence that resembled a heavenly mountain in size and shape. Since man was created to be ruler of the planet upon which he was placed, and yet initially was created lower than the angels (Heb 1:7), it stands to reason that Lucifer was the planetary ruler (or at least caretaker) of the planet which hosted this mountain shaped Emerald Eden on or above that planet. If an Emerald Eden on (or above) a planet in the first galaxy to emerge from the white hole is envisioned, so that this is when all these precious gems were first prepared as a covering for Lucifer (who was created and coroneted on the same day O.G.T.), then this neo-creational model is reasonable understanding of the text.

Obviously, this description of Lucifer in Eden does not match that of Adam in Eden. Two different pictures of Eden are pictured because two different Edens are involved. In commenting on Eze 28:13-14, Whitcomb (a young-earth creationist) provides the following explanation:

> It seems clear from a comparison with Daniel 2:45 and Isaiah 14:13 that "the holy mountain of God" must refer to the third heaven of God's immediate presence and not to an earthly [planetary] domain. It should be noted that Satan was "cast…from the mountain of God…*to the ground* (Ezek. 28:16-17, cf. Isa. 14:12)….It should also be noted that "Eden, the garden of God" was not a garden with trees, flowers, and streams. It was composed of precious stones and "stones of fire" (Ezek. 28:13, 14, 16). When we compare this with the description of the Holy City of Revelation 21:10-21, with its various precious stones, we conclude that Ezekiel's "garden of God" refers not to an earthly Eden back in Genesis 1:1, but to **a** heavenly one, from which Satan was cast down to earth. (Italics his, bold mine.)[1635]

This identification is correct insofar as it goes. Lucifer was a cherub who was on the holy mountain of God.[1636] What mountain could this be? What *mountain* would qualify as a *heavenly one* hosting an *Emerald Eden* like *the Holy City of Revelation*. Such clues are more than sufficient to make more than an educated guess. Yet the Scripture supplies another clue to seal the inference. Hebrews informs us that Abraham "was looking for **the** city which has foundations, whose architect and builder is God" (Heb 11:10). The Greek definite article informs us that Abraham was not merely looking for *some* heavenly city or *a* heavenly city. He was not merely looking for *something*—that just so happens to be a heavenly city or even the heavenly city. His aspirations were high and they were definite. He definitely was looking for the Holy City described in Revelation.

Of this conclusion, one need not have any doubt, despite the doubt of the commentators. Bruce tells us that we can be certain that the writer of Hebrews is allegorizing here (NIC). I would think, contrastively, that we can be certain that he is not allegorizing. He is speaking literally. Hebrews identifies this city as *Mount Zion, the Heavenly Jerusalem* that God has prepared for both OT and NT believers (Heb 11:16; 12:22). The writer of Hebrews tells us that we are seeking for this same city (Heb 13:14). This *seeking* (*epizeteo*) is clearly misthological and thus misthopological. In Phil 1:27 and 3:20, Paul exhorts us to *act as members of this heavenly city* (*politeuo*) in view of our *membership in that city* (*politeuma*). Being worthy of the gospel is tied inexplicably to this city by Paul. This city is the literal city of New Jerusalem, explicably described time and again in Revelation as a reward given to those who overcome (e.g., Rev 3:12; Rev 22:19).

Lucifer did not fall from just any heavenly city that just so happened to resemble the mountain city described by Hebrews and Revelation. Nor was Abraham blindly groping in the dark for some city that just so happens to turn out to be Heavenly Jerusalem. Lucifer fell from the same city to which Abraham aspired. Abraham was an early misthopoligist. He was not looking for some reward city. He was looking for **the** Reward City. Residence in that city is conditioned on obedience. Lucifer rebelled and lost his residence in that city. One day he will lose all access to that city. Abraham was seeking to gain residence in that city by being obedient. He was one extraordinarily motivated man because he knew what he was looking for. Therefore, I must amend Whitcomb's statement. Lucifer did not fall from *a* heavenly emerald city; he fell from *the* Heavenly Emerald City. Lucifer fell from it; Abraham was seeking to rise to it. Abraham intended to fill the vacancy and everything that went with it.

Lucifer was in the Heavenly City. He was cast from this Heavenly City to the ground below. God cast Lucifer from this Heavenly Eden to the ground of the planet below that satellite city. Just as a correlation is made between the king of Tyre and Satan, so a connection should be supposed between the Emerald Eden of that mountain and the Eden of Earth. The precious stones of the Eden on Earth (Gen 2:12) are only reminiscent of those of the Emerald Eden. Now the key question is, "Where was this Emerald Eden located in relation to Earth's Eden?"

Illustration 345. Three Possible Locations of the Emerald Eden

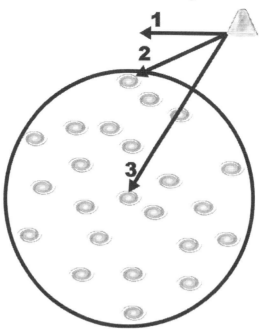

The first location of the Heavenly City (i.e., the Emerald Eden) to be considered would be in hyperspace outside the sphere of the material universe. Perhaps the city was located in hyperspace and Lucifer fell from hyperspace to space. Classical gap theorists do well to insist that the fall of Satan was to planet Earth. Yet they seem content to picture the heavens from which he fell to be a metaphysical arena. Although the diagram pictures this location as being to the north of the universe, it must be remembered that this location is in hyperspace. Therefore, it is not truly north. This location would not actually make sense if *north* means *north* and *clouds* mean *clouds* in the passage from Isaiah. Literal interpretation is to be preferred over symbolic interpretation when literal interpretation makes sense. Therefore, this first option is rejected herein as being in discord with Isaiah (Is 14:12-15) as well as with other possible references.

The second possibility is not so easily dismissed, however. As the first galaxies emerged from the white hole and the angels were (being) created and (being) given jurisdiction over the planets being created, one easily may propose that the galaxy to the furthermost north of the universe had a planet over which Lucifer was given authority and that the Emerald City was suspended in space above this planet. The capital city was over the capital planet. If this is the case, then when Lucifer fell he may have been cast to the ground of this unknown planet, which (for sake of discussion) will be called Planet X. His fall from the Emerald City to Planet X, just below the city, would have prefigured the fall of man from Eden to being cast just outside of Eden.* Later, when man fell, Lucifer gained rulership of the planet, which had been given to man.

More likely, though, the Emerald City was located above the Earth, at the center of the universe, by the time Lucifer fell. Although the city originally may have been located above Planet X (so option two), God moved it to above the new capital planet when He finished creation (so option three). Lucifer's capital planet was replaced by Earth as the new capital. The Emerald City was moved from the furthermost northern part of the universe to the furthermost northern part of Earth. If this conjecture is correct, the Heavenly City was in orbit above the North Pole of Earth when Satan was cast down from the Heavenly City to the Earth just below it. If so, both the classical and neoclassical models can accept this identification. Indeed, the best precreational model would also harmonize with this proposal. In any event, at the time of Lucifer's fall, the most reasonable inference is that this Emerald Eden was above this planet—Earth. Young-earth creationists Harry and John Morris matter-of-factly make this assumption.[1637]

Possibly, this city was *created* for the angels, at least in the sense of being their original habitation. But it *was prepared* for humanity (aorist of *hetoimazo*, Heb 11:16). This past phase of preparation may have been at the

---

* Alternatively, he might have been cast from the Emerald City all the way across the universe to Earth. But just as Adam and Eve were not ported to some remote location when they fell, it is doubtful that Lucifer was ported to some remote location when he fell. Thus, this theoretical possibility would be very doubtful typologically.

point of creation, in the sense of being the ultimate purpose for which the city was created. It was created/prepared for humanity as its misthological citizens. The ongoing preparations for the Bride (future of *hetoimazo*, Jn 14:2-3) indicate that the preparations have not yet been completed. Yet this phase of preparation will have been completed when the Bride comes down out of heaven (perfect of *hetoimazo*, Rev 21:2). Inversely, just as the Lake of Fire originally was prepared for Satan and his fallen angels (Mt 25:41) but ultimately will be co-inhabited with them by humanity, so the Heavenly city originally was prepared for humanity but ultimately will be co-inhabited with them by holy angels.

Illustration 346. Probably Location of Emerald Eden

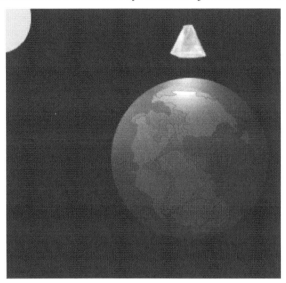

In the above model, the early Earth is pictured as having the supercontinent *Pangea* (*Pangaia*), meaning *all earth, all land*, also transliterated from Greek into English as *Pangaea*. Some creationists adopt this theory; some do not. Some who adopt it believe the supercontinent may have broken up in a post-Flood geological disaster (Gen10:25). The more prevalent position among those creationists who do accept the continental drift theory is to insist that the breakup would have occurred during the Flood. The reference to the dividing up of the Earth in the days of Peleg probably would refer to a patriarchal division or the incident regarding the Tower of Babel after the Flood. The working model adopted herein will be this latter creationist proposal. The continents were broken apart by the Flood.

Possibly, David makes an allusion to this very location of the Heavenly City during the time of the Food: *The Lord sat enthroned over the Flood* (Ps 29:10). Perhaps the Lord sat enthroned in the Heavenly City over the Earth during the Flood. Maybe Isaiah had a glimpse of the Lord sitting enthroned above this planet as the One *who sits above the sphere of the Earth* (Is 40:22). Plausibly, Noah saw this city from the ark during the time the ark was traversing the planet during the flood. To be sure, such suggestions are merely tentative, but how was it that Abraham was looking for a Heavenly City that has foundations and was built by God if he did not have any reason to believe that such a city exists (Heb 11:10)?

If the Pyramidal City was suspended above this planet as the sign of God's judgment and presence until the time of the Flood, and then was replaced by the rainbow in the clouds of this planet when the city returned to either the northernmost sector of the universe or to hyperspace, one might expect to find some faint echoes of that fact in early history, perhaps wrapped up in distortion within pagan myths. Mount Olympus would fit that bill. Might the pyramids of Egypt and the Mount Olympus of Greek mythology go back to a common racial memory of a pyramidal city above Earth where the gods dwelt?

Today, Christians strictly refer to these gods as angels. Yet the Bible repeatedly and inclusively refers to angels as *sons of God* (Gen 6:2,4; Job 1:6; 2:1; 38:7). Even Israel's human judges are said to be *gods, sons of the Most High* (Ps 82:1). To be sure, these humans were rulers in the sense of being given ruling authority as God's representatives. Still, they are called *gods*. It would not take much imagination to see how recollections of a mountain-shaped-city above Earth that was inhabited by God and by the sons of God (i.e., angels) could be misperceived and corrupted over time into the fabled Mount Olympus: the home of the gods with one supreme

God—Zeus.* Possibly, in his fall from Mount Olympus to Earth, Satan was perceived as becoming Hades, the god of the underworld. In mythology, this was misperceived to be his lot. The Bible, however, calls him the *god of this world* (2Cor 4:4).

Aside from the possible blend of fact and fiction, the most reasonable reconstruction is to conclude that Lucifer was cast out of the Heavenly City down to Earth. Most likely, the Heavenly City was above the Earth at that time. The city may have moved after Lucifer's fall, or after the fall of man, or at the time of the Flood. In any event, it was moved by the time of Job, when Satan, along with the rest of the sons of God, returned to the Heavenly City, apparently some distance from Earth, to give a periodical update of his activities. If this city is currently in hyperspace, then the same rules of time would not apply there as they do here. The earth day in which Satan appeared before God may have lasted much longer than twenty-four hours (E.S.T.). Job may not have aged more than a day while those events were going on, even if Satan had to wait years (O.G.T.) before having his turn to present himself before the Lord while away at the Heavenly City.

Illustration 347. Correlation of Expulsion

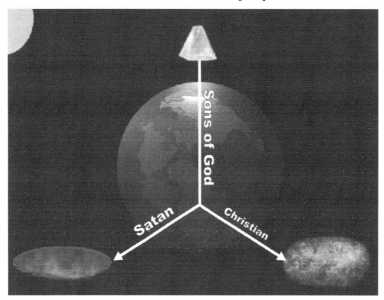

Even if some of the exact details must be left to the field of speculation, the broad strokes of the picture painted by Scripture strongly suggest a correlation between (1) Satan being cast out of the Heavenly City to this Earth and eventually to the Lake of Fire and (2) unfaithful Christians being cast out of the Heavenly City to this Earth and eventually to the outermost galaxies. The soteric expulsion of angelic sons of God provides a prototype for the mistholic expulsion of regenerate sons of God. In response to the question, "What is the outer darkness?" an answer that factors this correlation into consideration will have to acknowledge that in some ways, "The outer darkness will be what it was." What will happen to disobedient Christians shares a point of commonality with what has happened, and will happen, to Satan. The fallen cherub was cast out of the Heavenly City to the Earth below and eventually will be cast into the Lake of Fire. Fallen believers likewise will be cast out of the Heavenly City to the Earth below and eventually be ported to outer galaxies.

Conditional Security

Amidst these points of similarity, however, points of dissimilarity must not be ignored. Conditionalists challenge the affirmation of OSAS (in terms of *once a son always a son*) because Satan lost his sonship status. In doing so, conditionalists are guilty of a fallacy in making an equality between the sonship of Satan and that of the believer. Correlation is no justification for equalization. Fallen believers remain regenerate sons even when they fall from grace. To be sure, Paul says of the Galatian believers, "You are all sons of God **through faith** in Christ Jesus" (Gal 3:26). **However, they are not sons of God because of their current faith** (which is soteriologically defective, as Paul points out repeatedly) **but because of their original faith**. Their original saving response of faith to the gospel (as Paul originally had preached it to them) had been abandoned. This original response of faith

* For collaborating details, see *Like a Tree Planted by the Water.*

had resulted in their experiencing spiritual birth and becoming sons of God soteriologically. And they retain that original status of sonship in the present regardless of their failure to remain in grace.

Illustration 348. Fallen Sons are Still Regenerate Sons

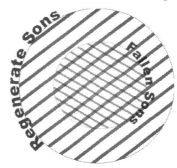

These fallen brethren had been made and continued to remain sons of God because of their past faith which they now had abandoned. Paul affirms that they retain their classification as sons of God, although they have abandoned their original faith. The Arminian contention that one must continue in faith in order to remain a son of God in this soteriological sense fails to do justice to the context. Static classification continues despite discontinuation in the means by which that classification was derived. Or stated differently, these regenerate unbelievers were still believers (in terms of being possessors of regeneration) because of the effects of their original belief.[*]

Yes, a correlation exists between (A) being cast soteriologically outside the city (like those who are categorically unclean) into the black darkness of the Lake of Fire and (B) being cast misthologically outside the city (as those who are characteristically unclean) into the planetary and then astral outer darkness. Nevertheless, the present book insists that those who move beyond the realm of correlation to make an equalization, or even equivocation, out of this correlation (so as to mislead others into thinking that salvation from these soteriological realities is conditioned upon performance) are teaching a false gospel. Acknowledging a correlation between soteric and mistholic realities provides no excuse for combining the two. Correlativity is not equivalency. One must not make a reward out of heaven. As always, entrance into the heavenly realm is free; rulership within the heavenly realm is costly.

Frontloading

The most serious flaw in Misslers' book is that it conditions soteric salvation on a commitment to perform better: "to be obedient to His commandments."[1638] The Misslers then add turning from one's sin to make this frontloading complete—a complete affront to the free offer of eternal life.[1639] This frontloading of the gospel is inexcusable, especially on the part of misthologists. Of all people, misthologists should know better than to condition soteriological salvation on performance because they realize that what is at stake for poor performance is not salvation from soteriological damnation in the Lake of Fire but misthological salvation from the outer darkness. At least the Misslers acknowledge that many regenerate believers "have *not* totally surrendered" their "lives to Christ" (emphasis theirs).[1640] Still, in view of their conditioning soteric salvation on turning and (partially) surrendering, they would have to be considered inconsistent Lordship Salvationists who are teaching a false gospel. Hopefully, in a future edition of their book, they will correct this tragically mistaken perspective.

Backloading

At the opposite end of the conditionalistic scale, Becker entertains the idea that perseverance in faith is a soteriological requirement to reach heaven. In doing so, she backloads the gospel.[1641] Much to her credit, nevertheless, she acknowledges that those who fall back into the world remain saved: "Are they lost then, since they failed to continue? No, they genuinely *believed*; therefore, their sins remain covered by the blood of Christ."[1642] I will pause only long enough to point out her implementation of the past tense. She correctly attributes their present blood-covered status to their past faith. However, in that case, the blood would cover the sin of failing to continue to believe. If moral apostasy is covered by the blood, then so is theological apostasy. Becker's conditional security is not only destructive, it self-destructs. Such a weakened view of conditional security as hers would have a tendency to reduce, at most, to soft unconditional security.

---

[*] See *Fallen from Grace but Not from Perfection* for further discussion of this illustration.

Conclusion

The basic premise of the theory of correlativity is that just as there are degrees of punishment in hell so there are degrees of punishment in heaven. A threshold exits in both realms: At ground level, heaven will be good, and hell will be bad. Many have acknowledged this theory in principle. The present work has formalized the theory and provided some particulars (P1, P2, etc.), adapting a diagram first suggested in rudimentary form by Crawford.[1643]

Illustration 349. Basic Principle of Correlativity

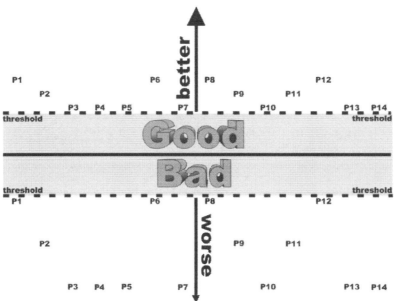

Investigation of the possible correlation between the Gizrah of Ezekiel's Temple and the outer darkness has led to the conclusion that the former provides a typological foreshadowing of the distance to the latter. Whatever positive, conjectural implications that might be derived from indentifying Gizrah with the West Building are not applicable to the outer darkness. Not only does Gizrah probably not include the West Building, Gizrah is not the outer darkness but rather the separating space between the holy places and the outer darkness. The outer darkness is pictured by the Outer Court of Ezekiel's Temple and would picture a place for punishment, not future remediation. To be limited to the Outer Court would be to fail to have access to the Inner Court, Holy Place, and Holy of Holies. Those serving in the outer darkness may perform lowly service for people and animals. But the opportunities for higher forms of service, to which they otherwise would have been entitled, will be taken away and given to those who have been faithful. Being limited to the Outer Court would be typologically parallel to being confined to the outer court of the palace and would have misthopological implications.

Consideration of these misthopological implications led to considering a misthopological cosmology. The most attractive proposal is to locate New Jerusalem above the New North Pole. One reason for this preference is because the Heavenly City originally was located to the north of this planet before Lucifer fell. Looking back to the past location of the city led to a consideration of various gap theories. Three primary gap theories were surveyed.

- Precreational: (GAP) → Gen 1:1
- Classical: Gen 1:1→ (GAP) → Gen 1:2
- Neoclassical: Gen 1:14 → (GAP) → Gen 1:31

Basically, a gap occurred before verse 1, between verses 1 and 2, or after verse 2. The neoclassical option was selected from a young-earth creationist model as the best option. However, it was noted that creationists perceive Lucifer as fallen from an Emerald Eden (namely, the Heavenly City) and classical gap theorists believe that he fell to this planet. Harmonizing these two perspectives was accomplished easily by locating the Heavenly City above the North Pole of this planet, possibly up through the time of the Flood.

A probable correlation was found to exit between the casting out of Lucifer from the Heavenly City and the casting out of unfaithful believers to the outer darkness. Surely, the fact that both Satan and believers, as *the sons of God*, are cast from the same city to the same planet is not merely coincidental or incidental. Just as importantly, though, neither is it identical. Correlativity does not imply equivalency. Important distinctions remain intact. Therefore, equating the outer darkness with the Lake of Fire or with the black darkness of Jude, for example, should be rejected most stringently.[1644]

Appendix 18.
Jewish Friend and Jewish Son(s)

Introduction

Within the body of the present book, the parable of the wedding guest has been interpreted as dealing with the church-age believer, called *friend*, who is thrown into the outer darkness because of his poor service in the present dispensation.[*] Various FG soteriologists would disagree with that assessment and argue instead that this friend represents a Jewish unbeliever living during the time of the tribulation.

Nation Options

Phillip Evans, for instance, commences his chapter *Outer Darkness* with a quotation from Mt 21:43 and then follows this quotation with that of Mt 22:1-14. His argument is that the kingdom was taken away from the unbelieving Jewish nation at that time to be given to the believing Jewish remnant at the end of time, which would be "the nation of Israel at the time of Christ's return, as composed of believing Jews, not unbelievers." Jesus is dealing exclusively with Israel in this parable. Supposedly, "the Church age is skipped over," Evans assumes, because eschatology was not sufficiently developed at the time Jesus gave this parable for Jesus' listeners to perceive this interadvent age. So the friend excluded from the feast is a hypocrite who claimed to be a believer. According to Evans, "the rejected wedding guest had to be shown into the banquet hall in order to illustrate why he was rejected."[1645]

John Philips, on the other hand, believes that in this parable "the nation of Israel is being set aside and, for the present age, the church is being called to take its place." Yet, like Evans, he believes that the friend thrown into the outer darkness is a lost hypocrite and that the nation to whom the kingdom will be given is the "new nation of Israel."[1646] For reasons already explained, I find the position taken by Phillips to be more persuasive as to the intervening church age and neither writer to be persuasive as to the unsaved status of the hypocrite—regardless as to which time period is in view. Even aside from exegetical evaluation, Evan's assessment that the hypocrite (if that is what the friend was) had to be allowed into the feast in order to show why he was ejected from the feast is open to objection. Why was this reputed hypocrite not met at the door and barred from entering the feast, if the feast represents the kingdom of God as Evans supposes? Why let the friend into the eschatological feast/kingdom in the first place since the point Evans envisions could have been illustrated by exclusion at the door? The foolish virgins were excluded at the door. Why could this foolish friend not be excluded at the door as well?[†]

As to the nation to whom the kingdom will be given, Haller (GNTC), like myself, adopts the misthological interpretation of the outer darkness and understands the guests at the feast to represent church-age believers. Unlike myself, though, Haller believes that the nation to whom the kingdom will be offered will be the future Jewish generation. Constable rejects the misthological interpretation and yet believes that the new nation to which the kingdom is offered is the church. Basically, dispensationalists are divided as to whether the nation to whom the kingdom will be offered is the church or the tribulational Jewish remnant. The misthological understanding of the outer darkness and the church-age understanding of the new nation are not tied inextricably to one another.

Illustration 350. New Nation

Writer	New Nation	Outer Darkness
Cauley	Church	Misthological
Constable	Church	Soteriological
Evans	Jewish Remnant	Soteriological
Haller	Jewish Remnant	Misthological
Phillips	Jewish Remnant	Soteriological/Misthological[‡]

Since FG theology is divided over how to best interpret this parable, and for the sake of interaction with my fellow FG writers who hold divergent points of view, I briefly will set aside my own preference (in part) and provide a concise, alternate, misthological interpretation of the parable that adopts the Jewish hypothesis for both

---

[*] See *Friend in the Outer Darkness (Mt 22:1-14)*, 421.
[†] In the case of Evans' hypothesis, the exclusion should have happened (1) at the door and (2) before the feast began.
[‡] Phillips takes the outer darkness to be soteriological in the parable of the wedding guests but misthological in the parable of the talents.

the *nation* and *friend* in order to further demonstrate that those adopting this perspective are operating on speculative grounds when they assume that this position nullifies a misthological interpretation of the friend thrown into the outer darkness.

Broad Context for Three Parables

The temple provides the setting (Mt 21:23-27) for three parables that Jesus provides in response to the antagonistic Jewish leaders pertaining to the temporary removal of the nation of Israel as the steward of the gospel of the kingdom. They demand to know by what authority He cleared out the temple. Jesus responds by asking if they acknowledge the authority of John the Baptist. A stalemate of sort results: "And answering Jesus, they said, 'We do not know.' He also said to them, 'Neither will I tell *you* by what authority I do these things'" (Mt 21:27).

First Parable

The stalemate is short lived as Jesus immediately launches an offense: "But what do *you* think? A man had two sons, and he came to the first and said, 'Son, go work today in the vineyard'" (Mt 21:28). The impression that one gets from Matthew's account of what follows is that Jesus addresses the first parable to the same group—the unbelieving Jewish leaders—with the word *you*. This impression is confirmed as being correct as one proceeds: "Truly I say to *you* that the tax collectors and prostitutes will get into the kingdom of God before *you*. For John came to *you* in the way of righteousness and *you* did not **believe** him; but the tax collectors and prostitutes did **believe** him; and *you*, seeing this, did not even feel remorse afterward so as to **believe** him" (Mt 21:31-32).

In this parable of the two sons, their father tells them to "go work" in his vineyard. The first son said that he would go and work, but in the end, this son neither went nor worked. Historically, this first son represents the unbelieving Jewish leaders, of course. The second son initially refused to go and work but eventually did so. This second son (evidently at one level at least) represents the Jewish tax collectors and prostitutes who came to saving faith and then repented of their works. This first parable can be understood as dealing exclusively with unbelieving and believing Jews. Might the same be said about the other two parables?

Before jumping to that consideration or conclusion, note that the point in the narrative where the kingdom is taken away from the Jewish nation has not yet actually been reached. To conclude that because the first parable is dealing with Jews that the second and third parable must be also would be premature. A parable dealing with Jews before the kingdom is taken away from the Jews would be expected to deal with Jews would it not? Whereas parables delivered after the kingdom is taken away from the Jews and given to another nation might be expected to deal with this subsequent nation. Additionally, even these Jewish sons could not work until they went. Going into the field may be taken as depicting coming into the kingdom via saving faith. The two-fold summons was to *go work*: (1) *go = believe*, (2) *work = repent*. One must be a believer in Jesus before one can be a worker in God's vineyard. Belief is foundational. As Matthew skillfully narrates, even before Jesus gives the triple emphasis on *believe* (Mt 21:32), Jesus' opponents realize that they cannot affirm John's authority without Jesus asking, "Why did you not believe?" (Mt 21:25)

Second Parable

Moving now to the second parable, the initial impression again is that it is addressed to these unbelieving Jewish leaders. Jesus tells them to "Listen to another parable" (Mt 21:33). The same group is being addressed.* Luke broadens the addressees, however, with additional details. The context not only reveals Jesus being in the temple with the Jewish leaders, the Jewish populace is present also: "While He was teaching the people in the temple and preaching the gospel, the chief priests and the scribes with the elders confronted Him" (Lk 20:1). Luke skips over the parable of the sons and goes directly to Matthew's second parable, that of the tenant farmers, and introduces it this way: "And He began to tell the people this parable" (Lk 20:9). Surely, some of those within the Jewish crowd standing there listening to Jesus were Jewish believers (cp. Mt 21:11,46). Yet within this parable Jesus informs His listeners that the vineyard would be rented to other vine-growers (Mt 21:41). Jesus interprets this detail for them: "The kingdom of God will be taken away from you, and be given to a nation producing the fruit of it" (Mt 21:43).

The Jewish antagonists correctly "understood that He was speaking about them" (Mt 21:45), in His reference to the first group of vine-growers who killed the owner's son. They knew He was referring to them.

---

* Mark uses *them* to convey the same impression: The *them* refers to the Jewish leaders who refused to answer His question (Mk 11:33; 12:1).

Therefore, Jesus is saying that the stewardship of the kingdom is taken away from that group of Jews and given to another nation. Because of the Jewishness of the context and because of prophecies regarding Israel in the future, Evans argues that all three parables must be dealing exclusively with Jews. From this premise he supposes that the friend thrown into the outer darkness must be a lost Jew. Such a conclusion does not necessarily follow, though, in that Haller shares much the same perception regarding the Jewishness of the section and yet believes that the friend thrown into the outer darkness is a believer. For that matter, all the writers charted above hold to the same basic understanding of the overall Jewishness of the context and the same overall dispensational understanding that the kingdom has been withdrawn only temporally from the Jewish people. Yet some of those holding this same generic framework would perceive an interim entrustment to the church as the new, present group of vine-growers. Since this matter is not crucial and for the sake of the present interaction, I will concede the possibility that the new set of vine-growers refers to the future generation of Jews during the tribulation. And I will use this as the working premise in this appendix in order to deal more directly with those holding this perception.*

Third Parable

Audience

Moving now to the third parable directed against these Jewish antagonists—the parable of the wedding feast, Matthew introduces this parable in an ambiguous fashion: "Jesus spoke to *them* again in parables" (Mt 22:1). To whom does *them* refer? Constable believes that the *them* refers to the Jewish leaders. However, this assumption is contestable for a number of reasons provided by Sapaugh.[1647]

The people is the nearest matching antecedent in Greek *for them*. This multitude is a key factor in the conversation that, up until this point, has been occurring between Jesus and His antagonists. Jesus drops the use of *you* in the third parable. Matthew may be alerting the reader implicitly to the possibility that this parable is no longer addressed to the antagonists but to *the people* referred to in the previous verse: "When they sought to seize Him, they feared *the people*, because *they* considered Him to be a prophet (Mt 21:46)." Apparently, Jesus switches to speaking to Jewish believers in the audience.

In fact, the leaders' fear of the multitude set the stage for all three temple parables (Mt 21:26). The reminder of this fear of the multitudes (who were present with them in the temple) comes at the conclusion of the second parable. The vocal interaction that Jesus has been having in the first and second parables ceases at this point, which is the same position in the Markan narrative where the antagonists leave. Mark adds this detail to the end of Matthew's concluding comment for the second parable: "And they [the Jewish leaders] were seeking to seize Him; and yet they feared the multitude; for they understood that He spoke the parable against them. *And so they left Him, and went away*" (Mk 12:12). His antagonists left the building. Where did they leave Jesus? In the temple. Doing what? Teaching *the people*, many of whom were Jewish believers. Given that the makeup of Jesus' remaining audience was composed of eager listeners (many of whom were believers), who were hanging on to Jesus' every word (Lk 19:48), one might expect that the focus of Jesus' teaching would shift to believers.

Granted, this positioning in the Markan narrative of the departure of the leaders is not conclusive since Mark does not include the parable that follows it. Nevertheless, their leaving at this point does coincide extremely well with the subtle Matthean indicators. The *they said*, which has been skillfully interwoven in Matthew's narration of the first and second parables, is absent from the third parable (Mt 21:27,31,38). Whereas the vocal interaction of the preceding two parables has been explicitly between Jesus and His antagonists, any reference to these antagonists is absent in the third parable.

The objection will be raised that Matthew delays the departure of the antagonists until the conclusion of the third parable: "Then the Pharisees went and counseled together how they might trap Him in what He said" Mt 22:15). Actually, however, the text does not say that they hung around to hear the third parable, only that after these parables Jesus' antagonists went to plot how they might find a way to trap Him in a statement.

In defense of Sapaugh's premise, I also would add a couple of other observations. Luke specifics that the second parable was spoken to the multitude: "And *to* [*pros*] the people He began to speak this parable: 'A man planted a vineyard and rented it out to vine-growers'" (Lk 20:9; TM). To be sure, the parable simultaneously is spoken *to/against/about* the antagonists, as we learn at the conclusion of the parable: "The scribes and the chief priests tried to lay hands on Him that very hour, and they feared the people; for they understood that He spoke this parable *against* [*pros*] them" (Lk 20:19). The antagonists need not be present in order for the third parable to be

---

* In this case, I would regard them as future tribulational Jewish believers. Yet this does not need to be made a major point of contention for the present purposes regarding this parable.

spoken *against/about* them. The speaking *to them* (i.e., to the antagonists) in Mt 21:24,27,31,42 gives way to *about* (*peri*) *them* (Mt 21:45). Jumping over the *about them* of 21:45 to equate the *to them* of 22:1 with the earlier references of *to them* is certainly open to question.

Not only are the *multitudes* the closer antecedent, Matthew introduces the third parable with an adverb that might suggest a change in the reference: Jesus "spoke to them *again* (*palin*) in parables" (Mt 22:1). In Mk 7:14, after refuting His antagonists, Jesus summons the multiple to Him *again* (*palin*) and began speaking in parables. * Probably, *palin* is used to mark such a transition on this occasion in Matthew.† *Parables* is plural in Mt 22:1. According to Matthew, Jesus spoke to them again in multiple parables in the opening verse of the third (and final) parable. Yet Matthew only records one more parable. Surely, the crowds, who hang on His every word, are the ones who stay in the temple to hear His every word. His antagonists, in contrast, leave the building in order to plot how they might trap Him in His teaching. These remaining parables (of which only one is recorded) were spoken to the remaining multitudes—to *the people* who stayed to listen.‡

Additionally, as also pointed out by France, the opening phrase of Mt 22:1 (*answered and said*) is not a reply, as such, but a Semitic formula used to introduce a significant new pronouncement/contribution when no preceding interpolation for the answer is provided.[1648] Yet despite such splendid observations, France assumes "the third parable is still spoken *to* the same audience of chief priests and elders/Pharisees."[1649] Why? Because Jesus was speaking *to them* previously—so France.

A much more consistent interpretation, though, would be to conclude that the parable was spoken *about* chief priests and elders/Pharisees *to* the crowd who remained to hear what Jesus had to say. The *them* to whom Jesus is speaking has changed to the (predominately believing) multitude at the beginning of the third parable. In addition to the three reasons supplied by Sapaugh, two additional considerations in favor of this conclusion have been supplied herein: the phrase and adverb used to introduce the parable. Mathematically, therefore, in terms of simply counting the arguments for and against this aspect of the interpretation, the odds are five-to-one in favor of Sapaugh's premise. Jesus is speaking to the multitudes, many of whom were believers.[1650]

In response to Evans' assertion that "the Church age is skipped over" and the corresponding question, "How do I know that the wedding parable is dealing only with Israel?" Evans responds, "First of all, He was speaking *to* the Jewish religious leaders."[1651] Contrary to Evan's assumption, Jesus is probably not speaking to the Jewish leaders. The much more plausible presumption is that they have left the temple, and Jesus is speaking the parable of the wedding feast to the crowd *about* the Jewish leaders and *about* other participants in the drama, such as themselves. The crowd (many of whom were believers) would be expected to find themselves in the parable.

Original Intent Versus Original Understanding

Next Evans proceeds with a dispensational explanation of the coming tribulational period in which he explains:

> These last prophets then will be the 144,000 Jewish believers that will spread the Gospel throughout Israel and the rest of the world. Since Jesus made it clear in 21:43 that unbelieving Jews will be rejected from the Kingdom of God, the wedding feast must be understood in this light. It is not the marriage supper of the Lamb. The eschatology of the people Jesus was speaking to would not have been developed enough to come anywhere near understanding this if this is what He was meaning.[1652]

---

* In Mk 10:1, Jesus begins to teach the multitudes after they *again* (*palin*) gather around Him.

† With France, I would think that Mt 13:44-50 was spoken to the crowds. Thus, the *palin* of Mt 13:44 (MT) marks this transition in audience much as it does in Mt 22:1. Again and again, *palin* occurs in Mt:13:45,47 in earmarking these thee parables as spoken to the crowd. This is not to say that *palin* is not used when presenting parabolic material to His disciples. Indeed, it is used in such capacity in Mt 19:24. For that matter, the implicit contrast is so mild in Mt 13:44-50 that many commentators think that this passage is spoken to the disciples. Regardless, in all these passages those who are sympathetic to Jesus' message are the ones to whom more light/teaching is being given, even if in parabolic form. I find it very doubtful that Matthew intends for us to understand Jesus as giving more light yet *again*, in the parable of the wedding feast, for the leaders who already had rejected the light He provided in the preceding two parables. Jesus's sympathetic listeners and Matthew's interested readers are the ones for whom this additional information is intended, and it will shed light on the future of Jesus' antagonists.

‡ *People* (*laos*) is singular in Lk 20:9,19. The plural *them*, which occurs in the latter verse, does not refer to the people but to the antagonists: "They feared the people; for they understood that He spoke this parable against *them*" (Lk 20:19). The *multitudes* (*ochlos*) in Mt 21:46, in contrast, are plural and thus a proper reference for the plural *them* in the following verse: "Jesus answered and spoke to *them*" (Mt 22:1).

How can Evans interject an explanation involving the 144,000, however, when this number is only revealed in Revelation, which had not yet been written? Ironically, Evans rejects an explanation involving the marriage supper of the Lamb from Revelation (because it allegedly was unknown) only to interject his own explanation (with a number from Revelation that also was unknown). If he can explain the parable in terms of the 144,000, then why can misthologists not explain the parable in terms of the marriage supper? Regardless, his assumption that a parable must be limited to the understanding of its original listeners is open to strenuous objection.[*]

Nation

Aside from his special pleading and questionable supposition, the impression Evans gives is that the rejection in Mt 21:43 will be at the time of the tribulation. Not so. The offer of the kingdom of God already has been withdrawn temporarily from the Jewish nation. Therefore, this offer can be made now to a new nation. The singular form of *nation* suggests that offer of the kingdom has now been extended to the church. Paul, quoting Moses no less, affirms that the new nation that God uses in the interim period is the church (Rom 10:19). In fact, Paul exclaimed that he would turn from the Jewish nation to the Gentiles since the Jews rejected his message (Acts 13:46; 18:5-6). Peter, likewise, confirms that the church is *a holy nation* (1Pet 2:9). A well developed eschatology is not necessary to read Moses. Although one might object to interjecting an interpretation derived from Revelation, might one not at least be allowed to derive eschatological implications from Moses? Surely, it is not wrong to think that Jews should be able to make such a deduction from their own OT! If Paul can anticipate the church from Moses' writings didactically, then Evans surely has overstated his case in thinking that Jesus could not do so parabolically.

Wedding Feast

The crux of the matter, however, is that Evans' equates the feast with the kingdom; thus "being rejected from the banquet is to be rejected from the kingdom altogether."[1653] Supposedly, Mt 8:11 and Lk 13:24-29 establish Evans' point. I have stated my counter case pertaining to those contexts and need not do so again here.[†] For present purposes, I simply will note that Evans had to leave the present context in order to make that allegation. The most natural impression from the actual parable is that to be cast out of the feast is to be cast out of the wedding feast, not to be cast out of the kingdom. A well developed eschatology is not necessary to make that parabolic observation.[‡]

The Wedding Canopy of Mount Zion

Even aside from Paul's use of the text from Moses to establish that the church is the future nation that God will use, might one not expect these Jews to be familiar with Is 4:5, in which the Lord spreads His wedding canopy over Mount Zion? Would these Jews not be aware that Is 25:6-9 talks about a lavish eschatological banquet on the Lord's holy mountain—Mount Zion? Might one not expect Jews to be familiar with Is 65:1, which talks about God being found by another nation? Indeed, this nation is the church (cp. Rom 10:20). Furthermore, in this very context, the messianic reign is compared to a feast on God's holy mountain (Is 65:13-25). According to the OT, the wedding feast is to occur on Mount Zion.

Will everyone in the kingdom live on this mountain? Of course not! Even the Jews of Jesus' day and the Evans of our day should be able to discern this from the OT:

> [2] Now it will come about that in the last days, the mountain of the house of the Lord will be established as the chief of the mountains, and will be raised above the hills; and all the nations will stream to it. [3] And many peoples will come and say, "Come, let us go up to the mountain of the Lord, to the house of the God of Jacob; that He may teach us concerning His ways, and that we may walk in His paths." For the law will go forth from Zion, and the word of the Lord from Jerusalem. (Is 2:2-3)

---

[*] See *Inductive Approach*, 8. Also, for example, see *Illustration 207. Parallels for Mt 7:21*, 599.

[†] See *Part 1. Chapter 18. Sons in the Outer Darkness (Mt 8:5-13)*, 429. For Lukan parallel, see *Illustration 153. Sequence and Significance of Casting*, 467; *Illustration 207. Parallels for Mt 7:21*, 599; *Table Exclusion*, 563; *Illustration 231. Last is not Least*, 683.

[‡] Additionally, even if it is assumed that the wedding feast is the kingdom, the misthological position is not necessarily nullified. Both ultraists and neo-ultraists would interpret the wedding feast to be the kingdom and still regard the outer darkness to be a misthological concept.

Such a message is worth repeating, especially since some expositors miss it:

> [1] And it will come about in the last days that the mountain of the house of the Lord will be established as the chief of the mountains. It will be raised above the hills, and the peoples will stream to it. [2] And many nations will come and say, "Come and let us go up to the mountain of the Lord and to the house of the God of Jacob, that He may teach us about His ways and that we may walk in His paths." For from Zion will go forth the law, even the word of the Lord from Jerusalem. [3] And He will judge between many peoples and render decisions for mighty, distant nations. Then they will hammer their swords into plowshares and their spears into pruning hooks; nation will not lift up sword against nation, and never again will they train for war. [4] And each of them will sit under his vine and under his fig tree, with no one to make them afraid, for the mouth of the Lord of hosts has spoken. [5] Though all the peoples walk each in the name of his god, as for us, we will walk in the name of the Lord our God forever and ever. [6] "In that day," declares the Lord, "I will assemble the lame, and gather the outcasts, even those whom I have afflicted. [7] I will make the lame a remnant, and the outcasts a strong nation, and the Lord will reign over them in Mount Zion from now on and forever. (Micah 4:1-7)

Many people living in the kingdom will live outside of Mount Zion. Thus, one cannot possibly equate living in Mount Zion with living in the kingdom. Moreover, a wedding feast on Mount Zion cannot be equated with living in the kingdom, not according to the OT or the NT. Yet, Evans makes the wild accusation:

> The free grace teachers are correct that unfaithful Christians will be without reward, but whether unfaithful Christians will be barred from the marriage supper of the Lamb or from the holy city, this parable is not addressing that issue....Free grace teachers are incorrect to state that the ousted wedding guest is a Christian in the Kingdom of God.[1654]

What are his grounds for such a sweeping rejection of such FG teachers? Basically, his primary arguments are: (1) The passage is dealing with Jews, not church-age believers. (2) Jesus would have limited Himself to the primitive eschatology of His Jewish audience. (3) Kingdom = banquet (Mt 8:11), so rejection from the kingdom = rejection from the banquet (Lk 13:24-29).

As to the first point, even if the passage is dealing with Jews, the friend may be a Jewish believer. As to points two and three, even in OT eschatology being present within the kingdom is not equatable with being present at Mount Zion or at a banquet on Mount Zion. Obviously, Mount Zion is a place within the kingdom, not the kingdom itself, and the feast is a privilege for those who live on Mount Zion. One need not turn to Revelation to destroy Evans' position. The OT will suffice. Nevertheless, before proceeding to additional OT evidence, since Evans conceded that "unfaithful Christians will be without reward," let it be pointed out that in doing so he has conceded the argument. Unfaithful Christians will be without the reward city—Mount Zion. They will be outside the city, not inside the city.

Kingdom Entrance Versus Possession

As to the OT witness, one should be able to make such a misthopological inference regarding Mount Zion even if one only had the OT and the Gospel of Matthew at one's disposal. Within the course of these three parables, Jesus stresses that entrance into the kingdom is conditioned on faith alone (Mt 21:31-32), not on producing the fruit of repentance. Entrance is granted to believers. However, possession of the kingdom is granted to those believers who produce the fruit of repentance (Mt 21:43). The kingdom was taken away from the Jews, before A.D. 70, and given to a new nation (i.e., to those believers) who produce the required fruit, namely repentance. The logical inference, even from Matthew alone (plus the OT), would be that if you are a believer and yet do not produce the required fruit of repentance, then you merely will enter the kingdom (and live within the kingdom) rather than dwell in Mount Zion (and rule the kingdom): OT + Mt = Misthopology.

Bridal Righteousness in Isaiah 61:10

Evans tries to shirk away from the misthopological overtones of the passage by making a pure assumption that the wedding garments refer to imputed righteousness "provided *freely* by the host. (Isaiah 61:10)"[1655] Let us read the Evans' poof-text from Isaiah together: "I will rejoice greatly in the Lord, My soul will exult in my God; for He has clothed me with garments of salvation, He has wrapped me with a robe of righteousness, as a bridegroom decks himself with a garland, and as a bride adorns herself with her jewels" (Is 61:10). Did you see the word *freely* anywhere in the biblical text? Neither did I. Evans interjects it. Martin rejects it (BKC). The OT context is decisively in favor of Martin's rejection.

Evans appeals to a favorite OT text found chapters away: "All our righteous deeds are like a filthy garment" (Is 64:6). Fair enough. This text establishes the need for imputed righteousness. Still, it does not nullify the need of imparted righteousness for misthological themes. For those who have been made imputationally righteous, the possibility of imparted righteousness becomes a valid possibility. In the context of Is 61:10, imputational righteousness is not the theme.

Jesus is the speaker in this chapter from Isaiah 61: "The Spirit of the Lord God is upon me, because the Lord has anointed me to bring good news to the afflicted; He has sent me to bind up the brokenhearted, to proclaim liberty to captives, and freedom to prisoners; to proclaim the favorable year of the Lord" (Is 61:1-2; cp. Lk 4:18-19). Therefore, as Lange notes in his commentary on Isaiah, the one being clothed with the garment of salvation and righteousness is Jesus and His Bride the church. Oops, Evans does not want to bring the church into the picture. So let us ignore the NT reference to the Lord sanctifying the church with what arguably would be practical sanctification (Eph 5:26). Instead, let it be noted simply that the Lord does not need imputed righteousness. Therefore, the supposition that the robe represents imputed righteousness is immediately suspect in the very verse Evans has chosen for his proof-text. In Isaiah, Jesus is the Bridegroom putting on the robe. The reasonable supposition is that the righteousness of His character will be manifested in the misthological righteousness of His robe, the nature of which is shared with His Bride (Zion). As Lang points out, "The connection is not that of a criminal being accounted righteous but that of a bridegroom and bride decking for the wedding....it is not a question of a person escaping penalty in a court of law."[1656]

The setting for this wedding is eschatological. In this future setting, the next verse affirms, "The Lord God will cause *righteousness and praise* to spring up before all the nations" (Is 61:11). Imputational *righteousness* is no more intended than imputational *praise*. Actual praise and manifest righteous are the obvious subject matter: righteous you can see, and praise you can hear. The next two verses confirm this point: "For Zion's sake I will not keep silent, and for Jerusalem's sake I will not keep quiet, until her righteousness goes forth like brightness, and her salvation like a torch that is burning. And the nations will *see* your righteousness, and all kings your glory" (Is 62:1-2). In that future day, Israel indeed will be righteous in deed (Is 54:14; 58:8; 60:21). A shining righteousness that is seen by others and that is associated with being a "crown of beauty" (Is 62:3) strongly suggests what the NT would call a "crown of righteousness" (2Tim 4:8). Crowns are not free. Misthological righteousness is the focus of this passage.

Regardless of all the above indications of misthological righteousness, which Evans simply ignores, is it not rather strange that Evans appeals to an OT text that talks about a bride dressing for her wedding as proof that guests are provided free clothing for the wedding? Even if the bride was furnished a free dress, how does this prove that the wedding attire of the guests is provided by the host? Evan's glaring inconsistency becomes even more acute when he correctly acknowledges that Rev 19:7-9 teaches that "Christ's bride has prepared herself with the righteousness of the saints (godly living). The bride has clothed herself with faithfulness, and so will be rewarded."[1657] Does Evans really intend to be taken seriously when he claims that the guests are given free clothing when he has admitted that the bride has to make her own clothing? Both Is 61:10 and Rev 19:7-9 picture the Bride of Christ. She clothes herself with the righteous deeds which her Bridegroom makes possible.

Free Clothing is a Myth

As for the Augustinian myth that the wedding robes worn by the wedding guests were provided by the host, France rejects such mythology and responds, "The clothing expected at the wedding was not a special garment (like our 'morning dress') but decent, clean 'white clothes such as anyone should have had available." Such Augustinian mythology regarding free clothing should be replaced with Marrowian misthology, thus acknowledging costly clothing.

Clothing of Conditional Security

Unfortunately, France falls short of fully carrying his observation to the appropriate conclusion. He rightly surmises, "The symbolism is of someone who presumes on the free offer of salvation by assuming that therefore there are no obligations attached." This assessment is splendid, if misthological obligations are intended. Regrettably, France interposes soteriological obligations instead: "Entry into the kingdom of heaven may be free, but to continue in it carries conditions." France interprets this parable as teaching conditional security and denies entrance into heaven to "someone whose life belies their [sic] profession: faith without works."[1658]

In a book that was supposed to be written to prove eternal security, Evans unwittingly aligns himself with conditional security as he comes to much the same conclusion: "Their complete lack of fruit during the tribulation will prove that they are lost."[1659] In such France-Evans theology, entrance into the kingdom might be given initially upon the singular condition of belief, but realization of that entrance will require that you prove your faith by your works. Such proveitistic soteriology, in the end, becomes salvation by faith and works.*

Garment of Repentance

Of these two conditionalists, France is the more consistent writer concerning the garments. He correctly deduces that the garments refer to the necessity of good works on the part of believers. Evans also perceives that the issue is "producing fruits of the kingdom."[1660] What Evans did not perceive, however, was that in making such a deduction he refuted his own argument that the garments refer to imputed righteousness. Far to the contrary, as France correctly observes, the salvation being spoken of here "depends on producing the 'fruit,' here symbolized by the wedding clothes."[1661] Both Evans and France are correct to conclude that fruit one must produce in Mt 21:43, in order to qualify for the promised kingdom, is the fruit of good works on the part of believers. Therefore, Evans is incorrect to think that the wedding garment refers to the free gift of imputational righteousness. Rather, the fruit = garment = repentance (cp. Mt 3:8). Jesus is seeking the fruit of repentance on the part of believers in these parables (Mt 21:29,32).

Two Promises

Salvation from the outer darkness is conditioned on the production of good works by believers. Those who equate the outer darkness with hell, of necessity, condition salvation from hell on the production of good works. The well-meaning attempt on the part of some to circumvent this inescapable conclusion by appealing to Augustine's fabrication of free garments does little, if anything, to offset the conditionality of the three parables. In parable one, the requirement is, "Go work" (Mt 21:28). Basically, in the second parable, the requirement is to *pay the fruit* (i.e., *produce the produce*). This fruit is not free; it is something you must pay/produce. What do you get in return? The kingdom of God. Once again let it be stressed that to enter a kingdom is one thing; to be given a kingdom is quite naturally another. Jesus speaks of both aspects in this context. (1) Those who believe will **enter** the kingdom (Mt 21:31-32). (2) Those believers who produce the fruit of repentance will be **given** the kingdom (Mt 21:43).[†]

The man in question entered the feast. So what is the feast? Limiting ourselves to simple contextual propositions leads to consistent conclusions. *The feast = some future wedding celebration within the future kingdom.* As a corollary, *the wedding hall = some place within the future kingdom where the future wedding celebration will take place.* Such deductions are not rocket science.

First Promise

As to Jesus' first promise, the man in question entered the wedding hall—a place where the wedding celebration will take place in the future kingdom. Obviously, the man had to enter the kingdom in order to be at this wedding since this celebration was within that future kingdom. Thus, we can conclude, purely on the basis of the context, that this man was a believer who had entered the kingdom.

Second Promise

As to Jesus' second promise, after initially being allowed into this wedding hall (i.e., a place within the future kingdom where this wedding will be taking place), the man was ejected from the wedding hall (again, from a place within the future kingdom where this wedding will be taking place). From the context, such ejection would be anticipated if a believer were to fail to produce the fruits necessary to be given the kingdom. The most such a fruitless believer could expect was entrance into the kingdom. Being given the kingdom itself would not be something that a fruitless believer could expect. Exclusion from the feast (where fruits/garments were expected and inspected) would be exclusion from being given this future kingdom (and thus from kingship). Exclusion from this

---

* For my book dedicated to the rebuttal of the fruit-proves-root theory, see *Woolly Wolves and Woolless Sheep.* Despite my criticism of Evan's assessment regarding the outer darkness, overall I would recommend his book. For the most part his soteriology is commendable. Granted, his chapter on the outer darkness is very disappointing. However, even this poor chapter on his part serves a useful purpose in demonstrating the inconsistencies of FG soteriology when FG misthology is rejected.

† Just as to be given a million dollars necessarily means to become a millionaire, to be given a kingdom anticipates that one is being given kingship.

future kingdom would not be at stake since one's presence in this kingdom was conditioned solely on one's entrance into this kingdom—a condition that this man already had met.

Feast = ≠ Kingdom

In contrast to such natural and self-consistent deductions, Evans wants to make two offsetting suppositions regarding the identity of feast: (1) *The feast = the future kingdom.* (2) *The feast ≠ the future kingdom.* When the guest is rejected from the feast, Evans claims that this means that the guest was rejected from the kingdom (i.e., feast = kingdom). Yet when it is pointed out that the guest was present in the feast, Evans responds that this does not mean that the guest was present within the kingdom (i.e., feast ≠ kingdom). Thankfully, the parable does not evidence the state of confusion found in Evans' exposition. The parable is capable of being understood variously, but it need not be interpreted in such a contradictory manner as that posed by Evans.

From the details of the parable, the most natural deduction is that to enter the feast and then subsequently to be excluded from the feast would refer to being excluded from an event within the kingdom and from the place where that event is taking place, not from the kingdom itself. The OT also suggests that eschatological exclusion from Mount Zion is based on performance (Eze 20:33-40).[*]

Levels of Detail

Some of the details within the parable are so apparent that they typically are handled in a rather summary fashion. A king "sent out his slaves to call those who had been invited to the wedding feast, and they were unwilling to come." (Mt 22:3). More servants are sent; some of these servants are killed by those originally invited to the feast. Accordingly, the *king* represents the *Father* who has sent His *servants* (the *prophets*) to the *invitees* (the *Jews*) time and time again to invite them to the *feast* (the *messianic feast*). The Jewish leaders resist and even kill the prophets with the result that Jerusalem will be burned by the Romans in A.D. 70. These murderous antagonists (culminating in those confronting Jesus in the temple) are killed and their city burned. These details are easily interpreted, at least at an elementary level.

Unfortunately, due to ease with which these detail are interpreted, some scholars make simplistic assumptions as a result. For example, Hindson and Borland state, matter of factly, that the setting of the city on fire is "an obvious reference to the coming destruction of Jerusalem in A.D. 70."[1662] True, but is that all that it is? No. A more careful articulation would clarify that the burning of the city is "at least a partial fulfillment" (NAC, ECNT). The richness of this multidimensional detail hints that it is to be interpreted as referring to more than one event. Moreover, this item may not be the only particular within the parable for which Jesus intends to convey dual application. Yet Hindson and Borland gloss over this parabolic richness because of their underlying hermeneutic: "A parable, as the saying goes, should not be made 'to walk on all fours.' Not everything in a parable is meant to have some particular meaning. The parable serves as an illustration of one basic meaning."[1663]

This statement about "all fours" is made a couple of pages earlier concerning the parable of the vineyard and, from their perspective, justifies not seeking anything very specific in the details. In actuality though, the very moment that Hindson and Borland concede that the burning of the city refers to something other than the basic eschatological judgment (which is the focus of the parable), they seriously weaken their argument that one should not look to the particulars for "some particular meaning." Their prejudice against the particulars is undermined even more once it is acknowledged that burning probably alludes to more than one event.

In addition to this obvious weakness in such an approach to parabolic details,[†] Hindson and Borland derail their own position when, concerning the wedding guest, they claim: "The garment must actually be worn on the heart, since nothing is made of the fact that the servants had not refused him entry."[1664] By means of an argument from silence (which is notoriously weak), they make this unwarranted conclusion about a missing detail! They interject their own inference, regarding a missing detail, and in doing so move beyond the text—way beyond the text. Perhaps one should quote to them their own words: "Not everything in a parable is meant to have some particular meaning." Better yet, one could respond with the words of the text, "The king came in to look over the dinner guests" (Mt 22:11). The king looked *over*, not *into*, his guest. He was looking for a form of righteousness that would be openly manifested, not only to himself but to everyone else in the room as well. The actual particulars of the parable counter the Hindson-and-Borland conjecture. Moreover, if this righteousness is imputed

---

[*] Also see *Like a Tree Planted by the Water*. As to this text from Ezekiel, this passing *under the rod* In Eze 20:37 deals with living Jews at the time of the Lord's return at the conclusion of the tribulation. That some (if not all) of those who pass under this rod are regenerate Jews is suggested by Dan 12:2 in which resurrected Jewish believers will, in a manner of speaking, pass under the rod as well.

[†] See *Deductive Approach*, 7; *Inductive Approach*, 8; *Adductive Approach*, 9.

righteousness, as Hindson and Borland allege, then why was the man let into the feast without imputed righteousness? This detail is well explained by misthopology, not by Hindson and Borland's soteriology.[1665]

Hindson and Borland feel free to disregard details that counter their interpretation. They regard such particulars as meaningless: "*Nothing* should be made of the fact that the owner of the vineyard, who represents God, says, 'They will respect my son.' This is not an indication that God was mistaken or that He does not have infinite knowledge of all future events."[1666] True, a limitation of God's precognition is not the intention of this parabolic verbalization. On the other hand, neither was this communication intended to mean *nothing*—to be a meaningless detail—as Hindson and Borland imagine. On the contrary, this statement from the mouth of God allows one to feel the heart of God and to see the moral right of God. Morally, God had a right to expect them to respect His Son. Additionally, for those not prone to parabolic insensitivity regarding particulars, the emotional intensity of this statement made from the heart of God should be apparent.

Parabolic details should not be assumed to be meaningless, nor even necessarily one dimensional, nor are the particulars so pliable so as to be assigned whatever meaning suites the interpreter. As another case in point, drawing from the parable of the vineyard, Turner correctly anticipates, "The detail of the son's being thrown out of the vineyard before being killed may implicitly refer to Jesus' being crucified outside Jerusalem's walls."[1667] This parabolic specification is not merely a cog in the parabolic machine without any significance of its own; rather, this component contributes to the richness of the parable and finds fulfillment in historical events. Jesus literally was killed outside of Jerusalem, and the Romans literally attacked Jerusalem in A.D. 70. Why not also affirm that the wedding guest literally will enter the Heavenly Jerusalem where the future wedding literally will take place?

Good and Bad

For a misthologist, the problem in trying to pin down what some details mean is that some details have multiple possibilities, each of which would be valid and consistent with FG misthology. For example, who exactly are the *good and bad* gathered from *the streets* (Mt 22:10): Jews, Gentiles, or both? From which time period do they come: the church age, tribulation, or both?

Certainly, the Jewish tax-gatherers and harlots listening to the parables would perceive themselves as being in that group, and rightly so (Mt 21:31-32). Yet this detail would make a natural transition to the Gentiles being included in this new nation—not to the exclusion of the Jews, of course, but with the inclusion of both Jews and Gentiles as a new entity, namely the church. Even so, Turner stresses the Jewishness of this new eschatological community as a Jewish remnant, which he terms, the "Matthean Christian Jewish community."[1668] He correctly surmises, "The man without the wedding clothes in this parable warns those within Matthew's community that they must focus on their own fidelity, not on the errors of the outsiders, the religious leaders."[1669] The warning and application intended to be drawn from the man without the wedding clothes pertains to insiders, that is, to those within the Matthean Christian Jewish community, to those inside the feast. What should be deduced, then, is that (genuine) believers within this Matthean Jewish Christian community who fail to produce the necessary fruit (of repentance) will not be allowed to participate in the festivities (associated with kingdom rulership). Misthological election is at stake (Mt 22:14).[*]

Thus, for various reasons, the proper conclusion is that these guests, whoever they are, represent believers. Evans thinks that Mt 22:9 "fast forwards to the time of the seven year tribulation, for since Jesus is only dealing with Israel here the Church age is skipped over."[1670] Misthologists can be charitable toward this aspect of his argument and allow this possibility. If so, the guests in the feast are tribulational believers. If one wants to insist that they are tribulational Jewish believers, this possibility can be entertained as well.

(Jewish) Friend

Similar options are possible for the *friend* without wedding clothes who is cast into the outer darkness. He may be one of the *good and bad* gathered from the street. If the church age is in view (or at least included), this guest would represent someone within the Matthean Jewish Christian community. Jewish believers within that community would find the warning applicable to themselves; Gentile believers would find the warning relevant to themselves. Yet the same assessment could be made for tribulational believers, whether they are Jews or Gentiles. Indeed, as some commentators specify, the intended application could *include the church age and go **through** the tribulational period.*

---

[*] Unfortunately, commentators tend to regard it as a soteriological election that makes good works a corresponding soteriological necessitation, and Turner is no exception.

Which particular group and time period Jesus intends to picture is difficult to pin down because the Lord may be using the details to include believers from both ethnic groups and both time periods. For those like Evans, who prefer to see this parable through a Jewish lens, accommodations can easily be made. For those who prefer a church-age lens, allowances are readily acceptable. Perhaps Jesus intends for us to be able to see the parable through multiple lens.

Illustration 351. Three Temporal-Ethnic Lens

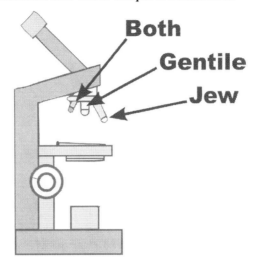

To use an illustration familiar to many, consider a three-lens microscope. At the lowest magnification, one may see characteristics that upon higher magnification can be separated. Broadly speaking, the Lord may not intend for the *good and bad* to be limited to believers of either the church age or the tribulational period. Yet upon closer examination, the parable is capable of being perceived as referring to one set of believers as opposed to another set of believers. One reason commentators are divided may be because multiple perceptions are intended.

If I had to view this parable through only one lens, then I would view the gathering of the *good and bad* as dealing with the rapture of church-age believers as Haller (GNTC) does. In that case, I would be inclined to agree with those interpreters, such as Hindson and Borland, who regard the *street* invitees as Gentile and the original invitees as Jewish: "The invited guests are the people of Israel, whereas those in the main highways are Gentiles."[1671] Further, the invitee called *friend* would most naturally be understood as being a member of the group to whom the original invitation was sent; not an unknown person from the street. The church is composed of both Jews and Gentiles, and the gospel is intended to go forth to the "Jew first and also to the Greek" (Rom 1:16; 2:9-10). Dogmatically identifying the *friend* as Jewish (as Evans attempts to do) is not advisable. But Jesus certainly has told the parable in such a way that encourages this identification at one level of magnification. I am certainly not averse to indentifying this friend as a Jewish Christian of the Matthean community. In fact, for simplicity's sake, this perspective is the one I adopted in the body of the present book. Nevertheless, this interpretation is not the only one possible and probably not the only one intended.

Let my fellow FG dispensationalists who share my preference for the above interpretation note carefully the absence of a very important person from the wedding celebration—the bride! Why is the bride absent from the wedding parables? In the parable of the virgins, the absence is easily explained dispensationally: The virgins are not the bride. That parable is dealing with tribulational believers rather than with church-age believers. However, by the same token, in the parable of the wedding feast, these church-age guests, if that is what they are, are not the Bride. Why does Jesus present a parable that distinguishes appropriately clothed church-age believers from the Bride? Perhaps, at least in part, the reason is because the Lord does not wish to limit the application to church-age believers. Using a broad temporal lens, Hindson and Borland surmise: "The kingdom of heaven must refer to the mediatorial aspect of the kingdom *in the Church Age and **through** the Tribulation period*."[1672] Here, two dispensational writers assert that the time period includes both the church age and tribulational period. If it includes both periods, at least at one level of magnification, then the absence of the Bride is quite understandable. At the same time, trying to zoom in at the Jewish level and insisting that it cannot have application at the church level (as Evans attempts to do) is ill-advised because (1) even Revelation does not make so sharp a division so that one could not picture being invited (and properly clothed) as a prerequisite to being the Bride (Rev 19:7-9), and (2) the *friend* is present in the wedding (not merely standing outside the wedding, as is the case of the foolish virgins who represent unfaithful Jewish tribulational believers).

Having briefly sketched a case for allowing mutual magnifications, I will now zoom in with different lenses at different magnifications so that the friend thrown into the outer darkness may be scrutinized more carefully. Some scholars simply regard the friend to be an invitee from the group of *good and bad* Gentiles. If so, he is a Gentile believer. However, some scholars have noted that his being called *friend* more likely would place him in the original group of invitees. As we turn the knob of our examination to this level of specification, the friend is identified as a Jew, in contrast to *good and bad* Gentiles. As the knob is turned on the microscope to an even stronger magnification though, one may observe that the distinction between Jews and Gentiles fades away. The man is no longer merely a Jew in contrast to the *good and bad* Gentiles, he is a Jewish believer in contrast to *good and bad* Jews! At last we have reached the level of specification requested by Evan's proposal in which both the friend and other guests are regarded as Jewish. At this level, the parable is dealing strictly with the offer of this wedding experience to Jews.

I appreciate the fact that Evans is consistent with identifying the nation to whom the kingdom is given as the Jews. Although I am in agreement with Haller (my fellow misthologist) that the friend is a believer and that the other guests gathered from the street are raptured church-age believers, Haller is inconsistent in identifying the nation to whom the kingdom is given as the Jews and the invitees as the Gentiles. Doing so is possible, but at different magnifications. *Nation* and *friend* should match at any given level of mutual magnification. Matching is no problem if one simultaneously examines both groups under the same lens.

On the other hand, Evans suffers from a major inconsistency in regarding this friend as a tribulation Jew in that the feast would not be a tribulational event but a post-tribulational event. The friend is in the post-tribulational event and, therefore, must be in the kingdom and thus a believer according to the context (Mt 21:31-32). But turning aside from this weakness in Evans' argument for the moment, allow me to turn the knob on the microscope even a little further and, through this ethical lens, examine the friend thrown into the outer darkness from this Jewish perspective at an even higher magnification.

As is commonly pointed out by the commentators, the Jewish leaders were the group that originally was invited to the feast who rejected and killed the prophets. The Jewish leaders are the villains in these three parables, and they knew it: "When the chief priests and the Pharisees heard His parables, they understood that He was speaking about them" (Mt 21:45). When the focus of this parable is perceived to be dealing exclusively with Jews, then the *friend* is best interpreted not merely to be a Jew, but a Jewish leader in contradistinction to the common Jew. When the Jewish officers came back from a failed attempt to arrest Jesus, the Pharisees (i.e., the Jewish leaders of these officers) rebuked them: "You have not also been led astray, have you? No one of the rulers or Pharisees has believed in Him, has he? But this [Jewish] multitude which does not know the Law is accursed" (Jn 7:47-49). The Jewish rulers distanced themselves from the Jewish crowds who hung onto Jesus' every word.

At this level of magnification some will jump to the conclusion that since the Jewish rulers did not believe in Jesus and since the friend thrown into the outer darkness was a Jewish leader, the friend must have been an unbeliever. Such a deductive assessment is defective because the major premise is faulty for multiple reasons. For one thing, the Jewish leaders were wrong to assume that none of the Jewish leaders were believers.

Even on the occasion when the Pharisees rebuked the officers who failed to arrest Jesus, "Nicodemus said to them (he who came to Him before, being one of them), 'Our Law does not judge a man, unless it first hears from him and knows what he is doing, does it?'" (Jn 7:50-51) Nicodemus was too timid to acknowledge that he believed in Jesus. His fellow leaders scoffed at Nicodemus on that occasion. That ridicule, coupled with intimidation, was enough to keep Nicodemus (and other like-minded rulers) too timid to confess Jesus. "Nevertheless many even of the rulers believed in Him, but because of the Pharisees they were not confessing Him, lest they should be put out of the synagogue; for they loved the praise of men rather than the praise of God" (Jn 12:42-43; TM).

From the details of the parable, the proper deduction at this level of magnification is that this man represents believing Jewish leaders who were unwilling to confess Jesus. These non-confessing Jewish leaders were regenerate believers. Nevertheless, they were in danger of the outer darkness. According to Jesus they had eternal life, but they were risking exclusion from the Messianic banquet on Mount Zion promised in their OT Scriptures. This man might represent a Jewish believer for other reasons also. However, before pursuing those options, let the importance of multiple lens or vantage points first be reiterated.

If the illustration of multiple lens is difficult to follow, perhaps a popular optical illusion will help clarify the probable intent of the parable. One may find this following frog-horse illustration on internet easily enough. For present purposes, let the perceptions be defined as follows:

1. Frog $\Rightarrow$ *Friend = (Jewish) Church-Age Believer*
2. Horse $\Rightarrow$ *Friend = Jewish Tribulational Believer*
3. Frog-Horse $\Rightarrow$ *Friend = (Jewish) Church-Age and Tribulational Believers*

Illustration 352. Primary Vantage Point

When I first looked at this picture, I only saw a frog. Similarly, when I first examined the parable of the wedding feast, the only realistic possibility I saw was that the friend thrown into the outer darkness represented a church-age believer—possibly, more specifically, a Jewish church-age believer. As to the picture, being told that a horse was in the picture, I kept trying to see the picture through the eyes of those making such a claim. Cocking my head to the right helped. I eventually saw the horse. Likewise, being told by others that they perceive the friend thrown into the outer darkness to be a tribulational Jew, I tried to see the parable from their vantage point. A careful examination of the context—specifically, the two parables leading up to it, among other things—helped supply that vantage point. Finally, I was able to see how the parable could also picture a Jewish tribulational believer thrown into the outer darkness. Unfortunately, some of those insisting upon the horse perspective have failed to see the frog perspective, so to speak. They insist the friend thrown into the outer darkness must be a tribulational Jew—a lost Jew at that! They have closed their eyes to the significance of some very important details. Insisting that a horse is the **only** animal in the picture and that it has its eye **closed** would be an analogous portrayal of their perception. Looking at the picture from their vantage point, I can allow that a horse is in the picture, but I would insist that the horse has its eye open and that those who misperceive the friend to represent a lost Jew should open their eyes.

Illustration 353. Secondary Vantage Point

When my brother, Phil, first saw the frog-horse picture, he only saw a horse. He wondered why the horse was drawn sideways. If the picture initially had been presented to him in the horse-oriented position, as has been done in the rotation above, then this horse orientation would have been the primary rather than secondary vantage point of the presentation. When you search for this image on the internet, you will find that some sites present the horse-oriented position as the primary vantage point. My perception is that the frog orientation, so to speak, is the primary vantage point of the parable intended for those in the present age. The servant is intended to be seen (at least initially and primarily) from the vantage of those now living in the church-age period as a church-age believer. Jesus and Matthew expected those living in the present dispensation to see the primary application as being made to church-age believers. However, the Lord and Matthew may have expected Jewish believers living in the tribulation period to see the primary application as being made to themselves. Quite possibly, the reason the Bride is not in the picture is because adding this detail would have limited the interpretation (and thus the intended direct application) to one group as opposed to another. Just as the frog's leg has been positioned so as to allow for a horse's eye, so the wedding participants clothed in appropriate attire have been so pictured so as to allow dual application.*

So which animal is portrayed by the picture: a frog, a horse, or both? The artist draws a composite and expects us to see a frog-horse of course. In like manner, what ethnic group and time period is represented by the servant in the parable? Does he represent a Jewish believer, a Gentile believer, or both? Further, is he a church-age believer or a tribulational believer? Jesus and Matthew intend for us to see how the servant (at various vantage points or levels of specificity) can represent both a church-age believer and a tribulational believer, both a Jew and a Gentile. So those commentators who see both can be commended.

The principle error made by most interpreters of this parable lies in thinking that the parable is dealing with unbelievers being cast into the outer darkness. This would be like insisting that both the frog and the horse have their eyes closed! Those insisting that the parable is intended to have application to both church-age servants and tribulational servants should open their eyes to see that believing servants are the ones in danger of being cast into the outer darkness. Believers do not need to serve in order to prove that they are believers any more than the servant must serve in order to prove that he is a servant. He is an entrusted servant. That is a statement of fact. Service needs to be rendered in order to prove one's service, not to prove that one is a servant. The question is not, "Is he a servant?" but, "Will this servant serve?" Servant/believers need to serve in order to prove that they are faithful servant/believers, not in order to prove that they are servant/believers.

Fire

At this point, many will stop zooming in any further, and perhaps rightly so. Notwithstanding, for the more inquisitively and adventurously minded, let me hesitantly turn the knob even further and, using the high-power Jewish lens, go back and reexamine the burning of the city in Mt 22:7. Before doing so, a quick review will help.

Illustration 354. Basic Magnification of Burning City

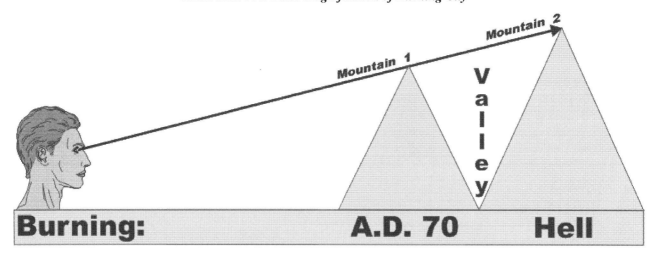

At the most basic magnification, this prophecy about the burning of the city pertains to what happened historically to Jerusalem in A.D. 70. At a slightly more detailed magnification, it also telescopically pictures an eschatological soteric judgment awaiting the lost in the fires of hell. These two levels of application have been well noted by many others. But might a third level of detail also be possible? As a matter of conjecture, I will now entertain an extreme magnification of the parabolic particular *fire* with this particular ethnic lens.

---

* See "A Frog-Horse Addendum" in *3D Unconditional Security.*

Illustration 355. Advanced Magnification of Burning City

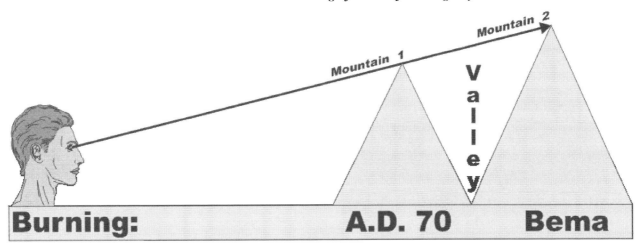

In another context at least, the burning of Jerusalem in A.D. 70 need not be limited to an eschatological picture of the fate awaiting unbelievers. Constable entertains the possibility that Heb 10:25 contains "an allusion to the destruction of Jerusalem in A.D. 70 for the original readers."[1673] Tanner finds this suggestion "doubtful," preferring an exclusively **eschatological** perspective, yet even he acknowledges, regarding the burning of God's adversaries in Heb 10:26, "a similar fate of God's **temporal** judgment could await New Covenant believers who rebel."[1674] Writing before A.D. 70, and being familiar with Jesus' warning of what was going to happen to Jerusalem, and warning his readers of the danger of going back to Judaism, certainly gave the writer of Hebrews the opportunity, means, and motive to include such a dual temporal-eschatological (frog-horse)[*] application within the scope of his warning. Whether or not he did so, Jesus may have done so—from at least two vantage points.

First, some of the rulers who kept silent about their faith in Jesus were probably present at Jesus' trial and, by keeping silent, were accomplices to the crime. By keeping their mouth shut, they had a hand in putting Jesus to death. Second, even if one did not want to zoom in at this level on the Jewish leaders, one might zoom out and simply regard those originally invited to the feast as Jewish people. Among the Jewish crowds who savingly believed in Jesus, some subsequently became disenchanted with His Messianic claims (cp. Jn 6:60-66). Perhaps some of these regenerate apostates even cried out for His death. In this parabolic warning, Jesus may have been including these regenerate Jewish apostates among those who could expect death in the upcoming events of A.D. 70. If so, the burning of the city represents three things: the **temporal** destruction that foreshadows the **soteriological** destruction of Jewish unbelievers and the **misthological** destruction of regenerate Jewish apostates. For the lost, the fire would represent hell. For the saved, the fire would represent the Jewish Bema.[†]

Jewish Typological Son

If one wishes to press the matter, even beyond this level of super Jewish magnification regarding the historical Jewish rulers who were believers, this same misthological conclusion is tenable for yet another reason. Typologically, the Jews represent God's redeemed people, not only as His servant (Is 44:21-22), but also as His son (Ex 4:22; Hos 11:1).[‡] If Jesus is allowing a typological perspective in which those Jews resisting Him are considered redeemed typologically (even though they may not be redeemed historically), then the *son* who says that he will obey his father and does not (Mt 21:29) is dealt with typologically as God's *redeemed child* (even though he may not have been so historically). Constable's comment on the parable of the two sons is suggestive of this very possibility: **"All the Jews, those with a privileged position and those with none, enjoyed being sons of**

---

[*] In this case, frog = temporal destruction; horse = eschatological destruction. A dual reference to the destruction occurs in Jn 2:19, where Jesus says, "Destroy this temple, and in three days I will raise it up." Borchert calls this *double level thinking* (NAC).

[†] For sake of technical accuracy, let it be clarified that church-age believers do not appear before the Christian Bema at the same time that OT and tribulational believers appear before the Jewish Bema. Not only are these two Bemas separated in time, they also may be separated in space, occurring in two (or three) different places: one for Christians, one for Jewish believers who lived through the tribulation, and another for Jews who had died in the OT or tribulation. Nevertheless, seeing how the casting into the outer darkness is a Bema event and can be used simultaneously, at different magnifications, to picture both the Christian Bema and Jewish Bema, the present book follows suite and does not always differentiate between the various Bemas awaiting various groups of believers.

[‡] See *Israel My Redeemed Servant*, 376; *Israel My Redeemed* , 376; *Israel My Redeemed Punished Servant*, 377.

God in the sense that God has chosen Israel as His son (cf. Hos. 11:1).”[1675] Typologically speaking, Israel, as God's redeemed son, was subject to severe temporal discipline and would be subject to misthological burning at the Jewish Bema.

Therefore, when Evans assumes that the *sons of the kingdom* must represent the unsaved because Jesus is using this parable to rebuke unsaved Jewish leaders, he has made an unwarranted assumption, even when given his underlying theological perception: *children* (*teknon*) in Mt 21:28 = ethnic Jews = *sons* (*huios*) in Mt 8:12. Although I challenge this common assumption in the present book, for present purposes I will theorize that at some level of magnification (perhaps at the typological level), Evans is justified in following commentators who gloss over these Matthean distinctions. In my own mind at least, I have to have some justification for following others in ignoring the distinctions Matthew has made in the Greek text between *children* and *sons*. Therefore, so that I may engage such assumptions at a level that is most congenial to those holding such antagonistic positions, I will allow Evans the possible legitimacy of such an equation at this magnification: *children* (*teknon*) = ethnic Jews = *sons* (*huios*).

Turner surmises that *sons of the kingdom* “is a Semitic idiom referring to those who would be the expected heirs to God's eschatological blessings.”[1676] France equates these *sons* (*huios*) with “the disobedient *son* [*teknon*] of 21:28-32; the defaulting tenants of 21:33-34, and those who despised their invitation to the feast in 22:1-10.” In other words, these commentators assume the above equation. Basically, the stock mentality is that the sons/son/tenants/invitees of the kingdom are ethnic Jews (represented by their unbelieving Jewish leaders) who will find the kingdom taken away from them (the anticipated heirs) and given to repentant Gentile believers (or to faithful Jewish believers, depending on which commentator is consulted). For sake of argument, let such equivalency be granted. At one zoom level at least, such a perspective can be entertained. Nevertheless, harmonization with a misthological perception is still reasonable, even highly probable.

Although the gospel of the kingdom was intended first and foremost to the Jews, the generation of ethnic Jews to whom Jesus spoke did indeed find the kingdom taken away from them and their city burned. The offer of the kingdom was withdrawn from them. This offer has been extended currently to the Gentiles, regardless of ethnicity, and will be extended once again ethnically to the Jews during the tribulation. Nevertheless, unregenerate Jews were never expected by God to inherit the kingdom. Unregenerate Jews may have had such expectations of themselves, based on their ethnicity and religiosity, but God never had such an expectation. Notwithstanding, ethnic Jews represent God's redeemed children typologically and thus may be expected to represent redeemed Jews parabolically. Although the antagonistic Jewish leaders historically were unbelievers, they may be used typologically and parabolically to represent unfaithful Jewish believers. The common misperception, that the contrast in Mt 8:11-12 is between Gentles with great faith and Jews with no faith, is historically accurate to some degree, yet it fails to take into consideration that, at the very least, the ethnic *sons of the kingdom* would represent Jewish **believers** typologically and parabolically. The typological contrast intended in Mt 8:11-12 is between Jew's with weak faith and Gentiles with great faith.

The common claim made by those who reject the misthological interpretation regarding the *sons of the kingdom* is that the contrast in that pericope is between *no faith* and *great faith*. Supposedly, within the range of *no faith* and *great faith*, no room exists for *weak faith*. Yet the Bible certainly makes allowances for the possibility of weak faith (Rom 4:19; 14:1-2). Notwithstanding, the typical assumption, unfortunately, is that the sons thrown into the outer darkness must be Jewish unbelievers. Among other things, this typical assumption fails to take *typological resumption* into account. Time and time again, the Jews are pictured as God's redeemed people in the OT. The NT resumes this perspective in this pericope.

Illustration 356. Typological and Historical Jews

Gentile with **great** faith	Jews with **weak** faith
Those from the east and the west (Gentiles)	Son's of the kingdom (**believing** Jews—typologically and historically)
At the **banquet** inside the kingdom	Outer darkness—excluded from the **banquet**
Reason for inclusion—**great** faith	Reason for exclusion—**weak** faith

In light of the above discussion, the above chart, which was given previously,* has been amended with the clarification that the *sons of the kingdom* **typologically refers to Jews who are believers historically** (whether past or future). Although the Jewish antagonists to whom Jesus was speaking (at the point in time in which He gave the pericope) were not believers, these Jews typologically represent (via the designation *sons of the kingdom*

---
* See *Illustration 146. Matthew's Kingdom Banquet*, 432.

used in the pericope) those redeemed Jews who will be cast into the outer darkness. Such redeemed, misthological outcasts would be understood to be weak in faith. The inference of weak faith is not made historically-typologically, but typologically-historically. Although the Jews who confronted Jesus on the historical occasion in which He gave the warning were unbelievers, the warning applied to them typologically because ethnically they typologically represent those who naturally would be expected to recline eschatologically at that banquet table. Historically, they had no faith at that past point in time. Typologically, they represent God's redeemed people and thus believers—yet believers with very weak faith—at that future point in time and thus in history future.

Before

A "little detail," as some would call it, that occurs at the end of Mt 21:31, may suggest a typological correspondence: "Truly I say to you that the tax-gatherers and harlots will get into the kingdom of God *before you*." Mounce glosses over this text by retranslating it as *instead of you*.[1677] Actually, *before you* (*proago*) means *before you* (BDAG). Nevertheless, the point that Mounce is trying to make (with this mistranslation) could be valid. Even though *before you* is the correct translation, Turner notes that commentators are divided as to whether the comparison signifies *exclusion* versus *precession*.[*] He thinks the latter is more likely since precedence is the usual meaning; thus, he thinks that Jesus "leaves room for the leader's eventual repentance." [1678] Both sets of commentators, however, are prone to error in regarding repentance (in terms of performance) a requirement for soteric entrance. In the very next verse, Jesus clarifies that the reason they did not enter was because they did not "repent so as to believe" (Mt 21:31; TM). The repentance that Jesus requires for kingdom entrance is repentance regarding disbelief. Repentance in terms of performance, that is, in terms of producing the fruit of repentance, is required for kingdom possession, not for simple kingdom entrance.

In light of that clarification, is Jesus holding out hope (or thinking wishfully) that these antagonists will repent of their disbelief so that they too will come to saving faith and enter into the kingdom? Not likely. Jesus is in the midst of prophetically projecting the response of these antagonists as being thoroughly negative. Jesus is clear: "The kingdom of God will be taken away from you" (Mt 21:43). Nevertheless, He seems to be equally clear (at least at one level of magnification) in entertaining the possibility that they will enter the kingdom: "Tax collectors and harlots *will enter* the kingdom of God *before you*" (Mt 21:31; TM). The most natural implication is that these Jewish antagonists will have some type of entrance into the kingdom *after* the publicans and prostitutes enter the kingdom. Mounce is correct to perceive a ranking here, an allusion back to Mt 20:16. That statement regarding first-and-last ranking within the kingdom applies, naturally, to those who are in the kingdom. This misthological ranking comes at the conclusion of a parabole regarding those who likewise are addressed as, "Friend" (Mt 20:13). How can these Jews, who historically rejected Jesus, be described as entering the kingdom as low-ranking friends?

Once again, an answer is readily available in typology. These Jewish leaders typologically represent redeemed sons of the kingdom who will be in the kingdom and yet cast into the outer darkness within the kingdom because they failed to believe misthologically. Historically, of course, these unregenerate Jews were unbelievers, who will burn in hell because they did not believe soteriologically in Jesus for eternal life. Typologically, however, they may be taken to represent the lowest ranking among God's redeemed people, who will be in the outer darkness within the kingdom because, as typological believers, they parabolically rejected Jesus. Evidently, all OT believers who had believed in the coming Messiah for eternal life eventually (if not immediately) believed in Jesus as they heard His message when He appeared on the scene. The fact that these leaders did not believe in Jesus indicates that they had failed to believe in the Messiah for eternal life before He appeared on the scene. Nevertheless, ethnically, these Jews are pictured as God's people by the OT and may be taken typologically (and thus parabolically) as picturing OT believers who failed to express mega faith in the Messiah when He appeared on the scene. Although they are not believers historically, they are believers typologically.

Opponents of misthology point out that these leaders, at this point in history at least, had no faith. Thus, these contemporary antagonists seek to reduce the subject matter to soteriology. Even so, misthologists can point out that Jesus places these Jewish leaders within the kingdom and thereby typologically uses them as examples of unbelieving believers. The reference to *sons of the kingdom* being thrown into the outer darkness would be limited to this (or some similar[†]) misthological frame of reference (to the exclusion of any soteriological dimension). On

---

[*] Jesus purposefully may have used ambiguity that would allow a neoclassical dualism in which *exclusion* would signify soteric entrance but *precession* would denote mistholic entrance. See *Neoclassical Exclusion-Precession*, 952.

[†] Another misthological vantage point which yields much the same result is to understand Jesus as referring to Jewish believers in Mt 8:12 who actually do believe (within the course of history, even presently at the time of His ministry) but who would be cast into the outer darkness as a warning to those Jews listening to Him that Jewish ethnicity does not qualify one for inheriting the kingdom.

the other hand, Jesus may have intended for *proago* also to apply soteriologically to these Jewish unbelievers, in which case the reverse would be true in this particular parable regarding that particular detail when viewed through that particular lens. In this case, *proago* would denote their soteriological exclusion from the kingdom, not just from the feast within the kingdom. In summary, at the historical level *proago* would denote soteriological *exclusion*; whereas, at the typological level it would depict misthological *precession*.

Multiple Vantage Points

Some securitists insist that the passages in question are dealing with Jews as God's entrusted servants during the tribulation. Those holding to a soteriological interpretation of the outer darkness, in all three passages pertaining to it, jump to the conclusion that if this soteriological premise is granted, then the outer darkness is not applicable to believers. This assessment is premature for a variety of reasons. First, even if those cast into the outer darkness are lost Jewish stewards of the future tribulational dispensation, the probability of a correlative applicability to present-day believers is still virtually certain. Second, even if all the passages regarding the outer darkness pertain to Jewish stewards during the tribulation, then, given the OT view of Israel as God's redeemed son, these entrusted servants surely represent regenerate Jewish believers typologically. Third, nothing precludes these Jewish stewards from being regarded outright as regenerate believers prophetically (i.e., during that future point in history). Fourth, even if some of the passages regarding the outer darkness pertain to Jewish stewards during the tribulation, it is exceedingly unlikely that all three passages could be explained in this manner.

Illustration 357. Three Views of the Outer Darkness

1. Tribulational Mt 8:12 	2. Church-Age & Tribulational Mt 22:13 	3. Church-Age Mt 25:30 

Specifically, the final parable regarding the outer darkness, that of the parable of the talents, is best regarded as having primary applicability to church-age believers who currently are serving their Master while He is gone for a "long time" (Mt 25:19). Jewish believers who will be serving Him for a relatively brief period during the tribulation are not in view, at least not primarily. In contrast, the first passage regarding the outer darkness plausibly might have primary application to Jewish believers during the tribulational period. Interestingly, the middle passage regarding the outer darkness quite possibly intends a mediating applicability to both church-age believers and Jewish tribulational believers.

Tribulational or church-age interpretations are not the only options. Some interpreters do not perceive this level of specificity and prefer to interpret the judgment being expressed in these passages as spanning both ages. To be sure, such an approach would be expected in amillennial circles; nevertheless, some dispensationalists show a propensity to reject dispensational precision in their treatment of these passages and thus to interpret the outer darkness in more generic terms. This perspective is permissible, as long as one does not insist exclusively on generality. In other words, the middle passage does not intend for us to see just a frog-horse. Rather, we are expected to see all three: a frog, a horse, and a frog-horse. The frog-horse allows the specificity of the frog and the horse to be merged into a composite unity having both specific and generic applicability. Regardless as to whether one holds to—(1) a tribulational interpretation, (2) a church-age interpretation, or (3) a more general interpretation—failing to perceive the misthological nature of the outer darkness is inexcusable.

Jewish believers (who were indeed believers at that point in history) needed to be warned of their need for great faith in order that they might recline at table and enjoy Messianic rulership.

Conclusion

At the broadest level, the *friend* thrown into the outer darkness might simply be perceived to represent believers, indiscriminately of ethnic identity or temporal locality. Consistency would dictate that the new nation be interpreted broadly at this level of investigation as well. When the details are interpreted more strictly, however, the friend is better identified as a church-age believer (perhaps a Jewish church-age believer) who is being dealt with after the rapture. The new nation, in turn, to whom rulership of the kingdom is given, would be perceived as church-age believers who have born the fruit appropriate to repentance. Alternatively, when the focus is on other details at an even more precise level, perceiving the friend to be a Jewish tribulational believer is reasonable. The assumption that Jesus intends to limit the interpretation to any one of these viable options is questionable. Commentators are divided in their preference, and probably justifiable so. To insist on any one perspective is probably to be guilty of posing a false trichotomy. The friend may be properly taken as: (1) a generic reference to unfaithful believers regardless of the time period, (2) a generic reference to unfaithful believers of either the church age or the tribulational period, or (3) an explicit reference to unfaithful Jewish believers of either the church age or the tribulational period. In each case, the outer darkness can only be understood appropriately as referring to table exclusion, not kingdom exclusion. When the focus is on the outer darkness, misthological exclusion from a place and experience within the kingdom, rather than from the eschatological kingdom itself, is entailed by the various details, regardless of the zoom level of this particular detail. Nevertheless, the OT background is very suggestive that when the outer darkness is examined in detail, this misthological exclusion pertains to Mount Zion and confirms the misthopological understanding of the darkness detailed herein.

In addition to *friend*, other related details are also capable of being understood from multiple vantage points, the most notable of which are: *sons of the kingdom, son, children, fire,* and *before.* Historically, even those Jews who rejected the gospel at that point in time may be considered redeemed children of God typologically. While such soteric Jewish unbelievers will burn eternally, they may also be used to illustrate the point typologically (and thus correlatively) that those who are mistholic believers will burn misthologically.

Illustration 358. Classical Gehenna Soteriology

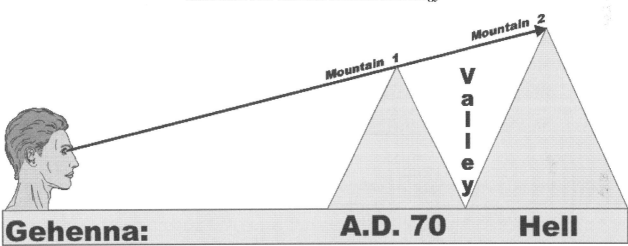

Undoubtedly, some misthologists will be quick to detect the possibility of a preteristic or purgatorial Gehenna at this level of detail. If the outer darkness is for those believers who simply fail to dress appropriately, then might the burning represent a worse fate for those believers who are guilty of apostasy? This purgatorial position is too fraught with problems to be given any further interaction in the present book. Moreover, the obvious purpose of the fire in this passage is to punish, not purge, those submitted to it.

The preteristic misthological Gehenna position, when enjoined with typology, on the other hand, is attractive within the confines of these three parables, especially when coupled with the potential temporal-eschatological duality of the A.D. 70 event as dually applicable to believers in Heb 10:26-31. If I were an ultraist, I certainly would wish to explore that possibility. My initial reaction to this proposition, though, is guardedly pessimistic in that the references to *unquenchable fire* (Mt 3:1), *furnace of fire* (Mt 13:42,50), and *eternal fire* (Mt 18:8; 25:41) seem to preclude preteristic Gehenna misthology.

Illustration 359. Preteristic Gehenna-Bema

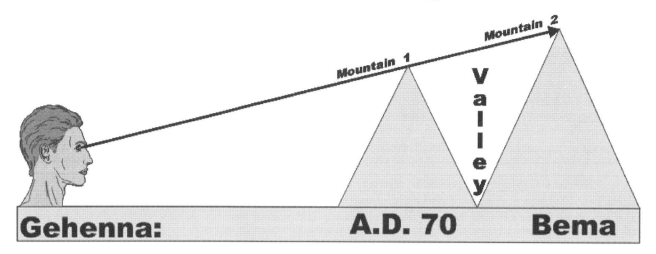

On the other hand, most (if not all) of these above fire-passages are probably eschatological and soteriological. The *fire* in Mt 22:7, in contrast, is temporal and potentially points (dualistically yet distinguishably) to both a soteriological and misthological conclusion (depending upon the zoom level). In admitting this possibility, allowance has been made, in harmony with the above passages regarding soteric burning, that those who historically are unbelievers are anticipated parabolically to burn eternally. At the same time, it must be admitted that the *fire* in Mt 22:7 is not said to be *eternal*. The inference that the fire in this context is eternal must be made deductively and is dependent upon the zoom level employed. When those suffering this temporal fire are perceived to be unbelievers, this fire is appropriately perceived to be temporal-soteriological (and thus eternal). The burning is eternal. When those suffering this temporal fire are interpreted to be believers, then this fire is fittingly understood to be temporal-misthological (and thus not eternal). The burning is not eternal, although the results of the burning are eternal.

According to some FG misthologists (e.g., Haller and Hodges), the bear-or-burn theme introduced in Mt 3:10 is temporal. Hodges, in fact, would include Mt 3:12 under this temporal umbrella. (Haller passes over this latter verse as to the nature of the fire.) For reasons explained elsewhere, however, although this temporal view of the fire is indeed plausible, the eternal view is more probable.[*] Therefore, I am left without this natural recourse to a preteristic cross reference for a possible preteristic misthological Gehenna in the above passages, unless, of course, one were to argue that both vantage points are possible, at least in Mt 3:10. When understood soterically, the fire would be understood to burn eternally. When understood temporally, the fire would perhaps be capable of also being understood as including a soteriological or misthological dimension, as the case may be, just as the fire in Mt 22:7 is applicable eschatologically to both unbelievers and believers, albeit pertaining to two distinct experiences. For those who would wish to explore preteristic Gehenna misthology though, Mt 5:29-30; 10:28; 18:9 provide ample motivation. As I am constantly reminded by some of my fellow misthologists, these passages are most naturally interpreted as addressing believers. One might attempt to find a dualistic possibility to these passages as well. Therefore, at least a speculative attempt will be made to broach that possibility in the next appendix.

---

[*] For these and other possibilities, see "Singular and Plural Fruit" in *Karpology: The Doctrine of Fruit.*

Appendix 19.
Neo-ultraistic and Neoclassic Entrance

Introduction

During the course of this book, I have interacted with various authors holding to a form of classical ultraism. However, if Curtis Tucker's new book *Majestic Destiny* is any indication of what is to come, a new form of ultraism may be on the horizon.[*] Written at the popular level, this book does not address critical issues and therefore fails to provide enough detail for sustained interaction. Yet its basic thesis is one shared by my good friend and fellow misthologist, Scott Crawford, who is assisting in the proofreading of this manuscript. Therefore, this topic is sufficient to spark our joint interest, even though it may be in embryonic form at this point. Although Curtis, Scott, and I surely will differ on some details as to what this neo-ultraism might look like when it is fully mature, interacting with this new and upcoming form of ultraism is not entirely premature in that Tucker already has broached the topic in his published book. Moreover, Neff has provided a splendid classical rejoinder to Tucker's position (as it pertains to the rich young ruler), in which Neff takes a conservative position, very much like the one presumed herein. Yet, among other things, Neff's failure to consider a neoclassical possibility prevents his response from being completely persuasive.[1679]

The mutual perspective shared by both Tucker and Crawford is that entrance into the kingdom in Mt 5:20 and 7:21 is a misthological entrance. For Crawford this would be entrance into kingdom rulership. Obviously, I am not opposed conceptually to such a possibility in that I adopt this perspective for Acts 14:22: "Through many tribulations we must enter the kingdom of God."[†] To *enter* means to *inherit* in this context. Moreover, *basileia* may be taken to denote *kingship*. An experience within the Messianic kingdom on earth during the millennial era is in view. Spatial exclusion from that kingdom is not a consideration. All believers will be in the millennial kingdom, but not all believers will enter/inherit the kingdom/kingship. The outer darkness does not refer to exclusion from the kingdom but to exclusion from rulership of the kingdom.[1680] On such particulars, I would be in agreement with Tucker on this particular passage in Acts. The question is, "How far do we proceed with applying this perspective to other NT texts?"

Tucker apparently would apply this perspective to the entire NT. In Tucker's estimation, new birth in Jn 3:3-5 is a precondition rather than condition to enter the kingdom.[1681] This perspective is certainly nothing new in that classical ultraists would concur. On the other hand, I regard punctiliar faith to be the singular condition for kingdom entrance in that context and thus would argue for soteric rather than mistholic entrance therein. As Tucker and I would both agree, however, the reason John does not use the word *repent(ance)* in his gospel is because he is not presenting the gospel of the kingdom. In contrast to the synoptic writers, John does not present the kingdom of God as being at hand. In further contradistinction to the synoptic writers, John avoids the use of the word *gospel* in order to clarify that he is not presenting the same message as that presented by the synoptic writers. Astute misthologists are aware of such matters. Also, in comparison to the synoptic writers, John has very little to say about the kingdom, other than that faith is the requisite and that Jesus' kingdom is *not of this world* (Jn 18:36). Whereas I would tend to see a spiritual dimension to that kingdom that is presently entered into by faith (Col 1:13), Tucker would insist that this kingdom is not otherworldly at all but entered into during the millennium by those who have met the prerequisite of faith and followed through with the requisite repentance. Tucker would say that Jesus is only acknowledging that His kingdom does not have this world as its source, not that it will "not take place on this planet."[1682] In effect, Jesus was telling Nicodemus that he could not skip first base (new birth by faith) if he wanted to reach home base (i.e., have a part in kingdom rulership). Therefore, what is at stake for a believer (i.e., for someone who has rounded first base) is failing to reach home base (in terms of kingdom rulership). According to Tucker, entrance into the kingdom is strictly a misthological theme (Mt 5:20; 7:13,21; 18:3; 19:23-30).[1683]

The most glaring problem with Tucker's proposal is that he fails to deal clearly, and certainly not adequately, with two glaring questions: "What about those believers who do not enter the kingdom? And what about Gehenna?" One might piece together an answer to the first question from Tucker's discussion and simply regard him as a conservative misthologist. Yet the second question is left untouched. Specifically, what about Mt 18:8-9? According to Tucker, "'eternal life' is a synonym for 'kingdom'" in the book of Matthew."[1684] If this is

---

[*] For a review of these various positions, see *Illustration 204. Two Mediating Neo-Misthological Positions*, 596; *Illustration 205. Neo-Mistholic Views*, 596.
[†] See *Limited Entrance*, 570; *Misthological Entrance*, 571; *Spatial versus Experiential*, 572.

the case, then in this passage Jesus certainly seems to be warning believers about two opposing possibilities: entrance into the kingdom as opposed to being cast into the eternal fire of Gehenna (hell), where their worm does not die and the fire is not quenched (Mk 9:44-48). The warning to the disciples about Gehenna in Mt 10:28 is coupled easily with this passage. At least classical ultraists attempt to reconcile such passages with unconditional security. Tucker makes no such attempt at reconciliation and therefore is completely lacking in persuasive punch. If it could be shown that these warnings refer (at least in part) to a *Preteristic Gehenna-Bema*, as I entertain in Mt 22:7* (insofar as it applies to believers), then Tucker's thesis would be far more appealing, and perhaps even a valid FG alternative to the position adopted herein. The neo-Dillowian perspective, as found in Dillow's newer writings, appears to make impressive strides in that area.

At its heart, misthology is a defense for unconditional security. The question at that juncture would be, "Which misthological perspective provides the most biblically consistent defense?" Conditional security is considered a strong position by its adherents. They argue for it from basically one of two competing theological perspectives: Arminianism or Calvinism. While both systems of thought cannot be true, nevertheless, both systems are seen as supporting the overarching schema of conditional security. The blend of these two formal systems into a less consistent Calminianism tends to fall under this same umbrella. Thus, conditional securitists are left with three broad options for their point of view. The same will probably turn out to be true for unconditional securitists also, except that unconditional security may have four primary options. The two established schools of thought in the Marrowism are (1) the *classical view* which regards entrance into the kingdom to be a gift and Gehenna to be a soteriological issue versus (2) the *ultraistic view* which regards entrance into the millennial kingdom to be a reward and Gehenna during the millennium to be a misthological concern as well. However, just as Calminianism is the theological birth child of Calminianism and Arminianism, so (3) *neo-ultraism* will be the birth-child of classical and ultraistic views. (4) *Neoclassicalism*, in turn, will be the birth-child of classicalism and neo-ultraism. At the broader level, unconditional security has an even broader range of advocates: soteriologists and misthologists.†

Just as at one level FG misthologists welcome FG soteriologists as fellow members of the FG fraternity defending unconditional security, so Marrowists, such as myself, who hold the classical view of Gehenna, will welcome ultraists and neo-ultraists as fellow defenders of misthology. For even though I do not find the neo-ultraistic perspective persuasive on all fronts, still, even before the conception of the neo-ultraistic movement, I found Acts 14:22 to be a misthological text, in harmony with the neo-ultraistic view of kingdom entrance. Briefly, then, in order to give some preliminary comments on any possible neo-ultraistic perspective that might be anticipated from what writings that are already available, a few observations will be in order regarding neo-ultraism.

Mt 18:9-10

By insisting that the *eternal* (*aionios*) fire in Mt 18:8 would only mean a fire that lasts a long time, perhaps for an age, neo-ultraism has a ready recourse by which to challenge the soteriological view of Gehenna. Not all scholars believe that the adjective form *aionios* necessarily means *eternal* every time *aionios* occurs in the NT. Therefore, the *Preteristic Gehenna-Bema* position (which I simply will term as the *neo-ultraistic* perspective) could follow the path taken by ultraism in arguing that it does not have that meaning here. If so, neo-ultraists will suffer the same setbacks as ultraists. However, neo-ultraism does not have to take this recourse, and it would be potentially inconsistent in doing so. Why take the fire to be a long time when the Bema will only be a short time? The Bema will not be an age-long experience for the individual standing before the Bema. Trying to make *aionios* mean *long time* or *age long* is not the best option for neo-ultraism. The better option would be to allow the eternal fire of Gehenna to represent the eternal consequences of the Bema. In the context, *whoever* causes one of these *little ones who believe to stumble*, and thus go *astray* and potentially *perish* (Mt 18:6,12-14), will be in danger of Bema fire, pictured by fiery Gehenna. Neither the believers who stumble nor the believers who cause them to stumble will be in danger of the Lake of Fire, but both will be in danger of Gehenna-Bema fire, the results of which are eternal. Salvation from the fiery Bema and from its consequent eternal outer darkness are at stake. The temporary experience of the Bema is eternal in its result. Jesus portrays this graphically with the Jewish garbage dump. The beauty of this approach is its simplicity.

To be sure, various details will have to be worked out, such as the entrance into the kingdom/life being juxtaposed with this misthological garbage dump. Even so, if this entrance is understood as misthological ranking in the kingdom, so as to contrast those who are least with those who are greatest (so Mt 18:1-4), then the context

---

* See *Illustration 354. Basic Magnification of Burning City*, 940; *Illustration 359. Preteristic Gehenna-Bema*, 946.
† See *Illustration 204. Two Mediating Neo-Misthological Positions*, 596.

suggests equating entrance into the kingdom with living as a king within the kingdom. Being devoid of life would be misthological death, not the second death in the Lake of Fire. Thus, the neo-ultraistic position does not need to run aground on the shores of that soteriological lake. "But what about the worms?" someone, such as myself, quickly would object, "And the unquenchable fire?" The same rejoinder could be offered. The worms and unquenchable fire are merely garbage-dump imagery depicting the permanent misthological loss of life. No indication of ongoing suffering within the flames of Gehenna is provided in the NT literature. Such importations are apocalyptic interpolations.[*]

Illustration 360. Neoclassical Gehenna

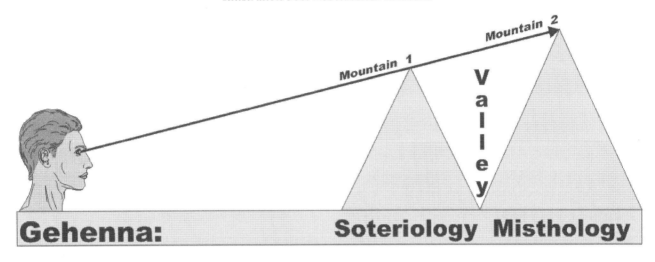

One might even dig deeper into this misthological garbage dump and find some soteriological refuse at the bottom. In this context, Gehenna is described as a place, "where *their* worm does not die, and *the* fire is not quenched. For *everyone* will be salted with fire" (Mk 9:48-49). *Everyone*, evidently lost and saved, will experience the fire of judgment. This clue, provided at the conclusion of this Gehenna passage, suggests that soteriological and misthological possibilities are merged at different levels in the Gehenna imagery, just as both dimensions are discernible at different zoom levels for the burning city (Mt 22:7).[†] Curiously, the Lord makes a contrast between *your* and *their* in this Markan passage. *Your* hand, *your* foot, and *your* eye are contrasted with *their* worm. Is this an incidental, meaningless detail? Perhaps not. *Everyone* would be a natural composite of *you* (second person) and *them* (third person). For *them* (i.e., unbelievers) the fire of Gehenna includes worms. The worms are for the unbelievers, not for the believers, thrown into Gehenna.[‡] For *you* (i.e., believers) the gnawing worms are omitted. Everyone will be salted by fire, but not everyone will be eaten by worms.

"But surely Jesus is doing nothing more than quoting Is 66:24!" a conservative misthologist, such as myself, would object, "So this fire is at least millennial in scope and simply deals with soteriological issues." Perhaps. But if so, why did the Lord change the pronouns? The OT reads, *their* fire and *their* worm. Why did Jesus change the OT phrase to *the* fire and *their* worm? Why contrast the fire applied to *everyone* with the worm applied just to *them*? Given that a change was made, evidently to clarify the intended application, why did the Lord not change

---

[*] See *Unquenchable Fire in the New Testament*, 819. Annihilation does not have recourse to the neoclassical distinction between the fire of Mt 13:42 as applied to unbelievers and the fire of Gehenna as applied to the believer. Ongoing suffering will exist in *that place*, that is, in the furnace of fire (Mt 13:42). But such suffering is not implicitly said to exist in Gehenna. Thus, the neoclassical possibility of a punctiliar suffering (of the loss of misthological life at Gehenna-Bema) is not out of question and may be contrasted with the linear suffering in the furnace. Moreover, the neoclassical view further would be able to suggest that Gehenna serves as a metaphorical picture for the unfaithful believer suffering the eternal loss of reward but a typological picture of unbelievers suffering in the furnace of fire (cp. Mt 23:15,33). Even so, the unfaithful believer will not suffer linearly in Gehenna, only linearly as a result of Gehenna in the neoclassical view. The NT purposefully does not mention linear suffering within Gehenna so that it might be used jointly, but in different capacities, to picture the fate of both unbelievers and unfaithful believers. For unbelievers, it pictures a place of suffering. For unfaithful believers, in contrast, it pictures a misthological loss of physical and soulical life: a place where you experience physical and misthological death, not soteriological suffering (Mt 10:28).

[†] See *Levels of Detail*, 935.

[‡] If so, the worms would apply to the vipers thrown into Gehenna (Mt 23:15,33), not to unfaithful believers thrown into Gehenna. Otherwise, the worms are just part of the garbage-dump imagery and need not denote suffering, only death. Believers, in any case, are not eaten alive by worms. What is being entertained is that their misthological dead bodies might be pictured as being eaten by worms—morbid perhaps, but then again, loss of rewards was never intended to look pretty.

the application of the warning to *you*—since He is speaking to *you* about *your* hand, foot, and eye? In order words, if He intended for the worm to apply to you, why not make this clarifying change: "Where *your* worm does not die, and *your* fire is not quenched"? Instead, the Lord universalizes the fire and particularizes the worm. The fire applies to *everyone*; the worm applies only to *them*—whoever *them* is in contrast to *you*. Nevertheless, the fire will not be a garbage-dump experience for you if you cut off your hand, foot, and eye. For those of Jesus' followers who yet needed to enter the kingdom soteriologically, understanding the cutting as dealing with soteriological preconditions is reasonable. For those of His disciples who already had entered soteriologically, but needed to be concerned about entering misthologically, understanding the cutting as dealing with misthological conditions is more practicable. If the Lord intends both levels of application, as the conclusion of the pericope itself suggests, then the classical and neo-ultraistic positions find common ground. A merger of these two perspectives into a neoclassical position might be feasible. Although as an advocate of the classical position I might not find an exclusively neo-ultraistic position probable, a joint neoclassical position would certainly be far less objectionable.

Illustration 361. Neoclassical Preteristic Gehenna-Bema

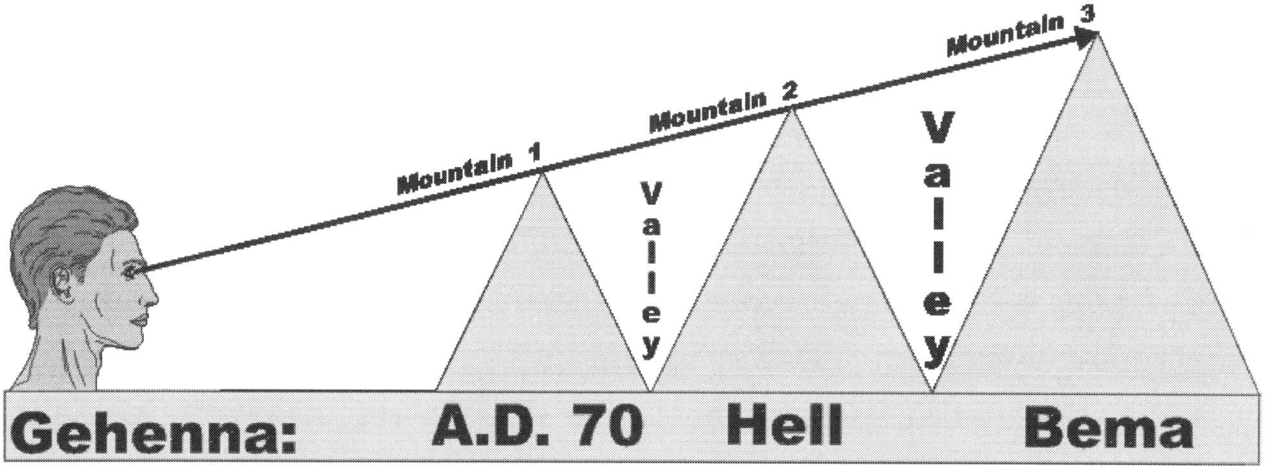

If this neoclassical hypothesis is correct, then the burning of the city in A.D. 70 not only preteristically prefigures the fire of Gehenna for unbelievers but also the fire of the Bema for believers, in a manner already anticipated by the principle of correlativity.* For unbelievers, eternal suffering in hell would be entailed. For believers, though, only a Preteristic Gehenna-Bema would be in view. The underlying principle for both is the same: This garbage dump is what your earthly life will look like in terms of eternal value if you have failed to do what is necessary to enter the kingdom/kingship of heaven. Unbelievers will fail to enter the kingdom; unfaithful believers will not enter the kingship. *Basileia* can be used to convey both senses, as the case may be. In Mt 18:9-10 at least, the neoclassical position seems preferable.†

Mt 10:28

As to the cross reference in Mt 10:28, the absence of specificity is apparent: "And do not fear those who kill the body, but are unable to kill the soul; but rather fear Him who is able to destroy both soul and body in hell [Gehenna]." Jesus does not say, "*Your* soul and *your body.*" Then again, neither does He say, "*Their* soul and *their* body." He might intend joint, neoclassical applicability. Gehenna will be the gateway to the second death for unbelievers cast into the Lake of Fire, but the entrance to misthological death for believers cast into the outer darkness. The loss of one's soul is certainly suggestive of misthological possibilities. The destruction of one's body could refer simply to temporal death, inclusive of the preteristic variety. This Gehenna-Bema position has an

---

* See *Theory of Correlativity*, 911.
† Also see *Joint Neoclassical Soteriology and Misthology*, 638. In other of my writings, when not examining the various misthological options, I simply may approach Mt 18:9-10 in a classical format. Although I may prefer to interpret the passage from multiple vantage points when explaining it in detail, for many discussions merely expounding the classical position suffices. After all, for the neoclassical interpretation of a passage to be valid, the classical interpretation must also be valid. The passage must be capable of reasonably sustaining a classical interpretation. Of course, contextual clues would cause one to suspect that a dual application is intended. Otherwise, the passage would not be interpreted neoclassically when explained fully. Still, a robust, independent argument should be possible for both the classical and neo-classical position for a text being considered as having both intended meanings.

advantage over the classical ultraistic position in not becoming embroiled in wild speculations about believers having to be raised so that they can be killed. The neo-ultraistic position avoids some very apparent pitfalls inherent in classical ultraism.

Mt 5:20-23

As to Mt 5:20, a joint neoclassical understanding of the verse could understand it as saying, "Unless your soteric righteousness surpasses that of the lost, you will not enter the kingdom soteriologically. And unless your mistholic righteousness surpasses that of the religious, you will not enter the kingdom misthologically." Just as the burning of the city (Mt 22:7) is to be understood preteristically-eschatologically, so the fiery Gehenna might be understood millennially-eschatologically: "Everyone who is angry with his brother shall be guilty before the court; and whoever shall say to his brother, 'Raca,' shall be guilty before the supreme court; and whoever shall say, 'You fool,' shall be guilty enough to go into the fiery hell" (Mt 5:23). A shameful, premature death in the fiery garbage dump would be a joint possibility for both believers and unbelievers during the millennium and foreshadow respective misthological and soteriological conclusions. Since this passage is millennial in its scope and since Is 66:24 is as well, enjoining these two passages is reasonable. "Then [during the millennium] they shall go forth and look on the corpses of the men who have transgressed against Me. For *their* worm shall not die, and *their* fire shall not be quenched; and they shall be an abhorrence to all mankind." A shameful, physical death in an open grave for anyone living in physical bodies during the millennium is the foreseen possibility if they rebel and transgress against the Lord. Joint correlative misthological and soteriological outcomes are foreseeable.

Mt 7:13,21

Similarly, the broad gate in Mt 7:13 might be taken as leading to soteriological destruction for unbelievers and to misthological destruction for believers. Unbelievers need to bear the singular good fruit of saving faith, while believers need to bear the plural good fruit of holy living. Unbelievers who fail to produce saving faith will depart into an eternal flame, while believers who fail to produce holy lives will depart into the outer darkness. As for the parallel in Lk 13:28, some neo-ultraists, such as Tucker, probably will prefer to see it as referring to being present misthologically in the kingdom. If I were a neo-ultraist I would be more inclined to maintain, as I do now as a classical misthologist, that soteriological exclusion is described in Lk 13:28, while misthological exclusion is depicted in Lk 13:29. Joint soteriological and misthological themes are present, but distinguished, in the verses. How else can one reasonably explain the presence of these evildoers in the kingdom? One cannot say that that they are in the kingship, sitting as rulers with the millennial kingdom, only to be excluded subsequently. Experiential misthological exclusion, which seems to be the only possibility entertained by Tucker, is thus not a reasonable conjecture. On the other hand, spatial exclusion might be a possibility, if an innovative neo-ultraistic can demonstrate that being excluded from the kingdom means only to be excluded from the Heavenly Jerusalem and the Promised Land (i.e., the land of Israel), but not from other surrounding kingdoms during the millennium. Otherwise, such a neo-ultraistic proposal appears unreasonable. Tucker needs misthopology, but it remains to be seen if even misthopology can be stretched to accommodate such misthology.

Wedding Feast

To further illustrate Tucker's need of misthopology, even for more conservative estimations, consider his equating the kingdom with the wedding feast in Mt 22:10-12.[1685] Misthologists frequently point out that any soteriological equation of the feast with the kingdom suffers from the fact that the ill-dressed man is in the banquet hall before being cast out of the feast into the outer darkness. Consequently, equating this feast with the eschatological kingdom is impossible. New birth is requisite for such entrance. Thus, this man is allowed into the eschatological kingdom while in a regenerate state. Surely, he was, and remains, a regenerate believer. His regenerate state (his spiritual life) is not taken away from him after the millennial kingdom has started. The feast must be an experience and/or place within the kingdom, not the kingdom itself. By misthologically equating the feast with the kingdom itself, Tucker has run amuck misthologically in the same place where conditionalists get stuck soteriologically. The classical misthological argument definitely has the advantage in arguing that the feast is not the kingdom. Correspondingly, entrance into the kingdom is not a misthological issue but is granted freely to the believer. This believer enters the kingdom freely but is excluded subsequently from the place from which kingdom rulership will be exercised (and thus from exercising such rulership). This misthopological exclusion is not from the kingdom but from the Promised Land and the Reward City within the kingdom. Misthopology trumps, rather than aids, neo-ultraism in this passage. For such reasons, I am not a kingdom exclusionist, though I am willing to entertain a limited neoclassical misthology that would allow a dual applicability of soteriological and misthological themes (to both unbelievers and believers respectively) in certain entrance-passages.

Impossible Camel

Perhaps the wedding feast might be considered a permissible exception to the neo-ultraistic premise that entrance is a misthological concept since entrance is only an inference in that context. This passage is missing the formula: *enter the kingdom.* Even so, neo-ultraists may not get off the hook so easily. The account of the rich young ruler contains back-to-back citations of this formula: "Jesus said to His disciples, 'Truly I say to you, it is hard for a rich man to *enter the kingdom* of heaven. And again I say to you, it is easier for a camel to go through the eye of a needle, than for a rich man to *enter the kingdom* of God'" (Mt 19:23-24). Tucker says, and rightly so, "Jesus told the disciples that it is hard (not impossible) for a rich man to enter the kingdom."[1686] Granted, entrance by the rich man is difficult, yet, even so, entrance by the camel is impossible. An entrance requiring imputational righteousness is suggested by the impossibility of the camel entering. The soteriological assessment of Haller (the GNTC Matthean commentator) on this passage seems to be right on target:

> Jesus is speaking literally of a hole in a sewing needle. There was no such thing in the city walls of that time as a small gate called "the eye of a needle" that camels could go through if they went on their knees. That is something possible, but Jesus is speaking of the impossible….If one is trusting in his or her riches as **proof** of one's righteousness, that person will fail to enter the kingdom. God will save by grace or not at all. Salvation is possible only through Him.[1687]

Performance wise, entering the kingdom was impossible (not merely hard) for the rich man. Merely trusting in God-enabled practical righteousness as (necessary) **proof** of soteriological righteousness places one in danger of being excluded soteriologically from the kingdom because one has trusted in God-enabled self-righteousness for kingdom entrance. Haller's point is well taken herein. Proveitists are in soteriological danger.

Illustration 362. Neoclassical Entrance

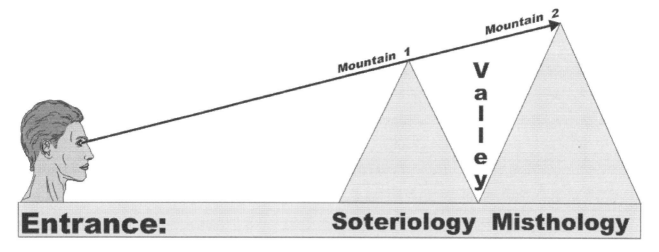

On the other hand, the Matthean context is dripping wet with misthological details. For example, Haller also correctly perceives that inheriting eternal life in Mt 19:29 is a misthological issue. The Markan and Lukan parallels could be taken as equating entrance into the kingdom with inheriting eternal life (Mk 10:17,24-25; Lk 18:18,24-25). Thus, a neoclassical view might prevail in which Jesus is dealing with both soteriological and misthological entrances into the kingdom. The parabolic impossibility indicates soteriology; the didactic difficulty (among other things) accents misthology.

Neoclassical Exclusion-Precession

As already noted, commentators are divided as to what it means for the publicans and prostitutes to *enter before* (*proago*)* the Pharisees into the kingdom of heaven (Mt 21:31), especially since the Pharisees do not enter

---

* See *Before*, 943.

the kingdom (Mt 5:20), apparently at all (Mk 10:15; Lk 18:17) and thus not soterically. When the complete exclusion of the Pharisees is perceived to be in view, the passage would be understood as conditioning soteric entrance exclusively on faith alone (Mt 21:32). After all, no ranking within the kingdom would then be implied if the Pharisees are not making it into the kingdom at all. On the other hand, when the Pharisees typologically are seen as entering the kingdom in a lower ranking position (i.e., second place, and thus last place), a misthological entrance would then be in view, in which case the repentant publicans and prostitutes earn the higher ranking position of first place.

The soteriological perception of the entrance is enhanced by the tense of the verb. Translations generally handle this present tense verb in one of three ways, translating it as (1) *go/enter* (ambiguous/punctiliar action), (2) *are going/entering* (present linear action), or (3) *will go/enter* (future punctiliar action).[*]

As to the first option, when this verse is understood as describing present soteric entrance (to the exclusion of the unbelieving Pharisees), then a punctiliar entrance (at least as far as each individual is concerned) is understood. Jesus attributes the Pharisees' lack of entrance to their lack of punctiliar repentance and lack of punctiliar faith: "For John came to you in the way of righteousness and you did not *believe* ⊙ him; but the publicans and prostitutes did *believe* ⊙ him; and you, seeing this, did not even *repent* ⊙ afterward so as to *believe* ● him" (Mt 21:32; TM). The externally punctiliar aspect is confirmed to be internally punctiliar by the aorist infinitive for the final occurrence of *believe*. The singular response of soteric faith qualifies one for entrance. In view of this punctiliar condition for entrance, present entrance would be punctiliar: "The publicans and prostitutes *go/enter* (•) before you." If one must insist on translating the verb linearly (as in the second option), then in this case (i.e., when understood soterically) it should be done so distributively: The publicans and prostitutes *go/enter* (⋯•⋯) before you."[†] Naturally, if understood soteriologically and translated futuristically (as in the third option), then a punctiliar action would be in view. As a soteriologist, I certainly am satisfied with this explanation.

Nevertheless, as a misthologist, I could at least entertain a neoclassical dualism in which Jesus intends to move beyond this level of detail to allow a typological portrayal of these antagonistic, redeemed Jewish sons[‡] as entering in last place because they do not believe their Messiah. They rejected the gospel of the kingdom. In contrast to the other entrance-passages which use *eiserchomai* for *enter into*, the Lord uses (the present tense of) *proago eis* for *go before into* on this singular occasion for kingdom entrance (Mt 21:31). One might suspect that in this verbal choice (and tense), Jesus purposefully is invoking a detail that could be taken as denoting linear action. Nolland is of the opinion that linear action is entailed:

> In Matthew's other uses, entry into the kingdom is always future.[§] Nonetheless, meeting the conditions for entry is a matter in the present time, in which the kingdom is being proclaimed. In light of the other instances, the imagery here would seem to be best taken as being well along the path that leads into the kingdom rather than of having already entered the kingdom.[1688]

As a soteriologist, I would object to part of what Nolland is stating. For one thing, entry is not always future. Present punctiliar entrance is suggested by the imagery surrounding the aoristic summons to enter the gate in Mt 7:13. Enter now! The present participle in the latter part of this verse, that contrasts those currently entering

---

[*] For sake of symmetry, I am treating the NAS and NLT *will get into*, the TNT *shall come into*, and DRA *shall go into* as *will go/enter into*.

[†] The gnomic articular present participle for *entering* (⋯•⋯) in Mt 23:13 is used in conjunction with an aorist infinitive for *enter* ●. As an aside, linearly not entering (→) points to a linear failure to enter (•) even once. Jesus is not insinuating that their problem is that they do not enter continuously, as if they enter occasionally. Rather, "you do not enter (•) nor permit those who are entering (⋯•⋯) to enter ●" (TM). Present soteric entrance is punctiliar. Although entering (⋯•⋯) the kingdom in Mt 23:13 is the only occurrence of the present tense being used for *eiserchomai* in Matthew in relation to entering the kingdom, this is not the only passage denoting present entrance. Significantly, though, punctiliar entrance (in relation to the individual) is the point being considered in all cases. The gnomic articular present participle is also used of those entering (⋯•⋯) the broad gate to destruction in Mt 7:13, where it is again juxtaposed with a punctiliar aorist. In this case, an aorist imperative is used to exhort punctiliar entrance ● through the narrow gate. The soteriologist has every right to perceive a punctiliar present soteric entrance as opposed to the lack of a punctiliar entrance. The question is, "Does the soteriologist have exclusive rights to this passage, or might the misthologist also have rights to perceive the path, to which the gate opens, to be a joint soteric or mistholic path so that Jesus purposefully is giving a dual correlative invitation to both unbelievers and believers?"

[‡] See *Israel My Redeemed Servant*, 376; *Israel My Redeemed Son*, 376.

[§] At this point he cites Mt 5:20; 7:21; 18:3; 19:23-24. Technically, the aorist subjective in Mt 5:20 does not refer to the future (since time is lost outside the indicative mood). Nevertheless, Nolland's point, for these particular passages at least, is well taken herein because the parallel in Mt 7:21 does use the future tense. As to the aorist subjunctive in 18:3, translations almost universally translate it futuristically (TNT being an exception).

through the broad gate, certainly indicates that current entrance into the narrow gate is being urged. Additionally, the aorist infinitive used to warn of the necessity to remove body parts in order to enter life the in Mt 18:8-9 could be well taken to denote the need for present punctiliar entrance, in which case the warning that one punctiliarly become like children in order to punctiliarly *enter* the kingdom in Mt 18:3 might be a logical future rather than an eschatological future. *Become* ● like children right now in order that you may *enter* ● right now into the kingdom. Might one also see a picture of the new birth in this punctiliar, inward transformation (in which one becomes a regenerate child and therefore qualified to enter the kingdom)? In any event, a soteriological process (or path of becoming or entering) is not in view in these *eiserchomai* passages. Whenever *eiserchomai* is used in Matthew to denote a present entrance into the kingdom, a punctiliar entrance is under consideration. For that matter, when a future entrance is in view, it is also punctiliar. Yet this future entrance may be mistholic: "Those who were ready entered into the feast with him" (Mt 25:10; TM). "Enter into the joy of your Lord" (Mt 25:21,23; TM). These parabolic passages picture an eschatological entrance at that point in time. Or future entrance into the kingdom may be soteric. But whether this future soteric entrance is a logical future (Mt 19:23) or eschatological future (Mt 7:21) is another consideration.

If the neoclassical view is correct, then those adopting this perspective can maintain that at the soteric level the previous points made about such passages are correct. Both the entrance and path are fully capable of being interpreted in a manner consistent with FG soteriology. The illustrations and arguments already made may be retained in their full force at this level of understanding since the neoclassic hypothesis would allow that Jesus intended for the imagery to be interpreted in this manner.[*] Neoclassicism does not need to jettison a thoroughgoing soteriological interpretation of the entrance and path. At the same time, a misthological dimension can be entertained at a deeper level. If a misthological perspective is perceived as being warranted as an additional part of the Lord's original intent at this level, then interpreting the passage is this manner is allowable. Whereas we might like to pigeonhole the Lord to an either-or-mentality, the possibility exists that His teaching was intended to be understood in a multidimensional manner, at least on occasion.

Illustration 363. Neoclassical Entrance and Path

---

[*] See *Illustration 216. Narrow Fruit*, 623; *Illustration 217. Narrow Gate*, 624; *Illustration 218. Broad Gate*, 624; *Illustration 219. Gate to Hell*, 625.

Erchomai/entrance onto the path does make a path out of the entrance. Entry is not a pathway. Although one might argue that entry by a gate unto a path is a soteriological entrance onto a misthological path, this point of entry onto the path is not to be confused with the path itself. The *erchomai* passages seem only to entertain the possibility of punctiliar entrance (or distributive entrance which is punctiliar for the individual), whether as an initial or final point of entry into the kingdom. Linear entrance into the kingdom is not under consideration. Contrastively, *proago* more readily allows both a punctiliar and linear aspect.

Illustration 364. Neoclassical Entrance and Path with Proago

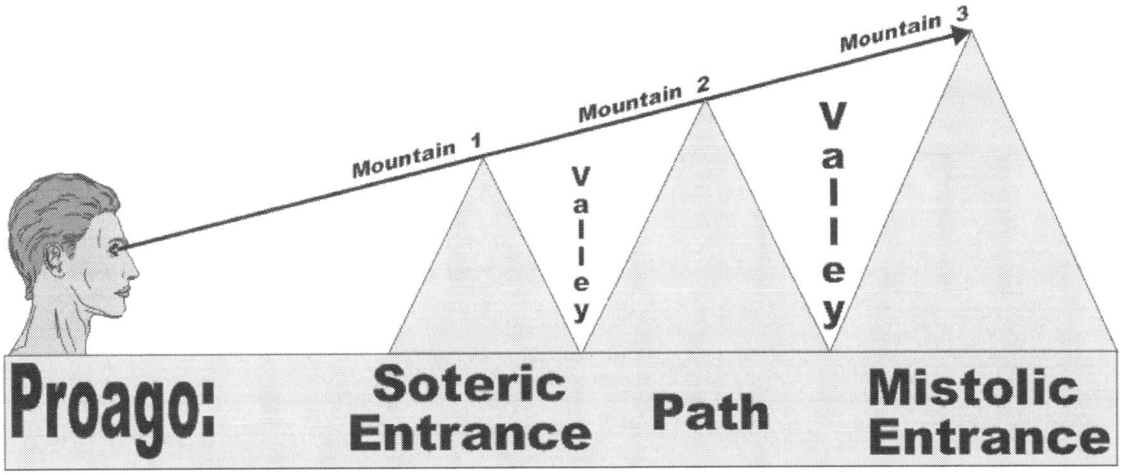

A misthological procession spanning from first to last is suggested by the verbal imagery invoked by *proago*. Since no gate is mentioned in Mt 21:31-32, *proago* might encompass all three elements: (1) the initial soteric gate (present *erchomai*), (2) the path, and (3) the final mistholic gate (future *erchomai*).

Summary

Although the present book has taken the classical view of Gehenna as being a soteriological theme and entrance-passages pertaining thereto in the same light, and thus has provided arguments against the ultraistic view of Gehenna, allowance conceivably might be made for a neo-ultraistic view that perceives a Gehenna-Bema and predominant misthological kingdom entrance. Even then, a thoroughgoing equating of entrance into the kingdom with rulership is doubtful. A more promising proposition would be to combine the classical and neo-ultraistic views into a neoclassical view that takes at least some of the passages in a dualistic manner, so that the Lord is understood as giving a principle that is intentionally applicable to both unbelievers and believers and that thus may be seen from one vantage point as being soteriological and from another vantage point as being misthological. In conjunction with my supportive writings elsewhere, the present book has sought to provide a mature, classical view on these issues. Nevertheless, not even I, as a classical misthologist regarding Gehenna and kingdom entrance, would try to put Acts 14:22 in the soteriological category. GNTC, on the other hand, is classical to a fault and even places this verse in the classical perspective, in which unqualified kingdom entrance is necessarily regarded as a soteriological entrance. I take exception to the classical position in that context. Nevertheless, I do not feel compelled to jettison the classical position taken by GNTC in similar such passages.

When a mature work devoted to the neo-ultraistic position becomes available, perhaps a neoclassical writer will use that book in conjunction with the present book to provide a more thorough synthesis for the classical and neo-ultraistic views into a neoclassical view than the brief sketch provided above. In anticipation of such mature works to follow, I would make the current projection as to relative probabilities of these and related views.

Illustration 365. Primary Kingdom Positions

View	Ranking	Notes
Classic	Probable	Acts 14:22 is an exception to soteriological applicability
Neoclassic	Plausible	Mt 22:10-11 and Lk 13:28 are exceptions to dual applicability
Neo-ultraistic	Possible	A thoroughgoing limitation to misthological entrance/Gehenna is unlikely
Ultraistic	Improbable	Spatial misthological exclusion so as to burn millennially is highly unlikely
Conditionalistic	Impossible	Burning eternally in the Lake of Fire is impossible for the believer

This above chart is a simple summation. However, a more detailed summation in the chart to follow might be helpful for quick review of some of the preferences taken by the present author in the present book regarding the primary texts under discussion as to which verses are soteric, and which verses are mistholic, and which verses are a combination of the two.

Illustration 366. Mediation between Classicalism and Neoclassicalism

Passage	Parallel	Sot.	Mis.	Text	Classification
Mt 5:19			✔	Least and greatest in the kingdom	Classic
Mt 5:20		✔		Not enter at all	Classic
Mt 5:23		✔		Whoever says fool is in danger of Gehenna	Classic
Mt 5:29-30		✔		Cut it off or be cast bodily into Gehenna	Classic
Mt 7:13		✔		Enter by narrow gate	Classic
Mt 7:21		✔		Enter the kingdom	Classic
Mt 7:23		✔		I never *knew* (*ginosko*) you. Depart from Me	Classic
Mt 10:28		✔		Fear Him who can cast bodily into Gehenna	Classic
Mt 18:3	Mk 10:15; Lk 18:17	✔	✓	Enter the kingdom by becoming like children	Classic?
Mt 18:4			✔	Greatest in the kingdom	Classic
Mt 18:8-9	Mk 9:47-48	✔	✔	Cut it off to enter kingdom/life	Neoclassic*
Mt 18:8-9	Mk 9:47-48	✔	✓	eternal fire of Gehenna	Classic?
	Mk 9:44,46,48	✔		worms of Gehenna	Classic?
Mt 22:12			✔	Friend, how did you enter this feast?	Classic†
Mt 19:14	Mk 10:14; Lk 18:16	✔	✔	For of such as children is the kingdom	Neoclassic‡
Mt 19:16	Mk 10:17; Lk 18:18	✔	✓	Obtain/inherit eternal life	Classic?
Mt 19:17		✔	✓	Enter into life	Classic?
Mt 19:23	Mk 10:24;§ Lk 18:24	✔	✓	Difficult for the rich to enter the kingdom	Classic?
Mt 19:24	Mk 10:25; Lk 18:24	✔	✓	Easier for a camel to enter	Classic?
Mt 21:31-32		✔	✓	Publicans and prostitutes will enter before you	Classic?
Mt 19:25	Mk 10:26; Lk 18:26	✔	✓	Then who can be saved?	Classic?
Mt 22:7		✔	✔	Burn their city	Neoclassic
Mt 25:12			✔	I do not *know* (*oida*) you	Classic
Lk 13:27		✔		I do not *know* (*oida*) you. Depart from Me	Classic
Lk 13:28		✔		Cast out of kingdom	Classic
Lk 13:29			✔	Recline at the feast in the kingdom	Classic
Lk 13:30			✔	Least and greatest in the kingdom	Classic
Jn 3:5		✔		You must enter the kingdom through new birth	Classic
Acts 14:22			✔	You enter the kingdom through tribulations	Not classic**

✔ = Primary   ✔ = Secondary   ✓ = Plausible   ✓ = Possible

---

* Although I am adopting a neoclassical view of the entrance, I am not necessarily compelled to adopt neoclassical view of the fire, much less the worms.

† To enter the feast within the kingdom, he first had to enter the kingdom. The classical distinction between misthologically entering the feast and soteriological entering the kingdom is maintained.

‡ Even the classical GNTC entertains a dualistic (and thus neoclassical view) here. Whereas, the Matthean and Markan GNTC commentators are simply classical (i.e., soteriological), the Lukan commentator suggests that Lk 18:16 deals with both entry into the kingdom and reward within the kingdom by those with childlike dispositions.

§ Mk 10:24 clarifies that the difficulty lies in trusting in one's riches (MT).

** Although this interpretation might be termed as neo-ultraistic, as a classical writer, my sympathies are more in harmony with neoclassical possibilities than neo-ultraistic ones. Thus, I am disinclined to summarize my interpretation of Acts 14:22 as neo-ultraistic. Rather, even as a classicalist, I think that the classical position is simply wrong in treating this verse as denoting soteriological entry. The classicalists should acknowledge their error, regard the text as dealing with misthological entry, and change their classical position to this new classical (thus neoclassical) position. Therefore, I really regard my understanding of Acts 14:22 as being neoclassical from that perspective. Yet to be consistent with my definitions of neoclassicalism as holding to both the soteric and mistholic possibilities for any given verse, I have not labeled my interpretation of this verse as being neoclassical within this particular chart from that definitional perspective.

A simpler recourse would be to treat all the entrance and/or Gehenna passages as either: classic, neo-ultraistic, or neoclassic. Understandably, some misthologists certainly will opt for such a refuge in the name of consistency. In fact, I am quite pleased that GNTC took a consistent classical approach. That is the place to start, especially in a FG commentary that one is using to introduce FG theology.

However, contextual sensitivity suggests that each passage should be allowed a weighted probability—which the above chart has sought to provide in the form of dark arrows, small arrows, and light arrows—when the full range of possibilities are being considered. FG misthologists have several valid options available, so dogmatically limiting oneself to one option is not always advisable. The above chart serves as a snapshot of my misthological preferences at the present time, which presents a mediation between contemporary classicalism and the neoclassicalism which is sure to follow.

Although the above chart serves as a conclusion to the present discussion, it will only provide a starting point for further consideration as misthologists weigh the probabilities among themselves in the years to come. Room for divergent opinions will have to be made as we probe the strengths and weaknesses of such options. Having multiple means of reasonably deriving a FG conclusion is a strength of the FG position. In anticipation of the neoclassical preferences that one might chose to pursue in one's ongoing investigation, an alternate ranking will be suggested below. Most of the above passages could be marked neoclassically (i.e., as having a check mark in both the soteric and mistholic columns). The following chart will provide that neoclassical preference and be followed by a word of warning to those neoclassicalists who may be tempted to a thoroughgoing neoclassicalism.

Illustration 367. Neoclassical Alternative

Passage	Parallel	Sot.	Mis.	Text	Classification
Mt 5:19			✓	Least and greatest in the kingdom	Classic
Mt 5:20		✓	✓	Not enter at all	Neoclassic
Mt 5:23		✓	✓	Whoever says fool is in danger of Gehenna	Neoclassic
Mt 5:29-30		✓	✓	Cut it off or be cast bodily into Gehenna	Neoclassic
Mt 7:13		✓	✓	Enter by narrow gate	Neoclassic
Mt 7:21		✓	✓	Enter the kingdom	Neoclassic
Mt 7:23		✓	✓	I never *knew* (*ginosko*) you. Depart from Me	Neoclassic
Mt 10:28		✓	✓	Fear Him who can cast bodily into Gehenna	Neoclassic
Mt 18:3	Mk 10:15; Lk 18:17	✓	✓	Enter the kingdom by becoming like children	Neoclassic
Mt 18:4			✓	Greatest in the kingdom	Classic
Mt 18:8-9	Mk 9:47-48	✓	✓	Cut it off to enter kingdom/life	Neoclassic
Mt 18:8-9	Mk 9:47-48	✓	✓	eternal fire of Gehenna	Neoclassic
	Mk 9:44,46,48	✓	✓	worms of Gehenna	Neoclassic?
Mt 22:12			✓	Friend, how did you enter this feast?	Classic
Mt 19:14	Mk 10:14; Lk 18:16	✓	✓	For of such as children is the kingdom	Neoclassic
Mt 19:16	Mk 10:17; Lk 18:18	✓	✓	Obtain/inherit eternal life	Neoclassic
Mt 19:17		✓	✓	Enter into life	Neoclassic
Mt 19:23	Mk 10:24; Lk 18:24	✓	✓	Difficult for the rich to enter the kingdom	Neoclassic
Mt 19:24	Mk 10:25; Lk 18:24	✓	✓	Easier for a camel to enter	Neoclassic
Mt 21:31-32		✓	✓	Publicans and prostitutes will enter before you	Neoclassic
Mt 19:25	Mk 10:26; Lk 18:26	✓	✓	Then who can be saved?	Neoclassic
Mt 22:7		✓	✓	Burn their city	Neoclassic
Mt 25:12			✓	I do not *know* (*oida*) you	Classic
Lk 13:27		✓	✓	I do not *know* (*oida*) you. Depart from Me	Neoclassic
Lk 13:28		✓	✓	Cast out of kingdom	Neoclassic
Lk 13:29			✓	Recline at the feast in the kingdom	Classic
Lk 13:30			✓	Least and greatest in the kingdom	Classic
Jn 3:5		✓		You must enter the kingdom through new birth	Classic
Acts 14:22			✓	You enter the kingdom through tribulations	Neo-ultraistic

✓ = Primary   ✓ = Secondary   ✓ = Plausible

Even if I were attempting to construct a more thoroughgoing neoclassical view, I would not mark all verses dually. Certain verses still would be an exception. As for the soteriological columnar exceptions, the lost are not in the eschatological kingdom, not merely least in it. So some verses could not be marked soteriologically: Mt 5:19;

Mt 18:4; Lk 13:30. Similarly, kingdom possession in Mt 19:14 is not a soteriological concept. The friend in Mt 22:12 is cast out of the feast, but at least he is still in the kingdom. Likewise, the virgins are outside the feast, not outside the kingdom (Mt 25:12). Soteriological exclusion from the kingdom is not in view. Obviously, reclining at feast in Lk 13:29 is strictly a misthological issue. I have not marked Acts 14:22 as being neoclassical in either chart in that I do not give any weight to the classical argument for this verse. Nevertheless, some might consider my *not-classical* assessment in the previous chart as being *neoclassical* in that it is a compromise between classicalism and ultraism. Notwithstanding, *neo-ultraistic* would be the more consistent term in that case. Since in this chart I am one more step closer to the neo-ultraistic position than in the previous chart, I have marked Acts 14:22 in a manner more consistent with this definitional perspective.

Warnings

Warning to Misthologists

As for the singular misthological columnar exception in the above chart, contrary to ultraists and some neo-ultraists, I would not regard Jn 3:5 as being anything other than soteric. Within the field of prophetic studies, the need to make allowance for telescopic phenomena is readily admitted. Possibly, within the fields of soteriology and misthology, a similar need will be discerned in which it will be perceived that free soteriological entrance into the kingdom is intertwined with costly misthological entrance in certain passages. Even if this should prove to be the case, however, to enjoin this duality into a costly-free soteric entrance would be a deadly mistake. Soteric entrance still would have to be seen as free; mistholic entrance as costly. Even if two different aspects to entrance are entertained in the same passage, discerning the separate components is a matter of life and death.

The Jews missed the kingdom altogether because they could not discern that two different aspects of the kingdom were telescoped together in the OT pictures of the Messiah's coming. Likewise, today, during the church age, many are missing the kingdom completely because they cannot discern two different aspects of the kingdom. As a neoclassical view is contemplated, making a clear distinction between the two perspectives will be crucial, even if both perspectives are merged in some contexts. That two advents were merged together into one passage prophetically does not provide an excuse for failing to distinguish two advents historically. As any misthologist would concede, if soteric and mistholic entrances are combined in some passages, this does not mean the soteric entrance is costly, or that mistholic entrance is free, or that the entrance is a singular costly-free entity.

For any neoclassical writer, I would further caution against marking Jn 3:5 as having dual applicability. Just as a classical writer, I give no weight to the classical interpretation of Acts 14:22, I would encourage those contemplating the feasibility of a neoclassical position to give no weight to a neoclassical interpretation of Jn 3:5. I have left Jn 3:5 alone in the chart, and I would advise neoclassicalists to leave Jn 3:5 alone also. To be sure, marking this verse neoclassically is not difficult. Taken independently of other considerations, a neoclassical position is possible. That is not the question. Rather, is it plausible? Moreover, even if it is plausible, is it probable? If not, then it is certainly not prudent. As a classicalist, I easily could have marked Acts 14:22 classically. Yet I have chosen not to do so because I do not believe doing so is the most prudent option, even for classicalists. I would urge neoclassicalists to show the same restraint by not marking Jn 3:5 neoclassically. Just because everyone else in our camp may want to mark these two respective verses in a manner consistent with camp mentality does not excuse us for following the crowd. If, as a classicalist, I am willing to stand my ground against my own camp regarding Acts 14:22, then certainly I have the right to ask those of you contemplating becoming neoclassicalists to do the same regarding Jn 3:5. Far more is at stake for you regarding Jn 3:5 than for me regarding Acts 14:22.

Illustration 368. Classic Jn 3:5

Taken together, these two verses pose a neoclassical entrance into the kingdom. But they do so by complementing one another. One verse deals with soteriological entrance into the kingdom via new birth; the other with misthological entry via tribulations. The Johannine verse stands as a clear, classical signpost that soteriological entrance into the kingdom is free to those who simply believe. Tamper with that signpost, by adding misthological themes to it, and you make a potentially grave mistake that could lead to your misthological grave.

Illustration 369. Misconstrued Neoclassic Jn 3:5

We would not excuse well-meaning conditionalists who make entrance into heaven a costly-free reward. I am not inclined to think that the Lord will excuse well-meaning misthologists who obscure the clear message that entrance into heaven is a gift just because they think that Jn 3:5 is not a go-to-heaven-when-I-die type of passage. A clear thinking misthologist would recognize the above signpost as a misrepresentation of the neoclassical presentation. But will the person in the pew who is being told that entrance into the kingdom in Jn 3:5 is both free and costly be able to discern the error? To be sure, as misthologists we can explain that soteriological entrance is free, and that misthological entrance is costly, and that there is no such thing as a costly-free soteriological entrance. The gift does not become a reward. Even so, one of our greatest resources in making that clear distinction is Jn 3:5. If you obscure the message in that verse, then where will you clarify the message with equal clarity? In my assessment, the Lord intends for this verse, within the GJ context, to be the watermark by which this distinction is most clearly maintained.

Given the strong soteric context of GJ, are you sure that you want to risk confusing the readers of that book by importing the gospel of the kingdom into such a crucial passage within that book, even when John purposefully has avoided presenting the gospel of the kingdom anywhere within his book? If John passed over presenting the gospel of the kingdom within his book, then what right do we have to impose that mistholic meaning within this essential passage? Be doubly sure and doubly cautious about marking Jn 3:5 neoclassically. As your friend, who is acquainted with your hermeneutical options and who is sympathetic with your misthological preferences, I nevertheless warn you that if you unintentionally confuse unbelievers by infusing a meaning into this verse that is not intended (and even purposefully avoided) by John, in the singular biblical book written evangelistically (and thus soteriologically) for unbelievers no less, then, by your own theology, you may have Gehenna to pay. Play with Jn 3:5, and you play with fire. Do not play with this fire, lest you risk getting burned.

Warning to Soteriologists

Having issued a warning to my fellow misthologists, fair play would advise that I do so to my fellow soteriologists as well. As I was concluding this book, I attended a FG Leadership Conference in July of 2012 in which I listened to a presentation by Robert Congdon. He asserted that all believers are elected corporately to be a part of the Bride of Christ. During the Q&A period at the end of the session, I asked if his position insulated believers from the results of the Bema. He responded that the Bema was merely educational, which he explained to mean that all believers will have the deficiencies in their understanding corrected at the Bema so that thereafter they can rule with Christ as members of his Bride. He indicated that he was familiar with bridal misthology but rejected it. A number of those attending his workshop session clapped at his response.

Needless to say, I was quite disappointed. I had driven about twelve hours to attend this FG conference but found this anemic teaching on rewards very discouraging. Thankfully, this was not the main point of his presentation, and the FG soteriology that he and the rest of the conference presented was refreshing. Still the disappointment lingered until two weeks later when I attended a kingdom Bible study lead by Scott Crawford. He played an excellent sermon by J. William Kanoy dedicated to the topic of rewards. (Scott had the message on CD and will post it on his website: www.wordoftruthclass.org.) At the end of his sermon, Kanoy stressed that *the children of Israel were not allowed to enter Canaan because they **disbelieved kingdom truth*** (cp. Heb 3:19).

While I was thinking about Kanoy's statement, several strands came together into a possible solution of an enigma that I had been contemplating. I discussed my proposal with Scott at the conclusion of the meeting. Two of those strands had to do with Esau and the prodigal son. Before the Bible study started, I had explained to my youngest son, Jonathan, who was at the Bible study and who had attended the FG conference with me, that I was still trying to determine how believers like Esau and the prodigal son could qualify for some degree of misthological blessing but fail to qualify for inheriting the kingdom. Simply picturing them as being in the outer darkness did not seem to do full justice to the biblical imagery, particularly regarding the prodigal son.

Occasionally, in the back of my mind, I had entertained the vague notion of some type of twilight zone. But I had not made an extrapolation as to what the nature of that intermediary darkness might look like, so that strand of thought was stranded. However, after mulling over Kanoy's statement, it occurred to me how these strands might come together and relate to Congdon's presentation. I drew a model on the board for Scott's consideration. He agreed with the plausibility of the theory. I would like to share this model (pictured below) with my fellow FG misthologists who, like me, may be discouraged by the treatment that misthology receives at the hands of some otherwise fine FG soteriologists.

Illustration 370. Twilight Zone

Naturally, wicked servants are cast into the *outer darkness* (OD) outside the city. This would include the slothful, abusive, legalistic, or licentious teachers. These conclusions are rock solid. Further, my extrapolation is that once they are cast into the outer darkness, they would never be able to re-inter the city. As to the licentious teachers, possibly those FG teachers who promote, even by logical implication, an anti-biblical antinomianism (in which it does not matter how you live) would be subject to the OD, even if they themselves do not adopt an antinomian lifestyle, because they have been a stumbling block to others and destroyed them with their reckless teaching. Residency in the city would require that one be an overcomer in both teaching and practice.

But what about those teachers who teach that the way you live matters only temporally, not eternally or even millennially? Their doctrine of rewards amounts to misthological antinomianism. This is the impression I got of Congdon's presentation. Everyone will be rewarded with bridal rulership. All believers will have this special intimacy with Christ. Contrary to the Bible, enduring is not necessary for ruling with Christ.

I am reminded of the animated movie, *The Incredibles*, in which the villain's ultimate objective is to make everyone special—which does not seem like a bad thing until you understand the plot. The villain wants to endow everyone with super powers so that he can do away with superheroes. For in the movie's perspective, *if everyone is special/super, then no one is*. Now while this perspective might be falsifiable in certain contexts, it certainly is villainous in the context supplied by Congdon. The biblical exhortation to *run to win* is met with the apathetic response: "Why bother? Everyone is going to win even if they don't run. So why run?"

If all believers are going to be considered winners even if they refuse to run, then the encouragement to run is easily replaced with discouragement. If the *special rewards* are given to everyone, even to those who show no interest in earning them, then what makes the rewards so *special*, comparatively speaking, for those who work to earn them? All the special rewards promised in Rev 2-3 for overcomers are given, by this villainous doctrine, to all believers—even to those believers who do not overcome (at least not in the sense provided in that context). The misthological incentive to overcome is nullified.

By replacing the judicial Bema with a purely educational Bema, Congdon domesticates the Bema. Imagine a college professor exhorting, "Study hard for the final exam because if you don't, then when you take it I will give you the answers so that you can ace it." Surely, apathetic students will remark to one another, "Why study if we are going to be given the answers anyway?" Possibly, the studious might decide to study hard anyway, but many of them would be discouraged by the realization that their classmates who do not study will be given the same grade.

Likewise, many teachers assert all believers will, for all practical purposes, be treated equally at the Bema. They think that the parable of the laborers establishes that point. I object. Those laborers labored. Surely, any teacher who uses that parable so as to discourage hardworking believers from laboring for the Lord ought to be dealt with harshly at the Bema (cp. Eze 13:22). If such teachers are not cast into the outer darkness, then they should at least be cast into some type of *twilight zone* (TZ). After all, the Bible has some rather harsh things to say about stumbling blocks and teachers who abuse the Scripture.

Accordingly, my theory is that those FG teachers who promote misthological licentiousness (i.e., that the way you live does not really matter in terms of heavenly rewards) will fail to inherit the kingdom. Even if they themselves do not stumble into licentiousness behavior, they will have placed a stumbling block before others that discourages them from being faithful. Consequently, such teachers will not qualify for bridal rulership. As a result of **disbelieving the kingdom message**, they will disqualify themselves from kingdom rulership. Misthological unbelievers will not be kingdom rulers.

Trying to make up for rejecting kingdom mythology by replacing it with a strong FG soteriology will not suffice for kingdom aristocracy. Just as the children of Israel tried to make up for rejecting the kingdom message by subsequently serving the Lord, so those securitists who reject the kingdom message and then try to make up for it by fervently serving the Lord in other ways will, nonetheless, place themselves in danger of being rejected for kingdom rulership.

Notwithstanding, my initial impression was that misthological antinomians who serve the Lord faithfully might be better off than those cast into the outer darkness. Serving the Lord faithfully, even after being rejected in terms of the gospel of the kingdom, still counts for something rather significant. Like the prodigal son, they still might be given a robe and ring and welcomed into the house, though not as having an inheritance. My original conjecture was that such teachers will be allowed to live in the Northern hemisphere where they can see the light of the city. Moreover, they will be allowed to enter the Reward City. Perhaps they will even compose (at least in part) the *kings of the earth* (Rev 21:24-26).

Their residency will be on Earth, but they will be allowed to enter the Heavenly City when they bring tribute from their territories on Earth. They bring their tribute *in order that they may enter* the city (TM; Hodgian MT). They do not have free access to the city. But as low ranking kings, they can at least enter the city when they bring tribute. Residency in the city is, of course, reserved for bridal overcomers who earned the right to live there. These low ranking earthly kings, in contrast, forfeited their opportunity to dwell in the city when they made being the Bride of Christ a common thing. As a result of having defaming and profaning the Bride when they were teachers on Earth, the most they can hope to do now is to bow before her feet when they bring tribute from their earthly territories into her city.

At this point, I would like to offer a clarification and reminder. First, I am not the Judge, and the nature of the data is too speculative for me to render judgment, especially on a particular individual for a few comments made at a conference. The reminder and warning by James (4:11-12) is applicable. I can only provide what, in my judgment, would be a reasonable hypothesis. Definitely, I am not able to render a definitive verdict or make such a specific application in such a particular case. The extrapolation is too tenuous. A conjecture as to possibilities is the most I can offer. Nevertheless, I will venture to make this proposal because I am also exhorted to encourage the brethren. Given the cold shoulder that misthologists typically get from soteriologists, I will offer this as a word of encouragement to my fellow misthologists. Do not be discouraged by those who marginalize you because they teach a *Toothless Bema*. They will find out soon enough that the Bema is not toothless when they are devoured by it. The educational experience they derive from the Bema will be to learn that it is not merely educational.

Second, my concerns are in no way applicable to everyone who rejects bridal misthology. Hodges, for example, has such a solid doctrine of rewards that charging him with misthological licentiousness would be ridiculous. Even though he believes that all believers will compose the Bride, he is simply being inconsistent with his otherwise splendid kingdom misthology. However, as for those who serve the Lord faithfully in every other capacity and yet reject the kingdom position because of their bridal misperceptions, certainly, at best, they would be in a prime position for the twilight zone. Like Kanoy, I do not believe that those preachers who reject the gospel of the kingdom will inherit the kingdom. Nevertheless, I am trying to be as charitable as possible in thinking that they might still live just outside the Promised Land on Earth and have some kingdom responsibilities. I am not sure, however, that Kanoy would have granted them even that much. And he might be right.

Those FG teachers who fall from grace into legalism, and thereby teach an accursed soteric gospel, will be in the OD. By turning the gift of God into a reward, they poison the gospel of grace and prevent many from receiving the gift of God. Their gospel is soteriologically deadly. Accordingly, their punishment is just. The darkest part of the outer darkness will be a fitting reward for such legalists who will lead many into hell with their false soteric gospel. However, just as hell is worse than the outer darkness, tripping someone up misthologically is not as bad as tripping them up soteriologically. Perhaps those FG soteriologists who turn the grace of God into licentiousness, by teaching a false mistholic gospel, might not be treated as harshly as FG legalists.

On the other hand, since by turning rewards into gifts, these FG antinomians unwittingly discourage believers from pursuing rewards from God, one must conclude that they have poisoned the gospel of the kingdom.[1689] After all, a misthologically accursed gospel can result in misthological death. How could such teachers possibly qualify as kingdom rulers in any capacity? A gift is not a reward (contra FG legalists), and a reward is not a gift (contra FG antinomians). Those FG teachers who cannot distinguish a gift from a reward are not apt to be fit kingdom rulers. The gospel of grace must not be confused with the gospel of the kingdom.

Therefore, a more reasonable supposition is that the prodigal son does not represent a teacher of an accursed mistholic gospel; rather, the repentant prodigal could represent a believer who repents of the licentious perspective he learned from a FG teacher. Suppose a modern-day prodigal were to conclude that rewards do not really matter (since his FG preacher told him that all believers would be given these rewards freely). However, years later, after this prodigal has squandered his opportunity to earn the reward of the inheritance, he hears a kingdom teacher who corrects his misperception of heavenly rewards. Earning the privilege of ruling with Christ in heaven is out of reach now. But perhaps he still might earn the right to live on the earth as a low ranking ruler. So he repents of his licentious behavior. Perhaps he can still qualify for earthly reign, although not as a bridal queen.

What will become of the FG preacher who misled the prodigal into thinking that rewards do not really matter, with the result that the prodigal spent most of his life in a licentious lifestyle and thus forfeited heavenly rulership? Will this FG preacher be a co-ruler with the repentant prodigal although the FG teacher is the one who, with his lukewarm teaching on the Bema, led the prodigal astray into the far country? In my original assessment, I tried to be charitable in thinking that such FG teachers might still do reasonably well at the Bema. More likely, though, the antinomian teacher would be cast into the OD while the repentant prodigal is allowed to rule in the TZ.

Those FG teachers who belittle kingdom theology can pick their poison. They can either teach an accursed soteriology and be cast into the darkest part of the OD, or they can teach an accursed misthology and be cast into the shadowy parts of the OD. In view of passages like Eze 33:6-9, I must issue this warning to FG teachers who trivialize the Bema. When FG teachers do not warn licentious believers of the misthological death awaiting them, then the Lord will require the blood of those believers from the hands of those teachers who failed to warn them, and they will share their fate. Both will die. Such a teacher would lose his soul/life. Likewise, by logical extension, if I were to fail to warn FG teachers who inadvertently promote licentious behavior by downplaying the doctrine of rewards, then the blood of those teachers would be on my hands, and I would share their fate—misthological death.

False prophets fail to warn God's people of God's judgment (Jer 23:16-17). If you, as a FG teacher, fail to warn licentious believers of the misthological death awaiting them, then the Lord will require their blood from your hands. If the Lord has told them, *You surely will die misthologically*, and you tickle their ears by saying, *You surely will **not** die misthologically*, then, misthologically, you are playing the role of the serpent, who likewise told Eve, *You surely will not die*. As a result, the serpent was cursed with death in the form of a crushed head. The serpent shared Eve's fate—death. If licentious believers are to die misthologically and you tell them the opposite, then you will share their fate—misthological death. Repent you misthological serpent! Stop being a false prophet with blood on your hands who minimizes the Bema; otherwise, you will forfeit your soul/life at the Bema. God called you as a watchman to warn believers about judgment, not to warn them about receiving an education!

Unlike some of my fellow misthologists, I do not believe that the "*ungodly persons who turn the grace of our God into licentiousness*" (Jude 1:3) were regenerate. Rather, the eternal black darkness reserved for them is hell rather than the outer darkness (Jude 1:13). Nevertheless, I do see a potential correlation between them and the *godly teachers who turn the grace of our God into licentiousness*. By denying the impact of the misthological warnings against licentiousness, such godly teachers place themselves in danger of the outer darkness with their ungodly teaching. Licentiousness results in darkness. Unregenerate promoters of licentiousness will be in the soteriological darkness. Regenerate promoters of licentiousness will be in the misthological darkness, even if they just promoted it by denying that the misthological darkness applies to licentiousness.

If you are not promoting the kingdom message, then you are demoting it.

If you are not with us, then you are against us.

Glossary

Active inheritance refers to a misthological entrance into the kingdom in which the mature child of God is recognized as His mature son and receives the honor of being co-glorified with Jesus as His co-heir and co-ruler of the kingdom as a result of his or her active obedience to the Lord.

Adductive method uses both deductive and inductive methodology but allows the nature of the material being examined to determine which methodology is given primacy. When interpreting parables, the initial inductive observations should be subsequently submitted to deductive analysis.

Amillennialists ("a" means "no") believe that there is no future millennial kingdom on earth.

Anarthrous is a term of Greek grammar which means that the word in question does not have a Greek article. If it had an article, it would be called an articular expression. For example, *the dog* is articular in English because it has the English article *the* in front of the noun *dog*.

Antinomian is derived from *anti+nomos* (*anti-law*) and refers to those who are against the law. They are also known as libertines—those liberated from the law. Legalists love to charge non-legalists with being antinomians (i.e. teachers of lawlessness). Since Paul was a non-legalist, he was reported slanderously as saying, "Let us do evil that good may come" (Rom 3:8). This defamatory trend still survives today. Some so-called Lordship Salvationists calumniously say that those who teach free grace are teaching that the way a person lives does not matter. This would be true only if rewards do not matter. Perhaps this is the background for some of the criticism. So-called Lordship Salvationists can appeal to the popular sentiment that rewards do not matter. For many, the only thing that matters is heaven versus hell. So if you stress that the doctrine of heavenly rewards provides a compelling reason to live a good life, then you have said (from their perspective) that the way you live does not matter. Nevertheless, biblical Christianity will remain a balance between legalistic and libertarian extremists.

Arminianism is a branch of conditional security which teaches that God contingently predetermines that those who persevere will be chosen (elected) for heaven.[*] Human perseverance is the condition for divine election. The free will of the believer is emphasized. In Arminianism, reaching heaven is conditioned on the believer's perseverance. (Arminians may be defined broadly at the popular level as those who believe that regeneration actually might be lost.) The Arminian order of conditional results is: perseverance, then predestination, then heaven. Arminianism is summarized by the acronym PEARS:

- **P**revenient Grace—means God's preparatory grace by which He takes the prerequisite step of providing mankind with the pragmatic ability to search for Him and find Him in saving faith.
- **E**lection on Condition—means that God conditionally has elected all mankind to salvation. However, God has only predestined that those who of their own free will respond in faith to this offer of salvation and persevere in this faith will be saved. Predestination is thus conditioned on persevering faith.
- **A**tonement for All—means that the atonement is available sufficiently for all mankind, and its efficaciousness is limited only by their response.
- **R**esistible Grace—means that God's prevenient grace may be resisted so that it does not result in salvation.
- **S**alvation through Perseverance—means that God's grace is not only resistible; it is also reversible. Believers may fall irremediably from the state of saving grace if they fail to persevere. Those who persevere are elected to salvation from eternal damnation as a result of persevering. Believers must persevere in order to be saved in the end. This doctrine also is popularly known as NOSAS, which stands for ***not** once saved always saved*. This form of NOSAS affirms that one **actually** may lose one's regeneration and cease to be saved if one does not persevere.

---

[*] Technically, some Arminians affirm the *unconditional corporate election* of those in Christ but make perseverance in faith the condition for remaining in Christ. Those particular individuals who persevere in faith are conditionally predestined for heaven. Hence, this approach simultaneously affirms *conditional particular predestination*. Other Arminians affirm the election of individual believers. Being elected is conditioned on being a believer. This latter Arminian approach is less convoluted. Either way, the bottom line remains the same: In Arminian theology, only those who persevere are elected for heaven. Consequently, Arminians may be described as teaching conditional election (in regard to the individual).

A-Theory of time is also referred to as the process or dynamic view: Events are in past, present, and future. *Now* is an objective state of reality. If the A-Theory is true, then God is temporal and experiences change. Otherwise, if God were atemporal, then He would be ignorant of some of A-Theory realities. It is possible to see the past or future, but not visit it (assuming the linear rather than circular view of time).

B-Theory of time is also referred to as the static/stasis view: Events are simply relative to one another (i.e., before, during, after). *Now* is a subjective state of mind. God is atemporal, so everything that happens in our time frame is an *eternal now* to Him. Time is spatial; therefore, time travel is at least theoretically possible since one is visiting a place that exists before or after his or her current location in the space-time plane and that is equally real.

Bema is a transliteration of the Greek word used in 2Cor 5:10 for the *Judgment Seat of Christ* and is used as an abbreviation for the judgment of believers. The unqualified use of *Bema* will be understood in the typical dispensational manner as referring to the *Christian Bema*—the judgment of church-age believers following the rapture. *Jewish Bema* will refer to a similar judgment of Jewish believers following the tribulation. *Gentile Bema* (also known as the *Judgment of the Sheep and the Goats*) will be used for the judgment of Gentile believers following the tribulation (after the Jewish Bema). Unbelievers are judged 1000 years after the tribulation at the *Great White Throne* (*thronos*) judgment of Rev 20:11.

Betrothal is similar to engagement. When someone accepts the Lord Jesus as their Savior, they are betrothed to Him in the first stage of the prenuptial engagement.

Calminianism = Calvinism + Arminianism. The term Calminianism was popularized by Norman Geisler in his endeavor to adopt a mediating position between Calvinism (TULIP) and Arminianism (PEARS). His Calminian approach basically takes the point of agreement between the two systems regarding the soteriological necessity of perseverance and replaces the Arminian S of PEARS with a synthesis of the Calvinistic P from TULIP.* The end result is an abbreviated **PS** Calminian acronym.[1690]

Regardless of the preferred full acronym for Calminianism, final salvation from hell comes through perseverance in all forms of Calminianism (as well as in Calvinism and Arminianism). By definition, then, **Calminianism is a mediation between Calvinism and Arminianism that, like its two predecessors, makes perseverance necessary for salvation from eternal damnation**. Since the present book does not make perseverance necessary for salvation from eternal damnation, it should be categorized separately from Calminianism. Contrary to Calminian claims otherwise, in making perseverance descriptively necessary, Calminianism also necessarily makes perseverance prescriptively necessary: both exegetically and logically. The present book rejects any and all Calminian attempts at harmonization in favor of a Marrowistic mediation which teaches that perseverance is necessary for rewards in heaven rather than for entrance into heaven itself.

Calvinism is a branch of conditional security which teaches that God sovereignly determines (i.e., elects) who will persevere and thus will make it to heaven. Divine election is the basis for human perseverance. The sovereignty of God is emphasized. The elect persevere because they are unconditionally predetermined by God to persevere so that they might reach heaven. Calvinists sometimes like to present themselves as advocates of unconditional security, but actually Calvinism is a failed attempt to enjoin unconditional security with conditional security. The Calvinist might assert that the believer is unconditionally assured of reaching heaven, but what a Calvinist actually means with such an articulation is that the believer is unconditionally assured of persevering, thereby reaching heaven. In Calvinism, reaching heaven is conditioned on the believer's perseverance. The Calvinistic order of conditions and result is: election, then perseverance, then heaven. Calvinism is summarized by the acronym TULIP:

- **T**otal Depravity—means total inability. Man is totally unable to believe the gospel unless God acts upon him with irresistible grace in regeneration. Regeneration, at least in its incipient form, must precede belief. God regenerates man so that man may believe in accordance with his new nature.
- **U**nconditional Election—means that God unconditionally elects who will believe and be saved. Man is not elected because he believes. Rather, he believes because he is elected. God predetermines who will believe and

---

* In S those who persevere are predestined, while in P those who are predestined persevere. Geisler attempts to reject any logical order between perseverance and predestination. Other Calminians do not necessarily reject a logical order.

be saved. It was never God's intention to save the nonelect. Election is selection. God pre-selects who will believe and causes them to believe. No one else genuinely can believe the gospel. No one else will persevere in saving faith. No one else can be saved.

- **L***imited Atonement*—means that the benefits of the atonement are extended only to the elect. In summary, Christ died only for the elect, not for the nonelect. God limited the available benefits of Christ's death to the elect. God never had any true intention of making salvation possible for everyone.

- **I***rresistible Grace*—means that God irresistibly causes the elect to become regenerate so that the elect will believe. Regeneration, therefore, precedes faith. Faith is a gift from God that the elect do not have the power to refuse.

- **P***erseverance of the Saints*—means that saints who persevere are preserved and thus saved, in the end, as a result of their perseverance. Only those who persevere are preserved. Preservation does not apply to those who do not persevere. Thus, perseverance of the saints is not to be confused with eternal security of the saints. Only the elect persevere, and they persevere because they are predestined to persevere. Yet they must persevere in order to reach heaven. From the perspective of unconditional election, this model teaches OSAS (once saved always saved). However, from the perspective of conditionality, this model teaches NOSAS (not once saved always saved). This form of NOSAS affirms that one **hypothetically** may lose one's regeneration and cease to be saved if one does not persevere.

Campbellites are followers of Alexander Campbell who started a separatist movement in 1807. Campbellism teaches that water baptism is essential to soteriological salvation. A split over the use of musical instruments among these followers gave rise to the Disciples of Christ and later to a more conservative branch called the Church of Christ.

Chiliasts is a Greek term used to describe those who believe in a literal return and reign of Christ on earth that will last for a literal thousand years. It is synonymous with *millennialists* (the Latin term).

Co-glorification salvation is misthological salvation with which only faithful believers will be rewarded, as God's mature obedient sons.

Comer is a coined expression used to refer to those who come to faith in Christ, that is, to the believer.

Common Election means to be chosen for service. Even Judas was chosen/elect in this capacity.

Common Grace is the universal enablement of God that enables human beings to exercise good will toward one another and perform socially good works. Its positive influence restrains evil and upholds civil justice. This universal level of grace is insufficient so as to enable the lost sinner to respond savingly toward God, much less to seek God or have stirring of good will toward God.

Common-Prevenient Grace[*] is a universal call to fallen humanity that begins as the individual's first stirring of good toward God in response to an internal, effective, general, supernatural call from God. This initiatory draw uses general revelation (i.e., nature, history, and conscience) as its instrument and enables the lost to respond positively toward God. This general call, however, is insufficient for salvation. If one responds to the initiatory stages of this prevenient grace so as to begin seeking God through enabling grace, one may advance to the point where God will give special revelation with the explicit message of salvation that is sufficient for salvation.

Alternately, upon final rejection of this universal prevenient draw, one potentially might reach a hardened state in which one could only grope for God in the sphere of *common-prevenient grace* without hope of finding Him—that is, without being able to ever enter (or re-enter) the sphere of *prevenient grace proper*. This later state, prevenient grace proper, is the necessary sphere for saving faith to occur. Therefore, even though one may search for God through the pages of Scripture (while in the sphere of common-prevenient grace), doing so is insufficient

---

[*] *Common-Prevenient Grace* is a coined term used herein to fill the gap created between common grace and prevenient grace by those libertarians (such as myself) who restrict prevenient grace to special revelation. Additionally, my belief that one may harden one's heart by rejecting God's drawing to the point where the possibility of responding in saving faith is effectively withdrawn, also necessitates the proposal of common-prevenient grace as an intermediate state.

to qualify for prevenient grace proper if common-prevenient grace is not sufficiently accompanied by the Spirit's inward draw to advance to prevenient grace proper. The general external draw effected by the explicit word of God is insufficient apart from the internal, cooperative, effective drawing of the Holy Spirit. One must have both in order to savingly believe the gospel.

Illustration 371. Common-Prevenient Grace

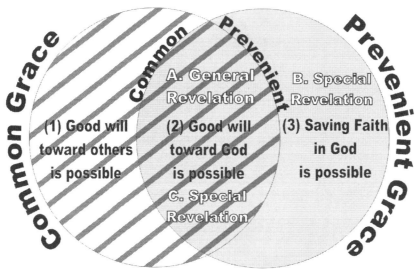

Compatibilism is an affirmation of divine determinism that believes that hard determinism is compatible with human freedom since compatibilism **defines freedom as the ability to act in accordance with one's prevailing internal desires** rather than being forced to take a particular course of actions by external control. This viewpoint, also known as soft determinism, actuality is no less deterministic than hard determinism. In the soft view, our internal desires are causally determined by the external factors leading up to those desires so that we could not desire to do otherwise. Secondly, we cannot do otherwise than what we desire to do. Stated jointly, we cannot do otherwise than what we do because we cannot do otherwise than what our external factors have compelled us to want to do. In other words, God made a complex array of dominos to control our desires and thereby control our actions. By knocking over (or pulling the rug out from under) the first domino, God has set in motion a sequence of events that causally determines our internal desires to the point of making us irresistibly respond in the manner in which we (desire to) do. God has remotely controlled our actions by putting in motion a chain of events that make it impossible for us to do otherwise than what we do. **God controls our internal desires, and our internal desires control us. In short, God controls us by controlling our internal desires.** God controls our character, and our character controls us.

Condign merit is performance that incurs reward because Christ won these rewards for us and contingently obligated Himself to us by promising these rewards to us on the basis of our derivative moral merit. Although the opportunity to earn the reward is not merited, the reward is merited. In short, **condign merit points to the obligatory nature of the reward**. Quantitatively, every reward is merited. Solely on the basis of God's gracious initiative, He makes it possible for us to earn rewards through His enabling grace: *grace-$\frac{merit}{grace}$-reward*.

Conditional security is the conviction that once a person believes in Christ for eternal life, that person is conditionally secure in Christ and conditionally assured of reaching heaven. According to conditional securitists, a believer must persevere in order to reach heaven. (Both proveitism and forfeitism advocate conditional security.)

Conditionalist refers to an advocate of *conditional security*—the conviction that once a person believes in Christ for eternal life, that person is conditionally secure in Christ and must persevere in order to reach heaven.

Congruent merit is performance that results in rewards that graciously, yet proportionally, outweigh any effort that we may have put into our character development or any improvement actually made in our character as a result of that effort. In short, **congruent merit points to the excessiveness of the reward**. Qualitatively, the scope of the reward far exceeds what we deserve. As an expression of God's grace, although all rewards are based on merit, God rewards our works with greater benefits than we deserve so that Marrowistic congruent merit is: *merit- $\frac{gracious\ reward}{works}$*.

Day of Christ is the time of blessing in **heaven** that begins with the rapture and ends with the revelation and thus would include the Bema and the marriage. It is referred to as *the Day of the Lord Jesus, the Day of the Lord Jesus Christ,* and *the Day of Christ* in Scripture.

Day of the Lord is the time of wrath and fulfillment on **earth** that begins with the rapture and thus would include both the tribulational period and millennial kingdom.

Deductive method ideally takes the central truth of a parable and then interprets the details on the basis of that central truth. Some interpreters unfortunately focus on the central truth of the parable with little regard for the details.

Divine determinism is the viewpoint that everything that happens, including the choices we make, must happen exactly as they do because the events and circumstances leading up to these actions are the sufficient conditions that God uses causally to determine what actions will take place. Our choices are governed by the *principle of universal causality*, according to which everything that happens is causally determined by a long unbreakable chain of sufficient conditions that cause us to respond in the manner in which we do. In other words, God made a complex array of dominos to control our actions and affections. By knocking over the first domino, He has set in motion a sequence of events over which we have no free will to do or desire otherwise than what God has determined that we will do and desire.

Divine Essentialism asserts that God wills something because it is good and right, because it is in accordance with the essence of His immutable good nature.

Divine Voluntarism in Calvinism means that something is right and good just because God wills it.

Di-Soul (dichotomous soul) refers to those usages of the word *soul* where it is used in a dichotomous contrast with the word *body* so that *soul* only denotes the immaterial portion of the person.

Di-Spirit (dichotomous spirit) refers to those usages of the word *spirit* where it is used in a dichotomous contrast with the word *body* so that *spirit* only denotes the immaterial portion of the person.

Elect refers to those chosen by God to reach heaven in both Arminianism and Calvinism. Biblically, the term may be used much more comprehensively than what is suggested by these two schools of thought, however.

Eschatology is derived from the Greek words *eschatos* (*last*) and *logos* (*teaching*); it refers to the doctrine of the last days, the end of time, and thus the millennial and eternal states.

Eternal salvation in popular (rather than biblical) usage refers to salvation from eternal damnation in hell. Popular usage generally is used in the body of this book.

Forfeitist refers to an advocate of conditional security who believes that those who do not persevere forfeit (i.e., lose) the gift of eternal life.

First Coming happens in two stages. The first stage already has taken place in that Jesus came to the earth to save it. In the second stage, He will come to earth to judge it.

Formal litotes is an understatement that implicitly indicates the opposite affirmation by means of explicit negation.

Free Grace is the group, movement, or understanding (commonly abbreviated as **FG**) which teaches that saving grace must be received as a free gift. From their perspective, unconditional security is guaranteed upon the recognition that the free gift of eternal life is offered freely to one who simply believes in the Lord Jesus for eternal life. The biblical requirement for salvation from eternal damnation is thus that one simply believes in the Lord

Jesus for eternal life. As a result one is granted unconditional security. This understanding is exemplified by the *Grace Evangelical Society* (**GES**) motto: *Faith Alone in Christ Alone.*

Free Grace Salvationists are those who insist that the biblical requirement for salvation from eternal damnation is that one simply believes in the Lord Jesus for eternal life. This understanding is exemplified by the *Grace Evangelical Society* (**GES**) motto: *Faith Alone in Christ Alone.* From their perspective, unconditional security is guaranteed upon the recognition that the free gift of eternal life is offered freely to one who simply believes in Jesus Christ for eternal life.

Free will (from the libertarian/incompatibilistic point of view) is the is God-given ability for free agency exercised by the freed agents that allows them to do otherwise than what their desires dictate, within God's parameters and time frames. Free will (from the soft-deterministic/compatibilistic point of view) is the ability to act in accordance with one's prevailing internal desires which, in turn, are predetermined by external factors. Free will is outright denied in hard determinism.

Functional litotes is an understatement that implicitly indicates the opposite affirmation by means of implied negation.

Glorification salvation is soteriological salvation that all believers will receive as God's children.

Grace Salvationists is an older term that is synonymous for Free Grace Salvationists, used in simple contradistinction to Lordship Salvationists.

GRAPE is a Marrowian acronym: (1) **G**ift is Free; (2) **R**ewards are Earned; (3) **A**bsolute Assurance; (4) **P**assive Persuasion; and (5) **E**ternal Security.

Hermeneutics refers to the scientific art of biblical interpretation. As a science it has rules which should be followed in performing an exegesis of the text. These rules are helpful in providing boundaries and limiting options when interpreting the text. But the application of these rules cannot be applied mechanically in such a way as to make one's deductions a foregone conclusion as a function of logic alone so as to rule out either the subjective necessity of weighing the various probabilities by one's God-given powers of reason or the need of depending upon the Spirit's insights, discernment, and wisdom conveyed to the interpreter through spiritual disposition, perception, and intuition.

Hol-Soul (holistic soul) refers to those usages of the word *soul* where it is used holistically in reference to the person as a whole and thus to both the material and immaterial (physical and metaphysical) components.

Illegitimate totality equivalence is the faulty contextual presumption of the hermeneutical equivalence of seemingly related texts due to partially overlapping sections of certain centrally perceived elements, to the exclusion of equally important incongruent details. In other words, it is to compare apples with oranges under the mistaken impression that their similarities render them the same.

Illegitimate totality transfer is the expression popularized by James Barr to describe the faulty lexical procedure of importing a word's full semantic range of meaning from multiple contexts into any given context.

Imminency refers to the teaching that the Lord may come at any moment. No signs are yet to be fulfilled before He comes at the rapture.

Inductive method determines what the central truth is from the details and what additional truth is being conveyed by the particulars.

Incompatibilism is the denial that free will is compatible with soft determinism (i.e., compatibilism) or with hard determinism. In short, it is the affirmation that one is freed (by the grace of God) not to act in accordance with one's prevailing desires.

Initial justification is the justification granted when a person first becomes a believer. ***Final justification*** is the justification necessary for a believer to reach heaven at the end of his or her life. According to conditional security, initial justification may be by faith alone but final justification necessarily includes perseverance in faith and faithfulness.

Insecuritist refers to an advocate of conditional security. Perseverance (in faith and/or faithfulness) is the postconversional condition for reaching heaven according to insecuritists.

Judicial hardening refers to God's conditional temporal hardening of a person or nation because of their negative response to Him. He hardens them after they harden themselves.

Karpology is a coined term derived from *karpos* (*fruit*), used to refer to the doctrine of fruitfulness. It is spelled as *carpology* in English. In accordance with my transliterational preference and to underscore that I am concerned about the biblical aspect of fruitfulness, I have chosen this alternative spelling.

Libertarianism is the true affirmation of human freedom in which prior factors are not seen as sufficient conditions to explain all of our choices. This does not mean that our actions are uncaused, of course. Rather, they are self-caused. A person's actions do not cause themselves; the person him or herself causes his or her own action. This viewpoint is synonymous with ***self-determinism***. From the libertarian perspective, a person must be free to do otherwise than what his or her internal and external factors dictate in order to be morally responsible for his or her actions. Free agents must be free to determine their own actions. This is not to say that their actions occur in a vacuum, but free agents sometimes act contrary to their desires, and, in doing so, they can have a dynamic effect upon our desires. Libertarian freedom is therefore the ability to act contrary to external and internal impulses.

When the Scripture commands us to "let your character be free from the love of money" (Heb 13:5), it thereby indicates that we have some control over our character. Not only does our character mold us, but we mold it (Rom 5:4). When the Bible says, "You shall not desire your neighbor's house" (Dt 5:21), it is taking libertarian freedom for granted in telling us that we have culpable control over what we desire. When Paul exhorts believers to "earnestly desire the greater gifts" (1Cor 12:31), he assumes that they are free to determine their own desires (cp. 1Cor 14:1). In fact, Paul gives believers a course of action which they may follow so that they will not have to carry out the desires of the flesh (Gal 5:16). They have a choice as to which desires they will obey: those of the flesh versus those of the Spirit. We choose what desires we will obey. Believers are not slavishly obedient to their strongest desires. Obviously, Paul is not a compatibilist, much less a hardcore determinist. It is possible, on occasion, to base our actions on our convictions and principles rather than simply on what we want to do.

Linear faith (➜) is ongoing faith that takes place over a period of time. Although linear aspect is represented frequently by a line (—) in Greek grammars, herein it is represented as an arrow so that a line can be used to represent a state in contradistinction to an ongoing action.

Litotetic is a coined adjectival equivalent for litotes.

Litotes is a positive or negative affirmation made by the explicit or implicit denial of its opposite.

Lordship Salvationists are those who maintain that some form or degree of surrender to Christ as Lord of one's life is biblically necessary for salvation from eternal damnation. Actually, from an exclusively logical and biblical standpoint, those (such as myself) who are opposed to today's so-called Lordship Salvation affirm that the only way to be saved from hell is to submit to the Lordship of Christ in terms of believing in Christ for eternal life. The Lord has commanded that we believe in Him for eternal life. Therefore, to believe in the Lord Jesus for eternal life is to submit to the His lordship in terms of what is necessary for eternal life. *Genuine Lordship Salvationists* correctly insist that one must submit to the Lord's will as it pertains to having eternal life by believing in Jesus (rather than one's performance) for eternal life.

As a theological term, however, the designation *Lordship Salvation* has come to be associated with those who condition salvation from eternal damnation on one's performance (or at least on one's intent to change one's performance). They frequently will be referred to as *pseudo Lordship Salvationists* in this book because they refuse to submit to what the Lord actually demands for this type of salvation—simple faith. Because of the popular association of the term *Lordship Salvationists* with these false advocates of Lordship Salvation, however, unless noted otherwise, the popular association will be adopted by default so that the unqualified term Lordship Salvation will be understood herein in the popular (rather than biblical sense) as denoting performance-based salvation.

Marriage Supper is the third stage of the marriage celebration and ends with the consummation. Although this feast is often referred to as the Marriage Supper, it must be kept in mind that it takes place over a period of time. Specifically, it is held on Earth after the revelation, lasts throughout the entire millennial age, and represents the joyous experience of ruling with Christ in the millennial kingdom.

Marriage refers to the period in which Christ takes overcomers of the church age as His Bride after the Bema but before the revelation in the marriage ceremony. It is the transfer of the bride to the bridegroom.

Marrowism is the present author's coined term for describing his mediating non-Calvinistic Free Grace theology, which is positioned between Arminianism (PEARS) and Calvinism (TULIP) and summarized herein by the author's acronym GRAPE. Historically, this movement was expressed in seminal form by the *Marrow Controversy*. In a number of key areas, the present author may be considered a modern-day Marrowist. The present book is an explanation of Marrowism as the present author has come to refine and define it. As used by the author, Marrowism refers to a defense of unconditional security consisting of soteriological and misthological consistency. Marrowism is summarized by the acronym GRAPE:

- **G***ift is Free*—means that the gift of eternal life is offered as a free gift and must be passively received as such.
- **R***ewards are Earned*—means that the distinction between unmerited gifts and merited rewards must not be blurred.
- **A***bsolute Assurance*—means that personal assurance of one's salvation from eternal damnation is the essence of saving faith.
- **P***assive Persuasion*—means that faith is a passive persuasion, not an active commitment.
- **E***ternal Security*—means that the person who trusts in Christ alone for eternal life immediately and eternally thereafter has eternal life and cannot experience eternal damnation. This doctrine of eternal security is known popularly as OSAS (*once saved always saved*) and is consistently and emphatically affirmed by GRAPE, in contrast to the conditional denunciation this doctrine receives in TULIP and PEARS. The affirmation of *eternal security* (E) is placed strategically at the end of the GRAPE acronym in order to contrast the most distinctive aspect of Marrowistic theology from the other two acronyms. Unlike Arminianism and Calvinism, Marrowism emphatically does not condition salvation from hell on the believer's perseverance. GRAPE affirms true eternal security, not some Arminian or Calvinistic imitation of security. Marrowistic eternal security is unconditional security.

Meiosis generally is used as an interchangeable term for litotes. If a distinction is to be made between the two terms, it is probably that a litotes actually states the negative, whereas a meiosis does not. Those who prefer this type of distinction may prefer to refer to the functional litotes as meiosis. However, the present work will use the terms interchangeably.

Midcomers is a coined term for those semi-faithful believers who have demonstrated a moderate amount of faith and faithfulness so that they are only qualified to sit at the lower end of the table.

Millennial form of the kingdom is the future eschatological kingdom into which only believers (and those who have not reached the age of accountability) will be allowed.

Millennium is based on the Latin translation for the *1000 years* in Rev 20:2-7.

Misthological salvation refers to salvation in terms of rewards in heaven.

Mistholic is an abbreviation for *misthological* (that has been shortened syllabically to match its counterpart *soteric*, which, in turn, is the abbreviation for *soteriological*).

Misthologist: refers to an advocate of unconditional soteriological security who has a sufficient degree of misthological competency so as to recognize that the biblical teaching regarding the outer darkness pertains to misthological themes so that salvation from the outer darkness depicts conditional misthological security.

Misthology is a coined term derived from the Greek words *misthos* (*reward*) and *logos* (*teaching*) and refers to the doctrine of temporal and eternal rewards but is used primarily in reference to eternal rewards.

Misthopology is a coined term derived from the Greek words *misthos* (*reward*) and *city* (*polis*) and refers to the study of the *reward city*. It is principally concerned with the capital city, that is, the bridal city. This city is properly called *Heavenly Jerusalem* during the millennium (when it hovers as a satellite city above the earth during the millennium) and *New Jerusalem* (when it comes down to rest upon the New Earth during the eternal state).

Monergism means *to work alone* and refers to the sovereign work of God in which He is the necessary and sufficient cause in regenerating the elect without dependency on their freewill synergistic cooperation. Although broader than Calvinism, this view is associated typically with Calvinism. Since synergism also affirms that regeneration is the work of God alone, the crux of the dispute between monergism and synergism narrows down to the fact that Calvinistic monergism places regeneration before faith so that it can attribute initial faith exclusively to God's work apart from freewill synergistic cooperation. In terms of salvation apart from works, however, this Calvinistic emphasis on saving faith being produced monergistically by God is largely beside the point. Since Calvinism conditions final salvation on the believer's synergistic perseverance in faith, Calvinists are synergists in relation to final salvation. Because Calvinism simultaneously teaches that the elect are unconditionally elected to final salvation apart from their cooperation, Calvinists have an irreconcilable tension created by their making perseverance conditioned on their cooperation. As a result, some Calvinists will even try to make perseverance a monergistic result.

Mystery form of the kingdom is the present form of the kingdom that is entered through profession of faith in Christ in which genuine and pseudo believers live together by virtue of their shared profession.

Mystical form of the kingdom is the spiritual kingdom that is entered through genuine spiritual birth. Genuine believers are members of both the mystery and mystical forms of the kingdom—the former by profession of faith and the second by possession of spiritual life.

Nikology is a coined expression derived from *nikos* (*victory*) and refers to the doctrine of the victorious Christian life. It is a cognate of the verb *nikao* (*overcome*). Overcomers are those who experience the Lord's victory.

Nomian is a coined expression from the Greek word *nomos* (*law*) and refers to legalists who believe that soteriological salvation is conditioned on performance.

Nonlateral is a term used herein in distinction to bilateral and unilateral to designate a consequence which has *no* remaining conditions.

Noncomer is a coined expression used to refer to a nonbeliever, that is, to someone who never comes to faith in Christ.

NOSAS is the popular acronym for *Not Once Saved Always Saved* (i.e., *conditional security*). Popularly, OSAS is not the same thing as unconditional security in that many proveitists believe in OSAS yet insist that one must persevere in order to reach heaven. This hybrid by the proveitist camp is not considered a valid form of OSAS in the present book.

Ontology is statement of what one *is* as opposed to what one *appears to be*. For example, believers are new creatures by virtue of having a new nature even if they act like unbelievers.

Ordo salutis is a Latin term meaning *order of salvation*. In theological discussions it pertains to the logical sequence of events that take place regarding conversion.

Outer darkness is the parabolic representation of the didactical reality that unfaithful believers will undergo in the permanent punitory (rather than preparatory or purgatorial) spatial experience of being in the millennial and eternal kingdom but never ever being allowed to enter the capital city, or the land of Canaan throughout eternity future, with the result that those submitted to this banishment will never ever be allowed to exercise rulership (or participate in any other misthological functions, roles, or privileges pertaining thereto) over any part, sphere, or aspect of the millennial or eternal kingdom during the millennial age or for any part of eternity future, forever.

Overcomer is a coined expression used to refer to those believers who overcome. Although the word *overcome* is used as a *statement* in Scripture to refer to the positional victory already achieved by all believers in the past, it sometimes is used in Scripture as an *exhortation*, urging believers to progress on to achieve experiential victory in the present. Finally, it is used futuristically as a *promise* of rewards to those relatively few believers who will be victorious in faithfulness until the end, thus urging experiential victory in the present. Its chief usage herein is as an exhortation and promise for believers to become what they are so that they may rule as such.

Panmillennialists is a colloquial designation for those who do not know what to believe about the millennium and who just say, "It will all *pan out* in the end."

Parousia is simply the transliteration of the Greek word *coming* and is used as a scholastic abbreviation to refer to the Second Coming of Christ.

Passive inheritance is the aspect of the inheritance for which believers are qualified unconditionally as a result of their passive response in saving faith to the gospel of grace. Soteriological entrance and glory are among such benefits.

PEARS is an Arminian acronym: (1) **P**revenient Grace; (2) **E**lection on Condition; (3) **A**tonement for All; (4) **R**esistible Grace; and (5) **S**alvation through Perseverance.

Pelagianism is a heterodox view of human monergism that asserts the natural and moral human ability to **initiate and consummate** salvation by exercising good will toward God apart from the grace of God.

Perfect sanctification refers to the future experience of believers in Christ when they will be fully in practice what they are now in position.

Performatist refers to someone who believes that good performance on the believer's part is necessary for entrance into heaven.

Positional righteousness is the righteousness that is imputed to believers legally as a gift. To be considered positionally righteous, one must be a believer.

Positional sanctification refers to the sinless position of believers in Christ, that is, who they are in Christ.

Postcondition is a coined term and refers to an item that may be considered a necessary result of having met a stated condition. Calvinists may argue that perseverance in faith is the necessary result of coming to faith. Whereas coming to faith is the condition for justification, persevering in faith is Calvinistically made the condition for salvation from eternal damnation.

Postmillennialists ("post" means "after") believe that Christ comes after the millennium.

Post-temporal election is election made in the eschatological future.

Practical righteousness is righteousness that is imparted to us experientially. To be considered practically righteous, a believer must be faithful.

Practical sanctification refers to our present experience in Christ, that is, to how we live in Christ.

Precondition is a coined term to refer to an item that may be considered a necessary means of meeting a stated condition. For example, hearing the gospel is a precondition to believing the gospel. But believing the gospel is the actual condition for having eternal life.

Premillennialists ("pre" means "before") believe that Christ comes before the millennium starts.

Pre-temporal election is election made in eternity past.

Prevenient Grace (proper) is the orthodox view of divine-human synergism in which God initiates a pre-regenerative enablement that makes it possible for a lost person to respond cooperatively in saving faith to the gospel and thereby experience regeneration (in the form of impartation of eternal life to one's spirit). This form of grace, therefore, logically precedes the regeneration of one's spirit in sequence, efficiently restores the lost person's ability to respond positively to God by breaking the initial and normative bondage of the enslaved human will to sin so that one no longer has to respond negatively to God, supernaturally prevents one's fallen will from making a positive free response to God impossible, sufficiently arouses the lost soul at the hearing of the gospel so that one can either resist the gospel call and stay asleep in unbelief or allow oneself to become fully awakened by the call to believe, partially opens one's eyes to the truth of the gospel so that one may either close one's eyes in disbelief or allow one's eyes to be opened in saving faith, directly restores free agency so that the constitutional free agent who is practically bound by sin pragmatically now becomes the freed agent who may respond freely, instrumentally exerts resistible persuasional force upon the intellect through the explicit gospel that will be successful unless resisted, and internally creates a desire and ability in one's soul to respond positively to the gospel.

Principle of correlativity is a subset of the broader field of correspondence that refers to a specific type of intentional correlation in which a broad soteric-mistholic or mistholic-soteric typological relation is perceived to exist between two different persons, events, or states. A mistholic-mistholic correlation, therefore, such as that which exists between the out-resurrection and the outer darkness or between the priests that serve in the outer courts versus their typological counterparts, would be outside the scope of the type of correlation being described by the principle of correlativity.

Possible examples of such soteric-mistholic correlations include: exclusion from kingdom inheritance based on classification versus characterization, the covering of one's bets by Judas and the servant, the lost and saved being thrown into the outer darkness, weeping and gnashing their teeth, being outside the city, categorically black dogs versus characteristically black sheep, metaphysical black darkness as compared to the metaphorical outer darkness, outer darkness as compared to exclusion from the city, being cast out of the kingdom as compared to being cast out of the feast, exclusion from the kingdom versus from the city, expulsion of both unfaithful angels and servants from the city, being cast into the fire, being condemned, being hurt by the second death, partaking of God's wrath, not being known, experiencing eternal torment versus enduring eternal shame, and being subject to soteriological death as opposed to misthological death.

Correlative applicability is not to be limited to or confused with metaphorical applicability in that being hurt correlatively by the Lake of Fire, for example, is not to be equated with being cast metaphorically into the Lake of Fire. The principle of correlativity does not deduce that unfaithful believers are cast metaphorically into the Lake of Fire. Rather, the casting of unbelievers into the Lake of Fire and unfaithful believers into the outer darkness can be said to have a soteric-mistholic typological relation. At most, being hurt by the second death would be a metaphorical picture of this correlation. Believers are not submitted to the Lake of Fire, although a direct correlation exists between the Lake of Fire and the Outer darkness. Even so, a direct correlation is not to be confused with a direct application. One should not confuse type and antitype.

The negative results meted out at the Bema can be compared in the broad typological sense to (but not literally or metaphorically equated with) the negative results poured out at the GWT. The typological correlation is **direct**: *Bema* $\cong$ *GWT*.

Principle of indirectivity is similar to the principle of correlativity in that both perceive a soteric-mistholic or mistholic-soteric relation. However, the principle of indirectivity does so through an intermediate link. This principle is sometimes used improperly. For example, unfaithful believers are falsely thought to be hurt indirectly by the second death in the Lake of Fire by the means of others. An improper intermediate link is posed: Bema-Others-Lake. Instead, the proper connection is: *Bema-Gehenna-Lake* so that *Bema* $\nearrow$ *Lake of Fire*. The misthological application of the Lake of Fire is reached indirectly by means of the typological *preteristic Gehenna Bema*. The negative results meted out at the Bema can be compared in the broad typological sense to (but not literally or metaphorically equated with) the negative results poured out at the GWT. The intermediate link is typological, and the typological correlation is **indirect**: *Bema* ↷ *GWT*.

Pri-Soul (phenomenal soul) refers to the *phenomenal* overlapping interchange of the flesh and *tri-soul* in which the soul remains organically sinless but functionally subject to sinful fleshly impulses since the soul's responses are not ontologically determined.

Pri-Spirit (phenomenal spirit) refers to the *phenomenal* overlapping interchange of the tri-soul and *tri-spirit* at a functional level of phenomenal experience, wherein the function of the tri-soul and tri-spirit overlaps in intellectual, volitional, and emotional functions.

Proveitists is a coined abbreviation for *prove-it-tists*: advocates of prove-it theology. Many proveitists will object to being calling Calvinists. Perhaps they are Calminians or closet Calvinists. In any event, the term proveitists is used broadly to denote those who (like Calvinists) maintain that the way a person lives proves whether that person is a genuine believer. Proveitism asserts that fruit in the form of perseverance is necessary proof of salvation: *If you do not have this fruit, then you were never saved initially*. Perseverance is necessary to prove that you are saved and to enter heaven. Calvinists, closet Calvinists, and Calminians would thus be included under the proveitistic umbrella.

Punctiliar faith (●) is a response of faith that takes place at a point in time.

Rapture is derived from Latin Vulgate translation (*rapere*) of the Greek word for *caught up* (*harpazo*) in 1Thess 4:17. It describes the first stage of the second coming. Christ will come in the clouds with the first part of the church (those who have died in Christ) for the rest of the church (those who are alive in Christ) to take them to heaven.

Reformed Arminian is someone who holds the views of Arminius himself and his original followers. It is debated as to whether Arminius himself actually affirmed that irremediable apostasy actually could take place for those who had experienced saving faith. In any case, his modern advocates certainly tend to deny OSAS in the case of willful irremediable apostasy. Basically, it would seem that Arminius' position leads to the conclusion that regenerate believers who persevere in the faith until the end of their lives become elect at that time and are chosen to go to heaven as a result. God predestines those whom He foreknows will persevere in the faith to reach heaven. If you fail to persevere, you lose your regenerate life and fail to reach final salvation. In Reformed Arminianism, you are predestined because you persevere. In Reformed theology itself, however, you persevere because you are predestined. Other than this particular matter, Reformed Arminianism tends to agree with Reformed theology on other issues, such as the penal nature of the atonement and justification by imputation.

Regeneration is the theological term used to describe the impartation of eternal life as a free gift (to one's spirit) which occurs when a person believes in Christ for eternal life. Such a person is said to be *born again* (i.e., given spiritual life in the form of eternal life as a free gift).

Revelation of Christ is based on the word *revelation* (*apokalupto*) in 2Thess 1:7 and Lk 17:30; both verses associate it with *fire* (*pur*). It refers to the second stage of the second coming in which He comes with all the church saints all the way to earth, not stopping in the clouds.

Revelation is used of both stages of the second coming. It will generally be used herein, as it is used in 2Thess 1:7 (*apokalupto*), to refer to the second stage of the second coming, that is, to the second coming itself in distinction to the rapture.

Saving faith is a theological term used to refer to the faith which results in salvation from hell. For an unconditional securitist, such faith is regarded as punctiliar (●). For the conditional securitist, such faith is regarded as linear (→). In other words, securitists believe that initial faith is sufficient for salvation from eternal damnation. Insecuritists, in contrast, teach that initial faith is insufficient since it must be followed by perseverance in faith in order to qualify for heaven.

Second Coming happens in two stages. In the first stage, Jesus returns to the clouds of earth. This stage is called the rapture. He comes to judge believers. In the second stage, He comes to judge everyone.

Securitist refers to an advocate of *unconditional security*—the conviction that once a person believes in Christ for eternal life, that person is unconditionally secure in Christ and is unconditionally assured of reaching heaven unconditionally.

Semi-Pelagianism is a heterodox view of human-divine synergism that asserts the sufficiency of natural and moral human ability to **initiate** (rather than consummate) salvation by exercising good will toward God apart from the grace of God. (Consummation of salvation requires the grace of God.)

Sensus Plenior is the belief that Scripture may be taken in plural senses. According to this perspective, Scripture may have many types of meanings, such as literal and spiritual. But this approach gives rise to allegorical interpretation in which Scripture is interpreted non-literally according to its hidden spiritual meaning. In order to avoid this excess, limitations were placed on *sensus plenior* in our text.

Shortcomer is a coined term for the believer who *comes short* (Heb 4:1; 12:15) of the level of misthological grace necessary to enter the kingdom rest by inheriting the kingdom.

Skotology is a coined term derived from the Greek word *skotos* (*darkness*) and used to refer to the study of darkness in the NT. A misthological skotologist would be one who finds darkness being misthologically applied punitively to believers.

Soteriological Election means to choose for salvation. It may be used in a *broad* sense to refer to justification salvation, sanctification salvation, and co-glorification salvation. Or it may be used in a *restricted* sense to refer to only one or two phases of salvation.

Soteriology is based on two biblical Greek words, *soteria* (*salvation*) and *logos* (*teaching*), and correspondingly refers to biblical teaching about salvation. Although the biblical concept of salvation includes many dimensions other than deliverance from hell, it is this aspect of salvation to which writers refer frequently when they use the word soteriology. Thus, salvation from hell (or more specifically, from eternal damnation in the Lake of Fire) will be referred to as **soteriological salvation** or **eternal salvation**. A soteriological interpretation of a passage thus would treat the passage as dealing with eternal salvation from the Lake of Fire (Rev 20:14-15).

Sovereign hardening refers to God's unconditional pre-temporal choice to harden a person or nation for no other apparent reason than that He chose to do so because it pleased Him to do so. From this Calvinistic perspective, God evidently is pleased to reprobate the lost to hell without giving them a chance to believe.

Strict merit refers to an equitable exchange between works and their attendant reward. Basically, the reward is the agreed-upon, fair-payment value for the service performed. The reward is **fully merited**. No appeal to grace occurs in this view: *merit-reward*.

Subcomer is a coined expression to describe believers who fail to overcome in the sense described in Revelation. That is, they are genuine believers who fail to overcome experientially and are consequently overcome by evil. They succumb (i.e., *subcome*, to use my terminology) to the world rather than overcome it. They are genuine believers who fail to overcome practically and misthologically and thus miss out on the rewards promised to overcomers.

Synergism is derived from the Greek verb *sunergeo* and means *to work together cooperatively with someone else to produce something that is a result of mutual work*. God works synergistically with the cooperative individual to bring the individual to the point of saving faith. The saving faith produced by this joint enterprise is the result of mutual work. Therefore, saving faith qualifies, by definition, as a synergistic response—a response produced by mutually cooperative work. Although saving faith is the result of work, saving faith itself, however, is not a work. Consequently, regeneration is not a synergistic result. Regeneration is produced exclusively by God, not jointly by God and cooperative human beings. (We do not give birth to ourselves.) The cooperative human being is regenerated by God on the condition of faith alone—apart from any human works. Because regeneration is not the result of mutual work, it is not a synergistic result. Regeneration is exclusively a work of God and therefore a monergistic result. The only thing contributed by the cooperative human being at the point of regeneration is the passive response of faith which is not a work.

Synoptic gospels refers to the gospels by Matthew, Mark, and Luke, since they describe Jesus' earthly ministry from a similar point of view.

Teleology is based on two biblical Greek words, *teleo* (*end*) and *logos* (*teaching*). Some writers prefer to use the word *teleology* and its derivatives to denote eschatological rewards. But *teleology* would appear to be better suited to describe the doctrine of the end time rather than a limited aspect of that period (e.g., rewards). But since *eschatology* is the word popularly used to describe the doctrine of the end of time, *teleology* is herein regarded as an inferior designation for the doctrine of eschatological rewards. My preference will be to use *misthology* to refer to eternal rewards.

Telology is a coined expression derived from *telos* (*end*) and refers to the doctrine of the end of time. It is the nominal cognate of the verb *teleo*. To avoid confusion, misthology has been used herein in preference to telology.

Temporal election is election made in the present time.

Temporal salvation is salvation in the present time.

Theology refers to biblical teaching about God. The derivation of the word is based on a combination of two biblical Greek words: *theos* (*God*) and *logos* (*teaching*).

Time bubble is a temporal sphere in time in which time may be experienced at vastly different rates by those in the sphere as opposed to those outside of it. Although the bubble may be restricted spatially to a certain location, it is not to be thought of as being a different place in time as if one spatially could visit another place in time, whether past or future, inside such a bubble. Nevertheless, it is probable that experiential time travel would be possible in such a bubble even though spatial time travel would not be.

Tri-Soul (trichotomous soul) refers to those usages of the word *soul* where it is used in a narrower trichotomist sense to designate only part of the immaterial portion of the person in contrast to the trichotomous *spirit*. The tri-soul is the center of our self-consciousness.

Tri-Spirit (trichotomous spirit) refers to those usages of the word *spirit* where it is used in a narrower trichotomist sense to designate only part of the immaterial portion of the person in contrast to the trichotomous *soul*. The tri-spirit is the ontological core of our innermost being that experiences regeneration.

TULIP—Calvinistic acronym: (1) **T**otal Depravity; (2) **U**nconditional Election; (3) **L**imited Atonement; (4) **I**rresistible Grace; and (5) **P**erseverance of the Saints.

Typology is derived from the Greek word *tupos* (*type*). The study of types is an important part of interpreting Scripture. The Scripture teaches that Adam is a type of Christ (Rom 5:15), and OT events are types for NT believers (1Cor 10:6). OT people and events illustrate NT truths.

Unconditional securitist is someone who believes that perseverance is not necessary to enter heaven.

Unconditional security is the conviction that once a person believes in Christ for eternal life, that person is unconditionally secure in Christ and *unconditionally assured of* reaching heaven *unconditionally*. Technically, this redundant articulation is superior to saying simply that a believer is *unconditionally assured* of reaching heaven. A Calvinist might affirm the latter but could not affirm the former.

Wesleyan Arminian is someone who follows the modifications made by Wesley to Arminianism. Most notably, this view believes that salvation can be lost by either apostasy or unconfessed sin. Nevertheless, regeneration may be restored by reconversion and repentance.

Endnotes

¹ Antonio da Rosa, "Definition of Eternal Life." Available at http://free-grace.blogspot.com/2006/11/definition-of-eternal-life.html. Accessed on November 24, 2006. "It is a fearful thing to fall into the hands of the living God." Available at http://free-grace.blogspot.com/2006/02/it-is-fearful-thing-to-fall-into-hands.html. Accessed on November 24, 2006.

² Carl G Johnson, *The Account Which We Must Give: Studies on the Judgment Seat of Christ* (Schaumburg: Regular Baptist Press, 1990), 72.

³ Bruce Wilkinson and David Kopp, *A Life God Rewards: Why Everything You Do Today Matters Forever* (Sisters: Multnomah Publishers, 2002). Robert N. Wilkin, *The Road to Reward: Living Today in Light of Tomorrow* (Irving: Grace Evangelical Society, 2003). Randy Alcorn, *Heaven* (Carol Stream, IL: Tyndale House, 2004). Idem, *The Law of Rewards* (Carol Stream, IL: Tyndale House, 2003). Zane C. Hodges, *Grace in Eclipse: A Study on Eternal Rewards*, 3rd edition (Irving, TX: Grace Evangelical Society, 2007).

⁴ David F. Wells, *No Place for Truth or Whatever Happened to Evangelical Theology?* (Leicester: Inter-Varsity Press, 1993).

⁵ Hampton Keathley IV, "The 'Outer Darkness': Heaven's Suburb or Hell?" Available at http://bible.org/page.asp?page_id=1044. Accessed on September 17, 2004.

⁶ One might consult the explanation by Forster as to why Jesus spoke in parables to hide the meaning. Forster's estimation might be surmised as saying that it was judicial but not absolute or irrevocable blinding. But even this explanation fails to account fully for the cryptic manner in which Jesus spoke to even His disciples. Roger T Forster and V. Paul Marston, *God's Strategy in Human History* (Wheaton: Tyndale House Publishers, 1973), 234-241.

⁷ Michael G. Huber, "The Concept of the 'Outer Darkness' in the Gospel of Matthew" (Th.M. thesis, Dallas Theological Seminary, 1978), 30-31.

⁸ James C. McClymont, Jr., "The Parable of the Talents" (Th.M. thesis, Dallas Theological Seminary, 1976), 35-39.

⁹ France, *Matthew*, NIC, 503.

¹⁰ Turner, *Matthew*, ECNT, 333.

¹¹ Zane C. Hodges, *Jesus: God's Prophet: His Teaching about the Coming Surprise* (Mesquite: Kerugma, 2006), 60. Jesus encoded His message in the details of the parables in order to reveal truths to insiders who were willing to put forth the effort to decode them and at the same time to conceal truths from outsiders who were not inclined to put forth the effort to decode them or who were inclined to decode them wrongly by interpreting them legalistically.

¹² Ronald Youngblood, ed., *Evangelicals and Inerrancy: Selections from the Journal of the Evangelical Theological Society* (Nashville: Thomas Nelson Publishers, 1984), 137-146. Norman L. Geisler, *Inerrancy* (Grand Rapids: Zondervan Publishing House, 1980), 267-276.

¹³ In his introductory chapter, in which Jeremias explains how he will interpret Jesus' parables, Jeremias launches an immediate attack against Mk 4:10-12, saying that the grouping is artificial, that the details are contradictory, that the explanation of the parable of the sower is not authentic to Jesus but was supplied by later tradition (p. 13). Jeremias alleges that Mark misunderstood Jesus' statement and erroneously applied Jesus' affirmation of obscurity to the parables, saying that it should have been applied to Jesus' teaching as a whole (pp. 17-18). More pointedly, Jeremias claims that the interpretation of the sower attributed by the Scripture to Jesus really should be attributed to the primitive church (pp. 55, 79) so that when interpreting parables the first thing one must do is "entirely disregard the context" (p. 56). Secondly, one must discard the details as being allegorical insertions made by the primitive church (p. 89). Conversely, and contrary to Jeremias, if the details are authentic, then the details count! Consequently, the way for conservatives who believe in inerrancy to discover the original meaning intended by Jesus is to pay attention to the details. See Joachim Jeremias, *The Parables of Jesus*, Revised Third Edition (London: SCM Press, 1972).

¹⁴ Gordon C. Olson, *Beyond Calvinism and Arminianism: An Inductive Mediate Theology of Salvation* (Global Gospel Publishers, 2002), 18.

¹⁵ Ibid., 33.

¹⁶ If one induces that the outer darkness refers to the judgment of believers and if one induces that the Lake of Fire refers to the judgment of unbelievers, then one would deduce that the outer darkness and the Lake of Fire are referring to two separate things. Correspondingly, if it is induced that the parable of the outer darkness refers to one time period and if it is induced the parable of the wheat and tares deals with another time period, then it would be deduced that they are dealing with two different judgments.

¹⁷ "Epistemological certainty can be acquired because in order to know some things about an object one does not have to know everything about it. If this were the case, then we would know nothing….Knowing with epistemological certainty is not to be equated with knowing exhaustively." Mark M. Hanna, "A Response to the Role of Logic in Biblical Interpretation," *Hermeneutics*, 866.

¹⁸ George Eldon Ladd, Herman A. Hoyt, Loraine Boettner, and Anthony A. Hoekema, *The Meaning of the Millennium: Four Views*, ed. Robert G Clouse (Downers Grove: InterVarsity Press, 1977), 7-40.

¹⁹ Laurence M. Vance, *The Other Side of Calvinism*, revised edition (Pensacola: Vance Publications, 1999), 37-68.

[20] David R. Anderson, "The Soteriological Impact of Augustine's Change from Premillennialism to Amillennialism: Part 1," *JOTGES* 15:28 (Spring 2002): 25-36. Also, see various sections of his book for interaction with Augustine. David R. Anderson, *Free Grace Soteriology* (Xulon Press, 2010), for example, 295-324. Both Augustinianism and Catholicism believe that entrance into heaven is merited by God-enabled works (pp. 106-107) and thus trust in their God-enabled legalism for entrance into heaven. More typically, Protestant performatists today attribute their positive performance to God but deny that it entails any human merit. Such arguments are still self-refuting in that they make the free gift of salvation a reward based on one's performance. Thus, it is not truly free. For example, Arrington (an Arminian) gives the typical disclaimers: "**Salvation is not a matter of human achievement**" (p. 49). "It is not a matter of earning salvation by works, but it is about Christ working through us" (p. 57). However, he refutes that statement in the next paragraph: "Believers can persevere, but perseverance **demands effort** in faith, which draws strength from God" (p. 57). Whose effort is demanded? Believers are the ones who must persevere in their effort to reach heaven. Necessarily, this effort entails work. Thus, Arrington is teaching that believers must work their way to heaven. Salvation is very much a result of God-enabled human effort in that case, a God-enabled human achievement. Somehow the gift becomes a reward conditioned on our continuous performance (p. 68). Christians gain "**salvation as their reward**" by their successful "struggle against sin, Satan, and the world" (p. 72). Inheriting the kingdom is equivalent to being saved from hell and is a reward for one's work (p. 115; cp. Col 3:23-25). "To do good work and receive salvation [as a result] means believers **must** remain faithful" (p. 135). Yet in the next paragraph, he adds, "We must hasten to add that this is not salvation by works" (p.135). Really? Then what is it? He is simply denying the logical outcome of his theology. Still, he continues on the next page, "Our responsibility is to cooperate with the Holy Spirit in bringing this blessing to fruition....Godly living is not simply a sign or fruit of salvation, but it is a condition for continuing salvation" (p. 136). Thus, you synergistically work your way to heaven which, of course, is salvation by works. "God's keeping power **must** be matched by **the believer's effort**" (p. 169). Your God-enabled effort keeps you saved. Yet supposedly, "salvation is an eternal gift of God" (p. 151). Somehow this salvation is a gift from start to finish, even though it ends up being a reward for your effort! Supposedly, though, such salvation does not "come by works" because "the Holy Spirit does the work" (p. 151). Immediately, he adds, "But we must commit ourselves to it [the work]" (p. 152). We are not saved by our works, but by our works, in other words. Arrington keeps waffling back and forth between affirming and denying that salvation is by works. The only thing missing from this waffle is the syrup. French L. Arrington, *Unconditional Security: Myth or Truth?* (Cleveland, TN: Pathway Press, 2005).

Illustration 372. The Compatibilism of A and non-A

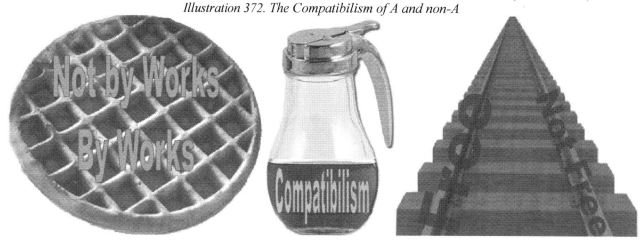

A couple of weeks before I published this book, a guest speaker at our church preached a very good sermon on 1Pet 1:6-9, in which he said that the benefit we are acquiring is progressively obtained. I will refer to this speaker as S.E. I agree with S.E in that assessment. After the service I asked S.E if he was basing his statement on the fact that *obtaining* (*komizo*) is a present participle in v. 9. He acknowledged that he was. I shared with him that I could follow the logic of that assessment since the verbal aspect would seem to be linear and the context progressive. One might also add, in harmony with his sermon, that the linear *testing* (*dokimazo*) of our faith in v. 7 results in an increasing pure faith in which the refiner would be able to see His reflection with increasing clarity. However, S.E. did not specify the nature of the salvation in v. 9. So I asked if the salvation in this verse was a gift or a reward. He responded that it did not matter because in the end a gift and reward merge into the same thing. I surmised that he was being Augustinian in that perspective. He acknowledged that he was. As an explanation for his perspective, he stated that he was a compatibilist. Understanding how this explanation would suffice from his perceptive (for how a free gift can amount to a costly reward) is not difficult. Within compatibilism, one imagines that free will is both free and not free. If the free will simultaneously can be both free and not free, then why can God's gift not simultaneously be both free and not free? Why can salvation from hell not be concurrently both by good works and not by good works? As expected, S.E added the typical explanation: God is the one doing the good works within us. Yet this explanation does not suffice. The Lord does not help us work our way to heaven. Moreover, Paul rules out making salvation from hell dependent upon our works—period.

At this juncture, S.E. asked me what I thought. I responded that I believe that Augustine was wrong and that I am an incompatibilist. I do not find it compatible to call that which is *free, not free*. I also believe that it is incompatible to call that which is *not free, free*. Nevertheless, I am well acquainted with that perspective. So in a matter of moments, I was able to surmise his position. I told S.E. that I would send him a copy of this book when it is finished if he was interested in reading it. He responded that he was. Let us hope that he does.

The appeal by S.E. to compatibilism reminds me of a quote of Spurgeon by Coate, in which Spurgeon compared God's sovereignty and our liberty to two straight lines that run "so nearly parallel" that we cannot perceive how they converge, but they do converge "somewhere in eternity." Micah Coate, *A Cultish Side of Calvinism* (Innovo Publishing, 2011), 35.

Briefly, Spurgeon missed the relationship. According to the law of non-contradiction (in which God tells us how things really are), *A* and *non-A* are not merely *nearly parallel*. Rather, if two related truths have this relationship, then they are *actually parallel*. They can never converge. Projecting them into eternity future will not help. Just as evolutionists imagine that evolution can occur if given enough time, such compatibilists imagine that contradictory statements are not contradictory if given enough distance. The imagery of a train track comes to mind. They imagine that the train tracks do merge, not merely optically, but actually. Try to imagine the train that is going to run on that track though! Even by evolutional standards, however, there is not enough time within its own model for it to explain all phenomena. For example, as I write this note, I went to Nasa.gov to see how large the universe is projected to be. An article there says that the light from a remote galaxy took 14 billion years to get here. However, if the universe is only 4.5 billion years old, then how did the light have 14 billion years to get here? Evolutionists need to recheck their math. Likewise, I would encourage S.E. to reconsider his position and hope that he will read this note when I send him this book. His interpretation of 1Pet 1:6-9 does not give him time to project the merger of a gift into a reward off into the distant future. In fact, his time is already up. We already are working to earn the future salvation being promised in 1Pet 1:9. That outcome already has undergone a transformation from being a gift into being a reward—if it ever was a gift. Just as it is incumbent upon evolutionist to prove that current species have emerged from previous ones, so S.E. must prove (not merely assume) that this reward evolved from first being a gift. Like a creationist, as a securitist I have proven (within the body of this book and my related books) that God's gift of eternal life does not evolve into a reward. I contend that the rewards we are trying to earn are not gifts that have mutated into rewards. Contrary to S.E., we are not progressively becoming more qualified to enter heaven. Entrance into heaven is a free gift, already granted permanently as a gift to those who have eternal life. Rather, what we are trying to obtain (by increasing the quality of our faith) is an increased quality of eternal life. If we are following the Lord in obedience, then we are becoming increasingly qualified for this benefit as a reward, and thus increasing our capacity to experience this life qualitatively. Peter describes this as an abundant entrance into the kingdom (2Pet 1:11).

See my discussion in *Breaking the Rocking Horse* and *Mere Christianity and Moral Christianity* for future discussion of compatibilism in relation to sovereignty and free will in which I explore Gracely rocking horse analogy. Daniel Gracely, *Calvinism: A Closer Look: Evangelicals, Calvinism, and Why No One's Answering the Problem of Evil*, revised and enlarged edition (Grandma's Attic Press, 2009).

[21] Ibid.

[22] Some within GES presume that the theology expressed herein necessarily requires a dispensational framework and could not be compatible with amillennialism. Although the present writer certainly holds a low view of amillennialism, it has not yet been demonstrated to his satisfaction that the perversion of Augustine's soteriology by his amillennial eschatology was a logical necessity. Theoretically at least, it would seem possible for an amillennialist to conclude that an abundant entrance into the eternal kingdom in 2Pet 1:11 is a misthological issue and yet regard basic entrance into the eternal kingdom a soteriological matter.

For the premillennial misthologist, the rewards that commence in the millennial kingdom would carry over into the eternal kingdom. For the amillennial misthologist, the rewards of the millennial kingdom may be regarded as heavenly rewards experienced in the eternal kingdom. Rewards would be regarded as eternal from both perspectives. Therefore, someone advocating a FG view from the amillennial perspective might be expected to deduce that since an abundant entrance is a reward and since ruling with Christ is a reward, topics such as being *worthy of* the kingdom or *fit for* the kingdom in passages such as Lk 9:62 and 2Thess 1:5 are also dealing with misthological themes. One does not need to be premillennial in order to believe that being worthy of kingdom rulership is a reward.

The misthological salvation in Mk 13:13 might also be regarded as salvation from the outer darkness rather than from hell. After all, some amillennialists in Baptist circles believe in OSAS. And the theology of GES is basically just a logically consistent defense of the stronger form of OSAS—unconditional security. Although unconditional security typically is defended from a dispensational perspective within the GES camp, any conclusion that amillennialism could be not be consistent with unconditional security (and thus with GES) is just theoretical speculation in the absence of theological or exegetical proof. An amillennial advocate of OSAS might find it easier to make the transition to unconditional security without necessarily having to adopt the dispensational arguments used in favor of that security. If so, there is no need to put eschatological stumbling blocks in the way of the amillennialists coming to believe in unconditional security and thus coming to saving faith. Nevertheless, in my review of three articles by Grant Howley, I concede that, pragmatically speaking, non-dispensationalism leads to a LS position. For my article, see http://misthology.org/wpcontent/uploads/2012/08/Eschatology_and_Soteriology.pdf. Grant Howley, "Dispensationalism and Free Grace: Intimately Linked—Part 1," *JOTGES* 24:46 (Spring 2011): 63-81. "Dispensationalism and Free Grace: Intimately Linked—Part 2," *JOTGES* 24:47 (Autumn 2011): 89-106. "Dispensationalism and Free Grace: Intimately Linked—Part 3," *JOTGES* 25:48 (Spring 2012): 21-36. Without doubt, FG should be promoting a consistent dispensationalism..

[23] Some in FG would question the extent of Calvin's Calvinism. In particular, four-point Calvinists would contend that Calvin did not teach a limited atonement. On this basis, Geisler asserts that "Calvin was not a Calvinist." Norman L. Geisler, *Chosen but Free*, second edition (Minneapolis: Bethany House Publications, 2001), 160. Perhaps it would be better to acknowledge that Calvin's views were anachronistic and inconsistent but not necessarily antagonistic to a limited atonement. Rather, his views appear sympathetic to the limited atonement, and it is not surprising that his followers, in seeking to be systematic and consistent in developing his views, came to this perspective as a foregone conclusion. See Vance, 459-473.

If I had followed the description of Calvin by Hunt, I would have stated that Calvin **was** a Calvinist, rather than say that Calvin **became** a Calvinist. Hunt pictures Calvin as being under the dominion of Augustinian Catholicism from the very beginning of Calvin's presumed conversion. Thus, the subsequent editions of Calvin's *Institutes* would have been an amplification of his initial edition rather than a radical modification of its key components. Dave Hunt, *What Love Is This? Calvinism's Misrepresentation of God* (Sisters, OR: Loya, 2002), 37-40.

Anderson, on the other hand, traces a development from Calvin's first edition (which only contained 6 chapters) through to his finished work (containing 80 chapters). David R. Anderson, "The Soteriological Impact of Augustine's Change From Premillennialism to Amillennialism: Part 2," *JOTGES* 15:29 (Autumn 2002): 23-39. Anderson's contention is that Calvin originally divorced justification and sanctification but subsequently remarried them under Augustine's influence (p. 24). Further, "Augustine never espoused assurance of salvation before death. Calvin did, but only initially" (p. 36). "John Calvin, who began teaching assurance is of the essence of faith, wound up teaching that no man could tell if he were elect or reprobate until he died" (p. 37). My description of Calvin at this particular point in my discussion follows the presentation by Anderson.

[24] Vance, 138-139.

[25] David R. Anderson, "Another Tale of Two Cities," *JOTGES* 18:35 (Autumn 2005): 60.

[26] M. M. Ninan, "Soteriology: Man, Sin, Salvation and God: Armanianism [sic]: The Five Points of Arminianism can be remembered by the acronym: PEARS." Available at http://www.acns.com/~mm9n/sot/Introduction/main.html. Accessed on September 24, 2004.

[27] Michael D. Makidon, "From Perth To Pennsylvania: The Legacy Of Robert Sandeman," *JOTGES* 15:28 (Spring 2002): 75-92. Idem, "The Marrow Controversy," *JOTGES* 16:31 (Autumn 2003): 65-77. Makidon's article is useful in showing divergences between Marrowism and the Reformers. For a historical analysis that focuses more on convergences, one may consult Thomas G. Lewellen, "Has Lordship Salvation Been Taught throughout Church History?" *BibSac* 147:585 (January 1990): 54-68.

[28] At its heart, Marrowism is a defense of unconditional security for the believer, with believer being simply defined as someone who has believed in Christ alone for eternal life. A personal perception of one's unconditional possession of a quality and quantity of spiritual life that cannot be forfeited is considered implicit within this definition. In other words, it is impossible for a person to believe in Christ for eternal life and yet not believe that he or she has eternal life in Christ. Saving faith is the assurance of one's own eternal security, conditioned only on one's initial faith in Christ alone for eternal life. One cannot have saving faith apart from assurance. Assurance is not optional.

Some within FG further will argue that the degree of such assurance must be absolute so that there must not be any doubt at the point of saving faith. One argument implemented in defense of this proposition is to claim that assurance is degreeless. While it is not denied herein that by definition assurance is the absence of doubt, it is maintained herein that a person can have assurance to various degrees. Hence, Marrowism, as the term is intended herein, does not demand that at the time of regeneration one must possess absolute assurance. It is sufficient that at the moment of conversion Christ alone is the object of one's faith for eternal life.

Others in FG will add one or more other contingencies, asserting that in order to experience saving faith one also must believe that Christ is: (1) divine, (2) risen from the dead, and (3) the only means of eternal life. Like many of those in FG, at one point or another I have considered such matters to be absolute theological necessities that God would require one to believe in order to come into the possession of eternal life. However, over the course of time, I have come to regard such matters more likely to be psychological necessities which some people may need to embrace in order to come to saving faith. Therefore, although these three principle truths clearly are affirmed within the present work, recognition of these truths nevertheless is considered a helpful means of bringing a person to saving faith rather than made a part of saving faith itself. Regardless, belief in Christ's aforementioned deity, reviviscency, and exclusivity are not performance issues, so I consequently would allow divergency under the Marrowistic canopy on these issues.

For example, explicit faith in Christ alone is the only means of regeneration (Jn 14:6; Acts 4:12), but this does not mean that a person necessarily must (as a theological contingency) believe that explicit faith in Christ alone is the only means of regeneration. Universalists can be saved despite their failure to recognize the exclusivity of Christ's soteriology. (See endnote 761.) As to reviviscency, if Christ were not raised from the dead, then a person's faith certainly would be worthless (1Cor 15:17). Even so, this does not necessarily mean that a person must believe that Christ is raised from the dead for his or her faith to be worthwhile. (See endnote dealing with 1Cor 15:2 in *Carnal Corinth*.) In regards to deity, if Christ were not God, then He could not offer us eternal life since the atoning value of His death which makes regeneration possible would be valueless apart from His deity and since the regeneration itself which He imparts is the life which He himself has (1Jn 5:11-13), albeit not independently of the Father. Still, this affirmation of Christ's *objective deity* (OD) does not necessarily mean that a person must recognize that Christ is God in order to receive eternal life from God. In other words, subjective affirmation of Christ's deity—*subjective deity* (SD)—may not be a soteriological necessity. (See endnote 690.) This clarification between the objective and subjective Deity of Christ (i.e., between OD and SD) is using similar abbreviations as those used for the distinction made between the objective and subjective Lordship of Christ (i.e., between OL and SL). To illustrate the difference between subjective recognition and objective ability, if a man were to offer you a million dollars, it would not be necessary that you believe that the man himself is rich in order for you to believe his offer was legitimate. You might simply believe that he was operating on behalf of someone else who was rich. Some might likewise mistakenly conclude that since Jesus is the intermediate agent offering eternal life that He is not Himself God. This subjective error need not, in and of itself, necessarily prevent them from believing in Jesus alone for eternal life.

GJ certainly stresses the deity of Christ, and it appears to do so evangelistically as a means of leading a person to faith in Christ for eternal life. To continue with the illustration, if the person offering you the million dollars claimed to be rich himself and made it clear to you that the million dollars he was offering you was his own money, then it would be psychologically necessary for you to believe that the person was rich in order for you to believe that his offer was legitimate. The person might demonstrate his wealth to you in order to enable you to believe in his wealth and thereby believe that his offer was valid. John demonstrates Jesus' deity with a wealth of literary material so that we might believe that Jesus' offer of eternal life is genuine. Yet just as the actual requirement is not that you believe that the person offering the money is himself rich in order to believe that his offer of a million dollars is true, so it is not theologically necessary that you believe that Jesus is Himself God in order to believe that the life He offers you from God is indeed His own. Nevertheless, for those who correctly perceive that GJ presents Jesus as God, it would be natural to expect that they would have to embrace that truth before they could trust in the message of GJ and find life in Jesus as the Son of God. As Christ, Jesus is the Son of God (Jn 20:31). The perspective adopted herein is that Jesus' converts did not necessarily fully grasp His deity when coming to saving faith in Him as the Christ and/or Son of God. What was necessary was that they believe in Jesus for eternal life.

This life is eternal and therefore cannot be extinguished or lost. It is secure. Soteriology and misthology are the two twins of security. Soteriology is the systematic study of unconditional security. Misthology is the systematic study of conditional security. As such, misthology (symmetrically and systematically) traces out the logical implications of conditional security in demonstrating that linear contingencies deal with rewards rather than with the possession of eternal life as a free gift.

The basic *possession* of eternal life (in both its *reception* and *retention*) is to be understood as freely bestowed on believers at the moment they believe in Christ alone for eternal life. So-called Lordship Salvationists are nothing more than conditional securitists who make the basic possession of eternal life (in either its reception or retention) contingent on one's performance. Marrowism thus is to be understood in both its intention and definition as the affirmation of the believer's soteriologically unconditional security and misthologically conditional security. Submission to the Lordship of Christ in the area of one's performance is explicitly limited in terms of theological necessity to the realm of misthology. *The Outer Darkness* is a systematic misthology in that it investigates the logical implications of biblical rewards and weaves these strands together into a logically harmonious defense of soteriological security.

[29] Stephen L. Andrew, "PROPER: A Free-Grace Alternative to Calvinism's TULIP and Arminianism's PEARS." Unpublished paper, 2001. PROPER refers to *Preeminent Grace, Responsible Agency, Ontological Freedom, Passive Faith, Eternal Security, Rewards for Obedience*. An online comparison of PROPER, TULIP, and PEARS can be found at: http://www.columbiabible.com/files/files/pears.pdf. Accessed January 27, 2010.

[30] EDBT, s.v. "Reward," by Wesley L. Gerig.

[31] EDT, s.v. "Reward," by H. Z. Cleveland.

[32] Ibid.

[33] UBD, s.v. "Reward."

[34] Ibid.

[35] Brian Schwertley, "Justification by Faith - Part V: Judgment According to Works." Available at http://www.glenwoodhills.org/article.asp?ID=96. Accessed on September 24, 2004.

[36] John Gerstner, "The Nature of Justifying Faith," in Don Kistler, *Justification by Faith Alone* (Morgan, PA: Soli Deo Gloria, 1995), 121. Cited by Schwertley.

[37] Schwertley, "Justification."

[38] Alcon, *Reward*, 124.

[39] John A. Martin, *Luke*, BKC (Wheaton: Victor Books, 1985), 248.

[40] Lenski, *Luke*, 873.

[41] Joseph C. Dillow, *The Reign of the Servant Kings: A Study of Eternal Security and the Final Significance of Man*, 2nd ed. (Hayesville, NC: Schoettle Publishing Co., 1993), 526-530.

[42] Schwertley, "Justification."

[43] John F. MacArthur, Jr. *Faith Works: The Gospel According to the Apostles* (Dallas: Word Publishing, 1993), 30, n. 5.

[44] Ibid., 30.

[45] Ibid., 52.

[46] Ibid., 47-48.

[47] Ibid., 70.

[48] Ibid., 53.

[49] Ibid., 114, 242.

[50] Ibid., 110, 114.

[51] Ibid., 182.

[52] Ibid., 185.

[53] Ibid., 243.

[54] Ibid., 242. They even go so far as to make sanctification as equally necessary as justification for soteriological glorification.

[55] Ibid., 236-237.

[56] Ibid., 207.

[57] James E. Rosscup, "The Overcomer of the Apocalypse," *GTJ* 3:2 (Fall 1982): 274, n. 18.

[58] David R. Reagan, "Eternal Security: Do Believer's Have It? How Does It Relate To Prophecy? A Review of the book, The Reign of the Servant Kings." Available at http://www.lamblion.com/other/religious/RI-18.php. Accessed on August 11, 2004.

[59] The booklet by George Bryson forms a particularly easy-to-digest introduction for the layperson. See his *The Five Points of Calvinism: Weighed and Found Wanting*. Costa Mesa, CA: The Word for Today, 2002. It is also available online at http://calvarychapel.com/library/bryson-george/books/fpocwafw.htm#01. Accessed on November 11, 2004.

[60] Donald Guthrie, *New Testament Introduction*, 3rd ed. (Illinois: InterVarsity Press, 1970), 957.

[61] Ibid., 955.

[62] W. A. Criswell, *Expository Sermons on Revelation* (Grand Rapids: Zondervan Publishing House, 1962), 177.

[63] Rev 1:19 reads, "*Ha **mellie** genesthai meta tauta*." Rev 4:1 reads, "*Ha **dei** genesthai meta tauta*." The wording is identical except for the word *must* which is synonymous; that is, *mellie* is synonymous with *dei*, and both may be translated as *must*.

[64] There are many interpretations concerning the identity of the elders. Johnson says, "There are at least thirteen different views." Alan Johnson, *Revelation*, vol. 12, EBC (Grand Rapids: Zondervan Publishing House, 1976), 462. However, the three identifiers of the twenty-four elders should be conclusive. Commentators such as Scott, Seiss, Tatford, and Walvoord do well in concluding that the twenty-four elders represent glorified believers in heaven. They also do well in noting the OT background for the significance of the number 24. It refers to all in that class. Their mistake lies in assuming that it refers to all believers or even all believers of the church age. This mistake is due to their earlier mistake of assuming that all believers are overcomers.

[65] Robert G. Gromacki, *New Testament Survey* (Grand Rapid: Baker Book House, 1974), 397. He also gives simplistic diagrams of the parallel and consecutive arrangements. House adopts Gromacki's diagrams. H. Wayne House, *Chronological and Background Charts of the New Testament* (Grand Rapids: Zondervan Publishing House, 1981), 146. Both men list the parenthetical sections. Larkin's diagram is a beautiful representation of the same position. Clarence Larkin, *The Book of Revelation* (Glenside, Pa.: Rev. Clarence Larkin Estate, 1919), 148.

The illustration for *Chronological Outline of Revelation* (in the present book) is in agreement with the presentations of the above interpreters concerning the seals, trumpets, and bowls. It also finds Larkin's conclusion of the seals at 18:5 (*Revelation*, 148) more reasonable than Gromacki's conclusion at 18:1 (*Survey*, 399). However, Gromacki's parenthetical break at Rev 19:10 is well taken (*Survey*, 399-400). Walvoord's statement that "from 19:1 to 21:8 a strict chronological order is preserved" (*Revelation*, 289) needs to be tempered with his statements that ch. 19 is parenthetical and "**does not advance** the narrative chronologically" (p. 225) versus his statement that there is little chronological development from the outpouring of the bowls "**until** chapter 19" (p. 186). References are to John F. Walvoord, *The Revelation of Jesus Christ* (Chicago: Moody Press, 1966). How can ch. 19 both advance and not advance the narrative? How can it be both parenthetical and not parenthetical? The answer is that it is both because the first half is parenthetical, and the second half is not. The first half does not advance the narrative; the second half does. Walvoord is inconsistent in including Rev 19:1-10 as part of the "strict chronological order" of 19:11-21:8. On the other hand, Blaising is content to uphold the strict chronology of 19:1-10 in his defense of dispensationalism (*Millennium*, 212-220).

Walvoord also goes on to say, "Many expositors would extend the chronological sequence [of 19:11-21:8] to the end of the book of Revelation" (p. 290). Yet such an approach is too stringent in its chronological analysis. I would agree that there is no recapitulation in ch. 21 of ch. 20. But it is far better to acknowledge the obvious parallelism in the conclusion of the book of ch. 21 by ch. 22 regarding the eternal state. The arguments against recapitulations concerning the seals, bowls, trumpets, and the millennium are sound enough without attempting to deny the obvious recapitulations concerning the New Jerusalem. The recapitulations are concerning the eternal state rather than the millennium.

[66] For alternate proposals to the telescopic view of seals, trumpets, and bowls adopted herein, the following oversimplification will give some sense of the various possibilities:

1. Seals → Trumpets → Bowls (cp. Walvoord, *Revelation*, BKC, 950.)

2. Seals/Trumpets → Bowls (cp. Claeys, 168-169.)

3. Seals → Trumpets/Bowls (cp. Hindson, *Revelation*, TFCBC, 76.)

Claeys follows Hodges. See John Claeys, *Apocalypse 2012: The Ticking of the End-Time Clock—What Does the Bible Say?* (Sisters, OR: VMI Publications, 2012), 161-172, 262, n. 1. Edward Hindson, *Revelation: Unlocking the Future*. Twenty-First Century Bible Commentary Series, ed. Mal Cough (Chattanooga, TN: AMG Publishers, 2002). J. E. Becker, *Rightly Dividing the Book of Revelation* (Enumclaw, WA: Winepress Publishing, 2004). Becker adopts the third view, which Hindson considers the most popular view. The present study has adopted the first view as its working model.

[67] Robert Mounce, *The Book of Revelation*, NIC, ed. F. F. Bruce. (Grand Rapids: Eerdmans Publishing Co., 1977), 292. Thus Mounce is justified in concluding: "The latter series is not a recapitulation of the former but an intensification of divine recompense which share its imagery" (p. 294).

[68] Some interpreters do indeed believe that the descriptions of the churches correspond to what has happened in the history of the church. Their interpretations are subjective and contradictory.

[69] Mounce, 44. Everett F. Harrison, *Introduction to the New Testament*, rev. ed. (Grand Rapids: Eerdmans Publishing Co., 1985), 465.

[70] For a discussion of these premillennial variations, see Walvoord, *Revelation*, 284.

[71] This argument is valid even if those being referred to in 19:14 are overcomers **and** angels. Mounce believes that those referred to in 19:14 are angels **and** faithful believers (*Revelation*, 146). He bases this conclusion on the parallel in 17:14. His comments there are very pertinent: "The armies of heaven share his victory as well (cf. Rev 19:14). Those who overcome will exercise the authority of the Lamb over the nations of the earth and will rule...success depends not only upon their divine election but also upon their corresponding loyalty" (p. 318). It takes more than election to rule; it also takes faithfulness. Lang also correctly believes that 17:14 refers to overcoming Christians, but he believes that angels are exclusively referred to in 19:14. G. H. Lang, *The Revelation of Jesus Christ* (London: Oliphants, 1945; reprint, Miami Springs: Conley and Schoettle Publishing Co., 1985), 329. Also see Ps 149:59; Eze 7:27; and Rev 2:26-27.

Unfortunately, although Lang previously had quoted Ps 58:10 (p. 49), he failed to interact with it in his identification of the armies in 19:14 (p. 329). In contrast to Mounce and particularly Lang concerning 19:14, Seiss says, "These armies are saints, and not angels." J. A. Seiss, *The Apocalypse: Lectures on the Book of Revelation* (Grand Rapids: Zondervan Publishing House, n.d.), 439. In support of his position, Seiss quotes 1Cor 6:2, but his quote and understanding of Ps 58:10 is more decisive. This army of saints washes its feet in the blood of the slain. Ps 58:11 specifically refers to this type of participation in this event as a reward.

Scott also argues that both Rev 17:14 and Rev 19:14 refer to saints "who have proved faithful in all and every relation of life." Walter Scott, *Exposition of the Revelation of Jesus Christ* (Grand Rapids: Kregel Publications, 1982), 355, 388-389. Johnson (*Revelation*, 575) believes that the reference in Rev 19:14 is to victors rather than angels since they "are riding on white horses of victory—something hardly true of angels"—and since their clothing "is identical to the bride's attire (cf. v. 8)." This position is superior. Their attire, action, and OT background distinguish them as rewarded overcomers, not angels or subcomers. Calvinistic interpreters who make such statements believe that all saints will persevere. However, if Calvinists were to acknowledge that not all believers are faithful, they would have to acknowledge that verses such as Rev 17:14 and Rev 19:14 do not refer to all believers. Such verses do not refer to subcomers. This is not to deny that subcomers will come with Jesus. They will come with Him but not be clothed in the same manner as overcomers and not exercise the judgment indicated.

[72] Walvoord, *Revelation*, 289.

[73] Ibid., 290.

[74] See Walvoord's discussion concerning parenthetical expressions and chronological advancement on pp. 139, 169, 175, 186, 187, 289-290, 317-318.

[75] Ibid., 292-293.

[76] Frederick A. Tatford, *The Revelation* (Minneapolis: Klock and Klock Christian Publishers, 1983), 376.

[77] The second *I saw* in the second sentence of the English translation or Rev 20:4 is not actually stated in the Greek text, but it is implied by the first *I saw* in the previous English sentence. John literally says, "I saw thrones…and the souls." John's statement that "the rest of the dead were not resurrected until after the millennium" is a common Johannine aside (i.e., a parenthetical remark, a footnote). Estimates of the number of footnotes in the Gospel of John run anywhere from one to two hundred. For my listing, see *John in Living Color*. Their number and function is discussed by Tom Thatcher, "A New Look at the Asides in the Fourth Gospel," *BibSac* 151:604 (October 1994): 428-439. John did not have the literary luxury of parenthesis and footnotes at the time of his writings. These literary devices must be supplied for him by his modern translators. Translators normally only indicate some of the more obvious ones with parenthesis. Rieu, on the other hand, sets a commendable example when he displays some of these asides as footnotes. His example has been followed herein. See E. V. Rieu, *The Four Gospels: A New Translation from the Greek* (Baltimore: Penguin Books, 1953). Such a layout would not be suitable for translations intended for public reading or for memorization, but it would be very helpful for a study Bible.

Anastasis in Rev 20:5 is describing *ezesan* (coming to life) regardless of whether it is describing the first or second occurrence of *ezesan*. Nevertheless, the first occurrence of *ezesan* is the one denoted as the first resurrection. **The reference to the first resurrection in v. 5 is referring to the first occurrence of *ezesan* because v. 6 makes it clear that those who participate in the first resurrection come to life at the beginning of the millennium in order to reign during the millennium.** The purpose of this particular aside in Rev 20:5 is to point out that the same thing that happened to the dead described in v. 4 before millennium happened to the rest of the dead after the millennium.

The use of the Latin-based derivative *millennium* for 1000 years is used in my translation but is not intended to deny that the 1000 years are a literal period of time. On the contrary, a careful analysis of Dan 9:24-27 would demonstrate that the tribulation is literally seven years long. Thus, half of the tribulation is 3½ years long, i.e., 3½ * 12 = 42 months long, or 3½ * 360 = 1260 days long. Correspondingly, John's repeated references to the second half of the tribulation as being 3½ years long (12:14) = 42 months long (11:2; 13:5) = 1260 days long (11:3; 12:6) should be taken literally. And if his repeated statements concerning the duration of the tribulation are taken literally, it would be reasonable to take his repeated statements concerning the duration of the millennium literally. Of course, if this is done, the amillennial position is ruled out.

[78] Boettner, *Millennium*, 47,150,202.

[79] Craig A. Blaising, Kenneth L. Gentry, Robert B. Strimple, *Three Views on the Millennium and Beyond*, eds. Darrell L. Bock and Stanley N. Gundry (Grand Rapids: Zondervan, 1999) 70-71.

[80] Ibid., 73.

[81] Ibid., 57. For a concise reference to their discussion see pp. 35-38; 57-59; 167-172; 189-191.

[82] Anthony A. Hoekema, *The Bible and the Future* (Grand Rapids: Eerdmans Publishing Company, 1979). There are some rather obvious weaknesses in Hoekema's arguments. (1) Hoekema said that Rev 20:11-13 is something distinct from what is presented in 20:4-6. On the contrary, the account in 20:11-13 is **descriptive** rather than **distinctive**. Rev 20:6 describes what happens to those who experience the first resurrection in 20:4. Rev 20:11-13 describes what happens to those who experience the second resurrection (indicated in the Johannine footnote). This is evident from the fact that v. 6 is discussing what happens before and during the millennium, while 20:7-15 is discussing what happens after the millennium. (2) *Ezesan* unquestionably refers to physical resurrection in 2:8, where it affirms that Jesus was dead and came to life. But Hoekema's assertion that it does not refer to resurrection in 13:14 is very questionable. The text says that the beast who had the wound of the sword came to life. And the wound described in 13:14 was stated as appearing mortal or fatal in 13:3. It would seem probable that it was a mortal wound in appearance and in fact (in terms of phenomenal language). (3) Hoekema's appeal to other forms of the verb *ezesan* in Rev 7:2 and 15:7, as referring to spiritual life rather than physical life, are hardly conclusive. These references do not refer to men but to God. The counter given by Ladd in response to Jn 5:25-29 also would deal with these two examples in Revelation as well.

[83] Not only do the text and context of Rev 20:4-5 and Rev 20:12-13) specifically refer five times to them as being *dead* (*nekros*) and picture the reality of this death in various images, in v. 5 it informs us that some of them had been beheaded. This literal death points to a literal resurrection.

[84] Blaising, *Millennium*, 224.

[85] Gentry, *Millennium*, 50.

[86] Seiss, *Revelation*, 454-472. The paragraph in my text is a summarization of Seiss' arguments. He even goes so far as to state that "no saints are crowned till 'the resurrection of the just'" (p. 466), but in doing so he probably overstates his case since the twenty-four elders probably represent crowned overcomers of the church age (Rev 4:10). Yet even in this case, his argument is valid that no unresurrected believer is crowned since the elders received their resurrected bodies at the time of the rapture.

[87] Craig L. Blomberg, "Degrees of Reward in the Kingdom of Heaven?" JETS 35:2 (June 1992), 166-167.

[88] Craig L. Blomberg, *Matthew*, vol. 22, NAC, gen. ed. David S. Dockery (Nashville: Broadman Press, 1992), 101.

[89] Blomberg, "Degrees," 172. For his affirmation that one "must" have these works to receive heaven as a reward, see *Matthew*, 102.

[90] Blomberg, *Matthew*, NAC, 100.

[91] Since some question the use of the LXX in NT studies, it is necessary to point out that the LXX was the form of the OT most commonly used in the churches and cited in the NT. As Kaiser asks and surmises: "What text type does the NT prefer when citing the OT? The substantial majority of these quotes and allusions reflect the Septuagint (hereafter LXX)" (p. 4). Walter C. Kaiser, Jr., *The Uses of the Old Testament in the New* (Chicago: Moody Press, 1985). He then continues on the next page: "That the LXX was the principle Bible of the early church can hardly be refuted if one is to judge on the basis of the text form of the OT most frequently used throughout the entire NT in quotations. D.M. Turpie concluded that the NT writers departed from the LXX far less than from the Masoretic text."

Gleason Archer likewise remarks: "It [the LXX] was virtually the only form of the Old Testament in the hands of Jewish believers outside of Palestine, and it was certainly the only available form for Gentile converts to the Jewish or Christian faiths" (p. ix). Gleason L. Archer and Gregory Chirichigno, *Old Testament Quotations in the New Testament* (Chicago: Moody Press, 1983). He then continues on that same page by further explaining:

> "Had the New Testament authors quoted those promises in any other form than in the wording of the LXX, they would have engendered uncertainty and doubt in the minds of their readers, for as they checked their Old Testament, the readers would have noticed the discrepancies at once—and would have objected, 'But that isn't the way I read it in my Bible!...They really had little choice but to keep to the LXX in all of their quotations of the Old Testament."

As a case in point as to why it is necessary to mention this commonly recognized implementation of the LXX in the NT, Daniel Wallace tried to discredit a FG blog by Antonio da Rosa in which the latter had demonstrated that the *salvation of the soul* refers to temporal salvation in the LXX about 98% of the time. Antonio da Rosa, "Lordship Salvation's 'Notorious' Error : Lexical Study of 'Save Your Souls' (James 1:21)." Available at http://free-grace.blogspot.com/2006/12/lordship-salvations-notorious-error.html. Da Rosa also had done an analysis of this phrase in the NT and found that it refers to temporal salvation about 61% of the time. This computation along with the OT background gave him the basis for concluding that the phrase probably refers to temporal salvation in Jam 1:21. Da Rose responded to Wallace and defended his use of the LXX. See "Response to Frank Turk's 'big gun' Expert: Part 1." Available at http://free-grace.blogspot.com/2006/12/response-to-frank-turks-big-gun-expert.html. See also "The Free Grace Rendering and Interpretation of James 1:21 is the Most Probable." Available at http://free-grace.blogspot.com/2006/12/free-grace-rendering-and.html. Accessed on December 24, 2006. And more recently, "Response to Dr. Wallace's Objections: Apostolic Fathers Analyzed." Available at http://free-grace.blogspot.com/2007/01/response-to-dr-wallaces-objections.html. Accessed on February 2, 2007.

The present writer would agree that the LXX provides a powerful foundation for the temporal understanding of the salvation of the soul. In fact, he supplied Da Rosa with additional references from Koine Greek to this effect. Josephus, for example, refers to the salvation of the soul in terms of preserving one's life (Ant 18:358). Philo also uses the term temporally (Spe 1:222). Nevertheless, the present writer would be very inclined to see an eschatological expansion into the misthological sphere in the NT as to the significance of this temporal salvation. He thus would have no quarrel with the quote itself from the apostolic father who says, "Now I do not think I have given you any light counsel concerning self-control, which if anyone do he will not repent of it, but will save both himself and me who counseled him. For it is no light *reward* [*misthos*] to turn again a wandering and perishing soul that it may be saved" (2Clem 15:1). The salvation of the soul is by-and-large a rewards concept in the NT. It is not soteriological. If one can distinguish the difference between a free gift and an earned reward, then a statement such as the one made by the apostolic father above is indeed correct. Some LS advocates, such as Wallace, argue that FG is mistaken in saying that the phrase is not soteriological since the phrase may have an eschatological dimension. It should be pointed out, however, that this criticism is not logical. Just because the phrase may be eschatological does not mean that it must be soteriological. It may be misthological instead.

[92] See Walvoord on 19:8, *Revelation*, 272.

[93] See Huber, "Concept," 50.

[94] Walvoord, *Revelation*, 296. And as Scott remarks, "The reign of angels is nowhere taught in the Scriptures, but rather the contrary...(Heb. 2:5)," *Revelation*, 400.

[95] J. Dwight Pentecost, *Things to Come: A Study in Biblical Eschatology* (Grand Rapids: Zondervan Publishing House, 1958), 207-209,253-258,407-411.

[96] Johnson, *Revelation*, 474-475.

[97] William MacDonald, *Once in Christ: In Christ Forever* (West Port Colborne: Gospel Folio Press, 1997), 144.

[98] For soteriological examples of coming to Christ as being equivalent to believing in Christ, see Mt 11:28; Lk 6:47; 14:26; 18:16; Jn 5:40; 6:35,37,44-45, 64-65; 7:37-38; 10:41-42. The Johannine parallels are particularly clear as to this equivalence. See the contexts of those references.

[99] George Zeller, "The Theology of Zane Hodges and Joseph Dillow and the Grace Evangelical Society." Available at http://www.middletownbiblechurch.org/doctrine/theology.htm. Accessed on August 13, 2004.

[100] Constable, *Revelation*, 66. Unfortunately, Constable's statement that the Greek text clearly indicates that the twenty-four elders are the ones *having* the harps in Rev 5:8 does not appear as "clear" as he indicates. Nor for that matter would one be able to say that the Greek clearly limits the masculine participle for *saying* in 5:9 to the masculine elders. My reason for not pressing Constable's statement about the grammar more fully to my advantage is because in Rev 19:4 the reverse order occurs: twenty-four (masculine) elders followed by the (neuter) four living creatures. But the same masculine participle for *saying* is used of both groups. They are both evidently *saying, "Amen. Hallelujah!"* Therefore, I have not implemented this grammatical remark in defense of my interpretation other than to note Constable's inconsistency in making this observation. However, it might be pointed out that the order of masculine-followed-by-neuter also occurs in Mt 22:4, but this time it is followed by a neuter participle: "My oxen and my fattened livestock are all butchered." Apparently, trying to press this grammatical point either direction would be ill-advised.

[101] Mounce, *Revelation*, 149

[102] Pentecost, 430-431.

[103] Eddie Chumney, *Who is the Bride of Christ?* Revised edition (Hagerstown: Serenity Books, 2001), 253-255, 393.

[104] In Ex 19:6, the LXX affirms that God's people *will be* (*eimi* future tense) His holy nation if they obey Him (cp. Ex 23:22 in LXX). The LXX also affirms that they *are* (*eimi* present tense) His holy people (Dt 7:6; 14:2). In Dt 7:6, they are chosen *to be* (present infinitive of *eimi*) His *special treasure* (Heb. *segullah*, Gr. *periousios*). In Dt 14:2, they are chosen *to be* (aorist infinitive of *ginomai*) His *special treasure* (Heb. *segullah*, Gr. *periousios*). In Dt 26:18, they are now declared *to be* (aorist infinitive of *ginomai*) His *special treasure* (Heb. *segullah*, Gr. *periousios*), because of their promise to perform as He has directed (Dt 26:17). Being God's *special treasure* (*periousios*) is conditioned on the performance of His people in the OT.

Granted, the word Peter uses for *treasured possession* in 1Pet 2:9 is *peripoiesis* (rather than *periousios*). Still, this word choice reaches out to encompass Mal 3:17, where God's children who serve Him are His special treasure (Mal 3:18). Undoubtedly, Peter intends to draw upon this rich OT material with this combined phraseology. Nevertheless, two questions must be posed. First, is Peter referring to being God's special treasure presently or futuristically? His leaving out the copula allows his readers to insert both dimensions from the OT background. "You *are* (*to be*) a chosen generation, a royal priesthood, a holy nation, God's special treasure" (1Pet 2:9; TM)

Secondly, is Peter speaking exclusively misthologically? One might think so, strictly from the OT background cited above, but ruling out a soteriological dimension is difficult because Peter immediately proceeds to explain: "You once were not a people, but now you are the people of God; you had not received mercy, but now you have received mercy" (1Pet 2:10). Peter has just affirmed that they have been redeemed (1Pet 1:18) and born again (1Pet 1:23) and are to approach his exhortation as newborn babies (1Pet 2:2). Surely, in this NT context they are people of God because they are children of God by virtue of soteriological mercy and by means of spiritual birth. They would be expected to understand that they are God's special treasure, at least to some extent, simply because of their relationship with Him as their Father (1Pet 1:17). Nevertheless, they are warned that the full realization of being God's special treasure is yet future and is contingent upon their performance. If this dual perspective is correct, then the Petrine usage of *peripoiesis* parallels the Pauline usage. Soteriologically, all believers are God's special treasure (Eph 1:14). Nevertheless, they are exhorted misthologically to acquire salvation and glory as their special treasure (1Thess 5:9; 2Thess 2:14). A duality is seen. Sensing a soteric bedrock upon which to build the mistholic superstructure also accords with Paul's usage of *periousios*: "Who gave Himself for us, that He might redeem us [soterically] from every lawless deed and [through practical sanctification] purify for Himself a people for His own *special treasure*, zealous for good deeds" (Tit 2:14; TM). Misthologically qualifying as God's special treasure is conditioned on the redeemed believer's behavior.

Regarding being God's *own possession* in 1Pet 2:9, Walls believes that Peter combines the phraseology found in Ex 19:5; Is 43:21; and Mal 3:17 (TNTC, 104). Lenski points out that Peter is repeating Is 43:21 regarding their proclaiming God's praise. According to Raymer, Peter's reference to *chosen* (*eklektos*) *people* specifically echoes Is 43:20. Thus, from three different vantage points, Is 43:20-21 is considered a cross reference. Yet, to this point in the present discussion, this oft cited passage has not been factored into consideration as to what Peter means in 1Pet 2:9. The verb used in Is 43:21 is *peripoieo*. Peter uses the noun form, as does Malachi: Those who fear the Lord are His "treasured possession" (Mal 3:17; ESV). The verbal form accordingly would be understood as: "This people I have acquired as My treasured possession" (Is 40:21). What people? The people of Israel—God's people. However, in this context they are being anything but obedient and reverent to the Lord (Is 40:22-27)! Therefore, in contrast to the other OT passages cited above, they are God's treasured possession despite their performance, not because of it, in this passage from Isaiah.

The Hebrew verb used in Is 40:21 is *yatsar* (*formed*). This verse is almost universally translated as: "The people whom I *formed* for Myself." The same verb is used in the opening verse: "But now, thus says the Lord, your Creator, O Jacob, and He who *formed* you, O Israel, 'Do not fear, for I have redeemed you; I have called you by name; you are Mine!'" (Is 43:1) Is it an accident that Peter links being redeemed with being God's special treasure in the passage he cites? Hardly! "Thus says the Lord your Redeemer, the Holy One of Israel, 'For your sake I have sent to Babylon, and will bring them all down as fugitives" (Is 43:14). "I, even I, am the one who wipes out your transgressions for My own sake; and I will not remember your sins" (Is 43:25). In this context God repeatedly reminds the disobedient people of Israel how precious they are to Him: "I give Egypt as your ransom" (Is 43:4). "Since you are precious in My sight, since you are honored and I love you, I will give other men in your place and other peoples in exchange for your life" (Is 43:4). All God's sons and daughters are included in these sweeping promises (Is 43:6). "Everyone who is called by My name, and whom I have created for My glory, whom I have *formed* [*yatsar*], even whom I have made" (Is 43:7). Being God's special treasure is not conditioned on being His obedient child in this context; rather, all His redeemed children qualify. Given that Peter certainly includes this passage in the mix and that this passage clearly conditions being God's special treasure on simply being His redeemed child, one must conclude that Peter's OT allusions are not limited to the misthological arena but encompass the soteriological spectrum as well.

Illustration 373. 3D Duality

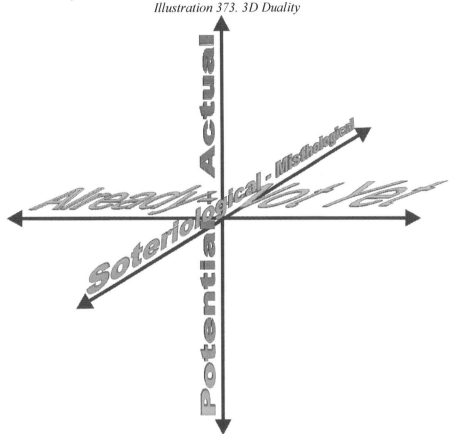

The multidimensional duality will be summarized using the following translation, "But you are (to be) a chosen people, a royal priesthood, a holy nation, God's special treasure" (1Pet 2:9; TM). They already are chosen soteriologically so that they might be chosen misthologically. They already are royal provisionally so that they might become royal misthologically. They already are holy so they are to be holy. They already are God's special treasure soteriologically, but they can become God's special treasure misthologically. The duality is multidimensional: (1) already versus not yet, (2) soteriological versus misthological, (3) potential versus actual. Because of this duality, my use of 1Pet 2:9 (within *Sealed and Secure*) in defense of unconditional security is justified. Yet misthological conditionality is also part of the scope as demonstrated here.

[105] Anthony B. Badger, "Tulip: A Free Grace Perspective, Part 3: Limited Atonement," *JOTGES* 17:32 (Spring 2004): 42.

[106] Believers are sinful in terms of their experience, when that experience is viewed in terms of what they do in the flesh. Contrastively, according to Johannine *anamartetology* (doctrine of sinlessness, cf. Jn 8:7), all believers are: judicially, positionally, ontologically, eschatologically, and relationally sinless. And those believers who walk in the

light are familially sinless. The fact that believers are both sinless and sinful parallels the Johannine teaching that believers are both overcomers and subcomers.

[107] Corner combines Lk 9:62 with Rev 22:3 to conclude that being unfit for (service in) the kingdom of God means to be unworthy to enter the kingdom since all "those who do enter God's kingdom will serve Him there." Daniel D. Corner, *The Myth of Eternal Security*, third edition (Washington, PA: Evangelical Outreach, 2005), 70. This combination of experiential and spatial dynamics is interesting but misplaced. Actually, such an argument regarding Rev 22:3 is better suited for misthopology rather than for kingdom exclusion since this text is talking about the city rather than the kingdom. The only servants noted in the city will be those who serve God; they also will rule with Him (Rev 22:5). Those servants cast into the outer darkness will be cast out of the city. They no longer will have opportunity to serve God, certainly not in the city, probably not in the kingdom. They will be excluded from service to God. (Perhaps they can serve animals in the kingdom instead.) As to the former text, experiential exclusion from kingdom rulership is the more reasonable inference. As in 2Thess 1:5, the objective is to be worthy of kingdom rulership by means of earthly service.

[108] Lang, *Revelation*, p. 335. G. H. Lang, *Firstborn Sons, Their Rights & Risks: An Inquiry as to the Privileges and Perils of the Members of the Church of God* (London: Samuel Roberts Publishers, 1936; reprint, Miami Springs: Schoettle Publishing Co., 1984), 72ff.

[109] John M. Sweigart, "Romans 6:23: A Pothole in the Romans Road," 3. Available at http://www.inthe beginning.org/kingdom/sweigart/pothole.pdf. Accessed on 11 November, 2005.

[110] Walvoord, *Revelation*, 303.

[111] Zeller, *Theology*.

[112] William E. Brown, "The New Testament Concept of the Believer's Inheritance" (Th.D. diss., Dallas Theological Seminary, 1984): 133. We are quoting from Morris, 1Corinthians, *TNTC*, 232.

[113] Ibid., 155.

[114] Ibid., 154.

[115] Ibid., 134, 154.

[116] Lenski, First Corinthians, 732-733.

[117] Zeller, *Theology*.

[118] J.D. Faust, *The Rod: Will God Spare It? An Exhaustive Study of Temporary Punishment for Unfaithful Christians at the Judgment Seat and During the Millennial Kingdom* (Hayesville: Schoettle Publishing Co., 2002), 250-262.

[119] In Forlines' assessment, infants are not innocent, cannot believe, are born with a depraved sin nature, and are racially guilty. I concur. But he further believes that Christ's death automatically took care of their racial guilt, as well as that of the rest of humanity, by virtue of His identification with humanity in His crucifixion, but personal guilt requires personal identification with Christ. Although infants cannot exercise the faith necessary for this identification, they are not considered personally responsible for their sins (i.e., their sin is not personally and legally imputed to them), until they reach the age of accountability, with its attendant realization that they have sinned against God (*Truth*, 208-215). While this view is attractive, it also seems to be defective in that infants apparently still enter heaven as innocents in his view, and personal identification with Christ and the corresponding imputation of Christ's righteousness is unnecessary. For this reason, I would prefer the viewpoint which believes that infants are given provisional entrance into heaven until such time as they come to personal identification with Christ through explicit faith. For other various views, see Radmacher, *Salvation*, 229-236. He would criticize this view because it entertains "a neutral state after death, before one's final destiny" is settled (p. 233). In response, I would ask, "If they can have a provisional state on earth, then why not in heaven?"

[120] Compare and contrast this position with Dillow, 79, 175.

[121] Regarding Is 65:20, Baughman comments:

> The rebellious are 'destroyed from among the people," perhaps at the end of each hundred years during the millennium. If this is the case, the rebels mentioned in Revelation 20:7-8 are those born during the last one hundred years of Christ reign on earth.
>
> The Jews today practice a ritual called Bar Mitzvah on the first Sabbath after a boy's thirteenth birthday....In the millennium, grace may be reached until the age of one hundred before judgment is exercised (p. 225).

An age of accountability that varies with the dispensation is certainly reasonable, if that is what Baughman means to suggest. However, even if the age of accountability is extended to age one hundred, this would not necessarily prove that all those who died as rebels were unregenerate. Capital punishment would be applicable to believers also if they rebel. In contradiction to these rebels who are killed, Eze 20:37 merely poses that rebellious Jews who are alive at the beginning of the millennium will not be allowed to enter the Promised Land. If, contrary to popular opinion, any regenerate Jews are in that number, then they would be candidates for the outer darkness. As to the rebels deceived by

Satan at the end of the millennium, what is to prevent one from thinking that some of those led astray are believers? If so, they will be devoured with fire from heaven. They, along with rest of the dead, will be raised afterward. Like other regenerate rebels killed every hundred years, they will be sentenced to the outer darkness.

[122] A complete discussion of the age of accountability necessarily would entail consideration of eschatological and embryonal implications. Therefore, my question for those who deny the *age of accountability* (AA) and prefer only accountability is: "Does this accountability begin at conception, or at birth, or later?" Since the assumption herein is that life begins at conception, it will be assumed that a denial of AA results in *gestational accountability* (GA), that is, accountability at the point of conception. Those who deny AA must, by logical necessity, believe that a person is morally accountable the moment that person comes into existence. Others who reject AA and who think that life begins at birth would be forced to affirm accountability at birth, that is, *birth accountability* (BA).

Assuming GA, what happens to pregnant believers when the Lord returns to set up His kingdom? Does He perform mass abortions so that He can throw their unborn children into hell? At the beginning of the millennium, abortions will have to be performed. There are two basic options. God will either have to take the unborn of unbelievers and provisionally allow them into the kingdom as infants, or He will have to take the unborn of believers and throw them into hell. AA can affirm the former; GA must affirm the latter.

Surely there will be pregnant women who are alive when the Lord returns who have taken the mark of the beast. Although the life of the mother cannot be saved, will the Lord perform an abortion as a rescue operation to save the life of the child, or will He cast their unborn children into hell also? I prefer the former point of view. Unfortunately, it would appear that many of these children will grow up resenting the fact that their mothers were sent to hell. Their resentment may give birth to the rebellion that occurs at the end of the millennium.

Since from an AA perspective I affirm that the unborn of unbelievers will be allowed provisionally into the kingdom, I certainly will conclude that the unborn of believers will be allowed provisionally into the kingdom as well. By logical extension, the same would be true of newborns, and by further extension, the same would be true of those who have not reached the AA. They will be allowed provisionally into the millennial kingdom then, just as those who die before the AA are allowed provisionally into heaven now. When they reach their *age of ability*, which varies for each person, they can believe. Since the *age of ability* naturally precedes the *age of accountability* (by a number of years), it would not be necessary for those provisionally allowed into the kingdom to believe immediately when they reach their subjective age of ability as long as they believe before they reach the objective age of accountability. Since the one naturally precedes the other, I will use numbers to further denote the logical and temporal order: The subjective *age of ability* (AA1) is followed by the objective *age of accountability* (AA2).

To use my children as object lessons, if AA1 for Jeremy was age 7, this would have been the age where his cognitive development was sufficient for him to believe the gospel. If AA1 for Jonathan was age 6, then this would have been the age where his cognitive development was sufficient for him to believe the gospel. But for the sake of example, if AA2 is age 20 for everyone (at least in the author's present time and culture), then my children had a gap of 13 to 14 years respectively before they would be accountable and sent to hell for dying in a state of unbelief. Since I believe that the age of ability precedes the age of accountability by a number of years, I was under no compulsion to try to make my children make a decision for Christ at as early an age as possible. Quite the opposite, my preference was to allow them to come to the point of persuasion in as an unperceptive manner as possible. My hope was that they would never know a point in their lives where they did not believe in Christ for eternal life so that their assurance would be tied to their persuasion rather than to a decision.

To be sure, there are other possibilities. Some would regard AA2 to be age 12 or 13. This is quite possible. In fact, AA2 might vary from one time period and culture to another. For example, suppose that during the tribulation some older teenagers will take the mark of the beast. Such teens will have nullified their opportunity to believe, so an AA2 of age 20 would not be applicable to them. God simply may drop AA2 to age 12 for everyone during that time period. Although it is unlikely that children will be required to take the mark of the beast, it is conceivable that older teens may be so required. Since God is aware of what will be the minimum age at which the mark will be applicable, He could set AA2 below this age. He might also lower AA2 during this time since the gospel will be proclaimed throughout the whole earth, thus making it readily assessable to people at a younger age. Some may wish to extend this argument to say that there can be a personalization even of AA2 so that if a teenager is murderously rebellious or rejects the gospel repeatedly, God might drop AA2 in individual cases in the present time period. Just as it is possible to reach an unpardonable state before death, so it is possible to reach an unpardonable state before AA2. Then again, God providentially may arrange things so that the mark will only be given to adults. Or again, God providentially (and mercifully) may kill youths who would be forced to take the mark of the beast before they actually do so. There are numerous possibilities open up to advocates of the age of accountability, especially for those who affirm AA2.

Others drop AA2 all the way down to AA1 so as to make AA1 = AA2. From their perspective, there is no grace period between the two. As soon as children come to a saving understanding, they must come to saving faith. The present author, of course, does not believe this to be correct. Otherwise, he would have worried about whether his children had come to a saving persuasion and would have wanted (pressured?) them to articulate it just as soon as possible. Others do not believe that AA2 exists. They would be under the same pressure.

Some would suggest that those who die before AA2 are allowed into something other than heaven at present and will be resurrected to live in the millennial kingdom and will have opportunity to come to explicit faith there. I am in agreement that explicit faith is necessary for regeneration but would point out that those taking this latter perspective still are allowing provisional entrance into the kingdom. So why not do the same for entrance into heaven?

However, those who deny AA cannot appeal to mystery in an attempt to avoid the logical outcome of their theology. If there is no AA, then there is no room for mystery. If AA and its attendant provisional entrance are denied, then the logical conclusion is that God will take the unborn and newborn and throw them into fires of hell at the beginning of the millennium. I object. Children are born to God and provisionally belong to God: "Moreover, you took **your** sons and daughters whom you had **borne to Me**, and you sacrificed them to idols to be devoured. Were your harlotries so small a matter? You slaughtered **My** children, and offered them up to idols by causing them to pass through the fire" (Eze 16:20-21). God objects. The heathen gods, not the Lord God, causes children to be thrown into fire. Children may not always be under God's temporal protection or covenantal protection, but they are universally under His provisional protection.

If there is no AA or provisional entrance into the kingdom, then one must logically deduce that God will take even the unborn and newborns of believers and throw them into hell. But if that were the case, why is God so upset with the Israelites supposedly following His example by throwing His children into fire? The implication is that God does not throw His children into fire, so the Israelites were not to throw their children into fire either. God objects to throwing children into fire. He expects His people to see the theological implications of what they are doing. We have no business throwing God's children into fire with our theology. The children born to us are born to God. They are God's children in the provisional sense of the word. God's children are not to be thrown into the fire.

[123] Wilkin, *Sure*, 92, n. 5.

[124] Idem, *Ten*, 164.

[125] Lang, *Revelation*, 361.

[126] Faust, *Rod*, 216.

[127] One ultraistic possibility for KJVO advocates is to posit three books of life: physical, misthological, and soteriological. The misthological Book of Life may is considered by some to be the book of millennial life and by others the book of soul life. In the case of the latter, the books accordingly would be labeled the books of physical, soulical, spiritual life and pertain respectively to the salvation of the body, soul, and spirit. Another possibility would be to assume multiple entries in one Book of Life. For example, it could be argued that just as the tree of life in Rev 22:19 has fruit that is limited to the overcomer in the city but leaves that are available to those outside the city, so the Book of Life might have double entries: one for those who (will) have eternal life as a gift and another for those who still are potentially qualified to inherit eternal life. The latter entry could be erased (Rev 3:5). Rather than suggest multiple books or multiple entries in one book, the present writer, believes the singular book (with exclusively soteriological entries) is being used in two senses in Revelation: soteriologically and misthologically (the latter litotetically).

[128] Robert N. Wilkin, "Are Believers Worthy of Entering the Kingdom? Luke 20:35," *GIF* (June 1989). Wilkin originally had accepted this misthological view for Phi 3:11 and Heb 11:35. Also see Robert N. Wilkin, "Has This Passage Ever Bothered You? Philippians 3:11; Is Our Resurrection Certain?" *GIF* (January 1988). Although Wilkin subsequently abandoned this view concerning Phil 3:11, he still acknowledges that the out-resurrection is earned and that the upward call in Phil 3:14 is still dealing with rewards, as is Heb 11:35. See Robert N. Wilkin, "Raised To Run - Philippians 3:11," *GIF* (August 1991).

[129] For a discussion of the out-resurrection from the misthological perspective adopted herein, see Dillow, *Reign*, 559-560. For an extended discussion of Phil 3:11 from this perspective see R. E. Neighbour, *If By Any Means....* (Elyria, Ohio: Gems of Gold, 1935; reprint, Miami Springs: Schoettle Publishing Co., 1985), 40-62. He perceptively concludes, "We cannot accept this [partial rapture]...Paul meant that *out of the saints who partake of the resurrection out of the dead, there will be some who will attain to a special 'placing;' this placing he called, the 'OUT-RESURRECTION out of the dead"* (pp. 57-58; emphasis his). Also see ch. 8 in Kenneth F. Dodson, *The Prize of the Up-Calling* (Baker Book House, 1969; reprint, Miami Springs: Schoettle Publishing Co., 1989), 111-120.

[130] Positive human merit in BDAG can be found in the following:

- *Agathopoiia*—*doing what is right* in 1Pet 4:19 is used of "persons of exceptional merit."
- *Agathos* (2.a.α)—*good* in Mt 12:35; 22:20; Lk 18:18; Tit 2:5, etc, is used of those who meet "**a high standard of worth and merit.**"
- *Axios* (see *kosmos* 6.a)—*worthy* (in Heb 11:38) is used of "persons of exceptional merit."
- *Amemptos*—*blameless* (in Phil 2:15, etc.) is used of "persons of exceptional merit."
- *Antilambano* (2)—*devoted to kindness* (in 1Tim 6:2) "suggests persons of exceptional merit."
- *Arete* (1)—*excellence of character* (in Phil 4:8; 2Pet 1:5) is used of "recognition of distinguished merit."
- *Exoutheneo* (1)—*to regard as worthless or without merit.* In 1Cor 6:11 Paul tells believers not to regard their brother in this manner.
- *Ergon* (1.a)—*work* is "frequently used to describe people of exceptional merit."

- *Martureo* (2.b)—*reputation/approval* (in connection with Acts 6:3) is used "of OT worthies *people of attested merit*" and that Abraham's "merit was gloriously attested." Compare Heb 11:2,4,39.
- *Oida* (6)—*respect, honor* (in 1Thess 5:12) means "to recognize merit."
- *Proistemi* (2)—*to give aid* (in Tit 3:8,14) gives "as indication of exceptional merit."
- *Stephanos* (3)—*prize, reward* (in 1Cor 9:25) provides "the imagery of the wreath [that] becomes less and less distinct, yet without loss of its primary significance as a symbol of exceptional merit."
- *Timios* (2)—*respected* (in Acts 5:34) indicates "**high status that merits esteem.**"

[131] Robert N. Wilkin, "Will You Be Counted Worthy of the Kingdom? 2 Thessalonians 1:5," *GIF* (May 1999).

[132] Robert N. Wilkin, *Confident In Christ: Living By Faith Really Works* (Irving: Grace Evangelical Society, 1999), 76.

[133] Faust, *Rod*, 195.

[134] Dillow, 373-379.

[135] James M. Ventilato, "A Scriptural Refutation of The Teachings of Zane Hodges, Joseph Dillow and the Grace Evangelical Society, with Respect to the Future Inheritance, Glory, and Destiny of the Church—Christ's Beloved Body & Bride," section 3, (19). Available at http://www.middletownbiblechurch.org/doctrine/hodgesjv.htm. Accessed on August 12, 2004. To interact with Ventilato's discussion, let it be assumed that he means that such expressions are unconditional for the believer. For example, when one talks about unconditional eternal security versus conditional eternal security, one is not saying that eternal security is unconditional in every sense of the word, only that such security is no longer conditional to one who has met the singular condition of punctiliar faith in Christ. In other words, believers are secure because they already have met the punctiliar condition when they believed. It will likewise be assumed that Ventilato means that all believers are the ones who are unconditional heirs and co-heirs.

[136] Ventilato, "Bride," Section 9, (9), (H).

[137] Ibid., Section 3, (9), (A).

[138] Ibid., Section 3, (19).

[139] Wilkin provides a personal example that well illustrates the difference between active and passive inheritance. Robert N. Wilkin, *The Ten Most Misunderstood Words in the Bible* (USA: Grace Evangelical Society, 2012), 196.

[140] The soteriological significance of the expression *sons of God* pertaining to eternal security is very strong when contrasted to tribulational wrath or soteriological slavery. Peter's describing being **born again** as being accomplished with **indestructible** seed in 1Pet 1:23 indicates that the life imparted is indestructible. It is eternally secure. Paul provides a link between becoming a son and receiving the Spirit in Gal 4:6. Sonship in this dimension would suggest sonship by birth. In birth, God imparts His life to us. This life is denoted as eternal life. Just as parents have imparted their genetic code to their children in giving them life, so God has imparted His type of life as well. Sonship, as an expression of the life that He has imparted to us as believers, is eternal. This impartation has implications as to both quality and quantity. It is eternal in quantity and moral in quality. Paul describes us as sons of light (1Thess 5:5). However, the context shows that sons of light are capable of living like sons of night, but they will not suffer the same wrath that the sons of night will suffer (1Thess 5:6-10). Again, such sonship does not guarantee daily performance, nor is it conditioned on daily performance. Quite to the contrary, such sons are promised that they will **not suffer wrath** even if their daily performance is of the night. Moral imperfection does not nullify static retention of regeneration.

Arminians object to basing eternal security on the sonship of a believer because in some passages sonship is conditional and because (in their assessment) affirmations of eternal security derived from this relation assume more than what was intended by this illustration. In response, it may be demonstrated that sonship has components that are both static and dynamic. One may squarely face the Arminian challenge: *Does Paul actually intend to affirm the believer's sonship despite severe moral and theological failure on the part of the believer?* and answer this question with an emphatic *Yes!*

Static soteriological sonship is permanent. True, there are passages in which sonship may be lost. Certainly, such passages exist and attest to the dynamic component of sonship. But such passages tend to contrast sonship with childhood. The static dimension is confirmed by the status as child, while the dynamic status is denoted by the description of potential sonship. At the same time, two passages use the word *son* itself to affirm its static permanence (1Thess 5:5; Col 3:26).

Paul *states*: "**You are all sons** of light and sons of the day" (1Thess 5:5). He then proceeds to *urge* these sons of light to live as sons of light, to be morally awake. He also *assures* them that they will be spared from God's wrath and live with Jesus even if they are morally asleep. This is an affirmation that they are and remain God's sons temporally and eternally even if they fail to demonstrate this reality dynamically. Static sonship provides the basis for dynamic sonship, but static sonship does not guarantee its dynamic expression, nor does dynamic failure dissolve the static relationship. In other words, the relationship denoted by sonship in this passage is permanent.

Further, it is proper to stress that Paul's affirmation of sonship is to **all** these believers, even the ones who are morally asleep. The same truth is stated again by Paul: "For **you are all sons** of God through faith in Christ Jesus" (Gal 3:26). Paul again applies this affirmation to the entire readership. This is astonishing! These believers were apostates (Gal 1:6-9; 3:1; 4:21; 5:4,7). They are deserting Christ for a false gospel (Gal 1:6-9). Yet Paul assures them that they are still indeed God's sons.

- You **are** all sons of God. (Gal 3:26)
- You **have been** severed from Christ. (Gal 5:4)
- You **have fallen** from grace. (Gal 5:4)

They all remain God's sons even though they have been severed from Christ and fallen from grace. Theological defection does not nullify static sonship. Conclusion, Paul does indeed intend to affirm the eternal security of the believer's relationship with God with the word *son* in these passages.

The Arminian response that Paul did not really mean to apply this affirmation to the apostates in the church is not persuasive. Paul is upset with the membership at large because of their apostasy. The point made herein in defense of eternal security does not require that every single individual in the church be guilty of apostasy. It would suffice to note the church in general had committed apostasy. Paul is exasperated with the church at large and says, "**You foolish Galatians**, who has bewitched you" (Gal 3:1). One example of a believer who remains a *son of God* in spite of his or her apostasy would suffice to prove that apostasy does not nullify sonship. Here, we find a whole church full of them.

The Arminian rebuttal that they only remain sons of God through **ongoing** faith in Christ does not do justice to the context. True, the rest of Gal 3:26 says, "For you are all sons of God through faith in Christ Jesus." But the full significance of this qualifier is not that it takes continuous faith to remain a *son of God* but that a previous faith had ongoing results. They are not sons of God because of their current faith. Paul demonstrates that their current faith is soteriologically defective (Gal 1:6-9; Gal 5:4). Rather, they are *sons of God* because of the faith they had exercised earlier. Their past faith has made them sons of God in the present. They have been permanently made *sons of God* because of their past faith which they had now abandoned. Paul still affirms that they are *sons of God* although they have abandoned their original faith. The Arminian contention that one must continue in faith in order to remain a *son of God* in this soteriological sense must be rejected. Apostasy does not nullify eternal security for the Galatians.

Paul stresses the ongoing reality of their past conversion. "For you **are** all sons of God through faith in Christ Jesus. For all of you who **were** baptized into Christ **have** clothed yourselves with Christ" (Gal 3:26-27). Through faith in Christ, they were baptized into Christ by the Spirit at regeneration. This past event has a present result. They are clothed with Christ and are *sons of God*. Being clothed with Christ is not dependent on the present performance. Earlier in this chapter, Paul affirmed that they were clothed with the new self. Then he exhorted them to cloth themselves with this self in terms of their performance. He urges them to be what they are. They have been clothed with a new self in Christ so act like it. All three verses use the verb *clothe* (*enduo*). Regardless of their current moral and theological failures, they are still sons of God and clothed with Christ soteriologically and ontologically. Thus, one may conclude: once a regenerate son of God always a regenerate son of God. In that sense, the OSAS statement is true: once a son always a son (OSAS).

[141] Dillow, 346, 368-369, 472. For an extended discussion of dual sonship, see 368-382.

[142] John A. Witmer, *Romans*, BKC (Wheaton: Victor Books, 1984), 462.

[143] Daniel B. Wallace, *Greek Grammar Beyond the Basics: An Exegetical Syntax of the New Testament* (Grand Rapids: Zondervan Publishing House, 1996), 690, n.12.

[144] Ibid., 692.

[145] Robert N. Wilkin, "*What is the Gospel? A Theological Debate with Dr. Darrell Bock and Dr. Bob Wilkin.*" Available at http://64.233.167.104/search?q=cache:tmkld6JGZ9EJ:www.faithalone.org/resources/debate.pdf+daisy+site: faithalone.org&hl=en. Accessed on September 30, 2004.

[146] GES News, vol. 4, num. 8 (August1989): 3. Used by permission.

[147] Biblical synonymity in general between the mind and heart is found in such passages as Ps 26:2; 73:21; Jer 17:10 (NKJ); Acts 2:46; Heb 8:10. However, more importantly, being *slow of heart to believe* (Lk 24:25) is contextually antonymous to having one's *mind opened to understand* (Lk 24:45). Likewise, the *full assurance* (*plerophoria*) is used with both *faith* and *understanding*: *full assurance* **of faith** (Heb 10:22); *full assurance* **of understanding** (Col 2:2). Understanding is a function of the intellect, and this corresponding intellectual faith is said to result "in a true knowledge of God's mystery, that is, Christ Himself." Moreover, Christians are urged to be fully persuaded/convinced (*plerophoreo*) in their minds (Rom 14:5). This full persuasion is used as a synonym for (mature) faith in Rom 4:21. In fact, it is translated as *faith* by the KJV in Lk 1:1. Likewise, the problem with unbelief is not that belief takes place in the head while unbelief occurs in the heart; the mind and heart both experience unbelief (Eph 4:17-18). After all, coming to faith is the result of changing one's mind. Faith is a mental persuasion.

To be sure, some passages of Scripture also describe faith as taking place in one's heart (Mk 11:23; 16:14; Lk 8:12; 24:45; Rom 10:9-10). However, in the latter passage, the contrast is between what happens internally in one's heart as opposed to what happens externally with one's mouth. There is no contrast in Scripture between the heart and head belief. In fact, those making this false distinction frequently do so in order to assert that there is necessarily a difference between understanding and believing. But in the Matthean parallel to the Lukan reference above, not believing is synoptically parallel to not understanding (Mt 13:19; Lk 8:12). Furthermore, Luke contextually equates not believing with not understanding (Lk 8:10). Matthew adds that they do not *understand with their heart* (Mt 13:15), but this is not contrasted with understanding in one's head! It is equated with not believing in one's heart. Saving faith is a function of one's understanding. Those who trying to shoot intellectual faith in the head are shot in the heart by their own compatriots who despise emotional faith. So what is the proper recourse? Rule out both the heart and the head as the locus of faith? No. Rather, it is to understand that an emotional experience does not constitute faith and that saving faith is more than just understanding that Christ offers eternal life to those who believe in Him. Saving faith is understanding that one is personally saved because he or she has believed in Christ alone for eternal life, whether that function is ascribed to the heart or head is not important.

[148] Faust, *Rod*, 24.

[149] See also R. T. Kendall, *When God Says, "Well Done!"* (Ross-shire: Christian Focus Publications, 1993), 202.

[150] In addition to the passages cited within the text, the following passages may also be consulted as references to misthological glory: Rom 2:5-10; 1Thess 2:12; 2Thess 2:14; 2Tim 2:10; 1Pet 1:7; 5:4,10. Likewise, Tit 3:7 should be added to the list of passages cited within the text as dealing with misthological hope. Admittedly, Dillow (p. 86) is correct in that certain passages teach a soteriological heirship that is unconditional for all believers (e.g., Rom 8:17a, Gal 3:29; 4:7). However, his including Tit 3:7 in this soteriological list is doubtful. Dillow earlier had acknowledged "every time eternal life is presented in Scripture as something to be obtained by work, it is always a **future** acquisition" (pp. 66-67), and he subsequently listed eleven passages presenting eternal life "to the believer as something to be earned or worked for" (p. 136). His discussion is excellent, but it would be best to add Tit 3:7 to this latter list of misthological passages since the eternal life promised in this verse is yet future and provides the contextual basis for the instruction in the next verse to believers "to be careful to engage in good deeds" (Tit 3:8). Paul is talking about inheriting eternal life as a futuristic hope (in contrast to having it as a present possession), and Paul implicitly indicates that it is obtained by good works. Of course, such contextual considerations are lost on Zeller who lumps proof texts together regardless of contexts. For example, concerning Tit 3:7 he claims: "Those 'justified by His grace' are 'heirs'" (Zeller, "Theology"). This is a considerable injustice to the text, much less the context. If the text actually said what Zeller pretends, then one would be forced to agree with Dillow concerning the verse. However, Zeller has oversimplified the verse to fit his own theology.

An interesting textual variant occurs in Tit 3:7 regarding the voice of *ginomai*. The CT reads *genethomen* whereas the MT reads *ginothomen*. The former is flagged by BibleWorks as being passive and the latter as middle deponent. This led to my inquiry at B-Greek concerning the potential difference and a subsequent discussion between the present writer and Carl Conrad, which is posted on the B-Greek site. See "GINOMAI: Middle or Passive in Tit 3:7?" Available at http://lists.ibiblio.org/pipermail/b-greek/2005-June/034893.html. Accessed on July 25, 2005.

Conrad has provided links to documents which summarize his previous discussions on B-Greek concerning the middle/passive use of *ginomai* in the NT. Carl W. Conrad, "New Observations on Voice in the Ancient Greek Verb: November 19, 2002." Available at http://www.ioa.com/~cwconrad/Docs/NewObsAncGrkVc.pdf. Accessed on July 25, 2005. "Active, Middle, and Passive: Understanding Ancient Greek Voice." Available at http://www.ioa.com/~cwconrad/Docs/UndAncGrkVc.pdf. Accessed on July 25, 2005.

The present writer expressed his preference for the middle form and asked, "**Does it mean to make yourself |an heir| through deliberate effort or to allow oneself to be made |an heir| through passive consent?**" Conrad responded that the meaning was not determined by form, since both forms have the same identical meaning. In fact, the passive form should be understood as having a middle meaning unless the context or syntax indicated otherwise. He explicitly rejected the notion, advanced by some, that the middle voice virtually had dropped out of use in the Greek NT except for a few frozen forms

His above documentation substantiates his claim. Concerning Tit 3:7, he concludes, "Although the middle voice doesn't require that the process of the verb be one in which the subject actively participates, I do think that in this instance the will and intention are clearly evident." The translations he suggests are: *in order to get to be heirs* or *in order to gain our inheritance*.

This translational approach is preferred herein. Nevertheless, for those who desire to be more traditional, the NKJ *become* as opposed to the NAS *be made* will do nicely. Believers were soteriologically justified by faith in order that they might **become** misthological heirs by works. These works are the condition for the realization of their inheritance. Believers are not passively made heirs but actively become heirs in this context. Believers actively, volitionally, and intentionally participate in the process of becoming heirs in v. 7 by doing the good works of v. 8. This is why they must be careful to perform the good works of the latter verse: to fulfill the hope of misthological heirship in the form of the future acquisition of eternal life.

Consequently, I would concur with Lavender (*Lavender*, 37-38), to a considerable degree, concerning the significance of the middle form of *ginomai* in texts such as Jn 1:12. They were passively born children of God because of something they did—receive Christ. They allowed themselves to be born of God. This might be regarded a permissive middle. But their cooperation should not be regarded as synergistic since the reception is through passive appropriation.

[151] Hodges makes the same point concerning 2Jn 1:8. "We can also learn from the apostle's concern that we need to have an active interest in those who succeed us in any given ministry, since the way in which *they* protect the work of

God can affect *our own* reward." Zane C. Hodges, *The Epistles of John: Walking in the Light of God's Love* (Irving: Grace Evangelical Society, 1999), 261.

[152] Quite probably, 1Pet 1:13 should be added to this list of passages regarding misthological hope. The misthological grace for which they hope in 1Pet 1:13 is the foretold misthological salvation of their souls (vv. 9-10). Also, Gal 5:5 might at least include the misthological dimension in its reference to *hope of righteousness*. The faith in Gal 5:5 is a loving, working faith (v. 6) that is necessary to inherit the kingdom (v. 21) as a result of being found misthologically righteous. This *hope of righteous* should be linked conceptually to the fruit of righteousness. Being filled with this fruit in Phil 1:11 is necessary to be found misthologically blameless (Phil 1:10). The reason for enduring discipline is because it produces the fruit of righteousness (Heb 12:11), which contextually is associated with realization of one's firstborn inheritance rights. Since Paul will refer to reaping eternal life in the next chapter, the OT background may come to mind: "The fruit of righteousness is a tree of life" (Prov 11:30).

Alternatively, in view of Gal 5:4, a soteriological reference to the final justification would be within the realm of possibility in Gal 5:5. By their linear soteriological seeking of final justification by works, the Galatians had fallen from grace. The only kind of performance that misthologically counts for anything, however, is that produced by a faith that realizes that final soteric justification is not by works (Gal 5:6).

[153] John M. Sweigart, "Philippians: Analytical Outline with Notes." (August 1997): 44. Available at http://www.inthebeginning.org/newtestament/philippians/philoutline.pdf. Accessed on August 12, 2004.

[154] Ibid., 40-46.

[155] The resurrection of Jesus (Acts 4:2; cf. 17:3) likewise is described as *the resurrection out from dead*, rather than as *the out-resurrection from the dead.*

[156] The preposition *ek* is spelled *ex* before a vowel. For the sake of those not familiar with this equivalence, these forms have been used interchangeably in the chart and discussion.

[157] R. C. H. Lenski, *The Interpretation of St. Paul's Epistles to the Galatians, to the Ephesians, and to the Philippians* (Minneapolis: Augsburg Publishing House, 1961), 844.

[158] Homer A. Jr. Kent, *Philippians*, vol. 11, EBC (Grand Rapids: Zondervan Publishing House, 1978), 146.

[159] Ibid., 142.

[160] Jac. J. Muller, *The Epistles of Paul to the Philippians and to Philemon*, NIC, ed. F. F. Bruce (Grand Rapids: Eerdmans Publishing Co., 1955), 118.

[161] The closest text that comes to using *ek nekron* as referring to a general resurrection is Acts 4:2, but not even it does so. The Sadducees did not believe in any type of resurrection. Therefore, for the disciples to proclaim that Jesus was raised *from* (*ek*) the dead (Acts 3:26) was a violation of the Sadducean dogma. Moreover, for the disciples to teach that believers in Jesus would also be raised *out from among the dead* further assaulted their Sadducean theology. The follow of logic was from particular to general. If a particular person, namely Jesus, could be raised *out from the dead*, then other particular people could be also. And if there could be a resurrection of particular people *out from among the dead*, this might be followed by a resurrection *of the dead*. Paul himself uses this type of approach in 1Cor 15:12-13. He contrasts the resurrection of Christ *out from the dead* with the resurrection in general. If Christ is raised *from* the dead, then one cannot deny that there is no resurrection of any of the dead. Conversely, if there is no resurrection *of* any of the dead, then there could be no resurrection of Christ *from the dead.*

Illustration 374. Resurrection of/from the Dead

[162] Dillow, 560. Gary T. Whipple, *Shock and Surprise Beyond the Rapture!* (Miami Springs: Schoettle Publishing Co., 1992), 43. Arlen L. Chitwood, *Judgment Seat of Christ* (Norman, Okla.: The Lamp Broadcast, 1986), 165-166. Abbreviated references to various editions of Chitwood's books will reference the year when more than one edition of that particular book is being cited within the present work.

[163] Neighbour, *Means,* 56-57; Dodson, 117.

[164] Faust, *Rod*, 191-193.

[165] Strimple, *Millennium*, 108.

[166] Blaising, *Millennium*, 151.

[167] Wilber B. Wallis, "The Problem of an Intermediate Kingdom in I Corinthians 15:20-28," JETS 18:4 (Fall 1975): 229-242.

[168] Zeller, "Theology."

[169] George Zeller, "Statement of Faith of the Middletown Bible Church." Available at http://www.middletown biblechurch.org/info/statemnt.htm. Accessed on 9 May, 2006.

[170] Wilkin, *John*, GNTC, 388-389.

[171] Zane C. Hodges, "Problem Passages In The Gospel Of John—Part 6: Those Who Have Done Good—John 5:28-29." *BibSac* 136:542 (April 1979): 161-162.

[172] See Dillow for similar comments on similar comparisons (pp. 73-75,477). Compare Hodges treatment ("Good") of absolutes in Jn 5:28-29.

[173] Hodges, *Eclipse*, 74-75. His endnote (p. 117) to this material adds:

> The Greek word *meros* (Rev. 20:6; Lk. 15:12) is used once in the Septuagint (Prov 17:2) to translate the Hebrew word *nahal* (inheritance, possession). The word *meris* is the one usually used in the Greek Old Testament to render *heleq* (portion), although *meros* stands for *heleq* once (Eccl 5:18). *Meris* is rare in the New Testament (5 times, all in Luke and Paul), while *meros* is common (about 40 times). It is highly probable that for the New Testament writers other than Luke and Paul *meros* has largely replaced *meris* in the sense of "portion" (= inheritance).

[174] Faust, *Rod*, 185-188.

[175] Dillow uses *partaker* as the distinctive label for the misthological position, and the last chapter of his book bears this label. See his entire discussion for further elaboration.

[176] Robert G. Gromacki, *Is Salvation Forever?* (Chicago: Moody Press, 1973), 168-169.

[177] For a scriptural evaluation of Simon, see Dillow, 327-328. Hodges, *Eclipse*, 87. James Inglis, "A Voice from the Past: Simon Magus," *JOTGES* 2:1 (Spring 1989): 45-54. R. T. Kendall, *Once Saved, Always Saved* (Chicago: Moody Press, 1983), 157.

[178] In Acts 26:18, the expression *have been sanctified by faith* is a perfect participle showing completed action and resulting state. It pertains to positional sanctification, not progressive sanctification.

[179] Kendall, *Saved*, 147-148.

[180] Zeller, "Theology."

[181] J.F. Strombeck, *Shall Never Perish* (Harvest House Publishers, Eugene: Oregon, 1982), 68.

[182] Kendall, *Saved*, 156.

[183] The misthological FG view initially held by the present author for 1Cor 5:5 was that it pictures the temporal destruction of the flesh, but (in agreement with Dillow) that it uses a result clause when referring to the soteriological salvation of the spirit (cp. 3:15), and (in contrast to Dillow) that 11:32 shows that being judged in this manner is necessary for salvation from soteriological condemnation. Such initial judgment was regarded as necessary proof of regeneration (Heb 12:8). See GNTC. But believers who reject this initial discipline will be disinherited misthologically. This preference has now been long abandoned in preference for the view articulated in the body of the text.

[184] Also see Robert Wilkin, "'The Day' is the Judgment Seat of Christ," *JOTGES* 20:39 (Autumn 2007), 5.

[185] Dillow, 321-323.

[186] The potential Arminian argument for 1Cor 5:5 is weak that insists that since the salvation of the spirit will occur soteriologically at that future moment in time, the individual cannot be saved soteriologically at this point in time. First, even if the individual were lost (when being submitted to this discipline) but did in fact come to Christ sometime subsequently in this life, the salvation Paul describes here still would not be experienced until the Day Of Christ—not the day the person comes to Christ. Consequently, this NOSAS approach, in which a believer loses his salvation and then regains it, does nothing to resolve the disagreement in time between the salvation one experiences on the day the individual comes to Christ versus the day that Christ comes for the individual. Second, Paul already had described this Bema salvation as yet future in 1Cor 3:15. In other words, just because this salvation is described as occurring in the future does not mean that the individual's spirit was not already saved (i.e., regenerate in the present). To the contrary, his spirit would not be saved soteriologically at the Bema—if it were not already saved soteriologically in the present (cp. 3:15). If the person were not already on the soteriological foundation in the present, then he would not find himself saved through fire at the future Bema.

Moreover, the Arminian may presume that Paul is saying that the person must yet come to Christ in order to experience salvation in the Day of Christ. But this is reading into the text something that is not there. The text actually states that what is necessary for this individual to be saved in the Day of Christ is that Satan destroys his flesh. This would be taken most naturally as a reference to a painful, premature death. Consequently, the person must already have come to Christ since only those who have come to Christ will be saved in the Day of Christ. Otherwise, one is left to imagine Satan leading this person to faith in Christ—a rather strange notion to say the least! Just as the person in 3:15 suffers the temporal loss of his soul but not the soteriological salvation of his spirit (which he already had because he was already on the soteriological foundation of Christ), so the individual in 5:5 suffers the loss of his flesh but not the salvation of his spirit (which he already had because he already has come to Christ for soteriological salvation). So why is the loss of his flesh necessary *in order to* experience the soteriological salvation of which he already is assured?

There are several options, one of which is to say that initial discipline is a necessary indicator that the individual is indeed a child of God (so 11:32, if that discipline is soteriological, which is the view held by GNTC and the view the present author previously held). Another option is to say that Paul is alluding to the truth he just enunciated in 3:15, which is to show that such temporal destruction now would have the same outcome as misthological destruction—only the person himself would be saved, that is, just his spirit would be saved. A more satisfactory explanation is to follow GNTC on 5:5, at least in enjoining a remedial destruction with a misthological salvation.

If *hina* is a **purpose** clause in 5:5, he will be saved because he was delivered over to Satan, not despite the fact he was handed over. The purpose (= *intended result*) of such discipline is to ensure the believer's soteriological salvation. This view is rejected in the discussion within the present text. However, the GNTC proposal is acceptable: The purpose (= *intended result*) of such discipline is to ensure the believer's misthological salvation. Notwithstanding this attractive GNTC understanding of 5:5, a **result** clause has been deemed more likely in the present treatment of 5:5. Dillow already has presented a good discussion of the arguments that could be advanced for both vantage points and stated his preference in favor of the result clause in 5:5 (see Dillow, 322-323). I will not repeat his argument here but only note my agreement. Also, the Bema result of *hina* in 5:5 perfectly matches the contrastive use of *de* in 3:15 (in showing a *guaranteed result*).

Should one also follow Dillow or Constable in rejecting soteriological condemnation in 11:32? Dillow believes that temporal condemnation for the unfaithful believer is in view (p. 301). Constable believes that premature death and misthological condemnation are entailed for such a believer (*1Corinthians*, 123). Following their lead in rejecting soteriological condemnation is necessary for the following considerations. If it is soteriological condemnation, then why is God's temporal discipline necessary in 11:32 to save us from hell? Is our response to this temporal discipline a factor in our salvation from hell? If so, the door is open to both Reformed LS and Reformed NOSAS. The Arminian also would argue that this is the intended goal rather than the assured result. If not, then a securitist might adopt a *soft disciple-oriented security* perspective. See SROS in *3D Unconditional Security*. Nevertheless, this securitist view is not the most intuitive option available for securitists.

Granted, condemnation can be soteriological (Mt 12:41-42; Mk 16:16; Lk 11:31-32; 8:34; Rom 8:3; Heb 11:7; 2Pet 2:6) or temporal (Mt 20:18; 27:3; Mk 10:33; 14:64; Jn 8:10-11; Heb 11:7; 2Pet 2:6). As such, the concept of condemnation may be applied to either the lost or the saved. A wordplay between *krino* and *katakrino* occurs in Rom 2:1, where the lost person may be self-condemned. In Rom 14:23, the saved person may also be self-condemned. In Rom 14:22, a wordplay occurs between the verbs *krino* and *katakrino*, which also picture a saved person as self-condemned. In Rom 5:16, a soteriological wordplay exists between the nouns: *krima* and *katakrima*. Even believers may be condemned (*katakrima*), if they do not walk according to the Spirit (Rom 8:1). *Krima* is applicable to believers in numerous texts: Mt 7:2; Rom 13:2; 1Cor 6:7; **11:29,34**; Gal 5:10; 1Tim 3:6; 5:12; Jam 3:1; 1Pet 4:17. Thus, when one encounters the wordplay in **11:32** between the verbs *krino* and *katakrino* (*krino* is for the purpose of preventing *katakrino*), one is lead to suspect that the condemnation is certainly applicable to believers.

In consideration of these factors, the present writer has found it preferable to modify his view on 11:32 so that it is understood as saying that (1) the world will participate soteriologically in God's condemnation and (2) the believers in Corinth, who were experiencing premature death as a result of God's temporal judgment (*krima/krino* in 11:29,34), would be subject to His severer misthological condemnation (*katakrino* in 11:32). In summary, those believers who do not respond rightly to the Lord's *krino* and *paideia* died prematurely and will be condemned misthologically to outer darkness. Unbelievers will participate in God's condemnation soteriologically; unfaithful believers will participate in it misthologically. A correlative relationship is entailed.

In view of the contingent nature of believer's salvation in 1Cor 15:2, Hunt (GNTC, 715) entertains the possibility of unfaithful believers jointly perishing temporally with the lost in 1Cor 1:18. Given my shared perspective with Hunt regarding 1Cor 15:2, I found his proposal of mutual perishing plausible. Yet I did not deem it probable—at least not initially. However, given the mutual condemnation of unbelievers and unfaithful believers in 11:32 (a view Hunt does not hold), his joint-perishing proposal in 1:18 becomes probable.

For those who are more technically inclined, I would like to address a potential problem with my proposed solution. The purpose of *dokimazo* in 11:28 and *diakrino* in 11:29,31 is to avoid the *krima* of 11:29,31. *Krima* resulted in sickness and premature death in 11:30. The purpose of *krino/paideuo* in 11:32 is that one not experience *katakrino* (11:32). But if premature death is a form of the *krino/paideuo* in 11:32, then how can it be said that *katakrino* is premature death or loss of rewards? In other words, it would appear that my approach leads to the conclusion that the purpose of premature death of *krino/paideuo* in 11:32 is to save believers from premature death or from loss of rewards. But neither alternative is acceptable herein.

At least three possibilities, however, still would render my overall approach plausible. One hypothesis could be that the temporal judgment *krino/paideuo* in 11:32 does not include premature death. God disciplines believers with weakness and sickness first (cp. 11:30) in hopes that they will repent before He finally culminates that punishment in premature death and misthological loss. If this approach is taken, then my view is equivalent to that of Constable regarding 11:32, although I still am disinclined to accept his conclusion concerning 5:5 (that this destruction is to save us from further loss of rewards).

Another alternative would be to take the *hina* of 11:32 as a result clause like I did in 5:5. The result of premature death in 5:5 is misthological loss (in that only the spirit rather than the soul is saved), and in 11:32 the result of premature death for the believer is misthological condemnation. Although this view is grammatically possible and certainly upholds my interpretation, my preference will be for the third theory below, since the result clause is rather rare and the immediate context opens up an extremely plausible position that also would be suitable for the corresponding text in Hebrews.

The third alternative that could be used to support the misthological view of condemnation for the believer in 11:32 is to recognize that Paul may be speaking about believers collectively in terms of groups rather than strictly as individuals. This understanding of the text is very attractive in view of the preceding chapter in which Paul had just described how God prematurely killed His own people in the OT (e.g., 1Cor 10:5,8-9). In the midst of that discussion, Paul says, "Now these things happened as examples for us, that we should not crave evil things, as they also craved" (1Cor 10:6; cp. v. 11). In other words, on those occasions God punished one group of His people with the premature death in order to dissuade another group of His people from following their example. Likewise, it could be said that God killed many of the believers in Corinth (11:30) so that the rest of the believers would be discouraged from following this sinful course of behavior. God punished some of His children with temporal judgment *krino/paideuo*, which included premature death in 11:32, so that the rest—(1) those who were weak and sickly but who had not yet died and (2) those who were being tempted to follow their sinful example but had not yet been struck down with sickness or premature death—would be spared from the misthological *katakrino* to which those believers who already had died prematurely would certainly be subject. In other words, it was God's goal that His temporal discipline (that already had sealed the misthological fate of some of His children in the outer darkness) would prevent the rest of His children from sharing the same fate. This latter alternative is the explanation preferred herein.

Unfaithful believers cannot share God's condemnation soteriologically *with the world*, but they can share it misthologically. God will judge both the lost and the saved on the basis of their works and jointly condemn the faithless and unfaithful as being unworthy of His kingdom. God will sentence the faithless to hell outside His kingdom and the unfaithful to the outer darkness inside His kingdom. The unfaithful will share the same condemnation but not the same sentence. This interpretation has a conceptual parallel in 1Tim 3:6. Believers who subcome to pride will fall into the same *condemnation* (*krima*) as the devil. They will be judged guilty of pride and suffer corresponding consequences but not in the same spatial location. See *Theory of Correlativity*, 911.

This approach also has the advantage of taking the related text in Heb 12:10 as showing the purpose or goal of God's discipline rather than the guaranteed result: "He disciplines us for our good, that we may share His holiness." As demonstrated in Heb 12:8, this chastisement does not infallibly accomplish its intended effect in that it may be resisted even to the point where the disobedient child is no longer subjected to corrective temporal discipline. I thus would agree with NOSAS that the **intended result** (= purpose) does not always accomplish its intended end. However, this must be understood in terms of the misthological (rather than soteriological) purpose of temporal chastisement. The misthological result is not guaranteed. OSAS is not impeded.

Thus, 1Cor 5:5 is a very strong verse in favor of OSAS rather than conditional security in that (assuming the failure of temporal discipline) the verse shows the **guaranteed result**. The soteriological result is guaranteed regardless of the outcome of the temporal discipline. In other words, the intended goal, and therefore the purpose, of the chastisement in 1Cor 11:32 and Heb 12:10 is that believers will respond positively to God's temporal discipline and thus have rewards. But 1Cor 5:5 is not merely describing the result in terms of the intended goal pending their positive response; rather, it depicts their actual result pending their negative response—a believer's spirit is still saved despite the loss of rewards.

Furthermore, since the believer's response to God's discipline determines his or her rewards, the individual's response is misthological and thus considered a work by God. Since soteriological salvation cannot be conditioned on works, soteriological salvation cannot be lost on the basis of one's response to God's chastisement. Otherwise, soteriological salvation would be salvation by works. The fact that it is a misthological result argues strongly in favor of OSAS.

Granted, 1Tim 1:20 uses this terminology of being delivered over to Satan for a remedial purpose. Nevertheless, in 1Cor 5:5 a different purpose is followed by a different result: (1) The intended purpose is the destruction of the believer's flesh (i.e., premature death and thus the temporal loss of his soul), and (2) the guaranteed result is the salvation of his spirit (and thus the misthological loss of his soul). That this result is guaranteed is deduced from several observations. One, it makes little sense to say that the person did not already have a regenerated spirit to which God already had imparted eternal life. Second, it would be exceedingly strange to take the premature killing of a wayward believer as a means of saving that believer from eternal damnation while that believer is living in a state of willful sin. Surely, salvation from such damnation would be the result rather than goal of implementing this punishment. The person's regenerate spirit will be saved despite his living in willful sin. Since the believer's spirit is saved regardless of his response, the result is unconditionally determined by God.

In conclusion, the believer's response to God's discipline determines whether God's discipline will achieve its *intended result*, which is conditioned on our positive response in 1Cor 11:32, 1Tim 1:20, and Heb 12:8-10. However, our response to God's discipline does not determine whether God's discipline will achieve its *guaranteed result*, which is not conditioned on our positive response in 1Cor 5:5. The salvation of the believer's spirit is guaranteed unconditionally despite his or her lack of positive response to God's discipline. A Marrowistic understanding of chastisement remains a very strong argument for eternal security. For further discussion of intended versus guaranteed results, see endnotes 466, 564. For a similar perspective on the mark of the beast, see endnote 1479.

[187] For an exposition at the popular level that considers the inheritance a reward, see Tony Evans, *The Kingdom Agenda: What a Way to Live!* (Nashville: Word Publishing, 1999), 140-158. For a more academic defense, see ch 13 of Michael Eaton, (*No Condemnation: A New Theology of Assurance* (Downers Grove: InterVarsity Press, 1995), 175-185. As to the opposing view, for a scholarly rejection of Hodges' position (according to which only faithful believers are overcomers and receive a special inheritance), see Brown, "Inheritance." Especially see his comments concerning the Johannine writings and his conclusion (pp. 199-226). Bing apparently agrees with Brown. See Charles C. Bing, *Lordship Salvation: A Biblical Evaluation and Response. Grace Life Edition* (Burleson: GraceLife Ministries, 1992), 145 n. 120, 149 n. 141. Although Bing rejects Lordship Salvation, he concurs with Brown concerning the identification of "inherit salvation" with soteriological possession of eternal life. Consequently, what is at stake is not necessarily correct soteriology but correct misthology, at least primarily. This is particularly true in Lopez's treatment in which he concedes to Brown concerning inheriting the kingdom of God but not to inheriting when used generically. Nevertheless, this weakened misthology results in a weakened defense against LS soteriology. René A. Lopez, "Do [Sic] The Vice List In 1 Corinthians 6:9-10 Describe Believers or Unbelievers?" *GES Conference CD* (2005).

[188] Brown, "Inheritance," 92-156.

[189] Ibid., 120-121,124,126.

[190] Zeller, "Theology."

[191] Wuest, in the NTET, translates the articular substantive (*hoi adikoi*) in 1Cor 6:1 as *those who are unrighteous* and the anarthrous substantive (*adikoi*) in 6:9 as *unrighteous individuals*. This is a commendable translation in that it alerts the English reader that the expression is different in these two verses and does not use an article on the second occasion. Unfortunately, many translations (but not all) simply render both verses as *the unrighteous*.

I have chosen Wuest's translation of *those who are unrighteous* for the anarthrous substantive in v. 9 and retained the rendering of *the righteous* for the articular substantive in v. 1. Certainly, if he can render the articular substantive in this manner, then rendering the anarthrous substantive in the same fashion should be worthy of consideration. Reserving this rendering for v. 9 gives the advantage of verbally showing the parallel with v. 9, which uses the verbal form. It is also true to Paul's articulation in Gal 5:21 to say that the verbal participation (*prasso*) in such behavior disqualifies believers from inheriting the kingdom. If it be objected that I have rendered the substantive as predicative by introducing the copulative *are*, then let it be pointed out that (1) I merely am following the precedent already set by Wuest, (2) I am on stronger contextual grounds than Wuest in doing so in v. 9 rather than v. 1 since Paul evidently uses the adjectival form in v. 9 to allude to the verbal form he just used in v. 8, (3) I am only making implicit what Paul made explicit in the Galatian parallel, (4) I am within bounds of Greek grammar in seeking to express the anarthrous substantive in a manner that denotes character in terms of behavior, and (5) anarthrous adjectives may be predicative. Lenski likewise states, "Since ἄδικος, as well as the entire list of sinners following, has no article, the quality is stressed: 'unrighteous people,' they **who are** such" (First Corinthians, 246, bold added).

Lopez (ibid., p. 4) assumes as his premise that *adikoi* is being used substantively in v. 9. Perhaps, but according to Wallace a substantival adjective normally will have an article to show that it is substantive (GGBB, 294). Paul has referred repeatedly to the categorical distinction between the saints and the unrighteous in the normal fashion in v. 1-2. Why does Paul abandon this normal usage in v. 9 if he wishes to be understood substantively? Even if v. 9 is a substantive, and thus functions as a noun, one would expect it to function as an anarthrous noun in showing quality rather than identify. Therefore, a reasonable expanded translation of *adikoi* in v. 9 would be: *those who are unrighteous in their character*.

[192] George Zeller, "Those Who Do Not Inherit The Kingdom....Are They Saved or Unsaved?" Available at http://www.middletownbiblechurch.org/doctrine/inherit.htm. Accessed on August 13, 2004. Ventilato, III, 23.

[193] Zeller, "Theology."

[194] Ibid.

[195] Dillow, 70-72.

[196] Lopez attempts to navigate a difficult course in taking the vice list passages, which discuss inheriting the kingdom of God, as dealing with soteriological issues (Gal 5:19-21, 1Cor 6:9-10; Eph 5:5). Yet, at the same time, Lopez maintains: "In other places, however, inheritance stresses only the reward concept (Acts 20:32; Col 3:24; Heb 6:12; 12:17)." Lopez recognizes that various writers from a variety of interpretive backgrounds connect v. 8 and v. 9:

Chitwood, Hodges, Dillow, Fee, and Lenski. Of course, this list could be expanded. Robertson (WPNT), for example, remarks in his comments on v. 9 that "the unrighteous (*adikoi*)" of v. 9 is used "to remind them of the verb *adikeô* just used" in v. 8.

Lopez, however, seeks to establish a categorical connection between v. 1 and v. 9 instead. The interpretation that Lopez prefers is *live like saints* as opposed to the *lose rewards view*. His dichotomization of these views into two separate interpretations is suspect in that they are not mutually exclusive. Paul is urging them to *be what you are* because otherwise *you will lose the reward of the inheritance.* Lopez would seek to remove the warning from the exhortation and simply make it *be what you are* because of *who you are.* While this approach is certainly Pauline, the misthological couplet is also, as even Lopez himself concedes concerning Col 3:24 and the related texts mentioned above. In undertaking to limit Paul's approach to psychology divorced of misthology, Lopez opens up his position to the same criticism expressed by the majority view of Hodges' minority view in regards to 1Thess 5:8, in which the majority view objected to Hodges' presentation since it was void of any warning. (See *Majority View*, 172). I strengthened Hodges' position in that discussion by offering a moderation that encompassed both exhortation and warning. The same fortification should be entrenched in the present Corinthian context, which is done easily in that Hodges and Dillow already have supplied the munitions. Despite his well-researched efforts otherwise, Lopez has not provided sufficient argumentation by which to dislodge the beachhead already entrenched by his FG counterparts for several reasons.

First, it seems rather unlikely that the anarthrous *hoti adikoi* would be equated categorically with the articular *ton aidikon.* Lopez's syntactical search is certainly of interest: "A *hoti* followed by a substantive nominative case never appears with an article out of the 113 occurrences…a *hoti* clause followed by an anarthrous substantive nominative appears as the normal expression of this Greek construction" ("Vice," 10). But is this correct? I would point out, in return, that *hoti* does appear to be followed by an articular substantive nominative in a number of places: *for the consecration* of the anointing oil (Lev 21:12); *for a multitude* (2Chron 30:18); *for the wicked* will perish (Ps 37:20); *for behold your enemies* (Ps 82:3; 91:10); *according to Your ordinances* (Ps 119:91); *because all things are vanity* (Ecc 2:17; 3:19); *that the Jews* (Ezra 4:12; Neh 3:34; Acts 23:20); f*or the wicked* surround the righteous (Hab 1:4); say *that my idol* has (Is 48:5); *for your waste and desolate places* (Is 49:19); *for the customs* (Jer 10:3); *for the ten* (Eze 45:14); *that these Galileans* (Lk 13:2); *that the goodness* of God (Rom 2:4); *that the older* will serve (Rom 9:12); *for the foolishness* of God is wiser (1Cor 1:25); *for the righteous man* will live by faith (Gal 3:11); *for the former things* have passed away (Rev 21:4). One might also compare the extra biblical text: *for what is pleasing* to God (Baruch 4:4). To use Lopez's own words for my counter observation, as seen from the examples just cited, there was nothing in the normal expression of this Greek construction to prevent Paul from using an articular form following *hoti* and thus to have linked it back with v. 1 had this been his intent.

More impressive and pertinent is the fact the Johannine soteriological vice list of Rev 22:15 is articular: "Outside are **the** dogs, and **the** sorcerers, and **the** immoral persons, and **the** murderers, and **the** idolaters, and all **the** people who love and practice lying" (TM). Those who are classified by the articular construction as following into these categories in the eternal state will burn in the Lake of Fire. If Paul's intent had been to classify those in 1Cor 6:9-10 as belonging to the same category as those described in v. 1, why did he abandon the articular construction to use one that readily could be understood as referring to behavior rather than classification? Why did he not use the same construction that John used and which he himself had just used in v.1? Presumably, if Paul actually had intended to provide a soteriological classification, then he would have implemented the article as John did in his vice list. The anarthrous nature of this Pauline vice list encompasses more than just the *hoti adikoi.* The entire remainder of the *neither-nor (oude…oude)* chain is not part of this construction, and yet it also bears witness to the anarthrous implications. Certainly, Paul would have been within bounds of contemporary usage to use *oude* followed by an article had he so desired (e.g., Ex 20:17; Dt 5:21; Ps 58:4; Dan 3:18; Jn 8:19; 9:3; Acts 2:31; 15:10; also see 1Esdras 4:21; Judith 7:4). In fact, earlier in this same epistle, Paul used the articular forms with *neither-nor (oude…oude)*: "So then *neither* **the** one who plants *nor* **the** one who waters is anything, but God who causes the growth" (1Cor 3:7). Here again we have articular classification. Yet Paul chooses to use anarthrous forms with his *neither-nor (oude…oude)* construction for the vice list in the next chapter. For these and other reasons, such as those below, I prefer to follow Dillow and others in understanding the anarthrous construction in 1Cor 6:9 as emphasizing their character and behavior rather than their soteriological classification or categorization.

The syntactical analysis, however, is not what causes my primary concern with Lopez's work. Rather, his endorsement of Brown's hermeneutical procedure is far more alarming. His first quote of Brown is: "Significantly, there are no degrees or levels of inheritance among the righteous. The inheritance of the wicked is also singularly described as a place of torment and destruction (2 Enoch 10:1-6)" (p. 13). From that point, Lopez will defer to Brown, in an excess of a dozen times, within the space of five pages in defense of this soteriological understanding. At the same time, Lopez refers to Enoch half a dozen times within the scope of that same discussion: 1En 5:7; 8:1-4; 40:9; 2En 9:1; 10:4-6; 34:1-2.

The latter two passages are of the greater significance and form the backbone of his argument that the NT writers adopted this vice list from Jewish literature to describe the characteristics of unbelievers: "2 Enoch 10:4-6 mentions a similar vice list of that in 1 Cor 6:9-10 and concludes that such will have their eternal inheritance with the wicked" (p.

17, n. 73). To be sure, Lopez sites other intertestamental literature as well, but my interest gravitates toward his Enochian appeals in that Enochian matter provides the major cross-reference for his argument. Further, I also provide my own chapter that focuses on the background of the outer darkness as found in Enoch. (See *Intertestamental Context of Outer Darkness*, 461.) Lopez has been overly attracted to Brown's thesis and the intertestamental literature in that Lopez has limited his understanding of inheriting the kingdom of God to the soteriological perception of Brown and the intertestamental period.

I counter: To adopt Enoch's soteriology is to reject NT soteriology. My discussion, particularly of 2 Enoch (p. 474), provides sufficient grounds for questioning the heart of Lopez's argument. He should have given more attention to Brown's admission: "Even if minimal the Apocrypha and Pseudepigrapha uses the concept of inherit in much the same way as in the OT (Sir 6:1; Jub 33:20; Jud 4:12; 8:22; 9:12; 13:5; Tob 4:12; 1 Macc 2:56; 6:24; 15:33; 2 Macc 2:17)" (p. 13, n. 52). Not a single Enochian passage is listed. Evidently, Lopez does not a have a single Enochian passage to fall back upon for his using the Enochian background to demonstrate a passive NT inheritance. This Pauline inheritance in 1Cor 6, like that of Enoch, is anything but passive. To the contrary, it is very proactive.

Perhaps the most glaring weakness in Lopez's treatment is his rejection of caution. He notes that "most interpreters think Paul warns his audience," but Lopez concludes that the passage merely presents a contrast between believers and unbelievers rather than a caution for believers not to live like unbelievers (p. 20, n. 89). Lopez sees this passage as an "exhortation instead of warning," lulling that "Paul exhorts the Corinthian believers instead of warning them" (pp. 19-20). Lopez concedes that Hodges "believes Paul warns believers of a possible lost of inheritance." To be sure, Lopez seeks to avert it with multiple claims: "This view impossible to harmonize with the strong contrast" (p. 20). "This exhortation does not involve a warning of a possible lost of salvation or rewards" (p. 22). Yet in doing so he subverts the nature of the admonition as is demonstrated by how Lopez handles Paul's exhortation: *Do not be deceived*. According to Lopez, this phrase is merely a rhetorical device. Paul urges: "Do not be deceived: 'Bad company corrupts good morals'" (1Cor 15:33). Lopez expects us **not** to see this as a warning that bad company may corrupt our good morals. Paul is simply speaking rhetorically; there is no danger according to Lopez.

Paul cautions, "Do not be deceived, God is not mocked; for whatever a man sows, this he will also reap. For the one who sows to his own flesh shall from the flesh reap corruption, but the one who sows to the Spirit shall from the Spirit reap eternal life." (Gal 6:7-8). Lopez's incaution is that there is no peril in this passage. There is a biblical parallel to Lopez's tranquilizing teaching: "While they are saying, 'Peace and safety!' then destruction will come upon them suddenly…and they shall not escape." (1Thess 5:3). While Lopez is soothing believers with assurances of soteriological safety, the passages (Gal 5:19-21, 1Cor 6:9-11; Eph 5:5-6) are screaming sirens, warning believers of their misthological destruction as a result of their moral corruption!

When Paul concludes the vice list by commanding, "Let no one deceive you" (Eph 5:6), one should understand Paul as issuing a warning. Bewilderingly, Lopez does also, contrary to everything else he has been saying:

> Likewise in Eph 5:1-2 Paul appeals to believers to walk as "imitators of God as dear children" on the basis of Christ's sacrifice. Then he contrasts believers with those who are characterized by their behavior in vv 3-5 who will not inherit the kingdom. Upon looking at v 6, these are described as unbelievers since the phrase "sons of disobedience" in 2:2-3 defines it as such. Finally, Paul **exhorts and warns**, "not to be partakers with them," because it logically follows they will also share in their present wrath of God (cf. Rom 1:18-32). (p. 20, n. 93).

Exhortation is coupled with warning. This admonition is clearly addressed to believers. How Lopez can admit that this is a vice list warning and yet assert that there is no warning in the vice list remains a mystery. There is no need for enigma here. Paul is warning believers that they may not inherit the reward of the kingdom. Translations, such as the NAS, are therefore correct to conclude the Galatian vice list by stressing Paul's warning to these believers: "I **forewarn** you just as I have **forewarned** you that those who practice such things shall not inherit the kingdom of God" (Gal 5:21). Granted, *prolego* could simply mean to *foretell* rather than to *forewarn*. But in the vice list context, L-N is most certainly correct in its lexical rendering of Gal 5:21 as: "to tell someone that some future happening is dangerous and may lead to serious consequences—'to warn.'" Precisely. Paul was not urging these believers not to be deceived into thinking that unbelievers would inherit the kingdom! Pauline believers already knew that unbelievers would not inherit the kingdom. Believers do not need to be warned of this fundamental truth. Enochian and Pauline soteriology are agreed on that simple matter. Instead, Paul is reminding these believers that as God's children they must live righteously or they themselves would not inherit the kingdom either.

Lopez's argument is subject to the same weakness already demonstrated in relation to Brown regarding 1Cor 15:50. As a fellow dispensationalist, Lopez would be forced to concur with the present perspective that there will be people who *enter* the millennial kingdom in flesh and blood bodies. If inheriting the kingdom were necessarily synonymous in Pauline thought with entering the kingdom, then Paul's statement in 15:50 that flesh and blood will not *inherit* the kingdom of God would be detrimental to the dispensational position. Lopez will need to dispense with dispensationalism or with his equation of entering the kingdom with inheriting it. On a less technical note, as already noted, the only way to inherit the kingdom is as a king. Having an inheritance in the kingdom is not to be equated with inheriting the kingdom. Or as James expresses it, being an heir of the kingdom is based on rich faith (Jam 2:5).

[197] Daniel D. Corner, *The Believer's Conditional Security: Eternal Security Refuted* (Washington, PA: Evangelical Outreach, 2000), 222.

[198] Ibid., 83

[199] Ibid., 223.

[200] Ibid., 229-230.

[201] Ibid., 519-520.

[202] Ibid., 223-224,338.

[203] Brown, 210, cp. 155.

[204] Ibid., 225.

[205] To further clarify my procedure for moving from clear texts to unclear texts in countering those within the Reformed and Arminian Camps who believe that we are saved by nonmeritorious works, Paul makes a semantic distinction: "Now to the one who works, his reward is not reckoned as a *gift* (*charis*), but as a debt" Rom 4:4; (TM). What is given in response to soteric faith is a gift. What is given in response to works is a reward. A reward is not a gift. Paul denies that what is given in response to faith in this passage is a reward. Likewise, in Eph 2:8-9, what is given in response to faith is a gift. What is given in response to such faith is not given in response to works. Therefore, what is given in response to saving faith is not a reward. In soteriological passages, faith is distinguished from works, and rewards are based on works rather than faith.

Despite these clear texts, some within the Reformed and Arminian Camps attempt to argue that believers are saved by nonmeritorious works. Texts such as Jn 6:29 and Jam 2:14ff are pressed into service to prove this point. Primary options concerning these ambiguous texts would be to assert:

1. Soteriological justification can be by nonmeritorious works in soteriological tests such as Jn 6:29. Faith as a nonmeritorious work is not ruled out by the denial of soteriologically meritorious works in Rom 4:4-5. I would counter that this position is popular but impossible. Semantic overlap is emphatically ruled out in soteriological texts. This option is thus falsified.

2. Misthological justification is exclusively by works in Jam 2:14ff, not by faith at all. My response is that this reaction, in contrast, is too restrictive. Faith can be a work. There is contextual room for semantic overlap in non-soteriological texts. This option is thus nullified.

3. Semantic overlap and distinction is determined contextually. To prove this point, using the analogy of faith, one properly starts with texts where overlap is clearly impossible (e.g., Rom 4:4-5); then using texts where overlap is clearly necessary, one demonstrates that faith can be a work. From this procedure, one should not conclude that there are two types of works: meritorious versus nonmeritorious. Rather, one should conclude that there are two types of faith: meritorious versus nonmeritorious. Meritorious faith is clearly capable of demonstration; nonmeritorious works are not. More specifically, faith, which is always passive persuasion, can have two different results and thus be roughly described by those results. In certain contexts faith results in receiving a gift, so faith is not a work in those contexts. Conversely, in contexts where faith results in receiving a reward, faith may be considered a work. This approach is adopted herein. Having demonstrated this distinction in clear texts, one moves out to ambiguous texts like Jn 6:29 and Jam 2:14ff in order to see if they fall in the overlap by checking the context first (which is king) and the theology second (which is the corresponding queen). This process leads to putting Jam 2:14ff in the semantic overlap where faith may be considered a work in the broad sense. Yet this method excludes regarding faith as a work in Jn 6:29 since:

    a. it is contextually questionable,

    b. it has no precedence elsewhere,

    c. it is clearly ruled out semantically elsewhere,

    d. it is ruled out theologically as well.

Those within the Reformed or Arminian Camps who would agree with this assessment are to be commended rather than their Reformed or Arminian counterparts. Works are meritorious, and believers are not saved from hell by works in any sense of the word.

[206] Zeller, "Theology."

[207] Johnson, *Account*, 113.

[208] After having believed in Jesus as Savior, they subsequently come to know that Jesus is the Savior (Jn 4:42). They not only believe, they also know, that Jesus is the Messiah (Jn 6:69). Those who believe in Jesus for eternal life may also know that they have such life (1Jn 5:13). A solidification of knowledge appears to result as an advanced level of belief. To know is a higher degree of faith (Jn 16:30). By faith we understand (Heb 11:3). This level of knowledge comes from faith. We believe in order to know and understand (Jn 10:38; cp. 1Cor 2:14). Nevertheless, a rudimentary understanding is necessary for saving faith to occur (Mt 13:19; cp. Lk 8:12). A prerequisite level of understanding enables an elementary level of faith, which in turn enables an advanced level of understanding, which results in mature faith, and so on. Understanding and faith build on one another.

[209] Pentecost, 216-217.

[210] Zane C. Hodges, "The Rapture in 1 Thessalonians 5:1-11," in *Walvoord: A Tribute*, ed. Donald K. Campbell (Chicago: Moody Press, 1982), 67-80. The on-line version is available at: http://chafer.edu/CTSjournal /journals/v6n4_2.pdf. Any quotations herein will be from the original version.

[211] The reference in Rev 16:15 is an exception to the rule that the thief in the night indicates Rapture rather than Revelation. In several passages the coming of the thief is said to be at a time unknown and unexpected by **believers** (Mt 24:43-4; Lk 12:39-40; Rev 3:3). Contrastively, in 1Thess 5:2-3, the thief (the Day of the Lord) comes when **unbelievers** do not expect him. In 2Pet 3:10, the Day of the Lord also comes unexpectantly. But this passage telescopes the Rapture, tribulation, Revelation, millennium, and creation of the new earth all together. The commencement of that day is imminent in both passages since it starts with the Rapture. In contrast to these references, Rev 16:15 refers to the Revelation, yet it does not say that the time is unknown or unexpected by believers. The first coming of the Lord (like a thief in the Rapture) is unexpected by everyone, lost and saved, and is imminent. The second time it is unexpected by the lost and is not imminent. Walvoord is correct: "The unifying factor in all these passages is that the coming in view results in loss for those who are not ready" (*Revelation*, 238). It results in the loss of opportunity for both believers and nonbelievers to obtain white garments and thus avoid nakedness and shame. Noncomers will not be clothed in imputed righteousness, and subcomers will not be clothed in imparted righteousness.

[212] Walvoord, *Rapture*, 90, 100, 107-110, 191.

[213] Whipple, Shock, 71.

[214] Ernest C. Reisinger, "The Carnal Christian." Available at http://www.peacemakers.net/unity/carnal.htm. Accessed on August 11, 2004.

[215] William W. Combs, "The Disjunction Between Justification And Sanctification in Contemporary Evangelical Theology," *DBSJ* 6 (Fall 2001): 40. Combs denies that justification can be divorced from progressive sanctification. He traces this distinction from Wesley through the Victorious Life teaching of the Keswick movement to Chafer and Ryrie and contemporary FG writers. His historical overview is interesting, but his arguments from Corinthians are as flawed as the ones he presents from Romans. According to Combs, Rom 6:2 means that Christians cannot practice sin (p. 35) because Christians reckon themselves dead to sin as a reflex action in Rom 6:11 (p. 36), and the conflict in Rom 7:14ff supposedly describes the normal Christian life.

These LS views are rightly rejected by FG commentator Lopez: "It strips Paul's use of imperatives of any real significance ([Rom 6] vv 12-13). Why command holy living if it will automatically occur?" (*Romans*, 125). "One should *not* understand this section [in Rom 7:14ff] as the normal Christian experience" (*Romans*, 152; emphasis his). The imperatival force of Rom 12:1-2 likewise short-circuits Combs' attempt (p. 36) to throw Ryrie's exegesis into the abused aorist garbage heap. Even if the aorist is not describing punctiliar action, it could still be ingressive. Paul is urging them to do something they have not yet done. In any event, Paul does not assure his readers that they are or will inevitably continue to present themselves to God. Rather, he urges them to do so. Lopez is quite correct to surmise that those Christians who do not heed his injunction "are carnal Christians" (*Romans*, 242). A gag reflex response is the appropriate reaction to Combs' attempt to make the interpreter swallow a merger of justification and practical sanctification. Practical sanctification is volitional, not inevitable. It is not an unconditional reflex action. It is conditioned on our free volition.

[216] Combs, 41.

[217] In response to the claim by MacArthur that carnal Christians do not exist even though they behave in a carnal manner, Pickering retorts:

> One is not going to make "carnal" Christians vanish simply by demanding that saving faith include surrender to the Lordship of Christ. If he did not do so, he would become a "carnal" Christian, walking according to the flesh and not the Spirit....
> ...we fail to see the difference between "behaving in a carnal way" and being a carnal Christian."

Ernest Pickering, *Lordship Salvation: An Examination of John MacArthur's Book, "The Gospel According to Jesus"*(Minneapolis: Central Baptist Seminary, n.d), 3. Of course, Reformed LS may counter that perseverance ensures progressive sanctification so that a Christian cannot remain in a carnal state, but then it does an about-face and admits that Christians may die in a carnal state in premature death. Premature death as a punishment for sin acknowledges the existence of premature Christians and thus carnal Christians. Reformed theology is self-defeating.

[218] Reisinger, "Carnal." In contrast, Hart sets forth the three basic hermeneutical options in Rom 7:14-15 as describing the experience of (1) natural person (i.e., unsaved) or (2) a spiritually mature believer or (3) a carnal believer. He argues in favor of the third interpretation. He finds it descriptive of an immature carnal believer living in defeat. John F. Hart, "Grace Theology and the Struggle of the Legalistic Christian Life: The Contributions of Romans 7," *GES Conference CD*, 2001. Hart also cites Fung as sharing this perspective. Ronald Y. K. Fung, "The Impotence of the Law: Toward a Fresh Understanding of Romans 7:14–25," in Scripture, Tradition, and Interpretation, ed. W. W. Gasque and W. S. LaSor (Grand Rapids: Eerdmans Publishing Co., 1978): 34-48. Newell likewise argues that Rom 7:14-25 does not refer to the struggle of a lost man. A lost man only has one nature, not two. He further agrees with Hart's assessment that

it does not describe Paul's present experience; rather, it probably refers to Paul's initial experience in Arabia after his Damascus Road conversion and regeneration. William R. Newell, *Romans: Verse by Verse* (Chicago: Moody Press, 1948), 280.

Since the *therefore* of Rom 8:1 draws upon the preceding context, a soteriological understanding of *condemnation* in Rom 8:1 would most naturally require a soteriological understanding of the preceding context in Rom 7:14-25. Newell correctly rejects the soteriological interpretation of Rom 7:14-25 but presumes a soteriological understanding of Rom 8:1 on the basis of eternal security (Newell, 289). But the rejection of soteriological understanding of the antecedent text makes a soteriological interpretation of Rom 8:1 exceedingly unlikely, even if the reading of the CT is accepted. Although Dillow uses the CT in Rom 8:1, he rightly rejects the soteriological interpretation and takes Hart's second option that Rom 7B describes the experience of the mature believer (Dillow, 358): Freedom from *penal servitude* (*katakrima*) to sin is now available for the believer. Of course, this does not mean that all believers experience this freedom (cp. Gal 5:1).

The present writer opts for Hart's argument in favor of the third position. The antecedent passage in Rom 7B is referring to the defeated experience of a carnal believer; therefore, the deliverance in view in Rom 8A is from that of a carnal experience. Even Paul could not pass from being lost to being spiritually mature without going through the carnal stage of immaturity during his sojourn in Arabia. Although Dillow opts for the second option in Rom 7B, he also adopts the experiential nature of the deliverance in Rom 8A. Despite the fact that Rom 8:1 popularly is used as a proof text for eternal security, it would be better suited for an explanation as to how to have present victory. In this regard, the *now* of Rom 8:1 may be considered a logical as well as temporal interjection. This verse is, therefore, nikological rather than soteriological. The exclamation of Rom 7:25 anticipates a temporal victory in the here and now. Logically, the same person described in Rom 7B can now have victory because of his union with Christ in His death and resurrection. As a result of the victory now available in Christ, those in Christ who walk according to the Spirit are no longer under a *death penalty* (*katakrima*). Those believers who walk according to the flesh are still subject to death: both nikologically and misthologically (Rom 8:6,13). Taken from this perspective, in Rom 8:1 Paul is affirming that there is no longer any misthological death penalty for those believers who are walking victoriously.

The requirement that one walk according to the Spirit to avoid being under condemnation in v. 1 is affirmed realistically by the CT in Rom 8:4 where believers fulfill the requirements of the law by walking according to the Spirit. This experiential righteousness is only possible to those who are spiritually alive because of the imputational righteousness in Rom 8:10.

[219] Hodges, *"Rapture,"* 76.

[220] The *Day of the Lord* refers to the beginning of the tribulational period, see Hodges, *"Rapture,"* 70. Pentecost, 229-231. Charles C. Ryrie, *A Survey of Bible Doctrine* (Chicago: Moody Press, 1972), 170. Also see his *Basic Theology* (Illinois: Victor Books, 1986.*Theology*), 486. Gerald B. Stanton, *Kept from the Hour: Biblical Evidence for the Pretribulational Return of Christ* (Miami Springs: Schoettle Publishing Co., 1991), 71, etc.

[221] Problems with 1Thess 3:13 are well stated in EBC. Its solution, however, is not very helpful. Understanding 3:13 as a reference to the second stage is better, not to standing before the Bema, which would be associated with the first stage. The results of the Bema at the return of the Bride and bridegroom (at the second stage) are in view.

[222] John F. Walvoord, *The Rapture Question*, revised and enlarged edition (Grand Rapids: Zondervan Publishing House, 1979), 116-120.

[223] Mark Hitchcock, *The Complete Book of Bible Prophecy* (Wheaton: Tyndale House Publishers, 1996), 190-191.

[224] Other proposals that postmillennialists make concerning the identity of the restrainer will not be discussed since postmillennialism already has been ruled out as a valid option. In any event, their alternative proposals are hardly convincing.

[225] Charles C. Ryrie, *Dispensationalism Today* (Chicago: Moody Press, 1965), 150-155.

[226] Ibid., 151.

[227] Stanton, 120-121.

[228] Robert L. Thomas, *2 Thessalonians*, vol. 11, EBC (Grand Rapids: Zondervan Publishing House, 1978), 320-321.

[229] Hitchcock, 207.

[230] Thomas Ice, "Salvation in the Tribulation: Revisited." Available at http://www.raptureready.com/featured/Salvation.html. Accessed on April 25, 2006. George Zeller, "If a Person Rejects Christ Before the Rapture, Can He Be Saved After the Rapture?" Available at http://www.middletownbiblechurch.org/proph/savetrib.htm. Accessed on April 25, 2006.

[231] See all of Stanton's chapter six, esp. 127-134.

[232] Hoekema, Future, 159-160.

[233] Ibid., 136.

[234] Ibid., 174.

[235] Archer, *Rapture*, 126.

[236] Ryrie affirms double and partial fulfillments. Charles C. Ryrie, *The Basis of the Premillennial Faith* (Neptune: Loizeaux Brothers, 1953), 45,79. See also Kaiser's affirmations of partial, double, and multiple fulfillments. Kaiser, *Uses*, 62, 94, 230.

[237] Strimple, *Millennium*, 99.

[238] Hodges, *Jesus*, 53.

[239] Ibid.

[240] Hoekema, 203-205.

[241] Ibid., 148-149

[242] Elliot E. Johnson, "Author's Intention," Earl D. Radmacher and Robert D. Preus, eds. *Hermeneutics, Inerrancy, and the Bible* (Grand Rapids: Zondervan Publishing House, 1984), 427. Arp simply expresses the matter in terms of *sensus plenior*: "Is it possible that a prophecy may have a deeper meaning or 'fuller' sense than the prophet envisioned?...This deeper or fuller meaning is called *sensus plenior*. The *sensus plenior* is that additional, deeper meaning, intended by God but not clearly intended by the human author." William Arp, "Authorial Intent," *JMT* (Spring 2000): 43.

[243] Walvoord, *Rapture*, 272.

[244] The reasons given herein for taking a pretribulational premillennial position have not been based on a thoroughgoing distinction between the church and Israel (which is the backbone of dispensationalism), on how one side treats hermeneutics, nor on the postponement of the kingdom. The pretribulational premillennial position can be advanced without taking positions on these matters as one's starting point. Potentially, consistency with the pretribulational premillennial position might require a specific position on these matters. For example, in regard to hermeneutics, both sides interpret some passages literally, and both sides take some passages symbolically, and probably some passages are interpreted by both groups as partially literal and partially symbolic. Even the inaugurated kingdom idea of the already-not-yet kingdom that Hoekema presents is attractive. Lightner points out that some taking a pretribulational premillennial position are open to this possibility. Robert P. Lightner, *The Last Days Handbook: A Comprehensive Guide to Understanding the Different Views of Prophecy. Who believes What about Prophecy* (Nashville: Thomas Nelson Publishers, 1990), 111-113, 198-199. See also Walvoord, *Rapture*, 110. Although the thoroughgoing identification between the church and Israel made by amillennialists must be rejected, it is perhaps questionable if the identification or separation between the church and Israel really must be a thoroughgoing approach. Agreement with dispensationalism on everything, or knowing everything, is not required for the pretribulational premillennial position at this introductory level.

[245] Walvoord, *Rapture*, 97-113.

[246] The wording in the body of the text is the present author's summation of Walvoord's words. His actual wording is, "The faithfulness of those watching is evidence of true faith...[works] are indicative of vital faith or its lack" (*Rapture*, 100). Compare this statement with his earlier comment, "Works are taken as evidence of salvation" (p. 90). And compare his later remarks, "All true Christians are waiting for Christ" (p. 109); "those who do not heed the message of Christ and ignore the warning are by so much demonstrating their fundamental lack of faith and salvation" (p. 109); "the evidence of salvation, good works, is pointed to as necessary to salvation" (p. 110); "those without works are not true believers" (p. 110). Accordingly, Walvoord mistakenly says concerning 1Thess 5:6, "The contrast here again is not between some believers who watch and other believers who do not....Those who sleep are *obviously* the unsaved" (p. 107). Actually, the opposite is obvious. Walvoord wrongly believes that all believers **will** live lives in keeping with their faith. He misrepresents his position when he tones it down to saying, "All believers **should** have lives in keeping with their faith" (p. 107; emphasis mine). Of course, they **should**, but Walvoord's entire argument requires that they **will**.

[247] Walvoord, *Rapture*, p. 110

[248] Ryrie's treatment is a soteriological counterbalance to this chapter on the partial rapture by Walvoord. Charles C. Ryrie, *So Great Salvation: What it Means to Believe in Jesus Christ* Illinois: Victor Books, 1989). And Ryrie's chapter, "Must Christ be Lord to be Savior?" is an outstanding classic. Charles C. Ryrie, *Balancing the Christian Life* (Chicago: Moody Press, 1969), 169-181. Although Walvoord and Ryrie are both strongly identified with Dallas Theological Seminary, Ryrie's writings are soteriologically superior.

[249] Jeremy D. Myers, "The Gospel Under Siege," *JOTGES* 16:31 (Autumn 2003): 43,48. In the same journal, Makidon discusses the historical shift in which Melanchthon compromised Luther's theology by making good works a necessary result of regeneration and, therefore, a necessary condition for glorification in his concession to Catholicism. Michael D. Makidon, "Marrow," 67. Therefore, when Shank allies himself with Melanchthon, those in FG are not surprised: "James' discourse (2:14-26)...serves, not to establish works as a means of salvation, but to qualify the kind of faith that saves. Melanchthon's dictum is an apt summary of James' contention: It is faith, alone, which saves; but the faith that saves is not alone" (*Life*, 7). Arminianism as well as Calvinism join hands with Catholicism in unholy tripartite matrimony when they claim that we are saved by faith alone but faith that saves is not alone. By making works an indispensable result of saving faith in such passages, soteriologically they are making works a necessary requirement for the final realization of salvation.

[250] Lang, *Sons*, 234.

[251] Walvoord, *Rapture*, 91.

[252] Ibid., 98.

[253] Walvoord, *Rapture*, 112.

[254] Pentecost, 161.

[255] Pentecost mistakenly applies these passages to Israel rather than the rapture of the church (pp. 154,175,231). Stanton's interpretation is to be preferred in taking it as a reference to the rapture, (p. 73). Lazarus, as well as other believers who saw Jesus and believed in Him during the time of His earthly ministry, will be resurrected at the rapture.

[256] Walvoord does a good job of dealing with key passages concerning the tribulation from a pretribulational viewpoint. For this reason, his book, *Rapture*, is a very good eschatological text. Stanton does a better job of developing concepts and terminology, so his work also should be consulted.

[257] Hoekema, *Future*, 165-166.

[258] There is disagreement as to where the transfer took place. Some believe it took place at the bride's house. Others believe it took place at the groom's house. Agreement on this detail is probably not necessary. The important point is that the transfer of the bride takes place before the marriage feast.

[259] Thomas R. Edgar, "Lethargic or Dead in 1 Thessalonians 5:10?" ***CTSJ*** 6:4 (October 2000): 36-51.

[260] Ibid., 37-38.

[261] Ibid. 47, n. 44.

[262] Ibid., 48.

[263] Hodges, *Walking*, 130.

[264] It might be possible to limit the salvation in 1 and 2 Thessalonians to glorification and take 1Pet 1:2 as referring to full salvation, but this also appears doubtful. Dillow has a good case concerning 1Pet 1:2. He takes it as referring to those who are already believers who need to obey and be sprinkled. Although the sprinkling imagery is used positionally by the writer of Hebrews, one may understand Peter as using it experientially, especially since the writer of Hebrews is urging those believers to avail themselves of the experiential benefit (i.e., the cleansing) of the positional sprinkling. Thus, 1Pet 1:2 may be regarded as urging believers to obey Jesus through continuing faith and faithfulness. The specific obedience called for in 1Peter is to obey the word, i.e., believe the word, to be a believer and continue to believe (1Pet 1:5,9).

[265] Whether the verb used in Lk 17:33 is *peripoieomai* is debatable. This reading is preferred in the Critical Text, and it is the reading used by Lang, which is the reason he believes that Lk 17:33 is an especially important cross reference for Heb 10:39 (p. 193). Both verses are talking about the same **destruction** (*apollumi/apoleia*—verb & noun forms of the same word) and the same **salvation** (*peripoieomai/peripoiesis*—verb & noun forms of the same word) of the same thing—the **soul** (*psuche*). Lk 17:33 uses the verbal forms and Heb 10:39 uses the noun forms of the same words (destruction and salvation) concerning the soul. The question is not really, "What does the destruction of the soul mean?" Obviously, it means to lose your soul (life) rather than to save it. Both verses are contrasting the two different possibilities of losing and saving your life (soul). The real question is, "Are the contexts referring to losing your soul temporally, eschatologically, or both?"

It is difficult to credit Zeller with being completely forthright in his treatment of the FG understanding of *apoleia* in Heb 10:39. Zeller rejects the treatment of Hodges and Dillow and makes the absurd claim: "The Bible consistently uses this term to describe eternal destruction in hell" ("Theology"). But Hodges references the Greek word *apoleia*, and Dillow devotes a paragraph to the discussion of this word in Heb 10:39 and lists examples where this Greek word "is not a technical term for hell." Dillow then repeats this entire paragraph verbatim later (pp. 337,466). So what does Zeller do with this discussion of the Greek term and the texts in which it does not refer to hell? He completely ignores them! Contrary to Zeller, the Bible does not consistently use *apoleia* to describe hell (e.g., Mt 26:8; Mk 14:4; Acts 8:20; 25:16 [MT]; 1Tim 6:9; Heb 10:39; Jam 4:12). It can refer to temporal, misthological, or soteriological destruction. And this list is just from the NT. Zeller's claim is all the more unreasonable because he made his claim regarding the entire Bible. The Greek OT (i.e., the LXX) is replete with numerous examples where the term does not refer to destruction in hell (e.g., Dt 4:26; 7:23; 8:19; 12:2; 30:18). Frequently, it refers to physical death. Just as Heb 10:39 contrasts destruction with the salvation of the soul, a similar case may be noted in the OT: "Whoever commits adultery with a woman lacks understanding; He who does so destroys his own soul" (Prov 6:32; NKJ). Is Solomon saying that his father David had his soul destroyed in hell because of his infamous adultery that resulted in Solomon's birth? If Zeller's premise were correct, then one would conclude this is indeed the case—David perished in hell. On the other hand, if the destruction is temporal rather than soteriological, then an entirely different conclusion is derived. David brought a lot of grief upon his soul—on his life—because of his adulterous affair. Solomon saw the tragic impact the adultery had upon his father. He is not teaching that his father, David, went to hell. Rather, he is sharing, from painful experience, that adultery has a destructive impact upon the lives of those who participate in it. This destruction is not necessarily experienced in the fires of hell. His father suffered because of his adultery, but he did not suffer in hell as a result of it. Solomon is not using *apoleia* to describe the destruction of David's soul in hell. Neither would one conclude that Daniel was praying that he and his friends would not go to hell in Dan 2:18. He was using *apoleia* in reference to physical destruction.

Perhaps, Zeller is ignoring the Greek text being used by Zane and Dillow in favor of an English translation that is better suited for his theology. If this is the case, though, then it is rather strange that he calls attention to the verbal cognate, *perish* and then cites Mt 10:28 and 2Cor 4:9 in his list of texts in which the underlying Greek *apollumi* is translated as *perish*, when in fact this verb is typically translated as *destroy* in these two texts (e.g., KJV). In other words, Zeller appears to be consulting the Greek text to pick out verses in defense of his argument and then ignoring references from the Greek text when they do not support his position. Even a quick glance at *apollumi* in a Greek concordance destroys Zeller's assertion that this word automatically means hell. Were Herod and the Pharisees trying to send Jesus to hell (Mt 2:13; 12:14)? Were the disciples drowning in hell (Mt 8:25)? Were the wine bottles perishing in hell (Mt 9:17)? Do weak Christians perish in hell when they are grieved by mature Christians (Rom 14:15; 1Cor 8:11)? Does gold go to hell (1Pet 1:7)? If so, what about the streets of gold in heaven! Zeller's statement that this verb refers so destruction in hell leads to some rather ridiculous conclusions.

This word, like its nominal counterpart, can refer to either temporal, misthological, or soteriological destruction. As a matter of fact, the verbal form is linked explicitly with the discussion of rewards in Mk 9:41. "For whoever gives you a cup of water to drink because of your name as followers of Christ, truly I say to you, he shall not *lose* [*apollumi*] his reward." Matthew also quotes the Lord using this same verb in discussing rewards (Mt 10:42). It is likewise associated with a reward by John: "Watch yourselves, that you might not *lose* [*apollumi*] what we have accomplished, but that you may receive a full reward" (2Jn 1:8). There is considerable NT precedence for understanding *apollumi* to refer to losing a potential reward, enough so that one certainly should be open to this possibility when discussing passages that use this verb to talk about losing one's soul (e.g., Mt 16:25; Lk 9:24-25). Such texts could very well be describing losing your soul in terms of potential rewards if the context indicates such, and the reader is encouraged to consult the contexts to confirm that this is indeed the case. An examination of either word in the Greek Bible destroys Zeller's claim that the Bible always uses these words in reference to hell. To save your soul means to preserve your soul. This is dealing with the doctrine of self-preservation as opposed to the salvation of the spirit, which concerns divine preservation (1Cor 5:5). The doctrine of eternal security deals with the divine preservation of the saints' spirits.

[266] Leon Morris, *The First and Second Epistles to the Thessalonians,* NIC, ed. F. F. Bruce (Grand Rapids: Eerdmans Publishing Co., 1959), 161.

[267] NIDNTT, s.v. "περιποιέομαι," by E. Beyreuther.

[268] Robert L. Thomas, *1 Thessalonian,* vol. 11, EBC (Grand Rapids: Zondervan Publishing House, 1978), 285.

[269] Apparently, Hodges may take Lk 17:33 and Heb 10:39 as referring exclusively to temporal misthology experienced in this life rather than eschatological misthology at the Bema. Zane C. Hodges, *The Gospel Under Siege: A Study on Faith and Works*, 2nd ed. (Dallas: Redención Viva, 1992), 80-81,169. In any event, his discussion is limited to the temporal aspect of this punishment, and he seeks to limit the salvation of the soul in Jam 1:21 and 2:14 to temporal loss rather than misthological loss at the Bema. Zane C. Hodges, *The Epistle of James: Proven Character Through Testing*, eds. Arthur L. Farstad and Robert N. Wilkin (Irving: Grace Evangelical Society, 1994), 41-42,61. (Contrast the present author's position on Jam 2:14.) In support of his conclusion, Hodges (*Gospel,* 169, n. 15) quotes from p. 193 of Lang's commentary on Hebrews to the effect that what is at stake is premature death. Hodges' quote is true to the immediate context of Lang's discussion. On the other hand, although Lang does argue for temporal punishment, he is very open to the possibility of eschatological punishment as well. Concerning *peripoiesis* of one's soul in Heb 10:39, Lang concludes that what is being referred to is the "possible punishment of one's life being cut short in judgment **and what further temporary penalty may follow upon this.**" See G. H. Lang, *The Epistle to the Hebrews*, 2nd ed. (Miami Springs: Schoettle Publishing Co., 1985), 194. Also, in his earlier discussion of Heb 10:29, Lang said that "there is therefore something possible after death, something to be feared" (p. 183). In continuing his discussion about the "prospect of punishment after death for some who are ultimately to be saved" (p. 185), Lang cites Col 3:25 as demonstrating that "the fulfillment of this warning lies beyond death" (p. 186). The context of Lang's previous discussion is dealing with the possibility of a believer being cast temporarily into Gehenna, thus, eschatological misthology. Therefore, although Hodges and I may disagree as to the time frame in which the punishment is experienced, we nevertheless are in agreement that *peripoiesis* is used in Heb 10:29 (and Lk 17:33) to describe a salvation that is obtained as a reward based on merit.

[270] Wilkin correctly notes that this soul salvation in 1Pet 1:9 is eschatological, not temporal: "The 'soul salvation' in view here is future, not present.…This salvation, whatever it is, is future." Wilkin, "Soul," 2.

[271] Ibid.

[272] Ibid.

[273] S.v. "possessions," by E. Beyreuther.

[274] Dillow, 329

[275] Although Luke uses *agrupneo* instead of *gregoreo* in Lk 22:36, Mark's use of *agrupneo* in Mk 13:33 is followed by three parallel usages of *gregoreo* in 13:34-37, which makes it clear that these words can be used interchangeably. In any event, Paul probably had Mark's account in mind.

[276] Mike Stallard, *First & Second Thessalonians: Looking for Christ's Return, TFCBC,* eds. Mal Cough and Ed Hindson (Chattanooga, TN: AMG Publishers, 2009), 97.

277 Ibid., 186-187.

278 Ventilato, section III, 23.

279 Dave Hunt, *What Love Is This? Calvinism's Misrepresentation of God.* (Sisters, OR: Loya, 2002), 211.

280 Forster, 147.

281 Zane C. Hodges, and Arthur L. Farstad, eds. *The Greek New Testament: According to the Majority Text*, second edition (Nashville: Thomas Nelson Publishers, 1985).

282 For additional information, see Gregory P. Sapaugh, "A Call to the Wedding Celebration: An Exposition of Matthew 22:1-14," *JOTGES* 5:1 (Spring 1992): 11-34. Michael G. Huber, "The 'Outer Darkness' in Matthew and Its Relationship to Grace," *JOTGES* 5:2 (1992): 11-25.

283 The "promise of eternal life" in 2Tim 1:1 corresponds to the "hope of eternal life" in Tit 1:2. Both verses refer to the potential of a futuristic acquisition of eternal life (cp. 1Tim 4:8; 6:19).

284 Wilkin, *Confident*, 258, n. 10.

285 Michael Eaton, *No Condemnation: A New Theology of Assurance* (Downers Grove: InterVarsity Press, 1995), 249, n. 9.

286 Lightner presents a diagram of the Pearly Gate illustration. Robert P. Lightner, *Sin, the Savior, and Salvation* (Thomas Nelson Publishers, 1991), 147. Wilkin concurs with this approach. Robert N. Wilkin, "Election and the Gospel: Can Only the Elect Accept Christ?" *GIF* (July 1989).

287 Curtis Hutson prefers the foreknowledge position: "God in His foreknowledge knows who will trust Jesus Christ as Saviour [sic], and He has predestined to see that they are justified and glorified." See his pamphlet, *Why I disagree with All Five Points of Calvinism* (Murfreesboro: The Sword of the Lord Publishers, 1980), 7. Stanford likewise states, "God FOREKNEW those who would believe and predestined the BELIEVERS to be conformed to the image of His Son. *He did not predetermine WHO would believe.* He predetermined what would happen to those who did believe" (emphasis his). A. Ray Stanford and Richard A. Seymour and Carol Ann Strieb, *Handbook of Personal Evangelism,* revised ed. (Hollywood, FL: Florida Bible College, 1975), 216. John Rice concurs, "It is not that predestination *causes* people to trust Christ and be saved….Predestination is based wholly on God's foreknowledge" (emphasis his). See John R. Rice, *Predestined for Hell? No!* (Murfreesboro: Sword of the Lord Publishers, 1958), 90. Hunt devotes a chapter to the defense of this position (*Love*, 219-234). The present writer shares Hunt's lack of satisfaction with the Pearly Gate illustration (*Love*, 28).

288 Thiessen, 106-108, 257-267.

289 Shank, *Life*, 292.

290 Samuel Fisk, *Election and Predestination* (Bicester: Penfold Book and Bible House, 1973), 71-83. Originally published as *Divine Sovereignty and Human Freedom* (Neptune: Loizeaux Brothers, 1973).

291 Fisk, 82-83.

292 Bryson, Dark, 301-302.

293 Although faith is not volitional, volition frequently has a role to play in our coming to faith.

294 Free will is the God-given ability to respond positively or negatively to opportunities God gives within His parameters and time frame. For example, God put Adam in a situation where he had a choice as to whether to eat of the tree of knowledge. Flying like a bird was not one of the choices. There were parameters on what choices Adam could make. Likewise, once Adam ate of the tree of knowledge, he no longer had a choice to stay in the garden and eat of the tree of life. That window of opportunity was slammed shut. It was in the past. However, Adam did not lose his free will when he ate the apple. God provided Adam with animal skins (foreshadowing the Promised Redeemer who would bruise the serpent's head by the sacrifice of Himself). Of his own free will, Adam chose to wear the skins. Since man retains free will, some would say that man can simply choose of his own volition to come to Christ without any help from God. This is not the position taken herein.

295 White, *Freedom*, 108.

296 Hendriksen, *John*, 212.

297 Barnes, *John,* 313.

298 Lenski, *John*, 887.

299 Ibid., 889.

300 Craig, *Wise*, 73.

301 Tenney, *John*, 133.

302 Thiessen, 107.

303 Ibid., 106.

304 Leo G. Cox, "Prevenient Grace – A Wesleyan View," *Journal of the Evangelical Theological Society* 12:3 (Summer 1969): 149.

305 Michael S. Horton, Norman L. Geisler, Stephen M. Ashby, and J. Steven Harper, *Four Views on Eternal Security*, ed. Matthew J. Pinson (Grand Rapids: Zondervan, 2002), 221.

306 Ashby, *Security*, 273.

[307] William Lane Craig, *The Only Wise God: The Compatibility of Divine Foreknowledge and Human Freedom* (Eugene; OR: Wipf and Stock Publishers, 2000), 137.

[308] Peterson and Williams, 37.

[309] Forster, 145.

[310] David R. Anderson, "Regeneration: A Crux Interpretum." *JOTGES* 13:2 (Autumn 2000): 63.

[311] Aldrich, *"Gift,"* 253.

[312] Zane Hodges, "Calvinism Ex Cathedra: A Review of John H. Gerstner's Wrongly Dividing the Word Of Truth: A Critique of Dispensationalism," *JOTGES* 4:2 (Autumn 1991): 65-66.

[313] C. Norman Sellers, *Election and Perseverance* (Miami Springs: Schoettle Publishing Co., 1987), 43.

[314] Gordon Olson, 240.

[315] Ibid., 140, 240.

[316] Ibid., 148.

[317] Godet, John, 901.

[318] James Montgomery Boice, *The Gospel of John* (Grand Rapids: Zondervan Publishing House, 1985), 439.

[319] Lewis Sperry Chafer, The "The Saving Work of the Triune God," *BibSac* 105:419 (July 48): 274, 283-284.

[320] Merrill C. Tenney, *The Gospel of John*, vol. 9, EBC (Grand Rapids: Zondervan Publishing House, 1981), 76.

[321] Frederic Louis Godet, *Commentary on John's Gospel* (Grand Rapids: Kregel Publications, 1978), 591.

[322] Dillow, 284-288.

[323] Vance, 513-521.

[324] GGBB, 334-335.

[325] Charles C Bing, "Why Lordship Faith Misses the Mark for Salvation." *JOTGES* 12:22 (Spring 1999): 31-32. Gary L. Nebeker, "Is Faith a Gift of God? Ephesians 2:8 Reconsidered," *GIF* (July 1989). Zane C. Hodges, *A Biblical Reply to Lordship Salvation: Absolutely Free!* (Grand Rapids: Zondervan Publishing House, 1989), 219. Gregory P. Sapaugh, "Is Faith A Gift? A Study of Ephesians 2:8," *JOTGES* 7:12 (Spring 94): 31-43. George Zeller, "What is the 'Gift of God'? A Study of Ephesians 2:8-9" (March 2000). Available at http://www.middletownbiblechurch.org/reformed/godgift.htm. Accessed 16 July, 2004.

[326] George Zeller, "Can A True Believer Depart from the Faith? Can a Saved Person Totally Abandon His Faith in Christ?" Available at http://www.middletownbiblechurch.org/doctrine/departff.htm. Accessed 7-24-04.

[327] Erwin W. Lutzer, *How You can be Sure that You will Spend Eternity with God* (Chicago: Moody Press, 1996), 79.

[328] Ibid., 81.

[329] Ibid.

[330] Ibid., 82.

[331] Ibid., 83.

[332] Ibid., 113-115.

[333] Anderson, *Soteriology*, 278. Apparently, some Calvinists would consider regeneration as the "holy rape of the soul." See Coate, 133.

[334] Lutzer, *Sure*, 54.

[335] Granted, even leading Arminians tend to acknowledge that saving faith is the instrumental means by which the merit of Christ is imputed to us. This soteric faith is the vehicle by which Christ's merit is brought to us—the condition as opposed to the cause, the instrumental cause as opposed to efficient cause, the means rather than grounds or basis—for our imputational righteousness. Saving faith has no merit (derivative or otherwise) in and of itself. Rather, saving faith is the condition for having the righteousness of Christ imputed to us. Paul simply uses faith as metonymy (of the instrumental cause for the effect) as a short-hand way of saying that Christ's righteousness is imputed to the person because of his or her faith.

Still, the most straightforward reading of the text is that faith is imputed (rather than infused). Paul does not hesitate to affirm the imputational nature of saving faith. Obviously, it does not have any forensic meritorious value. Soteric faith is only the boat by which the rich cargo is brought into the imputational port. Nevertheless, this faith is allowed into the imputational port. This cargo of Christ's righteousness was shipped in, so to speak, by the oil tanker of non-meritorious faith, not piped in via means of meritorious faith. The imputational language is applied to saving faith, not because of the intrinsic value of the ship, but because of the forensic value of its cargo.

Saving faith is the means by which Christ's righteousness is legally brought to the believer. The transmission is that of imputation rather than infusion. Calvinism throws the whole matter into a state of confusion when it fails to note that the imputational language prevents one from regarding saving faith as the gift. Soteric faith is not the cargo but the cargo ship. Faith is not the gift given to us, but the means by which the gift reaches us. Abraham's faith was imputed soteriologically to Abraham because of Christ's righteousness, not because of the righteousness of Abrahams' faith. If it had not been for Christ's righteousness, there would have been no soteric righteousness to impute to Abraham. Indeed, Abraham's container would have been empty. Likewise, our container is imputed to us as righteousness because of what it contains—Christ's alien righteousness. Nonetheless, faith is our container. What God gives us is the content (i.e.,

Christ's alien righteousness) and the legal transfer of this content to our account. God does not give us the container. We produce the container. Faith is not imparted. Faith is our part.

Even the misthological imputation of persevering faith does not regard such faith as infused or imparted to us independent of our cooperation. Faith remains our part. The instrumental means which is imputed to us as righteousness is not infused or imparted to us apart from our cooperation. In *soteriological imputation*, saving faith is imputed to us as the instrumental means of our **positional** righteousness. Saving faith has **no merit** but simply lays hold on the merit of Christ which is freely given to those who believe. In *misthological imputation,* persevering faith is imputed as the instrumental means of our **progressive** righteousness. Persevering faith has **derivative merit** (which it derives from Christ) and lays hold of that dimension of Christ's merit which is given to the faithful as a reward. Christ not only merited gifts for us but also rewards for us as well. Gifts and rewards are reckoned to our account but for different reasons. Imputed gifts are granted to us independent of any merit on our part. Imputed rewards are granted to us because of our derivative merit—the merit that our God-enabled performance derives from and in Christ. Faith is imputed as the means for the gift of righteousness and as the means for the reward of righteousness—but the same faith in not imputed in these two instances. The faith that is imputed as the instrumental means for the gift of righteousness is punctiliar. The faith that is imputed as an instrumental means for the reward of righteousness is linear. Persevering faith is credited toward our account in earning the crown of life (Jam 1:12), which Christ merited for us and offers as a reward to us on the basis of our God-enabled initiated obedience. Saving faith is credited toward our account (in receiving the free gift of eternal life) by being credited with Christ's perfect obedience as a gift.

[336] White, *Potter*, 324.

[337] NIDNTT, s.v. "Determine: λαγχάνω," by J. I. Packer.

[338] Aldrich, "Gift," 251.

[339] George Meisinger, "The Sufficiency of Scripture for Life and Godliness: 2 Peter 1:1-4," *CTSJ* 1:2 (Summer 1995): 6.

[340] Ryrie, *Balancing*, 98.

[341] Just as we have free will in regards to the exercise of out NT gifts, OT believers had free will in regards to their sacrifices. Some refused to offer the sacrifices they should in the way they should, however. God so values free will that He even gave latitude regarding certain types of OT sacrifices: *freewill offerings* (Lev 7:16; 23:38; Num 15:3; 29:39; Dt 12:6; Eze 1:4,6; 3:5; 8:28; Ps 118:108). The significance of this OT affirmation of freewill should not be brushed aside. Paul uses this same word in the NT when he explicitly affirms in Phlm 1:14 that he wanted Philemon's response to not be one of compulsion but of Philemon's own *free will* (hekousios). This concern is understandable in light of the Pauline teaching in 1Cor 9:17 that rewards are based on what we do of our own *free will* (hekon). Just as the OT believers gave of their own free will, so Paul is delighted when NT believers give *of their own accord*, that is, *of their own free will* (authairetos, 2Cor 8:3; cp. 2Cor 9:7). Indeed, Peter even uses the adverbial form of *hekousios* to affirm that service as an overseer is to be done *voluntarily*, that is, *of our own free will* (1Pet 5:2). From such evidence, it readily may be deduced that God is concerned that responses to Him be of one's own free will.

[342] In *Breaking the Rocking Horse*, for example, the quality of faith was stressed as a soteric requirement and the quantity of faith as a mistholic requirement. The richness of this theme is not exhausted by that two dimensional contrast, however. The quality of faith may be further broken down into a two dimensional representation. The faith refined by fire in 1Pet 1:7 is to be found in a life purified from sin by suffering and a faith from which doubt has been purged by trails. The exclusion of doubt and sin in such a mistholic faith qualitatively qualifies it for reward (2Pet 5-11). As always, soteric concerns are not with the degree of faith versus doubt but with the exclusivity of one's faith so that it is exclusively in Christ alone for eternal life.

Illustration 375. Dualistic Quality of Faith

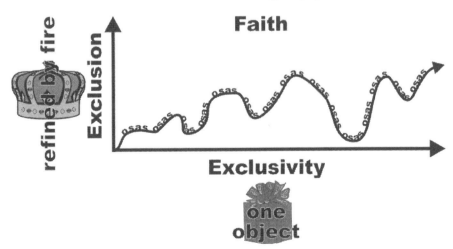

[343] As a converse of the beggar illustration, consider the *milk cow illustration*. Suppose you have to drive one mile to the store to buy milk for $2. Does the store give you a discount on the milk because you had to drive a mile to get it? No. The work you did in coming to purchase the milk may be a pragmatic necessity to obtain it, but it is not part of the grounds upon which the milk is offered nor part of the stipulated condition. The drive is a precondition. For this reason, your brother does not get a bigger discount if he has to drive two miles to obtain it. Neither of you get a discount. For your driving to the store is not taken into consideration as part of the condition upon which the milk is offered. The only condition taken into consideration is the $2. Likewise, God does not consider our work in coming to faith as part of the condition for our reception of eternal life.

Now, the reader is probably wondering why this illustration is called the *milk cow* illustration. It goes back to a discussion the author had with a Calvinist at the GES chat site. The Calvinist alleged that those of us in the FG movement were teaching salvation by works by refusing to acknowledge that faith is something that God sovereignly causes. From this Calvinistic perspective, if it is not God-caused, then it is self-caused and therefore a work. The present writer disagrees. Just because something is self-caused (i.e., caused by oneself) does not mean that it is a work. See "Not of Yourselves" in *Soteric and Mistholic Faith*. The Calvinist's accusation was that we were making false distinctions in FG theology between cause and condition and that those of us who accept the GES position are in fact making our faith a cause for salvation. His argument was that GES believes that there is one condition for the gift of eternal life, this condition must be considered the cause for the gift as well. (Never mind that even Calvin acknowledges that faith is an instrumental cause!)

The author used a twist of the above illustration to show the fallacy of this reasoning. If cause and condition are one and the same, then your $2 in the above illustration is what caused the store to sell you the milk (using cause in the popular sense, which might more technically be called the efficient cause). Neither the store owner or even his desire to make money was the cause for his selling you the milk. On the contrary, you caused him to have the desire to sell milk. Such an argument is ridiculous. (More technically, it confuses final cause with efficient cause.) This makes as much sense as saying that your $2 caused the cow to produce the milk! (This confuses final cause with instrumental cause.) GES, in contrast, would view your $2 as the condition for the milk, not the cause for the milk. This is not to say that all Calvinists fail to make a distinction between cause and condition. Far from it. But some of them certainly do. See "What is Work" in *Soteric and Mistholic Faith*.

For a confused scholastic defense of the Calvinistic position that faith is both a cause and condition and not a cause and condition, see Samuel T. Logan, Jr. "The Doctrine of Justification in the Theology of Jonathan Edwards," WTJ 46 (1984): 26-52. The idea is that God causes you to have faith and this God-caused faith is a noncausal condition for justification. The noncausal condition that was caused by God is not the cause for "the blessing" (p. 44). God is the sole cause, which is why He caused the fall of Satan. It is not supposed to bother us that this view of causation leads to the conclusion that God causes sin because He does so in order that He can accomplish a greater good—the end justifies the means in this type of approach (p. 46). And good works, such as feeding the poor, are conditions for justification, but this is not supposed to contradict Paul because Calvinism teaches that God is the sole cause of these good works (pp. 40,43-45). So we do not cause our salvation by meeting the condition of producing good works, God does. This is a very scholastic way of saying that the cow made you bring your $2 to the store. Or perhaps more accurately, you are the cow that God uses to produce faith. You have no real choice to do otherwise in the matter. In order to maintain their monergistic nonmeritorious works, Calvinists need to demonstrate that these works do not entail our cooperation and that they are not misthological. Calvinism fails on both accounts.

It is better to make and keep the distinction between cause and condition as is done in FG theology: cause ≠ condition (when cause is used to refer to grounds). The basis for God offering us the gift of salvation is because He wanted to save us as an expression of His grace. This is what caused Him to make salvation possible. Our faith certainly did not cause Him to make salvation possible! Our faith is not the cause. His love was the reason He built His milk store on the ground of grace as a source of salvation to those who would come drink.

Or as it turns out, He built a milk dispensary instead of a store so that He could freely offer the milk of salvation to all who are willing to drink it. He says, "You who have no money, drink!" (Is 55:1) The sole condition upon which the offer of receiving the milk is made is that we drink it. The fact that some of us have to drive a mile or two to get to the dispensary is not part of the reason the milk is offered or part of the means by which the milk actually is received. You receive the milk by putting the milk in your stomach, not by putting gas in your car. Not even your preconditional action of bringing the cup of milk to your lips is considered the condition for its appropriation. The reflexive response of the swallow is the singular stipulated condition.

[344] Much ado has been made over Gal 5:6. Chay and Correia provide a noteworthy scholastic interaction with Piper Luther, and others (*Faith*, 90-101). Basically, the Piperean position is that *faith working through love* is the condition for final justification. Chay and Correia contend instead that *faith working through love* is the condition for sanctification. These FG authors perceive the issue to be sanctification rather than justification—a rather standard FG counterargument (GNTC). In my assessment, these LS and FG positions are both half-right and half-wrong. This double error is attributable to a failure to deduce from Gal 5:4-6 that the Galatians were committing a double error. First, they were seeking present sanctification by the wrong means: by works of the law. Second, they were seeking future justification

for the wrong reason: as if it was salvation from hell. They were seeking final justification by means of sanctification, as if this future realization of justification was soteriological justification. When properly understood, sanctification is the means to final justification. The mistake that Piper makes is in thinking that this final justification to which Paul aspires is soteriological justification. The overreaction by the FG camp is to limit Paul's concern to the present (and thus to progressive sanctification). In terms of both progressive sanctification and mistholic justification, "neither circumcision nor uncircumcision means anything, but faith working through love" (Gal 5:6). See my *Race of Grace*.

[345] Dead faith does not have works: "Even so faith, if it produces no works, is dead, being by itself" (Jam 2:17; TM). Mature faith does have works: "The testing of your faith produces perseverance. And *let* perseverance produce perfect work, so that you may be perfect and complete" (Jam 1:3-4; TM). The testing of our faith will produce perfect work and perfect us in the process—if we *let* it. The production of works by faith is not automatic or inevitable but is contingent upon our freewill response. To have mature faith without works is impossible (cp. Jam 2:22). Works are absolutely essential to perfect one's faith, and works certainly will be expressed by perfect faith. Soteriological faith may be dead. But mature faith cannot be. Perfect faith is a working faith, so by definition, a mature faith is a faith that works. Just as breathing is both the necessary means and product of a mature life, so faith is both the means and product of a mature faith. If you cease to breath, you will die. If you stop exercising your faith, it will shrivel and die as well. In faith⟨⟩works, works are necessary to keep faith alive.

The testing of your faith produces perseverance, which in turn produces perfect work, which in turn produces perfect faith (Jam 1:2-6; 2:22). Perseverance in faith does not result in petrifaction in faith. This faith will produce works. Some in FG would question how works can be both a necessary means of developing mature faith and the necessary expression of such faith. How can the means be the result? Consider a sport's analogy. Is it not necessary to play basketball to be a basketball player? You have to play basketball to develop the maturity in skill level to play on the school team, for example. Also, you have to continue to play ball at the practices and games to remain a basketball player on that team. Suppose the coach were to say, "Go in and play." And the player were to respond, "No, I'll just sit here on the bench." Very likely, the result would be that such a player would no longer be a basketball player on the school team. Likewise, God says, "Go in and work." Some Christians say, "No, I'll just sit here on the bench." Such Christians are in danger of losing their maturity in faith. Over a period of time, if they persist in this attitude, their faith will dwindle and die. Instead of having mature faith, they will have dead faith. Just as heart damage can come in small degrees, so saying, "No," to God over the little details can damage a healthy faith and deaden it more and more.

Some in LS would counter that Jn 14:12 proves that all genuine believers will work and thus that good works are a necessary expression of saving faith: "Truly, truly, I say to you, he who believes in Me, the works that I do, he will do also." They would couple this promise with that made earlier: "Truly, truly, I say to you, he who believes in Me has eternal life" (Jn 6:47). LS thus claims that Scripture promises that all believers in Christ will have both eternal life and works. This faulty argument is due to ignoring the context in which both of these statements occur. The context of Jn 6:47 is soteriological. Jesus is encouraging unbelievers to believe in Him for eternal life. The context of Jn 14:12, in contrast, is firmly embedded in a discipleship context in which Jesus is attempting to get those who already have believed in Him for eternal life to now believe in Him for answered prayer, and for spiritual empowerment from on high, and to expect tremendous works as a result.

The Lord is privately talking to His eleven disciples and trying to deepen their faith and prepare it for the trials ahead: "From now on I am telling you before it comes to pass, so that when it does occur, you may believe that I am He" (Jn 13:29). Certainly, they already had believed this soteriological truth (Jn 8:24). Jesus wants their apprehension of this identification to grow. He exhorts them, "You believe in God, believe also in Me" (Jn 14:1; cp. 14:10-11,29; 16:30-31). They already had believed in Him in the sense described in Jn 6:47 and had been granted eternal life as a result. Now these believers are urged to believe in Him for something else and develop a mature faith. Jesus may be understood in this context as elaborating in Jn 14:12, "Whoever has believed in Me for eternal life and who now advances to believing in Me in the manner in which I am currently describing in this context will do stupendous works in terms of their fruitfulness, that is, he will bear much fruit." This is not a promise in 14:12 to immature believers, much less to unbelievers. In contrast, the promise in Jn 6:47 is to unbelievers that if they become believers, they will receive the free gift of eternal life. The promise in 14:12 is to believers that if they become mature believers, they will receive answered prayer and be fruitful (cp. Jn 15:7-8).

Those who believe in Christ for eternal life do not necessarily believe in Christ for the fullness of life available to them. That fullness includes answered prayer (Jn 14:13-14). These greater works will require a faith greater than the feeble soteric faith with which the new believer first embraces Christ as Savior. To believe in Christ in the manner described in Jn 14:12 moves on qualitatively to grasp the eternal life which the believer already posses quantitatively. To develop such faith takes time and maturity. Jesus is referring to the mature believer in Him who grasps the fuller promises. Those who believe in Christ for the fullness of life available to them will be part of a movement of the Spirit that will accomplish more than what Jesus did during His earthly ministry

[346] Although the law is a means of leading us to faith, we are not saved by the law and faith. We are not saved by works (of the law) and faith. The law is not considered part of the means by which we receive the gift of life. Let W = works; F = faith; G= gift; J = positional justification; S = practical sanctification, and H = heaven.

The LS position is: $F \Rightarrow J + S$. You cannot have F without receiving the entire package: $J + S$. But this results in: $F \Rightarrow J + S \Rightarrow H$. Entrance into H is conditioned on postconversional works as expressed in S. But S is MR (meritorious response) since S accrues (R) rewards. That is: $(S \Rightarrow R) \Rightarrow (S = MR)$.

Some in FG might grant the conceptual category NR (nonmeritorious response). Some might even claim that baptism is conceptually a nonmeritorious work in Acts 2:38.. However, it cannot be claimed that S is NR. Therefore, to make H dependent on S is to make it dependent on MR. These simplistic Arminian and Reformed articulations can be easily seen to condition entrance into heaven on meritorious works. This refutes the package argument used by Forlines to a considerable extent as well (*Truth*, 300). His argument is that retention of justification is only conditioned on perseverance in faith, not conditioned on works. Thus, he believes that he cannot be accused of teaching salvation by works (pp. 269, 275, 295, 298). However, this argument is false since such persevering faith is assigned MR value in the NT.

To Forlines' credit, however, it must be admitted that he presents a more sophisticated argument than just the package approach. His argument is that S keeps F alive. Believers are saved by faith alone, but works are necessary to maintain linear faith. If they resist's God's disciplinary efforts, they may reach the point where they commit apostasy and thereby lose their faith and lose eternal life as a result (p. 296). So in his view, tampering with sin (p. 296), rather than practicing sin (p. 300), may lead to apostasy and therefore to loss of regeneration. According to this perspective, those who practice sin already have committed apostasy, lost eternal life, and been taken out of Christ by the Father because they are no longer believers. A little sin indirectly causes one to lose salvation; a lot of sin proves that one already has lost it. Salvation is not lost because of sins but because of the resulting unbelief. This is a very interesting NOSAS argument. It is acknowledged herein:

FG Premise
$(W \Rightarrow F \Rightarrow G) \neq (W + F \Rightarrow G)$

The works used to come to faith are not considered part of the requirement to receive the gift. This argument may be modified to express a representation of Forlines' position as follows:

Forlines' Premise
$(W \Rightarrow F1 \Rightarrow J + S \Rightarrow F2 \Rightarrow H) \neq (W + F \Rightarrow G)$

In other words, (W) works that are necessary to come to (F1) *initial saving faith* are not part of the requirement to receive the package (J + S), but S is part of the condition necessary to experience (F2) *ongoing faith*. But since the W necessary to come to F1 is not a co-condition with F1 (as acknowledged by the FG premise), then by the same token it may be argued that S is not co-condition with F2 for (H) heaven. Preconditions such as W in coming to F1 and such as S for coming to F2 are not co-conditions. So H is conditioned on F alone. Forlines' logic appears to be sound as far as this mathematical representation. To his credit, he limits loss of salvation to departure from faith, whether that loss of faith is as a result of deliberation or deception.

My main problem with his reasoning is not with his logical deduction but with his exegetical inductions. I contend that $F2 \Rightarrow R$ so $F2 = MR$. That is, since linear faith may result in (R) rewards, F2 may be considered a (MR) *meritorious response*. Thus, $J + S \Rightarrow R$, which implies $J + S \Rightarrow F2 \Rightarrow R$. But Scripture also appears to consider the works to be necessary to maintain and develop F2 to be co-conditions rather than preconditions for R. So $F2 = MR$. And F2 may thus be considered a meritorious *work* at the conceptual level. Therefore, Forlines inadvertently still teaches that entrance into heaven is conditioned on works by making H contingent on F2.

In FG, salvation by faith alone in Christ alone refers to F1, not to F2. The singular and punctiliar condition to receive and retain the free gift of eternal life is the initial response of faith (F1). In addition to the misthological nature of F2, a number of reasons for deducing this as the nature of persevering faith from Scripture are available. Some believers, like Hymenaeus, are delivered over to Satan, yet they still are dealt with as God's children. Some believers have fallen from grace, yet they still are considered God's children even though they now believe a false gospel. Such considerations and the standard arguments for OSAS rule out taking F2 as necessary to reach H. Moreover, it appears that many of the NOSAS exegetical proof texts base soteriological salvation on performance and, therefore, would be better taken as describing misthological salvation rather than soteriological retention. Consequently, such texts are counterproductive to NOSAS theology. Any text showing that postconversional performance has misthological value makes it impossible to regard postconversional performance a soteriological condition for retaining our salvation. Misthology is a very formidable foe for NOSAS soteriology.

By way of broader response, in his chapter on Rom 9, Forlines appears to argue that the Jews believed that their soteriological election was maintained by soteriologically nonmeritorious works. But this admission is detrimental to Forlines' own position. Since the NT refuses to acknowledge that these works are nonmeritorious, and indeed rejects them as a possible means to salvation, these alleged nonmeritorious works must be regarded as meritorious. The NT rejects the notion that supposedly nonmeritorious works are necessary to stay saved. By assigning such works a function in retaining one's salvation, Forlines himself seems to play the role of the Pharisees as he has described them (see ch. 16, esp. 354-355). Conditioning one's salvation on what are nonmeritorious works in one's own eyes is still salvation by works in God's eyes.

[347] Lenski, *Hebrews*, 427.

[348] Donald R. Shell, "Making Sense of God's Election: An Overview of The Work." Available at http://www.nepaugchurch.org/SpecialTopics/divineElection.htm. Accessed on August 11, 2004.

[349] The LXX will be used unapologetically in this book to supplement discussion of the Hebrew OT: "Most if not all of the writers of the New Testament trusted the Septuagint as the version of the Scriptures that they read, studied, and memorized, much as modern American students of Scripture use English translations. And the writers of the New Testament undoubtedly colored, to greater or lesser extents, their theological understanding of terms by their use in the Septuagint." Fred Chay and John P. Correia, *The Faith that Saves: The Nature of Faith in the New Testament* (Hayesville, NC: Schoettle Publishing Co., 2008), 29-30.

[350] GGBB, 236, cp. 607.

[351] A. T. Robertson, A Grammar of the Greek New Testament in the Light of Historical Research (Nashville: Broadman Press, 1934), 777.

[352] Jac. J. Muller, *The Epistles of Paul to the Philippians and to Philemon*, The New International Commentary on the New Testament, ed. F. F. Bruce (Grand Rapids: Eerdmans Publishing Co., 1955), 71.

[353] Homer A. Kent, Jr. *Philippians*, vol. 11, EBC (Grand Rapids: Zondervan Publishing House, 1978), 119.

[354] Ralph P. Martin *Philippians*, vol. 11, TNTC, ed., R. V. G. Tasker (Grand Rapids: Eerdmans Publishing Co., 1959), 87-89.

[355] Concerning the oft cited Is 10:15, it is sometimes assumed that God uses us practically independently of our free volition. Rather than picturing us as Calvinistic puppets, it pictures us a Calvinistic ax, saw, rod, and club. By way of response, first of all, it seems that the point of the verse is that we cannot boast in putting ourselves in a position over God in how He uses us. The point is not that He takes away our free will so that He can do whatever He wants with us regardless of our synergistic cooperation. The verse is commending an attitude of humility, such as what is found in Lk 17:10. Synergistic service rules out human monergistic boasting. Second, the fact that Is 10:15 pictures the tools as boasting shows that autonomous boasting is possible. God is not the one causing the tools to boast. Third, even if God does use human beings as tools to perform actions, this does not necessarily mean that He does so independently of their free will. Through use of middle knowledge, God providentially can use their freewill responses (to their circumstances) to accomplish His objectives.

[356] Jon Tal. Murphree, *Divine Paradoxes: A Finite View of an Infinite God* (Camp Hill, PA: Christian Publications, 1998), 73. I would also highly recommend the treatment of the topic by Walls and Dongell.

[357] Ibid., 79.

[358] Wilkin, "Election."

[359] Zane C. Hodges, "Man's Role in Conversion," *GIF* (September-October 1993). Gordon Olson also makes a plausible argument that Paul is quoting the intensive form of *ekzeteo* from the LXX to deny that such men do not seek God diligently (pp. 102-103). The same verb is used in Heb 11:6, and certainly one would not expect the text to mean that God rewards half-hearted seeking. The OT background would confirm that the seeking God wants and rewards is seeking with the whole heart (Dt 4:29; 2Chron 15:12; Ps 119:2; Jer 29:13). Both *zeteo* and *ekzeteo* are used by the LXX in these passages. Multiple texts attest that man can seek God. The implication of Heb 11:6 is that such seeking is indeed synergistic. Human seeking results in a divine reward. Rewards require human effort. Humanity is able to cooperate with the Spirit's drawing to seek God. If they do so, God will reward them with the opportunity to believe the gospel, not through irresistible grace but through gospel proclamation. The multiple exhortations to seek demonstrate that seeking is not irresistible.

[360] Zane C. Hodges, "God's Role in Conversion," *GIF* (July-August 1993).

[361] Thiessen, 106.

[362] Robert E. Picirilli, *Grace, Faith, Free Will: Contrasting Views of Salvation: Calvinism and Arminianism* (Nashville: Randall House, 2002), 149.

[363] Ibid., 156. For additional discussion of the *influence response*, see Forlines' subject index in *Truth*.

[364] Picirilli, *Grace*, 167.

[365] Dave Hunt and James White, *Debating Calvinism* (Sisters, OR: Multnomah Publishers, 2004), 202.

[366] Hunt, *Debating*, 213.

[367] A related argument that asserts that those in the flesh are incapable of believing is to assert from Jn 6:63 that those in the flesh can do nothing positive since the *flesh profits nothing*. In response it may be noted that the person himself believes, not some aspect of his being, namely the flesh. In the response of faith, the flesh does not give any profit or receive any. The flesh is not the source of faith and is crucified as a result of faith.

[368] Alcorn, *Heaven*, 301.

[369] The future experience of regeneration anticipated for Israelites is assumed by some to confirm the fact that regeneration irresistibly will result in perseverance in practical sanctification for those in the church age now:

"Moreover, I will give you a new heart and put a new spirit within you; and I will remove the heart of stone from your flesh and give you a heart of flesh. And I will put My Spirit within you and *cause* (*asah*) you to walk in My statutes, and you will be careful to observe My ordinances" (Eze 36:26-27).

The impression from such translations of the Hebrew word *asah* (*cause*, *make*) is that God will use regeneration to provide an irresistible inner compulsion to do His will. This would accord with the Calvinistic understanding of regeneration. Lloyd Olson has a commendable defense of unconditional security from Eze 36:22-38; Jer 31:31-34; Heb 8:9-12 in which he conceives of OSAS as a one-sided contract on God's part (pp. 193-194). Unfortunately, he also thinks that "justification cannot exist without sanctification any more than light can exist without heat" (p. 113). The weakness in his proposal is that it only makes OSAS applicable to those who persist in practical sanctification. Limited applicability strongly suggests conditionality. Lloyd Olson, *Eternal Security: Once Saved; Always Saved* (Mustang, OK: Tate Publishing & Enterprises, 2007).

However, his proposal is not the only option available. An alternative translation suggests a different understanding: "And I will put my Spirit within you collectively, and I will do this **in order that** (Gr. *hina*) you **may** collectively walk in My statutes and may collectively be careful to observe My ordinances" (Eze 36:27; TM). Such a translation would be well suited to the Greek text and would take the *hina* as denoting intended *purpose* rather than guaranteed *result*. (The Hebrew would be understood as using the imperfect to show intended result.) If such a translation were adopted, this could be considered an influence-response of the majority rather than a mechanical reaction of each individual. Taken corporately, believers will be inclined positively to follow the Lord as a result of the ministry of the Holy Spirit in their midst. Even if the passage were understood as picturing regeneration and individual response, the verse still may simply be saying that God will take this action in order that those whom are regenerated will keep His commands, without necessarily guarantying that each individual will do so.

Additional support for understanding the passage as denoting *purpose* rather guaranteed *result* may be found earlier in the book, where Ezekiel describes this experience as:

> And I will give them one heart, and will put a new spirit within them. And I will take the heart of stone out of their flesh and give them a heart of flesh, **in order that** [Heb. *lemaan*; Gr. *hopos*] they **may** walk in My statutes and keep My ordinances, and do them. Then they will be My people, and I will be their God. (Eze 11:19-20; TM)

In this parallel passage, the Hebrew uses *lemaan* (*in order that*) to signify "the intended response" (TWOT). To be sure, Jeremiah pictures God as saying, "I will *make* (*cause*) them walk by streams of waters, on a straight path in which they shall not stumble" (31:9). But who would understand *makes* as meaning irresistibly *causes*, when David says, "He *makes me* lie down in green pastures"? Does *makes* mean that God forces David to lie down in green pastures? Probably not. So there is reason for thinking that one may translate Eze 36:27 as, "And I will put My Spirit within you, and I will *do this* (*asah*) **in order that** you may walk in My statutes and be careful to observe My ordinances and *do them* (*asah*)" (TM; cp. with the *so that* of NLT and YLT). What God *will do* is introduced with (*asah*), and what we *can* or *will do* as a result is likewise concluded with (*asah*).

While such a translation certainly would seem to be possible in Eze 36:27, many probably would consider it implausible. In any event, I will be content with the majority opinion and accept the prevalent view that the verse is saying that God will *cause* (or *make*) them keep His commandments. Does this mean that one must accept the Calvinistic conclusion that regeneration always irresistibly causes sanctification? Not hardly.

A dispensational understanding of the text can accommodate the Calvinistic translation without embracing the Calvinistic conclusion. The context is dealing with gathering Israelites from all the nations back into their own land (Eze 36:24). Even if the cleansing of 36:25 moves beyond justification to sanctification (cp. 36:27,29), it is eschatological. Constable notes, "This is a coming of the Holy Spirit on Israel in the future, not His coming on the church at Pentecost." Quoting from Cooper, he clarifies, "The temptation to find the fulfillment of the 'new heart' and 'new spirit' of 36:25-27 **exclusively** in Christian conversion in this age should be resisted. New Testament conversion is only a **preview** of the massive spiritual revival God has in store for all of true Israel and Gentiles who believe" (*Ezekiel*, 171).

Hodges notes that the author of Hebrews quotes the parallel "passage from Jer 31:31-34 in Heb 8:8-12. He treats the New Covenant as **fully** applicable to his Christian readers." Zane C. Hodges, "Regeneration: A New Covenant Blessing," *JOTGES* 18:35 (Autumn 2005): 44. Hodges appears to be correct regarding the **full** applicability of Jeremiah's **limited** description of the New Covenant; even so, the parallel in Jeremiah does not assert that the internal causation will result in practical sanctification. The passage is content simply to affirm internal transformation. The writer of Hebrews provides the further clarification that this inner transformation does not result in irresistible external compulsion. That is, those who have experienced this New Covenant blessing of regeneration may fail to follow through and keep God's commandments (Heb 10:19-38). The internal transformation of the New Covenant is "fully applicable" to believers today. But the external manifestation of that transformation is not yet fully visible in believers. So this modification (or more likely, simple clarification) of Hodges' articulation is in order.

Indeed, Hodges' own discussion suggests this clarification and limitation: "The law of God—His will—becomes part of the regenerate person's innermost experience" (p. 47). "Since God's law is written in his heart, his regenerate self never produces sin." Or as he states concerning 1Jn 3:9, "the regenerate person, as such, cannot sin." "It is the inner man that is transformed at new birth, not the outward man….the process will be completed when we meet the Lord in the air and receive **glorified bodies**" (p. 48).

Therefore, if we adopt a translation and interpretation that favors causation and individualization in the Ezekiel passage, we do so by affirming that the description of the New Covenant by Ezekiel is **not fully** applicable to the church. If this passage is teaching that practical sanctification is the inevitable outgrowth of regeneration, then applicability of this aspect of the affirmation of the New Covenant must await future fulfillment when all Israel will be saved.

If the passage is anticipating the result that the transformation will have on saved Jews who survive the tribulation as overcomers, as seems quite likely, and as both Hodges and Constable seem to agree, then it is describing a group of Jews who will be in **glorified bodies**. Consequently, these glorified Jews would no longer have a sin nature. After all, they could not inherit the kingdom in flesh and blood bodies (1Cor 15:50). Instead, they would be rewarded with the glory to rule the kingdom in glorified bodies animated by an ontologically sinless spirit. They would live sinlessly during the millennium (and throughout eternity for that matter) due to the internal compulsion generated by their regeneration in the absence of their sin nature. This is the interpretation adopted herein for the Ezekiel passage. It describes the irresistible and infallible, internal and external transformation of all Jews who enter the millennial kingdom in glorified bodies. Although it is individualistic, it is not Calvinistic.

So assuming this understanding, God will cause those in glorified bodies to walk in His statues. A similar affirmation occurs in Dan 9:24. Sin will end when the kingdom comes. Is this a condition for salvation? No. It is guaranteed result. So in this case, we might have a genuinely descriptive text, rather than prescriptive text, for that certain group of people. Does this mean that one can apply this text descriptively and Calvinistically to those in sinful bodies? No. Walking flawlessly is not guaranteed unconditionally to believers in flawed bodies. For example, consider people born in eternity future. They will be sinless. Their sinlessness is descriptive. Certainly, their salvation from hell is not conditioned on something they cannot do, that is, not sinning. Or for a less theoretical proposition, take people in heaven. If they were to sin, they would be punished. But they cannot sin, so they are not punished for sinning in heaven. Does this mean that their salvation from not being punished is conditioned on their not sinning in heaven? No. Their salvation from such punishment is not conditioned on their performance because their performance cannot result in such punishment. So the text may be taken as genuinely descriptive rather than prescriptive, but if so, it does not affirm that those in sinful bodies are so described.

Another possibility must yet be taken into consideration. It has been assumed in Eze 36:26 that God will do two things—the second by means of the first. Namely, (1) God will regenerate this group of people, and, by means of doing so, (2) He will cause them to keep His commandments. Thus, He will cause them to keep His commandments by an internal, irresistible impulse that comes from their regenerate nature. However, since the fulfillment of the passage awaits the future millennial kingdom, another possibility exists. It could be that God is affirming that He will do two things but not necessarily infallibly cause the second by means of the first.

If the passage is not limited to Jews who enter the kingdom in **glorified bodies**, then external causation becomes a real possibility. The Messiah and His servant kings will exercise very strict rulership during the millennium, ruling the nations with a rod of iron (Ps 2:9; Rev 2:27). Disobedience will not be tolerated (Zech 14:16-10). Anyone living in the millennial kingdom in flesh and blood bodies will be forced externally to follow carefully the law of God. At the end of the millennium, many of those in flesh and blood bodies will rebel against this iron yoke in the battle of Gog and Magog (Rev 20:8). But this rebellion, like any rebellion during the millennial reign, will be dealt with severely and quickly. If nonovercoming Jews enter the kingdom in flesh and blood bodies, they will be forced externally to follow carefully the resistible impulses of their regenerate nature and not yield to the sin nature that still resides in their flesh and blood bodies.

[370] The confirmation of elect angels in a state of perfect holiness seems to be built too much upon a Calvinistic view of election (1Tim 5:21). The basic idea is that God arbitrarily chose some angels to be sinless so they did not fall. They persevere because of their election. In this writer's estimation, it would better to say that they are elected because of their perseverance. This consideration gives rise to a more palatable variation which teaches that elect angels were confirmed in an immutable state of holiness after a period of probation. While the latter is not impossible, the present writer finds it improbable. If we are to rule over elect angels, then it would seem likely that we will be a higher order of being. While it is true that we will be like angels in many ways (Mt 22:30), there is no reason to suppose that they will be like us in every way. We are God's image-bearers. We were created to rule. They were not. They were created to serve us: "Are they not all ministering spirits, sent out to render service for the sake of those who will inherit salvation?" (Heb 1:14, cp. 2:5-10). The argument that it is impossible to mislead someone simply because that person is elect is false (Mt 24:24). Our confirmation is based on our regeneration, not on our election. Judas was elect (Jn 6:70), but this did not result in his confirmation. The elect are elected (Mk 13:20) but still can be lead astray (Mk 13:22). Conditional election (Eph 1:4; Jam 2:5) is not the basis upon which to build unconditional confirmation.

[371] Roger E. Olson, *Arminian Theology: Myths and Realities* (Downers Grove: InterVarsity Press, 2006), 99.

[372] Picirilli, *Free*, 61. See also Forlines, *Truth*, 325-328. White adopts the compatibilistic approach (*Debating*, 43,219). Feinberg notes that although "some Calvinists...have denied that humans are free," he in contrast adopts "*soft determinism or compatibilism*" (emphasis his). John Feinberg, Norman Geisler, Bruce Reichenbach, and Clark Pinnock, *Predestination & Free Will: Four Views of Divine Sovereignty & Human Freedom*, eds. David and Randall Basinger (Downers Grove: InterVarsity Press, 1986), 24. Geisler will have none of it and responds, "Feinberg's view really reduces to a strong Calvinistic determinism in which we are not actually free at all. According to this view, we cannot actually choose contrary to the desires which God gives us" (Ibid., 47). So although White may claim to be compatibilistic, it seems that his flat denial of free will is more to the point when he admits, "I do not believe in free will" (*Potter*, 335).

[373] John Murray, *The Epistle to the Romans*, NIC, ed. F. F. Bruce (Grand Rapids: Eerdmans Publishing Co., 1965), 287.

[374] Robert N. Wilkin, "The Lord Opened Her Heart: Acts 16:14," *GIF* (September-October 1995).

[375] R. Alan Cole, *The Epistle of Paul to the Galatians*, TNTC, ed., R. V. G. Tasker (Grand Rapids: Eerdmans Publishing Co., 1965), 51.

[376] Thomas L. Constable, *Notes on Acts*, CBSN, 241. All subsequent references to Constables notes on various books of the Bible will be to this series and be abbreviated to just that of the biblical name.

[377] John Calvin, "Romans 8:5-8," Commentary on Romans. Available at http://www.ccel.org/c/calvin /comment3/comm_vol38/htm/xii.ii.htm#_fnb5. Accessed on 8 August, 2004.

[378] Alternately, if *the people of Nineveh believed in God* salvifically, then Luther was correct to use Jonah 3:5 to support an *ordo salutis* that places saving faith before repentance (Hodges, *Free*, 22-223; n. 5).

[379] White, *Potter*, 110.

[380] Even Vance admits, "So in a sense, all men are predestinated to everlasting death, but not unconditionally" (p. 299). He goes on to argue that reprobation is based on man's response to the gospel, not on an unconditional eternal decree (e.g., pp. 302-305). I agree but would further point out that a conditional theological reprobation based on foreknowledge is not incompatible with his argument. Had Vance explored this theological possibility, he may have been able to do a better job handling Rev 3:5 and Rev 22:19. As it is, he believes these two verses, taken together, demonstrate that the elect can have their names erased from the Book of Life, and he calls it, "The reprobation of the elect" (p. 338). He does not explain how he reconciles this view with his belief in eternal security. Vance has a considerable handicap in adopting the KJV translation with its reference to *Book of Life* in Rev 22:19. This is probably the most difficult verse in the Bible for a KJVO advocate who believes in eternal security. The CT and MT read *tree of life*, which is a misthological concept. But the soteriological reading of *Book of Life* in the TR presents Vance with what well may be an insurmountable obstacle to his theology, leaving him with a choice between TR or eternal security. I choose eternal security.

[381] Forlines, *Truth*, 374.

[382] Stephen. Strehle, "Universal Grace and Amyraldianism." *WTJ* 51:2 (Fall 1989): 345-57.

[383] As Elwell summarizes, "Since no sinner is capable of coming to Christ on his own, God in grace wills to create faith." Walter A., Elwell, ed., Evangelical Dictionary of Theology (Grand Rapids: Baker Book House, 1986), s.v. "Amyraldianism," by B. A. Demarest. In Amyraldianism, it is not that people in general can believe; rather, specific people must believe.

[384] For translation of Justin Martyr's statement, see for example, chapter 42 (i.e., XLII): "Those who it was foreknown were to believe in Him." Justin Martyr. *Dialogue of Justin, Philosopher and Martyr, with Trypho, a Jew*. Available at http://www.ccel.org/fathers/ANF-01/just/justintrypho.html#Section42. Accessed on April 5, 2005.

[385] Thomas R. Edgar, "The Meaning of ΠΡΟΓΙΝΩΣΚΩ ("Foreknowledge")," *CTSJ 44* (Spring 2003): 49.

[386] Sellers, 56.

[387] Gordon Olson, 158.

[388] White, Debating, 145.

[389] Sellers, 58.

[390] Edgar, "Foreknowledge," 58-59.

[391] Gordon Olson, 161.

[392] For more *whosoever* passages see Jn 4:13; 6:40; 11:26; 12:46; Acts 2:41; Rom 9:33; 10:11 in the KJV. The *whosoever* is based on constructions identical with or similar to the *pas ho* [*whosoever*] employed in Jn 3:15-16.

[393] White, *Debating*, 297.

[394] Ibid., 322.

[395] John Calvin, "Chapter 2. Of faith. The definition of it. Its peculiar properties." Available at http://www.ccel.org/c/calvin/institutes/htm/iv.iii.iii.htm. Accessed on September 1, 2004.

[396] John Calvin, "Luke 17:11-21." Available at http://www.ccel.org/c/calvin/comment3/comm_vol32 /htm/xxxix.htm. Accessed on September 1, 2004.

[397] John Calvin, "Matthew 13:18-23; Mark 4:13-20; Luke 8:11-15." Available at http://www.ccel.org /c/calvin/comment3/comm_vol32/htm/xx.htm. Accessed on September 1, 2004.

[398] Abraham Kuyper, "Testimonies." Available at http://www.ccel.org/k/kuyper/holy_spirit/htm/vi.viii.viii.htm. Accessed on September 1, 2004.

[399] Loraine Boettner, "The Reformed Doctrine of Predestination. Chapter XIV. The Perseverance of the Saints," in *Reformed Doctrine of Predestination.* Available at http://www.ccel.org/b/boettner/predest/14.htm. Accessed on September 1, 2004.

[400] This is not to say that God is never pleased, in some sense of the word, to punish those who deserve it. While it is true that passages such as Eze 18:23 and 33:10-11 confirm that God does not derive any pleasure over the punishment of the wicked, Calvinists take recourse to passages such as Dt 28:23 and Prov 1:26 to show that it is possible to argue that the punishment of the wicked is indeed in accord with God's good pleasure. However, not even these latter passages are conducive to Calvinism. To the contrary, the logical structure of these verses is clearly: A ⇒ B. If (A) you rebel, then (B) God will take pleasure in destroying you. Your freewill response determines God's resultant emotion: A = your freewill response, and B = God's contingent response. God's pleasure is determined by, and therefore contingent upon, your obedience or lack of it. Calvinism inverts the logical order and teaches: if God is pleased to damn you, then you will rebel (B ⇒ A). If you are damned, then you will rebel. Conversely, if you are elect, then you will persevere. Your perseverance or lack thereof is contingent upon God's good pleasure in Calvinism. This is an inversion of the verse. Calvinism's inversion is a perversion of the contingent agency.

[401] White, *Potter*, 137-138.

[402] Hunt, *Love*, 364.

[403] Thiessen, 260.

[404] Walter, A. Elwell, ed. *Evangelical Dictionary of Theology* (Grand Rapids: Baker Book House, 1986), s.v. "Foreknowledge," by G. W. Bromiley.

[405] Edgar, "Foreknowledge," 69.

[406] Gordon Olson, 157ff. Also see Edgar, "Foreknowledge."

[407] Bromiley, "Foreknowledge."

[408] Peterson and Williams, 176-177.

[409] John F. Walvoord, *The Holy Spirit: A Comprehensive Study of the Person and Work of the Holy Spirit,* third ed. (Grand Rapids: Zondervan Publishing House, 1958), 126.

[410] Gordon Olson, 41.

[411] White, *Debating*, 17.

[412] Ibid., 18.

[413] Ibid., 260.

[414] Ibid., 265-268.

[415] White, Potter, 140.

[416] Hunt, *Love*, 255.

[417] Gordon Olson, 226.

[418] Vance, 447-448, 485-487.

[419] Guthrie, *Epistles*, 71.

[420] Sellers, 70.

[421] Ken Keathley, "Salvation and the Sovereignty of God: The Great Commission as the Expression of Divine Will," *JOTGES* 19:39 (Spring, 2006): 3.

[422] Ibid., 18.

[423] Ibid., 21.

[424] Sellers, 72.

[425] Ibid.

[426] Hodges believes that temporal destruction of the Tribulation is in view in 2Pet 3:9 (*Harmony*, 60).

[427] White, *Potter*, 147.

[428] Corner, *Security*, 434, 609.

[429] Dillow, 492.

[430] Shank, *Elect*, 181.

[431] Sellers, 74.

[432] R. C. H. Lenski, *The Interpretation of St. Luke's Gospel* (Minneapolis: Augsburg Publishing House, 1961), 416-417.

[433] William F. Arndt, *Luke*, CCC (St. Louis: Concordia Publishing House, 1956), 215.

[434] Vance, 272, 482-484.

[435] Dillow, 82, see also 131, 447, 452.

[436] Zane C. Hodges, *Hebrews*, BKC (Wheaton: Victor Books, 1984), 796-797. Also, see Zane C. Hodges "*Class notes on Hebrews,*" n.d., 138-142.

[437] David R. Anderson, "The National Repentance of Israel," *JOTGES* 11:21 (Autumn 1998): 17.

[438] Pentecost, 74.

[439] Anderson, *JOTGES*, vol. 11, num, 21, National, 17.

[440] Pentecost, Things, 74.

[441] Anderson, "National," 16.

[442] Ibid., 17.

[443] Pentecost, 87-88.

[444] Baughman also believes the covenant was expanded: "Not until Abram had separated from Lot, meeting the fourth condition—'from thy kindred'—did God promise to him and his seed the land forever ([Gen] 13:15)" (p. 23). For other possibilities that still affirm the unconditional core, see Paul N. Benware, *Understanding End Times Prophecy: A Comprehensive Approach* (Chicago: Moody Publications, 2006), 40-50.

[445] William E. Brown, "The New Testament Concept of the Believer's Inheritance," Th.D. diss. (Dallas Theological Seminary, 1984), 105-110.

[446] Everett F. Harrison *Romans*, vol. 10, EBC (Grand Rapids: Zondervan Publishing House, 1976), 51.

[447] Dillow, 88.

[448] *Logizomai* is a verbal derivative of *lego*, whereas *logos* is a nominal derivative, making *logizomai* and *logos* cognates of one another. In 2Tim 4:16, Paul evidently is alluding to the Bema and prays that the Lord will not hold this failure against his fellow believers. His statement at the beginning of the epistle is similar, where Paul uses the optative to expresses the prayer that the Lord grant Onesiphorus to find misthological mercy from the Lord at the Bema on that day (2Tim 1:16). Paul uses the optative to express the same desire on behalf of those who deserted him in 2Tim 4:16. Perhaps Paul anticipates that Onesiphorus will find mercy by virtue of his service to Paul and that Paul's friends will find mercy by virtue of Paul's prayer on their behalf. Or it may be that he prays that God will so influence these deserters so that they will repent and receive misthological forgiveness. In any event, although some commentators speculate that not all those who deserted Paul were unregenerate, it is still reasonable to assume that some of those who deserted Paul were believers. Certainly, not all of Paul's supporters were lost. Since God will judge all men, lost and saved, on the basis of their works, this reckoning has misthological applicability to believers.

As L-N notes, "The phrase εἰς λόγον in Php 4.17 is a technical expression referring to the settlement of an account and indicates that this is a credit to the account" (57.228). The fact that believers, as well as non-believers, must give an *account* (*logos*) of themselves is affirmed by Paul in Rom 14:12. Peter affirms the same truth (1Pet 4:5). For believers this will be a Bema event (Rom 14:10).

The writer of Hebrews also talks about believers having to give an account of themselves before God. The results will be unprofitable for those believers who have performed poorly (Heb 13:17; cp. 4:13). Jesus also discusses the necessity of believers giving account of themselves before God in parabolic form: "Give an account of your stewardship" (Lk 16:2). "For this reason the kingdom of heaven may be compared to a certain king who wished to settle accounts with his slaves" (Mt 18:23). "Now after a long time the master of those slaves came and settled accounts with them" (Mt 25:19). These texts portray misthological accountability.

The latter text is of particular significance since it is embedded in the last pericope concerning the outer darkness of Mt 25:30. This day of reckoning results in the unfaithful believer being found unworthy of the misthological entrustment with which he had been entrusted by his Lord. Consequently, the servant is condemned misthologically and held accountable for the previous entrustment, and future misthological entrustment is denied. In the first Matthean pericope, the servant is found to have the debt of the entrustment misthologically imputed (i.e., counted) against him. In the second, the interest he should have accrued is misthologically imputed (i.e., counted) against him. The notion that misthological imputation is simply before men rather than before God is patently false. This misthological imputation and corresponding justification or condemnation will take place before God at the Bema (Rom 14:10; 2Cor 5:10). Jesus requires misthological imputation of faith, forgiveness, and service before God in order to avoid misthological bereavement in the outer darkness. Paul likewise acknowledges the reality of misthological accountability before God and misthological imputation by God.

[449] Lopez, *Romans*, 34.

[450] Ibid., 51.

[451] Ibid., 97.

[452] Ibid.

[453] Ibid., 36, 297.

[454] René A. Lopez, "Is Faith a Necessary Gift to Receive Salvation?" 7-8. Available at http://www.scripture unlocked.com/pdfs/IsFaithaGift.pdf. Accessed on September 9, 2006.

[455] Ibid., 101.

[456] Hodges, *Hebrews*, 797.

[457] In commenting on the "steps of faith of our father Abraham" (Rom 4:12), Govett notes, "Abraham is *doubly* the father of believers" (emphasis his, 88). (1) He is the father of justification by faith for believers of course. (2) However, "after justification comes the *walk* of the justified—'*The obedience of faith*'" (emphasis his, 88). The exhortation to Abraham in Gen 17:1 to "Walk before Me, and be blameless" commences a chapter dealing with "the principle of *reward according to works*" (emphasis his, 100). Concerning Rom 4:22, Govett evidently

recognizes that the initial justification by faith was soteric (citing Gen 15:4-5) but the second justification by faith was mistholic (citing Gen 17:5). This latter justification by mistholic faith was granted subsequently because "Abraham under this new trial of his faith still stood firm" (p. 121). Proceeding to Rom 4:23-25, he points out that Abraham was (1) justified *by faith* and subsequently by (2) *works of faith* (p. 101). Robert Govett, *Govett on Romans* (Hayesville, NC: Schoettle Publishing Company, 2010).

[458] Eaton, 176-183

[459] Shank, *Life*, 110.

[460] Grammatically, I may be faulted for saying *should = could* to show potential. *Can* shows power or ability and *could* shows conditional power or ability. Additionally, one technical difference between *may* and *might* that is sometimes noted is that *may* is used with verbs that are present or future, whereas *might* is used with the past tense. Another possible grammatical distinction is to use *may* to show permission or possibility and *might* to show conditional permission or possibility. Therefore, to be grammatically correct, I should say that *should = may* or *might*. Nevertheless, this precision is not necessarily followed for the sake of interaction of similar meanings with similar sounds. *May* is a popular translation for Jn 3:16. NAB uses *might* in v. 16, but it uses *may* for the identical expression in v. 15. Some translations use *may* while many use *might* in Jn 3:17 for a potential conditional action. Technical distinctions are evidently not followed by the translators and are not followed in the current discussion. The point I make concerning flippant usage is based more on popular usage than grammatical distinction. In such cases, *may* might be just as unsuitable for conveying moral obligation.

[461] White, *Debating*, 41-42.

[462] White, *Freedom*, 48.

[463] Walls and Dongell, 132. See their entire discussion 125-134.

[464] Jn 3:16 and 6:40 are very close verbal parallels. "**Everyone who believes in Him** will not perish, but *will* **have eternal life**" (3:16; TM). "**Everyone who** beholds the Son and **believes in Him,** *will* **have eternal life**" (6:40). The NAU justifiably has changed the *may* of 6:40 to *will*. Having eternal life and not perishing are not mere possibilities or even probabilities: In the case of those who believe, they are certainties. The NAU also has changed Jn 12:46 from *may* to *will*, evidently due to its implicit certainty: "I have come as Light into the world, so that everyone who believes in Me **will** not remain in darkness." Every believer already has positionally passed out of death in life (Jn 5:24). Not only *should* believers be in the light, they *are* in the light. *Will* is a better translation than *should* in this verse. If the translational intent is to use *would* or an equivalent term when the context demands certainty, however, then the NAU is not entirely consistent with this methodology. For example, in Jn 17:2 the NAS has Jesus saying, "That to all whom You have given Him, He **may** give eternal life." Is there any doubt that Jesus will give eternal life to all whom the Father has given Him? If not, then is not *will* a better translation? It could be argued that *may* is best to convey the thought of enablement. The authority that Jesus has received from the Father enables Him to give eternal life. Even so, there is no doubt that He will give it, and *will* is superior. Jn 20:31 is another verse that combines enablement with certainty. "These have been written that you **may** believe that Jesus is the Christ, the Son of God; and that believing you **may** have life in His name." This verse contains two *hina* clauses, the first one is appropriately translated as *may* in order to express enablement. However, the second one should be translated *will* (or equivalent) to denote certainty. There is no doubt that those who believe actually have eternal life.

Other Johannine passages where NAU has abandoned *should* (e.g., in favor of the stronger rendition of *would/was*) include Jn 9:2,22; 11:50,57; 12:42; 13:1; 18:39; 19:31). In some of these examples, the first *hina* clause should be rendered differently than the second *hina* clause. (1) "These have been written so that you *may* believe that Jesus is the Christ, the Son of God; and that by believing you *would* have life in His name" (Jn 20:31; TM). The **intent** of the writing is so that the unbeliever *may* believe. The **guarantee** of the writing is that those who do believe *would/will* have eternal life. (2) "It is expedient for us that one man *should* die on behalf of the people so that the whole nation *would/will* not perish" (Jn 11:50; TM). As a result of His death the whole nation would not perish. For further examples, consider the translation of the phrase *that the Scripture may/should be fulfilled* versus *that the Scripture would be fulfilled*. See *The Race of Grace* for discussion on such examples.

Of course, such translational shifts (from purpose to result) are not limited to the *hina* construction. In Heb 3:18 the NAS changed from *should* to *would*. The NKJ likewise abandoned the *should* of the KJV for the better translation of *would* in this verse. The *should/would not* of Heb 3:18 is parallel to the *will not* of Heb 3:11 and 4:3. In other cases, NAU perhaps should have inserted *would* but failed to do so: "We have believed in Christ Jesus, that we **would** [not *may*] be justified by faith in Christ" (Gal 2:16). Those who have believed have already met the condition for justification by faith. "Others were tortured, not accepting their release, in order that they **would** [not *might*] obtain a better resurrection" Heb 11:35). Believers who endure suffering have met this condition for a better resurrection and are assured of the misthological result.

Tit 3:7 is debatable. The NAS has changed the *might* to *would*. "Being justified by His grace we would be made heirs according to the hope of eternal life." If this verse is talking about unconditional heirship (as Dillow believes, 86), then this is a correct rendition. However, is justification by faith the only condition, or is it just the initial qualification? If it is the single condition for being an heir, then Dillow is correct. On the other hand, it simply may be the qualification for earning the inheritance. Paul proceeds to confirm, "This is a trustworthy statement; and concerning these things I want you to speak confidently, so that those who have believed God may be careful to engage in good deeds" (3:8). The *trustworthy statement* is that heirship is possible to those who are justified by faith and that eternal life is a misthological hope. However, in order to obtain this heirship and misthological hope, they must be *careful to engage in good deeds*. Paul appears to be saying that believers may earn the inheritance by engaging in good works. For this reason, Tit 3:7 is best translated as *might, may*, or *should*. Believers may become heirs (and be recognized as such at the Bema) if they engage in good works.

[465] R. C. H. Lenski, *The Interpretation of St. John's Revelation* (Minneapolis: Augsburg Publishing House, 1963), 265, cp. 1398.

[466] Although Wallace uses the translation of *should* in Jn 3:16, he nevertheless acknowledges its "sure accomplishment." He considers it a *purpose-result* use of *hina* but says that even if it is merely a *simple-purpose*, "there is evidently no doubt about the accomplishment" (GGBB, 473). For this reason, I prefer rendering it as *would*.

I am mindful that White uses the purpose-result argument to try to limit *world* to the elect in Jn 3:17. In a nutshell, this argument is that God's purpose-result in sending His Son is the salvation of the world. Since the result is guaranteed, the word *world* must be limited to the elect since not everyone in the world will be saved. Roberts rightly calls White to task for overstating his syntactical argument. Yet Roberts then proceeds with an overly skeptical response to the syntax. On the basis of the nature of the subjunctive mood, Roberts states: "In some contexts, it can suggest a high level of probability, but seldom, if ever, absolute certainty of purpose." Don Roberts, "James White on John 3:14-18: An Examination by Don Roberts, B.A., M.Div." Available at http://www.twincentral.com/site/pages/articles/doctrines /beliefs/calvinism/jw_john3.shtml#21. Accessed on February 21, 2005.

White's discussion had given the misimpression that the syntax settles the issue and determines that a purpose-result clause is necessarily understood in Jn 3:17 as showing guaranteed result. Although, with Roberts, I reject White's assessment of Jn 3:17, I maintain that the purpose-result classification for Jn 3:16 as denoting a guaranteed result is valid when syntactical and contextual factors are taken together. In other words, just because we have *hina* plus an aorist passive subjunctive (which is the case in Jn 3:17), this does not prove that a purpose-result clause is involved or that a guaranteed result is certain. As is demonstrated by my discussion of 1Cor 5:5 and 11:32, both of which implement *hina* plus an aorist passive subjective, I do not necessarily regard this construction to be a purpose-result. In fact, although I regard 5:5 as showing guaranteed result, I do not take it as a purpose-result. Moreover, I agree with Arminians in 11:32 to the extent that this verse shows intended result rather than guaranteed result. Concerning the *eis* plus infinitive in the related passage in Heb 12:10, a construction which is commonly understood as denoting either purpose or result, I again prefer to take it as purpose clause—not a guaranteed result. My syntactical conclusions have been based on contextual considerations. Compare endnotes 186, 564.

Roberts overreacted to White by appealing to Robertson's *Short Grammar* in trying to limit the subjective mood to doubtful assertions and limiting absolute assertions to the indicative mood. In his full grammar, Robertson acknowledges that this statement in his short grammar is a generalization, admitting that these moods "overlap all along the line." Robertson then immediately goes on to describe the futuristic subjunctive. He calls it an "emphatic future" and most importantly clarifies: "The practical equivalence of the aorist subjunctive and the future indicative is evident in the subordinate clauses, particularly those with εἰ, ἵνα [*hina*], ὅς, ὅστις" (*Grammar*, 928). Put differently, the subjective can make a positive assertion about the certainty of the future event with just as much force as the indicative. Robertson refutes Roberts. Therefore, Roberts' claim that a purpose-result clause is "an alleged grammatical rule," "an unproven assumption," and "a questionable grammatical principle," is just as much an error in the direction of skepticism as White's treatment is in the way of positivism. Even Roberts' more restrained remark that this *hina* clause with the subjunctive "seldom, if ever, [suggests] absolute certainty of purpose" is more skeptical than is warranted. Wallace's discussion of the purpose-result clause may be consulted for further elaboration (GGBB, 473-474). The two examples he provides are Jn 3:16 and Phil 2:10-11. The latter text is uncontestable and Wallace's discussion is commendable. See *The Race of Grace* for additional examples.

Pertaining to the discussion of Jn 3:16, note that the phrase, "should not perish," in Jn 3:16 is equivalent in terms of absolute certainty to "shall never perish" in Jn 10:28. Both statements use the subjunctive to express absolute certainty for those who meet the stated condition in each respective context. To illustrate this certainty in terms of Robertson's statement, the aorist subjective of "shall not perish" is equivalent to the future indicative of "shall not snatch them out of My hand." The phrases are used in synonymous parallel within the same verse of Jn 10:28, a text which expresses absolute security in the certainty of safety. The guarantee of eternal life may also be seen in comparing the intended result expressed by the subjunctive in the phrase, "have eternal life," in 3:15-16 with the actual result expressed by the indicative in such passages as Jn 3:36; 4:14; 5:24. As believers, we not only should have eternal life, we actually have it. The intended result of eternal life for the believer is expressed by *hina* plus the subjunctive in 6:40 as "may have eternal life," but it is emphatically and immediately assured as being the actual result with the indicative as "has eternal life" in 6:47,54. Moreover, both v. 40 and v. 54 immediately go on to use the indicative to assure believers that they will be raised. Hence, I can do no other than deduce that the intended possession of eternal life by the believer is the guaranteed result by God.

The *intended result* (or intention or goal) normally is referred to simply as *purpose* in distinction to *result*. It refers to an action which may or may not actually occur. For an interesting diagram of the two in regards to participles, see Wallace chart (GGBB, 638). But one cannot simply conclude that Jn 3:16 is merely an intended result. Despite Roberts' skepticism concerning combining the purpose and result, by comparing equivalent subjective and indicative statements above, I have demonstrated (on Roberts' own terms and from Robertson's own grammatical assessment) that the intended result may indeed be a guaranteed result. What is intended for the world is guaranteed to the believer, namely, eternal life. The purpose and result combine in this particular case to give a divine guarantee that everyone who believes in the Son for eternal life actually has it. To say otherwise would be to call the Lord a liar. His promise in Jn 6:47 is too clear to conclude otherwise. In this case, the indicative result cannot be separated from the subjunctive intent. The Lord intends to give believers eternal life and has assured them that He not only will do so but has actually done so. On some occasions the Lord is not content merely to leave us with intentions; rather, He wishes to covey the certainty of what He intends (Is 14:24).

Lavender's criticism of White, and of Wallace for that matter, by and large, misses the mark because Lavender, like Roberts, overstresses the contingent nature of the subjunctive (*Freedom*, 27-29, 184-188). One must therefore agree with White ("Blinded"), when in this context, he says:

> The *hina* clause expresses God's purpose in the sending of the Son. It does *not* contain some kind of sense that "God did this which *might* result in that, *if* this happens...." While the subjunctive can be used in conditional sentences, it is also used in purpose/result clauses *without* the insertion of the idea of doubt or hesitant affirmation. The word "might" then is not to be read "might as in maybe, hopefully, only if other things happen" but "might" as in "I turned on the printer so that I might use it to print out this letter." Purpose, not lack of certainty.

Whether the purpose is simple or guaranteed is contextually determined. Of course, in agreement with Lavender, I would assert that White has strained this syntax in trying to make it result in a limited atonement. The guaranteed result is limited to whoever believes. *Whoever* is a subset of *world*.

Prince claims that those who have "substituted the word 'would' in Jn 3:16" are misquoting the Scripture and lying (p. 30). He evidences no knowledge of purpose-result constructions. Yet with such proofs (if I may call his overly optimistic assessments of his own arguments proofs), he says that he has "proven with absolute certainty that it [unconditional security] is wrong" (p. 105). His book exhibits the very pride that he attributes to the securitist camp, yet his book presents such an extremely weak case for conditional security that I cannot even recommend it as a worthy read for representation of that position. Benny D. Prince, *Once Saved, Always? The False Doctrine of Eternal Security* (Bloomington: Author House, 2007).

[467] Other passages where *may* or *should* are better translations than *would* include: Jn 5:34 (*may*—enablement), 5:40 (*may*—enablement) 11:15 (may—enablement), 11:42 (*may*—enablement), 19:35 (*may*—enablement); 20:31a (*may*—enablement); Acts 19:4 (*should*—moral obligation); 1Cor 9:24 (*may*—conditional); 1Cor 10:33 (*may*—enablement); Eph 5:26-27 (*may, may, may*—enablement); 1Tim 6:19 (*may*—conditional); 2Tim 2:10 (*may*—enablement), Heb 10:36 (*may*—conditional); 1Jn 3:23 (*should*—moral obligation). To its credit, the NAS does not render this as *would*.

[468] Some have tried to insist upon the use of *should* in Jn 3:16 on the basis of its future applicability. For example, some would say that the similar construction in Jn 6:40 is best translated as *may* have eternal life because it also applies to some future believers who have not yet believed. However, its futuristic fulfillment does not nullify its certainty. In the case of those who do believe in Him, the results are no longer contextually in question. This is even clear in an exclusively futuristic text such as Jn 11:26. The fact that they have not yet believed does not render the result uncertain once they believe.

Likewise, the syntactically parallel statement in Jn 16:2 should not be translated as, "the time is coming that everyone who kills you *should* think that he is offering God a service." Rather, it tells what they *will* think. The subjunctive should be translated as *will* because it describes the situation as it will be at that time. This is the same observation I am making regarding Jn 3:16 and 6:40. Whoever believes, whoever they are, *will* have eternal life at that time, not merely *should*. Again, some have tried to evade this conclusion by pointing out that Jn 3:16 and 6:40 are talking about *everyone*. But the syntax for all three verses is the same. The verses are saying *that everyone* (*hina pas ho*) *will*. Everyone who kills you will think he is doing God's work, and everyone who believes will have eternal life. The insecurity of Arminianism is just as unnecessary as the irresistibility of Calvinism. The *will* does not mean that God will cause them to kill or cause to think that they are doing His will when they kill in 16:2. Nor does *will* in 3:16 or 6:40 mean that God will cause them to believe.

[469] Ashby, a representative of soft Arminianism (i.e., the Reformed Arminianism, also called Classical Arminianism) provides an important clarification in contradistinction to strong Arminianism (i.e., Wesleyan Arminianism) which asserts that regeneration would be lost in the case of backsliding. According to Reformed

Arminians, "there is only way for a believer to lose salvation: a decisive act of apostasy" (p. 182-183). "Rejection of faith in Christ, and that alone, removes one from union with Christ" (p. 187).

I do not provide substantial interaction with Ashby in the present book on this particular variance of Arminian theology, but I do provide interaction with Forlines, whom Ashby repeatedly and rightly quotes in defense of this position as advocating this perspective. (See for example, endnote 346.) Forlines is an astute theologian. I provide more sustained interaction with his approach to NOSAS in my *Mere Christianity and Moral Christianity.* Suffice it to say here that trying to maintain this NOSAS is more difficult than one might initially suppose. Although in theory it sounds better than strong Arminianism, it is fought with exegetical difficulty. For example, would a Reformed Arminian actually allow that a believer could be saved from hell by dead faith? If not, their claimed allegiance to the theory of loss of regeneration only upon the grounds of theological apostasy can be shown to be fraudulent. Moral apostasy easily slips in as additional grounds to theological apostasy, even in the soft Arminian perspective. On the other hand, a soft Arminian like Becker might actually succeed, where even Forlines fails, and at least be able to limit loss of regeneration to loss of faith. Because I met Becker at a kingdom conference, where we exchanged books, I would infer that she holds to a strong doctrine of rewards. This goes with the territory at kingdom conferences. One would think that she would be able to affirm that dead faith saves from hell but not from the outer darkness. Consequently, she may be able to make a better case for the Reformed Arminian perspective than what I have encountered in Forlines. What he only has been able to do in theory, she might be able to do in practice—at least as much so as possible given the Reformed Arminian premises. Of course, as a kingdom advocate of unconditional security, I would be interested in defending that doctrine against a kingdom version of conditional security should Becker venture to put forth such an argument. But as it is, I already have pointed out an inconsistency in her limited argument for conditional security in the present book and see no point in pressing the matter further at this point since my other books, and even this one, provide substantial arguments for unconditional security that are more than a match for the arguments for conditional security that I thus far have encountered.

Also, if soft Arminianism be defined as affirming that believers only lose regeneration in the case of apostasy, then, by the same token, soft Calvinism would be defined as affirming that believers *would* only lose regeneration in the case of apostasy. The present work does interact with writers who do hold this view. See discussion of RFG2 and RFG3. Seymour, in particular, would make a good, potential example of someone who holds a kingdom version of what some would regard as conditional security from a soft Calvinistic perspective. However, given my labeling, I would not regard Seymour as a soft Calvinist. Since he successfully deals with the dead faith issue from an acceptable FG position and affirms that the outer darkness is a misthological issue, he is a valid representative of kingdom misthology. To be sure, his affirming eternal security from a perspective that denies that apostates were ever saved would qualify him as a representative of what some would call soft Calvinism. If so, he would be a better representative of soft Calvinism than Geisler.

For my part though, I would label Seymour as a *soft securitist* rather than a soft Calvinist. He apparently holds a purely descriptive view of perseverance in the faith (or better yet to a FG affirmation of the preservation of faith). By the same token, I would even regard Lutzer to be a strong securitist rather than a Calvinist regarding the issue of unconditional security. Although I lock horns with some of Lutzer's Reformed remarks in the present book, when it comes to addressing the issue of unconditional security, he certainly writes like a securitist (rather than a Calvinist). Basically, he would define *historic Calvinism* as conditioning security on perseverance. From his assessment (rather than mine), Calvinistic writers (such as Edwards and Pink) can be regarded as teaching unconditional security (even though they condition salvation on perseverance) because perseverance is grounded in unconditional election. In contradiction, I do not believe that someone who teaches conditional security can be called an unconditional securitist. *Other Calvinists*, to use Lutzer's repeated term, do not condition soteric salvation on perseverance and thus affirm that the apostate remains saved. To his credit, Lutzer seems to write from this *other* perspective. From that perspective, I would call him a *strong securitist* rather than a Calvinist. (See my *3D Unconditional Security.*) Even though I hold the view he describes as being associated with other Calvinists, I certainly would not describe myself as a Calvinist; in fact, I would resent that label. For his perspective, see Erwin Lutzer, *The Doctrines that Divide: A Fresh Look at the Historic Doctrines That Separate Christians* (Grand Rapids, MI: Kregel Publications, 1998), 225-239.

[470] Robert A. Peterson, "The Perseverance of the Saints: A Theological Exegesis of Four Key New Testament Passages," Presbyterion 17/2 (1991): 99, n. 17.

[471] Peterson and Williams, 77-79,90.

[472] Horton, *Security*, 24, see also, 27,29,36,37.

[473] Ibid., 57.

[474] Walls and Dongell, 57, n. 16. Geisler, *Chosen*, 121.

[475] Walls and Dongell, 13.

[476] Vic Reasoner, "Review of "The Believer's Conditional Security." Available at http://www.fwponline.cc /v16n1reasonerb.html. Accessed on August 25, 2007.

[477] Geisler, *Security*, 68.

[478] Ibid.

[479] Ibid.

[480] Gordon Olson, 318. If Olson merely is affirming the believer's preservation in the faith but not the believer's perseverance in the faith, then he qualifies as soft-shelled unconditional securitist. Indeed, Wilkin states that when he was at DTS, he "was was taught that the perseverance was guaranteed by God and was something that the believer would do whether he wanted to or not," but he "was never that told that eternal security was contingent upon that perseverance." Robert N. Wilkin, "Review of 'Grace and Warning in Paul's Gospel,'" *JOTGES* 24:40 (Spring, 20011), 13. I would call this preservation rather than perseverance. See *3D Unconditional Security*.

[481] By application the verse may be used in regard to seeking God soteriologically perhaps, but the interpretation of Heb 11:6 is dealing with rewards and thus misthological seeking.

[482] Geisler, *Security*, 76.

[483] Idem, *Chosen*, 124.

[484] Idem, *Security*, 76-77.

[485] Ibid., 86.

[486] Ibid., 103, n. 37.

[487] Hodges, "Legalism," 30-31. Wilkin also makes multiple assertions to the same effect: "Present sanctification is both possible and natural for every believer" ("Present Sanctification," 10). "Loving other Christians is a natural expression of who we are. Hating other Christians is not." Robert N. Wilkin, "Because We Love the Brethren: 1 John 3:14," *GIF* (November, 1994). "The normal Christian experience should be ever-increasing holiness." Robert N. Wilkin, "Letters to the Editor," *GIF* (May, 1990). Farstad was in harmony with expressing good works as the natural result of regeneration: "Bible-believing Protestants do indeed believe in good works as a normal *fruit* of salvation, but grace alone as the *root*" (emphasis his). Arthur L. Farstad, "We Believe In: Good Works," *JOTGES* 2:2 (Autumn, 1989): 3.

[488] Geisler, *Security*, 90.

[489] Ibid., 105.

[490] Ibid., 98.

[491] Ibid., 106.

[492] Ibid., 109. Geisler repeatedly denies that perseverance is a condition (pp. 86, 89).

[493] In FG theology, justification is not divorced from sanctification in that it makes sanctification possible, profitable, and natural. Forlines criticizes the FG view, explaining the relationship this way: "Sanctification is *dependent* upon justification. Justification is *not dependent* upon sanctification" (*Truth*, 217; emphasis his. See also, 241-242.). However, FG theology would agree with this statement but question Forlines' commitment to his own comment since he follows this statement by deriding FG theology as being cheap easy-believism of either a pseudo-Calvinism or non-Calvinistic variety. Yet if justification guarantees progressive sanctification, as he believes, then it would be impossible to lose salvation, which is contrary to his NOSAS claims! In his view, the **final** realization of justification **is** dependent upon progressive sanctification. Had he been consistent with his own issuing discussion, he would have acknowledged that regeneration results in internal changes that assert positive influence for external changes but not in a deterministic fashion that reduces us to passive puppets so that Rom 12:2 remains a command to free will agents rather than a promise to preprogrammed robots.

Lloyd Olson also has a chart that depicts FG between the Arminian and Calvinistic positions, but some of the groups he includes in the FG camp are open to question (*Security*, 212).). However, he did not make a distinction between strong and soft Arminians. A Free Will Baptist like Forlines would be better located in the Soft Arminian camp rather than in the FG camp.

[494] Ibid., 274.

[495] Shank, *Life*, 301.

[496] For an article that compares and contrasts Augustine to Owen on this matter of believers losing regeneration, see Henry Knapp, "Augustine and Owen on Perseverance," WTJ 62:1 (Spring 2000): 78-83. Augustine's major work on the topic is, *Rebuke and Grace*. Available at *http://www.newadvent.org/fathers/1511.htm*. Accessed on June 10, 2005. In ch. 9, Augustine answers objections from both the unregenerate and regenerate to this argument that perseverance is a gift only given to the elect. His answer to the regenerate nonelect is: "If, however, being already regenerate and justified, he relapses of his own will into an evil life, assuredly he cannot say, 'I have not received,' because of his own free choice to evil he has lost the grace of God, that he had received." Regeneration, like justification, will be lost by the nonelect by their own free will because God did not will to give them the gift of perseverance. Augustine continues to respond to this objection in ch. 11 with the rebuke that not receiving the gift of perseverance is not an excuse for not persevering. In ch. 18 of this work, Augustine marvels "that to some of His own children—whom He has regenerated in Christ—to whom He has given faith, hope, and love, God does not give perseverance also." The end result is that some of God's regenerate children lose their regeneration because God did not give them the gift of perseverance. God gave them the gift of life but not the gift of perseverance, so they fail to retain their regeneration. His related work, *Gift of Perseverance*, continues with the same train of thought. Available at http://www.truecovenanter.com/gospel /augustin_perseverance.html. Accessed on June 10, 2005. In explaining the defection of 1Jn 2:9, he expounds it as follows:

They were not of us; for if they had been of us, they would certainly have continued with us"?...had not both been called, and followed Him that called them? and had not both become, from wicked men, **justified** men, and both been **renewed by the laver of regeneration**?...Nevertheless, in respect of a certain other distinction, they were not of us, for if they had been of us, they certainly would have continued with us. What then is this distinction?...They were not of them, because they had not been "called according to the purpose;" they had not been chosen in Christ before the foundation of the world; they had not gained a lot in Him; they had not been predestinated (ch. 21).

His assumption of baptismal regeneration (i.e., regeneration by the laver) should not be a distraction from the fact that he asserts that believers who have been justified and regenerated can commit apostasy and thereby lose both justification and regeneration because they are not among the elect believers who have been predestined to have the gift of perseverance. Also see Anderson, "Cities," 60-61.

[497] John Jefferson Davis, "The Perseverance Of The Saints: A History Of The Doctrine" *JETS* 34:2 (June 1991): 213-228.

[498] Anderson, "Change," 33, n. 30.

[499] Davis, in his history of perseverance, includes what might be called an affirmation of ontological regenerational immutability as being representative of Reformed thought: "Calvin also differs from Luther in his understanding of regeneration. According to Calvin, once the Spirit brings a person to regeneration this reality cannot be lost" (p. 217). He bases this understanding of Calvin's theology on Calvin's exegesis of 1Jn 3:9. According to Calvin, regeneration not only enables us to believe but insures that we will continue to believe "so that inflexible perseverance is added to newness of life." Calvin anticipates the interrogative reaction:

> But here a question arises, Whether the fear and love of God can be extinguished in any one who has been regenerated by the Spirit of God? for that this cannot be, seems to be the import of the Apostle's words. They who think otherwise refer to the example of David, who for a time labored under such a beastly stupor, that not a spark of grace appeared in him. Moreover, in the fifty-first Psalm, he prays for the restoration of the Spirit. It hence follows that he was deprived of him. I, however, doubt not but that the seed, communicated **when God regenerates his elect, as it is incorruptible, retains its virtue perpetually**. I, indeed, grant that it may sometimes be stifled, as in the case of David; but still, when all religion seemed to be extinct in him, **a live coal was hid under the ashes**. Satan, indeed, labors to root out whatever is from God in the elect; but when the utmost is permitted to him, there ever **remains a hidden root**, which afterwards springs up. (See John Calvin, "1 John 3:7-10." Available at http://www.ccel.org /c/calvin/comment3/comm_vol45/htm/v.iv.iii.htm. Accessed on June 24, 2006.)

The present writer is in considerable agreement with Calvin on this matter but would stop short of affirming that this hidden life necessarily will spring back up in perseverance in this life. Even so, the present writer would concur that ontological immutability assures that the believer will continue to believe at the trichotomous core of his or her being. Though the coal of the regenerate spirit is hidden in the ashes of the apostate soul and even if the root fails to manifest any life to the person herself in her deadened soul or to others through her sinful body, the spirit still lives on incorruptibly and perpetually. Calvin himself has well expressed it above: "When God regenerates his elect, as it is incorruptible, retains its virtue perpetually." By virtue of the fact that our regeneration is with incorruptible seed, it must abide perpetually and immutably. Much in the same vein of thought, Davis continues by quoting from the Cannons of Dort:

> Even when believers commit serious sin, God **"preserves in them the incorruptible seed of regeneration"** and prevents it from perishing or being totally lost. 1 John 3:9 and 1 Pet 1:23 are cited as Scriptural support. This Calvinistic understanding of the nature of **regeneration as a permanent** state of the soul differs from both the Roman Catholic and Lutheran understandings (p. 222).

Regeneration is permanent because it is the product of incorruptible seed. Davis again makes the same claim from the Westminster Confession:

> The **final perseverance of the believer depends** not upon free will but **upon the immutability of** God's decree of election, the unchangeable love of God, the efficacy of Christ's intercession, and the abiding power of God's Spirit and **the seed of regeneration** (p. 223).

Perseverance depends on regeneration, not retention of regeneration upon perseverance. Chafer is to be commended also, it would seem, in deriving the same conclusion, given the parameters of his Calvinistic views of perseverance:

> If salvation is the creation of **a new being composed of unchangeable and imperishable elements**, and in every aspect of it is made to depend on the perfect and **immutable** merit of the Son of God, there can be no failure. [See Lewis Sperry Chafer, "The Eternal Security of the Believer: Part 1" *BibSac* 106:423 (July 1949): 267.]

Since the new nature is composed of elements that are unchangeable and imperishable and dependent solely on the immutability of God's Son, there can be no doubt but that Chafer regards the new nature as being unconditionally immutable, which is the perspective of the present writer as well. Chafer, Calvin, and the creeds are much better in their above articulation than the mainstream Calvinistic thought in making the retention of regeneration conditioned on perseverance. But one fears that the creeds are not necessarily consistent, so the mainstream thought can find fertile soil for conditional affirmations therein as well. The problem for Calvinists is that on the one hand they want to make regeneration result in perseverance, and on the other hand they make perseverance result in (i.e., preserve) regeneration. In the latter affirmation, they make perseverance **necessary** for the retention of regeneration. What they give with one hand they take away with the other. Even FG Calvinists typically only have limited success in affirming perseverance in faith as an infallible expression of regeneration without conditioning preservation on perseverance. Not surprising, then, LS Calvinists are unable to avoid making perseverance a necessary cooperative contingency with anything approaching FG consistency.

Nevertheless, a question arises from time to time as to what Reformed FG would look like. Wilkin gives three different types of FG, which I will abbreviate as: (1) antinomian (AFG), (2) basic (BFG), and (3) Reformed (RFG). The present writer holds to the basic position—in which apostasy is regarded as possible but punishable at the Bema. In RFG, as defined by Wilkin, the possibility of apostasy is typically denied. See Robert Wilkin, "Putting the Gospel Debate in Sharper Focus" *GIF* (May 1991).

Perhaps those in RFG would be better described, broadly speaking, as those who affirm TULIP, or at least TUIP. Wilkin's focus on P (perseverance), nevertheless, has merit in that TULI is not of decisive importance in FG soteriology. Instead, the P of this acronym is the paramount concern. Accordingly, like Wilkin above, I will consider those in FG holding to P as *Reformed FG* (*RFG*). As usual, the concern centers on what to do with Reformed P. The present writer would urge those in RFG to consider the merits of limiting P to perseverance in a state of grace (through ontologically immutable regeneration similar to Calvin above) rather than to try to broaden P to include perseverance in the expression of grace (as Calvinists typically do in their extended exegesis).

Despite this appeal, I am aware that many will wish to see just how far they can push the envelope in the Calvinistic direction and still be consistent with FG. With that in mind, the following categorization might be useful. Let *Reformed FG1* (RFG1) be broadly defined as those in FG who are in general agreement with TULIP and yet regard perseverance in the expression of grace simply as a misthological rather than soteriological concern. According to this view, a believer may commit genuine apostasy at the soulical level but not at the ontological level. Such a view of P would be in general accord with the BFG view and the thrust of Calvin's comments above. Whereas that hidden ontological belief naturally might be expected to spring up from time to time, this expectation would not be made a condition or necessary result. Specifically, it is not maintained that a believer must persevere in conscious faith in the end, much less until the end. In short, complete soulical apostasy is possible.

Let *Reformed FG2* (RFG2) be descriptive of those in FG who are in fuller accord with the Reformed view of perseverance in which genuine apostasy is regarded as impossible—a regenerate believer cannot cease to believe. To be sure, even in RFG2 it could be acknowledged that believers may commit volitional apostasy without actually committing intellectual apostasy. That is, even though a believer may get mad at God, deny Him, and claim to disbelieve in Him, nevertheless, in the believer's heart of hearts, even at the soulical level, he or she still assents to the truth of the gospel. Regeneration causes the believer to continue to believe, at least within the suppressed consciousness of one's soul (not just in the realm of his or her spirit). In harmony with RFG1, confessing and denying Christ are considered misthological rather than soteriological conditions. In short, if believers were to cease to believe completely at the soulical level, they would lose their regeneration. But regeneration makes such soulical apostasy impossible. (A mediating view between RFG1 and RFG2 might allow that believers would not lose regeneration if they ceased to believe but hold that such apostasy is impossible because of regeneration.)

Let *Reformed FG3* (RFG3) be the term employed for those in FG who are in fuller accord with the alternative Reformed view of perseverance in which genuine apostasy is hypothetically possible but pragmatically impossible in that regenerate believers could cease to believe but God's discipline prevents them from reaching this point in their lives. However, hypothetically speaking, if regenerate believers were to cease to believe, they would lose their regeneration. Therefore, retention of regeneration is conditioned on perseverance in faith. (See *Reformed View of Discipline*, 114.) In short, if believers were to cease to believe completely at the soulical level, they would lose their regeneration. But God's discipline makes such soulical apostasy impossible. (A mediating view between RFG1 and RFG3 might allow that believers would not lose regeneration if they ceased to believe but hold that such apostasy is impossible because of God's discipline.)

The present writer acknowledges that God's discipline will prevent believers from taking the mark of the beast during the tribulation. So the view adopted herein regarding the mark of the beast bears some similarity to RFG3. However, there is a marked difference. Hypothetically speaking, I believe that if a believer were to take the mark of the beast, the believer would still be saved. So the believer's salvation is not conditioned on his or her perseverance. Even so, God will not actually allow the believer to take the mark of the beast. **Most importantly, it must be clarified that, from my perspective, God's discipline does not keep believers saved because believers still would be saved even if (hypothetically speaking) they were to take the mark of the beast**. Yet it may be deduced prophetically that believers infallibly will not take the mark of the beast, but not because prophecy irresistibly prevents the believer from doing so, for prophecy is not causative. Rather, prophecy allows us to deduce that God will not allow believers to commit this particular sin. So although believers hypothetically might take the mark of the beast, doing so is prophetically impossible. (If God had intended to allow believers who live during the tribulation to take the mark of the beast, Revelation would have been written differently.) My view, therefore, is offered in contradistinction to RFG3 in that I do not believe that God's discipline is for the purpose of keeping believers soteriological safe. I reject RFG3 in favor of a strong view of unconditional security. Continuation in faith at the ontological level, much less at the soulical level, is not **necessary** for the retention of regeneration. As will be clarified below, *sufficient* causation is not to be equated with *necessary* causation. (Also see "Causation Cube" in *Logic Table and Diagrams*.) Petrification is a sufficient cause, but not necessary cause, to prevent a piece of wood from being used in a longbow.

Some might be tempted to take my combination of unconditional security with my limitation on the nature of sin that God will allow during the tribulation and try to reconcile it with the approach taken by some who claim that God will not allow a believer to persist in a sinful lifestyle today. However, they would be laboring under a considerable exegetical burden in that they would have to maintain (with exegetical consistency) that not practicing sin is not a condition for the final realization of soteriological salvation and that a believer would still remain saved even if God (hypothetically speaking from their point of view) allowed the believer to persist in a sinful lifestyle. Further, they would be refuted by a host of passages that indicate that some believers have in fact fallen into sin and fallen from the faith.

As for RFG2, the exegete would have to concede that no passage conditions soteriological security on cooperative perseverance; rather, perseverance is a promise at best and a misthological issue at worst. Perseverance in the expression of grace must be limited to a promise that is not exegetically or implicitly made a soteriological condition. Perseverance in faith itself must be promised without being soteriologically required or conditioned. Otherwise, one would voice the same objection for RFG2 that I already have stated concerning RFG3. Linear faith is not **necessary** for the retention of regeneration. It will be interesting to see if those in RFG3 who wish to push the envelope as far as possible in the direction of arguing that God will cause believers to persevere in faith are successfully able to make what appears to be a round square, exegetically and theological speaking, in avoiding making linear faith a necessary condition. Lutzer appears to have been rather successful in this venture, at least in regard to his cited herein. But he writes more so as a strong securitist (RFG1).

Seymour appears to hold a RFG2 position though. Richard A. Seymour, *The Gift of God*, second edition (LaGrange, WY: Integrity Press, 2007), 92-96,122. Willard Aldrich might also be regarded as a commendable example of RFG2 in that he insists that saving faith is punctiliar in its conditional aspect, even though he affirms: "While I believe that the saved one will continue to believe, it will not be *in order to* become saved, *but because* he has been saved that believers will persevere in faith" (emphasis his, p. 94). And I appreciate his effort to be consistent with his own position and with FG, when he goes on to try to explain 1Pet 1:5 as meaning:

> "Who are kept by the power of God through faith unto salvation ready to be revealed in the last time." The keeping power of God seems at first here to be limited by the "through faith," that is, He is able to keep only so long as the believer retains his faith. But, we have before showed that if the continued exercise of faith were essential to salvation, that God would have to guarantee it, for He has promised that "If any man eat, he shall live forever." Thus we may conclude that man and his exercise of faith is not the prime mover in this passage, but that the governing principle is found in the statement of the keeping power of God. The postulate that man's faith in this passage is no more than the intermediate agency over which God exercises control is supported by the Greek preposition (διά). [See Willard Maxwell Aldrich, "Is Salvation Probationary?" *BibSac* 91:361 (January 1934): 97.]

Valiant try, even if unsuccessful. That *dia* shows intermediate agency does not mean that it cannot show contingency. After all, we are saved *through* faith. If this Petrine passage is addressing soteriological concerns, then God is using our ongoing faith as the **necessary** intermediate means to keep us safe soteriologically. This observation is detrimental to Aldrich's entire article since he correctly denies that eternal life is probationary or conditioned on linear faith. So even an appeal to irresistible grace as the means by which God causes our linear faith appears very questionable since Aldrich rejects linear faith as being a linear contingency. Even if it were true that God causes us to continue in faith, it is false to conclude that just because God causes it that it cannot be necessary. If Aldrich simply were to acknowledge that the verse is describing misthological issues, then ongoing faith would be regarded as necessary for temporal protection and misthological salvation rather than for soteriological retention and salvation. This would be in complete harmony with his otherwise splendid article and tantamount to a RFG1 position. Still, I will not rule out the possibility that a carefully formulated RFG2 theology might indeed be tenable for those in FG who feel compelled to follow that path. (See my *3D Unconditional Security*.)

Even so, for those who wish to remain on the Reformed side of the tracks, RFG1 would appear to be the wiser and safer course to follow. Taking this line of defense allows one to draw upon the Arminian arsenal in demonstrating that genuine believers do commit apostasy. It also allows one to retain the best arguments for OSAS from the Reformed camp, such as ontological immutability. Of course, since this is also the perspective of BFG, those in RFG1 can draw upon FG scholarship as well without any incompatibility. Two exegetes from a BFG and a RFG1 perspective should be able to share the same hermeneutical foxhole with minimum irritability in a firefight opposing RT theology. Ryrie already has blazed the trail and Kendall has paved it for RFG1. For a compatible online representation, see Jason Engwer, "If you believe that salvation can be lost." Available at http://members.aol.com/jasonte2/law.htm. Also, see his related link, at http://members.aol.com/jasonte2/eternal.htm. Accessed on June 6, 2005.

Notwithstanding my preference for BFG as the best approach and RFG1 as the next best alternative, some in FG seek for as much harmonization as possible with the inferior RFG alternatives—RFG2 and RFG3 (which is last and least likely). For their sake, I offer the further elaboration for those in RFG2 who believe that God will cause them to continue to believe (in spite of themselves) via regeneration and for those in RFG3 who believe that they will persevere in faith because God would kill them before allowing them to commit apostasy and thereby lose their regeneration.

Like those in the LS camp who are going to hell because they believe that they must persevere in faith in order to reach heaven, RFG3 advocates likewise believe that they must persevere in faith in order to reach heaven. They both regard linear soulical faith as **necessary** to reach heaven. RFG3 turns what they consider to be a guaranteed result into a necessary condition. Why then does the one group go to hell while the other group is allowed into heaven despite their common mistaken perception? My tentative proposal is that the theology of LS requires that their faith logically be viewed as synergistic cooperation while the theology of the RFG3 does not. Both groups will deny that their perseverance in faith is a synergistic response, of course. From their joint perspective, their perseverance in faith is not a synergistic response. Notwithstanding their unified denial, however, both groups are mistaken. So the answer to the question as to why one group goes to hell while the other does not is not to be found simply in whether perseverance in faith is regarded as meritorious from their own perspectives. I will assume that both groups share the misguided view that their linear faith is not meritorious. Otherwise, they would stand self condemned.

My perception is that (from God's perspective) LS soteriological assurance via perseverance in faith is regarded as a meritorious response by God even though it is not so considered in their own eyes. Yet the faith of the RFG camp is not regarded by God as a meritorious response. God is able to overlook the logical inconsistency of the RFG group because their defective understanding allows them to *embrace* this dangerous perspective about P without His having to regard their actual *embrace* of this perspective as a meritorious response. (Although perseverance is actually meritorious, their *embrace* of this view in and of itself is not necessarily meritorious if their embracement can meet certain criteria to be considered below.) On the other hand, LS holds its position regarding P with a greater theological, exegetical, and logical consistency that makes it impossible for LS to believe in Christ for an unconditional security that is not contaminated with conditional security. (See *Illustration 248. Cross-Eyed Calvinism*, 709.) But those in RFG2 and RFG3 are able to believe in Christ for unconditional security (which is the essence of saving faith) because they are less consistent exegetically with their perseverance-based perspective, thereby making their embrace of P more tenuous, while that of LS is tenacious.

From the RFG2 perspective, regeneration is regarded as preventing believers from ceasing to believe (at the soulical level). Granted, some of those in RFG2 may believe that if they were to cease to believe (at the soulical level) they would lose regeneration. Nevertheless, they believe that regeneration guarantees the response of linear faith necessary for its own survival. Their regeneration is believed to produce their ongoing faith which in turn protects their regeneration apart from their cooperation. Although perseverance in faith may be regarded as a necessary condition for the retention of regeneration from their perspective, regeneration in and of itself guarantees perseverance in faith with the result that the condition of perseverance in faith ceases to be synergistically contingent on their cooperation. Soteriologically speaking, then, from their perspective, their perseverance in the faith functionally becomes a mere description of those who have experienced regeneration. Their view of perseverance in the faith is really nothing more than preservation in the faith. Logically, this preservation in the faith cannot be regarded as a synergistic condition from their perspective. **Their regeneration (rather than their cooperation) keeps them saved.** And God, in grace, soteriologically adopts their perspective because they were able to trust in Christ alone for an unconditional security that logically was not conditioned on their cooperation. Likewise, from the perspective of RFG3, believers could cease to believe (and thereby not cooperate with God) and lose their salvation, but God will kill them before allowing them to do so. **God's disciple (rather than their cooperation) keeps them saved.** They are able to believe in Christ alone for unconditional security. This is our working theory by which I affirm the salvation of those adopting these *inconsistent Free Grace (IFG)* perspectives. (See *Illustration 166. Inconsistent Frontloaders and Backloaders*, 499.) Also see endnote about FG Calminians in *Mere Christianity and Moral Christianity*. See my illustrations in *3D Unconditional Security*.

Although LS Calvinists will be quick to try and use the same rationale to persuade themselves and others that they are not soteriological synergists, even though they theologically and exegetically condition their eternal salvation on their logically cooperative perseverance, they have failed to persuade those of us in BFG that they are not in reality closet soteriological synergists. Their claim that a necessary condition is a mere description in their theology is falsified by the proof texts they employ which demand a cooperative response. Perseverance is in reality prescriptive, not merely descriptive, in their overall approach. (See *Calminian Perseverance in faith is a condition for salvation*, 273; *Illustration 239. Calvinistic Conditional Security*, 704; *Illustration 242. Simplistic Eternal Security*, 706; *Lost Grace & Sovereign Grace*, 854. Also see "Number Four—Parenthetical" in *Salvation: A Categorical Analysis* and "Key to Foreknowledge" in *Predestination and the Open View*. For juxtaposition of White's illegitimate use of the descriptive argument with a legitimate use, see descriptive argument in the endnotes of *Believe: An Aspectual and Metaphorical Analysis from the Gospel of John*. Also see endnote 369 herein for another possible example of legitimate usage.)

Those who hold a BFG position must, in turn, express a sincere warning toward those adopting the Calvinistic LS position that when these LS advocates are forced to come out of the closet and face up to the logical implications of their own position at the GWT, they will not be able to persuade God that they were not soteriological synergists. Whether a person's view of perseverance is regarded as synergistic cooperation **from God's perspective** thus becomes the key for determining who among those adopting the Calvinistic P will be sent to hell. Those who embrace perseverance in such manner that would require that God consider their faith a synergistic response will be sent to hell because they have embraced perseverance in such a way as to require that their ongoing faith be regarded logically as a cooperative synergistic soteriological condition **from God's perspective**, even though they failed to perceive it as such from their own perspective.

Those who embrace P with a theological or exegetical consistency that requires that P be considered a logical contingency (that they must meet cooperatively in order to reach heaven) will be sent to hell instead. The key, then, as to whether perseverance is regarded as soteriologically synergistic from God's perspective would naturally be whether it is logically (not admittedly) **cooperative** from their perspective. It is not necessary that those in LS who adopt a Calvinistic view of P actually admit that their perseverance in faith is cooperative. As a frequent rule, they will not. The determining factor is whether the manner in which they *embrace* perseverance in faith is logically cooperative. Pragmatically at least, this would appear to be the case. To the degree one's system of thought pushes one into finding one's assurance in one's perseverance rather than in Christ alone, one will be moved away from trusting in Christ alone for unconditional security. What I have deduced, accordingly, is that God pragmatically (and perhaps logically) is required to reject soteriologically those who pragmatically are induced by their own theological error to embrace P in such a way that it causes them to trust, in any degree, in their cooperative perseverance rather than in Christ alone for their entrance into heaven. Calvinistic LS turns the perseverance it regards as a guaranteed result into a necessary condition with sufficient logical consistency so as to make faith in Christ alone for unconditional security a logical impossibility and psychological improbability.

While many LS will take the classical approach and claim that God causes their perseverance through means of irresistible grace, this is by no means a safe approach. Some of those doing so will presume that God irresistibly causes them to cooperate willingly so that they believe that their perseverance is accomplished compatibilistically by means of their forced-willing cooperation. In such a case, they are still trusting in their cooperation. Others will attempt to bypass this objection by asserting that God irresistibly causes them to persevere in faith, independent of their cooperation. In doing so, they deceive themselves into thinking that they do not trust in their cooperation when, in fact, their exegesis of certain passages and their theology as a whole has caused them actually to trust (at least in part) in their participation in their preservation. They end up trying to save themselves by means of their perseverance and drown in their attempts. Despite their theological claims that perseverance is merely descriptive, biblical exegesis demonstrates that perseverance is, indeed, prescriptive. Consequently, their having psychological dependency in Christ alone for unconditional security is a practical impossibility. I suspect that very few theological escapologists will be able to pull a Houdini and pragmatically escape the logical restraints of their own system long enough to trust in God for unconditional security since they will be bound simultaneously by their interpretations of key passages to trust in their own conditional security. (Again, see *Illustration 248. Cross-Eyed Calvinism*, 709.) Perhaps, some like Aldrich may prove to be an exception to this rule. Perchance, some in RFG are tentatively able to hold P as a necessary condition with sufficient logical inconsistency so as to make faith in Christ alone for unconditional security a psychological possibility. In any case, those adopting a soteriological view of P are playing with fire, and many of those who play with it will get burned.

In contradistinction to RFG2 above, let dissimilarities not be lost amidst similarities. Those in RFG2 who believe that regeneration would be lost without perseverance in faith because regeneration is maintained through perseverance in faith have committed a logical fallacy found in the NOSAS camp: where it is believed that the means of our security must necessarily imply contingency and that we must make a choice between multiple means so that we are only left with one means (cp. Forlines, *Truth*, 292-293). They confuse *necessary* means with *sufficient* means. In contrast, I believe that multiple means of security do not prove that each means is necessary to guarantee that security. For example, if a tree branch were petrified, it would not bend. Likewise, if a tree branch were charcoaled, it would not bend. The petrified or charcoaled branch might be broken, but it could not be bent. It would be futile to try to make a longbow out of petrified or charcoaled wood. Either means—petrification or charcoalization—is sufficient to make the wood unbendable and, thus, both means are not necessary to make it unbendable. Correspondingly, God has made us secure in Christ through multiple means—justification and regeneration (just to name two). It would be false, even in principle, to claim that both are necessary to assure us of unconditional continuation in a state of grace. Far to the contrary, both means of guaranteeing our security are capable, in and of themselves, to assure us that we are unconditionally secure. Even if (hypothetically speaking) we were to lose one, the presence of the other would be sufficient to assure us of heaven. Furthermore, it is not unlike God to give us more than one means of absolute assurance (cp. Heb 6:18).

Just as fossilization or charcoalization are *sufficient*, in and of themselves, to guarantee that a piece of wood would not be suitable for use as a longbow, so justification and regeneration are sufficient, in and of themselves, to assure us of our suitability for heaven. We may liken this double assurance to finding a charcoaled piece of wood that subsequently had been petrified. This charcoaled fossil would not be suitable for a longbow. In like fashion, justified believers who have been regenerated are not suitable for hell. Either attribute—justification or regeneration—would be sufficient to make them unsuitable for eternal damnation. So unlike some of those in RFG2 (much less like those in the NOSAS camp) who believe that believers must continue in faith (which was the intermediate means of their becoming regenerate) in order to stay regenerate, I contend that there is no linear contingency for remaining regenerate. Ontologically, linear faith assures us that we will remain regenerate, but this linear faith is not necessary for us to remain regenerate. Linear faith is a *sufficient* means, not a *necessary* means, for our continued state of regeneration. Punctiliar faith and ontologically linear faith are thus two independent means of assuring our linear state. Whereas punctiliar faith is necessary, linear faith is merely sufficient, not necessary. Just as a petrified piece of wood does not have to stay submerged in order to stay petrified (although this submergence was the means of its initial fossilization and would continue to assure its petrification), so a believer does not have to continue in faith in order to stay regenerate.

Granted, it is true from the joint perspectives of both BFG and RFG2 that regeneration guarantees the response sufficient for its own continued state. But whereas RFG2 tends to believe this response is *necessary*, BFG merely consider it *sufficient*. (See "Causation Cube" in *Logic Table and Diagrams*.) Regeneration produces ongoing faith at the ontological level which, in turn, guarantees regeneration—just as remaining submerged in a petrifying environment would assure that a petrified piece of wood would remain petrified. This regeneration (at the ontological level) is assured by linear faith (at the ontological level). Nevertheless, from the BFG perspective being proposed herein, although perseverance in faith **at the ontological level** might be regarded as a sufficient condition for the ontological retention of regeneration, regeneration in and of itself guarantees the preservation of faith at this ontological level. The result is that the condition of continuing in faith at the ontological level ceases to be contingent synergistically on our cooperation. Moreover, this ontologically linear faith is merely a sufficient condition, not a necessary condition. Simply put, we do not have a choice as to whether our spirit believes because our spirit is persuaded by the presence of the Holy Spirit that we are regenerate. This ongoing internal persuasion that we are regenerate because we have believed in Christ for eternal life is, in and of itself, sufficient to assure us that we are regenerate, but this ongoing persuasion is by no means necessary for us to remain regenerate. Even if our spirit could cease to believe, it would still remain regenerate. Just as one can find petrified forests today that are no longer submerged in the Noachian deluge, the presence of those flood waters are no longer necessary to assure the presence of such forests. Yet if those flood waters still were present, they would be sufficient to assure the presence of such forests.

Of course, perseverance in faith at the soulical level remains a misthological condition for the salvation of the soul. Those who try to make linear faith, at the soulical level, a soteriological condition necessary to reach heaven are mixing elements together that were not intended to be mixed. This mixed up theology can be expected to be lethal in many (if not most) cases. I am simply seeking to explore the possible scenarios under which this concoction might not prove fatal. Certainly, even under the best of circumstances, this mixture would not be deemed advisable. Nonetheless, there are those in FG (like Strombeck and Seymour) whom the present writer certainly regards as fellow FG advocates who have adopted a view more in harmony with RT theology than his own BFG perspective, and he is merely sharing his assessment as to how it might be possible to reconcile their theology with his own while at the same time keeping both under the FG umbrella.

[500] A. W. Pink, *Eternal Security*, 6. Available at http://www.jaynesgarden.com/Spirit/A-W-Pink/eternal-security.pdf. Accessed on June 9, 2005. This work was originally published under the title, *The Doctrine Of The Saints' Perseverance*.

[501] Ibid., 21.

[502] Ibid., 57.

[503] Idem, *The Holy Spirit*. Available at http://www.pbministries.org/books/pink/Holy_Spirit/holy_spirit.htm. Accessed on June 6, 2005.

[504] Ibid.

[505] Ibid.

[506] Ibid.

[507] Ibid.

[508] Ibid.

[509] Ibid.

[510] Pink, *Security*, 82.

[511] Murray, *Romans*, 293-294.

[512] John F. MacArthur, Jr. "Perseverance of the Saints" *MSJ* 4:1 (Spring 1993): 13.

[513] Ibid., 17.

[514] Ibid., 12.

[515] Sellers, *Election*, 99.

[516] Hendriksen, *Romans*, 255.

[517] Matthew Henry, CWB (1706-1721), s.v. Rom 8:13. Via BibleWorks. For interested parties, the online edition is available at http://www.ccel.org/h/henry/mhc2/MHC00000.HTM. Quotations herein will be form the BibleWorks edition.

[518] John Owen, *The Holy Spirit: His Gifts and Power* (Michigan: Grand Rapids, 1954), 219.

[519] Idem., "The Doctrine Of Justification By Faith." Available at http://www.ondoctrine.com/2owe0109.htm. Accessed on June 14, 2005.

[520] Ibid.

[521] Ibid.

[522] Ibid.

[523] Tony Warren, "Perseverance of the Saints: Is it the Doctrine of Eternal Security?" Available at http://members.aol.com/twarren17/perseverance.html. Accessed on June 14, 2005. According to Warren, "we persevere because God by His Spirit has sealed or secured us eternally." Apparently, Warren is asserting that we persevere because we are regenerate. Still, in equating persevering in the state of grace with persevering in the expression of grace, he makes the expression of grace the necessary means of reaching heaven. You cannot have regeneration without practical sanctification in his estimation. The only options Warren gives are (1) to confess Jesus, keep His commandments, follow Him, never be deceived, do His will, and do not continue in sin or (2) to go to hell. Despite his best efforts, he ends up teaching a Reformed version of conditional security based on one's performance. Claiming that Christ does all the work for us and that these actions are not in any sense of ourselves does little to dampen this charge. Even if this were true, our security would still be conditioned on these subsequent, robotic actions. In any event, this type of evasive maneuver is incompatible with his claim that "the responsibility that is ours to walk in a manner which is consistent with the Word." How can the responsibility be ours if the response is not ours? These are our actions and therefore our works which Warren makes necessary to reach heaven.

[524] Corner, *Security*, 15.

[525] Ibid., 478.

[526] Pink, *Security*, 57.

[527] Ibid., 131.

[528] Peterson, "Perseverance," 95.

[529] Ibid., 97

[530] Ibid., 112.

[531] Thomas R. Schreiner, "Perseverance and Assurance: A Survey and a Proposal," 6. Available at http://www.sbts.edu/resources/publications/sbjt/1998/1998Spring4.pdf. Accessed on June 23, 2005.

[532] Ibid., 49.

[533] Ibid., 50.

[534] Ibid., 52.

[535] Ibid., 53.

[536] Peterson, "Perseverance," 99.

[537] Schreiner, "Perseverance," 56. Schreiner reinterprets Mk 13:22 to say that "deception of the elect is *impossible*" (emphasis his). For refutation, see *Apostasy of the elect*, 292.

[538] Ibid., 57.

[539] Ken Keathley, "Does Anyone Really Know If They Are Saved? A Survey of the Current Views on Assurance with a Modest Proposal." *JOTGES* 15:28 (Spring 2002): 58. To be sure, on this same page, the editor of *JOTGES* tries to pacify disgruntled GES readers by noting that Keathley "is not saying that good works certainly persist. Keathley holds the view that believers may backslide and even die in that state." If so, I would have liked to have read this affirmation by Keathley himself in his conclusion. Even so, I have heard this from enough Southern Baptist to assume that it is probably a correct assessment of Keathley's views. Nevertheless, even if Keathley does hold this watered-down position on perseverance, it is inconsistent with his statement that he himself makes as quoted in the text. Moreover, Keathley himself acknowledges that he is closer to the *tests-of-genuineness* view than the once-saved-always-saved view and is just presenting a variation of the former since he believes in "persevering faith" (p. 57).

[540] Bing is correct that Rom 6:23 is concerned primarily with the possibility of believers experiencing death or life in terms of their fellowship. Charles C. Bing, *Simply by Grace: An Introduction to God's Life-Changing Gift* (Grand Rapids, 2009), 112, 160. To clarify his statements, our static possession of eternal life as a gift in Rom 6:23b is not conditioned on our willingness to serve God. However, our temporal and misthological dynamic experience of this gift is conditioned upon such service (Rom 6:23a). The tension between death as a wage and life as a gift for the believer is resolved by noting that the wage can offset the gift temporally and misthologically but not soteriologically.

[541] Believers cannot be separated from God in terms of their relationship as a child of God. Their fundamental relationship with God cannot die. Their fellowship with God, on the other hand, both now and in the future, can die. Those believers who are cast into the outer darkness are separated from God in terms of fellowship. They do not share the joy of ruling with Him in heaven. To be sure, they will share the joy of being with Him in heaven, but this joy certainly will be impoverished compared to the life of those who rule as lords with Him who is Lord of lords.

[542] Lopez, *Romans*, 166.

[543] An ingenious suggestion has been made in FG circles to take *dwells in* (*oikeo en*) in Rom 8:11a experientially in terms of fellowship but regard *indwells* (*enoikeo*) in Rom 8:11b relationally as referring to regeneration: "If the Spirit of Him who raised Jesus from the dead [experientially; *oikeo en*] *dwells in* you, He who raised Christ Jesus from the dead will also give life to your mortal bodies through His Spirit who [ontologically; *enoikeo*] *indwells* you." This approach is attractive in the verse itself. Even so, it is not adopted herein since my perception is that *dwells in* (*oikeo en*) is used in 8:9 to make, or at least draw, a positive affirmation: "You are not in the flesh but in the Spirit, *since* indeed the Spirit of God dwells in you" (see Lopez, Romans, 165). Moreover, *dwells in* (*oikeo en*) is used of what is true by virtue of regeneration in 1Cor 3:16, and its use in Rom 7:18 is surely not to be limited to experiential truth. Further, if a distinction exists, it is *enoikeo* (rather than *oikeo en*) that appears to have experiential possibilities: Col 3:16; 2Tim 1:14(?).

[544] Dillow, 127-128.

[545] Blomberg, *Matthew*, NAC, 361.

[546] France, *Matthew*, NIC 917.

[547] Brad McCoy, "Secure Yet Scrutinized: 2 Timothy 2:11-13." *JOTGES* 1:1 (Autumn 1988): 31.

[548] Robert N. Wilkin, "We Believe In: Sanctification—Part 2: Past Sanctification," *JOTGES* 6:10 (Spring 1993): 6-7.

[549] Hodges wrote, "1 Peter 2:2," but this is evidently a typographical error referring to 1Pet 1:2. This is part of a personal correspondence (9-3-92) that will be discussed more fully latter.

[550] This type of sanctification (present sanctification) is discussed by Wilkin in a subsequent article. Robert N. Wilkin, "We Believe In: Sanctification—Part 3: Present Sanctification—God's Role in Present Sanctification," *JOTGES* 7:12 (Autumn 1994): 3-16.

[551] Fisk, 139-140.

[552] Forster, 146.

[553] Vance, 355-359.

[554] Fisk, 141.

[555] Nevertheless, both passages indirectly confirm the preconversion the sanctification of 1Cor 7:14. The same Spirit who sanctifies believers, by enabling them to live and walk by faith and take up the shield of faith, is also at work in the lives of unbelievers in drawing them to respond in faith to the gospel.

[556] Dillow, 297.

[557] Hodges' affirmation of unconditional election is certainly milder than that of Calvinists since he has argued that everyone can believe: "I say nothing in *Absolutely Free!* about the doctrine of unconditional election (the so-called second point of Calvinism). As a matter of fact, I hold to that doctrine, though probably not in a form to which Horton would give his approval." In actuality, what Hodges subscribes to is middle knowledge: "In my view, the approach designated 'middle knowledge' is superior to other views. In 'middle knowledge,' full account is taken of God's omniscience so that room is left for the biblical concept of human responsibility as well as of divine sovereignty. Zane C. Hodges, "The New Puritanism, Part 2: Michael S. Horton: Holy War With Unholy Weapons," *JOTGES* 6:11 (Autumn 1993): 25-38. For explanation, Hodges cites David Besieger's article, "Divine Control and Human Freedom: Is Middle Knowledge the Answer?" in the *JOTGES* 36 (1, March 1993): 55-64. The present writer is appreciative of the fact that Basinger does not advocate a form of middle knowledge that trades in irresistible grace for irresistible manipulation. God does not irresistibly manipulate our circumstances to cause us to believe. The entire Calvinistic notion of unconditional election is very questionable. See Philip F. Congdon, "Soteriological Implications of Five-Point Calvinism," *JOTGES* 8:15 (Autumn 1995): 55-68.

[558] Hodges, *Siege*, 101, 173.

[559] Idem, *Hebrews*, 792.

[560] Zane C. Hodges, "The Epistle of 2nd Peter: Shunning Error in Light of the Savior's Return," A verse-by-verse commentary, n.d., 13.

[561] Wilkin, *Confident*, 77-78.

[562] *Plousios* is translated as *rich(ly)* by the NAS in: Col 3:16; 1Tim 6:17; Tit 3:6.

[563] Dillow, 297.

[564] The purpose, and thus **intended result**, of our calling in 1Pet 2:21 is that we earn Gods grace in 2:20 by persevering while suffering: "For you have been called for this *purpose* [*eis*]...*in order that* [*hina*] you may." *Eis* and *hina* followed by a subjunctive is used to denote the intended purpose in both clauses (1Pet 2:21; 3:9). The conditional misthological intention of the calling in 3:9 is unmistakable: "Not returning evil for evil, or insult for insult, but giving a blessing instead; for you were called for the very purpose *in order that* you may inherit a blessing" (TM). The inheritance is not unconditionally guaranteed to believers. Likewise, in 1Thess 4:7, dual purpose clauses are associated with the calling: "For God has not called us *for* [*epi*] the purpose of impurity, but *for* [*en*] sanctification" (TM). BDAG notes *epi* is used as a dative of purpose in this verse. The same should be concluded for the dative use of *en* in this verse. Although the use of *en* to denote purpose is rare, this usage of *en* is acknowledged by UBS in its translation of *for* in this capacity. Practical sanctification is not a guaranteed outcome. For further discussion of intended result versus guaranteed result, see endnotes 186, 466.

[565] Louis A. Barbieri Jr., *Matthew,* BKC (Wheaton: Victor Books, 1984), 76.

[566] Arno C. Gaebelein, *Gospel of Matthew* (Neptune: Loizeaux Brothers, 1961), 467.

[567] Gaebelein, *Matthew*, 473.

[568] Mk 13:14-23 refers "to both the destruction of Jerusalem and the future Great Tribulation." John D. Grassmick, *Mark*, BKC (Wheaton: Victor Books, 1984), 171.

[569] Walter W. Wessel, *Mark*, vol. 8, EBC (Grand Rapids: Zondervan Publishing House, 1984), 748.

[570] Johnston M. Cheney, *The Life of Christ in Stereo* (Portland: Multnomah Press, 1969), 165-166.

[571] Incidentally, the beginning of the tribulation is described as *the beginning of birth pangs* (Mt 24:8; Mk 13:8), which Paul says, "will come upon them suddenly like birth pangs upon a woman with child" (1Thess 5:3). The Greek word used on all three occasions to associate the beginning of the tribulation with *birth pangs* is *odin*. Both Matthew and Mark record Jesus as using the same Greek word in describing the eschatological tribulation—*thlipsis*. This word is also used of a woman being in labor (Jn 16:21). Luke uses an entirely different word in this parallel section in referring to the intermediate distress that is to occur before the tribulation—*anagke*. While it might be said that *thlipsis* is used of the tribulational birthing of a new age, the same would not be true of *anagke*.

[572] Cheney, 165-166.

[573] Chitwood, *Olivet*, 18-20.

[574] Constable, *Luke,* 232.

[575] Idem, *Matthew,* 301.

[576] Timmy Ice, "The Destructive View of Preterism," *CTS* 3:10 (December 1999): 386-400. Ron J. Bigalke, Jr., "The Olivet Discourse: A Resolution of Time," *CTSJ* 9 (Spring 2003): 106-140.

[577] Bigalke, 122.

[578] Ice, "Preterism," 391.

[579] Robert L. Thomas, "The Doctrine of Imminence in Two Recent Eschatological Systems," *BibSac* 157:628 (October 2000): 457.

[580] Bigalke, 116-117, 124, 129.

[581] George Meisinger, "Judgment Seat of Christ: Loss of Rewards." *GES Conference CD* (2006), 25-28.

[582] Dillow, 79.

[583] Radmacher, "Forever," 31-35. He also uses this terminology in his forward to Dillow's book, *The Reign Of The Servant Kings*. More recently in his own book, *Salvation*, Radmacher elucidates this terminology. Unfortunately, he refers to future salvation that we inherit as glorification salvation (p. 144), and then defines this glorification salvation as salvation from the presence of sin (p. 219). This ambiguity is unfortunate and results from using glorification salvation to refer to both co-glorification (which is merited) and salvation from the presence of sin (which is unmerited). Radmacher acknowledges in his forward to Dillow's book that he is indeed using it to refer to both (p. xiii). Sellers, likewise, breaks salvation up into its past, present, and future aspects as salvation from the penalty, power, and presence of sin. He cites Rom 5:9 and 13:11 as examples of salvation from the presence of sin (p. 119). However, Rom 5:9 refers to salvation from the wrath of God, not from the presence of our sin nature. And Rom 13:11 is by no means a clear reference to salvation from the presence of sin in our lives either. Lightner, *Salvation*, (216-217) uses the same classification and cites 1Jn 3:1-2 and Rom 8:30 as examples of salvation from the presence of sin. But the word salvation does not appear in either verse. The present author agrees with these writers that all believers will be delivered from the presence of sin when they are conformed to the likeness of Christ. The question is whether the word *salvation* itself is used to denote this deliverance. Perhaps it could be contended that a verse like Mt 1:21 refers to full salvation from the penalty, power, and presence of sin. It is thus represented in the chart as referring to all aspects of spiritual salvation. Yet in response to LS which frequently chirps that Jesus came to save us from our sin rather than to leave us in our sin—with the thought in mind that if you are living in sin, then you are not really saved—it may be asked, "Does Jesus save us perfectly or imperfectly?" If perfectly, does this affirmation entail sinless perfection in the present? Most people realize that it does not. Our experience of present salvation is neither perfect nor unconditional; therefore, the LS deduction is nonsensical.

Likewise, the purpose of Jesus' coming is that we might attain the fullest measure of salvation. Yet doing so is not unconditionally guaranteed.

[584] Sellers, 120.

[585] John Phillips, *Exploring the Gospel of Matthew: An Expository Commentary* (Grand Rapids: Kregel Publications, 1999): 454-458.

[586] Sellers, 101.

[587] Chitwood, *Olivet*, 4. Mize, a kingdom exclusionist, of the partial rapture persuasion, also gives this same breakdown as Chitwood for the Olivet Discourse. See Mize's *Chapter 6. The Olivet Discourse.* Mize is a misthological moderate rather than ultraist in that he asserts: "'Outer darkness' in [Mt 22] verse 13 is not hell as is commonly thought. The phrase is an ancient oriental idiom that means to receive the displeasure of the master. It is a picture of the chastisement for unfaithfulness that Christians will receive at the Judgment Seat of Christ" (*Chapter 5. The Bride Of Christ*)." As to the Lake of Fire, his position is that carnal believers may have a part in the Lake of Fire (Rev 21:8) but not be cast into it (Rev 20:14-15). That is, carnal believers will lose their souls and their inheritance via the Lake of Fire and thus be misthologically hurt by it (Rev 2:11) but not actually be cast into it or spend the millennium there (*Chapter 2. The Judgment Seat Of Christ*). His identification of Gehenna as the Lake of Fire in ch. 2 is clear: "The baptism of fire will take place in the lake of fire (i.e., Gehenna) which is called the second death. This is the same place where the Antichrist, the False Prophet, and unbelievers will be cast for all eternity and disassociated with." And his disassociation of this location with the outer darkness is appreciated:

> "Outer darkness" is not the same as hell (i.e., Gehenna or the lake of fire). "Cast into outer darkness" is an ancient oriental idiom that means to receive the displeasure of the master. The three Scriptural references to "outer darkness" are in Matthew 8:12, 22:13, and 25:30 and all refer to the children of God. The unsaved are "cast into the fiery furnace." (Ch. 2).

Since believers are not actually cast into the Lake of Fire or Gehenna, the casting into Gehenna in a passage such as Mt 18:8 thus would be regarded as strictly soteriological and not for believers. Consequently, this position, which merely has carnal believers being misthologically hurt and passing *through* (*dia*; 1Cor 3:15) rather than being cast into the fire, should be distinguished from the ultraistic approach. Mize's approach would pose an alternate to the litotetic approach taken herein for Rev 2:11. Mize's chapters may be found in his online book. See Lyn Mize, *The Open Door*. Available at http://www.thefirstfruits.org. Accessed on August 2, 2005. Subsequently, Mize modified his approach and said that believers are experientially rather than spatially cast into Gehenna, where they only lose their souls rather than spend 1000 years, since he does not consider Gehenna a place. See "What are Hades, Tarteros, Gehenna and the Second Death?" which is an excerpt taken from an article by Lyn Mize. Available at http://www.wellofoath.com /home.asp?pg=Newsletter&toc=July+2003. Accessed on August 8, 2005. In personal correspondence on 8-5-2005, Mize confirmed the online excerpts present in his more recent position, via an attached document: "Gehenna vs. Life."

[588] Colin Hoyle Deal, *The Day and Hour Jesus will Return* (Rutherford College; NC: Colin H. Deal, 1988).

[589] George E. Meisinger, "The Parable of the Fig Tree: Matthew 24:32-36," CTSJ 2:2 (Fall 1996).

[590] Ibid.

[591] Sweigart, "Olivet" 5. For a thorough defense of the significance of the *peri de* as opening up a pretribulational interpretation of Mt 24:36-44, see John F. Hart, "Should Pretribulationalists Reconsider the Rapture in Matthew 24:36-44? Part 1 of 3" *JOTGES* 20:39 (Autumn 2007): 47-70; "Part 2 of 3" *JOTGES* 21:40 (Spring 2008): 45-63; "Part 3 of 3" *JOTGES* 21:41 (Autumn 2008): 43-64.

[592] Ibid.

[593] John Sweigart, "Matthew 24:45-25:30," 2. Available at http://www.inthebeginning.org/newtestament/matthew /mt25.pdf. Accessed on September 9, 2004.

[594] The reference to Walvoord concerning Mt 25:1-13 in the chart needs a word of explanation. Walvoord notes that some pretribulationalists like Chafer take the passage as referring to the elect in the tribulation (charted as W^C) while others like Ironside understand it as referring to the elect in the church age (charted as W^I). (Walvoord, *Rapture*, 103-104.) However, Walvoord does indicate his personal preference for considering the entire discourse in Mt 24-25 as referring to the second phase. (Walvoord, *Rapture*, 101,184,195.) But as Carson notes, the more prominent view among dispensationalists is to take part of the discourse as referring to the rapture and part of it as referring to the revelation. D. A. Carson, *Matthew*, vol. 8, EBC (Grand Rapids: Zondervan Publishing House, 1984), 494. The abbreviations on the chart may be rough approximations in some cases. For example, some dispensationalists split the passage in Mt 24:36-51 a little differently. Whereas I assign the entire passage to a judgment of believers, Gaebelein and Dillow assign 24:36-41 to a judgment on the world (Gaebelein, 540; Dillow, 386). Dillow's micro chiastic structure is interesting but not detailed enough for my purposes. On the other hand, the macro chiasm by Sweigart is too complex for present needs. John M. Sweigart, "Chiasmus Of Matthew 23:1—25:46," Available at http://www.inthebeginning.org/chiasmus /matthew/matthew23-25.pdf. Accessed on October 9, 2004. If his discussion were integrated with the QLM theory, the complexity of such a discussion could quickly become exponential. But it is difficult to believe that Matthew's major

discourses are merely steps in a much larger complex chiasm. If one takes this route, then, of course, certain questions must be addressed. For example, are all of the major Matthean discourses part of a larger chiasm? If not, why not? Do all the synoptic writers arrange their material in this manner? If not, why not? Does the chiasm approach explain the arrangement of the material in regard to the QLM hypothesis. Again, if not, why not? The mediating phase charting used in my approach offers a balance of simplicity and complexity that is sufficiently suitable for present purposes.

[595] **B** = Barbieri (BKC). **C** = Chitwood. See Arlen L. Chitwood, *Prophecy on Mount Olivet* (Norman, Okla.: The Lamp Broadcast, 1989). **D** = Dillow. **G** = Gaebelein (*Matthew*). **H** = Hodges (personal correspondence). **P** = Pentecost. **R** = Ryrie (*Premillennial*, Basic *Theology*). **S** = Stanton. **W** = Walvoord (*Rapture*).

[596] Personal correspondence 5-28-92.

[597] Personal correspondence 6-3-92.

[598] Ryrie, *Theology*, 493.

[599] I. Howard Marshall, *The Gospel of Luke*, NIC, eds. I. Howard Marshall and W. Ward Gasque (Grand Rapids: Eerdmans Publishing Co., 1986), 669.

[600] Norval Geldenhuys, *Commentary on the Gospel of Luke,* NIC, ed. F. F. Bruce (Grand Rapids: Eerdmans Publishing Co., 1983), 442.

[601] Barbieri, *Matthew*, 77-78.

[602] Ron J. Bigalke Jr., "Time," 108.

[603] Ibid, 130.

[604] John Sweigart, "The Olivet Discourse," 5. Available at http://www.inthebeginning.org/newtestament/matthew /mt24.pdf. Accessed on August 12, 2004.

[605] Compare the same use of the word *day* in 2Pet 3:10.

[606] Compare the use of hour in Rev 3:3 concerning the imminency of the rapture with Matthew's use of hour in Mt 24:36,42,44,50. Cf. also Mt 25:13; Lk 12:39-40,46.

[607] For judgment according to works, see Mt 16:27; Rom 2:6; 1Cor 3:8,13-15; 2Cor 5:10; 11:15; 2Tim 4:14; Rev 2:23; 18:6; 20:12-13. Also see "Appendix 1" of *Breaking the Rocking Horse*.

[608] The words Peter uses are: *judgment (krino/krima), salvation (sozo/soteria).*

[609] The fact that salt that becomes unsalty is good for nothing "except to be thrown out and trampled underfoot by men" might seem to limit the being *thrown out* to temporal reproach by men, but this is highly unlikely. Luke does not mention this exception (Lk 14:35). In addition to the famous Matthean exception clause regarding divorce, in this passage we have yet another example of a Matthean exception clause—this one misthological. The preceding verses and context are discussing rewards in heaven (Mt 5:12). The temporal expulsion is a picture of an eschatological limitation, or at the very least, being *cast out* is a picture of the exclusion that begins now and extends into the future.

The trampling underfoot by men happens after the casting out. Since men do not trample people under their feet in hell, this imagery is not conducive to soteriological motifs. Nevertheless, Lenski believes that it represents a man soteriologically thrown out of the kingdom after having entered it (*Matthew*, 200-201). This would accord well with the Arminian view in which a believer can lose his salvation. Marrowism rejects this interpretation theologically on the basis of eternal security and exegetically on the basis of the context. On the other hand, kingdom exclusionists who affirm eternal security could argue that the worthless Christian is misthologically thrown out of the kingdom. This assessment still seems excessive in that the context is talking about rewards in heaven (Mt 5:12): possessing the kingdom rather than merely entering it (Mt 5:3,10). Additionally, being trampled underfoot by men does not fit Gehenna misthology. Contextually, the most that can be said definitively is that being cast out represents being excluded from the promised rewards in heaven. Even so, the sequence of events leads to a plausible misthological hypothesis.

Being cast out is a picture of the outer darkness. The casting out of the banquet pictured by *ekballo* (into the outer darkness) is anticipated by *ballo exo* here in Mt 5:13. Just as one has to be in something before one can be cast out of it, so believers attending the wedding banquet are expelled from the banquet after it already has started. Participation in the banquet is the reward. Entrance into the kingdom (or even into the banquet for that matter) is not in view since entrance is given freely to believers. Worthless salt is *cast out* (*exo ballo*) in Lk 14:35. The outcast of the kingdom are not necessarily outcast from the kingdom. Rather, they are cast out of the banquet, which, among other things, represents being cast out of New Jerusalem during the millennium. They are not cast out of the kingdom itself.

All church-age believers will enter New Jerusalem, but those found unfaithful at the Bema will be expelled from the capital city at the commencement of the millennial kingdom. They will be cast out of the city and caused to dwell elsewhere on earth. Jesus affirms that this worthless salt still has a useful purpose. "It is good for nothing anymore, **except** to be thrown out and trampled under foot by men" (Mt 5:13). According to this Matthean exception clause, those cast out still serve a useful purpose, as Constable (*Matthew*, 77) notes: "In modern Israel weak salt still often ends up scattered on the soil that tops flat-roofed houses, which the residents sometimes use as patios. There it hardens the soil and so prevents leaks. God will use disciples either as vessels unto honor or as vessels unto dishonor (cf. Rom. 9:21; 2 Tim. 2:20)."

Just as tasteless salt has a useful function of being trodden underfoot on patios, so unfaithful believers would have a useful function in the millennial kingdom. They can be trodden underfoot in menial servitude to the nations (i.e., to men in flesh and blood bodies) during the millennial kingdom and eternal state. Luke mentions that this salt is not *fit* (*euthetos*) for "the soil or for the manure pile" (Lk 14:35). The only other time he uses *euthetos* is in Lk 9:62, where Jesus says, "No one, after putting his hand to the plow and looking back, is *fit* for the kingdom of God." There are three ways to take this verse. Such a believer is not fit for: (1) entrance into the kingdom, (2) service in the kingdom, or (3) rulership in the kingdom. I reject the first option, accept the second, but note that it extends into the third option. Again, I concur with Constable: "The disciple who does not continue following Jesus faithfully falls under divine judgment, not that he will lose his salvation but part of his reward, specifically the opportunity for further **significant** service" (*Luke,* 173).

There will be animals in the millennial kingdom. Perhaps subcomers will be given jobs shoveling manure or other such related insignificant chores. That would be a rather demeaning occupation for vessels of dishonor and would seem to accord very well with Mt 5:13 and 2Tim 2:20. At least the Lord and the kingdom will still be getting some good out of subcomers. Plausibly, Christians are faced with a choice of service ranging from ruling with Christ for eternity to shoveling manure for eternity. In any event, those Christians who trod Jesus under foot temporally (Heb 10:29) will themselves be trodden under foot eternally (Mt 5:13). Those believers who treat Christ with distain on earth will be given dishonorable service to perform in the kingdom.

[610] The reward of having a portion in the tree of life means to eat from the tree and have a right to the tree of life (Rev 2:7; 22:2,14). Correspondingly, the reward of having a portion in the Heavenly City (Rev 22:19) should be understood similarly as having the misthopological right to participate in and experience the city. The idea of entering the city but not being rewarded with the city would be as foreign as the notion of being given access to the fruit and being allowed to hold and lick it but not being allowed to eat it. Exclusion from one is best understood as exclusion from the other. Those who fail to overcome will not be allowed into the city or to the fruit.

[611] Phillip M. Evans, *Eternal Security Proved! Salvation not Probation* (LuLu.com, 2008), 38.

[612] Ibid., 93.

[613] See Bing's discussion of disciples that were curious followers. Charles C. Bing, "Coming to Terms with Discipleship," *JOTGES* 5:1 (Spring 1992): 41-42. See also Roy B. Zuck, "Cheap Grace?" *Kindred Spirit* (Summer 1989): 7.

[614] J. B. Phillips, *The New Testament in Modern English*, student ed. (New York: MacMillan Publishing Co., 1958).

[615] Arndt, *Luke*, 320. William Hendriksen, *Exposition of the Gospel According to Luke,* NTC (Grand Rapids: Baker Book House, 1978), 680.

[616] Conversely, *pistos* is best rendered as *believer* in Eph 1:1, but most translations fail their English readers by translating it as *faithful*. However, a few translations, such as the BBE, EDB, MRD, and TNT, correctly render *pistos* in this verse as "those who have *faith*," or some form of *believe*. The NTME is even better in that it also treats the *kai* as epexegetical: "*namely*, believing ones." The BKC likewise acknowledges that the phrase could be rendered as, "*that is*, the believers in Christ Jesus." The LEK specifies that the *kai* is epexegetical and renders it as, "saints *who are* believers." This understanding is preferred by Martin in the WBC. Barnes likewise adopts this view. Lenski and Hendriksen take similar approaches.

Briefly, *pistos* is a substantive united under one article with its substantive predecessor. Paul is not using *pistos* as an adjective to describe a subset of saints in Ephesus. Context, as well as grammar, makes that matter clear. Context also argues against taking *pistos* to refer to their behavior. This is the same group of people whom Paul urges to "**no longer** walk just as the Gentiles also walk (Eph 4:17; TM), and to "let him who steals **no longer** steal" (4:28; TM). Other such similar statements within the epistle lead one to suspect that Paul stops short of affirming that this group of believers has yet attained faithfulness. His three chapters of moral exhortations certainly make it impossible to assume that he believes that being a saint positionally necessarily means that a believer is a saint experientially. He primarily extols them for their position in Christ rather than their behavior in Christ.

To be sure, Eph 1:15 may be an exception to this rule, where Paul expresses a prayer of thanks to God for their love. But at the same time, one must question from his petitions in this same prayer as to whether that love had achieved mature expression. Their love would seem to be lacking mature stabilization, as evidenced from Paul's editorial *we* when he says, "We are **no longer** to be children, tossed here and there by waves" (Eph 4:14). This triple combination of *no longer* (*meketi*) causes one to conclude that they had not yet attained maturity. Not entirely surprising, then, years later John rebukes this church for having lost its first love (Rev 2:4). Moreover, John does not consider the loving church of Thyatira to be morally virtuous (Rev 2:18-20). John does not take it for granted that believers will be faithful (Rev 2:10). As shown in the parabolic material on the outer darkness, some believers are faithful and hear the words, "Well done," (Mt 25:23), while other believers are wicked and are called, "Lazy."

A better approach toward translating *pistos* in such contexts would be to understand Paul's designation in Eph 1:1 as a reference to the other reason for thanksgiving mentioned in Eph 1:15, that is, their *faith in the Lord Jesus*. He also uses the substantive participle for *believer* in 1:19. In the context, he is listing spiritual truths that are positionally applicable to them because they simply believed (1:13) rather than truths that apply because they are faithful. The saints of Eph 1:18 are defined as those who believe in 1:19

Those who adopt the substantive approach generally assume that Paul limits the phrase *believers in Christ* to its positional meaning so that *in Christ* denotes the spiritual sphere in which they are located rather than the object of their faith. This sharp distinction is unnecessary in this context. Paul certainly intends the positional meaning, but there is no reason to exclude the latter as well. Both senses are probably intended: Believers in Christ are in Christ. Those who have Christ as the sole object of their soteriological faith are in Christ as their soteriological sphere. As to a substantive taking an object, the substantive *believers of the truth* (1Tim 4:3) is not that far removed from the substantive *believers in Christ* (Eph 1:1). John uses substantive participles with Christ as the object of faith (Jn 6:35, 47 MT; 7:38; 11:25-26; 12:44,46; 14:12). Certainly, faith in Christ is a common Pauline theme (Rom 4:5; 9:33; 10:11; cp. v. 24; Gal 2:16; 3:26; Eph 1:15 (cp. v. 12); Phil 1:29; 3:9; Col 1:4; 2:5; 1Tim 1:16).

Therefore, the translation used herein is: "Paul, an apostle of Christ Jesus by the will of God, to the saints who are in Ephesus, that is, to believers in Christ Jesus" (Eph 1:1; TM). The Colossian counterpart would be translated similarly: "Paul, an apostle of Jesus Christ by the will of God, and Timothy our brother, to the saints who are in Colossae, that is, to believers, brethren in Christ" (Col 1:1-2; TM). These two verses should be added to the dozen NT passages in which the NAS translates *pistos* in terms of being a believer: Jn 20:27; Acts 10:45; 16:1; 2Cor 6:15; Gal 3:9; 1Tim 4:3,10,12; 5:16; 6:2; Tit 1:6; 1Pet 1:21. Note that the NAS treats the *pistos* in the last passage of this list as a substantive, which takes an object: *believers in God*. This Petrine parallel further specifies that *pistos eis theos* ("believers in God") are those who have *pistis eis theos* ("faith in God"). I likewise understand Eph 1:1 and Col 1:1 to refer to *believers in Christ*. Believers in Christ are positionally in Christ, not merely physically in Ephesus or Colossae. Paul brings this point to their attention. He addresses them as believers in regard to their physical location and reminds them of their spiritual position.

[617] Robert N. Wilkin, "Believers at the Judgment Seat of Christ: Well Done or Cut in Two?" *GIF* (September-October 2000). Also see Dillow (p. 389) for more references in favor of the position that *unfaithful* is the better translation.

[618] Alcorn, *Money*, 148.

[619] Karl E. Pagenkemper, "Rejection Imagery in the Synoptic Parables [Part 1]," *BibSac* 153:610 (April 1996): 191, n. 39.

[620] Earl D. Radmacher, gen. ed. *Nelson's New Illustrated Bible Commentary* (Nashville: T. Nelson Publishers, 1999), 1279.

[621] "And to whom did He swear that they should not enter His rest, but to those who were *disobedient* [*apeitheo*]? And *so* we see that they were not able to enter because of *unbelief* [*apistia*] (Heb 3:18-19). *Disobedient* (*apeitheo*) and *unbelief* (*apistia*) are used synonymously in this passage as referring to subsequent unbelief, as attested by Jude: "The Lord, after saving a people out of the land of Egypt, subsequently destroyed those who did not *believe* [*pisteuo*]" (1:5). Jude accurately expresses the LXX (Num 14:11; cf. Dt 1:32). These redeemed Israelites had enough faith to get them out of Egypt but not enough faith to get them into the promised rest. God destroyed them temporally as a result, providing a picture of misthological destruction of apostate believers.

[622] The position adopted herein is that only soteric unbelievers are classified as sinners in the eternal state. The articular construction In Rev 21:8, 27; 22:15 suggests this as an eternal classification. The objection will be made by conditional securitists that I should treat the articular *hoi apistos* (*the unbelievers*) in Lk 12:46 in the same fashion as I do in Rev 21:8 so that the Lukan verse is considered a soteriological text. Conversely, ultraists will object and insist that I treat these texts in Revelation as misthological as I have argued for Lk 12:46.

I counter that the classification in Lk 12:46 might only be for the purpose of judgment. The misthological classification does not extend into eternity future for the saints; only the misthological results remain. If this rejoinder seems too strained, then another possibility exists. Misthological classification is permanent. If a believer is classified as a hypocrite at the judgment, then that believer is classified a hypocritical believer throughout eternity. Just as the positive designation of *faithful* sticks so does the negate stigma of *unfaithful*. Faithful and unfaithful believers will be known as such throughout eternity.

Regardless of which of these two counter approaches are adopted, the articular classification does not necessarily indicate ongoing participation so that those so branded are still being unfaithful. If the anarthrous construction suggests behavior and character (as is generally expected), then one would not require Jesus to tell these unfaithful believers at this judgment that they would be assigned a place with those who still have this behavior and character! The articular construction is thus to be anticipated. In this context, in and of itself, the articular versus anarthrous construction proves nothing regarding the final state, as to whether it is soteric or mistholic. Context rules over syntax.

[623] Gaebelein, *Matthew*, 526.

[624] Chitwood, *Olivet*, 139.

[625] Gaebelein, *Matthew*, 526.

[626] Hodges, *Jesus*, 58-59.

[627] Ibid., 57.

[628] Chitwood, *Olivet*, 158.

[629] Hodges, *Jesus*, 57.

[630] Wall not only cites the Scripture for the open door policy but uses it in connection with other principles in finding guidance in earning rewards. See Joe Wall, *Going for the Gold, Reward and Loss at the Judgment of Believers* (Chicago: Moody Press, 1991), 131-139.

[631] For this threefold description of the wedding, see Theodore H. Epp, *Practical Studies in Revelation* (Lincoln, Nebraska: Back to the Bible Broadcast, 1969), 337-339. This is perhaps the most popular view.

[632] Pentecost, 227-228.

[633] Stanton, 261-262.

[634] Robert N. Wilkin, "The Mark of the Beast and Perseverance: Revelation 14:9-12," *GIF* (June, 1991).

[635] Personal correspondence, 8-20-93.

[636] Dillow, 175.

[637] Corner, *Security*, 504.

[638] Dillow, 175.

[639] Claeys, 146.

[640] Ibid., 260, n. 13.

[641] Ibid.,195, 203.

[642] Benware, *Prophecy*, 317.

[643] Claeys, 197. Also see his excellent discussion of Israel's need of repentance (p. 171).

[644] Hindson and Borland, *Matthew*, TFCBC, 209.

[645] Ibid., 221.

[646] John F. Walvoord, *Matthew: Thy Kingdom Come* (Grand Rapids: Kregel Publications, 1974), 197.

[647] Ibid., 220.

[648] John MacArthur, *Matthew 24-28,* MNTC (Chicago: Moody Press, 1989).

[649] G. Campbell Morgan, *The Pictures and Metaphors of Our Lord* (Old Tappan, NJ: Fleming H. Revell Company, n.d.), 133-134,157. For comments about passing through the tribulation, see G. Campbell Morgan, *God's Methods With Man* (Old Tappan, NJ: Fleming H. Revell Company, 1898), 177-178.

[650] Gaebelein, 536.

[651] Constable, *Mark*, 141.

[652] Chitwood, *Olivet*, 68-69.

[653] Epp, *Revelation*, 2:105. Becker, 220-221. Ryrie, *Revelation*, 69.

[654] Pagenkemper, "Part 1," 196.

[655] Ibid., 198.

[656] Claeys, 118.

[657] Ibid., 258, n. 9.

[658] Benware, *Prophecy*, 43.

[659] Randall C. Gleason, "The Old Testament Background of Rest in Hebrews 3:7-8," *BibSac* 157:627 (July, 2000): 281-303.

[660] During the window of time in which God was constituting a relationship with Israel by making them a nation, specifically His nation, they were not allowed to return to Egypt even though they wanted to return (Ex 13:17-18; Dt 17:16; Num 14:3-13; Acts 7:39). Thereafter, they permanently would be His nation, even if they were scattered aboard and even if He brought them back to Egypt or they sinfully returned to Egypt (Dt 28:68; 2Kgs 25:25-26; Hos 8:13-14; 9:3; Eze 29:15-16). That Exodus generation could not return. Typologically, the window of opportunity was closed for their apostasy (in either desire or intent) to culminate in an action that would picture them as returning to an unsaved state by returning to Egypt. Whatever action God might bring against the nation of Israel in the future would never dissolve the relationship He established with them in the Exodus experience, a relationship typologically pictured by the Exodus generation. Going back subsequently to Egypt (after this typological window closed) might typify God's punishment upon their apostasy (as they live as if they were unsaved after returning to Egypt), but even then it would not be the end of the story. In truth they would remain the people of God. Even apostasy and returning to Egypt after this typological window of opportunity had closed would not dissolve their relationship with God, thereby allowing Israel to remain a picture of unconditional security throughout the pages of history, both typologically and historically. They may go back to living and looking as if they were unsaved experientially, but they could not be unsaved soteriologically. If Israel chose to return to Egypt, death would follow them (Jer 42:13-19). However, they could not return to Egypt in the same way they left it in terms of passing through the Red Sea on dry ground. They could not completely undo their miraculous deliverance. Likewise, when believers choose to present themselves as experiential slaves to sin (Rom 6:13), death will follow them (Rom 6:16). Even then, death cannot separate them from the love of God in Christ (Rom 8:38-39).

Stretching the typological window to include Dt 28 poses a problem for both conditional security and unconditional security. Neither group would be inclined to argue that remaining in heaven is conditioned on subsequent obedience once one has arrived in heaven. If entrance into the Promised Land is pictured as entrance into heaven, then neither camp would want to press the point that subsequent performance was necessary to stay there, as if soteriological typology were involved. Therefore, the safest option is simply to regard this prophecy as being fulfilled literally in the various deportations that have happened to the Jews (so Constable). If hell is in the picture, then it is for lost Jews (WBC). Perhaps, this is the end of the story.

Then again, misthopology is open to a more encompassing typology. That Moses, the same writer who brought them out of Egypt, gives this warning is utterly amazing: "And the Lord will bring you back to Egypt in ships, by the way about which I spoke to you, 'You will never see it again!'" (Dt 28:68) Their desire to go back to Egypt pictures a desire to return to earthly pleasures rather than pursue God's treasure. If they did not overcome the world's allurements, the Promised Land of blessing (Dt 28:1-14) would become the Cursed Land of blasting (Dt 28:15-68). So it is with believers who fail to overcome the world's allurements. After being imported from the world into the Promised Land (the Heavenly Jerusalem), they will be deported from it back to the world. Only, comparatively, the world will not be filled with pleasure they thought they would find in it. Believers are not of this world, and they will be taken out of this world into Heavenly Jerusalem. Yet those who subcome to a love affair with this world will be cast out of the Heavenly Jerusalem back to the world they love so much. However, they will not find life here to be the quality of life they imagined.

If a typological parallel is valid, then Dt 28:15-68 (and following) may be one of the bleakest pictures of the outer darkness in all of Scripture. Elsewhere, Scripture pictures the Bema as a burning experience for those believers who do not overcome (Jn 15:6; 1Cor 3:15). Literal burning is not intended. Likewise, a literal correspondence to this possible misthological typology should not be pressed, just as we do not insist on carnal believers who are pictured typologically in the wilderness as being bitten by literal serpents. Nevertheless, in the same way as the Bema may be described as a fire, so these curses in Deuteronomy may be regarded as its ashes. Smell the lingering smoke as you walk through the charred remains typologically contained in these verses.

Indeed, the writer of Hebrews is walking through these ashes when he makes application to believers in Heb 10:30 of God's vengeance in Dt 32:35. Likewise, Heb 12:29 draws upon Dt 4:24 as a warning that would be applicable after they enter the Promised Land.

> So watch yourselves, lest you forget the covenant of the Lord your God, which He made with you, and make for yourselves a graven image in the form of anything against which the Lord your God has commanded you. For the Lord your God is a consuming fire, a jealous God. When you become the father of children and children's children and have remained long in the land, and act corruptly, and make an idol in the form of anything, and do that which is evil in the sight of the Lord your God so as to provoke Him to anger, I call heaven and earth to witness against you today, that you shall surely perish quickly from the land where you are going over the Jordan to possess it. You shall not live long on it, but shall be utterly destroyed. (Dt 4:23-26)

If the writer of Hebrews is making an eschatological application of these warnings as being applicable to believers and if this application depicts what happens to believers in the outer darkness (both of which certainly seem to be the case), then the supposition stands that these Deuteronomic curses, as to what will happen to God's people if they abandon the Lord after they qualify for entrance into the Promised Land, typologically foreshadow the outer darkness. They will not live long in the Promised Land, the Heaven Jerusalem, but be removed from it permanently.

If Numbers (ch. 14 and Ps 95:8-11) depicts what happens to carnal believers who fail to qualify for kingdom inheritance, then Deuteronomy depicts what happens to apostate believers who subsequently are disqualified for kingdom inheritance. Whereas Numbers pictures misthopological exclusion, Deuteronomy pictures misthological expulsion. In Numbers, God's people fail to enter the rest. In Deuteronomy they fail to stay there. One must overcome carnality in order to enter into the Promised Land; one must overcome apostasy in order to remain there. Initial faithfulness is required to qualify for entrance into the Promised Land. Subsequent faithfulness is required to remain qualified for dwelling in the Promised Land. Just as one can forfeit one's crown (Rev 3:11), so one can forfeit one's tenure in the capitol city (Rev 22:19). Those who think that life will be heavenly for those cast out of the city ought to consider carefully the typology of Deuteronomy. Like the servant cast out of the wedding after it was started and who did not get to stay at the celebration very long (Mt 22:11-13), these unfaithful Jews will find themselves removed from the Promised Land very quickly. I suppose that all those currently in Heavenly Jerusalem are able to eat presently of the tree of life. Just as these unfaithful Jews got to taste the Promised Land but once ejected would no longer be able to enjoy the fruits of the Promised Land, so those believers expelled from the Reward City will no longer be able to eat of the tree of life which grows in that city. Typologically, they would die misthologically.

[661] Even bridal slaves can rejoice in being unworthy-worthy slaves throughout eternity. The Bible encourages us to think of overcomers as the Bride of Christ. An imaginative personification of this bridal slave might be sketched as follows:

The Lord's Bride kneels before Lord Jesus as nothing more than a slave so that She may sit beside Him as nothing less than a Queen. In respect to Her having acknowledged that He is the Lord and as far as being under His complete authority, She is just a slave. She has no rights other than the rights He gives Her. In respect to being His co-regent, however, She is nothing less than a Queen.

His Queen may refer to Herself as a slave throughout eternity in order to magnify His Lordship, even calling Herself an unworthy slave on occasion. Perhaps even occasionally the Lord may refer to His Queen as a slave. But no one under His or Her authority would dare address her as a slave. She may refer to Herself as a slave, but her subordinates will not be permitted to do so. They will address Her as *your Majesty*.

Because She is *His* slave, not *their* slave, no one will address Her as a slave. She will not be treated or addressed as a slave by those over whom She rules. She may bow before Her Lord and acknowledge that She is nothing more than a slave (and from one limited perspective that is true). Yet He will have Her raise from Her knees to sit beside Him on His throne and point out that She is nothing less than a Queen (which is equally true from an alternate point of view).

She is the slave-Queen: the slave of Her Lord; the Queen of heaven. While on earth, She bowed before Her Lord as His slave in order that She might sit beside Him as His Queen in heaven. She still will be afforded the honor of bowing before Him in heaven and confessing Herself to be nothing more than a slave. Affectionately, He may even refer to Her occasionally as His *little slave*, but He also will have Her rise and sit with Him as His Queen.

Picture a possible scene. She stands before Her subjects and whispers in a soft, humble voice, "I am nothing more than a slave." They fall to their knees and respond in strong, unanimous refrain that sakes the ground, "And yet nothing less than our Queen!"

She turns, kneels before Her Husband-King, and confesses, "I am nothing more than a slave." He responds tenderly, "And nothing less than My Queen. Arise My *little slave* and sit beside Me as My Queen."

King Jesus has declared that anytime His Bride confesses Herself to be nothing more than a slave, all her subjects will kneel and exclaim that She is nothing less than their Queen. The King will allow Her to humble Herself by calling Herself a slave, but He will demand that Her subjects honor Her when She does so by calling Her their Queen.

Surely, the Lord will not allow Her to be treated as anything less than a Queen by Her subjects. For any subject to treat Her as a slave (or even call Her a slave to Her face) would be an unthinkable offense. No angel would dare commit such an atrocity. She is His slave, not their slave. No heavenly subject will dare call Her a slave, even though She may call Herself such. She is His slave, but She is their Queen. Most certainly, She will be honored as their heavenly Queen.

When She kneels before Her King and Lover, She coos, "I am an unworthy slave; I have done only that which I ought to have done" (Lk 17:10). He does not deny the truth of that statement. Truly, He has every right to expect Her to kneel before Him and to serve Him as Her Lord and Master. He taught Her to adopt that perspective on earth. She learned it well and still enjoys doing so in heaven. Yet He is certainly not content to leave the matter there, as He sweeps Her up into His arms and lovingly adds a refrain of His own, "And yet a worthy Queen!"

For such reasons, this woman actually relishes kneeling and bowing before Her Husband-Lord as His slave and calling Herself a slave. In fact, on rare occasions, when She publically bows before Him and confesses Herself to be His slave, He sometimes responds by asking, "Do You not resent being My slave?" She particularly enjoys those occasions. Those social events give Her the opportunity to shake her head, "No," as She shyly rises to her feet and with a coy smile on her face responds, "Because I am also, 'She who is Loved.'"

As everyone in heaven knows, on her left arm the Queen wears a golden bracelet that has the single word: *Slave*. Often She will wear a short-sleeve, white blouse with the matching title embroidered in golden thread: *Nothing more than a Slave*. This title shows just above the arm bracelet. On the other arm the Queen wears a matching golden bracelet with the single word: *Queen*. On the left sleeve is the corresponding title: *Nothing Less than a Queen*. Around Her neck She wears a diamond-studded, golden necklace which sparkles like a rainbow with the single word: *Loved*. Embroidered on the neckline of the blouse in golden thread is the title: *She who is Loved*.

Her subjects often will address Her by the title—*She who is Loved*. No one, however, would dare address her by the title—*Just a slave*. Addressing Her as *Slave* is love language reserved for Her by Her Lord. And even He only does so as a term of endearment. On those infrequent occasions, when He does address Her in this manner, He does so with such tenderness, body language, and facial expression that everyone knows that in all emotionally reality and irony He is addressing her as *She who is Loved*. Bystanders can feel the love practically dripping from His words when He uses His pet names for Her such as: *My little Slave*.

She is a slave of love to Him who is Love. And She loves it. She is the apple of His eye, and She knows it. So does everyone else. His referring to her as *Slave*, *My little Slave*, or *Just a Slave* does not change Her Queenly status one iota. *She who is Loved* loves being able to submit to Her Lord as His queenly slave.

As She bows on her knees before Her Lord as He sits on His throne and casts Her eyes downcast toward the ground, She whispers, "I am just a slave." He bends over, places His index finger under her chin, gently raises Her downcast eyes to meet His, and affirms, "Yes, that is all you are, just My slave." Then He takes her cheeks in His hands, tenderly kisses Her on the top of Her head, and whispers with equal tenderness, "Nothing but a Slave."

He often enjoyed using irony when He was living on earth to put His enemies in their place, and He enjoys using it inversely in heaven to elevate His Queen to Her place. The loving twinkle in His eye and the smile on His face are dead giveaways that He means quite the opposite. Being called *Nothing but a Slave* is just love language between them, one of His pet titles for Her that He uses on rare occasions to convey so much more than it actually says.

On those occasions, She does not rise to sit beside Him on Her throne. Instead, She responds, "Yes, My Lord, nothing but a slave," as She places Her hands on His knees and rises, not to sit on Her throne but to sit in His lap on His throne! On those opportune moments, She purposefully takes His promise to share His throne quite literally. When that happens, the ensuing love talk between them is almost comical. Holy chuckles and grins are common among the bystanders.

"Alright, *Nothing but a Slave*," He joking replies, "You are supposed to sit on your throne, not on My lap," amusingly imitating a reprimanding tone.

"But My Lord, I am nothing but a slave. What right do I have to sit on a queenly throne?" She inquisitively replies, with facetious sincerity.

Now that She is in His lap, She is in no hurry to leave. Plus, She always finds it interesting as to what witty response He might use to coax His *little Slave* out of His lap and onto Her throne. After all, She reasons, He would not have practically coaxed Her into His lap in the first place by affectionately acknowledging that She was nothing more than a slave if He did not want to have to sweet-talk Her out of His lap. He is Her Lord. For Her, *Lord = Lover*. He became Her Lord so that He might be Her Lover (Love-Her): a sovereign lover no doubt, nevertheless, a lover nonetheless. He is Her Lord-Lover as She is His Slave-Queen. Little wonder, then, that the heavenly Queen finds Her slavery to be heavenly.

[662] Paul Benware, *The Believer's Payday* (Chattanooga, TN: AMG Publishers, 2002), 208.

[663] Ibid., 17.

[664] Ibid., 173.

[665] Ibid., 92.

[666] Walvoord, *Matthew*, 198.

[667] France, *Matthew*, NIC, 955-956.

[668] Ibid., 955, n. 72.

[669] Walvoord, *Matthew*, 140.

[670] Ibid., 199.

[671] However, even if this position concerning the time is not accepted, the unworthy slave still could represent a genuine believer just as the foolish virgins do in the previous parable.

[672] Keathley IV, "Darkness," 1-2.

[673] Ibid., 4.

[674] Ibid., 3.

[675] Hodges, *Free*, 151.

[676] Hodges, *Harmony*, 31.

[677] Ibid., 32.

[678] Huber, Relationship, 13-14.

[679] Should it be challenged that these ethnic Jews conceptually are merely *sons of God* covenantally, this contention would be undermined lexically by the underlying Greek text. The word used for *sons* in the phrase *sons of the kingdom* is *huios* as opposed to *teknon* in Mt 21:28. This latter word is the word used inclusively of ethnic Jewish relationship to Abraham in the NT (e.g., Mt 3:9; 15:26; 23:37; 27:25; Lk 16:25; Jn 8:39; Rom 9:7; Gal 4:5). Thus, *teknon* might be used generically to represent someone who is either an ethnical or spiritual child of Abraham. Indeed, in some of these texts, the right of ethnic Jews even to call themselves *children of Abraham* is challenged. Moreover, in the Lukan text referenced, Abraham is speaking to his ethnic child who is in hell!

Contrastively, the phrases *sons of God* (Mt 5:9; Lk 20:36; Rom 8:14; 8:19; 9:26; Gal 3:26), *sons of your Father* (Mt 5:45), *sons of the kingdom* (Mt 8:12; 13:38), *sons of the Most High* (Lk 6:35), *sons of the Lord* (2Cor 6:18), and *sons of light* (1Thess 5:5) more restrictively implement *huios* (soteriologically and misthologically as opposed to ethnically). This Greek word (which more especially means *sons*) appears to be used intensively—when applied ethnically to Jews seeking to kill Jesus—as being *sons of hell* (Mt 23:15) and *sons of murders* (Mt 23:31). Admittedly, *sons of Israel* (Lk 1:16; Acts 5:21; Rom 9:27; 2Cor 3:13) might be used ethnically and nationally of Jews generically. Antagonists might argue that *sons of Israel ≈ ethnic sons of Abraham = generic sonship*, so *huios* conceptually is used ethnically for *sons of God*. This supposition breaks down, however, in that it begs the question: "Where is the missing link that equates these generic equations with sons of God so that sons of God are not necessarily saved?"

Furthermore, although Paul specifies that *sons of Abraham* are believers and thus *sons of God* (Gal 3:7; 26), and yet conceives of a sense in which legalistic sons of Abraham form an exception to being sons of God (Gal 4:22; 30), even here it cannot be maintained that sons of God may refer to unbelievers.

Opponents cannot appeal to Mt 21:28 to assert that sons of God may be unbelievers because this verse uses *teknon*, not *huios*! In this verse, the parabolic man (representing God) has two *children* (*tekna*). One will go on to believe (and thus implicitly become a *huios*); the other remains a *teknon* (who is not allowed to enter the kingdom because he did not believe and thus become a soteric *huios*). Or, if one looks at this passage through the mistholic lens, he was not allowed to enter the kingship because he failed to become a mistholic *huios*. (See discussion surrounding and following *Illustration 351. Three Temporal-Ethnic Lens*, 937.) But presuming the current lens is the vantage point, contrastively, in

Lk 15:11 the parabolic man (representing God) has two *sons* (*huioi*). His sons are already *huioi*. Unfortunately, the vast majority of English translations render **both** verses as: *The man had two sons.* Not so! In the Matthean parable (where ethnic Jews are included), *tekna* is used. The man had two *children*, evidently *boys*. In the Lukan parable (that of the Prodigal Son where spiritual Jews are in view), *huios* is used. The man had two *sons*.

Even more germane, the issue in this Lukan parable is, "Who is **worthy to be called** *sons* (*huios*) of God?" The repeated concern of the younger son is not that he is no longer a *huios* but that he is no longer worthy to be called such (Lk 15:19,21). Whereas English translations typically err in translating *tekna* as *sons* in Mt 21:28, some translations err inversely in rendering *tekna* in 1Jn 3:1 as if all believers are qualified unconditionally *to be called **sons*** (*huios*) *of God*. In actuality, the verse only affirms that all believers are qualified unconditionally *to be called **children*** (*tekna*) *of God*. Incontrovertibly, being **called** *sons* (*huios*) *of God* is a reward in Mt 5:9. Whereas Rom 9:26 might be an exception, thus preventing one from stating this to be a misthological rule; nevertheless, it is not an exception to the soteriological rule that within the NT *sons of God* always refers to believers. In any event, even this text in Romans need not be an exception to the misthological rule. That only Jews who qualify misthologically (as opposed to ethnically) comprise the remnant **called** *sons of God* does not necessarily mean that soteriological Jews are also **called** *sons of God* (*huios*).

Incidentally, the same Greek word for *call* (*kaleo*) is used in relation to being called a son in all three passages regarding: the rewarded believers (Mt 5:9), the Prodigal Son (Lk 15:9,21), and the remnant believers (Rom 9:26). Although *kaleo* (and any other verb for *call*) is omitted from Lk 19:9, when Jesus calls Zaccheus a son of Abraham, it is nevertheless apparent that Jesus is in fact calling him such.

GNTC is surely correct to conclude that Zaccheus had become a spiritual Jew before Jesus pronounced him to be a *son of Abraham* (Lk 19:9). Thus, GNTC regards this as a soteriological pronouncement. GNTC is also correct to regard being *sons of Abraham* (Gal 3:7) and *sons of God* (Gal 3:26) as soteriological affirmations. All three verses use *huios*. However, Zaccheus *being* **called** *a son of Abraham* by Jesus should probably not be limited to the soteriological spectrum.

Zaccheus had become a soteriological son of God (in the Pauline sense) by simple faith in Jesus for eternal life as a free gift—and thus a *child* (*teknon*) of God. But Zaccheus qualified to be **called** a son of God in the mistholic sense by going on beyond receiving eternal life as a gift to making a promise that (if followed through upon) would result in him also receiving eternal life additionally as a reward. So why would Jesus not misthologically call Zaccheus a son of Abraham? If being **called** *sons of God* is a mistholic theme (and according to Jesus it is) and if being *sons of God* can be used synonymously for being *sons of Abraham* (and according to Paul it can), then what is to prevent one from concluding that Jesus misthologically is encouraging Zaccheus (as a new believer) by rewarding him in bestowing this title upon him because Zaccheus promises to invest so heavily in heavenly things? Jesus purposefully and proleptically **calls** Zaccheus a *son of Abraham* as a misthological title to introduce His parable that previews the potential rewards to which Zaccheus will be entitled. His being **called** a *son of Abraham* is a foretaste of hearing, "Well done" (Lk 19:9).

[680] If it is objected that since spiritual gifts are forfeitable so the gift of eternal life must be forfeitable also, let it be remembered that spiritual gifts are not necessarily eternal (1Cor 3:8-10). The spiritual gift is not taken away before it has run its allotted course. The reward is in having the gift extend beyond its freely allotted time. For example, it is one thing for a firm to give an employee a car to use freely for an entire year. For the firm to transfer possession of that car over to the employee at the end of the year as a reward for exceptional service is quite another. The former might be considered a perk (perhaps even a gift); the latter definitely would be considered a reward, not a right for simply being an employee.

A spiritual *gift*, as such, is a God-given energization for service during the allotted time in which that gift is intended to be used freely in performing that service. Apparently, even those who had the gift of tongues, for example, lost the exercise of that gift within the course of their lifetime because the gift was not intended to run the course of their lifetime. The gift was expected to be in operation during their lifetime, not throughout their lifetime. What was given freely was the ability to exercise this gift for a limited period of time, not for an unlimited period of time.

Spiritual gifts cease to be gifts that may be used freely once they have run their intended course. Even the gift of teaching will cease once a Christian teacher dies or is raptured because the capacity to use this gift freely was limited to his or her time on earth during the present advent. Whether that capacity to teach is granted again in heaven will be contingent upon one's service on earth. If one has been a faithful teacher on earth, then one will be rewarded with increased ability and opportunity to teach in heaven. The talent that freely was given to be exercised on earth will be increased misthologically for exercise in heaven—if the believer has been faithful in the exercise of that talent on earth. Otherwise, that talent will be taken away and given to someone else.

It is not the spiritual *gift*, as such, which is taken away since the stage of that capacity to serve as a *gift* already will have ceased. Rather, what is taken away and given to another as a reward is the capacity to perform that function (that was previously a gift but that has now become a reward after its allotted time is up). As to tongues, presumably there will be no need of this gift in heaven in order to talk to men or angels. However, what about talking to animals? Even if some animals are able to talk in heaven, it is unreasonable to think that all animals will be able to speak with equal clarity. Some animals may need an interpreter. Believers who have been faithful in their exercise of the gift of tongues or interpretation during their lifetimes on earth may find that they are able to talk to some animals in the new earth that no one else is able to talk with. Could it be that the stars actually sing and the creation really groans (Job 38:7; Rom 8:21)? Perhaps these believers will be able to commune with nature at a level no one else can fathom.

[681] Keathley IV, "Darkness," 5.

[682] Hampton Keathley IV, "The Parables in the Olivet Discourse (Matthew 25)," 1. Available at http://bible.org /page.asp?page_id=1045. Accessed on September 17, 2004.

[683] Dillow, 349-350.

[684] Bigalke, 133.

[685] To be sure, Pagenkemper ("Part 1," 196) erroneously contends that the relationship is dissolved when the talent is taken away. Actually, the servants were servants even before they were entrusted, so the supposition (that the taking away of the talent dissolves his status as a servant) is flawed. In actually, what is taken away is his ability to serve his master in that capacity. Nothing would prevent his master from deciding to have him permanently serve the horses thereafter by mucking their stalls. Regardless, even given Pagenkemper's limited perspective, it would be false to conclude that the servant was not a believer since the believer's relationship with the Lord, supposedly, was not permanent. Even if Pagenkemper's argument were accepted that the possession of the talent proves whether the relationship is genuine, it would lead to the conclusion that what is being pictured is the loss of salvation since the talent was taken away. It cannot be a picture of a believer who proved to be a false believer in the end. His strained exegesis leads to Arminianism rather than Calvinism. Pagenkemper's argument is fallacious since the Scripture does not teach that the slave/master relationship is permanent; it is the child/Father relationship that is indestructible. A Christian who fails to serve loses the opportunity to serve but does not thereby cease to be a Christian.

[686] Tom Stegall, "Must Faith Endure for Salvation to be Sure? (pt. 5)." Available at http://www.duluthbible.org /g_f_j/Must_Faith_Endure2.htm. Accessed on 28, February 2005.

[687] France, *Matthew*, NIC, 951-952.

[688] Ibid., 956-957.

[689] Paul Copeland, *"That's Just Your Interpretation": Responding to Skeptics who Challenge Your Faith* (Grand Rapids: Baker Books, 2001), 32.

[690] Some within the FG camp understand passages such as Jn 8:24, 20:31, and Rom 10:9-13 as teaching that in order to be saved from hell a person must have a basic recognition as to Jesus' identity as Lord God. Others from the FG perspective do not believe that recognition of Jesus' deity is necessary; rather, what is exclusively necessary is belief in His ability to guarantee eternal life to those who simply trust Him for it. (See endnote 28.) From this latter perspective, it could be claimed that Jn 8:24 represents a psychological, rather than theological, requirement. These particular Jews being addressed could not be saved unless they accepted His deity because this was a stumbling block preventing them from trusting in Him as Messiah. Or it could be that Jesus simply is saying that they must believe that He is Christ/Messiah (cf. Jn 20:31). As Messiah/King, He has the right to determine who will enter His kingdom and has promised to give life in His kingdom to those who trust Him for it.

One criticism made by the *objective deity* (OD) view of the *subjective deity* (SD) view is that it is very difficult to define exactly what subjective degree of deity is soteriologically necessary from the traditional viewpoint. But this criticism may be subject to the degree fallacy. I will use an adaptation of Geisler's beard argument for this analogy (see *Reason*, 110).

Beard Argument
• *What degree of facial hair is necessary to constitute a beard? Since you cannot tell me the degree, no degree exists. There is no degree of facial hair that would constitute having a beard.*

OD Argument
• *What subjective degree of deity must necessarily be recognized in order to constitute saving faith? Since you cannot tell me the degree, no degree exists. There is no degree of deity necessary to constitute a saving faith.*

SD Objection
• *Why must one reject the first argument (which is obliviously false) but accept the second argument (which uses the same rationale)? Both arguments assume that the inability to define a relative degree proves that no absolute is possible. However, the first argument leads to the faulty conclusion that there is no absolute difference between having a beard and not having a beard. Since its conclusion is faulty, the inability to answer an objection based on degrees with exactitude does not necessarily prove that a distinction is invalid. The absurdity of the first argument calls into question the validity of the second.*

Certainly, those in LS will try to use this approach to question the FG criticism of LS. So I will respond to their anticipated objection. They could pose the following FG argument and then respond with a similar objection.

FG Argument
• *What degree of repentance or commitment is necessary to constitute saving faith? Since you cannot tell me the degree, no degree must exist. There is no degree of repentance or commitment that would constitute having saving faith.*

LS Objection
• *Our inability in LS to tell the exact degree does not invalidate the fact that some degree must exist. As seen in the SD rebuttal of the OD position, inability to specify a minimal degree does not prove that some degree cannot be required.*

Assuming the validity of the SD response, the LS argument must be refuted on some other ground. In this case, it is easy. FG can respond absolutely that requiring any degree of repentance or commitment (in terms of changing ones' performance) would nullify the freeness of the gift. So the LS faces a dual problem. It teaches a false gospel and also makes present assurance difficult. (LS makes linear assurance impossible.)

The problem of relativity is not limited to soteriology. While serving on a panel at a FGA conference, a question was posed as to how much one had to do in order to avoid the outer darkness. The author simply responded that meeting the terms for being an overcomer in Rev 2-3 would certainly suffice. The audience was by no means satisfied with this answer. But as the author went on to explain, giving a minimal degree is not possible because the Lord has given us individual talents and opportunities. What is a sufficient degree of loving faithfulness for one might not be for the other. It is highly ironic that at this same FGA conference, in which another panel had denied that it was possible to define the minimal content of the gospel necessary to escape hell, that the current author was expected to define the minimal content of the gospel necessary to escape the outer darkness! The former is certainly easier than the latter. In fact, many in GES would say that the former is possible, especially those who hold the OD position.

This is not to say that those who positively are inclined toward SD cannot have absolute assurance. To use the beard analogy, one may not be sure if a five o'clock shadow constitutes having a beard, but one certainly can be sure that having one inch of facial hair constitutes having a beard. Likewise, if one believes that (1) Jesus is the preexisting Son of God (who was God in the flesh), (2) who died for our sins and rose from the dead, and (3) who gives eternal life to those who simply believe in Him for it, then the believer has more than meet the minimal requirements for eternal life and may have absolute assurance of eternal life. This level of specificity more than qualifies one for eternal life. Just as one who has one inch of facial hair may be absolutely sure that he has a beard by societal standards, so those who have met these three requirements may be sure that they are saved by God's standards.

Therefore, although the present writer has migrated ever so slowly toward a OD view, he still retains considerable empathy with those holding the SD view and offers the above argument, which he himself has used in defense of that SD position, as solace for those still holding the SD view. Speaking only for himself, the consideration of sufficient means versus necessary means, in regards to universalism (see endnote 761), was the straw that broke the back of his insistence regarding the subjective recognition of the deity of Christ as theological necessity. Stressing Christ's deity still could be a useful psychological means of bringing people to saving faith. Certainly, Christ's objective deity is a soteriological necessity. Christ could not offer us His life as eternal life if He were not God. Nevertheless, it does not appear that acknowledging this theological necessity is a soteriological necessity unless it is as a psychological necessity. (Again, see endnote 28.) Contrary to some of my OD friends, and to use the words of Jesus' opponents, I believe that Jesus made Himself out to be the *Son of God*, and thus *God* (Jn 8:53,58; 10:33; 19:7), with sufficient clarity (1) that His statements can be used in a defense of Trinitarian precepts today and (2) with enough lucidity in that day that those who were inclined to believe in Him for eternal life were further encouraged to believe that He was capable of bestowing that life. Yet He implemented adequate ambiguity so as to impose (1) a considerable difficulty for those seeking to stone Him in His day [so much so that in exasperation they were forced to demand that He tell them plainly if He was even the Christ (Jn 10:14), much less God!] and (2) an ample formidability for those in our day that would claim that GJ clearly teaches that as a theological necessity one must believe that Jesus is God in order to believe in Him for eternal life.

After all, if Nathaniel's exclamation ("Rabbi, You are the Son of God; You are the King of Israel" in Jn 1:49) proves that all believers had a firm grasp of Jesus' deity when they first came to saving faith, then we are left with a puzzling enigma when they later ask, "*Who* then *is this*, that even the wind and the sea obey Him?" (Mk 4:41) It was not only Jesus' enemies who were asking Him, *Who are you?* (Jn 8:25) Believers in Jesus were grabbling with that very question and asking one another, *Who is this?* Or as Matthew relates it, "the men marveled, saying, "*What kind of a man is this*, that even the winds and the sea obey Him?" (Mt 8:27). Their amazement is utterly amazing if they already had deduced that Jesus was indeed God-man. Are we to conclude that these followers were not saved until the second time that He calmed the sea and they finally worshiped Him (Mt 14:33)? No. Certainly most of them were already believers long before then. Therefore, the fact that these believers had not yet deduced *what kind of man* Jesus was allows one to deduce that becoming a believer did not require that one grasp *what kind of man* Jesus was.

On the basis of progressive revelation, some in SD will insist that recognition of Jesus' deity became a soteriological requirement after the resurrection. One difficulty with such a proposal, however, is that Jn 8:24 is one of the strongest texts used to support the soteriological necessity for recognizing Jesus' deity, and it is a pre-resurrection text. If pre-cross texts, such as this one, do not establish the case for recognizing Jesus' deity as a universal soteriological necessity, then it is highly doubtful that post-cross texts will be able to do so, because the necessity could not be attributed to progressive clarity. Clarity may increase accountability, but there was sufficient clarity before the resurrection to establish necessity, if recognition of Christ's deity were in fact a necessity.

[691] Or as Radmacher has so bluntly stated: "The motivation to good works is the Judgment Seat of Christ" ("Bema," 38).

[692] Steven W. Waterhouse, *What Must I do to be Saved? The Bible's Definition of Saving Faith* (Amarillo, TX: Westcliff Press, 2000), 28.

[693] Ibid.

[694] Idem, *Not By Bread Alone: An Outlined Guide To Bible Doctrine*, revised edition (Amarillo, TX: Westcliff Press, 2003), 163-164.

[695] Brad McCoy, "Obedience Is Necessary To Receive Eternal Life," *GIF* (September 1994).

[696] Bob Wilkin, "Not Everyone Who Says 'Lord, Lord' Will Enter the Kingdom: Matthew 7:21-23," *GIF* (December 1988).

[697] Idem, "Obedience to the Faith: Romans 1:5," *GIF* (November 1995).

[698] Bing, *Salvation*, 22.

[699] Ibid., 24.

[700] Ibid., 25.

[701] Ibid., 58.

[702] Donald H. Bunge, *What Happened to the Word "Believe"?* (Omaha, NE: self published), 1985.

[703] Although *obedience* (*hupakoe*) to *the faith* need not refer to initial faith exclusively in Rom 1:5 and 16:26, certainly it does so inclusively. This also may be true of *hupakouo* in Acts 6:7. In any event, *hupakouo* probably refers exclusively to soteric faith in Rom 6:17 and certainly does so in 10:16. Even a LS Calvinist like MacDonald (pp. 56-57) admits:

> We must understand that the gospel is a message to be obeyed, and you obey it by believing on the Lord Jesus Christ....That is what Paul elsewhere speaks of as obedience of faith (Rom. 1:5; 16:26). And Luke speaks of a great many priests who were obedient to the faith (Acts 6:7). Their salvation experience was a single event, not a process."

Whether or not MacDonald is right in confirming the exclusive reference to soteric faith in these passages is open to debate. Lopez is probably correct that the Pauline *inclusio* is inclusive rather than exclusive in Rom 1:5 and 16:26 (*Romans*, 33-34). However, my argument does not require exclusivism in these passages, only inclusivism. Paul's use of *hupakouo* in a strictly soteric manner in Rom 10:16 should be acknowledged because it is part of his stair steps in Rom 10:14-15 in which the plank for faith in these stair steps is to be identified with the faith in Rom 10:10 for soteriological justification. Consequently, 10:16 is referring to the soteriological faith of 10:10 via the stair steps.

[704] Ibid., 26-27.

[705] Robert N. Wilkin, "The Free Grace Position Should Rightly Hold Claim to the Title *Lordship Salvation*," *GIF* (November-December, 2010).

[706] MacArthur, *Gospel*, 28.

[707] Gleason L. Archer, Paul D. Feinberg, Douglas J. Moo, Richard R. Reiter, *Three Views on the Rapture: Pre; Mid; or Post-Tribulation?* (Grand Rapids: Zondervan Publishing House, 1996), 78.

[708] Feinberg, *Rapture*, 74.

[709] Benware, *Prophecy*, 74.

[710] Constable, *Ezekiel*, 98.

[711] Betz, *Stage*, 321.

[712] Those unfaithful believers who live until the end of the tribulation will be disqualified, by the judgment following the tribulation, from inheriting the kingdom. Nevertheless, they will enter the millennial kingdom. Eventually, they will die. Certainly, at the end of the millennium, they will be resurrected and judged for their performance during the millennial kingdom. Thus, they will be judged twice. The judgment at the conclusion of the tribulation will disqualify them from inheriting the kingdom. They will not be able to overturn that judgment by their millennial performance. Still, they will have incentive to live obediently during the millennial age because they possibly can mitigate how severe their punishment will be in the outer darkness during the eternal state by their repentant obedience during their remaining years of earthly life during the millennial age, knowing that they will be judged a second time, not for their works performed before the millennium (for which they already were judged) but for their works that are performed subsequently during their remaining lifetime within the millennial period. For example, Noah was not cast back into the flood because of his post flood drunkenness in Gen 9:21. By his righteousness before the flood, he gained God's favor and was spared the flood. Even if he incurred God's displeasure by his drunkenness after the flood, it did not undo the results of his previous judgment, although God will judge Noah for his behavior after the flood.

[713] R. T. Kendall, *The Complete Guide to the Parables: Understanding and Applying the Stories of Jesus* (Grand Rapids: Chosen Books, 2004), 342, 347.

[714] Zeller, "Theology."

[715] If your faith is even partially in your works as **necessary** proof of the soteriological sufficiency of your faith, then you are viewing your works as a condition to reach heaven and will be left behind to endure the tribulation as a result. Such faith is not saving faith. To be delivered from tribulation, your faith must be in Christ alone. Just as the soteriological separation of believers from unbelievers via the rapture occurs before the judgment of believers at the Bema, so the soteriological separation of the sheep from the goats proceeds the misthological pronouncements made to the sheep and goats.

716 Sapaugh, "Wedding," 24-25.

717 Idem., "Interpretation," 34.

718 Irenaeus, writing between A.D. 182 and A.D. 188, identifies the wedding garment as our conduct, our works of righteousness, saying that those without it will be cast into the outer darkness ("Against Heresies," 4:36:6). Available at http://ccel.org/fathers2/ANF-01/anf01-62.htm#P7979_2198226. Accessed on 9 September, 2004. Other church fathers of this Ante-Nicene period (i.e., the period of time until the first General Council which was held at Nice in A.D. 325) also concur with this position.

719 Karl E. Pagenkemper, "Rejection Imagery in the Synoptic Parables [Part 2]," *BibSac* 153:611 (July 1996): 315, n. 27.

720 Some would appeal to texts such as Zech 3:1-5 as being a picture of the soteriologically white garments with which all believers are clothed and thus suppose that all believers meet the NT requirement of being clothed in white. There are at least three problems with this supposition. In that OT passage, the Lord is the one who does the clothing. The recipient of the clothing does not cloth himself. Thus, the parallel to the NT is not complete in that the NT Bride clothes herself. Moreover, the overcomers are to wash their garments to make or keep them white. Even if Zech 3:1-5 refers to garments that are initially clean by virtue of imputed righteousness, the admonition in Zech 3:6-7 might be taken as an indication that keeping one's garments white is necessary to exercise the rulership to which one otherwise naturally would be entitled by virtue of the initial cleansing. Lastly, it is not clear if Zech 3:1-5 is referring to soteriological rather than misthological purity. The parallel with Lev 8:7-9 would suggest that misthological purity may indeed be understood. The washing and clothing here do not picture regeneration, which had been pictured long before in their passing through the Red Sea. Rather, this was a washing and clothing to perform priestly service. Satan may reasonably be seen as accusing believers of not being worthy to govern the Lord's house, or to have charge of the Lord's court, or to have unhindered access to the Lord along with His other ruling officials in v. 6. These matters are contingent upon the recipient's obedience. Hence, it is more natural to understand the status of having white garments and ruling as being conditioned on practical righteousness. Misthological blamelessness will be conferred upon those believers who do not soil their garments. They, and they alone, will walk in white and be clothed misthologically in white (Rev 3:4-5). Nothing in Zech 3:1-7 causes one to suspect otherwise.

721 Keathley IV, "Darkness," 7.

722 R. T. France, *Matthew*, vol. 1, TNTC, ed., R. V. G. Tasker (Grand Rapids: Eerdmans Publishing Co., 1985), 313.

723 Keathley IV, "Darkness," 8.

724 Ibid., 33.

725 Huber, "Concept," 50.

726 Zane Hodges and Robert Wilkin, "Matthew 22:1-14 (The Parable of the Wedding Feast." Available at http://www.faithalone.org/Audio/mp3/Matt_22_1-14.m3u. Accessed on May 26, 2006.

727 Ibid., 23-24.

728 Keathley IV, "Darkness," 3.

729 Phillip L. Simpson. "A Biblical Response to the Teachings of Zane Hodges, Joseph Dillow, and the Grace Evangelical Society (Called the 'Free Grace' Movement)." Available at http://phils-page.blogspot.com/2006/03/response-the-free-grace-movement.html. Accessed on April 4, 2006.

730 Ibid.

731 Pagenkemper, "Part 1," 188.

732 Huber, "Relationship," 13-14.

733 Zeller, "Theology."

734 Pagenkemper, "Part 1," 183. Although I disagree with Pagenkemper's conclusion, I appreciate his caution in acknowledging that the meaning of the phrase *weeping and gnashing of teeth* must be found in its NT context since the idiom is not used in the classical Greek literature or the LXX. Unfortunately, after weighing the options between various interpretations, Constable seems to throw caution to the wind as he rejects the misthological interpretation because he claims:

> The term "weeping and gnashing of teeth" as Jesus used it elsewhere seems to describe hell, the place where unbelievers go (cf. 8:12; 13:42, 50; 24:51; 25:30; Luke 13:28). This term was a common description of gehenna, hell (4 Ezra 7:93; 1 Enoch 63:10; Psalms of Solomon 14:9; Wisdom of Solomon 17:21)."

Giving preference to intertestamental texts over NT contexts is fraught with danger. I have illustrated why this is the case in regard to the outer darkness. Nevertheless, since Constable has allowed the meaning of the phrase *weeping and gnashing of teeth* within these intertestamental texts to determine his NT exegesis, one might choose to interact with these texts to see what the term means in intertestamental literature at least, if it were not for one small problem—the phrase does not occur in any of the intertestamental proof texts that Constable has cited!

France supplies only two intertestamental references for the phrase: 1En 108:3,5; 2En 40:12 (*Matthew*, NIC, 319). At least these texts use the imagery of *weeping and crying* in hell. So I can understand why Jesus' original listeners (being the works-righteous Jews that they were) and why their contemporary counterparts (being the conditionalistic legalists that they are) jump to the conclusion that Jesus is talking about weeping and gnashing one's teeth in hell because of poor performance. Still, I will pass over examining the phrase *weeping and gnashing of teeth* in intertestamental literature in the present book because the references provided above do not have the phrase, and even if they did, they would not be a controlling factor of the NT context for those who perceive Jesus as teaching something other than works-righteousness.

[735] Pagenkemper, "Part 1," 185

[736] Pagenkemper, "Part 2," 308.

[737] Keathley IV, "Darkness," 3.

[738] Ibid., 4.

[739] Pagenkemper, "Part 1," 183, n. 15.

[740] Ibid., 186, n. 24.

[741] Keathley IV, "Darkness," 3.

[742] Ibid., 7.

[743] Ibid., 1.

[744] Ibid., 2.

[745] As to Mt 11:12 and Lk 16:16, one may understand these passages as teaching that the kingdom suffers violence at the hands of those seeking forced entry into the kingdom by means of good works. They take it by force rather than receive it by grace. They abused the law by seeking unlawful means of entry through legalism and, consequently, only enter the mystery form of the kingdom rather than the mystical form.

[746] Faust, *Rod*, 99-101.

[747] France, NIC, *Matthew*, 542-543.

[748] Dillow, 20.

[749] Zane Hodges, "The New Puritanism Part 1: Carson on Christian Assurance," *JOTGES* 6:10 (Spring 1993): 19-20.

[750] Alexander Roberts and James Donaldson, eds. *The Ante-Nicene Fathers*, 10 vols., American Reprint (Grand Rapids: Eerdmans Publishing Co., 1967). All references to writers of the Ante-Nicene period are made to this series and references to volume and page number are cited in the text.

[751] Lewis Sperry Chafer, *Salvation: A Clear Doctrinal Analysis* (Grand Rapids: Zondervan Publishing House, 1955), 73. Also compare his discussion in *Systematic Theology* (Dallas: Dallas Seminary Press, 1948), 5:133-134.

[752] Curtis Hutson, *Salvation Crystal Clear*, 2 vols. (Murfreesboro: Sword of the Lord Pub., 1987), 2:62.

[753] Seymour, *Gift*, 62, 99. Kendall also renders a split application in which the passage pertaining to the wedding feast is interpreted as picturing an unbeliever thrown into the outer darkness while the passage pertaining to the unfaithful servant is interpreted as picturing a believer thrown into the outer darkness (*Parables*, 236, 316). The principle of correlativity would allow this soteric-mistholic approach to the outer darkness. So my disagreement with my fellow misthologists so as to interpret all three outer darkness passages as dealing with believers must find its resolution in exegesis.

[754] Alexander Campbell, *Five Discourses on Hell! Being an Exposure and Refutation of Universalism: In Reply to Rev. Theodore Clapp*, 31. Available at http://www.cimmay.com/pdf/discourse.pdf. Accessed on July 21, 2005.31.

[755] Ibid., 33.

[756] Fredrick W. Morris, "Universal Salvation in Origen and Maximus," *Universalism and the Doctrine of Hell*, ed. Nigel M. de S. Cameron (Grand Rapids: Baker, 1992): 35-72.

[757] Ibid, 48.

[758] Ibid., 49.

[759] Ibid., 50.

[760] Ibid., 56.

[761] Can a universalist who trusts in Christ alone for eternal life be saved? I would theorize so (just as I believe that those in IFG, RFG2, or RFG3 might possibly be saved despite their logical inconsistencies, as long as they trust in Christ alone for eternal life). To be sure, in passages such as Jn 11:25-27, Jesus makes it implicit that *only* those who believe in Him *alone* for eternal life will be saved. Through means of progressive revelation, we know from a comparison of Paul's writings that one must explicitly trust in Christ *alone* for eternal life. One cannot trust in Christ plus works. We likewise may infer that one cannot trust in Christ plus someone else (whether it be Buddha or Bubba) for eternal life. Therefore, we may deduce that the implicit element within Christ's promises that limits the offer of eternal life to those who believe in Him must carry with it an exclusion of those who believe in Christ plus anyone or anything else. However, I cannot be equally certain that the implicit *only* (which is made explicit in other texts such as Mt 7:13; Jn 14:9; Acts 4:12) necessarily excludes those, for example, who mistakenly think that implicit or postmortem faith in Christ qualifies for saving faith. Texts which promise eternal life to *whosoever* and *everyone* who believes in Christ seem to be using this

universal language to invite a personal application. Thus, when Jesus asks Martha in effect, "Do you believe that *everyone* who believes in Me has eternal life?" one is not surprised to hear her answer in effect, "Yes, Lord. *I* believe in you for eternal life." John expects the reader to reason on the basis of the exclusivity stressed by Jesus later in Jn 14:9 that:

1. *Everyone* who believes in Christ (implicitly *alone*) for eternal life is given eternal life.
2. Martha believes in Christ (implicitly *alone*) for eternal life.
3. Therefore, Martha has eternal life.

The universality of the offer emphasized by the word *everyone* (*pas*) encourages the reader to make personal application, not to make the reader erroneously assent to two propositions:

1. Everyone who believes that one is saved *only* by faith in Christ *alone* is given eternal life.
2. Martha believes that one is saved *only* by faith in Christ alone.
3. Martha believes in Christ *alone*.
4. Therefore, Martha has eternal life.

Although I am confident that the implicit affirmation that we are saved only by faith in Christ is clear enough from the repeated promises of eternal life based on faith (even to the point where I believe that this faith excludes works in Jn 6:29), I am not necessarily convinced that this implicit affirmation is a theological necessity that must be included in a dual affirmation as to what composes saving faith. It may serve instead as a functional utility to bring people to saving faith. We are to show people that they can be saved only by faith in Christ alone in order to bring them to faith in Christ alone. Logically, however, we cannot simply assume that this means that they must necessarily be persuaded that they can be saved only by faith in Christ alone in order to believe in Christ alone. In other words, if they can actually embrace their own personal salvation through faith in Christ alone, their faith is valid even if they took an invalid path in reaching that conclusion. Possibly, some would regard their faith in Christ as a sufficient means rather than necessary means of receiving eternal life. Nonetheless, their mistaken impression would appear to be sufficient for saving faith. Although saving faith is actually the necessary means rather than merely sufficient means of reaching heaven, it would appear sufficient that a person take that means rather than recognize the necessity of that means. This means that even if Martha hoped that a good Pharisee like Nicodemus might somehow finally reach heaven (even though as far as she knew he had not trusted in Christ alone for new birth), she would still receive eternal life as long as she herself trusted in Christ alone for eternal life.

Like Peter who, upon hearing Jesus' instructions to follow Him, turned around and asked Jesus, "What about this man?" (Jn 20:21) many want to ask, "What about the universalists? What about the infants? What about the heathen who never heard?" We would do well to do what Jesus has told us to do (which is tell them that faith alone in Christ alone is the only way to receive eternal life) and leave such matters to Him. If some of them personally become inclined to accept the proposition that they could be saved by faith alone in Christ alone without following our logical path in doing so, we would do well to hesitate before trying to prevent them from trusting in Christ alone for eternal life by insisting that they must first follow our logical path (cp. Mk 9:38). One is saved by faith in Christ alone, not by logical consistency in nonessential areas. Logical consistency only becomes a soteriological necessity when lack of that consistency prevents one from trusting in Christ alone for eternal life. For example, those who think that they are trusting in Christ alone for eternal life when in fact they are trusting partially in their performance must be shown their logical inconsistency before they can come to saving faith because their logical inconsistency is preventing them from logically trusting in Christ alone for eternal life.

[762] Origen's *both* is indicated by references to "all men" and "not only men alien from piety, but also some of the believers" (10:499).

[763] Origen is correct in assuming that practical righteousness is required to enter Zion. However, in contrast to Origen's soteriological position concerning the gates of Zion, a better position would be a misthological interpretation that unrighteous believers will not enter Zion, much less enter it by its gates; rather, they will be confined to other parts of the kingdom outside of Zion (i.e., the outer darkness).

[764] Origen's states, "There would seem to be some little ones among those who believe in God who can be made to stumble" (10:486). But this statement must be understood in light of his previous discussion:

> [A1] Every one that gives his adherence to Jesus as the Son of God according to the true history concerning Him, and by deeds done according to Gospel, is on the way to living the life which is according to virtue, **is converted** and is on the way towards becoming as the little children; and it is **impossible for him not to enter into the kingdom of heaven**. There are, indeed, many such [who are really saved]; **but not all, [A2] who are converted with a view to becoming like the little children, have reached the point of being made like unto little children**; but each wants so much of the likeness

to the little children, as *he falls short* of the disposition of little children towards the passions, of which we have spoken [= really lost]. **In the whole multitude, then, of believers, are also** [B1] **those who, having been as it were, just converted in regard to their becoming as the little children, at the very point of their conversion, that they may become as the little children, are called little** [= truly saved believer]; **and** [B2] **those of them, who** are converted that they may become as the little children, but *fall far short* of having **truly** become as the little children, **are capable of being caused to stumble**; each of whom *falls so far short* of the likeness to them, as *he falls short* of the disposition of children [= really lost believer]....they cause to **stumble** one of the little ones pointed out by Jesus, who are **believers** in Him. (10:485)

Following Origen is not easy here, but he apparently is saying that if you have orthodox belief concerning Jesus and live a life in harmony with that belief, you are converted and definitely will enter heaven. If you are truly converted, you are eternally secure. But not all who are converted are fully converted. Some fall short of true conversion. (A1) Not everyone who gives his adherence to Jesus is a genuine convert. (A2) Some of these fall short of genuine conversion. They are distinguished by the quality of their faith, lives, and dispositions. (B) To speak in terms of belief, (1) those who are genuinely converted are genuine believers at the point of their conversions. They exercise saving faith. Their practice will match their position. They are called *little* at the moment they believe. Their practice will not fail to match their title; they will become in practice what they already are in title. (2) On the other hand, those believers who fall short of being *little* will fail to become *little*. They fall short of truly believing and are the ones who can be made to stumble. Those believers who stumble were never saved to start with.

[765] All references to Saint Jerome are cited in the text and refer to Philip Schaff and Henry Wace, eds., *A Select Library of Nicene and Post-Nicene Fathers of the Christian Church*, second series, vol. 6, *St. Jerome: Letters and Select Works* (Grand Rapids: Eerdmans Publishing Co., 1892).

[766] Robert N. Wilkin, "Repentance and Salvation Part 1: The Doctrine of Repentance in the Old Testament." *JOTGES* 2:1 (Spring 1989): 13.

[767] Thomas F. Torrance, *The Doctrine of the Grace in the Apostolic Fathers* (Eugene, OR: Wipf and Stock Publishers, 1948), 24-25.

[768] Lavender, *Freedom*, 70, 112, 127-140.

[769] Jacques Le Goff, *The Birth of Purgatory* (Chicago, Illinois: The University of Chicago Press, 1986), 61. Cited by Jason Engwer, "Catholic, But Not Roman Catholic—Archive 05." Available at http://www.ntrmin.org /catholic_but_not_roman_catholic_05.htm. Accessed on August 8, 2005. John Campbell, "Forgiveness in the Age to Come (1)." Available at http://www.affcrit.com/pdfs/2004/01/04_01_wr.pdf. Accessed on August 8, 2005.

[770] J.N.D. Kelly, *Early Christian Doctrines* (San Francisco, California: HarperCollins Publishers, 1978), 484. Engwer, Catholic.

[771] Philip Schaff, *A Select Library Of The Nicene And Post-Nicene Fathers Of The Christian Church: Saint Chrysostom: Homily VI*, vol. 9., n. 1318. Available at http://www.ccel.org/ccel/schaff/npnf109.xix.viii.html #fnb_xix.viii-p59.3. Accessed on August 8, 2005. The quote within the body of the text is from the online version. For Campbell's discussion, see "Forgiveness," 58.

[772] Le Goff, 61. Quoted by Engwer, "Catholic." Much the same quote can be found in Ambrosiaster's comments on 1Cor 3:15.

> To suffer loss is to endure reproof. For what person, when subjected to punishment, does not lose something thereby? Yet the person himself may be saved. His living soul will not perish in the same way that his erroneous ideas will. Even so, however, he may suffer punishments of fire. He will be saved only by being purified through fire.

Gerald Bray, ed., *Ancient Christian Commentary on Scripture, New Testament VII: 1-2 Corinthians* (Downers Grove: InterVarsity Press, 1999), 33.

[773] Laurence M. Vance, "Faust, J.D.—The Rod: Will God Spare It? Second Edition." Available at http://www.faithalone.org/journal/bookreviews/faust.htm. Accessed on August 8, 2005.

[774] Faust, *Rod*, 90. He also provides the same quote from Ambrosiaster as included in the body of the present text (*Rod*, 166).

[775] Bray, *1 Corinthians*, 5-6. Many of the following quotes are also cited by Matt, a Catholic apologist, at http://matt1618.freeyellow.com/fathers.html#G)%20Ambrosiaster. Accessed on 8 August, 2005. Matt's primary rebuttal is that concerning Rom 1:11 Ambrosiaster said,

> For the mercy of God had been given for this reason, that they should cease from the works of the law, as I have often said, because God, taking pity on our weaknesses, decreed that the human race would be **saved by faith alone, along with the natural law** (*Romans*, 23).

To be sure, this is an unusual statement, but the statement by Matt hardly seems warranted:

> He says 'works of the law' do not justify. Any Catholic would agree to that. In fact he specifically says faith alone, **along with the natural law**. Thus, when he uses the term faith alone, he only terms it as salvific only when it is in conjunction *with* the natural law. (Emphasis his.)

It is doubtful that this ambiguity is enough to offset the clarity that one finds latter in Ambrosiaster's statements from Romans from this same commentary. "They are justified freely because they have not done anything nor given anything in return, but by faith alone they have been made holy by the gift of God" (3:24; p. 101); "in Christ God put forward, i.e., appointed, himself as a future expiation for the human race if they believed" (3:25; p. 102); "he had promised that he would justify those who believe in Christ, as he says in Habakkuk: *The righteous will live by faith in me*. Whoever has faith in God and Christ is righteous (3:26; p. 103); "no one is justified before God except by faith" (3:27; p. 103); "without work or any keeping of the law, they are justified before God by faith alone" (4:6; p. 113). See Gerald Bray, ed., *Ancient Christian Commentary on Scripture, New Testament VI: Romans* (Downers Grove: InterVarsity Press, 1998).

Matt seeks to buttress his claim that Ambrosiaster would be more in line with Catholicism than Protestantism by providing quotes which show that Ambrosiaster taught that good works are necessary to inherit the kingdom as a reward and that such works are also necessary for the final realization of eternal life as a reward. However, Ambrosiaster's belief that the inheritance is a reward in Tit 3:7 is in harmony with Marrowistic misthology. Furthermore, misthology is in agreement with Ambrosiaster's comments on Rom 2:7 as well: "Those who seek eternal life are not merely those who believe correctly but those who live correctly as well" (*Romans*, 59).

[776] Warren Wiersbe, *The Bible Exposition Commentary*, 2 vols. (Wheaton: Victor Books, 1989), 1:92. Unfortunately, in a subsequent writing Wiersbe retreats into a hesitant acceptance of a soteriological position concerning the third servant by saying, "It is doubtful whether the third servant can be called a Christian." But at least he does not rule out the possibility. See his *Wiersbe's Expository Outlines on the New Testament* (Wheaton: Victor Books, 1992), 91. To a considerable extent, Chumney appears to anticipate the *Principle of Correlativity* and its misthopological implications when he writes:

The term "*outer darkness*" in the Bible has two meanings and applications. To the unbeliever who has not accepted Jesus as their [sic] personal Lord and Savior, "*outer darkness*" is a reference to hell and damnation. To the carnal Christian, "*outer darkness*" refers to not being the Bride of Christ and abiding with God in the "*Holy of Holies*" thereby suffering a lack of the highest spiritual rewards in heaven. (Emphasis his, 160.)

[777] Spiros Zodhiates, *Hebrew-Greek Key Word Study Bible: Key Insights into God's Word*, NASB revised edition, eds. Warren Baker and Joel Kletzing (Chattanooga, TN: AMG Publishers, 2008), 1270-1271. I would like to extend credit to the Misslers for having alerted me to this extensive quote from Zodhiates regarding the outer darkness in their book. This quote was impressive enough that I checked it out for myself. However, by the same token, I must note a correction regarding their citation of Wuest as sharing a misthological perspective of the outer darkness because of his expanded translation of Mt 8:12, which I quote here from Wuest: "But the sons of the kingdom shall be thrown into the darkness, that darkness which is outside of the King's banqueting house. There, in that place, there shall be audible weeping and lamentation and gnashing of the teeth" (Wuest, WNT, 18). The Misslers misquote Wuest as saying, "The outer darkness is the darkness that is outside of the King's banqueting house" (*Kingdom*, 89). As one may see, the Misslers correctly have conveyed the sense of what Wuest is saying, but they should not have put it in quotes since they have given a modified summation. Nor is this the only occasion in which I perceive them as modifying quotes. Aside from this minor correction regarding proper citation practices, however, let me also point out that the Misslers immediately go on to add: "In other words, it is not hell!" Granted, one would think that this is the logical implication of Wuest's translation, but interpreters are not always logically consistent. In his comments on Heb 4:14, Wuest comments: "As it is the same sun that melts the wax which hardens the clay, so it is the same Word of God that leads some on to salvation, and turns others who will have none of it away into outer darkness" (via E-sword). I also consulted my printed copy of WNT and found E-Sword accurate. A soteriological understanding of the outer darkness is certainly implied by Wuest in this comment on Heb 4:14. The Misslers have interpreted Wuest's translation of Mt 8:12 in a logically consistent manner and wrongly attributed that logical consistency to Wuest himself. Proof that this is the case comes in the earlier quotation provided by the Misslers: "Kenneth Wuest in his *Greek New Testament* said, 'This darkness is **simply** the darkness that is outside the King's banqueting house. It is *not* hell'" (italics theirs, 62). In this early rendition of their quote from Wuest, they interject the word, "simply" (which is not in the original) and then include their own assessment, "it is not hell," as part of the quote, as if Wuest had made this statement, when in fact this is their interpretation of Wuest translation, not part of what Wuest himself has said. One might attribute the placement of the quotation mark to a simple typographical error, but the interjection of the word simply is not so easily overlooked.

[778] H. L. Ellison, *Matthew: A New Testament Commentary*, ed. G. C. D. Howley (Grand Rapids: Zondervan Publishing House, 1969), 169.

[779] Alexander Balmain Bruce, *The Parabolic Teaching of Christ* (New York: A. C. Armstrong & Son, 1892), 207. In the same paragraph, Bruce mistakenly implies that Calvin prefers a mild or minimum (i.e., misthological) interpretation of the outer darkness. He is followed in this error by George A. Buttrick, *The Parables of Jesus* (New York: Harper & Brothers, 1928), 249. Although Bruce and Buttrick present the misthological position as a valid option, Calvin assumes that the outer darkness is a soteriological issue.

In his discussion of the outer darkness in Mt 25:29-30 (cf. 2:289), Calvin refers the reader back to his discussion concerning the use of the term in Mt 8:12. In his discussion of that passage, he says that those cast into the outer darkness are "not truly" saved; they are false professors (1:251, 291). See David W. Torrance and Thomas F. Torrance, eds., *Calvin's Commentaries: A Harmony of the Gospels*, trans. by A. W. Morrison (Grand Rapids: Eerdmans Publishing Co., 1972). "Thus, outside all joy, power, and the other goods of the Heavenly Kingdom, condemned to eternal darkness and eternal punishment [Matt. 8:12; 22:13], they will be eaten by a deathless worm." See John Calvin, *Institution of the Christian Religion*, trans. by Ford Lewis Battles (Atlanta: John Knox Press, 1975), 88. The bracketed Scripture references are not mine.

[780] Henry Alford, *The Greek Testament,* vol. 1, *The Four Gospels* (London: Deighton, Bell, & Co., 1863), 253.

[781] Ibid., 79. In view of his comments on p. 253 about the "outward diligence" and putting on the imputed righteousness by baptism and a living faith, it reasonably may be inferred that Alford intends that the garment that the guest was to provide himself with in Mt 22:11-12 is to be understood as the practical expression of imputed righteousness (see pp. 219, 220). In other words, the garment refers to practical righteousness.

[782] This summation of Alford's position is based in part from an argument from silence, which is weak by its very nature. He does not actually state that the outer darkness is not damnation or that it does not refer to exclusion from the kingdom. He does not explicitly state that it is a reward concept. However, the implication of his writing is that this is the position he is advocating. The following page references are to his work, *The New Testament for English Readers* (Chicago: Moody Press, n.d.).

Alford clearly expresses his Arminian preference in discussing Heb 6:4-6 (p. 1495-1496) and 10:26-30 (p. 1547-1548), which he interprets as referring to regenerate believers who commit apostasy by abandoning the faith and who consequently suffer eternal damnation. Likewise, in dealing with Mt 24:47-51 (p. 171), he does not hesitate to state that the evil slave is a believer who did not abandon his faith but abandoned his faithfulness and is thus condemned with nonbelievers. Therefore, for Alford, regenerate believers will fail to achieve salvation in the case of unfaithfulness or apostasy. However, in dealing with the parables of the virgins and talents, he states that they are both dealing with the same issue and that "there is no question of apostasy, or unfaithfulness" here (p. 171). The virgins, all of them, are "not hypocrites, but *faithful*" (p. 172; emphasis his). He further goes on to state that the foolish virgins do not have a dead faith (p. 172) since the lamps of all ten were burning initially and even when the call goes forth the lamps of the foolish are still burning (p. 173). And he makes it clear that Jesus' statement that He does not know them in Mt 25:12 is "very different" from that in Mt 7:23 (p. 173). They are dealing with different circumstances, times, and judgments. Further, he states that the lazy servant of Mt 25:26 is "not to be confounded with the *wicked servant*" in Mt 24:48 who was damned (p. 174).

Admittedly, he does seem to think that the virgins will be judged twice, once at the beginning of the feast and then at the Great White Throne judgment at its conclusion (p. 173). But this does not necessarily mean that he believes they will be cast into the Lake of Fire, since according to Alford the books will determine at that time whether those who stand before that judgment are saved (p. 1931). "What purpose would be a judgment, *if all were to be condemned?*" (p. 177, emphasis his.) Moreover, his subsequent comment appears to demand that even if the foolish virgins are present at the Great White Throne judgment, the issue is not their salvation:

> This proceeding [in the parable of the talents] is *not*, strictly speaking, *the last judgment*, but still *the same as that in the former parable* [the parable of the virgins]; *the beginning of judgment at the house of God*—the judgment of the *millennial advent*. This to the servants of Christ (*his own servants*, ver. 14), is *their* final judgment—but not that of the rest of the world. (p. 174; emphasis his.)

This understanding of his words would harmonize with his statement in Jn 5:24,

> *Judgment* being the *separation,*—the effect of which is to gather out of the Kingdom *all that offendeth,*—and thus regarding especially the *damnatory* part of judgment,—he who believes *comes not into*, has no concern with, judgment....The reckoning which ends with "*Well done, good servant,*" [i.e., the parable of the talents] is not *judgment: the reward is of free grace.* (p. 508; emphasis his.)

Since the lazy servant's **final** judgment is the judgment of Christians (cf. pp. 151, 1813), rather than the final judgment of the nations, the lazy servant does not come into judgment where the issue is being cast out of the kingdom or damnation. Likewise, the issue for the virgins is rewards, not judgment (in Alford's limited sense of the word). For this reason, his comment is important that the parables of the virgins and talents deal with the judgment of

"*Christians*...and *both these had reference to that first resurrection and millennial Kingdom*...during which *all Christians* shall be judged" (p. 176; emphasis his). Alford clearly maintains that the outer darkness is the final judgment for genuine Christians and deals with the issue of entrance into, or exclusion from, the wedding feast. The implication of his writing is that this means that it deals only with entrance or exclusion in relation to the feast, not the kingdom. The outer darkness is by implication a misthological concept, not a soteriological one.

[783] T. Francis Glasson, "The Last Judgment—In Rev. 20 and Related Writings," *NTS* 28 (1982): 530. Seiss also notes that Alford, like Olshausen and others, takes a misthological position concerning the parable of the foolish virgins. Joseph A. Seiss, *The Parable of the Virgins: In Six Discourses* (Philadelphia: Smith, English & Co., 1873), 110.

[784] Huber, "Relationship." 11-25. Huber, "Concept" (Th.M. thesis, Dallas Theological Seminary, 1978). Sapaugh, "Interpretation." Sapaugh, "Wedding." Anthony T. Evans, *Bible Prophecies Through the Ages: The Best is Yet to Come* (Chicago: Moody Press, 2000), 156. Evans, "Rewards for Christians" *Tim LayHaye Prophecy Study Bible* (AMG Publishers, 2000): 1234. Charles Stanley, *Eternal Security: Can You Be Sure?* (Nashville: Thomas Nelson Publishers, 1990), 120-130. Hodges, *Eclipse*, 91-102. Frank D. Carmical, "The Coronation of the King: An Annotated Work of Fiction: Part 1" *JOTGES* 2:2 (Autumn 1989): 53-68. Dillow, 347-350. Erwin W. Lutzer, *Triumph and Tears at the Judgment Seat of Christ: Your Eternal Reward* (Chicago: Moody Press, 1998), 55, 77-80.

[785] Personal correspondence with Hodges 6-3-92.

[786] Herman Olshausen, *Biblical Commentary on the New Testament*, American ed. (New York: Sheldon, Blakeman & Co., 1857), 4:269-270. Compare 1:917 in his first German edition. In the American edition, the editor, A. C. Kendrick, adds this note at the bottom of the page: "It is not light (the opposite of darkness) in which the children of darkness are punished, but fire." Subsequent references to Olshausen's work are to the American edition.

[787] Ibid., 4:270.

[788] Olshausen did not do as well concerning Matthew's first two parables concerning the outer darkness, apparently assuming that they were simply soteriological in scope (Ibid., 1:347; 2:172).

[789] Ibid., 1:582. It is not absolutely clear in Olshausen's discussion of these passages as to what happens to believers after they are cast into the outer darkness. He is careful to state that the unfaithful servant in Mt 25:30 is not an apostate who has fallen entirely from the faith since "he has not dissolved his connection as a servant, or squandered his talent" (2:268). Yet concerning Mt 10:33, he merely states that apostasy and denial are possible and result in the extinction of their faith and their exclusion from the kingdom (1:408-409). What happens afterward? Exclusion is the same punishment which he proposes for both the unfaithful and those who lose their faith.

Olshausen's Arminian views are clearly seen in his comments concerning two types of believers. Concerning believers who adopt an antinomian lifestyle in Eph 5:6-7 he says: "They [unbelievers] are, therefore, not merely shut out from the kingdom of God, but they also fall into Gehenna. Paul therefore warns his readers [Christian believers] against community with them, for *that* also brings with it a like fate." (5:126; emphasis his.) According to Olshausen, Christian believers who fall into this decree of unfaithfulness are not merely excluded from the kingdom but suffer the additional punishment of eternal damnation in Gehenna as well. It is not surprising that he also believes the same punishment awaits those believers who commit the even graver sin of apostasy. Concerning Gal 3:4 he says: "If they fell away altogether from the faith and lost Christ, then it *was* all in vain" (4:540; emphasis his). Although Olshausen believes it is possible for believers to lose their salvation in the most serious cases of failure, he does not suppose that this is the case in the parables of the wicked servant (Mt 24:43-51), the foolish virgins (Mt 25:1-3), nor the lazy servant (Mt 25:14-30). These three parables represent believers who are excluded from the kingdom but who do not necessarily suffer damnation.

Concerning the weeping and gnashing of teeth on the part of the wicked servant, he clarifies: "It does not appear that the words can be understood here as denoting eternal perdition; they merely designate exclusion from the kingdom of God which begins with the advent of the Lord, and the torment which results from the consciousness of having deserved it" (2:261). He continues to discuss the relationship of the parables to one another:

> The expressions *virgin, servant*, plainly indicate a special relationship to the Redeemer; hence, in the first and second parables, the referenced is not to men without distinction, but to children of the kingdom, concerning whose vigilance and fidelity, judgment is passed. In the third, on the contrary, all nations appear before the Judgment Seat of Christ, with the exception of true believers. (2:262; emphasis his.)

Olshausen goes on to distinguish between the general resurrection with its final judgment and the resurrection of the just (i.e., believers; cf. Rev 20:4) with their preliminary judgment.

> The establishment of the kingdom of God is connected with a sifting of those who belonged to the earthly church (comp. Rev. xx. 4, about preliminary judgment); "all who stand that [preliminary] trial are members of the kingdom, and participants in the marriage of the Lamb, but those who cannot endure it, although they certainly are excluded from the kingdom of God, are not as **yet** eternally condemned. The final decision respecting them also takes place at the general judgment of the world (Rev xx. 12). (2:262)

His statement here seems to be in potential conflict with his proceeding statement that "true believers" will not appear at the general judgment. However, in view of the context of his remark, the two statements can be harmonized partially by supposing that he is referring to believers who have been *true* in the sense of being *faithful* rather than genuine. His entire argument is that the issue is the distinction between genuine believers who have been faithful or unfaithful. For example, he definitely believes that the foolish virgins represent true (i.e., genuine believers) who have been untrue (i.e., unfaithful) in terms of their service (2:264-265):

> The foolish virgins are merely to be viewed as representing minds that seek that which is pleasing and sweet in the service of the Lord, instead of following him in right earnest, and hence neglect to labor after thorough renewal [i.e., after regeneration], and to build in the right way upon the foundation that is laid (1 Cor. iii. 15).

His comments concerning the fate of the foolish virgins in Mt 25:12 are even more explicit (2:266):

> *I know you not* (ver. 12) **cannot denote eternal condemnation**; for, on the contrary, the foolish virgins are **only excluded from the marriage of the Lamb** (Rev. xix. 7); hence they must be viewed as parallel with the persons described, 1 Cor. iii. 15, whose building is destroyed, but who are not thereby deprived of eternal happiness. These virgins possessed the general condition of happiness, faith…but they **lacked the requisite qualification for the kingdom of God**, that sanctification which proceeds from faith (Heb. xii. 14).

Seiss (*Virgins*, 110), like Olshausen, argues for a misthological interpretation concerning the foolish virgins, and he correctly cites this above passage from Olshausen in support of his argument. Olshausen's statement that the foolish virgins are "**only** excluded from the marriage" supper means that exclusion from the kingdom is their only punishment. They do not experience "eternal condemnation," nor are they "deprived of eternal happiness." The only requirement for salvation from eternal condemnation is "faith." The additional requirement for entrance into the kingdom of God is "sanctification." The conclusion that must be drawn from these passages where Olshausen clearly expresses himself is that, although these believers may be cast into the outer darkness and thereby excluded from the marriage supper and the kingdom, they are nevertheless saved from the eternal fire and condemnation of Gehenna; they will experience happiness rather than fiery torment in eternity.

Nevertheless, an ambiguity still remains with his statement quoted above: "Although they certainly are excluded from the kingdom of God, are not as **yet** eternally condemned. The final discussion respecting them also takes place at the general judgment of the world" (2:262). Does this mean that **some** untrue (i.e., unfaithful) believers who are cast in the outer darkness will be eternally condemned? Apparently so, and this would correspond with his Arminian views. On the one hand, he says (2:271): "Believers shall not come into judgment (comp. John iii. 18, v. 24; 1 Cor. xi. 31)." Further, he defines the *nations* in the final judgment (the sheep and the goats) as "denoting all men, with the exception of true believers—*that is, all unbelievers*…[believers] do not come into judgment at all, but at the resurrection of the just enter into the joy of the kingdom of God; but this act of shutting out must not be confounded with the general judgment" (2:272).

In both the text and footnote, he makes it clear that he believes that only unregenerate non-Christians will be judged at the final judgment. Nevertheless, his comment above that some regenerate Christians are not "**yet** eternally condemned" but will have their final fate determined "at the general judgment of the world" leads one to suspect that he is being inconsistent. His view may be summarized by saying that those believers who are excluded from the kingdom in the outer darkness will be eternally damned if they do not repent as a result of their exclusion. Their degree of guilt determines the likelihood of their repenting. The outer darkness is a place for regenerate believers who have been untrue. If they repent as a result of being in the outer darkness, they will truly be treated as believers in that they will not come into damnation. His comments concerning 1Cor 11:31 seem to be a fitting summary of his position: "Death, in a frame of mind verging towards apostasy, consequently appeared to him to preclude all participation in Christ's kingdom; while yet precisely this forfeit, as a divinely inflicted penalty, might in effect prove the means of awakening the fallen for eternal life" (4:336).

[790] Neighbour, *Means*, 74, 80, 88, 105-111, 126. Also see I. M. Haldeman, *Satan as an Angel of Light* (New York: The Book Stall, n.d.), 17-18. Haldeman, *Sermons*, 356-361. Alexander Patterson, *The Greater Life and Work of Christ: As Revealed in Scripture, Man and Nature* (New York: Christian Alliance Publishing Co., 1896), 318. Edwin A. Wilson, *Selected Writings of A. Edwin Wilson*, 3rd ed., ed. Arlen L. Chitwood (Schoettle Publishing Co. 1981), 377-390. Among other citations, Wilson notes these additional ones: A. B. Bruce wrote that the outer darkness refers to the fatal consequences experienced by some believers; John J. Morey believed it refers to believers who have to live outside the kingdom among the millennial nations; G. Campbell Morgan believed that the outer darkness does not refer to believers

going to Gehenna but through the tribulation. David W. Dyer, *Thy Kingdom Come* (Rochester: "A Grain of Wheat" Ministries, 1984), 123-125; for his Lordship salvation perspective, see pp. 22-24, 80-89.

[791] Robert Govett, *Entrance into the Kingdom: Reward According to Works*, 2nd ed. (Miami Springs: Schoettle Publishing Co., 1978.). See p. 147 for millennial exclusion from the kingdom and p. 229 for the suffering of believers in Gehenna. Also see his chapter, "Will All Believers Enter the Millennial Kingdom," 1-68. The printing of the first publication ranges from 1870 to 1895. Govett affirms that believers can fail to confess Him [Christ] openly, or to the end" and even "give up their faith in" Christ. And he denies that the Lake of Fire in Rev 21:8 applies to them. Rather, the Lake of Fire is reserved for unbelievers. See Robert Govett, *Govett on Revelation*, 2 vols. (London: Bemrose and Sons, 1891; reprint, Miami Springs: Conley and Schoettle Publishing Co., 1981), 2:360-362.

[792] G. H. Pember, *The Great Prophecies of the Centuries Concerning the Church* (New York: Fleming H. Revell Comp., n.d.), 96-116. Panton, *Judgment*, 75-76. Lang, *Hebrews*, 180-186. Lang, *Revelation*, 96-97. Watchman Nee, *The Gospel of God*, (Anaheim, CA.: Living Stream Ministry, 1990), 3:441-462. Witness Lee, *The New Testament: Recovery Version*, revised ed. (Anaheim: Living Stream Ministry, 1991), 210-211. S. S. Craig, *The Dualism of Eternal Life: A Revolution in Eschatology* (Rochester: Du Bois Press, 1916), 139, 187, 210, 231, 233. Gary T. Whipple, *Shock and Surprise Beyond the Rapture!* (Miami Springs: Schoettle Publishing Co., 1992). Tom W. Finley, *Worth of the Kingdom*, 66-67, etc. Available at http://www.seekersofchrist.org/download/Worthy%20of%20the%20Kingdom%20040622.pdf. Accessed on August 13, 2004.

Some ultraists equate Gehenna with the Lake of Fire (e.g., Lang, *Revelation*, 354). Although Lang acknowledges that some who also equate the two believe the Lake of Fire is "the place of temporary punishment after death for evil-living Christians," he himself actually is hesitant to take this position, even though he is open to it (Lang, *Hebrews*, 184; cf. *Revelation*, 96). Pember, however, is not hesitant to take this position (*Prophecies*, 113-115). In other words, subcomers will be punished temporarily in the Lake of Fire. This could be called an *exceptional ultraistic position* in contrast to the *mild ultraistic position* in that Gehenna is not to be equated with the Lake of Fire, and it is the former rather than the latter where believers may be punished temporarily (e.g., Lang, *Hebrews*, 180-186; Whipple, *Shock*, 166-170). But it is beyond the scope of this study to delve into the differences of opinion within the three ultraistic subgroups. Suffice it to say that (1) some ultraists distinguish the outer darkness from Gehenna and the Lake of Fire; (2) some distinguish Gehenna from the Lake of Fire, and (3) some equate all three.

[793] In other words, the designations are: Conservatives (inside), Moderates (outside), and Ultraists (outside-inside).

[794] J.D. Faust, "Answers to George Zeller (#1)." Available at http://www.kingdombaptist.org/zeller1.cfm. Accessed on August 4, 2004.

[795] Soteriological salvation is *not by works*: Jn 6:28-**29**; Rom 3:20-4:6 (esp. 3:**28**; 4:5); 9:32; 11:**6**; Gal 2:**16**-3:11; Eph 2:**8-9**; 2Tim 1:9; Tit 3:**5** (cf. Ps 14:1,3; 53:1,3; 143:2; Eccl 7:20; Is 53:6; 64:6; Rom 3:10,23; Jam 2:10). These passages are reinforced by others. Salvation from hell is *by grace*: Lk 7:41,42; Rom 3:**24**; 4:**16**; 5:2; **15-17**; 11:5-**6**; 2Cor 8:9; Gal 1:6,15; 2:**21**; 5:**4**; Eph 1:**6**-7; 2:**4-9**; 2Tim 1:9; Tit 3:**7**. Salvation from hell is *by faith*: Mt 9:2,22; 21:31-32; Mk 2:5; 5:34; 10:52; Lk 5:20; 7:48-**50**; 8:**12**,48; 17:19; 18:42; Jn 1:7,12; 3:**15-18**,36; 4:39-42; 5:**24**,45-47; 6:**29,35,40,47**; 7:31,**38-39**; 8:**24**,30; 9:**35-38**; 10:24-26; 11:15,**25-27**,42; 12:11,**36**,46; 13:19,48; 14:1; 16:7-**9**; 17:**20**-21; 19:35; 20:**29-31**; Acts 3:16; 4:**4**,32; 8:**12**-13,**37**; 9:42; 10:**43**; 11:**17**,21; 13:12,**39**; 14:1,23,27; 15:7-**9**; 16:**31**; 17:4 (KJ),11-12; 18:8,27; 19:4; 20:21; 21:25; 26:18; Rom 1:**16**-17; 3:**21-4:16**,23-**24**; 5:**1**-2; 9:30-33; 10:4-11; 11:20,32 (KJ); 15:13; 1Cor 1:**21**; 2Cor 4:4; Gal 2:**16-3:11**,14,**21-26**; Eph 1:**13**,19; 2:**8-9**; Phil 1:29; 3:**9**; 1Thess 1:7; 2:10; 4:14; 2Thess 1:10; 2Tim 1:12; 3:**15**; Heb 6:1; 11:6-**7**,**31**; Jam 2:23; 1Pet 1:21; 2:**6-7**; 1Jn 5:**1,4-5,10-13**; Jude 1:5. Also see Gen 15:6 (cf. Rom 4:1-25 & Gal 3:6-14); Hab 2:4 (cf. Rom 1:17). Soteriological salvation is a *free gift*: Jn 4:**10**; Rom 3:**24**; 5:15-17; 6:**23**; Eph 1:6; 2:**8**; Rev 21:6; 22:17 (cf. Is 55:1). Numerous Johannine synonyms for believe could be added to the latter list.

[796] Michael E. Stone, "Apocalyptic Literature," in *Jewish Writings of the Second Temple Period*, ed. M. Stone (Philadelphia: Fortress Press, 1984), 393-394.

[797] Collins gives the following broad definition of apocalypse, which is the one most widely used, and discusses its shortcomings: "A genre of revelatory literature with a narrative framework, in which a revelation is mediated by another worldly being to a human recipient, disclosing a transcendent reality which is both temporal, insofar as it envisages eschatological salvation, and spatial insofar as it involves another, supernatural, world." John J. Collins, "Apocalyptic Literature," in *Early Judaism and Its Modern Interpreters*, eds. Robert A. Kraft and George W. E. Nickelsburg (Philadelphia: Fortress Press, 1986), 346-347.

[798] The apocalyptic section of 2 Esdras/Ezra (chs. 3-14) is referred to as 4 Esdras/Ezra. It was written by a Jew in the first century after the destruction of the temple in A.D. 70. (Chapters 1-2 and 15-16 of 2 Edras were added later by Christians.) Although 4 Ezra may give a valuable window into the Jewish thought world of the first century, it is still at best contemporary with the writings of the New Testament, if not later. It was not composed in the intertestamental period.

[799] Collins, "Literature," 358.

[800] David W. Suter, "Weighed in the Balance: The Similitudes of Enoch in Recent Discussion," *RSR* 7 (1981): 217.

[801] E. Isaac, "1 (Ethiopic Apocalypse of) Enoch," in *The Old Testament Pseudepigrapha*, ed. James H. Charlesworth, vol. 1 (New York: Doubleday, 1983), 7.

[802] George W. E. Nickelsburg, "The Bible Rewritten and Expanded," in *Jewish Writings of the Second Temple Period*, ed. M. Stone (Philadelphia: Fortress Press, 1984), 90.

[803] Although Charles dates the first five chapters of 1 Enoch as the latest of the book, Frost says, "Their theology is no more advanced than the rest of the First Book." Stanley B. Frost, *Old Testament Apocalyptic: Its Origins and Growth* (London: Epworth Press, 1981), 169, n. 13.

[804] Isaac, "1 Enoch," 10.

[805] F. I. Andersen, "2 (Slavonic Apocalypse of) Enoch," in *The Old Testament Pseudepigrapha*, ed. James H. Charlesworth, vol. 1 (New York: Doubleday, 1983), 97.

[806] Ibid., 96. Andersen's soteriological comment concerning ethics is in harmony with Charles' general observations: "Apocalyptic was essentially ethical....it was rooted and grounded in ethics...based on the essential righteousness of God" (p. 191) and "to every Jewish apocalyptic writer the Law was of eternal validity....devotion to the Law is the note that characterizes apocalyptic from its earliest beginnings" (pp.194-195). See R. H. Charles, *Eschatology: The Doctrine of a Future Life in Israel, Judaism and Christianity* (New York: Schocken Books, 1963). Quotations of 2 Enoch will be from the longer recension, J, since it appears to be original. The shorter recension appears to be a condensed, disjointed, drastic revision. See Andersen, "2 Enoch," 94.

[807] Collins and other scholars have concluded that Charles and his collaborators rather freely posited interpolations and multiple sources. This assessment is not a denial that there are interpolations and distinguishable sources, but they are not distinguishable to the degree that Charles and his followers have claimed in pointing out the inconsistency and lack of coherence found in these apocalyptic writings. See Collins, "Literature," 348-349; he also states that "the quest for sources has often distracted scholars from the inner coherence of apocalyptic literature in its own right" (p. 356). Rowley notes that although many scholars have held that the Similitudes have Christian interpolations, their interpolation hypothesis is precarious, and he believes that it would be better to give the supposed interpolations the benefit of a doubt and treat them as genuine (p. 57). Rowley makes a further summarization that applies to all these writings, "In general I share the skepticism with which these dissection hypotheses are viewed....throughout the apocalyptic literature, there is far too ready a disposition to resort to dissection whenever some minor inconsistency is found" (p. 143). After expressing this skepticism of Charles' source analysis based on inconsistencies, Rowley immediately gives an example of inconsistency in Charles' own writing. Yet no one would conclude two different authors or sources for Charles' work! See H. H. Rowley, *The relevance of Apocalyptic: A Study of Jewish and Christian Apocalypses from Daniel to the Revelation*, 2d ed. (London: Lutterworth Press, 1947). Just as a study of Matthew is to be given precedence over a study of his sources and just as the theology of Matthew is more important than the theology of the hypothetical Q, it is more important that this study of 1 Enoch and 2 Enoch give preference to treating and examining them as completed works.

[808] Pagenkemper, "Part 1,"e.g., 182, 186-187.

[809] David C. Sim, "Matthew 22:13a and 1 Enoch 10:4a: A Case of Literary Dependence?" *Journal for the Study of the New Testament*, 47 (1992): 5.

[810] Ibid., 6.

[811] Ibid., 10.

[812] Ibid., 12-13.

[813] Mt 13:42 does not help Sim's case even though it deals with the wicked who are gathered out of the kingdom and then cast into the fire. *Gathered out* is not the same as *cast out*, that is, gathered out ≠ cast out. Further, there is no proof that those *cast out* (*ekballo*) are cast out of the kingdom itself.

[814] The argument that those in Mt 7:22 had to be saved because they cast out demons is rather shortsighted in that Jesus indicates that Jewish exorcists had some success in casting out demons (Mt 12:27; Lk 11:19). Although it may be countered that they were not able to do so in the name of Jesus (Acts 19:13), this passage is insufficient grounds for concluding that this reaction would be encountered on every occasion when an unbelieving exorcist attempted to use the name of Jesus to perform the exorcism. Satan probably uses various strategies in responding to exorcism. For example, a higher ranking demon (a religious demon) might prompt unbelieving religious exorcists to cast out demons and command the lower ranking demon to leave so that the seemingly apparent exorcism might give credibility to the ministry of the higher ranking demon. There may be some conflict in the demonic ranks when such engagements take place, but demonic commitment to the overall strategy may be assumed. They are not a house divided although there may be skirmishes within that house.

[815] Keathley IV, "Darkness," 6.

[816] Ibid., 6.

[817] The one thing required to do the will of the Father concerning entering heaven is to believe (cp. Mt 7:21 with Mt 21:31-32 and Jn 6:40).

[818] The Matthean account in Mt 8:12 is focused on great-faith. The Lukan parallel in Lk 13:28, if it be contrastively called parallel, appears to be focused on non-faith. A different emphasis as well as a different sequence is seen in the two accounts. Nevertheless, some assert that since the outer darkness is non-parabolic in Mt 8:12 but parabolic in the other two Matthean passages, the non-parabolic occurrence is a closer match to Lk 13:28. This is unlikely, however, in that the

parabolic teaching concerning the outer darkness eventually leads to a literal exclusion when the implications of the outer darkness are traced out in the OT and NT. Therefore, the literal-parabolic distinction is of no decisive consequence. In fact, the *ekei* signifies the spatial significance: *"There* [spatially], there [experientially] will be weeping and gnashing of teeth"* (Mt 8:12; 22:13; 25:30; Lk 13:28). In comparing the Matthean parable of the talents with the Lukan parable of the minas, note that the Lukan account includes the soteriological category of the enemies, but the Matthean account is focused exclusively on misthological concerns. Thus, it should occasion no surprise if the same emphasis repeats itself in a comparison between the accounts represented in Mt 8:12 and Lk 13:28.

[819] D. Edmond Hiebert, "An Exposition of Jude 12-16," *BibSac* 142 (1985): 244-245.

[820] Henry H. Tucker, *The Gospel in Enoch* (Philadelphia: J. B. Lippincott, 1869), 195.

[821] Conzelman considers the outer darkness as a place "on the edge of the world" or "beneath" the ground. He equates Matthew's outer darkness with its background and ignores its context. He also equates Matthew's outer darkness with the darkness in 2 Pet. 2:17 and Jude 1:13. Gerhard Kittel, ed., *Theological Dictionary of the New Testament*, trans. Geoffrey W. Bromiley (Grand Rapids: Eerdmans Publishing Co., 1967), s.v. "σκότος," by G. Hans Conzelman.

[822] Hiebert, "Jude," 240.

[823] Zeller misidentifies the ship of eternal security as the "ship of faith" ("Theology"). The essence of his argument is based on an analogy between the soteric guarantee of not being lost and the promise Paul made to those aboard the ship with him that they would not be lost temporally. God had promised Paul: "There shall be no loss of life among you, but only of the ship" (Acts 27:22). Yet Paul subsequently warned the centurion and his soldiers that they would be killed if they let the sailors abandon ship (Acts 27:31). From this perceived parallel, Zeller concludes that despite God's promise of salvation believers **must** persevere in the faith in order for those promises of security to be realized. Zeller then seeks to turn this apparent Arminian proof text into a Calvinistic one by claiming that genuine believers **will** heed the warnings and stay on ship. Regardless of which approach is taken, Zeller's analogy advocates conditional security. Had the sailors not stayed on the ship there would have been a loss of life. If believers do not stay on Zeller's ship of faith, they will be lost in hell. Their salvation is conditioned on their staying on the ship of faith (i.e., remaining in the faith) according to Zeller.

Marrowists do not share Zeller's belief that the passage pictures soteriological salvation for the simple reason that we affirm unconditional security rather than conditional security. If one must express eternal security in terms of a ship, then the Marrowistic ship is Christ. Whereas Zeller trusts in his persevering faith to save him from hell, Marrowists trust in Christ. Whenever a person trusts in Christ alone for his or her salvation, that individual enters into Christ positionally and cannot abandon this ship positionally. This is not to say that a believer's experience necessarily is in Christ or that a believer cannot abandon Christ experientially.

Zeller is sensitive to the inconsistency his theology creates: "It may seem contradictory how God can promise us eternal safety and yet at the same time issue strong warnings that if we abandon the faith we are not safe! But keep in mind that God uses these warnings as a means of keeping us on the ship of faith" ("Theology"). The believer's safety is contingent upon the believer's stability in the faith. Perseverance is our means of reaching heaven. Zeller sees no problem in such contingent safety because he believes in the perseverance of all genuine believers in the faith.

In response, one would naturally ask, "Do the warnings represent a real threat?" Of course they do. If the sailors had not stayed on ship, then lives would have been lost. The warnings reveal real danger. Likewise, it must be a real possibility for real believers to abandon the faith and shipwreck their faith. In fact, the Bible is not only replete with warnings concerning this reality, but provides examples of this very thing happening as well.

Paul says in 1Tim 1:19 that some rejected a good conscience and had "their" faith shipwrecked as a result. "The faith" that was shipwrecked was "their faith." Robertson clarifies, "The article here [is] used as a possessive pronoun, a common Greek idiom" (WPNT). Their objective apostasy was also a subjective apostasy. In abandoning a good conscience, they had destroyed *their* faith. The contexts of these Pastoral Epistles make it clear that faith is not invincible. Departure from the faith is widespread. What is at stake in keeping "the faith" is rewards. Only believers can keep the faith (2Tim 4:7-8). For an excellent discussion of the grammatical and logical implications of Hymenaeus' faith, see Tom Stegall, "Must Faith Endure for Salvation to be Sure? (pt. 6)." Available at http://www.duluthbible.org/g_f_j/Must_Faith_Endure2.htm. Accessed on February 28, 2005. Parts 7 and 8 of his series are also commendable in their overall misthological treatment of apostasy in the passages in 1 and 2 Timothy.

Briefly, as Stegall explains in more detail, Hymenaeus presents a very difficult problem for advocates of perseverance. Obviously, Hymenaeus had to have genuine faith to have committed apostasy. Calvinistic counters are completely unpersuasive, either grammatically or logically. Arminians fare little better in their view of apostasy. In the Reformed Arminian camp, apostasy is irremediable. Once salvation is lost it cannot be regained. Yet here is an example of Paul hoping for a remediable conclusion to their apostasy. The Wesleyan Arminian fares no better. In their view, salvation may be lost and regained. But the verb used to describe their discipline is (*paideuo*). This type of discipline is proof that the individual in question is God's child (Heb 12:6-7). God may use the devil as a belt to discipline His children, but the wayward child remains a child of God. Since the type of discipline implemented proves that Hymenaeus remained a child of God, the Wesleyan Arminian position is disproven.

- 1Tim 1:5-6   Some have strayed from genuine faith and have turned aside.
- 1Tim 1:19   Some have rejected a good conscience and had their faith shipwrecked as a result.
- 1Tim 4:1   Some will fall away from the faith.
- 1Tim 5:8   Some have denied the faith and are worse than unbelievers.
- 1Tim 5:15   Some already have turned aside to follow Satan.
- 1Tim 6:10   Some have wandered away from the faith.
- 1Tim 6:21   Some have gone astray from the faith.
- 2Tim 1:15   All turned away from Paul.
- 2Tim 2:14   Those listening to false teaching are subverted (destroyed) by it.
- 2Tim 2:18   Hymenaeus and Philetus have gone astray from the truth.
- 2Tim 2:18   Hymenaeus and Philetus overthrow the faith of others.
- 2Tim 4:4   They turn away from the truth and will turn aside to lies.
- 2Tim 4:10   Demas has deserted Paul.
- 2Tim 4:16   Everyone deserted Paul.
- Tit 1:11   Whole families were overthrown.
- Tit 1:14   They turn away from the truth.

Acts 27:31 is indeed an interesting text. Barnes deals with the problem it creates with Acts 27:22 at length and takes it to mean that God has ordained the means (staying on the ship) as well as the result (salvation). They necessarily stayed on the ship because God predetermined that they would. See Albert Barnes, *Acts*, vol. 10, Notes on the New Testament, ed. Robert Frew (Grand Rapids: Baker Book House, 1884-1885, 366. Fisk cites Fuller's objection to this Necessarian doctrine as being superficial and then seeks to explain the passage in Acts by saying, "*God's promises to his children are always conditional on their obedience to His will.*" (Fisk, 88-89; emphasis his.) Zeller has evidently taken a Necessarian approach in which God has predetermined the salvation of all genuine believers and has conditioned attaining such salvation upon their perseverance in the faith, yet He has made Himself responsible to see to it that they do in fact persevere with the result that their perseverance or lack of it is ultimately His responsibility and will correspondingly result in His glory rather than theirs. They are the puppets, and God irresistibly pulls the strings. His warnings are just one of the many strands of the strings that He pulls. God threatens His children with hell in order to scare them from going to hell, but they cannot really go to hell because He will make certain that He scares the hell out of them with such warnings. Perseverance is conditionally necessary yet unconditionally guaranteed.

In contrast to Zellerian puppet theology, the overall view of election taken herein allows a simple alternative. God's promise to Paul in Acts 27:22 was based on the foreseen positive response that God saw that the soldiers would make to Paul's warning concerning the sailors. The Lord foresaw rather than foreordained that they would cut the ropes and stay aboard. The promise is based on prescience. On the other hand, Fish overreacts when he says that God's promises to His children are always conditional. Not so. The rapture, entrance into heaven, eternal security, and many other promises are guaranteed unconditionally by the Lord to all His children. Nevertheless, Fish is correct that the promise of safety in Acts 27:22 is conditional, although this was not clearly stated at the inception. The clarification came subsequently. But subsequent passages concerning certain promises, such as eternal security, make it clear that these promises are not conditioned on post-regenerational performance or on staying on the ship of faith. See *Sealed and Secure*.

[824] Carroll D. Osburn, "1 Enoch 80:2-8 (67:5-7) and Jude 12-13," *CBQ* 47 (1985): 302.

[825] Sim, "Dependence," 6. Additional passages cited by commentators such as Pss Sol 14:9 & 15:10 (sinners inherit darkness) and Sib Ora 4:43 (he will send them "down into the gloom in fire") have less to commend them as parallels than the Enoch passages. However, the passages in Pss Sol about inheriting darkness do provide a possible parallel to Rev 21:8. Revelation makes it clear that noncomers (i.e., the lost, Rev 21:8), subcomers (Rev 22:19), and overcomers (Rev 20:6) will each have different portions/inheritances (*meros*).

[826] Radmacher refers to the distinctions as justification salvation and glorification salvation. See Radmacher, "Forever," 31-35, and his "Bema," 31-43. Many in FG acknowledge that James (2:14) teaches salvation by works and that he is referring to temporal and/or misthological salvation (not salvation from hell—eternal salvation). Other passages that teach temporal and/or misthological salvation by works include: Mt 10:22; 24:13; Mk 8:35; 13:13; 16:16; Lk 9:24; Acts 2:21; Rom 10:9-10,13; 13:11; 1Cor 15:2; 2Cor 1:6; 7:10; Phil 1:19,28; 2:12; 1Thess 5:8-9; 2Thess 2:13; 1Tim 2:15; 4:16; 2Tim 2:10; 4:18; Heb 1:14; 2:3; 9:28; 1Pet 1:5,9; 2:2; 3:21; 4:18; and Jude 1:23.

[827] An examination of the verbs for *justify* (*dikaioo*) and *condemn* (*katadikazo*) reveals an example of misthological condemnation in Lk 6:37—where misthological judgment, condemnation, and forgiveness are determined by how we treat others. Likewise, the justification and condemnation in Mt 12:37 applies soteriologically to the lost and misthologically to the saved. The principle is that judgment, whether it results in condemnation or justification, is always based on works. Believers and nonbelievers come into two different kinds of judgments. The lost will come into soteriological judgment and experience soteriological condemnation. The saved will come into misthological judgment and experience either misthological condemnation or misthological justification. 1Cor 4:4-5 is an example of the latter

type of judgment and justification. Paul acknowledges that he is not justified by his own judgment; rather, his justification will be determined by God's judgment of his actions and motives. Paul affirms justification by works. He teaches a misthological justification before God based on works. Paul also admits that Abraham experienced justification by works in Rom 4:2. "*Since* **Abraham was justified by works**, he has something to boast about, but not before God" (TM). This is a first class conditional sentence and assumes the reality of the premise; the *if* may appropriately be translated as *since*. James also teaches the misthological justification of believers based on their works (Jam 2:21,24-25).

[828] Sim, "Dependence," 17.

[829] F. Andersen, *2 Enoch*. Longer recension, manuscript J. Available at http://www.marquette.edu/maqom /slavonicenoch.html. Accessed on December 26, 2009.

[830] Andersen, Enoch, 120, n. r.

[831] Ibid., 96.

[832] Lopez, "Vice," 14-15.

[833] Ibid.,

[834] David B. Guralnik, *Webster's NewWorld Dictionary of the American Language,* 2nd college edition (New York: Simon and Schuster, 1982), s.v. "litotes."

[835] GGNT, 1205. Myers and Mickelsen head their discussion of litotes as "Litotes or Meiosis." A. Berkeley Mickelsen, *Interpreting the Bible* (Grand Rapids: Eerdmans Publishing Co., 1963), 193. Edward P. Myers, "Interpreting Figurative Language," in *Biblical Interpretation: Principles and Practices*, eds. F. Furman Kearley, Edward P. Myers, and Timothy D. Hadley, (Grand Rapids: Baker Book House, 1986), 97.

[836] James L. Boyer, "The Classification of Subjunctives: A Statistical Study," *GTJ* 7:1 (Spring 1986): 3-19. Boyer evidently regards the *ou me* construction with the future indicative as a litotes, which would include his Johannine references to, Jn 4:14; 6:35; 10:5; and Rev 9:6; 18:14. See especially Jn 6:35 in which the construction is used in the same sense with both the subjective and future indicative. If the subjunctive is a litotes in this verse, then certainly the future indicative is also.

[837] See E. W. Bullinger, *Figures of Speech Used in the Bible* (Grand Rapids: Baker Book House, 1898), 155.

[838] Ibid.

[839] Gideon. Burton, *The Forest of Rhetoric: Silva Rhetoricae*. Available at http://rhetoric.byu.edu:16080/. S.v. "Litotes." Available at http://rhetoric.byu.edu/Figures/L/litotes.htm. Accessed on September 17, 2004. S.v. "Meiosis." Available at http://rhetoric.byu.edu/Figures/M/meiosis.htm. Accessed on September 17, 2004.

[840] Compare Jn 5:38 with Jn 5:40 and 1Jn 4:3 with 1Jn 2:22-23. For references see R. C. H. Lenski, *The Interpretation of St. John's Gospel* (Minneapolis: Augsburg Publishing House, 1961), 57, 419, 465, 639, 647. Lenski refers to the expression in 1Jn 4:3 as being both a "meiosis and litotes." See his *The Interpretation of the Epistles of St. Peter, St. John, and St. Jude* (Minneapolis: Augsburg Publishing House, 1961), 488. Idem, *Revelation*, 134, 141, 664, 1268. William Hendriksen, *The Gospel of John*, 2 vols., New Testament Commentary (Grand Rapids: Baker Book House, 1985), 1:74, 210, 234-235; 2:54, 62, 150. Hodges, *Eclipse*, 116-117; *Gospel*, 138-140, 183. Dillow, 485, 556-558. D. Martin Lloyd-Jones, *Romans Chapter 8:17-39: The Final Perseverance of the Saints* (Grand Rapids: Zondervan, 1976), 314ff. Bullinger, 157-158. Richard R. Benedict, "The Use of Νίκαω in the Letters to the Seven Churches of Revelation" (Th.M. thesis. Dallas Theological Seminary, 1966), 14, 31. Robert Wilkin, "I Will Not Blot Out His Name," *GIF* (March-April 1995). David B. Curtis, "Smyrna, The Suffering Church." Available at www.bereanbiblechurch.org/transcripts/eschatology/2_8-11.htm. Accessed on July 29, 2004. Idem, "The Church at Sardis." Available at www.bereanbiblechurch.org/transcripts/eschatology/3_1-6.htm. Accessed on July 29, 2004. J. Hampton Keathley III, *Studies in Revelation: Christ's Victory Over the Forces of Darkness* (Biblical Studies Press, 1997), 47-48, 69, 340. Available at http://www.bible.org/assets/worddocs/jhk3_rev.zip. Accessed on September 17, 2004. Sweigart, "Revelation," 13-14, 20. Thomas L. Constable, *John*, 106; *Revelation*, 29-30, 39. Although the NIBC does not use the term litotes, it is clearly advocating that interpretation (pp. 1738, 1740). The same is true of Tatford, *Revelation*, 124-125, 187-189. Robert Vacendak (*Revelation*, GNTC).

[841] Benedict appears to be straining his argument when he says that subcomers can be hurt indirectly by the second death through others in terms of rewards. See Benedict, "Letters," 15. Chitwood contends that subcomers **metaphorically** can: be hurt by the second death (Rev 2:11), be under the power of the second death (20:6), and have their part in the second death (21:8) without literally being cast into the Lake of Fire which is the second death (20:14). The Lake of Fire only has literal application to unbelievers. See Chitwood, *Judgment* (2011), 89-103. Keathley III also entertains a similar possibility or litotes as the best interpretation, *Relation*, 47-48. However, it would seem best to apply Rev 21:8 to the lost and consider 2:11 and 20:6 as litotes, which are not intended to be thrown into reverse.

[842] Hodges, *Eclipse*, 81-82, 127.

[843] Faust, *Rod*, 148.

[844] Lang, *Revelation*, 96.

[845] Harold Barker, *Secure Forever* (Neptune: Loizeaux Brothers, 1974), 134.

[846] This litotetic distinction might also be represented by logistic illustration. It may be contrapositionally affirmed from $P \Rightarrow \Diamond Q$ that $\Diamond P \Leftarrow Q$ (i.e., $Q \Rightarrow \Diamond P$). Meeting the (P) condition that you overcome will solidify the promise (Q)

that you are not hurt by the second death. One would state this logically as: P ⇒ ⊘Q. The contraposition may also be assumed as true: If you are hurt by the second death, then you are not an overcomer: Q ⇒ ⊘P. However, one cannot logically assume that if someone does not overcome, then that person is hurt by the second death: ⊘P ⇒ Q.

847 Lenski, *John*, 465.

848 Hendriksen, *John*, 234.

849 Ibid., 235. His italicized emphasis has been replaced with a bold emphasis.

850 Hendriksen says, "The doctrine of the **preservation (hence, perseverance)** of the saints is surely implied in the very term *everlasting life*" (Ibid., 235; bold mine; italics his).

851 Some have imagined that Jn 10:28-29 only prohibits external forcible extraction so that being snatched out against God's will is impossible but leaving by your own free will is not prohibited. On the contrary, freewill expulsion is rendered just as implausible and perhaps even more so. Not only must one be stronger than God to get out, one must also be stronger than Satan. If someone who is stronger than you (namely Satan) cannot take you out, then how can you take yourself out. How can the weaker force accomplish what the greater force could not? An argument from greater to lesser renders this Arminian argument invalid. Additionally, if you were to leave of your own volition, then it would not be independent of Satan's temptation. Satan would be able to take credit for taking you out of God's hand. Your squirming out and Satan taking you out are not mutually exclusive. If Satan cannot take you out against God's will, then he cannot take you out by appealing to your will because God's will is that Jesus loses none of those who have been given to Him for safe keeping (Jn 6:39).

The only means of departure entertained by the passage is that of being taken by force. To suggest that there are other means of departure is to introduce an element into the text that is foreign to the text and context. The text suggests no other means of departure. As to context, the safety of the sheep is the responsibility of the shepherd, not the sheep. If the sheep wander into danger of their own free volition, then the shepherd is still at fault.

The Arminian appeal to freewill expulsion is an argument from silence. The implications of the passage render it impossible since believers are not only not snatched, they are promised eternal life and litotetically assured that they will not perish. This triple security leaves no wiggle room for insecurity. If someone were to seal you in a bank vault and tell you that no one could take you out, you would be foolish to conclude that this means that you can take yourself out. The clear intention is to prohibit extraction, not merely to exclude forcible extraction. God is not saying, "I hold you in My hand, but I might change My mind." He proves this with the guarantee of eternal life and never perishing. Nor is it as if Satan can walk up to God and say, "Pretty, please, let me have this believer," and expect God to say, "Well, since you asked nicely and did not try to snatch him, ok." No! The intent of the text is not merely to exclude a forcible removal but any removal. By denying the possibility of successful forcible extraction, the text has denied all possibilities of extraction since the only way God would let go is by force.

852 Lavender, *Freedom*, 19.

853 Ibid., 31.

854 The first interpretation is the one preferred by Walvoord. He attempts to avoid this charge of salvation by works claiming that salvation secures perseverance rather than perseverance secures salvation (*Revelation*, 82). However, from this Calvinistic perspective of perseverance, a person cannot enter heaven apart from perseverance. Perseverance is required for salivation from the Lake of Fire.

855 J. William Fuller, "I Will Not Erase His Name From The Book of Life (Revelation 3:5)." *JES* 26:3 (September 1983): 299.

856 Ibid., 306.

857 Ibid., 298.

858 For conditionalists who suppose that God will blot out names of those believers who do not overcome (Rev 3:5), let the following question be posed: "Does God blot out the blot out in Col 2:14?" *Exaleipho* is the Greek word used for *blot out* in both verses. If *all* (Col 2:14) sins are blotted out at the point in time we believe, then the sin of not overcoming was also. So how could God blot out of names for not overcoming when He already has blotted out our not overcoming. For God to blot out our names for not overcoming, He would first have to blot out His blot out of our sin of not overcoming.

859 Lloyd-Jones, 314.

860 Lenski, *Revelation*, 134.

861 Ibid., 148.

862 Walvoord, *Revelation*, 63-64.

863 H. E. Dana and Julius R. Mantey, *A Manual Grammar of the Greek New Testament* (New York: MacMillan Publishing Co., 1957), 250.

864 GGBB, 671.

865 Corner, *Security*, 60, n. 10.

866 Ibid.

867 Picirilli, *Free*, 11-12. For the citation of the same quotation from non-Calvinists, see Hunt *Love* (77), and Vance *Calvinism* (130).

868 Ibid., 198.

869 Ibid.

870 See Ryrie, *Salvation*, 98-99.

871 Ibid., 137.

872 Robert N. Wilkin, "An Exegetical Evaluation of the Reformed Doctrine of the Perseverance of the Saints" (Th.M. thesis, Dallas Theological Seminary, 1982). Likewise, Dillow deals very thoroughly with the topic. See his indices.

873 Charles C. Ryrie, *The Ryrie Study Bible: New American Standard Translation* (Chicago: Moody Press, 1978), 1897.

874 Ryrie, *Theology*, 154.

875 Ibid., 28.

876 Ibid., 31.

877 Ibid., 33.

878 Ryrie repeats this two-coupon analogy about saving faith practically verbatim in *Theology*, 300.

879 Charles C. Ryrie, *What you Should Know about Inerrancy* (Chicago: Moody Press, 1981), 15.

880 Ibid., 17.

881 Dillow, 10-13.

882 According to LS arguments, repentance is a resolution or decision to turn from sin. Repentance is made out to be the root not fruit, so it is supposedly not a work. Thus, the LS argument is that to condition salvation on repentance is not to teach salvation by works. The same argument is made concerning faith. It is commitment to Christ. It is the root of the good works to follow, but saving faith itself is not a work. Thus, to teach that salvation is conditioned on the mere willingness to commit good works and turn from bad works is not to teach salvation by works. Therefore, even if taking up one's cross and following Jesus is a work, the mere willingness to do so is not.

Of course, FG can counter with definitions, contexts, and by showing that the promise is conditioned on the fruit not just the root. Nevertheless, for the sake of argument, let these considerations momentarily be set aside. Let us engage the LS contention that commitment to work is not a work and willingness to turn is not a turn by pointing out that judgment is not only based on our actions but also on our motives and intentions (Gen 6:5; 50:20; Prov 21:27; Is 29:20; Acts 8:22; 1Cor 4:5; Heb 4:12). To look a woman with the intent of lusting for her is sin (Mt 5:28). If the action arising from the intent has (negative) meritorious value, then so does the intent. The intent to order mustard is not evil. But the intent to kill someone for ordering mustard is evil. If killing someone for ordering mustard is evil, then so is the intent to do so. Since taking up one's cross has misthological value, the mere willingness to do so must also. Further, since perseverance in faith has misthological value, the intent to persevere in faith has misthological value. So regeneration cannot be conditioned on the intent to persevere in faith. Those who teach that a person must be willing to turn from sin, or commit his or her life, or persevere in faith in order to be saved are teaching salvation by works. Likewise, if the motive of their heart is to serve Christ in order to reach heaven, then their motive is legalistic and their service contemptible.

883 Lybrand's entire book is dedicated to the study of a cliché that was first formally in Calvin's writings as: "It is therefore faith alone which justifies, and yet faith that justifies is not alone." Lybrand suspects that cliché goes back to Martin Luther, although Strong attributes it to Melanchthon. Fred R. Lybrand, *Back to Faith: Reclaiming Gospel Clarity in an Age of Incongruence* (Xulon Press, 2009), 4-5. Some of the short comings that he points out concerning the cliché are that Calvin and other Reformers acknowledged that unbelievers can produce good works and that believers do not necessarily produce good works. Therefore, trying to discern who is a believer by the works they produce is a logically flawed methodology (pp. 38-39). Stipulating that all believers will produce some fruit given enough time does nothing to help the claim that you can discern believers by their works (p. 189). Supporters of the cliché necessarily embed postconversional works in the initial faith which justifies (just like a plant in its seed) so that such works are required for both initial and final justification (p. 59). He devotes a chapter to Piper's implementation of the cliché (pp. 195-235). In this chapter, Lybrand correctly perceives that Piper and Edwards have conditioned final justification on postconversional performance. This perception should be linked to his assessment that those within the Reformed camp are importing those postconversional works into what is required for initial justification. See my *Mere Christianity and Moral Christianity* for demonstration as to how Jonathan Edwards and John Piper, like two peas in a pod, make this virtual importation with a seed-tree analogy.

884 George Zeller, "Saved By Grace: A Clarification of the Lordship Salvation Issue." Available at http://www.middletownbiblechurch.org/doctrine/sbgrace.htm. Accessed on August 13, 2004.

885 Zeller, "Theology."

886 Rosscup, "Overcomer," 261-286.

887 Ibid., 279.

888 Ibid., 263.

889 Ibid., 270.

890 Ibid., 271.

[891] Zeller, "Theology."

[892] Epp, *Revelation*, 2:81.

[893] William R. Ross, Jr., "An Analysis of the Rewards and Judgments in Revelation 2 and 3" (Th.M. thesis, Dallas Theological Seminary, 1971), 8.

[894] Ibid.

[895] Donald G. Barnhouse, *Revelation: An Expositional Commentary* (Grand Rapids: Zondervan Publishing House, 1971), 68, 412.

[896] Ross, "Revelation," 12-16.

[897] Barnhouse, 43-44.

[898] Ibid., 49.

[899] Rosscup, 262-263. The same criticism should be made concerning Ross' work.

[900] Barnhouse, 408.

[901] Ralph D. Richardson, "The Johannine Doctrine of Victory" (Th.M. thesis, Dallas Theological Seminary, 1955).

[902] Ibid., 28.

[903] Ibid., 12-13.

[904] Robert Gromacki, *Is Salvation Forever?* (Chicago: Moody Press, 1973).

[905] Ibid., 74.

[906] Ibid., 159.

[907] Ibid., 176.

[908] Ibid., 161-162.

[909] Ibid., 92.

[910] Ibid., 93.

[911] Ibid., 120.

[912] For a FG Calvinistic defense of eternal security that does not manifest the Calvinistic weakness of perseverance, see Kendall who devotes ch. 1 of his book to a discussion of perseverance. R. T. Kendall, *Once Saved, Always Saved* (Chicago: Moody Press, 1983), 19-33.

[913] See ch. 8, "For Those Who Stop Believing," in Stanley, *Security*, 73-83.

[914] See Harlen D. Betz, "The Nature of Rewards at the Judgment Seat of Christ" (Th.M. thesis, Dallas Theological Seminary, 1974), 28-35. Also see Richard R. Benedict, "The Use of Νίκαω in the Letters to the Seven Churches of Revelation" (Th.M. thesis, Dallas Theological Seminary, 1966). A brief survey of the various positions concerning Rev 3:5 can be found in Robert N. Wilkin, "I Will Not Blot Out His Name," *Grace in Focus* (March-April 1995). Hodges devotes the last chapter of his book to this topic (*Eclipse*, 103-118) and chapter 11 to Rev 3:20 (*Free*, 129-140). Dillow has a rather exhaustive treatment. See his indexes in *Reign*. Keathley III, *Revelation*, Lessons 5-11, and *Appendix 3. Who are the Overcomers?* Chitwood devotes chapters 4-12 to this perspective of Revelation. See Arlen L. Chitwood, *Judgment* (2011), 53-176. Vacendak (GNTC). John Philips, *Exploring Revelation: An Expository Commentary* (Grand Rapids: Kregel Publications, 1987).

[915] Daniel K. K. Wong, "The Pillar and the Throne in Revelation 3:12, 21," *BibSac*, 156:623 (July 1999): 304.

[916] Robert N. Wilkin, *JOTGES*, 23:107. See John Niemelä, "For you have kept My Word: The Grammar of Revelation 3:10," *CTSJ* 6:1 (January - March 2000): 1-25.

[917] John Niemelä, "For you have Kept My Word: The Theology of Revelation 3:10 (Part 2 of 2)" *CTSJ* 6:4 (December 2000): 65.

[918] There are three possible interpretations of 2Cor 5:20. (1) It is addressed to lost people in the church. (2) It is addressed to lost people in the world. (3) It is addressed to saved people in the church. The last position is the one adopted herein.

[919] Rev 22:19 is a warning addressed to believers because unbelievers do not have a portion in the book/tree of life to lose. Eternal security rules out a soteriological warning to believers, leaving only misthological possibilities. Fuller's misthological interpretation in Rev 3:5 is inherently weak since the references to the Book of Life in 13:8 and 17:8 stress the permanence of the name; it is one of over 60 Johannine litotes; and it appears to be intertwined with prescience. The name cannot be removed. Since the promise of Rev 3:5 is a litotes that builds upon immutability of the name, it would be illogical for John to attack this foundational understanding in Rev 22:19. Consistency would demand that the name itself cannot be removed. This coincides nicely with Johannine soteriology in that the name represents those who have eternal life and who consequently cannot come into soteriological judgment (Jn 5:24). Moreover, the presence or absence of the name is undoubtedly soteriological in 20:12,15. Granted, Rev 21:27 could be taken to be either soteriological or misthological, but the contrast with those who are considered sinners in the eternal state would suggest a soteriological contrast. In summary, no clear evidence in Revelation advances the notion that a believer's name can be removed. Clear confirmation exists to the contrary, however. In contrast, the tree of life is definitely a misthological item (Rev 2:7; 22:14) and would accord much better in this misthological verse. The combined testimony of the CT and MT against the TR are conclusive due to the context and Johannine theology as reflected by the reading of the oldest manuscripts and

majority readings. What is at stake is the right of believers to partake of the tree of life, not the presence of their names in the Book of Life.

[920] Daniel K. Wong, "The Pillar and the Throne in Revelation 3:12, 21." *BibSac* 156:623 (July 1999): 297-307, 304.

[921] Ibid., 305.

[922] Shank, *Life*, 280-281.

[923] Corner, *Security*, 114.

[924] Wong, 306-307.

[925] Dillow, 362-363.

[926] Lopez, citing Moo, affirms that Rom 5:17 is a logical future (*Romans*, 119). A logical future, as opposed to a true future, has been entertained also on B-Greek (and elsewhere) as a reasonable recourse to avoid teaching universalism in Rom 5:19. Lopez rightly considers Rom 6:14 a logical future: "The future tense here does not function as a promise or command but as a logical-future stating what is naturally expected. Logically, Christians that obey Paul's command of v 13 will experience the truth contained in v. 14" (Romans, 135).

[927] Ibid., 416.

[928] What does this warning of death in Rom 8:13 mean for the Christian: "If you live according to the flesh, you must/will die"? Various alternatives have been suggested.

1. Die prematurely (Kendall, *OSAS*, 189; Constable)
2. Die temporally (Dillow, *Reign*, 365-368; Kendall, *OSAS*, 189; Constable; BKC; NIBC, Hodges, Secrets, 10-16)
3. Die misthologically (Sweigart, *Pothole*, 3)
4. Die hypothetically (Calvinists)
5. Die spiritually (Arminians)

According to Arminians, if believers do not persevere, they will die spiritually. That is, they will lose eternal life and go to hell. To be sure, this verse describes the potential death of born-again *believers*, who are referred to as *brethren* in v. 12. Calvinists frequently will admit that the verse is dealing with genuine believers. Then they will argue that it is only portraying the hypothetical possibility of such death. But this first class conditional sentence is firmly rooted in reality. It cannot be shuffled to the outer stratosphere of mere potentiality, belonging to classes further removed from reality.

After all, if this death were not a real possibility, the warning would be nonsensical. Simply put, those believers who walk according to the flesh will die. Those believers who walk according to the Spirit will live. The possibility of death is no more hypothetical than the possibility of life. The other Calvinistic counter sometimes offered is that these *brethren* are merely professing believers. But the context shows otherwise. Moreover, one must have spiritual life in order to be in danger of spiritual death. You cannot threaten a spiritually dead person with spiritual death. Such a person is already dead. Therefore, it must be concluded that these are regenerate *brethren* who are being warned of dying.

Does this mean that retention of regeneration is at stake? According to both Arminians and Calvinists, the answer is, "Yes." Perseverance is necessary to reach heaven in both of these soteriological systems. If a believer were not to persevere, then the believer would lose the eternal life imparted at regeneration. From their perspective, eternal life is a dynamic, life-giving stream flowing from one's union with Christ. If a believer is severed from Christ (Gal 5:4), the believer will wither and die and lose eternal life. For both the Calvinist and Arminian, soteriological security is at stake.

Since the Calvinistic interpretation merges into the Arminian outcome, the specific interest in this present survey deals with this Arminian explanation. The first three interpretations, in contrast, are non-soteriological and preferred by FG interpreters. From the FG perspective, since life and death are not dependent upon the way believers live in Rom 8:13, life and death do not refer to soteriological truths. FG does not understand Paul as teaching soteriological security based on works. Soteriological possession of life is not conditioned on the way a believer lives. Possession of eternal life is static in that there is no fluctuation in our possession of eternal life at the soteric level. However, our experience of life and death is conditioned on the way we live and is, therefore, open to dynamic variation. This distinction between possession and experience, therefore, leads to the conclusion that eternal life has both static and dynamic dimensions. The result of sin is death, even for the believer. By definition of what is meant by static possession, the FG interpretation will limit this death to the dynamic experience of such life.

The potential death of believers is described in Rom 8:13, who are referred to as *brethren* in v. 12. Those believers who walk according to the Spirit will live. Those believers who walk according to the flesh will die. Since this life and death are dependent upon one's walk, they do not refer to soteriological truths. Soteriological possession of life is not premised on the way one lives. However, the experience of life and death is so conditioned. The result of sin is death, even for a believer.

Paul has set the stage for this conclusion earlier in describing the present walk in life versus death for the believer (Rom 6:4,16,21,23; 7:10,13,24; 8:2,6,11). Or as Paul said elsewhere, believers who live according to the flesh are dead even while they live (1 Tim 5:6). They are the living dead. Although such believers have both physical and spiritual life, their experience is one of death.

They are dead in terms of their spiritual experience and in terms of their fellowship with God. Death is separation from God, who is life. Such believers are separated from God in terms of fellowship and in terms of empowerment. Tragically, such believers will also experience misthological death. Death is the absence of life. Just as life can be experienced at multiple levels, so can death.

Those believers who have eternal life at the soteriological level may fail to experience eternal life temporally at the filial level and eternally at the misthological level. They will not reign in life (Rom 5:17). Rather, their temporal and misthological experience will be one of death. They will not share this reign in life with God; instead, they will be separated from this experience with God as a result of their sin and have an impoverished experience both now and in the future. Believers cannot be separated from God in terms of their relationship. Their fundamental relationship with God cannot die. In sharp contrast, their fellowship with God both now and in the future can die. Those believers who are cast into the outer darkness are separated from God in terms of fellowship. They do not share the joy of ruling with Him in heaven and will be separated from the crown of life and tree of life. Misthological death for them will be separation from life with God at its fullest potential. Sweigart comes to much the same conclusion via a different route by following the research of Wyngaards: "'Dead' means 'loss of dominion' in addition to being a separation metaphor. We can easily see this is the life of Adam and Eve who, not only were separated from God by being driven out of the Garden, but also lost their dominion over creation in the same judgment" ("Pothole," 3). Chitwood also believes that the death expressed by Rom 8:13 is a metaphorical picture of misthological death (*Revelation*, 487)

To be sure, unfaithful believers will share the joy of being with God in heaven, but this joy certainly will be an impoverished experience compared to the life of those who rule with God. The wages of sin is death: temporal and misthological death in the case of the believer. In contrast to the wages of sin, the gift and reward of God is eternal life. At the static level, eternal life is a gift. At the dynamic level, it is a reward (Rom 6:22-23).

Both death and life in Rom 8:13 are referring to the believer's potential present experience. There is no need to shove this death off ultraistically to the future and teach that the Lord physically will kill believers at the Bema as Faust does (*Rod*, 121-133). Nor is there any need to move beyond experiential death to ontological death as the Arminians do. The passage is not describing the death of the believer's regenerate trichotomous spirit but the soulical death of believers who fail to experience the flow of life from their regenerate trichotomous spirit. Of course, temporal soulical death will result in one losing one's soul misthologically and thus result in misthological death.

[929] In his customary fashion, Corner misrepresents FG theology when he claims that FG denies that the Lord will deny unfaithful believers (*Security*, 117). Marrowists affirm misthological denial. This acknowledgement was affirmed explicitly in the very first journal of GES by McCoy, *Secure*, 25-29.

[930] Wong, 305.

[931] D. A. Carson, *Exegetical Fallacies* (Grand Rapids: Baker Book House, 1984), 86.

[932] Wong, 300.

[933] Dillow, 530-532.

[934] Hodges, *Eclipse*, 88.

[935] Stanley, *Security*, 127,128.

[936] Chitwood, *Olivet*, 291.

[937] Faust, *Rod*, 113.

[938] The popular usage of the phrase *eternal salvation* (rather than the biblical usage of Heb 5:9) is generally used in this manuscript. Therefore, unless indicated otherwise, eternal salvation is used herein to refer to salvation from hell in accordance with popular usage.

[939] Whipple, *Shock*, 173,174.

[940] Colin Brown, gen. ed. *The New International Dictionary of New Testament Theology* (Grand Rapids: Zondervan Publishing House, 1975). S.v. "Time: αἰών," by J. Guhrt. For online discussion from similar perspective about Mystery of Aion, see Tom Logan, "'Aionios'—A Lexical Survey." Available at http://www.1john57.com /aionios.htm. Accessed on July 5, 2005. William E. Wenstrom, Jr. "Aion." Available at http://prairieviewchristian.org/Acrobat%20files/Aion.pdf. Accessed on July 5, 2005.

The classic response to universalism is to argue that the understanding *aion* and *aionios* in terms of eternity is within the semantic range of both words. Next, one argues that this meaning is applicable to the nature of the life imparted to believers so that they quantitatively have received eternal life. Finally, one shows that this meaning is used in synonymous juxtaposition with the punishment inflicted upon the lost so they suffer eternal damnation in contrast to the eternal bliss of the saved. The YLT translation is a favorite among those seeking to deny the eternality of this word group, so it will be used below for reference.

In Eph 3:21, the YLT reads, "To Him is the glory in the assembly in Christ Jesus, to all the generations of *the age* (sg. *aion*) *of the ages* (pl. *aion*)." Other translations typically will translate this phrase in terms of eternity. The plural understanding is to be preferred in that it would be most unreasonable to suppose that Paul means to say that God is glorified only for one temporal age, as if then we stop glorifying God. In Heb 1:8, the YLT apparently tries to limit Christ's rulership: "Thy throne, O God, is to the age of the age." It is sometimes asserted by age advocates that Christ will cease to rule when He turns the kingdom over to the Father (1Cor 15:24-25). But the Lamb is seen co-ruling with His Father at the commencement of the eternal state (Rev 22:1).

Furthermore, even YLT acknowledges that Lk 1:33 explicitly affirms, "He shall reign over the house of Jacob to the *ages* (pl. *aion*); and of his reign there shall be no *end* (*telos*)." These plural ages are equated with eternity future in regard to the length of Christ's reign. *Aion* in the plural is thus used to refer to the eternal future. The argument that *aion* never necessarily refers to everlasting duration is thus invalidated. This is not to say that the plural form of *ages* always refers to eternity. There are texts in which the plural may refer to a limited duration (Heb 9:26; 1Cor 2:7; 10:11). But it should be noted that Heb 9:26 and 1Cor 10:11 jointly use *telos* and a cognate to describe the "end of the ages." *Ages* may have an *end* (*telos*). Although one might argue that this is a reference to eternity past in these two passages and eternity future in 1Cor 2:7, such a position will not be taken herein. It will suffice for present purposes to note that Lk 1:33 uses the plural of *aion* in a context that specifies that there will "be no end" to the Messianic Kingdom. In this verse, the Lord's reign "to the ages" will have "no end." These terms are practically synonymous. The original recipients were anticipating a physical kingdom to be sure, but this does not mean that they were awaiting a temporary kingdom. These *ages* are the inauguration of eternity, not separate from it. This usage establishes that the plural form of *aion* has eternal as part of its semantic domain.

BDAG (2b) notes that singular and plural of *aion* can be essentially equivalent. Not surprising, the singular is used in Is 9:7 (LXX) with the same meaning: "To the increase of the princely power, and of peace, there is **no end**, on the throne of David, and on his kingdom, to establish it, and to support it, in judgment and in righteousness, henceforth, **even unto the age**, the zeal of Jehovah of Hosts doth this" (YLT). If there is no end to this age, then it is endless and thus eternal. The passage is stressing the continuity between the inauguration and continuation of this rule and the age to come as an expression of eternity. His princely power and peace will have no end. Consequently, even the singular form of *aion* may mean eternal.

Even YLT translates the singular of *aion* singular as eternity more than once (Is 45:17; 57:15). The latter verse is interesting in that it describes God as "the high and exalted One, inhabiting eternity" (YLT). How does one limit *aion* to the millennial age? Is this verse only affirming that God inhabits the millennial age? Surely not! Furthermore, since the verse is dealing with the Greek word, it may be worthwhile to note the Greek present tense. Accordingly, if one seeks to limit *aion* to mean age, then Isaiah is saying that God inhabits the present age. Little wonder, then, that the YLT abandoned its translating preference for age and adopted *eternity*, even for *aion* in the singular!

Amazingly, however, YLT does not shrink back from translating Dt 32:40 as God saying, "I live to the age!" What? Does God only affirm that He lives to the millennium age? What happens at that point? Does He die? The absurdity of this translation is apparent. The Hebrew *olam*, like its Greek counterpart *aion*, can mean *forever*. The God who spoke of Himself as the eternally self-existent *I AM* in Ex 3:14 expressed Himself as *the One Who Eternally Is* in Dt 32:40. Those who say that God cannot speak to humanity in terms of eternity are going to have to explain why humanity can do what God cannot. Why is humanity able to speak about eternity and God unable to communicate to humanity in terms of eternity? We worship a Lord who has revealed Himself to us as eternally God: *aionos* God (Rom 16:26), *aion* God (1Tim 1:17).

God is from everlasting to everlasting, from eternity past to eternity future, from *aion* to *aion*, (1Chron 16:36; Ps 41:13; 90:2; 103:17; 106:48; cp. Ps 10:16; 93:2; 145:13; Is 57:15; Hab 1:12). It is ridiculous to assert that the Bible only asserts that God is age-lasting in such texts. To the contrary, He is the everlasting King (Jer 10:10; *olam*) who lives and reigns forever (Dan 4:34; *alam*). One might also note that Ps 102:106-107, quoted in Heb 1:11-12, is affirming God's eternality.

It is dumbfounding when one encounters arguments from those who oppose endless punishment and who claim that *aion* does not refer to eternity in Hellenistic Greek when, in fact *Aion*, was the Greek name for their god of eternity in the Hellenistic period! The Bible takes this term and applies it to the Christian God to assert that He, not Aion, is the God of eternity.

Most importantly, in terms of soteriology, this life, which God has shared with His Son (Jn 5:26), is not merely qualitative (cp. Ex 3:14; Jn 8:58). This life, which is also shared with us, is also quantitatively everlasting (Jn 5:24). To doubt the durative nature of the life offered would be to doubt the nature of the offer itself. The life that the Father has is the very same life that the Son has, and it is this life that is given to the believer and called *aionios* (Jn 5:24,26). This is the life that is offered in the next chapter, where even the YLT translates Jesus as promising, "I am the bread of the life; he who is coming unto me may not hunger, and he who is believing in me may not thirst—**at any time**" (Jn 6:35). If there is no subsequent time after which those who partake of Jesus thirst, then one drink from Jesus is an everlasting thirst quencher. Jesus also insinuates the shared nature of that life between the Father, Son, and believer in that context as well (Jn 6:57). Paul is straight to the point when He affirms that Christ is our life (Col 3:4). This life, which the Father has given us, is none other than Christ Himself. To limit it to an age would be to limit Christ to an age. But is not Christ ageless?

The YLT likewise has difficultly hiding the contrast between the temporary and the eternal in 2Cor 4:18, where it reads, "We are not looking to the things seen, but to the things not seen; for the things seen are **temporary**, but the things not seen are **age-during** (*aionios*)." *Age-during* is used in antonymous juxtaposition with what is *temporary*. Thus, *age-*

during is used to refer to what is eternal in this passage. Likewise, the rewards promised to us are permanent (1Cor 9:25; 1Pet 1:4; 5:4). The kingdom, which we are to receive, cannot be shaken in terms of being removed (Heb 12:27-28). But how can the rewards and kingdom promised to us be eternal and the promise of life in that kingdom not be eternal as well? How can our rulership be eternal and Christ's rulership only be millennial?

At the very least, the contrast in Mk 3:29 between *aion* and *aionios* indicates that the latter is eternal, "But whoever may speak evil in regard to the Holy Spirit hath not forgiveness—to the *age* (*aion*), but is in danger of *age-during* (*aionios*) judgment" (YLT). Attempts to limit *to the age* (*eis ton aiona*) to the "here and now," or to some terminus point in the future, is certainly questionable in that one would not maintain that the same expression used elsewhere only means that God's word and the life imparted by God's word only last to the end of the age and then ceases (1Pet 1:23,25). Peter is not affirming that God's word will last until the next age and then come to an end. Are we to understand Ps 119:89 as saying that God's word is only settled in heaven until the millennial age (sg. *olam*/sg. *aion*) and that His name only endures till the next *age* (sg. *olam*/pl. *aion*)?

Sometimes those wishing to picture *aion* and *aionios* as being devoid of eternal ramifications do so by stipulating that, had the biblical writers wished to express eternity, they would have done so with *aidios*. To be sure, one of only two places where YLT uses the word *eternal* (*aidios*) is in Rom 1:20. But YLT translates *aidios* as meaning *everlasting* in Jude 1:6. This latter passage presents a problem for those wishing to limit punishment to an *age* since the word for eternity is *aidios*, which seems contextually synonymous with *aionios* in the next verse (Jude 1:7). Apparently, Greek speakers could use the two terms interchangeably if they wished: "By the **eternal** (*aionios*) **destruction** of the tyrant, and by the **everlasting** (*aidios*) **life** of the pious, I will not renounce our noble family ties" (4Macc 10:15). Not only are *aionios* and *aidios* used in synonymous juxtaposition in this verse in regard to duration, they are used in antonymous juxtaposition regarding the contrasting fates of destruction versus life. So when a Greek scholar like Robertson says *aidios* is synonymous with *aionios* (WPNT, s.v. Jude 1:6), his assessment is factual. One of the more interesting parallels is when Ignatius, within the space of five verses (i.e., 1Ep 18:1; 19:3), uses *aidios* and *aionios* to refer to life: "But to us salvation and life *eternal* [*aionios*]…God Himself being manifested in human form for the renewal of *eternal* [*aidios*] life." Even the apostolic fathers could use the two Greek words for eternity as synonyms when speaking of the eternal life that God gives to us. Clearly, from Hellenistic literature, one can see a synonymity between these two words.

The Messianic age is but the first phase of eternity. It is the door into the eternal state. Since the lost will be cast into the Lake of Fire at the conclusion of the millennial age, their punishment certainly cannot be limited to that age. Trying to limit their punishment to the millennial age is self-defeating.

[941] Gary T. Whipple, *The Matthew Mysteries: A Revelation of the Higher Wisdom Concerning the Church, Israel and the Gentiles in Prophecy* (Hayesville: Schoettle Publishing Co., 1995), 247.

[942] Ibid., 51.

[943] Ibid., 125-127,164,249.

[944] Idem, *Shock*, 152-161.

[945] Faust, *Rod*, 230-231.

[946] UBD, s.v. "Gehenna."

[947] Dillow, 94.

[948] Ibid., 95.

[949] Hodges, *Hebrews*, 811.

[950] The soteriological reception of the kingdom in Mk 10:15 and Lk 18:17 uses *dechomai*, but the reception of the kingship in Lk 19:12,15 uses *lambano* (cf. Rev 17:12), and the misthological reception of the kingship in Heb 12:28 uses a compound of *lambano* (*paralambano*). For other misthological usages of *lambano*, see 1Cor 9:24-25 (in which it is used synonymously with winning a crown) and Jam 1:2 (where it is used in regard to obtaining the crown of life).

[951] The Greek word rendered by the NASB as *gratitude* in Heb 12:28 is actually the Greek word for *grace* (*charis*). We not only are saved by grace, we should also live by grace. This is known as enabling grace.

[952] Dillow, 95, 101.

[953] Nee, *Gospel*, 3:436-440.

[954] Ibid., 439.

[955] Ibid., 439, cf. p. 461.

[956] Ibid., 457.

[957] Sauer, *Arena*, 29.

[958] Witness Lee, *A Brief Definition of the Kingdom of the Heavens* (Anaheim: Living Stream Ministry, 1986), 38, 48, 56-58.

[959] Brad McCoy, *CTSJ*, 5:3 (July–September 1999): 8-9.

[960] See Dillow, 599-600.

[961] Ibid., 471-478

[962] Ibid., 478.

[963] Ibid., 476.

[964] See Dillow, 471; Lang, *Sons*, 122.

[965] Lang, *Revelation*, 377.

[966] Ibid., 379.

[967] Ibid., 379.

[968] Rev 21:8,27; 22:15 are recapitulations of the judgment of **noncomers** described in 20:11-15; Rev 22:17 is a recapitulation of the **comers** described in Rev 21:6 (and some comers will be subcomers—Rev 22:19), and Rev 22:3-5,14 are recapitulations of the **overcomers** of Rev 21:7. Thus, I agree with Wilkin's conclusion that Rev 22:15 describes the nonelect outside the eternal kingdom. See Robert N. Wilkin, "Who are the Outsiders? Revelation 22:14-17," *GIF* (November-December 1993).

[969] Rev 22:1-2 is a recapitulation of the New Jerusalem described in Rev 21:1-2,10-26.

[970] Lang, *Revelation*, 380-381. Unfortunately, Lang shies away from adopting a literal view of the Heavenly City (p. 372); nevertheless, he beautifully describes it as a wedding canopy above the earthly Jerusalem (pp. 364-365). He would correctly consider this Heavenly City to be a regal reward for the triumphant Bride (p. 379).

[971] Wilkin, "Outsiders."

[972] Lang, *Revelation*, 381, 384.

[973] Whipple, *Matthew*, 194.

[974] See Gary Hill, *The Discovery Bible: New American Standard New Testament*. Reference Edition (Chicago: Moody Press, 1987), 515.

[975] Chitwood, *Judgment* (1986), 173; Whipple, *Shock*, 158-160.

[976] Robert N. Wilkin, "Regeneration in the OT?" *GIF* (March-April, 2004).

[977] Robert A. Peterson, *Hell on Trial: The Case for Eternal Punishment* (Phillipsburg: Presbyterian and Reformed Publishing Company, 1995), 33-34.

[978] Nee, *Gospel,* 3:460-461.

[979] Lang, *Revelation*, p 113.

[980] Walvoord, *Revelation*, BKC, 987.

[981] Baughman, 120, 127, 186-187, 195.

[982] Haller correctly notes that "the duration and severity of hell are congruous with sin against the infinite holy God" (*Matthew*, GNTC, 121). The quality and quantity of punishment are congruent with nature of the Person against whom the sin is committed and thus eternal. The same observation, however, would lead one to conclude that the sins committed by a believer against an infinite Person would have eternal consequences if dealt with in judgment. For the same reason, on the positive side, service to an infinite Person would have eternal positive value.

[983] Chitwood, *Olivet*, 291.

[984] Keathley IV, "Darkness," 8-9.

[985] Ray E. Baughman, *The Kingdom of God Visualized* (Birmingham, AL: Shepherd Press, 1972), 243.

[986] The circumference of the Earth is 24901.55 at the equator, which I will round off to 25000 miles. The base of the city is 1500 miles. With these figures, one easily can compute the base of a scaled model of the city to some scaled model of the Earth, such as a basketball or globe. The ratio of the model/city = globe/Earth. The circumference of a basketball is 30 inches. So the model = (globe x city)/Earth. In the case of a basketball, the computation therefore is: model = (30 x 1500)/25000. The base of the model is 1.8 inches. One may use this computational procedure to calculate what the base length should be for some other globe so that one can change the scale of the model of the city accordingly. For the twenty-nine inch globe which the author used for example, it would round off to 1 ¾ inches.

[987] Alcorn, *Heaven*, 242, 467-476.

[988] Ibid., 56.

[989] Ibid., 248-249.

[990] Tatford, *Revelation*, 629.

[991] Lenski, *Revelation*, 650-651.

[992] Tanner, *Hebrews*, GNTC, 1046.

[993] Petterson, *Hell*, 176.

[994] Chitwood, *Olivet*, 291.

[995] See Dillow's treatment of the tree of life, crown of life, and Book of Life. These expressions concerning life are misthological. To his list, one should also add the water of life in Rev 7:17.

[996] John A. Martin, *Isaiah* (Wheaton: Victor Books, 1985), 1074.

[997] For an easy to read abbreviated presentation of Huber's thesis, see his "Relationship."

[998] Huber, "Concept," 6, 18-19, 26.

[999] For an abridged rewriting of Sapaugh's thesis, see his "Wedding."

[1000] Sapaugh, "Interpretation," 17.

[1001] Ibid., 37-38.

[1002] Martin, *Isaiah*, 1073.

[1003] Ibid., 1074.

[1004] According to Dillow, to the faithful believer at the Bema, the Lord promises: "There will be no more tears and no more pain" (p. 518). But for the remorseful believer thrown into the outer darkness, the wiping will be a 1000 years later: "When the eternal state begins, every tear is wiped away" (p. 531).

[1005] Pagenkemper, "Part 1," 188, n. 29.

[1006] Martin, *Isaiah*, 1117.

[1007] Hendriksen, *Matthew*, 270-271.

[1008] Dillow, 85.

[1009] Govett, *Revelation*, 474.

[1010] Arlen L. Chitwood, *The Time of the End: A Study About the Book of Revelation* (Norman, Ok: The Lamp Broadcast, 2011), 484-485.

[1011] In Luke's condensed thematic arrangement of Judas' placement at the Passover meal, it appears that Judas was at the Lord's Supper. When one produces a harmony of the gospels, however, it is clear that he left the Passover meal before the Lord's Supper. As a result, Lk 22:21-23 is a representation of thematic insertion rather than chronological progression. See Cheney, *Stereo*, 174-175. L. Robert Thomas and Stanley N. Gundry, *A Harmony of the Gospels: with Explanations and Essays* (San Francisco: Harper & Row, 1978): 208-209,212.

[1012] Constable, *Matthew*, 342.

[1013] *Anaklino* is the verb also used to describe the multitudes *reclining* on the green grass to eat (Mk 6:39). They did not bring chairs with them on which to *sit*. There were no chairs.

[1014] The following brings a number of logically related deductions together. The *if you* means *if you as a result of your regeneration*:

$(A \& B \Rightarrow C \& D)$
If you have undergone (A) a moral transformation and (B) an eschatological transformation,
then you will be (C) immortal (D) heirs of the kingdom.
See 1Cor 6:8-10; 15:50-58.

$(B \Rightarrow C)$
If you have undergone (B) an eschatological transformation,
then you will be (C) immortal.
See 1Cor 15:51-56

$(A \& B \Rightarrow C \& D \& E)$
If you are (A) worthy and (B) resurrected,
then you will be (C) immortal, (D) unmarried (E) sons of God.
See Lk 20:35-36

$(B \Rightarrow D)$
If you are (B) resurrected,
then you will be (D) unmarried.
See Mt 22:30; Mk 12:25

$(A \& B \Rightarrow C \& D \& E)$
If you have undergone (A) a moral transformation and (B) an eschatological transformation,
then you will be (C) immortal, (D) tearless (E) heirs of the kingdom.
See 1Cor 6:8-10; 15:50-58; Is 25:8; Rev 7:17; 21:4

$(B \Rightarrow C)$
If you have undergone (B) an eschatological transformation,
then you will be (C) immortal.
See 1Cor 15:51-56

Regeneration is the nonmeritorious precondition. It is important to note that when multiple co-conditions are promised to result in multiple co-benefits, each individual co-benefit is not necessarily limited to those who meet all the co-conditions. (Multiple conditions are not necessarily related in the same way to the singular conclusion, much less to multiple conclusions.) Thus, although Paul makes the statement that all believers will be immortal (as part of his proof that faithful believers who meet the co-conditions of moral and eschatological transformations will be entitled misthologically to the co-benefits of being immortal and inheriting the kingdom), this affirmation of unconditional immortality is but a building block in his overall argument, not the building itself. This unconditional part of his proof is but a corollary to his main point to which he is building up to—that inheriting the kingdom necessarily entails victory over death.

Similarly, when Luke teaches that believers who meet the co-conditions (of being resurrected and worthy) experience multiple results (of being immortal, unmarried, sons of God), it cannot be inferred necessarily that each three co-results are limited to those believers who meet both the co-conditions. Rather, from Paul's statements above, it may be deduced that all believers will be immortal. Accordingly, immortality is not limited to those believers who have met the requirement of morality. Likewise, from parallels in Matthew and Mark, it may be deduced that being unmarried is not conditioned on the believer's morality.

In similar fashion, the promises made to overcomers about their being immortal, tearless, heirs of the kingdom do not necessarily limit each of the co-benefits to overcomers. It can be necessarily inferred, from Paul's argument concerning inheriting the kingdom and from John's conclusion in which death is thrown into the lake of fire, that even subcomers will be immortal.

[1015] GGBB, 414, 417, 424.

[1016] These labels are used in reference to the standard position concerning the doctrine of eternal rewards. They have no correlation with labels used elsewhere concerning the doctrine of inspiration. Concerning that doctrine, the present writer would not label himself a conservative-moderate, conservative, or moderate. He has, in fact, labeled himself as a fundamentalist concerning that particular doctrine in his article, "Southeastern & Termination," *Baptist Banner*, 6:6 (1993): 7-9. His definition in that article concerning that doctrine was, "A fundamentalist is a conservative with backbone!"

[1017] Carmical, "Part 1," 57.

[1018] For example, Panton, *Judgment*, acknowledges the difference between being a heir and joint-heir (p. 52), but he does not distinguish between inheriting the kingdom and entering the kingdom.

[1019] Dillow, 580.

[1020] Dillow, 78.

[1021] Lee, *Definition*, 49.

[1022] Ibid., 13.

[1023] Ramey, "Feast."

[1024] *Dei* in Acts 14:22 denotes the necessary condition that one *must* meet in order to enter the kingship, just as in Jn 3:7 *dei* is used to provide the condition under which one must enter the kingdom (Jn 3:5). One must be born again to enter the kingdom of God, and one must successfully pass through tribulations to enter the kingship of heaven.

[1025] For example, see Panton, *Judgment*, p. 36.

[1026] According to Govett, all believers enter the present mystery form of the kingdom but not its future manifestation (*Entrance*, 20).

[1027] Panton, *Judgment*, 76.

[1028] Concerning Hades, compare Govett, *Entrance*, 5.

[1029] Govett, using popular language, says that believers are cast into hell-fire in *Reward*, "Enter," 20-21, but the texts he cites are the Gehenna texts and misthological tests, not the lake of fire texts.

[1030] Personal correspondence 6-23-92.

[1031] Hodges wrote "1 Peter 2:2," but this is evidently a typographical error referring to 1Pet 1:2.

[1032] Personal correspondence 9-3-92.

[1033] Hodges is astute to question the syllogisms, since syllogisms are not always accurate representations of the text. For example, Carson criticizes Hodges' interpretation of 1Jn 3:6,9 by reducing Hodges' argument to syllogisms. Carson concedes that the habitual interpretation cannot be defended on the basis of tense alone, and admits it must be based on the context (*Fallacies*, 102-104). He even admits that Hodges' argument is not limited to the tense, but Carson portrays Hodges' position syllogistically as:

1. The present indicative is not always durative.
2. The verbs in 1Jn 3:6,9 are present indicative
3. Therefore, these verbs in 1Jn 3:6,9 "do not have durative force."

In the last statement, Carson misrepresents Hodges' argument, as if Hodges had said that the tense **never** has a durative force. This is overstatement and, therefore, misrepresentation of Hodges' position. According to Hodges, helping words or context determines whether the verb conveys durative force. Accordingly, tense advocates cannot prove their point from the tense alone, since the tense does not **necessarily** convey the durative force apart from contextual clues or grammatical assistance. In fact, Hodges dedicated an entire paragraph to this clarification. Carson fails to mention this fact, acting instead as if Hodges had made an absolute denial.

Nor is this the only misrepresentation of Hodges in Carson's work. A few pages earlier (pp. 96-97), Carson had quoted a distinction that Hodges made between the offer of eternal life as a free gift and the demand of discipleship. In response, Carson rejects a disjunction between the gift and the demand, claiming that a person must give evidence of regeneration if such a person is truly saved. His insistence, on meeting the demand of discipleship and providing evidence in terms of the way one lives life, is tantamount to requiring works as a subsequent requirement for final salvation and thus to conditioning entrance into heaven on the way one lives. Considering Carson's syllogistic summation of Hodges' argument, perhaps making a similar summation of Carson's own counterargument is in order.

1. Hodges teaches salvation by faith apart from works.
2. Carson rejects Hodges teaching.
3. Therefore, Carson teaches salvation by faith and works.

Hopefully, the bridal syllogisms employed herein will be much more accurate descriptions of the biblical text than Carson's were of Hodges' text. In any case, the bridal syllogisms are bolstered by extended discussion to demonstrate their compatibility with the biblical context.

[1034] Dillow, 458.

[1035] John S. Lanham, "Who Is the Bride of Christ?" Available at http://www.inthebeginning.org/kingdom/lanham/bride.pdf. Accessed on August 10, 2004

[1036] Dillow, 203.

[1037] "Bikini Believers at the Bema" is certainly possible, as Radmacher's sermon title suggests ("Bema," 41). But a bikini Bride is not possible.

[1038] Ibid., 41.

[1039] See Dillow, 202-204.

[1040] Dillow, 203.

[1041] G. H. Lang, *Pictures and Parables: Studies in the Parabolic Teaching of Holy Scripture*, third edition (Miami Springs: Conley and Schoettle Publishing Co., 1985), 346-352.

[1042] Ibid., 346-347.

[1043] This is evident within Eph 5 itself. The universal church is meant in Eph 5:25-27. The "she" of 5:27 = the "we" of Eph 1:4 = all believers. The "we" of Eph 5:30 = all believers. All members form His body, but not all members form His Bride.

[1044] Lanham, "Bride."

[1045] Gromacki, *Salvation*, 63.

[1046] Lang, *Revelation*, 391.

[1047] Wilson, *Writings*, 102-103.

[1048] Ibid., 105.

[1049] Govett, *Ephesians*, 258.

[1050] Whipple, *Shock*, 99-100.

[1051] William F. Roadhouse, *Seeing the Revelation* (Toronto: Overcomer Publishers, 1932), 175.

[1052] Ibid., 178.

[1053] Chitwood, *Judgment* (1986), 21.

[1054] Walvoord, *Revelation*,272.

[1055] Hodges demonstrates his expertise in Greek when he refuses to overstate the significance of the aorist tense. If the verb does have its punctiliar sense, as appears to be the case here, it may be explained on the basis of the imagery (e.g., a bath rather than a swim). The use of the aorist tense in Rev 7:14 for wash, however, does not necessarily denote a punctiliar once-for-all action. Mounce is incorrect (NIC). This aorist verb is in the indicative mood and thus is indecisive as to the punctiliar nature of the action. Likewise, Mounce overstates the present tense of wash in Rev 22:14 since it is an articular participle; it does not necessarily prove continual action. If the verbs are punctiliar, it is because the imagery of the context demands it—a washing. If they are linear, it is because the meaning of the context demands it—a washing that denotes faithfulness.

[1056] Gary Derickson and Earl Radmacher, *The Disciplemaker: What Matters Most to Jesus* (Salem: Charis Press, 2001), 169.

[1057] Hodges, *Gospel*, 89-90.

[1058] The phrase, "day of Christ," is found in Phil 1:6,10; 2:16. It is typically translated as "until the day of Christ" in the first two verses (Phil 1:6,10). This is inconsistent. The first verse uses *achri* (*until, till*). But both the latter two verses (Phil 1:10; 2:16) use *eis* (*in, on*). This identical expression using *eis* should be translated consistently in both verses as *in* or *on* to convey the futuristic nature of the blamelessness, not as *till* or *until*, as if the verses were talking about present blamelessness. To the credit of the NRS, it is consistent in that it uses the futuristic renditions in both verses (*in* for Phil 1:10 and *on* for Phil 2:16) to convey more clearly the fact that Paul is referring to being found pure and blameless at that future point in time. Accordingly, Phil 1:6 looks at the present progress of practical sanctification on earth until the Bema. But Phil 1:10 and 2:16 look at the future outcome of practical sanctification in heaven at the Bema. Believers are to become righteous and blameless now in their behavior (Phil 1:11; 2:14) so that they may be considered blameless at the future Bema (Phil 1:10; 2:26).

The word I have translated as *pure* in Phil 1:10 is *eilikrines*. According to TY, there are two competing theories as to the type of purity: (1) "found pure when unfolded and examined by the sun's light, (2) "properly, sifted and cleansed by rapid movement or rolling to and fro, *pure, unsullied, sincere*." A number of translations use *sincerity* (so BDAG). But L-N expresses the sincerity in terms of purity: "Being sincere in the sense of having pure motivation." Paul is concerned about pure motives at the Bema (1Cor 4:5), and believers certainly would want to be regarded as sincere rather than insincere at the Bema. S*incere* is a suitable translation, but the translation of *pure* more clearly conveys the fact that misthological, rather than temporal, assessment is in view and thus shows the thematic association with bridal purity.

This need for purity is further underscored in the next verse: "So that you may **approve** the things that are excellent, in order that you may be found pure and blameless **in** the day of Christ; **having** been filled with the fruit of righteousness which comes through Jesus Christ, to the glory and praise of God" (Phil 1:10-11). If Christians hope to be found pure and blameless in that day at the Bema, they must previously, and thus temporally, have born much righteous fruit while on earth (cp. Jn 15:5,8). Believers become pure and blameless "by" having been filled with fruit of practical righteousness. R. C. H. Lenski, *The Interpretation of St. Paul's Epistles to the Galatians, to the Ephesians, and to the Philippians* (Minneapolis: Augsburg Publishing House, 1961), 721. This is the only way believers can attain such purity (Muller, 47). Their being pure and blameless in that time period is contingent upon their practical righteousness in the present time period.

The NKJ is superior to the NAS in translating the second person plural subjunctive of *eimi* in Phil 1:10 as, "you may be," rather than as an infinitive, "to be." Still, in deference to the NAS in other situations, I further suggest that the word *found* be included in the NKJ translation to show the thematic connection with 2Pet 3:14, where the Greek word for being *found* (*heurisko*) is used explicitly in connection with *blameless* (*amemptos*). The NAS translates the similar phrase *ginomai amemptos* as *found blameless* (Phil 3:6). The NKJ strangely fails to translate the verb (*ginomai*) on this occasion; I therefore must show preference for the rendition of *found* for *ginomai* by the NAS. Compare also with Rom 3:4 in which the NAS translates *ginomai* to say that God is *found* true. *Ginomai* is used on this occasion, not because God becomes true at some point in the future, but because He turns out to be true when examined; He is proven to be true or found to be true. The translation *found* is in substantial corroboration with BDAG (*ginomai*, 7) at any length. So there is considerable precedence for translating *ginomai* (*to be*) as meaning *found to be*.

Likewise, the NAS translates *eimi* (*to be*) as *found* diligent in 2Cor 8:22. Here is an instance in which *eimi* is translated as *found*. I suggest that *eimi* also be translated as *found* in Phil 1:10. The same suggestion could be made for *ginomai* in Phil 2:15 of course: "In order that you may be *found* blameless and innocent" (TM). The present tense in 1:10 is used to describe a futuristic state of righteousness where it is stated explicitly to be "in the day of Christ." The aorist of 2:15 indicates that this blamelessness is granted at a punctiliar point in time. That point of time is associated with misthological glory "in the day of Christ" (2:16); therefore, it would refer to being found blameless at the Bema. The present subjunctive of *eimi* in 1:10 could be seen as describing the futuristic enduring result of the Bema, while the aorist subjunctive of *ginomai* could be regarded as alluding to the event of the Bema. Thus, the closely related verbs of *eimi* (*to be*) and *ginomai* (*to become*) could be translated identically in such cases with the understanding, on the basis of tense and basic semantic differences, that believers are to live holy lives so that they may be pronounced misthologically blameless at the Bema and then be regarded as misthologically blameless throughout eternity.

Further corroboration for this misthological understanding could be derived from the verb *approve* (*dokimazo*) used in the beginning of Phil 1:10. Believers are to approve the correct things now so that they may be found approved then. Paul is using *eimi* as a gentle reminder that the testers are to be tested. Whether they pass God's test and are found blameless at the Bema will be dependent on what has passed their test on earth. Compare this misthological usage of *dokimazo* with that of 1Cor 3:13 and 1Pet 1:7, or with the misthological use of its adjectival form (*dokimos*) in 2Tim 2:15 and Jam 1:12. Whether they are approved in that day will be based on what they approve in this day and age. Therefore, *to be* (*eimi*) pure and blameless in the Day of Christ means to be found approved misthologically rather than *disapproved* (*adokimos*; 1Cor 9:27). This would suggest that Phil 1:10 could also be translated: "So that you may approve the things that are excellent, in order that you may be **approved** pure and blameless in the day of Christ." Such a translation would show the sense of the verse, but I have chosen to follow the NAS precedence for *found* rather than use *approved* to show that a different verb (*eimi* rather than *dokimazo*) is being used by Paul to express this meaning. My interpretation of the passage, of course, does not require that either *found* or *approved* be inserted into the translation. Yet the insertion is plausible and does help clarify Paul's thought for the reader and thus is recommended.

Alternatively, the middle form of *ginomai* in Phil 2:15 can be understood readily as *become* in the sense of *in order that you may get to be*. See endnote 150. They are to "Do all things without grumbling or disputing" in v.14, *in order that they may* (1) *be found*, (2) *become*, or (3) *get to be misthologically blameless* in v. 15. This same meaning should be carried over to the parallel in Phil 1:10.

[1059] Robert N. Wilkin, "He Is Able To Keep You From Stumbling! Jude 24." *Grace in Focus* (January-February 1994).

[1060] Hodges, Hebrews, 803.

[1061] Sapaugh, *Wedding*, 24-25

[1062] Ibid.,25, n. 50.

[1063] Chumney, 158.

[1064] In addition to the ultraistic authors already mentioned (such as Govett, Lang, Panton, Pember, Lee, Nee, and Whipple), the works by Finley and Faust should be consulted as concise presentations of the ultraistic position. These works will be the ones primarily referred to in this presentation as representative of the ultraistic position.

[1065] Dillow, 149.

[1066] Ibid., 348, 368.

[1067] Joseph Dillow, "Discipleship in the Sermon on the Mount: A Review of Some Problem Passages." *GES Conference CD*, 2003.

[1068] As expected, Dillow's scholarship is evident in his presentation. For this reason, his argument probably will find advocates in the FG camp and make a modification of the ultraistic position appealing. However, rather than complicate matters even more by interacting with Dillow's new position, the present book will be content to deal with published works of those using similar arguments. Attempting to take Mt 5:20 as denoting a soteriological entrance but regarding 5:22 as dealing with a misthological Gehenna would appear to be a strained approach. Taking both verses misthologically, as the ultraists do, or both verses soteriologically, as the conservatives tend to do, would be more natural.

[1069] Hodges, *Eclipse*, 26-29.

[1070] Hodges, personal correspondence, November 26, 2004.

[1071] See Robert N. Wilkin, "Whoever Says 'You Fool!' Shall Be in Danger of Hell Fire: Matthew 5:22," *GIF* (September 1997).

[1072] First and last place at the table is distinguished from least in the kingdom. In the passages in which first versus last place are used, the context is in reference to the kingdom table. If so, there are three categories of believers: first, last, and least. All three are in the kingdom. The first two are at the table in the kingdom. If so, then the three groups are: faithful, semi-faithful, and unfaithful. In Mt 8:10-12 the contrast is between first and least, not first and last.

[1073] Finley, 62.

[1074] An interesting site that depicts the different mansions pictorially may be found at http://www.raptureme.com/photo/mansions/mansions.html. Accessed on December 14, 2004. Perhaps it would have been better to picture the quitter in a pup tent.

[1075] Alcorn, *Money*, 175.

[1076] Seymour, *Gift*, 166.

[1077] Hodges, *Eclipse*, 97.

[1078] Ibid., 105.

[1079] Tenney, *John*, 143.

[1080] Chumney, 60.

[1081] An objection can be raised from Jn 17:24 regarding my identification of the futuristic place denoted by Jesus as *where I am* as a place of reward. Securitists tend to use Jn 17:24 in defense of eternal security. Indeed, the present book follows this trend. Doing so presents a problem in terms of consistency. If Jn 17:24 unconditionally guarantees that all believers will be with Jesus in this where-I-am place (in heaven or the millennial kingdom), then how can being with Jesus in the same where-I-am place in Jn 14:3-4 be conditional for believers? This question is not easy to answer succinctly because there are a variety of ways to interpret the Lord's Prayer in Jn 17.

[1082] The accounts are combined in order to urge abundant entrance, that is, justification salvation and glorification salvation (Lk 13:23).

[1083] Dillow, 395, n. 23.

[1084] Ibid., 194-199. Hodges, *Eclipse*, 19-23.

[1085] For examples of the misthological usage of *destruction* (*apoleia*), see Acts 8:20; 1Tim 6:9; and Heb 10:39. For soteriological examples, see Mt 7:13; Jn 17:12; Rom 9:22; 2Thess 2:3; and Rev 17:8,11. That *apoleia* can be used both ways is acknowledged by Hodges (*Hebrews*, 807) and Dillow (*Reign*, 337), although they stress the temporal rather than eschatological aspects of its misthological usage.

[1086] Matthew himself has indicated that entrance into the kingdom is based on faith rather than works with sufficient clarity in Mt 21:21-32. The same is probably true in Mt 18:3 as well when it is compared with Mt 19:14 and Mk 10:14-15 (cf. Lk 18:16-17).

[1087] Bing, *Salvation*, 41.

[1088] Pagenkemper, "Part 2," 310. Pagenkemper considers fruit to be a reference to good works due to the emphasis on works in the other separation parables (p. 311). Such an assumption is hardly decisive, however. If some of these parables are describing misthological separation (rather than soteriological separation) and if Mt 7:15-23 is soteriological, then the parallels with the misthological parables are not very decisive. Further, even the soteriological parables (such as the sheep and the goats and the wheat and the tares) entertain the possibility that the sheep and wheat are saved because of what they are (sheep and wheat), not because of what they do. Further, even if it be insisted that a correspondence exists between what they are and what they do (so that fruit refers to works in the present parable), then the possibility still remains of treating this parable like that of the other two (or perhaps even Jn 5:28-29) so that a FG soteriological interpretation of the passage in terms of works might still be possible; although, this is not the hermeneutical course chosen herein.

[1089] R. C. H. Lenski, *The Interpretation of St. Matthew's Gospel* (Minnie-polis: Augsburg Publishing House, 1943), 301-302.

[1090] Picirilli, *Free*, 205.

[1091] Pagenkemper, "Part 2," 319.

[1092] Ibid., 322.

[1093] Ibid., 326.

[1094] Ibid., 328.

[1095] Ibid., 330.

[1096] Ibid., 330-331.

[1097] Keathley IV, "Olivet," 7-8.

[1098] Ibid., 6.

[1099] In addition to the material cited in the text that he borrowed from Pagenkemper, see for example, Keathley IV, "Darkness," 6.

[1100] Pagenkemper, "Part 2," 329.

[1101] Ibid., 329, n. 78.

[1102] Ibid.

[1103] Shank, *Life*, 281.

[1104] Ibid., 15-17.

[1105] When the present author joined GES (in May 1989), one of the first things he did was to consult with Wilkin regarding assurance (personal correspondence, February 1990). The present writer took a three-source approach to assurance, with objective assurance (perhaps in the form of infallible **moral** certainty) being directly derivable from the Word. At that time, the author entertained the idea that subjective secondary assurance by the Spirit could potentially increase this assurance to absolute **formal** philosophical certainty through the supernatural medium of our spirit, and that secondary experiential confirmation was possible as we manifest the fruit of the Spirit. Even if we quench the Spirit and fail to experience the fruit of the Spirit, we still would retain logical assurance in the form of moral certainty. The author's epistemology still allows degrees and types of certainty. Although he would today be more inclined to take a dualistic view and regard the Word as both the objective means to **moral** certainty (through the instrumentality of logic) and the subjective means to **formal** certainty (through the witness of the Spirit). True, it is said that only God can have formal certainty. But since the Spirit can bear witness directly to our spirit that we are saved, this immediate spiritual certainty would be grounded in formal certainty and, therefore, be arguably greater than moral certainty. See Norman L. Geisler, *Baker Encyclopedia of Christian Apologetics* (Grand Rapids: Baker Book House, 1999), s.v. "Certainty/Certitude." Geisler, *Inerrancy*, 344-354. On the other hand, this formal certainty within our spirits cannot be communicated to our consciousness with formal certainty since demonic spirits can impart moral certainty to those who wrongly believe that they are saved. Psychologically, the formal certainty within our spirit would be reduced to moral certainty within our soul during the transmission of this certainty to our consciousness.

Pragmatically, biblically, and logically, the present writer has ceased to find any secondary confirmatory value in either his works or feelings. Works and feelings can give false assurance and conversely cause false doubt. Any secondary value works and feelings may have is theoretical, philosophical, and highly technical. Even worse, secondary soteriological assurance based on works is potentially very dangerous. Our faith should be based exclusively on what the Bible expresses in promises such as Jn 6:47. If we instead ascribe secondary value to works and feelings, we open ourselves up to the temptation to base our assurance, at least in part, on those works and feelings. But soteric assurance based on works leads to faith in works. And faith in works to any degree is the soteriology of an accursed gospel.

Moreover, logically it must be acknowledged that works and feelings may be counterfeit. Even the supposed formal/spiritual certainty can be counterfeited demonically. But absolute certainty is still possible because, although works and feelings are not reliable witnesses, the Bible remains an infallible witness. So the author has come to base his assurance exclusively on the Word and to give no soteriological value to secondary witnesses from works and feelings. His absolute moral certainty that he is saved is completely devoid of any psychological doubt and is grounded directly in God's moral immutability via logical certainty. Logically, there is no room for soteric doubt in FG theology. While the present writer would allow the presence of psychological doubt on the part of those coming to saving faith, since their psychological experience may not be necessarily consistent with the logical certainty they possess, he would hasten to point out that this logical certainty can give stability to their psychological certainty so that there is no need for psychological doubt. Whereas moral doubt is logically necessary for those who are logically consistent outside the FG camp, moral doubt is logically impossible for those who are logically consistent within the FG camp. As one's psychological certainty within the FG camp comes to reflect one's logical certainty, absolute moral certainty will certainly be the result.

The author inferred from Wilkin's comments in *Secure and Sure* that Wilkin had come to a similar understanding: "works play no role" (p. 18); introspection "has no place" (p. 24); "works and feeling play no role" (p. 25). In a personal correspondence (July 30, 2005), the author asked Wilkin if it was not time to change the older GES affirmation, which affirmed that works may have a secondary role. Wilkin agreed, and this assertion regarding the secondary role of works in regard to assurance was dropped from the revised affirmation. See *http://www.faithalone.org/about/beliefs.html*.

[1106] Those living for Jesus tend to use Mt 7:20 as a litmus test to doubt the salvation of those not living for Jesus. However, the context intends the opposite application. The context tends to doubt the salvation of those living for Jesus. As a general rule, those living for Jesus point to their works as (necessary) evidence that they belong to Jesus and thereby reveal that they do not belong to Jesus. The next time you hear someone remark that because so-and-so did such-and-such (such as commit apostasy) this **proves** that so-and-so was never saved, you might remark (with considerable exegetical justification) to the person making the remark that such a remark would tend to prove that he or she is a Proveitist and that the passage was written as a warning to Proveitists. The intent of Mt 7:20 was not to give consolation to tares who question the salvation of those believers who resemble the wheat that sprang forth from the rocky ground or the salvation of the wheat that was choked by the thorny ground. This verse provides no grounds for tares to question the salvation of the wheat. The weed does not have the right to question the regeneration of the wheat.

[1107] If it is objected that the leaven we are to beware of in Lk 12:1, as opposed to Mt 16:11-12, is hypocrisy rather than teaching, one may respond that the most natural place to evaluate the Matthean focus is from Matthew. Second, BKC equates their hypocrisy with their teaching. This harmonizes well with the Lucan context which contrasts what believers are publicly on the outside (which is revealed by their works) with what they are privately on the inside (which is revealed by their words). Quite possibly, Luke intends for his readers to understand hypocrisy in the narrow sense.

[1108] Congdon, "Calvinism," 59.

[1109] While F = J + W is equivalent mathematically to F - W = J, the two statements are not the same theologically in that sequence matters. For a simple chart, see Ken Neff and David Bast, *Hold Fast: Against Christian Myths* (St. Augustine, FL: Leader Quest, 2010), 149.

[1110] Zeller, "Theology."

[1111] Since we are to love our brothers in Christ and yet consider those who teach a false gospel accursed, perhaps we are to love those who name the name of Christ and who yet teach a false gospel as accursed brethren. For all we know, they might be werewolves—genuine sheep who have become wolfish in their behavior or doctrine—instead of genuine wolves. According to Anderson (*Joy*, 223-225), the implication of 1Jn 4:20-21 is that we are required to love anyone who **professes** to be a Christian and not base our love on fruit inspection. Given that we cannot be certain that a professing believer is not a functional wolf rather than an ontological wolf, perhaps we should at least functionally love them as potential brothers. Our love is to function under the premise that they actually may be brethren. Surely, we must do so pragmatically if we are to worship with them in a community in which FG theology virtually does not exist. Better to err on the side of caution and love them as brethren than to risk not loving genuine brethren, I suppose. This would seem to be a biblical recourse when the churches in one's community are full of such creatures. True, Paul has commanded us (collectively) to consider false teachers as accursed (Gal 1:8-9). But when you are the only one in the community who believes in FG, obeying this command collectively is impossible. To be sure, there are commands to *come out* (2Cor 6:17; Rev 18:4), and there are times for separation. But such commands are more clearly applied when matters are black and white, as in the case of worshiping with those who do not name the name of Christ. At other times, it may be necessary to stay put, worship with professing Christians, and morally and doctrinally keep one's own garments clean (Rev 2:24-25; 3:4). The best I have been able to do in such cases is love them as brethren, even if it looks like there is a strong possibility that they will only turn out to have been functional brethren. Our job, as believers, is to love them, not to determine if they are merely functional brethren rather than ontological brethren. Until He comes who separates the wheat from the tares, we (the wheat) will have to love some tares as if they were wheat since we cannot be certain that they are not wheat.

[1112] Whipple, *Matthew*, 104.

[1113] Both passages were spoken to a combination of believers and nonbelievers. Mt 18 explicitly mentions life whereas Mt 5 does not. Nevertheless, both passages are giving an invitation to discipleship.

[1114] When asked for a definition of eternal life, the author supplied this one:

Eternal life is

... a gift and yet a reward.
... a possession and yet an experience.
... a promise and yet a guarantee.
... a future hope and yet a present possession.
... static and yet dynamic.
... quality and yet quantity.
... infinite and yet measured in degrees.
... in Christ and yet is Christ.
... knowing God and yet had by those who do not know God.
... the seed planted and yet the harvest reaped.

... not the result of works and yet something one must work to lay hold of.
... a liquid that cannot be lost and yet a solid that may be taken away.
... a present which must be received and yet which cannot be returned.

Eternal life is quality of existence in that it may be had abundantly. Eternal life is a quantity of existence in that it never ceases. Yet the lost will have endless existence, but they will not have eternal life because eternal life is not just a endless quantity of existence but simultaneously a quality of existence. Living one's entire life for 90 years as a blind beggar is the same quantity of life as one who lives his entire life for 90 years in the lap of luxury. Yet the quality of life is much different. That Jesus guarantees us both qualitative and quantitative life results in eternal security.

Eternal life is as infinite in qualitative height as it is in quantitative length. Our participation in either planar dimension is measured by what point in time we became saved and thus temporally and ontologically entered into this super-temporal flow of eternal existence pictured as the water of life. It is also measured in terms of our experience, by the capacity we misthologically have to participate in the qualitative height and depth of this divine attribute portrayed as the crown and tree of life. Unconditional quality without guaranteed quantity results in conditional security. The same is true of unconditional quantity without guaranteed quality. Eternal life is everlasting quality of existence. Eternal life is eternal and therefore quantitative. Eternal life is life and therefore qualitative.

[1115] Many in OSAS would succumb to the NOSAS argument that Heb 13:5 is limited to temporal security for the faithful (cp. Josh 24:20; 1Chron 28:9; 2Chron 15:2). The emphatic *ou me* thus would be understood as limited in applicability to these faithful believers: "I will never leave you [who are faithful], nor will I ever forsake you [who are faithful]." The reason that OSAS would cave in on this verse is because of its OT background. Corner believes that this phrase is taken from Deuteronomy, and he very well may be correct:

"He will never *leave* (*raphah*) you nor *forsake* (*azab*) you"
(οὐ μή σε ἀνῇ οὔτε μή σε ἐγκαταλίπῃ; Dt 31:6).

"He will never *leave* (*raphah*) you nor *forsake* (*azab*) you"
(οὐδὲ μὴ ἐγκαταλίπῃ σε μὴ φοβοῦ μηδὲ δειλία; Dt 31:8).

"I will never leave you nor forsake you"
(οὐ μή σε ἀνῶ, οὐδ' οὐ μή σε ἐγκαταλείπω; Heb 13:5).

If Dt 31:6,8 does provide the background, then the context of those verses strongly suggests a conditional understanding such as: "I will never forsake you if you never forsake Me" (cp. Dt 31:16-18). But as the reader can see, these parallels are not identical. Morris (EBC) supplies a number of other biblical parallels (e.g., Gen 28:15; 1Chron 28:20; Is 41:17) but thinks that the closest one may be Josh 1:5. To be sure, this parallel uses the first person rather than third person, and if one follows the Hebrew, Morris may be correct.

"I will never *leave* (*raphah*) you nor *forsake* (*azab*) you"
(οὐκ ἐγκαταλείψω σε οὐδὲ ὑπερόψομαί σε, Josh 1:5).

Interestingly, Philo uses this identical phrase in Greek. "On which account an oracle of the all-merciful God has been given, full of gentleness, which shadows forth good hopes to those who love instruction, in these terms: *I will never leave you nor forsake you*" (οὐ μή σε ἀνῶ, οὐδ' οὐ μή σε ἐγκαταλίπω; Philo, Lin 1:166). So Morris speculates that both the writer of Hebrews and Philo may be quoting from a version of the LXX that was current at the time. In fairness to the NOSAS understanding, it should be noted that Philo is limiting the application of this identical phrase to those *who love instruction*, which apparently could be equated with the *faithful*. That said, the present writer finds it unlikely that this is the intent of Heb 13:5 for a number of reasons.

First, it would have posed no difficulty for the writer of Hebrews to have quoted Dt 31:6 or 31:8 verbatim had he intended to signify this as the passage he explicitly had in mind. Instead, he uses a generalization that is not so explicitly linked with contingency. Second, although the phrase is capable of application to the faithful, as Philo indicates, it need not necessarily be limited to the faithful or contingent upon the future faithfulness of the one receiving the promise as seen in Gen 28:15. Third, the context argues against a contingency of faithfulness. The assurance of Heb 13:5 results in the confidence found in Heb 13:6: "We confidently [not cautiously or contingently] say, 'The Lord is my helper, I will not be afraid. What shall man do to me?'" This confidence would seem to rule out human contingence. Otherwise, one would retort from Heb 13:4 that others can temp us to commit fornication, with the result that we will find God to be our judge rather than helper. Balaam and Balak serve as such reminders. Surely, the writer of Hebrews is not so shortsighted so as not to have perceived this possibility if he were talking contingently. Fourth, even if the background does show temporal contingency, it is not absolute contingency. Even though Israel did indeed abandon the Lord, just as Moses predicted, the Lord did not utterly abandon them, as Paul reminds us (Rom 11:1-5). We might likewise move from national to personal application by affirming that even if God temporally and misthologically forsakes a believer, He will not do so soteriologically. There will be a soteriological remnant saved in that believer's life, namely the salvation of his spirit as opposed to his soul, even though the bulk of his or her life is forfeited misthologically. Fifth, this affirmation of soteriological security is in harmony with the affirmations made in Hebrews of Christ sufficiency in permanently taking away our sins once for all. Sixth, limiting Heb 13:5 to temporal prosperity would be very much out of harmony with the use of the OT background being made by the writer of Hebrews who brings out the eschatological applicability of these promises. Let us be assured that the Lord will not leave us soteriologically. As a corollary, since we can have unconditional soteriological assurance and misthological conditional confidence pertaining to the hereafter, we need not think that we must go for the gusto in this present life.

[1116] Bing, "Discipleship," 41.

[1117] Although Wilkin says that both interpretations are possible, he prefers the second. Robert N. Wilkin, Self-Sacrifice and Kingdom Entrance: Part 2 of 2: Matthew 5:29-30," *GIF* (September 1989).

[1118] Finley, 70.

[1119] Wessel, *Mark*, 713.

[1120] Finley, 66.

[1121] The phrase, "of such is the kingdom," is generally assumed by commentators to be a possessive genitive as denoted by their interpreting it in terms of possession. Arndt explicitly calls it a possessive genitive (*Luke*, 382).

[1122] The position taken herein is that to *receive a kingdom* necessarily entails becoming a kingdom *ruler* (Dan 7:18; Lk 19:12; Heb 12:28; Rev 17:12). However, it might be objected that the requirement to enter the kingdom at all is to receive the kingdom like a child (Mk 10:15; Lk 18:17). Syllogistically, this objection might be expressed as:

1. To receive the kingdom is to rule the kingdom.
2. Only those who receive the kingdom will enter the kingdom at all.
3. Therefore, only those who rule the kingdom will enter the kingdom at all.

In this objection, entrance is practically equated with rulership: *enter ≈ rule*. Conditionalists and ultraists might stipulate that only those believers who overcome and thus qualify for kingdom rulership will qualify for kingdom entrance. Or neo-ultraists might argue that only those who receive the kingship now in childlike humility will enter the kingship then.

One problem with such an objection is that it fails to fully appreciate the distinction between receiving a kingdom presently versus eschatologically. Even if the present participle of Heb 12:28 is understood as conveying some sense of inaugurated misthology so that we are occurring receiving a kingdom, it would only be predominately in a potential sense, such as being pictured as already having crowns. These crowns, as well as one's possession of this kingdom, can be forfeited (cp. Rev 3:11). All believers have received the kingdom, in the sense of the potential to rule in the future kingdom, by virtue of having embraced the message of the kingdom, which has as its core the message of grace in which kingdom entrance is conditioned only on childlike faith (depicted by childlike dependency). Children are not called dependents for nothing. Their humility is seen in their dependency. Whether as babies (so Luke) or children, they depend upon (trust in) others to meet their needs. Even babies trust in their mothers for milk. For simplicity sake, one might say that children enter the kingdom because they receive the message of the kingdom in childlike faith. What is literally being received is the kingdom message rather than the kingdom itself: "Whoever does not receive *the message of* the kingdom of God like a child shall not enter it at all." Jesus is using children to refer to present receptivity of the kingdom message as the sufficient condition for future kingdom entrance.

Otherwise, if one insists upon a more technically correct articulation, to receive the kingdom presently is to receive it provisionally and potentially. Only those who receive the kingdom presently (and thus provisionally and potentially) will enter the kingdom eschatologically. The eschatological realization of receiving a kingdom necessarily entails eschatological rulership: no rulership, no kingdom. This does not mean that those who presently, like children, are in a state of humility have not yet received the kingdom provisionally and potentially. Rather, receiving a kingdom in present humility does not nullify its eschatological reality or regality. The eschatological realization of receiving a kingdom necessarily involves living like royalty. To receive a kingdom necessarily entails becoming a kingdom ruler when the time of exercising that rulership comes. Even the nobleman in Lk 19:12 who went into the far country to receive a kingdom was given that kingdom before he returned and exercised the reality of that rulership. So Christ and children of the kingdom already have received the kingdom in one sense, although they are not yet exercising the rights pertaining thereto.

Present childlike reception of the kingdom (by faith) qualifies for kingdom entrance. However, not all who presently have received the kingdom, and thus are qualified to rule the kingdom, will realize that potentiality eschatologically. Those who have received the kingdom in the present will enter the kingdom in the future even if they fail to exercise rulership in that kingdom. Present reception of the kingdom does not assure future rulership. Even so, the statement is still true that the only way to be given a kingdom is as a king. Yet if this kingdom is only given potentially, then so is the kingship. Retranslating *kingdom* as *kingship* does not detract from the fact that those who currently are receiving this kingship are not exercising it. A tension still remains between present reception and future entrance.

Reception of the kingship cannot be equated simplistically with entrance into the kingship. Once again, present reception of the kingship does not assure future entrance into that kingship: *receive now ≠ rule then*.

Thus, Jesus may be understood as saying, "Whoever does not become potentially qualified to be a kingdom ruler now by childlike faith will not enter the kingdom at all then" (Mk 10:15; Lk 18:17). A soteriological entrance then is not to be equated with potential mistological rulership now: *entrance ≠ rulership*. A classical distinction between entering the kingdom and being qualified as a kingdom ruler can be maintained. To be consistent with my preference to regard the *ou me* entry passages as soteric, this classical position is the one adopted here.

Otherwise, a neoclassical position would be preferred, in which case Jesus would be understood as saying, "Whoever does not receive the potential kingship now in childlike humility will not enter the kingship at all then." This neoclassical position in Mk 10:15 and Lk 18:17 would be attractive in that in the previous verse Jesus had just said of the children, "The kingdom of God belongs to such as these" (Mk 10:14; Lk 18:16). The account of the rich young ruler follows immediately, which is quite possibly a neoclassical text. Even given my classical preference, Mk 10:14-15 and Lk 18:16-17 are both neoclassical in that the first verse in each pair is mistholic and the second verse in each pair is soteric. Simultaneous soteric-mistholic dimensions of the kingdom are being discussed. A classic kingdom entrance plus a classic kingdom possession yields a neoclassic composition. The question is not if the passage is neoclassic but if the entrance is neoclassic. I am inclined simply to interpret the entrance classically and to leave the neoclassic impression to the joint presentation of both verses taken together.

1123 Faust, *Rod*, 78.

1124 Pentecost, *Come*, 580.

1125 Larkin, *Revelation*, 206-207.

1126 Walvoord, *Revelation*, 327.

1127 Watson, *Saints*, 114-115.

1128 Patterson, *Work*, 387-388.

1129 The Bride of Christ is composed of the rulers in the New Creation. That Craven believes that the Bride is composed of only overcomers is deduced from his comments that the Bride is probably identical with the 144,000 of Rev 14:1. "Into that glorious company it is probable that only those who have been partakers of Christ's humiliation and suffering...shall be received" (391, n. 5). In short, the Bride is composed of only such partakers. In support of this position, he lists Lk 22:28-30; Phil 3:10-11; 2Thess 1:5; 2Tim 2:12; Rev 2:10,26; 3:12,21; 6:9-11; 19:4-6. By such citations, he indicates that the Bride is composed of overcomers who endure and thus rule with Christ. He continues, "These are they who sit on Christ's Throne, who are united with Him in authority,—who, as *related to* Him constitute the Kingdom, i.e., the governing power" (p. 391, n. 5). Concerning the 144,000 he believes that they were those who had the seal on their forehead (Rev 14:1) and that thus they "constitute a peculiar portion of the redeemed, eminent for faithfulness and nearness to Christ:

> "They are the *first-fruits*, the ἀπαρχή, unto God and to the Lamb" (ch. xiv. 3-5). This fact seems to be indicated by the *number*, which is one of *perfection*, which may well indicate, not merely completeness as to number, but the peculiar excellence, both in character and condition, of the whole body. They are selected from the tribes, the denominations, of the nominal Israel, the visible Church of God (possibly the Jewish as well as the Christian—the latter being the legitimate successor of the former, Rom. xi. 17). By the *sealing* the writer [Craven] understands (probably) a peculiar Christlikeness impressed upon the sealed by the sanctifying influences of the Holy Ghost (p. 193).

"The writer [Craven] expresses no decided opinion as to whether the *Bride*, the subjects of the First Resurrection, will consist of the martyrs; or the whole body of the redeemed; or a select portion including martyrs—the ἀπαρχή, (see p. 193). "He inclines, however, to the last mentioned view" (p. 391). That is, Craven believes the Bride is composed of a select portion of the redeemed rather than all the redeemed. Therefore, his earlier comment that the Bride refers to "the whole body of the saints (the quick and the dead), at the Second Advent of the Lord" (p. 337) should not be understood as indicating that the Bride refers to all the redeemed but that the Bride is composed of both the living and the dead. In short, Craven believes that the Bride is not composed of all believers but only those believers who overcome (regardless of the time period in which they live). One need not necessarily agree with his early observations on all points in order to accept his conclusion. It is not necessary to identify the Bride with the 144,000 or with the overcomers of all ages in order to accept the fact that the Bride is only composed of overcomers. That all overcomers will rule does not, in and of itself, prove that all overcomers are called the Bride. All page references are to John Peter Lange, *Revelation* vol. 24, Commentary on the Holy Scriptures, ed. Philip Schaff (Grand Rapids: Zondervan Publishing House, 1960). All emphases are his.

1130 Lange, *Revelation*, 388, 391.

1131 Paterson, *Life*, 392. Quoting Bickersteth, *Yesterday, To-day, and For Ever*, book 12, line 1482.

1132 Paterson, *Life*, 402. Quoting Bickersteth, *Yesterday, To-day, and For Ever*, book 12, line 6002.

1133 Patterson, *Work*, 386-408.

[1134] Pentecost, *Come*, 563.

[1135] Seiss, *Revelation*, 506.

[1136] Ibid., 491-492.

[1137] Patterson, *Work*, 386.

[1138] Seiss, *Revelation*, 511.

[1139] Govett, *Revelation*, 475-476. For further defense of this position, see his discussion on pp. 349,382-383,433, 441.

[1140] Although the stars are evidently finite in number (Ps 147:4; Is 40:26), they may continue to grow in number throughout eternity as the population continues to grow in number throughout eternity. In the blink of an eye, I would suppose that God could double the number of stars, perhaps even create another spherical universe in addition to our own in hyperspace. The possibilities of growth are infinite.

[1141] Seiss, *Revelation*, 483.

[1142] Ibid., 486-487.

[1143] In Ps 33:11, from generation to generation [NASV] = all generations [ASV].

[1144] Larkin is close to this perception when he says, "As the duration of God's Covenant with Israel was extended in Deut. 7:9 to a 'Thousand Generations' or 33,000 years, we have an intimation that the 'Dispensation of the Fullness of Times' will last for at least that length of time" (Larkin, *Revelation* 202). However, the phrase is figurative rather than literal, but not in the sense of referring to figurative generations. It does not refer to a literal 1000 generations or a literal 33,000 years. Rather, eternity is measured in terms of infinite literal generations.

[1145] Kenneth S. Wuest, *Word Studies in the Greek New Testament*, vol. 4: *The New Testament: An Expanded Translation* (Grand Rapids: Eerdmans Publishing Co., 1984), 453.

[1146] Alcorn, *Heaven*, 257.

[1147] Dillow, 562.

[1148] Lutzer, *Reward*, 157.

[1149] Keathley III, *Revelation*, 297.

[1150] Alcorn, *Heaven*, 224. If Alcorn is correct that there will be talking animals in the eternal state, it should not be supposed that their reproduction will constitute an increase in human government. If animals also talked before the fall, as Alcorn suggests, then the fact that Adam and Eve were to be fruitful and multiple in order to exercise dominion over these talking animals certainly requires that we affirm (via the principle of continuity) that humans will have to reproduce to govern the increase in the animal population. The number of overcomers who are available to rule will be finite. However, the number of subordinate humans could expand infinitely.

[1151] William F. Beirnes, *The Bride, The Lamb's Wife* (Tequesta The Midnight Cry, n.d), 96.

[1152] See Frank D. Carmical, *The Omega Reunion* (Dallas: Redención Viva, 1986).

[1153] Evans, *Best*, 272-273.

[1154] Govett, *Revelation*, 428-430.

[1155] Ibid., 468.

[1156] Patterson, *Work*, 400.

[1157] Baughman, 256.

[1158] Ibid., 247.

[1159] Patterson, *Work*, 387, 392. Govett, *Revelation*, 424-429, 491.

[1160] Seiss, *Revelation*, 501.

[1161] Baughman, 248.

[1162] Govett translates 1Kgs 4:21 as kings rather than kingdoms and appeals to 2Chron 9:26 (*Revelation*, 425).

[1163] Ibid., 274-286).

[1164] Robert Govett, *The New Jerusalem: Our Eternal Home* (Miami Springs: Conley and Schoettle Publishing, Co., 1985), 72,80-81

[1165] Tatford, Revelation, 639. A Google search for *enter by the gates into the city* brought up several on-line works adopting a similar translation: Mungo Ponton, *Glimpses of the Future Life: With an Appendix on the Probable Law of Increase of the Human Race*, 1873 (p. 127). *The Expositor*, vol. 8, 1903 (p. 338). Ernst Wilhelm Hengstenberg, *The Revelation of St John: Expounded for Those who Search the Scriptures*, 1852 (p. 370).

[1166] Even though the *right* to eat of the tree of life is a reward given only to overcomers, might some of those visiting the city in flesh and blood bodies be *allowed* to eat of the fruit (on occasion) without having the right to do so (only any occasion)? Likewise, might subcomers currently living in the city be allowed to eat the fruit until such time that they are rejected from the city?

[1167] Betz, *Stage*, 288.

[1168] When the author's children were young, they would often say, "Uppy Daddy, Uppy." Sometimes, after shopping with their mother for an extended period of time, they would add that their feet were tired and implore their father to pick them up and carry them, adding that they wanted to go home. This intimacy carried over into the family devotions in the desire to see the Lord in the rapture and be held in His arms as His child. The author often sung this song to his boys as a lullaby when he tucked them in at night, teaching them to love the Lord's appearing by picturing the rapture as the Lord Jesus picking them up in His loving arms. During that time frame, one of the author's co-workers asked him, "Do you think of God as above, or beyond, or within?" The author's response was simply, "I think of Him as Daddy."

[1169] A. Sproule, "'Judgment Seat' or 'Awards Podium'?" *Spire* (Spring 1984).

[1170] J.D. Faust, "A Response to Robert L. Sumner's Review of [The Rod]." Available at http://www.kingdom baptist.org/article836.cfm. Available on 4 August, 2004.

[1171] Samuel L. Hoyt, "The Judgment Seat of Christ in Theological Perspective—Part 1: The Judgment Seat of Christ and Unconfessed Sins," *BibSac* 137:545 (January 1980): 32.

[1172] For sake of argument, the assumption has been entertained that these texts relate to soteriological forgiveness. Some of them certainly do. Others may have application to soteriological forgiveness; nevertheless, the primary application is not soteriological. For example, Ps 103:12 is extolling the forgiveness given to obedient believers because of their obedience. Their sins are forgiven *as far as the east is from the west*. The passage is talking about how God deals with those who *fear Him*, which contextually is equated with keeping His commandments:

- So great is His mercy toward *those who fear Him* (Ps 103:11; TM).
- So the Lord has compassion on *those who fear Him* (Ps 103:13).
- The mercy of the Lord is from everlasting to everlasting on *those who fear Him* (Ps 103:17; TM).
- *To those who keep His covenant* and remember His precepts to do them (Ps 103:18).

His children who obey Him are those who fear Him and the ones to whom the benefits expressly and especially apply. The child-Father relation is presumed, yet so is the obedience of the children: "Just as a father has compassion on his children, so the Lord has compassion on those who fear Him" (Ps 103:13). The context is praising God for how He deals with His obedient children. The obedience of all His children is not assumed. How God deals with His disobedient children who do not reverence Him by keeping His commands is not the subject matter of this Psalm. Thus, to assume that all God's children fearfully obey Him goes beyond the Psalm and against other texts that clearly assert otherwise.

Consider the first two benefits listed: "Who pardons all your iniquities, who heals all your diseases" (Ps 103:3). This passage does not deny that God sometimes heals the disease of those who are not His children. God does not necessarily withhold healing from the lost on all occasions. Nevertheless, His obedient children rightly look to Him more confidently for healing. Suppose that when David had an affair with Bathsheba, God afflicted him with diseases, and subsequently when David repented, God removed the diseases. David might well praise God as healing all diseases for those who fearfully obey Him. Even then, however, one cannot regard this praise as an assurance that God always will remove every disease when His children repent. That He does so on some occasions does not guarantee that He will do so on all occasions. Similarly, that God may heal all diseases without distinction does not mean that He necessarily heals all diseases without exception in the present life. Ultimately, God will heal all diseases without exception for His children. Even then, though, experiencing a super abundance of health may be a reward reserved for His obedient children.

As to the first benefit, God sometimes pardons the sins of unbelievers in terms of not bringing temporal calamity upon them. For example, they may repent and avoid some disaster and perhaps even experience some degree of estranged fellowship with God—yet not as His children. Even in the case of believers, some believers have more forgiveness than others. All believers are forgiven of all their sins in regard to being a child of God on their way to heaven. All their sins are forgiven in terms of their relationship with God. Nonetheless, only obedient children have all their sins forgiven in regard to fellowship with God, which is the case here (and in 1Jn 1:7). Accordingly, while it might be said that all God's children have all their sins permanently forgiven *as far as the east is from the west* in terms of their relationship with God, only obedient children have their sins contingently forgiven *as far as the east is from the west* in terms of their fellowship with God. The contingent nature of this forgiveness is presented parabolically in Mt 18:23-35. Only those believers who are obedient to the end of their lives will find their sins removed *as far as the east is from the west* misthologically.

Some might seek to counter and assert that the passage cannot be talking about misthological (or temporal) benefits based on one's performance because it states that God "has not dealt with us according to our sins, nor rewarded us according to our iniquities" (Ps 103:10). However, this counter is nullified by the fact that the very next verse explains that the *us* refers to *those who fear Him,* which in this context would be His children who obey Him. Not being rewarded negatively with what one deserves because of one's positive performance is itself a reward. Therefore, these verses are describing misthological *mercy* (*chesed,* vv. 1,4,8,11,17). Without doubt, the Lord shows mercy even on disobedient unbelievers and perhaps even more so on disobedient believers. Even so, this passage advances beyond these lower forms of mercy to *great mercy*: "For as high as the heavens are above the earth, so *great* is His mercy toward those who fear Him" (Ps 103:11; TM). This Davidic concept of merited mercy has its roots in earlier OT passages. According to Moses, God promises, "I will have mercy through a thousand generations on those who have love for me and keep my laws" (both Ex 20:6 and Dt 5:10 in BBE; cp. Dt 7:9; Dan 9:4). Those believers who lovingly keep God's commandments will be shown the fullest expression of God's mercy as a result. This *great* mercy is described as being as *high as the heavens are above the earth* in v. 11. In v. 4, the soul (who contextually fears the Lord) is described as being *crowned* (*stephanoo*) with mercy. Significantly, this verb was used earlier in a well known Psalm: "You have crowned him with glory and honor" (Ps 8:5; NAU). The NT affirms that Jesus is crowned in this capacity (Heb 2:9), and mankind has the same potential (Heb 2:7). Psalms affirms that this experience denoted by *stephanoo* is available to those who are (experientially) righteous (Ps 5:12). Mercy is available as a crowning reward to God's children who fearfully obey Him. Indeed, *stephanoo* is translatable as *reward*. Thus, Ps 103:4 could be translated appropriately as: "Who *rewards* you with mercy" (TM). Mercy is a reward in this context. Surely, God gives undeserved mercy to the lost on occasion and even to His disobedient children. This passage is not saying that all expressions of God's mercy are limited to God's obedient children. Nevertheless, the *great, crowning, heaven-reaching* dimension of grace being described in this context is a superlative experience of God's mercy bestowed on God's obedient children.

Just because a father loves his own wife and children more than his neighbor's wife and children does not mean that he is a bad father. Indeed, one might well question if he really is a good father if he did not have a special affinity for his own family. Likewise, he is not to be criticized if he has a special love for his children who manifest his godly character. Nor is God to be esteemed lowly just because He especially loves His children who esteem Him fearfully: "The Lord favors those who fear Him, those who hope in His *mercy*" (*chesed*, Ps 147:11; TM). If you want to be shown misthological mercy so that your sins are *as far as the east is from the west* at the Bema, then fearfully keep God's commandments, especially His commandment to show mercy.

[1173] Miles J. Stanford, "Dispensational Disintegration (Part 1)—The Reign of The Servant Kings: A Study on Eternal Security and the Final Significance of Man." Available at http://withchrist.org/MJS/reign.htm. Accessed on August 11, 2004.

[1174] Ibid.

[1175] Ibid.

[1176] Hoyt, "Perspective," 37.

[1177] Stanford, "Part 1."

[1178] Zane C. Hodges, "Justification: A New Covenant Blessing," *JOTGES* 19:37 (Autumn 2006): 83.

[1179] Major W. Ian Thomas, *The Saving Life of Christ* (Grand Rapids: Daybreak Books, 1961), 43.

[1180] Ibid., 37-38.

[1181] Ibid., 25.

[1182] Ibid., 52. Thomas thinks that those who think they are holy are lost, but his understanding of Rom 8:1 inconsistently requires that one be holy to be saved.

[1183] To be worthy of the resurrection (Lk 20:35) means more than just to experience the resurrection, after all even the unrighteous will experience a resurrection (Jn 5:29; Acts 24:15). To be worthy of the resurrection refers to the superlative experience of the out-resurrection. If *worthy* (*kataxioo*, MT) is the correct translation of Lk 21:36, then the meaning is much the same. All believers will appear before the Bema, but only faithful believers will be considered worthy of the event. Similarly, in 2Thess 1:5 faithful believers may be considered misthologically worthy of the kingdom.

[1184] Sauer, 60.

[1185] Ibid., 52.

[1186] Dillow, 412.

[1187] Radmacher, *Disciplemaker*, 179. See also 177, 180.

[1188] Dillow, 520.

[1189] John Niemelä, "If Anyone's Work Is Burned: Scrutinizing Proof-Texts." *CTSJ* 8:1 (January - March 2002): 35-39.

[1190] Lutzer, *Reward*, 63.

[1191] Lutzer might be called an ultra-conservative misthologists in that he correctly discerns the misthological nature of many passages rather than treating them as threats to professing believers (as his fellow Reformed interpreters are so prone to do), yet he fails to affirm that the outer darkness is consistently a misthological term. On the one hand, he will consider the outer darkness as misthological in Mt 25:30 (*Reward*, 55,75-80), but elsewhere he considers it soteriological (p. 168). Albeit, due to the principle of correlativity, I do not find this dual perspective objectionable theologically, only exegetically. Nevertheless, Lutzer's theological shortcomings are evident in various places since he considers our good works to be a gift (p. 14) and our faith to be a gift (p. 24, 99). He conversely considers the gift of our salvation to be a reward for our faith (p. 42) and our rewards to be gifts (p. 144). Too much Reformed theology is left over in his misthology for him to be fully consistent. To his credit, however, even he can affirm that believers are punished at the Bema (p. 78).

[1192] If our workmanship is burned (1Cor 3:15) and we are God's workmanship (Eph 2:10), then is God's workmanship burned? The Calvinist would seem to have to answer, "Yes." I answer, "No." To the degree we respond to God's will, our workmanship represents His workmanship.

[1193] Hodges, *Walking*, 199.

[1194] If last place at the banquet in Lk 14:9 indicates that the believer in question is still allowed to dine at the table rather than be cast into the outer darkness, then one may simply acknowledge that there will be degrees of shame. Those last at the table will not experience as great a shame as those least in the kingdom.

[1195] Samuel L. Hoyt, *The Judgment Seat of Christ: A Biblical and Theological Study* (Milwaukee, WI: Grace Gospel Press, 2011), 108, 144.

[1196] The context of Jam 4:4 shows a reciprocal hostility. On the one hand, they have "hostility toward God," and on the other hand, God is opposed to the proud among them. These proud, self-centered believers should morn for the calamity that awaits them from God. This reciprocating action upon God's people may also be seen in Heb 10:27. Here, they are called *adversaries*, whereas in Jam 4:4 they are called *enemies* (*echthros*). Certainly, one will not have to look far in the OT to find examples of God dealing with his people in an adversarial manner (Num 16:9-10). The basic principle of God dealing with His enemies in fiery wrath is stated clearly in the OT (Is 26:11). As to possibility of a believer being called an *enemy*, it should occasion no surprise that believers behaving in such a manner would be so regarded. After all, Jesus' complimentary statements teach that we are either for Him or against Him (Mt 12:30; Mk 9:40; Lk 9:50; 11:23). There is no neutral ground. The fact that this principle applies to the lost enemy in Lk 19:27 does not mean that only the lost can be an enemy. Understandably, the lost are not excluded from the application of this principle. In fact, Constable is probably right in regarding the *enemies* (*echthros*) of the cross in Phil 3:18 to include both lost and saved antinomians. The need of reconciliation is not limited to the unregenerate. Many of the regenerate stand in need of familial reconciliation with their Father as well.

[1197] Hodges, *Siege*, p. 80.

[1198] Ibid., 77-81.

[1199] Dillow, 139, 452-453, 458-466. Concerning Heb 6:8 he states, "While the immediate reference is certainly to divine discipline in time, the writer of the epistle **probably** has the future consequences of this cursing in mind **as well**. He often speaks of the need to persevere and hence receive our reward" (p. 452). Concerning Heb 10:28-29, "**No doubt** the writer views millennial disinheritance and a failure to enter rest as more severe than physical death." His conclusion concerning the warning in Heb 10 is, "**The most severe punishment**, however, **is** that God will have 'no pleasure in Him [sic].'" When the carnal Christian stands before His Lord **in the last day**, he will not hear Him say, 'Well done, good and faithful servant. Enter into the joy of your Lord'" (p. 466). Dillow does not limit the Hebrew warnings to temporal consequences but believes that the severe punishment "no doubt," or at least "probably," encompasses "millennial disinheritance" "in the last day" "as well."

[1200] Ibid., 453.

[1201] Dillow does not overlook the eschatological nature of the rest since concerning the warnings of Heb 10, he states, "No doubt the writer views millennial disinheritance and a failure to enter the rest as more severe than physical death as well" (p. 462).

[1202] J. Paul Tanner, "A Severe Warning Against Defection: Hebrews 10:26-31," *GES Conference CD* (2006), 13.

[1203] Ibid., 14.

[1204] Ibid., 26.

[1205] Stephen G. Miller, "The Ancient Basis for the Modern Nemean Games." Available at http://ist-socrates .berkeley.edu/~clscs275/Games%20folder/basis.htm. Accessed on December 31, 2004.

[1206] Woodrow Michael Kroll, *It will be Worth it All: A Study in the Believer's Rewards* (Neptune, NJ: Loizeaux Brothers, 1977), 34, 109.

[1207] After all, if there is even one passage that teaches that God may deal with believers punitively, then the PJ position is proven. God may, in fact, deal with believers punitively, and the Bema correspondingly may be punitive and not simply equated with an awards podium.

[1208] One argument employed by partial rapturists is to regard Rev 3:10 and 22:18 as the end pieces of a tribulational sandwich of which believers are warned they may have to partake if they are unfaithful. The first verse is taken as a implicit threat that subcomers will have to undergo the tribulation, and the latter verse is taken as an explicit warning that anyone (including believers) who add to the Scripture will have to suffer the plagues of the tribulation, supposedly by undergoing the tribulation.

In contradistinction, I understand the first passage as a litotetic promise to overcomers, and the nature of litotes is such that it is unsafe to assume that they can be thrown into reverse. In fact, given that Lang is considered one of the ablest proponents of the partial rapture position, his concession made concerning the nature of litotes (in his comments on Rev 2:11) are monumental: "It is not safe to reverse divine statements and draw a negative inference from a positive statement, as is done by inferring here that a believer who does *not* overcome *will* be hurt of the second death" (*Revelation*, 96; emphasis his). Even partial rapturists acknowledge that throwing litotes into reverse is unwise!

As to Rev 22:18, Constable's response is probably adequate: "What Jesus meant was that anyone who perverts the teaching of this book will experience judgment from God that is similar to the judgments that will come upon the earth-dwellers during the Tribulation" (*Revelation*, 216). For a partial rapturist to limit the warning concerning the tribulational plagues of the book to the actual plagues which take place during the tribulation would also entail limiting *anyone* so that it no longer means *everyone*: "I testify to everyone who hears the words of the prophecy of this book: if anyone adds to them, God shall add to him the plagues which are written in this book" (Rev 22:18). Does this warning not apply to those believers who already have died? Yet they will not be alive at the time of the tribulation to undergo the tribulation on earth. So if the plagues must be limited to the actual plagues of the tribulation, most unfaithful believers would be exempt. However, the text suggests no limitation. This suggestion of tribulational wrath is thus not the most natural understanding of the text.

This threat should be understood similarly to that of Dt 7:15, where God assures His children that, if they obey Him, they will be spared the "diseases of Egypt" which they had seen. Instead, He would afflict their enemies with these diseases. Should the Lord implement this punishment, He would certainly not have to take them to the land of Egypt in order to do so—much less back in time! This temporal affliction could be put in effect anytime, anywhere. *The plagues of this book* like *the diseases of Egypt* should be taken as conceptual parallels which refer to plagues that could be effected temporally anytime, not just during the tribulation, and be recognized as bearing the stamp of their respective predecessor or successor based on their similarity. A foretaste of the future plagues of the tribulation are a danger for believers living now in the same way in which an aftertaste of the past plagues of Egypt remained a danger for God's people living then.

[1209] Blomberg, "Degrees," 161.

[1210] Lon Gregg, Gregg, Lon "Model Faith for Christian Service: Matthew 19:28-20:14," *JOTGES* 19:36 (Spring 2006): 26-31.

[1211] Blomberg, "Degrees," 163.

[1212] Ibid., 168-169.

[1213] Ibid., 170.

[1214] Ibid., 172.

[1215] Pagenkemper, "Part 1," 188, n. 30.

[1216] Idem, "Part 2," 327.

[1217] Keathley IV, Olivet, 4.

[1218] The texts from which Ryrie tries to prove universal fruitfulness in *Salvation* include: Lk 15:10 (p. 46); Rom 5:1? combined with Gal 5:22? (p. 46); 1Cor 4:5 (pp. 46, 63); Mt 13:8 (p. 59); Rom 6:7 (p. 132); Heb 12:11? (p. 152). As to Lk 15:10, God's joy in heaven is not identified as our fruit. Even if it were, the text does not need to be taken as a soteriological text. Thus, it would not necessarily be applicable to all believers. Ryrie convolutes *peace with God* and *peace of God*. Peace with God, which all believers have, is not a fruit of the Spirit in the sense described by Paul. Peace with God is a result of regeneration that all believers have regardless of whether they are walking by the Spirit or experiencing the peace of God. Ryrie's assumption from Mt 13:8 presupposes that all genuine believers are good ground, which is false. The fact that sin is no longer our master does not prove that we will no longer live like sin is our master. Ryrie, of all people, should not have used this proof text since he is aware of the significance of the aorist in the related context. The fruit of righteous in Heb 12:11 is produced only in the lives of those believers who submit to God's disciple. Some refuse to submit and become "without discipline" (Heb 12:8) and therefore are without fruit. The passage, in reality, is another passage which indicates that all believers are not fruitful.

Ryrie's understanding of 1Cor 4:5 is grammatically unnecessary and contextually impossible. The contrast of two separate categories in 1Cor 3:11-15 makes it impossible to affirm that Paul is saying that even those believers who are saved *so as through fire* are praised for their workmanship. Further, Niemelä's contextual analysis ("Burned," 35-39) indicates that Paul is not referring to each Christian in 1Cor 4:5, but only to himself and Apollos (cf. 1Cor 4:6). Even so, Paul is not claiming that even he and Apollos will receive praise unconditionally. Instead, he acknowledges that even he himself will be disapproved at the Bema if he does not persevere (1Cor 9:27). Niemelä's attention to the pronouns and contrasts between *we* and *you* should be read in conjunction with the discussion of the present author concerning the exclusive *we* in 1Corinthians (in *Carnal Corinth*). But even aside from such detailed analyses, Paul's statement in 1Cor 4:5 means that each believer will get the praise he or she deserves from God. If they do not deserve any, then they will not receive any. The verse is not a promise that every believer will be praised regardless of the way he or she lives.

[1219] Hodges, *Free*, 215. In general agreement with the basic point both writers are making, the present sectional heading within the text has been adapted from that made by Ryrie ("The Theory of Relativity") in his chapter defending this position, *Salvation*, 47.

[1220] Robert N. Wilkin, "Are Good Works Inevitable." *GIF* (February 1990), 1.

[1221] Zane C. Hodges, "We Believe In: Assurance of Salvation." *JOTGES* 3:2 (Autumn 1990): 7.

[1222] Ibid, 9. See also his comments in *Free*: "Finally, we must add that there is no need to quarrel with the Reformer's view that where there is justifying faith, works will **undoubtedly** exist too. This is a reasonable assumption for any Christian unless he has been converted on his death bed! But it is quite wrong to claim that a life of dedicated obedience is guaranteed by regeneration, or even that such works as there are must be visible to a human observer. God alone may be able to detect the fruits of regeneration in some of His children."

[1223] Wilkin, *Sure*, 147, n. 2.

[1224] Ryrie, *Salvation*, 45. Zeller, "Theology."

[1225] Ryrie, *Salvation*, 52-54.

[1226] Dillow, 308. For the most disappointing statements from Dillow, consider the following: "True faith…cannot coexist with an attitude of determination to continue in sin" (p. 10). If Dillow means that a person cannot continue smoking, drinking, or overeating and still be saved, then I must voice disagreement. Dillow proceeds to say (p. 21): "A man who claims he is a Christian and yet never manifests any change at all has **no** reason to believe he is justified (Mk 4:5,16-17)." On the contrary, in the parable of the sower, the seed produced life without any fruit whatsoever in some of the soil. Not only has Dillow based his misperception on Scripture, he has failed to take into account that the fruit might only be manifest to the Lord rather than to others or even to the believer himself. Dillow continues, "We would have serious doubts about the salvation of a man who claims he is a Christian and gives little or no evidence of it in his life. We could not give assurance of salvation to such an individual" (p. 23). No assurance apart from visible manifestation of transformation! Not hardly. Ryrie's theology is, at times, better than his own exegesis, whereas Dillow's exegesis is, at times, better than his own theology. An ideal blend would be to combine Ryrie's theology of relativity with Dillow's exegetical ability. Dillow again stresses,

> It is impossible to become a Christian and at the same time harbor ideas that one is going to "continue in sin." Becoming a Christian involves repentance….it is *biblically, psychologically,* and spiritually impossible to…cherish ideas of intending to persist in some known sin….The presence of a purpose to continue in sin is incompatible with saving faith. (p. 151)

I am willing to make a limited concession to Moyer at the psychological level. (See endnote pertaining to psychological necessity in *Salvation: A Categorical Analysis.*) Nevertheless, I must ask, "Where is the evidence requiring one to do so at the biblical arena?" Dillow again expresses a theological opinion rather than an exegetically derived result when he says, "Everyone who is born again will necessarily manifest some fruit" (p. 237). "A determination to disobey or to continue in a known disobedience is contrary to saving faith" (p. 279). He appeals to 1Jn 3:10 to find an exegetical basis for his *karpology* (doctrine of fruitfulness): "Since a life of good works reveals who the children of God are, one can only wonder about the genuineness of a man's faith if that man reveals no good works" (p. 308). This sounds like he is asserting that good works determine whether one is saved. It is far better to say that good works reveal the children of God for who they are rather than to say that good works reveal who are children of God. There is no need to turn this text into a soteriological litmus test.

[1227] Robert N. Wilkin, "The Litmus Test of True Believers? First Corinthians 12:3." *Grace in Focus* (January-February 1993).

[1228] Dead works are works done by dead men. Works done by those who are dead in their trespasses and sins in an attempt to gain eternal life as a free gift would be dead works (cp. Eph 2:1; Heb 6:1). Faith without works is dead (Jam 2:20,26). So, too, works without faith are dead. A dead battery is a battery that cannot fulfill its purpose. Dead works cannot fulfill their purpose of gaining soteriological life. Dead faith cannot fulfill its purpose of gaining misthological life.

[1229] Govett, "The Laborers in the Vineyard," *Govett on the Parables* (Miami Springs: Schoettle Publishing Co., 1989): 31-32.

[1230] Zeller, "Theology."

[1231] Niemelä, "Burned," 4-5.

[1232] Keathley IV, "Darkness," 7-8.

[1233] Charles Stanley, *The Wonderful Spirit-Filled Life* (Nashville: Thomas Nelson Publishers, 1992), 107.

[1234] Ibid., 110

[1235] James Dobson, *When God Doesn't Make Sense* (Wheaton: Tyndale House Publishers, 1993), 10.

[1236] Ibid., 40.

[1237] Wilkin, *Confident*, 257, n. 3.

[1238] Bill Gillham, *Lifetime Guarantee* (Eugene: Harvest House Publishers, 1993), 149.

[1239] Alcorn, *Heaven*, 300.

[1240] Corner, *Security*, 184, 188.

[1241] Evasive maneuvers by those seeking to avoid a misthological understanding of Jam 2:5 include taking the preposition *in* (Gr. *en*) to denote rich *in* the sphere or domain of faith. Brown, for example, discounts the qualitative use of *in* and prefers this locative approach. His claim is that faith puts you in a soteriological sphere which automatically makes you rich by making you an heir of the kingdom. He concludes, "there is no higher position or greater wealth an individual can acquire than to become an heir of God through faith in Christ." (*Inheritance*, 161, 226.) The Calvinistic spin on this verse, then, is that *rich in faith* simply means *believer*. Allegedly, God has unconditionally chosen the poor to become believers. Then Calvinists have to explain that *the poor of this world* actually means *the elect of this world*, which is a rather gratuitous assumption. According to this soteriological approach, simple faith, rather than rich faith, is supposedly what makes one rich by virtue of making one an heir of the kingdom. However, Brown's quote of Lk 12:21 to substantiate his point is poorly chosen since the context of that verse indicates that being rich in God's eyes and receiving the kingdom is contingent upon laying up one's treasures in heaven (Lk 12:33-34).

Rich in faith is conceptually antonymic to being *weak in faith* and, therefore, impossible to harmonize with this Calvinistic rhetoric. Some believers are weak in faith; some are strong in faith. In fact, James had just addressed this problem in the previous chapter, where he said that the believer who wavers in faith should not "expect that he will receive anything from the Lord" (Jam 1:7). So why think that such believers will receive the inheritance of the kingdom in Jam 2:5! This is especially true in an epistle that is devoted to showing the necessity of developing a mature, working, living faith so that believers may realize the promised benefits (Jam 1:3-4; 2:17,22). God has contingently predestined, that is, providentially (i.e., circumstantially) predisposed, the poor of this world to trust Him, as opposed to the rich who are more inclined to trust in their riches. The arguments that Hodges gives for a quantitative view of faith in Jam 2:5, therefore, are to be preferred (*James*, 51). It will take a great faith to inherit the kingdom.

[1242] Arminians will sometimes use translations that leave out *to be* in Jam 2:5. And to be sure, the words *to be* are not actually stated by the Greek text. Most translations concur, however, that this verbal affirmation is implied by the text. Aside from such translational considerations, the Marrowistic understanding of this text as a contingent misthological affirmation finds confirmation in other factors as well. The parallelism to Mt 5:3 and Lk 6:20 is apparent. The contexts of both of these parallels confirm that misthological blessings are in view, explicitly confirming this fact with the word *reward* (Mt 5:12; Lk 6:23). The *great* (*polus*) reward in the kingdom of heaven in these contextual parallels will be correspondingly for those who have a *rich* (*plousios*) faith in Jam 2:5. Both words are used quantitatively. Further note that James refers to being *rich in faith*, not to being *rich in the faith*. The thought is not that they are rich merely because they are *in the faith*; rather, they are personally *rich in faith*, and for that reason they are heirs of the kingdom. They are rich because of the personal quantitative quality of their faith, not merely because they belong to the class of those who hold the faith.

This qualitative understanding of James' use of this anarthrous construction is reinforced by the only other time he uses *in faith*, which is in Jam 1:6. Here, James again leaves out the article before faith: "Let him ask *in faith*, without any doubting." The quality of this faith is stressed as not being a faith that is not mixed with any doubting. According to James, the quality of a believer's faith qualifies him or her for answered prayer in the present and for heirship of the kingdom in the future.

Articular constructions, in contrast, can be found in various places: *sound in the faith* (1Cor 16:13), *if you are in the faith* (2Cor 13:5), *sound in the faith* (Tit 1:13), *in the faith which is yours* (2Pet 1:5). This latter reference is personalized by means of the possessive pronoun. This is not to say the anarthrous construction cannot be translated as *in the faith*. Indeed, *in the faith* would seem reasonable renditions for 1Tim 1:2; 3:13; Tit 3:15. But these are the exception rather than the rule. Had James wished to objectify faith, he certainly could have indicated such with the articular construction. As it is, one would presume that he is being consistent with his subjective usage in both 1:6 and 2:5.

[1243] Anderson, "Tale," 71.

[1244] Vic Reasoner, "Golden Chain or Iron Padlock?" Available at http://www.fwponline.cc/v20n1reasoner.html. Accessed on December 21, 2005.

[1245] Some Arminians try to avert the golden-chain argument for OSAS by pointing out that both PEARS and TULIP require perseverance to reach heaven, so TULIP advocates cannot use the chain to avert the necessity of perseverance. While true, this NOSAS response is beside the point if TULIP is in error. This NOSAS counter is meaningless to those who reject TULIP. Other Arminians attempt to offset the individual soteriological applicability of the chain by limiting it to corporate election or by denying that the glorification is eschatological. The cooperate limitation is nullified by the fact that Arminians believe the warning in Rom 8:13 has individual application. The individual believer who lives according to the flesh will die. Therefore, even on Arminian terms, the plurality of the pronouns (we/you) does not prevent an individuality in the application of the warning. Therefore, it cannot be used to limit the applicability of the promises. This election is just as much particular as it is cooperate. As to the attempt to limit the glorification to a temporal affirmation (i.e., we simply have glory in the present as being God's children), the context refutes this feeble claim with its emphasis on the eschatological nature of the glorification.

The superior Arminian response to the golden chain would follow Arminius' argument that election is based on perseverance. As noted in my initial discussion of the chain (see *Illustration 89. Golden Chain of Rom 8:29-30*, 236), the more common Arminian claim about the chain is that those who *stick to it* will be glorified soteriologically. More specifically, **those who persevere are foreknown to do so and are thus assured of glory**. God's election (Rom 8:33) is limited contextually to those elected according to God's purpose who correspondingly love God (Rom 8:28) and who conform to the moral image of Jesus (Rom 8:29). In short, the elect are those who persevere (Rom 8:25). In this estimation, this soteriological glory is limited to those who persevere in their love for God and moral likeness of Christ.

In response, OSAS may rightly object that it is impossible to reconcile the logical order of placing progressive sanctification before *initial* justification in the Arminian chain. One would have to argue for *finial* justification instead. However, a finial justification conditioned on progressive sanctification would necessarily be a misthological justification. If misthological justification were intended in Rom 8:30, then the justification in Rom 8:33 would in turn be misthological. Taking this approach would produce a chain-reaction of turning the chain, and the entire passage in which it is embedded, into an affirmation of misthological security for those who persevere as follows:

The co-sufferings co-heirs are enduring are to result in a co-glory with Christ (Rom 8:17b). This present suffering will be followed eschatologically with the misthological glory that is to be revealed to them as misthological heirs (Rom 8:18) who wait for misthological adoption as sons (Rom 8:23) by persevering (Rom 8:25). God causes all things to work together for the good of misthological heirs because they love Him and walk according to His purpose (Rom 8:28). For whom God foreknew would persevere, He also misthologically predestined to become conformed to the moral and misthological image of His Son, so that Jesus might be the first-born among many misthological brethren. And whom God misthologically predestined, these He also misthologically elected. And whom God misthologically elected, these He also misthologically justified. And whom God misthologically justified, these He also misthologically glorified (Rom 8:29-30). How will God not also graciously give us (i.e., the misthological heirs) all things? (Rom 8:32) Who will bring a misthological charge against God's misthological elect? God is the one who misthologically justifies (Rom 8:33). Who is the one who misthologically condemns God's misthological elect? (Rom 8:34) Who will misthologically separate God's misthological elect from the love of Christ? In all these things misthological heirs overwhelmingly conquer through Him who loved them (Rom 8:37). Nothing will be able to separate misthological overcomers from the misthological love of God, which is in Christ Jesus our Lord (Rom 8:39).

Taken in this manner, the passage could be understood as teaching a perseverance-based election and justification. If so, it affirms misthological security rather than soteriological insecurity. It simply becomes a misthological passage and an exclusively misthological chain. Some of my fellow misthologists may opt for such an approach. But this option would not be available to NOSAS. If perseverance is a misthological issue, then it cannot be a soteriological issue. If it is teaching that perseverance results in co-glorification as a reward, then perseverance is a work in the rewardable sense of the word and as such cannot be a condition for entrance into heaven. Hence, the passage would still provide an indirect affirmation of OSAS. I have not adopted this approach in that I see the passage as an amplification of both parts of Rom 8:17, not just the misthological latter half of the verse. Misthological links are found within the soteriological chain. Regardless as to whether the chain is exclusively soteriological or partially soteriological, Marrowists find the passage to be a direct, rather than indirect, affirmation of OSAS. Nevertheless, I have taken time to point out the alternative of an exclusively misthological chain in order to show that NOSAS has no logically consistent recourse in interpreting the passage.

[1246] As contradictory as it may sound (and actually is), Waterhouse is a FG proponent of conditional security who affirms eternal security. Concerning 1Cor 15:1-2 and Col 1:21-23, two conditional texts, he sells out to conditional security: "Biblical calls to continue in the faith are quite consistent with the security of believers. God uses such Scriptural commands to keep believers in the faith and thereby keep them in salvation" (p. 45). He likewise deduces: "In a hypothetical sense one might lose faith and salvation where it not for God's work of persevering a believer in the faith" (p. 32). "Commands to remain in faith in Christ are one means God uses to keep believers secure" (p. 33). Although he acknowledges that most unconditional securitists would regard 1Pet 1:5 as referring to initial (and thus punctiliar faith), he prefers to side with Arminians in regarding it as referring to ongoing faith as necessary for future soteric salvation. Both he and Arminians are conditional securitists. The major difference being that whereas he thinks that the possibility of losing eternal life is only hypothetical, Arminians insist that it is actual.

Waterhouse's argumentation is the same employed by strong Calvinists who insist that God commands us to persevere (and threatens us with hell if we do not) as a means of keeping the elect saved. One has to preserver in both faith and faithfulness in order to make it to heaven. Entrance into heaven is conditioned on perseverance. Rather than being a blessed assurance, though, this so-called assurance becomes a source of doubt. How can you know that you are elected to persevere? Not by your present faith. For if you are not elected to persevere, your faith will not last. Waterhouse's blessed assurance is not so blessed. See Steven W. Waterhouse, *Blessed Assurance: A Defense of the Doctrine of Eternal Security* (Amarillo: TX: Westcliff Press, 2000). Perhaps a better title for his book would be: *Blessed Hope: A Defense of Soft Calvinism*. See *Illustration 99. Eternal Security—The Rose Between the Thorns*, 271.

To be sure, Waterhouse soft-pedals the conditional nature of his argument as much as possible, even to the point of logical inconsistency. Whereas his above interpretations require that one regard him as a conditional securest, he attempts to offset that conclusion by insisting, "Endurance of persecution in the Tribulation will not earn or retain salvation, but it does demonstrate it" (p. 23). Not so, if one adopts his above interpretations. According to Waterhouse, God commands believers to preserver in faith because their perseverance is His means of enabling them to retain their salvation from hell. Supposedly, not practicing sin is only "practical evidence that a person has never possessed salvation" (p. 42). Such a statement would be more consistent with strong Calvinism in that it makes reaching heaven conditioned on not practicing sin. Again, he downplays the conditional nature of his own position by acknowledging that one cannot use his position to make a categorical denial that professing believers who practice sin are lost. (For some believers practice sin more than unbelievers!) Thus, one may leave him in the soft Calvinistic camp. The point that Waterhouse is most emphatic about is that genuine believes will never deny Christ in their hearts, although they may deny Him with their mouths (p. 25).

In response, the passages mentioned above (1Cor 15:1-2; Col 1:21-23; 1Pet 1:5) do teach conditional security. Waterhouse was correct in this assessment. Where he erred was in regarding them as dealing with soteric security rather than mistholic security. As to the mark of the beast, Marrowists agree that genuine believers will not take the mark. If you are living during the tribulation and take the mark of the beast, this will prove that you are not a genuine believer. This poses a problem for assurance of salvation from Waterhouse's model in that the only way you can know that you are saved is to persevere. If you fail to persevere, then this will prove that your faith was not genuine.

The securitist model does not suffer from this defect. If you are a genuine believer, then you can know you are a genuine believer because your faith is in Christ alone for unconditional security—a security not conditioned on your not taking the mark of the beast. The assurance of your salvation has nothing to do with whether you take the mark of the beast. However, given the conditions of the tribulation, if you are a believer living in that time period, you will be able to deduce that if you succumb to the desire to take the mark of the beast, then God will kill you before you actually have a chance to carry out that course of action. Does He do so in order to keep you saved from hell? No. He does so because He has determined that no child of His will go to hell and that no one who takes the mark of the beast will go to heaven. Further, because He has determined that the salvation of His children is not conditioned on their not taking the mark of the beast, He has conditioned the preservation of their physical life (and misthological life) on their not taking the mark. The mark of the beast does not have the power to send a child of God to hell, but it does have the power to send him or her to the outer darkness. Those believers who succumb in intent to the mark will spend eternity in the outer darkness.

In this sense, the mark of the beast has the power to hurt the child of God misthologically. Even today, sin has the power to hurt the child of God misthologically. Sin hurts. More than many of God's children realize. Most of God's children have learned that sin can hurt very badly in this life. They need to realize that it can hurt profoundly in the life to come. Neither the practice of sin nor this particular form of sin have the power to hurt the child of God soteriologically; nevertheless, the child of God can be hurt severely by sin.

As to Waterhouse trying to water down his conditional security by only insisting that believers will never cease to believe in their hearts, I would remind the reader that some believers have become atheists. Surely, at one time some of them thought that they were genuine believers who would never fall into atheism. Yet the Bible warns: "Therefore let him who thinks he stands take heed lest he fall" (1Cor 10:12). Does Waterhouse suppose that he is immune to falling? In any case, as a securitist I would acknowledge that although the danger of falling into sin is real (hence I need to seek the God-appointed ways of escaping it, 1Cor 10:13), my salvation from hell is not conditioned on my not falling into sin. I can know with absolute assurance that I am God's child despite my prone-to-wander heart. At the same time, I know that at the core of my being I cannot sin (the proper understanding of 1Jn 3:9). Also, I may further deduce that I cannot deny Christ in my spirit. My spirit with the Holy Spirit will continue to bear witness that I am a believer (Rom 8:16). For a more positive theoretical assessment of what Waterhouse is trying to do, see soft securitists in 3D *Unconditional Security*. Perhaps Waterhouse might be pictured in the gray zone. Even so, he is too gray to be pictured as falling within the sphere of unconditional security.

[1247] Geisler, *Security*, 68,76, 86, 109, 110.

[1248] Gordon Olson, *Calvinism*, 320, 344.

[1249] Ibid, 302.

[1250] Ibid, 316.

[1251] Ibid, 318.

[1252] Ibid, 233.

[1253] John Calvin, "Chapter 23. Refutation of the Calumnies by which this Doctrine is Always Unjustly Assailed." Available at http://www.ccel.org/ccelcalvin/institutes.v.xxiv.html. Accessed on August 25, 2007.

[1254] C. S. Lewis, *Mere Christianity: A Revised and Amplified Edition With a New Introduction of the Three Books: Broadcast Talks, Christian Behavior, and Beyond Personality*, Harper Collins edition (Harper San Francisco, 2001), 9-10.

[1255] Ibid., 47-48.

[1256] Peterson and Williams, 136-138.

[1257] Ibid., 148.

[1258] Ibid., 156.

[1259] Ibid., 158-160.

[1260] The appeal by Peterson and Williams to dual agency is beside the point (p. 152). They already had acknowledged that libertarians affirm it (p. 140). As it pertains to the inspiration of Scripture, Geisler explains it in terms of primary versus secondary efficient causes. Doing so allows Geisler to account for the fall of Lucifer as well (*Reason*, 176-177). As to the latter, his second chapter in *Chosen* is a classic (see also p. 182).

[1261] Ibid., 64.

[1262] Ibid., 96.

[1263] Ibid.

[1264] Ibid., 104.

[1265] Ibid., 98.

[1266] Ibid.

[1267] Walls and Dongell, 132.

[1268] Corner, *Security*, 618.

[1269] Idem, 658.

[1270] Ibid.

[1271] Shank, *Life*, 278.

[1272] Constable, *Jude*, 19.

[1273] Neil T. Anderson, *Victory over the Darkness*: with Study Guide (Oxford: Monarch Books, 2007), 278.

[1274] Ibid., 52.

[1275] The proposition Marrowism affirms is: (P1) "You must believe in OSAS." Some mistakenly think that this means that Marrowists affirm a second proposition: (P2) "You must believe that you must believe in OSAS." In other words, you would have to believe in the necessity of believing that belief in OSAS is necessary. Many in GES affirm the (P1) *first proposition*, and I will refer to this group as P1 respectively. Yet, to my knowledge, no one affirms the (P2) *second proposition* since it is one step farther removed from the logical consistency necessary to believe Christ's offer. Christ requires that we believe that He has given us eternal life, as opposed to conditional life, by simply believing in Him for the prolific offer. Since the second proposition is one step further removed from what is necessary, the second proposition is not necessary: P1 is necessary; P2 is not.

However, many in FG who believe in OSAS would counter that even P1 is one step further removed from what is necessary. Therefore, they would argue that there are (P0) *zero propositions* concerning OSAS that must necessarily be affirmed for saving faith: "You do not have to believe in OSAS." Such FG advocates believe in OSAS but do not believe that this belief is necessary for saving faith.

- P0   FG view which affirms OSAS as true but unnecessary.
- P1   FG view which affirms OSAS as true and necessary.
- P2   FG view which affirms the necessity of affirming OSAS as true and necessary.

Both P0 and P1 believe in OSAS, and neither group denies the salvation of the other group. P0 does not believe that believing in OSAS is necessary. P1 believes that believing in OSAS is necessary. Thus, in P1 the requirement is that you believe in OSAS, not (P2) that you believe in the necessity of the belief in OSAS. So the salvation of those in P0 is affirmed by P1 since P0 affirms OSAS.

Those in P0 believe that OSAS can be deduced logically but do not see it as imperatively necessary. Both P0 and P1 acknowledge that the imperative is that we believe in Christ for eternal life. From a P1 perspective, since the imperative is that one believes in Christ for eternal life, if one believes in Christ for conditional life instead of eternal life, then one has failed to believe in Christ for eternal life. Consequently, one has failed to meet the stated condition and consequently has failed to receive eternal life.

As to P1, not only can OSAS be deduced logically, but the necessity of believing in OSAS can be logically deduced also. Since a person cannot logically believe in Christ for salvation from hell and still believe that he or she might still go to hell, P1 perceives P0 as teaching nonsense. Thus, P1 rejects the P0 notion that it is possible to believe in Christ for probation and be given salvation instead. Moreover, since NOSAS asserts that a person must persevere in order to make it to heaven, P0 logically is asserting that one can believe in this false gospel of salvation by works and still become saved. P1, in contrast, does not believe a person can be saved by believing in this false gospel.

Thankfully, P0 advocates do not accept this false gospel themselves since they themselves believe in OSAS. Nevertheless, the permissive attitude P0 takes toward NOSAS fails to confront those taking the wide road leading to destruction with the fact that NOSAS actually results in a defective form of the gospel that cannot save. P0 is leaving the NOSAS proponent with the false perception that getting to heaven can be based on one's performance, specifically perseverance in faith. This accursed form of the gospel leads to hell. Those in P0 will be saved from hell because those in P0 have accepted the OSAS serum. But by failing to insist that others take this OSAS serum and by making it optional, P0 is giving the false impression to those infected with NOSAS that they can make it to heaven while still trusting in their performance. Many of those fatally infected with NOSAS may fail to take the OSAS serum because P0 promised them that it was optional. Therefore, the blood of those NOSAS causalities may very well be found on the hands of those in P0.

[1276] When one trusts in a medic, one naturally trusts in the medic's medicine. Conversely, when one trusts in this medicine, one naturally trusts in the medic. Likewise, saving faith in Christ is to trust in Him for eternal life.

[1277] As explained more fully in my introductory level writings. Jesus could not die in the sense of completely losing eternal life. Technically, Jesus could lose eternal life only to a certain extent. Certainly, He could not lose eternal life in the sense of losing an attribute that is essential to His existence as God. However, the basic possession of eternal life is, by its very nature, permanent. Thus, not even His possession of eternal life could drop below a certain threshold. A correlation exists between His threshold and ours. The line of eternal life quantitatively stretches linearly into eternity future and must be graphed with an unbroken line because there is a soteriological threshold.

Illustration 376. Did Jesus Lose Eternal Life?

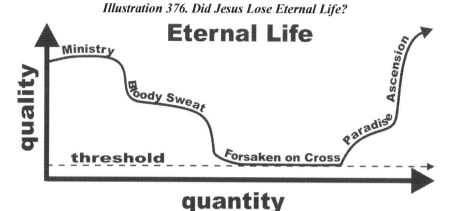

Jesus lost eternal life qualitatively in that experience on the cross. Even so, His loss of eternal life could not drop below the qualitative threshold (and neither can ours). Since spiritual death is defined as separation from God, one might even say that Jesus experienced spiritual death on the cross. Nonetheless, not even in that experience could He experience the complete death of eternal life. His static possession of eternal life remained intact. He could give up His dynamic personal exercise of that attribute but not His static possession of such an attribute.

Illustration 377. Threshold Between Gift and Reward

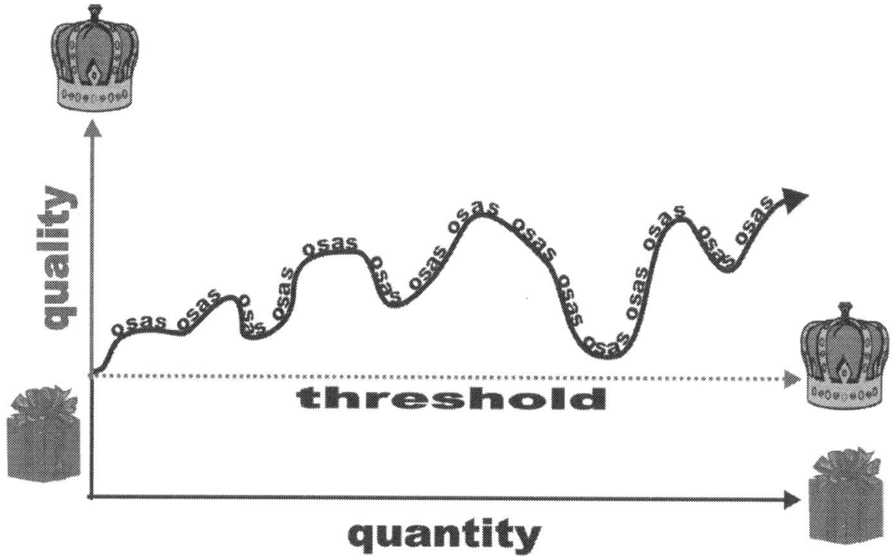

Qualitatively, eternal life can be a reward once the reward dimension of eternal life passes beyond the basic soteriological threshold. The quantitative (horizontal) aspect should be self-apparent: Eternal life is eternal. Thus, if you have eternal life, you cannot lose it in the sense that it could dip below the soteric threshold and so nullify having the gift of eternal life.

Illustration 378. Extrapolation of Misthological Death

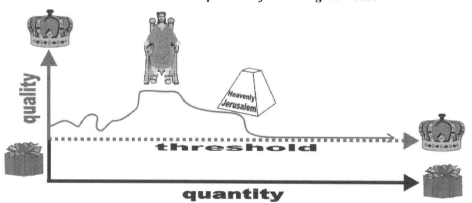

Misthological death occurs when the effects of the Bema are carried out. When unfaithful believers are expelled from Heavenly Jerusalem (to live in more remote locations of the kingdom) and are excluded from the privilege of ruling with Christ throughout eternity, their qualitative experience of eternal life will flat line into misthological death. Qualitatively, in terms of having misthological life, these believers will reap misthological death (cp. Rom 8:13). Nevertheless, in terms of retaining their quantitative possession of eternal life as a free gift and entering the kingdom and living within it, their experience of eternal life cannot drop below the soteriological threshold. For further discussion and illustrations of this threshold as it impacts misthology, see *Sheep and Goats: Four Misthological Interpretations.*

[1278] In order to receive these consequences, a person must at least come to the basic OSAS realization for at least one such proposition (such as: regeneration, justification, or salvation). In other words, OSAS is the lowest common denominator for all three propositions concerning soteriologically having regeneration, justification, and salvation. The essence of the gospel of grace is OSAS. Eternal security is the objective, soteric content of the gospel. It cannot be fragmented and still perform its saving function.

[1279] I acknowledge that dispensationalists, such as Chafer, who were instrumental in developing the recent articulation of FG theology may have believed that all believers will perseverance in faith and that they stressed security rather than perseverance. Nevertheless, the dispensational cleavage to this Calvinistic baggage cannot be logically maintained without serious compromise to the gospel and theological consistency. Notwithstanding, I do place soft securitists within the sphere of unconditional security. See *3D Unconditional Security.*

[1280] Randy C. Alcorn, *Money Possessions and Eternity* (Wheaton: Tyndale House Publications, 1989), 125, 130.

[1281] Alcorn, *Rewards*, 116.

[1282] Faust, *Rod*, 36.

[1283] Dillow, 592.

[1284] Matt Perman, "The Joy of Heavenly Rewards." Available at http://www.geocities.com/Athens/Delphi/8449/reward.html. Accessed on April 27, 2005.

[1285] Hodges, *Eclipse, 50.*

[1286] Zane C. Hodges, "We Believe In: Rewards." *JOTGES* 4:2 (Autumn 1991): 7.

[1287] Alcorn, *Rewards*, 106.

[1288] Dillow, 529, 554.

[1289] Faust, *Rod*, 30, 36.

[1290] In a television interview, in which the atheistic author of *Good Without God* was espousing the virtues of humanism, he said that it is kind of sad when someone believes that the only reason we should live a good life is because of hope for divine reward. He retorted that compassion is the center of humanism. As I was watching the interview with my family, I burst out laughing as the speaker continued to explain that the best way to help oneself is to help others. In that statement, the speaker unwittingly confessed the desire for rewards interwoven in his own personal motivation to help others. The logical basis of his appeal was: *Help others to help yourself. Help others because of the help one derives for oneself.* Apparently, the speaker meant that the way we help ourselves feel better about ourselves is by helping others. The atheistic reward one gets for helping others is a better feeling about oneself. Even in the act of denying rewards as a proper motivation for behavior, this atheist refuted himself by making rewards an appropriate motivation for compassion. Both Christians and this atheist are motivated by the desire to feel pleasure. Christians believe that they will feel pleasure for eternity, atheists believe that they will only experience this pleasure temporarily. Christians are motivated by eternal pleasure, atheists by fleeting pleasure.

For a philosophical acknowledgement that atheists can be good, see Copan's two chapters ("We can be Good Without God," chs. 17-18). God's existence and mankind being made in the image of God makes it possible for even atheists to be good. Paul Copan, *True for You but Not for Me*, revised edition (Bloomington, MN: Bethany House, 2009), 98-108. Also see my "Good Without God" in *Woolly Wolves and Woolless Sheep* for the addition of common grace as a means of enablement. Copan makes the same point (p. 138).

[1291] NIDNTT, s.v. "Recompense: μισθός," by P. C. Böttger.

[1292] Ron Barnes, *A Hero's Welcome: A Dissertation on the Doctrine of Future Rewards with Special Emphasis on the Bema Seat of Christ* (Graphic Business Solutions, 1997), 256.

[1293] Barnes, 285.

[1294] Böttger.

[1295] Constable, *Psalms*, 205.

[1296] Likewise, Ecc 5:19 is not an example of a reward being called a gift; rather, the opportunity to earn the reward is a gift. Thus, the reward is an example of condign merit: "As for every man to whom God has given riches and wealth, He has also empowered him to eat from them and to receive his *reward* and rejoice in his labor; this is the *gift* of God." This verse is not saying: reward = gift. Rather, gift → reward. The reward follows the gift. The *potential* to experience reward from one's labor *is a gift*. This does not detract from the fact that the reward ≠ gift.

[1297] Böttger.

[1298] Ibid.

[1299] Ibid.

[1300] D. M. Panton, *The Judgment Seat of Christ* (Miami Springs: Schoettle Publishing Co., 1984), 7.

[1301] Leon Morris, *Hebrews*, vol. 12, EBC (Grand Rapids: Zondervan Publishing House, 1976), 134.

[1302] Donald Guthrie, *Hebrews*, vol. 15, TNTC, ed. R. V. G. Tasker (Grand Rapids: Eerdmans Publishing Co., 1983), 251.

[1303] R. C. H. Lenski, *The Interpretation of the Epistle to the Hebrews and the Epistle of James* (Minneapolis: Augsburg Publishing House, 1966), 428-429.

[1304] M. Haldeman, *Ten Sermons on the Second Coming of Our Lord Jesus Christ* (Chicago: Fleming H. Revell Co., n.d.). 351-352.

[1305] Erich Sauer, *In the Arena of Faith* (Grand Rapids, Wm. B. Eerdmans Publishing Company, 1955), 24.

[1306] Radmacher also addresses this issue: "I run into some people who say, 'Well, I don't believe you ought to work for reward, I believe you ought to work for the Lord.' I want to submit something to you. It's impossible for you to work for the Lord *without* working for reward because the delight of the heart of Jesus Christ will be to give out all the rewards that He can possibly fairly give out" (p. 41). "The motivation to good works is the Judgment Seat of Christ" (p. 38). Earl D. Radmacher, "Believers and the Bema," *JOTGES* 8:14 (SPRING 1995): 31-43.

[1307] Alcorn, *Rewards*, 107.

[1308] NIDNTT, s.v. "Infant Baptism: Its Background and Theology," by R. T. Beckwith.

[1309] NIDNTT, s.v. "Baptism," by G. R. Beasley-Murray.

[1310] Chitwood, *Judgment* (1986), 173-177.

[1311] Leon Morris, *The Gospel According to John*, NIC, ed. F. F. Bruce (Grand Rapids: Eerdmans Publishing Co., 1983), 218, n. 35.

[1312] Chitwood, *Judgment* (1986), 174.

[1313] The case for temporal wrath is so strong that some claim that it (*orge*) is never used of soteriological wrath in the NT, meaning it never refers to hell. Indeed, the instances of *wrath to come* could refer to the temporal wrath of the tribulation. Admittedly, even the wrath in Jn 3:36 is one that presently, and therefore temporally, abides on the unbeliever. On the other hand, the temporal expression of this wrath in Jn 3:36 does not appear to limit it to the present period since it is equated with not having eternal life by faith. Consequently, this temporal wrath, at least in this one verse, is best understood as having soteriological dimensions. As usual, context determines what range of meaning is intended.

[1314] Donald Guthrie, *John*. NBC, ed. D. Guthrie and J. A. Motyer (Grand Rapids: Eerdmans Publishing Co., 1970). 936. Cited by Zane C. Hodges, "Problem Passages in the Gospel of John—Part 3: Water and Spirit—John 3:5," *BibSac* 135:539 (July 1978): 212.

[1315] From Hodges' perspective, Jesus is saying in Jn 3:5 that one must be born "of water and wind," which "can serve as a double metaphor for the work of the Holy Spirit as that work is reflected in the Old Testament Scriptures" ("Water," 218). Indeed, the word for *Spirit* can be translated as *wind*, as indeed is the case in Jn 3:8. Although writing concerning Pentecost, Watson's words support Hodges' observation: "I have examined every passage in the Bible which compares the operations of the Spirit to wind, or to breath, and I find in every passage the reference is exclusively to giving life. The wind is never a type of sanctification, or bestowment of power, but the impartation of life; as: 'God breathed into his nostrils the breath of life,' and 'Come, O wind, upon these slain, that they may live.'" George D. Watson, *The Bridehood Saints* (Cincinnati: God's Revivalist Office, 1913), 89.

[1316] NIDNTT, s.v. "Discipline: πορνεύω," by H. Reisser.

[1317] Morris, John, 216. In contrast, Hodges surmises, "The materials Odeberg collects are certainly interesting, but fail to carry conviction in respect to the Johannine passage." Hodges, "Water," 212, n. 12.

[1318] Morris, *John*, 216. He supports this interpretation from the grammar "in that neither noun has the article and the one preposition governs both" (p. 216, n. 29).

[1319] Hugo Odeberg, The Forth Gospel Interpreted in Its Relation to Contemporaneous Religious Currents in Palestine and the Hellenistic-Oriental World (Uppsala: n.p., 1929; reprint ed., Chicago: Argonaut Publishers, 1968), 49, cf. 48-71.

[1320] Also, recall that the seed sprang up in Mt 13:5 and Mk 4:5 and thus produced life. One point of the parable is that some believers who have been born again (germination picturing regeneration) may fail to produce good fruits. Spiritual life does not inevitably result in spiritual fruits, much less in perseverance in producing spiritual fruits.

[1321] Odeberg, *Gospel*, 48-49, 67.

[1322] Zeller, "Theology."

[1323] Robert N. Wilkin, "Christians Who Lose Their Legacy: Galatians 5:21." *JOTGES* 4:2 (Autumn 1991): 23-37.

[1324] NIDNTT, s.v. "King," by B. Klappert. Unfortunately, it appears that Klappert has mistakenly cited the LXX as using nominal *basileia* in Ex 19:6 when, actually, it is the adjectival *basileios*. But his argument still appears to be intact, and I omitted the errant part of his statement from my quotation.

[1325] Ernest Best, *1 Peter*, NCB (London: Oliphants Ltd., 1971), 108.

[1326] Personal correspondence, Finley, 8/16/1995.

[1327] Dillow (p. 75) also uses the same argument that Hodges does when he implies that, since inheriting the kingdom suggests more than merely entering it, many will enter it who will not inherit it (i.e., *inherit > enter*).

[1328] Ibid., 78,99.

[1329] Ibid., 99-102.

[1330] Ibid., 99.

[1331] Ibid., 100.

[1332] Some ultraists (and moderates) reject the conservative argument concerning Jn 3:5 by either arguing that the entrance in Jn 3:5 is millennial entrance merited through discipleship (i.e., baptism), or they take Lee's position that Jn 3:5 is referring to present unmerited entrance into the kingdom by faith but then stipulate that entrance into the millennial kingdom is merited by discipleship.

[1333] Faust, *Rod*, 67-69.

[1334] It is beyond the purpose of my chart to differentiate between the mystery, mystical, and millennial forms of the kingdom. But to summarize the definitions that have been stated previously, the mystery form is the present form which includes both professing believers and believers. The mystical form is the present form into which only believers enter. The millennium form is the future form into which only believers will enter.

[1335] Mershon entertains an interpretation of Mk 1:15 similar to what I have adopted and yet rejects it in favor of opting for a faith which has the misthological offer of the kingdom in focus (*Mark*, GNTC, 142). His assessment is attractive and perhaps preferable. Nevertheless, I retain the soteriological dimension because of Jn 1:7.

[1336] This passage in Mt 5:6 is sometimes used unwittingly by some in FG to argue that only those who acknowledge their sin and desire righteousness can be saved. The author will slip his old LS shoes back on momentarily to demonstrate how this FG perspective is incompatible with FG theology.

LS might stipulate that if you want to have the satisfaction of having imputed righteousness, then you must hunger and thirst for practical righteousness. Genuine brokenness over one's sinfulness must produce a corresponding desire for behavioral righteousness. Lack of desire to change one's sinful behavior, therefore, is proof that one does not genuinely meet the prerequisite for the appropriation of soteriological righteousness. In short, only those who really want to change their behavior can be saved from hell, and this salvation will necessarily entail a change in behavior as Jesus has promised here: Those who thirst for righteousness will be satisfied. Imputed righteousness cannot be divorced from practical righteousness. Justification cannot be had apart from sanctification. The gift of salvation is a package which entails both. This LS argumentation can also be buttressed by noting that Jesus only promises soteriological freedom from sin to those who not only believe in Him but who acknowledge their sin and abide in Him. The desire to live in sin prohibits one from being saved from sin and will result in one dying in one's sins (Jn 8:30-36). Only those who desire escape from sin are genuine believers.

Now, stepping back into my FG shoes, it may be countered that the context of Mt 5:6 evidences that misthological, rather than soteriological, blessings are in view. Believers who long for experiential righteousness will be satisfied with the crown of righteousness (2Tim 4:8). This verse is not demanding that one desire righteousness in order to be saved from hell. As to the auxiliary support, those who believe in Jesus are freed soteriologically from the penalty of sin (Jn 8:24), whereas those believers who abide in Jesus experience a temporal victory over the power of sin (Jn 8:32). Experiential freedom is neither *equated with* nor *automated from* its underlying soteriological freedom.

Whether the recognition of one's own sinful dilemma is a theological necessity at the hypothetical level, it is certain that in many cases it is a psychological necessity. A self-righteous Pharisee, or his modern LS counterpart, in all reality cannot be brought to the point of trusting in Christ without first recognizing his sinful quandary and thus abandoning all trust in self-effort. However, the biblical requirement is only that one simply desires the water of eternal life and drinks it by trusting in Christ alone (Rev 22:17). Technically, it would seem, a grasp of *hamartiology* (the doctrine of sinfulness from the Greek word *hamartia*) is not a universal necessity in order to partake of this benefit. The small child, the poorly informed, or the mentally handicapped—who hear the message that God loves them and has made it possible for them to live with God forever in heaven by simply trusting in His Son, Jesus Christ, for eternal life—may be assured that he or she will live with God forever in heaven. On the other hand, for stubborn mules that are lead to the water of life but refuse to drink, the doctrine of hamartiology is a good way to salt their oats and create a thirst; as a practical necessity, this may be the only means by which they will be brought to the point of taking a drink.

[1337] What is the crown of righteousness (2Tim 4:8)? Evidently, an increased ability and capacity to experience and manifest the specific benefit bestowed is entailed by each respective crown. Those believers who receive the crown of life, for example, will have a greater qualitative experience of life than those believers who do not (Jam 1:12; Rev 2:10). The benefits bestowed by this crown are rather easy to picture because one may easily associate it with the tree of life and special access to the fountainhead of the water of life. Similarly, those believers who receive the crown of rejoicing will rejoice more subjectively and have more to rejoice over objectively than those believers who do not receive this crown (1Thess 2:19). This crown is also called the soul-winners crown and thus easily pictured as having a greater degree of joy in heaven because of the souls one has won for the Lord. Those believers who receive the crown of glory will have more glory than others (1Pet 5:4). This crown is not difficult to picture because we are accustomed to thinking of some believers receiving more glory than other believers and manifesting that differentiation in glory like stars

(1Cor 15:41). But what is to be made out of the crown of righteousness? What mental imagery should be used for this crown? From the fact that righteousness is rewarded to a select group of believers, as opposed to all believers, it must be deduced that, although all believers will be sinless, some believers will be more righteous than others.

One person being more righteous than another is certainly nothing new in Scripture (Gen 38:26; 1Sam 24:17; 1Kings 2:32; Jer 3:11; Hab 1:13). While on the one hand it might be said that none are (absolutely) righteous practically speaking (Rom 3:10), on the other hand it may be said that some are (comparatively) righteous practically speaking. The crown of righteousness cannot refer to the imputation of soteric righteousness. For in that capacity, no believer is unrighteous to any degree. A practical, comparative righteousness must be intended by Scripture by means of the crown. The Scripture does not fail to provide tantalizing clues as to what the crown of righteousness may entail. Being crowned with the crown of righteousness as a reward would seem to be very much akin to being clothed with the robe of righteousness (Is 61:10)—a righteousness that shines brightly (Is 62:1) and can be seen by others (Is 62:2). Being given a crown of righteousness by God would go hand in hand with being declared righteous by works before God and being called a "friend of God" (Jam 2:21,24-25).

An increased ability to administer justice (1Kgs 3:28; Jer 21:12) would seem to be a natural reward for those who hunger and thirst for personal and social righteousness (Mt 5:6). Their increased capacity to live and rule rightly before God will allow them to be entrusted with opportunities to display that supernaturally enhanced ability. This righteousness is not a gift, but a reward. Every day as I pray through the Ephesian armor, I ask in regard to the breastplate of righteousness (Eph 6:14) that the Lord will do, say, think, desire, and write the right thing in and through me and to deliver me from error in what I do, say, think, desire, write, and pray so that I may live in His will and pray in His will. Yet I am ever mindful that my ability to do so is conditioned to a considerable degree on my diligence (2Tim 2:15). Surely, my desire to do, say, think, desire, and write the right thing will be rewarded, in accordance with my diligence, with an increased ability to do, say, think, desire, and write the right thing when I stand before His Bema. Those who can combine right interpretation with right application and implement the conclusion in proper action will make better kingdom rulers than those believers who are unpracticed in these areas (Heb 5:14). Jesus exhorts: "Do not judge according to appearance, but judge with righteous judgment" (Jn 7:24; cp. Dt 16:18). One would expect that the crown of righteousness awarded by the righteous Judge would entail the ability to judge righteously. God will mark those who are competent to rule righteously with a crown denoting that ability.

[1338] Karen Hinckley, ed., *A NavPress Bible study on the books of: 1, 2 & 3 John.* LCS (Colorado Springs: NavPress, 1988), 84.

[1339] MacArthur, *Gospel*, 251.

[1340] See Robert N. Wilkin, "Do Born Again People Sin? 1 John 3:9." *GIF* (March 1990). In doing so, he is evidently following the lead of Kubo, who likewise rejects the habitual interpretation. See Sakae Kubo, "1 John 3:9: Absolute or Habitual?" *AUS* 7 (1969): 47-56. Hodges (BKC) cites Kubo's article and commentaries by Dodd and Marshall in support of rejecting the habitual interpretation. To this list should be added the commentaries by Raymond Brown and Stephen Smally. The question is not, "Is the habitual argument wrong?" It most certainly is. The real question is, "Which of the competing counter solutions is most viable?" Although the present writer finds Kubo's ideal interpretation to be unsatisfactory, the problems Kubo points out for the habitual interpretation are sound.

[1341] LCS, *1 John*, 83.

[1342] Personal correspondence 3-22-90.

[1343] To be sure, Miller tries to circumvent the FG interpretation of Jn 15:4 by attempting to turn the command to abide into unconditional assurance and encouragement by Jesus, in other words, a promise. Keith J. Miller, "What Does Abiding Have to Do with Being a Christian? The Theological Significance of John 15." Available at http://gesot1.compsupport.net:8080/upload/Paper%20on%20John%2015.pdf. Accessed on March 21, 2005. But the imperative of this verse is reinforced by the imperatival command to *abide* (*meno*) in Jn 15:9. That this type of abiding remains fully conditional for those who already have become believers is seen in 8:31. Therefore, there is no reason to try to circumvent the conditional nature of this abiding for believers in 15:6-7,10. Third class condition is used in each case. The combination of an imperatival command with a third class conditional promise occurs in 1Jn 2:24. The imperative to abide is also addressed to believers in 1Jn 2:28, with the warning of misthological shame if they do not. Rather than being portrayed as assured result of regeneration, experiential abiding is conditional and imperatival. Unloving believers experientially abide in death (1Jn 3:14) and do not have eternal life experientially abiding in them (1Jn 3:15). Abiding in the experience of God's love is conditioned on loving one another with good works (1Jn 3:17; cp. 4:12). The condition for mutual indwelling is keeping His commandments (1Jn 3:24) and loving (1Jn 4:16). Therefore, the argument that indwelling is unconditional in Jn 15:6 because it is mutual is futile.

Jesus' exhortation to believers for them to continue in His love in Jn 15:9 is conditioned on their keeping His commandments in Jn 15:10. If you want to continue to experience this dimension of His love, you must obey Him. In short, if you want Jesus to love you in the manner He describes, then you must love Him in the manner He describes. Believers are being exhorted to keep themselves dynamically in Jesus' love. Likewise, Jesus' half brother exhorts: "Keep yourselves in the love of God" (Jude 1:21). If you want God to keep loving you in this manner, then you must keep loving Him. This is the only way to continue to experience this loving fellowship with God.

While all believers have the Son ontologically and soteriologically (1Jn 5:12), not all believers have either the Father or the Son abiding in them in terms of their experience or fellowship (1Jn 2:23; 2Jn 1:9). Some believers may be out of touch with God doctrinally, morally, experientially, energetically, familially, and cooperatively—not having God with them in what they do. They do not have the life of God as an abiding experience (1Jn 3:15). To abide experientially in Jesus and His love, the believer must keep Jesus' commandments (Jn 15:4-10). This conditional abiding is not to be confused with the unconditional abiding promised to the believer (in Jn 6:56). This multidimensionality for *abiding* (or *having* in terms of *abiding*) as anthropologically ranging from ontological to experiential considerations, and aspectually from eternal to temporal dimensions, and contingently from unconditional to conditional possibilities does not show logical inconsistency but semantic flexibility.

Union is free; communion is not. John made it clear that having God in terms of an abiding fellowship is conditional for the believer (Jn 14:23). Similarly, Paul indicates (in 1Cor 6:17-19 and Eph 5:17) that all believers have the Spirit of Christ in their spirits (union), but not all believers have Christ in their hearts (communion). A believer may have God in one sense but not the other. The Johannine and Pauline perspectives can be combined in a paraphrase: "Any believer who goes too far does not have God in his heart. The believer who abides in the teaching has both the Father and Son abiding in his heart" (2Jn 1:9). A trichotomist might state it this way: "All believers have God in their spirits, but not all believers have God in their souls."

[1344] A person's name was understood to represent the person; thus, to be kept in the Father's name would mean to be kept in Him. Due to the unity of the Father and the Son, to be in one is to be in the other.

[1345] Also see; Jam 1:18; 1Pet 1:23; Tit 3:5.

[1346] Paul urges those who are new creatures ontologically (2Cor 5:17) to be reconciled to God experientially (2Cor 5:20).

[1347] Eph 5:8 is a beautiful Pauline parallel to the Johannine truth of Jn 12:35-36.

[1348] NOSAS will respond that relationships are not necessarily permanent since God is pictured as divorcing Israel in Jer 3:8 (cp. Is 50:1). Some in OSAS would counter by pointing out that God says, "I am [still] married unto you" (Jer 3:14; KJV), despite the bill of divorce. But this translational solution is open to question in that the imagery may be interpreted otherwise. More likely, God's people can be disowned, disinherited, or divorced in certain senses but not in other senses. Jer 3:8 is apparently temporal and temporary. Although Jer 3:8 (like Rom 11:22) has individual application, the point that still remains to be proven by NOSAS is that such renunciation is soteriological. Other imagery and passages would suggest that it is not (Ps 137:5; Is 49:15; Jer 23:39).

[1349] The best interpretation of Jn 8:42 is to accept Wilkin's "parenty by example" idiom as the proper interpretation **and** understand love in its full force. Thus, it could be paraphrased as, "If God were the Father of your behavior, you would love Me." Or it could be restated as, "If God were your Father, you would love Me; since you do not love Me, God is not the Father of your behavior nor the nature that produced that behavior" (cp. 1Jn 3:8). Thus, Jesus intends the primary application of this rebuke to be addressed to unbelievers to reveal that the father of their behavior and nature is Satan. However, He likely intends a secondary application to the silent believers in the audience as well (cf. Jn 8:30-32). He challenges them not to live according to their old nature and to realize that their silence stems from that old nature and, thus, from Satan. When anyone, lost or saved, fails to love Jesus, God is not the Father of his or her behavior or of the nature producing that behavior. When God is the Father of someone's behavior and nature, he or she loves Jesus.

Mt 5:45 is similar in thought. We are to love our enemies in order that we may be children of God experientially and become children of God misthologically. We are to love in order that God may be the Father of our behavior, so that we may behave like children of God. Behavioral sonship results in misthological sonship (Mt 5:9; Rev 21:7). That all believers are relationally and ontologically sons of God (e.g., Gal 4:4-7) does not guarantee that all believers will be experientially and misthologically sons of God. The Bible speaks of both aspects of sonship.

When unbelievers fail to love Jesus, they show their true nature—the only nature they have. When believers fail to love Jesus, they hide their true nature—their regenerate nature. Since believers have two natures, they may fail to love Jesus. That genuine believers may fail to love Jesus is illustrated repeatedly in the NT. It is implicitly demonstrated by the fact that carnal believers do not keep the Lord's commandments. Consequently, Jesus denies that they love Him (Jn 14:15). John also says that if a believer does not love his brother in Christ, he does not love Christ (1Jn 3:16-18; 4:20-21). That some believers do not love Jesus is stated explicitly in Rev 2:4, where John describes believers who have left their first love for Jesus. Their problem is not that they were never saved or never had loved Jesus the way they should. Rather, they left the love that was associated with the early stages of their conversion. In Jam 1:12, Jesus' half-brother, James, concurs with John and points out that the crown of life is given to those believers who love Jesus. Since all believers do not receive crowns, all believers do not love Jesus.

[1350] In comparing the believers of Jn 12:42-43 who loved human honor with the nonbelievers in Jn 5:44, it is evident that the saved can display the same satanic desires and nature as do the lost. Further, the Greek word in both Johannine passages is *doxa* (*glory, praise*). Unfortunately, the NAS renders it as *glory* in 5:44 but *approval* in 12:43. This is the only place in the NT where it renders it as *approval*. This translational preference on this isolated occasion sounds suspiciously like it is theologically motivated, especially since *doxa* is rendered some form of glory or honor 162 times, which comprises practically every other occasion, except three. On those three instances, it is not used of humans. This unusual rendering may covey the false impression that it is soteriological approval. I have no problem with the translation if the reader understands it as misthological approval, which is the case for the NAS translation for *martureo* in Heb 11:2,39. But as a precaution, I point out this translational inconsistency in Jn 12:43. "Their problem wasn't that they were motivated by praise. It was that they were working for praise from the wrong source—men, rather from God" (Alcorn, *Rewards*, 109).

[1351] Brad McCoy, "Chiasmus: An Important Structural Device Commonly Found in Biblical Literature," *CTSJ* 9:2 (Fall 2003): 21. William D. Ramey, "The Literary Structure of 1 John 1:1-5:21." Available at http://www.inthe beginning.org/chiasmus/xfiles/x1jn.pdf. Accessed on August 28, 2004.

[1352] These verses are marked by the *stop symbol* in *The Discovery Bible.* Other verses addressed to believers that are so marked include the following injunctions to **STOP:** being arrogant (Rom 11:18); being conceited (Rom 11:20); being conformed to this world (Rom 12:2); cursing (Rom 12:14); being wise in your own estimation (Rom 12:16); making provisions for the lusts of the flesh (Rom 13:14); regarding with contempt (Rom 14:3); judging (Rom 14:3); tearing down (Rom 14:3); judging (1Cor 4:5); being deceived (1Cor 6:9); depriving (1Cor 7:5); worrying (1Cor 7:21); misc. (1Cor 7:23,27); being idolaters (1Cor 10:7); grumbling (1Cor 10:10); misc. (1Cor 10:28); being children (1Cor 14:20); being deceived (1Cor 15:33); sinning (1Cor 15:34); being bound with unbelievers (2Cor 6:14); misc. (2Cor 6:17); being deceived (Gal 6:7); sinning (Eph 4:26); letting the sun go down on your anger (Eph 4:26); giving the devil an opportunity (Eph 4:27); stealing (Eph 4:28); speaking filth (Eph 4:29); grieving the Holy Spirit (Eph 4:30); letting immorality, impurity, and greed be named among them (Eph 5:3); being deceived (Eph 5:6); being partakers with sons of disobedience (Eph 5:7); participating in the unfruitful deeds of darkness (Eph 5:11); being foolish (Eph 5:17); getting drunk (Eph 5:18); provoking your children (Eph 6:4); being anxious (Phil 4:6); being judged (Col 2:16); being defrauded (Col 2:18); lying (Col 3:9); exasperating your children (Col 3:21); quenching the Spirit (1Thess 5:19); despising prophetic utterances (1Thess 5:20); letting the lazy eat (2Thess 3:10); regarding a brother as an enemy (2Thess 3:15); neglecting your spiritual gift (1Tim 4:14); burdening the church (1Tim 5:16); receiving an unsupported accusation (1Tim 5:19); laying hands too hastily (1Tim 5:22); misc. (1Tim 5:23); being disrespectful (1Tim 6:2); lightly regarding God's discipline (Heb 12:5); fainting (Heb 12:5); neglecting to show hospitality to strangers (Heb 13:2); being carried away by strange teachings (Heb 13:9); neglecting doing good and sharing (Heb 13:16); expecting anything when asking in doubt (Jam 1:9); saying that God is tempting you (Jam 1:13); being deceived (Jam 1:16); showing favoritism (Jam 2:1); carelessly becoming teachers (Jam 3:1); being arrogant (Jam 3:14); lying (Jam 3:14); speaking against your fellow believer (Jam 4:11); complaining against your fellow believer (Jam 5:9); swearing (Jam 5:12); being surprised by suffering for righteousness (1Pet 4:12); suffering as a murderer, thief, evildoer, or meddler (1Pet 4:15); loving the world (1Jn 4:15); marveling when hated by the world (1Jn 3:13); believing every spirit (1Jn 4:1); receiving false teachers (2Jn 1:10); greeting false teachers (2Jn 1:10); imitating evil (3Jn 1:11); fearing (Rev 2:10). The New Testament writers repeatedly use the negation of the present imperative to urge believers to stop their sinful practices.

Unfortunately, the *Discovery Bible* did not mark negations of the present subjunctive with the *stop symbol.* These passages could be added as well. **STOP:** judging (Rom 14:13), having divisions (1Cor 1:10), acting immorally (1Cor 10:8), trying the Lord (1Cor 10:9)—these two references are sandwiched in-between the stop commands of vv. 7 & 10 that are correctly marked with the stop symbol by *The Discovery Bible* since they are imperatives, but the subjunctives have the same force. **STOP:** being judged for abusing the Lord's supper (1Cor 11:34). The problem with the believer in 1Cor 13:1 is not that he never loved but that he stopped loving (cp. Rev 2:4). The same is true in 1Cor 13:2 and 1Cor 13:3. **STOP:** trusting yourself instead of God (2Cor 1:9); living for yourself (2Cor 5:15); exalting yourself (2Cor 12:7); being boastful, challenging, and envying (Gal 5:26); being weary (Gal 6:9); being children (Eph 4:14; cp. this subjunctive *no longer* [NAS] with the imperative *no longer* in 4:28); being deluded (Col 2:4); sleeping morally (1Thess 5:6); loving in word and tongue (1Jn 3:18).

Critics of this perspective will smirk, "Why should you stop being drunk with wine if you can be drunk with wine and yet filled with the Spirit while you are drunk?" In other words, if the present imperative urging believers to be *filled* (*pleroo*) means *continue to be filled* with the Spirit in Eph 5:18b, how can the negation of the present imperative urging believers not to be *drunk* (*methusko*) in Eph 5:18a mean *discontinue being drunk*? Why would Paul command them to stop being drunk if being drunk was not preventing them, thus far, from being filled with the Spirit?

Three immediate problems are apparent in such a reductionistic perspective. First, Paul may not necessarily be indicting the whole church of getting drunk. That part of the congregation that is getting drunk may find it necessary to stop being drunk so that they may join the rest of the congregation in being filled with the Spirit. Second, the exhortation to *stop getting drunk* does not necessarily mean that they were *staying drunk*. On those occasions when they got drunk, they would no longer be filled with the Spirit. However, upon confession of such sin, they could return to their state of being filled with the Spirit. The exhortation to be filled continuously with the Spirit (as opposed to getting drunk occasionally) would make sense. Surely being filled with the Spirit would not be a completely new experience for them. The present imperative makes sense. Thirdly, context, context, context!

In Eph 4:14, Paul says that they are "*no longer* [*meketi*] to be children" doctrinally and morally (Eph 4:14). This means they are to *stop* being morally immature. They are *no longer* [*meketi*] to walk morally just as the Gentiles walk.

Bond correctly comments: "Paul charges [these] believers to *no longer* live as unbelievers [4:17]....The believers in Ephesus were once like that (2:1-5). They were now to *stop* living that way." J. B. Bond, *Ephesians*, GNTC, 879. "Let him who steals steal *no longer* [*meketi*]" in Eph 4:28 means *stop* stealing! If Paul can use *meketi* with the present tense to say *stop* your present sinful course of action (three times in quick succession), then there is every reason to believe that when he uses *me* with the present impetrative a few verses later, he means *stop* getting drunk.

Of course, this is just a small sampling of one type of biblical evidence that believers practice sin. To the above evidence should be added passages where believers are accused of sinful practices, described as engaging in sinful practices, or warned against sinful practices, or told to put away sinful practices. Additionally, sins of omission should not be overlooked (Jam 4:17). Exhortations to start performing a practice they should have been performing would indicate the practice of sin.

[1353] Hodges, *Epistles*, 127.

[1354] Anderson, *First John*, 154-156.

[1355] Ibid., 155.

[1356] If A then B (A $\Rightarrow$ B) does not necessarily imply its **inverse** B $\Rightarrow$ A. However, A $\Rightarrow$ B does logically result in its **negative inverse** $\oslash$B $\Rightarrow$ $\oslash$A (also known as a contrapositive). See endnote 1371. For example, consider the statement: If you hit the ball, it will move (hit $\Rightarrow$ move). Its inverse does not necessarily follow: If the ball moves, it was hit (move $\Rightarrow$ hit). The ball could have been kicked or thrown rather than hit. However, the negative inverse is true. If the ball does not move, it was not hit ($\oslash$move $\Rightarrow$ $\oslash$hit).

Logically, Lenski is in error when he says, "If I do not the righteousness, it is evident that I am not born of God [$\oslash$A $\Rightarrow$ $\oslash$ B]; but if I do it, there is evidence that I am so born [A $\Rightarrow$ B]" (*1John*, 446). Semantically, though, he may be correct if this expression is an evidence-inference. Conversely, Hodges is logically correct in BKC when he says, "The converse of John's statement does not follow, namely, that everyone who is born of God does righteousness." (*1John*, 893). This is easily conceived if one thinks of it in terms of subsets. A $\subset$ B does not mean that A $\supset$ B, as shown in *Illustration 280. Produces Righteousness $\subset$ Born of God*, 778.

Hodges rejects the inverse of this syntax in 1Jn 2:29. Marshall, in dealing with the similar syntax in 1Jn 4:7, also disapproves of the inversion because it "would have the effect of laying an obligation on the readers. Rather he is making parallel statements....John is here concerned with definition, not with exhortation" (*1John*, 211). As to the chiastic parallelism of 1Jn 4:7-8, I picture it as:

> for love is from God
> > lovers are born of God and know God
> > non-lovers do not know God
> for God is love.

Trying to read the second phrase in reverse would throw it out of harmony with the third phrase. White, nevertheless, will insist that this construction be read in reverse because loving God is a present participle and born, which is one of the main verbs, is a perfect. But present participles are normally contemporaneous with the main verb. Moreover, there are too many exceptions to this rule to make it dependable, especially concerning substantival present participles. See endnote 1370. Also, see the endnote pertaining to 1Jn 5:1 in *Believe: An Aspectual and Metaphorical Analysis from the Gospel of John*. What is more, in the present verse there are two main verbs, *born* and *know*, the latter of which is in the present indicative. One would expect the present participle to be contemporaneous with the present indicative. Thus, I am very comfortable with my conclusion.

Nevertheless, I will entertain alternatives for 1Jn 4:7 and find it plausible to regard it in terms of equivalence. See *Equivalence* in *Believe: An Aspectual and Metaphorical Analysis from the Gospel of John*. This would not be incompatible with the above parallelism if both the second and third phrases are regarded as convertible equivalence. However, with regard to 1Jn 2:29, I prefer noncausal *Evidence-Inference*. See my discussion by that title in *Believe: An Aspectual and Metaphorical Analysis from the Gospel of John*. From the evidence of seeing a believer who lives righteously, one can draw the inference in terms of experimental confirmation and knowledge that such a believer is born of God.

This is not to say that a case cannot be made for equivalence. Briefly, it could be argued that since the substantival participle does not necessarily convey linear force, practical righteousness is not necessarily in view. The phrase *everyone who produces righteousness* is found in only two verses in the NT, and both of these occurrences are in this context (1Jn 2:29; 3:7; cp. 3:9). Everyone who legitimately may be classified as a doer/producer of righteousness is born of God (2:29) and just as righteous as God (1Jn 3:7). Absolute righteousness is thus in view. An expanded translation of verse 29, along this line of thought, might be: "If you *know* (in the sense of being able to deduce logically) that God is righteous, then you should also *know* (through deductive logic) that everyone who is a doer of righteousness (in the absolute sense) is born of God since the only reason they could be just as righteous as God is because they are born of God" (cp. 3:9). If *ginosko* (the second *know*) is taken like *oida* (the first *know*), as referring to some type of intuitive or logical nonexperiential deduction, then such an approach would make sense. This discussion paves the way for those Marrowists who may prefer to use the equivalence interpretation consistently in all these verses (2:29; 4:7; 5:1) and take the phrase absolutely in 2:29 and 3:7. Suffice it to say, that Marrowistic theology does not limit one's exegetical options. However, in my treatment, I am not taking these verbs in the same sense in 2:29, and I am taking *being a doer of righteousness* in a relative sense in 2:29 and absolute sense in 3:7. My preference for this view is not based on theological necessity but contextual sensitivity.

[1357] The phrase *everyone (pas) also who practices* (1Jn 2:29) uses a relative *all (pas)*, which is limited contextually to believers and is followed by a substantival present participle. Contrary to the misperception of many, such participles do not necessarily denote linear action. However, this does not mean that they cannot, if the context so warrants, and in the present context, this would seem to be the case.

[1358] Walter Martin, *The Kingdom of the Cults* (Minneapolis: Bethany House Publishers, 1985), 109.

[1359] Hodges, *Walking*, 130.

[1360] The transition from first and second person to third person does not prove that a transition occurs in subject matter from the author and his readers, who are saved, to someone who is not saved. In other words, it does not prove that the author has moved from a discussion of fellowship to relationship. Both paragraphs are dealing with the similar claims made by both groups. Both passages are dealing with believers who make a false claim to be walking with the Lord in fellowship. The problem in the second paragraph is how a believer responds to *his brother* (stated three times in 1Jn 2:9-11). The statement, *his brother*, seals the relationship between them—they are both saved. The first, second, and third person are used interchangeably in the second paragraph, with the same exhortations and applications being addressed to each group. The indefinite pronoun "anyone" used in 1Jn 2:1 does not deny the relationship of those to whom the reference is being made. The same pronoun is used in 1Jn 2:15 without questioning their relationship, since the intended application of both verses is to the readership, whose salvation clearly is confirmed in 1Jn 2:12-14. These two verses (1Jn 2:1,15) combine to teach that if anyone sins (e.g., by loving the world), that believer has an Advocate with the Father even though he or she does not have the love of the Father. In other words, you cannot love the Father and love the world. Jesus' advocacy is adequate for those believers who love the world and who thus fail to love the Father.

Although John is generally pleased with this congregation, he *gently* (given his positive assessment of their performance from the context) can tell them to *stop loving the world* (1Jn 2:15; TM; *me* + present imperative). Love for God and the world is experienced in various degrees. To the degree they love the world, they do not love the Father. Conversely, to the degree they love the Father, they do not love the world. Regeneration is not by degrees, but practical sanctification is dynamic. Even though they had progressed well, there was still room for further development. John does not condone a little sin; he condemns all sin, in whatever degree it is experienced.

[1361] Eaton, *1,2, 3 John*, 49-51, 62-63.

[1362] The parallel contingency in 1Jn 2:3 is we *have come to know* (●—→) Him, if we *keep* (→) His commandments. The Calvinistic tests-of-regeneration would stress that in 1Jn 3:9 the perfect precedes the present tense so that those who *have been born* (●—→) of God do not *practice sin* (→). They thus would argue that the linear aspect in the joint symbol (●⃗) in this case represents result rather than condition. The Arminian could try to counter by stating that staying in a state of being born of God is conditioned on not sinning. Doing so would be difficult since John uses *hoti (because)* rather than *ei (if)* to clarify the relationship in 1Jn 3:9. In short, the Arminian tests-of-regeneration wins the argument over the Calvinist in 1Jn 2:3, and the Calvinistic tests-of-regeneration wins over the Arminian in 1Jn 3:9. Both lose when it is realized that John is not contradicting himself. John is not saying that everyone who has been born of God keeps God's commands as a result and that keeping God's commandments is a condition for staying born of God. John is not confusing condition with result. To the contrary, he is talking about two different things: experience versus existence. 1Jn 2:3 is experiential; 1Jn 3:9 is ontological.

Eaton does very well in rejecting the linear understanding of the present tense for sin in 1Jn 3:4 since it is an unmarked tense (*1John*, 95-96). He would have done well to apply that same observation to the rest of his discussion of that Johannine paragraph. An additional verb such as *practices* should be omitted in 1Jn 3:9. John is not stressing the linear practice of sin in this verse. Moving in the opposite direction, one could mark the relationship as (●⃗): No one who *has been born* (●—→) of God *sins at all* (●). In this case, the adverbial phrase *at all* is used to mark the punctiliar aspect. Alternatively, one might leave it unmarked as (●⃗): No one who *has been born* (●—→) of God *sins* ( ). The *at all* is omitted and the liner expression is deemphasized.

[1363] Eaton says that the elect can be lead astray "but only for a short time" (*1John*, p. 50). So if you do not persevere, you are not one of Eaton's Calvinistic elect. "The intruders [in 1Jn 2:19] had never been converted....Their breakaway made it clear that they had never been a part of the church" (p. 76). "False teachers may throw the Christian off balance for a while, but the false teacher cannot persuade the Christian to adopt a heretical 'gospel.'" "The elect cannot be deceived at this point." The elect to whom John is writing had "never been fully persuaded that the gnostics were right" (pp. 78-79). This typical Calvinism midrash denies that the elect can fall fully or finally from the faith. Regarding 1Jn 2:23, Eaton states that those who "deny the deity of Jesus...lose the Father's presence. It is to lose His protection, His promises and His provision, and finally to forfeit heavenly glory and thus to lose His paradise" (p. 82). In this Calvinistic schema, those believers who become caught up in a cult and deny the deity of Christ will lose their salvation. Obviously, Eaton would deny that the elect could do so—because if the elect were to do so, they would lose their regeneration. Eaton is unwittingly teaching conditional security from the Reformed perspective. The only way you can know if you are one of the Calvinistic elect is to persevere in the faith. Persevering in the faith is also a condition to reach heaven. Eaton implicitly makes moral performance necessary to reach heaven when he concludes from 1Jn 2:29 that only those who live a loving life are born of God (p. 87). Yet he nullifies his own argument when he concludes that some believers will shrink back in shame before the Lord in 1Jn 2:28. John is not stressing that loving believers may be put to shame at the Bema in this epistle. Rather, unloving believers are in misthological danger. Contrary to Eaton, adopting the tests-of-conversion interpretation for this epistle cannot be used to discern the salvation of others without teaching conditional security and personal introspection for oneself. Salvation from damnation is not conditioned, in whole or in part, on whether one is fully, versus partially persuaded, by a false gospel after coming to saving faith.

[1364] Hodges, *Epistles,* 77.

[1365] Ibid., 90, n. 4.

[1366] Anderson, *1 John*, 75.

[1367] Ibid., 74. Although Anderson does not specify the article, he is evidently thinking of McKay's 1981 article in Nov. T. 23: "On the Perfect and Other Aspects in New Testament Greek." Also see McKay's grammar (NSVNT, 33).

[1368] The perfective stative is translated properly as: *so that your/our joy may be **be** full* (in Jn 16:24; 1Jn 1:4; and 2Jn 1:12). As Robertson notes, the perfect in this case emphasizes "the abiding and permanence of the joy," "stressing the state of completion…remain full" (WPNT). The present state is stressed; the past is omitted. There is no *have.* The aorist is used in Jn 15:11 and better translated there as: *so that your joy made be **made** full.* The action, rather than state, is expressed.

[1369] The negation of an *if-then* ($\Rightarrow$) statement may or may not be true. The simple negation of the condition in John's statement does not prove that unloving people are lost. $A \Rightarrow B$ does not prove $\lozenge A \Rightarrow \lozenge B$. *Love* $\Rightarrow$ *born & know* does not prove $\lozenge love \Rightarrow \lozenge born$ & $\lozenge know$. *If you hit the ball, it will move* does not prove that *if you do not hit the ball, it will not move.* It could still be kicked. A negation of condition is to be differentiated form an inversion of negation. For further symbolic summation, see endnote dealing with Jn 8:42 in *Believe: An Aspectual and Metaphorical Analysis from the Gospel of John.*

[1370] Hodges has an interesting footnote concerning the perfect tense of *know* in 1Jn 3:6. See *Siege*, 165, n. 13. He quotes Zerwick to the effect that the prefect is presenting the present state of affairs, albeit as a result of a past action. One may see Wallace (GGBB, 573) for the same citation from Zerwick. Thus, what is denied is that such a believer currently sees or knows God rather than has never seen or known God. Hodges again stresses that the focus of the perfect is on the present rather than the past in his commentary, citing the research done by Louw (*Walking*, 135-136). Indeed, the use of the perfect tense for *know* in 1Jn 2:3-4 would harmonize with his statements that the perfect "is not a past tense but a present one. One might thus regard this as an intensive (i.e., resultative) perfect which correspondingly is emphasizing the existing present result rather than the past action.

However, the tense used for know in 1Jn 4:8 is an aorist indicative, so extending this discussion regarding *know* to the past is permissible, although only on the basis of the context. To use the perfect as proving either past or present aspects could be dubious since it may have both or either. Although the present writer agrees with Hodges that John is not ruling out that there is a sense in which an unloving person can know God (e.g., a saved person may be unloving and yet know God as Father), there does not seem to be any compelling reason to restrict an unloving person's lack of knowing God to the present. Lack of love always shows an absolute lack of intimate knowledge of God. Yet to the degree we fail to love, we absolutely fail to have fellowship with God.

John may be using the perfect tense to show the absolute sense in which this is true. For example, the tense used for *born of God* in 1Jn 3:9 and 1Jn 4:7 is the perfect. Birth cannot be experienced in degrees. John evidently is not using the perfect to restrict the aspect of the new birth he has in mind to the present experience of that birth. Rather, if the tense be pressed, it probably indicates the absoluteness of the statement. He allows the nature of the verb (not its tense) to determine whether it can be experienced to various degrees. Additionally, he may be using the tense of the verb to indicate that the degree to which it is experienced is absolute.

To the degree we abide, we are absolutely sinless. To the degree we sin, we absolutely do not know Him. Sin has no part in our fellowship with Him or obedience to Him. To the degree we fail to love, we fail to know Him—we fail to have fellowship with Him. Oil and water do not mix, although they may exist in the same container. *Abide, sin, know,* and *love* are verbs that obviously can be experienced in degrees. But this observation does not rule out the possibility of their being used absolutely as well, depending on the context.

If Jn 17:3 is used to assert that it is impossible for believers not to know God, it must be pointed out that knowing God and having eternal life can both be dynamic experiences. They need not necessarily be taken as static soteriological concepts in every passage. Granted, it is true that you either know God as your Savior or you do not. You are either lost or saved. Additionally, it is also true that you either have eternal life or you do not at the soteric level. Knowing God and having eternal life can be taken absolutely. Equally evident, eternal life can be had at various experiential degrees by those who already have it at its absolute level. Eternal life is not only a gift; it is a temporal and eschatological reward. Those believers who already have received the gift of eternal life have eternal security. Their possession of eternal life at this soteric level is static; it cannot change. On the other hand, those who already have eternal life at the static level may progress to enjoy eternal life at a dynamic level. Possession of eternal life at the static level is required for salvation from hell. Possession of eternal life at the dynamic level is required for the abundant life, the crown of life, and the tree of life. Further, it should be self-evident that some believers know God better than other believers. Still, according to Jesus in Jn 17:3, eternal life is knowing God. Consequently, those believers who know Him best have more eternal life (in terms of a greater dynamic experience) than those believers who fail to meet the multifaceted requirements for knowing Him in a mature manner.

[1371] The negation or the inverse of an *if-then* ($\Rightarrow$) statement is not necessarily true, that is, $A \Rightarrow B$ does not necessarily imply either $\varnothing A \Rightarrow \varnothing B$ or $A \Leftarrow B$. However, the combined negative inverse (i.e., the contraposition) of such a statement is true: $(A \Rightarrow B) \Rightarrow (\varnothing A \Leftarrow \varnothing B)$ is necessarily true. See endnote 1356.

[1372] This does not rule out positional abiding. If we completely abide in Him (which is true of every believer positionally), then we are completely sinless (which is true of every believer positionally). To the extent we abide in Him, we are absolutely sinless. However, although John's statement is true positionally, he probably intends for it to refer primarily to our experience in this verse.

[1373] Jam 1:15 might be used to argue that the devil can be viewed as giving birth to the dead sin nature of the lost: "When lust has conceived, it gives birth to sin; and when sin is full-grown, it gives birth to death" (TM). James uses surprising imagery when he pictures sin as giving birth to death. Since the imagery of birth can be associated with the impartation of death, the devil might be pictured as giving birth to the dead sin nature of the human race. It might also be argued that the devil can impart life since he will be allowed to "give life to the image of the beast" (Rev 13:15; TM). Even then, the devil has to be permitted to give life. This is an exceptional occurrence. Likewise, the imagery invoked by James is surprising because of its shocking twist of imagery. Had John desired to invoke such imagery for his purposes, he could have done so easily enough by entertaining the possibility of being *born of the devil*. As it is, he avoids the term, leading one to suspect that he is using birth in its normal sense in association with life.

[1374] The Navigator's rejection (LCS, 83) of Hodges' position was based on the fact that concerning 3:6 Hodges had stated that a believer is sinless "insofar as" he abides in Christ (BKC, 894). The Navigator's objected that there is not an "insofar as" in 3:9. Even so, as has been shown, 3:6 should be understood in terms of degrees, or as Hodges articulated, "insofar as." Conversely, 3:9 is not to be understood in terms of degrees. Nevertheless, both verses teach absolute sinlessness. The Navigator's objection is pathetically superficial and woefully adequate. If one must have an "insofar as" in verse 9, then here it is: "*Insofar as* believers are viewed in terms of who they truly are, people born of God, believers are completely sinless." The reason it was not necessary to speak of degrees, or levels, or "insofar as" in 3:9 is because in that verse John is viewing believers exclusively in terms of who they truly are. "Insofar as" a person is viewed as having been born of Him, or abiding in Him, that person is sinless. Therefore, when a person is viewed exclusively in terms of his or her new birth, or abiding in Christ (as in 3:6,9), that person is completely sinless.

[1375] Zeller, "Theology." He says, for example, "The expression 'NOT OF GOD' means that the person has never been born of God" (emphasis his). Actually, the texts he cites do not make this assertion.

[1376] Zane C. Hodges, "2nd Peter," 5. So also Gangel in BKC.

[1377] It is perhaps ironic that Hodges is inclined to take the *hina* plus aorist subjunctive in 2Pet 1:4 as ingressive and, therefore, experiential but inclined to take it as soteriological and punctiliar in Eph 5:26; whereas, the present author leans in the opposite direction, due in part to the desire to maintain consistency with his treatment of this construction in Johannine soteriological texts, such as Jn 20:31a. The problem is that the aorist subjective is not aspectually decisive in and of itself apart from any and all contextual and conceptual considerations. This is why it was necessary to augment Robertson's aspectual quotation with corroborating discussion in the metaphorical analysis of *believe* in regard to the Johannine texts. Like Hodges, as noted in his comments on Eph 5:26, the present writer's propensity is to take the aorist subjunctive as denoting punctiliar action unless the context or concept strongly indicates that an ingressive aspect would be preferable on that specific occasion.

[1378] Meisinger, "Sufficiency," 9.

[1379] If 2Pet 1:4 is taken as indicating that, at the point of regeneration, we ontologically became partakers of the divine nature and simultaneously escaped the metaphysical corruption, then 1:5 is exhorting that we should become in practice what we already have become in nature. This approach still might be possible, even if the escape refers to an antecedent action in that, at the point of regeneration, we logically are crucified with Christ before we are raised with Christ in newness of life. Verse five would still mean, "You are a new creature, so live like it." Be what you are. Alternately, if a temporal sequence occurs in 1:4, then Peter is acknowledging that *having escaped* ontologically in regeneration, we morally and logically should now escape experientially by heeding his injunction in 1:5ff. If this is the case, then the latter approach is to be preferred. Logically, the partaking is ingressive because it is experiential and subsequent to the regenerational escape they already have experienced. (See option two in endnote 1382.) In other words, an expanded translation of v. 4 from this latter perspective (that incorporates elements from the context) would be: "For by His own glory and excellence, He has granted to us His precious and magnificence misthological promises pertaining to life and godliness, in order that by the motivation provided by such contingent promises you might now become experiential partakers of the divine nature by adding moral excellence to your faith since you already have escaped moral defilement ontologically by regeneration."

[1380] A case could certainly be made for Hodges' interpretation of 2Pet 1:4 based on the middle voice of *ginomai*. If this is more than a *permissive middle* (so that we become righteous by actually participating in the process rather than merely giving intellectual assent to it), then an ingressive understanding of the aorist would be preferred with the result that we are to become experientially righteousness in this verse. Likewise, in 2Cor 5:21 the middle could be taken as referring to our becoming experientially righteous This approach, concerning *hina ginomai* for the aoristic middle, would be in substantial harmony with my discussion of the middle/passive of the aorist subjunctive of Tit 3:7 (cp. 1Cor 9:23). However, I still would prefer punctiliar aspect even in these two texts. The realization of our misthological hope of being a partaker awaits the future punctiliar conference of this benefit at the Bema. The textual variant between the aorist and future middle of Jn 15:8 in the CT and MT might suggest that being found at the Bema to be Christ's disciples, in more than name only, is the subject matter.

Granted, the argument could be made that since the Greek is an aorist loving language and since *hina ginomai* occurs frequently in the aorist but only rarely in the present tense, the distinction should not be overly pressed. On the other hand, the general disposition that the aoristic *hina ginomai* refers to punctiliar action accords reasonably well with my expectations. For example, the proposed command for the stones to become bread does not presuppose a drawn out process in the transformation (Mt 4:4). The expectation that a disciple will be like his teacher (Mt 10:25), rather than expressing a linear aspect in becoming like his teacher, could refer to the end of the process so that he is *found to be*, or *turns out to be*, like his teacher (cp. BDAG 7).

[1381] GGBB, 473, 476.

[1382] Three positions concerning 2Pet 1:4 are available. (1) The aorist and perfect are both used experientially; (2) the aorist is experiential and the perfect is ontological; (3) the aorist and perfect are both used ontologically. Hodges and Gangel take the first position; however, they both acknowledge that the experiential participation presumes the ontological participation. The present author prefers the third position but finds the second option very attractive in this particular context. (See latter discussion in endnote 1379 for explanation of this second option.)

As to the preference herein for the third option, the combination of aorist and perfect in 1:4 seems to be Peter's way of stressing the ongoing result. This is certainly the case when Peter says that God "condemned (aorist) the cities of Sodom and Gomorrah to destruction by reducing them to ashes, *having made* them *an example* (perfect) to those who would live ungodly thereafter" (2Pet 2:6). Obviously, the aorist-perfect combination of *condemned...having made* does not mean that God made them an example before He condemned them. Rather, He made them an example at the same time He condemned them. Being made an example is the ongoing result of their having been reduced to ashes. The subsequent perfect aspect is used to stress the linear state that resulted from the punctiliar action of the aorist. Likewise, one should not assume from the typical translation of the *aorist...perfect* in 1:4 as *become...having escaped* that the perfect action took place before the aorist. Instead, the perfect may be used to highlight the resultant state of the punctiliar aorist. The thought appears to be that those who became partakers of the divine nature (at the moment of regeneration) have (as of that moment and even into the present time) escaped the corruption that is in the world by lust. The immutability of our sinless new nature appears to be affirmed as an ongoing reality.

Something similar occurs in 1Pet 4:1: "He who *suffered* (aorist) in the flesh *has ceased* (perfect) from sin" (TM). Granted, the perfect (*has ceased*) in this verse is the main verb, and the aorist participle generally portrays action that is antecedent to the main verb and, therefore, is rendered frequently as *has suffered* in this verse. But if this is Peter's way of reiterating the truth in Gal 2:20—that Paul had used to publicly refute Peter "to his face" (Gal 2:11, cp. v. 14)—it may be Peter's way of stating that the one who has been crucified to sin cannot be resurrected to sinfulness. (Or as John relates in 1Jn 3:9, the one born of God cannot sin.) The believer's crucifixion with Christ is permanent. When Christians died with Christ, they died to sin (cp. Rom 6:7). Even though Peter found some of what Paul wrote to be "hard to understand" (2Pet 3:16), I suspect that Peter eventually got Paul's point, at least on this occasion. Peter certainly would have taken time to ponder on that stinging public rebuke that he had received to his face from Paul in Gal 2:20. Believers have suffered with Christ in the flesh (i.e., they have been crucified with Christ). Therefore, in terms of that completed and irreversible suffering/crucifixion with Christ, they have ceased to sin. That is what Peter is acknowledging in 4:1. In the next verse he goes on to exhort, "So (*eis*) as to live the rest of the time in the flesh no longer for the lusts of men, but for the will of God" (1Pet 4:2). This practical manifestation (of v. 2) is the intended result of the internal transformation (of v. 1). After all, Peter himself indicated the immutability of their sinless internal transformation when he said that they had purified their souls at the time of regeneration by being born again of a seed that was incorruptible (1Pet 1:22-23). Although the soul may be corrupted phenomenally at the level of the pri-soul, the metal of the soul cannot be tarnished. See creeping vine illustration in "Purification" in *Trichotomy*.

[1383] *The Discovery Bible* marks each of the three verbs in question with the start symbol.

[1384] This is not to say that Peter looks exclusively at the person's nature. Peter also has the person's life and the person him or herself in view. Note his repeated use of *us* and his use of *you*.

[1385] It is difficult to decide if *by this* in 1Jn 3:10 refers to what has preceded or what follows. In either case the sense remains the same since what proceeds is a restatement of part of what has preceded from a different angle. Nevertheless, since what follows is talking about being *of God* rather than being *born of God* or being a *child of God*, and since what follows only deals with the manifestation of what is *not of* God rather than what is *of God*, it seems probable that it refers to the preceding discussion in which both types of children are manifested. It seems best to take 10a-c as referring to the preceding discussion and 10d-e as concluding the discussion. Since 10d-e concludes the discussion, it also refers to 10a-c, which is part of that discussion. The net result is that *by this* refers not only to what follows but what precedes. This is the case even if the opposite is assumed. If *by this* is referring to 10d-e, then it is referring to the conclusion of the preceding discussion so that it also refers to the preceding discussion.

[1386] The last part of verse 10, *and the one not loving his brother,* is transitional.

[1387] Jesus does the keeping—according to NAS, following CT. However, this is exceedingly unlikely. *Born of God* repeatedly describes believers, never Jesus, in this epistle (1Jn 2:29; 3:9; 4:7; 5:1, 5:4,18). The MT reading of 5:18 is accepted herein: The believer keeps *himself* (*heatou*). Precedence for this reflexive action is found in 1Jn 3:3: The believer purifies *himself* (*heatou*). If this verse is talking about ontological purification, at least inclusively as seems likely, then it is almost an exact match for 1Jn 5:18. Regardless, it shows that John is open to a sinlessness effected by the believer upon him or herself. In 1Jn 5:18, the believer's new nature results in the believer being absolutely sinless at all times (1Jn 3:6,9). Believers keep themselves perfectly sinless ontologically by means of their ontological composition—that is, their sinless nature.

[1388] Unless otherwise noted, all quotations and citations of *AJ* are derived from Frederik Wisse, "The Apocryphon of John," in *The Nag Hammadi Library*, gen. ed. James M. Robinson (San Francisco: Harper & Row, 1978), 98-116.

[1389] Pheme Perkins, "Ireneus [sic] and the Gnostics: Rhetoric and Composition in Adversus Haereses Book One," *VC* 30 (1976): 197.

[1390] B. A. Pearson, "Jewish Sources in Gnostic Literature," in *Jewish Writings of the Second Temple Period*, ed. Michael E. Stone (Philadelphia: Fortress Press, 1984), 458.

[1391] ERE, s.v. "Valentinianism," by E. F. Scott.

[1392] Parrot, writing from the literary-dissection perspective, believes AJ was originally a Gnostic writing that was Christianized; certainly, it was not a Christian writing that was de-Christianized. Instead of merely dressing up their Gnostic doctrines in Christian clothing, their Gnostic faith was transformed by Christianity as they unsuccessfully tried to hold on to their old faith and embrace the Christ of the Christian faith. See Douglas M. Parrott, "Evidence of Religious Syncretism in Gnostic Texts from Nag Hammadi," in *Religious Syncretism in Antiquity*, eds. Walter H. Capps and Charles H. Long (Missoula: University of Montana, 1975), 173-190. Parrot's conclusion is accurate to a considerable degree, but his dichotomy is false. Although the document would not have been transformed from a Christian document to a Gnostic document, its author may have been transformed from a Christian to a Gnostic. Whether the document is viewed as a literary unity, it may well reflect the struggle of a Christian trying to reconcile his new faith (Gnosticism) with his old faith (Christianity).

[1393] Robert M. Grant, "Two Gnostic Gospels," *JBL* 79 (1960): 4. It may have been added because of the quotation of Philip and the Gnostic tradition in *Pistis Sophia* that said that Philip recorded the secret post-resurrection words of Jesus. Thus, it is possible that *GP* was regarded as post-resurrection sayings. See Floyd V. Filson, "New Greek and Coptic Gospel Manuscripts," *BA* 24 (1961): 11.

[1394] Unless otherwise noted, all citations and quotations in reference to the Gospel of Philip (*GP*) are from Wesley W. Isenberg, "The Gospel of Philip," in *The Nag Hammadi Library*, gen. ed. James M. Robinson (San Francisco: Harper & Row, 1978), 131-151.

[1395] D. H. Tripp, "The 'Sacramental System' of the Gospel of Philip," in vol. 17, pt 1 *Studia Patristica*, ed. Elizabeth A. Livingstone (Oxford: Pergamon Press, 1982), 251.

[1396] Michael A. Williams, "Uses of Gender Imagery in Ancient Gnostic Texts," in *Gender and Religion: On the Complexity of Symbols*, ed. Caroline W. Bynum, Stevan Harrell, and Paula Richman (Boston: Beacon Press, 1986), 205.

[1397] Robert M. Wilson, "Second Thoughts: XI. The Gnostic Gospels from Nag Hammadi," ET 78 (1966): 40.

[1398] W. C. Van Unnik, "Three Notes on the 'Gospel of Philip,'" *NTS* 10 (1964): 465.

[1399] Robert M. Wilson, "The New Testament in the Nag Hammadi Gospel of Philip," *NTS* 9 (1963): 293-294. Although Wilson is certainly correct in his assessment that the author GP's "theology is not that of the New Testament," he is being somewhat speculative when he conjectures that "the document gives the impression that he knows the language without having penetrated very deeply into the content of Christian thought" (p. 293). Previous to this statement, Wilson admits that "the allusions vary from explicit quotations to echoes…which are worked into the context and give the impression of a man steeped in the Scriptures, to whom their language and phrases came as the natural vehicle for the expression of his own ideas" (p. 292). Having acknowledged such a grasp of New Testament on the part of the author of *GP*, it seems rather strange that Wilson believes that *GP*'s author had not penetrated very deeply in thought of the NT. Is Wilson's opinion based on a theological prejudice that determines beforehand that someone who abandons the Christian faith was not a genuine believer to start with? Perhaps not, at least not wittingly.

In his commentary on *GP*, Wilson makes the same comment that *GP's* author knew the NT language but had not penetrated very deeply into its thought; however, Wilson immediately proceeds to explain that in this lack of perception the author of *GP* "was perhaps a man of his time. The proper standard of comparison is not the theology of the Reformation, or of the later Fathers, much less any theology of to-day. It is the theology of the second century." Robert M. Wilson, *The Gospel of Philip: Translated from the Coptic text, with an Introduction and Commentary* (New York: Harper & Row, 1962), 12. As to the extent of the author *GP's* citations and allusions to the NT, Wilson gives a chart (*Gospel*, 197-198): from Matthew (17), Mark (4), Luke (5), John (13), Romans (4), 1 and 2 Corinthians (9,1), Galatians (8), Ephesians (3), Philippians (1), Colossians (2), 1 Thessalonians (1), Hebrews (4), 1 Peter (3), and 1 John (5).

These 80 references from such a variety of the NT certainly demonstrate that *GP's* author was familiar with the thought of the NT. Any lack of penetration of his insight into the NT thought can be attributed to the time of his writing but perhaps not just for the reason Wilson supposes. Not only was it written in the second century, it was also written after the writer had moved from genuine Christianity to Gnostic Christianity. Lack of insight, when not attributable to the second century date, might in reality point to an abandonment of insight rather than lack of it. *GP* author's perspective had changed from the time when he was Christian to the time when he wrote *GP* as a Gnostic Christian.

[1400] Isenberg translates this as: "Through the Holy Spirit we are indeed begotten again, but we are begotten through Christ in the two. We are anointed through the Spirit" ("Philip," 141). Catanzaro translates it as: "Through the Holy Spirit we are, indeed, born anew, and we are born through the Christ a second time, we are anointed by the Spirit." Carmino Joseph De Catanzaro, "The Gospel According to Philip," *JTS* 13 (1962): 52. Wilson's translation is, "Through the Holy Spirit we are indeed born, but we are born again through Christ. In the two we are anointed through the Spirit" (*Gospel*, 137). Wilson suggests two interpretations: (1) Only Gnostic Christians are born by the Spirit and then by Christ; (2) all men have natural birth through the Spirit, but only Gnostic Christians have new birth by Christ (p. 137). In view of the opening of the book, in which the "we" is identified as Christians, it seems best to adopt a modification of interpretation number one. *GP's* author is claiming that as Christians we are born again by the Spirit, but only Gnostic Christians are then born again by Christ.

Buckley suggests that "the two" refers to the two parents. The mother of the Hebrew orphans is the Spirit who receive a Father when they become Christians. Jorunn Jacobsen Buckley, "'The Holy Spirit is a Double Name': Holy Spirit, Mary, and Sophia in the *Gospel of Philip*," in *Images of the Feminine in Gnosticism*, ed. Karen L. King (Philadelphia: Fortress Press, 1988), 220-221. Compare Jeffrey S. Siker, "Gnostic Views on Jews and Christians in the Gospel of Philip," *NovTes* 31 (1989): 277.

[1401] Grant, "Gospels," 10.

[1402] Siker, "Jews," 281. Hylic, psychic, and pneumatic refer to the three Valentinian levels of human existence described in this Valentinian document (p. 280).

[1403] Ibid., 278, n. 5. Siker incorrectly cites the source of his quotation as p. 86 of Wilson's book. Actually, it is p. 68. Wilson goes on to say in the same reference that this may "provide some confirmation for the view which traces the origins of Gnosticism to Jewish-Christian circles." See Wilson, *Gospel*, 68.

[1404] Ibid., 286.

[1405] Wilson says, "The 'Hebrews' represent an earlier and less advanced stage from which the Gnostic has emerged, so that here he appears to be superior even to the apostles" (*Gospel*, 82). In calling the apostles "Hebrews," the author of *GP* is not denying that they are Christians; he is saying that he and his readers have progressed further than their Jewish-Christian heritage. The progression remains: Hebrew → Christian → Gnostic.

[1406] Ibid., 22. Wilson originally gave the backbone of Siker's view in his commentary that perhaps Gentile = material man, Hebrew = psychic, and Christian = Gnostic. But Wilson then went on to acknowledge that this assessment is not explicitly stated, and thus that there is always a danger of reading more into the text than it actually says (p. 66).

[1407] Grant, "Gospels," 6.

[1408] Siker, "Jews," 276-279.

[1409] Ibid., 281.

[1410] Ibid., 283.

[1411] Gerald L. Borchert, "Insights Into the Gnostic Threat to Christianity as Gained Through the Gospel of Philip," in *New Dimensions in New Testament Study, ed. R. Longenecker* (Grand Rapids: Zondervan Publishing House, 1974), 93.

[1412] Ibid., 84.

[1413] Ibid., 90. Borchert uses Marcus and Simon to prove the "immoral and fraudulent" claims of Gnosticism (p. 91). Evidently, he believes that immorality proves his claim that they are fraudulent Christians. The present writer does not share this perspective. In any case, Borchert thinks that Gnostics claimed eternal security for themselves while denying it for Christians and claims that since Gnostics believed themselves eternally secure, they could participate in loose living (p. 89). However, his statements concerning the eternal security and immorality of these Gnostics are open to attack on the basis of what has been shown in the Apocrypha of John concerning their eternal security and morality and from the moral tone of the Gospel of Philip.

[1414] McCasland says, "Although Justin attacks the followers of Simon, Menander and Marcion, with all his power, he nevertheless admits in Apol. I.26.6 that their followers are called Christians. So we have to assume, not only that Simon became a Christian, but that he remained one." IDB, s.v. "Simon Magus," by S. V. McCasland. However, although the biblical data itself demands that Simon be considered a genuine believer, the claim that he remained a genuine believer is exceedingly doubtful in light of tradition. He apostatized from the faith with his gnostic perversion of the faith. In view of prevalent theological presuppositions, it must be pointed out that this admission is not a denial of eternal security. Losing one's faith does not result in soteriological exclusion from the kingdom.

[1415] Buckley believes that Jesus kissing Mary in public in this manner was a prelude to physical intercourse in the privacy of the bridal bed ("Double," 216-217, 225). However, there is a long-standing debate as to whether the *GP* advocates physical or spiritual marriage or uses ambiguity to avoid taking a stand on this issue. See Elaine H. Pagels, "The 'Mystery of Marriage' in the *Gospel of Philip* revisited" in *The Future of Early Christianity*, ed. Birger A. Pearson (Minneapolis: Fortress Press, 1991), 446. Craig Evans and Elaine Pagels were two of the offsetting scholars in the National Geographic documentary on the Gospel of Judas.

In appearances on the John Ankerberg show, which are obtainable from http://www.johnankerberg.org, Evans clarifies that there is no evidence that Jesus was married and that the most interesting details are in the lacunae: "And the companion [ ] Mary Magdalene. [   ] her more than [ ] the disciples [   ] kiss her [   ] on her [   ], more than all his students." This is typically assumed to mean: "And the companion [is] Mary Magdalene. [Jesus loved] her more than [all] the disciples [and used to] kiss her [often] on her [face], more than all his students." He may have been kissing her on the hand or forehead. In that society, kissing denoted affection, not necessarily romantic involvement.

It is perhaps unfortunate that some online versions of Isenberg's translation fails to note the lacunae for *mouth* or that the second reference to *disciples* is in the lacunae: "And the companion of the [...] Mary Magdalene. [...] loved her more than all the disciples, and used to kiss her often on her **mouth**. The rest of the **disciples** [...]. They said to him 'Why do you love her more than all of us?'" Available at http://www.gnosis.org/naghamm/gop.html. Accessed on May 27, 2006. *Mouth* is bracketed in the printed edition used herein. However, a translation by Paterson Brown renders it as follows: "And the Consort of the [Christ] is Mariam the Magdalene. The [Lord loved] Mariam more than [all the (other)] Disciples, [and he] kissed her often on her **[mouth]**. The other [**women**] saw his love for Mariam, they say to him: Why do thou love [her] more than all of us?" Available at http://www.metalog.org/files/philip1.html. Accessed on May 27, 2006. Here, by the presence of the bracket, it is noted that mouth is a guess, but the translation fails to bracket *often*. The text is infamous as a very early source for the idea expressed in the *Da Vinci Code* that Jesus married Mary Magdalene. But at best this is but a guess at what this unholy holey text meant to suggest.

Even if one were to fill in the blanks in the manner necessary to give the Da Vinci theory any credibility, it still would be necessary to suppose that physical rather than spiritual intercourse is implied for the Da Vinci plot. Yet the text is more interested with the spiritual realm and spiritual ramifications of the kiss: "All who are begotten in the world are begotten in a natural way, and the others in a spiritual way" (58:26-28). "For it is by a kiss that the perfect conceive and give birth. For this reason we also kiss one another. We receive conception from the grace which is in one another" (59:1-6) Or if we use Brown's translation: "[Grace comes] forth by him from the mouth, the place where the Logos came forth; (one) was to be nourished from the mouth to become perfect. The perfect are conceived thru a kiss and they are born. Therefore we also are motivated to kiss one another—to receive conception from within our mutual grace."

All we have as to any supposed evidence that Mary Magdalene was Jesus' cohort in any possible sexual capacity is in a fictional portrayal by a late document that has no historical credibility in a Gnostic system in which they kissed one another so that they might impart grace in the form of spiritual birth in order to be "always begotten" (58:23) or "continually born" (so Brown). Even if the document is picturing Jesus as frequently kissing Mary on the mouth, it also alleges that He kissed the other disciples in this same manner. Further, other disciples also kissed each other on the mouth to impart this spiritual grace to one another. Whether the kissing on the mouth was to retain or continuously experience the spiritual birth they already had is hard to determine. In any event, sexual intercourse should be considered a skeptical recourse.

As Evans stated in his interview on the Ankerberg show, there is no evidence that Jesus was married to Mary. This was the same conclusion presented on the National Geographic documentary regarding the *Da Vinci Code*. Although some might consider the suggestion that Jesus married Mary blasphemous, the present author is content to consider it ridiculous. As Evans noted, there was no reason, as far as the early church was concerned, that Jesus could not have married Mary. The church would have celebrated the event, rather than try to keep it secret. Surely, if Jesus had married Mary, the NT writers would have mentioned this fact. As it is, the only bride they have to pose for Christ are faithful believers who endure to the end. If they had had a historical parallel in Mary Magdalene by which to illustrate this beautiful event, surely they would have done so.

[1416] See De Catanzaro, "Philip," 62.

[1417] Borchert, "Threat," 82. According to Filson, "no one can claim seriously that we learn anything authentic about the ministry and teaching of Jesus by the use of the *Gospel of Philip*" ("Manuscripts," 13). *GP* inconsistently denies the virginal conception of Jesus. See Brian McNeil, "New Light on Gospel of Philip 17," *JTS* 29 (1978): 146. Nor is this the only means in which *GP* distorts the nature of Christ, since it teaches that we can become Christs as well. The perversion is not limited to the nature of Christ but also involves the nature of salvation. Buckley challenges the long-lived view that Gnosticism teaches "automatic salvation" based on the so-called "Gnostic nature" and argues instead that in *GP* the practice of the bridal-chamber sacrament is "the *means* toward achieving salvation." Jorunn Jacobsen Buckley, "A Cult-Mystery in The Gospel of Philip," *JBL* 99 (1980): 578. The moral exhortations in 83-84 are addressed to Gnostics who on the basis of knowledge are morally free, not to live immorally; rather, they are free in the NT sense of having the power to live morally. See Wilson, *Gospel*, 169- 170. Compare Pagels, "Marriage," 452. Segelberg defines five sacraments in *GP* that are necessary for salvation: three are initiation rites, two are repeated acts. Eric Segelberg, "The Coptic-Gnostic Gospel According to Philip and Its Sacramental System," *Numen* 7 (1960): 199. Here again, we have a double perversion of the gospel. The nature of Christ has been changed, and works have been added. Thus, Jn 20:31 has been abandoned, and the Galatian curse has been invoked.

[1418] Compare Wilson, *Gospel*, 86.

[1419] Constable, *Jeremiah*, 59.

[1420] J. Preston Eby, "The Saviour of the World Series: The Lake of Fire." Available at http://www.kingdom life.com/eby/s7.htm. Accessed on August 4, 2004.

[1421] Constable, *Ezekiel*, 100.

[1422] Ibid.

[1423] Constable, *Isaiah*, 291

[1424] Jack Van Impe, "Hell," in *Tim Lahaye Study Bible*, 1112.

[1425] Evans, "Rewards," 1234.

[1426] Frank D. Carmical, "The Coronation of the King: An Annotated Work of Fiction: Part 2," *JOTGES* 3:1 (Spring 1990): 60.

[1427] Ibid., 69, n. 12. Carmical's reference to Is 65:24 is an obvious typographical error, actually referring to Is 66:24.

[1428] Carmical, "Part 1," 58.

[1429] Ryrie, *Bible*, 1113.

[1430] Gleason L. Archer, *Isaiah*, WBC (Chicago: Moody Press, 1990), 654.

[1431] Martin, *Isaiah*, 1120.

[1432] Constable, *Isaiah*, 283-284.

[1433] Archer, *Isaiah*, 653.

[1434] NIDNTT, s.v. "Quench," by R. K. Harrison and C. Brown.

[1435] John F, Walvoord, William Crockett, Zachary Hayes, and Clark Pinnock. *Four Views on Hell*, ed. William Crockett (Grand Rapids: Zondervan Publishing House, 1992), 18.

[1436] Ibid., 20.

[1437] Buis' book is more helpful as a historical overview rather than a lexical analysis, however. Harry Buis, *The Doctrine of Eternal Punishment* (Pennsylvania: The Presbyterian and Reformed Publishing Company, 1957).

[1438] Wuest, *Treasures*, 38.

[1439] Constable, *Romans*, 160.

[1440] Peterson, *Hell*, 132.

[1441] Faust, *Rod*, 264.

[1442] Constable, *Daniel*, 137.

[1443] Edward W. Fudge, *The Fire that Consumes: The Biblical Case for Conditional Immortality* (Carlisle: The Paternoster Press, 1994).

[1444] Millard J. Erickson, "Is Hell Forever?" *BibSac* 152:607 (July 1995): 267.

[1445] Augustine, *The City of God*, 23.21. Available online at: http://www.ccel.org/fathers/NPNF1-02/Augustine/cog/t121.htm. Accessed on January 20, 2005.

[1446] Ibid., 270.

[1447] Fudge, *Fire*, 122.

[1448] Erickson, "Hell," 271. Citing John A. T. Robinson, *In the End, God* (New York: Harper and Row, 1968), 131, n. 8. Erickson's article is also available online at http://www.theologicalstudies.org.uk/article_hell_erickson.html. Accessed on August 8, 2004. This statement by Robinson is also reproduced in an online theology. W. Robert Cook, "Chapter 54. The Eternal State," *The Christian Faith: a systematic theology.* Available at http://www.moulton.to /theology/html/c54.html. Accessed on August 14, 2004.

[1449] Faust, *Rod*, 403.

[1450] Ibid., 401.

[1451] Ibid., 402.

[1452] Robert A. Peterson, "Does the Bible Teach Annihilationism?" *BibSac* 156:621 (January, 1999): 17.

[1453] See Pentecost, *Things*, 559. Constable, *Matthew*, 330. Lang, *Parables*, 325; *Revelation*, 358.

[1454] Govett, *Parables*, 30.

[1455] Hodges, *Eclipse*, 28. His position in regarding *Gehenna* as a millennial possibility is attractive in view of Is 66:24 and Rev 19:20. If the lost who speak abusively are in potential danger of being cast into Gehenna during the millennial kingdom, then there is no temporal reason that the lost goats in Mt 25:41 cannot be cast into Gehenna at the commencement of the millennium.

Constable, like Hodges, associates Gehenna with the Lake of Fire, but in contrast Constable expresses a common dispensational sentiment that the goats in Mt 25:41,46 do not enter Gehenna until the end of the millennium: "*The goats (unbelievers) will go into eternal punishment in hell eventually instead of entering the messianic kingdom (cf. 7:21-23; 13:40-43). Immediately they will enter Hades, the place of departed spirits, until God resurrects them at the end of the millennium and sends them to hell*" (*Matthew*, 330).

This wholesale rejection of Hodges' contention fails to deal adequately with the data. The information that we have about Gehenna requires at least some type of millennial applicability to Gehenna. The position taken herein is that Gehenna will be the temporal terrestrial mouth of Hades during millennial and that Mt 25:41 should be taken as proleptic present, referring to the eventual punishment in the celestial Lake of Fire during eternal state. However, the temporal utilization of Gehenna may be used telescopically and typologically to refer to the future Lake of Fire. So although technically the lost are not cast into the Lake of Fire at this time, they nevertheless are cast into terrestrial Gehenna as the millennial representation of that Lake of Fire at this point in time.

Gehenna is not always sharply distinguished from Hades or from the Lake of Fire since it is the mouth for one and the picture of the other. Just as digestive tract includes mouth, stomach, and intestines, so Gehenna can be used to refer, in a comprehensive or general manner, to God's soteriological wrath regardless of which particular aspect of that wrath actually is being implemented. Those swallowed by the mouth of Gehenna will pass on to its stomach and finally to its intestines to be eaten alive by the teeth, acid, and wormlike bacteria. Finally, they will be eliminated, not from conscious torment, but from the conscious thought of those in heavenly bliss.

Because Mt 10:28 states that both the soul and body go to Gehenna, it is best taken as referring to the place of final punishment and thus to the Lake of Fire. Since (1) the goats apparently are cast bodily into Gehenna in Mt 25:41 at the beginning of the millennium, and since (2) the beast and false prophet are also cast bodily into the Lake of Fire at the beginning of the millennium in Rev 19:20, and since (3) unbelievers can be cast into Gehenna during the Millennium in Mt 5:21-22, Hodges believes that Gehenna and the Lake of Fire are one and the same and that unbelievers can be cast into it during the millennium. Those cast into Gehenna/Lake of Fire at the commencement of the millennium and during the course of the millennium will be removed from it long enough at the conclusion of the millennium to stand before the Great White Throne Judgment before being cast back into it. Hodges position is certainly attractive due to its logical consistency and simplicity.

On the other hand, the present writer has been attracted more so to a typological and telescopic understanding due to the OT background, particularly Is 66:24, and has concluded that **the torment in the presence of the Lamb during the tribulation is typologically and telescopically merged with the torment to be experienced throughout eternity away from His visible presence**. Hodges, in contrast, believes that Jesus is using the OT imagery differently than the manner Isaiah employed them. The present writer concurs but explains this difference in terms of telescopic typology. In any event, in these two similar approaches, conservative misthology possesses two plausible alternatives to ultraistic misthology. As to the ultraistic position on Mt 5:22, Hodges well clarifies in this series of correspondences:

> There is no good reason to think that a regenerate person can be sent there even temporarily. The words "his brother" are to be understood in the Jewish sense of that term (as in Lev. 19:17-18 and many, many places in the Law) since this is a discussion about fulfilling the Law (Mt. 5:17)....
>
> ...As Govett admits in one of his books, his doctrine about a temporary "hell" for believers arose from Mt. 5:22, which he misunderstood as a reference to a Christian brother. The resulting doctrine is an enormous theological heresy. (Personal correspondence, 26 November, 2004.)

To summarize a rather complex discussion, there are multiple opinions concerning Gehenna being evaluated in the FG camp. Hodges and the present writer take a similar but not identical avenue to regarding Gehenna as a literal soteriological issue. Dillow has more recently suggested a metaphorical misthological interpretation. Faust advocates a literal misthological approach. The complexity is compounded by trying to determine if Gehenna is temporal, millennial, eternal, or some combination of these options. Basic observations leading up to the option taken herein would include the following:

- Is 66:24 indicates a literal millennial fulfillment for the display of unbelievers' corpses who were slain in Armageddon.
- Mt 5:22,29-30 confirms that Gehenna is a place for the whole body.
- Mt 10:28 confirms that Gehenna is for the metaphysical soul and physical body.
- Mt 18:9 implies that Gehenna is for the whole body.

- Mt 23:15,33 indicates that Gehenna is a soteriological issue.
- Lk 12:5 is unusual in that Gehenna seems to go beyond death of body to punishment of disembodied soul and is thus apparently equivalent to the subterranean Hades.
- Jam 3:6 is used metaphorically.
- Mt 18:8 parallels Gehenna of 18:9 with the eternal fire of Mt 25:41 and appears to picture the eternal state in 25:41.

The conclusions I have reached include taking Gehenna as a literal millennial fulfillment for the bodies of the lost who are slain at the commencement of the millennial kingdom (Is 66:24). This usage typologically foreshadows the NT terrestrial usage and telescopically merges this usage with the NT celestial usage. Gehenna is also used of the literal subterranean imprisonment of the disembodied souls of the lost in Hades (Mt 10:28; Lk 12:5). Gehenna is also a millennial indictment that is inclusive of the eternal punishment of the lost (Mt 18:8-9; cp 25:41). The nature of this eternal punishment, coupled with its usage in Mt 23:15,33, requires that it be taken soteriologically rather than misthologically.

[1456] See Pentecost, *Things*, 559. Constable, *Matthew*, 330.

[1457] Charles C. Ryrie, *Revelation: New Edition*, EBC (Chicago: Moody Press, 1996), 104.

[1458] Constable, *Revelation*, 134.

[1459] Peterson, "Annihilationism," 17-18.

[1460] Fudge, 155, n. 31.

[1461] Charles L. Quarles, "The Ἀπό of 2 Thessalonians 1:9 and the Nature of Eternal Punishment," *WTJ* 59:2 (Fall 1997): 201-211.

[1462] Morris, *Second Thessalonians*, 206.

[1463] Peterson, "Annihilationism," 18.

[1464] Henry M. Morris, "Biblical Eschatology and Modern Science: Part IV," *BibSac* 125:500 (October 1968): 298-299.

[1465] C. T. Schwarze, "The Bible and Science on the Everlasting Fire: A Radio Broadcast By Professor C. T. Schwarze," *BibSac* 95:377 (January 1938): 102-112.

[1466] Morris, *Second Thessalonians*, 205.

[1467] Fudge, 180.

[1468] Peterson, *Hell*, 85.

[1469] Forster, 72.

[1470] BECA, s.v. "Pharaoh, Hardening of."

[1471] Forster, 73.

[1472] Hunt, *Love*, 267.

[1473] Forster, 75.

[1474] BECA, "Pharaoh."

[1475] Vance, 327.

[1476] Ibid., 273.

[1477] Gleason L. Archer, *Encyclopedia of Bible Difficulties* (Grand Rapids: Zondervan Publishing House, 1982), 187-188.

[1478] Hodges, *James*, 27.

[1479] A common view held by some soft securitists is that God's discipline keeps a believer saved. See endnote 186. Some take this to mean that God will not allow a believer to sin too badly or so long that it would result in the believer losing salvation. For example, God will kill a believer before He lets the believer commit apostasy. One problem with this view is that it conditions security on not committing apostasy. Second, apostasy is biblically possible. Nevertheless, the present book acknowledges that God will kill a believer during the tribulation before God would allow a believer to take the mark of the beast. The sin of taking the mark of the beast is off limits to believers. But with technical finesse, it is added that God's not allowing them to take the mark does not mean that if they did take the mark, they would become lost. As a strong securitist, I reject the soft notion that God's temporal or misthological discipline keeps the believer saved. Rather, God disciplines the believer temporally and misthologically because the believer is eternally saved and, therefore, cannot be subjected to soteriological discipline.

Because a believer cannot become unregenerate and since God wishes to limit the mark of the beast to the unregenerate, God implements temporal discipline to prevent believers from taking the mark of the beast (1) since regeneration will not prevent believers from subcoming to the mark of the beast and (2) since subcoming to take the mark of the beast will not cause believers to lose their regeneration. Preservation is not using perseverance as a means of preservation. Hypothetically speaking, even if God had decided to allow a believer to take the mark of the beast, the believer still would remain soteriologically saved. However, since God has decided that He will not allow a believer to take the mark of the beast, it is impossible for a believer to take the mark of the beast. Those believers who fail to persevere in intent will still be saved, even though they will be prevented by premature death from subcoming in action to taking the mark. In other words, had God decided differently regarding the mark of the beast, the book of Revelation would have been written differently. But since Revelation reveals what will actually take place rather than what merely could take place hypothetically, it may be deduced that genuine believers cannot take the mark of the beast. Hypothetically, even if believers could take the mark, they would not lose their regeneration. Realistically, they cannot take the mark because God has decided that they cannot, not because their regeneration or forfeiture of regeneration prevents them from doing so. Also see my *3D Unconditional Security*.

[1480] For a similar diagram from an ultraist, see Whipple, "The Moving of Paradise," *Mysteries*, 117. For his discussion, see p. 93. Also, see his *Shock*, 213.

[1481] The six basic options concerning 1Pet 3:18-19 may be summarized into three realistic possibilities. (1) It may be referring to the pre-incarnate Christ descending to earth and spiritually energizing Noah in his proclamation. (2) Or it may be describing the post-crucified Christ descending into Hades and making proclamations of condemnation and liberation to the unrighteous and righteous respectively. (3) Then again, it might refer to the post-resurrected Lord's announcement of victory to the demonic spirits who had cohabited with women in the days of Noah (and perhaps their offspring).

[1482] Archer, *Difficulties*, 350-351, 367.

[1483] Faust, 273-276.

[1484] Barbieri, *Matthew,* 47.

[1485] Grassmick, *Mark*, 117.

[1486] Lane, *Mark*, 145, n. 101; 146.

[1487] Morris, *Luke*, 211.

[1488] Lenski, *Mark*, 154.

[1489] Hendriksen, *Matthew*, 529.

[1490] Berkhof, 352-354.

[1491] Hutson, *Salvation*, 1:128.

[1492] Stanley, *Security*, 133.

[1493] Robert N. Wilkin, "Christians and the Unpardonable Sin," *GIF* (March-April 1997).

[1494] Crawford, personal correspondence, 9-27-2009.

[1495] Tanner, "Thorns," 29. Tanner believes that the reference to *eternal judgment* in Heb 6:2 is not part of the elementary teaching; rather, it evidently serves as a bridge from the elementary soteriological teachings to the mature misthological theme to be exhorted in Heb 6:4-8. This term *eternal judgment* is transitional since it encompasses both the soteriological and misthological results for all those who are raised from the dead. *The resurrection of the dead* mentioned immediately before the reference to eternal judgment in v. 2 certainly would include believers. This being the case, the writer of Hebrews wants his readers to advance from a simple understanding of eternal judgment in soteriological terms to a mature grasp of the misthological dimensions also embedded in that term. The eternal misthological salvation in 5:9 is to be preceded by an eternal misthological judgment in 6:3-8.

Granted, Kendall shares this overall theological perspective but does not believe that misthological judgment is part of the *eternal judgment* in Heb 6:2. R. T. Kendall, *Are You Stone* Deaf *to the Spirit or Rediscovering God?* (Ross-shire: Christian Focus Publications, 1994), 79-80. Thus, his reservation is not based on a theological objection but an exegetical one. The resurrection is *of* the dead, not *from* the dead. Kendall is of the opinion that if it were the judgment of believers, then it would be the judgment of those raised *from* the dead. Although Kendall concurs that there is a two-fold resurrection, he does not believe the writer of Hebrews has this in mind in this particular passage. Kendall's consistency (in limiting the meaning of resurrection and judgment) and his sensitivity to the text are appreciated. However, it appears that he is guilty of making an overly stringent refinement in his appeal to the meaning of the preposition in this instance. After all, we would not say that the resurrection *of* the dead in Mt 22:31 is limited to unbelievers would we? Further, the resurrection *from the dead* (Acts 17:31) can be equated simply with resurrection *of the dead* (Acts 17:32; cp. 24:21). Paul equates the resurrection *of* the dead with *from* the dead in 1Cor 15:**12**-13,21,42.

Kendall misspeaks when he says that the writer of Hebrews "wants his readers to leave the subject of judgment" (p. 80). On the contrary, the author of Hebrews wants his readers to advance beyond the subject of the judgment of the lost to the judgment of the saved (e.g., Heb 10:27,30). In light of Kendall's treatment of the topic, this is evidently what he meant to say. But if so, this brings him one step closer to agreement with Tanner. The writer of Hebrews wants them to advance beyond a foundational understanding of eternal judgment to a mature understanding that recognizes the potentially severe eternal misthological ramifications that judgment holds for believers. Yet as Kendall has demonstrated so eloquently, the writer of Hebrews wants them not only to have a mature understanding of the Bema, he wants them to realize that if they persist in the direction they are heading, then severe punishment at the Bema will be inevitable. Such believers' hearts may become so hardened that there is no longer any possibility whatsoever of their repenting. Tanner agrees (p. 34). Misthologists are justified in concluding that such believers will be misthologically guilty of an eternal sin. They will reach this state before they die. Such believers misthologically commit the unpardonable sin.

[1496] Pagenkemper, "Part 1," 187-188.

[1497] Jesus is speaking to a hostile crowd of unbelievers; they are implicitly and explicitly identified as such in the context of Jn 8:21-46. Jesus makes a parenthetical statement to the new believers within this crowd in vv. 31b-32. John makes a parenthetical remark in vv. 30-31a to clarify that Jesus' words spoken in 8:31b-32 are intended for the new believers dispersed among the hostile crowd at large.

These hostile unbelievers do not understand, hear, or believe Jesus' words. His word has no place in them. They have completely rejected and misunderstood it. They want to kill Him. Their generation and nature are strictly from the world and of the world. So why in the midst of this argument did Jesus invite them to abide/remain in His word when they never had received His word at all? John explains, with a parenthetical insert, that this invitation is addressed to a small subgroup who did believe.

Address to Hostile Crowd (Jn 8:21-29)
He said therefore again to them, "I go away, and you shall seek Me, and shall die in your sin; where I am going, you cannot come." And He was saying to them, "You are from below, I am from above; you are of this world, I am not of this world. I said therefore to you, that you shall die in your sins; for unless you believe that I am He, you shall die in your sins"...

Parenthetical Insert by *John* and **Jesus** (Jn 8:30-31)
As He spoke these things, many came to believe in Him. Jesus therefore was saying to those Jews who had believed Him, **"If you abide in My word, then you are truly disciples of Mine; and you shall know the truth, and the truth shall make you free."**

Response of Hostile Crowd (Jn 8:33ff)
They answered Him, "We are Abraham's offspring, and have never yet been enslaved to anyone; how is it that You say, 'You shall become free'?"... "I know that you are Abraham's offspring; yet you seek to kill Me ...Why do you not understand what I am saying? It is because you cannot hear My word. You are *of your father the devil* ...you do not believe Me. Which one of you convicts Me of sin? If I speak truth, why do you not believe Me?"

[1498] Not surprisingly, Zeller ("Theology") equates the soteriological occurrence of passing from death into life in Jn 5:24 with the experiential usage in 1Jn 3:14 to conclude that if your experience does not prove that you are saved, then you are not saved. However, it would seem rather inconsistent to affirm that 1Jn 3:14 is referring to our experience of love and yet deny that knowledge is likewise experiential, especially since it is coupled with the highly experiential concept of abiding (also see 1Jn 3:15). Yet in this same discussion, Zeller appeals to 1Jn 2:9,11 as proof that believers are not in the darkness. To the contrary, the passage is referring to a believer's *walk* (i.e., experience) rather than to a believer's position (v. 11). The phrase *in the darkness* is parallel to *walks in the darkness*; thus, *in* is being used experientially. And both verses are talking about a believer since both verses explicitly say, "His brother." Further, John had mentioned earlier the possibility of believers walking in the darkness and clarified that he was talking about fellowship rather than relationship (1Jn 1:6). Believers who claim to be experientially in the light nullify that claim if they hate their brother in Christ and thereby show that they are experientially in the darkness. Those believers who love one another can know that they are experientially in the light. Zeller's position is disproven by the texts he cites in that they confirm that believers may be experientially in the darkness (1Jn 2:9,11; 3:14); although, they are positionally in the light (Jn 5:24). The promise of passing from death to life in Jn 5:24 is conditioned on being a believer. It is thus positional. The passing from death to life in 1Jn 3:14 is conditioned on being a loving believer. It is thus experiential. Unloving believers are darkened in their walk and thus in their experience (1Jn 2:11).

[1499] Practicing Mt 5:16 and 1Tim 4:15 are sometimes hard to do when one has not reconciled them with Mt 6:1-6. When I was in a church that had AWANA, I posed this question on the AWANA web site:

There are people in our church who are opposed to using rewards to motivate children to memorize Scripture. Too be sure, I do not share their perspective since the Bible uses a variety of rewards, both temporal and eternal, to motivate godly behavior. In preparing a response to their seemingly atheistic mindset that discourages the use of rewards in favor of the intrinsic value of the behavior itself, there is a biblical matter that causes me concern, however. Certainly, this is an apprehension that you have pondered, and I am hoping that you will share your insights with me.

The Lord warns us in Mt 6:1-6 that certain types of godly behavior are to be practiced secretly. Otherwise, the reward of human praise we get on earth will be all that we get. We will be disqualified from receiving rewards in heaven for the righteousness we practice publicly for human praise.

If I might paraphrase this Matthean passage in a manner from the viewpoint of this objection, it would be as follows: "Beware of memorizing your verses for the AWANA program to be noticed by and praised by the people in your church; otherwise, you will have no reward in heaven." Thus, someone could use this passage to discredit the use of AWANA trophies, patches, and bucks to encourage the children in memorizing Scripture. Participation in AWANA public praise system disqualifies one from heavenly rewards.

Your help in formulating a response to this type of objection would be most deeply appreciated, as I am sure that you have dealt with this type of mentality before. How do you biblically justify using public rewards to motivate memorization?

The response I received was helpful in formulating an insert that I included in the AWANA notebooks I created for the children. The thrust of my response was as follows:

God commands Scripture memorization (Deut 6:6-9), and He rewards it (2Tim 2:15). This second verse provides the acronym for AWANA: **A**pproved **W**orkman **A**re **N**ot **A**shamed. The Greek word for *approved* in 2Tim 2:15 is *dokimos*. It is the same Greek word that James uses to say that those believers who are *approved* will be rewarded with the crown of life (Jam 1:12). God gives crowns to approved workmen, and AWANA gives them trophies! Such rewards are not given to all believers. A believer can be *unapproved* (*adokimos*) and ashamed at the Judgment Seat of Christ (1Cor 9:27; 1Jn 2:28). Crowns, like trophies, must be earned.

Memorizing verses simply to be noticed by and praised by others is discouraged (Mt 6:1-6). We will be disqualified from receiving rewards in heaven for the righteousness we practice publicly for human praise. But in this very passage Jesus expects us to be concerned about and motivated by heavenly rewards, to seek heavenly payment. Jesus is not discouraging seeking rewards. In this same chapter He commands us to lay up treasure for ourselves in heaven (Mt 6:20). God wants to be thought of as a "rewarder" (Heb 11:6). We do not encourage memorizing Scripture for the purpose of human praise but for the purpose of hearing the heavenly praise, "Well Done." The doctrine of heavenly rewards is used to purify earthly motives.

At the same time, the Bible also commands us to encourage one another while on earth. We are to come together for the purpose of encouraging one another and considering how to motivate one another in the Lord (Heb 10:24-25). We reward Scripture memorization in order to follow the Lord's example and encourage one another to obey the Lord's command. Would we tell our pastor that he is not entitled to reward for studying the word? Not hardly! Paul says that those who work hard in the word are entitled to both honor and pay (1Tim 5:17-19). To use Paul's analogy, if we are not to muzzle an ox while it is working, what makes us think that we have the right to muzzle our children when they are memorizing? The working ox, as well as the approved workman, should be rewarded. Diligent study is expected to be publicly evident, esteemed, and appreciated (1Thess 5:12-13; 1Tim 4:15). If God tells us to honor such behavior in this manner, then who are we to tell God, "No"? Teaching children to obey God and giving positive reinforcement for positive behavior and attitudes is not bribery.

Children should be encouraged to memorize Scripture, and part of that encouragement should include public recognition and reward. They should be taught that such recognition is the tool of encouragement rather than the goal of memorization. We memorize to encourage one another rather than to be better than others. Additionally, as fathers, we are to train our children in the Lord's instruction and yet seek to do so in such a way that will not provoke them to anger (Eph 6:4). How happy would you be with your boss if he expected you to work for free? Would you be angry? Jesus pays us according to our works (Rev 22:12). Would it not be better to follow the Lord's example of paying for services rendered? Perhaps a quarter or even a fifty-cent piece for each new verse your children memorizes would help convey the heavenly value that both you and God put on such activity and help them avoid resentment. Have them quote their verses to you. Doing so will show that you care. Children are also more prone to do what you inspect rather than what you merely expect. Inspection resulting in reward would be a great time to reinforce the positive truths pertaining to the *Bema*.

[1500] Miles J. Stanford, "Dispensational Disintegration (Part 2)—Grace in Eclipse: A Study on Eternal Rewards." Available at http://withchrist.org/MJS/zane.htm. Accessed on August 11, 2004.

[1501] Ibid.

[1502] Pentecost, 121-128.

[1503] Paul R. Schmidtbleicher, "Balancing the Use of the Old Testament. *Chafer Theological Seminary Journal* 8:3 (July - September 2002).

[1504] Pentecost, 532-546.

[1505] Ibid., 543.

[1506] Ryrie, *Dispensationalism*, 198-203.

[1507] Ventilato, "Refutation," section I, 10.

[1508] Ibid., II, 5.

1509 Ibid., II, 8.

1510 Ibid., II, 9.

1511 Ibid., II, 9, B.

1512 Ibid., II, 9, F.

1513 NIDNTT, S.v. "Crown, Sceptre, Rod," by C. J. Hemer.

1514 Richard Chenevix. Trench, *Synonyms of the New Testament,* seventh edition, revised and enlarged (London: MacMillian and Co., 1871), 74-77.

1515 Hemer, "Crown."

1516 Ventilato, "Refutation," section II, 9, H..

1517 Ibid., section III, 13.

1518 Wilkin, *Confident*, ch. 19. Also see his online article: "Does Hell Await Those Who Fall? 2 Peter 2:18-22" *GIF* (May 1988).

1519 *The way of truth* (2Pet 2:2) will be scandalized by two different groups of apostates in this context and, thus, by two different forms of apostasy: objective and subjective. Both types of apostasy are introduced in 2:1-3 and then expounded upon in the context. In the opening verses, *the way of truth* will be maligned by unbelieving teachers who introduce destructive heresies that lead mature believers astray into sensuality.

The first type of apostasy explicitly dealt with is the objective apostasy by the false teachers from *the way* (2Pet 2:15). These teachers never had any saving knowledge of the way. Their knowledge of the way was, therefore, superficial and impersonal. They never had personally embraced the faith. Numerous details from the text lead to this conclusion.

For one thing, Peter says, "They have no knowledge" (2:12). That is, they are *agnoeo;* they are completely ignorant (*agnoeo* is an antonym of *ginosko*). Their lack of even basic *gnosis* (*knowledge*) *of the way of the truth* itself indicates that they do not have saving knowledge of *the way.* Therefore, their departure from *the way* reflects objective apostasy from the Christian body of truth which they never personally had embraced as true.

Additionally, these *unrighteous* and *ungodly* men are contrasted with *righteous* and *godly* Lot (2:5-9). Now if Lot represents a carnal believer in Scripture, as seems evident, then these men rank even lower than carnal believes and, therefore, most naturally would represent unbelievers. Abraham asked, "Wilt Thou indeed sweep away the righteous with the wicked?" (Gen 18:23) Lot and his family were spared, yet we do not assume that they were spared because of their ethical righteousness. Far to the contrary, Lot's wife turned back and was turned into a pillar of salt, and his daughters got him drunk so that they could become pregnant by him. It is best to understand that they were spared because of their judicial righteousness, and this righteousness provides the grounds for the infrequence that we find evidenced in verse 8: "For by what he saw and heard that righteous man, while living among them, felt his righteous soul tormented day after day with their lawless deeds."

These false teachers in 2:15, who forsake *the way* are contrasted (with Lot) as being *unrighteous*, meaning they are unregenerate. They are described in 2:12 as "*born (gennao)* as creatures of instinct to be captured and killed," rather than as having experienced the *new birth* (*anagennao*) Peter had described previously (1Pet 1:3,23). They never had embraced the truth subjectively. They never came to *gnosis*, much less *epignosis* (cp. 2Tim 3:7). They never had experienced the *deliverance* (*rhuomai*) that immature Lot did in 2:9 or the *escape* (*apopheugo*) that mature believer experienced in 2:20.

Contrastively, the second type of apostasy expounded in the passage by those who personally had embraced the faith is certainly subjective apostasy. Not only had they experienced saving knowledge, they had advanced to mature saving knowledge. The false teachers will scandalize *the way of the truth* by not only abandoning it themselves but by causing *many* to do so as well. It will be scandalized both by objective apostasy on the part of the false teachers and additionally by the derivative subjective apostasy on the part of those whom they lead astray. As a result, the blasphemy in this passage is the result of the dualistic apostasy of the false teachers and their dupes. Both the original and derivational apostasy will result in criticism of *the way of the truth.*

1520 Another misperception that has led some to assume these false teachers were saved is the fact that they are called *accursed children* in 2Pet 2:14. It is assumed that they were children of God who became accursed. However, the text does not say that they were children of God. Instead, as frequently noted in the commentaries, the text literally says that they were *children of a curse*. This is a Hebraism meaning that they are the *objects of God's curse.*

Just as the parallel in Eph 2:3 of being *children of God's wrath* is not equatable with being *children of God*, so neither is being *children of God's curse* synonymous with being *children of God.* And lest one try to avoid this conclusion by saying that *children of obedience* in 1Pet 1:14 refers to all those who are ontologically *children of God*, let it be noted that being children of *wrath* (or of a *curse* or of *obedience*) does not mean that such children are born by wrath (or by a curse or by obedience or by *disobedience* for that matter in Eph 2:2 or 5:6). Yet being a *child of God* can mean to be *born of God* (e.g. Jn 1:12). So making a simple equation between being a *child of God* and being a *child of obedience*, regardless of the context, would be ill-advised since one may be an ontological *child of God* without being an experiential *child of obedience*. Although this idiom can be used of one's character, one cannot press this idiom to mean that children of God are necessarily obedient in their character. For that matter, being *born of God* (which is an ontological affirmation) cannot necessarily be equated with being *children of God* (which may be a idiomatic identification as it is in Phil 2:15). In terms of idiomatic disparity, not all those who are born of God are children of God, although conversely we affirm that all children of God are born of God. Or to use mathematical notation to represent it more simply: children of God ⊂ born of God. See "Pater (Father)" in my *Drawing and Appointment.*

According to Lenski, this genitive used in 1Pet 1:14 and its parallels "describes the constitution and character of these children, which is impressed upon them from their very birth, belongs to their very nature" (*First Peter*, 54). Even so, it cannot be maintained that this disposition makes it impossible for those described by this idiom to act contrary to their nature since, in 1Pet 1:14 itself, Peter is urging believers to be children of obedience in their behavior. This is all the more apparent in yet another parallel that Lenski provides in Eph 5:8, where Paul is exhorting believers who are *light in the Lord* to *walk as children of Light*. Obviously, this Semitism cannot be pressed to mean that the new birth constitutionally guarantees such behavior on the part of the believer. I will be content, therefore, to understand *accursed children* in 2Pet 1:14 to simply mean that these lost teachers are *objects of God's curse* just as the parallel in Eph 2:3 refers to the lost who by nature are *objects of God's wrath.*

[1521] Bryson, *Dark*, 160-164.

[1522] Gordon Olson, 134; Bryson, *Dark*, 140-142.

[1523] Andrew D. Chang, "Second Peter 2:1 and the Extent of the Atonement," *BibSac* 142:565 (January 1985): 52-61.

[1524] Simon Escobedo III, "2 Peter 2:1 and Universal Redemption." Available at http://www.aomin.org /2PE21.html#_ednref20. Accessed on June 20, 2005.

[1525] Gordon Olson, 118.

[1526] Lenski, *Romans*, 118.

[1527] Idem, *2 Peter* 332-333.

[1528] Wilkin, *Confident*, 165-166.

[1529] Ryrie, *Balancing*, 180.

[1530] Ventilato, "Refutation," addendum 5.

[1531] Ibid., 3.

[1532] Ashby, *Security*, 129.

[1533] Corner, *Security*, 352-353.

[1534] Shank, *Life*, 200, cp. 190.

[1535] Ibid., 258.

[1536] Ibid., 264.

[1537] Ibid., 265.

[1538] Craig Blomberg, "Degrees," 163.

[1539] Keith R. Krell, "Will You Be Approved On That Day? 1 Corinthians 9:24-27." Available at http://www.faithalone.org/sermons/approved.htm. Accessed on August 10, 2004. Wilkin and Tanner point out that *adokimos* is used of believers in Heb 6:8. Robert N. Wilkin, "No Second Repentance? Hebrews 6:4-8." *Grace in Focus* (July-August 1992). J. Paul. Tanner, "'But If It Yields Thorns And Thistles': An Exposition Of Hebrews 5:11–6:12," *JOTGES* 14:26 (Spring 2001): 19-42 This word is also used of believers in 2Cor 13:5. See Robert N. Wilkin, "Test Yourselves to See If You Are in the Faith: Assurance Based on Our Works? 2 Corinthians 13:5." *GIF* (October 1989).

[1540] Ashby, *Security*, 129.

[1541] Zeller, "Theology." Compare, Hodges, *Eclipse*, 73-74.

[1542] Litfin, *Titus*, 763. Lenski, *Titus*, 904. Hendriksen, *Titus*, 355.

[1543] Guthrie, *Titus*, 190.

[1544] Wilkin, *Confident*, 81-88, n. 7, 259.

[1545] Zeller, Theology."

[1546] Ibid.

[1547] Clarence E. Mason, Jr. "A Study of Pauline Motives: As Revealed in 2 Corinthians 4:16-6:4a," *BibSac* 111:443 (July 1954), 219.

[1548] Dillow, 300.

[1549] Scott Crawford, "Hebrews: Five Warnings For Believers." Available at http://www.wordoftruthclass.org /articles/fivewarnings.pdf. Accessed on July 7, 2007.

[1550] Barker, *Secure*, 144-145.

[1551] Lang, *Hebrews*, 98.

[1552] Kendall, *Deaf*, 85.

[1553] Dillow, 447.

[1554] Dillow, 446. A. Duane Litfin, *2 Timothy* BKC (Wheaton: Victor Books, 1984), 755.

[1555] The Greek is ambiguous in Rom 1:28 as to whether they refused to *have* or *hold* God in a mature level of knowledge. The former would indicate that they never had *epignosis*; the latter would indicate that they had it but failed to hold on to it. Translations are split over the difference. Those favoring the latter point of view include: *keep* (BBE), *retain* (KJV, NKJ, NIB, NIV, RWB, WEB), *any longer* (NAS, NAU). However, even if it were understood as saying that they did not see fit to have *epignosis*, this would indicate that they not only had *gnosis* but that they were in a position to move on to *epignosis* and chose not to do so. In this case, it would be like Israel standing on the brink of entering the Promised Land but refusing to do so. Otherwise, it would be like Esau who already was entitled to the full inheritance but lost it. In either case, it is easier to explain how believers would be in a position to reject this mature understanding of God than it is to theorize that unbelievers somehow could have a saving knowledge (*gnosis*) of God and then be rejected because they failed to press on to, or hold on to, a mature knowledge.

[1556] David A. deSilva, "No Confidence In The Flesh: The Meaning and Function of Philippians 3:2–21," *TrinJ* 15:1 (Spring 1994): 50.

[1557] Eaton, 159.

[1558] DeSilva, 44.

[1559] Robert A. Pyne, "The Role of the Holy Spirit in Conversion," *BSac* 150:598 (April 1993): 214.

[1560] Henry W. Holloman, "The Relation Of Christlikeness To Spiritual Growth," *MTJ* 5 (Spring/Fall 1994): 63.

[1561] Martin, *Cults*, 484.

[1562] Norman Geisler and Ron Rhodes, *When Cultists Asks: A Popular Handbook on Cultic Ministries* (Grand Rapids: Baker Books, 1997), 98.

[1563] Michael J. Wilkins, *Matthew*, The NIV Application Commentary: From biblical text . . . to contemporary life, gen. ed. Terry Muck (Grand Rapids: Zondervan, 2004), 229.

[1564] Wilkins, 236. But Wilkins (not to be confused with Bob Wilkin of GES) blows Mt 5:20 royally by insisting that the righteousness necessary to enter heaven is "justification (imputed righteousness) and sanctification (imparted righteousness)"—the latter being described as inner transformation (pp. 234-235). And he is by no means alone in this error. Contrary to Wilkins, and those like him, our entrance into heaven is conditioned on imputational righteousness alone.

[1565] Leon Morris, *The Gospel according to Matthew* (Grand Rapids: Eerdmans Publishing Co., 1992), 108.

[1566] John MacArthur, *Matthew 1-7*, MNTC (Chicago: Moody Press, 1985), 256.

[1567] Craig L. Blomberg, *Matthew,* vol. 22, NAC, gen. ed. David S. Dockery (Nashville: Broadman Press, 1992), 104.

[1568] See Wilkins, *Matthew*, 236, n. 21.

[1569] R. T. France, *Matthew*, TNT, 115.

[1570] Kuhatschek, *Applying*, 54. This simplified version of the principlizing approach is described more in-depth by Hayes with additional steps. See J. Daniel Hays, "Applying the Old Testament Law Today," *BibSac* 158 (January-March, 2001): 21-35.

[1571] I would also add, "Is it prophecy that is yet to be fulfilled?" If so, then, although the direct application awaits the future, proceed through the pyramid to discover its indirect application for today. For example, although Mk 13:13 is referring to being saved as a result of enduring the future tribulation, it certainly has application for today.

[1572] Compare Kuhatschek, 75.

[1573] Although Martin demonstrates that the NT practice is to worship on Sunday, he nevertheless makes allowances for Sabbatarians (such as Adventists) to worship on Saturday on the basis of Rom 14:5-6 (p. 470). Accepting the council of Kuhatschek and Martin in regarding the day as a variable would appear reasonable as long as the proper motivation is maintained and the Galatian error is avoided. However, since Adventists seek to retain the justification through such observance, they fail to avoid falling from grace into legalism with their sabbatical observance.

[1574] Geisler and Rhodes provide a very helpful illustration to explain how "the moral principles embodied in the Commands" are "still binding on believers today" without placing believers under the law: "The fact that we are bound by similar moral laws against adultery, lying, stealing, and murder no more proves we are still under the Ten Commandments than the fact that there are similar traffic laws in North Carolina and Texas proves that a Texan driving in Texas is under the laws of North Carolina" (p. 98). So how do we reconcile this perspective with Paul who affirms that all the OT law has been abolished (Eph 2:15) and Jesus who announces that He did not come to abolish the Law. Morris is correct: "Jesus firmly disclaims any intention of doing away with any part of the Bible" (*Matthew*, 107-108). By fulfilling the requirements of the law for us, Jesus not only delivered us from the direct application of the law but also from the price of obedience soteriologically demanded by the law. That price is no longer demanded from us—either directly or indirectly. The law's demand for soteric righteousness from us has ended because it has been fulfilled for us by Christ (Rom 10:4).

Adventists are by no means alone in thinking that the moral law remains intact. Mainline interpreters such as MacArthur and Hendriksen also share this error. Hendriksen "insists that *every* commandment of that [the greatest commandments] which is truly God's moral law...must be kept" (italics his). Hendriksen, *Matthew*, 292. MacArthur acknowledges that Jesus has fulfilled the moral, judicial, and ceremonial law for us. By His life, Christ fulfilled the moral demands of the law. And by His death, He fulfilled the judicial and sacrificial demands of the law. Yet MacArthur strangely concludes that although the latter two ended and were set aside because they were fulfilled, the moral law is still being fulfilled by Jesus' disciples (*Matthew 1-7*, 257-259). Besides being inconsistent, his distinction is artificial and superficial. His inconsistency grows even worse, even if he is just following WCF, when he regards keeping the Sabbath part of the moral law as part of the law that was completed along with the judicial and ceremonial law (p. 262). How he can pick and choose what parts of the so-called moral law is to be set aside is left a mystery. As to the part of the moral law that MacArthur still deems to place believers under, he says it is "just as valid" and yet "no longer binding" and calls this a "paradox" (p. 272). What happened to Jam 2:10? MacArthur says that Christians "are no longer under the ultimate penalty of the law." Yet elsewhere he will conclude that God does not keep us apart from our perseverance. (For documentation, see my book *Mere Christianity and Moral Christianity*.) Such a perspective certainly makes it sound like MacArthur regards the moral law as soteriologically binding!

To his credit, however, MacArthur does address Mt 5:20 very well in his commentary by describing it exclusively as imputed righteousness. Splendid! In defense of his treatment of this verse, I will point out although the moral *principles* (rather than *laws* themselves) of the OT are still applicable to us (albeit not soterically) and need to be fulfilled by us, this pericope in Mt 5:17-20 conditions our entrance into the kingdom on *our* righteousness (v. 20) as produced by *Jesus'* fulfillment of the law. Entrance is not based on *our* righteousness as produced by *our* obedience of the law. The righteousness in view in this immediate context is produced *for* us rather than *by* us or *through* us. Nor is it righteousness *displayed by* us. Righteousness produced by us, or through us, or displayed by us results in rewards for us. Entrance is free; rewards are not. Imputed righteousness is exclusively in view in 5:20, not imparted righteousness or manifestative righteousness.

[1575] Martin, 485-486, 490. One cannot simply chop those 10 commandments out of the 613 commandments (from the first five books of the Bible) and claim to have discovered applications for moral principles that are still operable today.

[1576] For documentation, see my book *Mere Christianity and Moral Christianity*.

[1577] See Hodges, "Law," and Wilkin, "Fool." The only modification to Hodges' article that I would suggest is to clarify that those in the millennial kingdom (the future *then*) are not placed directly under the OT law (back *then*). After all, the millennial prohibition against murder will modify the OT Law so that it will have application to anger. This super-strict enforcement of the in-depth implications of the OT Law would be better considered the Millennial Law than a return to the OT Law.

[1578] Virgil V. Porter Jr., "The Sermon on the Mount in the Book of James, Part 1," *BibSac* 162:647 (July 2005): 344-360. Unfortunately, in his second article, when discussing the mutual soteriology of the Sermon on the Mount (pp. 479-481), Porter appears to adopt the popular view point that one must have good works as the necessary and natural expression of one's faith in order for such faith to be saving faith. Virgil V. Porter Jr., "The Sermon on the Mount in the Book of James, Part 2," *BibSac* 162:648 (October 2005): 470-482. Such an approach logically and tragically results in making final soteric justification conditioned on faith and works. Porter overlooks the mistholic nature of such salvation. Both Jesus and James are talking about rewards as the outcome for the believers' works! Exclusion from the kingdom and rulership of the kingdom is based on performance. Entrance into the kingdom is not based on works. To those (unbelievers) who are seeking kingdom entrance by means of their performance, Jesus says, "Depart from Me" (Mt 7:23). To those (believers) who are seeking rewards in the kingdom by means of their performance, Jesus says, "Blessed" (Mt 5:3-12).

[1579] For commentators affirming that the issue is kingdom ranking rather than kingdom exclusion in Mt 5:19, see Carson, Greene, MacArthur, Morris, Mounce, Nolland, Wilkins. Oliver B. Greene, *The Gospel According to Matthew*, vol. 1, chapters 1-5 (Greenville; SC: The Gospel Hour, 1971). Some commentators, in contrast, believe that Mt 5:19 refers to ranking in the present kingdom. France, for example, believes that it is a ranking of last in terms of the quality of discipleship rather than in terms of future rewards. Blomberg also believes that it is ranking in the present kingdom, and on the basis of Mt 20:1-16, he is doubtful that there will be ranking in the future kingdom. See *Workers in Vineyard (Mt 20:1-16)*, 683.

For sake of interaction with Bloomberg's principle arguments against misthological ranking in Mt 5:19 that may be gleaned from its closest parallels, however, let it be granted for sake of argument that Jesus is describing someone in Mt 11:11 who is presently least in the inaugurated kingdom as having a greater privilege (rather than a greater reward) than John the Baptist: "He who *is* least in the kingdom of heaven *is* greater than he." The present tense is emphasized. Because John did not live to see the actual inauguration, a believer living during the inauguration would see things that John did not see, being lesser or greater in the kingdom in Mt 11:11 would not refer to a misthological ranking within the kingdom but to the privilege of seeing certain events unfold. Thus, from this perspective, Blomberg's interpretation of Mt 11:11 is reasonable regarding present privilege.

Likewise, let it be assumed that the present tense in 18:1,4 is addressing present greatness in the kingdom, that Jesus' mention of greater versus lesser in regard to the kingdom is lurking in the back of the disciples' minds from Jesus' earlier references in 5:19 and 11:11, and that Jesus is addressing present greatness: "Who then *is* greatest in the kingdom of heaven?....Whoever then humbles himself as this child, he *is* the greatest in the kingdom of heaven." Even so, if one is not to play favorites with the tense, then it should be acknowledged, by the same token, that Jesus' use of the future tense in 5:19 is referring to a future greatness: "Whoever then annuls one of the least of these commandments, and so teaches others, *shall be* called least in the kingdom of heaven; but whoever keeps and teaches them, he *shall be* called great in the kingdom of heaven." The most natural correlation would be to associate that future greatness with millennial status during the millennial administration described in Mt 5:22: "But I say to you that everyone who is angry with his brother *shall be* guilty before the court; and whoever shall say to his brother, 'Raca,' *shall be* guilty before the supreme court; and whoever shall say, 'You fool,' *shall be* guilty enough to go into the fiery hell."

Accordingly, the future tense of Mt 5:20 would be regarded as dealing with entrance into this future kingdom (to be consistent with the tense argument Blomberg is using): "For I say to you, that unless your righteousness surpasses that of the scribes and Pharisees, you *shall not* enter the kingdom of heaven." Consequently, that future tense would correspond with the misthological ranking in 5:19. The matching entrance in Mt 18:3 would also pertain to the eschatological future: "Unless you are converted and become like children, you *shall not* enter the kingdom of heaven."

To correlate the present and future tenses, I propose that while the disciples were so concerned over which of them was *currently* the greatest in the kingdom and would therefore be qualified for sitting on His left and right in the *future* expression of that kingdom (cp. Mt 20:21), Jesus was concerned with the fact that some of them (e.g., Judas) had not yet even entered the kingdom presently and, therefore, were disqualified for entrance into that kingdom eschatologically. A sharp dichotomy between initial and final entrance into the kingdom is unwarranted. Likewise, denying a correlation between present and future ranking would be unwise. Their concern over present status would not be mutually exclusive with their concern over future status. Therefore, their inquiry regarding present ranking was in anticipation of their misthological ranking. Their present ranking would determine their future ranking and positions of rulership. Present ranking and its corresponding future rulership is what they were concerned about—it is what **they** had in mind (Lk 22:22). Even if current ranking was not foremost on Jesus' mind, it was foremost in their minds. Blomberg's theory that Mt 5:19 refers to present ranking is rendered implausible even by his own tense argument since the most reasonable hypothesis is that these future tenses are allusions to the future kingdom and that the preoccupation with current status on the part of His disciples was in anticipation of future ranking. Jesus stresses that present greatness, via childlike humility, is the present means (Mt 18:4) to gain this future status they had lurking in their minds from His previous confirmation of future kingdom ranking (Mt 5:19).

Undoubtedly, Blomberg would reply that his argument is not only based on the tense but the sense of the passage to which he is appealing for confirmation in Mt 18:1-4, where he observes: "The criterion for greatness is precisely the criterion for entrance." Blomberg, "Degrees," 166. Indeed, one may strengthen his argument by augmenting it with the parallel from Lk 18:9-14, in which Jesus again uses children to illustrate the necessity of humility for soteric justification and entrance into the kingdom. So let us be charitable to Blomberg and allow that the humility of childlike dependency is necessary for both entrance into the kingdom and for greatness within the kingdom. Does doing so necessarily require that we follow Blomberg's example in equating entrance with greatness and misconstruing heaven to be a reward? Not logically. Not biblically.

The Lukan parallel incorporates both soteric and mistholic themes, but it does not necessarily equate them. To be sure, humility is necessary not only for soteric justification but also for mistholic exaltation: "I tell you, this man went down to his house justified [soteriologically] rather than the other; for everyone who exalts himself shall be humbled, but he who humbles himself shall be exalted [misthologically]" (Lk 18:14). Humility is necessary for soteric kingdom entrance: "Whoever does not receive the kingdom of God like a child shall not *enter* it at all" (Lk 18:17). It is also required for mistholic kingdom possession: "Permit the children to come to Me, and do not hinder them, for the kingdom of God *belongs* to such as these" (Lk 18:16). Nevertheless, the shared necessity for humility both to enter the kingdom and inherit the kingdom does not mean that humility is the condition per se for entrance. Instead, humility may be a necessary precondition for faith, and faith itself the necessary condition for kingdom entrance (Mt 21:31-32). This distinction between precondition and condition accords quite well with the Matthean context, which otherwise could be misconstrued as having one earning entrance into heaven by chopping off one's hand (Mt 18:8). This demarcation also accords quite well with the Lukan context in which the rich young ruler had to sell his possessions as a precondition for saving faith and as a condition for rewards in heaven (Lk 18:22). This distinction allows one to affirm, in contrast to Blomberg, that one does not buy heaven.

The mistholic nature of humility is confirmed by Jesus: "He who humbles himself shall be exalted" (Lk 18:14). Jesus already had associated this exaltation with table ranking and thus with kingdom status at the wedding feast (Lk 14:8-11). Therefore, when Peter applies this same principle to believers, years later, he is not telling them how to earn kingdom entrance but how to obtain exalted kingdom ranking: "Humble yourselves, therefore, under the mighty hand of God, that He may exalt you at the proper time" (1Pet 5:6). Humility is a virtue. We are not saved from hell by virtue of our virtue. Therefore, we are not saved from hell by our humility. Rather, faith is the sole condition for our salvation from hell.

Granted, even faith can be a virtue. Saving faith, however, cannot be a virtue. See my book, *Mere Christianity and Moral Christianity*. The reason saving faith is not a virtue is because it is a passive, punctiliar persuasion and therefore not rewardable as a work. Virtuous faith, on the other hand, is emboldened and enlivened by works and is itself considered a work since it is rewarded as a work. The virtue of humility is required for one to come to saving faith, but this virtue is distinguishable from saving faith, just as a precondition is differentiable from a condition. Those, like Blomberg, who cannot tell the difference between a precondition and a condition, end up inadvertently teaching salvation by works. Blomberg's attempt to make heaven a reward that he receives because of his humility turns out to be a claim that he will be exalted to heaven because of the virtue of his humility. Humility has been lost when those who profess it think that they have enough of it to justify their reaching heaven. The publican's humility should not be turned into Pharisaical humility. The publican humbled himself by giving up all attempts to justify himself. He did not seek to justify himself by virtue of his humility. Let us follow his example. If we will do so, then not only will we qualify for kingdom entrance, but we also will be useful for humble kingdom service that can qualify us for a high kingdom ranking. Jesus is demonstrating that we need to be presently humble as His disciples if we wish to obtain a high ranking in the future kingdom.

Like Blomberg, Lenski believes that Mt 5:19 is referring to ranking in the present kingdom; however, in contrast to Blomberg, Lenski at least acknowledges that there will also be similar ranking in the future kingdom. Lenski does, nonetheless, pose an interesting dilemma. If being least is the most that can happen to those disciples who trifle with the least commandments, then what would happen to those disciples who set aside the greatest commandments. In other words, if a person can be sent to hell for just calling someone a fool in Mt 5:22, then what will be the outcome for those believers who actually commit murder. As an advocate of NOSAS, Lenski believes that any disciple who did so would "cease to be a disciple and would forfeit the kingdom" (p. 211). MacArthur responds to such type of thinking by saying, "Jesus does not refer to loss of salvation" (*Matthew 1-7*, 271). MacArthur's statement is true but inadequate since Lenski concurs that the present passage does not refer to the loss of salvation. The real question is, "What would happen if a believer were to violate the greater commandments?" Something worse than being least in the kingdom would be required since the worse violators would have to be punished with greater punishment than the least violators. So how could the worse violators be made lower than the least? As advocates of OSAS, misthologists would contend that entrance into the eternal kingdom cannot be lost. At least two options are possible. Ultra misthologists would argue that such believers would forfeit the millennial kingdom. On the other hand, Wilkin's article may be consulted for a more conservative misthological approach. See *Illustration 206. Same Crime—Different Penalties*, 597.

My dispensational interpretation of Mt 5:19 leads me to suspect that breaking the least commandments and so teaching others will be among the greatest types of offenses that will be committed during the course of the millennial kingdom. (The rebellion at the end of the millennial kingdom is thus not included in this consideration.) Since the lion is to lay down with the lamb, this kingdom is to be characterized by peace. Proposing that its inhabitants actually will commit murder seems rather ludicrous. Those deemed murderers during the span of this kingdom will be those who simply express murderous emotions. They will be subject to removal from the kingdom via capital punishment (Mt 5:22). Alternatively, one might suggest that even if it were possible for someone actually to commit murder during the course of this kingdom administration, such a person would be subjected to capital punishment and thus removed from the kingdom. (It must be remembered that those who enter the millennial kingdom in flesh and blood bodies will still be subject to death.) Therefore, the greatest infringement that one could commit and still be allowed to live in the millennial kingdom would be of the type described by Jesus in Mt 5:19 and would result in one being least in the millennial kingdom. Those committing greater offenses will not be allowed to remain in the millennial kingdom (so Mt 5:22).

Under these circumstances, I am willing to concede to my ultraistic friends that temporary kingdom exclusion (via death) for believers who commit greater crimes during the course of the millennial kingdom is at least a theoretical possibility. Even so, even Mt 5:22 indicates that such believers would not be subject to Gehenna. As for my dispensational application to the present church age, I would equate being least in the kingdom with being cast into the outer darkness. Therefore, spatial exclusion from the millennial kingdom is not even a remote possibility for church-age believers since they would at least still be in the kingdom. The greatest offense that a present-day believer could commit would be dealt with in terms of kingdom status, not in terms of kingdom exclusion.

[1580] Wayne Baxter, "The Narrative Setting Of The Sermon On The Mount" TrinJ 25:1 (Spring 04), 35. Nevertheless, Baxter's presentation is less than stellar. He makes final (i.e., eschatological) entrance into the kingdom (Mt 7:21-23) conditioned on one's postconversional performance and thus relates Mt 5:20 more so to sanctification rather than to justification (p. 36). By basing eschatological entrance into the kingdom on one's allegiance in following Jesus, Baxter is basing entrance on good works. Yet he denies that the entrance is based on good works. Evidently, he does not know what good works are—mistakenly thinking that they are only works done "apart from Jesus" (pp. 36-37). Baxter fails to grasp the significance of Jesus' sermonic stress on rewards and even fails to list this mistholic evidence in his list of reasons (on pp. 36-37) as to why it must be concluded that Jesus is concerned with more than just entrance into the eschatological kingdom. To set the record straight, **a good work is an action or attitude that results in a positive or negative reward or increases or decreases those rewards**. Jesus is not only demonstrating that entrance into the kingdom (and thus that final soteric justification) cannot be a reward for our behavior; rather, He is also demonstrating that rewards in heaven are based on our performance. The paradox as to why we cannot merit entrance into heaven but can merit rewards in heaven is easily explained: The righteousness which enables us to enter heaven is imputed; the righteousness which entitles us to rewards in heaven is imparted.

[1581] Warren Wiersbe, *Matthew*, Wiersbe's Expository Outlines on the New Testament, vol. 1 (Wheaton: Victor Books, 1992), 22.

[1582] Tim LaHaye and Thomas Ice, *Charting the End Times,* (Eugene, OR: Harvest House Publishing, 2001), 94. Baughman also indentifies Gizrah (the *separate space*) as the West Building. However, he erroneously projects the priestly chambers into the Gizrah surrounding the temple (p. 228). He poses no positive function for Gizrah, thinking that "it is probably used for the disposal of refuse from the sacrifices and other unclean things" (p. 231).

[1583] Frances Brown, S. R. Driver, and Charles A. Briggs, *A Hebrew and English Lexicon of the Old Testament: With an Appendix Containing the Biblical Aramaic, trans. Edward Robinson* (Oxford: Clarendon Press, 1951), 160.

[1584] Wayne ODonnell, "Matthew / Romans: Expository Bible Surveys with 1 John, 1 Cor 11, Ezek 40-48 on Justification, Sanctification, Glorification, the Messianic Kingdom, Headcovering, Role of Women, and Ezekiel's Temple." Available at http://bible.ag/en/mr4web.html#EZanchor-anchor. Accessed on December 26, 2011.

[1585] Chuck and Nancy Missler, *The Kingdom Power, & Glory: The Overcomers Handbook,* new and revised edition (Coeur d' Alene, ID: The King's High Way Ministries, 2007), 144.

[1586] Ibid., 50.

[1587] Ibid., 63.

[1588] Ibid., 90.

[1589] Ibid., 144.

[1590] Ibid., 322.

[1591] Ibid., 146.

[1592] Sapaugh, "Wedding," 30.

[1593] Ibid.

[1594] Missler, 146.

[1595] Chumney equates the outer darkness with the outer court of the tabernacle. Initially, I did not find his argument compelling. Yet, now having concluded that the outer darkness is the outer court of the temple, I would be more inclined to reconsider the plausibility of his argument by working my way backward to the typological connection between the temple and tabernacle (*Bride*, 160, 334-335).

[1596] Missler., 149. In other words, the present writer does not believe that the unfaithful OT Levitical priests will be raised from the dead and physically allowed to minister, even in these lowly positions, within the millennial temple (Eze 44:10-13). Rather, their descendents who enter the millennial kingdom in flesh and blood bodies will be allowed to serve in the temple and typologically represent the unfaithful OT Levitical priests (who are raised from the dead but banished to the outer darkness where they can serve the people by taking care of their animals). After all, someone has to take care of the manure and muck the stalls for all those horses. In this way, consistency may be maintained with the perspective that unfaithful believers are not allowed into the Promised Land. If this perspective is thought to be too restrictive, then even if unfaithful resurrected OT Levitical priests are thought to be able to minister in lowly positions within the temple, they still would be excluded from the Holy Place and the Holy of Holies and from the spiritual realities and spatialities therein represented. In a parade, those following the horses and shoveling up the feces have their role to play. So if those cast into the outer darkness actually do have access to Mount Zion in some similar such capacity, it would be in line with some such responsibility rather than as their residency. But my perception is that they will not even have this access. Rather, those living in flesh and blood bodies will take care of the flesh and blood animals within the restricted regions of the Promised Land and earthly Mount Zion. Typologically, they might be used to represent the service performed by the resurrected servants thrown outside of these regions into the outer darkness.

[1597] Baughman likewise believes that "the church and other resurrected believers probably will not minister in this earthly temple, but in the New Jerusalem" (p. 235).

[1598] TPC, via e-Sword.

[1599] Ibid.

[1600] Amazingly, despite writing a book defending rewards, the Misslers despise being motivated by rewards! They claim that we should be motivated by love instead: "Some Christians protest that it is wrong to be motivated by the reward of inheritance in the future kingdom. They believe we should be motivated only by our love for God. We agree wholeheartedly" (p. 167). I disagree wholeheartedly. Even the Misslers acknowledge, "God's reward for this kind of faith and obedience is more of His Love" (p. 212). If the Misslers' statements are taken at face value, their logic is rather straightforward: (1) We should not be motivated by rewards. (2) God's love is a reward. (3) Therefore, we should not be motivated by God's love.

Hopefully, the Misslers would object to such a deduction even though it logically follows from their own statements. Therefore, the proper deduction is that the Misslers' major premise is false. Consequently, we should be motivated by rewards. So contrary to the Misslers repeated statements that we should not seek to earn rewards (pp. 214-216,234), we certainly should seek to earn rewards, even God's love at the misthological level. We run to win the prize; we do not run for the sake of running. Running to win is not wrong. And what we are running to win is the reward.

[1601] J. E. Becker, *Rightly Dividing the Book of Revelation* (Enumclaw, WA: Winepress Publishing, 2004), 118.

[1602] Ibid., 118. As to subcomers being limited to the lower city, see pp. 522-524. Her sentiment the subcomers will have access to the tree is refuted by her own acknowledgement that access to the tree is a reward for overcomers (p. 40).

[1603] Ibid., 163-177. See also: 204-205,214-222, 224-229, 233-235, 249, 267-268, 287-292, 380-382, 390, 469-476, 483-488, 532-534.

[1604] Walvoord, *Revelation*, 136-137.

[1605] Becker, 495-497.

[1606] Ibid., 501, 547.

[1607] Missler, 268.

[1608] Becker seems to think that all believers, even those who do not overcome, will mature and rule: "Those beginning their ABCs in the lower city will mature and take on more authority. All His servants will serve Him" (p. 524). Not so! The morally apostate OT Levitical priests will not *serve Him*; they will only serve the people (Eze 44:9,12). These priests represent those cast into the outer darkness and form an exception to the maturation-to-rulership hypothesis for those who reside in the lower level.

[1609] Ibid., 514-515.

[1610] Ibid., 40.

[1611] Ibid., 538.

[1612] Ibid., 507.

[1613] Ibid., 507.

[1614] Ibid., 507.

[1615] For some, my desire for continuity pertaining to the city between the millennial kingdom and the eternal state will seem strange. "What difference does it make where the city is located in the millennial kingdom as opposed to the eternal state since the present earth is to be destroyed by fire before the new heavens and new earth commence?" will be the question going through the minds of some. My principle reason for desiring continuity is that the earthly Jerusalem is evidently to bask in the light of the Heavenly Jerusalem during both the millennial kingdom and eternal state. Thus, the earthly Jerusalem would have to move to the north pole before the millennial kingdom starts. Becker believes this will happen during the tribulation. She also has substantial reason for believing that the fiery transition to the new heavens and new earth (and the heavens passing away with a roar) occur during the tribulation also. This theory is attractive and provides a scientific basis for the phenomenal language. It also has the advantage of explaining why the new heavens and new earth are already present at the beginning of the millennial kingdom (Is 65:17). As Baughman observes, this text along with other considerations do not correlate with picturing the earth as burning like a marshmallow on a stick (pp. 186-198).

[1616] Becker, 508.

[1617] Ibid., 508.

[1618] Ibid., 515-516.

[1619] Baughman does not believe that the trees described by Ezekiel are the same as the tree of life in Revelation: "The trees, although described as being good for food, are not called the tree of life. This description is not the same as the description in New Jerusalem, but the earthly one is a type of the heavenly. Or expressed differently, Ezekiel's description is a reflection of what will be found in New Jerusalem" (p. 246).

[1620] The water of life is free outside the gates. But how can this water of life be offered freely to those on the other side of the planet or even on other planets? One possibility is that teleportals may allow free access, particularly to other planets. The water flowing from Ezekiel's temple expands rapidly—miraculously. Within the space of a few thousand cubits, the water expands from an ankle-deep trickle to a river that could not be forded (Eze 17:1-5). Even one teleportal from Earth to another planet would suffice to start a chain of teleportals conveying living water from this planet to every inhabitable planet throughout the universe.

For sheer sake of illustration, suppose that just as living water flows from inside the Heavenly City through twelve gates to those outside the city, so each of these twelve portals will flow to some other location in the eternal state. After all, if the city is suspended in outer space or in the atmosphere, to where does the water flow when it exits those city gates if not through a hyperspace portal? In any event, a portal could be placed anywhere along any of the rivers of living water inside the city. In fact, one of these portals could lead from the Heavenly City to Ezekiel's Temple, thus explaining the presence of the same water flowing from this earthly city as from the Heavenly City. Otherwise, two independent sources of living water would have to be hypothesized. Proposing one source seems preferable. This singular source of living water represents Jesus (who is the singular source of eternal life) and flows through these portals to other planets where, in turn, it produces rivers of living water. Just as a believer who drinks the living water becomes a spring of living water (Jn 4:14), even to others, so those planets to which the living water flows become the source of living water for other planets through the means of such portals.

[1621] Becker, 524.

[1622] D. Russell Humphreys, *Starlight and Time: Solving the Puzzle of Distant Starlight in a Young Universe* (Green Forest, AR: Master Books, 1994), 11. During the Creation Mega Conference of 2005, Jason Lisle noted that GTD (Gravitational Time Dilation) is a very popular young earth option but also posed ASC (Alternative Synchrony Convention) as a competing model. The former would pose that the universe gets older as you travel from earth, the former that it gets younger. "Are the remotest galaxies older or younger in appearance as seen from Earth?" is a question allowing these models to be tested. For DVD, see Jason Lisle, *Distant Starlight: Not a Problem for Young Universe* (Hebron, KY: Answers in Genesis, 2006). Lisle points that GTD is based on good, solid, well-tested physics. Further, he acknowledges, that if you believe that God would not have created galaxies already in the process of collision, then GTD is the preferable model. GTD is the model adopted herein. For ASC preference, see Jason Lisle, "Distant Starlight: Anisotropic Synchrony Convention." Available at http://www.answersingenesis.org/articles/am/v6/n1/distant-starlight. Accessed on August 13, 2012.

[1623] Missler, 305.

[1624] Technically, the universe does not end at the wall of ice: "For some unspecified distance beyond those waters there exists more space of the same sort as interstellar space, but empty of matter" (Humphreys, 99). Nevertheless, for sake of simplicity, the fabric of space will be rounded off, so to speak, in the present discussion as ending just beyond the wall of ice.

[1625] Humphreys, 35-36.

[1626] Ibid., 37.

[1627] Ibid., 98.

[1628] Although Carmical provides references for a number of scholars holding the gap theory, he rejects it in favor of Waltke's precreational model. Still, Carmical's fascinating fictional reconstruction presupposes the existence of the material universe (before the fall of Lucifer) that becomes ruined because of Lucifer's fall and before the recreation of the world.

Illustration 379. Modified Precreational Gap

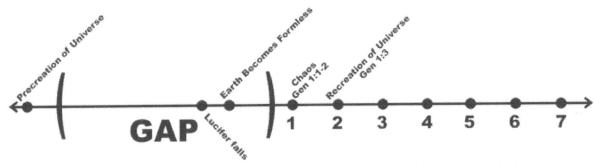

His account still reads basically like a presentation of the gap theory, though Carmical technically places the Luciferian fall before Gen 1:1 and in conjunction with our space and affecting our solar system. Carmical, "Part 2," 72, n. 1.

[1629] Merrill F. Unger, "The Old Testament Revelation of the Beginning of Sin," *BibSac* 114:456 (October, 1957): 327.

[1630] Unger, 331.

[1631] John C. Whitcomb, *The Early Earth*, revised edition (Grand Rapids, MI: Baker Book House, 1986), 154.

[1632] Ron Rhodes, "How did Lucifer fall and become Satan?" Available at http://www.christianity.com /Christian%20Foundations/Theological%20FAQ/11557519. Accessed January 17, 2012.

[1633] Terry takes Is 14:12-15 as an example of apostrophe. Milton S. Terry, *Biblical Hermeneutics: A Treatise on the Interpretation of the Old and New Testaments,* second edition (Grand Rapids: Zondervan, n.d.), 252. Technically, it would not be considered an example of typology when types are narrowly defined to be OT inferior objects that are intended by God to represent (foreshadow) some future (i.e., NT) superior antitypes with a notable point of resemblance amidst dissimilarities (pp. 334-346).

Virkler takes much the same perspective as Terry and gives this exercise: "Isaiah 14:12-15 has often been interpreted as a typological allusion to Satan. Discuss the hermeneutical pros and cons of such an interpretation. Henry A. Virkler, *Hermeneutics: Principles and Processes of Biblical Interpretation* (Grand Rapids: Baker Book House, 1981), 209. Two notable cons are readily apparent: (1) The allusion moves from present to past (instead of from past to future), and (2) the scope of the allusion is within the OT (instead of between the testaments). Therefore, given the restrictive definition posed by both Terry and Virkler, one may object to considering this a type.

On the other hand, the *type (tupos)* in Heb 8:5 indicates that typology should not be viewed in such a narrow fashion. The tabernacle is a shadowy type of the heavenly sanctuary. If this heavenly sanctuary is understood as representing the Heavenly City (the *true tabernacle* of Heb 8:2) that already was in existence at the time that the earthly tabernacle was prepared, then a broader typology is understood than that allowed by Terry and Virkler. The antitype can come after the type in time. A more feasible approach would be to broaden typology more inclusively when a physical entity is used to picture a metaphysical reality. Normally the predictive element of typology is claimed to set it aside from being a symbol. However, the fall of Lucifer is not merely symbolized, but typified, by the passage in question.

[1634] Unger, "Beginning," 328.

[1635] Whitcomb, 154.

[1636] The working hypothesis adopted herein is that the Luciferian fall as described in Is 14:12 and Eze 28:17 took place in the past, after the creation was completed and before the fall of Adam. Timing this with the war in heaven described in Rev 12:7-12 is problematic. Because Satan still has access to the Heavenly City (Job 1:6; 2:1), Claeys believes that the Luciferian fall described in each of these passages is future (pp. 114, 257, n. 4). I would pose that Satan no longer has his residence in the Heavenly City, and he may not even have access to the very top of the city. So the OT texts still may portray a past event. Pember seems to perceive the matter similarly to myself in that he regards the ejection in Rev 12:10 as future and yet believes that the Luciferian Eden in Ezekiel predates the Adamic Eden on Earth. He further calls attention to the resemblance between the Luciferian Eden and New Jerusalem where overcomers are to live. I conclude that they are one in the same: Emerald Eden. G. H. Pember, *Earth's Earliest Ages: And Their Connection with Modern Spiritualism, Theosophy, and Buddhism* (Grand Rapids: Kregel Publications, 1975), 50-53.

Regardless of the differences between Claeys and myself, we both subscribe to Hodges' layover theory (pp. 23; 242, n. 9) in which it is posed that Jesus does not make a U-turn and return to heaven at the rapture. Thus, all that one would have to do in order to harmonize with the Luciferian fall hypothesis in relation to this planet is simply locate the Heavenly City in the atmosphere to the north of this planet during the tribulation: a positioning that is probable anyway. Consequently, the principle of correlativity would still hold true, as well as the major points made herein regarding the casting of Satan from the Emerald City to the north of this planet down to the ground of this planet.

[1637] Henry D. Morris and John D. Morris, *Scripture and Creation*, vol. 1, The Modern Creation Trilogy (Green Forest, AR: Master Books, 1996), 52-53.

[1638] Missler, , 39, cp. 285.

[1639] Ibid., 286.

[1640] Ibid., 136.

[1641] Becker, 51-53, 87.

[1642] Ibid., 40; cp. 59.

[1643] For sake of *Illustration 349. Basic Principle of Correlativity* (p. 926), let P1 = not inheriting the kingdom, P2 = being cast into the outer darkness, P3 = being hurt correlatively by the second death. Let each value be plotted as being less positive (at least descriptively speaking) in terms of heavenly rewards, with the last value approaching the threshold, below which no misthological value can be plotted in the positive quadrant. If so, then the correlating values in the negative quadrant would reflect the same ranking relative to one another but be plotted at greater vertical divergences since the negative range does not transverse as far from the threshold as does the positive range. Although heaven will get infinitely better, hell will not get infinitely worse. Suffering in hell is qualitatively finite but quantitatively infinite. Basically, the second death (-P3) is as bad as it gets. Although there will be degrees of punishment in the Lake of Fire, once that degree of punishment is reached, that degree of punishment will stagnate for eternity. The variation in degree of hellish suffering for any given being will become essentially static, at least objectively, when the maximum negative value for that being is reached. However, for overcomers, the positive degree of heavenly reward will be exponentially dynamic. Heaven will get better and better for a heavenly ruler. This observation is indicated by the much darker arrow pointing in the positive direction along the vertical axis. Correlatively, the values for the nonovercomer would be static. Contrastively, the subcomer values would not be static, at least relatively speaking, if they were plotted on a time graph and compared to the values of an overcomer. In that case, the distance between the two set of positive values would become increasing greater as time progresses. The divergence between being an overcomer and subcomer will become ever greater as overcomers become rulers over ever increasing areas.

[1644] Some misthologists will wish to pursue this theory of correlation so as to suggest that subcomers may be hurt in a correlative sense by the second death (Rev 2:11). According to this perspective, since a correlation exists between being hurt by the second death and misthological death, the promise in Rev 2:11 is meant to convey the assurance that there will be no such correlation for the believer who overcomes. Conceptually, such a possibility may be granted; however, more likely, John simply is speaking litotetically, at least at this particular point in the narrative upon the initial reading of the epistle. Nevertheless, the possibility exists that he is speaking dualistically, that is, litotetically and correlatively. If the theory of correlativity has genuine applicability to both the Lake of Fire and the outer darkness as proposed herein, then a correlation between the second death and misthological death is intended by Scripture. The question, then, is not whether such a correlation exists, but whether John wished to signify the cessation of such correlativity for the one who overcomes in Rev 2:11. That the text allows such an interpretation does not necessarily prove that it intends it. The distinction being made at this juncture is between interpretation and application. Just because a correlation could be applied appropriately to this text does not prove that John should be interpreted as having this correlation in mind as a principle.

With that clarification in mind, one can be charitable toward Wall when, in reference to Rev 2:11, he allows the possibility that "a believer could be harmed, though not destroyed, by the second death" (p. 114). Yet he leaves the question unanswered as to **how** a believer might be hurt by the second death. After affirming the litotetic interpretation,

Benedict allows a dual possibility in which believers can be hurt by those heading on their way to the second death (p. 15). From this perspective, the second death might be said to hurt the believer **indirectly** through the instrumentality of the unbeliever. While it is true that believers can be hurt by those on their way to the second death, this is probably not the point John is seeking to make. This particular implementation of the *principle of indirectivity* is too weak to be persuasive. On the other hand, the ultraistic opinion that believers will be submitted **directly** to the metaphysical Lake of Fire, which is the second death (Rev 20:14; 21:8), is too aggressive in its interpretation. Granted, Wall and Benedict are not approaching the passage ultraistically in trying to find applicability to believers. Even so, neither these writers nor the ultraists prove to be persuasive in the application of the second death that they depict John as making in 2:11. Wall is too ambiguous, Benedict's argument is too weak, the ultraistic position asserts too much. Finding any misthological porridge that seems "just right," to use the words of Goldilocks, is difficult.

Wilson simply **equates** being hurt by the second death **with** suffering at the fiery **Bema** in Jn 15:6; 1Cor 3:11-15; and Heb 6:8 (pp. 133-134). Granted, (A) these three texts do describe the plausibility of being hurt misthologically by the metaphorical fire of the Bema, and (B) being hurt by the second death could be taken as being hurt misthologically in some manner by the Lake of Fire. Still, for technical reasons, I must disagree with the manner in which Wilson has derived his conclusion. His assumption seems to be: A $\Rightarrow$ B. I would allow both A and B, but I fail to see that the relation is: A $\Rightarrow$ B. I derive B by other means.

Similarly, Chitwood reasons that believers can be hurt misthologically by the second death. I agree with this conclusion but would disagree with some of his statements and would derive the connection differently. He believes that nonovercoming Christians **metaphorically** will have their portion in the Lake of Fire (in Rev 21:8) and be cast metaphorically into the Lake of Fire (*Revelation*, 483-487). Whereas the lost literally have their portion in the Lake of Fire and literally are cast into it, nonovercomers will only metaphorically have their portion in it and be cast metaphorically into it. His argument would be something like this: Given (A) preteristic Gehenna Bema misthology and (B) that Rev 21:8 is describing the fate of unfaithful believers during the millennial kingdom, it follows that (C) the Lake of Fire has *metaphorical* applicability to nonovercoming believers.

In his *Mysteries* (1998 edition, pp. 164-167) and *Judgment* (2001 second edition, 95-103), Chitwood seemed to argue that nonovercoming believers literally would spend the millennium in the Lake of Fire. My initial impression was that in his original edition of *Judgment Seat of Christ* he believed that unfaithful believers would be within the millennial kingdom, but I thought he abandoned that position in his 1998 *Mysteries* (pp. 164-167) and his 2001 *Judgment* (pp. 95-103) and came to believe that nonovercoming believers literally would spend the millennium in the Lake of Fire. My impression was that in these latter writings he was taking the outer darkness and Gehenna as metaphorical depictions of the millennial punishment of unfaithful believers in a place literally pictured very much like the Lake of Fire. The primary difference between the suffering of unfaithful believers and unbelievers in the Lake of Fire would be one of duration, not of degree. Thus, I concluded that he had adopted a kingdom-exclusion position. My understanding (or misunderstanding as the case may be) was that he believed unfaithful Christians would be cast into a literal Lake of Fire and remain there for 1,000 years. I reasoned that he was using the outer darkness and Gehenna as metaphors of this literal reality.

When I approached Chitwood with a series of correspondences in February of 2012 about changes he had made in the 2011 editions of *Revelation* and *Judgment*, I was presuming that he was abandoning the kingdom exclusion position (i.e., ultraism) that he had demonstrated in his 1998 and 2001 writings. He informed me that this was a misunderstanding on my part, shared by others as well, in that he actually never had adopted the kingdom exclusion position (i.e., the ultraistic position regarding the Lake of Fire). Therefore, I will take his explanation at face value and assume that I was mistaken in holding an ultraistic impression of his second edition. Most importantly, in the 2011 edition of *Judgment* he clearly has stated: **"All Christians, faithful and unfaithful alike, will be in the [millennial] kingdom"** (p. 100). Moreover, he clarified that to the best of his knowledge Wilson would agree with this position also, considering subcomers as subjects rather than sovereigns within the kingdom. With this clarification, it would appear, then, that the three of us are what I have described herein as *progressive moderates*.

Chitwood has revised his position in his *Revelation* (2011 edition, 483-488) to clarify that the Lake of Fire only has metaphorical applicability to such believers. In his first edition (1986), he had said that believers could not be cast into the Lake of fire (*Judgment*, first edition, 59-60). In this clarified edition, he affirms that nonovercomers can be cast metaphorically into the Lake of Fire. To be sure, his revised position is commendable in clarifying a metaphorical over literal applicability of the Lake of Fire to unfaithful believers and is consistent with his take on Rev 21:8. Nevertheless, I do not share his view that Rev 21:8 was written with primary application to nonovercomers in view. Thus, I do not believe that John intends for nonovercoming believers to be understood as metaphorically having their portion in the Lake of Fire or metaphorically being cast therein. However, I would allow that the Lake of Fire has *misthological* applicability to such believers. Moreover, John expects us to make that connection.

The repetition of John's rejection of any application of the second death to the overcomer (this time in Rev 20:6) give grounds for thinking that John intends a correlation between the second death and misthological death for those believers who do not overcome, at least by the time one reaches this point in the narrative. The understanding adopted herein is that **the second death has the power of correlatively over the subcomer**. With this second litotetic reference to the second death, John probably intends for one to see this correlation when one reaches this point in his discussion. Once having made this litotetic-correlative connection in this subsequent context, he would intend for the reader to see how Rev 2:11 would be understood litotetically and correlatively as well. **Being hurt by the second death and under its power could be described as metaphorical pictures of this correlation.** In technical contradistinction to Chitwood, I would perceive being cast into the Lake of Fire or having a portion in the Lake of Fire to be strictly correlative rather than metaphorical events for the nonovercomer. The unfaithful believer is not pictured as being metaphorically cast into the Lake of Fire, but being hurt by the second death might be said to be a metaphorical recasting of the correlative relationship as it applies to the unfaithful believer.

While the second death is the antitype of physical death for the unregenerate, the second death is the antitype (in terms of severity) of misthological death for the unfaithful believer. Just as physical death is the separation of the metaphysical spirit from the body in another dimension and just as the second death is separation of the unregenerate spirit from God in the Lake of Fire, so misthological death is the separation of the unfaithful believer from God in the outer darkness. Just as the type is not to be confused with the antitype, so physical death is not to be confused with the second death, and the second death is not to be confused with misthological death. The second death is to be cast literally into the literal Lake of Fire. Nonovercoming believers will not literally experience the second death. Nor are they metaphorically cast into the Lake of Fire. Nevertheless, they might be said to be hurt metaphorically by the Lake of Fire in terms of this correlation and thus correlatively under its power. The Lake of Fire is literal, and unbelievers literally will be cast literally into it. Nonovercomers, on the other hand, can only be hurt metaphorically/correlatively by that literal Lake of Fire.

Unlike Govett, who thinks that a promise like Jn 11:25-26 means that believers *shall not die forever* (*Revelation*, 261), so as to pose that they may die in the Lake of Fire for a 1000 years, my translation of that Johannine passage (and others like it), as supplied in *John in Living Color*, emphasis that *whoever ever believes will never ever die*. No believer will ever dip so much as one toe in that metaphysical Lake of Fire. These litotes do not have to be thrown into reverse to derive this theory of correspondence. Some litotes can be thrown into reverse; some cannot be. Nevertheless, the correlation being made herein is not derived by reversing the litotes regarding the second death.

Regarding those soteriologically outside the city as the antitype of being misthologically outside of the city is not based on litotetic reversal. Although a possible correlation is allowable, the notion that John expects his litotes to be thrown into reverse in order to derive that correlation is doubtful. John stops far too short of explicitly asserting that believers will be hurt by the second death or be under its power for one to conclude that he would expect such a crass treatment of these litotes. His correlation is much more subtle and refined, so much in fact that he would not expect us to see the correlation when thinking exclusively in terms of litotes. And he certainly intends for us to see Rev 2:11 and 20:6 as litotes. To see the correlation, at least as perceived herein, these passages must be seen dualistically as litotetic-correlative, not as a litotes read in reverse. For years I missed being able to affirm any correlation between the second death and misthology because I rejected the attempts of others see these litotes as simply moving forward and backward at the same time. Such attempts are completely unnecessary and non-persuasive. To throw these litotes into reverse would lead to an ultraistic conclusion and indicate that believers literally can be hurt by the second death. Because this ultraistic position is rejected herein, for many years I opted for an exclusively positive litotetic interpretation and made no application at all of the second death to nonovercomers. However, when seen as part of a greater web of literary correlativity, the literary genius of the Writer can be appreciated more fully so as to allow a duality.

These litotes should not be read in reverse so as to think that believers literally or directly can be submitted to the second death or the Lake of Fire. Just as typology insists that antitypes not be confused with types, so the principle of correlativity demands that similarities not be changed into equalities. No believer will be hurt by the second death in terms of being cast into the Lake of Fire. However, a correlation between being hurt by the second death and being hurt by misthological death can be said reasonably to exist. The denial of any such correlation for the overcomer strongly hints at the affirmation of such a correlation for the subcomer. That such a correlation is intended is suggested by other such similar indications.

Illustration 380. Traditional Litotes

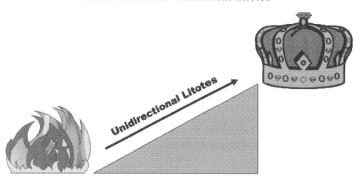

The traditional litotetic approach to Rev 2:11 and 20:6 affirms that believers who overcome will obtain the crown of life as opposed to the second death. Not all believers will overcome, but the litotes should not to be read in reverse so as to suggest that those believers who fail to overcome will be hurt by the second death. The litotes are unidirectional. Some traditionalists might allow that believers can be hurt by the second death in some undefined or indirect manner. Still, even in that case, whether that point is intended by the passage is questionable. In any event, whatever being hurt by the second death means for the unfaithful believer, it does not entail a believer being cast into the Lake of Fire. A unidirectional promise is intended.

Illustration 381. Ultraistic Litotes

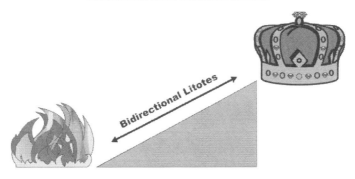

The ultraistic approach affirms that believers who overcome will obtain the crown of life as opposed to the second death. However, since not all believers will overcome, the litotes are bidirectional and readable in reverse so as to indicate that those believers who fail to overcome will be hurt literally by the second death, even to the point of being cast into the Lake of Fire for one thousand years. In the ultraistic camp, a bidirectional threat-promise is perceived.

Illustration 382. Correlative Litotes

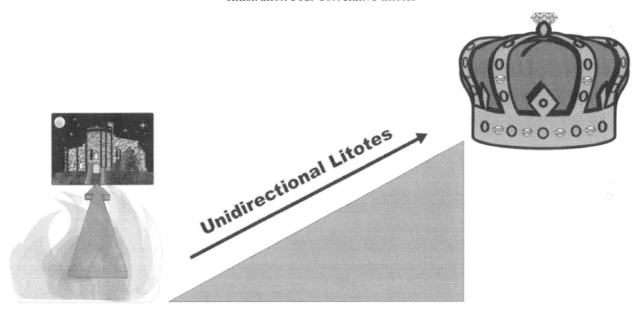

The correlative approach to Rev 2:11 and 20:6 would affirm that believers who overcome will obtain the crown of life as opposed to the second death. Not all believers will overcome, but the litotes should not to be read in reverse so as to suggest that those believers who fail to overcome will be hurt either literally or directly by the second death. The second death, which exists at the opposite end of the litotetic spectrum is but a shadowy pointer to the misthological death that awaits believers who fail to obtain the crown of life. Just as the death penalty that was inflicted upon those who disobeyed God in the past is held out as an *example* (*tupos*) to believers warning them not to disobey God in the present (1Cor 10:6), so the death penalty imposed upon those who disbelieve God and who are cast into the black darkness of the Lake of Fire is set before believers warning believers not to turn back from God and be cast into the outer darkness of the kingdom. In the same way, the second death is an *example for us* that misthological death awaits us if we fail to persevere in the faith (cp. Heb 4:11). These litotes are not to be thrown into reverse so as to equate the second death with misthological death. The litotes are unidirectional in that regard. Nevertheless, the second death is allowed to serve as a *example for us* (and in this sense as a *type*) so that we should not shrink back from the faith. In terms of severity, the Lake of Fire might be called the antitype, but in the sense of serving as an example, it may be called the type. Broadly speaking, then, the Scripture allows a typological parallelism in this sense between the second death and misthological death. Those believers who fail to overcome will be hurt by the second death typologically, not literally or directly. Correlatively, to be *hurt* by the second death would correspond to the Bema (Rev 2:11), whereas to be under the *power* of the second death would correspond to the outer darkness (Rev 20:6). Jointly in terms of correlativity, the Lake of Fire is to the unbeliever what the Bema and outer darkness are to the unfaithful believer. Classically, I can correlate to ultraism. Neoclassically, I can relate indirectly to ultraism. In neither approach do I relate directly to ultraism. Believers can be hurt correlatively and indirectly by the second death, but not directly.

- Believer hurt by second death ≅ Bema.
- Believer under power of second death ≅ Outer Darkness.
- Unbeliever cast into Lake of Fire ≅ believer cast into outer darkness.
- Second death ≠ outer darkness
- Lake of Fire ≠ outer darkness.

[1645] Philip Evans, 145-147.
[1646] Philips, *Matthew*, 415-416.
[1647] Sapaugh, "Wedding," 12, n. 3.
[1648] France, *Matthew*, NIC, 439, n.1; 820, n. 1.
[1649] Evans, *Security*, 821.
[1650] Commenting on Mt 21:1, Haller believes that the parable of the wedding feast was addressed to the Jewish leaders, "but there were some believers in the crowd. They understood His true identity and believed on Him (cf. 21:11,46)" (*Matthew*, GNTC, 100). Sapaugh, on the other hand, believes that the Jewish leaders left before Jesus spoke this parable. Nevertheless, both Haller and Sapaugh are agreed that the parable is spoken to a crowd, many of whom were believers. Sapaugh specifies that they "believed Jesus to be **the promised Messiah.**" His justification for this assessment is,

> According to Matt 21:46, the crowd considered Jesus to be a prophet. Previously, at the triumphal entry, the crowds *called* Jesus a prophet (Matt 21:1) and proclaimed Him as the Son of David (21:9). This directly ties back to the testimony in 20:30-31 of the two blind men on the road out of Jericho: "Have mercy on us, O Lord, Son of David." This entire episode is full of messianic implications." (Emphasis his.)

Sapaugh adds: "The recognition by the crowd that Jesus was **a prophet** probably alludes to **the prophet** to come of Deut 18:15-19" ("Wedding," 12-13). Sapaugh is thus saying: *a prophet = the prophet = Messiah.* However, I am not so certain that this equation necessarily will hold up. *The prophet Jesus from Nazareth* (21:11) seems to be merely *a prophet* (21:46) in the minds of this crowd, rather than the Messiah (cp. Mt 16:13-16). If this counter assessment is accurate, then it raises the question, "If some in this crowd of Jews listening to Jesus believed in Him for eternal life and yet simply believed that He was merely a prophet, would they have been granted eternal life?" This question leads to others: "If so, can Jews today who believe that Jesus was merely a prophet be saved if they believe in Him for eternal life?" If one wants to press the issue, the question might be posed, "Can those today who believe that Jesus was merely a good man be saved, if they believe in Him for eternal life?" Theoretically at least, the answer would seem to be, "Yes." If they could, they would. Of course, this does not prove that they can.

Illustration 383. Levels of Specificity Concerning Jesus Identity

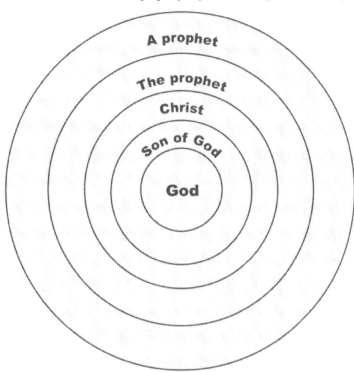

Since the subjective recognition of the deity of Christ (SD) is not a theological requirement for saving faith, it would seem that recognition of His Messianic identity would not be required theologically either. If that is the case, then believing in Jesus as the Christ would be a useful vehicle to lead a person to believe in Him for eternal life. If one accepts the NT claims regarding His Messianic identity, then one should believe in Him for eternal life (Jn 20:30-31). Yet to stipulate that they must have believed in Jesus as the Christ in order to receive eternal life may be going beyond the NT evidence as to what was soteriologically necessary, at least at that point in history. In any event, at the present point in history, my belief is that we should follow the example of the Gospel of John in not only presenting Jesus as the Christ, the Son of God, but as God Himself in our evangelistic endeavors.

Still, at the point in time of Jesus' earthly ministry, those who believed in the message of this mere prophet (and thus in this prophet) for eternal life would have received eternal life from the message of this Prophet. Although they misperceived Jesus to be a prophet, this misperception did not prevent them from exercising saving faith if they believed in Jesus' message (and thus in Jesus) for eternal life. Therefore, although I am not persuaded that Sapaugh is correct in attributing Messianic perception to all believers within the crowd, I do share his perception that many in the crowd were genuine believers. The Galilean-supporter hypothesis notwithstanding, perhaps some of these (Judean) believers in the crowd (who lived in Jerusalem) shortly became disenchanted with Jesus' Messianic claims and were part of the crowd who cried out for His crucifixion. Such apostates literally would be crucifying to themselves the Son of God (cp. Heb 6:6). The fires of Mt 22:7 would apply to them literally and historically and also parabolically and misthologically (cp. Heb 6:8). If Jesus knew that this crowd, many of whom included believers, would soon be turning on Him, why think that He necessarily would exclude them from the parabolic burning? I would not be surprised if some of those in the crowd who had just finished crying out *Hosanna* when Jesus entered Jerusalem (Mt 21:9), and who were with Him in the temple when He spoke these parables, were believers who soon thereafter turned on Him and cried out, *Crucify Him*! Surely, some of these apostates suffered a fate worse than a quick death when the Romans entered Jerusalem and crucified them! Their cries from their Roman crosses would be temporary, however, compared to their cries from the outer darkness.

If this hypothesis is correct, then some of these apostate believers probably were thrown physically into Gehenna by the Romans in A.D. 70. This might lead some to theorize as to the possibility of a preteristic Gehenna, in which Jesus was warning Jewish believers of His day that if they (along with the rest of the Jews) did not repent, then they would find themselves in danger of being thrown into this Valley of Hinnom in A.D. 70. I have not found such a simple preteristic Gehenna hypothesis necessary, probable, or even possible, however, in the texts where it would be most attractive, such as Mt 18:9, because of its association with *eternal* fire in Mt 18:8 and undying worm in Mk 9:44-48. Certainly, I would concede that the results of the Bema are eternal, but to say that the burning of the Bema is eternal is contrary to the imagery given elsewhere (1Cor 3:11-15). However, when preteristic Gehenna misthology is enjoined with correlative misthology, the combination becomes a formidable option.

[1651] Evans, *Security*, 145.

[1652] Ibid., 146.

[1653] Ibid., 147.

[1654] Ibid., 144.

[1655] Ibid., 148.

[1656] Lang, *Parables,* 309.

[1657] Evans, *Security*, 147.

[1658] France, *Matthew*, NIC, 827.

[1659] Evans, *Security*, 149.

[1660] Ibid.

[1661] France, *Matthew*, NIC, 823.

[1662] Hindson and Borland, *Matthew*, TFCBC, ed. Mal Cough (Chattanooga, TN: AMG Publishers, 2006),197.

[1663] Ibid., 195.

[1664] Ibid.

[1665] Rather than quibble over whether the wedding garment refers to imputed and or imparted righteousness, Hendriksen thinks the solution is to bind these two forms of righteousness seamlessly together into one robe (*Matthew*, NTC, 799). Such sentiment reminds me of France's quip that entrance into the kingdom is free but continuance therein is costly (*Matthew*, NIC, 827). Taken together, one could make the typical conditionalistic party line: Entrance into the kingdom is granted freely on the condition of imputational righteousness, but continence in the kingdom is stipulated expensively on the condition of impartational righteousness. Initial salvation is by grace; final salvation is by works. Heaven is a reward for good behavior, not a gift to the simple believer. The Pharisaical spirit is alive and well on planet earth and in Protestant writings.

[1666] Hindson and Borland, *Matthew*, TFCBC, 194.

[1667] Turner, *Matthew*, ECNT, 515.

[1668] Ibid., 519.

[1669] Ibid., 521.

[1670] Evans, *Security*, 145.

[1671] Ibid., 198.

[1672] Ibid., 197.

[1673] Constable, *Hebrews*, 89.

[1674] Tanner, *Hebrews*, GNTC, 1075.

[1675] Constable, *Matthew*, 273.

[1676] Turner, *Matthew*, ECNT, 233.

[1677] Mounce, *Matthew*, NICB,

[1678] Turner, *Matthew*, ECNT, 509. BDF 245a is cited by Turner in his citation of Morris, but Morris actually specifies BDF 245a[1]. One might site 245 also, where a positive for comparative does not necessary "provide for degree at all."

[1679] Ken Neff, *Choose to Live: Distinguishing Possessing Eternal Life from Experiencing Eternal Life* (St. Augustine, FL: LeaderQuest, 2012). Although I highly recommend Neff's book as an excellent presentation of the conservative view and very much in harmony with my own assessment in my book *Salvation*, some of his statements are open to question. For example, "we should assume that" since the rich young ruler (RYR) and the testing lawyer both asked Jesus the same question, "either both men were believers or both were unbelievers" (p. 36, cp. 53). I would prefer to be more guarded in my assumptions from their shared perspective. Second, as he admits in connection with Jn 12:42, many religious believers believed in Jesus (p. 38). Therefore, I question his seeming assumption that in Luke the religious leaders necessarily portray unbelievers (p. 123). Rather, I would assume that the Pharisee who invited Jesus to dine with him (and whom was being addressed personally by Jesus about the possibility of gaining rewards in terms of table ranking in Lk 14:12-14) was a believer. GNTC regards the Pharisee who invited Jesus to supper in Lk 7:36-50 was a believer, though he only believed Jesus to be a prophet (Lk 7:16), and was even struggling with that (Lk 7:39)! The RYR likewise could have been a believer in Jesus for eternal life who only perceived Jesus to be a prophet (see endnote 1650). Jesus is seeking to increase his perception as to His true identity by pointing out that only God is truly good. Nevertheless, this deficiency in RYR's understanding need not prevent him from believing in Jesus savingly. As to his trusting riches, this is a problem for rich NT believers that could prevent them from gaining eternal life as a reward (1Tim 6:17-19). Certainly, the RYR might be an example. Just as it is impossible for a camel to enter through the eye of a needle, so it is impossible (not merely difficult) for rich believers who trust in their riches to inherit the kingdom. Thirdly, and most importantly, Neff stresses that one "must choose the one correct explanation" (p. 133), "remembering that there is *only* one correct interpretation" (p. 135, emphasis his) so that "one or none is correct" (p. 140).

However, if my neoclassical perception is correct, then the biblical writers may indeed intend for us to see this account from more than one perspective.

Illustration 384. Neff's Options with a Neoclassic Addition

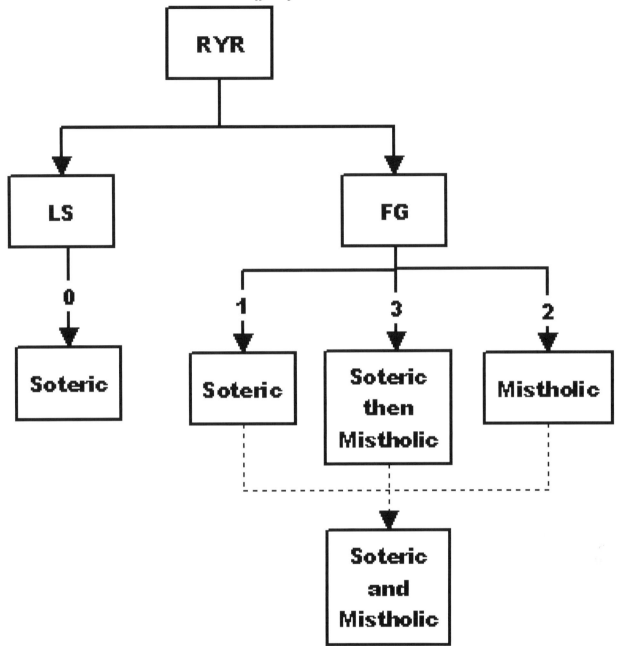

This is my summary chart of Neff's options (p. 197). I have assigned relative values for hermeneutical probabilities. Neff could only give four options since he believes that one must chose only one option at each branch. Neoclassically, I added a fifth option in which the branches come back together. See the dashed lines.

[1680] Seemingly, Tucker simply equates *entrance* with *full inheritance* (pp. 152, 231). Failure to enter on the part of a believer pertains only to forfeiture of misthological inheritance (p. 139). He takes a very conservative misthological assessment of the outer darkness, apparently seeing it merely as exclusion from the experience of ruling within the kingdom, certainly not hell (p. 282). If by this statement he intends to rule out possibility of millennial Gehenna for the unfaithful believer, which seems to be the case (p. 139), then he has opted for what I have termed neo-ultraism in contradiction to the more prevalent classical form of ultraism which puts the worst offending believers in Gehenna for the millennium. Curtis H. Tucker, *Majestic Destiny: Kingdom Hope is Rising* (Redmond, OR: Last Chapter Publishing, 2011).

[1681] Ibid., 131.

[1682] Ibid., 125.

[1683] Ibid., 245, n. 25.

[1684] Ibid., 100, n. 57.

[1685] Ibid., 207.

[1686] Ibid., 270.

[1687] Haller, *Matthew*, GNTC, 88-89.

[1688] Nolland, *Matthew*, NIGNT, 863.

[1689] Just as most LS teachers emphasize grace and yet abuse the gospel of grace by teaching a mistaken view of grace, so some FG teachers promote the Bema and yet abuse the gospel of the kingdom by teaching a mistaken view of the Bema. Just as the former will miss entry into the kingdom, the latter will miss rulership of the kingdom. Just as not everyone talking about living in heaven is going to be living there, so not everyone talking about reigning in heaven is going to be reigning there. If those teaching a false gospel of grace are to be excluded from living there, what is the preclude one from thinking that that those who teach a false gospel of the kingdom are to be excluded from ruling there? Those teaching a *Toothless Bema* may very well find themselves devoured by it.

[1690] Geisler enjoined S with P by claiming that God *determinately knows* who will persevere. Geisler's *determinate election* results in a conditional security in which the result is positively guaranteed. Therefore, in terms of results, Geisler's Calminianism looks more like PEAR*P*. This might be the best acronym by which to describe Calminianism. Since the perseverance is guaranteed in TULIP, the security of the elect is also. They will not lose their regeneration since they will persevere. Therefore, this security is both guaranteed and conditional. Geisler's approach results in the same outcome and, therefore, is best considered a modification in which the S in PEARS has been replaced with a synthetic form of P in TULIP to yield PEAR*P*.

Alternatively, since the acronyms for Calvinism and Arminianism both teach that perseverance is necessary to reach heaven, the Calminian mediating position forged by affirming the soteriological necessity of perseverance from the S of PEARS and the P of TULIP might be better described by a combination of S + P. Because Geisler affirmed this core doctrine of perseverance from a TULIP perspective but rejected the rest of TULIP in preference for an approach more in harmony with PEARS, his Calminian position may be described appropriately as somewhat analogous to a PEARS**+P** since he affirms the TULIP form of P. Conversely, some Calvinists frankly acknowledge that Calvinistic retention of regeneration is conditioned on perseverance. This stress might be regarded by some Calvinists to be TULI**P+S**, at least in terms of stress. The Arminian S+P and the Calvinistic P+S forms of Calminianism might be represented by the acronyms PEAR**PS** and TULI**PS** respectively. From the viewpoint of predestination, perseverance is guaranteed in both forms of Calminianism. Since the majority of Calminians seem to affirm the body of the PEARS, the best recourse is to either describe them in terms of PEAR*P*, PEAR**PS**, or just stress the tail-end agreement with PS.

Bibliography

Originally, this was a bibliography of cited sources. However, when it became necessary to parse the size of this book down to about half its original size so that it would be more manageable, much of the material referencing the following works was moved to approximately twenty smaller supplemental books. Rather than parse the bibliography down to the works cited in the present two volumes, the original bibliography has been retained since these works are highly integrated within the composite discussion. Taken together, these books will interact with all the works listed in this bibliography (plus whatever additional works are cited in my supplemental books). Thus, the present bibliography is more than a reference of *cited works* but less than reference of *consulted works*. As always, if a short title is used within the notes, it is shown by bold type within the entry, unless it is a commentary, in which case the short title is self apparent.

Bibles

Darby, John Nelson. *The English Darby Bible*. Online Bible Foundation and Woodside Fellowship of Ontario, 1890.

Lee, Witness. *The New Testament: Recovery Version*, revised ed. Anaheim: Living Stream Ministry, 1991.

Phillips, J. B. *The New Testament in Modern English*, student ed. New York: MacMillan Publishing Co., 1958.

Wuest, Kenneth S. *Word Studies in the Greek New Testament*. Vol. 4: *The New Testament: An Expanded Translation*. Grand Rapids: Eerdmans Publishing Co., 1984.

Dictionaries and Encyclopedias

Brown, Colin, gen. ed. *The New International Dictionary of New Testament Theology*. Grand Rapids: Zondervan Publishing House, 1975. S.v. "Baptism," by G. R. Beasley-Murray.

_____. S.v. "Crown, Sceptre, Rod," by C. J. Hemer.

_____. S.v. "Discipline: πορνεύω," by H. Reisser.

_____. S.v. "Fight: νικάω," by W. Günther.

_____. S.v. "Grace, Spiritual Gifts," by H. H. Esser.

_____. S.v. "Gift, Pledge, Corban," by O. Becker.

_____. S.v. "Infant Baptism: Its Background and Theology," by R. T. Beck-with.

_____. S.v. "King," by B. Klappert.

_____. S.v. "**Possessions**: περιποιέομαι," by E. Beyreuther.

_____. S.v. "Recompense: μισθός," by P. C. Böttger.

_____. S.v. "Reconciliation" by H. Voränder and C. Brown.

_____. S.v. "Quench," by R. K. Harrison and C. Brown.

_____. S.v. "Time: αἰών," by J. Guhrt.

Burton, Gideon. *The Forest of Rhetoric: Silva Rhetoricae*. Available at http://rhetoric.byu.edu:16080. Accessed on September 17, 2004

Buttrick, George A. *The Interpreter's Dictionary of the Bible*. Nashville: Abingdon Press, 1962. S.v. "Simon Magus," by S. V. McCasland

Elwell, Walter A., ed. *Evangelical Dictionary of Biblical Theology*. Grand Rapids: Baker Book House, 1996. Available at http://bible.crosswalk.com/Dictionaries/BakersEvangelicalDictionary/. Accessed on September 17, 2004. S.v. "Reward," by Wesley L. Gerig.

_____. *Evangelical Dictionary of Theology*. Grand Rapids: Baker Book House, 1984. S.v. "Amyraldianism," by B. A. Demarest.

_____. S.v. "**Foreknowledge**," by G. W. Bromiley.

_____. S.v. "Freedom, Free Will, and Determinism," by N. L. Geisler.

_____. S.v. "Reward," by H. Z. Cleveland.

Geisler, Norman L. *Baker Encyclopedia of Christian Apologetics*. Grand Rapids: Baker Book House, 1999. S.v. "Essentialism, Divine."

_____. S.v. "Certainty/Certitude."

_____. S.v. "**Pharaoh**, Hardening of."

Guralnik, David B. *Webster's NewWorld Dictionary of the American Language*, 2nd college edition. New York: Simon and Schuster, 1982.

Hastings, James, gen. ed. *Encyclopedia of Religion and Ethics*. New York: Charles Scribner's Sons, 1951. S.v. "Valentinianism," by E. F. Scott.

Kittel, Gerhard, ed. *Theological Dictionary of the New Testament*. Trans. Geoffrey W. Bromiley. Grand Rapids: Eerdmans Publishing Co., 1967. S.v. "σκότος," by G. Hans Conzelman.

Unger, Merrill. *Unger's Bible Dictionary*, 3rd edition. Chicago: Moody Press, 1985.

Linguistic Tools

Blass, E. and A. Debrunner. *A Greek Grammar of the New Testament and Other Early Christian Literature.* Trans. Robert W. Funk. Chicago and London: University of Chicago Press, 1961. [Citations are to sections rather than pages.]

Brooks, James A. and Carlton L. Winbery. *Syntax of New Testament Greek* Lanham: University Press of America, 1979.

Brown, Frances, S. R. Driver, and Charles A. Briggs. *A Hebrew and English Lexicon of the Old Testament: With an Appendix Containing the Biblical Aramaic. Trans. Edward Robinson.* Oxford: Clarendon Press, 1951.

Burton, Ernest DeWitt, *Syntax of the Moods and Tenses in New Testament Greek.* Via BibleWorks. [Citations are to sections rather than pages.]

Dana, H. E. and Julius R. Mantey. *A Manual Grammar of the Greek New Testament.* New York: MacMillan Publishing Co., 1957.

Danker, Frederick William, ed. *Greek-English Lexicon of the New Testament and Other Early Christian Literature,* second edition. Chicago: University of Chicago Press, 2000.

Fanning, Buist M. *Verbal Aspect in New Testament Greek.* Oxford: Clarendon Press, 1990.

Friberg Timothy and Barbara. *Analytical Lexicon to the Greek New Testament,* 1994. Via BibleWorks.

Hill, Gary. *The Discovery Bible: New American Standard New Testament.* Reference Edition. Chicago: Moody Press, 1987.

Hodges, Zane C. and Arthur L. Farstad, eds. *The Greek New Testament: According to the Majority Text,* second edition. Nashville: Thomas Nelson Publishers, 1985.

Kurt Aland, Matthew Black, Carlo M. Martini, Bruce M. Metzger, and Allen Wikgren, eds. *The Greek New Testament,* 4th ed. Stuttgart: German Bible Society, 1994. Via BibleWorks.

Leedy, Randy. *BibleWorks New Testament Greek Sentence Diagrams.* Via BibleWorks, 2006.

Louw, J. P and E. A. Nida, eds. *Louw-Nida Greek-English Lexicon of the New Testament Based on Semantic Domains,* 2nd ed., 1988. Via BibleWorks.

Lust, J. A, E. Eynikel, and K. Hauspie, with the collaboration of G. Chamberlain *Greek-English Lexicon of the Septuagint,* German Bible Society, 1996. Via BibleWorks.

MacDonald, William G. Greek *Enchiridion: A Concise Handbook of Grammar for Translation and Exegesis.* Peabody: Hendrickson Publishers, 1986.

McKay, K. L. *A New Syntax of the Verb in New Testament Greek: An Aspectual Approach,* vol. 5. Studies in Biblical Greek, gen. ed. D. A. Carson. New York: Peter Lang, 1994.

Moule, C.F.D. *An Idiom Book of New Testament Greek,* second ed. New York: Cambridge University Press, 1959.

Moulton, J. H. and G. Milligan. *Vocabulary of the Greek Testament.* Peabody: Hendrickson Publishers, 2004.

Mounce, William D. *Greek for the Rest of Us: Mastering Bible Study without Mastering Biblical Languages.* Grand Rapids: Zondervan Publishing House, 2003.

Newman, Barclay "A Concise Greek-English Dictionary of the New Testament," in *The Greek New Testament,* 3rd ed., eds. Kurt Aland, Matthew Black, Carlo M. Martini, Bruce Metzger, and Allen Wikgren. West Germany: United Bible Societies, 1983.

Robertson, A. T. *A **Grammar** of the Greek New Testament in the Light of Historical Research.* Nashville: Broadman Press, 1934.

_____. *Word **Pictures** in the New Testament,* 6 vols. Grand Rapids: Baker Book House, 1931. Via BibleWorks.

Thayer, Joseph. *A Greek-English Lexicon of the New Testament.* Grand Rapids: Baker Book House, 1977.

Trench, Richard Chenevix. *Synonyms of the New Testament,* seventh edition, revised and enlarged. London: MacMillian and Co., 1871.

Wallace, Daniel B. *Greek Grammar Beyond the Basics: An Exegetical Syntax of the New Testament.* Grand Rapids: Zondervan Publishing House, 1996.

Young, Robert. *Young's Analytical Concordance to the Bible.* Grand Rapids: Eerdmans Publishing Company, 1970.

Books and Essays

Adams, Jay E. *From **Forgiven** to Forgiving.* Wheaton: Victor Books, 1989.

_____. *Ready to Restore: The Layman's Guide to Christian Counseling.* Phillipsburg: Presbyterian and Reformed Publishing Co., 1981.

Alcorn, Randy C. *Heaven.* Carol Stream, IL: Tyndale House, 2004.

_____. ***Money** Possessions and Eternity.* Wheaton: Tyndale House Publications, 1989.

_____. *The Law of **Rewards**.* Carol Stream, IL: Tyndale House, 2003.

Alford, Henry. *The New Testament for English Readers.* Chicago: Moody Press, n.d.

Arrington, French L. *Unconditional Security: Myth or Truth?* Cleveland, TN: Pathway Press, 2005.

Andersen, F. I. "2 (Slavonic Apocalypse of) **Enoch**." *The Old Testament Pseudepigrapha,* ed. James H. Charlesworth, Vol. 1, 91-213. New York: Doubleday, 1983.

Anderson, David R. *Free Grace Soteriology*. Xulon Press, 2010.

Archer, Gleason L. *Encyclopedia of Bible Difficulties*. Grand Rapids: Zondervan Publishing House, 1982.

_____. And Gregory Chirichigno. *Old Testament Quotations in the New Testament*. Chicago: Moody Press, 1983.

_____. Paul D. Feinberg, Douglas J. Moo, Richard R. Reiter, *Three Views on the Rapture: Pre; Mid; or Post-Tribulation?* Grand Rapids: Zondervan Publishing House, 1996.

Augustine, *Gift of Perseverance*. Available at http://www.truecovenanter.com/gospel/augustin_perseverance.html. Accessed on June 10, 2005.

_____. *Rebuke and Grace*. Available at http://www.newadvent.org/fathers/1511.htm. Accessed on June 10, 2005.

_____.*The City of God*, Available at: http://www.ccel.org/fathers/NPNF1-02/Augustine/cog/t121.htm. Accessed on January 20, 2005.

_____. *The Trinity*, trans. Edmund Hill. Vol. 5. *The Works of Saint Augustine*, ed. John E. Rotelle. Brooklyn: New City Press, 1991.

Bailey, Mark. *To Follow Him: The Severn Marks of a Disciple*. Sisters: Multnomah Publishers, 1977.

Barker, Harold. *Secure Forever*. Neptune: Loizeaux Brothers, 1974.

Barnes, Ron. *A Hero's Welcome: A Dissertation on the Doctrine of Future Rewards with Special Emphasis on the Bema Seat of Christ*, Graphic Business Solutions, 1997.

Barr, James. *The Semantics of Biblical Language*. Oxford: Oxford University Press, 1961.

Baughman, Ray E. *The Kingdom of God Visualized*. Birmingham, AL: Shepherd Press, 1972.

Beirnes, William F. *The Bride, The Lamb's Wife*. Tequesta: The Midnight Cry, n.d.

Benware, Paul. *The Believer's Payday*. Chattanooga, TN: AMG Publishers, 2002.

_____. *Understanding End Times Prophecy: A Comprehensive Approach*. Chicago: Moody Publications, 2006.

Bell, M. Charles. *Calvin and Scottish Theology: The Doctrine of Assurance*. Edinburgh: The Handsel Press, 1985.

Berkhof, Louis. *Systematic Theology*. 4th ed. Grand Rapids: Eerdmans Publishing Co., 1938.

Betz, Harlan D. *Setting the Stage for Eternity*. Kingwood, TX: Falcon Publishing LTD, 2006.

Bing, Charles C. *Lordship Salvation: A Biblical Evaluation and Response*. Grace Life Edition. Burleson: GraceLife Ministries, 1992.

_____. *Simply by Grace: An Introduction to God's Life-Changing Gift*. Grand Rapids, 2009.

Blaising, Craig A., Kenneth L. Gentry, Robert B. Strimple. *Three Views on the Millennium and Beyond*, eds. Darrell L. Bock and Stanley N. Gundry. Grand Rapids: Zondervan, 1999.

Borchert, Gerald L., "Insights Into the Gnostic Threat to Christianity as Gained Through the Gospel of Philip." *New Dimensions in New Testament Study*, ed. R. Longenecker. Grand Rapids: Zondervan Publishing House, 1974.

Boyd, Gregory A., William Lane Craig, David Hunt, and Paul Helm. *Divine Foreknowledge: Four Views*, eds. James K. Beilby and Paul R. Eddy. Downers Grove: InterVarsity Press, 2001.

Bruce, Alexander Balmain. *The Parabolic Teaching of Christ*. New York: A. C. Armstrong & Son, 1892.

Bryson, George. *The Dark Side of Calvinism: The Calvinist Caste System*. Santa Ana, CA: Calvary Chapel Publishing, 2004.

_____. *The Five Points of Calvinism: Weighed and Found Wanting*. Costa Mesa, CA: The Word for Today, 2002. [Also available at http://calvarychapel.com/library/bryson-george/books/fpocwafw.htm#01. Accessed on November 11, 2004.]

Buckley, Jorunn Jacobsen. "'The Holy Spirit is a Double Name': Holy Spirit, Mary, and Sophia in the *Gospel of Philip*." *Images of the Feminine in Gnosticism*, ed. Karen L. King, 211-227. Philadelphia: Fortress Press, 1988.

Buis, Harry. *The Doctrine of Eternal Punishment*. Pennsylvania: The Presbyterian and Reformed Publishing Company, 1957.

Bullinger, E. W. *Figures of Speech Used in the Bible*. Grand Rapids: Baker Book House, 1898.

Bunge, Donald H. *What Happened to the Word "Believe"?* Omaha, NE: self published, 1985.

Buttrick, George A. *The Parables of Jesus*. New York: Harper & Brothers, 1928.

Calvin, John. *Institution of the Christian Religion*, trans. by Ford Lewis Battles. Atlanta: John Knox Press, 1975.

_____. "Chapter 2. Of faith. The definition of It. Its Peculiar Properties." Available at http://www.ccel.org/c/calvin/institutes/htm/iv.iii.iii.htm. Accessed on September 1, 2004.

_____. "Chapter 23. Refutation of the Calumnies by which this Doctrine is Always Unjustly Assailed." Available at http://www.ccel.org/ccelcalvin/institutes.v.xxiv.html. Accessed on August 25, 2007.

Campbell, Alexander. *Five Discourses on Hell! Being an Exposure and Refutation of Universalism*: In Reply to Rev. Theodore Clapp. Available at http://www.cimmay.com/pdf/discourse.pdf. Accessed on July 21, 2005.

Carmical, Frank D. *The Omega Reunion*. Dallas: Redención Viva, 1986.

Carson, D. A. *Exegetical Fallacies*. Grand Rapids: Baker Book House, 1984.

_____. And John D. Woodbridge, eds. *Scripture and Truth*. Grand Rapids: Zondervan Publishing House, 1983.

Chay, Fred and John P. Correia. *The Faith that Saves: The Nature of Faith in the New Testament*. Hayesville, NC: Schoettle Publishing Co., 2008.

Chafer, Lewis Sperry. *Salvation: A Clear Doctrinal Analysis*. Grand Rapids: Zondervan Publishing House, 1955.

_____. *Systematic Theology*. Dallas: Dallas Seminary Press, 1948.

Charles, R. H. *Eschatology: The Doctrine of a Future Life in Israel, Judaism and Christianity*. New York: Schocken Books, 1963.

Cheney, Johnston M. *The Life of Christ in Stereo*. Portland: Multnomah Press, 1969.

Chitwood, Arlen L. **Judgment** *Seat of Christ*. Norman, Okla.: The Lamp Broadcast, **1986**.

_____. **Judgment** *Seat of Christ*, revised edition. Norman, Okla.: The Lamp Broadcast, **2001**.

_____. **Judgment** *Seat of Christ*, revised edition. Norman, Okla.: The Lamp Broadcast, **2011**.

_____. *Mysteries of the Kingdom*. Norman, Okla.: The Lamp Broadcast, 1998.

_____. *Prophecy on Mount **Olivet***. Norman, Okla.: The Lamp Broadcast, 1989.

_____. *Salvation of the **Soul***. Norman, Okla.: The Lamp Broadcast, 1983.

Chumney, Eddie. *Who is the Bride of Christ?* Revised edition. Hagerstown: Serenity Books, 2001.

Clark, Gordon. H. *Faith and Saving Faith*. Jefferson, The Trinity Foundation, 1983.

Claeys, John. *Apocalypse 2012: The Ticking of the End-Time Clock—What Does the Bible Say?* Sisters, OR: VMI Publications, 2012.

Cloud, David W. *The Calvinism Debate*. Port Huron, Way of Life Literature, 2006.

Cocoris, Michael G. *Evangelism: A Biblical Approach*. Chicago: Moody Press, 1984.

Collins, John J. "Apocalyptic **Literature**." *Early Judaism and Its Modern Interpreters*, eds. Robert A. Kraft and George W. E. Nickelsburg. Philadelphia: Fortress Press, 1986.

Copan, Paul. *"That's Just Your Interpretation": Responding to Skeptics who Challenge Your Faith*. Grand Rapids: Baker Books, 2001.

_____. *True for You but Not for Me*, revised edition. Bloomington, MN: Bethany House, 2009.

Craig, S. S. *The Dualism of Eternal Life: A Revolution in Eschatology*. Rochester: Du Bois Press, 1916.

Craig, William Lane. *The Only **Wise** God: The Compatibility of Divine Foreknowledge and Human Freedom*. Eugene, OR: Wipf and Stock Publishers, 2000.

Corner, Daniel D. *The Believer's Conditional **Security**: Eternal Security Refuted*. Washington, PA: Evangelical Outreach, 2000.

_____. *The Myth of Eternal Security*, third edition. Washington, PA: Evangelical Outreach, 2005.

Dagg, John L. *Manual of Theology*. Harrisonburg, VA: Gano Books, 1982.

Deal, Colin Hoyle. *The Day and Hour Jesus will Return*. Rutherford College; NC: Colin H. Deal, 1988.

Dillow, Joseph C. *The Reign of the Servant Kings: A Study of Eternal Security and the Final Significance of Man*. 2nd ed. Hayesville, NC: Schoettle Publishing Co., 1993.

Derickson, Gary and Earl Radmacher. *The **Disciplemaker**: What Matters Most to Jesus*. Salem: Charis Press, 2001.

Dobson, James. *When God Doesn't Make Sense*. Wheaton: Tyndale House Publishers, 1993.

Dodson, Kenneth F. *The Prize of the Up-Calling*. Baker Book House, 1969; reprint, Miami Springs: Schoettle Publishing Co., 1989.

Duty, Guy. *If Ye Continue: A Study of the Conditional Aspects of Salvation*. Minnesota: Bethany Fellow, 1966.

Dyer, David W. *Thy Kingdom Come*. Rochester: "A Grain of Wheat" Ministries, 1984.

Eaton, Michael. *No Condemnation: A New Theology of Assurance*. Downers Grove: InterVarsity Press, 1995.

Erickson, Millard J. *Christian **Theology***. 3 vols. Grand Rapids: Baker Book House, 1983-1985.

Evans, Anthony T. *Bible Prophecies Through the Ages: The **Best** is Yet to Come*. Chicago: Moody Press, 2000.

_____. "**Rewards** for Christians," in *Tim LayHaye Prophecy Study Bible*. AMG Publishers, 2000.

_____. *The Kingdom Agenda: What a Way to Live!* Nashville: Word Publishing, 1999.

Evans, Phillip M. *Eternal **Security** Proved! Salvation not Probation*. LuLu.com, 2008.

Faust, J.D. *The **Rod**: Will God Spare It? An Exhaustive Study of Temporary Punishment for Unfaithful Christians at the Judgment Seat and During the Millennial Kingdom*. Hayesville: Schoettle Publishing Co., 2002.

Feinberg, John, Norman Geisler, Bruce Reichenbach, and Clark Pinnock. **Predestination** *& Free Will: Four Views of Divine Sovereignty & Human Freedom*, eds. David and Randall Basinger. Downers Grove: InterVarsity Press, 1986.

Finley, Thomas W. *Worth of the Kingdom*. Available at http://www.seekersofchrist.org/download/Worthy%20of%20the%20Kingdom%20040622.pdf. Accessed on August 13, 2004.

Fisk, Samuel. *Election and Predestination*. Bicester: Penfold Book and Bible House, 1973. Originally published as *Divine Sovereignty and Human Freedom*. Neptune: Loizeaux Brothers, 1973.

Forlines, F. Leroy. *The Quest for **Truth**: Answering Life's Inescapable Questions*. Nashville: Randall House, 2001.

Forster, Roger T. and V. Paul Marston. *God's Strategy in Human History*. Wheaton: Tyndale House Publishers, 1973.

Friesen, Gary and J. Robin Maxson. *Decision Making and the Will of God*. Sisters: Multnomah Publishers, 1980.

Frost, Stanley B. *Old Testament Apocalyptic: Its Origins and Growth*. London: Epworth Press, 1981.

Fudge, Edward W. *The Fire that Consumes: The Biblical Case for Conditional Immortality*. Carlisle: The Paternoster Press, 1994.

Hanna, Mark M. "A Response to the Role of Logic in Biblical Interpretation." Earl D. Radmacher and Robert D. Preus, eds. *Hermeneutics, Inerrancy, and the Bible*. Grand Rapids: Zondervan Publishing House, 1984.

Hoyt, Samuel L. *The Judgment Seat of Christ: A Biblical and Theological Study*. Milwaukee, WI: Grace Gospel Press, 2011.

Jeffrey, Grant R. *The New Temple and the Second Coming*. Colorado Springs: WaterBrook Press, 2007.

Gracely, Daniel. *Calvinism: A Closer Look: Evangelicals, Calvinism, and Why No One's Answering the Problem of Evil*, revised and enlarged edition. Grandma's Attic Press, 2009.

Geisler, Norman L. ***Chosen but Free***, second edition. Minneapolis: Bethany House Publications, 2001.

_____. ***Inerrancy***. Grand Rapids: Zondervan Publishing House, 1980.

_____. And Ronald M. Brooks. *Come Let Us Reason: An Introduction to Logical Thinking*. Grand Rapids: Baker Book House, 1990.

_____. And Ron Rhodes, *When Cultists Asks: A Popular Handbook on Cultic Ministries*. Grand Rapids: Baker Books, 1997.

_____. And William E. Nix. *A General Introduction to the **Bible**: Revised and Expanded*. Chicago: Moody Press, 1986.

Gillham, Bill. ***Lifetime*** *Guarantee*. Eugene: Harvest House Publishers, 1993.

_____. *What God **Wishes** Christians Knew About Christianity*. Eugene: Harvest House Publishers, 1998.

Gromacki, Robert G. *New Testament Survey*. Grand Rapid: Baker Book House, 1974.

_____. *Is **Salvation** Forever?* Chicago: Moody Press, 1973.

Govett, Robert. ***Entrance*** *into the Kingdom: Reward According to Works*. 2nd ed. Miami Springs: Schoettle Publishing Co., 1978.

_____. *Govett on the Parables*. Miami Springs: Schoettle Publishing Co., 1989.

_____. *The New Jerusalem: Our Eternal Home*. Miami Springs: Conley and Schoettle Publishing, Co., 1985.

_____. ***Reward*** *According to Works*. 4th ed. Miami Springs: Schoettle Publishing Co., 1989.

Guthrie, Donald. *New Testament **Introduction***. 3rd ed. Illinois: InterVarsity Press, 1970.

Haldeman, I. M. *Satan as an Angel of Light*. New York: The Book Stall, n.d.

_____. *Ten **Sermons** on the Second Coming of Our Lord Jesus Christ*. Chicago: Fleming H. Revell Co., n.d.

Haley, W. John. *An Examination of the Alleged Discrepancies of the Bible*. Grand Rapids: Baker Book House, 1977.

Harrison, Everett F. *Introduction to the New Testament*, rev. ed. Grand Rapids: Eerdmans Publishing Co., 1985.

Helm, Paul, Alan G. Padgett, William Lane Craig, and Nicholas Wolterstorff. *Four Views: God & **Time***, ed. Gregory E. Ganssle. Downers Grove: InterVarsity Press, 2001.

Hitchcock, Mark. *The Complete Book of Bible Prophecy*. Wheaton: Tyndale House Publishers, 1996.

Hoekema, Anthony A. *The Bible and the **Future***. Grand Rapids: Eerdmans Publishing Company, 1979.

Hodges, Zane C. *A Biblical Reply to Lordship Salvation: Absolutely **Free**!* Grand Rapids: Zondervan Publishing House, 1989.

_____. *Did Paul Preach Eternal Life? Should We?* Mesquite: Kerugma, 2007.

_____. *Grace in **Eclipse**: A Study on Eternal Rewards*, 3rd edition. Irving, TX: Grace Evangelical Society, 2007.

_____. ***Harmony*** *With God: A Fresh Look at Repentance*. Dallas: Redención Viva, 2001.

_____. *Jesus: God's Prophet: His Teaching about the Coming Surprise*. Mesquite: Kerugma, 2006.

_____. *Six **Secrets** of the Christian Life: The Miracle of Walking with God*. Redención Viva, 2004.

_____. *The Gospel Under **Siege**: A Study on Faith and Works*, 2nd ed. Dallas: Redención Viva, 1992.

_____. "The **Rapture** in 1 Thessalonians 5:1-11." *Walvoord: A Tribute*, ed. Donald K. Campbell. Chicago: Moody Press, 1982. Although the newer version is available on-line from CTSJ, any quotations herein will be from the original version.

Horton, Michael S., Norman L. Geisler, Stephen M. Ashby, and J. Steven Harper. *Four Views on Eternal **Security***, ed. Matthew J. Pinson. Grand Rapids: Zondervan, 2002.

House, Wayne H. *Charts of Christian Theology and Doctrine* Grand Rapids: Zondervan Publishing House, 1992.

_____. *Chronological and Background Charts of the New Testament*. Grand Rapids: Zondervan Publishing House, 1981.

Humphreys, D. Russell *Starlight and Time: Solving the Puzzle of Distant Starlight in a Young Universe*. Green Forest, AR: Master Books, 1994.

Hunt, Dave. *What **Love** Is This? Calvinism's Misrepresentation of God*. Sisters, OR: Loya, 2002.

_____. And James White, ***Debating*** *Calvinism*. Sisters, OR: Multnomah Publishers, 2004.

Hutson, Curtis. *Is Water Baptism Essential to Salvation?* Murfreesboro: Sword of the Lord Publishers, 1988.

_____. ***Salvation*** *Crystal Clear*. 2 vols. Murfreesboro: Sword of the Lord Publishers, 1987.

_____. *Why I disagree with All Five Points of Calvinism*. Murfreesboro: The Sword of the Lord Publishers, 1980.

Impe, Jack Van. "Hell," in *Tim LayHaye Prophecy Study Bible*. AMG Publishers, 2000

Ironside, H. A. *Full **Assurance***, revised ed. Chicago: Moody Press, 1937.

Isaac, E. "**1** (Ethiopic Apocalypse of) **Enoch**." *The Old Testament Pseudepigrapha*, ed. James H. Charlesworth, vol. 1 New York: Doubleday, 1983.

Isenberg, Wesley W. "The Gospel of **Philip**." *The Nag Hammadi Library*, gen. ed. James M. Robinson. San Francisco: Harper & Row, 1978.

Jeremias, Joachim. *The Parables of Jesus*, revised third edition. London: SCM Press, 1972.

Johnson, Carl G. *The **Account** Which We Must Give: Studies on the Judgment Seat of Christ*. Schaumburg: Regular Baptist Press, 1990.

Kaiser, Walter C., Jr. *The **Uses** of the Old Testament in the New*. Chicago: Moody Press, 1985.

Kendall, R. T. *Are You Stone **Deaf** to the Spirit or Rediscovering God?* Ross-shire: Christian Focus Publications, 1994.

_____. *Calvin and English Calvinism to 1649*. Oxford: Oxford University Press, 1979.

_____. *Once Saved, Always Saved*. Chicago: Moody Press, 1983.

_____. *The Complete Guide to the Parables: Understanding and Applying the Stories of Jesus*. Grand Rapids: Chosen Books, 2004.

_____. *When God Says, "Well Done!"* Ross-shire: Christian Focus Publications, 1993.

Kroll, Woodrow Michael. *It will be Worth it All: A Study in the Believer's Rewards*. Neptune, NJ: Loizeaux Brothers, 1977.

Kuhatschek, Jack. *Taking the Guesswork out of Applying the Bible*. Downers Grove: InterVarsity Press, 1990.

Ladd, George Eldon, Herman A. Hoyt, Loraine Boettner, and Anthony A. Hoekema. *The Meaning of the **Millennium**: Four Views*, ed. Robert G. Clouse. Downers Grove: InterVarsity Press, 1977.

Lash, Dan. *The Plan of Salvation Through the Ages*. Available at http://www.danlash.net/Dad's%20sermon %20notes/Consistantly%20of%20Saving%20Faith%20through%20the%20Ages.doc. Accessed on September 7, 1995.

Lang, G. H. *Firstborn **Sons**, Their Rights & Risks: An Inquiry as to the Privileges and Perils of the Members of the Church of God*. London: Samuel Roberts Publishers, 1936; reprint, Miami Springs: Schoettle Publishing Co., 1984.

_____. *Pictures and **Parables**: Studies in the Parabolic Teaching of Holy Scripture*, third edition. Miami Springs: Conley and Schoettle Publishing Co., 1985.

LaHaye, Tim and Thomas Ice. *Charting the End Times*. Eugene, OR: Harvest House Publishing, 2001.

Lavender, Malcolm L. *The Potter's Freedom to Love the World*. Port Huron, MI: Crisis Publications, Inc., 2005.

Lee, Witness. *A Brief **Definition** of the Kingdom of the Heavens*. Anaheim: Living Stream Ministry, 1986.

Lewis, C. S. *Mere Christianity: A Revised and Amplified Edition With a New Introduction of the Three Books: Broadcast Talks, Christian Behavior, and Beyond Personality*, Harper Collins edition. Harper San Francisco, 2001.

Lovett, C. S. *Dealing with the Devil*. Baldwin Park: Personal Christianity Chapel, 1981.

Lightner, Robert P. *The Last Days Handbook: A Comprehensive Guide to Understanding the Different Views of Prophecy. Who believes What about Prophecy*. Nashville: Thomas Nelson Publishers, 1990.

_____. *Sin, the Savior, and **Salvation***. Thomas Nelson Publishers, 1991.

Luther, Martin. *De Servo Arbitrio "On the Enslaved Will" or The Bondage of Will*. Available at http://www.ccel.org /ccel/luther/bondage.html.

Lutzer, Erwin W. *How You can be **Sure** that You will Spend Eternity with God*. Chicago: Moody Press, 1996.

_____. *The Doctrines that Divide: A Fresh Look at the Historic Doctrines That Separate Christians*. Grand Rapids, MI: Kregel Publications, 1998.

_____. *Triumph and Tears at the Judgment Seat of Christ: Your Eternal **Reward***. Chicago: Moody Press, 1998.

MacArthur, John F., Jr. *The **Gospel** According to Jesus: What is Authentic Faith?* Revised and expanded anniversary edition. Grand Rapids: Zondervan, 2008.

_____. *Faith **Works**: The Gospel According to the Apostles*. Dallas: Word Publishing, 1993.

MacDonald, William. *Once in Christ: In Christ Forever*. West Port Colborne: Gospel Folio Press, 1997.

Martin, Jobe. *The Evolution of a Creationist: A Laymen's Guide To The Conflict Between The Bible and Evolutionary Theory*. Rockwall, TX: Biblical Discipleship Publishers, 2004.

Martin, Walter. *The Kingdom of the **Cults***. Minneapolis: Bethany House Publishers, 1985.

Martyr, Justin. *Dialogue of Justin, Philosopher and Martyr, with Trypho, a Jew*. Available at http://www.ccel.org/fathers/ANF-01/just/justintrypho.html#Section42. Accessed on April 5, 2005.

McDowell, Josh and Don Stewart. *Handbook of Today's Religions: Understanding the **Occult***. San Bernardino: Campus Crusade for Christ, 1982.

Mickelsen, Berkeley. *Interpreting the Bible*. Grand Rapids: Eerdmans Publishing Co., 1963.

Missler, Chuck and Nancy. *The Kingdom Power, & Glory: The Overcomers Handbook,* new and revised edition. Coeur d' Alene, ID: The King's High Way Ministries, 2007.

Mize, Lyn. *The Open Door*. Available at http://www.thefirstfruits.org. Accessed on August 2, 2005.

Morgan, G. Campbell. *God's Methods With Man*. Old Tappan, NJ: Fleming H. Revell Company, 1898

_____. *The Pictures and Metaphors of Our Lord*. Old Tappan, NJ: Fleming H. Revell Company, n.d.

Morris, Fredrick W. "Universal Salvation in Origen and Maximus," in *Universalism and the Doctrine of Hell*, ed. Nigel M. de S. Cameron, 35-72. Grand Rapids: Baker, 1992.

Morris, Henry D. and John D. Morris. *Scripture and Creation*. Vol. 1. The Modern Creation Trilogy. Green Forest, AR: Master Books, 1996.

Murphree, Jon Tal. *Divine Paradoxes: A Finite View of an Infinite God.* Camp Hill, PA: Christian Publications, 1998.

Myers, Edward P. "Interpreting Figurative Language" in *Biblical Interpretation: Principles and Practices*, eds. F. Furman Kearley, Edward P. Myers, and Timothy D. Hadley. Grand Rapids: Baker Book House, 1986.

Nee, Watchman. *A Living Sacrifice.* New York: Christian Fellowship Publishers, 1972.

_____. *The Gospel of God.* Vol. 3. Anaheim, CA.: Living Stream Ministry, 1990.

_____. *The Spiritual Man.* 3 vols. New York: Christian Fellowship Publishers, 1963.

Neff, Ken and David Bast. *Hold Fast: Against Christian Myths.* St. Augustine, FL: Leader Quest, 2010.

Neff, Ken. *Choose to Live: Distinguishing Possessing Eternal Life from Experiencing Eternal Life.* St. Augustine, FL: LeaderQuest, 2012.

Neighbour, R. E. *If By Any Means...* Elyria: Gems of Gold Publishing Co., 1935; reprint, Hayesville: Schoettle Publishing Co., 1985.

Neighbour, Ralph W. *The Touch of the Spirit*, prologue by Jack Taylor. Nashville: Broadman Press, 1972.

Nickelsburg, George W. E. "The Bible Rewritten and Expanded," in *Jewish Writings of the Second Temple Period*, ed. M. Stone. Philadelphia: Fortress Press, 1984.

Olson, Gordon C. *Beyond Calvinism and Arminianism: An Inductive Mediate Theology of Salvation.* Global Gospel Publishers, 2002.

Olson, Lloyd. *Eternal Security: Once Saved; Always Saved.* Mustang, OK: Tate Publishing & Enterprises, 2007.

Olson, Roger E. *Arminian Theology: Myths and Realities.* Downers Grove: InterVarsity Press, 2006.

Owen, John. *The Holy Spirit: His Gifts and Power.* Michigan: Grand Rapids, 1954.

Pagels, Elaine H. "The 'Mystery of Marriage,' in the *Gospel of Philip* revisited." *The Future of Early Christianity*, ed. Birger A. Pearson, 442-454. Minneapolis: Fortress Press, 1991.

Panton, D. M. *The Judgment Seat of Christ.* Miami Springs: Schoettle Publishing Co., 1984. [Also available at http://www.gbcne.org/authors/judgmentseat/judgmentseat.htm. Accessed on August 8, 2005.]

Parrott, Douglas M. "Evidence of Religious Syncretism in Gnostic Texts from Nag Hammadi," in *Religious Syncretism in Antiquity*, eds. Walter H. Capps and Charles H. Long. Missoula: University of Montana, 1975.

Patterson, Alexander. *The Greater Life and Work of Christ: As Revealed in Scripture, Man and Nature.* New York: Christian Alliance Publishing Co., 1896.

Pearson, B. A. "Jewish Sources in Gnostic Literature," in *Jewish Writings of the Second Temple Period*, ed. Michael E. Stone, 443-482. Philadelphia: Fortress Press, 1984.

Pentecost, J. Dwight. *Things to Come: A Study in Biblical Eschatology.* Grand Rapids: Zondervan Publishing House, 1958.

Pember, G. H. *Earth's Earliest Ages: And Their Connection with Modern Spiritualism, Theosophy, and Buddhism.* Grand Rapids: Kregel Publications, 1975.

_____. *The Great Prophecies of the Centuries Concerning the Church.* New York: Fleming H. Revell Comp., n.d.

Peterson, Robert A. *Hell on Trial: The Case for Eternal Punishment.* Phillipsburg: Presbyterian and Reformed Publishing Company, 1995.

Picirilli, Robert E. *Grace, Faith, Free Will: Contrasting Views of Salvation: Calvinism and Arminianism.* Nashville: Randall House, 2002.

Prince, Benny D. *Once Saved, Always? The False Doctrine of Eternal Security.* Bloomington: Author House, 2007.

Radmacher, Earl D. *Salvation*, gen. ed. Charles R. Swindoll. Nashville: Word Publishing, 2000.

Rice, John R. *Predestined for Hell? No!* Murfreesboro: Sword of the Lord Publishers, 1958.

Rieu, E. V. *The Four Gospels: A New Translation from the Greek.* Baltimore: Penguin Books, 1953.

Roberts, Alexander and James Donaldson, eds. *The Ante-Nicene Fathers*, 10 vols., American Reprint. Grand Rapids: Eerdmans Publishing Co., 1967. All quotations from writers of the Ante-Nicene period are from this series, and references to volume and page number are cited in the text.

Rowley, H. H., *The Relevance of Apocalyptic: A Study of Jewish and Christian Apocalypses from Daniel to the Revelation*, 2d ed. London: Lutterworth Press, 1947.

Ryrie, Charles C. *A Survey of Bible Doctrine.* Chicago: Moody Press, 1972.

_____. *Balancing the Christian Life.* Chicago: Moody Press, 1969.

_____. *Balancing the Christian Life*, anniversary edition. Chicago: Moody Press, 1994.

_____. *Basic Theology.* Illinois: Victor Books, 1986.

_____. *Dispensationalism Today.* Chicago: Moody Press, 1965.

_____. *So Great Salvation: What it Means to Believe in Jesus Christ.* Illinois: Victor Books, 1989.

_____. *The Basis of the Premillennial Faith.* Neptune: Loizeaux Brothers, 1953.

_____. *The Ryrie Study Bible: New American Standard Translation.* Chicago: Moody Press, 1978.

_____. *What you Should Know about Inerrancy*. Chicago: Moody Press, 1981.

Sauer, Erich. *In the Arena of Faith*. Grand Rapids, Wm. B. Eerdmans Publishing Company, 1955.

Schaff Philip and Henry Wace, eds. *St. Jerome: Letters and Select Works*. Second Series. Vol. 6. A Select Library of Nicene and Post-Nicene Fathers of the Christian Church. Grand Rapids: Eerdmans Publishing Co., 1892.

_____. Saint Chrysostom: Homily VI. Vol. 9. Available at http://www.ccel.org/ccel/schaff/npnf109.xix .viii.html#fnb_xix.viii-p59.3. Accessed on August 8, 2005.

Seiss, Joseph A. *The Parable of the Virgins: In Six Discourses*. Philadelphia: Smith, English & Co., 1873.

Sellers, C. Norman. *Election and Perseverance*. Miami Springs: Schoettle Publishing Co., 1987.

Seymour, Richard A. *All About Repentance*. Hollywood; FL: Harvest House Publishers, 1974.

_____. *The Gift of God*, second edition. LaGrange, WY: Integrity Press, 2007.

Scriven Darryl. *Eternal Security Revisited: A Dialogue with Charles Stanley*. Lincoln, NE: iUniverse, Inc, 2004.

Shedd, William G. T. *Dogmatic Theology*, reprint ed., 2 vols. Grand Rapids: Zondervan Publishing House, n.d.

Shank, Robert. *Elect in the Son: A Study of the Doctrine of Election*. Grand Rapids: Baker Book House, 1989.

_____. *Life in the Son: A Study of the Doctrine of Perseverance*. Minneapolis, MN: Bethany Fellowship, 1989.

Showers, Renald. *The New Nature*. Neptune: Loizeaux Brothers, 1986.

Stanford, A. Ray and Richard A. Seymour and Carol Ann Strieb. *Handbook of Personal Evangelism,* revised ed. Hollywood, FL: Florida Bible College, 1975.

Stanley, Charles. *Eternal Security: Can You Be Sure?* Nashville: Thomas Nelson Publishers, 1990.

_____. *The Wonderful Spirit-Filled Life*. Nashville: Thomas Nelson Publishers, 1992.

Stanton, Gerald B. *Kept from the Hour: Biblical Evidence for the Pretribulational Return of Christ*. Miami Springs: Schoettle Publishing Co., 1991.

Stevenson, Tim. *The Bema: A Story about the Judgment Seat of Christ*. Gainesville: Fair Havens Publications, 2000.

Stone, Michael E. "Apocalyptic Literature," in *Jewish Writings of the Second Temple Period*, ed. M. Stone, 383-441. Philadelphia: Fortress Press, 1984.

Strombeck, J.F. *Shall Never Perish*. Harvest House Publishers, Eugene: Oregon, 1982.

Terry, Milton S. *Biblical Hermeneutics: A Treatise on the Interpretation of the Old and New Testaments,* second edition. Grand Rapids: Zondervan, n.d.

Thiessen, Henry Clarence. *Lectures in Systematic Theology*. Revised by Vernon D. Doerksen. Grand Rapids: Eerdmans Publishing Company, 1979.

Thomas, Major W. Ian. *The Saving Life of Christ*. Grand Rapids: Daybreak Books, 1961.

_____. *The Saving Life of Christ* and *The Mystery of Godliness*. Grand Rapids: Zondervan Publishing House, 1988.

Thomas, L. Robert and Stanley N. Gundry, *A Harmony of the Gospels: with Explanations and Essays*. San Francisco: Harper & Row, 1978.

Torrance, Thomas F. *The Doctrine of the Grace in the Apostolic Fathers*. Eugene, OR: Wipf and Stock Publishers, 1948.

Tripp, D. H. "The 'Sacramental System' of the Gospel of Philip," in vol. 17, part 1 *Studia Patristica*, ed. Elizabeth A. Livingstone. Oxford: Pergamon Press, 1982).

Tucker, Henry H. *The Gospel in Enoch*. Philadelphia: J. B. Lippincott, 1869.

Unger, Merrill F. *Demons in the World Today*. Wheaton: Tyndale House, 1971.

Vance, Laurence M. *The Other Side of Calvinism*, revised edition. Pensacola: Vance Publications, 1999.

Virkler, Henry A. *Hermeneutics: Principles and Processes of Biblical Interpretation*. Grand Rapids: Baker Book House, 1981.

Wall, Joe. *Going for the Gold, Reward and Loss at the Judgment of Believers*. Chicago: Moody Press, 1991.

Walvoord, John F, William Crockett, Zachary Hayes, and Clark Pinnock. *Four Views on Hell*, ed. William Crockett. Grand Rapids: Zondervan Publishing House, 1992.

_____. *The Holy Spirit: A Comprehensive Study of the Person and Work of the Holy Spirit*, third ed. Grand Rapids: Zondervan Publishing House, 1958.

_____. *The Rapture Question*, revised and enlarged edition. Grand Rapids: Zondervan Publishing House, 1979.

Warfield, Benjamin Breckinridge. *The Inspiration and Authority of the Bible*, ed. Samuel G. Craig. Phillipsburg: Presbyterian and Reformed Publishing Company, 1948.

Waterhouse, Steven W. *Blessed Assurance: A Defense of the Doctrine of Eternal Security* (Amarillo: TX: Westcliff Press, 2000)

_____. *Not By Bread Alone: An Outlined Guide To Bible Doctrine*, revised edition. Amarillo, TX: Westcliff Press, 2003.

_____. *What Must I do to be Saved? The Bible's Definition of Saving Faith*. Amarillo, TX: Westcliff Press, 2000.

Watson, George D. *The Bridehood Saints*. Cincinnati: God's Revivalist Office, 1913.

Wells, David F. *No Place for Truth or Whatever Happened to Evangelical Theology?* Leicester: Inter-Varsity Press, 1993.

Whipple, Gary T. *Shock and Surprise Beyond the Rapture!* Miami Springs: Schoettle Publishing Co., 1992.

_____. *The Matthew **Mysteries**: A Revelation of the Higher Wisdom Concerning the Church, Israel and the Gentiles in Prophecy*. Hayesville: Schoettle Publishing Co., 1995.

Wilkin, Robert N. **Confident** *In Christ: Living By Faith Really Works*. Irving: Grace Evangelical Society, 1999.

_____. *The Road to Reward: Living Today in Light of Tomorrow*. Irving: Grace Evangelical Society, 2003.

_____. *The **Ten** Most Misunderstood Words in the Bible*. USA: Grace Evangelical Society, 2012.

Wilkinson, Bruce and David Kopp. *A Life God Rewards: Why Everything You Do Today Matters Forever*. Sisters: Multnomah Publishers, 2002.

Williams, Michael A. "Uses of Gender Imagery in Ancient Gnostic Texts," in *Gender and Religion: On the Complexity of Symbols*, ed. Caroline W. Bynum, Stevan Harrell, and Paula Richman, 196-230. Boston: Beacon Press, 1986.

Wilson, Edwin A. *Selected **Writings** of A. Edwin Wilson*, 3rd ed., ed. Arlen L. Chitwood. Schoettle Publishing Co. 1981.

Wilson, Robert M. *The **Gospel** of Philip: Translated from the Coptic text, with an Introduction and Commentary*. New York: Harper & Row, 1962.

Wisse, Frederik. "The Apocryphon of John," in *The Nag Hammadi Library*, gen. ed. James M. Robinson. San Francisco: Harper & Row, 1978.

Whitcomb, John C. *The Early Earth*, revised edition. Grand Rapids, MI: Baker Book House, 1986.

White, James R. *The Potter's **Freedom**: A Defense of the Reformation and a Rebuttal of Norman Geisler's Chosen But Free*. New York: Amityville, Calvary Press Publishing, 2000.

Wuest, Kenneth S. "**Treasures** From the Greek New Testament," in *Wuest's Word Studies: From the Greek New Testament for the English Reader*. Vol. 3. Grand Rapids, Eerdmans Publishing Company, 1942.

_____. "Untranslatable **Riches**," in *Wuest's Word Studies: From the Greek New Testament for the English Reader*. Vol. 3. Grand Rapids, Eerdmans Publishing Company, 1942.

Youngblood, Ronald, ed., **Evangelicals** *and Inerrancy: Selections from the Journal of the Evangelical Theological Society*. Nashville: Thomas Nelson Publishers, 1984.

Zodhiates, Spiros. *Hebrew-Greek Key Word Study Bible: Key Insights into God's Word*, NASB revised edition, eds. Warren Baker and Joel Kletzing. Chattanooga, TN: AMG Publishers, 2008.

Commentaries

Adamson, James B. *The Epistle of James*. The New International Commentary on the New Testament, ed. F. F. Bruce. Grand Rapids: Eerdmans Publishing Co., 1976.

Alford, Henry. *The Greek Testament*. Vol. 1, *The Four Gospels*. London: Deighton, Bell, & Co., 1863.

Archer, Gleason L., *Isaiah*. The Wycliffe Bible Commentary, eds. Charles F. Pfeiffer and Everett F. Harrison. Chicago: Moody Press, 1990.

Arndt, William F. Arndt. *Luke*. Concordia Classic Commentary Series. St. Louis: Concordia Publishing House, 1956.

Barbieri, Louis A., Jr. *Matthew*. The Bible Knowledge Commentary, eds. John F. Walvoord and Roy B. Zuck. Wheaton: Victor Books, 1984.

Barnes, Albert. *Acts*. Notes on the New Testament, ed. Robert Frew. Grand Rapids: Baker Book House, 1884-1885.

_____. *James*. Notes on the New Testament, ed. Robert Frew. Grand Rapids: Baker Book House, 1884-1885.

Barnhouse, Donald G. *Revelation: An Expositional Commentary*. Grand Rapids: Zondervan Publishing House, 1971.

Barrett, C. K. *The First Epistle to the Corinthians*. Harper New Testament Commentaries, ed. Henry Chadwick. New York: Harper & Row Publishers, 1968.

Barth, Markus. *Ephesians: Introduction, Translation, and Commentary on Chapters 1-3*. Vol. 34. The Anchor Bible. New York: Doubleday & Company, 1974.

_____. *Ephesians: Translation and Commentary on Chapters 4-6*. Vol. 34A. The Anchor Bible. New York: Doubleday & Company, 1974.

Becker, J. E. *Rightly Dividing the Book of Revelation*. Enumclaw, WA: Winepress Publishing, 2004.

Best, Ernest. *1 Peter*. New Century Bible. London: Oliphants Ltd., 1971.

Blomberg, Craig L. *Matthew*. Vol. 22. The New American Commentary: An Exegetical and Theological Exposition of Holy Scripture, gen. ed. David S. Dockery. Nashville: Broadman Press, 1992.

Boice, James Montgomery. *The Gospel of John*. Grand Rapids: Zondervan Publishing House, 1985.

Bray, Gerald ed., Ancient Christian Commentary on Scripture, New Testament VII: 1-2 Corinthians (Downers Grove: InterVarsity Press, 1999),

_____. *New Testament* VI: Romans (Downers Grove: InterVarsity Press, 1998).

Brown, Raymond, D. *The Gospel According to John*. Vol. 29. The Anchor Bible. New York: Doubleday & Company, 1986.

Bruce, F. F. *The Epistle to the Hebrews*. The New International Commentary on the New Testament, ed. F. F. Bruce. Grand Rapids: Eerdmans Publishing Co., 1964.

Calvin, John. *A Harmony of the Gospels*. Calvin's Commentaries, eds. David W. Torrance and Thomas F. Torrance, trans. by A. W. Morrison. Grand Rapids: Eerdmans Publishing Co., 1972.

_____. "Commentary on Matthew, Mark, Luke," vol. 1, p. 153. Available at http://www.ccel.org/ccel/calvin /calcom31.pdf. Accessed on August 15, 2009.

_____. "1 John 3:7-10." Available at http://www.ccel.org/c/calvin/comment3/comm_vol45/htm/v.iv.iii.htm. Accessed on June 24, 2006.

_____. "Eph 2:8-10." Available at http://www.ccel.org/ccel/calvin/calcom41.iv.iii.iii.html. Accessed on February 2, 2005.

_____. "James 2:20-26." Available at http://www.ccel.org/c/calvin/comment3/comm_vol45/htm/vi.iii.vii.htm. Accessed on December 3, 2006.

_____. "*John 6:41-45*." Available at http://www.ccel.org/c/calvin/comment3/comm_vol34/htm/xii.vii.htm. Accessed on August 19, 2004

_____. "Luke 17:11-21." Available at http://www.ccel.org/c/calvin/comment3/comm_vol32/htm/xxxix.htm. Accessed on September 1, 2004.

_____. "Matthew 13:18-23; Mark 4:13-20; Luke 8:11-15." Available at http://www.ccel.org/c/calvin /comment3/comm_vol32/htm/xx.htm. Accessed on September 1, 2004.

_____. "Romans 8:5-8," Commentary on Romans. Available at http://www.ccel.org/c/calvin/comment3 /comm_vol38/htm/xii.ii.htm#_fnb5. Accessed on August 8, 2004.

Carson, D. A. *Matthew*. Vol. 8. The Expositor's Bible Commentary, eds. Frank E. Gaebelein and J. D. Douglas. Grand Rapids: Zondervan Publishing House, 1984.

Chitwood, Arlen L. *The Time of the End: A Study About the Book of Revelation*. Norman, Ok: The Lamp Broadcast, Inc., 2011.

Cole, R. Alan. *The Epistle of Paul to the Galatians*. The Tyndale New Testament Commentaries, ed., R. V. G. Tasker. Grand Rapids: Eerdmans Publishing Co., 1965.

Constable, Thomas L. *Dr. Constable's Bible Study Notes*, 2004 ed. Available at http://www.soniclight.com /constable/notes.htm. Accessed on September 14, 2004.

Criswell, W. A. *Expository Sermons on Revelation*. Grand Rapids: Zondervan Publishing House, 1962.

Ellison, H. L. *Matthew: A New Testament Commentary*, ed. G. C. D. Howley. Grand Rapids: Zondervan Publishing House, 1969.

Epp, Theodore H. *Practical Studies in Revelation*. Lincoln, Nebraska: Back to the Bible Broadcast, 1969.

Fee, Gordon D. *The First Epistle to the Corinthians*. The New International Commentary on the New Testament, ed. F. F. Bruce. Grand Rapids: Eerdmans Publishing Co., 1987.

France, R. T. *Matthew*. Vol. 1. The Tyndale New Testament Commentaries, ed., R. V. G. Tasker. Grand Rapids: Eerdmans Publishing Co., 1985.

Gaebelein, Arno C. *Gospel of Matthew*. Neptune: Loizeaux Brothers, 1961.

Gangel, Kenneth O. *2 Peter*. The Bible Knowledge Commentary, eds. John F. Walvoord and Roy B. Zuck. Wheaton: Victor Books, 1984.

Geldenhuys, Norval. *Commentary on the Gospel of Luke*. The New International Commentary on the New Testament, ed. F. F. Bruce. Grand Rapids: Eerdmans Publishing Co., 1983.

Godet, Frederic Louis. *Commentary on First Corinthians*, Grand Rapids: Kregel Publications, 1977.

_____. *Commentary on John's Gospel*. Grand Rapids: Kregel Publications, 1978.

Govett, Robert. *Govett on Revelation*, 2 vols. London: Bemrose and Sons, 1891; reprint, Miami Springs: Conley and Schoettle Publishing Co., 1981.

_____. *Govett on Romans*. Hayesville, NC: Schoettle Publishing Company, 2010.

Grassmick, John D. *Mark*. The Bible Knowledge Commentary, eds. John F. Walvoord and Roy B. Zuck. Wheaton: Victor Books, 1984.

Greene, Oliver B. *The Gospel According to Matthew*. Vol. 1. Chapters 1-5. Greenville; SC: The Gospel Hour, 1971.

Grosheide, F. W. *Commentary on the First Epistle to the Corinthians*, The New International Commentary on the New Testament, ed. F. F. Bruce Grand Rapids: Eerdmans Publishing Co., 1953.

Guthrie, Donald. *Hebrews*. Vol. 15. The Tyndale New Testament Commentaries, ed. R. V. G. Tasker. Grand Rapids: Eerdmans Publishing Co., 1983.

_____. *The Pastoral Epistles*. Vol. 14. The Tyndale New Testament Commentaries, ed. R. V. G. Tasker. Grand Rapids: Eerdmans Publishing Co., 1957.

Harrison, Everett F. *Romans*. Vol. 10. The Expositor's Bible Commentary, eds. Frank E. Gaebelein and J. D. Douglas. Grand Rapids: Zondervan Publishing House, 1976.

Hendriksen, William. *Commentary on 1 Timothy*. New Testament Commentary. Grand Rapids: Baker Book House, 1979.

_____. *Commentary on Titus*. New Testament Commentary. Grand Rapids: Baker Book House, 1979.

_____. *Exposition of Paul's Epistle to the Romans*. New Testament Commentary. Grand Rapids: Baker Book House, 1981.

_____. *Exposition of the Gospel According to Luke.* New Testament Commentary. Grand Rapids: Baker Book House, 1978.

_____. *Exposition of the Gospel According Matthew.* New Testament Commentary. Grand Rapids: Baker Book House, 1973.

_____. *The Gospel of John*, 2 vols. New Testament Commentary. Grand Rapids: Baker Book House, 1985.

Hengstenberg, E. W. *Commentary on the Gospel of St. John.* 2 vols. Minneapolis: Klock and Klock Christian Publishers, 1865.

Henry, Matthew. *Commentary on the Whole Bible* (1706-1721). Via BibleWorks.

Hinckley, Karen, ed. *A NavPress Bible study on the books of: 1, 2 & 3 John.* Life Change Series. Colorado Springs: NavPress, 1988.

Hindson, Edward and James Borland. *Matthew: The King is Coming.* Twenty-First Century Bible Commentary Series, ed. Mal Cough. Chattanooga, TN: AMG Publishers, 2006.

_____. *Revelation: Unlocking the Future.* Twenty-First Century Bible Commentary Series, ed. Mal Cough. Chattanooga, TN: AMG Publishers, 2002.

Hodges, Zane C. *The Epistle of James: Proven Character through Testing*, eds. Arthur L. Farstad and Robert N. Wilkin. Irving: Grace Evangelical Society, 1994.

_____. *The Epistles of John: Walking in the Light of God's Love.* Irving: Grace Evangelical Society, 1999.

_____. *Hebrews.* The Bible Knowledge Commentary, eds. John F. Walvoord and Roy B. Zuck. Wheaton: Victor Books, 1984.

Hughes, Philip E. *The Second Epistle to the Corinthians.* The New International Commentary on the New Testament, ed. F. F. Bruce. Grand Rapids: Eerdmans Publishing Co., 1982.

Johnson, Alan. *Revelation.* Vol. 12. The Expositor's Bible Commentary, eds. Frank E. Gaebelein and J. D. Douglas. Grand Rapids: Zondervan Publishing House, 1976.

Kent, Homer A. Jr. *Philippians.* Vol. 11. The Expositor's Bible Commentary, eds. Frank E. Gaebelein and J. D. Douglas. Grand Rapids: Zondervan Publishing House, 1978.

Keathley III, J. Hampton. *Studies in Revelation: Christ's Victory Over the Forces of Darkness.* Biblical Studies Press, 1997. Available at http://www.bible.org/assets/worddocs/jhk3_rev.zip. Accessed on September 17, 2004.

Kistemaker, Simon J. *Exposition of the Epistle to the Hebrews*, New Testament Commentary. Grand Rapids: Baker Book House, 1996.

Lang, G. H. *The Epistle to the Hebrews*, 2nd ed. Miami Springs: Schoettle Publishing Co., 1985.

_____. *The Revelation of Jesus Christ.* London: Oliphants, 1945; reprint, Miami Springs: Conley and Schoettle Publishing Co., 1985.

Lange, John Peter. *Hebrews.* Commentary on the Holy Scriptures, ed. Philip Schaff. Grand Rapids: Zondervan Publishing House, 1960.

_____. *Revelation.* Commentary on the Holy Scriptures, ed. Philip Schaff. Grand Rapids: Zondervan Publishing House, 1960.

Larkin, Clarence. *The Book of Revelation.* Glenside, Pa.: Rev. Clarence Larkin Estate, 1919.

Lenski, R. C. H. *The Interpretation of St. John's Gospel.* Minneapolis: Augsburg Publishing House, 1961.

_____. *The Interpretation of St. John's Revelation.* Minneapolis: Augsburg Publishing House, 1963.

_____. *The Interpretation of St. Luke's Gospel.* Minneapolis: Augsburg Publishing House, 1961.

_____. *The Interpretation of St. Matthew's Gospel.* Minneapolis: Augsburg Publishing House, 1943.

_____. *The Interpretation of St. Paul's Epistle to the Romans.* Minneapolis: Augsburg Publishing House, 1961.

_____. *The Interpretation of St. Paul's Epistles to the Colossians, Thessalonians, Timothy, Titus, and Philemon.* Minneapolis: Augsburg Publishing House, 1961.

_____. *The Interpretation of St. Paul's Epistles to the Galatians, to the Ephesians, and to the Philippians.* Minneapolis: Augsburg Publishing House, 1961.

_____. *The Interpretation of St. Paul's First and Second Epistles to the Corinthians.* Minneapolis: Augsburg Publishing House, 1963.

_____. *The Interpretation of the Epistle to the Hebrews and the Epistle of James.* Minneapolis: Augsburg Publishing House, 1966.

_____. *The Interpretation of the Epistles of St. Peter, St. John, and St. Jude.* Minneapolis: Augsburg Publishing House, 1961.

Litfin, A. Duane. *2 Timothy.* The Bible Knowledge Commentary, eds. John F. Walvoord and Roy B. Zuck. Wheaton: Victor Books, 1984.

_____. *Titus.* The Bible Knowledge Commentary, eds. John F. Walvoord and Roy B. Zuck. Wheaton: Victor Books, 1984.

Lloyd-Jones, Martin. Romans Chapter 8:17-39: The Final Perseverance of the Saints. Grand Rapids: Zondervan, 1976.

Lopez, René A. *Romans Unlocked: Power to Deliver.* Springfield: 21st Century Press, 2005.

MacArthur John. *Matthew 1-7.* The MacArthur New Testament Commentary. Chicago: Moody Press, 1985.

_____. *Matthew 24-28*. The MacArthur New Testament Commentary Chicago: Moody Press, 1989.

MacLaren, Alexander. *Hebrews*. Vol. 10. Expositions of Holy Scripture. Grand Rapids: Eerdmans Publishing Co., 1952.

Marshall, I. Howard, *The Gospel of Luke*. The New International Greek Testament Commentary, eds. I. Howard Marshall and W. Ward Gasque. Grand Rapids: Eerdmans Publishing Co., 1986.

Martin, Ralph P. *Philippians*. Vol. 11. The Tyndale New Testament Commentaries, ed., R. V. G. Tasker. Grand Rapids: Eerdmans Publishing Co., 1959.

Martin, John A. *Luke*. The Bible Knowledge Commentary, eds. John F. Walvoord and Roy B. Zuck. Wheaton: Victor Books, 1985.

_____. *Isaiah*. The Bible Knowledge Commentary, eds. John F. Walvoord and Roy B. Zuck. Wheaton: Victor Books, 1985.

Morris, Leon. *The First and Second Epistles to the Thessalonians*. The New International Commentary on the New Testament, ed. F. F. Bruce. Grand Rapids: Eerdmans Publishing Co., 1959.

_____. *The Gospel according to Matthew* (Grand Rapids: Eerdmans Publishing Co., 1992

_____. *Hebrews*. Vol. 12. The Expositor's Bible Commentary, eds. Frank E. Gaebelein and J. D. Douglas. Grand Rapids: Zondervan Publishing House, 1976.

_____. *The Gospel According to John*. The New International Commentary on the New Testament, ed. F. F. Bruce. Grand Rapids: Eerdmans Publishing Co., 1983.

Mounce, Robert. *The Book of Revelation*. The New International Commentary on the New Testament, ed. F. F. Bruce. Grand Rapids: Eerdmans Publishing Co., 1977.

_____. *Matthew*. New International Commentary, ed. W. Ward Gasque. Peabody: Hendrickson Publishers, 1991.

Moyer, Larry R. *Free and Clear: Understanding and Communicating God's Offer of Eternal Life*. Grand Rapids: Kregel, 1997.

Muller, Jac. J. *The Epistles of Paul to the Philippians and to Philemon*. The New International Commentary on the New Testament, ed. F. F. Bruce. Grand Rapids: Eerdmans Publishing Co., 1955.

Murray, John. *The Epistle to the Romans*. The New International Commentary on the New Testament, ed. F. F. Bruce. Grand Rapids: Eerdmans Publishing Co., 1965.

Neighbour, R. E. *If They Shall Fall Away: The Epistle to the Hebrews Unveiled.* Miami Springs: Conley and Schoettle Publishing Co., 1984.

Newell, William R. *Romans: Verse by Verse*. Chicago: Moody Press, 1948.

Nolland, John. *The Gospel of Matthew*. The New International Greek Testament Commentary, eds. I. Howard Marshall and Donald A. Hagner. Grand Rapids: Eerdmans Publishing Co., 2005.

Nygren, Anders. *Commentary on Romans*. Philadelphia: Fortress Press, 1949.

Odeberg, Hugo. The Fourth Gospel Interpreted in Its Relation to Contemporaneous Religious Currents in Palestine and the Hellenistic -Oriental World. Uppsala: n.p., 1929; reprint ed., Chicago: Argonaut Publishers, 1968.

Olshausen, Herman. *Biblical Commentary on the New Testament*, American ed. New York: Sheldon, Blakeman & Co., 1857.

Phillips, John. *Exploring the Gospel of Matthew: An Expository Commentary*. Grand Rapids: Kregel Publications, 1999.

_____. *Exploring Revelation: An Expository Commentary* (Grand Rapids: Kregel Publications, 1987).

Pink, A. W. *Eternal Security*. Available at http://www.jaynesgarden.com/Spirit/A-W-Pink/eternal-security.pdf. Accessed on June 9, 2005.

_____. *The Holy Spirit*. Available at http://www.pbministries.org/books/pink/Holy_Spirit/holy_spirit.htm. Accessed on June 6, 2005.

Quarles, Charles L. "The Ἀπὸ of 2 Thessalonians 1:9 and the Nature of Eternal Punishment," *WTJ* 59:2 (Fall 1997): 201-211.

Pickering, Ernest. Lordship Salvation: An Examination of John MacArthur's Book, "The Gospel According to Jesus." Minneapolis: Central Baptist Seminary, n.d.

Radmacher, Earl D., gen. ed. *Nelson's New Illustrated Bible Commentary*. Nashville: T. Nelson Publishers, 1999.

Roadhouse, William F. *Seeing the Revelation*. Toronto: Overcomer Publishers, 1932.

Ross, Allen P. *Genesis*. The Bible Knowledge Commentary, eds. John F. Walvoord and Roy B. Zuck. Wheaton: Victor Books, 1978.

Ryrie. Charles C. *Revelation: New Edition*. Everyman's Bible Commentary. Chicago: Moody Press, 1996.

Scott, Walter. *Exposition of the Revelation of Jesus Christ*. Grand Rapids: Kregel Publications, 1982.

Seiss, J. A. *The Apocalypse: Lectures on the Book of Revelation*. Grand Rapids: Zondervan Publishing House, n.d.

Smith, R. Payne. *1 Samuel*, Pulpit Commentary, eds. H. D. M. Spence and Joseph S. Exell. McLean, Virginia: MacDonald Publishing Company, n.d.

Stallard, Mike. *First & Second Thessalonians: Looking for Christ's Return*. Twenty-First Century Bible Commentary Series, eds. Mal Cough and Ed Hindson. Chattanooga, TN: AMG Publishers, 2009.

Stott, John R. W. *The Epistles of John* The Tyndale New Testament Commentaries, ed., R. V. G. Tasker. Grand Rapids: Eerdmans Publishing Co., 1960.

Tatford, Frederick A. *The Revelation*. Minneapolis: Klock and Klock Christian Publishers, 1983.

Tasker, R. V. G. *The Second Epistle of Paul to the Corinthians*. Vol. 8. The Tyndale New Testament Commentaries, ed. R. V. G Tasker. Grand Rapids: Eerdmans Publishing Co., 1963.

Tenney, Merrill C. *The Gospel of John*. Vol. 9. The Expositor's Bible Commentary, eds. Frank E. Gaebelein and J. D. Douglas. Grand Rapids: Zondervan Publishing House, 1981.

Thomas, Robert L. *1 Thessalonians.* Vol. 11. The Expositor's Bible Commentary, eds. Frank E. Gaebelein and J. D. Douglas. Grand Rapids: Zondervan Publishing House, 1978.

_____. *2 Thessalonians.* Vol. 11. The Expositor's Bible Commentary, eds. Frank E. Gaebelein and J. D. Douglas. Grand Rapids: Zondervan Publishing House, 1978.

Trueblood, Elton. *The Humor of Christ*. San Francisco: Harper & Row, 1964.

Turner, David L. *Matthew*. Baker Exegetical Commentary on the New Testament, eds. Robert W. Yarbrough and Robert H. Stein. Grand Rapids: Baker Academic, 2008.

Walvoord, John F. *Matthew: Thy Kingdom Come*. Grand Rapids: Kregel Publications, 1974.

_____. *The **Revelation** of Jesus Christ: A Commentary*. Chicago: Moody Press, 1966.

_____. *Revelation*. The Bible Knowledge Commentary, eds. John F. Walvoord and Roy B. Zuck. Wheaton: Victor Books, 1984.

Wessel, Walter W. *Mark*. Vol. 8. The Expositor's Bible Commentary, eds. Frank E. Gaebelein and J. D. Douglas. Grand Rapids: Zondervan Publishing House, 1984.

Wiersbe, Warren. *The Bible Exposition Commentary*, 2 vols. Wheaton: Victor Books, 1989.

_____. *Wiersbe's Expository Outlines on the New Testament*. Wheaton: Victor Books, 1992.

Wilkin, Robert N. The Gospel According to John: Special Prepublication Edition. Grace Evangelical Society, 1993.

Wilkins, Michael J. *Matthew*. The NIV Application Commentary: From biblical text . . . to contemporary life, gen. ed. Terry Muck. Grand Rapids: Zondervan, 2004.

Witmer, John A. *Romans*. The Bible Knowledge Commentary, eds. John F. Walvoord and Roy B. Zuck. Wheaton: Victor Books, 1984.

Articles

The URL for the following articles will be cited here rather than for each potential (published versus online) entry: *CTSJ* (http://chafer.edu/CTSjournal), *GIF* (http://faithalone.org/news), *JOTGES* (http://www.faithalone.org/journal), and the author's articles (www.misthology.org).

Aldrich, Roy L. "The **Gift** of God." *Bibliotheca Sacra* 122:487 (July 1965): 248-253.

Aldrich, Willard Maxwell. "Is Salvation Probationary?" *Bibliotheca Sacra* 91:361 (January 1934): 87-100.

Anderson, David R. "Another *Tale* of Two Cities," *Journal of the Grace Evangelical Society* 18:35 (Autumn 2005): 51-75.

_____. "The Nature of Faith." *Chafer Theological Seminary Journal* 5:4 (September-December 1999): 1-26.

_____. "Regeneration: A Crux Interpretum." *Journal of the Grace Evangelical Society* 13:2 (Autumn 2000): 43-65.

_____. "The **National** Repentance of Israel." *Journal of the Grace Evangelical Society* 11:21 (Autumn 1998): 13-37.

_____. "The Soteriological **Impact** of Augustine's Change from Premillennialism to Amillennialism: Part 1." *Journal of the Grace Evangelical Society* 15:28 (Spring 2002): 25-36.

_____. "The Soteriological Impact of Augustine's **Change** From Premillennialism to Amillennialism: Part 2." *Journal of the Grace Evangelical Society* 15:29 (Autumn 2002): 23-39.

Arp, William. "Authorial Intent," *The Journal of Ministry & Theology* (Spring 2000): 36-50.

Badger, Anthony B. "Tulip: A Free Grace Perspective, Part 3: Limited Atonement," *Journal of the Grace Evangelical Society* 17:32 (Spring 2004): 33-59.

Basinger, David. "Divine Control and Human Freedom: Is Middle Knowledge the Answer?" *Journal of the Evangelical Theological Society* 36:1 (March 1993): 55-64.

Baxter, Wayne. "The Narrative Setting Of The Sermon On The Mount" Trinity Journal 25:1 (Spring 04), 27-37.

Berkhof, Louis. "Chapter XVIII: Calling and Regeneration." *Summary of Christian Doctrine.* Available at http://www.mbrem.com/shorttakes/berk19.htm. Accessed on May 7, 2005.

Blomberg, Craig L. "**Degrees** of Reward in the Kingdom of Heaven?" *Journal of the Evangelical Theological Society* 35:2 (June 1992): 159-172.

Bigalke, Ron J., Jr. "The Olivet Discourse: A Resolution of **Time**." *Chafer Theological Seminary Journal* 9 (Spring 2003): 106-140.

Bing, Charles C. "Coming to Terms with **Discipleship**." *Journal of the Grace Evangelical Society* 5:1 (Spring 1992): 35-49.

_____. "Does Philippians 1:6 Teach Perseverance?" *Grace in Focus* (February 1991).

_____. "The Condition for Salvation in John's Gospel." *Journal of the Grace Evangelical Society* 9:16 (Spring 1996): 25-36.

_____. "Why Lordship Faith **Misses** the Mark for Salvation." *Journal of the Grace Evangelical Society* 12:22 (Spring 1999): 21-35.

Boettner, Loraine. "The Reformed Doctrine of Predestination. Chapter XIV. The Perseverance of the Saints," in Reformed Doctrine of Predestination. Available at http://www.ccel.org/b/boettner/predest /14.htm. Accessed on September 1, 2004.

Boyd, Jeffrey H. "One's Self-Concept and Biblical Theology." *Journal of the Evangelical Society* 40:2 (June 1997): 207-227.

Boyer, James L. "The Classification of Subjunctives: A Statistical Study." *Grace Theological Journal* 7:1 (Spring 1986): 3-19.

Buckley, Jorunn Jacobsen. "A Cult-Mystery in The Gospel of Philip." *Journal of Biblical Literature* 99 (1980): 569-581.

Campbell, John. "Forgiveness in the Age to Come (1)." Available at http://www.affcrit.com/pdfs/2004 /01/04_01_wr.pdf. Accessed on August 8, 2005.

Carmical, Frank D. "The Coronation of the King: An Annotated Work of Fiction: **Part 1**." *Journal of the Grace Evangelical Society* 2:2 (Autumn 1989): 53-68.

_____. "The Coronation of the King: An Annotated Work of Fiction: **Part 2**." *Journal of the Grace Evangelical Society* 3:1 (Spring 1990): 55-70.

Cauley, Marty. "Anaphoric Faith." Revised (July 2007).

_____. "Southeastern & Termination." Baptist Banner, 6:6 (1993).

_____. "Work of God. Revised (June 2007).

Chafer, Lewis Sperry. "Anthropology: Part 4." *Bibliotheca Sacra* 101:401 (January 1944): 8-29.

_____. "The Eternal Security of the Believer: Part 1" *Bibliotheca Sacra* 106:423 (July 1949): 260-290.

_____. "The Saving Work of the Triune God." *Bibliotheca Sacra* 105:419 (July 48): 261-286.

Chang, Andrew D. "Second Peter 2:1 and the Extent of the Atonement," *Bibliotheca Sacra* 142:565 (January 1985): 52-61.

Cloud, David W. "Calvinism's Proof Texts Examined." Available at http://www.wayoflife.org/database /calvinismprooftext.html. Accessed on July 26, 2009.

Cocoris, G. Michael. "The Error of John MacArthur's 'Lordship Salvation.'" *The Bible for Today* (1989).

Coile, Freddie. "What about James 2?" Available at http://bestnews.gracenet.org/WhatAboutJames2.htm. Accessed 27 July, 2004.

Combs, William W. "The Disjunction Between Justification And Sanctification in Contemporary Evangelical Theology." *Detroit Baptist Seminary Journal* 6 (Fall 2001): 17-44.

Congdon, Philip F. "Evangelical/Roman Catholic Agreement on the Doctrine of Justification and its Ramifications for Grace Theologians." *Journal of the Grace Evangelical Society* 13:1 (Spring 2000): 11-23.

_____. "Soteriological Implications of Five-Point **Calvinism**." *Journal of the Grace Evangelical Society* 8:15 (Autumn 1995): 55-68.

Cook, W. Robert. "Chapter 21. The Constitution of Man." *The Christian Faith: A Systematic Theology*. Available at http://www.moulton.to/theology /html/c21.html. Accessed on July 29, 2004.

_____. "Chapter 54. The Eternal State." *The Christian Faith: A Systematic Theology*. Available at http://www.moulton.to/theology/html/c54.html. Accessed on August 14, 2004.

Cox, Leo G. "**Prevenient** Grace - A Wesleyan View." *Journal of the Evangelical Theological Society* 12:3 (Summer 1969): 143-149.

Crawford, Scott. "Chapter 2. The Earned Prize from God." Available at http://www.wordoftruthclass.org/articles /The%20earned%20prize%20from%20God.pdf. Accessed on August 17, 2006.

_____. "Hebrews: Five Warnings For Believers." Available at http://www.wordoftruthclass.org/articles /fivewarnings.pdf. Accessed on July 7, 2007.

Curtis, David B. "Smyrna, The Suffering Church." Available at www.bereanbiblechurch.org/transcripts /eschatology/2_8-11.htm. Accessed on July 29, 2004.

_____. "The Church at Sardis." Available at www.bereanbiblechurch.org/transcripts/eschatology/3_1-6.htm. Accessed on July 29, 2004.

Davis, John Jefferson. "The Perseverance Of The Saints: A History Of The Doctrine." *Journal of the Evangelical Theological Society* 34:2 (June 1991): 213-228.

Dean, Robert, Jr. "Abiding in Christ: A Dispensational Theology of the Spiritual Life (Part 3 of 3)." *Chafer Theological Seminary* 8:1 (January - March 2002): 43-61.

De Catanzaro, Carmino Joseph. "The Gospel According to **Philip**." *Journal of Theological Studies* 13 (1962): 35-71.

Deffinbaugh, Robert L. "Lesson 9: Authentic Apostleship (2 Cor. 5:20–6:10)." Available at http://www.berean biblechurch.org/transcripts/eschatologee/3_1-6.htm. Accessed on July 29, 2004.

_____. "Lesson 21: Paul's Closing Argument, Appeal, and Blessing (2 Cor. 12:11-13:14)." Available at http://www.bible.org/docs/nt/books/2co/deffin/2cor-17.htm. Accessed on July 29, 2004.

DeSilva, David A. "No Confidence In The Flesh: The Meaning and Function of Philippians 3:2–21," *Trinity Journal* 15:1 (Spring 1994): 27–54.

Da Rosa, Antonio. "Definition of Eternal Life." Available at http://free-race.blogspot.com/2006/11/definition-of-eternal-life.html. Accessed on November 24, 2006.

_____. "It is a fearful thing to fall into the hands of the living God." Available at http://free-grace.blogspot.com/2006/02/it-is-fearful-thing-to-fall-into-hands.html. Accessed on November 24, 2006.

_____. "Response to Dr. Wallace's Objections: Apostolic Fathers Analyzed." Available at http://free-grace.blogspot.com/2007/01/response-to-dr-wallaces-objections.html. Accessed on February 2, 2007.

Dyer, Sidney D. "The Salvation of Believing Israelites Prior to the Incarnation of Christ." *Journal of the Grace Evangelical Society* 14:26 (Spring 2001): 43-55.

Eby, J. Preston. "The Saviour of the World Series: The Lake of Fire." Available at http://www.kingdomlife.com/eby/s7.htm. Accessed on August 4, 2004.

Engwer, Jason. "Catholic, But Not Roman Catholic—Archive 05." Available at http://www.ntrmin.org/catholic_but_not_roman_catholic_05.htm. Accessed on 8 August, 2005

_____. "If you believe that salvation can be lost." Available at http://members.aol.com/jasonte2/law.htm. Accessed on June 6, 2005.

Escobedo III, Simon. "2 Peter 2:1 and Universal Redemption." Available at http://www.aomin.org/2PE21.html#_ednref20. Accessed on June 20, 2005.

Edgar, Thomas R. "**Lethargic** or Dead in 1 Thessalonians 5:10?" *Chafer Theological Seminary Journal* 6:4 (October 2000): 36-51.

_____. "The Meaning of ΠΡΟΓΊΝΩΣΚΩ ("**Foreknowledge**")." *Chafer Theological Seminary Journal* 44 (Spring 2003): 43-80.

Erickson, Millard J. "Is **Hell** Forever?" *Bibliotheca Sacra* 152:607 (July 1995): 259-272.

Farstad, Arthur L. "We Believe In: Good **Works**," *Journal of the Grace Evangelical Society* 2:2 (Autumn, 1989): 3-12.

_____. "We Believe: Jesus is **Lord**." *Journal of the Grace Evangelical Society* 2:1 (Spring 1989): 3-11.

Faust, J.D. "Answers to George Zeller (#1)." Available at http://www.kingdombaptist.org/zeller1.cfm. Accessed on August 4, 2004.

_____. "A Response to Robert L. Sumner's Review of [The Rod]." Available at http://www.kingdombaptist.org/article836.cfm. Available on 4 August, 2004

Filson, Floyd V. "New Greek and Coptic Gospel **Manuscripts**." *Biblical Archaeologist* 24 (1961): 2-18.

Fuller, J. William. "I Will Not Erase His Name From The Book of Life (Revelation 3:5)." *Journal of the Evangelical Society* 26:3 (September 1983): 297-306.

Grant, Robert M. "Two Gnostic **Gospels**." *Journal of Biblical Literature* 79 (1960): 1-11.

Gregg, Lon "Model Faith for Christian Service: Matthew 19:28-20:14." *Journal of the Grace Evangelical Theological Society* 19:36 (Spring 2006): 23-34.

Glasson, T. Francis. "The Last Judgment—In Rev. 20 and Related Writings." *New Testament Studies* 28 (1982): 530.

Gleason, Randall C. "The Old Testament Background of Rest in Hebrews 3:7-8," *Bibliotheca Sacra* 157:627 (July, 2000): 281-303.

Hart, John F. "Does Philippians 1:6 Guarantee Progressive **Sanctification**? Part 2" *Journal of the Grace Evangelical Theological Society* 9:17 (Autumn 1996): 33-60.

_____. "How to Energize Your Faith: Reconsidering the Meaning of James 2:14-26," *Journal of the Grace Evangelical Society* 12:22 (Spring 1999): 37-66.

_____. "Should Pretribulationalists Reconsider the Rapture in Matthew 24:36-44? Part 1 of 3" *Journal of the Grace Evangelical Society* 20:39 (Autumn 2007): 47-70.

_____. "Should Pretribulationalists Reconsider the Rapture in Matthew 24:36-44? Part 2 of 3" *Journal of the Grace Evangelical Society* 21:40 (Spring 2008): 45-63.

_____. "Should Pretribulationalists Reconsider the Rapture in Matthew 24:36-44? Part 3 of 3" *Journal of the Grace Evangelical Society* 21:41 (Autumn 2008): 43-64.

_____. "The Faith of Demons: James 2:19." *Journal of the Evangelical Society* 8:15 (Autumn 1995): 39-54.

_____. "Why **Confess** Christ? The Use and Abuse of Romans 10:9-10." *Journal of the Grace Evangelical Society* 12:23 (Autumn 1999): 3-35.

Hays, Daniel. "Applying the Old Testament Law Today," *Bibliotheca Sacra* 158 (January-March, 2001): 21-35.

Hiebert, D. Edmond. "An Exposition of **Jude** 12-16." *Bibliotheca Sacra* 142 (1985): 244-245.

Hodges, Zane C. "Calvinism Ex Cathedra: A Review of John H. Gerstner's Wrongly Dividing the Word of Truth: A Critique of Dispensationalism." *Journal of the Grace Evangelical Society* 4:2 (Autumn 1991): 59-70.

_____. "Eternal Salvation in the Old Testament: The Salvation of Samuel." *Grace in Focus* (May-June 1994).

_____. "Eternal Salvation in the Old Testament: The Salvation of Saul." *Grace in Focus* (July-August 1994).

_____. "Justification: A New Covenant Blessing." *Journal of the Grace Evangelical Society* 19:37 (Autumn 2006): 79-85.

_____. "God's Role in Conversion." *Grace in Focus* (July-August 1993).

_____. "How to Lead People to Christ: Part 1 The Content of Our Message." *Journal of the Grace Evangelical Society* 13:25 (Autumn 2000): 3-12.

_____. "How to Lead People to Christ, Part 2: Our Invitation to Respond." *Journal of the Grace Evangelical Society* 14:26 (Spring 2001): 9-18.

_____. "**Law** and Grace in the Millennial Kingdom." *Journal of the Grace Evangelical Society* 20:38 (Spring, 2008): 31-38.

_____. "Legalism: The Real Thing." *Journal of the Grace Evangelical Society* 9:17 (Autumn 1996)): 21-32.

_____. "Man's Role in Conversion." *Grace in Focus* (September-October 1993).

_____. "Problem Passages in the Gospel of John—Part 2: Untrustworthy Believers—John 2:23-25." *Bibliotheca Sacra* 135:538 (April 1978): 139-153.

_____. "Problem Passages in the Gospel of John—Part 3: **Water** and Spirit—John 3:5." *Bibliotheca Sacra* 135:539 (July 1978): 206-220.

_____. "Problem Passages In The Gospel Of John—Part 6: Those Who Have Done Good—John 5:28-29." *Bibliotheca Sacra* 136:542 (April 1979): 158-166.

_____. "Regeneration: A New Covenant Blessing," *Journal of the Grace Evangelical Society* 18:35 (Autumn 2005): 43-49.

_____. "The New Puritanism Part 1: Carson on Christian Assurance." *Journal of the Grace Evangelical Theological Society* 6:10 (Spring 1993): 19-31.

_____. "The New Puritanism, Part 2: Michael S. Horton: Holy War With Unholy Weapons." *Journal of the Grace Evangelical Theological Society* 6:11 (Autumn 1993): 25-38.

_____. "We Believe In: Assurance of Salvation." *Journal of the Grace Evangelical Society* 3:2 (Autumn 1990): 3-17.

_____. "We Believe In: Rewards." *Journal of the Grace Evangelical Society* 4:2 (Autumn 1991): 3-11.

_____. "What Do We Mean By *Propitiation*? Does It Only Count If We Accept It?" *Journal of the Grace Evangelical Society* 19:36 (Spring 2006): 35-42.

_____. And Robert Wilkin. "Matthew 22:1-14 (The Parable of the Wedding Feast." Available at http://www.faithalone.org/Audio/mp3/Matt_22_1-14.m3u. Accessed on May 26, 2006.

Hoeksema, Herman "Regeneration." Available at http://www.prca.org/articles/regeneration.html. Accessed on May 7, 2005.

Holding, James Patrick. "Fallacious Faith: Correcting an All-too-Common Misconception." Available at http://www.tektonics.org/whatis/whatfaith.html. Accessed on March 21, 2009.

Holloman, Henry W. "The Relation Of Christlikeness To Spiritual Growth," *Michigan Theological Journal* 5 (Spring/Fall 1994): 57-85.

Howley, Grant. "Dispensationalism and Free Grace: Intimately Linked—Part 1." *Journal of the Grace Evangelical Society* 24:46 (Spring 2011): 63-81.

_____. "Dispensationalism and Free Grace: Intimately Linked—Part 2." *Journal of the Grace Evangelical Society* 24:47 (Autumn 2011): 89-106.

_____. "Dispensationalism and Free Grace: Intimately Linked—Part 3." *Journal of the Grace Evangelical Society* 25:48 (Spring 2012): 21-36.

Hoyt, Samuel L. "The Judgment Seat of Christ in Theological **Perspective**—Part 1: The Judgment Seat of Christ and Unconfessed Sins" *Bibliotheca Sacra* 137:545 (January 1980): 32-39.

Huber, Michael G. "The 'Outer Darkness' in Matthew and Its **Relationship** to Grace." *Journal of the Grace Evangelical Society* 5:2 (1992): 11-25.

Hughes, Philip E., "Book Reviews—Fall 1976." *Westminster Theological Journal* 39:1 (Fall 1976): 149-151. Citing Robert H. Gundry: *SOMA in Biblical Theology, with emphasis on Pauline Theology*. Cambridge, London, New York, Melbourne: Cambridge University Press, 1976.

Ice, Tommy. "The Destructive View of **Preterism**." *Conservative Theological Journal* 3:10 (December 1999): 386-400.

_____. "The **Filling** of the Holy Spirit: A Quality of Life." *Chafer Theological Seminary Journal* 2:1 (Spring/Summer 1996).

_____. "Salvation in the Tribulation: Revisited." Available at http://www.raptureready.com/featured /Salvation.html. Accessed on April 25, 2006.

Irenaeus. "Against Heresies," 4:36:6. Available at http://ccel.org/fathers2/ANF-01/anf01-62.htm#P7979_2198226. Accessed on September 9, 2004.

Inglis, James. "A Voice from the Past: Simon Magus," *Journal of the Grace Evangelical Society* 2:1 (Spring 1989): 45-54.

Johnson, Elliot E. "Author's Intention." Earl D. Radmacher and Robert D. Preus, eds. *Hermeneutics, Inerrancy, and the Bible*. Grand Rapids: Zondervan Publishing House, 1984.

Johnson, S. Lewis. "Jesus Praying for Himself: An Exposition of John 17:1-5." *Emmaus Journal* 7:2 (Winter 1998): 211.

Kaiser, Walter C., Jr. "A Neglected **Text** in Bibliography Discussions: I Corinthians 2:6-16." *Westminster Theological Journal* 43 (Spring 1981): 301-319.

Keathley, Ken. "Does Anyone Really Know If They Are Saved? A Survey of the Current Views on Assurance with a Modest Proposal." *Journal of the Grace Evangelical Society* 15:28 (Spring 2002): 37-59.

_____. "Salvation and the Sovereignty of God: The Great Commission as the Expression of Divine Will." *Journal of the Grace Evangelical Society* 19:39 (Spring, 2006): 3-22.

Keathley IV, Hampton. "The 'Outer **Darkness**': Heaven's Suburb or Hell?" Available at http://bible.org /page.asp?page_id=1044. Accessed on September 17, 2004.

_____. "The Parables in the **Olivet** Discourse (Matthew 25)." Available at http://bible.org /page.asp?page_id=1045. Accessed on September 17, 2004.

Knapp, Henry. "Augustine and Owen on Perseverance." *Westminster Theological Journal* 62:1 (Spring 2000): 65-87.

Krell, Keith R. "Will You Be Approved On That Day? 1 Corinthians 9:24-27." Available at http://www.faith alone.org/sermons/approved.htm. Accessed on 10 August, 2004.

Kubo, Sakae. "1 John 3:9: Absolute or Habitual?" *Andrews University Seminary Studies* 7 (1969): 47-56.

Kuyper, Abraham. "Testimonies." Available at http://www.ccel.org/k/kuyper/holy_spirit/htm/vi.viii.viii.htm. Accessed on September 1, 2004.

Lanham, John S. "Who Is the Bride of Christ?" Available at http://www.inthebeginning.org/kingdom/lanham /bride.pdf. Accessed on August 10, 2004.

Lisle, Jason. "Distant Starlight: Anisotropic Synchrony Convention." Available at http://www.answersin genesis.org/articles/am/v6/n1/distant-starlight. Accessed on August 13, 2012.

Lewellen, Thomas G. "Has Lordship Salvation Been Taught throughout Church History?" *Bibliotheca Sacra* 147:585 (January 1990): 54-68.

Lindstrom, Hank. "Faith Without Works." Available at http://hank.dkat.com/basearch.php3?action=full&mainkey= FAITH+WITHOUT+WORKS. Accessed on August 10, 2004.

Logan, Samuel T. Jr. "The Doctrine of Justification in the Theology of Jonathan Edwards," *Westminster Theological Journal* 46 (1984): 26-52

Logan, Tom. "'Aionios'—A Lexical Survey." Available at http://www.1john57.com/aionios.htm. Accessed on July 5, 2005.

Lopez, René A. "Do Believers Experience the Wrath of God?" *Journal of the Grace Evangelical Society* 15:29 (Autumn 2002): 45-66.

_____. "Do [Sic] The Vice List In 1 Corinthians 6:9-10 Describe Believers or Unbelievers?" *Grace Evangelical Society Conference CD*, 2005.

_____. "Is Faith a Necessary Gift to Receive Salvation?" Available at http://www.scriptureunlocked.com /pdfs/IsFaithaGift.pdf. Accessed on September 9, 2006.

Lyons, Eric and Kyle Butt. "Taking Possession of What God Gives: A Case Study in Salvation." Available at http://www.apologeticspress.org/rr/rr2004/r&r0407a.htm. Accessed on August 13, 2004

Makidon, Michael D. "From Perth To Pennsylvania: The Legacy Of Robert Sandeman." Journal of the Grace Evangelical Society 15:28 (Spring 2002): 75-92.

_____. "The **Marrow** Controversy." *Journal of the Grace Evangelical Society* 16:31 (Autumn 2003): 65-77.

_____. "Soteriological Concerns with Bauer's Greek Lexicon." *Journal of the Grace Evangelical Society* 17:23 (Autumn 2004): 11-18.

MacArthur, John F., Jr. "Perseverance of the Saints" *Master's Seminary Journal* 4:1 (Spring 1993): 5-24.

Malick, David. "An Argument Of First Corinthians." Available at http://www.bible.org/page.php?page_id=1829. Accessed on June 24, 2007.

Mason, Clarence E. Jr. "A Study of Pauline Motives: As Revealed in 2 Corinthians 4:16-6:4a," *Bibliotheca Sacra* 111:443 (July 1954): 213-228.

McCoy, Brad. "Chiasmus: An Important Structural Device Commonly Found in Biblical Literature." *Chafer Theological Seminary Journal* 9:2 (Fall 2003): 18-34.

_____. "Obedience Is Necessary To Receive Eternal Life." *Grace In Focus* (September 1994).

_____. "Secure Yet Scrutinized: 2 Timothy 2:11-13." *Journal of the Grace Evangelical Society* 1:1 (Autumn 1988): 21-33.

_____. "The Parable of The Sower." *Chafer Theological Seminary Journal* 5:3 (July–September 1999): 2-11.

McNeil, Brian. "New Light on Gospel of Philip 17." *Journal of Theological Studies* 29 (1978): 143-146.

Meisinger, George E. "Divine Emotion." *Chafer Theological Seminary Journal* 4:2 (April 1998): 11-20.

_____. "The Parable of the Fig Tree: Matthew 24:32-36." *Chafer Theological Seminary Journal* 2:2 (Fall 1996).

_____. "The **Sufficiency** of Scripture for Life and Godliness: 2 Peter 1:1-4." *Chafer Theological Seminary Journal* 1:2 (Summer 1995): 5-10.

Merryman, Ron. "Election & Acts 13:48." Available at http://www.duluthbible.org/g_f_j/Election.htm. Accessed on August 8, 2004.

Miller, Keith J. *What Does Abiding Have to Do with Being a Christian? The Theological Significance of John 15.* Available at http://gesot1.compsupport.net:8080/upload/Paper%20on%20John%2015.pdf. Accessed on March 21, 2005.

Miller, Stephen G. "The Ancient Basis for the Modern Nemean Games." Available at http://ist-ocrates.berkeley.edu/~clscs275/Games%20folder/basis.htm. Accessed on December 31, 2004.

Moo, Douglas J. "'Law,' 'Works of the Law,' and Legalism in Paul." *Westminster Theological Journal* 45:1 (Spring 1983): 73-100.

Morris, Henry M. "Biblical Eschatology and Modern Science: Part IV." *BibSac* 125:500 (October 1968): 291-299.

Myers, Jeremy D. "The Gospel Under Siege." *Journal of the Grace Evangelical Society* 16:31 (Autumn 2003): 43-48.

Nebeker, Gary L. "Is Faith a Gift of God? Ephesians 2:8 Reconsidered." *Grace in Focus* (July 1989).

Niemelä, John. "For You have Kept My Word: The Grammar of Revelation 3:10." *Chafer Theological Seminary Journal* 6:1 (January - March 2000): 1-25.

_____. "For You have Kept My Word: The **Theology** of Revelation 3:10 (Part 2 of 2)" *Chafer Theological Seminary Journal* 6:4 (December 2000): 52-68.

_____. "James 2:24: Retranslation Required (Part 1 of 3)." *Chafer Theological Seminary Journal* 7:1 (January - March 2001): 1-24.

_____. "If Anyone's Work Is **Burned**: Scrutinizing Proof-Texts." *Chafer Theological Seminary* Journal 8:1 (January - March 2002): 22-42.

Ninan, M. M., "**Soteriology:** Man, Sin, Salvation and God: Armanianism [sic]: The Five Points of Arminianism can be remembered by the acronym: PEARS." Available at "http://www.acns.com/~mm9n/sot/Introduction/main.html. Accessed on September 24, 2004.

ODonnell, Wayne. "Matthew / Romans: Expository Bible Surveys with 1 John, 1 Cor 11, Ezek 40-48 on Justification, Sanctification, Glorification, the Messianic Kingdom, Headcovering, Role of Women, and Ezekiel's Temple." Available at http://bible.ag/en/mr4web.html#EZanchor-anchor. Accessed on December 26, 2011.

O'Rourke, John. "Asides in the Gospel of John." *Novum Testamentum* 21 (July, 1979): 210-219.

Osburn, Carroll D. "1 Enoch 80:2-8 (67:5-7) and Jude 12-13." *The Catholic Biblical Quarterly* 47 (1985): 296-303.

Owen, John. "The Doctrine Of Justification By Faith." Available at http://www.ondoctrine.com/2owe0109.htm. Accessed on June 14, 2005

Pagenkemper, Karl E. "Rejection Imagery in the Synoptic Parables [**Part 1**]." *Bibliotheca Sacra* 153:610 (April 1996): 179-198.

_____. "Rejection Imagery in the Synoptic Parables [**Part 2**]." *Bibliotheca Sacra* 153:611 (July 1996): 308-331.

Perkins, Pheme, "Ireneus [sic] and the Gnostics: Rhetoric and Composition in Adversus Haereses Book One." *Vigiliae Christianae* 30 (1976): 193-200.

Perman, Matt. "The Joy of Heavenly Rewards." Available at http://www.geocities.com/Athens/Delphi/8449/reward.html. Accessed on April 27, 2005.

Peterson, Robert A. "Does the Bible Teach **Annihilationism**?" *Bibliotheca Sacra* 156:621 (January, 1999): 13-27.

_____. "The **Perseverance** of the Saints: A Theological Exegesis of Four Key New Testament Passages." Presbyterion 17/2 (1991): 95-112.

Picirilli, Robert E. "Foreknowledge, Freedom, and the Future." *Journal of the Evangelical Theological Society* 43:2 (June 2000): 259-271.

_____. "The Meaning Of The Tenses In New Testament Greek: Where Are We?" *Journal of the Evangelical Theological Society* 48:3 (September 2005): 533-555.

Porter Jr., Virgil V. "The Sermon on the Mount in the Book of James, Part 1." *Bibliotheca Sacra* 162:647 (July 2005): 344-360.

_____. "The Sermon on the Mount in the Book of James, Part 2." *Bibliotheca Sacra* 162:648 (October 2005): 470-482.

Pyne, Robert A. "The Role of the Holy Spirit in Conversion." *Bibliotheca Sacra* 150:598 (April 1993): 203-218.

Radmacher, Earl D. "Believers and the **Bema**," *Journal of the Grace Evangelical Society* 8:14 (Spring 1995): 31-43.

_____. "Saved Yesterday, Today, **Forever**." *Decision* (April, 1992): 31-35.

Ramey, William D. "The Literary Structure of 1 John 1:1-5:21." Available at http://www.inthebeginning.org/chiasmus/xfiles/x1jn.pdf. Accessed on August 28, 2004

_____. "The Parable Of The Marriage **Feast**: Matthew 22:1-14." Available at http://www.inthebeginning.org/newtestament/matthew/feast.pdf. Accessed on September 6, 2004.

Reagan, David R. "Eternal Security: Do Believer's Have It? How Does It Relate To Prophecy? A Review of the book, The Reign of the Servant Kings." Available at http://www.lamblion.com/other/religious/RI-18.php. Accessed on August 11, 2004.

Reasoner, Vic. "Golden Chain or Iron Padlock?" Available at http://www.fwponline.cc/v20n1reasoner.html. Accessed on December 21, 2005.

_____. "Review of "The Believer's Conditional Security.'" Available at http://www.fwponline.cc /v16n1reasonerb.html. Accessed on August 25, 2007.

Reisinger, Ernest C. "The **Carnal** Christian." Available at http://www.peacemakers.net/unity/carnal.htm. Accessed on August 11, 2004.

Robbins, John W. "The Biblical View of Truth," *Journal of the Grace Evangelical Society* 18:34 (Spring 2005): 49-69.

Roberts, Don. "James White on John 3:14-18: An Examination by Don Roberts, B.A., M.Div." Available at http://www.twincentral.com/site/pages/articles/doctrines/beliefs/calvinism/jw_john3.shtml#21. Accessed on February 21, 2005.

Rhodes, Ron. "How did Lucifer fall and become Satan?" Available at http://www.christianity.com /Christian%20Foundations/Theological%20FAQ/11557519. Accessed January 17, 2012.

Rokser, Dennis. "Seven Reasons NOT to Ask Jesus into Your Heart!" Available at http://www.duluthbible.org /seven_reasons.htm. Accessed on August 11, 2004.

Rosscup, James E. "The **Overcomer** of the Apocalypse." *Grace Theological Journal* 3:2 (Fall 1982): 261-286.

Sapaugh, Gregory P. "A Call to the **Wedding** Celebration: An Exposition of Matthew 22:1-14." *Journal of the Grace Evangelical Society* 5:1 (Spring 1992): 11-34.

_____. "Is **Faith** A Gift? A Study of Ephesians 2:8." *Journal of the Grace Evangelical Society* 7:12 (Spring 94): 31-43.

Schmidtbleicher, Paul R. "Balancing the Use of the Old Testament. *Chafer Theological Seminary Journal* 8:3 (July - September 2002).

_____. "Forgiveness: Believers Forgiving One Another." *Chafer Theological Seminary Journal* 4:2 (Spring 1998).

Schwarze, C. T. "The Bible and Science on the Everlasting Fire: A Radio Broadcast By Professor C. T. Schwarze." *BibSac* 95:377 (January 38): 102-112.

Schwertley, Brian. "The New Birth." Available at http://www.reformedonline.com/view/reformedonline /newbirth.htm#F17. Accessed on May 7, 2005.

Segelberg, Eric. "The Coptic-Gnostic Gospel According to Philip and Its Sacramental System." *Numen* 7 (1960): 189-200.

Shell, Donald R. "Making Sense of God's Election: An Overview of the Work." Available at http://www.nepaugchurch.org/SpecialTopics/divineElection.htm. Accessed on August 11, 2004.

Siker, Jeffrey S. "Gnostic Views on **Jews** and Christians in the Gospel of Philip." *Novum Testamentum* 31 (1989): 275-288.

Sim, David C. "Matthew 22:13a and 1 Enoch 10:4a: A Case of Literary **Dependence**?" *Journal for the Study of the New Testament* 47 (1992): 3-19.

Simpson, Phillip L. "A Biblical **Response** to the Teachings of Zane Hodges, Joseph Dillow, and the Grace Evangelical Society (Called the "Free Grace" Movement)." Available at http://phils-page.blogspot.com /2006/03/response-the-free-grace-movement.html. Accessed on April 4, 2006.

Smith, Charles R. "Errant Aorist Interpreters." *Grace Theological Journal* 2:2 (Fall 1981): 205-226.

Snoeberger, Mark A. "The Logical Priority of Regeneration to Saving Faith in a Theological *Ordo Salutis*," *DBSJ* 7 (Fall 2002): 49–93.

Sproule, A. "'Judgment Seat' or 'Awards Podium'?" *Spire* (Spring 1984).

Spurgeon, Charles H. "All of Grace, Chapter 8: Faith, What is It?" Available at http://www.spurgeon.org /all_of_g.htm#Faith,%20What%20Is%20It? Accessed on August 11, 2004.

Stagg, Frank "The Abused Aorist." *Journal of Biblical Literature* 91 (1972): 222-31.

Stanford, Miles J. "Dispensational Disintegration (**Part 1**)—The Reign of The Servant Kings: A Study on Eternal Security and the Final Significance of Man." Available at http://withchrist.org/MJS/reign.htm. Accessed on August 11, 2004.

_____. "Dispensational Disintegration (**Part 2**)—Grace in Eclipse: A Study on Eternal Rewards." Available at http://withchrist.org/MJS/zane.htm. Accessed on August 11, 2004.

_____. "The Adamic Natures." Available at http://www.withchrist.org/MJS/adamic.htm. Accessed on August 11, 2004.

Stegall, Tom. "Must Faith Endure for Salvation to be Sure?" Available at http://www.duluthbible.org /g_f_j/GFJ_Article_Series.htm. Accessed on February 28, 2005.

_____. "The Tragedy of the Crossless Gospel Pt. 1." *The Grace Family Journal* (Spring 2007): 6-16.

_____. "The Tragedy of the Crossless Gospel Pt. 2." *The Grace Family Journal* (Summer 2007): 10-17.

Strehle, Stephen. "Universal Grace and Amyraldianism." *Westminster Theological Journal* 51:2 (Fall 1989): 345-57.

Suter, David W. "Weighed in the Balance: The Similitudes of Enoch in Recent Discussion." *Religious Studies Review* 7 (1981): 217-221.

Sweigart, John M. "Chiasmus Of Matthew 23:1—25:46." Available at http://www.inthebeginning.org/chiasmus /matthew/matthew23-25.pdf. Accessed on 9 October, 2004.

_____. "Matthew 24:45-25:30," 1-6. Available at http://www.inthebeginning.org/newtestament/matthew/mt25 .pdf. Accessed on September 9, 2004.

_____. "Philippians: Analytical Outline With Notes." (August 1997): 1-56. Available at http://www.inthe beginning.org/newtestament/philippians/philoutline.pdf. Accessed on August 12, 2004.

_____. "Romans 6:23: A **Pothole** in the Romans Road." Available at http://www.inthebeginning.org/kingdom /sweigart/pothole.pdf. Accessed on November 11, 2005.

_____. "The **Olivet** Discourse." Available at http://www.inthebeginning.org/newtestament/matthew/mt24.pdf. Accessed on August 12, 2004.

_____. "Understanding the Book of **Revelation**: An Outline of the Literary Form of Revelation." Available at http://www.inthebeginning.org/newtestament/revelation/revelation.pdf. Accessed on August 12, 2004.

Tanner, J. Paul. "'But If It Yields **Thorns** And Thistles': An Exposition Of Hebrews 5:11–6:12." *Journal of the Grace Evangelical Society* 14:26 (Spring 2001): 19-42.

Tanton, Lanny Thomas. "The Gospel and Water Baptism: A Study of Acts 2:38." *Journal of the Grace Evangelical Society* 3:1 (Spring 1990): 27-52.

Tenney, Merrill C. "The Footnotes of John's Gospel." *Bibliotheca Sacra* 117:468 (October 1960): 350-364.

Thatcher, Tom. "A New Look at the Asides in the Fourth Gospel." *Bibliotheca Sacra* 151:604 (October 1994): 428-439.

Thomas, Robert L. "The Doctrine of Imminence in Two Recent Eschatological Systems." Bibliotheca Sacra 157:628 (October 2000): 452-467.

Townsend, James A. "Grace in the Arts: G. K. Chesterton: The Theology of Philip Yancey's Favorite Writer," 15:29 *Journal of the Evangelical Theological Society* (Autumn, 2002): 67-91.

Turner, Allan. "The Foreknowledge Of God" (November 23, 19). Available at http://allanturner.com/calbk_4.html. Accessed on August 19, 2007.

Unger, Merrill F. "The Old Testament Revelation of the **Beginning** of Sin." *Bibliotheca Sacra* 114:456 (October, 1957): 326-333.

Unnik, W. C. Van. "Three Notes on the 'Gospel of Philip.'" *New Testament Studies* 10 (1964): 465-469.

Young, Ed. "Revealing the Revelation." Available at http://www.second.org/absolutenm/anmviewer .asp?a=14&z=2. Accessed on October 4, 2004.

Ventilato, James M. "A Scriptural **Refutation** of The Teachings of Zane Hodges, Joseph Dillow and the Grace Evangelical Society, with Respect to the Future Inheritance, Glory, and Destiny of the Church—Christ's Beloved Body & Bride." Available at http://www.middletownbiblechurch.org/doctrine/hodgesjv.htm. Accessed on August 12, 2004.

Vance, Laurence M. "Faust, J.D.—The Rod: Will God Spare It? Second Edition." Available at http://www.faithalone.org/journal/bookreviews/faust.htm. Accessed on August 8, 2005.

Wallis, Wilber B. "The Problem of an Intermediate Kingdom in I Corinthians 15:20-28." *Journal of the Evangelical Theological Society* 18:4 (Fall 1975): 229-242.

Warren, Tony. "Perseverance of the Saints: Is it the Doctrine of Eternal Security?" Available at http://members.aol.com/twarren17/perseverance.html. Accessed on June 14, 2005.

Walvoord, John F. "Premillennialism and the Tribulation: Part V: Partial Rapture Theory." *Bibliotheca Sacra* 112:447 (July, 1955): 193-208.

Wenstrom, William E. Jr. "Aion." Available at http://prairieviewchristian.org/Acrobat%20files/Aion.pdf. Accessed on July 5, 2005

White, James. "A Lavender Attempt Around John 6." Available at http://aomin.org/index.php?itemid=490. Accessed on August 12, 2005.

_____. "A Lavender Attempt Around John 6 (Concluded)." Available at http://www.aomin.org/index .php?itemid=491. Accessed on August 12, 2005.

_____. "**Blinded** By Tradition: An Open Letter to Dave Hunt: Regarding His Newly Published Attack Upon the Reformation, *What Love Is This? Calvinism's Misrepresentation of God*." Available at http:// www.aomin.org/DHOpenLetter.html. Accessed on August 26, 2004.

Wilkin, Robert N. "An Enormous Debt Forgiven: Part 1." *Grace in Focus* (January-February 2002).

_____. "An Enormous Debt Forgiven: Part 2." *Grace in Focus* (May-June 2002).

_____. "A New View on Acts 13:48 "As Many as Were Prepared for Eternal Life Believed," *Grace in Focus* (January-February 2007).

_____. "Are Believers Worthy of Entering the Kingdom? Luke 20:35." *Grace in Focus* (June 1989).

_____. "Are Esau and Cain in Heaven or Hell?" *Grace in Focus* (September-October, 2007).

_____. "Are Good Works Inevitable." *Grace in Focus* (February 1990).

_____. "A Review of R. C. Sproul's Grace Unknown: The Heart of Reformed Theology." *Journal of the Grace Evangelical Society* 14:27 (Autumn 2001): 3-19.

_____. "As Many as Were Devoted to Eternal Life Believed." *Grace in Focus* (May 2004).

_____. "Because We Love the Brethren: 1 John 3:14." *Grace in Focus* (November, 1994).

_____. "Believers at the Judgment Seat of Christ: Well Done or Cut in Two?" *Grace in Focus* (September-October 2000).

_____. "Beware of Confusion About Faith," *Journal of the Grace Evangelical Society* 18:34 (Spring 2005): 3-13.

_____. "Christians and the Unpardonable Sin." *Grace in Focus* (March-April 1997).

_____. "Christians Who Lose Their Legacy: Galatians 5:21." *Journal of the Grace Evangelical Society* 4:2 (Autumn 1991): 23-37.

_____. "Do Born Again People Sin? 1 John 3:9." *Grace in Focus* (March 1990).

_____. "Do Demons Really Believe? James 2:19." *Grace in Focus* (November-December 1992).

_____. "Does Being New Creatures in Christ Guarantee Good Works in the Lives of Believers? 2 Corinthians 5:17." *Grace in Focus* (January 1990).

_____. "Does Hell Await Those Who Fall? 2 Peter 2:18-22" *Grace in Focus* (May 1988).

_____. "Does Your Mind Need Changing? Repentance Reconsidered." *Journal of the Grace Evangelical Society* 11:20 (Spring 1998): 35-46.

_____. "Do You Know Our View on Assurance of Salvation?" *Grace in Focus* (March-April 2008).

_____. "**Election** and the Gospel: Can Only the Elect Accept Christ?" *Grace in Focus* (July 1989).

_____. "He Who Keeps His Word Won't See Death – John 8:51," *Grace in Focus* (July-August 1998).

_____. "Has This Passage Ever Bothered You? Philippians 3:11; Is Our Resurrection Certain?" *Grace in Focus* (January 1988).

_____. "He Is Able To Keep You From Stumbling! Jude 24." *Grace in Focus* (January-February 1994).

_____. "If it's Free, Why Would Anyone Need to Strive to Enter? Luke 13:24" *Grace in Focus* (November 1991).

_____. "I Will Not Blot Out His Name." *Grace in Focus* (March-April 1995).

_____. "Letters to the Editor." *Grace in Focus* (May, 1990).

_____. "The Free Grace Position Should Rightly Hold Claim to the Title *Lordship Salvation.*" *Grace in Focus* (November-December, 2010).

_____. "The Mark of the Beast and Perseverance: Revelation 14:9-12." *Grace in Focus* (June, 1991).

_____. "No Second Repentance? Hebrews 6:4-8." *Grace in Focus* (July-August 1992).

_____. "Not Everyone Who Says 'Lord, Lord' Will Enter the Kingdom: Matthew 7:21-23." *Grace in Focus* (December 1988).

_____. "Obedience to the Faith: Romans 1:5." *Grace in Focus* (November 1995).

_____. "Putting the Gospel Debate in Sharper Focus." *Grace in Focus* (May 1991).

_____. "Raised To Run - Philippians 3:11." *Grace in Focus* (August 1991).

_____. "Remember the Bereans (Acts 17:11)." *Grace in Focus* (November-December, 2007).

_____. "Repentance and Salvation Part 1: The Doctrine of Repentance in the Old Testament." *Journal of the Grace Evangelical Society* 2:1 (Spring 1989): 11-20.

_____. "Repentance and Salvation **Part 2**: The Doctrine of Repentance in the Old Testament." *Journal of the Grace Evangelical Society* 2:1 (Spring 1989): 13-26.

_____. "Repentance and Salvation **Part 4**: New Testament Repentance: Repentance in the Gospels and Acts." *Journal of the Grace Evangelical Society* 3:1 (Spring 1990): 11-25.

_____. "Regeneration in the OT?" *Grace in Focus* (March-April, 2004).

_____. and Kerry Gilliard. "Resolved; Repentance Isn't a Condition of Eternal." Available at http://www.faithalone.org/debate.html. Accessed on 5 May, 2005.

_____. "Review of 'Grace and Warning in Paul's Gospel.'" *Journal of the Grace Evangelical Society* 24:40 (Spring, 20011): 3-20.

_____. "Saving Faith Is Not Like Sitting in a Chair." *Grace in Focus* (March-April 1993).

_____. "**Self-Sacrifice** and Kingdom Entrance: Part 2 of 2: Matthew 5:29-30." *Grace in Focus* (September 1989).

_____. "'**Soul** Salvation,' Part 5, Suffering Which Results in Abundant Life," *Grace in Focus* (May-June 1992).

_____. "Test Yourselves to See If You Are in the Faith: Assurance Based on Our Works? 2 Corinthians 13:5." *Grace in Focus* (October 1989).

_____. "'The Day' is the Judgment Seat of Christ." *Journal of the Grace Evangelical Society* 20:39 (Autumn 2007): 3-15.

_____. "The Litmus Test of True Believers? First Corinthians 12:3." *Grace in Focus* (January-February 1993).

_____. "The Lord Opened Her Heart: Acts 16:14." *Grace in Focus* (September-October 1995).

_____. "We Believe In: Sanctification—Part 2: Past Sanctification." *Journal of the Grace Evangelical Society* 6:10 (Spring 1993): 3-18.

_____. "We Believe In: Sanctification—Part 3: **Present Sanctification**—God's Role in Present Sanctification." *Journal of the Grace Evangelical Society* 7:12 (Autumn 1994): 3-16.

_____. "Who are the **Outsiders**? Revelation 22:14-17." *Grace in Focus* (November-December 1993).

_____. "Whoever Says 'You **Fool**!' Shall Be in Danger of Hell Fire: Matthew 5:22." *Grace in Focus* (September 1997).

_____. "Will You Be Counted Worthy of the Kingdom? 2 Thessalonians 1:5." *Grace in Focus* (May 1999).

_____. *"What is the Gospel? A Theological Debate with Dr. Darrell Bock and Dr. Bob Wilkin."* Available at http://64.233.167.104/search?q=cache:tmkld6JGZ9EJ:www.faithalone.org/resources/debate.pdf+daisy+site:faithalone.org&hl=en. Accessed on September 30, 2004

Wilson, Robert M. "The New Testament in the Nag Hammadi Gospel of Philip." *New Testament Studies* 9 (1963): 291-294.

_____. "Second Thoughts: XI. The Gnostic Gospels from Nag Hammadi." *Expository Times* 78 (1966): 36-41.

Woodcock, Eldon "The **Seal** of the Holy Spirit." *Bibliotheca Sacra* 155:618 (April-June 1998): 139-63.

Wong, Daniel K. K. "The Pillar and the Throne in Revelation 3:12, 21." *Bibliotheca Sacra* 156:623 (July 1999): 297-307.

Zeller, George. "Can A True Believer Depart from the Faith? Can a Saved Person Totally Abandon His Faith in Christ?" Available at http://www.middletownbiblechurch.org/doctrine/departff.htm. Accessed 7-24-04

_____. "If a Person Rejects Christ Before the Rapture, Can He Be Saved After the Rapture?" Available at http://www.middletownbiblechurch.org/proph/savetrib.htm. Accessed on April 25, 2006.

_____. "Saved By Grace: A Clarification of the Lordship Salvation Issue." Available at http://www.middletownbiblechurch.org/doctrine/sbgrace.htm. Accessed on August 13, 2004.

_____. "Statement of Faith of the Middletown Bible Church." Available at http://www.middletownbiblechurch.org/info/statemnt.htm. Accessed on May 9, 2006.

_____. "The **Theology** of Zane Hodges and Joseph Dillow and the Grace Evangelical Society." Available at http://www.middletownbiblechurch.org/doctrine/theology.htm. Accessed on August 13, 2004.

_____. "Those Who Do Not Inherit The Kingdom....Are They Saved or Unsaved?" Available at http://www.middletownbiblechurch.org/doctrine/inherit.htm. Accessed on August 13, 2004.

_____. "What is the 'Gift of God'? A Study of Ephesians 2:8-9." (March 2000). Available at http://www.middletownbiblechurch.org/reformed/godgift.htm. Accessed 16 July, 2004.

Zuck, Roy B. "Cheap Grace?" *Kindred Spirit* (Summer 1989).

Zeolla, Gary F. "Study of Acts 13:48 (Part Two)." Available from http://www.dtl.org/calvinism/study/acts-13-48/pt-2.htm. Accessed on August 28, 2004.

Theses and Unpublished Works

Andrew, Stephen L. "PROPER: A Free-Grace Alternative to Calvinism's TULIP and Arminianism's PEARS." Unpublished paper, 2001.

Benedict, Richard R. "The Use of Νίκαω in the **Letters** to the Seven Churches of Revelation." Th.M. thesis. Dallas Theological Seminary, 1966.

Betz, Harlen D. "The Nature of Rewards at the Judgment Seat of Christ." Th.M. thesis, Dallas Theological Seminary, 1974.

Bing, Charles. "Cross-Threaded Spirituality: The Lordship View of the Spirit-filled Life." *Grace Evangelical Society Conference CD*, 2001.

Brown, William E. "The New Testament Concept of the Believer's Inheritance." Th.D. diss., Dallas Theological Seminary, 1984.

Bryant, Robert. "Eternal Security: Do You Have To Believe It?" *Grace Evangelical Society Conference CD*, 2005.

_____. "How Were People **Saved** before Jesus Came?" *Grace Evangelical Society Conference CD*, 2001.

_____. "The Secret Believer in the Gospel of John." Th.M. thesis. Dallas Theological Seminary, 1975.

Christianson, Richard W. "The Soteriological Significance of Πιστευω in the Gospel of John." Th.M. thesis. Grace Theological Seminary, 1987.

Cocoris, Michael G. "John Macarthur, Jr.'s System of Salvation: An **Evaluation** of the Book, The Gospel According to Jesus." Unpublished paper, 1989.

Derickson, Gary W. "The Meaning Of John 20:31." 2002 Annual Meetings of the Evangelical Theological Society.

Dillow, Joseph. "Discipleship in the Sermon on the Mount: A Review of Some Problem Passages." *Grace Evangelical Society Conference CD*, 2003.

Huber, Michael G. "The **Concept** of the 'Outer Darkness' in the Gospel of Matthew." Th.M. thesis, Dallas Theological Seminary, 1978.

Meisinger, George E. "Judgment Seat of Christ: Loss of Rewards." *Grace Evangelical Society Conference CD*, 2006.

McClymont, James C., Jr. "The Parable of the Talents." Th.M. thesis, Dallas Theological Seminary, 1976.

Nicholas, Timothy R. "Commands to Believe: An Objection to Passive Faith?" A paper presented at the National Teaching Pastor's Conference, 2001. Available at http://www.gracenow.org/~tnichols/PassiveFaith-FurtherReadings.pdf. Accessed on March 17, 2006.

_____. "Is Faith a Decision?" A paper presented at the National Teaching Pastor's Conference, 2002. Available at http://www.gracenow.org/~tnichols/PassiveFaith-urtherReadings.pdf. Accessed on March 17, 2006.

Ralph D. Richardson. "The Johannine Doctrine of Victory." Th.M. thesis, Dallas Theological Seminary, 1955.

Ross, William R., Jr. "An Analysis of the Rewards and Judgments in **Revelation** 2 and 3." Th.M. thesis, Dallas Theological Seminary, 1971.

Sapaugh, Gregory P. "An **Interpretation** of Matthew 22:1-14." Th.M. thesis, Dallas Theological Seminary, 1991.

Shipley, Steven F. "**Belief**: False or True? An Appeal for Consistent Interpretation of Biblical Soteriological Terminology." M.Div. thesis, Grace Theological Seminary, 1985.

Hart, John F. "Grace Theology and the Struggle of the Legalistic Christian Life: The Contributions of Romans 7." *Grace Evangelical Society Conference CD*, 2001.

Hodges, Zane C. "***Class*** *notes on Hebrews*," n.d.

_____. "The Epistle of **2nd** **Peter**: Shunning Error in Light of the Savior's Return." A verse-by-verse commentary, n.d.

Tanner, J. Paul. "A Severe Warning Against Defection: Hebrews 10:26-31," *Grace Evangelical Society Conference CD*, 2006.

Wilkin, Robert N. "An Exegetical Evaluation of the Reformed Doctrine of the Perseverance of the Saints." Th.M. thesis, Dallas Theological Seminary, 1982.

Indexes

Italic, regular, and bold fonts have been used for page numbers within the indexes to rank entrees in terms of emphases as: *minor*, medium, **major**.

Author Index

Subject Index

Extrabiblical Index

Hebrew Index

Slavonic Index

Scripture Index

Greek Index

52099365R00351

Made in the USA
San Bernardino, CA
10 August 2017